12TH EDITION

CRIMINAL INVESTIGATION

CHARLES MIKE R. SWANSON
University of Georgia

NEIL C. CHAMELIN
Assistant State Attorney, Leon County,
Florida (Retired) and Attorney at Law

LEONARD TERRITO
Saint Leo University

ROBERT W. TAYLOR
The University of Texas at Dallas

Mc
Graw
Hill
Education

CRIMINAL INVESTIGATION, TWELFTH EDITION

Published by McGraw-Hill Education, 2 Penn Plaza, New York, NY 10121. Copyright © 2019 by McGraw-Hill Education. All rights reserved. Printed in the United States of America. Previous editions © 2012, 2009, and 2006. No part of this publication may be reproduced or distributed in any form or by any means, or stored in a database or retrieval system, without the prior written consent of McGraw-Hill Education, including, but not limited to, in any network or other electronic storage or transmission, or broadcast for distance learning.

Some ancillaries, including electronic and print components, may not be available to customers outside the United States.

This book is printed on acid-free paper.

1 2 3 4 5 6 7 8 9 LWI 21 20 19 18

ISBN 978-0-07-802657-7 (bound edition)
MHID 0-07-802657-1 (bound edition)
ISBN 978-1-259-86794-1 (loose-leaf edition)
MHID 1-259-86794-3 (loose-leaf edition)

Portfolio Manager: *Jamie Laferrara*
Product Developer: *Erika Lo*
Marketing Manager: *Nancy Baudean*
Content Project Managers: *Ryan Warczynski, Katie Reuter, Sandra Schnee*
Senior Buyer: *Susan K. Culbertson*
Content Licensing Specialist: *Brianna Kirschbaum*
Cover Image: *©anthonysp/Getty Images*
Compositor: *MPS Limited*

Library of Congress Cataloging-in-Publication Data

Swanson, Charles R., 1942- author.
Criminal investigation / Charles R. Swanson [and three others].
12th edition. | New York, NY : McGraw-Hill Education, [2019] |
   Includes index.
LCCN 2017050892 | ISBN 9780078026577 (alk. paper)
LCSH: Criminal investigation. | Criminal investigation–United
   States.
LCC HV8073 .S84 2019 | DDC 363.25–dc23 LC record available
at https://lccn.loc.gov/2017050892

mheducation.com/highered

From Charles Mike R. Swanson: For my siblings, Chris, Randy, and the oldest, Pat, who has gone ahead. Thank you for a lifetime of love, friendship, laughter, and wise counsel.

From Neil C. Chamelin: For my wife, Vicki, sons, Chris and Todd, daughter-in-law, Heidi and granddaughters, Tally, Casey, Laney, and Jessy.

From Leonard Territo: For my wife, Elena, the kindest and sweetest woman I have ever known, and our children, Lorraine, Kseniya, and Ilia, and my grandchildren, Matthew, Branden, and Alexander.

From Robert W. Taylor: For my beautiful wife Mary and parents, Rosemary and Harvey Taylor, and Elizabeth and R.H. Perez.

Charles R. "Mike" Swanson has extensive experience in designing promotional systems and tests for state, county, and municipal public safety agencies, including the Kentucky State Police, the Georgia Bureau of Investigation, the Alabama State Troopers, and the Georgia State Patrol. He has conducted over 60 job-analysis studies and written more than 125 promotional tests. He has designed and implemented at least 75 assessment centers, as well as written their exercises. Mike has trained assessors from 18 different states and has testified in federal court as an expert witness on police promotional matters.

Mike enlisted in the Marine Corps when he was 17 years old and then joined the Tampa Police Department, working as a uniformed officer in the highest crime areas of the city before being promoted to detective. Subsequently, he worked as the senior police planner and later as the acting deputy director of the Council on Law Enforcement in the Office of the Florida Governor. While working in Florida, Mike earned his bachelor's and master's degrees in criminology from Florida State University. After a teaching stint at East Carolina University, Mike accepted a faculty position at the University of Georgia's Institute of Government, where he received a Ph.D. with an emphasis on public administration and rose through the administrative ranks, retiring as the interim director in late 2001. While at the Institute Mike trained over 10,000 law enforcement officers from 42 states in advanced courses such as homicide investigation and police agency leadership. He remains active as a consultant

to law enforcement agencies and has written more than 200 technical reports for them.

In addition to this book, Mike has coauthored four others, including *Police Administration: Structures, Processes, and Behavior,* (9th edition 2017), and *Terrorism, Intelligence, and Homeland Security* (2nd edition, 2018). He has authored or coauthored a number of monographs, articles, and conference papers pertaining to policing. In 2003 he received the O. W. Wilson Award for Outstanding Police Scholarship. Mike has received multiple awards from the governors of three states and from the Georgia Association of Chiefs of Police, who recognized his 20 years of service to their association by making him the first Honorary Chief of Police. The University of Georgia twice recognized Mike for "extraordinary work with law enforcement agencies." In 2017, he was selected as a Distinguished Alumnus of Florida State University.

Neil C. Chamelin retired as an assistant state attorney, Second Judicial Circuit, Leon County, Florida. Previously he served as the hearing officer for the Florida Division of Motor Vehicles, Department of Highway Safety and Motor Vehicles; director of Criminal Justice Programs for Troy State University, European Region; director of the Florida Police Standards and Training Commission; and division director for the Standards and Training Division, Florida Department of Law Enforcement. He also served as a police officer in Sarasota, Florida. Neil is a co-author of *Essentials of Criminal Law,* formerly, *Criminal Law for Police Officers;*

Introduction to Criminal Justice; and *Police Personnel Selection Process*. He is currently retired and now lives in Deland, Florida.

Leonard Territo is presently a distinguished professor in the Department of Criminal Justice at Saint Leo University, Saint Leo, Florida, and professor emeritus in the Department of Criminology, at the University of South Florida, Tampa, Florida. He was previously the chief deputy (undersheriff) of the Leon County Sheriff's Office in Tallahassee, Florida. He also served for almost nine years with the Tampa, Florida Police Department as a patrol officer, motorcycle officer, and homicide detective. He is the former chairperson of the Department of Police Administration and director of the Florida Institute for Law Enforcement at St. Petersburg Junior College, St. Petersburg, Florida.

In addition to writing nearly 50 articles, book chapters, and technical reports, he has authored, co-authored, and edited twelve books, including *Police Administration* (9th edition); *International Sex Trafficking of Women and Children: Understanding the Global Epidemic* (2nd edition); *Criminal Investigation of Sex Trafficking in America; The International Trafficking of Human Organs: A Multi-Disciplinary Perspective; Crime and Justice in America* (6th edition); *Stress Management in Law Enforcement* (3rd edition); *Police Civil Liability; College Crime and Prevention and Personal Safety Awareness; Stress and Police Personnel; The Police Personnel Selection Process; Hospital and College Security Liability;* and a crime novel, *Ivory Tower Cop*, which was inspired by a true story. His books have been used in more than a thousand colleges and universities in 50 states, and his writings have been used and referenced by both academic and police departments in 15 countries including Australia, Barbados, Canada, Chile, China, the former Czechoslovakia, England, France, Germany, Israel, the Netherlands, Poland, Saudi Arabia, South Korea, and Spain.

His teaching awards include being selected by the Florida Criminal Justice Educators Association from among 200 Florida criminal justice educators as the Outstanding Criminal Justice Educator of the Year. He was also selected as the Outstanding Teacher of the Year by the College of Social and Behavioral Sciences at the University of South Florida. He has been given awards by both the Florida Police Chiefs Association and the Tampa Police Academy for his years of teaching and meritorious services; he was given an award for Distinguished Scholarly Publications by Saint Leo University; he has been selected for inclusion in *Who's Who in American Law Enforcement*; and he has recently been given a Lifetime Achievement Award from the Department of Criminology at the University of South Florida.

Robert W. Taylor is currently a full professor in the Criminology Program at The University of Texas at Dallas. Before that he was the founding Executive Director of the W. W. Caruth, Jr., Police Institute, an executive training and police research center funded through a $9.5 million grant embedded in the Dallas Police Department. For the past 30 years, Bob has studied police responses to crime and terrorism. He has traveled extensively throughout the Middle East, Europe, and Far East Asia. He currently serves as a consultant to numerous federal, state, and local agencies on policing issues and practices, intelligence analysis, police use-of-force, and terrorism. Bob has been a retained expert witness relating to the quality of police processes and investigative techniques on a number of high profile murder cases including the JonBenet Ramsey murder and several Innocence Project cases. In 2008 the Academy of Criminal Justice Sciences presented him with the O. W. Wilson Award "in recognition for his outstanding contribution to police education, research and practice," and in 2003 the University of North Texas presented him with the Regent's Lecture Award for his outstanding work on terrorism in the Middle East.

Bob also has written extensively in the area of law enforcement management and administration, community policing, and public policy. He served as a sworn police officer in Portland, Oregon, for six years, three of which were as a major crimes detective. Aside from this work, Bob has coauthored five additional books: *Police Administration: Structures, Processes, and Behavior* (Pearson, 2017); *Terrorism, Intelligence, and Homeland Security* (Pearson, 2018); *Juvenile Justice: Policies, Programs, and Practices* (McGraw-Hill, 2015); *Cyber Crime and Cyber Terrorism* (Pearson, 2018); and *Police Patrol Allocation and Design* (Pearson, 2009).

BRIEF CONTENTS

| CONTENTS

(©A.Ramey/PhotoEdit)

6
FIELD NOTES AND REPORTING 166

7
THE FOLLOW-UP INVESTIGATION AND INVESTIGATIVE RESOURCES 187

8

THE CRIME LABORATORY   222

9

INJURY AND DEATH INVESTIGATIONS   252

(©Steve Kohls/BrainerdDaily Dispatch/AP Images)

(©Robert Nickelsberg/Getty Images)

16
VEHICLE THEFTS AND RELATED OFFENSES   469

(©Ken Tannenbaum/Shutterstock RF)

20
RECOGNITION, CONTROL, AND INVESTIGATION OF DRUG ABUSE   592

(©Charles Reed/U.S. Immigration and Customs Enforcement/Getty Images)

As with the previous editions, the first purpose of this book is to provide a useful tool for those on law enforcement's front lines. Thus, *Criminal Investigation* is once again filled with practical "how to" information, case studies, and color photographs that illustrate important points and checklists that can be adapted to the needs of local agencies.

We have scrutinized all aspects of the book, downsizing and deleting some content while elsewhere adding new cutting-edge topics. Many portions of chapters have been substantially or totally rewritten. These and other changes are more fully identified shortly.

Criminal Investigation continues to differ from other texts, and the differences are again reflected throughout this edition. First, criminal investigation generally has been conceived of, and touted as, an art. This approach depreciates the precision required to conduct inquiries; it denies the existence of, and adherence to, rigorous methods; and it associates criminal investigation with unneeded mysticism. Criminal investigation is in large part a science. The fact that criminals are not always apprehended does not make it less so. The rational scientific method is, of necessity, supplemented by initiative and occasional fortuitous circumstances, but it is the application of the method rather than shrewd hunches that most frequently produces results. The most successful investigators are those who know how to apply the rational scientific method; therefore, it is this method that we consistently use in *Criminal Investigation.*

A second major difference between this text and others arises from our belief that writing about techniques takes on more substance if one understands something of the nature of the event being investigated. Thus we have discussed typologies—including offenses, offenders, and victims—in depth, so that our readers not only take away a more comprehensive understanding of criminal investigation than they would from another textbook but also have substantial information to use later as a reference.

Third, because crime-prevention technology has been a significant milestone for both the police and the public, we have inserted short sections on prevention in chapters where appropriate. The complexity of crime prevention dictates that it is a specialization within police departments. Yet at the scene of a crime, the investigator may be in a unique position to make a few helpful, if rudimentary, suggestions to a victim on how to avoid further loss. *Criminal Investigation*'s crime-prevention sections give investigators the tools to accomplish this task.

Finally, most investigative books tend to blur the distinction between the roles of uniformed officers and detectives; we draw this line distinctly. Although everyone may not agree with our dichotomizing, the uniformed officer's role must be recognized for the contribution it makes to the ultimate success of an investigation.

THE TWELFTH EDITION

Criminal investigation is always evolving owing to scientific, legal, and social developments, as well as to changes in the behavior of criminals. Although many investigative techniques are fundamental and remain basically the same over time, significant changes also occur on a continuing basis. In addition to having updated photographs, tables, figures, and citations, we have added new case studies and two new features: box items and quick fact boxes, which contain short statements with information relevant to the content of the chapter, but may not have an exact relationship to the content being discussed.

• **Chapter 1, "The Evolution of Criminal Investigation and Forensic Science,"** a historically oriented chapter, has a revised introduction that provides a definition of the investigator and the investigation, as well as an emphasis on the fundamental purpose of investigation and forensic science and its role in discovering the truth. New information on biometrics and forensic phenotyping has been added to this chapter.

• **Chapter 2, "Legal Aspects of Investigation,"** addresses legal topics that uniformed officers and investigators encounter on a daily basis and that are essential for the successful resolution of every criminal case. New feature materials have been added on "Fundamental Fairness, Due Process and Brady Violations," and "Stop and Frisk in New York City." New content has been added on arrest warrant scams, traffic enforcement and racial profiling, and warrantless trunk vehicle searches. Plus new material has been added on stop-and-identify statutes in the U.S., as well as a new Internet Activity focusing on the search and seizure of digital evidence by police officers in the future.

• **Chapter 3, "Investigators, the Investigative Process, and the Crime Scene,"** includes updated information on the disease risks officers face from Hepatitis A, B, C, Ebola, Zika, and tuberculosis infections. The chapter continues to emphasize its strong crime scene and preliminary investigation focus.

• **Chapter 4, "Physical Evidence,"** has been thoroughly revised and streamlined and includes new material on "geoforensics," as well as updated sections on forensic palynology, impression evidence, glass, fingerprints, forensic odontology, hair, and blood.

• **Chapter 5, "Interviewing and Interrogation,"** includes a new section on the most efficient way to interview people with disabilities. This includes those who are blind or visually impaired, deaf or hard of hearing, mobility impaired, or have cognitive disabilities.

- **Chapter 6, "Field Notes and Reporting,"** has been substantially re-written, including information about digital audio recorders and body worn cameras and the extent to which officers can use those recordings when writing reports. Also included are online public reporting systems, and a discussion of handling field contacts with different genders, races/ethnicities, and LGBT individuals.

- **Chapter 7, "The Follow-Up Investigation and Investigative Resources,"** has been thoroughly updated and includes a new section on Field Contacts and Field Interviews; a revised section on the Bureau of Alcohol, Tobacco, and Firearms; a completely updated section on surveillance; and an updated section on Guidelines for Conducting Show-ups, Photo Arrays/Lineups, and Live Lineups. Also you will find a new discussion on the Innocence Project and completely revised sections on Cold Case Investigation and Intelligence Analysis and Crime Analysis.

- **Chapter 8, "The Crime Laboratory,"** includes updated and expanded material on new technologies that have revolutionized the crime lab. As such, information on fingerprints and the law, and on CODIS (including new DNA quantitation, mitochondrial DNA, non-human DNA, sperm detection and separation, and Y-Chromosome analysis), is presented. A new section on "Biometrics and Next Generation Identification (NGI)" also highlights the chapter as well as added material on problems and scandals within crime laboratories (e.g., dissolution of the FBI's Hair Analysis and Bite-Mark Analysis section, and reforming state and local crime labs).

- **Chapter 9, "Injury and Death Investigations,"** includes a new discussion of the differences between spree killings and mass murders. For example, the spree killer is an individual who embarks on a murder rampage and the killings take place over a given period of time. The mass murder typically involves the intentional killing of a group of people at one time and usually occurs in a public place.

- **Chapter 10, "Sex-Related Offenses,"** includes an updated section on best practices for sexual assault investigation with new material on rape and sexual assault investigation and preliminary victim interviews, minimal fact interviews, victim-centered responses and trauma-informed responses, and follow-up interviews by detectives and/or officers. The chapter also presents new presentations on contemporary issues facing sex-related offense investigations, such as police sexual violence, transgender victims of sexual assault, drug and alcohol-facilitated sexual assault, and date rape (sexual assault) on college and university campuses.

- **Chapter 11, "Crimes Against Children,"** contains new and updated material on the impact of social media on crimes against children, such as investigative tools using Facebook, Twitter, and Snapchat in cases involving cyberbulling, sexting, and sextortion. The chapter also has a new and updated analysis of school shootings that continue to plague the U.S.

- **Chapter 12, "Human Trafficking,"** has been extensively modified with many of the previous topics expanded and new ones added. This includes the discussion of sex trafficking of American children and their demographics. We also discuss the Stockholm syndrome; recruitment; pimp control; the role played by customers (johns); programs for demand reduction; and the role of the law enforcement Multi-Agency Task Force.

- **Chapter 13, "Robbery,"** includes a discussion of the dramatic increase in the robberies of smartphones in recent years and how best to investigate them as well as prevent them in the first place. We have also discussed efforts by police to set up "Safe Zones" to prevent robberies which involve sales generated by Craig's List.

- **Chapter 14, "Burglary,"** was substantially rewritten, including new information on possession of burglary tools and lock picking's emergence as a competitive sport, profiles of burglaries, burglar motivations, gender differences, and the acquisition of information about potential targets, including the use of drones.

- **Chapter 15, "Larceny"** includes an expanded discussion of shoplifting and crime prevention tips for employees. We have also added new information which addresses the problem of bicycle theft. This includes a discussion of the typical methods employed by bicycle thieves as well as developing a profile for both the thief and potential victims.

- **Chapter 16, "Vehicle Theft and Related Offenses,"** includes updated statistical information relating to auto, airplane, motorcycle, and "big rig" (18-wheeler) vehicle theft. There are also new informational items on auto component and accessary theft, cybercrime and cars, the use of stolen vehicles by terrorists, odometer fraud, the transport of stolen vehicles to Mexico, and preventing vehicle theft through the use of new technologies.

- **Chapter 17, "Cybercrime,"** addresses one of fastest growing areas of criminal investigation confronting the police. There is new section on the "The Evolution of Cybercrime: From Teen Hackers and Script Kiddies to Sophisticated Criminal Organizations, International Espionage, and Cyber Terrorism," which provides detailed discussion of today's major threats from criminal organizations to foreign espionage groups. There are also a number of informational items that focus on high-level cybercrime threats and attacks, including discussion on Stuxnet and Flame, and Advanced Persistent Threat 1 (APT-1). The chapters also has a major new section on digital forensics that includes common digital evidence found in traditional crimes as well as securing evidence on mobile devices.

- **Chapter 18, "Agricultural, Wildlife, and Environmental Crimes,"** includes a discussion of the causes of wildfires and how investigators can go about determining whether they are accidental, intentional, or natural. We have also added an entirely new section dealing with agroterrorism, which is defined as the deliberate introduction of animal or plant disease for the purpose of generating fear, causing economic loses, or creating social instability. We have also added a discussion about the roles of outfitters, guides, and landowners in trophy poaching.

- **Chapter 19, "Arson and Explosives,"** includes an expanded discussion of the role played by the U.S. Bureau of Alcohol, Tobacco, Firearms, and Explosives (ATF) in the collection, storage, and analysis of explosives. New material also includes the consolidation of the FBI's Automated Incident Reporting System with the ATF's Bomb Arson Tracking System (BATS).

- **Chapter 20, "Recognition, Control, and Investigation of Drug Abuse,"** has new material on the major paradigm shift relating to the legalization and decriminalization of marijuana in the United States. There are also new informational items relating to the impact of the arrest, escape, and re-arrest of Joaquin "El Chapo" Guzman in Mexico, celebrity drug use focusing on the deadly effects of the heroin-cocaine mixture known as a "speedball," police use of Naloxone (Narcan), and new drug mixtures such as "el diablito" containing heroin and fentanyl.

- **Chapter 21, "Terrorism,"** has received a number of updates to reflect the changes in terrorist organizations, structures, and threats confronting the police. As such, there is new material on the Islamic State and the importance of Abu Musab al-Zarqawi in the development of the Islamic State in Iraq and Syria (ISIS). There are also new discussions relating to Sheikh Anwar al-Awlaki and his impact on radical Islam, and the terrorist attacks in San Bernardino (CA) by Syed Rizwan Farook and Tashfeen Malik and the Orlando (FL) attack of the gay *Pulse* nightclub by Omar Mateen. The chapter also has new informational items on recent attacks in Burkina Faso conducted by al-Qaeda in the Islamic Maghreb-AQIM, and the Malheur National Wildlife Refuge occupation in Central Oregon in 2016. The chapter concludes with new material focusing on the future of terrorism in the United States.

- **Chapter 22, "The Trial Process and the Investigator as a Witness,"** has seen all statistical data updated. New features have been added on "Expert Opinion and the *Daubert Standard*"; "Lying and Officer Credibility as a Witness"; "Scientific Jury Selection"; "49 Wrongfully Convicted People Who Were Exonerated in 2015"; and "Prima Facia Cases and Evidence." New Internet Activities added as well.

LEARNING AIDS

Working together, the authors and the editors have developed a format for the text that supports the goal of a readable, practical, user-friendly book. In addition to the changes already mentioned, we have added a host of new photographs, figures, and tables to reinforce and expand the text coverage. A visual presentation of the book's many lists—which are so critical in a text that teaches professionals and future professionals "how to" investigate crime—makes this material easy to digest. The learning aids in the edition go beyond these visual elements, however:

- **Chapter-opening photographs, outlines, and learning objectives** draw readers in and serve as a road map to the chapter.

- **Chapter-opening overviews** provide readers with a snapshot of the entire chapter and are excellent review tools for readers who are preparing for exams.

- **Detailed captions accompany photographs,** clarifying precisely what readers should be looking for and learning when examining each piece of art.

- **End-of-chapter review sections featuring key-term lists, review questions, and Internet activities** make preparing for exams easier than ever.

As mentioned, we have retained our plentiful, widely acclaimed "cases" within every chapter, ensuring that the twelfth edition is not only the most current, definitive text on criminal investigation but also the most practical and relevant. And with the enhancements we have made to the learning aids, *Criminal Investigation* is, simply put, the most mastery-oriented text available for the course.

SUPPLEMENTS

connect The 12th edition *Criminal Investigation* is now available online with Connect, McGraw-Hill Education's integrated assignment and assessment platform. Connect also offers SmartBook for the new edition, which is the first adaptive reading experience proven to improve grades and help students study more effectively. All of the title's ancillary content is available through Connect, including:

- A full Test Bank of multiple choice questions that tests students on central concepts and ideas in each chapter.
- An Instructor's Manual for each chapter with full chapter outlines, sample test questions, and discussion topics.
- Lecture Slides for instructor use in class and downloadable RAP forms.

ACKNOWLEDGMENTS

Without the kindness of many people throughout the country—literally from Alaska to Maine—this book could not have been written. We are grateful for the support of our colleagues around the country who have contributed case histories, reviewed portions of the manuscript within their areas of expertise, written sections for inclusion in the book, contributed photographs, forms, and other illustrations, or otherwise gone out of their way to be helpful. Our continuing concern in writing these acknowledgments is that, inadvertently, we may have omitted someone. If this is so, let us know so that we may correct this oversight, and also please accept our apologies. Our acknowledgments include persons who have contributed to this edition and those who helped with earlier editions. Some of the people identified have retired or taken on new responsibilities since assisting

 **connect®**

Homework and Adaptive Learning

- Connect's assignments help students contextualize what they've learned through application, so they can better understand the material and think critically.

- Connect will create a personalized study path customized to individual student needs through SmartBook®.

- SmartBook helps students study more efficiently by delivering an interactive reading experience through adaptive highlighting and review.

Over **7 billion questions** have been answered, making McGraw-Hill Education products more intelligent, reliable, and precise.

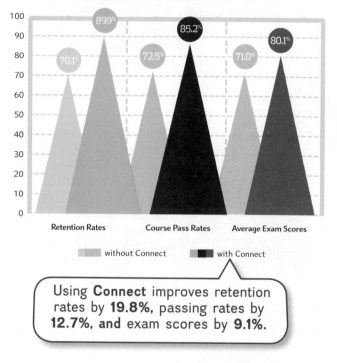

Connect's Impact on Retention Rates, Pass Rates, and Average Exam Scores

- Retention Rates: 70.1% (without Connect), 89.9% (with Connect)
- Course Pass Rates: 72.5% (without Connect), 85.2% (with Connect)
- Average Exam Scores: 71.0% (without Connect), 80.1% (with Connect)

without Connect | with Connect

Using **Connect** improves retention rates by **19.8%**, passing rates by **12.7%**, and exam scores by **9.1%**.

73% of instructors who use **Connect** require it; instructor satisfaction **increases** by 28% when **Connect** is required.

Quality Content and Learning Resources

- Connect content is authored by the world's best subject matter experts, and is available to your class through a simple and intuitive interface.

- The Connect eBook makes it easy for students to access their reading material on smartphones and tablets. They can study on the go and don't need Internet access to use the eBook as reference, with full functionality.

- Multimedia content such as videos, simulations, and games drive student engagement and critical thinking skills.

©McGraw-Hill Education

Robust Analytics and Reporting

- Connect Insight® generates easy-to-read reports on individual students, the class as a whole, and on specific assignments.

- The Connect Insight dashboard delivers data on performance, study behavior, and effort. Instructors can quickly identify students who struggle and focus on material that the class has yet to master.

- Connect automatically grades assignments and quizzes, providing easy-to-read reports on individual and class performance.

©Hero Images/Getty Images

Impact on Final Course Grade Distribution

without Connect		with Connect
22.9%	A	31.0%
27.4%	B	34.3%
22.9%	C	18.7%
11.5%	D	6.1%
15.4%	F	9.9%

More students earn **As** and **Bs** when they use **Connect**.

Trusted Service and Support

- Connect integrates with your LMS to provide single sign-on and automatic syncing of grades. Integration with Blackboard®, D2L®, and Canvas also provides automatic syncing of the course calendar and assignment-level linking.

- Connect offers comprehensive service, support, and training throughout every phase of your implementation.

- If you're looking for some guidance on how to use Connect, or want to learn tips and tricks from super users, you can find tutorials as you work. Our Digital Faculty Consultants and Student Ambassadors offer insight into how to achieve the results you want with Connect.

www.mheducation.com/connect

us, but, unless otherwise requested, we include their organizational affiliation and status at the time of the original contribution, since we feel that the agencies then employing them are also deserving of continued recognition.

Colleagues who have contributed photographs, forms, and other illustrations are identified beginning on page xxiii; thank you one and all. We would also like to thank another group of individuals who helped out in a variety of ways: Bryanna Fox led a research team studying burglary behavioral patterns in Florida. She received her doctorate in psychological criminology from the University of Cambridge (England). Dr Fox is a former FBI agent, a consultant to law enforcement agencies, and presently a faculty member in the College of Criminology and Criminal Justice, University of South Florida, Tampa. She and her research team graciously agreed to allow us to use portions of her ground breaking research in the burglary chapter. This research has been widely recognized, including the Excellence in Law Enforcement Research from the International Association of Chiefs of Police.

Ross Gardner reviewed the new section of forensic mapping and made helpful suggestions, as did Captain John P. Slater (retired), Training Director, National Institute for Truth Verification with respect to the CVSA II System. Special Agent, Joe Navarro, FBI (retired) was kind enough to provide us with most of the information discussing the detection of deception. Chief Jack Lumpkin and Sgt. David Leedahl, Athens Clarke County (Georgia) Police Department; Chief Dwayne Orrick, Cordele (Georgia) Police Department; Chief Rick Boren, Lt. Ronnie Griffin, and Sgt. Doug Shafer, Columbus (Georgia) Police Department; Major Tolbert and Lt. Zapal, Savannah Police Department; Bob Hopkins, Hillsborough County, Florida, Sheriff's Office gave us information to strengthen the section on follow-up investigations; Commander Michael Frazier, Phoenix, Arizona, Police Department, was helpful with information on arson and explosives, as were Chief Richard Pennington and Officer R. Bonelli from the New Orleans Police Department; Chief Lee Donahue and Major William Gulledge, Honolulu, Hawaii, Police Department; Kenneth V. Lanning, Supervising Special Agent of the Federal Bureau of Investigation and the National Center for Missing and Exploited Children allowed us to reprint in Chapter 11 ("Crimes against Children") from his previously published material on the topics of child molestation and child pornography. Major Andy Garrison and Frank Broadrick, Northeast Georgia Police Academy, reviewed the chapter on report writing and made good suggestions for its revision. Steven Gottlieb, executive director of the Alpha Group Center for Crime and Intelligence Analyst Training, allowed us to adopt portions of his textbook to explain the critical role of crime analysis in law enforcement investigations. Ron French of the Ecorse, Michigan, Fire Department provided updated commentary on where and how fires start, as well as on fire setting and related mechanisms. Leigh Herbst from the University of Nebraska helped with the new chapter-opening and closing material.

Chief Robert Davis, Lt. Rick Martinez, and Police Artist Gil Zamora, San Jose California Police Department, provided photographs for the robbery chapter. Lt. Anthony Traina, Paterson (NJ) Police Department, provided information and a photograph on using street surveillance cameras to prevent street robberies.

Gene Lazarus, Florida State Fire College, Ocala, and Steve Mraz, formerly with the Pinellas County, Florida, Fire Academy, reviewed and contributed to the arson chapter. Bob Quinn, Tom Costigan, Mike Rendina, Jim Wilder, and Richard Frank, presently or formerly with the Drug Enforcement Administration. Richard Souviron, Chief Forensic Odontologist, Dade County Florida, Medical Examiners Office, was an early major contributor of material dealing with bite marks and dental evidence. Dr. Wally Graves, Medical Examiner for Lee, Henry, and Glades Counties, Florida, provided information on dental evidence. John Valor, forensic artist and photographer, provided illustrations for the dental section. Dick Williams of the FBI Crime Laboratory read the questioned-documents section and made a number of suggestions to clarify and strengthen it. Don Hampton of the Springfield, Missouri, Police Department did the same for parts of the crime scene chapter. We benefited also from the reviews and research materials provided by Jim Halligan, formerly with the Florida Department of Law Enforcement and then a professor at Florida State University's School of Criminology. He was a superb teacher and a real friend.

Special thanks to Lt. Greg Terp, commander of the Miami-Dade Auto Theft Task Force, and to some special people with the National Insurance Crime Bureau—Special Agent Lawrence "Dave" Dempsey; Regional Manager Ron Poindexter; Vice-President and General Counsel Robert H. "Bob" Mason; and Member Relations Manager Ed Sparkman.

Thanks to professor Gail Anderson of Simon Frazer University in Burnaby, B.C., Canada, for providing us with updated information on forensic entomology. Robert Aristarco, Assistant Vice President for Corporate Communications, American Re-Insurance Company in Princeton, New Jersey, allowed us to reprint material on arson investigation published by his company. Linda Brown and Robyn Royall of Help A Child, Inc. and SAVE (Sexual Assault Victim Examination Program) in Pinellas Park, Florida, provided us with all the material they use to collect the physical evidence of sexual assault cases. Dave Crosbie of the Burnsville Minnesota Fire Department provided us with photos for the "Arson and Explosives" chapter. Michael Dorn of Dorn's, Inc. provided us with current information on crimes in schools. Dr. Thomas B. Kelley of Florida State University in Panama City (Department of Criminology and Criminal Justice) provided us with both narrative information on underwater crime scene investigation and photographs. Debbie Lewis, Records Custodian, William A. Pellan, Director of Forensic Investigations in Pasco and Pinellas Counties, Largo, Florida, and John R. Thogmartin, M.D. provided numerous photographs for Chapter 9 ("Injury and Death Investigations") and Chapter 10 ("Sex-Related Offenses"). Sergeant Jim Markey of the Sex Crimes Unit of the Phoenix, Arizona, Police Department supplied us with information on how to reopen cold case sex crimes; he also provided us with a photograph. Robert Parker, Director, and Major Raul M. Ubieta, Miami-Dade (Florida) Police Department, supplied us with their agency's Robbery Standard Operating Procedure along with model form letters sent to robbery victims. Greg C. Pauley of the Temple Terrace,

Florida, Police Department provided us with a computer-generated composite image as well as a police mug shot of a robbery suspect at the time he was arrested. Lieutenant Ted Snodgrass of the Las Vegas, Nevada, Metropolitan Police Department Robbery Section supplied us with considerable information about his agency's "Team Approach" in dealing with robbery cases. Detective David Spraggs of the Boulder, Colorado, Police Department provided us with material used in the discussion of opening a cold case homicide investigation, along with several photographs. Laurie A. Ward, Crime Scene Administrator, Laura Sheffield, Forensic Artist, and Sheriff Grady C. Judd, Jr., all of the Polk County Sheriff's Department Office in Barstow, Florida, provided us with information on the use of forensic artists to re-create images of a robbery suspect along with a picture of the suspect at the time he was arrested. Sergeant Scott Whittington of the Colorado Springs, Colorado, Police Department supplied us with a video photo of a robbery in progress. Maryellin Territo and Sal Territo devoted long hours to researching sources for the most current information relating to all facets of criminal investigation.

A special thank you is extended to Mr. Ed Hueske for his invaluable help and assistance on the Physical Evidence and Crime Laboratory chapters. His forensics expertise was instrumental in helping acquire photographs and addressing new techniques in the area. Also, a very special thanks to Ms. Jennifer Davis for her hard work, research, and assistance in developing the book. She was an important coauthor on the "Crimes against Children" chapter. Chief Jimmy Perdue, North Richland Hills, Texas Police Department; Gregory Allen and Assistant Chief Peter Pacillas, El Paso, Texas Police Department; Chief Robert Lehner, Elk Grove, California Police Department; and Chief David O. Brown, Dallas Police Department, provided opportunities within their departments for acquiring photographs and learning new techniques in the investigative process. Dr. Kall Loper has coauthored the "Computer Crime" chapter in previous editions, and some of his work was continued in this edition. Special Agent Corey Monaghan, Florida Department of Law Enforcement (Tampa Region) reviewed two important chapters in this book: Chapter 17 on Cybercrime and Chapter 11 on Crimes Against Children. His insight and remarks proved invaluable to this edition . . . Thank you Corey! Dr. David Carter, Michigan State University, Dr. Richard Holden, University of North Texas at Dallas, and Mr. Greg Smith, Institute for Law Enforcement Administration-ILEA, offered important information throughout the book. And, Dr. John Worrall, Dr. Sarah Maxwell, Dr. Tom Brunnell, and Dr. Galia Cohen, University of Texas at Dallas, all provided "valuable input, moral support, and encouragement" to Bob during the writing of this project.

We also would like to thank Sharon Ostermann for graciously and cheerfully typing up major portions of this edition. Her constructive criticism, research skills, and editing greatly improved the final product.

The book benefited from a counsel of reviewers. Thanks to:

Clare Armstrong-Seward, *Morrisville State College*
Lee Ayers, *Southern Oregon University*
Preston Baity, *Milwaukee Area Technical College*
Geriann Brandt, *Maryville University*
Tyler Brewer, *Southwestern College*
John Brooks, *University of Arkansas*
Michael Brown, *Southeast Missouri State University*
Ruben Burgos, *Milwaukee Area Technical College*
Steven Chavez, *Western New Mexico University*
Stephen D'Arcy, *California State University, Sacramento*
Gene Evans, *Camden County Community College*
Anita Bledsoe Gardner, *Cleveland Community College*
Don Haley, *Tidewater Community College*
Daniel Hebert, *Springfield Technical Community College*
Edward Jackson, *Baltimore City Community College*
William Kemper, *University of South Florida, Sarasota*
Dwayne Marshall, *Lock Haven University of PA*
Glenn McKiel, *Middlesex Community College*
Joe Morris, *Northwestern State University*
James Parlow, *Winona State University*
Dave Pauly, *Methodist University*
Scott Pray, *Muskingum College*
Cecilia Spellman-Frey, *Suffolk County Community College*
William Vizzard, *California State University, Sacramento*
Charlene Weitzeil, *Olympic College*
Donna Gaughan Wilson, *Prince George's Community College*

Finally, a few words about the hard-working people who helped make this a better book: We would like to thank our development team, ansrsource, led by editors Anne Sheroff, Reshmi Rajeesh, and Erin Guendelsberger; the team at McGraw-Hill: Portfolio Manager Jamie Laferrera, Product Developer Erika Lo, and Content Production Manager Ryan Warczynski; and finally; photo researcher Jennifer Blankenship, who found us photos and obtained permission to use them in a timely manner.

Charles R. "Mike" Swanson
Neil C. Chamelin
Leonard Territo
Robert W. Taylor

We are grateful to our colleagues from around the country who have been kind enough to contribute photographs, forms, and other figures to the text. The inclusion of such material helps ensure the relevancy and usefulness of the text for all readers in all states. For this, we are indebted to the following individuals, departments, and agencies:

Alaska

State of Alaska Scientific Crime Detection Laboratory

Arizona

Phoenix, Arizona, Police Department

California

California Bureau of Livestock Identification
Kern County, California, Sheriff's Department
Los Angeles County Sheriff's Department
Riverside County, California, Sheriff's Department
San Bernardino County, California, Sheriff's Department
San Diego County Sheriff's Department
San Jose Police Department
Santa Ana, California, Police Department
Santa Barbara County, California, Sheriff's Department

Colorado

Westminster, Colorado, Police Department

Delaware

Delaware State Police

Florida

Big Bend Bomb Disposal Team, Tallahassee, Florida
Dade County Medical Examiner Department, Miami, Florida
Florida Department of Law Enforcement
Leon County Sheriff's Department, Tallahassee, Florida
Miami-Dade Police Department
Pinellas County, Florida, Public Health Unit, Sexual Assault Victim Examination Program
Pinellas County, Florida, Sheriff's Office
Polk County Sheriff's Office
Port Orange, Florida, Police Department
St. Petersburg, Florida, Police Department
Tallahassee Regional Crime Laboratory, Florida Department of Law Enforcement
Tampa, Florida Fire Department
Tampa, Florida Police Department

Georgia

Athens-Clarke County, Georgia, Police Department
Atlanta Police Department
Cordele, Georgia, Police Department
Columbus, Georgia, Police Department
Georgia Bureau of Investigation
Savannah Police Department

Idaho

Idaho Bureau of Investigation

Illinois

Chicago Crime Laboratory
Chicago Police Department
Cook County, Illinois, Sheriff's Department
Illinois Environmental Protection Agency
Illinois State Police

Indiana

Indiana State Police

Iowa

Iowa Criminalistic Laboratory, Department of Public Safety
State Historical Society of Iowa

Kansas

Wichita, Kansas, Police Department

Kentucky

Kentucky State Police

Maine

Lewiston, Maine, Police Department

Maryland

The SANS Institute

Massachusetts

Massachusetts Environmental Police
National Fire Protection Association

Michigan

Ecorse, Michigan, Fire Department
Sterling Heights, Michigan, Police Department

Minnesota

Minneapolis, Minnesota, Police Department
Minnesota Department of Health

Missouri

Regional Criminalistics Laboratory, Metropolitan Kansas City, Missouri
Springfield, Missouri, Police Department
St. Louis County, Missouri, Police Department
St. Louis Police Department

New Jersey

New Jersey State Police
Paterson Police Department

New York

Nassau County, New York, Police Department
New York City Police Department

North Carolina
North Carolina Bureau of Investigation
SIRCHIE Fingerprint Laboratories, Inc.

Ohio
Geauga County, Ohio, Sheriff's Department

Pennsylvania
Pennsylvania State Police
Philadelphia Police Department

South Carolina
Georgetown, South Carolina, Police Department

Tennessee
Nashville Police Department
Tennessee Bureau of Investigation

Texas
Austin, Texas, Police Department
Dallas Police Department
Forensic Training and Consulting, LLC
Texas Department of Public Safety (Garland
   Crime Lab)
Texas Parks & Wildlife

Utah
Utah Department of Public Safety, Bureau of
   Forensic Sciences

Virginia
Alexandria, Virginia, Police Department
Fairfax County, Virginia, Police Department

Washington
Clark County Sheriff's Office, Vancouver, Washington

Washington, D.C.
Police Executive Research Forum
Virginia Department of Forensic Services

Wisconsin
Madison Police Department
Milwaukee County Department of Social Service

Wisconsin Crime Laboratory
Wisconsin State Police

Wyoming
Lincoln County, Wyoming, Sheriff's Office
Wyoming State Crime Laboratory
Wyoming Game and Fish Department
Wyoming State Archives and Historical Department

National & Federal Agencies
Bureau of Justice Statistics, U.S. Department of Justice
Centers for Disease Control
Chester A. Higgins, Jr., and the U.S. Department of
   Justice, Office of Justice Programs
Drug Enforcement Administration
Environmental Protection Agency
Federal Bureau of Investigation
Federal Emergency Management Agency
Immigration and Naturalization Service, Forensic
   Document Laboratory
National Automobile Theft Bureau
National Center for Missing and Exploited Children
National Drug Intelligence Center
National Institute of Justice
National Insurance Crime Bureau
National Park Service
Office of Justice Programs, National Institute of Justice
Pinkerton's Archives
U.S. Customs Service
U.S. Department of Justice
U.S. Department of the Treasury, Bureau of Alcohol,
   Tobacco, and Firearms
U.S. Forest Service
U.S. Public Health Service
U.S. Secret Service

International Agencies
London Metropolitan Police
Royal Canadian Mounted Police
Turkish National Police

CRIME SCENE DO NOT CROSS

1

THE EVOLUTION OF CRIMINAL INVESTIGATION AND FORENSIC SCIENCE

CHAPTER OBJECTIVES

1. Define "investigator."
2. Define the most fundamental purpose of investigation.
3. State four additional objectives of the investigative process.
4. Explain the importance of the Bow Street Runners.
5. Discuss the contribution of Sir Robert Peel's reform to early policing in the United States.
6. Explain the history and contributions of the Pinkerton National Detective Agency.
7. Identify the first major federal investigative agencies and their responsibilities.
8. Explain the Supreme Court's "due process revolution" and its impact on policing.
9. Discuss Bertillon's method of anthropometry.
10. Summarize the historical development of fingerprint identification.
11. Explain touch DNA.
12. Describe DNA phenotyping.

An investigator is someone who systematically gathers, documents, and evaluates evidence and information. This is accomplished through the process of investigation. The most fundamental purpose of criminal investigation and forensic science is to discover the truth. By making this purpose the cornerstone of their behavior, investigators can remain faithful to their oath of office and the accompanying ethical standards. Four additional objectives of the investigative process are to (1) establish that a crime was actually committed; (2) identify and apprehend the suspect(s); (3) recover stolen property; and (4) assist in the prosecution of the person(s) charged with the crime.

JURISDICTION

The authority of law enforcement officers is limited by such factors as the Constitution, court decisions, federal and state laws, departmental policies, and jurisdiction, which can be thought of as both a *geographic area* and the laws for which an agency has *enforcement responsibility.*

The general rule is that the *geographic jurisdiction* of police officers is limited to the area governed by their employer. Officers employed by states, counties, cities, and consolidated police agencies, follow this general pattern. Depending on the state, sheriffs' deputies and county police departments usually patrol the unincorporated portions of a county, although by contract they may also provide law enforcement services to municipalities. There is some variation across states whether Sheriff's deputies have jurisdiction outside of their home counties.

Investigations beyond the geographic boundary of an officer's employer, sometimes called the primary jurisdiction, are ordinarily conducted with the assistance of the appropriate law enforcement agency. However, some states have statutorily extended the primary jurisdiction of officers to a wider area with the authority to (1) continue investigating serious crimes originating in their primary jurisdiction, (2) make warrantless arrests, and (3) provide assistance to another law enforcement officer.

The Federal Bureau of Investigation (FBI) provides a good illustration of *enforcement responsibility.* It has primary enforcement responsibility for all federal criminal laws, except cases for which responsibility is by statute or otherwise assigned specifically to another agency. As a practical matter the enforcement responsibility of the FBI is limited to roughly 200 laws.

CRIMINAL INVESTIGATION AND FORENSIC SCIENCE

For present purposes, the roots of criminal investigation can be traced back to England in the eighteenth century, a period marked by significant social, political, and economic changes. These changes were important to the development of the first modern detective force, the **Bow Street Runners.** In addition, London was the home of the first police reformer, Robert Peel. Both of these factors contributed to the subsequent development of police organizations and criminal investigation in the United States.

Forensic science draws from diverse disciplines, such as geology, physics, chemistry, biology, and mathematics, to study physical evidence related to crime. If it is suspected that a person has died from poisoning, for example, a toxicologist, who specializes in identifying poisons and their physiological effects on humans and animals, can assist in the investigation. Experts in other areas, such as botany, forensic pathology, entomology, and archaeology, may also provide helpful information to criminal investigators.

Over hundreds of years many people have made contributions to the fields of criminal investigation and forensic science. To recognize all of them is beyond the scope of this chapter and requires setting some limits. This chapter presents a brief history of criminal investigation and forensic science. Many volumes have been written about these entwined topics, but the space that can be devoted to them here is limited. However, sufficient broad perspectives and supporting details are provided in this chapter to enable readers intrigued by these subjects to independently pursue their interests.

THE EVOLUTION OF CRIMINAL INVESTIGATION

THE IMPACT OF THE AGRICULTURAL AND INDUSTRIAL REVOLUTIONS

During the eighteenth century, two events—an agricultural revolution and an industrial revolution—began a process of change that profoundly affected how police services were delivered and investigations were conducted. Improved agricultural methods, such as the introduction in 1730 of Charles Townshend's crop rotation system and Jethro Tull's four-bladed plow, gave England increased agricultural productivity in the first half of the eighteenth century.[1] Improvements in agriculture were essential preconditions to the Industrial Revolution in the second half of the eighteenth century, because they freed people from farm work for city jobs. As the population of England's cities grew, slums also expanded, crime increased, and disorders became more frequent. Consequently, public demands for government to control crime grew louder.

THE FIELDINGS: CRIME INFORMATION AND THE BOW STREET RUNNERS

In 1748, **Henry Fielding** (Figure 1-1) became chief magistrate of Bow Street and set out to improve the administration of justice. In 1750, he established a small group of volunteer, non-uniformed home owners to "take thieves." Known as the **"Bow Street Runners,"** these Londoners hurried to the scenes of reported crimes and began investigations, thus becoming the first modern detective force.

QUICK FACTS

Henry Fielding

Although Fielding began professional life as a playwright, *The History of Tom Jones, A Foundling* earned him recognition as the "father of the English novel." In later life he suffered greatly from gout and traveled to Portugal hoping the sunshine would give him some relief. However, Fielding died 9 days after he arrived and is buried in the British section of the Lisbon cemetery.

▲ **FIGURE 1-1 Henry Fielding**
Educated at Eton College and later a barrister, Henry Fielding became the innovative magistrate at Bow Street. In a time when magistrates were not paid and made their living from fines and bribes, Fielding conducted his affairs in an exemplary manner. (©Chronicle/Alamy)

By 1752, Fielding began publishing *The Covent Garden Journal* as a means of circulating the descriptions of wanted persons. On his death in 1754, Henry Fielding was succeeded by his blind half-brother, **John Fielding,** who carried on Henry's ideas for another 25 years.[2] Under John Fielding, Bow Street became a clearinghouse for information on crime, and by 1785 at least four of the Bow Street Runners were no longer volunteers but paid government detectives.[3]

THE METROPOLITAN POLICE ACT OF 1829

In 1816, 1818, and again in 1822, England's Parliament rejected proposals for a centralized professional police force for London as different political philosophies clashed. One group argued that such a force was a direct threat to personal liberty. The other group—composed of reformers such as Jeremy Bentham and Patrick Colquhoun—argued that the absence, rather than the presence, of social control was the greater danger to personal liberty. Finally, in 1829, owing in large measure to the efforts of **Sir Robert Peel,** Parliament passed the **Metropolitan Police Act,** which created a metropolitan police force for London. Police headquarters became known as "Scotland Yard," because the building formerly had housed Scottish royalty. Police constables were referred to as **"Bobbies,"** a play on Peel's first name.[4]

Because French citizens had experienced oppression under centralized police, the British public was suspicious of, and at times even hostile to, the new force. In response to the high standards set for the police force, there were 5,000 dismissals and 6,000 forced resignations from the force during the first three years of operations.[5] This record was a clear indication to the public that police administrators were requiring officers to maintain high standards of conduct. Within a few years, the London Metropolitan Police had won a reputation for fairness, and it became the international model of professional policing (Figure 1-2).

Despite the growing popularity of the uniformed Bobbies, however, there was fear that the use of **"police spies"**—detectives in plain clothes—would reduce civil liberties.

> ### QUICK FACTS
>
> **Sir Robert Peel**
>
> Peel was a major figure of his time. Twice, he served as England's Prime Minister and also championed limitations on how many hours per day that women and children could be required to work. Peel died from injuries caused by the horse he was riding falling on him.

In the years immediately following 1829, some Metropolitan Police constables were temporarily relieved from patrolling in uniform to investigate crimes on their beats.[6] As the distinction between the use of uniformed constables to prevent crime and the use of plainclothes detectives for investigation and surveillance became clear, the public became uneasy. Illustratively, in 1833, a **Sergeant Popay** was dismissed following a parliamentary investigation that revealed that he had infiltrated a radical group, acquired a leadership position, and argued for the use of violence. In 1842, a regular detective branch was opened at **Scotland Yard** (Figure 1-3), superseding the Bow Street force.[7] Initially, the detective force was limited to no more than

▲ FIGURE 1-3   New Scotland Yard in 2016
Concerns about annual operating costs and the security of their current building, along with the desire to more easily use technologies, caused the London Metropolitan Police to seek a new facility. The Curtis Green Building was selected. Although completed in 1940, it was redesigned for "Metro" and occupied in 2016. It will continue to be known as New Scotland Yard.
(Courtesy of Allford Hall Monaghan Morris LLC)

16 investigators, and its operations were restricted because of a distrust of "clandestine methods."[8]

AMERICAN INITIATIVES

The success of Peel's reform in England did not go unnoticed in the United States. **Stephen Girard (1750–1831)** bequeathed $33,190 to Philadelphia to develop a competent police force. In 1833, Philadelphia passed an ordinance creating America's first paid, daylight police force. Although the ordinance was repealed just three years later, the concept of a paid police force would reappear as American cities staggered under the burdens of tremendous population growth, poverty, and massive crime. In 1836 New York City rejected the notion of a police force organized along the lines advocated by Peel. The committee studying the idea concluded it was better in emergencies to rely on citizens than "despotic governments."[9]

▶ FIGURE 1-2
London Metropolitan Police Officers, C. 1850
London Metropolitan Police officers standing outside of Catford Police Station in Southeast London. Their "stovepipe" hats with flat crowns were popular in that era. Their uniforms are trimmed with brightly polished buttons and belt buckles, giving them a disciplined and confident appearance.
(©Chronicle/Alamy)

▲ **FIGURE 1-4**
An 1887 New York Police Department Patrol Wagon.
It is unclear whether officers are (1) being dropped off at the beginning of a shift or picked up at its end, (2) patrolling an area in the manner depicted, or (3) responding to a large event.
(©Bettmann/Getty Images)

Thus, before the mid-1800s, few American cities had police service, and those that existed were inadequate. Many cities had paid police departments only at night or treated day and night police services as entirely separate organizations. In 1844 the New York state legislature created the first unified police force in the country, although New York City did not actually implement the measure until a year later. Other cities rapidly followed New York's lead: Chicago in 1851, New Orleans and Cincinnati in 1852, and Baltimore and Newark in 1857. By 1880 virtually every major American city had a police force based on England's Peelian reforms of 1829 and pioneered in this country by New York City (Figure 1-4).

QUICK FACTS

Stephen Girard as Patriot

In 1776, Frenchman Stephen Girard couldn't get past the British blockage of New York City's harbor. Instead, he sailed up the Delaware River to Philadelphia, just as Thomas Jefferson was putting the finishing touches on the Declaration of Independence. Nearly immediately, Girard supported the revolution and became an American citizen two years later. During the War of 1812 with Great Britain he personally loaned the new cash-poor government $8 million to keep it functioning.

If one of the problems of the London Metropolitan Police had been getting the public to accept some constables' working out of uniform as detectives, in the United States the problem was getting the police to wear uniforms in the first place. American officers believed that a uniform made them easy targets for public harassment and made them look like servants. Only after the Civil War did the wearing of a uniform—invariably Union blue—become widely accepted by American police officers.

PINKERTON'S NATIONAL DETECTIVE AGENCY

America needed reliable detectives for several reasons: (1) graft and corruption were common among America's big-city police officers; (2) the jurisdiction of sheriffs' offices and municipal officers was limited; and (3) there was little information sharing by law enforcement agencies. Thus, offenders often fled from one jurisdiction to another with impunity. Information sharing has vastly improved in the last 150 years but is an area that still requires further development.

In 1846, seeing the need for reliable investigators, two former St. Louis police officers formed the first recorded private detective agency.[10] However, the major private detective agency of the nineteenth century was formed by **Allan Pinkerton** (1819–1884, Figure 1-5). In 1850, after working as a Chicago detective and a U.S. mail agent,[11] Pinkerton formed a private detective agency with attorney Edward Rucker.[12]

The Pinkertons enjoyed such enormous success in the United States and throughout the world that some people thought "Pinkerton" was a nickname for any American government detective.[13]

The list of achievements by Pinkerton is impressive. Pinkerton reportedly discovered and foiled an assassination attempt on President elect Lincoln in Baltimore.[14]

At the outbreak of the Civil War in 1861, Pinkerton organized a Secret Service Division within the army (not to be confused with the U.S. Secret Service) and worked closely with General McClellan (Figure 1-6).[15] He infiltrated Confederate lines in disguise on several occasions and usually functioned as a military analyst.[16] Following the Civil War, the Pinkertons were primarily

We never sleep

▲ **FIGURE 1-5**
The Pinkerton National Detective Agency Logo
Pinkerton's trademark was an open eye above the slogan "We never sleep."[17] The trademark gave rise to the use of the term "private eye" in reference to any private investigator.[18]
("We Never Sleep", "Pinkerton National Detective Agency" and the "open eye" logo are trademarks of Pinkerton Consulting and Investigations, Inc. and are used by permission. All other rights are reserved.)

▲ **FIGURE 1-6 Pinkerton at work**
Allan Pinkerton, President Lincoln, and General McClellan at Antietam, Maryland, about October 3, 1862. Born in Scotland, Allan Pinkerton was the son of a police sergeant. He found employment as a barrel maker and advanced to supervisor. At the same time, this red-headed, strong-willed man advocated more voice in government for ordinary people, a position that resulted in him becoming a wanted man. Narrowly avoiding arrest on his wedding day, Pinkerton and his wife fled to America, surviving a shipwreck while en route. He started a successful barrel-making company. While owner of that business, his initiative led to the arrest of counterfeiters. This gave him an appetite for police work, his father's profession, and changed his life and American policing forever. (Source: Prints & Photographs Division, Library of Congress, LC-B8171-7949)

▲ **FIGURE 1-7 Butch Cassidy's Pinkerton record**
Note the "P.N.D.A." initials on the first line, which stand for Pinkerton National Detective Agency. Pinkerton agents were highly successful in combating the bank and train robbers of the Old West, such as the Hole in the Wall gang, so named because of the small opening through rocky walls that led to the valley in Johnson County, Wyoming, used as their hideout. As many as 40 bandits may have lived there in six cabins. Butch Cassidy and the Sun Dance Kid were both members of the Hole in the Wall gang at various times. ("We Never Sleep", "Pinkerton National Detective Agency" and the "open eye" logo are trademarks of Pinkerton Consulting and Investigations, Inc. and are used by permission. All other rights are reserved.)

engaged in two broad areas: (1) controlling a discontented working class, which was pushing for better wages and working conditions, and (2) pursuing bank and railroad robbers.[19]

Unrestricted by jurisdictional limits, Pinkerton agents roamed far and wide pursuing lawbreakers. In a violent time, they sometimes used harsh and unwise methods. As an illustration, suspecting that they had found the hideout of Jesse James's gang, Pinkerton agents lobbed in a 32-pound bomb, killing a boy and injuring a woman.[20]

Pinkerton understood the importance of information, records, and publicity and made good use of all of them (Figure 1-7). For example, in 1868, Pinkerton agent Dick Winscott took on the Reno gang. Winscott located Fred and John Reno and, after a drinking bout, persuaded them to let him photograph them.[21] He sent the photographs to Pinkerton files, and within a year the Reno gang was smashed.[22] Pinkerton also collected photographs of jewel thieves and other types of criminals and photographed horses to prevent illegal substitutions before races.[23] The Pinkertons also pushed Butch Cassidy (Robert Parker) and the Sun Dance Kid (Harry Longabaugh) into leaving the United States for South America, where they were reportedly killed by Bolivian soldiers at San Vincente in 1909 (Figure 1-7.) Because of their better-known antilabor activities, the Pinkertons' other work often is overlooked. But they were the only consistently competent detectives available in this country for over 50 years[24] and provided a good model for government detectives.

THE EMERGENCE OF MUNICIPAL DETECTIVES

As early as 1845 New York City had 800 plainclothes officers,[25] although not until 1857 were the police authorized to designate 20 patrol officers as detectives.[26] In November 1857 the New York City Police Department set up a **rogues' gallery** (Figure 1-8)—photographs of known offenders arranged by criminal specialty and height—and by June 1858, it had over 700 photographs for detectives to study so that they might recognize criminals on the street.[27]

Photographs from rogues' galleries of that era reveal that some offenders grimaced, puffed their cheeks, rolled their eyes, and otherwise tried to distort their appearance to lessen the chance of later recognition.

To assist detectives, in 1884 Chicago established this country's first municipal Criminal Identification Bureau.[28] The Atlanta Police Department's Detective Bureau was organized in 1885 with a staff of one captain, one sergeant, and eight detectives.[29] In 1886 Thomas Byrnes, the dynamic chief detective of New York City, published *Professional Criminals in America,* which included pictures, descriptions, and the methods of all criminals known to him.[30] Byrnes thereby contributed to information sharing among police departments. To supplement the rogues' gallery, Byrnes instituted the **Mulberry Street Morning Parade.** At 9 o'clock every morning, all criminals arrested in the past 24 hours were marched before his detectives, who were expected to make notes and to recognize the criminals later.[31]

BOX 1-1 | THOMAS BYRNES, THE "THE THIRD DEGREE," WEALTH, AND RESIGNATION

Byrnes was very successful and heavy handed. He allegedly coined the term "the third degree" to describe his harsh methods when questioning suspects. Byrnes became Chief of the New York City Police Department (NYPD) and was later forced from office by future president "Teddy" Roosevelt, a reformer police commissioner, amid whispers of corruption. Although nothing was ever proved, Byrnes did become a wealthy man while serving on the NYPD.

◄FIGURE 1-8
NYPD rogues' gallery
Uniformed officers of the New York City Police Department maintaining a rogues' gallery in the detective bureau, circa 1896. Police departments have used rogues' galleries since the late 1850s. (Source: George Granthan Bain Collection, Prints & Photographs Division, Library of Congress, LC-USZ62-90825)

FEDERAL AND STATE DEVELOPMENTS

From its earliest days, the federal government employed investigators to detect revenue violations, but their responsibilities were narrow and their numbers few.[32] In 1865 Congress created the U.S. Secret Service to combat counterfeiting. In 1903—two years after President McKinley was assassinated by Leon Czolgosz in Buffalo—the previously informal arrangement of guarding the president was made a permanent Secret Service responsibility.[33]

In 1905 the California Bureau of Criminal Identification was set up to share information about criminal activity, and Pennsylvania governor Samuel Pennypacker signed legislation creating a state police force. Widely regarded then by labor as "strikebusters on management's side," (Figure 1-9), the Pennsylvania State Police nevertheless was the prototype for modern state police organizations. New York and Michigan in 1917 and Delaware in 1919 adopted the state police concept. Since then, state police forces have assumed the function of providing local police with help in investigations.

Although Virginia, Kentucky, and Arkansas have a State Police, there are none in the deep South. To a large degree, their use in that area has been foiled by politically potent sheriffs seeking to maintain autonomy.

Where State Police agencies do not exist, a common arrangement is to have a department that focuses primarily on traffic enforcement and another for criminal investigation—for example, in Alabama, Florida, Georgia, Mississippi, and North Carolina there are both state highway patrol and non-uniformed state investigation agencies. In such arrangements the crime laboratory may be a separate department or part of the state investigative agency. Similarly, casino gaming enforcement may be a function of a state police agency or a state gaming commission.

After Prohibition was adopted nationally in 1920, the Bureau of Internal Revenue was responsible for its enforcement. Eventually the ranks of the bureau's agents swelled to a massive 4,000.[34] Because the Bureau of Internal Revenue was lodged in the Department of the Treasury, these federal agents were referred to as T-men.

In 1908 U.S. Attorney General Charles Bonaparte created the embryo of what was later to become the Federal Bureau of Investigation (FBI) when he ordered that investigations were to be handled by a special group. In 1924 J. Edgar Hoover (1895–1972) assumed leadership of the Bureau of Investigation; 11 years later Congress passed a measure giving the FBI its present designation. Hoover served as its director until his death in 1972.

When Prohibition was repealed by the Eighteenth Amendment to the U.S. Constitution in 1933, many former bootleggers and other criminals turned to bank robbery and kidnapping.[35] During the Depression, some people saw John Dillinger, "Pretty Boy" Floyd, and Bonnie and Clyde (Figures 1-10 and 1-11) "as plain folks" and did not grieve over a bank robbery or the kidnapping of a millionaire.[36] Given the restricted roles of other federal investigative agencies, it became the FBI's role to deal with these criminals.

▲ FIGURE 1-10   Bonnie Parker
Texas-born Bonnie Parker (1910–1934) was part of the murderous Barrow gang, which robbed and murdered its way across Oklahoma, Missouri, Texas, and New Mexico. In 1930, she smuggled a gun into the Waco (Texas) County Jail, helping Clyde Barrow and a companion to escape. From 1932 until 1934, Bonnie and Clyde left a deadly trail before they were stopped. (Source: Federal Bureau of Investigation)

▲ FIGURE 1-9   Arrest of a striking union man
In Pittsburgh on September 22, 1919, Pennsylvania State Police arrest a striking union man. The Pinkertons and State Police earned the enduring anger of unionists, who saw them as willing tools of the owners. By January 1920, the strike was over.
(Source: George Granthan Bain Collection, Prints & Photographs Division, Library of Congress, LC-USZ62-23690)

▲ FIGURE 1-11   Clyde Barrow

Clyde Barrow (1909-1934) was captured after his escape from the Waco County Jail and served two years in prison. Upon his release, he and Bonnie began their rampage. Outside of Black Lake, Louisiana, they were killed by law enforcement officers who had pursued them tirelessly. (Source: Federal Bureau of Investigation)

The Harrison Act (1914) made the distribution of nonmedical drugs a federal crime. Enforcement responsibility was initially given to the Internal Revenue Service, although by 1930 a separate Federal Bureau of Narcotics (FBN) was established in the Treasury Department. In 1949 a federal commission noted that federal narcotics enforcement was fragmented among several agencies, including the Border Patrol and Customs, resulting in duplication of effort and other ills. In 1968 some consolidation of effort was achieved with the creation of the Bureau of Narcotics and Dangerous Drugs (BNDD) in the Department of Justice, and in 1973, with the creation of its successor, the **Drug Enforcement Administration (DEA).**

Today the DEA devotes many of its resources to fighting international drug traffic. Like the FBI, the DEA trains state and local police in investigative work. The training focuses on recognition of illegal drugs, control of drug purchases, surveillance methods, and handling of informants.

In 2002 several federal agencies were consolidated to form Immigration and Customs Enforcement (ICE) in the Department of Homeland Security (DHS).

THE POLICE AND THE U.S. SUPREME COURT

As the highest court in this country, the Supreme Court is obligated to review cases and to make decisions that often have considerable impact. From 1961 to 1966, a period known as the "due process revolution," the Supreme Court became unusually active in hearing cases involving the rights of criminal suspects and defendants. Its decisions focused on two vital areas: (1) search and seizure and (2) the right to legal representation. Among those cases was *Miranda* v. *Arizona* (1966), which established the well-known "Miranda rights." *Miranda* and other decisions infuriated the police, who felt that the Supreme Court had "tied their hands."

So what did the due process revolution and subsequent Supreme Court decisions really change? Questionable and improper police procedures and tactics were greatly reduced. In turn, this created the need to develop new procedures and

Under Hoover, who understood the importance and uses of information, records, and publicity as well as Allan Pinkerton had, the FBI became known for investigative efficiency. In 1932, the FBI established a crime laboratory and made its services available free to state and local police (Figure 1-12). In 1935 it started the **National Academy,** a training course for state and local police. In 1967 the **National Crime Information Center (NCIC)** was made operational by the FBI, providing data on wanted persons and property stolen from all 50 states. Altogether, these developments gave the FBI considerable influence over law enforcement throughout the country. Although some people argue that such federal influence is undesirable, others point out that Hoover and the FBI strengthened police practices in this country, from keeping crime statistics to improving investigation.

BOX 1-2 | NEW BUILDING FOR FBI HEADQUARTERS

The current FBI Headquarters in Washington, D.C., was completed in 1974 at a cost of $126,108,000. In 2016, the location for a new headquarters was narrowed to three sites, all outside of the District. Whichever site is selected would cause traffic problems.

The federal General Services Administration (GSA) proposed to trade the existing headquarters for construction of the new one or payment of up to $1.8 billion. The current headquarters is inadequate for current staff, the use of advanced technologies, and it has security problems.

In the end, the project was killed because of the proposed cost. It appears that a FBI new headquarters building is not on the near horizon.

▶ **FIGURE 1-12**
FBI crime laboratory
In 2003 the FBI occupied its 463,000 square foot state-of-the-art crime laboratory, which cost $130 million.
(©Charles Dharapak/AP Images)

tactics and to make sure that officers were well trained in their uses. To no small extent, this cycle has hastened the continuing professionalization of the police while also asserting the principle that the action of police officers anywhere may be subject to close scrutiny by the Supreme Court.

HISTORICAL MILESTONES OF FORENSIC SCIENCE

Criminalistics or forensic science is the use of knowledge of natural and physical sciences and scientific techniques to answer questions of importance to administrative, civil, and criminal law. The origins of criminalistics or forensic science are largely European. The first major book describing the application of scientific disciplines to criminal investigation was written in 1893 by **Hans Gross,** a public prosecutor and later a judge from Graz, Austria.[37] Translated into English in 1906 under the title *Criminal Investigation,* it remains highly respected today as the seminal work in the field.

The Frenchman **Edmond Locard** established the first forensic laboratory in Lyon in 1910. All crime scenes are searched on the basis of Locard's exchange principle, which asserts that when perpetrators come into contact with the scene, they will leave something of themselves and take away something from the scene, for example, hairs and fibers. Expressed somewhat differently, Locard's exchange principle states that there is something to be found. He is also recognized as the father of poreoscopy, the study of pores and for advocating that if there were 12 points of agreement between two compared fingerprints the identity was certain.

Forensic science enjoys periods of stability, but on the whole it is dynamic and in constant progress. To illustrate this principle of dynamic change, the histories of two commonly used services—traditional methods of personal identification and firearms identification—are traced in the sections that follow.

THREE HISTORICAL BIOMETRIC METHODS OF PERSONAL IDENTIFICATION

In the early 1900s, biometry and **biometrics** referred to methods of analyzing biological data, "Biometrics" is derived from the Greek and means life measurement. In forensic science there are three historical biometric approaches to establish individual identity: (1) anthropometry, (2) dactylography, and (3) deoxyribonucleic acid (DNA) typing. The first was relatively short lived. The second, dactylography, or finger print identification, remains in use today throughout the world. The third, DNA, is a relative youngster, approaching 40 years of age. Newer approaches to biometric-based individual identification are discussed in a subsequent section.

Anthropometry

Anthropometry was developed by **Alphonse Bertillon** (1853–1914), who is rightly regarded as the father of criminal identification (Figure 1-13). The first method of criminal identification that was thought to be reliable, **anthropometry** "was based on the fact that every human being differs from every other one in the exact measurements of their body, and that the sum of these measurements yields a characteristic formula for each individual."[38] Figure 1-14 depicts a New York City police detective taking one type of measurement used in the "Bertillon system."

QUICK FACTS

Anthropometry

The root words for Anethropometry come from the Greek words for "human" and "measuring of."

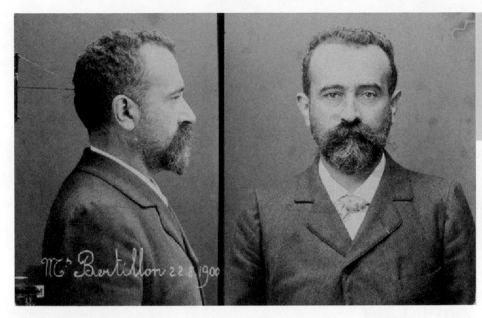

◀**FIGURE 1-13 Bertillon**
Alphonse Bertillon (1853–1914), the father of personal identification. In 1882, he began using his system on those incarcerated in Paris's Palais de Justice. (Source: https://commons.wikimedia. org/wiki/File:Bertillon_selfportrait.jpg)

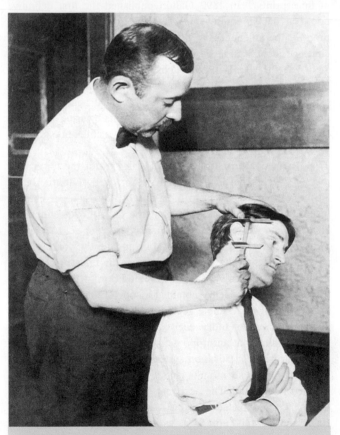

▲ **FIGURE 1-14 Taking a Bertillon measurement**
A New York City Police detective taking a Bertillon measurement of the right ear, one of the 11 measurements that made up anthropometry. This photograph was taken around 1896. Note in this photo and the one that immediately follows that the right ear is consistently part of the measurements made. (Source: George Granthan Bain Collection, Prints & Photographs Division, Library of Congress, LC-USZ62-50069)

There was little in Alphonse Bertillon's early life to suggest that he would later make significant contributions. He was the grandson of a well-known naturalist and mathematician and the son of a distinguished French physician and statistician, who was also the vice president of the Anthropological Society of Paris.[39] Despite the advantages Bertillon had, he failed in a number of jobs. He was, therefore, able to obtain only a minor position in 1879, filing cards on criminals for the Paris police, because of his father's good connections.[40] The cards described criminals so vaguely that they might have fit almost anyone: "stature: average . . . face: ordinary."[41]

Bertillon wondered why so many resources were wasted on a useless system of identifying criminals.[42] He began comparing photographs of criminals and taking measurements of those who had been arrested.[43] Bertillon concluded that if 11 physical measurements of a person were taken, the chances of finding another person with the same 11 measurements were 4,191,304 to 1.[44] His report outlining his criminal identification system was not warmly received. After reading it, the chief said "your report sounds like a joke."[45]

Yet in 1883 the "joke" received worldwide attention, because within 90 days of its implementation on an experimental basis, Bertillon correctly made his first criminal identification. Soon, almost all European countries adopted Bertillon's system of anthropometry. In 1888 Bertillon's fertile mind produced yet another innovation, the *portrait parlé* or "speaking picture," which combines full-face and profile photographs of each criminal with his or her exact body measurements and other descriptive data onto a single card (Figure 1-15).

After the turn of the century, many countries abandoned anthropometry and adopted the simpler and more reliable system of fingerprints instead. Bertillon himself was not insensitive to the potential of fingerprints. In 1902, he solved the murder of Joseph Riebel when he discovered the prints of Henri Scheffer on the pane of a glass cupboard.[46] Yet Bertillon's rigid personality would not allow him to acknowledge the clear superiority of

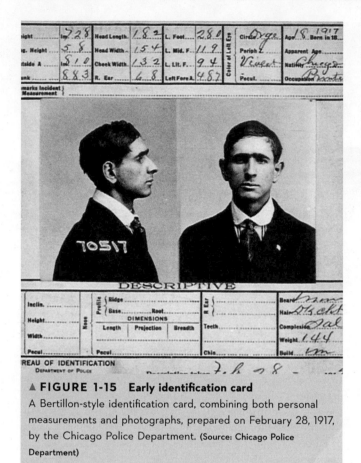

▲ **FIGURE 1-15 Early identification card**
A Bertillon-style identification card, combining both personal measurements and photographs, prepared on February 28, 1917, by the Chicago Police Department. (Source: Chicago Police Department)

dactylography to anthropometry. Even so, Bertillon's place in history is secure as the father of criminal identification.

Dactylography

Dactylography is the study of fingerprints. Fingerprints were used on contracts during China's T'ang Dynasty in the eighth century as well as on official papers in fourteenth-century Persia and seventeenth-century England.[47] In the first century, the Roman lawyer Quintilianus introduced a bloody fingerprint in a murder trial, successfully defending a child against the charge of murdering his father.[48]

In a scientific context, in 1684 in England, Dr. Nehemiah Grew first called attention to the system of pores and ridges in the hands and feet.[49] Just two years later, Marcello Malpighi made similar observations.[50] In 1823, John Perkinje, a professor at the University of Breslau, named nine standard types of fingerprint patterns and outlined a broad method of classification.[51] Despite these early stirrings, it was not until 1900 that a country, England, used dactylography as a system of criminal identification.

The Herschel-Faulds Controversy. Beginning in 1858 William Herschel, a British official in India, requested the palm prints and fingerprints of those with whom he did business, thinking that it might awe people into keeping agreements.[52] Over the next 20 years, Herschel noted from his records that the patterns of the lines on the fingerprints never changed for an individual. Excited by the prospects of applying this knowledge to the identification of criminals, Herschel wrote in 1877 to the

inspector general of the prisons of Bengal. The reply made it clear that the inspector general was not interested. Discouraged, Herschel made no further efforts to pursue his discovery. Henry Faulds, a Scottish physician at the Tsukiji Hospital in Tokyo, had been interested in fingerprints for several years before 1880. When a thief left a sooty print on a whitewashed wall, Faulds was able to tell that the person in police custody was not the thief[53] and to match another suspect's fingerprints with those on the wall.[54] Faulds reported his findings in the journal *Nature* in 1880. Herschel read the account and published a reply, claiming credit for the discovery over 20 years before. A controversy broke out that was never resolved to anyone's satisfaction. Because there was also no official interest in using fingerprints, both Herschel and Faulds were even further frustrated.

Galton's and Vucetich's Systems. In 1888 **Sir Francis Galton** (1822–1911) turned his attention to criminal identification.[55] When Galton contacted the editor of *Nature* for both Herschel's and Faulds's addresses, he was by chance sent only Herschel's. Contacted by Galton, Herschel unselfishly turned over all his files in the hopes that this revived interest would lead to practical uses of fingerprints.[56] In 1892 Galton published the first definitive book on dactylography, *Finger Prints*. It presented statistical proof of the uniqueness of fingerprints and outlined many principles of identification by fingerprints.[57] In Argentina, in 1894, **Juan Vucetich** (1858–1925) published *Dactiloscopia Comparada*, outlining his method of fingerprint classification. In 1892 a disciple of Vucetich's, Inspector Alvarez, obtained South America's first criminal conviction based on fingerprints by using Vucetich's system to convict a woman of beating her two children to death.[58]

The Henry System. The final breakthrough for the fingerprint method of personal identification was made by **Edward Henry**. At the age of 23 he went to India and by 1891 had become the inspector general of police of Nepal, the same province in which Herschel had worked some 15 years earlier.[59] Subject to many of the same influences as Herschel, but apparently working independently, Henry developed an interest in fingerprints[60] and instituted Bertillon's system with the addition of fingerprints to the cards. In 1893, Henry obtained a copy of Galton's book and began working on a simple, reliable method of classification. The governor general of India received a report from Henry in 1897 recommending that anthropometry be dropped in favor of Henry's fingerprint classification system. It was adopted throughout British India just six months later.[61] In 1900 Henry's system was adopted in England. The next year, Henry enjoyed two personal triumphs, the publication of his *Classification and Use of Finger Prints* and his appointment as assistant police commissioner of London,[62] rising to the post of commissioner two years later.

QUICK FACTS

The Assassination Attempt

In 1912, a cab driver who had been denied a license went to Edward Henry's home and shot him once in the abdomen. Henry survived, but the wound was to trouble him for the rest of his life.

Faurot and "James Jones." In 1904 New York City Detective Sergeant Joseph Faurot was sent to England to study fingerprints, becoming the first foreigner trained in the use of the Henry classification system. Upon Faurot's return, the new police commissioner told him to forget about such "scientific notions" and transferred him to walking a beat.[63] In 1906 Faurot arrested a man dressed in formal evening wear but not wearing shoes, as the man crept out of a suite in the Waldorf-Astoria Hotel.[64] Claiming to be a respectable citizen named "James Jones," the man demanded to see the British consul and threatened Faurot with nasty consequences.[65] Faurot sent the man's fingerprints to Scotland Yard[66] and got back a reply that "James Jones" was actually Daniel Nolan, who had 12 prior convictions of hotel thefts and who was wanted for burglarizing a home in England. Confronted with this evidence, Nolan confessed to several thefts in the Waldorf-Astoria and received a sentence of seven years.[67] Newspaper stories about the case advanced the use of fingerprints in this country.

The West Case. Despite the fame achieved by Faurot, the most important incident to advance the use of fingerprints in this country was the **West case** (Figure 1-16). In 1903, Will West arrived at the U.S. penitentiary at Leavenworth, Kansas. While West was being processed in through identification, a staff member said that there was already a photograph and Bertillon measurements for him on file. But a comparison of fingerprints showed that despite identical appearances and nearly identical Bertillon measurements, the identification card on file belonged to a William West, who had been in Leavenworth since 1901. The incident accelerated the recognition that fingerprints were superior to anthropometry as a system of identification.

Rivalry of Vucetich's and Henry's Systems

Vucetich's book on fingerprint classification was published in 1894, seven years before Henry's, but Henry's system has become much more widely used. However, some experts think that Vucetich's system was superior.[68] The rivalry between partisans of the two classification systems deserves attention.

In 1911 the provincial government of Buenos Aires passed a law requiring fingerprint registration for all adults subject to military service and eligible to vote.[69] By 1913 Vucetich had completed the task and decided to travel. In his travels, he was showered with decorations for his classification system. But when he visited Bertillon to pay his respects to the father of criminal identification,[70] Bertillon kept Vucetich waiting and finally opened the door just long enough to yell, "Sir, you have done me great harm," before slamming it shut again.[71] They were never to meet again. On his return to Argentina, Vucetich was to face further humiliation. When Buenos Aires planned an expansion of fingerprint registration, there were strong protests. In 1917 the Argentine government canceled registrations, seized Vucetich's records, and forbade him to continue his work.[72] In 1925 much as Bertillon had in 1914, Vucetich died a disappointed man. Although Vucetich's system is in use in South America today, Vucetich did not live long enough to see the vindication of his life's work.

In contrast, Henry became the head of what was then the world's most prestigious police organization and enjoyed the support of his government. These advantages, coupled with Vucetich's loss of support in his own country, meant that the Henry classification would become adopted virtually throughout the world.

	William West	Will West

Bertillon: Measurements (in centimeters)		
Height	177.5	178.5
Outstretched arms	188.0	187.0
Trunk	91.3	91.2
Head length	19.8	19.7
Head width	15.9	15.8
Cheek width	14.8	14.8
Right ear	6.5	6.6
Left foot	27.5	28.2
Left middle finger	12.2	12.3
Left little finger	9.6	9.7
Left forearm	50.3	50.2

▲ **FIGURE 1-16 The Two Wests**
William West had been in Leavenworth Prison since 1901; Will West arrived two years later. Given their similar appearances and nearly identical anthropometry measurements, one can understand the confusion created upon Will West's arrival. (**Source:** Federal Bureau of Investigation)

DNA

DNA as "Blueprint"

Although **deoxyribonucleic acid (DNA)** was discovered in 1868, scientists were slow to understand its role in heredity.[73] During the early 1950s, James Watson and Francis Crick deduced the structure of DNA, ushering in a new era in the study of genetics.[74] Such developments were seemingly of peripheral interest to forensic scientists until 1985, when research into the structure of the human gene by Alec Jeffreys and his colleagues at Leicester University, England, led to the discovery that portions of the DNA structure of certain genes can be as unique to individuals as are fingerprints.[75] According to Jeffreys, the chance of two persons having identical DNA patterns is between 30 billion and 100 billion to 1.[76]

In all life forms—with the exception of a few viruses—the basis for variation lies in genetic material called DNA.[77] This DNA is a chemical "blueprint" that determines everything from hair color to susceptibility to diseases[78] (Figure 1-17). In every cell of the same human that contains DNA, this blueprint is identical, whether the material is blood, tissue, spermatozoa, bone marrow, tooth pulp, saliva, or a hair root cell.[79] Thus, with the exception of identical twins, every person has distinctive DNA.

The Enderby Cases

The first use of DNA in a criminal case was in 1987 in England.[80] In 1983 Lynda Mann, age 15, was raped and murdered near the village of **Enderby.** This case was unsolved. Three years later, another 15-year-old, Dawn Ashworth, was a victim in a similar offense. Comparing the DNA "fingerprints" derived from semen recovered from both victims' bodies, investigators realized that the same man had raped and killed both women. A 17-year-old man was initially arrested and a sample of his blood was subjected to DNA analysis. This man's innocence, however, was clearly established by the lack of a DNA match, and he was released. Subsequently, all males in the Enderby area between 13 and 30 years of age were asked by the police to voluntarily provide blood samples for DNA typing. Of 5,500 men living in the area, all but two complied with the request. A man then came forward and told the police

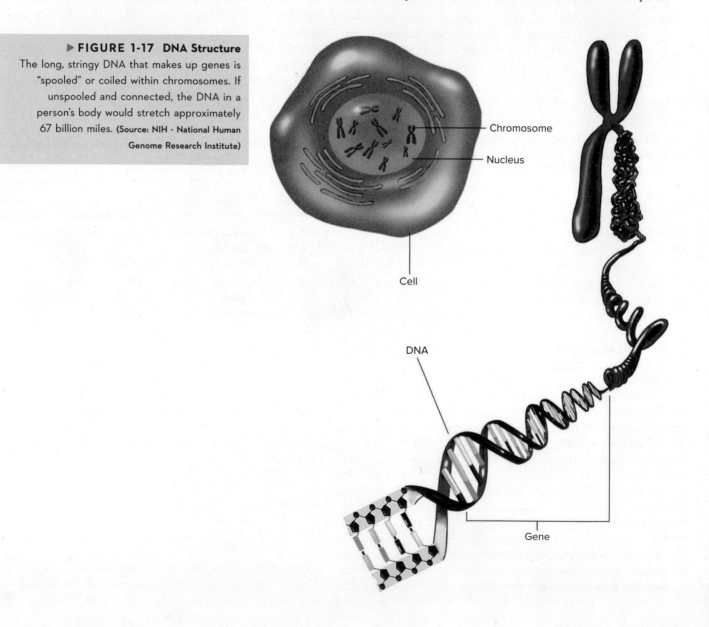

▶ **FIGURE 1-17 DNA Structure**
The long, stringy DNA that makes up genes is "spooled" or coiled within chromosomes. If unspooled and connected, the DNA in a person's body would stretch approximately 67 billion miles. (Source: NIH - National Human Genome Research Institute)

Chromosome

Nucleus

Cell

DNA

Gene

that he had used false identification to supply a blood sample in the name of a friend. This friend, Colin Pitchfork, was subsequently arrested and convicted of Ashworth's murder, with DNA evidence playing a crucial role in the prosecution's case.

The Orlando Cases

During 1986 a series of rapes and assaults occurred in Orlando, Florida, that resulted in the first use of DNA in criminal investigation cases in this country.[81] The crimes shared a common pattern: the attacks occurred after midnight, in the victims' homes, by a knife-wielding perpetrator. The perpetrator was quick to cover the eyes of the victims with a sheet or blanket, so none of them could give detailed descriptions of their assailant. During early 1987, investigators staking out a neighborhood in which it was believed the rapist might strike saw a blue 1979 Ford speeding out of the area. They followed the car for a short distance before it crashed into a utility pole while making a turn.

The suspect, Tommie Lee Andrews, lived just 3 miles from the home of the first victim, who identified him at a photographic lineup the next morning. The prosecutor's case was certainly not ironclad. The identification rested on the victim's having seen the defendant for 6 seconds in a well-lit bathroom nearly a year before the photo lineup. Standard forensic tests comparing characteristics of the suspect's blood with characteristics derived from the semen found on the victim suggested that only Andrews could have committed the offense; but 30% of the male population of the United States shared these same characteristics. In short, there was enough evidence to prosecute, but a conviction was by no means a certainty. However, on learning about the Enderby cases, the prosecutor secured DNA processing of the evidence and Andrews was convicted.

DNA Analysis

In 1988 the FBI became the first public-sector crime laboratory in the United States to accept cases for DNA analysis.[82] Private firms also offer DNA testing, including DDC Forensics, LabCorp, and NMS Labs.

Although DNA analysis of blood and other evidence from humans in criminal investigation cases is widely understood and used, there was no application of "genetic fingerprinting" to plant evidence in criminal cases until the 1992 **palo verde seedpod case** in Phoenix, Arizona.[83] Joggers found the body of a female who had been strangled. At the scene, investigators found a beeper, which led them to a suspect. The suspect admitted that (1) he had been with the victim the evening she disappeared, (2) the victim had been in his vehicle, (3) he and the victim had had sex, and (4) he and the victim had struggled. However, the suspect also maintained that the victim had run off with his beeper when he refused to help her to get drugs and that he had not been anywhere near the place the body was found in 15 years. Investigators had found two seedpods from a palo verde tree in the bed of the suspect's truck. A University of Arizona plant geneticist was asked to determine if the seedpods came from a palo verde tree at the scene. The Maricopa County Sheriff's Office collected a total of 41 samples of palo verde seedpods from the crime scene and the surrounding region. The geneticist was able to exactly match the seedpods from the bed of the

suspect's truck with those seized from the crime scene as part of the sample of 41 seedpods. Additionally, none of the 41 seedpods exactly matched another. This evidence was admitted at the trial. The defense attacked the evidence, properly arguing that the findings from a study based on 41 trees had substantial limitations and did not establish conclusively that the suspect could have gotten the seedpods only at the crime scene. However, along with other evidence, the testimony given by the geneticist had sufficient weight for the jury to convict the suspect.

FIREARMS IDENTIFICATION

Biometric-based personal identification grew as several rival systems. Anthropomorphy lost credibility; Henry's system of fingerprint identification substantially eclipsed Vucetich's, and DNA remains widely used. In contrast, firearms identification moved forward in a series of successive steps.

In the United States, the frequency of shootings has made firearms identification extremely important.[84] As a specialty within forensic science, firearms identification extends far beyond the comparison of two fired bullets. It includes identification of types of ammunition, knowledge of the design and functioning of firearms, restoration of obliterated serial numbers on weapons, and estimation of the distance between a gun's muzzle and a victim[85] when the weapon was fired.

In 1835 **Henry Goddard,** one of the last of the Bow Street Runners, made the first successful attempt to identify a murderer from a bullet recovered from the body of a victim.[86] Goddard noticed that the bullet had a distinctive blemish on it, a slight gouge. At the home of one suspect, Goddard seized a bullet mold with a defect whose location corresponded exactly to the gouge on the bullet. When confronted with this evidence, the owner of the mold confessed to the crime.[87]

Professor Lacassagne removed a bullet in 1889 from a corpse in France. On examining it closely, he found seven grooves made as the bullet passed through the barrel of a gun.[88] Shown the guns of a number of suspects, Lacassagne identified the one that could have left seven grooves. On the basis of this evidence, a man was convicted of the murder.[89] However, any number of guns manufactured at that time could have produced seven grooves. There is no way of knowing whether the right person was found guilty.[90]

In 1898 a German chemist named Paul Jeserich was given a bullet taken from the body of a man murdered near Berlin. After firing a test bullet from the defendant's revolver, Jeserich took microphotographs of the fatal and test bullets and, on the basis of the agreement between both their respective normalities and abnormalities, testified that the defendant's revolver fired the fatal bullet, contributing materially to the conviction obtained.[91]

QUICK FACTS

A Missed Opportunity

Unknowingly at the doorstep of scientific greatness, Jeserich did not pursue this discovery any further, choosing instead to return to his other interests.

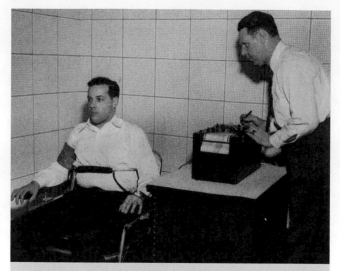

▲ FIGURE 1-18 Polygraph
In 1936 at Northwestern University, John Larson demonstrates the use of the polygraph he invented 15 years earlier.
(©Pictorial Press Ltd/Alamy)

Gradually, attention began to shift from just bullets to other aspects of firearms. In 1913 Professor Balthazard published perhaps the single most important article on firearms identification. In it, he noted that the firing pin, breechblock, extractor, and ejector all leave marks on cartridges and that these vary among different types of weapons. With World War I looming, Balthazard's article was not widely read for some years.

Calvin Goddard (1858–1946), a U.S. physician who had served in the army during World War I, is the person considered most responsible for raising firearms identification to a science and for perfecting the bullet-comparison microscope. To no small degree, Goddard's accomplishments were contributed to heavily by three other Americans—Charles Waite, John Fisher, and Phillip Gravelle—working as a team on firearms identification. In 1925, Goddard joined Waite's team and upon Waite's death a year later, Goddard became its undisputed driving force and leader.[92]

Like those of many pioneers, Waite's contributions are often overlooked. He had been interested in firearms since 1917, and from 1920 on he visited firearms manufacturers to get data on those manufactured since 1850. Because of Waite, the first significant cataloged firearms collection in this country was assembled. Nonetheless, ultimately it was Goddard who raised firearms identification to the status of a science.

OTHER EARLY CONTRIBUTORS

There are many other early contributors to the evolution of investigation and forensic science. For example, in 1910 **Albert Osborn** (1858–1946) wrote *Questioned Documents,* which is still regarded as a definitive work. **Leone Lattes** (1887–1954) developed a procedure in 1915 that permits blood typing from a dried bloodstain, a key event in forensic serology. Although more an administrator

and innovator than a criminalist, **August Vollmer** (1876–1955), through his support, helped **John Larson** produce the first workable polygraph in 1921 (Figure 1-18), Vollmer established America's first full forensic laboratory in Los Angeles in 1923.

In 1935, **Harry Soderman** and **John O'Connell** coauthored *Modern Criminal Investigation,* the standard work for the field for decades until the publication of *Crime Investigation* by **Paul Kirk** in 1953. A biochemist, educator, and criminalist, Kirk helped develop the careers of many criminalists.

THE CONTINUING EVOLUTION OF CRIMINAL INVESTIGATION AND FORENSIC SCIENCE

Science continues to provide tools for criminal investigation and forensic science, enhancing existing capabilities and creating new ones. In this section there are five topics: (1) what we know about touch DNA as it nears 20 years of use, (2) the perils of using touch DNA, (3) the new biometrics, (4) forensic phenotyping, which made its first investigative appearance in 2015, and (5) the increasing forensic interest in microbial communities.

TOUCH DNA AT 20

Despite the great usefulness innovations provide, there are often accompanying unintended side effects, an example of this is **touch DNA.** In 1997, it was established that items which a suspect handled could yield sufficient DNA for analysis. By the early 2000s, the number of crime and private labs certified to do the necessary analysis began proliferating. Touch DNA serves to exonerate some and help prosecute others. In 2008, touch DNA cleared the family of Jon Benet Ramsey in her murder. In 1996, the six-year-old child beauty pageant queen's body was found in the basement of her parents' home. Despite years of investigation the case remains unsolved.

QUICK FACTS

Understanding Touch DNA

1. Of the 400,000 skin cells lost daily, most are dead, but some will bear sweat or other properties that enable DNA analysis.
2. Touch DNA can be accumulated. If a person handles an item multiple times, the opportunity to find DNA is increased.
3. Touching other parts of the body, e.g., picking the nose, loads the finger with DNA material.
4. Touch DNA cannot determine *when* objects, such as an envelope or knife, were handled.
5. From just touch DNA analysis, it cannot be determined *how* an object was used, e.g., a stabbing motion.

6. The time it takes for touch DNA to be deposited is variable. Studies show glass, fabric, wood, wallets held for 60 seconds can leave DNA. Other studies reveal DNA can be found on plastic and cotton after being held for only 15 seconds. Older studies state longer times for transfers, up to 15 minutes.

   However, as DNA extraction techniques have become more sensitive, the time required to create transfers has dropped.

7. The action resulting in a transfer can be as simple as a handshake. There are high and low DNA skin shedders. However, a person does not consistently fall into one category or another. This may be a situational rather than a personal characteristic. For example, how recently people washed their hands reduces the likelihood of their leaving measurable touch DNA.

8. Touch DNA does not leave a visible residue and might be present on some objects for as long as two weeks outside and six weeks inside.

9. The number of suitable cells needed for analysis may be as low as 75 to 100 and some estimates are even lower.

10. Touch DNA has been found in pocket linings, shoe-strings, food, and even a victim's mouth from the tongue of the assailant.

11. Generally, touch DNA is best collected by (1) lightly moistening two swabs with sterile water and submitting one of them as a control sample, (2) gently wiping the area involved with a moistened swab, and (3) repeating the action in step 2 with a dry swab. Using only two swabs in a case with no other alternatives, the sticky portion of Post-It notes was used with good results.

12. Although touch DNA analysis costs vary, private laboratories may charge around $1,000 per analysis.[93]

Demands for touch DNA analysis quickly accumulated because a suspect could have touched many possible items at a crime scene. For a vehicle theft, where a car is subsequently abandoned and recovered, it is logical for investigators to swab the steering wheel and limited other places for touch DNA, e.g., door handles and controls for an audio system. In contrast, for the burglary of a home where all rooms are ransacked by a perpetrator looked for drugs, jewelry, money, and other valuables, investigators often must submit a large number of items for analysis.

As a result of numerous and also indiscriminate requests for touch DNA analysis, backlogs quickly grew, creating a need to set priorities. In response to this situation, crime labs developed policies that limited the conditions under which they would honor such cases; for example, they would only accept those involving violent crimes or when there was no other means of obtaining probative evidence, which could prove a major case.

THE PERILS OF TOUCH DNA

The purpose of criminal investigation and forensic science is to establish the truth. Although touch DNA is science, its use is not without perils and it is not infallible.[94] Science can be misapplied, misinterpreted, and misunderstood by investigators, jurors, and others. Touch DNA can also be accidentally transferred, resulting in wasteful misdirection of investigations and creating the potential for grievous injustices:[95]

1. In 2009, American Amanda Knox was convicted in an Italian Court of murdering her British female roommate. A key piece of evidence was a knife on the handle of which Amanda's touch DNA was found, although none of her roommate's blood was found on the blade. The knife was handled when Amanda cooked meals. After a series of court actions, Knox was finally exonerated in 2015.

2. In a 2012 California case, police arrested a homeless man, Anderson, in the murder of Kumra. Although Anderson had a police record, it did not include any violent acts. Anderson's DNA was found under the fingernails of Kumra. However, things were not as they seemingly appeared: (1) Anderson was in a hospital at the time of the murder and (2) the paramedics who earlier had brought Anderson to the hospital also later had brought Kumra to the hospital. In doing so, they inadvertently placed the oxygen-monitoring device used on Anderson on Kumra's hand, accidently creating a transfer of Anderson's DNA to Kumra.

Around 2015, secondary transfers of touch DNA garnered more attention from forensic scientists. Cale conducted experiments that began with two people shaking hands for two minutes.[96] When only one of the handshakers subsequently touched the handle of a knife, the other person's DNA was also found on it in 85% of the analyses. The great peril is that someone who was not involved in a murder and had never seen the involved gun could end up being charged.

An unreplicated 2016 study claims that it is possible to distinguish in a majority of cases between primary and secondary DNA deposits on items.[97] Presently, there is significant concern that secondary and even subsequent DNA transfers could have been a key factor in the conviction of innocent persons. Some cases are under review. In the meanwhile, the increasing forensic sensitivity to progressively smaller amounts of DNA make this a concern that cannot be easily dismissed. The takeaway for investigators is that laboratory reports should be considered in the totality of evidence and not produce a tunnel-vision fueled rush to judgment about culpability.

THE NEW BIOMETRICS

Historically, biometrics was thought of narrowly, with a tight focus on measurements limited to those taken from the body itself. **Biometrics** is now defined as the measurable and automated physiological or behavioral characteristics that can be used to verify the identity of an individual (see Table 1-1). It is

TABLE 1-1	Physiological and Behavioral Characteristics (FYI: By Swanson)	
PHYSIOLOGICAL CHARACTERISTICS	**BEHAVIORAL CHARACTERISTICS**	
1. Iris or retime	1. Signature, e.g., writing pressure	
2. Retina	2. Computer keystrokes	
3. Fingerprint, palm print, and nails	3. Voice	
4. Geometry of hands, knuckles, palms, and ears	4. Gait	
5. Vascular patterns		
6. Facial		
7. Voice		
8. DNA		
9. Odor, earlobes, sweat pores, lips, and blood vessels		

sometimes called "the new profiling." The new definition is more expansive in three ways: (1) a larger number of characteristics are being used or investigated for suitability for identification; (2) a set of behavioral characteristics has been added, although there is long-standing experience with using handwriting analysis to establish identification; and (3) automation is being used to establish individual identification.

The FBI established a Biometric Center of Excellence to explore and advance biometric technologies and capabilities.[98] Some physiological characteristics are sufficiently well established that 110 countries use one or more of them on passports.[99]

FORENSIC PHENOTYPING

A study of cold cases in Washington, D.C., revealed new information from witnesses or information from new witnesses was the most prevalent reason for a cold-case clearance.[100] However, phenotyping, a method first used in an actual criminal investigation in 2015, shows great promise as another valid reason to reopen some old cases.

Essentially, a forensic DNA phenotyping (FDP) is a twenty-first century composite sketch of a person of interest.[101] However, the image is not formed by a description from a witness, but from a person's DNA found at the scene of a crime. Where DNA analysis can lead to the individual identification of the perpetrator, **DNA phenotyping** provides a genomic-based, probabilistic estimation of the image of a person of interest. Producing this image, called a 'snapshot" by pioneering phenotyping firm Parabon NanoLabs, requires substantial databases. To illustrate, there are over 700 genetic variants linked to height, but only 15% of them helped explain variation in height from one person to another.[102]

A genotype is the actual sequence of 1.4 million nucleotides that make up the roughly 23,000 genes that constitute each individual human's unique "genetic fingerprint."[103] A phenotype is how an individual's genes combine to express themselves in an observable way[104] (Figure 1-19). FDPs can estimate the likely face shape, hair color, skin pigmentation, iris color, freckling, and adult height with accuracy rates approaching a combined 70%,[105] although one company claims a combined 80%. The ability to predict hair composition with a reasonable degree of accuracy is on the near time horizon. Gender and biogeographic ancestry, the portion of a suspect's ancestry that can be attributed to each continent, can be predicted with 100% accuracy, even with DNA from a mixed-race person. The age of a person of interest cannot presently be determined by phenotyping, so Parabon NanoLabs provides a "Snapshot" as the person might appear at two different age intervals.

There could be a reluctance to use FDP because it may appear to be a variant of racial profiling in terms of its ancestry component, which could seem to be unfairly targeting minority and immigrant populations. In addition, medical ethicists have raised concerns about misuse of the technology and people's medical records being compromised for the sake of "science." Major scientific breakthroughs will be subject to criticisms and will have to stand the test of time to overcome them. Even then, some critics will remain.

Elsewhere, the view is that with no other options, snapshots can reduce the suspect pool; for example, it can determine with 100% accuracy that the suspect does not have brown eyes or certain other features, which may productively refocus investigative effort. Snapshots are regarded as "persons of interest" and not suspects.

MICROBIAL COMMUNITIES

Microorganisms, often shortened to "microbes," are one-cell organisms so small that millions of them can fit in the eye of a needle. There may be as many as two to three billion species of microbes, such as bacteria, fungi, protozoa, and viruses. They live everywhere; microbes are in air, water, rocks, soil, plants, food, animals, and us. Some microbes need oxygen, and others do not. They thrive in the heat of deserts and the freezing cold. They are the oldest life-forms on Earth; microbe fossils 3.5 billion years old were found in Australia.[106] Some cause diseases, most are beneficial, and some are harnessed for medicine.

Life without any microbes would eliminate diseases such as tuberculosis, Ebola, malaria, ulcers, syphilis, the common cold, leprosy, pneumonia, athlete's foot, cholera, and other maladies.[107] The celebration would be short lived, however, as the negatives quickly emerged. The production of alcohol, butter, tea, coffee, tobacco, and some antibiotics would no longer be possible.[108] Dead animal and plant material wouldn't decay, eliminating the recycling of biomass. Living plant and animal food sources would be difficult to find. Human and other types of waste would accumulate. Oxygen levels would drop by 50%. Small pockets of humans might exist for decades, but long-term survival of the species would be doubtful.[109]

Forensic scientists have taken note of the ubiquitous microbes and have begun studying how they might be helpful to investigations. The most well developed inquiry is their application usefulness in determining the postmortem interval (PMI), the time after death. There are various ways to do so, for example, algor

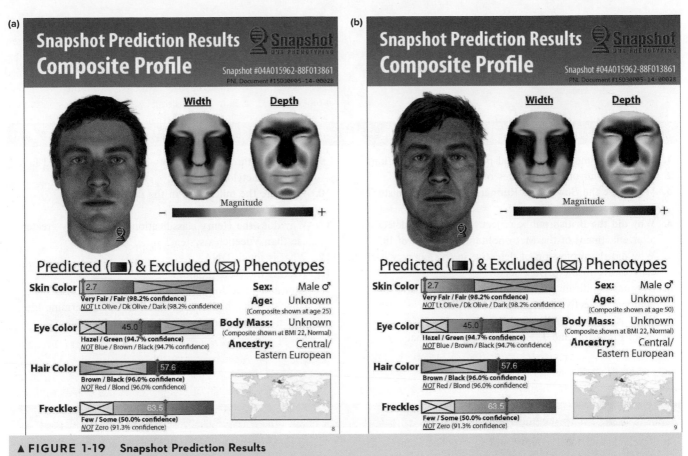

▲ FIGURE 1-19   Snapshot Prediction Results

In 1988, an eight-year-old girl was killed in Fort Wayne, Indiana. She left a friend's house and was not found until two days later in a ditch. The suspect as he may have appeared (a) in 1988 at age 25 and (b) at 50 in 2013. (©Parabon NanoLabs, Inc.)

mortis (body temperature), rigor mortis (body stiffening), livor mortis (blood pooling), and the presence of certain insects such as blowflies. However, as discussed in Chapter 9 "Injury and Death Investigations", all these ways have limitations on their utility; for example, seasonal climate variations can eliminate the possibility of using insects to determine the PMI.

In 2015, a joint study involving the University of Colorado-Boulder and the University of California–San Diego established that **microbial communities** tick along in a predictable, clocklike succession following death.[110] This characteristic allows forensic science to reliably estimate the PMI within 2 to 4 days over 25 days of decomposition. Microbial communities may also be useful in determining if a body was moved from its original resting place to another location. In the joint study, the results are reportedly not effected by types of terrain or soils. However, another study suggests that seasonal variations may affect the rate at which microbial communities progress.[111] Inquiries are also being conducted in the possibility of microbial communities on shoe soles, and articles laid down could have forensic possibilities.

KEY TERMS

anthropometry
Bertillon, Alphonse
biometrics
Bobbies
Bow Street Runners
dactylography
deoxyribonucleic acid (DNA)
Drug Enforcement Administration (DEA)
Enderby cases
Fielding, Henry

Fielding, John
forensic science
Galton, Francis
Girard, Stephen
Goddard, Calvin
Goddard, Henry
Gross, Hans
Henry, Edward
investigator
Kirk, Paul

Larson, John
Lattes, Leone
Locard, Edmond
Metropolitan Police Act (1829)
Mulberry Street Morning Parade
National Academy
National Crime Information Center (NCIC)
O'Connell, John
Osborn, Albert
palo verde seedpod case

Peel, Robert
phenotyping
Pinkerton, Allan
"police spies"

Popay, Sergeant
rogues' gallery
Scotland Yard
Soderman, Harry

Touch DNA
Vollmer, August
Vucetich, Juan
West case

REVIEW QUESTIONS

1. What is the most fundamental purpose of investigation?
2. What are four other objectives of investigation?
3. Who were the Bow Street Runners, and of what historical importance are they?
4. Why did the British public object to the use of detectives after enactment of the Metropolitan Police Act of 1829?
5. Why did the profession of detective in this country basically evolve in the private sector?
6. Of what significance is the work of Pinkerton and his National Detective Agency?
7. What is a rogues' gallery?
8. Allan Pinkerton and J. Edgar Hoover have what similarities?
9. What is anthropometry, and why was it abandoned in favor of dactylography?
10. What are the milestones in the development of dactylography?
11. Why does the Henry classification system enjoy greater use than Vucetich's system?
12. What is touch DNA?
13. What is the New Biometrics?
14. How and what does DNA Phenotyping produce?
15. How are microbial communities used to determine the post mortem Interval?

INTERNET ACTIVITIES

1. Research your local, county, and state police agencies. Do these agencies have a criminal investigation unit? Do "general investigators" investigate all types of crimes? Or, in contrast, is there investigative specialization—for example, a homicide unit? How many investigators are assigned to such units? Do officers have to meet a certain criteria to be assigned to these units? How are officers selected? Is there any history on the creation of these units?
2. Find out more about the FBI's Biometric Center of Excellence (BCOE) by visiting *www.biometriccoe.gov.*

Design Element: (crime scene tape): ©UpperCut Images/Getty Images RF

◄ Officers arrest two suspects after a brief chase in downtown Los Angeles. Both suspects were armed and wanted on separate warrants. These types of arrests are often the initial point of investigator involvement as both suspects need to be interviewed regarding their criminal activity in the area.
(©Robert Nickelsberg/Getty Images)

2

LEGAL ASPECTS OF INVESTIGATION

CHAPTER OBJECTIVES

1. Explain the historical evolution of the laws of arrest and search and seizure from the Bill of Rights through the Fourteenth Amendment.

2. Describe and diagram the flow of constitutional rights to a defendant in a federal criminal trial and a defendant in a state criminal trial.

3. Outline the requirements of a valid arrest warrant.

4. Describe whether a "John Doe" arrest warrant is ever valid, and if so, under what circumstances.

5. Define probable cause.

6. Describe the evolution of the Exclusionary Rule.

7. Explain the "Silver Platter" doctrine.

8. Describe the reasons for a search incident to a lawful arrest.

9. Explain the limitations on the search of a motor vehicle incident to an arrest.

10. Describe at least five circumstances that justify a search under exigent circumstances.

11. Define the law enforcement policy issue that determines whether an inventory search is lawful.

12. Identify the primary requirement that makes a plain view seizure lawful.

13. Describe the limitations of a stop-and-frisk encounter.

14. Explain the circumstances that would cause application of the "Fruits of the Poisonous Tree" doctrine.

All law enforcement officers, uniformed and plainclothes, conduct investigations. That is a statement of fact. There are, of course, differing concentrations of the investigative process and varying responsibilities among different units and different people.

Every law enforcement officer must have a working knowledge of the criminal laws that he or she is charged with enforcing. The greater the knowledge, the better overall job one can do as an investigator. This will become apparent throughout the remainder of this text. It will be reinforced over and over because the criminal law is the foundation on which every investigation is built.

Criminal law is divided into two major components that are interrelated yet serve different functions. The **substantive criminal law** deals with those elements that describe and define a crime. When an investigator has the needed proof to satisfy the particular elements of an offense, it can then be said that the crime did occur.

The other component of criminal law is **procedural criminal law.** It is not enough to know whether a crime has been committed. The investigator must understand what and how things need to be done with the people involved in an investigation, be it a victim, a witness, an informant, or a suspect. Thus, the procedural part of criminal law defines what can and cannot be done with, or to, people. The procedural law changes much more rapidly than does the substantive criminal law. Procedural law deals with processes of arrest, search and seizure, interrogations, confessions, admissibility of evidence, and testifying in court. Some of these topics will be discussed in other portions of this book because they are relevant to specific subject matter covered. For example, legal matters dealing with interrogations and confessions are dealt with in detail in Chapter 5, Interviewing and Interrogation. Rules regarding admissibility of evidence and testifying in court round out the book in Chapter 22, "The Trial Process and The Investigator as a Witness" because they come into play when an investigation is completed and the case is submitted for prosecution. This chapter concerns the concepts of arrest and search and seizure. But knowing the current case law on these topics is not enough. The student must also understand the historical constitutional principles that got us to where we were, where we are, and, perhaps, where we are going tomorrow.

CHAPTER OUTLINE

THE BILL OF RIGHTS AND THE STATES

An examination of constitutional history reveals that the powers yielded by the states were specifically granted for the purpose of establishing a national government. However, final ratification of the new constitution was delayed because some states wanted guarantees that individual liberties would be safeguarded from potential oppression by the newly formed government. This desire was based on the experiences of the colonists who supported the Declaration of Independence and fought the revolutionary war that won independence and created the United States of America, all of which occurred because the King of England was oppressing the colonies. The guarantees came in the form of the first ten amendments to the Constitution known as the Bill of Rights (Figure 2-1).

THE BILL OF RIGHTS

Amendment I

Congress shall make no law respecting an establishment of religion, or prohibiting the free exercise thereof; or abridging the freedom of speech, or of the press; or the right of the people peaceably to assemble, and to petition the government for a redress of grievances.

Amendment II

A well regulated militia, being necessary to the security of a free state, the right of the people to keep and bear arms, shall not be infringed.

Amendment III

No soldier shall, in time of peace be quartered in any house, without the consent of the owner, nor in time of war, but in a manner to be prescribed by law.

Amendment IV

The right of the people to be secure in their persons, houses, papers, and effects, against unreasonable searches and seizures, shall not be violated, and no warrants shall issue, but upon probable cause, supported by oath or affirmation, and particularly describing the place to be searched, and the persons or things to be seized.

Amendment V

No person shall be held to answer for a capital, or otherwise infamous crime, unless on a presentment or indictment of a grand jury, except in cases arising in the land or naval forces, or in the militia, when in actual service in time of war or public danger; nor shall any person be subject for the same offense to be twice put in jeopardy of life or limb; nor shall be compelled in any criminal case to be a witness against himself, nor be deprived of life, liberty, or property, without due process of law; nor shall private property be taken for public use, without just compensation.

Amendment VI

In all criminal prosecutions, the accused shall enjoy the right to a speedy and public trial, by an impartial jury of the state and district wherein the crime shall have been committed, which district shall have been previously ascertained by law, and to be informed of the nature and cause of the accusation; to be confronted with the witnesses against him; to have compulsory process for obtaining witnesses in his favor, and to have the assistance of counsel for his defense.

Amendment VII

In suits at common law, where the value in controversy shall exceed twenty dollars, the right of trial by jury shall be preserved, and no fact tried by a jury, shall be otherwise reexamined in any court of the United States, than according to the rules of the common law.

Amendment VIII

Excessive bail shall not be required, nor excessive fines imposed, nor cruel and unusual punishments inflicted.

Amendment IX

The enumeration in the Constitution, of certain rights, shall not be construed to deny or disparage others retained by the people.

Amendment X

The powers not delegated to the United States by the Constitution, nor prohibited by it to the states, are reserved to the states respectively, or to the people

◄FIGURE 2-1 **The Bill of Rights**
The Bill of Rights incorporates the first ten amendments to the U.S. Constitution, limiting governmental power and ensuring the protection of individual liberties.
Source: United States' Bill of Rights, I-X.

BOX 2-1 | FUNDAMENTAL FAIRNESS, DUE PROCESS, AND BRADY VIOLATIONS

In a landmark 1963 case (*Brady* v. *Maryland*),[1] the U.S. Supreme Court ruled that the suppression of any evidence by the prosecution favorable to the accused violates the premise of fundamental fairness through the due process clauses of the Fourth and Fourteenth Amendments of the Constitution. As a result, prosecutors are compelled to disclose to the defense any and all evidence that might be exculpatory for the accused—meaning any evidence that could possibly clear the suspect must be presented to the defense. Such evidence could include confessions (as in the Brady case), physical evidence, fingerprints, DNA, photographs, and the like, that conflicts with the prosecutor's evidence, and any evidence that could impeach the credibility of a prosecution witness.

More importantly, in a follow-up case, *Giglio* v. *United States* (and other Brady progeny cases),[2] the Court extended that obligation to share exculpatory information with the defendant to include information concerning the credibility of the prosecution's witnesses, including individual police officers. Police agencies must disclose to the prosecution, who must disclose to the defense, any exculpatory or impeachment evidence that demonstrates that a witness is lying about specific facts in a case or is generally unworthy of belief, including the credibility of individual police officers and/or investigators. Evidence of this nature is often referred to as "Brady material." Failing to disclose such evidence is a **"Brady" violation** that can lead to dismissal of the criminal case and civil (U.S. Code 42, Section 1983) cases brought against the individual prosecutor, the police department, and the officer for violation of the suspect's constitutional rights. Detectives often discover or are keenly aware of "Brady material" as they go about their duties investigating a case. It is imperative that detectives and investigators (and any other police officer involved in a case) realize that they have an affirmative duty to disclose any exculpatory material within their investigation and convey it to the prosecutor for their legal determination of what information must be disclosed to the defense.[3]

In providing the reason for their decision in the Brady case, the Supreme Court wrote the following key passage that clearly points to the concept of fundamental fairness guaranteed to the accused and embodied within the U.S. Constitution:

> We now hold that the suppression by the prosecution of evidence favorable to an accused upon request violates due process where the evidence is material either to guilt or to punishment, irrespective of the good faith or bad faith of the prosecution . . . Society wins not only when the guilty are convicted, but when criminal trials are fair; our system of the administration of justice suffers when any accused is treated unfairly.[4]

The Bill of Rights, however, restricts actions only by the federal government. It does not apply to, nor guarantee, the same protections from state governments. In addition, the Bill of Rights does not protect people from abuses by others who are not government officials or working on behalf of government officials. Thus, a private citizen could conduct an unreasonable search and seizure, then turn the results over to a government agency for use in court. Despite the fact that the seizing person may be criminally or civilly liable, the evidence seized could be used in court.[5]

The liberties protected by the specific clauses of the Bill of Rights are not exhaustive. One clause of the Fifth Amendment has been interpreted to leave the door open for additional protections. The **due process clause** provides: ". . . nor [shall any person] be deprived of life, liberty or property without due process of law." **Due process** is one of those concepts that has long been the subject of judicial controversy and has no universally accepted definition. The American concept of "fairness" is probably the closest one could get to an acceptable definition, in layperson terms, without burdening the effort with reams of judicial history and philosophy. Thus the Supreme Court has the latitude to interpret the Constitution in any manner it deems to be fair and just under the American judicial system.[6]

During this time period and until the last part of the nineteenth century, the federal courts could ensure fairness only in federal criminal proceedings.

EVOLUTION OF THE FOURTEENTH AMENDMENT

The Civil War was over. Slavery had been abolished. The Thirteenth, Fourteenth, and Fifteenth Amendments were all designed to guarantee the freedoms and equal protection of the laws for all citizens, especially the former slaves.

Interpretations given portions of the Fourteenth Amendment provide the foundation for much of modern criminal procedure in the United States today. The relevant portions of the Fourteenth Amendment read:

> No state shall make or enforce any law which shall abridge the privileges and immunities of citizens of the United States; nor shall any state deprive any person of life, liberty, or property, without due process of law; nor deny

any person within its jurisdiction the equal protection of the laws.

The first three words of this quote provide the cornerstone to the foundation. Until this amendment was ratified in 1868, the people of the United States had never before granted the federal government the power to tell the states what they could or could not do. This section contains the Fourteenth Amendment's due process clause. This shift in power and authority was enhanced by another part of the Fourteenth Amendment. The first clause of Section 1 of the amendment reads:

All persons born or naturalized in the United States, and subject to the jurisdiction thereof, are citizens of the United States and the state wherein they reside.

This wording creates what is commonly referred to as "dual citizenship" and gives the federal government the power to tell the states they cannot abuse the freedoms of those people—us; all of us.[7]

A few years after ratification of the Fourteenth Amendment, the United States Supreme Court was asked to determine the meaning of that amendment's due process clause. In the 1884 case of *Hurtado* v. *California*,[8] the defendant urged the Supreme Court to declare that the due process clause of the Fourteenth Amendment incorporated all the guarantees of the first eight amendments to the Bill of Rights. Hurtado was charged with a capital offense in the state court upon an Information filed by the District Attorney. He was convicted and sentenced to hang. The Fifth Amendment expressly requires that capital cases must be based on an indictment or presentment by a grand jury, but because Hurtado was being tried in a state court on a state charge, the Fifth Amendment was not applicable, as it would have been if he were being tried for a federal offense in federal court. He urged the high court to provide him the same guarantees in state court. This attempt to require carte blanche application of the first eight amendments to the states through the due process clause of the Fourteenth Amendment was rejected by a majority of the Court in this case and in many cases that followed. This attempted process became known as the "shorthand doctrine." The Supreme Court in rejecting the "shorthand doctrine" said that if the people and the states had intended for the Fourteenth Amendment to encompass the rights protected in the Bill of Rights and make them mandatorily applicable to the states, this would have been specified in the wording of the Fourteenth Amendment.[9]

Instead of adopting the "shorthand doctrine," the Supreme Court has reviewed cases on a case-by-case basis, determining whether the particular issue of the case calling into question a clause of the Bill of Rights should be made mandatorily applicable to the states through the due process clause of the Fourteenth Amendment. Although the Supreme Court rejected the quick way, the truth is, today, it doesn't matter anymore, because virtually everything in the first ten amendments has been ruled to apply to the states through the due process clause of the Fourteenth Amendment.

Let's now look at some of these processes as they have evolved.

THE FOURTH AMENDMENT

In part, the Fourth Amendment reads:

The Right of the people to be secure in their persons, houses, papers, and effects, against unreasonable searches and seizures, shall not be violated, and no warrants shall issue, but upon probable cause, supported by oath or affirmation, and particularly describing the place to be searched, and the persons or things to be seized.

It is a common misconception that search and seizure is the sole topic covered by the Fourth Amendment. However, the authority for the laws of arrest is also derived from this amendment, as is seen in the last clause that provides: "*and the persons . . . to be seized.*"[10]

By strict construction of the Fourth Amendment, the only time an arrest can be made or a search and seizure be conducted is under the authority of a warrant. However, the courts have not been that stringent in their interpretation of this amendment.

ARREST

There are a number of definitions of the term **arrest.** They range from "any interference with a person which, if not privileged, would constitute false imprisonment," to "interfering with the freedom of a person who is suspected of criminal conduct to the extent of taking him to the police station for some purpose," to "the taking of custody upon sufficient and proper evidence for the purpose of prosecution."[11] Each of these definitions is valid and depends on context. For example, what may appear to be a simple street stop or field interrogation may, in fact, constitute an arrest according to the first definition. Taking a person to the police station or sheriff's department for interrogation may fit the second definition. When an investigator intends to incarcerate and charge a person with a crime, the third definition applies.

INGREDIENTS OF ARREST

There are three essential ingredients of an arrest (Figure 2-2):

1. Intention
2. Authority
3. Custody

The officer must have the intention of taking the suspect into custody. This factor distinguishes an arrest from a lesser form of detention, but actual or expressed intention is not always the controlling factor. The intention may be inferred by a court if its estimate of all the conduct and circumstances indicates that an arrest occurred, despite any contrary intent on the part of the law enforcement officer.

▲ FIGURE 2-2

On the 2015 anniversary of Michael Brown's fatal shooting by a Ferguson, MO, police officer, some protestors blocking Interstate 70 outside of Ferguson were arrested. Note the different genders and races among those arrested.

(©Scott Olson/Getty Images)

The officer must have real or assumed legal authority for taking the person into custody. The officer must have the actual authority to make a legal arrest or at least believe this to be the case. For example, an investigator may make an arrest under a defective warrant but not know about the defect. The third ingredient is that the person arrested must come within the custody and control of the law. This element can be satisfied either by physical restraint or by the arrestee's voluntary submission to the custody and control of the arresting officer.

ARREST DISTINGUISHED FROM DETENTION

Detention is a temporary and limited interference with the freedom of a person for investigative purposes. Sometimes called investigative detention, it is also commonly referred to by law enforcement as a "street stop" or "field interrogation." In this instance, police are justified in employing **"stop-and-frisk"** measures—patting down the outer clothing—if they suspect that the person being questioned may be armed and their safety is in jeopardy.[12] This issue of "stop and frisk" is covered later near the end of the search and seizure section of this chapter.

There is a fine line between detention and arrest. Because an officer does interfere with the freedom of the individual stopped, even for only a few minutes, some theorists view any such action as constituting arrest. Most people and most courts recognize the validity of street stops and uphold them as not being arrests if conducted properly.

A valid detention must be brief and made for good reason. The officer must limit questioning and investigation and must then either release the subject or decide to arrest. Detention for an undue length of time could be construed as an arrest if later challenged in court.

BOX 2-2 | "STOP-AND-FRISK" QUESTIONED

The "stop-question-and-frisk" program developed in New York City in the 1990s as part of the "zero-tolerance" program was aimed at reducing public drinking, public urination, graffiti and vandalism, and various other street crimes in the core business center. The program was built around the landmark 1968 court cases of *Terry* v. *Ohio*, *Sibron* v. *New York*, and *Peters* v. *New York*, in which the Supreme Court granted approval to frisks conducted by officers lacking probable cause for an arrest to search for weapons. The primary concern was officer safety; however, the practice has become a hot issue as protests relating to racial bias in policing have emerged nationally. Data collected in 2011 revealed that the NYPD program resulted in a record 685,724 stops made under the program; the vast majority (81.5%) of those stopped were African-American or Latino; over half were aged 14 to 24 years; 46,785 were women; however, only 16,000 were actually frisked. Most importantly, guns and other weapons were discovered in less than 1% of all stops; raising serious question to the stops as an officer safety practice.[13] Even though the number of stop-and-frisk encounters has dramatically declined since 2011 with only 46,235 stops conducted in 2015, the issue remains an important and controversial topic as it became a centerpiece argument during the 2016 presidential election with Donald Trump supporting the practice by police and Hillary Clinton calling for serious police reform in New York City.[14]

▲ FIGURE 2-3

Thousands of people marched in New York City in silent protest of the NYPD's stop-question-and-frisk program. (©Tony Savino/Corbis/Getty Images)

ARREST DISTINGUISHED FROM CHARGING

As noted earlier, one definition of arrest is to interfere with the freedom of a person suspected of involvement in a crime to the extent that the person is taken to the police station. But investigators do not always intend to prosecute or have the ability to prosecute at that time. Formally **charging** a suspect with a crime does not automatically flow from an arrest. Charging follows a decision to prosecute. This decision may be made by the police, the prosecutor, or both. But they may also decide not to bring charges. For example, the evidence that justified the arrest may not be sufficient to warrant formal charges, because the prosecutor believes he or she cannot prove the case beyond, and to the exclusion of, every reasonable doubt. Perhaps additional information may come to light after the arrest that points to the accused's innocence. Maybe an arrest was unlawful or evidence was obtained in violation of constitutional standards.

ARREST PROCEDURES

The laws of most jurisdictions permit an arrest in at least three and sometimes four types of situations:

1. When a warrant has been issued.
2. When a crime is committed in the presence of an arresting officer.
3. When an officer has probable cause to believe that the suspect being arrested has committed a felony.
4. In statutorily created instances.

THE ARREST WARRANT

The preferred method of effecting an arrest is under the authority of a warrant. In fact, if one were to read the constitutional requirements in their strictest sense, arrests can be justified only if made with a warrant. Of course, the courts have chosen to be more liberal in their interpretation so that warrantless arrests can be made in certain situations. But there are sound reasons for both the warrant requirements and the exceptions created by judicial case law, and, in some instances, by legislation. In the U.S. constitutional system, the functions of government—executive, legislative, and judicial—are each the responsibility of a separate branch. The police function is an executive one, whereas the judicial responsibility obviously belongs to the courts. Although the mechanism of arrest is an executive function, it is subject to judicial scrutiny and review. This position is supported by the very wording of the Fourth Amendment to the U.S. Constitution:

> . . . and no warrant shall issue, but upon probable cause, supported by oath or affirmation, and particularly describing the . . . person . . . to be seized.

The two major benefits derived from securing prior judicial approval for arrests through the warrant process are that the approval relieves law enforcement of the burden of proving the legality of the arrest—so that officers need not fear charges of false arrest, malicious prosecution, or other civil suits—and getting a warrant provides for an independent evaluation of the evidence.

Even the most objective, well-trained, and well-intentioned investigators sometimes become so involved in a case that their involvement may affect their ability to evaluate the case's merits objectively. Presenting the case before a qualified judge has the benefits of allowing an independent third party, with no emotional involvement in the investigation and with the knowledge of legal standards that must be met, to assist the investigator in determining whether those standards have been achieved. It is also logical to assume that the validity of an arrest made after this review and the issuance of a warrant is more likely to be upheld if later challenged in court than an arrest based solely on an officer's own determination of the sufficiency of the evidence. The wise law enforcement officer recognizes the value of obtaining a warrant whenever practical. The word "practical" has significance with regard to the propriety of securing an arrest warrant. The law recognizes that the innumerable situations encountered by law enforcement officers in daily activities and the variety of conditions inherent in the nature of the law enforcement function make it impossible and unrealistic to expect an officer to obtain a warrant in every situation before effecting an arrest—hence, the exceptions to the warrant requirement.

The procedure required for obtaining a warrant is often time-consuming and inconvenient. Frequently, the process in major felony cases requires that the investigator seek out the prosecutor; present the facts, which will be reduced to paper in affidavit form for a probable cause determination; find a judge who is authorized to issue warrants; present the case again for a determination of the sufficiency of the grounds for arrest; and then wait for the warrant to be typed up and signed. In many cases, the procedure can take several hours, even during the normal workday. On weekends and late at night, it may take even longer, as the prosecutor, judge, or both are located or roused from bed. As a consequence, officers sometimes tend to take the easy way out by making a warrantless arrest, hoping they are right and believing they have sufficient grounds to act. By conducting themselves in this manner, they neglect the basic rule of thumb—get a warrant—and its underlying rationale. But the warrantless arrest is not always a shortcut. As clear as the law may appear to be on the need for warrants, each case must rest on its own facts. There are relatively few cases in which it is obvious that an arrest can be made without a warrant. Similarly, the clear-cut instances for which a warrant is absolutely needed are relatively few. The majority of cases fall within that vast plane requiring evaluation of the merits of each case. An arrest without a warrant, however, does not save time. In reality, the time an officer spends on justifying this decision in motion hearings demanded by the defense attorney will equal or exceed the time it would have taken to get a warrant in the first place. The potential consequence is that the case may be dismissed for want of a valid arrest or that important evidence, seized as a result of the arrest, may be suppressed.

The investigator is not relieved of all responsibility for the legality of the arrest simply because a warrant was obtained. The investigator must be aware of what constitutes a valid warrant to ensure that the one he or she possesses permits a legal arrest.

▲ FIGURE 2-4 Swearing or affirming to contents of affidavit for arrest warrant
When the judge is satisfied that the arrest warrant affidavit is in order, and probable cause to arrest exists, he places the investigator under oath and the affidavit becomes a sworn document. (©Mikael Karlsson/Alamy)

An **arrest warrant** is a judicial order commanding the person to whom it is issued or some other person to arrest a particular individual and to bring that person promptly before a court to answer a criminal charge. The arrest warrant generally must be written. By legislation, some jurisdictions allow for verbal authorization supported by written authorization in warrant form that is issued later (Figure 2-4).

In most cases, particularly major felonies, the warrant must be issued by a judge who personally reviews the facts to determine the existence of reasonable grounds as required by the Constitution. The warrant must be supported by an **affidavit**—a written statement of the information known to the officer that serves as the basis for the issuance of the warrant. In major cases, the requirements vary on whether the warrant must be issued in the county in which the offense occurred, but once issued, major case warrants can be served anywhere in the state.

The form and contents of an arrest warrant usually include:

1. The authority under which the warrant is issued (the name of the state).
2. The person who is to execute the warrant (generally addressed to any peace officer of the state).
3. The identity of the person to be arrested.
4. The designation of the offense.
5. The date, time, and place of the occurrence.
6. The name of the victim.
7. A description of the offense and how it occurred.

Blank warrants are not constitutionally valid. Before a warrant can be issued, the identity of the perpetrator must be known. The mere fact that a crime has been committed by someone unknown will not support a warrant's issuance. The Constitution requires that the warrant contain a particular description of the suspect. This description must be specific enough to permit an officer not acquainted with the case to identify the person to be arrested with reasonable certainty. Aliases may be used. If the suspect's name is not known, "John Doe" may be used provided there are other methods of describing the person to be arrested, such as place of residence, occupation, and a physical description.

A reprint of an Associated Press story appeared on the web on August 8, 2004, reporting that in Boston, prosecutors found a way to prevent the 15-year statute of limitations from destroying the possibility of bringing rapists to trial. In cases that have DNA evidence, prosecutors are obtaining indictments against "John Does" based on their DNA profiles. Massachusetts followed the lead of Wisconsin that started doing this in 1999. New York has also begun using the process. In a Wisconsin appellate case challenging the constitutionality of the statute claiming that the indictment does not specifically name the defendant, the court said that DNA evidence was the best method of identification available.

Herring v. *United States*[15] involved a warrant issued on erroneous information that the police did not know was in error.

Officers in one Alabama county arrested Herring based on a warrant that was listed in a neighboring county's database. Search incident to arrest yielded drugs and a gun. It was then learned that the warrant had been recalled months earlier but someone forgot to remove the warrant from the neighboring county's database. Herring was tried on federal gun and drug possession charges. The federal district court refused to suppress the evidence, and Herring was convicted. The U.S. Supreme Court held: When police mistakes leading to an unlawful search are the result of isolated negligence leading up to the search, rather than systematic error or disregard of constitutional requirements, the exclusionary rule does not apply.

QUICK FACT

Arrest Warrant Scams

In 2016, the IRS reemphasized its effort to warn taxpayers of phony arrest warrant scams. While there are many variations on the scam, most victims receive a phone call from a person posing as an official from the IRS, FBI, or a local law enforcement agency threatening some form of court action, license revocation, deportation, or arrest if they do not pay an outstanding tax bill or fine associated with a phony arrest warrant. The caller aggressively threatens the victim demanding that a payment be made immediately by a credit card, wire transfer, or certified check to avoid "immediate arrest" or the issuance of a "federal arrest warrant." Since October 2013, over 5,000 victims have paid collectively over $26.5 million as a result of the scam.

Source: IRS Bulletin, "Phone Scams Continue to Be a Serious Threat During the 2016 Filing Season," February 2, 2016. See: https://www.irs.gov/uac/newsroom/phone-scams-continue-to-be-a-serious-threat-remain-on-irs-dirty-dozen-list-of-tax-scams-for-the-2016-filing-season.

Crime Committed in Presence

Any offense committed in the presence of an officer, whether felony or misdemeanor, can be the basis of an arrest without a warrant. The in-presence requirement is usually thought of in the narrow context of sight. However, to satisfy the legal requirements, perception of some or all of the elements of an offense as they occur, through the use of any or all of the five senses—sight, hearing, taste, touch, or smell—can justify a warrantless arrest.

PROBABLE CAUSE

The third major category in which a lawful arrest is generally permitted involves offenses not committed in the officer's presence and for which a warrant has not been issued. The law allows an officer to make warrantless arrests in felony cases provided reasonable grounds or probable cause exists to make the arrest (Figure 2-5). (As previously noted, probable cause also must be shown in an affidavit to support the issuance of a warrant.)

Probable cause is a difficult term to define, because in no two instances are circumstances identical. One acceptable definition of **probable cause** is that it is more than suspicion but less than actual knowledge. It is suspicion plus facts and circumstances that would lead a reasonable person exercising ordinary caution to believe that a crime has been, is being, or is about to be committed (Figure 2-6).

Probable cause may be based on a number of sources of information, not all of which have to be the kind of evidence admissible at trial. However, if prosecution is an aim of the arrest, there must also be sufficient evidence to take the case to court. In addition, the probable cause must exist at the time the arrest is made and may not be developed by subsequently acquired evidence.

Mere suspicion is not enough to justify an arrest; there must be supporting facts and circumstances. Certain factors may help to decide the existence of probable cause. The most common is the personal knowledge of the officer/investigator. Information

◀**FIGURE 2-5**
Placing felon under arrest
Arapahoe County deputy sheriffs arrest a 16-year-old male in a parking lot for possession of narcotics, robbery, and carrying a concealed weapon, in downtown Aurora, Colorado.
(©Andy Cross/The Denver Post/Getty Images)

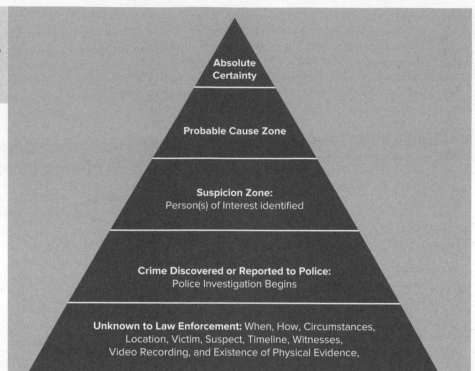

▶ **FIGURE 2-6 Probable cause**
(Source: Chamelin, Neil C., Fox, Vernon B. and Whisenand, Paul M. *Introduction to Criminal Justice*, 2nd Ed. Saddle River, NJ: Pearson Education.)

obtained from informants also may be of value, although that information may not be admissible at a subsequent hearing or trial. The investigator must be able to establish the reliability of the information and the informant by indicating the length of time the investigator has known or dealt with the informant, the general character and reputation of the informant, the number of tips received from the informant in the past, the accuracy of previous information, whether the informant is paid for the information, and the informant's motives for volunteering the information. One of the current common instances is the use of confidential informants to make drug buys.

Other sources of probable cause include information from a police department or from other law enforcement agencies, such as notice of outstanding warrants, the past criminal record of the suspect, physical evidence found at the scene of the crime, other evidence detected in the follow-up investigation, crime laboratory analyses, and reports of victims and eyewitnesses.

There is a third exception to the warrant requirement for a valid arrest. By legislation, states allow officers to make arrests in nonfelony cases even though the offense is not committed in the officer's presence. Examples include domestic violence situations, violations of injunctions against domestic violence, and cases of battery.[16]

SEARCH AND SEIZURE

The evolution of the law of **search and seizure** illustrates the relationship described earlier between federal and state court systems and between the Bill of Rights and its application to the states through the due process clause of the Fourteenth Amendment.[17]

Under early English common law, an illegal search and seizure that produced incriminating evidence was allowed, and the evidence obtained was admissible in court. Surprisingly, federal law enforcement officers in the United States were permitted to follow the same rule until 1914. Up to that time, the search and seizure practices of federal officials had not been scrutinized in light of the wording of the Fourth Amendment. In 1914 the case of *Weeks* v. *United States*[18] was decided by the United States Supreme Court. Weeks was charged by federal agents with using the mails for transporting materials that represented chances in a lottery. After his arrest for this federal offense, Weeks's room was searched twice without the authority of a valid search warrant. But Weeks had been arrested at his place of employment, not his home. During the **search,** the agents found and seized various incriminating papers and articles. This evidence was admitted at his trial for the federal violation, and Weeks was convicted. On appeal to the U.S. Supreme Court, the Court established what became known as the "Federal Exclusionary Rule." The Court ruled that any evidence unreasonably obtained by federal law enforcement officers could no longer be admissible in federal prosecutions. The Court made it quite clear that, because this was a federal case, the decision was applicable only to federal law enforcement officers and federal courts and was in no way applicable to the states. But this decision, as do many Supreme Court decisions, left a number of unanswered questions. Out of one question arose the "Silver Platter Doctrine." The *Weeks* decision prohibited federal officers from illegally seizing evidence, but it did not prevent law enforcement officers of the states from illegally seizing the evidence and handing it over to federal agents on a "silver platter" for use in federal courts. This method of circumventing the Federal Exclusionary Rule remained unchallenged until 1960. In that year, the Supreme Court prohibited the introduction in federal courts of all illegally seized evidence obtained by state officers in violation of the Fourth Amendment.[19]

After the *Weeks* decision, very few states adopted their own exclusionary rule applicable within their own state. It was not until 1949 that a serious attempt was made to seek mandatory application of the exclusionary rule to the states through the due process clause of the Fourteenth Amendment. In *Wolf* v. *Colorado,*[20] the defendant was charged with abortion. Based on suspicion of similar prior offenses, officers searched Wolf's office, arrested him, and seized certain documents that were later admitted into trial. Wolf appealed his conviction contending that the unreasonable search and seizure was a denial of due process under the Fourteenth Amendment, as it would be under the Fourth Amendment had he been in federal court. The Supreme Court held that unreasonable searches and seizures by state officials in state cases did not constitute a denial of Fourteenth Amendment due process but added that the Court did have the authority to rule otherwise if the Justices so desired. The interesting point in this case seemed to be that the Court was giving the states fair warning that they disapproved of unreasonable searches and seizures by state authorities and that sooner or later they would rule in favor of incorporating the Fourth Amendment protection in the due process clause of the Fourteenth Amendment. Many states took the hint.

By 1961 only 18 states had not adopted an exclusionary rule. In that year, the warning that the Supreme Court had given 12 years earlier in the *Wolf* case came to pass. In May 1957 three Cleveland police officers arrived at Dolree Mapp's residence in that city with information that a person who was wanted for questioning in a recent bombing was hiding out in her home and that there was a large amount of gambling paraphernalia being hidden in the home. The officers knocked on the door and demanded entrance, but Ms. Mapp, after telephoning her attorney, refused to admit them without a search warrant. The officers advised their headquarters of the situation and undertook a surveillance of the house. Some three hours later, the officers, with reinforcements, again sought entrance. When Ms. Mapp did not come to the door immediately, one of the doors was forcibly opened and the officers gained entry. Ms. Mapp demanded to see the search warrant. One of the officers held up a paper that he claimed was the search warrant. She grabbed the paper and stuffed it down the front of her dress. A struggle ensued in which the officers recovered the piece of paper and handcuffed Ms. Mapp for her "belligerency" in resisting the attempt to recover the "warrant." A subsequent widespread search of the entire premises disclosed obscene materials. Ms. Mapps was convicted for possession of these materials. No search warrant was ever produced at the trial.

Following Ms. Mapp's conviction and the denial of her appeals in the state courts, her case was appealed to the United States Supreme Court. *Mapp* v. *Ohio,*[21] decided in 1961, established the rule that any evidence unreasonably searched and seized would no longer be admissible in any court—state or federal. The Exclusionary Rule was now applicable in all courts at all levels.

Among the many unanswered questions created by the *Mapp* decision, the crucial question revolved around the definition of the word **unreasonable.** It did not take the state courts long to find the loophole. In order to avoid applying the decision in the *Mapp* case to instances arising in state courts, state officials merely called previously unreasonable searches and seizures reasonable searches. Because no standards had been set for determining what constitutes a reasonable or unreasonable search, many of the state courts felt free to make their own determination on this issue. In effect, *Mapp* had little impact on these states. However, within two years of the *Mapp* decision, the Supreme Court had the opportunity to rule on this matter. The Court held in *Ker* v. *California*[22] that the state court judges were still free to determine the reasonableness of searches but that in making those determinations they would now be guided by the same standards as had been followed in the federal courts, which were established in the line of cases decided since the *Weeks* case in 1914. In essence, the Court said that states would be held to federal standards in search and seizure matters.

The long line of cases evolving since *Mapp* and *Ker* have essentially revolved around the single issue of what constitutes a reasonable search in instances where law enforcement officers act with or without a warrant.

LEGAL SEARCHES AND SEIZURES

As is true for arrests, the Fourth Amendment also recognizes searches and seizures only by government agents under the authority of a warrant. The United States Supreme Court recognizes judicially created exceptions. Thus, legal searches and seizures can be made:

1. when a warrant has been issued;
2. with consent;
3. incident to an arrest;
4. of a motor vehicle;
5. when an emergency (exigent circumstances) exists;
6. to conduct an inventory.

There are two additional areas that are closely related but can't truly be called searches and seizures—plain view seizures and stop-and-frisk encounters. These will also be covered.

SEARCH WITH A WARRANT

A **search warrant** is a written order, in the name of the state, signed by a judicial officer, exercising proper authority, and directing a law enforcement officer to search for certain specific property and bring it before the court. To be valid, the warrant must be signed by one who is authorized to sign. Normally, this is a judicial officer. In rare instances, state law may allow a prosecutor or law enforcement officer to sign the warrant to expedite the process but only after the facts and circumstances have been reviewed over the telephone by a judicial officer, being later subject to that judicial officer's signature. In no case is a prosecutor or law enforcement officer permitted to sign a warrant without that judicial review. The independent impartial review is what provides the warrant with validity.

A warrant to search must be based upon probable cause. In this instance, probable cause can best be defined as facts and circumstances that would lead a reasonable person to believe that the place to be searched and the things to be seized are to be found. The probable cause is established by a written affidavit prepared by the law enforcement officer/investigator, stating all those known facts and circumstances. As is true for an arrest warrant, probable cause may be established by any number of sources, including information supplied by informants. In drug cases, probable cause is often established by confidential informants who make repeated drug buys from a specific house or store. The affidavit is then presented to the judicial officer, who independently evaluates it and, if she or he finds it sufficient, issues the warrant. As is pretty evident from the process described so far, probable cause must be established before the warrant is issued. Anything found as a result of the service of the warrant cannot be used to establish the probable cause.

The search warrant must particularly describe the place to be searched. Although the Constitution does not define "particularly," the description must be sufficient to distinguish the place from all others. Normally, one might think of a building on a piece of property as a place to be searched. Using the legal description is not necessary; however, a street address may not be sufficient. There are many appellate cases involving invalid warrants because the address failed to distinguish between two identical numbers on houses on "Main Street" because one was on "North Main" and the other on "South Main." In addition, numbers may be missing from the house or mailbox causing problems. What happens when a warrant is issued for "999 Main Street" but the numbers have come loose and flipped over at "666 Main Street" and now read "999"? Have investigators ever served a warrant at the wrong location? The appellate cases are full of examples. The warrant should contain information such as the color of the house, the type of floor plan (for example, ranch style home); apartment on the third floor, east side of a brownstone tenement; cream colored, vinyl siding, one story house with green trim, green shutters, an American flag on a pole in the front yard, and so forth.

The phrase "particularly describe" also applies to the things to be seized. This governs the extent of the search. For example, if the affidavit and warrant are for the search and seizure of drugs in a house, the search can be pretty extensive. Thus, it would be permitted to search closets, under beds, in dresser drawers, in medicine cabinets, and in kitchen cupboards—and anything found, even evidence of other crimes, may be properly seized and considered admissible. For example, the search turns up a firearm; but the occupant of the house, being a previously convicted felon, is not allowed to possess firearms. The discovery of the weapon could be the legal basis for adding a charge of illegal possession of a firearm. But if the warrant is based on the belief that the house contains stolen tires, the places that can legally be searched in that same house are significantly reduced. A search of dresser drawers, kitchen cupboards, and medicine cabinets would be improper, and, if the firearm in the previous example is found under the pillow on the bed occupied by the suspect, its seizure would be improper unless the investigator could convince the court, during a hearing on a motion to suppress the seizure of the firearm, that the investigator reasonably believed there might have been a stolen tire under the pillow.

In another example, a law enforcement officer went outside the scope of his authority to search when, with consent, while searching for a stolen boat motor and a shotgun, picked up and opened a tackle box that contained drugs and drug paraphernalia. This served as the basis for charging. The court stated there was no reasonable belief the boat motor or shotgun was in the tackle box.[23]

Normally, investigators should include in their affidavits in support of a search warrant the justification for searching persons found at the place where the warrant is to be executed and the search conducted. In the absence of such authority in the warrant, persons found on the scene may not be searched unless they are first lawfully arrested.

Once issued, a warrant must be executed within whatever time limits the law of the state requires; time of day/night limits are applicable. In some instances, the warrant may specify that it may be served at nighttime if the probable cause supporting the warrant can justify that the specific criminal activity only occurs at night. Until recently, state laws required officers/investigators executing warrants to knock, announce their purpose and the fact that they were in possession of a warrant, and giving the occupants a reasonable time to answer and open the door (Figure 2-7). In 2006 the Supreme Court ruled in *Hudson* v. *Michigan*[24] that violation of the knock and announce requirement for the service of a search warrant will no longer result in the suppression of evidence found during execution of the search warrant. The Court said the social cost

▲ FIGURE 2-7
A California Special Weapons and Tactics (SWAT) Team moves into position to execute an arrest warrant on a wanted subject.
(©Al Schaben/Los Angeles Times/Getty Images)

of applying the exclusionary rule to knock and announce violations was considerable.

During the search, particularly if several investigators are involved, one investigator should be designated the property custodian. A detailed record must be kept of each piece of evidence, with a specific description, where it was found, and by whom. This list then becomes part of the return on the warrant that must be brought back and presented to the judge for review. It, of course, also becomes part of the case file (Figure 2-8).

In 2005, in *Muehler* v. *Mena*,[25] the Supreme Court held that officers executing a search warrant of a house seeking weapons and evidence of gang membership in the wake of a drive-by shooting acted reasonably by detaining the occupants of the house in handcuffs during the search, especially since there were only two officers to watch over four people.

SEARCH WITH CONSENT

One of the most common situations arising today is when a uniformed officer, in encountering a citizen during a traffic stop or other routine activity, asks the person if he/she has any weapons or drugs on his/her person or in the vehicle. Sometimes the person says yes, and that might lead to an immediate arrest. Often the person says no, and the officer may then ask if he/she can search the person and/or the vehicle. If the person gives affirmative consent, the search may be conducted. If the person denies consent, which he/she has the right to do, no search may be made unless there is probable cause to conduct a search under one of the other exceptions to the warrant requirement. A refusal to allow a search, standing alone, does not constitute probable cause to justify any further action.

The crux of a consent search is that the consent must be voluntarily given. It can't be based on intimidation or threats of any kind.

A person may give consent to the search of his/her home, but in the case where there are roommates living in the same house or apartment and each has his/her own bedroom, an occupant may give consent to the search only of his/her private room and any area shared in common by the roommates, such as the kitchen or living room.

Once consent is given for search of a home, car, office, or any other place, it may be withdrawn at any time by the person who had the authority and gave the consent. When consent is withdrawn, the search must stop. Any incriminating evidence found after consent is withdrawn is illegally seized and is not admissible.

It is always wise to get documentation of the consent to search. Figure 2-9 is a generic form that may be used.

SEARCH INCIDENT TO ARREST

The courts have regularly recognized the right of law enforcement officers to search people who have been arrested without a warrant. Such searches are justified for officer safety and to preserve evidence.[26] In 1969 the U.S. Supreme Court limited the scope of a search when it ruled in *Chimel* v. *California*[27] that a warrantless search of the defendant's entire house, following his lawful arrest in the house on a burglary charge, was unreasonable. This case set the benchmark for searches incident to a valid arrest by holding that such searches may be made of the person arrested and the area under his/her immediate control from which he or she might obtain a weapon or destroy evidence. Initially, searches were reasonable only if conducted in conformity with *Chimel*. Over the years, case law has expanded the allowable area of search following a legal arrest, particularly as applied to automobile searches, but as to searches of an arrestee's home, *Chimel* is still followed closely. In *Maryland* v. *Buie*,[28] a 1990 case, the Supreme Court reported that:

Two men committed an armed robbery. The police obtained warrants for their arrest. Buie was one of the people to be arrested. The officers went to Buie's home to arrest him.

▶ FIGURE 2-9
Generic consent-to-search form

PERMISSION TO SEARCH AND SEIZE

I, _____, agree to permit members/officers
of the _____ to search my
             (agency name)
vehicle(s)/apartment/house/other structure(s) or other areas as described below, which
are in my control.

Area to be Searched: Located At:

_____

And I further agree to permit members/officers of the_____
                                                              (agency name)
_____ to remove from the above listed areas any item(s) of
property they deem relevant to their investigation. It is further understood that I will
receive a receipt for any and all items removed by the_____
                                                                (agency name)
_____.

I am giving this written permission to the _____
                                                            (agency name)
freely and voluntarily, without any threats or promises having been made to me, and
after having been informed that I have a right to refuse to permit this search and
seizure. I further understand that any item(s) seized, may be used in a court of law
during a criminal procedure/prosecution.

Signed: _____

Address: _____

Date: _____ Time: _____

Witness: _____

Witness: _____

When they entered, they found Buie coming from the basement. That is where he was arrested. One of the officers went into the basement, allegedly on a protective sweep, to make sure no one else was down there. While in the basement he saw "in plain view" a red running suit that matched the description of clothing that witnesses said one of the robbers was wearing. The officer seized the suit and it was used in evidence to help convict Buie.

The Supreme Court said that:

. . . as an incident to the arrest of the accused, the officers could, as a precautionary measure and without a search warrant, probable cause, or reasonable suspicion, look in closets and other spaces immediately adjoining the place of arrest from which an attack could be immediately launched . . .[29]

As to conducting protective sweeps, the Supreme Court went on to say:

. . . beyond that, the Fourth Amendment permits a warrantless protective sweep in conjunction with an in-home arrest—extending only to a cursory inspection of those spaces where

a person may be found, lasting no longer than is necessary to dispel the reasonable suspicion of danger, and in any event no longer than it takes to complete the arrest and depart the premises—when the searching officer possesses a reasonable belief based on specific and articulable facts which, taken with the rational inferences from those facts, would warrant a reasonably prudent officer in believing that the area to be swept harbors an individual posing a danger to those on the arrest scene.[30]

The Court made it clear that the officers had the right, pursuant to the arrest warrant, to search anywhere in the house, even the basement, until they found Buie.[31]

SEARCH OF A MOTOR VEHICLE

The search of a motor vehicle, sometimes referred to as the automobile exception to the requirement that a search be conducted with a warrant, really involves two distinct legal issues under modern law. The first can be traced back to a 1925 Supreme Court case. In *Carroll* v. *United States*,[32] the Court created the "moveable vehicle" rule. The Court held that if there was sufficient probable cause to get a warrant, but, because the vehicle was moveable, it might be gone if time were taken to get a warrant, a warrantless search was justified. In this case, the vehicle was moving and contained bootleg whiskey during Prohibition. The search of the entire vehicle, including the trunk was justified in this case.

In *Chambers* v. *Maroney*[33] a service station was robbed by two armed men. About the time of the robbery, two teenagers saw a blue station wagon circling the block around the service station and later sped off with four men. The service station attendant described one of the robbers as wearing a green sweater and the other wearing a trench coat. Sometime after, a vehicle fitting the description, carrying four men, one of whom was wearing a green sweater, was stopped. A trench coat was seen in the car. The occupants were arrested, and the car was searched without a warrant. The money, guns, and other evidence of the robbery were found. The Supreme Court approved of the search under the motor vehicle exception. The motor vehicle exception is still very viable.

In *Maryland* v. *Dyson,*[34] the Supreme Court continued to follow the ruling in *Carroll*. But it is not necessary that the vehicle actually be moving to justify such a warrantless search. Early on, the Supreme Court held that where a car was legally parked, agents did not have to speculate as to when the owner would return and whether there was time to obtain a search warrant.[35]

The second issue involves the search of a vehicle incident to a lawful arrest. Keeping in mind the foundation principle of the *Chimel* case, that a search may be made of the area under the arrestee's immediate control, the Supreme Court ruled in the 1981 case of *New York* v. *Belton*[36] that when a police officer makes a lawful custodial arrest of the occupant of an automobile, the officer may search the vehicle's passenger compartment as a contemporaneous incident of arrest. The right to search includes any open or closed containers found in the passenger compartment. It does not include the trunk.

QUICK FACT

Traffic Enforcement, Motor Vehicle Searches, and Racial Profiling

A 2016 report analyzing traffic enforcement in the City of San Diego, California, during 2014 and 2015, once again raised the issue of racial profiling. Racial profiling, or the discriminatory practice by police of using an individual's race, ethnicity, religion, or national origin as a predictor of criminal activity, is illegal in the United States. The most common example of racial profiling is the use of race to determine which drivers to stop for minor traffic violations (commonly referred to as "driving while black or brown"), or the use of race to determine which pedestrians to search for illegal weapons and/or contraband.

The report reflected national trends: While there were no disparities between black and/or hispanic, and white drivers and no meaningful difference in the rate at which drivers from each racial/ethnic group were arrested, there were differences relating to search patterns. Black and hispanic drivers were more likely than white drivers to be searched, including their vehicles, following a traffic stop. While this certainly is not evidence of racial profiling, it does indicate differences in police behavior that may be accounted for in variants of community crime and violence, demeanor of the suspect driver, previous contact with the driver, and/or previous observation of the driver by the police before the stop. Unfortunately, this study, as well as others, pointed to the difficulty of drawing significant conclusions, especially relating to individual police behavior, from aggregate data. Further, the study recognized the continued tension nationally between the police and certain minority community members.

Source: American Civil Liberties Union (ACLU), "Racial Profiling: Definition." See https://www.aclu.org/other/racial-profiling-definition; Joshua Chanin, Megan Welsh, Dana Nurge, and Stuart Henry, "Traffic Enforcement in San Diego, California: An Analysis of SDPD Vehicle Stops in 2014 and 2015." Unpublished report, 2016.

On May 24, 2004, the Supreme Court decided *Thornton* v. *United States.*[37] In 2001 Officer Nichols was driving behind Thornton's Lincoln town car. He ran the town car's license plate. The response from the Department of Motor Vehicles (DMV) reported that the tag belonged on a 1982 Chevrolet. Before Nichols had a chance to pull the car over, Thornton drove into a parking lot, parked, and got out of his car. Officer Nichols saw Thornton leave his vehicle as he pulled in behind him. The officer parked, got out of his car, and accosted Thornton. He asked Thornton for his driver's license and told Thornton that the license plate did not match the vehicle to which it was properly attached. Nichols then asked Thornton if he could pat him down. Thornton agreed. Nichols felt a bulge in Thornton's left front pocket and again asked him if he had any illegal narcotics on him. This time Thornton said that he did and pulled out two bags, one containing marijuana and the other crack cocaine. The officer handcuffed Thornton, informed him that he was under arrest, and put him in the back seat of the patrol car. Officer Nichols then searched the vehicle and found a 9-mm handgun under the driver's seat. Thornton was charged with federal firearms and drug offenses. He was convicted. His case was affirmed on appeal by the district court of appeals and then was appealed to the Supreme Court.

In brief, the Supreme Court said that the right to search the passenger compartment of a car still exists even if the officer does not make contact until the person arrested has left the vehicle (Figure 2-10). The issue in this case asked the question on the reasonableness of the search whether the defendant was inside or outside the vehicle when first contacted and subsequently arrested. The opinion points out that the length of time the person had been out of the car and how far away from the vehicle the person was may all come into play in determining reasonableness of a search. Interestingly, in this case, the defendant had already been secured and was in the back seat of the patrol car when this search took place. This, of course, was pointed out by the dissenting Justices, who said there was no longer any chance to obtain a weapon or destroy evidence and the officer should have obtained a warrant before searching.

Five years after *Thornton* and 28 years after *Belton,* the Court seemed to revert to the *Chimel* foundation. In *Arizona* v. *Gant,*[38]

▲ **FIGURE 2-10**
Police officer searching car's compartment finds over one kilo (2.2 pounds) of powder cocaine. (©Mikael Karlsson/Alamy)

the Supreme Court said that *Belton* had been expanded beyond what the Court intended. Although the majority opinion doesn't specifically overrule *Belton* and *Thornton,* the holding severely limits the situations in which law enforcement may search incident to a lawful arrest. Gant was arrested for driving with a suspended license. He was handcuffed and locked in the back seat of a patrol car. Two other individuals were with Gant. They were also secured in patrol vehicles. Then the passenger compartment of his vehicle was searched and officers found cocaine in the pocket of a jacket in the back seat. Gant was charged and convicted of possession of cocaine and a related charge. The Supreme Court held that once the scene was secured, that is, the driver was handcuffed and locked in the back of a patrol car, he could no longer reach a weapon to harm an officer or reach to destroy any potential evidence. Consequently, a search and seizure, without a warrant, under these circumstances would be reasonable. However, the Court waivered slightly by concluding "that circumstances unique to the automobile context justify a search incident to arrest when it is reasonable to believe that evidence of the offense of arrest might be found in the vehicle." Thus, when a person is arrested on a traffic charge and secured, there would be no evidence in the vehicle related to the charge. But if the vehicle driver is arrested on a drug charge, there may be evidence in the vehicle related to that charge and a search may be reasonable even though the driver is secured in the back of a patrol car. In *Belton,* there were four people in the vehicle. They were separated and were away from the vehicle at the time of the search but were not secured and not under arrest. That was the narrow context in which the Court intended *Belton* to be applicable. The Court pointed out that at least eight states followed the narrow interpretation based on state constitutional provisions. The states were Vermont, New Jersey, New Mexico, Nevada, Pennsylvania, New York, Oregon and Wyoming. In *Thornton,* the driver was away from the vehicle when arrested on a drug charge after a consent pat down. Thornton was secured and placed in a patrol car, but, because this was a drug case, search of the vehicle incident to arrest was reasonable and evidence found was admissible.

A vehicle search is not reasonable if conducted pursuant to stopping a vehicle for a traffic violation and writing a citation. A citation is not an arrest and no right to search arises. Does the same rule hold true if an officer issues a summons (sometime called a Notice to Appear)? Generally, the answer is yes; but consider the case of *Virginia* v. *Moore,*[39] decided by the Supreme Court in 2008. Moore was arrested for driving on a suspended license. He was searched and cocaine was found on his person. He was charged with the possession of cocaine and convicted. The kink in this story is that Virginia law specified that when officers stopped the vehicle Moore was driving, he should have been given a summons. Had that been done, there would not have been a search. But when they arrested him instead, they searched incident to the arrest. The Supreme Court held that police did not violate the Fourth Amendment by arresting Moore instead of following state law requiring the issuance of a summons, thereby making the search and seizure reasonable.

QUICK FACT

Can an Officer Search the Trunk of a Car without a Warrant?

An oft-asked question by drivers being stopped for a routine traffic ticket is, "Can the officer search my car and the trunk of my car without a warrant?"

There are two conditions in which the officer can search the inside of the car, including the trunk. The first is that permission is given by the owner or driver. The second is if the officer has probable cause to believe that contraband or evidence of a crime is within the confines of the vehicle. There are a number of ways in which probable cause can be developed. For instance, the officer can legally search your vehicle including the trunk if the officer smells marijuana as he or she walks up to the car or observes illegal items (such as drugs or a gun) that are within plain view that would lead a reasonable officer to believe that a crime exists, if an informant (such as a passenger in the vehicle) states that there are other drugs in the car, if a drug dog reacts when sniffing the trunk of the car, or if there is any other suggestion that a crime may exist. It is important to remember that because the car is a "movable vehicle," the search requirement is lower than for a residence or domicile.

There are also a number of notable exceptions to the need for a warrant as discussed in this chapter:

- **Consent.** If someone agrees to be searched, the police do not need a warrant.
- **Exigent circumstances.** Circumstances that include ongoing emergencies, dangerous situations and/or the like. For instance, the driver committed a felony by evading arrest and did not stop when the officer turned on the overhead lights and siren.
- **Plain view.** If an object is clearly visible, it does not need to be described in a warrant to be seized. For instance, a gun is observed on the front seat of the car next to the driver.
- **Administrative searches.** A search conducted for any purpose other than law enforcement. For instance, any vehicle at an airport can be searched for security purposes (for example, weapons and explosives) by police personnel.
- **Stop and frisk.** Police can generally stop someone based on a hunch, ask a few questions, and if that hunch develops into reasonable suspicion, pat the suspect down for weapons. This includes the driver and passenger of a vehicle during a traffic stop.
- **Incident to a lawful arrest.** If the driver of a vehicle is lawfully arrested during the traffic stop and taken into custody, the officer can conduct a search for weapons or contraband of the vehicle including the truck.

Source: Mathew Izzi, "Can Police Search My Trunk?" *LegalMatch. Com.* See http://www.legalmatch.com/law-library/article/can-police-search-my-trunk.html.

EMERGENCY (EXIGENT CIRCUMSTANCES)

The **exigent circumstances** exception recognizes that a warrantless entry by law enforcement officials may be legal when there is a compelling need for official action and no time to get a warrant. The exception covers several common situations including: danger of flight or escape, loss or destruction of evidence, risk of harm to the public or police, mobility of a vehicle (discussed earlier), and hot pursuit.[40] In *Warden* v. *Hayden,*[41] two taxi drivers reported seeing an armed robber run into a residence. Police arrived within minutes, entered the house without a warrant, found the defendant in an upstairs bedroom where he was arrested, and then conducted a search. They found and seized a shotgun and a pistol in the adjoining bathroom flush tank. They also seized a jacket and pants that were of the type witnesses said the robber was wearing. Hayden was convicted, and when the case reached the Supreme Court, it held the search and seizure was legal. The Court said that speed was essential to find out if other people were in the house who might be in danger and to protect the officers themselves by ensuring they had possession of all weapons that could be used against them or to effect an escape. In all cases of exigent circumstances, there must be an emergency that justifies the warrantless search.

Officers responded to a residence after receiving two 911 calls saying that there was loud arguing and numerous shots had been fired. On arrival, a husband and wife were on the porch of their mobile home. Officers, while behind their vehicle doors and with weapons drawn, ordered the people off the porch and told them to lie down with their palms facing up. After finally getting compliance and securing the pair along with a neighbor who appeared from the side of the house, officers entered the house to see if anyone was inside and hurt. In the process, when stepping on the porch, they found a shotgun leaning against the side of the mobile home about 3 feet from where the defendant had been standing and a number of expended shells on the porch and ground nearby. These were seized. The defendant was convicted of possession of a firearm by a convicted felon. He challenged the officers' actions of stepping on the porch as an illegal search.

When the case finally reached the Supreme Court, the search and seizure was upheld under exigent circumstances. The Court reasoned that there certainly was a reasonable belief by the officers that there might be injured people inside the home based on the multiple calls that shots had been fired. This emergency justified the warrantless entry and the seizure of the weapon that formed the basis of the charge.[42]

In *Brigham City* v. *Stuart,*[43] the Supreme Court held that law enforcement officers may enter a home without a warrant when there is an objectively reasonable basis to believe that an occupant is seriously injured or imminently threatened with serious injury.

In *Michigan* v. *Fisher*[44] officers arrived at Fisher's home in response to a call for service by a couple who reported that Fisher was "going crazy." The officers found the homestead trashed and a pickup truck in the driveway was smashed. There was blood on the hood and on clothes inside the truck. Fence posts along the side of the property were damaged, and three windows to the house were smashed. Through the window, officers could see Fisher smashing things in the house. The back door was locked and Fisher had pushed a couch against the front door. The officers knocked but Fisher would not answer the door. The officers saw a cut on Fisher's hand and asked him if he needed medical attention. Fisher told officers to get a search warrant. One officer forced his way in but he retreated when Fisher pointed a rifle at him. Officers entered the house and finally subdued Fisher. He was charged with assault with a deadly weapon and possession of a firearm in the commission of a felony. Fisher argued that the entry of the police was an unreasonable search and seizure and anything he said to a police officer should not be admitted. The trial court agreed, and the State appealed. After several remands and reversals, the case ended in the U.S. Supreme Court. The Court cited the *Brigham City* case for the proposition that an "emergency aid" exception exists justifying an entry into a residence without warrant. The State courts in this case found that an "emergency" did not exist. The Supreme Court, however, said that officers did not need iron-clad proof that a serious injury had occurred. There was ongoing violence and an objective basis for believing that medical attention was needed. Therefore, the officers were justified in entering without a warrant. The case was remanded, and the trial court was required to deny the defendant's motion to suppress the statements made by the defendant to officers who entered his home.

Conducting an Inventory

Law enforcement agencies have not only the right but also the obligation to inventory property taken from a person arrested. This includes property taken from the person and from their presence, such as a motor vehicle. The inventory is done for the purpose of protecting the property of the person arrested and documenting what was found with a receipt given to the person arrested. In this manner, law enforcement can prevent accusations of stealing an offender's money or property. Similarly, law enforcement should inventory a vehicle that was impounded pursuant to an arrest. This includes the contents of the trunk (Figure 2-11). If contraband or evidence of a crime are found by virtue of a valid inventory search, the results are admissible. To justify admissibility of the fruits of an inventory search, the agency must have a standing policy that specifies the inventory in all cases. If such a policy does not exist, but this particular vehicle was inventoried, it will be ruled a pretext for a warrantless search and will be deemed unreasonable.

PLAIN VIEW SEIZURES

If an investigator/officer is lawfully in a place and sees contraband or evidence in plain view, the investigator may seize the evidence, and it will be admissible. For example, investigators were called to a hotel room door, because the occupant wanted to turn himself in on an outstanding warrant. When the defendant opened the door, officers could see crack cocaine lying on the counter inside the room. Their entry and seizure was lawful. Investigators are not required to turn their backs on a crime being committed in their presence. It is critical that the officer has a lawful right to be where she/he can see the evidence in plain view. An investigator on the street outside a house who looks in a window and sees contraband can legally seize it, but if that same investigator is standing on a box, peering inside a window overlooking the backyard, he/she cannot expect any subsequent seizure to be upheld.

▶ **FIGURE 2-11**
In 2015, two killers escaped from the Clinton Correctional Facility in Dannemora, New York. At roadblocks, law enforcement officers from multiple agencies searched car compartments and trunks for the pair. For 23 days an extensive manhunt was conducted. One of the killers was killed in a gun battle with police, and the last prisoner surrendered. (©Seth Wenig/AP Images)

Consider this example: The men's restroom in a local club, frequented by young adults, is known for drug use. Users go in the stalls, lock the doors, and ingest cocaine. Off-duty, uniformed officers check out the whole club, including the men's room. Underneath the stall door they see an individual's feet turned sideways to the toilet. It's pretty obvious that the person is not using the toilet for its intended purpose. The officer looks through a crack between the stall door and the frame and sees the individual snorting cocaine. The officer tells the man to open the door, then arrests him for possession of cocaine. Whether this is a plain view seizure depends on two things. First, is a person in a public bathroom stall entitled to an expectation of privacy? Second, was the officer in a place where he had a lawful right to be when he viewed the offense? The answer to the first question is yes. A person does have a right to expect privacy in a bathroom stall. That's why there are stalls with doors on them. It doesn't matter that it was a restroom used by the public. The answer to the second question is a little trickier. If the opening between the door and the frame was small and, in order for the officer to see what was going on, he had to get right up to the door and peek in through the small space, this will likely be found to be an unwarranted invasion of privacy and in violation of the Fourth Amendment. However, if the space was large enough that anyone walking by might see what the accused was doing from a couple of feet away from the stall, there is no reasonable expectation of privacy, and a subsequent seizure would be reasonable.

STOP AND FRISK

Earlier in this chapter, the stop-and-frisk topic was mentioned to distinguish arrest from detention. There is, of course, a search and seizure aspect to this concept. In *Terry* v. *Ohio*[45] (Figure 2-12), Cleveland Police Officer McFadden observed three men walking back and forth in front of a jewelry store. Believing the men were casing the store for commission of a crime, he approached them. The defendant, one of the three, was acting strangely and the officer, concerned for his own safety, patted down the defendant's outer clothing for weapons. The officer removed a pistol from the defendant's overcoat pocket. Over the defendant's objection, the weapon was introduced in evidence. The appellate process took the case to the Supreme Court. The defendant's challenge was that the officer conducted an unreasonable search because he did not first arrest Terry and there was no probable cause or exigent circumstances justifying a search. The Court ruled that under circumstances where a person is acting suspiciously and the officer is concerned about his own safety when approaching such an individual, the officer may pat down the outer clothing to determine if the person has a weapon even though there was no arrest. If a weapon is found, it may be seized, and, if its possession is a violation of the law, it is admissible in a subsequent proceeding. The Court said that officer safety in a detention situation justifies the frisk. The Court held that an officer cannot frisk for illegal drugs but only for weapons. If, however, the officer feels something that she/he believes might be a weapon but turns out to be contraband, it is admissible. However, if it is readily apparent that the item is not a weapon, its seizure is unreasonable. To illustrate, in the case of *Minnesota* v. *Dickerson*,[46] officers stopped the defendant whose actions were evasive when approached by police just after he left a building known for cocaine traffic. One officer conducted a pat down and found no weapon, but he did feel a lump in the defendant's jacket pocket. After feeling it and examining it with his fingers, the officer believed it to be crack cocaine. He reached into the pocket and withdrew a bag containing cocaine. The Supreme Court held that even though the detention and frisk were lawful under the *Terry* doctrine, it was obvious to the officer that the lump in the pocket was not a weapon. Therefore, the seizure of the cocaine was based on an unlawful search and should not have been admitted into evidence.

◄ **FIGURE 2-12**
Officer frisking a suspicious person
An officer conducts a stop and frisk of the outer clothing of a man to determine if he is armed and poses a significant danger to the officer, as authorized by *Terry v. Ohio*. This individual was walking erratically in the street and causing a traffic problem; police were called to the scene to investigate the problem. (©Michael Matthews/Police Images/Alamy)

► FIGURE 2-13
Investigator checking identification
An investigator checks the identification of a young person in an abandoned house. Originally thought to be burglary suspects, these youths, it was discovered, were looking for a place to smoke marijuana. (©Kwame Zikomo/ SuperStock RF)

In a similar manner, police do not have the right to seize a cell phone during a routine frisk unless probable cause exists to believe evidence of a crime is on the device. In such cases, the cell phone can be seized by the officer on probable cause, not stop and frisk.

In an interesting collateral issue to a *Terry* stop, the Supreme Court, in 2004, upheld a conviction under a Nevada statute that requires a person to identify himself, when so requested, during a *Terry* stop. When the defendant refused to identify himself after 11 requests by the officer, he was arrested and charged with violating the statute.[47] In *Hiibel* v. *Sixth* Judicial District Court of Nevada (2004), the court found that Hiibel had no reasonable belief that his name would be used to incriminate him, and hence his name disclosure to a police officer during a Terry stop did not violate his Fifth Amendment right against self-incrimination. As a result, the court listed the following 20 states with legal "Stop and Identify" statutes: Alabama, Arizona, Arkansas, Colorado, Delaware, Florida, Georgia, Illinois, Indiana, Kansas,

Louisiana, Missouri, Montana, Nebraska, Nevada, New Hampshire, New Mexico, New York, North Dakota, Ohio, Rhode Island, Utah, Vermont, and Wisconsin[48] (Figure 2-13).

FRUITS OF THE POISONOUS TREE

A final point is necessary to fully comprehend the consequences of an unreasonable search and seizure. The **fruits of the poisonous tree doctrine** provides that evidence obtained from an unreasonable search and seizure cannot be used as the basis for learning about or collecting new admissible evidence not known about before. Not only is the evidence obtained from the unreasonable search and seizure inadmissible; any evidence resulting from the unreasonably seized evidence is also tainted and is not admissible as fruits of the poisonous tree. This doctrine resulted from a 1963 decision of the high court in which a confession was obtained from the defendant after evidence was produced that had been obtained unreasonably.[49]

KEY TERMS

affidavit	due process	search
arrest	due process clause	search and seizure
arrest warrant	exigent circumstances	search warrant
Brady violation	fruits of the poisonous tree doctrine	stop and frisk
charging	procedural criminal law	substantive criminal law
detention	probable cause	unreasonable

REVIEW QUESTIONS

1. Define *arrest*.
2. Distinguish arrest from detention.
3. Distinguish arrest from charging.

4. What are the benefits to a police officer and the case if an arrest is made under the authority of a warrant?

5. Is a "John Doe" arrest warrant valid under any circumstances? Explain.

6. Define and describe *probable cause*.

7. During an ongoing criminal investigation, what factors must the criminal investigator consider in deciding whether to make an arrest and when to make it?

8. Explain how the laws of arrest and search and seizure flow from the Bill of Rights.

9. Distinguish the effects of the Fifth and Fourteenth Amendments on defendants in criminal cases.

10. List the requirements of a valid arrest warrant.

11. What is the Exclusionary Rule, and how did it evolve?

12. Describe the "Silver Platter" Doctrine. Is it still followed? Why or why not?

13. Under what circumstances may a search be conducted without a search warrant?

14. For what reasons do the courts allow searches incident to a lawful arrest?

15. What limitations have judicial cases placed on the search of a motor vehicle incident to a lawful arrest?

16. Give five examples justifying a search under exigent circumstances.

17. How does a law enforcement agency's policy affect the lawfulness of an inventory search of a motor vehicle?

18. What is meant by a plain view seizure, and what are the requirements for conducting such a seizure by a law enforcement officer?

19. What are the limitations on a law enforcement officer conducting a stop and frisk?

20. Explain the "fruits of the poisonous tree" doctrine.

INTERNET ACTIVITIES

1. Locate the requirements in two states for the legal issuance of a search warrant. These requirements can be found as a list or on a blank search warrant form. How alike or unalike are the two? What explanation do you have for your conclusion?

2. In this country and abroad, newspaper stories about defendants alleging unlawful arrest by police are not uncommon. Take three such stories from this country and three from foreign countries and compare the fact situations for the arrest. Are there common denominators? For example, in some countries people are arrested because their speaking or writings are critical of a totalitarian government or "strong man" regime or they advocate for greater civil rights for citizens.

3. We now live in a world never imagined by our forefathers and the writers of the Constitution. A world filled with cell phones, personal tablets, and PCs accessing social network sites like Facebook, Instagram, and SnapChat millions of times a day. Visit the National Institute of Justice website at http://www.nij.gov/topics/forensics/evidence/digital/pages/welcome.aspx. How is search-and-seizure law evolving and different for evidence and property that is digital in nature? What do you see occurring in the future relating to the seizure of such evidence?

► Crime scene technician working location where police officer was stabbed by knife wielding subject. Officer wounded the assailant, who was apprehended. Both the officer and the assailant were hospitalized in serious, but stable condition.

(©Bernard Weil/Toronto Star/Getty Images)

3

INVESTIGATORS, THE INVESTIGATIVE PROCESS, AND THE CRIME SCENE

CHAPTER OBJECTIVES

1. Understand the skills and qualities needed by investigators.
2. Identify the objectives of crime scene investigation.
3. Distinguish between the preliminary and follow-up investigations.
4. Explain the importance of crime scene coordination.
5. Explain the factors that may affect crime scene processing plans.

6. Discuss three broad categories of evidence.
7. Explain the "rules" for crime scene investigators.
8. Identify crime scene health issues.
9. Summarize the four major considerations that dominate the crime scene search.
10. Identify different methods of visually documenting the crime scene.

Although crime is a national problem, its control is primarily the responsibility of local government. When officials cannot prevent or deal effectively with crime, other problems are created. First, if individuals commit crime and escape prosecution, future illegal acts are encouraged. Second, unchecked crime requires that resources, which could be devoted to other social problems, be diverted to crime control, resulting in further entrenchment of such ills as poverty and substandard housing. Third, as crime increases, our system of government faces the real possibility of a crisis of confidence in its ability to maintain public welfare. Finally, crime tears the fabric of social relations and living patterns. People become fearful of strangers and of being on the streets after dark, homes become fortresses, and families move to new locations in search of a secure life. A terrible reality is that until significant inroads are made in controlling crime, the overall quality of life is lower than it could be.

Certain qualities are common to successful investigators, such as good communication skills, strong ethics, initiative, and resourcefulness. All crimes assigned to investigators must be investigated effectively and thoroughly. This responsibility includes not only complete preliminary and follow-up investigations but also understanding the importance of physical evidence in a criminal investigation. The contributions of physical evidence to an investigation are diminished primarily by the inability, unwillingness, or failure to locate, properly collect, mark, and preserve the evidence, and by the drawing of improper conclusions from its analysis.

Although rare, there have also been cases of forensic examiners simply submitting reports on forensic tests that were never actually performed. In 2016, a New Jersey State Police lab technician produced a report for a marijuana test that was never conducted, throwing into question the other 7,827 criminal cases on which he worked.[1]

TYPES OF OFFENSES

A **crime** is the commission (doing) of any act that is prohibited or the omission (failing to do) of any act that is required by the penal code of an organized political state. There can be no crime unless there is advance notice that the conduct is prohibited or required.

Legislatures enact criminal laws that distinguish between felonies and misdemeanors. In most states, a **felony** is an act punishable by imprisonment for a term of one or more years, or by death. Generally, violations of the criminal code that are not felonies are designated as **misdemeanors,** lesser offenses that may be punishable by a fine, ordinarily not to exceed $500, and/or imprisonment for no more than a year. Some states have a third crime category called **violation** (for example, criminal littering), which is punishable only by a fine, usually no more than $250.

THE INVESTIGATOR AND THE IMPORTANCE OF INVESTIGATION

In the search for truth, the most important skill of an investigator is the ability to converse equally well with a wide range of people, from corporate executives to the homeless. This is essential because much of what we learn during an investigation comes from people. The competent investigator is aware of the difference between knowing things and doing things. Such an investigator will therefore consistently translate his or her special knowledge into actual investigative behaviors.

The investigation of any crime places significant responsibilities on the investigator. These responsibilities are particularly heavy during an arrest for a violent felony, since the investigator may have to use deadly force: investigators cannot legally use such force prematurely, but from a tactical standpoint they cannot be even a split second too late in responding to deadly force directed at them. When a person is arrested, whether for a felony or a misdemeanor, the arrest is often publicized, and the person, even if not convicted, incurs economic and/or social costs. The more heinous the charge, the greater these costs will be. If a criminal charge is sustained, the person may suffer any of the penalties authorized for conviction of a felony, misdemeanor, or violation, which run from a fine to execution. This means that investigators must evaluate information accurately and use sound judgment in making investigative decisions.

ESSENTIAL QUALITIES OF THE INVESTIGATOR

Some investigators have a reputation of being lucky, and good fortune sometimes does play a role in solving a case. Most often, however, the "lucky" investigator is someone with strong professional training and solid experience who, by carefully completing every appropriate step in an investigation, leaves nothing to

chance. By doing so, he or she forfeits no opportunity to develop evidence. In addition, successful investigators:

1. Invariably have a strong degree of self-discipline. It is not the presence or absence of a supervisor that causes them to get things done.
2. Use legally approved methods and are highly ethical.
3. Have the ability to win the confidence of people with whom they interact.
4. Do not act out of malice or bias.
5. Include in their case documentation all evidence that may point to the innocence of the suspect, no matter how unsavory his or her character.
6. Know that investigation is a systematic method of inquiry that is more science than art.
7. Realize that successful investigations are not always produced by rote application of the appropriate steps and therefore supplement the investigative procedures with their own initiative and resourcefulness.
8. Have wide-ranging contacts across many occupations.
9. Are not reluctant to contact experts from many different fields to help move the investigation forward.
10. Use both **inductive** and **deductive reasoning.** Inductive reasoning moves from the specific details to a general view. It uses the factual situation of a case to form a unifying and logically consistent explanation of the crime. In contrast, deductive reasoning creates a hypothesis about the crime. The explanation is tested against the factual situation. If the fit is not good, the hypothesis is reformulated and tested again. The process is repeated until everything "fits together."
11. Know that inductive and deductive reasoning can be distorted—by untenable inferences, logical fallacies, the failure to consider all alternatives, and bias—and self-monitor themselves to ensure effective use of these reasoning processes.
12. Learn something from every person with whom they come into contact, knowing that the wider their understanding of different lifestyles, occupations, vocabularies, views, and other factors, the more effective they will be.
13. Have the empathy, sensitivity, and compassion to do their job without causing unnecessary anguish (for example, when interviewing a rape victim).
14. Avoid becoming calloused and cynical from their constant contact with criminals, keeping in mind that the criminal element does not represent everyone. The failure to keep this distinction in mind can be the precursor of unethical behavior.

ORGANIZATION OF THE INVESTIGATIVE PROCESS

The major events in the investigation of crime are depicted in Figure 3-1. These elements provide an overview of the investigative process and introduce concepts covered in greater detail in subsequent chapters.

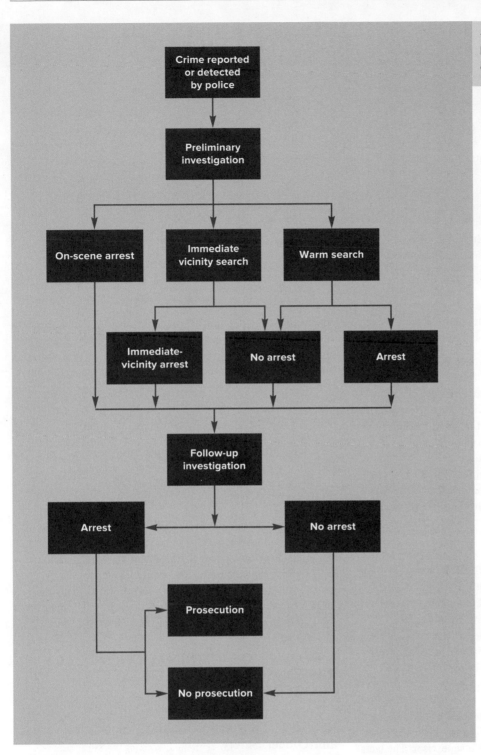

Once a criminal offense has been committed, three immediate outcomes are possible; it may: (1) go undetected, as in the case of a carefully planned and conducted murder by organized-crime figures, in which the body is disposed of in such a way that it will remain undiscovered; (2) be detected, but not reported, for example, because the loss is minor or the victim wants to avoid contact with the police, or (3) come to the attention of the police through their observation, a complaint by the victim or witnesses, or a tip.

Regardless of the outcome, a crime has occurred in each of the three preceding instances. However, only in the last case, when it is both detected and reported, is the offense of concern to the investigator, because only at that time does it become subject to formal processing.

THE PRELIMINARY INVESTIGATION MINDSET OF OFFICERS ASSIGNED CALLS

Although other responsibilities merit great respect, the most important thing officers do is protect human lives, including their own. Because of its sanctity, human life is unique in the

BOX 3-1 | A LAPSE OF BEING TACTICALLY SOUND

A woman was in her dark bedroom around midnight on a New Year's Eve. The bedroom window faced across an alley that ran behind a one-story strip mall. Hearing sounds outside, she got up to see what was happening. She saw a man and a woman breaking into a dress shop through its rear door. She called 911, which gave the call to two patrol units as a burglary in progress, two subjects observed entering the premises.

A motorcycle officer who was returning to the station at the end of his shift heard the call and voluntarily swung by as a backup because he was close to the scene. The woman, still connected to 911, gave a running account of what happened next.

The motorcycle officer arrived first and pointed his motorcycle lights toward the rear door. Instead of maintaining his position and waiting for the arrival of the patrol units, he walked to the open rear door and stopped, framed from behind by his own headlights. The male subject fired six times, hitting the officer with five .38 caliber bullets. Despite being mortally wounded, the officer courageously returned fire, wounding his killer. Less than a minute later, patrol units arrived at the scene and arrested the two suspects. Both were wanted on one murder and several felony warrants in nearby states.

degree of reverence it commands. Whether patrolling or assigned to calls, officers must keep two things at the front of their minds:

1. *Respect for the sanctity of life.* This does not require officers to needlessly or recklessly endanger their own lives. An uncomfortable truth is that sometimes the situation immediately requires the use of deadly force. Respect for the sanctity of life requires not getting to the point of using any and particularly deadly force prematurely, e.g., using conflict deescalation techniques.
2. *Being tactically sound.* Arguably, being tactically lax, such as not having a person take their hand out of their outer coat or rear pockets, is an invitation for some to violently assault officers.

QUICK FACTS

The Fatal Funnel

Tactically, choke points like doorways and halls are called the "fatal funnel" because there is no room for officers to maneuver or find cover, protection, from shots fired at them. Therefore, officers are at a tactical disadvantage if someone suddenly initiates the use of deadly force.

On "routine" calls law enforcement agencies usually dispatch one patrol unit. If it is a crime- in-progress, the usual initial deployment is two patrol units and often a supervisor. The facts of the situation at a scene will dictate the level of the police response. Consider the following actual examples: (1) a city's NFL team had just won the Super Bowl. Fans spontaneously flooded the streets to celebrate. Suddenly, the crowd turned violent. (2) An elderly woman called to report aliens had just landed in her yard and she wanted the police to tell them to leave her property. (3) Three notorious killers escaped sometime in the last three hours from a maximum security prison. (4) A man complained that teenagers living in the apartment above him were playing music loudly and yelling.

Although all calls are important to citizens, most often they are simply another "routine" unit of work for officers to handle

courteously. Therein lies a potentially deadly detail. Because "nothing usually happens," some officers get lured into a false sense of security by their own experience. Thinking this way commits the logical fallacy that the past will be linear in the future: It will continue to repeat itself. Even the experience of nothing happening in many tactical situations contributes, for lack of a better term, to officers developing a potentially deadly "cognitive disconnect" with being tactically sound. When this happens, officers don't do the things they should and they do things they shouldn't, even though they know better (see Box 3-1).

THE PRELIMINARY INVESTIGATION

The actions taken by the first officer to arrive at the scene of a crime after its detection and reporting are collectively termed the **preliminary investigation.** The **follow-up investigation** is the police effort expended after the initial incident report is completed until the case is ready for prosecution. Normally the preliminary investigation is conducted by a uniformed officer from the Patrol Division and consists of the following steps:

1. RECEIPT OF INFORMATION, INITIAL RESPONSE, AND OFFICER SAFETY PROCEDURES

Receipt of Information, Initial Procedures, and Officer Safety

a. *Note all dispatch information:* Record the time/date the call was received, when the officer arrived at the scene, the location and names of parties involved, their descriptions, past history of incidents at the location, and if known, the numbers and types of weapons involved.[2] **Field notes** must be made intermittently throughout the preliminary investigation. In those notes the condition and placement of people and things at the scene are recorded. To illustrate, where was the victim, assailant, and witnesses? What were they saying and doing? What types and numbers of weapons were where? The comments, statements, and spontaneous exclamations made by people at the scene may turn out to be key evidence. A dying

BOX 3-2 | DOMESTIC DISTURBANCE QUICKLY ESCALATES

A solo unit was dispatched to a domestic disturbance in progress. The caller reported that it involved a man and a woman arguing on the small porch of a home. A backup was also dispatched. When the primary unit arrived, a woman was sitting on the porch steps, facing the street. As the officer walked toward the loudly arguing couple, the man, who was facing the woman lunged forward, his right arm outstretched. She cried, "O Lord! You've killed me."

The man turned to run away from the house, saw the officer, took two quick steps, and slashed the officer's face from along under one eyebrow, across the bridge of the nose, and straight across his second eyebrow. Blood in his eyes, the officer tried to draw his weapon as he backed up, stumbled, and fell on his back.

The backup officer saw the stabbing and was running forward when the primary officer was slashed and stumbled. Faced with this second officer, the perpetrator abandoned his attack and turned to run, when the backup officer issued a command, "Stop or I'll shoot." The suspect looked at a forested area some 30 yards away and glanced back at the second officer as though assessing his chances to get away. The officer ordered him to drop the knife and get on his knees. He did so slowly. The woman died at the scene before the EMTs could arrive. Had they been at the scene when she was stabbed ,it would have made no difference. The 2″ blade on the knife, had severed her aorta, the largest artery in the body.

BOX 3-3 | MURDER OF WIFE STAGED AS ROBBERY

A badly wounded man called the police and reported an assailant had tried to rob him and his pregnant wife and that she had been shot in the head. With two victims, no gun at the scene, and no witnesses, the husband's version of events initially held up. However, there were lingering questions about what the two victims were doing in that area late at night. The wife died in the hospital as the investigation continued. Ultimately, the investigation established that the husband had been the shooter. His brother reportedly took the gun from the scene. When the husband's story unraveled, he committed suicide.[3]

declaration from a victim is ordinarily admissible as an exception to the hearsay rule. Comments and exclamations from the victim, suspects, and others at the scene should also be faithfully recorded.

b. *In all calls, field notes should be made only after higher priority tasks have been handled, such as getting medical assistance for wounded persons.* Examples conditions to record include: What lights are on? Is there evidence of a forced entry? Were the drapes/blinds open or shut? How many used/unused dinner plates were on the table? Is there evidence that suggests the possibility of a struggle, such as overturned furniture and broken vases? Is there lipstick on glasses? Did someone rummage through a desk? Are there blood-soaked towels in the hamper? Are toilet seats up or down? Are there items there that don't belong, e.g., a wallet of someone who is not a household member? These are examples and not an exhaustive list that must be followed strictly on a checklist.

c. Often, the type of call to which officers are dispatched is actually what happened at the scene. However, people who call 911 may be high, confused, misinformed, have a speech impediment, have only a rudimentary command of the English language, be injured, have wounds, or be lying Furthermore, background noise can degrade communications between the caller and the dispatcher. In addition to having only partial or misinformation, important events may have occurred between the time officers are

dispatched and when they arrive. For such reasons, officers must be open to the possibility there may be a difference between what the dispatcher tells them and the actual situation at the scene. Additionally, *before the primary unit arrives at the scene, the call sometimes turns into something different (See Box 3-2) or never have been what the dispatcher was told (See Box 3-3).*

d. *Some law enforcement policies give officers the discretion of responding to an emergency/crime in progress without using flashing lights and/or a siren.* It may allow an officer to arrive at the scene and arrest suspects who are unaware of how close the police are or it could provoke a hostage situation. Using lights and siren may also interrupt a criminal act, causing a perpetrator to flee before any more property is lost or someone is killed. Some states require an emergency vehicle to use both an audible signal and flashing lights while others require one or the other. At least one state allows officers to operate without lights or audible sound if it is important to the investigation of a suspected or actual criminal violation. Officers must be clear about what equipment must be in operation in order to have the protection of their state's emergency vehicle operation statute.

e. *Do not deviate from going to the call to which you are assigned, except for the most compelling reasons.* Examples of such reasons are being fired on or discovering a violent crime in progress. Where cars are equipped with cameras, departmental policies direct turning them on when getting closer to the scene. Overwhelmingly, what "getting closer" means is left to

▶FIGURE 3-2
Crime scene odor
A quiet neighborhood was plagued with strong stench. Ray's Sausage Shop, next to this house, was first thought to be the source of the odor. The drainpipe was flushed and a sewer line replaced. Still, the smell persisted. Investigators searching the house, where a convicted sex offender lived, discovered the bodies of 11 murdered women. Note the investigator at the left covering his nose and mouth. (©John Kuntz/The Plain Dealer/Barcroft Media)

the officers' discretion. In a random sample of 25 law enforcement agency policies, only one department specified a distance: 1/4th of a mile. As the first arriving unit, officers must quickly prioritize the sequence of their actions. These priorities may change as officers get additional information.

f. *Approach the scene cautiously, especially when there is thought or known to be a crime in progress.* Think about the location to which you are going and where lookouts might be posted. Always consider the possibility of there being more than one perpetrator. Continue to think that the crime could be on-going until you can conclude it is not. If additional units will be arriving you need to be able to direct them to positions that help contain the situation and where they are not unnecessarily exposed.

g. *Take time to look, listen, and smell (Figure 3-2) and evaluate what is going on.* Be alert for people and cars at, near, or leaving the crime scene or in its immediate proximity and note descriptions and tag numbers. For crimes-in-progress, perpetrators may not have had time to flee the scene, their pickup driver may have panicked and left them at the scene, her car won't start, or a lookout may have accidentally gotten stranded. Officers may recognize known criminals who may or may not be involved. At an in-progress scene, the statement that the armed robbers have left the scene should be carefully evaluated. The source of that information could be a perpetrator. Even if it comes from the store owner, consider the possibility that a spouse or an employee is being held hostage inside and the claim the alarm was set off accidently is based on a suspect's order to "get rid of the cops." One way to get some idea of the situation is to ask, "How many people are working today?" Then ask the store owner to call all of them outside.

Sometimes what is missing turns out to be crucial. A veteran police officer pulled into a 24-7 convenience store. The clerk was not behind the counter or anywhere else in view. Two men in a car with a very distinctive appearance were just exiting the store's parking area. The clerk was found tied up and tied to the toilet in the men's room. A description of the distinctive car

and some minimal information about the two men was broadcasted. It was enough to locate them and they subsequently pled guilty to the robbery.

h. Are there special hazards? If there's been an explosion, are there one or more backpacks on the ground that may contain bombs? Is a chemical/biological/nuclear event a possibility? What are people and any casualties doing, e.g., from where/what do they appear to be running and what physiological symptoms are apparent?

QUICK FACTS

Sarin?

If officers arrive at a scene where there is a large crowd and people are running away panicked, while others are stumbling around or laying on the ground, confused, nose running, drooling, coughing, and rubbing their eyes as if to eliminate blurred vision, officers should remain in their cars, immediately turn off their air conditioning, keep their windows tightly closed, and personally rapidly evacuate the scene far enough to hopefully observe at least part of it. While evacuating, officers must take into consideration the direction in which the wind is blowing: They may be witnessing a Sarin attack. Officers must be upwind to avoid the Sarin being blown in their direction.

Sarin is a colorless, odorless, high-potency nerve agent that begins to work in seconds. In a scene where people are down, a natural instinct is to rush in and help. However, as the first responding units, the responsibility of officers is to warn others of what is, or may be, happening and request appropriate units, e.g., bomb squad, EMTs, and Hazardous Material Units. Officers cannot warn or inform others if they become casualties too.

i. *Officers who get too close to the scene and are seated in their car are at a significant tactical disadvantage.* Officers may have gotten so close to a robbery in progress that they are faced on the front with a perpetrator while behind is another member of the robbery team.

QUICK FACTS

It Wasn't a Nun

A police officer ran past a nun and toward a bank robbery in progress. The nun was actually a backup gunman who was part of the robbery team and he shot the officer in the back. Lesson: Ordinary-looking people may be dangerous.

---

j. Officers must follow departmental policies for requesting additional assistance, such as a crime scene technician or the specialized units mentioned early in this section. Officers should wait for backup before attempting any clearing of a building. Supervisory approval is usually needed to call a canine team to help with this process. If large areas must be searched and multiple teams are used, there should be a briefing emphasizing each team's area of responsibility and how to avoid a "blue on blue" exchange of gunfire. The arrest of one suspect does not mean there isn't another one or even several more. Once inside a building, stop, allow your eyes to become adjusted to whatever the light conditions are, be still, and actively listen for slight sounds. In clearing the building look for evidence of the crime, keeping in mind the possibility of a staged scene and insurance fraud. As the search begins, the canine officer and dog go first, covered by other officers. Once an area potentially holding a suspect is identified, the other officers take the lead from the canine team.

k. If the suspect is still at the scene, arrest him/her, conduct a search of his/her person, seize weapons, drugs, fruits of the crime, and other evidence (Figure 3-3). Legal rules apply as to just how far you may search a person beyond his or her actual person (for example, the immediate area, other rooms, and any vehicle involved). Make sure you know and follow such rules. If you intend to interrogate suspects, make sure they are given their Miranda warnings and document this action. In some situations (for example, a growing hostile crowd or the presence of angry relatives of the victim), you will need to have suspects immediately removed from the scene.

2. EMERGENCY CARE

a. If there are no satisfactory options to causing or allowing the contamination or destruction of evidence, remember that *saving the victim's life has a higher value than preserving physical evidence.*

b. *Assess level of injuries to the victim and request any needed medical assistance,* which is usually provided by emergency medical technicians (EMTs). You may need to provide first aid, taking appropriate precautions, to the victim until EMTs arrive.

c. *Point out potential evidence to medical personnel,* and ask them to have no contact with it or to have minimum contact with it. Instruct emergency personnel to preserve all clothing and personal effects; do not allow them to cut clothing through or along bullet holes or knife openings. Document all movement of people and items (for example, furniture and blankets, weapons) by medical personnel. Also make note of things EMTs may have added to or left at the scene, such as hypodermic needles and bandage wrappings, as well as personal items, such as jackets. Restrict the movement of the EMTs to areas at the scene where they are actually needed. Depending on the condition of the scene, crime-scene technicians may want to take the fingerprints and get shoe impressions from EMTs who entered the scene for elimination purposes.

d. *Obtain as much information as possible from the victim before he/she is moved to the hospital by EMTs.*

e. *Do not allow EMTs to clean the scene,* because eradicate trace or larger types of evidence.

f. *Get the names of attending medical personnel, as well as their locator information,* including their employer, telephone numbers,

◄FIGURE 3-3
Conducting a search of a suspect
The investigator in the right foreground is handing a weapon discovered on the subject he is searching to the investigator at his immediate left. Note that he carefully keeps his finger outside the trigger guard. However, the proper action to take is to have the partially visible covering investigator at the left side of the picture approach the investigator who found the weapon, who would hand it directly back to him. The action depicted distracts both investigators and keeps an unsecured weapon near the suspects, making the situation more dangerous.
(©Mikael Karlsson/Alamy)

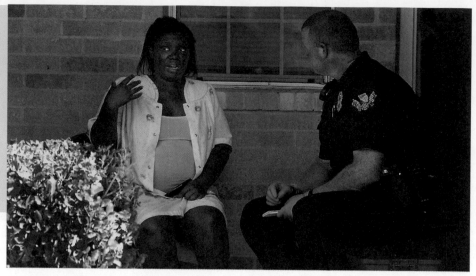

▶ FIGURE 3-4
Crime scene interview
A Nacogdoches (Texas) Police Department officer interviews one of two victims of a home invasion robbery. The other victim was shot in the back of his head by one of the two offenders. Home Invasion robberies annually represent about 15–17 percent of all robberies reported to the Federal Bureau of Investigation. (©Andrew D. Brosig/The Daily Sentinel/AP Images)

and email addresses. Find out to which hospital the victim will be taken and send an officer, whenever possible, in the ambulance with the victim to get additional information. If that is not possible have an officer check with the transporting EMTs regarding any statements made by the victim or suspect. If this is not done on a timely basis, it may be 24 hours or more before the EMTs are available to be interviewed and valuable information could be lost.

g. *If there is a chance that the victim may die, attempt to get a dying declaration.* Also document other statements, comments, and spontaneous exclamations by victims, suspects, EMTs, and witnesses.

h. *In some instances, officers may also have to rescue or provide first aid to suspects.* Examples include rescuing a would-be burglary from the chimney in which he was stuck, pulling a suspect from a burning car and another from a car sinking in an icy reservoir. Sometimes, offenders flee so desperately that they bring about their own deaths, most commonly in automobile accidents, but by other means as well. (See Box 3-4)

3. SECURE SCENE AND CONTROL PERSONS AND EVIDENCE

a. *As rapidly as possible, identify the boundaries of the crime scene and secure it* (Figure 3-5). Establishing the boundaries could entail checking an open field for additional bodies and physical evidence or all the rooms in a structure to determine if there are multiple scenes. A classic example of multiple scenes occurred in 1966 in a Chicago townhouse, where Richard Speck killed eight student nurses in different rooms. Checking for multiple scenes may also identify other victims who are still alive and require medical attention. On rare occasions, such victims or witnesses may have hidden themselves in closets or elsewhere, fearing the return of their assailant, as did a ninth nurse who eluded Speck. Crime scene control is also covered in different contexts, for example, dealing with the news media, in subsequent portions of this chapter.

b. *In defining the scene, officers must make sure that they also identify possible or actual lines of approach to, and flight from, the scene and protect them also.* These lines may contain shoe or tire impressions or residues, weapons, discarded fruits of the crime on which fingerprints or touch DNA may have been left, or other things which may provide investigative leads.

c. *Maintaining **crime scene control** is a crucial element in the preliminary investigation.* To the extent possible while meeting emergency care and other responsibilities, prevent individuals at the scene from committing any acts of theft, altering/destroying evidence, or attacking others. Identify all individuals at the scene, such as suspects, victims, bystanders, family, and friends.

Do not delay medical treatment for victims to identify them or accomplish other investigative tasks. Occasionally,

BOX 3-4 | BURGLARY SUSPECT HIDING FROM COPS ENDS BADLY

A man told his girlfriend that he would be in a nearby Florida town to commit burglaries with someone he knew. Subsequently in that town, the police responded to calls about two men dressed in black walking behind homes. Both men ran when the police arrived. While searching for them that night the police heard yelling, but could not determine the location. The next day, one of the burglars was reported missing.

More than a week later, the body of the man reported missing was found in a nearby lake with wounds appearing to be from an alligator attack. Divers recovering the body were confronted by an aggressive alligator roughly 11 feet long, which was euthanized. Inside were body remains consistent with the wounds on the recovered body.[4]

◀FIGURE 3-5
Crime scene control
Four gunmen entered Gomez's, a family owned bar in Murreo, Louisiana, and in a botched robbery, the owner, his brother, and two customers were killed. Gomez's was known to periodically keep large amounts of money on hand to cash their customers' paychecks. Crime scene control has not yet been achieved and uniformed officers, investigators, and civilians are comingled. (©Susan Poag/The Times Picayune/ Barcroft Media)

safety reasons will dictate seizing evidence before it is photographed (see Box 3-5).

d. *Separate any potential combatants* to avoid violence; *separate persons arrested* so they cannot "get their story together"; and *separate witnesses* so they don't contaminate each other's recollection.

e. *Set up a physical barrier to protect the scene, prevent the contamination or theft of evidence and for your own safety.* Use yellow crime scene tape or employ natural barriers such as doors, walls, gated areas, request additional personnel as needed. Cover fragile evidence with a box or other container that will not disturb or contaminate the evidence.

f. *Maintain a crime scene entry log of persons coming to and leaving the scene* (Figure 3-6). Brief those entering on the situation and any special conditions or hazards.

4. ISSUE A BE-ON-THE-LOOKOUT

Whenever possible, an APB/ BOLO should include the following points: number of suspects, age, race, sex, height, weight, build, coloration, birthmarks, hair color and length, condition of teeth, mustaches and beards, names and/or nick-names, clothing, hats, scars, marks, tattoos, jewelry worn, deformities (for example, missing finger), any prosthesis, and accent, as well as whether the suspects were unarmed or armed, numbers and descriptions of weapons, the method and direction of flight, and a full description of their vehicle, including year, make, model, color, stickers, damage,

things hanging from the mirror, and loud mufflers. There is an imperative to get a first APB/BOLO out quickly, sometimes called a "preliminary pickup order." As quickly as possible thereafter, forms shown in Figures 3-7 and 3-8 may be used to gather more detailed information to broadcast to all units in the field. These forms are normally attached to the incident reports. They can also

QUICK FACTS

BOLO Nets Robbery Suspect

A convenience store was hit by an armed robber. The first responding officer determined that a toy gun may have been used and that the suspect's vehicle had a white "hard hat" on the rear shelf. This information was included, along with a description of the suspect and his vehicle on the BOLO. Another officer found a vehicle matching the suspect's behind a tavern. A toy gun box was found on the rear floorboard, and a white hard hat was on the rear shelf. The bartender said a man matching the suspect's description had entered the tavern, called a taxi, had a quick drink, and left in the taxi when it arrived. The cab company reported that the fare was taken to the airport. There it was learned that he had boarded a flight to another city, where he was arrested when he got off of the plane.

BOX 3-5 | GUN SEIZED IMMEDIATELY

An officer arrived at a bar where a shooting had just occurred. The victim was lying on the cement floor and had been shot several times in his upper thighs and lower groin area by a small caliber pistol, which was lying on the bar. Two seats down the bar, his girlfriend was having a drink. When she saw the officer she spontaneously said, "Yea, that's right, I shot the son-of-a-bitch, caught him with another woman and me working and paying all the bills." Friends of the victim and the shooter were shouting back and forth and emotions in the crowd were running high. The officer immediately seized the weapon.

▶ FIGURE 3-6
Crime scene entry log sheet
(Crime Scene Entry Log, from "Crime Scene Investigation: A Guide for Law Enforcement" (2013) ©NFSTC. Reprinted with permission.)

CRIME SCENE ENTRY LOG

CASE NUMBER:		OFFENSE LOCATION			CRIME OFFENSE	
OFFICER IN CHARGE OF CIRME SCENE		FROM (DATE AND TIME)		TO (DATE AND TIME)	RELIEVED BY	
OFFICER PROVIDING SECURITY		FROM (DATE AND TIME)		TO (DATE AND TIME)	RELIEVED BY	

#	INDIVIDUAL NAME	TIME/DATE IN AND OUT	REASON FOR ENTRY	AUTHORIZED BY (NAME, BADGE)
		IN		
		OUT		
		IN		
		OUT		
		IN		
		OUT		
		IN		
		OUT		
		IN		
		OUT		
		IN		
		OUT		
		IN		
		OUT		
		IN		
		OUT		
		IN		
		OUT		
		IN		
		OUT		
		IN		
		OUT		
		IN		
		OUT		
		IN		
		OUT		
		IN		
		OUT		
		IN		
		OUT		
		IN		
		OUT		
		IN		
		OUT		
		IN		
		OUT		
		IN		
		OUT		
		IN		
		OUT		

An entry is to be made for every person who is allowed into the boundaries of the Crime Scene (including officers, Supervisors, and Civilians). Each entry must be authorized by the Officer in charge of the scene at the time the entry is made. Officer in charge of security will make entries into this log. Each person making entry into the scene will initial above, giving consent to submit samples of hair, blood, fingerprints, etc. Each person entering the Crime Scene may be asked to submit to a supplemental report and to testify in a court of law.

BOX 3-6 | THE BURGLAR WAS A NEIGHBOR

On a Sunday morning, a residential burglary resulted in the theft of $3,800 in rare coins. The uniformed officer making the original investigation received permission to conduct the neighborhood canvass. Usually the follow-up investigator did the canvass, but it was a slow day so the uniformed officer was allowed to do it. The victim's home was situated on a cul-de-sac along with four other homes with some view of the victimized premises. There were no homes to the rear of the victim's residence. After interviewing residents of the four neighboring homes, including a teenage boy, the uniformed officer recorded the identities and statements of those with whom he had talked in his report. All indicated they had seen nothing. Because of the value of the property taken, the case was referred for follow-up investigation.

The investigator assigned to the case recently had been transferred from the Youth Services Bureau to the Burglary Section and recognized the name of the teenager identified in the interview section of the uniformed officer's report as an individual with an extensive juvenile record for breaking and entering. Investigation revealed that the youth had committed the offense, and all coins taken were recovered.

SUSPECT DESCRIPTION FORM (Conclusion)

CASE #: _____ DATE: _____ OFFICER: _____

14. FACE SHAPE
- ☐ Oval
- ☐ Square
- ☐ Diamond
- ☐ Thin
- ☐ Long
- ☐ Fat
- ☐ Wide

15. SKIN
- ☐ Tan
- ☐ Pale
- ☐ Healthy
- ☐ Freckled
- ☐ Moles
- ☐ Acne
- ☐ Rough

16. FACIAL HAIR
- ☐ Clean-shaven
- ☐ Moustache
- ☐ Sideburns
- ☐ Beard
- ☐ Goatee
- ☐ Stubble

17. NECK
- ☐ Tan line
- ☐ Long neck
- ☐ Short neck
- ☐ Adam's Apple
- ☐ No neck/Thick
- ☐ Hairy
- ☐ Dirty

18. SCARS/TATTOOS
DESCRIBE: _____

19. HANDS/NAILS
- ☐ Long fingers
- ☐ Short fingers
- ☐ Ring
- ☐ Watch
- ☐ Scars on hand Describe: _____
- ☐ Dirty nails
- ☐ Long nails
- ☐ Chipped nails
- ☐ Painted nails Color: _____

20. CLOTHING DESCRIPTION

HAT (Knit cap, Baseball, Cowboy, etc.): _____

GLASSES (Sunglasses, Tinted, Wire-rimmed, Dark): _____

COAT (Trenchcoat, Ski-jacket, Raincoat, Leather, Windbreaker, Sports-team): _____

SHIRT (Long-sleeved, Short-sleeved, Tank top, T-shirt, Button-up, Pullover, Hooded): _____

PANTS (Sweatpants, Jeans, Shorts, Slacks): _____

BELT (Leather, Buckle:Gold/Silver, Cloth, Logo): _____

SHOES (Logo/Running, Boots, Sandals, Dress): _____

SOCKS (None or Color): _____

GLOVES (Leather, Knit, Color): _____

JEWELRY (Watch, Earring(s) L/R ear, Diamond, Hoop) NECKLACE (Chain, Gold/Silver): _____

MASK (Ski mask, Other/Color): _____

CLOTHING NOTES: _____

ANYWHERE POLICE DEPARTMENT
SUSPECT DESCRIPTION FORM

COMPLAINANT: _____ CASE #: _____

DATE: _____ OFFICER: _____

Sex: Male ☐ Female ☐

Race: _____ Age: _____ Height: _____ Weight: _____

1. BUILD
- ☐ Slender
- ☐ Medium
- ☐ Heavy
- ☐ Fat
- ☐ Muscular

2. HAIR
- ☐ None
- ☐ Long
- ☐ Short
- ☐ Curly
- ☐ Wavy
- ☐ Straight
- ☐ Dirty
- ☐ Oily

3. HAIR COLOR
- ☐ Black
- ☐ Brown
- ☐ Lt. Brown
- ☐ Blonde
- ☐ Red
- ☐ Grey
- ☐ Other: _____

4. FOREHEAD
- ☐ Small
- ☐ Large
- ☐ Lines
- ☐ Scars
- ☐ Other: _____

5. EYEBROWS
- ☐ Thick
- ☐ Bushy
- ☐ Thin
- ☐ Arched
- ☐ Plucked
- ☐ One brow

6. EYE SHAPE
- ☐ Almond
- ☐ Round
- ☐ Small
- ☐ Dark Circles
- ☐ Bags
- ☐ Wrinkled Corner
- ☐ Heavy Lids

7. EYE COLOR
- ☐ Brown
- ☐ Dark Brown
- ☐ Hazel
- ☐ Grey
- ☐ Green
- ☐ Blue
- ☐ Bright Blue

8. CHEEKS
- ☐ High Cheekbones
- ☐ Fat Cheekbones
- ☐ Dimples
- ☐ Fat Cheeks
- ☐ Pock Marks
- ☐ Pimples
- ☐ Freckles
- ☐ Hollow

9. NOSE
- ☐ Long
- ☐ Hooked
- ☐ Crooked
- ☐ "Broken"
- ☐ Wide
- ☐ Flat
- ☐ Pugged

10. LIPS
- ☐ Harelip
- ☐ Full
- ☐ Thin
- ☐ No Upper Lip

11. MOUTH
- ☐ Small
- ☐ Large
- ☐ Wide
- ☐ Bow-shaped

12. TEETH
- ☐ Yellow/Stained
- ☐ Gaps
- ☐ Crooked
- ☐ Large
- ☐ Small
- ☐ Braces
- ☐ Missing Teeth

13. CHIN
- ☐ Cleft
- ☐ Dimpled
- ☐ "No chin"
- ☐ Pointed
- ☐ Double
- ☐ Round
- ☐ Square
- ☐ Long

▲ **FIGURE 3-7 Anywhere Police Department Suspect Description Form**

(Courtesy of the Sacramento Police Department; drawing of man and badge: ©McGraw-Hill Education)

53

▶ **FIGURE 3-8**
Anywhere Police Department Vehicle Description Form
(Courtesy of the Sacramento Police Department.)

ANYWHERE POLICE DEPARTMENT VEHICLE DESCRIPTION FORM

COMPLAINANT: _____

_____ CASE#: _____

DATE: _____ OFFICER: _____

COLOR:	
YEAR:	
MAKE:	
MODEL:	
LICENSE PLATE:	
STATE OF LICENSE:	
DIRECTION OF TRAVEL:	
TIME ELAPSED:	
BUMPER STICKERS:	
BODY DAMAGE:	
TINTED WINDOWS:	
UNIQUE CHARACTERISTICS:	

be handed out when there are multiple witnesses, with each person directed to complete them without the need to talk to anyone else.

5. CONDUCT NEIGHBORHOOD AND VEHICLE CANVASS

A **neighborhood canvass** is an attempt to locate witnesses who may have heard, seen, or smelled something of investigative importance. The "neighborhood" may be other tenants in an apartment building, business owners and their employees in a commercial district, or some similar grouping. The neighborhood canvass may be conducted by uniformed officers, investigators, or some combination thereof. It may occur while the crime scene is still being processed. If not conducted at the time of the preliminary investigation, the investigator assigned to do the follow-up will determine whether the fact situation warrants one. All results of the canvass, both positive and negative, should be carefully recorded because information that seems unimportant to the canvasser may have significance to someone else (Figure 3-9).

Interviews should be conducted first at businesses or dwellings with a clear view of the crime scene then along and the suspect's avenues of approach and flight. When there are substantial numbers of locations involved, several teams of officers canvassing simultaneously are helpful.

If the crime was committed near a public transit system, visit the system at the same time and on the same day of the week as the time and day of the crime. If victims and witnesses have been intimidated or otherwise dissuaded from testifying investigators should notify their supervisors and protective services considered.

It is estimated that a systematic neighborhood canvass soon after the commission of an offense results in information of investigative value in approximately 20% of all cases. The extent of the canvass depends on variables such as the type of offense, time of day, and characteristics of the crime scene. The timing of a neighborhood canvass is an important consideration. People not only move randomly through areas but also ebb and flow on a variety of schedules. To mistime a neighborhood canvass by 30 minutes, for example, may mean eliminating the possibility of locating persons who regularly catch a bus at a particular time and who, on the day of an offense, might have seen something of considerable investigative value.

Offenders may have parked near to the scene to commit their crimes, but not have had sufficient time to get back to their car afterwards. Alternatively, the co-conspirator who was to drive the suspect from the scene may have panicked as he/she saw or heard police cars approaching and walked away from the "getaway" car. The **vehicle canvass** makes a record of all vehicles in the area to provide another investigative avenue (Figure 3-10). The address or location of each vehicle must be recorded, as well as its description and plate/tag number. Anything unusual about a vehicle should be noted, such as bullet holes; blood; odd appearance of the interior; damage; stickers; unusual articles;

BUILDING / NEIGHBORHOOD CANVASS

AGENCY: _____

INCIDENT #: _____

INSTRUCTIONS: Document whether or not all occupants of the residence were interviewed. Document locations where no persons were contacted. If available, list pager and / or cellphone numbers in the remarks column. Use the back side of this sheet for notes.

MULTIPLE UNIT OCCUPANCY: Address _____ Number of Units _____

(List only unit numbers below)

ADDRESS (indicate residence, business, etc.)		PERSON CONTACTED/DOB	TELEPHONE NUMBERS			REMARKS (pager / cell phone)
			CELL	HOME	WORK	
	# OF OCC.					☐ FOLLOW-UP RQ'D ☐ NOTES ON BACK
	# OF OCC.					☐ FOLLOW-UP RQ'D ☐ NOTES ON BACK
	# OF OCC.					☐ FOLLOW-UP RQ'D ☐ NOTES ON BACK
	# OF OCC.					☐ FOLLOW-UP RQ'D ☐ NOTES ON BACK
	# OF OCC.					☐ FOLLOW-UP RQ'D ☐ NOTES ON BACK
	# OF OCC.					☐ FOLLOW-UP RQ'D ☐ NOTES ON BACK
	# OF OCC.					☐ FOLLOW-UP RQ'D ☐ NOTES ON BACK
	# OF OCC.					☐ FOLLOW-UP RQ'D ☐ NOTES ON BACK
	# OF OCC.					☐ FOLLOW-UP RQ'D ☐ NOTES ON BACK
	# OF OCC.					☐ FOLLOW-UP RQ'D ☐ NOTES ON BACK
	# OF OCC.					☐ FOLLOW-UP RQ'D ☐ NOTES ON BACK
	# OF OCC.					☐ FOLLOW-UP RQ'D ☐ NOTES ON BACK
	# OF OCC.					☐ FOLLOW-UP RQ'D ☐ NOTES ON BACK
	# OF OCC.					☐ FOLLOW-UP RQ'D ☐ NOTES ON BACK
	# OF OCC.					☐ FOLLOW-UP RQ'D ☐ NOTES ON BACK
	# OF OCC.					☐ FOLLOW-UP RQ'D ☐ NOTES ON BACK
	# OF OCC.					☐ FOLLOW-UP RQ'D ☐ NOTES ON BACK

CANVASSING OFFICER (Print): _____

INITIALS: _____

DATE: _____

START TIME _____

TIME END: _____

▲ FIGURE 3-9 Building/neighborhood canvass

(Courtesy of Imprimus Forensic Services, LLC.)

VEHICLE INFORMATION CANVASS

AGENCY: _____

INCIDENT#: _____

INSTRUCTIONS: Document all vehicles in the area you have been assigned. Include vehicles parked in the streets, driveways, alleyways and yards. Under "Remarks" list anything unusual noted about the vehicle (manner of parking, warm engine, fresh damage, etc.)

For vehicles without license plates, enter the VIN in the "Remarks" column.

ADDRESS (indicate alley, driveway, street, etc.)	MAKE	MODEL	COLOR	PLATE	REMARKS (VIN)

CANVASSING OFFICER (Print): _____

INITIALS: _____ DATE: _____ START TIME _____ TIME END: _____

▲ **FIGURE 3-10 Vehicle information canvass**
(Courtesy of Imprimus Forensic Services, LLC.)

items hanging from the rearview mirror, and whether the car is hot, warm, cold, muddy, or clean.

6. ADMINISTRATIVE PROCEDURES FOR PROCESSING CRIME SCENES

Procedures for handling specific types of evidence are discussed in Chapter 4, "Physical Evidence." This section discusses the administrative procedures for crime scene processing.

a. In smaller departments that do not have specialists, roughly those with 20 or fewer sworn personnel, the responding officer must recognize and identify physical evidence, document its location through sketching and photographs, collect it and mark it, package it (Figure 3-11), and take it to the station for storage in the evidence room, where a written receipt for it will be given to the officer. This receipt is then attached to the incident/offense report, which the officer subsequently writes. When serious crimes are committed in smaller jurisdictions, assistance with the crime scene may be available through mutual aid agreements with larger agencies or from the state investigative agency.

b. At all stages of handling the evidence, the chain of custody or control of it must be established. The **chain of custody** (Figure 3-12) is the witnessed, unbroken, written chronological history of who had the evidence when. It also accounts for any changes in the evidence, noting, for example, if any portion was used for laboratory analysis.

c. In larger agencies that have sworn and/or civilian crime scene technicians, these specialists will process the crime scene. More detailed information about this subject is presented later in this chapter.

d. One or more plainclothes investigators may also come to the scene, depending on the severity of the crime. If they do, the first responding officer has the following crime scene turnover responsibilities: (1) briefing the personnel taking charge, (2) assisting in controlling the scene, (3) turning over responsibility for starting another crime scene entry log, and (4) remaining at the scene until relieved.

7. THE INCIDENT/OFFENSE REPORT

The officer assigned to the call must prepare an **incident/offense report** on his or her part in the investigation. (Additional information on this subject is presented in Chapter 6, "Field Notes and Reporting.") A supervisor reviews and approves the incident report; the case may be retained in the patrol division for further investigation, referral to the investigative division for follow-up, or inactivated and receive no further investigative effort unless new information is received. Both manual and electronic incident report systems are discussed in Chapter 6.

TYPES OF CRIME SCENES

From Chapter 1, "The Evolution of Criminal Investigation and Forensic Science" we recall that the fundamental assumption on which crime scene searches are carried out is **Locard's exchange principle:** which can be simplified to there is something to be found. We usually think of a crime scene as one particular place. Although this is often true, consider the 1988 terrorist bombing of Pan Am Flight 103 over Lockerbie, Scotland. Among the dead were 259 people on the plane and 11 people on the ground. Evidence from the explosion rained down over 800 square miles. In one of the greatest investigations ever, evidence was collected that led to the identification, arrest, and conviction of the bomber, who was a former Libyan intelligence officer.

Crime scenes vary in regard to the amount of physical evidence that is ordinarily expected to be recovered, for instance, a murder scene will yield more than a yard from which a lawn mower was stolen. At the most basic level, a **crime scene** is the location where the offense was committed. As discussed earlier, the search of the

ANYWHERE POLICE DEPARTMENT

PROPERTY RECORD NUMBER: _____

EVIDENCE CHAIN OF CUSTODY TRACKING FORM

CASE NUMBER: _____ OFFENSE: _____

SUBMITTING OFFICER (NAME/ID#): _____

VICTIM: _____

SUSPECT: _____

DATE/TIME SEIZED: _____ LOCATION OF SEIZURE: _____

DESCRIPTION OF EVIDENCE

ITEM #	QUANTITY	DESCRIPTION OF ITEM (Model, Serial #, Condition, Marks, Scratches)

CHAIN OF CUSTODY

ITEM #	DATE/TIME	RELEASED BY (SIGNATURE & ID#)	RECEIVED BY (SIGNATURE & ID#)	COMMENTS/LOCATION

EVIDENCE CHAIN-OF-CUSTODY TRACKING FORM
(Continued)

CHAIN OF CUSTODY

ITEM #	DATE/TIME	RELEASED BY (SIGNATURE & ID#)	RECEIVED BY (SIGNATURE & ID#)	COMMENTS/LOCATION

FINAL DISPOSAL AUTHORITY

AUTHORIZATION FOR DISPOSAL

Item(s)#: _____ on this document pertaining to (suspect): _____

is(are) no longer needed as evidence and is/are authorized for disposal by (check appropriate disposal method)

☐ Return to Owner   ☐ Auction/Destroy/Divert

Name & ID# of Authorizing Officer: _____ Signature: _____ Date: _____

WITNESS TO DESTRUCTION OF EVIDENCE

Item(s) #: _____ on this document were destroyed by Evidence Custodian: _____

ID#: _____ in my presence on (date): _____

Name & ID# of Witness to destruction: _____ Signature: _____ Date: _____

RELEASE TO LAWFUL OWNER

Item(s) #: _____ on this document was/were released by Evidence Custodian: _____

ID#: _____ to: _____

Name _____

Address: _____ City: _____ State: _____ Zip Code: _____

Telephone Number:(___) _____

Under penalty of law, I certify that I am the lawful owner of the above item(s).

Signature: _____ Date: _____

Copy of Government-issued photo identification is attached: ☐ Yes   ☐ No

This Evidence Chain-of-Custody form is to be retained as a permanent record by the Anywhere Police Department.

▲ FIGURE 3-12 Evidence Chain of Custody Tracking Form

◀FIGURE 3-13
Crime scene investigation
Officers from the Salt Lake City Police Department search for the body of murder victim Lori Hacking. Her body was eventually found three months after her death. Her husband subsequently pleaded guilty in the case. (©George Frey/Getty Images)

crime scene for physical evidence must include a wider area, such as the perpetrator's lines of approach to, and flight from, the scene.

The basic definition of a crime scene works well for many crimes, such as a burglary or a robbery at a liquor store. But where was the crime scene for Pan Am Flight 103? On a much smaller geographic scale, consider the example of a victim who is abducted from a mall parking lot and raped by one accomplice while the other one drives the van from one county to another. Later, the victim is taken to a secluded area, removed from the van, further abused, and executed, and her body is dumped into a ravine in yet another jurisdiction. Clearly, we need additional ways to think about what a crime scene is.

1. Criminal incidents may have more than one crime scene. The **primary scene** is the location where the initial offense was committed; the locations of all subsequent connected events are **secondary scenes.**[5] Illustrating this statement is a Utah case in which a husband shot his wife while she was sleeping. He disposed of the body in a trash bin that ended up in a landfill. After 33 days of picking through 4,600 tons of compacted garbage up to 20 feet deep, investigators located the body (Figure 3-13)[6].

2. On the basis of size, there are macroscopic and microscopic scenes.[7] A **macroscopic scene** is the "large view." It includes such things as the relevant location(s), the victim's and the suspect's bodies, cars, and buildings. The **microscopic scene** consists of the specific objects and pieces of evidence that are associated with the commission of the crime, including knives, bite marks, hairs and fibers, shoe and tire impressions, cigar butts, blood, and so on.[8]

3. Other useful ways of thinking about crime scenes are based on the type of crime (larceny versus aggravated assault), the location (indoors or outdoors), the condition of the scene (organized or disorganized), and the type of criminal action (active or passive). Some further breakdown of these types may also be useful, such as if outside, whether the body is on the surface, buried, or underwater.[9]

The usefulness of having several frames of reference for crime scenes is that they can help organize your thinking about how to approach and process a crime scene. If there are multiple crime scene locations, the primary and secondary scenes may be located in different legal jurisdictions, a situation requiring a high level of

cooperation and informational exchange between agencies. In cases where a serial offender is active and working across several jurisdictions, the case may be assigned to a standing interagency investigative task force, or a special one may be created. In such situations, it is important that departmental jealousies, the issue of who is going to get credit for solving the case, and other factors do not impede the success of the operation.

ORGANIZATION OF THE CRIME SCENE INVESTIGATION

Crime scene investigation is purposeful behavior and is intended to accomplish specific objectives:

1. Establish what happened; for example, was the purpose of the murder to kill the home owner or did she surprise a burglar when she came home unexpectedly? Or, more difficult, to often impossible, to determine, was it a murder-suicide versus an accidental discharge followed by a remorseful suicide?

2. Determine the sequence of events.

3. Find out what the suspect did or didn't do at the scene.

4. Establish the modus operandi, the method of operation, used by the suspect.

5. Determine what property was stolen and what articles were left by the suspect.

6. Note inconsistencies. For example, if the crime appears to be a home invasion that resulted in a murder, why wasn't the victim's cash and jewelry taken? Did the perpetrator panic and flee the scene before taking them, or is something else at work, such as a love triangle?

7. Locate and interview witnesses.

8. Document and recover physical evidence.[10]

9. Provide investigative leads.

Some of these objectives may not be attainable during the crime scene investigation phase and will require the services of specialists. At a complex scene with multiple victims and considerable evidence, determining the sequence of events, for example,

▶ **FIGURE 3-14**
The need for scene coordination
Maine State Police searching multiple sites for human remains in a forest. Without coordination, the investigative effort can lose focus and fail to capitalize on opportunities for locating physical evidence. (©Bill Trotter, Bangor Daily News)

in what order were the victims killed, may only be possible when autopsy and lab reports are available. Even then, the subsequent services of a crime scene reconstructionist may be needed. Lurking behind Point 6 in the preceding list is the determination of the motive for the crime, ordinarily the work of a specialist in criminal profiling. (Crime scene reconstruction and criminal profiling are discussed in Chapter 7, "The Follow-up Investigation and Investigative Resources.")

To achieve the objectives of crime scene investigation, the work at the scene is divided into three major functions: (1) overall coordination of the scene, (2) forensic services, and (3) investigative services.

OVERALL COORDINATION

The senior criminal investigator assigned to a case usually has overall responsibility for what happens at a crime scene. In order to fulfill this responsibility he/she must conduct a visual

inspection, the "walk through," of the scene and develop a preliminary plan for its investigation. Members of the investigative team typically know their jobs and little direct "standing over their shoulder" supervision is required or desired, although the senior investigator may direct that additional processing be done or otherwise provide investigative direction.

A crucially important task for the senior investigator is coordination (Figures 3-14, and 3-15). It is usually accomplished by the senior investigator as he/she moves from one point to another. Some scenes may be so large or victims so numerous that layers of coordination may be needed, which may require using a mobile incident command van or a temporary "headquarters" such as a tent or a building.

The senior investigator at the scene is also responsible for requesting whatever types of additional resources are needed—for example: (1) obtain a search warrant; (2) if there is a dead body, the medical examiner or the coroner must be called to the scene. Generally, this official has jurisdiction over a dead body, which

▶ **FIGURE 3-15**
A mobile command center
The Albemarle County (VA) Sheriff coordinates a search for a missing University of Virginia 18-year-old British-American female student. Weeks later, her body was found on abandoned property. Video cameras in downtown Charlottesville showed a man following her the night she disappeared. Based on forensic and other evidence the man was charged with murder and he pled guilty to avoid the death penalty. (©Ryan M. Kelly/The Daily Progress/AP Images)

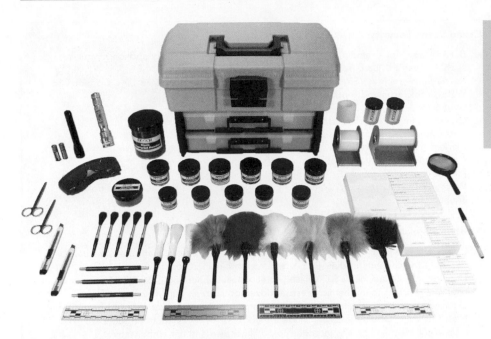

◀FIGURE 3-16
Latent fingerprint kit
A latent fingerprint kit, which includes different color powders, several types of brushes, scales, clear lifting tape, and cards to which the lifted prints are affixed. (Courtesy of EVIDENT, Inc.)

should not be searched or removed from the scene without his/her prior consent;[11] (3) fire truck ladders may be needed to search rooftops for evidence; (4) transportation of vehicles to impound lots; (5) aerial photography of scene; and (6) personnel with specialized knowledge and experience, such as being able to interpret gang graffiti/tattoos/markings.

The senior investigator must ensure that all the members of the crime scene team are briefed simultaneously so that everyone hears and knows the same thing. The senior investigator is also responsible for ensuring that there is a continuous flow of information between members of the team as evidence is recovered. Other duties include making his/her own evaluation of potential safety issues, reviewing the actions of the person who conducted the preliminary investigation, allocating resources among the primary and any secondary scenes, establishing a secure area for the temporary storage of evidence, and establishing a command post and

media function if the situation warrants them. The senior investigator also does a walk through of the scene with those responsible for forensic services to make sure there is a common understanding of how the scene will be approached and processed.[12]

FORENSIC SERVICES

Forensic services is the responsibility of the senior representative of the department's central crime laboratory or a crime scene processing unit. He/she may arrive to process the scene carrying one or more crime scene investigation kits (Figure 3-16) or have the more substantial resources carried in a crime scene van (Figure 3-17). Some jurisdictions also have a mobile crime laboratory in which technicians can carry out limited scientific tests.

Figure 3-18 is a list of supplies and equipment that are available for crime scene processing. Although law enforcement

◀FIGURE 3-17
Police department mobile crime scene unit
The inside of a crime scene van; note the portable Kawasaki generator on the left and the light on the right. The balance of the van is filled with various types of equipment needed at crime scenes, such as gunshot residue, blood, fingerprint, and other collection kits. Many departments buy prepared evidence kits; others assemble kits to better meet their specific needs and capabilities. (Courtesy of Athens-Clarke County Police Department)

▶ **FIGURE 3-18**
Crime scene supplies and equipment

Crime Scene Security

- Barrier tape—for example, "Police Line Do Not Cross," in locally spoken languages, such as Spanish, "La Linea de la Policia No Cruza"
- Scene flags—such as "Sheriff's Line Do Not Cross" and "BioHazard Line Do Not Cross"
- Waterproof tarps and tents
- Sawhorses
- Chalks—standard/reflective/fluorescent spray/assorted colors
- Spray paint/standard/fluorescent/assorted colors
- Marked police vehicles
- Cord, rope
- Flares, chem-lites
- Preprinted signs—such as "Command Center" and "Media Relations" and poles
- Traffic cones

Safety/Personal Protection Equipment (PPE)

- PPE is often divided into different classes, and many law enforcement agencies have designed the contents of their PPE kits. For example, In 2016, the Tucson Police Department's kit includes a full splash protection suit, inner and outer gloves, an armband, chemical-resistant tape, chemical-resistant overboots, an air-purifying respirator with chemical and biological filters that provides protection from a wide range of hazards, but not all of them. Other agencies include a Mark 1 NAAK nerve agent antidote kit. The equipment identified here is intended to be illustrative and not authoritative.
- Reflective vests and gloves
- Neoprene, Latex, nitrile (synthetic latex), polyvinyl, and cut/puncture resistant gloves, such as TurtleSkin, HexArmor, and Blackhawk
- Disposable air-filtering masks/respirators
- Safety glasses/chin length face shield/coveralls/shoe covers
- First responder spray—such as MyClyns™ for potential pathogenic exposures
- EPA registered wipes/spray (for example, Sporicidin) and bleach (for instance, Ultra Clorox Germicidal Bleach). Note that they are both general use and special use germicidals. The latter are engineered for specific use against such diseases as HIV, Ebola, and Hepatitis C.
- Chemical/Biological/Radiological/Nuclear (CBRN) threat environments require specialized PPEs
- First aid kit/insect repellant

Washington County (Maine) Sheriff's Deputy searching underwater for stolen guns using a metal detector.
(©Diana Graettinger, Bangor Daily News)

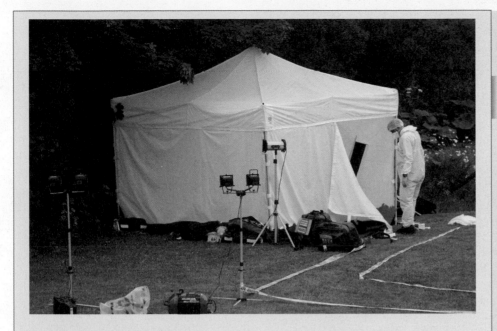

◄FIGURE 3-18
Crime scene supplies and equipment (continued)

An investigator in Rothbury, England, examines the scene where a fugitive shot himself, dying later in a hospital. The tent shields public observation of the process. Note the high-intensity lights, the carefully lined path, and the coveralls, hair net, gloves, and air-filtering mask being worn. Gun ownership rates are low in England, and suicide by them there is therefore rare.
(©Dan Kitwood/Getty Images)

Telecommunications

- Cell/smart phones
- Fax machine
- Tablet/netbook/laptop/computers
- Copier/printer
- Teleconferencing capability
- Departmental handheld radios
- Key telephone numbers/telephone directories

Miscellaneous Equipment

- Audio recorder
- Consent search forms
- Large magnet
- Handheld Global Positioning System (GPS)
- Magnetic compass
- Portable generator
- High-intensity lights—for example, two 750-watt halogens/telescoping arm/adjustable legs
- Evidence refrigeration capability
- Flashlights/spare batteries
- Numbered evidence location marking cones/tents/flags
- Metal detectors
- Thermometers
- Logbooks
- Tents/tarps to protect evidence/personnel/equipment from inclement weather
- Extension cords/adapters
- Ladders
- Privacy/body screen
- Area map
- Pruning shears/wood saws/axes to clear vegetation from core search area
- Rakes/shovels/trowels/paintbrushes
- Soil probe
- Business cards

Equipment for Basic Crime Scene Photography

- Digital single-lens reflex (DSLR) camera for still photography, at least 12 megapixels
- Backup digital camera
- 1 Gigabyte flash card, plus backup
- Detachable flash/flashlight/backups
- Photo logs/pens
- Gray card/other color checker
- External flashes and cords

▶ **FIGURE 3-18**
Crime scene supplies and equipment (*continued*)

- Remote shutter release
- Lens/camera cleaning supplies
- Various lenses, macro/normal/wide-angle/telephoto
- Lens filters
- Supplemental light meter
- Digital video recorder
- Tripods
- External rechargeable battery packs/extra batteries
- Auxiliary lighting
- Scales/adhesive scales/rulers
- Owner's manuals for cameras
- Stepladder
- Numbered evidence location marking cones/tents/flags

Equipment for Basic Crime Scene Sketching/Diagramming

- Sketching/drafting board
- "T" square, assorted transparent triangles: 45/90 and 30/60 degrees
- Drafting compass/dividers/protractor/straight-edge rulers
- Paper/tape/pencils/pens
- Several retractable tape measures, 6- to 100-feet lengths, steel, and fiberglass
- Distance measuring wheel with visible reader for longer distances up to 1,000 feet
- Laser/ultrasonic measuring device
- Magnetic compass
- Laptop computer/crime scene diagramming software, for example, The Crime Zone
- Sketching templates

▶ **Sketching templates**
Two types of templates used in sketching crime scenes: the Human Figure Template (*left*) and the Crime Scene Template (*right*).
(Courtesy Lynn Peavey Company)

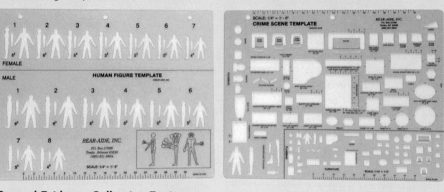

General Evidence Collection Equipment

- Stainless steel/disposable tweezers/forceps/hemostats/metal probes/scalpel
- Hard-metal scribes
- Tongue depressors
- Nets for flying insects
- Framed sifting screens and tubes
- Utility knife/scissors
- Assorted tools, wire and bolt cutters/hacksaw, extra blades/hammers/screwdrivers/wood and metal chisels/pliers/wrenches/pry bar/vise grips/drills, bits
- Mirror with telescoping arm
- Magnifying glasses

Specialized Evidence Collection Kits and Material

- Sexual assault
- Gunshot residue (GSR)
- DNA/biological evidence
- Laser trajectory
- Entomology/insect
- Latent fingerprint
- Trace evidence vacuum
- Latent fingerprint
- Blood spatter
- Presumptive field tests, for example, blood and drugs
- Body excavation
- Electrostatic lifting for dust and residue prints

- Forensic light source(s)/goggles
- Adjustable casting frames for foot/shoe/tire impressions
- Casting preparation materials/dust, sand, and dirt hardeners/wax hardener for snow impressions/snow print powder (red) to contrast impression to be photographed with surrounding snow
- Casting materials, for instance, Durocast, silicone, dental stone, low-density impression foam such as BioFoam, and AccuTrans, a silicone product, which won an innovation award. The silicone is dispensed from a caulk-gun-like nozzle and, dries in four minutes. It is highly flexible and tear resistant after drying and captures fine details. Self-contained kits for casting tire and shoe impressions, such as Shake-N-Cast, are also gaining in popularity. The Shake-N-Cast kits contain dental stone and a water vial in the same pouch; the vial is broken while inside of the pouch and the kit massaged, producing the same correct consistency to pour into an impression each time.

Evidence Packaging Materials

- Evidence tags/general identification labels
- Evidence control/chain of custody labels
- Sharpie permanent markers, assorted colors
- Assorted sizes of Kraft paper evidence envelopes/bags
- Rolls of Kraft/butcher paper
- Assorted adhesive/"sticky" labels—for example, "Biohazard" and "Latent Print Evidence"
- Weapons and other sized boxes
- Clear plastic tubes for syringes and knives
- Clear plastic jars, assorted sizes
- Transparent glassine envelopes
- Antistatic bags for computer and other digital evidence
- Nylon bags and metal cans for arson evidence
- Evidence sealing tape, sensitive to tampering efforts, ½" to 3" wide
- Document sleeves
- Polyethylene evidence tubing
- Assorted sizes of evidence bags and pouches
- Heat sealer for polyethylene/nylon bags
- Sterile swabs/swab boxes
- Blood tubes, with, and without, preservative coating
- "Peel and Seal" evidence bags, which cannot be opened without destroying the bag

Source: Content drawn from Technical Working Group on Crime Scene Investigation, *Crime Scene Investigation* (Washington, D.C.: U.S. Department of Justice, 2013), pp. 150–155; and Henry C. Lee, Timothy M. Palmbach, and Marilyn T. Miller, *Crime Scene Handbook* (San Diego: Academic Press, 2001), pp. 321–324; and additional content from the authors.

◀ **FIGURE 3-18**
Crime scene supplies and equipment (*concluded*)

agencies are varied, the core tasks that need to be completed at scenes dictate that they will use many of the supplies and equipment listed, but there will also be some variation in what is actually used. Because at least 92% of all law enforcement agencies in this country use **digital cameras**[13] their use is specified in Figure 3-18.

Advanced methods of crime scene documentation, laser scanning, and panoramic cameras are discussed later in this chapter.

Evidence located in areas that are "open-view" to the public are ordinarily processed first. Similarly, fragile evidence should be documented and collected before more durable physical evidence. The open-view "rule" is especially important when bodies are in plain sight because common talk and potential news media photography will cause family members and friends great pain (Figure 3-19).

The forensic services function includes (1) establishing a central point to collect trash generated by processing the scene, including biohazard bags for the collection of disposable evidence equipment and personal protection equipment (PPE); (2) establishing a decontamination point as needed; and (3) carrying out the identification, documentation, collection, marking, packaging, and transmission of physical evidence to the evidence room or the crime laboratory.

A variety of factors shape the initial plan for processing crime scenes. The initial plan and any revisions are effected by a variety of factors, including:[14]

1. Remote or difficult terrain—for example, steep ravines, swamp areas, and forested areas with thick underbrush. A man walking his dog found the remains of murder victim Chandra Levy in a remote part of Washington D.C.'s 2,000-acre Rock Creek Park. The Federal Bureau of Prisons intern had disappeared a year earlier. Based on information in the victim's computer, police thought she may have disappeared in the park. Although the

► FIGURE 3-19
Use of privacy screen to shield body
St. Tammany Parish, Louisiana, Sheriff's Office investigators use a privacy screen to shield the body of a homicide victim from morning rush hour traffic. A second victim was found on the same highway, two miles away. Gunshots killed both victims and investigators proceeded on the theory of a double homicide. (©David Grunfeld/The Times Picayune/Barcroft Media)

police had twice searched much of it, they did not search the park's most remote area, judging it unlikely to yield results.

2. Physical hazards that imperil crime scene technicians—for instance, downed power lines, unsafe structures, and booby traps.
3. A hostile crowd.
4. Human remains that are widely scattered because of animal predation.
5. Weather, including rain/sleet/snow, extreme heat/cold temperatures (Figure 3-20), blowing sand/dust, and nearby lightning strikes.
6. Potential presence of chemical/biological/radiological/ nuclear (CBRN) weapons agents—for example, following the attacks on September 11, 2001, a biological agent, anthrax, was mailed to several dozen recipients, including two members of Congress.

7. Presence of dangerous chemicals and vapors—for example, at meth labs or from fields recently sprayed with agrichemicals.
8. Limited personnel or the availability of additional personnel—such as cadets from a police academy.
9. Infectious disease risks, which have led some law enforcement agencies to require crime scene investigators to undergo health screening twice each year as a precaution. (Infectious disease risks and the precautions investigators should take regarding them are discussed in detail later in this chapter.)

INVESTIGATIVE SERVICES

Investigative services include: (1) interviewing witnesses; (2) conducting and documenting the neighborhood canvass; (3) a field interrogation of the suspect if he or she is in custody; and (4) carrying out and recording the results of a vehicle canvass.

► FIGURE 3-20
Maine State Police, Department of Inland Fish and Wildlife wardens, and officers from several municipalities reach a small island on which a light plane had just crashed, unsure if their mission is rescue or body recovery. Aluminum canoes were the safest choice to cross the water because of increasing ice in it. In extreme cold, hypothermia is a risk factor for investigators. Part of the overall coordination of a scene like this is making sure crime scene workers, rescue workers, EMTs, and survivors have hot beverages, food, water, cots, blankets, and warming tents.
(©Kevin Bennett, Bangor Daily News)

TYPES OF EVIDENCE

There are three broad categories of evidence in which investigators have a particular interest: (1) corpus delicti, (2) associative, and (3) tracing. The task of developing such evidence is spread across the three main crime scene functions, but the data from the different types of evidence are combined to create a larger and more unified picture of the crime. This picture helps determine, to a large extent, how the follow-up investigation will be conducted.

CORPUS DELICTI EVIDENCE

Each criminal offense contains a distinct set of elements whose commission or omission must be demonstrated to have occurred in order to prove a case; **corpus delicti evidence** substantiates these elements. Thus, at each crime scene the investigator must keep in mind the unique requirements of proof for the case and attempt to locate related evidence.

ASSOCIATIVE EVIDENCE

Associative evidence is bidirectional in that it connects the perpetrator to the scene or victim, or connects the scene or victim to the suspect. A case history illustrates this:

QUICK FACTS

He Wasn't Just Walking By

A silent burglar alarm was triggered at a bar in a high-crime area. Officers responding to the scene found a point of forced entry at a rear window of the building. An individual was detected hiding in a small shed attached to the building. His statement was that when walking up the alley, he suddenly saw police cars, panicked, and hid in the shed. The search of this person following his arrest revealed the presence of valuables and materials taken from the burglarized premises, connecting the suspect with the scene.

TRACING EVIDENCE

The identification and location of the suspect are the goals of **tracing evidence;** corpus delicti and associative evidence may also serve these purposes:

QUICK FACTS

Easy ID of Indecent Exposer

A 20-year-old female was at a laundromat washing her clothes. A male loitered nearby, observing her. When the woman was alone, he walked rapidly to the laundromat and entered the men's room. A few minutes later, with his pants and underwear around his ankles, he approached the woman, shook his genitals at her, pulled up his clothing, and ran off. The officer who responded to the call found a man's wallet on the floor of the men's rest room. A records check on the identification contained in it revealed that the owner of the wallet had a history of sex offenses and lived in the neighborhood of the laundromat. When the victim identified the suspect from a series of photographs, a warrant for the suspect's arrest was obtained.

TYPICAL CRIME SCENE PROBLEMS

Although the procedures to be followed at a crime scene investigation may be neatly delineated in theory, any number of conditions may render their accomplishment a good bit less orderly than the ideal. In a perfect world, every crime scene would be fastidiously processed. In reality, the scenes of misdemeanor offenses receive a cursory examination and even the thoroughness with which felony crime scenes are processed is frequently affected by the severity of the offense. A crime scene processing unit cannot be called out to process every crime scene. To victims, the crime committed against them is important regardless of the severity. To investigators, that crime may be important or "just another report to fill out." Regardless of the situation, officers must convey a genuine interest in the complainant's situation.

At the scenes of violent crimes, especially those that are interracial, emotions may run high. Even a small crowd may add considerable confusion to the process of ascertaining what has happened and along what lines the investigation should proceed. In such situations, it is not unusual for witnesses to be lost, for their versions and perceptions of what occurred to be altered by contamination through contact with the crowd, or even for so-called witnesses to be added. In this last circumstance, a bystander may hear actual witnesses talking and suddenly believe they personally know something they should tell the police.

Police officers and supervisors occasionally make investigations more difficult when they drop by to see if they "can be of help," when in reality they are simply curious. Too many people at the scene can lead to confusion of assignments or the accidental alteration or destruction of evidence.

RULES FOR THE CRIME SCENE INVESTIGATOR

Regardless of the type of crime involved, five fundamental rules must be observed.

MAINTAIN CONTROL

Although mentioned previously in this chapter, the issue of control is so important that it warrants further elaboration.

Without control, a life might be lost, evidence destroyed, assignments overlooked, or the investigation conducted in a generally haphazard manner. How the police relate to the news media is of critical importance. Broadly, police policies usually grant news media members broader access to noncriminal incidents, for example, when covering disasters. For reasons more fully examined below, crime scene access is more tightly regulated for sensational crimes like bank robberies, murders of public figures, and terrorist attacks. Nonetheless, incident commanders at some point may allow limited access by the news media to an outer portion of the crime scene, while maintaining a secure inner perimeter.

Often, law enforcement agencies will cordon off a safe staging area near crime scenes for use by the news media. Reporters should be advised when a public information officer (PIO) will arrive and be briefed on the situation and then provide the news media with releasable information. Two imperatives are at work: (1) the need for the news media to quickly get as much information as possible and (2) the need for the police to provide medical care for victims; ensure the safety of victims, witnesses, officers, and others at the scene; prevent actions that may compromise the right of suspects to a fair trial; and conduct a through investigation. On comparatively rare occasions these two imperatives unpleasantly collide. Great restraint should be exerted to avoid the arrest of a news reporter. As Mark Twain famously said, "Don't pick fights with people who buy ink by the barrel."

Members of the news media typically arrive shortly after the investigation begins and immediately attempt to quickly obtain information and/or videotape investigators, witnesses, or bystanders to meet their deadlines. Unless properly handled, this situation has the potential to create both confusion and complicate the investigative process (Figure 3-21). All investigators must have a thorough knowledge of their agency's media relations policy, and related state and/or federal laws, as well as any applicable portions of collective bargaining agreements, for example, provisions not to discuss departmental policies or cases with the news media.

Although some states have enacted "shield laws" so that news media personnel are not required to divulge their sources, as a general matter reporters have no legal rights beyond those granted each citizen. Although news officials may be permitted to enter certain types of scenes, even that may be restricted by measures such as home owner's privacy rights that trump the reporters' First Amendment claims.

With respect to a crime investigation, the policies of many police departments identify information that may not be released without the prior approval of the chief executive or a designee and information that may routinely be released by the PIO, unless there is some unusual situation. Examples of each of these types of information include:[15]

EXAMPLES OF IMPERMISSIBLE RELEASES

1. The identity of a suspect prior to arrest unless it would aid in apprehending the suspect or serve to warn the public of potential danger.

▲FIGURE 3-21 Investigations and the media
Washington, D.C. Police Chief Cathy Lanier speaks at a press conference following the 2009 shooting attack at the Holocaust Museum, which resulted in the death of a security guard. A persistent question is whether news media coverage helps or hinders investigations. The answer is that it all depends on the fact situation, but that excessive details revealed in the news media can hamper investigations or imperil a fair trial for the defendant. (©Alex Wong/Getty Images)

2. The refusal of a defendant to make a statement or to submit to any tests or examinations or alibi offered.
3. The results of any tests or examinations.
4. The identity of victims and witnesses, if such releases could substantially impair investigation (e.g., leads, identifiable MOs, and contents of note) or place them in personal danger.
5. The identity of any critically injured or deceased person before the next of kin is notified.
6. The identities of victims of child abuse, child neglect, domestic violence, or a sex crime or any information which conceivably could lead to them being identified.
7. The home address, telephone number, email address, or any other information about a departmental employee that could lead to them being contacted.
8. Any information about the employer of a person of interest, suspect, or defendant.
9. Identities of juveniles, except when they are being charged as an adult, or a misdemeanor violations of the traffic code.
10. Descriptions of physical evidence.
11. Whether an undercover officers or confidential informer was involved in the case.

12. Characterizations of the defendant's innocence or guilt.
13. Disclosure that a defendant led them to the fruits of the crime, a weapon used, or the remains of a victim.
14. Speculation about the credibility of someone who may or has been called as a witness.
15. Specific cause of a death unless determined by a medical examiner.
16. Photographs of arrested suspects in custody when other suspects involved are still at large or there are collateral investigations which could be adversely effected.
17. The names of the hospitals to which victims, witnesses, and suspects are being or have been taken.[15]
18. Require suspects to pose for photographs or reenact the crime.
19. Describing a suspect's character, any prior criminal record, or reputation, such as a "no-good."
20. If a juvenile is involved, information about their parents/legal guardians shall not be released.

EXAMPLES OF PERMISSIBLE RELEASES

1. Age, name, and marital status of adult accused of a crime.
2. A basic description of the incident, including time and place of arrest, and whether pursuit, weapons or resistance were involved.
3. The amount of bond, scheduled court date, and where the suspect is being held.
4. How the incident came to the attention of the police.
5. When an officer arrived at the scene.
6. Number of officers currently at the scene.
7. The number of suspects and victims involved.
8. When an adult is arrested and booked into the jail, their name, age, gender, race, city of residence, and alleged offense.
9. In very broad terms, medical condition of persons involved may be released. Detailed medical conditions cannot be released, such as prognosis, or severity of wounds.
10. The name and unit of the arresting officer if it does not hinder the investigation or place the officer at risk.
11. The identities of any other agencies participating in the Investigation.

CONCEPTUALIZE EVENTS

A 24-year-old man was shot five times and killed outside of a nightclub. Other shots were also fired. By conceptualizing how the crime was committed, Washington State Police officers believed that the front side of the club might contain places where bullet evidence could be recovered, but which they could not see. They called in for a bucket truck and were successful in locating important evidence. Law enforcement agencies also use drones to check areas of interest (Figure 3-22).

Without the investigator's thoughtful examination of the crime and reconstruction of how the perpetrator may have acted, that lower portion of the door would not have been dusted for fingerprints because it would have been illogical to expect to find a fingerprint there. Consequently, the most important piece of evidence would never have been located.

Assumptions that are made must be checked for accuracy as quickly as possible. The failure to do so may result in an offender's escaping prosecution and in embarrassment for the investigator and the department. It may also produce confusion in, or misdirect, the investigation:

QUICK FACTS

Assumption Dead Wrong

A woman was murdered in her apartment. The investigators assumed that the woman's husband had thoroughly searched the apartment for their missing infant child when he first arrived and found his wife's body. Thus, they further assumed that the baby had been kidnapped. Some four days later the baby's body was found by the grandmother in the apartment under a sofa cushion.[16]

Human behavior is rich in its variety; in reconstructing the crime, investigators must be alert to the danger of imparting their own probable motives or actions to the perpetrator unless there are solid grounds for so doing. Alternatively stated, this proposition dictates that simply because, under the same or a similar set of circumstances, we would not have acted in a particular fashion does not preclude the possibility that the perpetrator may have acted in that way. Two cases illustrate the importance of this point:

Case One

In Woodbridge, New Jersey, a series of burglaries was solved when it was established that two inmates had been breaking out of a correctional facility to commit the offenses, and then returning nightly to the facility.[17]

Case Two

In Palm Beach, Florida, a guard at a bank was surprised one night by an intruder who took $50,000 in gold coins. Unable to find a point of entry, investigators were puzzled until they received an anonymous tip that the intruder had shipped himself into the bank in a crate and broken out of it after the regular employees had gone home.[18]

Large physical evidence, such as a handgun used in a criminal homicide, is often easily found at the crime scene and requires little in the way of conceptualization. However, there is the possibility that much smaller types of evidence are also present; these will be located only if the investigator is able to conceptualize events:

▶ FIGURE 3-22
A Deputy Sheriff hand launches a fixed-wing Falcon drone
Drones can be useful in searching for lost children, hikers, elderly people who have wandered away, surveillance of illegal activities, and observing marches and counter marches where violence may erupt. In 2015, North Dakota became the first state to allow police to weaponize their drones, but only with "less than lethal" means, such as tear gas, pepper spray, tasers, and mace. No state has approved police use of lethally armed drones, although a fierce battle over whether to do so erupted in the Connecticut legislature in 2017, as this book was sent to the printer.
(Source: Kyle Allen, Comunity Oriented Policing Services (COPS), U.S. Department of Justice)

QUICK FACTS

Detail Trips Suspect

A university student claimed that several hours previously she had been raped at her date's apartment. This had been their second date. In addition to being able to identify her assailant, the victim showed the investigator a digital photograph taken on her phone earlier in the evening of her and her assailant. In examining the photograph, the investigator noticed that the victim was wearing a sorority pin in the photograph, but the victim's pin was now missing. Believing that the pin could have been lost at the crime scene, the investigator went to the suspect's apartment. The suspect's version of events was that he told the victim he no longer wanted to date her and she swore to get even for "being dumped." The suspect also said that the woman had never been in his apartment and consented to a search. The investigator found the missing sorority pin in the perpetrator's bedroom, and the suspect subsequently gave her a confession.

It does not take a great deal of conceptualization to recognize larger items of evidence at a crime scene. Where this ability pays substantial dividends is in locating **trace evidence,** which is present in extremely small or limited amounts. Such evidence may be, but is not exclusively, microscopic in size.

Often this trace evidence is located using **alternative light systems (ALSs)** (Figure 3-23). Illustrations include the Polilight,

BlueMaxx, and Luma-Lite. As illumination from ALSs sweep over a crime scene, the various lights cause many types of evidence to fluoresce. Trace evidence that reacts to such illumination includes fingerprints, bodily fluids, hairs, fibers, drugs, glass and metal fragments, bite marks, bruises, human bone fragments, and gunshot residues. The value of ALS is illustrated by the use of a Luma-Lite at a burglary scene:

A small leaf was found on the windowsill where a bare foot suspect entered a building. A portion of the offender's footprint was recovered. Confronted with this and other evidence the suspect plead guilty.[19]

Portable **trace-evidence vacuums** are also quite useful in locating very small items of evidence. To prevent the accidental contamination of the evidence, the nozzle and the evidence filter unit (which sits on top of the vacuum's nozzle) is packaged and sealed at the factory's "clean room." At the crime scene, as each different area is vacuumed, the nozzle and the filter are detached and sealed as evidence. These systems are particularly effective in gathering hairs, fibers, and certain types of drug evidence, such as cocaine. Thus, trace-evidence vacuum systems can often be effectively used in assault, rape, and some drug cases. If clothing is seized as evidence and fiber, hair, or other evidence from the suspect or victim may be on it, crime laboratories generally prefer that the clothing not be vacuumed at the scene but instead

◀FIGURE 3-23 Forensic light
Forensic light illuminating latent finger
fingerprints. Chapter 4, "Physical
Evidence," contains a major section on
fingerprint evidence. Such illumination
helps to find fingerprints that might
otherwise be overlooked. (Courtesy of
Athens-Clarke County Police Department)

be sent to the laboratory for processing to prevent the possibility that other valuable evidence may be lost during the vacuuming.

PROCEED WITH CAUTION

Many crime scenes provide an immediate focus; in criminal homicide, for example, there is a tendency to move directly to the body. Such action, when the person is obviously deceased, has a number of disadvantages. In approaching the point of focus, small but extremely important evidence may be altered or destroyed, the area to be searched may be too rapidly defined, and other areas that might be fruitfully explored are overlooked or given only a cursory examination.

APPLY INCLUSIVENESS

The rule of inclusiveness dictates that every available piece of evidence be obtained and, where there is a question as to whether a particular item constitutes evidence, be defined as such. The rationale is that mistakes made in excluding potential evidence often cannot be rectified. One cannot always return to the crime scene and recover evidence. Sound judgment is required in applying the rule of inclusiveness. If you pick up everything that remotely could have some evidentiary value, scarce laboratory resources are going to be wasted.

The rule of inclusiveness also requires that standard samples and elimination prints always be obtained when appropriate. If, for example, a burglary has been committed and a safe inside the building successfully attacked, exposing the insulation of the safe, then standard samples of the insulation should be obtained. This will ensure that if at some future time a suspect is identified, comparisons can be made between the standard sample of safe insulation and any traces of safe insulation that might be recovered from the soles of the suspect's shoes or his or her car floor mat.

Elimination prints are useful in determining whether a latent fingerprint found at a crime scene belongs to the suspect. In the case of a residential burglary, for example, if a latent print was discovered inside the house on the window ledge where the perpetrator entered, the residents of the household should be fingerprinted and a comparison made between the latent fingerprint and those of the residents. If the latent fingerprint does not belong to any of the residents, it may belong to the perpetrator. In some instances, the fingerprint might belong to someone having authorized access to the dwelling. In cases where this is found to be true, however, the possibility cannot be overlooked that the person with authorized access may be the perpetrator. An example of this is the case of a licensed real estate dealer operating in the Washington, D.C., area who may have entered more than 100 homes that were being offered for sale, stealing furs, tape recorders, silverware, and other valuables worth between $200,000 and $300,000.[20]

MAINTAIN DOCUMENTATION

Documentation of the crime scene is a constant activity, starting with the rough, shorthand record created by field notes. Other types of documentation that need to be maintained include:

1. The **crime scene entry log,** which was shown in Figure 3-6.
2. The **administrative log,** which is the responsibility of the crime scene coordinator and details such things as who is assigned to what function at the crime scene and the sequence of events at the scene, including its release.
3. **Assignment sheets,** which are completed by each individual who is given specific work to do and which document the results—both positive and negative.
4. The **incidence/offense report,** which is the responsibility of the first officer on the scene.
5. **Photographic logs,** detailing who took which shots, from where, when, and under what circumstances, for example, type of lighting (Figure 3-24). Separate logs are kept for each camera used.

▶ **FIGURE 3-24**
Photo Log Sheet
(Courtesy Imprimus Forensic Services)

PHOTO LOG SHEET Supplement to Evidence Report		CASE NO:
	INCIDENT:	VICTIM:

DATE OF PHOTOS:	TIME OF PHOTOS:	SUBJECT:

LOCATION PHOTOS TAKEN:

PHOTOGRAPHER:	ASSISTED BY:

SLATE ID#:	DIGITAL: ☐ VIDEO ☐ FILM: ☐ ISO: 100 ☐ 200 ☐ 400 ☐ 800 ☐

PHOTO #(s)	NOTES

SUBMITTED BY:	STAR #:	SUPER:	PAGE:1 OF ☐

6. The rough sketch of the crime scene; the data used to prepare the finished or final diagram, which may be drawn by hand or by computer.
7. The **evidence recovery log,** which lists each item of evidence; the names of the collector and witness; the location, date, and time of the collection (Figure 3-25).
8. Emergency medical personnel documents.
9. The **lifted-prints log,** which contains the same type of basic information as the evidence recovery log.
10. If applicable, the consent search form or search warrant.

In lesser offenses, a single officer may be the only representative of the police department at the scene. Thus, everything that is learned will be a result of his/her investigation. In such cases,

the only documentation that may exist is the officer's field notes and the incident/offense report.

INFECTIOUS DISEASE RISKS AND PRECAUTIONS FOR INVESTIGATORS

Investigators are at risk of exposure to infectious pathogens (disease-causing agents), such as HIV, Hepatitis A, B, and C, Ebola, the Zika virus, and tuberculosis. These pathogens can be more than a medical inconvenience. They may also end both

ANYWHERE POLICE DEPARTMENT

PROPERTY RECORD #: _____

EVIDENCE CHAIN OF CUSTODY TRACKING FORM

CASE #: _____ OFFENSE: _____

SUBMITTING OFFICER (NAME/ID#): _____

VICTIM: _____

SUSPECT: _____

DATE/TIME SEIZED: _____

LOCATION OF SEIZURE: _____

DESCRIPTION OF EVIDENCE

ITEM #	QUANTITY	DESCRIPTION OF ITEM (Model, Serial #, Condition, Marks, Scratches)

CHAIN OF CUSTODY

ITEM #	DATE/TIME	RELEASED BY (SIGNATURE & ID#)	RECEIVED BY (SIGNATURE & ID#)	COMMENTS/LOCATION

FINAL DISPOSAL AUTHORITY

AUTHORIZATION FOR DISPOSAL

Item(s) #: _____ on this document pertaining to (suspect): _____

is(are) no longer needed as evidence and is/are authorized for disposal by (check appropriate disposal method)

☐ Return to Owner ☐ Auction/Destroy/Divert

Name & ID# of Authorizing Officer: _____ Signature: _____ Date: _____

WITNESS TO DESTRUCTION OF EVIDENCE

Item(s) #: _____ on this document were destroyed by Evidence Custodian: _____

ID#: _____ in my presence on (date): _____

Name & ID# of Witness to destruction: _____ Signature: _____ Date: _____

RELEASE TO LAWFUL OWNER

Item(s) #: _____ on this document was/were released by Evidence Custodian: _____

ID#: _____ to: _____

Name _____

Address: _____ City: _____ State: _____ Zip Code: _____

Telephone Number: (____) _____

Under penalty of law, I certify that I am the lawful owner of the above item(s).

Signature: _____ Date: _____

Copy of Government-issued photo identification is attached: ☐ Yes ☐ No

This Evidence Chain-of-Custody form is to be retained as a permanent record by the Anywhere Police Department.

▲ **FIGURE 3-25 Evidence Chain of Custody Tracking Form**

(Courtesy Imprimus Forensic Services)

careers and in some instances lives. Officers should know their department's applicable policies, maintain their personal protective equipment (PPE), use it as needed, and take other appropriate precautions. Some prescribed medications, such as certain steroids and prescriptions for asthma, can comprise your immune system. This makes you generally more vulnerable to pathogens. Before accepting a prescription, consider asking your doctor whether it poses any risk to your immune system.

HIV/AIDS

The **human immunodeficiency virus (HIV)** is a pathogen that is present in the body fluids of a person with HIV, such as blood, pre-ejaculation fluid, semen, and vaginal secretions. In the United States it is commonly transmitted by vaginal and anal intercourse, without using a condom or taking medications to prevent or treat HIV, as well as sharing injectable drug equipment, such as needles. Mothers can infect babies during pregnancy, at birth, and while breast feeding.[21]

In some very rare cases, deep open mouth kissing between those who have sores in their mouths and/or bleeding gums has transmitted HIV. There is a very small number of cases in which a person bitten by someone who is HIV infected also became infected. All these cases involved severe trauma with extensive tissue damage exposed to infected blood. On the average, drug users sharing a HIV infected needle results in one new HIV infection per 159 shared instances, while skin-piercing accidental sticks with an HIV infected needle occurs only once every 495 times.[22]

The risk of getting HIV is low for those receiving blood transfusions and organ transplants because of rigorous testing standards. Dried blood may contain limited HIV. Although the risk of infection from dried blood is remote, it should be handled with care. There are no reported cases of HIV infections from tattooing or body piercing. although it could happen if equipment is reused without sterilization or if it is improperly sterilized.[23]

HIV transmission is not believed to be possible from swimming, toilet seats, telephones, closed mouth kissing, air, pets, biting insects, door knobs, drinking fountains or casual contract, such as hugging or shaking hands.[24]

If HIV progresses into acquired immunodeficiency syndrome (AIDS), the body's natural defenses against many types of infections are substantially reduced, leaving victims open to "opportunistic diseases," such as pneumonia, from which AIDS patients may eventually die.[25]

HIV is insensitive to extreme cold. Its survival outside of the body is variable. Factors affecting its survivability include how much air flows over it, the temperature, the concentration of the virus, how much sunlight it receives, and whether it is in a fluid or dried blood. Under favorable conditions, HIV may persist in a needle for as many as 42 days. However, the Centers for Disease Prevention and Control notes that the general rule is that it does not survive well outside of the body.[26]

HIV/AIDS and Investigator Precautions. While the general risk of being infected by an HIV-contaminated needle stick is low, investigators who have regular contact with prostitutes and intra-venous drug users may be at a higher risk, because of repeated exposure. The greatest danger to officers arises when they are making arrests, seizing drug-related evidence, and processing crime scenes and accidents where blood and other bodily fluids are exposed, as well as engaging in risky personal life styles. At all crime, accident, and other scenes with potential or known HIV risks, investigators should take appropriate precautions.

If investigators have a suspected exposure, it should be immediately reported to their supervisor and all departmental protocols immediately followed. If the exposure is caused by a sharps, many departments require that it be placed in a rigid container and entered into the evidence room, refrigerated, and sent for medical examination. (See Quick Fact Box HIV Post-Exposure–Prevention (PEP)) Many departments endorse the following practices:

1. Be cautious when conducting all types of searches. Never put your hands where you cannot see. Instead, use a mirror, or probe with a flashlight, pen, wooden dowel, or metal rod. Always carry a flashlight to see in dark areas during the day. Be aware of what you touch, for example, clipboards. Do not touch your body parts or clothing. Disinfect these items immediately after using them.

2. The most important protective barrier against HIV infection is intact skin. Even the slightest opening in the skin can be a portal through which HIV enters the body. Protect skin wounds, abrasions, and openings with 360-degree fluid-proof bandages.

3. In the United States roughly 10 percent of AIDS patients develop raised, purple/brown/red-colored lesions (Kaposi's sarcoma (KS)), which may be present anywhere on the body (Figure 3-26). Men who have sex with other men are more likely to contract Kaposi's Sarcoma. Most commonly these are seen on the head, neck, and oral cavity. Some of these are "weeping lesions" that let out an HIV-carrying fluid. You should be particularly careful around such lesions. Another condition, pseudo–Kaposi's sarcoma, or acroangiodermatitis, has a similar appearance but is not HIV related.[27]

QUICK FACTS

HIV AND AIDS: INFECTIONS AND MORTALITY

Since the HIV epidemic began in the early 1980s, through 2016, 1.2 million people have received an HOV diagnosis. In 2016, 18,160 people received a HIV diagnosis.[28] As information about HIV initially spread, policies focused on protecting officers and that should continue to be so. As an example, at least four New York Police Department officers became HIV infected on the job and were given disability pensions. According to the Centers for Disease Control and Prevention, there is also a low percentage of officers who have contracted it by risky off-the-job-behaviors.[29]

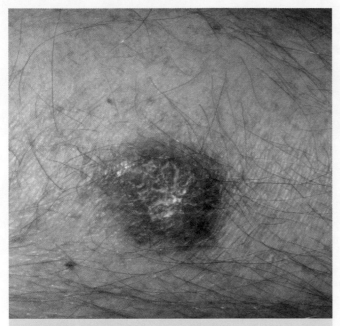

▲ FIGURE 3-26

Kaposi's sarcoma (KS) of an AIDs patient. As noted in the chapter, KSs may appear in one of several colors.

(©SPL/Science Source)

4. If you are bitten by a suspect, have a medical assessment made immediately if you have trauma to the tissue and blood is exposed. Do not place your mouth to the bite area. As previously noted, the risk of HIV infection is general remote, but other types of infections can be transmitted. The Quick Facts Box: HIV Post-Exposure-Prevention summarizes the protocol for HIV post-exposure prevention (PEP).

5. Bites, needle sticks, cuts, or similar incidents resulting in broken or punctured skin, however slight, should be washed immediately with soap in warm running water. Use soap from a dispenser, not a shared bar of soap. The Environmental Protection Agency (EPA) recommends using a germicidal wipe. There is no evidence that squeezing or "milking" wounds reduces the risk of HIV. Do not wash hands with single-use gloves on because this can break down the glove. Scrub your hands at least to the wrist, paying particular attention to the web between fingers, under the nails, and the cuticles. Rinse with clean water and dry with paper towels. Dry off the water using paper towels as a barrier. Washing with pure bleach may cause severe damage. If washing is not an option, clean your hands with 70% isopropyl alcohol, followed by washing when accessible.

6. If splashed in the eyes or on mucous membranes (for example, inside the nose), flush the area for 15 minutes using water, sterile water, or a saline solution.

7. Do not attempt to recap hypodermic needles seized as evidence. Use care when seizing any other sharp items (for instance, knives, razor blades, broken glass, scissors, and metal pieces) at crime scenes. When handling sharp objects, use disposable tongs or forceps and place the objects in appropriate rigid, puncture-resistant containers.

8. The use of latex or nitrile gloves significantly reduces exposure from body fluids and may reduce the amount of blood transferred by an accidental needle stick by 50%. To prevent the possibility of piercing your gloves, remove any rings before placing them on your hands. When wearing gloves, check them frequently for wear and tear; replace them often. When you remove gloves, wash your hands and use an approved germicidal wipe on them. High risk/cut-resistant gloves further reduce chance of accidental needle sticks and other wounds.

9. In addition to gloves, other **personal protection equipment (PPE)** may be necessary at high-risk scenes with exposed body fluids. Examples of such equipment are listed in Figure 3-27.

10. All disposable worn PPE should be placed in a red biohazard waste bag when you have completed your work at a crime scene. When removing PPE, do so in a manner that does not contaminate your clothing. Clean your hands in the appropriate manner immediately afterward.

11. It may be necessary to have departmental equipment sanitized also, such as handcuffs, badges, whistles, and batons. They should be packaged according to departmental policy.

12. In a medical emergency where rescue breathing is needed, use medical oxygen, a bag valve mask, or portable pocket mask with a one-way valve. Avoid mouth-to-mouth or mouth-to-nose contact.

13. Departmental policy should consider using disposable breathalyzer masks.

▶ **FIGURE 3-27**
Essential /Basic PPE for First Responders

ESSENTIAL /BASIC PPE FOR FIRST RESPONDERS

Initial responding officer(s) must have the following items readily available:

Assorted-size paper bags and other evidence containers

Consent/Search and incident report forms

Bindle paper, clean paper of various sizes suitable for folding to reliably holding trace or other evidence

Red Bio-hazard bags

Crime scene barricade tape

Crime scene markers, e.g., number cones

Evidence containers and seals/tapes

Flares

Flashlight and extra batteries

First aid kit

Forensic ruler

Insect repellent

Markers (e.g., chalk, spray paint, or some other marker to place by noted evidence items)

Measuring tape

Permanent black marking pens

Notebook

Paper bags

Several outer single-use gloves, cut-resistant glove liners, hair covering, filtered, full-face mask, helmet for falling objects/working in

Low overhead areas, goggles for eye protection, and some scenes will require a respirator with a fully sealed facemask

Some combination of fluid-proof pants, gowns, shoes, shoe coverings/booties, overalls, and apron

EPA-registered bleach, germicidal disinfectants, and wipes

14. Make sure you understand federal and state confidentiality laws that pertain to disclosing suspect information about HIV and other medical conditions to others, including the news media.[31]

HEPATITIS A, B, AND C

Hepatitis means inflammation of the liver. In the United States, the most common variants are hepatitis A, B, and C. The liver processes nutrients, filters the blood, and fights infections. When the liver is inflamed or damaged, its function can be affected. Heavy alcohol use, toxins, some medications, and certain medical conditions can cause hepatitis. However, hepatitis is most often caused by a virus.[32]

Hepatitis A (HAV)

In 2014, there were an estimated 2,500 acute HAV cases in the United States. Despite the low number of cases, law enforcement officers need to be aware of it.[33]

HAV is a highly contagious viral liver disease that causes mild to severe symptoms lasting a few weeks to several months. Symptoms may appear 2 to 6 weeks after being exposed. Common symptoms are fever, fatigue, loss of appetite, nausea, joint and abdominal pain, dark urine, clay-colored bowel movements, and jaundice. You cannot get HAV twice.[34] It is usually spread when it is taken into the mouth from contact with objects, food, and drinks contaminated from the stool of an

QUICK FACTS

HAV and Law Enforcement Officers

A 26-year-old HAV positive, drunken woman in a Tyler, Texas, mall resisted arrest and hit her face on the floor, then spit bloody HAV infected blood onto an officer's face, including his face, eyes, nose, and mouth. The officer is being periodically tested to see if he is infected.[35]

infected person. The mode of transmission is close personal contact with an infected person who does not wash his/her hands after using the bathroom and touches objects and food. It can also be transmitted by sexual activity, contaminated water, blood, infected needles, some legal drugs, and certain clotting agents. Additionally, HAV is spread by eating or drinking food or water contaminated with the virus, which can include frozen or undercooked food. This is more likely to occur in countries where hepatitis A is common and in areas where there are poor sanitary conditions and/or poor personal hygiene. The food and drinks most likely to be contaminated are fruits, vegetables, shellfish, ice, and water. In the United States, chlorination of water kills hepatitis A virus that enters the water supply.[36]

Twinrix is a combination vaccination for HAV and Hepatitis B that requires three shots, which are given (1) initially, (2) after one month, and (3) on the third month. Anyone traveling to an undeveloped country should consider getting the vaccination.

Hepatitis B (HBV)

HBV is the most common serious disease in the world and is the leading cause of liver cancer; about 500,000 people die annually from liver cancer and another 5,000 from chronic HBV and associated complications.[37] It also results in cirrhosis (scarring) of the liver and liver failure. Symptoms include appetite loss, fatigue, nausea, vomiting, pain over the location of the liver, stools that are pale gray or clay colored, and dark urine with a tea or cola color. Since 1982, there has been a safe and effective HBV vaccine.

HBV is a major health concern. It is spread by contact with infected needles, the blood or body fluids of an infected person, for example, blood to blood contact; unprotected sex; and sharing earrings, nail-clippers, toothbrushes, razors, and infected needles. Well- regulated acupuncture, tattooing, and body-piercing services are not viewed as a serious risk. In the absence of precautions, officers are 100 times more likely to contract HBV than HIV.[38]

Hepatitis C (HCV)

This virus may be transmitted from an infected woman to her newborn during delivery. Also at risk are persons with an HIV infection, accidental needle sticks, recipients of blood transfusions and organ transplants before 1992, and chronic hemodialysis patients.

QUICK FACTS

Police Officer Mother Passes HCV to Newborn Son

In 2016, a Portland, Oregon, Police Department police officer passed HCV to her newborn son. She had spent substantial time working assignments that resulted in a total of seven accidental needle sticks, at least three of which were from IV drug users who reported having "Hep C."[39]

There is no vaccine for HCV. Unless effective new therapies are developed, deaths due to HCV will double or even triple over the next 15 to 20 years simply because 80% of those infected have no signs or symptoms and therefore may have been infected for a long time without knowing it.[40] The symptoms are similar to those of HAV and HBV: jaundice, the yellowish coloring of the skin and whites of the eyes; dark urine; fatigue; abdominal pain; nausea; and loss of appetite.[41] There is no vaccine for HCV, although one is under development. Neither HBV nor HCV is spread by casual contact.

Ebola Virus Disease (EVD)

EVD is a rare and deadly disease. Between 2014 and 2016, there were four EVD cases and one death from EVD in the United States. That includes patients sent to this country for treatment, people who traveled in Africa and arrived with only the initial relatively mild symptoms, or health care workers taking care of EVD patients.[42] In 2015, a law enforcement officer was thought to be at risk. However, after thorough evaluation, it turned out not to be so. The risk of an EVD outbreak in the United States is very low. Nonetheless, given its deadly nature, police departments are being proactive, providing EVD information and training to personnel. EVD is not spread by casual contact; it is not airborne, nor is it transmitted by mosquitoes.

As a viral illness, EVD can only be transmitted person to person through direct contact with blood or body fluids (saliva, vomit, feces, urine, mucous, tears, sweat, breast milk, as well as semen and vaginal fluids) of a symptomatic individual. Individuals that are not symptomatic are not infectious. Symptoms are consistent with the flu: fever, headaches, nausea, vomiting, diarrhea, stomach pain, and unexplained bleeding/bruising. Symptoms may appear 5 to 10 days after being infected and may take up to 21 days to present. Illness can cause delirium, with erratic behavior by carriers that can place officers at risk of infection (e.g., flailing or staggering).[43]

Law enforcement personnel should fundamentally use the same EVD precautions as they would with someone who is possibly HIV infected, as well as taking other measures:

1. Wear PPE, including a facemask.
2. Do not handle items that may have been in contact with the body or fluids of a person with EVD.
3. Do not touch the body of a person who has died from EVD.
4. Do not have contact with the semen of a man who has recovered from EVD; this includes not having oral, anal, or vaginal sex.
5. Do not touch bats or nonhuman primates (apes and monkeys) or their blood or other fluids. Do not touch or eat raw meat prepared from these animals.
6. As a matter of information, if traveling, avoid hospitals in West Africa where patients with EVD are being treated.
7. Be aware that a high risk exposure includes all of the following: needle stick, mucous membrane exposures to blood or body fluids from a patient with EVD, direct skin contact with or exposure to blood or fluids without PPE.
8. Getting closer than 3 feet to a person infected with EVD without appropriate PPE.[44]

There is no vaccine for EVD or a protocol equivalent of the HIV PEP. The course of treatment is to treat the conditions that exist or can possibly be forestalled or eliminated.

Zika Virus Disease (ZVD)

The Zika virus was discovered in monkeys during 1947, in Uganda's Zika Forest. Five years later, the first Zika mosquito bite infecting a human was reported. Today, ZVD nearly spans the globe and has been identified in 70 countries. Between January 1, 2015, and December 7, 2016, the Centers for Disease Control and Prevention reported 4,682 ZVD cases from travel abroad and 217 cases that originated in the United States. Florida contributed 211 cases and Texas the remaining 6. During this time range, there

☐ *Aedes aegypti* ☐ *Aedes albopictus*

▲ **FIGURE 3-28 The August 2, 2016, Estimated Range of Zika-Carrying Mosquitos**
Continental U.S. range of the *Aedes aegypti* and *Aedes albopictus* mosquitos. A. *aegypti* is the major carrier of ZVD. It is an aggressive daytime biter, but also bites at night. A. *albopictus* can transmit ZVD but is much less likely to do so. The maps only suggest the presence of these mosquitos, not their numbers or medical cases. (Source: Centers for Disease Control and Prevention).

were 38 cases of sexually transmitted ZVD in this country. The range for ZVD-carrying mosquitos is roughly portions, or all, of 26 states, starting with mid-California and continuing to the south, the lower mid-west and northeastern states (Figure 3-28). A total of four south Florida law enforcement officers have contracted ZVD. There are no documented deaths due to ZVD.[45]

ZVD is transmitted primarily by *Aedes aegypti* mosquito bites and vaginal, anal, and oral intercourse, as well as the use of sex toys. Mothers may infect their children during pregnancy or at birth. During pregnancy, ZVD may result in the a child having microcephaly, which manifests itself by a smaller than expected head and life-long intellectual and developmental disabilities. There are no cases of breastfeeding or blood transfusions causing ZVD. There is no vaccine or specific medicines for ZVD. It is known that ZVD stays in semen and vaginal fluids for a longer period than a recovery.[46]

ZVD can be passed through sex even (1) if the person does not have symptoms at the time, (2) before their symptoms start, (3) while they have symptoms, (4) after their symptoms end, and (5) by those infected with the virus but who never develop symptoms. Transmission by blood transmission is considered possible but is unconfirmed in the United States.[47]

Testing blood, semen, vaginal fluids, or urine is not recommended to determine how likely a person is to pass ZVD through sex. Because ZVD can remain in semen longer than blood, someone might have a negative blood test but a positive semen test. The results of the semen and vaginal fluid tests are difficult to interpret. A sexual exposure is having sex without a condom in an area where there are known populations of the *A. aegypti*. Male and female condoms and dental dams reduce, but do not eliminate, the possibility of an infection. Pregnant couples should always use condoms from start to finish or refrain from sex during pregnancy in areas where the *A. aegypti* is known to exist. There is hope that a

vaccine for ZVD might become available by 2018, although that is by no means certain. It often takes a decade to develop a vaccine.[48]

QUICK FACTS

Protecting Yourself from Zika

Follow your department's protocols. The Centers for Disease Control and Prevention recommends you use the Environmental Protection Agency's (EPA's) search capability to learn more about Zika transmission and protecting yourself. In addition, the site has information on organic and nonorganic insect repellant. Any repellant should not be sprayed directly on the skin, not under outer clothing. If using sunscreen, apply it first, before the repellant. Wear long-sleeved shirts and pants.

Treat items such as boots, pants, and socks with permethrin or buy clothing treated with it. Treated clothing will protect you over several washings. Do not apply permethrin products directly on your skin. In some areas, such as Puerto Rico, permethrin has been used for years and mosquitos have become resistant to it. For all products you use, follow the manufacturer's directions. Mosquitos lay eggs near water. To protect your family, empty sources of water, such as tires laying on the ground, pots, toys, birdbaths, and flower pots weekly and scrub them out.[49]

Tuberculosis (TB)

About one-third of the world's population is infected with TB. Globally in 2015, 1.8 million people died of TB, making it one of the world's deadliest diseases. That year also saw 9,557 new cases in the United States and roughly 500 deaths.[50] TB is a chronic bacterial infection that is spread by air. When a person with active TB speaks, coughs into the air, or sings, infectious droplets are released. If breathed in, TB may be transmitted.[51] Exposure to the droplets can cause the disease. People who eat consistently healthy diets and lead healthy lifestyles are less at risk than others when such exposure occurs. Latent TB (when a person has TB but is not symptomatic) is responsible for more deaths worldwide than any other infectious disease; it usually infects the lungs, although other body parts may be involved, such as the spine, brain, and kidneys. One-third of the world's population is infected with TB, although most will never know it.[52] This is because their symptoms are latent or invisible.[53] Officers should recognize that certain populations pose higher risks for transmitting TB, including alcoholics; IV drug users; those infected with HIV; those who are long-term residents of facilities, such as homeless shelters, drug treatment centers, and correctional facilities; people in poor health; and those from countries with a high prevalence of TB.[54] Carriers often have been running a fever, have a loss of appetite and weight, feel unusually tired or weak, have night sweats, and have three or more weeks of a productive cough.[55]

Some departments recommend using as a respirator when in contact with a suspected or known carrier, as well as immediately reporting the contact as required by departmental policy.

QUICK FACTS

One Carrier Exposes 15 Colorado Police Officers to TB

Fifteen police officers had contacts with a 71-year-old man with active pulmonary TB in Pueblo, Colorado. The Police Chief believes the officers are not likely to be infected with TB. "However, we had each officer complete a workmen's compensation claim. They have also given blood samples to provide baseline information."[56]

The BCG vaccine is given to infants in some parts of the world where the disease is common; the effectiveness of BCG in adults varies widely, and in the United States its general use is not recommended. Several drug therapies are available for people who have a high risk of developing active TB, that are, those who are in close contact with persons who are infected with TB or have active TB.

The Americans with Disabilities Act

Investigators who contract the infectious diseases discussed previously may be covered by the federal Americans with Disabilities Act (ADA). Under this act, it is illegal to discriminate against an otherwise qualified employee in regard to employment actions—such as assignments and promotions—solely because the employee is thought to have, or actually has, a covered disability. Employers may be required to make "reasonable accommodations" for such employees. Reasonable accommodations include redesigning jobs, offering part-time hours, and modifying equipment and facilities. The legal provisions of ADA are broad and cover more than just infectious diseases; additional information is readily obtainable in personnel offices, from police unions, and on the Internet.

As a final note, some police agencies have taken the view that if an officer cannot fully perform all the functions required of a certified peace officer, she or he may be separated from the service or placed on involuntary medical retirement, depending on the situation. Other police departments have chosen to inventory their positions each year to determine how many of them could, with reasonable accommodations, be staffed by persons covered by ADA.

THE CRIME SCENE SEARCH

The purpose of the crime scene search is to obtain physical evidence useful in establishing that an offense has been committed, identify the method of operation, reduce the number of suspects, and provide leads or evidence of who the perpetrator was. Four major considerations dominate the crime scene search:

1. BOUNDARY DETERMINATION

In terms of the boundary of the crime scene, it is useful to think of an inner perimeter and an outer perimeter. The inner perimeter delineates the area where the specific items of evidence are known to be, along with the suspect's known or likely lines of approach to, and departure from, the scene. The outer perimeter extends outward from the inner perimeter and helps establish control of entry into the scene. The crime scene coordinator is responsible for deciding the positions of the inner and outer perimeters. Along the lines of approach and departure the perpetrator may have accidentally left or dropped valuable evidence, such as items taken from the scene, the perpetrator's wallet or distinctive jewelry, matches from an establishment he or she works at or frequents, a water bottle the perpetrator drank from while waiting for the victim, and the butt from a cigarette he or she smoked. Saliva traces from the bottle and the butt could yield DNA evidence. For an indoor crime scene, the physical limitations of the building can help determine where the inner and outer boundaries should be. More problematic is determining the boundaries for an outdoor crime scene. As a general rule, in such situations, it is better to establish the perimeters more broadly. Although doing so may result in some "wasted" search effort, items of evidence are occasionally found. A key consideration for the crime scene coordinator is determining whether there is any transient or fragile physical evidence that requires priority collection; for example, its value could be diminished or eliminated altogether because a heavy rain storm is approaching the outdoor crime scene.

2. CHOICE OF SEARCH PATTERNS

There are five basic crime scene search patterns from which the crime scene coordinator may choose:

1. The spiral, depicted in Figure 3-29(a) is usually employed in outdoor scenes and is normally executed by a single person. The searcher walks in slightly decreasing, less-than-concentric circles from the outermost boundary determination toward a central point. This pattern should not be operated in the reverse—beginning at some central point and working toward the perimeter of the crime scene in increasing, less-than-concentric circles—as there is a real danger that some evidence may be inadvertently destroyed while walking to the central point to initiate the search.

2. The strip/line search, diagrammed in Figure 3-29(b), involves the demarcation of a series of lanes down which one or more persons proceed. On reaching the starting point, the searchers proceed down their respective lanes, reverse their direction at the end of their lane, and repeat the process until the entire area has been covered. Whenever evidence is found, all searchers should be stopped and briefed about what was found to keep everyone informed.

3. The grid search is a variation of the strip/line pattern and is depicted in Figure 3-29(c). After completing the strip pattern, the searchers double back perpendicularly across the area being examined. Although more time-consuming than the strip search, the grid offers the advantage of being more methodical and thorough; examined from two different viewpoints, an area is more likely to yield evidence that might otherwise have been overlooked.

4. Figure 3-29(d) shows the zone/quadrant search pattern, which requires that an area be divided into four large quadrants, each of which is then examined using any of the methods already described. If the area to be searched is particularly large, each of the quadrants can be subdivided into four smaller quadrants.

5. The pie/wheel search, shown in Figure 3-29(e), entails dividing the area into a number of pie-shaped sections, usually six. These are then searched, usually through a variation of the strip method.

   In practice, both the spiral and the pie search patterns are rarely employed. When the area to be searched is not excessively large, the strip or grid pattern is normally used. When the crime scene is of significant size, the zone search pattern is normally employed.

3. INSTRUCTION OF PERSONNEL

Although instruction of personnel was mentioned earlier in the chapter, its importance requires some further elaboration. Even when the same type of criminal offense has been committed, the variation among crime scenes may be enormous, for example, the murder weapon may be recovered at the scene or in a distant body of water (Figure 3-30.) These variations are due to such factors as the physical settings, the manner and means that the perpetrators used to execute the offenses, and the lengths to which they may have gone to eliminate or destroy evidence. Thus, it is of paramount importance that the crime scene coordinator call together all the individuals who will be, in various capacities, processing the scene and share with them all the

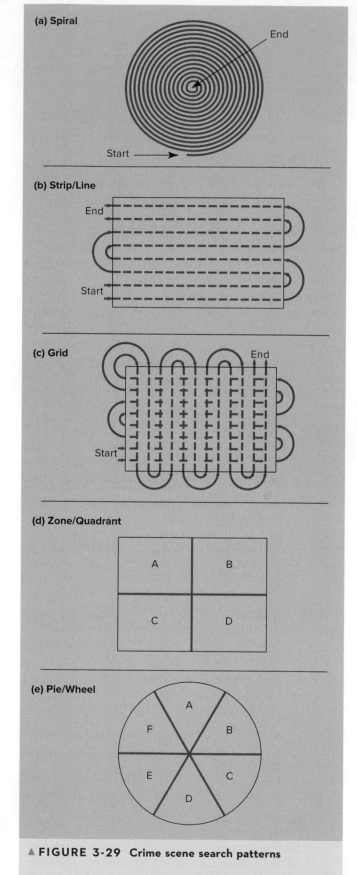

▲ FIGURE 3-29 Crime scene search patterns

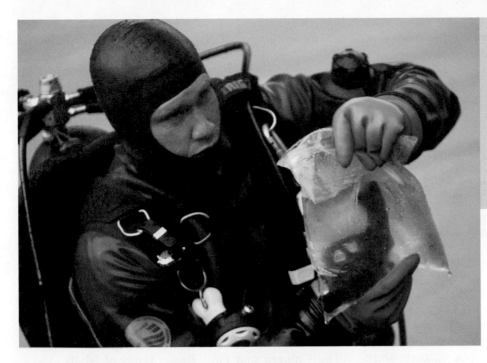

◄**FIGURE 3-30**
Police diver finds evidence
Police scuba diver with pistol used in murder case that was recovered from a lake. It is kept in the same type of water in which it was found until it arrives at the crime laboratory to be properly processed, preventing the accidental destruction or contamination of the evidence.
(©Paul Kuehnel/York Daily Record)

available information concerning the case. Doing so serves to minimize the possibility of excluding any available evidence. On receipt of this information, the members of the crime scene processing team may then begin their work.

4. COORDINATION

As discussed earlier, one of the most important responsibilities of the person in charge of the crime scene is integrating the efforts of those assigned to the technical and investigative service functions, along with ensuring the timely flow of pertinent information. For example, if a suspect is in custody and the interrogation yields information concerning the weapon or tool that may have been used, or where it may be located, then the crime scene coordinator should rapidly relay this information to those involved in crime scene processing so that they will be alert to specific possibilities for the recovery of physical evidence. Conversely, as significant physical evidence is recovered, the information should be conveyed to the crime scene coordinator, who can then transmit it to other investigators so they can move toward apprehending a suspect or use the information during the interrogation of a possible perpetrator already in custody.

SUSPENDED SEARCHES, DEBRIEFING, AND RELEASE OF THE SCENE

Occasionally, it may be necessary to suspend an operation temporarily. In one of the most common situations, a priority crime with evidence subject to decay requires the temporary diversion of personnel from another scene where delayed processing will not result in any loss of physical evidence. If it becomes necessary to stop the examination of a scene for a time, that scene should be secured in such a fashion that there is no possibility of contamination, alteration, or accidental destruction of any evidence that may exist.

Immediately before the **crime scene release,** the coordinator calls all team members together. In addition to ensuring that assignments were properly executed, the coordinator checks to make sure that all equipment brought to the scene has been retrieved and that all trash generated in processing the scene has been removed. Because each participant shares information during the debriefing, additional opportunities to develop evidence may be identified allowing all parties to leave the scene with a common understanding of the crime and of what the next steps are going to be. When the scene is finally released, the name of the party to whom it is released and his/her locator information should be noted in the administrative log.

Once a scene is released, the person to whom it is released will usually clean it up. Additionally, if the person is living there, the countless small things he/she does each day will alter and contaminate the scene, so that returning to it for further processing is not a viable option. Therefore, the decision to release a scene must be well thought out. An absolute must is to photograph the scene again just before it is turned over to the responsible party. These photos will counter claims that the police "tore my sister's house apart when they were there."

COLLECTION AND CARE OF EVIDENCE

The location of physical evidence during the crime scene search merely marks the first step in its long journey toward presentation in court. The chain of custody is how an item of evidence to be presented in court is authenticated as being the item that was seized at the crime scene. To satisfy legal requirements related to its introduction in a judicial proceeding, investigators must be able to:

1. Identify the evidence, and who found it where;
2. Verify its presence at the scene by video, photographs, sketches, or notes;
3. Describe how they collected, marked and packaged it;
4. State how evidence security was provided at the scene
5. State whom they gave the evidence to and for what reason
6. State who took the evidence to the station and where was it maintained and under what conditions
7. Identify who took the evidence to and from the laboratory
8. Identify the laboratory personnel who handled the evidence, what tests were conducted, and how testing changed the evidence
9. Identify who brought the evidence to the courtroom and how was security of it maintained.[57]

The essence of packaging any evidence is to do it in a way that will make any tampering with it clearly evident. For example, if evidence is placed in a plain Kraft envelope, the envelope should be sealed with tamper-evident evidence tape. As a further measure, when the officer signs her or his initials or signature, the writing can start on the envelope, cross the tape, and go back onto the envelope. Using a preprinted label or otherwise just writing on the envelope, the following information should be provided: type of offense and agency case number; the item number, the date recovered/received; and the investigator's name and badge number/departmental identifier. The entries made on evidence, and strong evidence room procedures, such as the use of bar codes to track evidence handling, can eliminate many barriers to introducing evidence in a courtroom.

VISUAL DOCUMENTATION OF THE CRIME SCENE

Occasionally, the value of an otherwise excellent investigation is reduced by improper or inadequate visual documentation of the scene. People process information differently, so the more ways a crime scene is properly documented, the greater the likelihood that other people will accurately understand the scene and what happened there.

This section examines three basic methods of documenting crime scenes: (1) digital still photography, (2) videography, and (3) sketching and mapping. In general, the methods should be used in that order with documentation progressing from the general to the more specific. More advanced crime scene digital imaging techniques are discussed later in the chapter.

DIGITAL STILL PHOTOGRAPHY

Photographs are taken in such a manner as to provide clear, undistorted high-quality images that document the condition of the crime scene, evidence, and persons related to a criminal investigation.

Objectives of Still Photography

The objectives of still photography are to:

1. Record the condition of the scene before alterations occur
2. Record the location of the scene
3. Record the position and condition of evidence
4. Document the point of view of the persons involved and witnesses
5. Document the spatial relationships of pertinent items
6. Convey the look of the scene to investigators, attorneys, and jurors who will not have the opportunity to view the scene first hand
7. Use as a tool for crime scene reconstruction efforts
8. Assist in portraying an accurate picture of the crime scene during courtroom testimony
9. Refresh the photographer's memory of the scene[58]

The Camera and Four Basic Types of Shots

Digital Single Lens Reflex (DSLR) cameras are used most often for still photographs of the crime scene. The camera should have at least a 12-megapixel image sensor, which allows photographs to be blown up to 1-in by 20-in size for court exhibits.[59] The policies of many law enforcement agencies is to list the equipment to be taken to photograph the scene, including an extra camera, batteries, cords, filters, flash, assorted lenses and filters, light meter, tripod, and flashlight. To protect cameras from inclement weather, an equipment list should include rainproof gear in which to place the equipment in that will still allow the camera to be used, such as rain sleeves and capes, as well as Storm Jacket Camera covers. Although videography (digital video recordings) capture images, it is a supplemental to still photography and not a substitute for it.

There are four categories of still photographs that are often taken, commonly in the following sequence:

1. Orientation: long-range shots, general views of the entire scene.
2. Relationship: medium-range photos of evidence and their positional relationship to each other (Figure 3-31).
3. Identification: close-ups that show specific features, such as the serial number on a firearm.
4. Comparison: close-up photographs should include shots of the item without and with a ruler. Include a ruler to provide the exact size of individual items of physical evidence. These photographs are necessary to produce an accurate one-to-one photographic reproduction to use for examinations or comparisons. Photographs that must contain a scale include those of latent prints, impressions, blood spatter, projectiles, defects from projectiles, tool marks, and injuries to skin. Scaled photographs should also be taken anytime the relative size and location of an item needs to be documented. Scales may be made of plastic, be magnetic, or one-time adhesives.[60]

◄FIGURE 3-31
Police officer photographing the body of a 29-year-old mother of six who was found murdered in a parking lot. The words on the yellow crime scene tape are hard to read because they are printed on the opposite side, but they can be plainly seen by people approaching the crime scene. (©Pablo Alcala, Lexington Herald)

The following rudimentary points illustrate commonly accepted practices for crime scene still photography:

1. Move though the crime scene without disturbing evidence; use the designated safe route if one has been established.
2. After developing a sense of the scene, form a plan for the photography.
3. Exclude people working at the scene from photographs.
4. Avoid magnetic fields.
5. Keep lenses clean for sharper images.
6. Take photographs before placing out any evidence cones, scales, placards, or other equipment.
7. Fill out your photo log as you work.
8. At any point in time, only a single case should be recorded on one media card.
9. If a photo is unacceptable, take another. Do not delete any photographs taken.
10. Photograph the crime scene as soon as possible; shoot a panoramic view, 360 degree overlapping photographs, and also the ceiling and floor if applicable.
11. Photograph the most fragile items/areas at the crime scene first.
12. Photograph the condition of evidence before recovery. Take one shot from medium distance to show its relationship to other aspects of the scene and, as needed, another for comparison.
13. Photograph from eye level to represent the normal view.
14. Photograph all parts of the crime scene investigation.
15. Photograph are evidence and should be handled according to the department's protocol for that type of evidence. Policies require the original media on which the images were made to be entered into a forensic digital management system in a format that prevents it from being altered in any way. The original images should never be edited. A copy of the original images is made so

an investigator may have access to them. On these copies changes may be made to make images sharper, resize them, or for other purposes. All those alterations must be carefully detailed.[61]

Some law enforcement agencies have concluded that although many crimes committed do not warrant full crime scene processing, there is still a need to supplement some reports with photographs—for instance, a misdemeanor assault that produces visible injuries. In those departments low-end "point and shoot" digital cameras are issued to officers or to their Sergeants.

DIGITAL VIDEOGRAPHY

Using **digital videography** to document the crime scene offers several advantages. Such cameras are relatively inexpensive, they incorporate audio, their use can be quickly learned, and the motion holds the attention of viewers. Videographs also give prosecutors a much better sense of the scene than just still photographs can.

Scenes that are commonly videographed include questionable deaths, homicides, suicides, major violent crimes, terrorism incidents, industrial and natural disasters, crowd control, riots, mass-transit accidents, interviews/interrogations, officer involved use of force/shootings, and weather-related incidents.[62]

By common sense, many of the commonly accepted practices discussed in the still photography section apply equally to videography and need not be repeated here, for example, moving through the crime scene without disturbing physical evidence.

1. Take multiple battery packs and battery chargers for the camera and portable lights, bring extension cords, and use high-quality recording media. Use the camera's title generator, and make sure that the time/date indicators are correct before recording begins.

2. The recording should begin with a narration that includes the identification of the location, case number, type of offense, camera operator's name, and the names of others at the scene and other pertinent information.

3. After the narration ends, a dummy microphone plug should be inserted in the camera to avoid recording unwanted and potentially embarrassing extraneous comments being recorded.

4. Once recording of the scene begins, the camera should be kept running; gaps may be hard to satisfactorily explain to jurors.

5. Most crime scenes can be documented within 30 minutes. Pan each area in 360 degrees.

6. The use of a rolling tripod or shoulder brace with the camera will produce smoother, less jerky images.

7. Avoid zooming in or out too fast. It is jarring to viewers. Likewise, move the camera smoothly in one direction. Do not sweep left and then right, back and forth. It may confuse viewers, is amateurish, and could cast doubt on how well the investigation was done. The same comments apply to videoing up and down a wall several times.[63]

CRIME SCENE SKETCHING AND FORENSIC MAPPING

A **crime scene sketch** is a basic diagram of the scene showing important points, such as the locations where various pieces of physical evidence were located. Often, the sketch is not drawn to scale. Sketches made by hand in the field are called **"rough sketches"** as opposed to the more polished **"smooth or finished" sketches** typically drawn in the office. Finished sketches may also be drawn by hand, although it is often done using specialized computer software. Although there is a learning curve with any software, once the package is mastered computer generated sketches produce substantial reductions in the time required to make them—perhaps 75%–versus traditional sketching methods.

Forensic mapping is the process of taking and recording the precise measurements of items of evidence to be drawn or "fixed" on the sketch.[64] In theory, a crime scene sketch and associated mapping data should allow someone to return to the crime scene and place an item of evidence in exactly the same place as it was recovered. As a practical matter, it allows the positioning of the evidence back into its original location with a reasonable degree of accuracy because there is some variation in the precision of sketching methods. The process of mapping the scene inherently intrudes into the scene, because the investigator must move through and around the scene taking and recording measurements.[65] This process requires a degree of caution in order to prevent the accidental moving, alteration, or destruction of physical evidence, all of which have the potential to confuse or misdirect the investigation.

It is critical that the entries on the sketch be as accurate as possible. Errors noted call into question not only the accuracy of the sketch but also the investigation as a whole. For example, distances should not be paced off and then recorded as so many feet and inches. Distances may be measured using rulers or tape measures, as well as by using more sophisticated methods, such as laser devices. Sketching and mapping methods are covered in the sections that follow.

TYPES OF SKETCHING AND METHODS OF FORENSIC MAPPING

Types of Sketches

Sketching is simply creating a depiction or drawing of a crime scene using any of several methods. Forensic mapping is taking the measurements that locate items of evidence or of investigative relevance and entering them into one of the appropriate types sketches. Beyond the basic distinction between rough and smooth sketches, there are four basic types of sketches: (1) bird's-eye, (2) elevation, (3) exploded or cross-projection, and (4) perspective. Ordinarily, mapping data is not entered into a perspective sketch.

1. *Bird's-eye sketch.* Also called the overview, floor plan, or overhead sketch (Figure 3-32). In this type of sketch you are looking down at a horizontal plane.

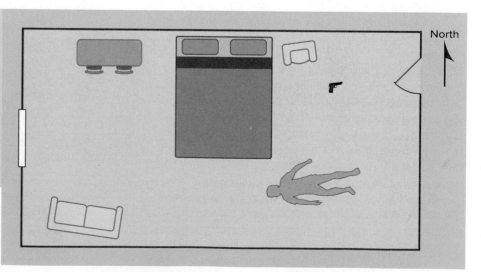

▶ **FIGURE 3-32**
Overhead or bird's-eye view of a crime scene
No measurements are included in this sketch because it is intended merely to portray the overhead or bird's-eye view. Occasionally it is also called a floor-plan sketch. As a convention, North is usually oriented toward the top of the sketch.

North

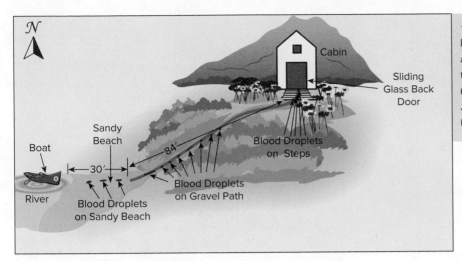

◀FIGURE 3-33 An Elevation Sketch
In this illustration a path of blood droplets
are shown going from the cement deck at
the top of the incline down to the river.
(Source: Adapted from Wisconsin Department of
Justice, State Crime Laboratory, Physical Evidence
Handbook, 2017, p. 49)

2. *Elevation sketch.* A vertical view of an object or area of investigative importance (Figure 3-33). Examples include a blood-splattered wall and bullet holes in windows.

3. *Exploded or cross-projection sketch.* While points of interest in a wall can be shown in an elevation sketch, the advantage of using the cross-projection method (Figure 3-34) is that when there are multiple points of interest in several different walls, they can be displayed simultaneously in one sketch, as opposed to having to make and refer to multiple elevation sketches.

4. *Perspective sketch.* Without some artistic ability this sketch is the most difficult to make because it requires drawing the object of interest in three dimensions (Figure 3-35).

Common Methods of Forensic Mapping

Investigators take measurements to add them to a sketch. The combination of a sketch and forensic mapping measurements provides precision to where a particular piece of evidence was found.[66] The common methods of forensic mapping: are (1) rectangular coordinates, (2) triangulation, (3) baseline coordinates, (4) polar coordinates, and (5) the grid system.

1. Rectangular coordinates are the best method to use with scenes having clear and specific boundaries, such as interior walls. In Figure 3-36, the investigator took two straight measurements at *right angles* from the center mass of a pool of blood, to the two nearest walls and did the same from where the cutting edge of the knife's blade joins the handle.

2. Triangulation is useful both for interior scenes in buildings, as well as for outdoor scenes, where measurements must spring from distinct, "permanent" features or landmarks, such as the corner of a home, telephone, mailbox and lighting poles, fences, stop sign posts, the intersections of paved driveways and roads, and other similar features (Figure 3-37). Each pair of

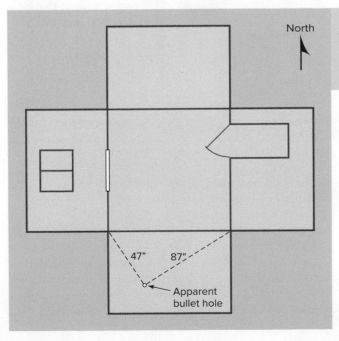

◀FIGURE 3-34
The Exploded or Cross-projection view of a crime scene
The cross-projection, or "exploded," view "lays" the walls down flat, as though the room had been unfolded like a box.

▶ FIGURE 3-35 The Perspective Sketch

Source: National Forensic Science Technology Center, Crime Scene Investigation (Washington, D.C.: Bureau of Justice Assistance and National Institute of Justice, 2013, p. 21, https://www.ncjrs.gov/app/publications/abstract.aspx?ID=265675, accessed April 19, 2017)

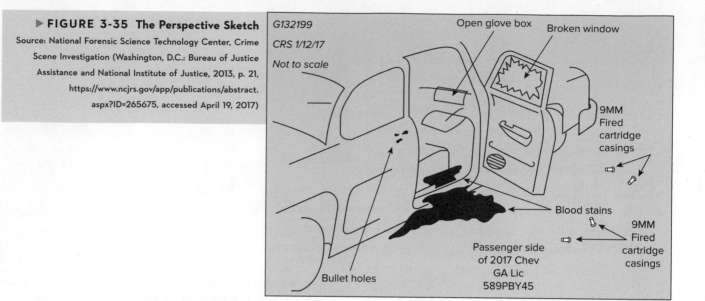

▶ FIGURE 3-36
Rectangular coordinates

In this example the legend block is blank, because the two items of evidence were drawn in the sketch. If numbers or letters had been used to indicate the locations of the evidence, then the legend would read: 1, pool of blood, and 2, knife with blood on blade. Some investigators prefer to use letters rather than numbers to indicate the location of evidence, because letters are more easily differentiated from the measurements that appear in the sketch.

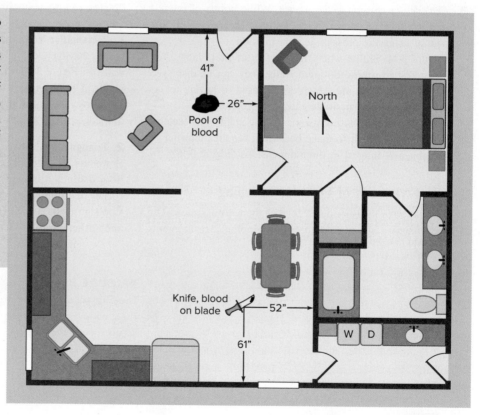

measurements is anchored by a reference point (RP), forming two sides of the triangle.[67] In Figure 3-37, two measurements from separate points were made to the:

(1) top of the foremost portion of the gun barrel and (2) nearest portion of the grip, fixing the location of the gun with precision.[68]

In the aftermath of the 1992 Ruby Ridge, Idaho, shootout involving the Weaver family and the FBI, they were criticized for not using triangulation to memorialize the location of

physical evidence, a remark that failed to take into account the limitations of using it when the terrain is very uneven.

3. Baseline coordinates may be used indoors and outdoors. Inside of a building (Figure 3-38), use chalk string or a chalk reel to draw a straight line on the floor between two *fixed* points. For example, from one corner of a room to the opposing corner that separates the room into two triangles or from the same edge of two exactly opposing windows or doors. At a right angle to the baseline, run a straight line to the middle of the

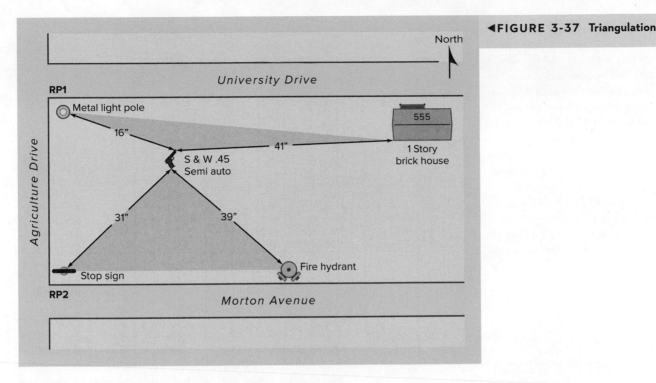

evidence and measure that distance. Also measure from the nearest end of the baseline to where the right angle begins.

Outdoors, an investigator might draw the baseline between the midpoints of two trees/telephone poles or from the center of a manhole cover to a particular edge of a house. Measurements are made in the same way described above. As a rule of thumb, when using the baseline outside using basic equipment, the lines leading from the baseline to the evidence shouldn't exceed 30 feet because the further you go, the greater the likelihood of introducing measurement error. Multiple lines can lead from each baseline, and at a large outdoor scene, there could also be several baselines in the same sketch.

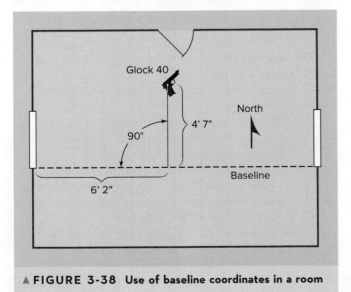

▲ **FIGURE 3-38 Use of baseline coordinates in a room**

4. The **polar** method is an excellent choice for many outdoors crime scenes (Figure 3-39) and has several variations. The method described here is the most basic and doesn't require specialized technological equipment. When using basic equipment, the item to be mapped must be viewable from the point the mapping begins. Thus, the polar is not a good choice for heavily forested areas or fields where crops or bushes are roughly more than waist high.[69]

In Figure 3-39, triangulation is used to identify the datum point, the starting point from which the forensic mapping will be made. At the datum point, place a protractor flat on the ground. Center the hole at the bottom of the protractor exactly on the datum point. Measure the distance down the angle to the evidence article of evidence, and record that measurement and the angle.[70] Repeat as needed for additional evidence items. If a two-wheel rolling measuring device is used, its accuracy should be checked by also measuring the same distance with a steel tape. Some departments drive a metal stake in the ground at the datum point,[71] which can later be reestablished by use a metal detector to locate it.

If there are no fixed positions to help plot a datum point, a Global Positioning System (GPS) can be used. There are 30 American-owned satellites constantly orbiting Earth. At any given time, there are six overhead which can be used to provide your location on Earth within 5 millimeters, which is one-fifth of an inch. For forensic mapping purposes, the most important GPS data provided is longitude, latitude, elevation, and time.

5. A **grid system** (Figure 3-40) is an excellent tool to use when there is a large outdoor scene without any significant features or landmarks.[72] For many years archaeologists have used this system to record where artifacts and other notable discoveries were made.

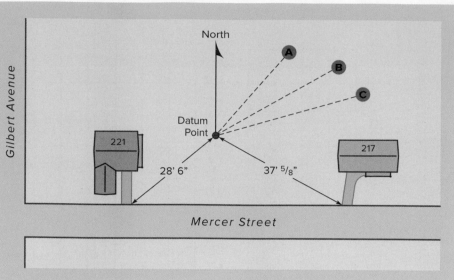

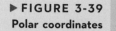
▶ **FIGURE 3-39**
Polar coordinates
The datum, or starting point, is established by triangulation using the points at which two paved driveways intersect with Mercer Street to form the base of the triangle. In this example: (1) no elevation measurements were taken. Elevation is measured as the difference between the elevation of the datum point and each item of evidence. (2) The angles and the distance from the datum point down each angle to the items of evidence (A, B, and C) have not yet been entered on the sketch.

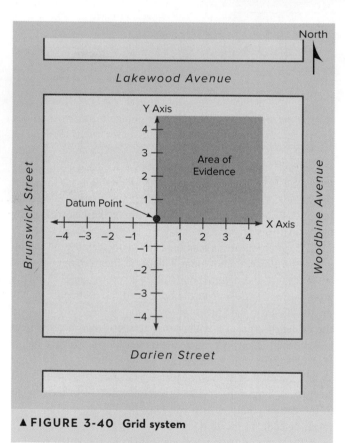

▲ **FIGURE 3-40 Grid system**

During the mid-1980s, there was a noticeable transfer of this technology to law enforcement to help process buried body scenes.[73] Individual grids have uniform sides of any size, but are often 3 meters to 10 feet when human remains are in compact areas or 30 feet or more when they are dispersed over a wider area.[74]

The boundary of each grid is fixed by a metal or wooden stakes; smaller sized grids may be connected using twine, although this may be impractical with large grids. If several search teams are working, each should be responsible for certain grids and as

they find physical evidence, information about it should be immediately communicated to all other search teams. Laying out the grids and marking the boundaries of each is time consuming, but essential;[75] evidence may be fixed within the grids by employing whatever method is most useful; this is an exception to the earlier guideline that typically each crime scene sketch uses only one mapping method; another exception is the use of triangulation to establish the datum point for the polar coordinates method.

Forensic Mapping of Crime Scenes

Digital still photography, videography, sketching, and forensic mapping are the predominant methods of crime scene documentation. However, because of technological advances over the past 15 years, rapid, automated, and extremely accurate measurements of crime and traffic accidents scenes have become possible. Other enhancements have also emerged, such as the ability to create 3-D images of scenes. The fusion of different scientific capabilities is a dynamic force that is shaping the field of forensic mapping.

The fusion of **laser scanning** and panoramic cameras (Figures 3-41 and 3-42) has produced extraordinary capabilities and advantages:

1. The systems can easily be deployed; setup time can be as little as 10 minutes.
2. Scenes can be documented very rapidly and more thoroughly.
3. The 3-D models and panoramic images created are easily stored and can be referred to days after a scene has been released up to years later.
4. The results can be accessed by investigators working similar cases at a distant precinct or across the country.
5. Questions that were not fully explored or contemplated at the scene can be carefully studied later.
6. In 3-D models investigators can "walk" through the virtual crime scenes to any location for any viewpoint.
7. Bullet and blood spatter trajectories can be inserted.
8. Victims can be imaged and displayed at the precise location and positions in which they were found.

▲ FIGURE 3-41   3-D Laser Scan

A DeltaSphere 3-D laser scan model of a mock crime scene with mannequins as two victims. The white lines above the woman's head show the major axes of the blood spatters on the wall. The blue line is perpendicular through their point of intersection. The red lines are the blood spatter trajectory. Where the red and blue lines intersect appears to be the woman's position when she was shot. In a working model, a click on the "Officer A" annotation at the left of the image would produce the same field of view the first arriving responder had. (Courtesy of 3rdTech Inc.)

9. Animation of the actions of the assailant and victim can be created.

10. With a DSLR, hundreds of still photographs could be taken and still not produce the complete coverage of these newer techniques.

11. If an investigator points at and clicks on any two different points, their precise distance apart is calculated and shown as if the scene still existed.

12. In addition to being powerful tools for courtroom presentations and training, they are being used by some agencies as part of the interrogation process.

13. Although a number of advantages are discussed above, the actual advantages actually created will depend on the actual equipment acquired.

Laser Scanning

Training for use of the DeltaSphere is conducted over a three-day period. The first half-day is devoted to setting up and using the equipment, that is, capturing the data, and the remaining time is spent using the associated SceneVision 3-D software building the 3-D computer graphics model, annotating the model and images with measurements and notes, making diagrams, linking close-up photographs, and preparing viewpoints, and the "walk through." The final step is creating the finished presentation.

Panoramic Cameras

A **panoramic camera** provides an unbroken, continuous view of the area that encircles it. The PanoScan rotates a full 360 degrees as it takes high-resolution photographs of the crime scene, a process of about 11 minutes. Individual photographs can be studied or they can be viewed as a seamless image of the entire the scene. Investigators can scene, pan left and right, and zoom in on features (Figure 3-42). Return to Scene (R2S) software bundles the ultra-high resolution images with full

◄FIGURE 3-42 PanoScan

These images were captured by the PanoScan panoramic camera and include a general view as well as a demonstration of the ability to zoom in on an evidence item. Note that the zoomed in on area has a cartridge case in it. (Courtesy of Panoscan Inc.)

measurement capabilities. Users can insert "hotspots" into the images to indicate the position of relevant features, for example, fingerprints and other forensic evidence, and links to associated files, such as laboratory reports.

SUBMISSION OF EVIDENCE TO THE CRIME LABORATORY

Faced with exploding demands for service, the FBI has a policy limiting acceptance to only those state and local law enforcement requests for evidence examinations that involved violent crimes and to virtually cease accepting property crimes evidence (Figure 3-42).

FBI FORENSIC SERVICES: CASE ACCEPTANCE POLICY

The successful investigation and prosecution of crimes require, in most cases, the collection, preservation, and forensic analysis of evidence. Forensic analysis of evidence is often crucial to determinations of guilt or innocence. The FBI has one of the largest and most comprehensive forensic laboratories in the world, and the FBI Laboratory is accredited by the American Society of Crime Laboratory Directors/Laboratory Accreditation Board.

The forensic services of the FBI Laboratory Division are available to the following: FBI field offices and legal attachés; U.S. attorneys, military tribunals, and other federal agencies for civil and criminal matters; and state, county, and municipal law enforcement agencies in the United States and territorial possessions for criminal matters.[76]

All forensic services, including expert witness testimonies, are rendered free of cost; however, the following limitations apply: No examination will be conducted on evidence that has been previously subjected to the same type of examination. Exceptions may be granted when there are reasons for a reexamination. These reasons should be explained in separate letters from the director of the laboratory that conducted the original examination, the prosecuting attorney, and the investigating agency. Exceptions require the approval of the Laboratory Director or a designee. No request for an examination will be accepted from laboratories having the capability of conducting the examination. Exceptions may be granted upon approval of the FBI Laboratory Director or a designee. No testimony will be furnished if testimony on the same subject and in the same case is provided for the prosecution by another expert. No request for an examination will be accepted from a nonfederal law enforcement agency in civil matters. No requests will be accepted from private individuals or agencies. In addition, when submitting evidence to the FBI Laboratory, contributors acknowledge the following: FBI examiners will choose appropriate technical processes to address the contributor's request for examination, including additional testing as initial testing results warrant. Depending on the caseload of the Laboratory and the needs of the contributor, evidence examinations may be subcontracted at FBI expense. An FBI Laboratory Report of Examination may contain the opinions and/or interpretations of the examiner(s) who issued the report. 1 Handbook of Forensic Services 2013 Additional Case Acceptance Guidelines.

The FBI accepts evidence related to all crimes under investigation by FBI field offices; however, it accepts from other federal, state, and local law enforcement agencies only evidence related to violent crime investigations. The FBI does not routinely accept evidence from state and local law enforcement agencies in cases involving property crimes unless there was personal injury or intent to cause personal injury. These guidelines help to ensure that the FBI continues to provide timely forensic assistance to law enforcement agencies investigating crimes of violence or threatened violence. Additional restrictions may be imposed on case acceptance to achieve this goal.

At the discretion of the FBI Laboratory Director or a designee, the FBI may accept evidence from property crime cases. Such exceptions will be considered on a case-by-case basis and should not be regarded as setting a precedent for future case acceptance. All accepted cases will be afforded the full range of forensic services provided by the FBI. The following are examples of property crimes that are not routinely accepted for examinations: Arson of unoccupied residential and commercial buildings and property (unless terrorism, such as an environmental terrorist attack, is suspected). Explosive incidents and hoaxes targeting unoccupied residential and commercial buildings and property (unless terrorism, such as an environmental terrorist attack, is suspected). Vandalism and malicious mischief directed toward residential or commercial buildings and property. Nonfatal traffic accidents involving headlight examinations except in cases involving law enforcement and government officials. Hit-and-run automobile accidents not involving personal injury. Automobile theft, except automobile theft rings or carjackings. Breaking and entering. Burglary. Minor theft (under $100,000). Minor fraud (under $100,000).

When a heart artery becomes clogged and narrowed, new blood vessels, collateral arteries, develop to help circulate the blood. Much like collateral arteries, when the FBI reduced the scope of its services state and local units of government developed new capacities for the analysis of forensic evidence, creating stronger central laboratories at the state level and smaller regional ones, reducing their dependence on the FBI. In the longer view, the FBI's policy shift was a positive development.

The result is that procedures for submitting evidence for examination are similar, but varied, across the country. Evidence submitted to a crime laboratory is most often transmitted by courier, air express, or registered mail. In the ideal situation, the investigator most knowledgeable about the case takes it to the laboratory so he/she can discuss the case with appropriate examiners. Given the caseloads all crime laboratories have, this situation is the exception. In general, the method of transmitting evidence is determined by the nature of the evidence and the urgency of getting an analyst's conclusions.

Rules established by federal and state agencies regulate how some special classes of evidence must be sent. Examples of these classes are chemicals, blasting caps, flammable materials, and biological and chemical agents. Check with laboratories before submitting these types of evidence.

Unsurprisingly, many state and local laboratories leverage resources through the use of Laboratory Information Management Systems (LIMS) software for various tasks, including the automated tracking of physical evidence and reporting examination results. Laboratory internet sites provide information useful to investigators, such as an *Evidence Handbook* on acceptable procedures for collecting, marking, and packaging evidence and guidance on submitting it.

Laboratories may have one "universal form" or separate forms for different types of evidence on their Internet site and/or require a letter on agency letterhead stationary formatted in a specific way. Either way, an investigator submitting evidence will need to provide the following information:

- The investigator's name, badge number, agency, address, telephone number, and email address.
- Copies of any previous correspondence about the case, including any pertaining to other evidence that was examined earlier.
- The type of criminal act and the basic case facts related to each item of evidence.
- The name(s) and descriptive data about the individual(s) involved (subject, suspect, victim, or a combination of those categories) and the agency-assigned case number.
- A list of the evidence being submitted.
- What type(s) of examination is requested.
- Where the evidence should be returned and where the laboratory report should be sent.
- A statement if the evidence was examined by another expert in the same field, if there is local controversy, or if other law enforcement agencies have an interest in the case.
- Any reason(s) justifying an expeditious examination request.
- The name and locator information for the assigned prosecutor, if designated already.[77]

Some law enforcement agencies maintain a list of crimes that the Patrol Division may retain for follow-up investigation. This list adds variety to patrol duties, creates skills that will be useful if the officers become detectives, and preserves the resources of the Investigative Division. If cases are retained for further investigation by the Patrol Division, the submission of evidence to the lab usually requires the approval of a supervisor. For cases referred for follow-up investigation, the assigned investigator often makes that decision. If submission to a private lab for analysis is contemplated a supervisor's approval is typically required because of the cost involved.

INVESTIGATIVE SUCCESS

The public thinks an investigation is a success when the perpetrator is arrested, property recovered, and the perpetrator convicted. However, law enforcement considers a case successful if it can be administratively classified in one of two different ways:

TABLE 3-1	Crimes Cleared by Arrest or Exceptional Means

OFFENSE	PERCENTAGE CLEARED
Murder/Non-negligent Manslaughter	59.4%
Rape (revised definition)	36.5
Rape (legacy definition)	40.9
Robbery	29.6
Aggravated assault	55.3
Burglary	13.1
Larceny-theft	20.4
Motor vehicle theft	13.3

Source: Federal Bureau of Investigation, *Crime in the United States—2016* (2017).

1. **"Cleared by exceptional means,"** meaning that the offender has been identified; enough evidence has been gathered to support an arrest, make a charge, and turn the offender over to the court for prosecution; and the offender's exact location has been identified so the suspect could be immediately taken into custody. However, circumstances beyond the law enforcement agency's control may prohibit it from doing so; for example, the offender is dead, is under the control of another jurisdiction that declines to extradite the suspect, or the victim refuses to cooperate with the prosecution. Two common reasons for one state declining to extradite a suspect to a second state are he/she will be tried on more serious charges in state one or is already incarcerated there on serious charges.

2. **"Cleared by arrest,"** meaning that the perpetrator has been arrested, charged with the commission of the offense, and turned over to the court for prosecution. Note that this definition of success does not require a conviction.

Table 3-1 shows that many types of crimes committed do not result in arrest and conviction. This is frustrating to investigators who want to take violent, predatory, and other offenders off the street. In these situations, police have to accept the fact that some crimes are simply not going to be solved because of insufficient evidence or legal restrictions. In such situations, investigators have to draw comfort from knowing they did their best, pursued all lines of inquiry, and then go on to the next case. Ultimately, time is on the side of law enforcement and eventually many suspected offenders will commit acts for which they can be arrested. The tragedy, of course, is the harm they do between when they first come to the attention of investigators and when they are ultimately arrested.

If investigators allow case disappointments to get the best of them, they run the risk of slipping into cynicism, an unattractive trait, and over a period of years will become vulnerable to engaging in unethical behavior, such as planting evidence or committing perjury.

KEY TERMS

administrative log
All Points Bulletin (APB)
alternative light sources (ALSs)
Americans with Disabilities
   Act (ADA)
assignment sheet
associative evidence
baseline coordinates
be-on-the-lookout (BOLO)
chain of custody
cleared by arrest
cleared by exceptional means
corpus delicti evidence
crime
crime scene
crime scene control
crime scene entry log
crime scene release
crime scene search patterns
crime scene sketch
cross-projection view
datum point
deductive reasoning

digital camera
digital videography
elimination prints
evidence recovery log
felony
field notes
follow-up investigation
forensic mapping
grid system
hepatitis B (HBV)
hepatitis C (HCV)
human immunodeficiency
   virus (HIV)
incident/offense report
inductive reasoning
laser scanning
lifted-prints log
Locard's exchange principle
macroscopic scene
microscopic scene
misdemeanor
neighborhood canvass
overhead or bird's eye view

panoramic cameras
personal protection
   equipment (PPE)
perspective
photographic log
polar coordinates
preliminary investigation
primary scene
rectangular coordinates
rough sketch
secondary scenes
smooth or finished sketch
trace evidence
trace-evidence vacuums
tracing evidence
triangulation
tuberculosis (TB)
vehicle canvass
violation

REVIEW QUESTIONS

1. What skills and qualities are needed by investigators?
2. What are the objectives of crime scene investigation?
3. How would you describe the "lucky" investigator?
4. What are preliminary and follow-up investigations?
5. How are inductive and deductive reasoning used in investigation?
6. Why is crime scene coordination so important?
7. What factors can shape or impact a plan to process a crime scene?
8. What are the three broad categories of evidence?
9. How is a crime scene entry log properly used?
10. What is a neighborhood canvass?
11. What are the "rules" for crime scene investigators?

12. What four considerations dominate the crime scene search?
13. Define *primary scene* and *secondary scene(s)*.
14. What are macroscopic and microscopic scenes?
15. What infectious disease risks are faced by crime scene investigators?
16. What methods are available to visually document the crime scene?
17. Draw a rough crime scene sketch of your bedroom, assuming that there are two shell casings on the floor and one bullet hole in the west wall.

INTERNET ACTIVITIES

1. Visit the website of five law enforcement agencies that have their policy manuals on it. What common features are there for conducting the preliminary investigation?
2. On the internet, visit five forensic laboratories and five law enforcement agencies serving a population of at least 50,000 people. The labs must have a publication roughly titled "Physical Evidence Handbook." The law

enforcement agency may have a similarly titled publication, but it's more likely the information you need will be in its policy manual.

   With respect to concern about officer safety when making arrests and collecting and handling physical evidence, do the publications have a good level of information about protection from infectious diseases?

Design Element: (crime scene tape): ©UpperCut Images/Getty Images RF

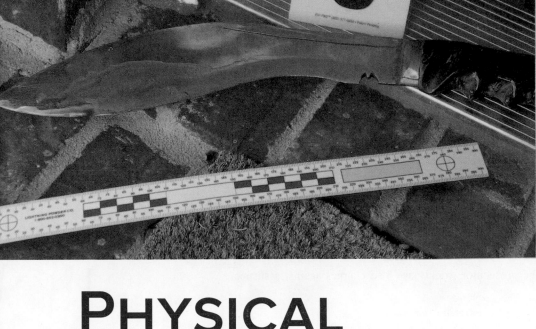

◄ Weapons are often found at the scene of a crime. Here, a large "bolo" type knife is found at the exit of the front door leading to the living room where a young woman was murdered in a domestic quarrel. This is the eighth piece of physical evidence found at the scene. A rigid ruler is included to give an indication of size and proportionality.
(Courtesy of Robert Taylor and The Dallas Police Department)

4

PHYSICAL EVIDENCE

CHAPTER OBJECTIVES

1. Distinguish between class and individual objectives.
2. Explain questioned samples.
3. Identify two major categories of impression evidence
4. Describe how to cast a shoe impression using dental stone "from scratch."
5. Explain how a fracture match is made.
6. Differentiate between radial and concentric glass fractures.
7. Explain what minutiae, ridges, and furrows are.
8. Define forensic odontology.
9. Describe an avulsed bite.
10. Explain the use of luminol.
11. Compare bore and caliber.
12. Define questioned document.

If physical evidence is to be useful in exonerating the innocent and pursuing suspects it must be treated in accordance with its importance. The evidence must be located, its position documented, be collected, be identified by marks/writing on it and/or on the package in which it is placed, and be transmitted to the evidence room or the crime laboratory. The chain of custody is the unbroken chronological history of who had possession of the evidence from the time it was received, through and including all other possessions.[1] This chapter describes the proper protocols of dealing with various types of physical evidence. Adherence to approved procedures maintains the potential that the evidence can be a powerful part of the investigative process and avoids the embarrassment that careless handling is sure to bring. Even more serious is the possibility that but for the careless handling of evidence the prosecutor would have filed charges against a suspect.

CHAPTER OUTLINE

CLASS VERSUS INDIVIDUAL CHARACTERISTICS

To fully appreciate the potential value of physical evidence, the investigator must understand the difference between class and individual characteristics. Characteristics of physical evidence that are common to a group of objects or persons are termed **class characteristics.** Regardless of how thoroughly examined, such evidence can be placed only into a broad category; an individual identification cannot be made because there is a possibility of more than one source for the evidence.[2] Examples of this type of evidence include all unworn Nike athletic shoes of a particular model, and the new, unmarked face of a manufacturer's specific type of hammer. In contrast, evidence with **individual characteristics** can be identified, with a high degree of probability, as originating with a particular person or source (Figure 4-1).[3] The ability to establish individuality distinguishes this type of physical evidence from that possessing only class characteristics. Some examples of evidence with individual characteristics are fingerprints, palm prints, and footprints.

Conceptually, the distinction between class and individual characteristics is clear. But as a practical matter, the crime scene technician or investigator often may not be able to make this differentiation and must rely on the results yielded by crime laboratory examination (Figure 4-1). Thus, although the investigator must recognize that physical evidence that allows for individualization is of more value, he or she should not dismiss evidence that appears to offer

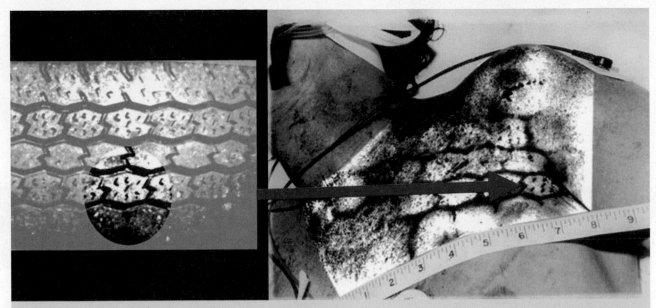

▲ FIGURE 4-1 Individual class evidence

A suspect was identified in a fatal hit-and-run case. The tread pattern from the tires was collected (L) and compared with those left on the victim (R). A positive identification was made, tying the suspect's car tires to the victim. (Courtesy of Forensic Digital Imaging, Inc.)

only class characteristics, because it may show individual characteristics through laboratory examination. Furthermore, a preponderance of class-characteristic evidence tying a suspect (or other items in the suspect's possession) to the scene strengthens the case for prosecution. Note also that occasionally class-characteristic evidence may be of such an unusual nature that it has much greater value than that ordinarily associated with evidence of this type. In an Alaska case, a suspect was apprehended in the general area where a burglary had been committed; the pry bar found in his possession contained white stucco, which was of considerable importance, since the building burglarized was the only white stucco building in that town.[4] Finally, class-characteristic evidence can be useful in excluding suspects in a crime, resulting in a more effective use of investigative effort.

COMPARISON SAMPLES

Much of the work of forensic science involves comparing various types of samples. Special terms are used to refer to these samples, and you must know what they mean to communicate with the laboratory and understand its reports. At the most general level, comparison samples may be from unknown or questioned sources or from known sources; each of these two main categories has three subcategories.

Unknown or Questioned Samples

1. *Recovered crime scene sample whose source is in question:* This evidence may have been left, for example, by either victims or suspects. A typical question is "Whose fingerprints are on the window used as the point of entry?"

2. *Questioned evidence that may have been transferred to an offender during the commission of a crime and been taken away by him or her:* When compared with the evidence from a known source, this evidence can be used to link the suspect to a person, vehicle, tool, or weapon. For example, the question might be "Do any of the hairs combed from the suspect's hair match those of the victim?"

3. *Evidence from an unknown or questioned source that can be used to link multiple offenses:* This material might link crimes that were committed by the same person, tool, or weapon. Assuming that a suspect is arrested at a murder scene with a pistol in his overcoat, the question raised could be "Did this gun fire the bullets recovered from the victims of a double homicide a week ago?"[5]

Known Samples

1. *Standard or reference sample:* This is material from a known or verifiable source. It is compared to similar material from an unknown source to determine whether an association or linkage exists between a crime scene, a victim, and the offender. For example, a sample of blood is taken under medical conditions from the suspect so that it can be compared with blood on the victim's shirt.

2. *Control or blank sample:* This is material from a known source that was uncontaminated by the crime (for example, carpet fibers taken from the far corner of a room in which a body was found). It is used to make sure that the material on which evidence was deposited—for instance, carpet fibers, under the body, on which there is blood, does not interfere with laboratory testing.

3. *Elimination sample:* This type of sample is taken from a source known to have had lawful access to the crime scene, such as a police officer, medical technician, or the occupant. It is compared with unknown samples of the same type from the scene so that matches can be eliminated, thereby highlighting non-matches. An example is elimination prints. If latent fingerprints recovered at a crime scene do not match the fingerprints of those who have lawful access to the area, they immediately become of investigative interest in terms of determining whose prints they are.[6]

SOIL AND POLLEN

The study of soils is within the purview of forensic geology, "geoforensics." Soil consists of loose aggregates of accumulations of natural elements, such as rocks, bacteria, minerals, pollen, fungus, and plant material.[7] Soil may also contain a variety of other things, including blood, chips from bricks, gasoline, fertilizers, pesticides, leaching from landfills or industrial sites, paint, and pieces of glass and metals. Because of its widespread occurrence and tendency to adhere to most materials, soil is commonly present on physical evidence. Examinations are performed to characterize, identify, and compare soil evidence, which may help to establish an association between individuals, objects and/or locations.[8]

Although long thought of as class characteristic evidence and compared based on color, composition, and texture, there is growing evidence that within soil there are microbial communities that essentially create their own distinctive DNA signatures.[9] Soil is poised to make a transition to being individual characteristic evidence. Its analysis can help focus investigations and discredit alibis.

BOX 4-1 | SOIL AND THE ALIBI

An elderly woman was robbed and murdered in a Washington, D.C., park, and her body was found under a park bench. Within a short time, a suspect was apprehended as a result of a description given by a witness who had seen the person leaving the park on the night of the murder. It was obvious that the suspect had been involved in a struggle and had soil adhering to his clothing and inside his trouser cuffs. He claimed to have been in a fight in another part of the city and gave its location. Study of the soil near the park bench and of that collected from the scene of the alleged fight revealed that the soil from the suspect's clothing was similar to soil near the park bench but did not compare favorably with samples from the area of the described fight. These comparisons strongly suggested that the suspect had been in contact with the ground in that area and cast strong doubt on his statement that he had not been in the park for years. Furthermore, the lack of similarity between the clothing soil samples and those from the area in which he claimed to have been fighting questioned the validity of his alibi.[10]

Forensic palynology is the discipline that studies pollen and spores. The literature on it is relatively small, and fragmented.[11] Despite the fact it can be a powerful investigative tool, it is extremely underutilized, because it is labor intensive and requires considerable expertise and experience.[12] The value of pollen and spores lies in their abundance and the great diversity of plants, even in microhabitats.[13] Additionally, pollen and spores are easily transferred to nasal passages, hair, clothing, shoes, hands, equipment, and other places.

BOX 4-2 | POLLEN GIVES NEW CLUE IN 40-YEAR-OLD COLD CASE MURDER

On September 12, 1976, Baltimore County, Maryland, Police Officers found the body of a woman wrapped in a white sheet near a cemetery in the unincorporated area of Woodlawn. For the next 40 years the victim was known As Woodlawn Jane Doe. Recently, the police decided to see if pollen on her body could be of any help. The mixture of cedar and mountain hemlock led them to Boston's Arnold Arboretum. A likeness of the victim was created and her case publicized in news media and other outlets with information, including that she was possibly in her mid-20s at death, had short brown hair, and the tattoo "JP" on her right arm. Among the remarkable factors in this case is that pollen had the potency to be useful after four decades.[14]

LOCATING AND HANDLING SOIL EVIDENCE

Soil residues and smears on such surfaces as clothing, people, and vehicles may not be of sufficient quantity for analysis. Unless the suspects were apprehended at the scene or in very close proximity to it, the soil on their feet/shoe soles and the tires of their cars may have been contaminated, and therefore may not be of evidentiary value.[15]

Soil evidence may be important when the suspect drives or walks on unpaved areas, since it is picked up by tire treads or the bottom of shoes and the cuffs of pants. It may also be recovered in a number of other places, such as on the floorboard of the subject's car or on articles in the trunk of the vehicle, including shovels and blankets. In an unusual case, a solid soil sample, roughly in the shape of a triangle with 3-inch sides was found on the roadway. Later, it was substantially matched to a space on the underside of the suspect's vehicle. The guidelines shown next should be followed in handling soil evidence:

1. Soil conditions at the scene can change, so gather the soil as quickly as sound action permits.

2. Collect soil not only from the crime scene but also from the logical points of access to, and escape from, the scene. Place the samples in clean plastic vials and labeled with the date, time, name of the crime scene technician, and the case number, if known.

3. Collect soil samples where there are noticeable changes in color, texture, and composition.

4. Collect soil samples from a depth that is consistent with the depth at which the questioned soil may have originated. In most cases, samples will be a tablespoon of material taken no more than ½ inch from the surface.

5. When possible, collect soil samples from alibi areas, such as the worksite, yard, or garden of the suspect.

6. Make a detailed drawing or map documenting where and at what depth you collected each soil sample.

7. Do not remove soil adhering to shoes, clothing, and tools. Do not process tools for latent prints at this time. Air dry the soiled garments and package them separately in paper bags. Avoid jostling and transport to the crime lab for analysis and further processing.

8. Ship unknown or questioned soil and known samples to the lab separately in leak-proof containers such as film canisters or plastic pill bottles. Avoid the use of paper envelopes or glass containers. If there are lumps in the soil, pack it in a way that keeps the lumps intact.[16]

9. In packaging soil or other types of evidence, take care to avoid **cross contamination** of the samples. Cross contamination is the unwanted transfer of materials between two or more evidence samples. For example, you risk cross contamination in a rape case when in a package to the crime lab you include samples of both the victim's and the suspect's pubic hairs.

10. Soil impressions should be photographed to scale and cast before any soil samples are taken.

11. At indoor crime scenes, special vacuums may be used to collect soil samples from carpets and floors that may have been introduced by the suspect(s).[17]

IMPRESSION EVIDENCE: FOOTWEAR AND TIRES

Shoe and tire impressions are often present at crime scenes and are frequently overlooked by investigators.[18] Examination of impressions can potentially provide the investigator with important information, such as how many people were at the scene, where they walked at the scene, a possible sequence of events, how they exited the scene, the direction in which they traveled, the type and brand of shoes and tire, and the type of vehicle involved. Although European agencies report collecting footwear evidence in over 70% of their cases, it's much less in this country, perhaps due to a lack of awareness of the contributions that impression evidence can make.[19]

QUICK FACTS

Footwear and Tires as Individual Class Evidence

While footwear and tires began "life" as individual class evidence, they are at the beginning of a journey that is likely to take them to individual class evidence. Both will begin to show the results of their use. Tires can develop cracks, they may be cut somewhat when making contact with a curb, they may develop wear patterns because the wheels are out of alignment, and pieces of glass or other material may become embedded in them. Footwear is similarly affected by use. Cumulatively and collectively, these marks produce imperfections that can form the unique wear patterns of individual class evidence.

Images of footwear impressions from scenes can be submitted to the laboratory for search in the SICAR (Shoeprint Image Capture and Retrieval) database for make/model determination and comparison to impressions from other scenes.[20] Tire impressions

BOX 4-3 | O.J. SIMPSON AND HIS BRUNO MAGLI SHOES

Following a career as a running back, O.J. Simpson was inducted into the Pro Football Hall of Fame in 1985. He also was the central figure in perhaps the most famous case involving shoeprints, the 1994 murders of Nicole Brown Simpson and her friend, Ronald Goldman.

Bloody shoeprints found on the walkway in front of Nicole Brown Simpson's condominium received worldwide media attention. Upon forensic examination, they were identified as from a pair of size-12 Bruno Magli shoes. Information from the manufacturer indicated that only 299 pairs of this size-12 shoe were sold in the United States. Two of these pairs were sold at a Bloomingdale's store in New York where Simpson was known to have shopped. However, Simpson denied ever owning a pair of these shoes. In a controversial 1995 criminal trial, where the defense essentially put the evidence on trial, Simpson was acquitted.

However, in the 1996 wrongful death civil trial, pictures surfaced of Simpson at a Buffalo Bills football game wearing a pair of black Bruno Magli shoes of the same style that left the bloody shoeprints. This was key evidence in the civil trial that led to the judgment against Simpson.[21]

can likewise be searched at their own specialized databases. Moreover, when impression evidence from two or more crime scenes match, it links cases and all their respective data together.

CATEGORIES OF IMPRESSION EVIDENCE

Impression evidence is divided into two major categories: surface impressions and three-dimensional impressions.[22]

Surface Impressions

Surface impressions (SIs) are two-dimensional. They have a length and width and by definition lack any appreciable height. They are often called "prints" or "residual prints." They are formed when the soles of footwear or tires are contaminated with foreign matter such as blood, oil, or dust and leave a print on a firm base, such as a linoleum floor, a piece of paper, or cloth. They may also be found on doors that have been kicked in during burglaries and home invasion robberies.

Preserving Surface Impressions.

The following crime scene guidelines apply to SIs:

1. If they can be collected without damage, photograph them with and without a two-dimensional scale. Package them so SIs cannot rub against their containers (Figure 4-2).

▲ **FIGURE 4-2 Footwear impression photography**
A crime scene technician documenting a footwear impression. The impression runs left to right, roughly between the front legs of the tripod. The white slip of paper "North" of the impression has the case number and other information on it.
(Courtesy of the Nassau County Police Department, New York)

2. A basic crime scene rule is to always photograph evidence before attempting to collect it. If the camera used is not high resolution, the images will be of limited value for comparisons.

3. Surface impressions may not be immediately apparent. Shinning a flashlight obliquely on the surface being examined may help find them. Oblique lighting should also be used to enhance details when making photographs.

4. Take overlapping photographs if the surface impression is very long.

5. There are several well-established methods for collecting surface impressions:

   a. An electrostatic dust print lifter (Figure 4-3) can be used to recover an SI. It must be photographed as soon as recovered because the image is not permanent. Electrostatic lifters are a good choice for lifting dry dust or dry residue SIs from clean porous or nonporous surfaces.

   b. Adhesive and tape lifters work well for lifting SIs on nonporous surfaces that have been enhanced with fingerprint powder (Figure 4-4).

   c. For lifting SIs on porous and nonporous wet or dry surfaces, black, white, or transparent gelatin lifters are good performers and are also used to lift fingerprints; for example, if a crime scene technician dusts for fingerprints with a dark powder, a white or transparent lifter is used to collect it (Figure 4-5).

   d. Mikrosil forensic silicone is used for casting powdered SI, particularly on textured or uneven surfaces. Like fingerprint dust and lifters, Mikrosil silicone comes in different colors. It also produces excellent details when casting tool impressions, which are three dimensional.

   e. Electronic shoeprint scanners are positioned directly over the SI and captures detailed digital images for comparison use.[23]

Three-Dimensional Impressions

Three-dimensional impressions (3DI) are those that have a significant depth, in addition to having a length and width. 3DI may be found impressed into soil, sand, snow, or other materials (Figure 4-6). The level of detail is affected by the material in which the impression is made, as well as its degrading due to weather, contamination, or other conditions. Casting is an effective method of collecting 3DIs, and they should always be photographed prior to casting. Photographs, however, are not considered a substitute for a cast. If a lengthy tire track is encountered, an attempt should be made to cast a section at least 3 feet in length. Debris that is part of the impression or was present when the impression was made should not be removed before casting.[24] Plaster of Paris is no longer used for casting.

PRESERVING THREE-DIMENSIONAL IMPRESSIONS

Casting 3

The first step in casting is the preparation of the impression. The rule is that the impression cannot not be disturbed. Thus,

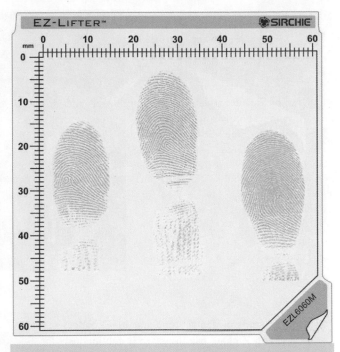

▲ **FIGURE 4-4**
Transparent adhesive lifter with metric measurements included on lifter
Once the SI is lifted, it is put on a backing of contrasting color. Lifters come in different sizes and are also commonly used to lift fingerprints. (Courtesy of Sirchie® www.sirchie.com)

▲ **FIGURE 4-3**
Use of electrostatic dust print lifter (EDPL)
(*top*) A lifting mat is laid over a shoe dust print and electrically charged using the high voltage power supply unit on the right side of the mat. An insulated roller systematically is moved across the silver side of lifting mat. (*bottom*) The dust print is transferred to the dark-colored underside of the lift mat.
(*Both:* Courtesy of Sirchie® www.sirchie.com)

▲ **FIGURE 4-5   Gelatin lifter**
A gelatin (Gel) lifter being picked up from floor where it captures a shoeprint. (©Arrowhead Forensics)

release agent or hairspray over the impression, being careful not to disturb the details of the impression.

Using Dental Stone

In Chapter 3, "Investigators, the Investigative Process, and the Crime Scene" Shake-N-Cast was mentioned. It has all needed materials preassembled in one bag. This section covers preparing and using dental stone "from scratch" to cast an average-sized shoe impression in nonsnow conditions.

if twigs, leaves, or other materials are stuck in the impression, they should remain there. Only loose material lying on the impression, such as leaves, should be moved. In loose or sandy soil, dental-stone use requires a preparation of the impression. Without disturbing the details of the impression, spray a silicone

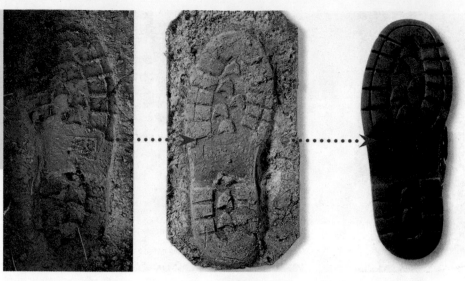

▶ **FIGURE 4-6**
Footwear impression
A footwear impression is found in the dirt, a cast is made, and its examination holds the potential to provide important investigative information or evidence, such as matching the footwear of someone in custody. (Courtesy of Sirchie® www.sirchie.com)

1. Mix 2 pounds of dental stone and 10-12 ounces of water in a gallon Ziplock bag. Massage it continuously for 3-5 minutes to produce a smooth consistency akin to thick paint, pancake batter or heavy cream.

2. Pour the mix *alongside* the impression, and allow it to flow or spill over the impression as opposed to pouring it directly on the impression. Once the impression is covered, the remaining dental stone can be gently poured onto the impression. Make sure you pour the mix smoothly; otherwise, there will be a lap mark in the cast that is likely to cause a loss of detail. On a warm day, dental stone will dry in 20-30 minutes and longer when it's cool or cold. Soil evidence should only be collected from the bottom of the impression after the cast is removed.

3. If there is standing water in the impression, the following steps should be taken: (a) place a casting frame around the impression so that a cast 2-inches deep can be made; (b) using a flour sifter, gently let dental stone drift directly into the impression to a depth of about 1 inch; (c) add enough mixed dental stone to form a second 1-inch layer; and (d) allow the cast to set, which will take longer because of the water. On a warm day ,drying may take an hour or more.

4. Casts should be carefully extracted to avoid damaging or breaking them, using a gentle rocking motion.

5. When the cast is firm but still soft, identifying marks can be scratched into the back. Alternatively, a permanent marker can also be used when the cast has dried.[25] A good practice is to also indicate on the cast the direction of north.

6. Never wrap a cast in plastic to protect it; use paper instead and then place it in a box with packaging around it. Each box should only contain one cast.

Casting in Snow: Dental Stone and Sulfur

Snow can be difficult. It may dissipate, be soft, dirty, or in the process of being covered up by additional snowfall. Its reflective quality and lack of contrast are a challenge for good photography. The state of the snow will dictate how to get more contrast:

1. If the impression is frozen, use a colored spray paint, dispersing it from 2-3 feet so the force of the aerosol does not damage the impression. Direct a light spray at a 30-45 degree angle so the paint only strikes the high points of the impression. Highlighted portions of the impression absorb heat from the sun and must be shielded; for example, place a box over it, until photographed and cast to prevent melting.

2. If the snow is soft or slushy use Snow Print Wax (Figure 4-7) to keep the snow from collapsing when you add the dental stone.[26]

CASTING IN SNOW WITH DENTAL STONE

To compensate for the limited heat generated by dental stone, one or more layers of Snow Print Wax should be sprayed on the impression. For the same reason, place the Ziplock bag with the dental-stone mix on the snow and allow it to cool to the temperature of the snow. Add snow to the mixing water to the cold dental stone until a slight amount of slush is present, but no ice crystals. To accelerate the curing process, add one tablespoon of potassium sulfate. Massage the bag until the content is the consistency of thick pancake batter. After the dental stone is in the impression, allow about an hour for it to harden.

Casting in Snow with Sulfur

Sulfur has long been used to cast impressions in snow (Figure 4-8). Despite the preparation and safety measures it takes versus dental stone, sulfur continues to be used. The following guidelines are not a substitute for being fully versed with sulfur casting:

1. Sulfur comes in powder and pellet form, both requiring heating to make it into a liquid. Sulfur melts at 110 degrees Celsius (°C) and has a flashpoint at 207°C and an ignition point of 248°C.

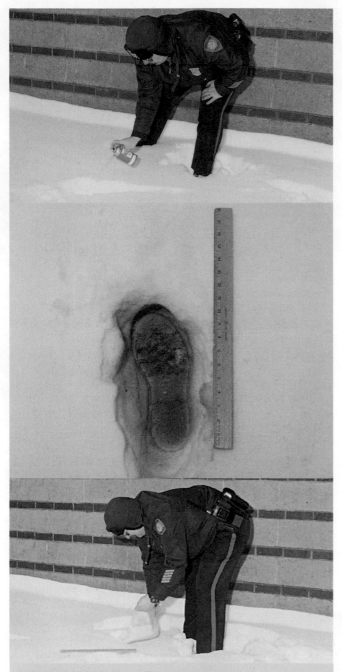

▲ FIGURE 4-8
Framed shoeprint liquid sulfur use
A Wisconsin Crime Laboratory Bureau technician pours liquid sulfur into a framed shoeprint in the snow. (Source: Wisconsin Department of Justice)

▲ FIGURE 4-7 Snow Print Wax use
Having already photographed the shoe impression in the snow, the officer sprays red-colored Snow Print Wax on the impression (*top*); the impression is rephotographed (*middle*); and the dental-stone mix is poured from a plastic pouch onto the impression (*bottom*). (*All:* Courtesy of Lewiston Maine Police Department)

2. Melting sulfur must be done outside in a well-ventilated area while one is wearing a dust/mist respiratory mask to prevent inhalation of the sulfur fumes.

3. Snow impressions cast with sulfur do not need a buffer of Snow Print Wax before casting, but a light application of Snow Print wax or a black spray paint, used in the manner previously described, can be used to enhance details for photography.

4. Framing the impression is important because melted sulfur is thin and free flowing. However, sulfur solidifies on contact with snow and ice, which helps to limit its movement.

5. Allow the sulfur to cool somewhat before applying to the impression; otherwise the impression will be destroyed.[27] Using a separate snow area to test the readiness of sulfur to be used is recommended. This is somewhat parallel to the carpenter's adage of measure twice, cut once. The sulfur can be applied by pouring it onto a deflector before it meets the impression.

6. Reinforce the cooled sulfur impression by smoothing a thick dental-stone mixture over the entire *back* of the sulfur cast. Hot liquid sulfur retains heat for a period of time after being poured. Do not attempt to lift the cast until it has completely hardened and cooled.[28]

PAINT

Paint evidence may be encountered in many types of investigation, but perhaps most commonly it is transferred from one source to another in burglaries and hit-and-run accidents. Paint is transferred as fresh smears, dried chips, or "chalking" from old, dry paint. Many burglaries involve a tool that was used to pry a door or window open, transferring paint from the building to the suspect's tools or clothing. In hit-and-run accidents, paint from the fleeing vehicle may be found on a pedestrian or another car.

In hit-and-run cases, the make and model of the involved vehicle might be identified by comparing paint evidence to the records in the 40,000 FBI's National Automotive Paint File on original-manufacturer finishes. **Paint Data Query (PDQ),** is a global automotive paint database, based on original manufacturer finishes. PDQ is used by 102 labs in 24 countries. Each country has a single point of contact with PDQ. In the United States and Canada it is, respectively, the FBI and the

BOX 4-4 | PAINT CHIP AND PEDESTRIAN HIT-AND-RUN DEATH

A 53-year man was hit by an unidentified vehicle and dragged more than 200 feet, dying from his injuries. No witnesses were present, and the police did not have any other leads regarding the suspect vehicle. A gold metallic painted plastic fragment recovered from the scene was sent to the lab, along with the victim's clothing containing gold metallic paint particles.

The PDQ system found one color, Aztec Gold, which closely matched the paint particles recovered from the victim's clothing. It was used on 11,000 Ford Mustangs made in 1997. Only two of these vehicles were registered in the jurisdiction of the offense. An officer located a 1997 Aztec Gold Ford Mustang with

scratches on its hood and a piece of painted plastic missing from the flair molding on the left side. The flair molding and paint samples were collected from the vehicle and submitted for comparison to the materials recovered from the scene and victim's clothing. The painted plastic piece was physically fitted together with the flair molding and the recovered gold metallic paint particles were consistent with paint samples taken from the suspect vehicle.

Although these results provided some closure to the victim's family, the suspect had been deported for other reasons several days before the vehicle was located.[29]

Royal Canadian Mounted Police (RCMP). The value of paint evidence is seen in the case study of Box 4-4.

Usually, paint is class-characteristic evidence, although in some cases it can reach the level of individual evidence. If the chips are large enough, it may be possible to make a fracture match between a questioned and a known source (Figure 4-9). A fracture match, a physical fit like putting a piece in a puzzle, occurs when it is established that two physical items were once co-joined. For example, if a paint chip recovered from a tool in a burglary suspect's possession fits exactly into a missing paint area where entry was forced into the business, the tool and that area were co-joined at some point. A new forceps or tweezer should be used to collect each paint chip to avoid contamination.

If a building or car has been painted multiple times, then the layer structure of a questioned sample can be compared to a known source as to the number of layers, their colors, the sequence of colors, the relative thickness of each layer, their

texture, and the chemical composition of each layer of paint (Figure 4-10).[30] Therefore, when taking standard paint samples, it is important to go all the way to the base surface.[31] If there are layers of paint, chip or cut them loose; never collect layered paint samples by scrapping them. However, smeared paint evidence may be collected by scraping if the entire item cannot be taken as evidence.[32]

If standard paint samples are collected from a burglary's point of entry, the samples should be collected from the area immediately adjacent to the area damaged by the suspect forcing entry.[33] Any surface or 3DI impressions would be photographed and collected. Additionally, standard samples should be taken from areas that are visually different, for example, paint color and numbers of layers.[34] Standard samples should be at least nickle-sized.[35] One rule of thumb is to collect four such samples around each area involved, which must be packaged individually. Likewise, paint evidence and paint samples should never be

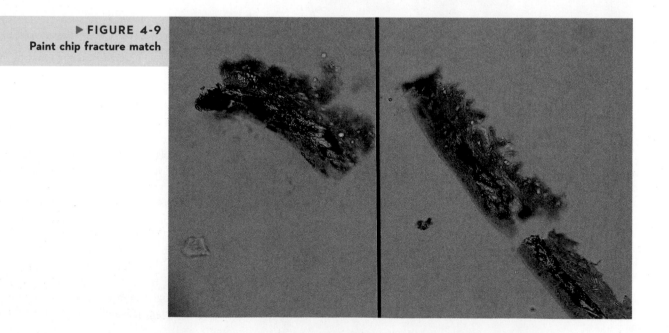

▶ **FIGURE 4-9**
Paint chip fracture match

▲ **FIGURE 4-10**
Side view of a multilayered paint chip
(Source: Wisconsin Department of Justice)

packaged together. Samples should be placed in carefully sealed folds of paper or in small envelopes and protected outside of that to prevent breaking paint chips.

QUICK FACTS

Taking Paint Samples from Damaged Vehicles

When taking standard paint samples from a damaged vehicle, you do so in the same manner as described above. There is also the possibility of paint transfers, fabric impressions, blood, or other evidence at the points of collision, which will also be collected as evidence.

Burglary tools that may contain paint evidence should be carefully wrapped in paper, packaged separately, and submitted to the lab without disturbing the evidence. Similarly, the clothes of a burglary suspect arrested at the scene or in its vicinity and the clothes of a pedestrian hit-and-run victim should be submitted to the lab without attempting to collect paint evidence. Paint smears may also be useful, and it is desirable to submit the item on which the smear is found—for example, a car's bumper, to the laboratory.

Do not collect paint chips or particles with transparent tape or use it to fix the evidence to a card. Paint chips and particles should not be placed in plastic bags, because they will develop a static electrical charge that makes them hard to handle. Placing paint chips in cotton is not good practice, because separating them is difficult and they are often fragile. A clear solid plastic container is ideal for packaging a paint chip, because it can be seen. Paper envelopes are acceptable if they are properly sealed and protected from being bent or compressed.

The sheets placed under and over hit-and-run victims in the ambulance while they are being transported may also be a good source of paint evidence; the clothing and sheets may have fresh blood on them. These items should be allowed to air dry naturally in properly ventilated lockers. Before hanging these items in the lockers or an other secure place, place fresh paper under the items so any evidence that falls as the drying occurs can be recovered. When dried, place the items separately in their own paper bag and submit them to the laboratory.

GLASS

Generally, glass is class-characteristic evidence, although in some fact situations it may become individual class. Glass is important as physical evidence because it is so common. It may be overlooked as important evidence because of this. Glass evidence is seen in many types of crimes, including hit-and-run accidents involving pedestrians and vehicles; carjackings; burglaries of cars and structures; home invasion robberies; felony assaults, for example, someone deliberately gets hit with a beer bottle in a bar fight; and robberies. Victims and suspects may both have glass evidence from the same incident. It may be embedded in their shoes, clothing, skin, and hair. Glass may have increased evidentiary value if decals, paint, tints, or other material is on it.[36]

Laboratory examination of glass may be able to determine:

1. The type of glass, such as tempered or container.
2. The direction of force used to break the glass, for example, inside or outside (Figure 4-11). When direction is an issue, use a permanent marker to write "inside" and "outside" on the appropriate sides of the glass. Figure 4-13 illustrates the characteristic impact effect of a bullet fired through glass.
3. The direction and sequence of shots fired through a closed glass window.
4. Similarity between evidence glass and standards.
5. A fracture physical match, establishing that pieces were formerly joined (Figure 4-12).[37]

As revealed by the discussion following Box 4-5, determining the direction of force can help reconstruct events and evaluating what witnesses are saying.

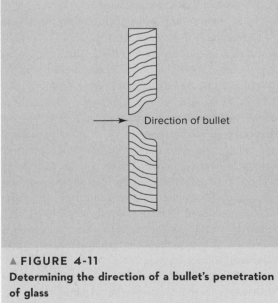

Direction of bullet

▲ **FIGURE 4-11**
Determining the direction of a bullet's penetration of glass

▶ **FIGURE 4-12**
Glass fracture match of a rear tail light and assembly
Pieces of red tail light were found at the scene of a hit-and-run and matched with pieces still intact in the tail light assembly when the suspect vehicle was located. (Courtesy of Forensic Training and Consulting LLC)

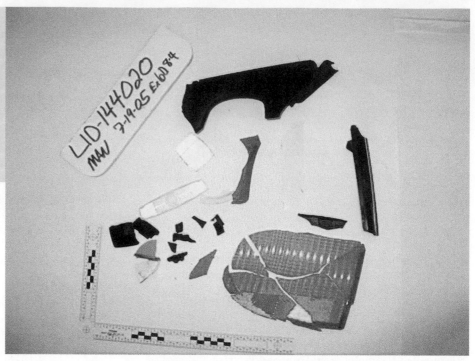

Police were called to a home where the occupant alleged that while standing in the living room someone standing outside of the house fired a shot at him. The complainant dropped to the floor, crawled to a nearby desk, and retrieved his revolver. After a short time he stood up and the person outside fired a second and third time. At that point the complainant fired a single shot at the outsider, whom he recognized as a man who lived nearby. The alleged shooter had a different version of events. He was walking past the complainant's house and was shot at three times before he shot once in self-defense at the man in the house.

Figure 4-13 illustrates the four bullet holes found in the window by the police. When a glass window is broken by a shot, both radial fracture and **concentric fracture** lines may develop. Radial fractures move away from the point of impact; concentric fracture lines more or less circle the same point. From Figure 4-11 we know that shot B came before shot A, because the radial and concentric fracture lines of shot B stop those of shot A. From 4-13, we know nothing of the relationship of holes C and D. However, as shown in Figure 4-10, we can determine the direction from which a bullet penetrated glass: on the side opposite the surface of initial impact, there will be a characteristic cone-shaped area. In the case being illustrated, shots A, B, and D all contained a cone-shaped characteristic on the inside of the window, indicating that these three shots had been fired from the outside. Shot C had the cone-shaped area on the outside, revealing that it had been fired from inside the house. Thus the physical evidence substantiated the complainant's statement.

It is essential that the crime scene technician and investigator understand the ways in which glass reacts to force. Often this knowledge is critical in determining whether a crime has been committed, establishing the sequence of action, and evaluating the credibility of statements given by parties at the scene. Before any glass or window pane is moved at all, it should be photographed in detail to reflect the exact features of the existent glass fractures. Moving the evidence may cause fracture extensions that could change the conclusions of the investigator and

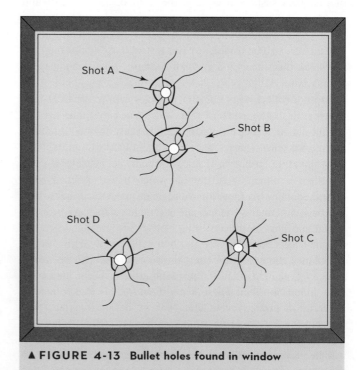

▲ **FIGURE 4-13 Bullet holes found in window**

BOX 4-5 | THE PHYSICAL EVIDENCE DIDN'T SUPPORT THE MAN'S

Walking a beat in a downtown business section in the late evening hours, a uniformed officer heard an alarm go off and saw an individual round the corner and run toward him at full speed. On seeing the officer, the individual started to double back the other way and then stopped. As the office approached, the man started to flee, but he stopped when commanded to do so. The man then told the officer that he had observed two people standing in front of a jewelry store window take a brick from a shopping bag and throw it through the window. The person said that, on seeing this, he became frightened and ran. Subsequent investigation revealed that the person who had rounded the corner was in fact the perpetrator of the offense and that he had fled before obtaining any material from the display window, because a lookout had seen a police car responding to a call in an adjacent block and had given warning. Processing of the perpetrator's clothing revealed pieces of glass in the cuff of his pants sufficiently large to make fracture matches with glass at the scene.

laboratory analyst. At crime scenes involving automobiles, the utility of glass evidence may be compromised by rescue personnel working to free occupants and wreckers pulling involved vehicles to the side of the road.

This example underscore the importance of the investigator's paying particular attention to determining what occurred between the time of the crime and the time he/she arrived at the scene. A key question that the investigator must attempt to answer with glass and other types of evidence is whether the position and characteristic of evidence could have been altered by the suspect, a witness, the victim, emergency medical personnel, or another officer. Stated differently, do not assume that the position of evidence you locate is in its original position.

HANDLING GLASS EVIDENCE

Ordinarily, if glass evidence is to be processed for fingerprints, it will be done in the laboratory. Tape should not be used to collect glass evidence in the field because it interferes with laboratory processing. As with other types of evidence, photography precedes the collection of glass evidence.

The physical properties used for comparison of known and questioned glass specimens are color, fluorescence, thickness, surface features, and curvature.[38] There are tests of optical properties, such as the refractive index, which measures the speed of light in a lab environment, which may also be conducted. A forensic glass analysis is typically a comparison of two or more glass fragments in an attempt to determine if they originated from different sources. Less frequently, the question of the end use of the glass needs to be identified; for example, is this broken glass from a light bulb?[39] Only a physical match of pieces of glass allows for their association to the exclusion of all other sources.[40] If glass is being submitted for comparison purposes, that is, to determine whether the particles may have originated from a common source, they are ordinarily small, and the following precautions should be taken: (1) glass in hair may be shaken or combed out over clean paper; (2) clothing and shoes should be packaged separately, and in no case should the victim's and suspect's items be comingled in any way; (3) if clothing items are wet, air dry them in the manner previously described; (4) glass may be embedded in the skin and open wounds of victims and suspects, and recovery by qualified medical personnel may be required; (5) submit weapons and tools without disturbing glass evidence; (6) samples of laminated glass—for example, windshields, should be labeled "inside" and "outside" and separately packaged in leak proof containers; (7) if a vehicle is involved, use a vacuum to collect the glass from each area of the vehicle; evidence collected from different areas should be packaged separately, and a new vacuum bag should be used for each new area processed; and (8) known and questioned glass samples, and evidence from victims and suspects, should be shipped separately to avoid contamination. These types of evidence should be wrapped in clean paper and sealed in a rigid container, such as a box, or if sufficiently small, a plastic container. Do not submit the evidence in a glass container.[41]

If door, window, or other framed glass is to be submitted for possible fracture matches, submit the entire frame in which all glass originally existed, marking the sides of the frame to show which way is inside and outside, along with marking it "top," "bottom, "left," and "right." Broken pieces should be carefully packaged in separate containers to avoid breakage in transit. Depending on the sizes involved, it may be necessary to place the glass between sturdy pieces of cardboard or plywood.[42]

FIBERS, CLOTH FRAGMENTS, AND IMPRESSIONS

Fibers are of value as evidence because they incorporate such variables as material type, number of fibers per strand, number of strands, thickness of fibers and strands, amount and direction of twists, dye content, type of weave, and the possible presence of foreign matter embedded in them. When something

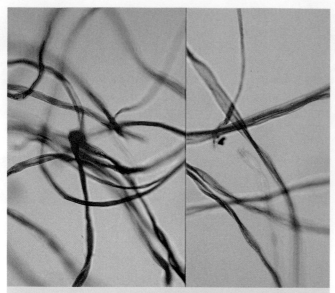

▲ **FIGURE 4-14 Comparison of cotton fibers**
The victim, who was wearing a red shirt, was stabbed by a man. Fibers from the victim's shirt (*above*) were compared to fibers collected from the assailant's pants (*right*). The two sets of fibers were consistent in all respects, although this finding does not exclude other sources for the fibers on the assailant's pants.
(Courtesy of Chicago Police Department)

composed of fibers, such as clothing, comes into contact with other clothing or objects, there is the opportunity for the exchange or transfer of fibers. Fibers may also be located on the body of the victim or the suspect, serving to connect one to the other (Figure 4-14).

Cloth fragments may be found at the scene of violent crimes or along the perpetrator's point of approach to, or exit from, a crime scene (Figure 4-15). They may be found on such diverse points as a chain fence, the splintered edge of a wooden building, or protruding nails. In hit-and-run offenses, cloth fragments

▶ **FIGURE 4-15 Fabric match**
Physical matching (sometimes called *physical* fit or *jigsaw* fit) is powerful and incontrovertible evidence. Shown here is a fragment from a victim's clothing found in the grille of the suspect's vehicle involved in a hit-and-run case. The fabric fragment fitted the victim's raincoat and conclusively established the contact between the suspect's vehicle and the victim. (©The McGraw-Hill Companies/Keith Eng, photographer)

may be found in the grille or undercarriage of the striking vehicle. Cloth impressions are found infrequently in investigations, usually on wet paint or some surface of a vehicle involved in striking a pedestrian.

Both fibers and cloth fragments should be packaged in a pillbox or in folded paper that is taped shut. Only on rare occasions will it be possible to obtain a cast of a cloth impression. This effort, however, should invariably be preceded by the taking of several photographs; at least one of these photos should show a scale to allow for comparisons at some future date.

STRING, CORD, ROPE, AND TAPE

String, cord, rope, and tape evidence is usually found in robbery, murder, rape, and kidnapping cases. It is also associated with accidental hangings by children and accidental sexual asphyxiations. String, cord and rope have essentially the same characteristics and share some characteristics of fibers. Known samples of these types of evidence can be compared to crime scene evidence on the basis of composition, diameter, color, and construction; if a tracer is present, it is possible to identify the manufacturer. There is some preliminary evidence if string, cord, and rope is made from plant material, and contains cells from the plant of origin, then DNA analysis techniques can exclude or include as a source remnants found in a suspect's possession as compared to a length used to bind a victim.[43]

In instances where the victim was tied, it may be possible to match the ends of the string, cord, rope, and tape with the rest of the roll in the suspect's possession (Figure 4-16). When rope evidence is removed from a victim or from anyplace, knots should never be severed. Instead, a place away from the knot should be cut and a piece of twine used to loop the two ends together. A tag should be attached to indicate that the investigator has cut the rope. Evidence about knot tier handedness and use of habitual knots has been scarce and conflicting. A study of 562 subjects did reveal differences in patterns of knot tying between left and right handers.[44] Ordinarily, because of its resilient nature, the packaging of this type of evidence poses no particular problem when standard procedures are followed.

FINGERPRINTS

Fingerprint identification and collection goes on in what are fundamentally two different universes. In the first universe, most of the fingerprint work is done by a lone patrol officer who may be investigating something like a home burglary where someone raised a window at the back of the house when no one was home; took the change jar from the kitchen counter, some prescription pills from a medicine cabinet in the master bathroom, and a Coke from the refrigerator; and left the way he/she entered. The officer is going to select a fingerprint powder to use from the two or three types in his/her briefcase, use a brush that costs from $3.50 to not more than $11.00, dust the promising areas, perhaps lift it with wide Scotch Tape, put it on a card, make some notations on it, and leave after talking with the complainants. The officer has done a good job.

However, when that officer catches a murder call, a jewelry store burglary where $330,000 in merchandise has been taken, or a messy domestic aggravated assault where a spouse used a kitchen knife on a cheating partner, trained crime scene technicians from the second universe are going to be there. In many smaller departments, those technicians may be from a larger neighboring agency or the State Police or State Investigative Agency who have not only the training, equipment, and technology, but also valuable experience. This section is for the men and women in the first universe.

Several different parts of the body—such as palms, fingers, toes, and the soles of the feet—have friction ridges that can form a "fingerprint." All such prints are collected, preserved, and identified using similar methods. But it may not be immediately

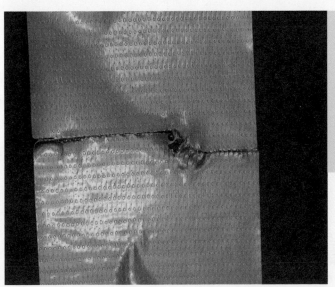

◀FIGURE 4-16 Tape match
In a particularly violent rape, the suspect used gray duct tape to tie the victim's hands and cover her mouth. The victim was left for dead, but she managed to crawl out an open window and seek help. The top portion of the photograph is the filament tape recovered from the victim's face covering her mouth. The bottom part of the photograph is the end of the tape roll found in the suspect's pocket. By showing that these two ends of the duct tape match, a physical match is established. (Courtesy Portland, Oregon Police Bureau)

apparent which part of a body made the print; as used here, "fingerprint" includes all prints made by friction ridges. Basically, a fingerprint is a replica of the **minutiae** or friction ridges that touched the surface on which the print was found. **Ridges** are the raised portions of the finger skin, atop which are miniscule sweat pores. **Furrows** are the low area between the ridges, sort of miniature valleys.

With just a few exceptions—persons with birth defects or amputations—everyone has fingerprints. This universal characteristic is a prime factor in establishing a standard of identification. Since a print of one finger has never been known to duplicate exactly another fingerprint—even of the same person or an identical twin[45]—it is possible to identify an individual with just one impression. The relative ease with which a set of fingerprints can be taken as a means of identification is a further reason for using this standard. Despite such factors as aging and environmental influences, a person's fingerprints do not change. This unchanging pattern is a permanent record of the individual throughout life.

Fingerprints are also being studied chemically and can provide some determinations about drug use.

BASIS FOR IDENTIFICATION

Fingerprint examiners follow the ACE-V guideless: Analysis, Comparison, Evaluation, Verification. The general rule is that identifications are checked by a second analyst to determine their accuracy. The basis for identification are ridge characteristics of which there are as many as 175 in an averaged-sized fingerprint.[46] The major fingerprint patterns are shown in Figure 4-17. About 60-65% of the population have loops, roughly 30-35% have whorls, and about 5% have arches.[47]

To make an identification, analysts study the fingerprint of an unknown suspect that was collected at a crime scene. They use the ridges to locate specific "points" on the print that give it its individuating quality and compare it to parallel-level information from a known source's fingerprint. If enough points are the same, there is an identification.

Although points are discussed in greater detail later in this section, it is sufficient to note here that in the United States there is no standard for the minimum number of points that a fingerprint must have to establish individual identity. That is left to each fingerprint examiner. However, positive identification of an individual cannot be made when an unexplained difference appears, regardless of how many other points there are.

Some persons erroneously believe that the points used for identification of the fingerprint occur only in the pattern area of the finger. In fact, all the different types occur outside the pattern area on the finger as well as on the first and second joints of the finger and the entire palm of the hand. They are also present on the toes and the entire sole of the foot; they may be found in any area where friction ridges occur.

There is no requirement for a fingerprint to be of a certain size to be used as a basis of identification. If a single partial fingerprint recovered at the scene is compared to a complete print of a suspect and the partial contains enough points of agreement, an individual identification can be made.

There is also no requirement for a certain number of points of agreement to exist. In the *United States of America v. Byron Mitchell*, appellant (45 F. 3rd 572 3d Cir, 1998) a fingerprint expert testified that he had never made an identification on less than seven points of agreement. In Mitchell, he testified on the basis of nine points of agreement. In 1924, England adopted the requirement of 16 points of agreement, which was later relaxed. In the United States, each individual examiner makes his/her own decision. For example, if there is a partial print that is smeared, an examiner might require more points than if it was a full, clear print. Impressionistically, in the United States examiners seem comfortable in making an individual identification if there is a minimum of 8-12 points of agreement.

There is no reliable method for judging the age of latent fingerprints (LFPs), although the context in which they are found may provide some information. However, both here and in England over roughly the last decade or more, promising research on age-dating fingerprints has been carried out. Being

► **FIGURE 4-17**
Fingerprint patterns
Fingerprints are initially classified into one of the major classifications shown here. (Source: Federal Bureau of Investigation)

Plain Arch

Tented Arch

Ulnar Loop

Radial Loop

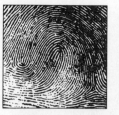

Plain Whorl

Central Pocket Loop

Double Loop Whorl

Accidental Whorl

able to date when fingerprints were deposited would allow investigators to rule out some as being too old to be relevant or fix the time of a crime more precisely.[48] Those involved in fighting terrorism would likely know when terrorists left their fingerprints to give them some idea of who or what they are targeting on a reconnaissance or the intelligence that could be gained by potentially seeing who had built a bomb or handled documents seized in special operations raids. Relatedly, at some point could we have the technology to tell us the age of a fingerprint's donor, akin to the use of DNA?

PLASTIC, LATENT, AND PATENT FINGERPRINTS

Fingerprints can be found on almost any solid surface, including the human body. Fingerprints are classified into three major groups:[49]

1. **Plastic prints** are finger impressions left in pliable, soft surfaces, such as wax, soap, wet paint, or fresh caulk, putty, and explosives (Figure 4-18). Those surfaces give the print the quality of being three dimensional.

2. **Latent prints** is an elastic term with two different meanings. (1) It can broadly refer to any fingerprint found at the scene or elsewhere on an item of interest, for example, a gun recovered from a pond, or (2) it can refer specifically to a fingerprint at the scene which is hidden or unseen to the eye. In this immediate section, we are using the latter term. Elsewhere, the context in which "latent" is stated, we will reveal which meaning is being used.

   A latent print can be invisible for several reasons, including their lack of contrast with the surface on which they are located or because the surface was only touched lightly. Sometimes, they can be found by shining a flashlight obliquely on the surface being examined.

At other times, specialized techniques or equipment must be used (Figure 4-19). One illustration of this is a specialized alternative light source (ALS), which illuminates the crime scene, potentially revealing not only fingerprints but a variety of other evidence, such as body fluids, hairs, and fibers. Shined on someone, an ALS reveals things such as bruises, bite marks, and gunshot and explosive residues. In Figure 4-20, a Ruvis SceneScope is being used. Its two primary applications are locating untreated fingerprints and those developed by Super Glue (cyanoacrylate) fuming.

Once located, LFPs are made visible by developing them with fingerprint powders and other techniques described later in this chapter. Most fingerprints are developed using traditional powder and brush. Perhaps the most common mistake made when first attempting to develop a print is putting too much powder on the brush, which fill up the furrows with finger powder, making the print useless.

Latent prints are created when the small amounts of body perspiration and oil that are normally found on the ridges are deposited on surfaces that are touched. The smoother and less porous a surface is, the more likely it is that any latent prints present can be found and developed.

3. **Patent prints** may immediately be wholly visible, or they may be latent. Visible/residue patent prints form when blood, dirt, ink, paint, etc., is transferred from the surface of a finger or thumb to another surface. Patent prints can be left on many surfaces, including smooth or rough and porous (such as paper, cloth, or wood) or nonporous (such as metal, glass, or plastic). Patent prints become latent prints when the fingerprint is not formed by residue, but by the body's natural oils and sweat on the skin that are deposited onto another surface.

◀ **FIGURE 4-18 Plastic print**
A suspect left this print in a child's "silly putty" while keeping his victims at bay during a home invasion robbery.
(©The McGraw-Hill Companies/Jill Braaten, photographer)

QUICK FACTS

Develop LFP or Swab for DNA First?

Everything someone touches may be a source of DNA because they may leave behind cells that have sloughed off on contact. With respect to a LFP and the possibility of there also being DNA evidence, this creates a question like the classical "Which came first, the chicken or the egg?"

If a crime scene fingerprint is developed, potentially that process could eliminate the possibility of DNA analysis. Conversely, swabbing for DNA might destroy the fingerprint. In the Wisconsin State Crime Laboratory, Hujet and Tabor analyzed data from actual evidence submitted to their lab for examination. Based on the data shown below, the sequence should be to attempt to recover DNA first and then develop the latent fingerprint.[50]

Telephone Record Matrix for "Crazy Joe's" Home Telephone			
SEQUENCE/ RESULTS	NO PRINTS OR DNA (%)	PRINTS AND NO DNA (%)	DNA AND NO PRINTS (%)	PRINTS AND DNA (%)
DNA first	24	34	18	24
Fingerprint first	25	43	13	19

However, if the print is recognized as an unusable smudge, should investigators still collect it for its potential DNA?

▶ **FIGURE 4-19 Locating prints**
A crime scene technician uses protective equipment while dusting for fingerprints. Several developed prints can be seen in the area the technician is dusting. (Courtesy of the Nassau County Police Department, New York)

CONDITIONS AFFECTING THE QUALITY OF LATENT FINGERPRINTS

Among the conditions affecting the quality of fingerprints are:

1. The surface on which they are deposited:
   A. *Porous surfaces*, including paper, cardboard, cigarette butts, and untreated wood. Surfaces of this type quickly absorb water and water-soluble deposits in the sweat

quickly. This quality makes prints durable, and the probability of getting usable prints is usually high. Development (visualization) begins with spraying the item with the chemical DFO. Spray DFO on the item, or submerge it in the solution for 5 seconds. Let it dry under a fume hood, and repeat this process. It quickly develops a reddish print. DFO fluoresces under a blue-green light. Ninhydin, another chemical, is also used on the

The **double swab** method is used before any attempts to develop an LFP. It maximizes the possibility of recovering useful biological evidence. Moisten the first swab with sterile distilled water. Using medium pressure, wash the area for 7–10 seconds. Immediately thereafter, with light pressure, run the second swab over the same area. Keeping the swabs separate, let them air dry at room temperature before submitting them to the lab. The two swabs should not be in the same container. They should be analyzed as soon as practical. The swabs may be kept at room temperature for 4–6 hours, but refrigerated after that.

The development of identifiable LFPs on the skin of dead bodies and living victims can be done, but it is difficult. Various approaches have been tried and reported in the literature. Some of the studies reported conditions that inhibited getting results, such as amounts of body hair, temperature, body temperature, and the lapse of time since the latent prints were on the body.

Two volunteers placed 150 fingerprints on 10 dead bodies as part of a clinical study. Thereafter, attempts were made to develop them using black fingerprint powder. Twelve prints (8%) of those developed had at least seven points of identification. Those prints were from the shin, chest, ulna, femur, and ankle area. After 3 hours, no more recoveries were made.[55] A clinical test on living subjects noted that recovery of LFPs was not possible after 15 minutes, although their impressions remained visible for a total of 30.[56]

In an experiment, the German Federal Criminal Police (FCP) tried developing 1,000 single latent prints that had been deliberately placed on dead bodies. As visualization agents, the FCP used the three types of powder identified in Table 4-1. The prints developed and lifted were divided into four categories based on number of identification points: (1) 12 or more, (2) 7–11, (3) 4–6, and (4) less than 3. Using seven or more points as a cut-off, Table 4-1 reveals just how difficult getting usable prints off of dead bodies can be.[57]

At a death crime scene, the medical examiner should be requested to release the body to investigators for the purpose of immediately processing it for LFPs at the scene. If this is not possible, the investigator should request they be allowed to go directly the morgue to do so before the body is refrigerated, which interferes with processing.

While there are other processes, Super Glue fuming is commonly used to develop LFPs on dead bodies. Although some have suggested super gluing the entire body, the consensus view is to use an ALS to identify specific sites. Skin is nonporous, and a Super Glue wand is suitable to process sites in 10–15 second bursts. When this procedure is completed, the latent prints should be sprayed with Basic Yellow 40, Rhodamine 6G, or Basic Red 20 to enhance the print for photography, with and without scales.

Recovering LFPs from living victims is very difficult. The safety and comfort of victims must be carefully considered. Investigators must prepare the victim by explaining whatever process they propose to use and answer the victim's questions before proceeding. The safest process is the direct transfer method. Depending on where the LFP is, a female technician may be needed. The victim must be instructed to remain absolutely motionless during the process or instead of a potential print there will only be a smudge. A clean, nonporous hard surface is selected, such as a glass plate or similar medium, and is pressed directly, evenly, and firmly against the area of the LFP. Remove the plate directly away without any sideward movement. Super Glue and develop it in the same manner as previously described with dead bodies.

COLLECTING AND PRESERVING LATENT PRINTS

Occasionally items such as beer cans or glasses that have condensation on them need to be processed for prints. Heat lamps or any other source of artificial heat should not be used to dry the object quickly. Such objects should be allowed to air-dry naturally. Similarly, articles that have been frozen and need to be processed for prints must be allowed to thaw and dry naturally. Whenever reasonable to do so, the actual item on which the print is located should be submitted for developing in the laboratory.

Once a print is found it should be photographed immediately with a rigid scale in view. The ruler allows a one-to-one, or actual-size, picture of the print to be made. This provides a permanent record of the print in the event that it is accidentally altered or destroyed while attempting to collect or transporting it.

Most latent prints are lifted with a clear strip of tape, 1½–2 inches wide, or with clear flap lifter after they have been developed with powders. One end of the clear tape is placed on the surface just before the latent print appears. Pressure is then applied to progressively lay the tape over the print, taking care not to leave air bubbles. If air bubbles are accidentally created, the tape should be carefully smoothed over to eliminate them. The tape may be left on the object if the object is to be submitted to the laboratory.

TABLE 4-1	FCP Study of Fingerprint Development on Corpses		
DATA/AGENT	GREEN FLUORESCENT MAGNETIC POWDER	BLACK MAGNETIC POWDER	BLACK POWDER
Sample size	498	322	180
Total prints lifted	32 (6.4%)	34 (10.6%)	33 (18.3%)
Categories 1 and 2	15	15	17

Alternatively, the pattern of the print is lifted by pulling up the tape, starting at one end and moving progressively to the other end. Now the powder that shows the print pattern is stuck to the sticky side of the tape. This tape is then laid back down on an appropriately colored backing card. For example, assume that a latent print on a glass window is developed with dark powder.

MARKING AND IDENTIFYING PRINT LIFTS

When a latent print has been developed, lifted, and placed on a card, the card must be properly identified. Information recorded on the card should include the date, type of case, case number, address of the crime scene, name of the officer who made the lift, exact place of the lift, and type of object from which the print was lifted. Regardless of how well the latent print was developed and lifted, if the card is not properly marked with all the data required or if the fingerprint specialist is not furnished with the information required, the entire process may be wasted effort. In describing the exact place that the lift was made, it is sometimes helpful to draw a simple sketch of the object. The sketch should be made on the fingerprint card that is sent to the laboratory. The inclusion of corresponding numbers on both the lift and the sketch establishes the location of the latent print.

FORENSIC ODONTOLOGY

Forensic odontology (FO) has been defined as the intersection of dentistry with criminal and civil laws. For present purposes, it is a medical specialty relating dental evidence to investigation. FO can make significant contributions in the following circumstances:

1. *Identifying missing/unidentified persons.* For example, hunters find a human skull, but investigation finds no other remains or a decomposing or skeletonized body is discovered. Human remains found in remote areas, clandestine graves, abandoned buildings, or under similar circumstances may be in very "rough" condition and may have been subject to animal predation and their remains scattered over a wide area. Although teeth are the most durable part of the body, some may become scattered, and investigators should try to find as many as possible. The addition of an experienced forensic anthropologist to the investigative team should be given consideration when buried and skeletonized remains are found.

2. *Recognition and analysis of bite marks.* In sexual assault, child/elder abuse, domestic violence, and homicide cases bite marks are important in determining what happened. In rare cases, a bite mark may be self-inflicted as part of a staged crime.[58] Children sometimes bite themselves, and that possibility must be considered. Alternatively, another child may have inflicted the bite. Although bite marks are most frequently found on skin and in human tissue, they may also be found on objects at crime scenes, including pencils, Styrofoam cups, food (Figure 4-23), and other objects.

3. *Recognition and evaluation of orofacial trauma in victims of violence.* This trauma occurs on the face and mouth. Symptoms appear as a result of blood being outside of a vessel. A new injury usually appears red and scan look somewhat like a rash. It typically fades into a bruise. Other symptoms include lacerated lips, damage gums, and loosened or lost teeth. It may the result of an accident or violence. Children just learning to walk may exhibit signs from falling or it could also be child abuse (See Chapter 11, "Crimes Against Children").[59]

4. *Identifying mass casualties of attacks and natural and industrial disasters.* Examples include 9/11; the Indian Ocean tsunami (2004), which may have killed as many as 250,000 people; and the 1,836 deaths caused by Hurricane Katrina (2005). In Thailand, 75% of the 2004 tsunami victims were identified by forensic odontology.[60]

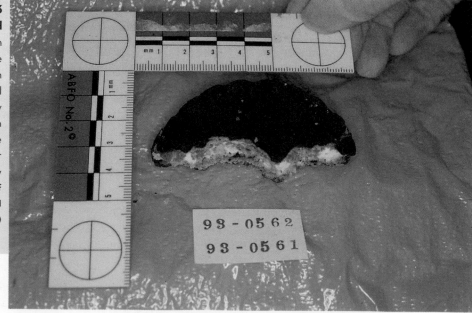

▶ **FIGURE 4-23**
Bite mark in food
A partially eaten "Moon Pie" bitten by one of the suspects in a double homicide. From the bite marks it can be determined that the individual making them had two non-equally protruding upper front teeth. Such information can play an important role in determining probable cause for arrest and/or search warrants. (Courtesy of Dr. Richard R. Souviron, DDS, ABFO, Chief Forensic Odontologist, Dade County Medical Examiner Department, Miami, Florida)

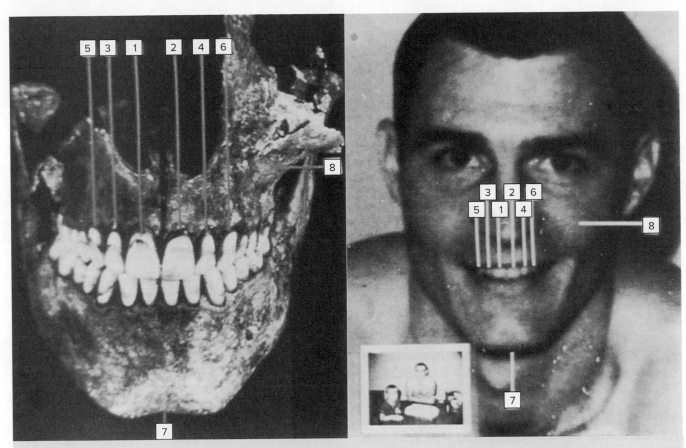

▲ FIGURE 4-24 Dental comparison

The left photo shows upper and lower jaws of an unknown white male. Some bone loss (pyorrhea) and tobacco staining
are evident. There were no fillings, decay, or missing teeth and no evidence of any dental treatment. The right photo is an
enhancement and enlargement of a photo of the victim at his son's birthday party. His kidnappers/killers were sentenced to life terms.
(*Both:* Courtesy of Dr. Richard R. Souviron, DDS, ABFO, Chief Forensic Odontologist, Dade County Medical Examiner Department, Miami, Florida)

IDENTIFICATION OF MISSING AND UNIDENTIFIED REMAINS

Dentition is the arrangement of a person's natural and artificial
teeth. Like a fingerprint, dentition is individual class evidence.
The FO dentition identification process includes the comparison of a person's postmortem or after-death dental remains with
antemortem or predeath records, including the written notes of
a dentist, radiographs/X-rays, casts, bridges, fillings,[61] and dental
restorations. Morphological (shape and form) peculiarities of
teeth can also help establish identities.

Some dentures are marked and can be traced to a particular
owner. Forensic dentists have established individual identity on the
basis of **smiling photographs** for remains for which there is no
identity. Assume an appeal in the news media for information
results in a family member or friend coming forward with a possible identity. The person possibly identified has no dental records,
but the family member has one of more photographs of the person
smiling. The smiling identification made in Figure 4-24 was made
on dental parameters, such as shape, dimensions, and alignment.[62]

Sources of dental records include the military, health insurance carriers, local dentists, and community health clinics for
indigent and low-income persons and families. In some cases, it
is useful to have a forensic artist prepare a likeness of the
deceased, as he/she may have appeared in life and solicit public
help in making an identification, which would then have to be
confirmed.

Searches for dental records may not be productive, because
(1) some number of individuals under the age of 30 have no
dental decay, and (2) individuals with decayed or missing teeth
may never have sought treatment. In either case, there are no
records of antemortem dental restorations that can be compared
with the postmortem dental features of a victim.

BITE MARKS

Most bite marks usually involve humans and are easily distinguished from those inflicted by animals. Victims may be alive
or dead. Investigators must be particularly alert to the possibility that bite-mark evidence exists, particularly when they are
working sexual assault, child/elder abuse, and homicide cases.
Female victims are most often bitten on the breast, buttocks,
and legs during a sexual assault, whereas male victims are more

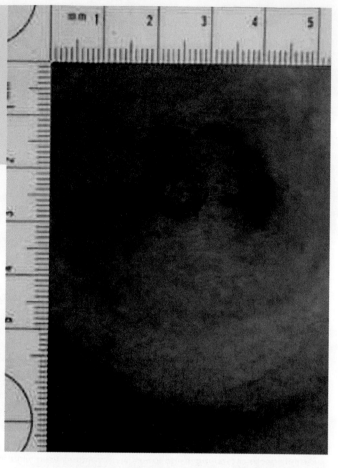

▶FIGURE 4-25 Bite mark on breast and nipple
Bite marks are often found on victims of sexual abuse, rape, and violence. It is not uncommon that the suspect bites the victim as part of the sexual sadist ritual. Here, a bite mark is reflected on the breast and nipple of a sexual assault victim. First swab the area for traces of the suspect's saliva, which may yield DNA evidence. Photograph the bite mark and follow other guidelines set forth by the ABFO relating to bite mark evidence collection and preservation.

likely to be bitten on the arms and shoulders. Bite marks on the arms and hands are usually defensive wounds caused when a person holds up his/her arms to ward off an attacker.[63]

Facial hair associated with bite marks may be transferred between attackers and victims; it should be collected consistent with the guidelines in the next major section, "Hair." In 99% of all violent rapes, victims are bitten at least once by their attacker (Figure 4-25).[64] An **avulsed bite** is so forcible that a portion of the body is detached. This may be a finger, a chunk out of someone's arm, or some other portion of the body. Although common, avulsed bites are seen on women's breasts in sadistic sexual assaults.

QUICK FACTS

Bite Results in Tissue Transfer

In two different cases, women were assaulted and bit their assailants, resulting in small fragments of the perpetrators' skin being wedged between the victims' teeth. Discovered during the postmortem oral examinations, the skin fragments recovered matched the perpetrators' injuries and identifications were made, which were subsequently confirmed by the DNA test results.[65]

The collection of bite mark evidence from victims, when reasonably possible, should be left to a forensic dentist because bite marks may be mistaken for bruises, abrasions, indentions, or lacerations (Figure 4-26); most have an overall ovoid appearance. One or both arches of teeth may be present, and there may be multiple, overlapping bites at the same location. Bite marks on skin should be processed quickly because they may be degraded

▶FIGURE 4-26
Hand laceration by teeth
Laceration at base of suspect's thumb area caused by victim's defensive bite. Suspect grabbed victim from behind, trying to gag her with his hand.
(Source: Los Angeles Police Department)

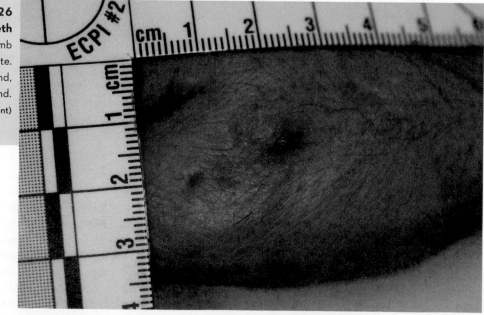

by skin elasticity, the postmortem position of the body, and skin dehydration. The follow procedures are recommended when collecting bite mark evidence from deceased victims:

1. Take orientation photographs.
2. Take two sterile saliva swabs from each bite mark using the double swab method.
3. Take close-up digital photographs, with, and without an ABFO scale. Consider additional photographs using infrared, ultraviolet, or an ALS to supplement the conventional images taken.
4. It may be beneficial to take a series of photographs over time with a living or deceased victim.
5. With proper authorization, the tissue at the deceased's bite site may need be excised, removed entirely, and preserved.
6. If the bite mark has three dimensional properties, an impression of it should be made.[66]

In some agencies over the last several years, there has been a shift away from casting certain 3D items. Among those are impressions and 3D bite marks. In a number of places, highly accurate laser scanners are being used to record bite marks, replacing casting. It is a time-saving measure that also yields greater detail. If investigators develop a murder suspect, they can get a search warrant to make casts of the shoes he/she is wearing and an analyst can compare the cast to the 3D photographs.

CHEILOSCOPY AND RECONSTRUCTED IDENTIFICATION

These tools of identification are not well known but are important. Therefore, investigators need to know about them and their potential contributions.

Cheiloscopy is the identification of individuals based on the pattern of wrinkles on their lips, which has individual characteristics. They are unique for life, even among twins.[67] It is defined as a method of identification of a person based on characteristic arrangement of lines appearing on the red part of lips and is an auxiliary method of identification referred to as lip prints.[68]

They can most frequently appear in sexual assaults, burglaries, and murders and may be co-located with tooth marks/bite marks. Lip prints are trace evidence and may be hard to locate, but coffee cups, glasses, food products, doors, photographs, letters, and plastic bags are among places that are good candidates.[69]

To get a sample from living subjects, ask the subject to press their lips against a glossy porous surface or a hard, nonporous surface. The sample provided should be allowed to air dry, or you can dry it with the use of a heat source. Using a magna fingerprint brush with an appropriately colored *magnetic* fingerprint powder, photograph and recover the print. With deceased victims, Super Glue fuming is a good choice.

Relatedly, **ear marks** may be useful in making comparison that excludes or includes a person as a possible suspect. However, its place in individual identification is still subject to some questions and debate. While the debate goes on, efforts to digitally automate comparisons are under way.

RECONSTRUCTED IDENTIFICATION

Sometimes called dental profiling, this tool is used when other means of identification are not available for a body. A forensic dentist may work with a forensic anthropologist to develop a profile of the person. Depending on how complete a set of teeth and cranium are, a forensic dentist may be able to offer opinions as to age, age at death, gender, membership in one of the major race categories, smoking, and alcohol consumption, personal habits such as pipe smoking, and, by the absence or presence of dental care, social class.[70]

HAIR

Hair evidence is often found because both victims and suspects can transfer it to each other or the scene; hair is easy to locate and recover, and durable.[71] It may be found on ski masks used by offenders, in head and pubic hairs of assailants and victims, as well as their clothing, hats, and wigs. It may also be clutched in the hands and under the finger nails of victims. Hair evidence is primarily associated with violent crimes.

A number of useful conclusions are possible from the examination of hair:

1. Human or nonhuman origin.
2. Limited determination of animal species.
3. Determination of classic racial characteristics of the donor.
4. Body area origin of the hair, for example, eyelashes, pubic, scalp, and beard.
5. Indication of how it was removed; for instance, if hair has an anagen/active growth root, it suggests forcible removal.
6. Damage to the hair, for example, by putrefaction, blunt force trauma, or burn.
7. Types of drugs ingested and how recently.
8. Presence of hair contaminates, including blood, semen, soil, pet hair, and soil; contaminates *may* suggest an occupation; for instance, automotive spray paint particles might indicate working in a body shop.[72]
9. Hair treatment, including bleaching, shampoo residues, and dyes.[73]
10. Determination of whether known and questioned hair samples could have a common origin (Figure 4-27).
11. Whether the hair is diseased.
12. Whether suitable for microscopic examination or DNA analysis.

While hair is growing (anagen phase), 10%–20% of it is resting (telogen phase). When growing, there are living cells, the presence of root tissue is common, and it is a good candidate for nuclear DNA (nDN) analysis to establish individual identity because it is inherited from both parents. Teleogen hair is not well suited for nDN. It is suited for mitochondrial DNA (mtDNA) examination, which is only inherited from the maternal line. MtDNA cannot establish individual identity because other people along the same maternal lines share it. There is also the possibility of a random match. In contrast, some mtDNA is so rare that it is seen only once even in very

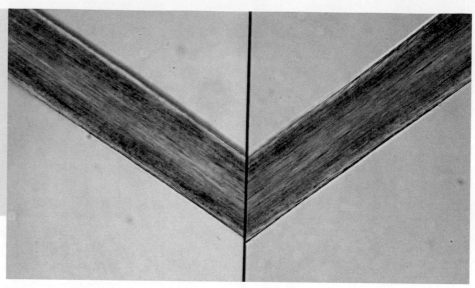

▶ **FIGURE 4-27 Hair Analysis**
Photomicrograph of hair found inside a rape suspect's vehicle (*left*) is matched with a sample of hair from the victim (*right*). Note the darker shading of brown near the outside of each strand as a result of color added to the victim's hair. These types of peculiarities provide matches between the characteristics of hairs but not to the exclusion of a donor other than the victim.

large DNA databases. MtDNA can be used to exclude suspects, establish that the victim is not from a particular lineage (or that he/she is), all of which helps to focus investigative effort.[74]

When collecting hair standards, at least 30 should be collected from various portions of the head (front, back, top, and each side) to ensure that all variations of texture, color, and length have been properly sampled.[75] At each site, half of the hairs should be pulled and the rest combed lightly onto clean paper. Gloves should be worn and a clean comb used on each area of the body. All areas of the pubic or other area should be thoroughly combed to dislodge foreign hairs and other materials.[76] In some cases, such as a missing person, it may be necessary to collect hair samples from a secondary source, such as a hair brush. Hair samples can be placed in a clean envelope, which is sealed and labeled. Pill boxes and other tightly sealed containers are also acceptable in many labs.

Known and questioned samples should be packaged separately when submitted to the laboratory. The investigator should be present when qualified medical personnel collect samples.[77] Before the process begins, the investigator should verify that the medical person understands the proper collection and packaging of samples.

Hair collection at the crime scene requires a different set of considerations regarding known and questioned samples:

1. Document by photos, the evidence log, and by diagram where the hairs were recovered.
2. Do not submit wet hairs to the lab; they should be allowed to air dry.
3. If they are firmly attached to an object, leave the hairs intact and submit the object.
4. When visible hairs are not firmly attached to an object or the object is too large to submit to the lab, carefully remove them with clean tweezers.
5. If hairs were possibly transferred to the victim's and/or suspect's clothing, keep their clothes apart. Package each article of clothing separately and submit to the laboratory separately.
6. Do not overlook the potential probative value of animal hair; if a victim's pets were present at the time of the offense, samples should be pulled from them and handled in the usual manner.

7. Combed and pulled hairs should always be packaged separately.
8. Because of the potential of cross-contamination, the same person should not collect hair from the victim and a suspect. For the same reason that person should not handle the clothing of the victim and suspect.

A recent experiment involving a new technology analyzed one hair provided by 13 different people.[78] The results correctly identified the gender of all 13 participants, as well as their race. Participants were limited to three different racial groups and the researchers are working to broaden that base. Analysis time was a lightening quick 85 seconds. If the technology does reach general use, forensic science will have another important analytical tool.

BLOOD

Blood was class-characteristic evidence until the introduction of DNA analysis in the early 1980s. Since then, there have been advances in how fast analyses can be completed. The Parbon NanoLab's Snapshot DNA Phenotyping services, discussed and illustrated in Chapter 1, "The Evolution of Criminal Investigation and Forensic Science" is an example.

There is additional ongoing research on blood-identification techniques that if they become viable for use will give law enforcement agencies and crime labs important new capabilities. Examples include:

1. On nonhumans, bloodstain pattern analysis is in its infancy with regard to being able to predict what part of the body blood stains came from using markers in the blood stain.[79]
2. Textiles with blood stains on it can help piece together events at a violent crime scene. Interpreting that evidence is still difficult. Researchers have experimented with various types of textiles to determine how blood acts when it lands on it because the effect of blood on cloth is variable and is also affected by the position of the victim, for example, standing or lying down.[80]

TABLE 4-2	Sources of DNA Evidence	
EVIDENCE	**POSSIBLE LOCATION OF DNA ON THE EVIDENCE**	**SOURCE OF DNA**
Baseball bat or similar weapon	Handle, end	Sweat, skin, blood, tissue
Hat, bandanna, or mask	Inside	Sweat, hair, dandruff
Eyeglasses	Nose or ear pieces, lens	Sweat, skin
Facial tissue or cotton swab	Surface area	Mucus, blood, sweat, semen, earwax
Dirty laundry	Surface area	Blood, sweat, semen, vomit
Toothpick	Tips	Saliva
Used cigarette	Cigarette butt	Saliva
Stamp or envelope	Licked area	Saliva
Tape or ligature	Inside or outside surface	Skin, sweat
Bottle, can, or glass	Sides, mouthpiece	Saliva, sweat
Used condom	Inside or outside surface	Semen, vaginal or rectal cells
Blanket, pillow, or sheet	Surface area	Sweat, hair, semen, urine, saliva, dandruff
"Through and through" bullet	Outside surface	Blood, tissue
Bite mark	Person's skin or clothing	Saliva
Fingernail or partial fingernail	Scrapings	Blood, sweat, tissue

Source: www.dba.Gov/Basics/Evidence_Collection/Identifying, January 5, 2011.

3. Blood trajectories and patterns can provide key information in crime scene reconstruction. Research continues in this area with increasingly accurate ability to know the location of participants in an event, their location, weapons type, and number of blows.[81]

Taken together, this research will help interpret crime scene events and sequences more accurately and to discriminate between different versions of events as described by participants. As an unexpected finding of a study asking crime scene investigators to process staged blood-splattered events, the researchers were impressed that although there was a great deal of blood evidence to be collected, the crime scene investigators did not get diverted or neglect gathering all types of evidence.

On average, an adult's body contains about 5–6 quarts of blood, and even small cuts can produce a lot of blood. At crime scenes, blood may be encountered in amounts ranging from small drops to large pools, in states ranging from fresh to dried, and in almost any place, including on floors, walls, ceilings, clothes, weapons, the suspect's and victim's bodies, and the exterior and interior of vehicles.

Because of the frequency with which blood is encountered and the fact that DNA analysis can provide individual identification (Table 4-2), officers need to be alert to locating and protecting this type of evidence. Moreover, they should wear appropriate PPE and take the other kinds of protective measures discussed in Chapter 3, "Investigators, the Investigative Process, and the Crime Scene."

THE APPEARANCE OF BLOODSTAINS

If blood at the crime scene is fresh and relatively uncontaminated, identifying it as blood is not difficult. If it is in some other condition, identifying blood merely by "eyeballing it" becomes increasingly difficult. Blood may appear as a rust-colored stain or have gray, black, green, or blue tints. It may also be mixed with earth, grease, paint, or other substances, making it difficult to see.

Very small drops of blood can be located by viewing the surfaces concerned at an oblique angle close to the plane of the surfaces. If the light is not strong or if the scene is dark, viewing the surfaces will be enhanced by shining a flashlight beam at the same oblique angle. Blood is naturally fluorescing and may be detected by the use of a FLS.

The drying time of blood depends on a number of factors, including whether it is on a porous or nonporous surface, its size and thickness, and the presence or absence of a fan or breeze. Higher temperatures hasten the drying time of blood, whereas increased humidity decreases it. Drying first appears at the edges of a bloodstain and works toward its center. A dried bloodstain will begin to pucker and crack from the edges inward after further drying. Research on estimating the age of a blood stain (From the time of its deposit) appears to be increasing and several different approaches are being tested. Although some approaches are promising, none are on the near horizon for widespread implementation.[82]

▶ **FIGURE 4-28**
Directionality of blood droplet
To visualize or demonstrate directionality in a droplet, the analyst simply draws a line down the long axis of the stain, splitting it into two equal parts. This line is oriented to the scallops, spines, or satellite stains. (Source: Tom Bevel and Ross M. Gardner, *Bloodstain Pattern Analysis: With an Introduction to Crime Scene Reconstruction* 2nd ed. [Boca Raton, FL: CRC Press, 2002], p. 146.)

When presented with a stain, the analyst simply visualizes a line through the center of the stain, which is aligned with the spines or satellite stain.

In circular stains, the directionality is not as distinct or clear to us.

In elliptical stains, the directionality is much clearer. The spines and satellite spatter help in making this alignment.

USING BLOODSTAINS TO RECONSTRUCT THE CRIME

Bloodstains (known as blood spatter) may take many forms at a crime scene. These forms are not random but are produced by such factors as the type, location, and number of wounds inflicted; the type of weapon involved; movements by the victim while trying to escape, defend himself/herself, or attack the offender; changes in the location of the victim's body owing to its being moved by the offender or someone; and continuing postmortem violence to the body by the offender, suggesting that the killer was in a state of rage and possibly knew the victim.

By studying bloodstain and spatter evidence, the investigator can learn significant facts that facilitate reconstruction of the crime. These facts include:

1. Direction in which blood droplets were traveling when they were deposited on the surface (Figure 4-28).
2. Distance from the source of the blood to the surface on which the droplets were found (Figure 4-29).
3. Angle at which the droplets impacted (Figure 4-30).
4. Direction and relative speed of blood trails.
5. Nature of the object used as a weapon.
6. Number of blows struck.
7. Relative locations of other persons, surfaces, and objects having droplets on them.
8. Sequence of events, if multiple events are involved.
9. Interpretation of blood-contact or blood-transfer patterns.
10. Estimation of the elapsed time for the event and the volume of bloodshed.[83]

LOCATING BLOOD EVIDENCE

The places at which the investigator will find bloodstains are virtually unlimited. For example, if a criminal homicide occurred indoors, blood might be found not only on the floor but perhaps also on the walls or even the ceiling. Ordinarily when perpetrators of violent crimes get blood on their bodies or clothing, they will attempt to rid themselves of it immediately. In some instances, they may be so repelled by the sight of blood on their

▶ **FIGURE 4-29**
Distance between bloodstain and source
Increasing diameter of bloodstains as a function of increasing distance fallen by single drops of blood from fingertips onto smooth cardboard (Source: Stuart H. James and William G. Eckert, *Interpretation of Bloodstain Evidence at Crime Scenes*, 2nd ed. [Boca Raton, FL: CRC Press, 1998], p. 21.)

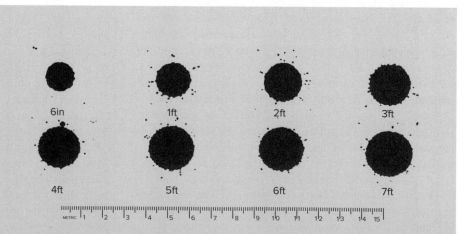

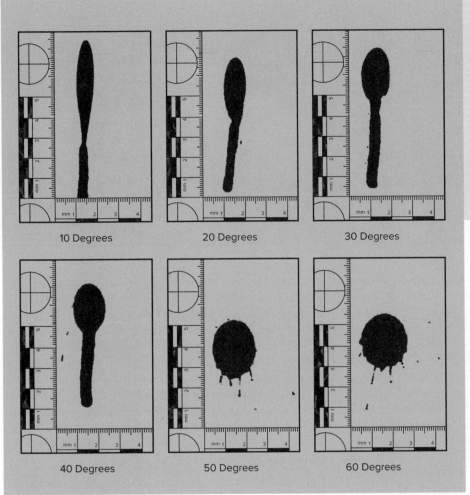

10 Degrees 20 Degrees 30 Degrees

40 Degrees 50 Degrees 60 Degrees

◀ **FIGURE 4-30**

Impact angle and stain shape

The range of droplet shapes that result from the varying impact angles. The more elliptical the stain, the more acute the angle of impact. Round stains indicate that the impact angle was closer to 90 degrees. (Source: Tom Bevel and Ross M. Gardner, *Bloodstain Pattern Analysis: With an Introduction to Crime Scene Reconstruction*, 2nd ed. [Boca Raton, FL: CRC Press, 2002])

hands that they will impulsively wipe it on a piece of furniture, such as a stuffed chair; if the fabric is multicolored or sufficiently dark, the stain may escape detection by the unobservant investigator. They may also attempt to clean bloodied hands before leaving the scene by using such surfaces as the reverse side of a small throw rug or the undersides of cushions on a couch.

At bloody scenes it is not uncommon for the suspect to have left a shoeprint on some hard, smooth surface. In turn, it is likely that some of the blood may be found in the cracks and crevices of the suspect's shoe soles. This is important evidence, because it can tie the suspect to the scene with great certainty, particularly if DNA evidence from the blood can positively link the suspect to the scene.

Another way of locating blood evidence is use of a presumptive or preliminary field test (Figure 4-31). Luminol, a water-based spray, locates trace amounts of blood within 30 seconds, creating a blue glow after the lights are turned out. Luminol's disadvantages are that the glow is short lasting; it doesn't differentiate between human and animal blood, and it reacts to copper, some alloys, and certain bleaches. **Hemident** also does not distinguish between human and animal blood. In the presence of blood, it

▲ **FIGURE 4-31 Use of BlueStar forensic**

Mop used by assailant in an effort to clean up blood from scene of an attack. The BlueStar reagent was sprayed on the mop, revealing presence of blood invisible to naked eye.

(Courtesy of BlueStar Forensic)

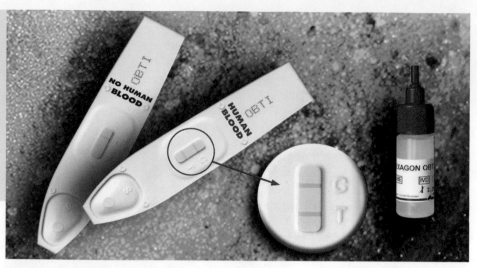

▶ FIGURE 4-32 Hexagon OBTI
Blood is placed in the white collection tube, followed by the addition of the reagent in the red-capped bottle at right. If the test is functioning properly, but there is no human blood detected, a single blue line appears in the window. Two single blue lines denote the presence of human blood.
(Courtesy of BlueStar Forensic)

produces a dark blue/green appearance within seconds. Hexagon OBTI (Figure 4-32) distinguishes between animal and human blood in two to three minutes; however, it also displays sensitivity to the blood of higher primates. To have legal significance, all three of these presumptive tests must be confirmed by more elaborate testing procedures in the laboratory. Some presumptive tests for blood may interfere with DNA analysis, and so investigators need to determine whether the one they are contemplating using does so.[84] If yes, the collection of blood samples from the scene should precede presumptive testing. Alternatively, a small blood sample can be collected and tested.

Occasionally, in an indoor homicide, the perpetrator will remove the body to an outdoor area to avoid discovery and then will return to the scene and attempt to eliminate all traces of the crime. Typically, this involves washing hands and scrubbing or mopping the floor on which the body had lain:

QUICK FACTS

It Wasn't the BBQ

An aggravated assault occurred between two friends who mutually agreed to misrepresent it as an accident. When the victim appeared at the local hospital for treatment, the police were summoned owing to the nature of the wounds and their locations, which suggested to the doctor that they were not accidentally inflicted. Investigators went to the scene and were told the accident happened outside while barbecuing. Granted permission to look inside the house, they found fresh blood underneath the faucets at the kitchen sink. Trace amounts of blood were found on the recently mopped floor between the back door and the kitchen sink. The location of the blood evidence was particularly pertinent, because the people involved alleged that the "accident" had happened in the backyard while they were barbecuing and that they had gone directly to the hospital. Although a solid investigation was conducted, no prosecution resulted due to a lack of cooperation from the victim and witnesses.

Before handling any blood evidence, investigators must document its location and physical state (for example, fresh) by some combination of notes, diagrams, video recording, and photographs. Other details may be pertinent to record as well, such as the temperature, humidity, or existence of multiple severe wounds but little blood. The last condition suggests that the person was killed somewhere else or that an attempt was made to clean the victim and/or scene, an action possibly indicating that the perpetrator had an attachment to the victim.

Blood Samples from a Known Source

Only qualified medical personnel should collect blood samples from a person. The following guidelines apply:

1. Draw two 5-milliliter samples of blood in purple-stoppered tubes, the insides of which are coated with EDTA, a preservative used to prevent coagulation.
2. If drug or alcohol testing is to be done, collect a 10-milliliter sample in a gray-stoppered tube, which contains a sodium fluoride (NaF) preservative.
3. Identify each tube with the date, time, collector's name, case number, subject's name, location at which drawn, and evidence number.
4. Do not freeze blood samples; the tubes may break. Refrigerate them, and use cold packs, not dry ice, to pack them for shipment to the laboratory.
5. Pack the blood tubes in special bubble packs, or wrap them in the same type of material.
6. After sealing the outer container or box, label it "Keep in a Cool Dry Place," "Refrigerate on Arrival," and "Biohazard."
7. Submit the samples to the laboratory as soon as possible.[85]

Fresh or Dried Blood on a Person

If there is fresh blood, absorb it on a clean cotton cloth or swab. If the blood is clotting or has dried, use distilled water to moisten a cotton cloth or swab and then absorb the blood with the moist surface. Leave a portion of the cloth or swab unstained as a control or blank sample. Let the cloth or swab air dry naturally. Do not place it in direct sunlight or next to a heat source, and do not use a hair dryer on it. These actions could cause the evidence to begin decomposing, thus reducing or eliminating its evidentiary value. Wrap the evidence in clean, dry paper, or place it in an envelope with sealed corners; plastic or airtight containers should not be used.

Fresh Blood on Surfaces or in Snow or Water

The procedure for collecting fresh blood from most surfaces is the same as that previously described for blood on a person. However, when blood is in a filled bathtub or some other body of water or when it is on snow, a different approach is required. For blood in water, recover the sample from the thickest concentrations of blood and clots whenever possible. When gathering blood from snow, eliminate as much snow as possible from the sample. Freeze it in a clean, airtight container, and submit the sample to the laboratory as rapidly as possible.[86]

Fresh or Dried Bloodstains on Garments and Objects

Allow fresh bloodstains on garments to air dry naturally; then fold the clothing with the crusts intact. Do not fold clothing in a way that creases bloodstains, since the creases may cause them to become dislodged. As you fold the clothing, place clean paper between each layer. Usually, bloodstained garments are found at the crime scene or retrieved from a hospital's emergency room.

Fresh bloodstains on a small movable item, such as a weapon, lamp, or door, should also be allowed to air dry naturally. The item is then submitted to the laboratory for processing; pack the item in clean paper in such a way that the paper does not rub against the bloodstains, since rubbing could alter or eradicate the bloodstain pattern.

When bloodstains are on a large immovable object, they can be collected, if fresh, by using the cotton cloth or swab technique or by cutting a large sample from a dried stain. If there are multiple stains on the object, use a new cloth or swab each time you switch from one stain to another; likewise, thoroughly clean the scalpel, razor blade, or knife you are using to cut dried samples when you switch from one collection area to another. In some cases, it may be necessary to cut a section out of the immovable object and transport it to the laboratory; do not forget the need for a control or blank sample.

Other Considerations in Handling Blood Evidence

During warm weather, especially during daylight hours, blood evidence should not be locked in car interiors or trunks, because heat could rapidly degrade the evidence. If dried-blood evidence is not submitted to the laboratory immedi-ately the garments, objects, and/or samples taken should be refrigerated.

LABORATORY DETERMINATIONS

Under ordinary conditions, laboratory examination of blood evidence can determine the following characteristics about the source of the blood:

1. Species (human, dog, horse, and so on).
2. Gender.
3. Blood type and DNA profile.
4. Use of drugs or alcohol by the blood source.
5. presence of certain types of illnesses (for example, venereal disease).
6. Presence of carbon monoxide.
7. Whether the source was a smoker.

The importance of such determinations was highlighted when labor leader Jimmy Hoffa disappeared in 1975. He had told people he was meeting that night with organized crime figures. It was thought that someone close to Hoffa betrayed him because of bloodstains found in that person's car. However, laboratory examination confirmed the person's statement that the bloodstains were from fish he was taking home. Hoffa was declared dead in 1982; his body was never found.

COSMETICS APPLICATORS AND DNA

In missing and unidentified remains cases, obtaining a DNA sample may be crucial. Cosmetic applicators can be a potential source, including eyeliner smudges, pencils, eye shadow sponges, mascara and lip gloss wands, face makeup sponges, pads, brushes, lipsticks, and balms. The actual applicators should be submitted for analysis to the lab. In one study, the face makeup sponge provided the most DNA samples.[87]

FIREARMS

Firearm evidence is commonly encountered and includes single- and double-action revolvers, semi-automatic handguns, rifles, scopes, shotguns, rim- and center-fire ammunition, bullets, shot pellets and slugs, shell cases, gunshot residues, clips and magazines, firing-pin impressions, and extractor and ejector marks. There may also be blood, tissue, and/or fingerprints on firearm evidence, making it even more important to a case. Investigators must acquire a broad, working knowledge of firearm evidence for three primary reasons: (1) the frequency with which they will encounter it; (2) your personal safety and that of others. Never assume that a firearm is unloaded, no matter who brings it to you, or where it is; that assumption could get you or someone else killed; and (3) the value of such knowledge in a gunfight situation.

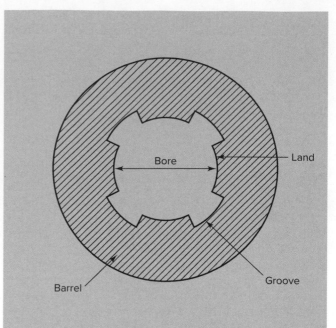

▲ **FIGURE 4-33   Rifled barrel**
Important features of a rifled firearm's barrel

LABORATORY DETERMINATIONS

The laboratory examination of firearm evidence may be able to provide answers to a number of important investigative questions.

1. Was This Bullet Fired from This Weapon?

Shotguns are smooth-bore weapons, but pistols and rifles have **rifling**. The **caliber** is the diameter of a bullet, whereas the **bore** (Figure 4-33) is the diameter of the barrel's interior between its opposing high sides, or **lands**. The low sides of the barrel's interior are called **grooves**. When a cartridge is fired, its bullet portion separates from it and passes through the barrel. Because the bullet's caliber is somewhat larger than the bore, the rifling grips the bullet, causing it to rotate, usually in a right-hand direction. The rotation increases the range and accuracy of the bullet (Figure 4-34.)

This rotation also creates striations on the bullet. Marks are also left on fired bullets from manufacturer defects and the use of a firearm. The combination of these distinctive scratches creates a "signature" on a bullet as it passes down a rifled barrel.

▲ **FIGURE 4-34   Barrel rifling**
Cross-section photograph of the barrel of a 9-mm pistol with traditional rifling. Note how the lands and grooves "twist" to the right, spinning the bullet as it is propelled through the barrel of the weapon. Rifling allows the bullet to be much more aerodynamic, improving the accuracy and stability of the bullet in flight. (Courtesy of Forensic Training and Consulting LLC)

A bullet recovered from a body can be compared to one fired from a suspect's firearm in a laboratory (Figure 4-35). Identification, however, is affected by the condition of the gun and that of the bullet or fragments. Although it is ideal to have the firearm, bullets themselves can yield important data. By matching striations on bullets recovered at different crime scenes, investigators can tie together information from several cases; the combined data may produce new leads and result in the clearance of the case.

In some cases, the striations on a bullet recovered from a decomposed body can be negatively affected by the interaction between the bullet material and the body tissue.[88] Conversely, an older revolver with a cylinder that microscopically does not fully align may sheer off a portion of the bullet when fired, creating distinctive markings. Other aspects of how individual-class firearm evidence is produced are discussed later in this section.

2. What Else Can Be Learned from the Bullet?

A fired bullet yields evidence of the class characteristics of the weapon that fired it with respect to the number of lands and grooves as well as their height, depth, and width. The class characteristics of a firearm are the design specifications to which it was manufactured; weapons of a given make and model will have the same class characteristics. The individual characteristics of the bore are found in the striae along the fired bullet. Examination of a fired bullet will suggest the type of weapon from which it was fired, whether the bullet is a hard-nose or soft-nose projectile, and the pitch and direction of twist within the barrel. Additionally, if the fired bullet is recovered in sufficient size, it may be possible, through weighing and measurement, to determine its caliber. Since bullets are often recovered as fragments, the caliber may only be implied; for instance, the weight may rule out smaller calibers. Although it is possible to determine the caliber of the bullet, some caution must be taken with respect to determining the bore of the weapon from which it was fired, since a smaller-caliber bullet can be fired through a larger-bore weapon.

Fired bullets are ordinarily damaged on impact. In some cases, you can see fabric impressions on the bullet's nose that were made as the bullet passed through the victim's outer garment. Additionally, there may be minute traces of blood, tissue, bone, fabric, or other such materials (Figure 4-36). Great care must be taken by the investigator not to destroy or in any way alter such evidence. When the fired bullet is to be recovered from the victim, the investigator should alert the attending medical personnel, if there is any doubt about their familiarity with proper handling procedure, as to the irreparable damage that can be wrought by the careless application of forceps or other such instruments in removing the bullet.

Note that it is ordinarily not possible to make a positive identification as to whether pellets were fired from a particular shotgun. However, in extraordinarily rare circumstances involving smooth-bore firearms, it may be possible to make an individual identification on the basis of gross defects in the barrel.[89]

3. What Determinations Can Be Made from Cartridge Cases?

In contrast to a bullet, which is typically acted on only by the barrel, a cartridge case is subject to a number of different forces that make marks on it, any of which can produce individual-class evidence. Such marks include:

1. Striations made on the outside of cartridge case as it is loaded into the chamber in preparation for firing; these striations may be caused by the action of the magazine or by the slide action of the firearm.
2. A firing-pin impression made on the base of the cartridge case, which is created when the weapon is fired (Figure 4-37).

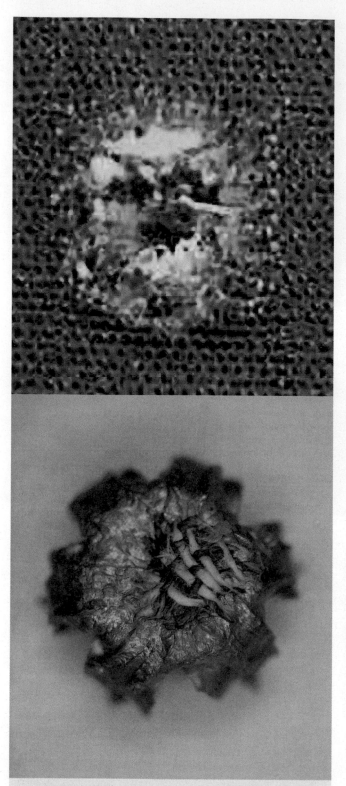

▲ FIGURE 4-36 Fabric traces in spent bullet
In some cases, the fabric of the garment being worn by the victim can be found attached to the bullet. In this unique homicide, the fibers from the sweater of the victim (*top*) are found inside the flattened "mushroom" of the bullet (*bottom*) recovered from the body. (Courtesy of Forensic Training and Consulting LLC)

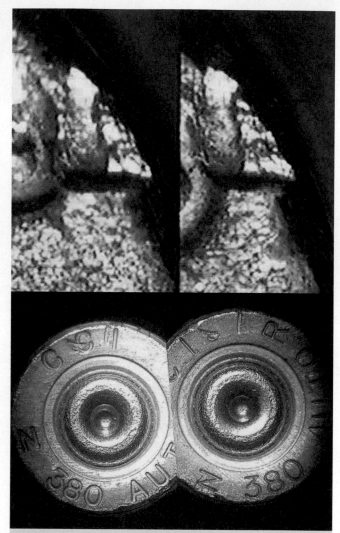

▲ FIGURE 4-37 Firing pin impressions
(*Top*) Photomicrograph showing comparison of questioned and known firing-pin impressions of .22-caliber rim-fire cartridge cases. (*Bottom*) Photomicrograph showing comparison of questioned and known firing-pin impressions on .380-caliber center-fire cartridge cases. Note the significant differences between a rim-fire and a center-fire cartridge: on the center-fire cartridge, the pin must strike the center of the primer to ignite the powder; however, on the rim-fire cartridge, contact may be anywhere around the face of the cartridge. (Courtesy of Forensic Training and Consulting LLC)

▲ FIGURE 4-38 Breach-face markings
Photomicrograph of the breach-face markings on two Speer 9-mm cartridge cases that were recovered at different locations at the scene of a murder. The victim was scheduled to testify in the trial of a drug dealer the next day. The murder is unsolved and under active investigation. (Courtesy of Tennessee Bureau of Investigation)

What Miscellaneous Determinations Can Be Made by Examination of Firearms Evidence?

If a firearm is received at a crime laboratory, several determinations beyond those mentioned may be possible. Does the weapon function properly, including safety features? Has it been modified to discharge in a manner other than designed, for example, for automatic fire? What was the shot trajectory? If the trigger pull on a weapon is of the "hair" nature, requiring only the slightest pressure to pull it, this would indicate that an accidental shooting was possible. Laboratory examination might reveal that a firearm is constructed—or malfunctioning—in such a way that it could discharge if dropped on its hammer, thereby giving more credibility to a claim that a shooting was accidental. Furthermore, even though invisible to the naked eye, obliterated serial numbers can sometimes be restored by the laboratory, thus providing an additional investigative lead.

COLLECTING FIREARM EVIDENCE

A cardinal rule in handling weapons at the scene of a crime is that they should never be picked up or moved until they have been photographed and measurements have been made for the crime scene sketch. As in the case of many rules for criminal investigations and as discussed in an earlier chapter, there are several exceptions: (1) if rapidly deteriorating weather conditions, for instance, a driving rain/sleet/snow storm or quickly rising water, threaten the potential to recover fingerprint or DNA evidence from a firearm located outside, move it to a sheltered area; (2) at the scenes of aggravated assaults and murders, feelings run high, and there is a danger that an emotionally charged person may suddenly attempt to pick up a weapon and shoot another party; or (3) there may be some compelling safety need, such as un-cocking a weapon that is in potential danger of falling and discharging.

Following documentation, the process of collecting firearms evidence includes:

1. Noting the position of the hammer and the slide, and safety, if applicable.
2. Recording the description of rounds and empty chambers in a revolver (Figure 4-38).
3. Removing cartridges from a revolver and packaging them individually.
4. Noting for semi-automatic/automatic weapons whether there is a misfeed/jam, a chambered cartridge, an inserted magazine, and the number and description of each round in the magazine in their exact sequence.
5. Removing any chambered round in a semi-automatic or automatic weapon and releasing the magazine—do not remove any cartridges from the magazine.
6. Recording the serial number, not to be confused with patent or model numbers—to avoid manual transcription errors, some law enforcement agencies and labo-

3. Marks are left on the cartridge case as the exploding gases that propel the bullet forward force the casing outward against the chamber wall and backward against the breach face of the weapon (Figure 4-38). The breach face is the mechanism that holds the bullet in the chamber.
4. Extractor marks made when the case is pulled out of the chamber and ejector marks made when the case is "kicked out," both of which are associated with semiautomatic and automatic weapons.

Markings made on cartridges by self-loading pistols can vary somewhat over a series of discharges. In laboratory tests, the first and 250th cartridges fired by the same auto-loader were identifiable as being made by the same weapon, but some differences in individual characteristics were observed.[90] Fingerprints left on cartridges loaded into a gun are subject to heat and friction when the cartridges are fired. Still, it may be possible to recover the prints.

ratories recommend dusting and lifting the serial number.

7. Allowing any fresh blood on a weapon to naturally air dry.

8. Placing metal objects recovered from water into a container filled with water from the same source.

In no case should a pencil or similar object be placed into the barrel of the gun to pick it up; this can dislodge evidence that may be in the barrel, such as tissue, blood, hair, or other trace evidence, and it can contaminate the barrel, thereby confusing the laboratory examiner.

To enhance the recovery of blood, tissue, and fingerprints, firearms evidence should be handled as little as possible consistent with the need to process it and "safe" the firearm. A victim is often the donor of blood and tissue on a firearm. Although a victim may grab a gun barrel and leave fingerprints, the more usual case is any fingerprints developed on a weapon or other firearms evidence are from the shooter, unless the victim's own gun has been used against him/her.

In rare situations it may not be possible to "safe" a firearm because of mechanical failure or damage, and in this case the laboratory should be contacted for guidance. The lab may recommend transporting the malfunctioning/damaged gun loaded, which is otherwise not done. Lacking such guidance, one can check with other resources, such as the local ATF office or a military installation.

MARKING AND PACKAGING FIREARM EVIDENCE

The FBI and many state crime laboratories do not recommend marking directly on firearms evidence. A gun should be tagged and placed in an approved firearms box. To secure the gun, place a strap over the barrel and another at the base of the hammer. Straps should never be placed inside the trigger guard. Magazines are another type of firearms evidence that is tagged. Smaller items—for example, cartridges and bullet fragments—should be placed separately in paper envelopes, sealed, and then put into a rigid container. Plastic wrapping or bags are not used with firearms evidence. If there is dried blood on any firearms evidence, a "Biological Hazard" sticker should be placed on the outside of the container.

TOOL MARKS

Tool mark evidence is commonly, but not exclusively, seen in burglaries at the point where a suspect attempted or achieved a forced entry. Figure 4-39 shows a case in which a pry bar was used as a murder weapon. In a rare case, a clod of soil at a gravesite had substantial details left by the digging tool. Later, when a suspect was identified, a mattock was found in the trunk of his car that examiners concluded was used to dig the grave.[91]

A mattock has a wooden handle of roughly 36–42 inches and a metal head, one end of which is a pointed "spike" and the other end looks like a hoe.

There are three categories of tool marks: 1) impressions, caused by a perpendicular force acting against an object, e.g., a hammer strike; 2) scrapes, produced by an instrument move laterally across a surface, such as a prybar. On wood, the same action would create an impression; and 3) pinching/shearing actions created by bolt cutters, cutting pliers, and related tools.[92] When a tool and a softer surface come into contact with each other, the softer surface yields (Figure 4-40). The tool may create an impression in the softer surface, produce striations on it, holes through it, or cut/shear the item. Tools often leave microscopic markings that can be class or individual class characteristic evidence (Figure 4-41). Additionally, contaminants on the tool and/or the surface affected may be transferred. Tools may simply require "elbow grease" to use or have a designed action, such as scissors or a bolt cutter. Tool mark examination includes locks and keys, for example, when an unauthorized implement is used to "pick" the lock.

Tool mark examinations are made to:

1. Identify what type of tool made the mark;
2. Determine if the tool has evidentiary value;
3. Establish the motion associated with using the tool;
4. Describe the size and other characteristics of the tool;
5. Identify unique features, e.g., a partially broken prybar tip;
6. Determine if two portions of the tool were ever joined (Figure 4-42);
7. Determine whether the toolmark has characterstics uniue to the suspect tool. Alternatively, the examiner might report that the evidence is inconclusive or exclude the tool as a source for making an impression or mark.[93]

In collecting evidence of tool marks, make every effort to obtain and submit the actual area for direct comparison. When this is not possible, a cast should be made. There are several good choices for casting tool marks, including Mikrosil. Tool marks should be photographed to establish their locations; however, the images have no forensic identification value. In no event should the investigator place a tool against a tool mark for size evaluation; doing so could lead to accidental cross contamination or result in the accidental destruction of evidence. When a tool is to be submitted to the crime laboratory for examination, the actual tool should be submitted; the making of test impressions or cuts is a function of qualified technicians in the laboratory. The importance of this last point is illustrated by the fact that under test conditions in the laboratory examiners found that when there was more than a 15-degree difference between the vertical angle at which a screwdriver was actually used and the comparison mark made in the laboratory, an improper finding of no identity from the same tool could result.[94]

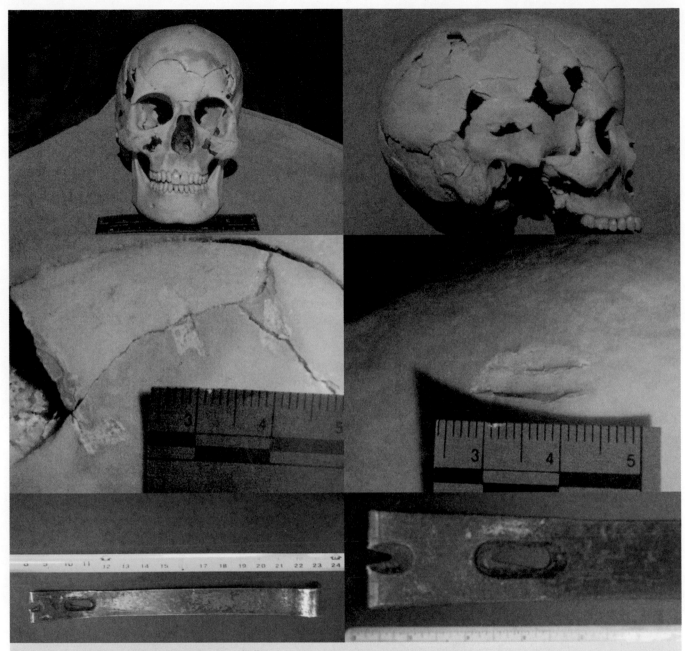

▲ **FIGURE 4-39 Tool marks on human skull**
A murder case in Arizona represents a unique tool match with wounds to the skull of the victim. The severely fractured skull and body of a young female victim were found in a freezer, presumably left there by the killer some two years before. Several tools were also found in the suspect's garage. By reconstructing the skull and carefully noting the unique types of wounds and marks, investigators determined that a pry bar was the murder weapon. Confirming the tool mark comparison and match were microscopic pieces of bone found on the prongs of the bar. (Courtesy of Forensic Training and Consulting LLC)

QUESTIONED DOCUMENTS

Loosely defined, a document is anything on which a mark, symbol, or writing is made for the purpose of transmitting a meaning. The mark, symbol, or writing may or may not be visible to the naked eye and may appear on surfaces other than paper. A disputed or **questioned document** is one whose origin or authen-ticity is in doubt.[95] The typical questioned document submission involves the comparison of a questioned document with a known sample[96]—for example, was this suicide note written by the deceased?

It is likely that white-collar crimes generate most requests for handwriting examinations. These tests typically involve checks, credit cards, and other financial and legal documents (Figure 4-43). Although in a lesser volume, handwritten documents, such as

▲ FIGURE 4-40 Screwdriver marks
The photomicrograph on the left depicts microscopic striae on the head of a woodscrew left by a burglar attacking a door. The right side is a known or test impression made by the laboratory examiner using the screwdriver seized in the suspect's custody. Note that black-and-white photography is often used to highlight the striae. (Courtesy of Wyoming State Crime Laboratory)

produce are also within the purview of document examiners—for example, check writers, scanners, facsimile machines, photocopiers, computer printers, and, less frequently, typewriters.[97] Some mechanical means of printing are central to counterfeiting items such as receipts, driver's licenses, ski lift and sporting event tickets, academic transcripts and degrees, social security cards, and passports.

HANDWRITING SAMPLES AND EXAMINATIONS

Handwriting samples may be requested or nonrequested. Some state/regional laboratories provide booklets for collecting requested samples of signatures and extended writings. If such a tool is not available, there are some basic guidelines:

1. For requested samples, if only a signature is being sought, 15 to 20 should be collected from an individual, one to a page.
2. If there is an extended questioned sample, for example, an extortion demand or death threat, the investigator should dictate the contents, obtaining at least five repetitions. No instructions as to format or other aspects of writing should be given—for instance, assistance with spelling words or punctuation—except if the questioned sample is printed or handwritten, the known sample should also be. The questioned samples are never shown to the person providing the known samples. As each page is completed, have the subject initial it; separate from those initials the investigator should add his/her own initials, identifying number, and the date and time, and he/she should number the pages sequentially as they are completed.
3. Collect requested writings with the same class/type of writing instrument as was used in the questioned samples. If this is not known, use a black ballpoint pen.

schedules, plans, checklists, and bank robbery and ransom notes, may be part of the execution of violent crimes.

Document examiners analyze non-handwritten evidence as well, including writing instruments, inks, paper, and rubber stamps. Mechanical means of printing and the writings they

▶ FIGURE 4-41
Comparison of plier marks
After breaking in, a suspect used pliers to dismantle copper tubing to sell for scrap metal. This image compares marks found on the copper tubing at the scene with test marks made in the laboratory with pliers found in the suspect's possession. (Courtesy of Wyoming State Crime Laboratory)

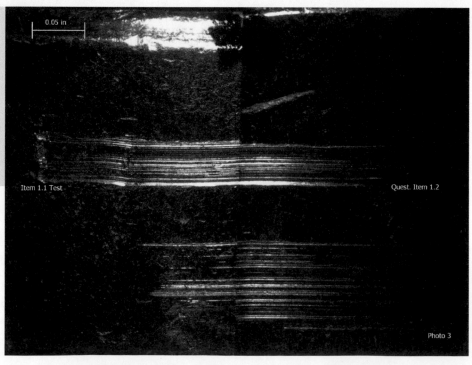

0.05 in

Item 1.1 Test

Quest. Item 1.2

Photo 3

Fracture-match tool

While trying to pry open a window during an attempted burglary-rape, the suspect broke the kitchen knife he was using as a tool, leaving the end of the knife embedded in the window sill. The suspect was later found walking in a nearby park with the broken knife and handle in his pocket. A fracture match of the knife tip was made with the remainder of the knife handle. (Courtesy of the Albuquerque Police Department)

◄**FIGURE 4-43**

A counterfeit marriage license

Note the differences between the "M" in "Robert M. Webster" and the "M" in "May," "March," and "Minister." Also, note the differences between the "3" and "4" in Webster's age and the same numbers elsewhere in the document. The differences in the type fonts as well as the gaps in the lines under the changed letters, left by whiting out the original entry, indicate a counterfeit document. (Source: Immigration and Naturalization Service, Forensic Document Laboratory)

If the questioned is on lined paper, paper of the same size should be used to collect the known. As each signature or extended writing is completed it should be removed from the person's sight.

4. Nonrequested samples should be collected from existing documents created/signed closest to the time the questioned document was executed, because handwriting evolves over time. Among the sources for nonrequested samples are signatures on Miranda warnings; suspects'

statement; notes to jailers; credit, employment, employment, insurance, and mortgage applications; messages written on greeting cards given to others; and workers' compensation claims.

Nonrequested writings were not executed with the thought they would be scrutinized and therefore ordinarily are not disguised in any way. Disguised handwriting is problematic for document examiners, and it attracts more misleading and inconclusive rates of authorship opinions; one study concluded that the error rate for examiners in labeling a writing genuine or disguised was 4.3%.[98] A difficulty with nonrequested samples is locating sufficient high-quality signatures and extended writing material from the same time frame as the questioned samples.

Document examination is partially automated, using software such as CedarFox. Its capabilities include comparison of samples and searching handwriting databases to find potential matches, both of which must be confirmed by the examiner.[99]

LABORATORY DETERMINATIONS

In addition to the possibility of determining whether handwriting can be attributed to a particular person, laboratories *may* be able to:

1. Determine whether a document is authentic or counterfeit. In 1983, 62 volumes of diaries attributed to Adolph Hitler were purchased by a German publisher. Three handwriting experts concluded Hitler wrote them, although others disagreed. However, forensic analysis established the method used to produce the paper on which the diaries were written was not available until 1954, and the ink used was first manufactured in 1982.

2. Recover indented writing; if not visible to the eye, indented writings may be located by an electrostatic detection apparatus (ESDA).

3. Identify the class/type of the writing instrument, such as a ballpoint, felt-tip pen, or pencil.

4. Determine whether the inks of known and questioned samples have consistent characteristics—the Secret Service and the Internal Revenue Service maintain the International Ink Library with more than 9,500 samples.

5. Decipher charred, burned, or water-soaked documents.

6. Match the ends of cut/torn paper. A man handed a bank teller a note, "This is a robbery." He left with money, but she retained the note. A week later, police executed a search warrant at the suspect's home, finding "This is a robbery" in indented writing on a pad. A portion of paper remaining in the pad also matched one end of the robbery note.[100]

7. Establish the source of paper through watermarks and other features.

8. Detect erasures, obliterations, and alterations to documents.

9. Determine whether one or more pages in a document were added subsequently to its original production.

10. Establish the relative age of a document.

11. Determine whether an office machine—for example, scanner, photocopier, typewriter, fax machine, or computer printer—is associated with a particular document. Often, the machine must have a defect or some unusual attribute to be distinguishable. However, there is substantial interest in developing "signatures" for scanners, printers, and digital cameras. One line of inquiry is looking at their intrinsic features to identify unique attributes; the alternative method is to embed microscopic codes, such as a serial number, on each page of output.

COLLECTING AND PACKAGING EVIDENCE

In many respects, all evidence collection is like the first rule of physicians: do no harm. Investigators should not attempt to reassemble torn or shredded documents; write on, trace, highlight, or underline portions of them; or make repairs to or fold them. Documents should be collected and processed using the following guidelines:

1. Wear gloves and use clean tweezers to handle documents.

2. Handle the documents as little as possible.

3. Use a transparent envelope if possible; otherwise, use a manila paper one.

4. Before placing the document in the envelope, fill out all required blocks of information on it and then slip it in the evidence and seal it.

5. Processing for latent prints and DNA is a laboratory responsibility.

6. Keep documents in a cool, low-humidity environment, out of the sunlight, until submitted to the lab.

KEY TERMS

bore	forensic odontology	ridges
caliber	fracture match	residue prints
class characteristics	grooves	rifling
concentric fracture	Hemident	smiling photographs
cross contamination	individual characteristics	surface impression
dental stone	known samples	three-dimensional impression
double swab	lands	unknown (questioned) samples
forensic palynology	latent prints	
furrows	patent prints	
forensic light source	PDQ	

REVIEW QUESTIONS

1. What are class and individual characteristics?
2. How is a questioned sample explained?
3. There are two major categories of impression evidence. What are they?
4. How do you cast a shoe impression using dental stone "from scratch"?
5. What is a fracture match?
6. Radial and concentric glass fractures differ in what way?
7. What are minutiae, ridges, and furrows?
8. How is forensic odontology defined?
9. An avulsed bite has what characteristic?
10. Luminol is used to detect what at a crime scene?
11. Bore and caliber differ in what way?
12. How is "questioned document" defined?

INTERNET ACTIVITIES

The FBI and other federal agencies have been working for more than 20 years to advance forensic standards and techniques. One mechanism to achieve these goals has been the creation of scientific working groups (SWGs) and technical working groups (TWGs). Altogether, there are perhaps 15 SWGs and TWGs, whose membership include both federal and state/local law enforcement agencies that have produced important publications. Visit SWGs and TWGs at *www2.fbi.gov/hq/lab/html/swg.htm*.

▶ Police officers interviewing suspects arrested for possession of cocaine outside a house where a search warrant has been served. Interview questions focus on suspects' knowledge of the drug-related activities occurring inside the house. (©A.Ramey/PhotoEdit)

5

INTERVIEWING AND INTERROGATION

CHAPTER OBJECTIVES

1. Explain the similarities and differences between interviews and interrogations.

2. Discuss the objectives of interviewing and interrogations as well as the qualifications of interviewers and interrogators.

3. Understand the importance of selecting the right place and time for conducting an interview or interrogation.

4. Explain how an investigator should prepare for conducting an interview or interrogation.

5. Understand the importance of witnesses' motivations, perceptions, and barriers.

6. Understand the most effective methods for interviewing people with disabilities.

7. Assess the reliability of eyewitness identification.

8. Discuss witness intimidation and what can be done to effectively deal with it.

9. Explain the psychological dynamics that cause some people to confess.

10. Identify the principal reasons why false confessions occur.

11. Understand the limitations related to the use of admissions and confessions at trial.

12. Explain the impact of *Miranda* v. *Arizona* and other past and current landmark Supreme Court cases on law enforcement interrogation.

13. Discuss the best indicators of detecting deception or truthfulness.

14. Understand the value of using technological instruments to detect deception.

In every criminal investigation process, interviewing and interrogation are among the most important means of obtaining needed information about a crime. Both require a combination of artistry and skill that must be cultivated and practiced. However not all people who possess information needed by the investigator are willing to share it. This is true in both interviews and interrogations. Witnesses may have various motivations and perceptions that can influence their responses during an interview. Their motivations and perceptions may be based on either conscious choices or subconscious stimuli. In addition, gaining information from specific demographic groups such as the elderly, those who do not speak English, and persons with physical infirmities requires unique skills on the part of the investigator. Situational characteristics such as the time and place of the interview or interrogation may also create challenges to eliciting information about a particular case. Each of these conditions must be effectively addressed in both interview and interrogation settings. The successful interviewer or interrogator must fully understand the techniques of both and be able to evaluate the psychological reasons why people are willing or reluctant to impart information. In this chapter we also examine many other important elements in the interviewing and interrogation process including witness protection, false confessions, and the most recent U.S. Supreme Court rulings regarding the admissibility of confessions and the most effective methods for **detection of deception.**

THE SIMILARITIES AND DIFFERENCES BETWEEN INTERVIEWS AND INTERROGATIONS

The success of an interview or interrogation depends on a number of personal characteristics and commitments of the investigator. Planning for and controlling the events surrounding both interviews and interrogations are important but are generally viewed as more critical to the success of an interrogation. Establishing **rapport,** asking good questions, listening carefully, and keeping proper documentation are elements common to both forms of obtaining information. Table 5-1 illustrates the similarities between interviews and interrogations.

Besides the difference in purpose between interviewing and interrogation, many other distinctions exist. Of paramount importance are the myriad legal requirements that pertain to interrogations but are absent in interviews. Because of the criticality of confessions and their use in obtaining convictions, it

TABLE 5-1	Similarities between Interviews and Interrogations
INTERVIEWS	**INTERROGATIONS**
Planning important	Planning critical
Controlling surroundings important	Controlling surroundings critical
Privacy or semiprivacy desirable	Absolute privacy essential
Establishing rapport important	Establishing rapport important
Asking good questions important	Asking good questions important
Careful listening	Careful listening
Proper documentation	Proper documentation

is not surprising that numerous legal guidelines and standards apply in interrogations that would not be needed in interviewing witnesses or victims. These are all discussed in greater detail

CHAPTER OUTLINE

later in this chapter. Also, it is far more likely that a hostile and adversarial relationship will exist between an interrogator and a **suspect** than between an interviewer and a **victim** or **witness**. The differences between interviews and interrogations are noted in Table 5-2.

OBJECTIVES OF INTERVIEWING

Interviews are conducted in criminal cases for the purpose of gathering information from people who have, or may have, knowledge needed in the investigation. The information may come from a victim or from a person who has no other relationship to the criminal activity other than being where he or she was. But interviewing is not a haphazard process consisting of a list of questions. It is a planned conversation with a specific goal.

The job of the investigator-interviewer is to elicit from the witness information actually perceived through one or more of the witness's five senses—sight, hearing, smell, taste, and touch. In any given case, any or all of a witness's senses may be involved. For example, in a case involving a drug-related killing, a witness may see the perpetrator pull the trigger, hear the victim scream, smell the pungent odor of marijuana burning, taste the white powdery substance later identified as heroin, and touch the victim to feel for a pulse.

Because, as suggested earlier, witnesses report perceptions based on their own interests, priorities, and biases, obtaining accurate and sometimes even voluntary information is not as easy to obtain as it may first appear. Investigators must always be sensitive to any of the psychological, physical and environmental influences as well as the motivations affecting witness perceptions.

At the outset of the interview, the person to be interviewed must satisfy three requirements of being a witness: presence, consciousness, and attentiveness to what was happening.[1] Presence and consciousness are relatively easy to establish in the

TABLE 5-2 Differences between Interviews and Interrogations	
INTERVIEWS	**INTERROGATIONS**
Purpose is to obtain information	Purpose is to test information already obtained
Minimal or no preinterview legal requirements; no rights warning	Extensive preinterrogation legal requirements; rights warning required
Cooperative relationship between interviewer and subject likely	Adversarial or hostile relationship between interrogator and subject likely
No guilt or guilt uncertain	Guilt suggested or likely
Moderate planning or preparation	Extensive planning and preparation
Private or semiprivate environment desirable	Absolute privacy essential

Source: John Fay, unpublished notebook, American Society for Industrial Security, Workshop in Criminal Interrogation (Jacksonville, FL: ASIS, 1991), p. A1-1.

interview process; attentiveness is more difficult. Yet all three elements are important to establishing the accuracy of a witness's perception.

OBJECTIVES OF INTERROGATION

Interrogation as opposed to interviewing is designed to match acquired information to a particular suspect in order to secure a **confession.** While interviewing is primarily for the purpose of gaining information, interrogation is the process of testing that information and its application to a particular suspect.

There are four commonly recognized objectives in the interrogation process:

1. To obtain valuable facts.
2. To eliminate the innocent.
3. To identify the guilty.
4. To obtain a confession.

As the investigator moves from the preliminary task of gathering valuable facts to the concluding task of obtaining a confession, there is an increase in the difficulty of acquiring information. That difficulty, however, is rewarded by an increase in the value of the information. Figure 5-1 illustrates these relationships. In attempting to obtain a confession from a suspect, the interrogator also gains information about the facts and circumstances surrounding the commission of an offense. In seeking such information, the investigator must be concerned with asking the basic questions that apply to all aspects of the investigative process: Who? What? Where? When? How? and Why?

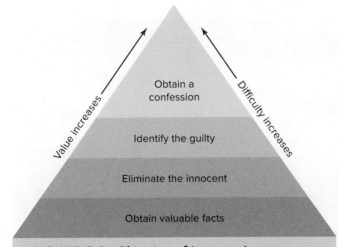

▲ FIGURE 5-1   Objectives of interrogation

Source: John Fay, unpublished notebook, American Society for Industrial Security, Workshop in Criminal Interrogation [Jacksonville, FL: ASIS, 1981], p. A2-1.

QUALIFICATIONS OF INTERVIEWERS AND INTERROGATORS

The effective interviewer or interrogator must be knowledgeable in the art and science of criminal investigation and know how to use psychology, salesmanship, and dramatics. Persuasiveness and perseverance are also essential to success. The interviewer or interrogator must make himself or herself easy to talk to. By the appropriate use of vocal inflection, modulation, and emphasis, even the *Miranda* warnings (discussed later in this chapter) can be presented to a suspect in a manner that does not cause the suspect to immediately assume a defensive posture. The words can be spoken without creating an adversarial atmosphere. The interviewer or interrogator must have a flexible personality and must be able to convey empathy, sympathy, anger, fear, and joy at appropriate times, but must always remain objective. The interviewer or interrogator must keep an open mind and be receptive to all information, regardless of its nature.

A positive, firm approach, an ability to inspire confidence, and knowledge of a broad range of topics of general interest all help establish dominance or control in an interview: Behavior—not words—that shows confidence, determines dominance.[2]

During an interrogation, the investigator must carefully evaluate each development while studiously avoiding the pitfall of underestimating the capabilities of the subject being interrogated. Screaming or shouting, belittling the subject or the information, sneering, and other such unplanned and uncontrolled reactions most often adversely affect the interrogation. The investigator must at all times maintain control of the interrogation without being openly domineering, by being a good active listener, by being serious, patient, and, most important, by being persistent and persuasive.[3] An ability to categorize the psychological and emotional traits being manifested by the suspect helps the investigator react in a manner that increases the possibility of conducting a successful interrogation, for it is the job of the interrogator to make it easy for a suspect to confess.

TIME, PLACE, AND SETTING OF INTERVIEWS AND INTERROGATION

Law enforcement officers conduct interviews in a number of situations. The most common is the on-the-scene interview. Whether it is a routine traffic accident investigation or a major felony case, officers who respond to the scene should, at the earliest possible moment, seek out and identify individuals who may have knowledge of the event and whose information may contribute to the investigation. Such individuals, of course, include victims and other participants as

▲ **FIGURE 5-2**

Officers interviewing witnesses at scene of accident

Individuals should be questioned separately; this includes victims and other participants as well as uninvolved witnesses. Note that the officers have separated the parties involved as they are being interviewed; however, they should not be in such close proximity that the conversations can be overheard. (©Ellen F. O'Connell/Hazleton Standard Speaker/AP Images)

well as uninvolved witnesses. Once witnesses have been identified, they should be separated from one another and, as much as possible, isolated from other people who may be loitering in the area (Figure 5-2). This prevents the witnesses from seeing or hearing irrelevant matters that may taint their actual knowledge. All witnesses should be interviewed as soon as practical, while their memory is still fresh, but this rule must be applied with discretion to take into account all circumstances.

Although convenience of the witness is important to a successful interview, the interviewer need not relinquish the

psychological advantage in selecting the time and place of the interview. It is not a good practice, for example, to rouse a witness from bed in the middle of the night. However, there are certain psychological advantages to questioning a witness at a law enforcement agency rather than in the witness's own home or office. A witness may feel in a better position to control the interview in familiar surroundings. The investigator cannot let this happen; he or she must be fair but always be in command of the situation.

After taking into account the factors of immediacy, privacy, convenience, and control, and weighing the importance of each in the context of the total circumstances, the investigator may decide to interview witnesses at their homes or places of business. As a matter of courtesy, the investigator should attempt to make an appointment to ensure convenience, particularly for professional and businesspeople. Others, such as salespeople, office workers, and laborers, may be interviewed during working hours with approval of their supervisors.

Privacy is of the utmost importance in conducting interviews (Figure 5-3). Distractions tend to have an adverse effect on the interview and its results. The interviewer should insist on as much privacy as possible, but the circumstances of on-the-scene interviews often have to be recognized as a fact of life for the investigator, who can be expected to perform only to the best of his or her ability in the given case. Similarly, investigators are often called on to canvass neighborhoods and interview residents. In these instances, investigators often are in no position to influence the conditions under which the interview takes place. Noisy children, blaring television sets, nosy neighbors, and similar factors must be accepted.

The physical and emotional states of the witnesses are important when one is conducting or determining whether to conduct an interview. Cold, sleepy, hungry, physically uncomfortable, or intoxicated people generally prove to be unsatisfactory witnesses.[4] Similarly, persons suffering noticeable emotional

▶ **FIGURE 5-3**

Interviewing a witness

This woman saw a purse-snatching incident occur about an hour before this photo was taken. She is with one of the investigating officers giving a statement about what she witnessed, including a description of the man who stole the woman's purse. (©Mikael Karlsson/Alamy)

problems can give, at the most, highly questionable information. Most investigators can recognize this state and will wisely choose to wait until the witness becomes lucid before conducting the interview. Age is also an important factor to consider when conducting the interview of a witness.

QUICK FACTS

Effects of Crime on Older Victims

When older people are victimized by crime, they may suffer worse physical, psychological, and financial injuries than other age groups. For example, when victims who are 65 years of age or older are injured in a violent crime, they are about twice as likely to suffer serious physical injury and to require hospitalization as any other age group.[5] Because the psychological process of aging brings with it a decreasing ability to heal after an injury, older people may also never fully recover physically or psychologically from the trauma of their victimization. In addition, this trauma may be worsened by their financial situation. Many older people live on fixed incomes and may be unable to afford the services that could help them in the aftermath of a crime.

Reinterviewing witnesses should be avoided if the reinterview is likely to produce nothing beyond the information given in the initial statement. Reinterviewing tends to become less and less convenient for witnesses, even though they may be friendly and cooperative. There may also be a tendency for reinterviewed witnesses to feel that the investigator does not know his or her job or was not prepared during the initial interview. To avoid this problem, the investigator should first tell the witness that the purpose of the interview is not to rehash old information and should then explain what new information is being sought. The investigator should ask for the information in a manner that does not elicit a repetition of the previous interview. But investigators should not hesitate to conduct follow-up interviews when necessary, whether there was lack of skill in obtaining an initial statement, new information has developed, or the time or setting of the initial interview did not elicit the full attention of the witness.

Unlike the interview, which may take place in any number of different locations and at various times—which may or may not be advantageous to the investigator—interrogation is a process controlled by the interrogator. The interrogator is in command of the setting and governs the number and kinds of interruptions. The most critical factor in controlling the interrogation is to ensure privacy and to guarantee that any distractions, planned or otherwise, are controlled by the interrogator. Privacy may be used as a psychological tool; suspects may feel more willing to unload their burden of guilt in front of only one person.

THE INTERROGATION ROOM

The traditional interrogation room should be sparsely furnished, usually with only two chairs. There should be no physical barriers, such as tables or desks, between the investigator and the suspect. From the officer's standpoint, such barriers may create an unwanted feeling of psychological well-being on the part of the suspect.

If there is a table or desk in the room, the chairs should be corner to corner rather than on opposite sides. This arrangement permits the interrogator to move both chairs away from the table and eliminate the barrier (Figure 5-4).[6]

Proximity in an interrogation can also be important. The suspect and the interrogator should be close enough to touch without being too close, without having any object easy to move in order to eliminate the table as a barrier. "It seems, for example, that around 27 inches is the limit of proximity for white American middle-class males . . . If you move closer, people become uncomfortable . . . farther away than 27 inches, you can't read a person's face well."[7] There are however considerable differences in the comfort zones of various ethnic groups, and interrogators must make it a point to know as much as possible about the unique psychological and cultural characteristics of the individuals they are most likely to encounter both in interviews as well as interrogations.

The two-way mirror, although still a useful tool for allowing others to observe the interrogation, is widely known and may cause some subjects to refuse to cooperate in the interrogation. If a two-way mirror is to be used, it should be small and unobtrusive. As a standard practice, the interrogation room should be equipped with a video or audio system that includes a recording device, unless prohibited by state law. The use of electronic recording in interrogation is discussed later in this chapter.

▲ **FIGURE 5-4 Interrogation room**
Note that the table and chairs can be easily moved so the table does not separate the interrogator from the suspect.
(©A. T. Willett/Alamy)

Although the traditional interrogation room just described is designed to ensure control and domination over the interrogation because of its privacy, security, and aura of authority, this approach does not impress the habitual or experienced offender, who understands the rules and standards of conduct of the classical interrogation room. If the offender is skilled and intelligent, he or she not only can cope with the psychological influences such a setting is designed to foster but perhaps also can become the dominant force, or at least be on the same psychological level as the interrogator. When this occurs, the skills of the interrogator become even more important.

PREPARATION FOR THE INTERVIEWS OR INTERROGATIONS

The success of the interviewer or interrogator and of the interview or interrogation often will be determined by the time and dedication committed to preparing for the conversation. The interviewer must become familiar with the facts of the case under investigation and with the victim. To carry out the four objectives listed earlier, the interrogator must learn as much as possible about the offense, the victim(s), and the suspect through the process of collecting, assessing, and analyzing data and theorizing about the motivations and thought processes of the suspect. This begins the formulation of a profile that will then dictate the initial approach the interrogator will take upon first contacting the suspect.

THE WITNESS

If the interview is to be conducted with a witness other than the victim, the interviewer should find out as much about the witness as possible before the interview. This includes learning about the witness's motivations and perceptions and any barriers that might exist. In some cases it might be advantageous to determine if a witness has a previous criminal record.

THE OFFENSE

It is necessary that the interviewer know specifically what crime or crimes were allegedly committed. This knowledge includes a working familiarity with the elements of each offense and some understanding of the kind of information necessary to prove each. Accurate information on the date, time, place, and method of the crime—including tools used, points of entry and exit, method of travel to and from the scene, complete description of any property involved, weapons used, modus operandi, and physical evidence recovered—is essential. The interviewer should also obtain a full description of the crime scene and the surrounding area. In addition, any and all possible motives should be identified.

THE VICTIM

The interviewer should learn as much as possible about the victim's background, the nature of the injury or loss, attitudes toward the investigation, and any other useful information, such as the existence of insurance in a property crime case. If the victim is an organization or a business, a determination of any practices that would make the organization a criminal target could be extremely valuable. If relevant, the interviewer should determine whether the business is insured against losses.

THE SUSPECT

The interrogator must evaluate the circumstances surrounding the conduct of the interrogation and must begin to evaluate the suspect. An effective interrogator understands that a successful interrogation cannot be organized and compartmentalized into a neat, orderly, step-by-step package. Rather, it is a combination of personality, behavior, and interpersonal communication skills between the interrogator and suspect. It is made up of verbal processes and the way they are communicated, nonverbal actions including **body language,** (discussed later in this chapter) and personality characteristics that together might be characterized as a psychological fingerprint.[8] Only by understanding the interaction of all these variables can the interrogator effectively evaluate the interrogation process as it will be initiated and as it will be modified during the interrogation.[9] To begin the preparation, the interrogator should review the offense report, statements of witnesses, laboratory reports, all file information pertaining to the suspect, and other related data. It is also essential that the interrogator know all the elements of the offense involved. Failure to possess this information may preclude obtaining a complete confession, which, by definition, must contain **admissions** by the suspect to the commission of each and every element of the crime.

The investigation should reveal as much personal background information on the suspect as can be obtained (Figure 5-5). This should include aliases, Social Security number, date and place of birth, education, marital status, employment history, financial history and current circumstances, prior offenses, past and present physical and mental health, any drug or alcohol abuse or addiction, relationship to the victim or crime scene, possible motive, biases and prejudices, home environment, sexual interests (if relevant), and hobbies. Additionally, the investigation and preparation for an interrogation should determine whether the suspect had the capability and opportunity to commit the offense and should confirm or disprove an alibi.

The interrogator should also obtain as much information as possible from other people involved to determine the suspect's attitude. This will enable the interrogator to anticipate levels of hostility or cooperativeness during the interrogation.

▲ FIGURE 5-5

Investigator preparing for interview/interrogation

This investigator is reviewing her notes one last time to ensure she has all available information on and statements of witnesses, information and statements of the victim, lab reports, investigative materials, a knowledge of the elements of the offense, and as much information as is available about the probable suspect before beginning her interviews or interrogation. (©Spencer Grant/PhotoEdit)

WITNESSES' MOTIVATIONS, PERCEPTIONS, AND BARRIERS

There are many types of witnesses, and each has different motivations and perceptions that influence his or her responses during an interview. The motivations and perceptions may be based on either conscious choices or subconscious stimuli. The interviewer must learn to recognize, overcome, and compensate for these factors.

There is no way to categorize all personalities, attitudes, and other character traits. The variables are too numerous and individualized; the combinations are as complex as the human mind. Nevertheless, there are some basic groupings that can be mentioned:

- Some witnesses may be honest and cooperative and desire to impart information in their possession to the investigator. Despite these admirable qualities, however, the information may still be affected by other factors that influence all witnesses, such as age, physical characteristics, and emotions. It may be wise in most circumstances to inter-

view this type of witness first to obtain basic information that can then be compared with later-acquired stories.

- Some witnesses may desire not to give any information in an interview regardless of what they know. Some may simply not want to get involved, while others may fear any contact with a law enforcement agency, especially if they have had some earlier negative experiences with law enforcement. This is especially true of immigrants who have come from developing countries in which the police may have been corrupt, or in some cases may be in the country illegally and are fearful of being deported. Others may not understand the significance of information they have, and some may not want to do anything that would aid law enforcement.

- Some witnesses may be reluctant to cooperate or be suspicious of the motives of the interviewer until a rapport is established and the investigator can assure the witness of his or her good intentions.

Because some witnesses may be deceitful and provide incorrect information, it is a basic principle that an investigator should never take a witness's explanation totally at face value but, rather, should obtain supporting information or evidence.

There may be other barriers that must be overcome in order to successfully interview someone who has knowledge of the circumstances under which a crime was committed. Language barriers, which may not initially be recognized as significant, may prevent the interviewer from obtaining any useful information; however, some people may be so talkative and provide so much information that their motives should be questioned, along with the information they provide. A potential witness who may be under the influence of alcohol or drugs may or may not have information that could be used at trial; thus the condition of the witness is a major factor to be considered in assessing the value of any information obtained.

INTERVIEWING PEOPLE WITH DISABILITIES

There are literally millions of individuals living in the United States who have special needs and law enforcement officers must be aware of the most effective means of interviewing such individuals as well as two federal laws that address the requirements on the part of law enforcement on how to deal with these types of crime victims.

QUICK FACTS

Two Federal Laws Regarding the Accommodation of Crime Victims with Disabilities

Two federal laws—the Americans with Disabilities Act of 1990 (ADA) and Section 504 of the Rehabilitation Act of 1973—prohibit discrimination on the basis of disability. Title II of the ADA applies to state and local government entities. Section 504 applies to recipients of federal assistance, including recipients of grants from the U.S. Department of Justice (DOJ).

An individual with a disability is defined by the ADA and Section 504 as a person who (1) has a physical or mental impairment that substantially limits one or more major life activities, (2) has a record of such an impairment, or (3) is regarded as having such an impairment.

Law enforcement officers must provide for equally effective communication with victims who have a disability and are required to make reasonable modifications to policies, practices, and procedures where needed to accommodate crime victims who have a disability, unless doing so would fundamentally alter the service, program or activity the agency provides.[10]

Within the special-needs groups are individuals who are blind or visually impaired, deaf or hard of hearing, mobility impaired, speech impaired or have cognitive disabilities.

The following are some suggestions that will assist law enforcement officers in dealing with individuals they encounter who have special needs thus ensuring the retrieval of the maximum amount of information that is available.

INTERVIEWING INDIVIDUALS WHO ARE BLIND OR VISUALLY IMPAIRED

- Speak to the individual when you approach him or her.
- State clearly who you are; speak in a normal tone of voice.
- When conversing in a group, remember to identify yourself to the person to whom you are speaking.
- Never touch or distract a service dog without first asking the owner's permission.
- Tell the individual when you are leaving.
- Do not attempt to lead the individual without first asking. Also, allow the person to hold your arm, thus allowing the person to control his or her own movements.
- Be descriptive when giving directions; verbally give the person information that is visually obvious to individuals who can see. For example, if you are approaching steps, mention how many steps.
- If you are offering a seat, gently place the individual's hand on the back or arm of the chair so that the person can locate the seat.[11]

INTERVIEWING INDIVIDUALS WHO ARE DEAF OR HARD OF HEARING

- Before speaking, get the person's attention with a wave of the hand or a gentle tap on the shoulder.
- Face the person and do not turn away while speaking.

- Try to converse in a well-lit area.
- Do not cover your mouth or chew gum.
- If a person is wearing a hearing aid, do not assume he or she can hear you well.
- Minimize background noise and other distractions whenever possible.
- When you are communicating orally, speak slowly and distinctly. Use facial expressions to reinforce what you are saying.
- Use visual aids whenever possible such as pointing to printed information on a citation or other document.
- Generally, for those who are deaf or hard of hearing, only one-third of spoken words can be understood by speech reading.
- When communicating in writing, keep in mind that some individuals who use sign language may lack good English reading and writing skills.
- If someone with a hearing disability cannot understand you, write a note to ask them what communication aids or service are needed.
- If a sign language interpreter is requested, be sure to ask via a note which language the person uses. American Sign Language (ASL) and Signed English are the most common.
- When interviewing a witness or a suspect or engaging in any complex conversation with a person whose primary language is sign language, a qualified interpreter is usually needed to ensure effective communication.
- When using an interpreter, look and speak directly to the deaf person and not to the interpreter.
- Talk at your normal rate or slightly slower if you normally speak fast.
- Only one person should speak at a time.
- Use short sentences and simple words.[12]
- If you telephone an individual who is hard of hearing, let the phone ring longer than usual. Speak clearly and be prepared to repeat the reason for the call and who you are.
- If you do not have a Text Telephone (TTY), dial 711 to reach the national telecommunications relay service, which facilitates the call between you and the individual who uses a TTY.

INTERVIEWING INDIVIDUALS WITH MOBILITY IMPAIRMENTS

- If possible, put yourself at the wheelchair user's eye level.
- Do not lean on a wheelchair or any other assistive device.
- Never patronize people who use wheelchairs by patting them on the head or shoulders.
- Do not assume the individual wants to be pushed—ask first.
- Offer assistance if the individual appears to be having difficulty opening a door.

- If you telephone the individual, allow the phone to ring longer than usual to allow extra time for the person to reach the telephone.

INTERVIEWING INDIVIDUALS WITH SPEECH IMPAIRMENTS

- If you do not understand something the individual says, do not pretend that you do. Ask the individual to repeat what he or she said and then repeat it back.
- Be patient. Take as much time as necessary.
- Try to ask questions that require only short answers or a nod of the head.
- Concentrate on what the individual is saying.
- If you are having difficulty understanding the individual, consider writing as an alternative means of communicating, but first ask the individual if this is acceptable.[13]

INTERVIEWING INDIVIDUALS WITH COGNITIVE DISABILITIES

About 3 out of every 100 people have developmental disabilities, so it is likely that a law enforcement office will at some point come in contact with an individual who has this disability. A successful interaction with a person who has developmental disabilities can yield accurate and useful information while, at the same time, protecting his or her rights as an individual.[14]

- If you are in a public area with many distractions, consider moving to a quiet or private location.
- Be prepared to repeat what you say, orally or in writing.
- Offer assistance completing forms or understanding written instructions, and provide extra time for decision making. Wait for the individual to accept the offer of assistance; do not "overassist" or be patronizing.
- Be patient, flexible and supportive. Take time to understand the individual, and make sure the individual understands you.[15]

ESTABLISHING THE COMPETENCY OF A WITNESS

The term *competency* refers to a witness's personal qualifications for testifying in court. Competency must be established before a witness is permitted to give any testimony. The witness's personal qualification depends on circumstances that affect his or her legal ability to function as a sworn witness in court. Competency has nothing to do with the believability of a witness's information.

Among the factors an investigator must evaluate in determining the competency of a witness are age, level of intelligence, mental state, relationship to individuals involved in the case, and background characteristics that might preclude the testimony of the witness from being heard in court. For example, in many jurisdictions, a young child cannot be a witness unless it can be shown that the child knows the difference between truth and imagination and understands the importance of being honest. Similarly, any person whose intelligence or mental state prevents him or her from understanding the obligation of telling the truth is not permitted to testify, regardless of the information he or she may possess.

Relationships among individuals involved in a case may also affect a witness's competency. Husbands and wives need not testify against each other, nor may attorneys testify against clients, doctors against patients, or ministers against penitents. Privileges vary by state. Background characteristics also may preclude a witness's testimony from being accepted in court. For example, some state laws forbid a convicted perjurer from testifying.

Possibilities such as those described in the preceding paragraphs mean the investigator must learn as much as possible about the witness before and during the interview.

THE RELIABILITY OF EYEWITNESS IDENTIFICATION

Eyewitness identification and other information provided by eyewitnesses to a criminal event are relied on heavily by both law enforcement and courts in the investigative and adjudication stages of our system of justice,[16] yet research indicates that eyewitness testimony is the most unreliable form of evidence and causes more miscarriages of justice than any other method of proof[17, 18] (Figure 5-6).

Research and courtroom experience provide ample evidence that an eyewitness to a crime is being asked to be something and do something that is not easily accomplished. Human perception is sloppy and uneven.[19] Existing research does not permit precise conclusions about the overall accuracy of the eyewitness identifications that are a common feature of criminal prosecutions, but research does lead us to conclude that identification errors are not infrequent.[20] Such errors are borne out by case studies in which the use of DNA evidence exonerated people who had been convicted on the basis of eyewitness identification.[21]

Many factors influence an individual's ability to accurately recognize and identify persons, and all of them depend on the circumstances under which the information is initially perceived and encoded, stored, and retrieved.[22] Eyewitness identifications take place in a social context[23] in which the witness's own personality and characteristics, along with those of the target observed, are as critical as factors relating to the situation or environment in which the action takes place.

Thus, human perception and memory are selective and constructive functions, not exact copies of the event perceived. The gaps will often be filled in by the observer in order to produce a logical and complete sequence of events. A person is motivated by a desire to be accurate as he or she imposes meaning on the overabundance of information that impinges on his or

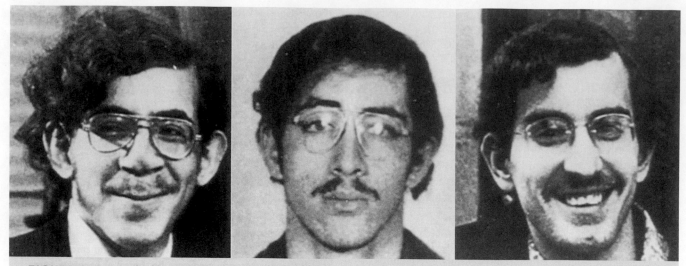

▲ FIGURE 5-6   Look-alikes

Mistaken identifications led to the arrests of two innocent men: Lawrence Berson (*left*) for several rapes and George Morales (*right*) for a robbery. Both men were picked out of police lineups by victims of the crimes. Berson was cleared when Richard Carbone (*center*) was arrested and implicated in the rapes. Carbone was convicted. He later confessed to the robbery, clearing Morales.

(Source: The New York City Police Department)

her senses, but also by a desire to live up to the expectations of other people and to stay in their good graces. The eyes, the ears, and other sense organs are, therefore, social organs as well as physical ones.[24]

Agreeing with this theory of eyewitness perception, one observer notes:

Studies of memory for sentences and pictures indicate that when we experience an event, we do not simply file a memory, and then on some later occasion retrieve it and read off what we've stored. Rather, at the time of recall or recognition we reconstruct the event, using information from many sources. These include both the original perception of the event and inferences drawn later, after the fact. Over a period of time, information from these sources may integrate, so that a witness becomes unable to say how they know a specific detail. In the end they only have a single unified memory.[25]

The gender, age, expectations, intelligence, race, and facial recognition skills of the witness are factors that individually may or may not influence the eyewitness identification process but collectively or in combination with other variables are likely to have a bearing.[26] Facial attractiveness and distinctiveness, disguises, facial transformations, and the gender and race of the target (the person identified) are factors likely to influence identification.[27] Situational factors include such things as the presence of weapons, duration of the exposure, and significance of the event in relation to all surrounding circumstances.[28]

Experts distinguish a number of factors that limit a person's ability to give a complete account of events or to identify people accurately. The following are among those factors:

- *The significance or insignificance of the event.* When an insignificant event occurs in the presence of an individual, it does not generally motivate the individual to bring fully into play the selective process of attention.
- *The length of the period of observation.* If ample opportunity is not provided for observation, the capability of the memory to record that which is perceived is decreased.
- *Lack of ideal conditions.* In situations where ideal conditions for observation are absent, the ability of the witness to perceive details is significantly decreased. Distance, poor lighting, fast movement, or the presence of a crowd may significantly interfere with the efficient working of the attention process.
- *Psychological factors internal to the witness.* A witness under stress at the time of observation may find this to be a major source of unreliability in his or her observations.
- *The physical condition of the witness.* If the witness is injured or intoxicated, this condition will affect his or her ability to provide complete and accurate information.
- *Lack of familiarity with members of another race or ethnic group.* Some of the most egregious cases of misidentification have occurred in those crimes which are interracial or interethnic in nature. These occur because in some cases the victim is not accustomed to dealing with members of the race or ethnic group of the assailant and is unable to distinguish important variation in facial characteristics. The more contact the victim has had with members of that race or ethnic group the less likely it is that a misidentification will occur.

- *Expectancy.* Research has shown that memory recall and judgment are often based on what psychologists term *expectancy.* This concept means that an individual perceives things in the manner in which he or she expects them to appear. For example, a right-handed eyewitness to a homicide might, in answer to a question and without positive knowledge, state the assailant held the gun in his right hand, whereas a left-handed person might say the opposite. Biases or prejudices are also illustrated by the expectancy theory, as is the classic problem associated with stereotyping.[29]

WITNESS INTIMIDATION

Citizens who witness or are victimized by crime are sometimes reluctant to report incidents to the police or to assist in the prosecution of offenders.[30, 31] Such reluctance may be in response to a perceived or actual threat of retaliation by the offender or his or her associates, or may be the result of more generalized community norms that discourage residents from cooperating with police and prosecutors. In some communities, close ties between witnesses, offenders, and their families and friends may also deter witnesses from cooperating; these relationships can provide a vitally important context for understanding witness intimidation. Particularly in violent and gang-related crime, the same individual may, at different times, be a victim, a witness, and an offender.[32] Historically, witness intimidation is most closely associated with organized crime and domestic violence, but has recently thwarted efforts to investigate and prosecute drug, gang violence and other types of crime.

FORMS OF WITNESS INTIMIDATION

Witness intimidation takes many forms, including:

- Implicit threats, looks, or gestures
- Explicit threats of violence
- Actual physical violence
- Property damage
- Other threats, such as challenges to child custody or immigration status
- Confronting witnesses verbally
- Sending notes and letters
- Making nuisance phone calls
- Parking or loitering outside the homes of witnesses
- Damaging witnesses' houses or property
- Threatening witnesses' children, spouses, parents, or other family members
- Assaulting or even murdering witnesses or their family members

Threats are much more common than actual physical violence and are in fact just as effective in deterring cooperation.[33] Although some witnesses experience a single incident of intimidation, it may also involve an escalating series of threats and actions that become more violent over time.[34] Other witnesses do not experience intimidation directly, but rather believe retaliation will occur if they cooperate with police. Either way, they are deterred from offering relevant information that might assist the police and prosecutors. Particularly in communities dominated by gang and drug-related crime, residents have seen firsthand that offenders are capable of violence and brutality. Many witnesses also believe offenders will return to the community after relatively brief periods of incarceration or will be able to arrange for intimidation by others while they are incarcerated. In many cases the experience of actually having witnessed violence by the perpetrators or groups of individuals in the community lends considerable credibility to any threats and creates a general sense of fear that discourages cooperation with police.

RESPONSE STRATEGIES FOR ADDRESSING WITNESS INTIMIDATION

The following response strategies provide a foundation for addressing witness intimidation.

- *Form multi-agency partnerships.* The appropriate party to address the threat of witness intimidation may change as a case moves through the criminal justice system. For example, the police may be responsible for protecting or supporting witnesses at the outset a case, but the responsibility might later shift to the prosecutor when the case goes to trial.
- *Strengthen ties between police and the community.* Fostering cooperation on the part of reluctant witnesses is a natural extension of community policing and community prosecution, which focus on engaging residents in preventing and responding to crime.[35] For example, mobile precincts can increase police visibility after a high-profile gang-related crime in an area where intimidation is likely to occur. Storefront precincts can increase the level of contact with residents and make it easier to provide encouragement and support.
- *Minimize the risk of witness identification when reporting crime or offering statements.* This is particularly true in neighborhoods where communitywide intimidation is a factor and residents may hesitate to cooperate with police at the scene of a crime, because they fear being labeled as an informant or a "rat." As a result, methods for reporting crime or offering witness statements that do not make cooperation obvious to observers are sometimes needed.[36]
- *Reduce the likelihood of contact between witnesses and offenders.* Most often, acts of intimidation are committed at a witness's home, workplace, or school, or during the normal course of the witness's daily activities. Minimizing the opportunities and avenues by which witnesses come into contact with offenders can reduce the incidence of intimidation. For example, wherever practical witnesses can alter their normal routines by varying the

routes taken to work or school and making their schedules irregular and unpredictable.[37]

- *Transport witnesses to and from work and school.* Many witnesses feel vulnerable when traveling to and from work or school, or while attending to their business in the community. Police escorts during these times can deter offenders from making contact. However, such protection schemes consume significant police resources and may not be feasible for broad application.

- *Keep witnesses and defendants separated at the courthouse.* Other than at home, witnesses are most often intimidated in the courthouse, both while waiting to testify and while in the courtroom giving testimony. Not only must witnesses endure a face-to-face encounter with the defendant, but they may also be apprehensive about contact with the defendant's family and friends. Key danger areas include courthouse entrances, hallways, elevators, waiting areas, refreshment areas, and restrooms. Separate waiting rooms and entrances for witnesses and defendants can be useful.

- *Relocate witnesses.* Because it is unusual for offenders to travel outside their neighborhoods to intimidate witnesses, simply moving a witness to another location may effectively protect him or her from harm. Of course, the key to this strategy is to ensure that the new location remains confidential. Out of boredom, or because they are reluctant to sever ties with friends and family, the witnesses may unwittingly compromise the secrecy of their new locations.

DETERRING INTIMIDATORS

The following responses focus on actions that can be taken to deter intimidators.

- *Admonish intimidators.* When witnesses or victims tell police they are afraid or have experienced direct intimidation, police can visit the offender and his or her family and friends to caution them regarding their behavior and to explain the laws concerning witness intimidation and obstruction of justice. In court, judges should be vigilant about threatening gestures or actions and should admonish defendants or spectators who display such behaviors. Some jurisdictions educate judges about the types of courtroom intimidation that are exhibited by gang members, such as courtroom packing or wearing specific gang colors.[38]

- *Request high bail and no contact orders.* In cases in which the risk of intimidation is significant, prosecutors can seek high bail to keep defendants in jail and away from witnesses. Where this strategy is used, bond hearings cannot be a mere formality; witness statements and risk assessments should be prepared in advance and presented in court. Prosecutors should seek release conditions that forbid contact with

witnesses and victims and make sure that the consequences for violating such conditions are clearly articulated.

DOCUMENTING INTERVIEWS

Note-taking during an interview raises two primary concerns for the interviewer. First, it may occasionally be distracting or suspicious to a witness; witnesses may be reluctant to give information knowing it is being documented. Consequently, the investigator should tell witnesses that notes will prevent the need for subsequent interviews owing to lapses of the investigator's memory. This explanation usually reduces the reluctance of the witness. Second, the interviewer should avoid becoming preoccupied with taking notes, for this creates the appearance of inattentiveness. As important as notes may be, the interviewer should treat them as less important than conversation with the witness. Note-taking during the interview should be kept to a minimum, recording only salient details. As soon as possible after the interview, the investigator should complete the notes, before their memory wanes.

In many instances, it is desirable for witnesses to write or sign statements concerning the events of which they have knowledge. In many jurisdictions, law enforcement officers are authorized to administer oaths so that such statements are sworn to or affirmed. The theory is that a victim or witness would be more inclined to be truthful if they are under oath and aware that charges of perjury could be lodged against them at a later date if they were determined to be lying.

The best form of documentation is electronic sound recording or a sound-and-visual recording of the interview. Visual recordings are generally not practical when the interview is held anywhere other than at a law enforcement agency, where equipment can be permanently situated. Audio recorders, however, are inexpensive, portable, and helpful in the majority of cases. The recorded interview has many significant advantages: All information is recorded in the witness's own words, details are not left to be recalled by human memory, concerns about detracting from the interview by note taking are absent, interviewers may listen to the verbatim conversations over and over at a later time to be sure they have understood completely and accurately what was said, and the taped interview might avoid unnecessary reinterviews. The advantages and disadvantages of each type of documentation are shown in Table 5-3.

DOCUMENTING INTERROGATIONS

Documenting an interrogation consists of three main phases: note taking, recording, and obtaining written statements. All three phases are geared to accomplishing two basic functions: first, retaining information for the benefit of the interrogator and

TABLE 5-3	Comparison of Types of Interview Documentation	
TYPE	**ADVANTAGES**	**DISADVANTAGES**
Memory	Quick and easy	Limited absorption and recall
	Captures salient details	Most information lost shortly afterward
	Prevents need for reinterviewing	
Note-taking by interviewer	Sufficient in most cases	May distract or offend witness
	Captures salient details	May preoccupy interviewer, creating appearance of inattentiveness
	Prevents need for reinterviewing	
Handwritten or signed statements by witness	Useful if witness cannot testify	Request may be offensive to witness
	Can be used to impeach if witness changes story in court	Not necessary in routine cases
Electronic sound or sound-and-visual recordings	Relatively inexpensive	Not necessary except in the most important cases
	Some equipment portable	Generally not practical
	All information recorded in witnesses' own words	
	Does not rely on inaccuracies of memory or another's notes	
	Does not distract	
	Prevents unnecessary reinterviews	

the continued investigation and, second, securing a written statement or confession from the accused for later use as evidence in court.

THE USE OF ELECTRONIC RECORDINGS FOR INTERROGATIONS

The methods of keeping notes of interrogations is the same as described for interviews. Electronic recording of an interrogation is the best means of documentation. Audio, video, or a combination of both may be used, but case law and local requirements should be checked.

At present, 238 law enforcement agencies in 38 states currently record custodial interviews of suspects in felony investigations. They are located in every area of the United States and are quite diverse in size and individual practices. Following are some of the elements addressed in their respective policies as it relates to the use of electronic recordings for interrogation.[39]

- *Mandatory or discretionary.* Most agencies leave the recording decision to the discretion of the investigator in charge, although recordings are customarily made by the investigators in cases covered by discretionary policies.
- *When to begin recordings.* Most departments use either audio and/or video recording devices to record interrogations of persons under arrest in a police facility starting from the point when the *Miranda* warnings (discussed

later in this chapter) are given until the interview is ended, with no intentional breaks or omissions in the recordings.

- *Crimes under investigation.* Most departments record only in "major" or "serious" felony investigations, such as homicide, sexual assault, armed robbery, and other crimes against persons and those involving weapons. Many also record interviews in DUI, child abuse, and domestic violence investigations.
- *Equipment.* Some departments use multiple cameras from different views, while others use a single camera focused on the suspect.[40] Many departments are acquiring digital technology in order to improve picture resolution and conserve storage space.
- *Suspect's knowledge.* State eavesdropping laws govern whether suspects must be told they are being recorded. "One-party consent" laws allow the police to record without informing the suspects. "Two-party consent" laws require the police to obtain the suspects' consent. Most state laws permit police to record surreptitiously, although sophisticated suspects and repeat offenders may be aware without being told. Most departments inform suspects that the session will be recorded and/or place the recording equipment in plain view, although most of them are not required by state law to do so. Almost all investigators turn the recording devices off if the suspect declines to talk while being recorded.

BENEFITS OF RECORDING FOR POLICE OFFICERS AND PROSECUTORS

An electronic recording of suspect interrogation has proven to be an efficient and powerful law enforcement tool. Audio is good, but video is better. Both methods create a permanent record of exactly what occurred. Recordings prevent disputes about the investigator's conduct, the treatment of suspects and the voluntariness of statements they made. Investigators are not called on to paraphrase statements or try later to describe suspects' words, actions, and attitudes. Instead, viewers and listeners see and/or hear precisely what was said and done, including whether suspects were forthcoming or evasive, changed their versions of events, and appeared sincere and innocent or deceitful and guilty. An electronic record is law enforcement's version of instant replay.

Experience also shows that recordings dramatically reduce the number of defense motions to suppress statements and confessions. The record is there for defense lawyers to see and evaluate: if the officers conduct themselves properly during the questioning, there is no basis to challenge their conduct or exclude the defendants' responses from evidence. Officers are spared from defending themselves against allegations of coercion, trickery, and perjury during hostile cross-examinations.

The use of recording devices, even when known to the suspect, does not impede investigators from obtaining confessions and admissions from guilty suspects. When suspects decline to talk if recorded, the investigators simply turn the recorder off and proceed with taking handwritten notes.

Recordings permit investigators to focus on the suspect rather than taking copious notes of the interview. When investigators later review the recordings they can often observe inconsistencies and evasive conduct which they overlooked while the interview was in progress.

Electronic recording forces investigators to better prepare for conducting interrogations by:

- Clarifying whether an interrogator missed something that requires further questioning
- Giving prosecutors a better understanding of cases, thereby fostering better charging decisions, plea-bargaining options, and case preparation
- Minimizing challenges by defense attorneys about the accuracy of the electronic recordings and the completeness of written confessions
- Reducing doubts about the voluntariness of confessions
- Refreshing the investigators' memories when they are testifying

In addition, tapes can be reviewed and used as training aids for less experienced investigators who are attempting to develop their interrogation skills.[41]

THE WRITTEN STATEMENT

After the use of such recordings, the next-best form is a signed statement written in the first person by the suspect in his or her handwriting. Frequently, however, it is not possible to convince a suspect to prepare such a statement. Or perhaps the suspect cannot write.

Other forms in which statements may be admitted into evidence, listed in descending order of the credibility with juries, are:

- A typed or handwritten statement by someone else that is signed in the accused's own hand
- A typed or otherwise prepared statement that the accused does not sign but that is acknowledged in front of witnesses
- The oral testimony of a person who was present and overheard the subject give a confession or admission

In the last case, even though admissible, the testimony is likely to carry little weight with the jury. Table 5-4 lists the types of documentation in descending order of preference and the advantages and disadvantages of each.

The form and content of a written statement should include a heading, which incorporates the data identifying the circumstances under which the statement was taken, the body of the statement, and a verification. The statement should open with an indication of the time and place where it was taken, and an identification of the person giving the statement that includes his or her name, address, and age. The heading must also include a definite statement to the effect that the subject is giving the statement freely and voluntarily after having been appropriately advised of his or her constitutional rights.

The body of the statement, which acknowledges the subject's involvement in the crime under investigation, should, if possible, be phrased in the first person, allowing the suspect to include his or her own ideas in a free-flowing manner. However, if this is not possible or practical, then the question-and-answer format is permissible. The terminology used should include the words, grammar, idioms, and style of the person making the statement. The body of the statement should be arranged so that its content follows the chronological order of the subject's involvement in the case under investigation.

At the end, the statement should indicate that the suspect has read the statement or has had it read to him or her, that its contents and implications are understood, and that the suspect attests to its accuracy.

Other suggestions for the interrogator to keep in mind include:

- Each page of the statement should be numbered consecutively with an indication that it is page _____ of _____ pages. If the pages get separated, they can later be easily restored to order.
- The interrogator should ensure that each page is initialed by the subject. If the subject is unwilling to sign, the statement should be acknowledged by him or her. If the subject cannot write, another identifying mark may be used.
- On occasion an interrogator may encounter someone who says, "I'll tell you what I've done, but I'm not writing anything and I'm not signing anything." In such circumstances, the interrogator can explain that the

TABLE 5-4	Comparison of Types of Confession Documentation (in Descending Order of Believability to Juries)	
TYPE	**ADVANTAGES**	**DISADVANTAGES**
1. Electronic video-audiotape or movie	May be required by legislative or judicial directive Shows all, including fairness, procedures, and treatment Easy to do Can be relatively inexpensive	May face legal constraints
2. Audio recording	Can hear conversations Can infer fairness	Some words or descriptions may be meaningless without pictorial support Necessitates identifying people and things involved
3. Statement written and signed in suspect's own handwriting	Can be identified as coming directly from suspect	Can't see demeanor or hear voice inflections Suspect may not agree to procedure
4. Typed statement signed by suspect	Signature indicates knowledge of and agreement with contents of statement	Less convincing than methods described above
5. Typed unsigned statement acknowledged by suspect	Contents of confession or admission are present Acknowledgment helps show voluntariness	Reduced believability of voluntariness and accuracy of contents
6. Testimony of someone who heard confession or admission given	Contents admissible	Carries little weight with juries

suspect confessed and the interrogator or some other person who heard the confession can go into court and testify about it. By preparing or signing a statement, the suspect protects himself or herself against the interrogator's testifying to something more damaging by changing the story in court (another good reason for electronic recording).

- If the suspect cannot read, the statement must be read to him or her, and the interrogator must ensure the suspect understands its contents before the suspect is allowed to attest to its accuracy.
- All errors in the statement should be corrected on the final copy and initialed by the suspect. The interrogator may accommodate the suspect by allowing small errors if this will help obtain the suspect's initials on each page of the statement.
- The interrogator should make sure the suspect understands all the words used in the statement. If some words are confusing, their meanings should be explained to the suspect and the suspect should be required to explain them back in front of witnesses in order to confirm this understanding.
- During the process of drafting and attesting to a statement derived through interrogation, there should be at least one additional witness who can testify to the

authenticity of the statement and the circumstances under which it was obtained. After the suspect signs the statement in ink, the witnesses should sign their names, addresses, and positions.[42]

WHY PEOPLE CONFESS

It is human nature to talk. Most people cannot keep a secret. It has been estimated that 80% of all people will confess to a crime. There are two basic categories of people who tend to confess to crimes: (1) guilty parties who psychologically need to "get it off their chest," and (2) persons who are not guilty but who act under some urge to confess. It is to protect the latter category of people that some procedural safeguards are provided. For example, a conviction cannot be based solely on a confession. There must be some other independent corroborating evidence to support the conviction.

The psychological and physiological pressures that build in a person who has committed a crime or who suffers from feelings of guilt concerning any other type of conduct are best alleviated by communicating. Talking is the best means of communicating. Therefore, in spite of having been advised of certain protections guaranteed by the Constitution, some people feel a need to confess. Even confirmed criminals sometimes suffer from the same pangs of conscience as first-time offenders. However, fear of the potential punishments that await them contributes to their silence. Those who confess rarely regret it, for doing so gives them peace of mind. It permits them to look at themselves and life differently and to live with themselves. Most guilty individuals who confess are, from the outset, looking for the proper opening during an interrogation to communicate their guilt to the interrogator. The good interrogator will seek out and be able to recognize individuals who desire to confess and will approach the interrogation in such a way as to provide the accused with the proper opening and reason for the relief of the psychological and physiological pressures that have built up.[43] If it is human nature to talk, and if people cannot generally keep secrets, then the job of the interrogator is to make it easy for a suspect to confess.

FALSE CONFESSIONS

A false confession is an admission of guilt followed by a narrative statement of what, how, and why the confessor committed the crime. Over the years, confessions have been proven false in a number of ways, as when it is discovered that the confessed crime was not committed; when new evidence shows it was physically impossible for the confessor to have committed the crime; when the real perpetrator, having no connection to the defendant, is captured and implicated; and when DNA and other scientific evidence affirmatively establishes the confessor's innocence. Through these methods, and contrary to the widespread belief that people do not confess to crimes they did not commit, the pages of American history reveal large numbers of men and women who were wrongfully prosecuted, convicted, imprisoned, and sometimes sentenced to death on the basis of false confessions.[44]

Although many researchers have discovered large numbers of false confessions in recent years, it is not possible to project from these cases the frequency with which innocent people in general confess to crimes they did not commit. First, within the U.S. criminal justice system, the postconviction cases discovered by the Innocence Project[45] and others do not include the numerous false confessions that are disproved subsequent to arrest but before trial, those that result in a false guilty plea, those to minor crimes that attract no postconviction scrutiny, and those that involve juveniles in which confidentiality provisions are in place.[46]

In a North American survey of 631 police investigators, respondents estimated from their own experience that 4.78% of innocent suspects confess during interrogation.[47]

Over the years, researchers have reported on numerous accounts of proven false confessions, producing a vast literature of case studies. As reported in books, newspapers, TV documentaries, and analyses of actual case files, these stories reveal false confessions occur with some unknown frequency, they share certain common features, and they seem more likely to occur in some types of people and under some conditions than others. From these descriptive analyses of specific instances and associations, one cannot draw conclusions about the causes of false confessions. Nevertheless, case studies of this nature have proven invaluable in the development of this area. By comparing and contrasting several known cases throughout history, for example, Kassin and Wrightsman[48] introduced a taxonomy that distinguished among three types of false confessions: voluntary, **coerced-compliant,** and coerced-internalized.

VOLUNTARY FALSE CONFESSIONS

Voluntary false confessions are those in which people claim responsibility for crimes they did not commit without prompting or pressure from police. Often this occurs in high-profile cases. For example, when Charles Lindbergh's infant son was kidnapped and killed in 1932, an estimated 200 people volunteered confessions. When "Black Dahlia" actress Elizabeth Short was murdered in 1947, more than 50 people confessed. In 2006 John Mark Karr confessed to the unsolved murder of JonBenet Ramsey. Researchers have not systematically studied these types of false confessions, in part because they are typically disproved at the outset by the confessor's ignorance and inability to furnish corroborating details about the crime. There are several reasons why innocent people might volunteer confessions, such as a pathological need for attention or self-punishment; feeling of guilt or delusions; the perception of tangible gain; or the desire to protect a parent, child, or someone else.

COERCED–COMPLIANT FALSE CONFESSIONS

In contrast, people may be induced to confess through the processes of police interrogation. In false confessions, the suspect capitulates in order to escape a stressful custodial situation, avoid physical or legal punishment, or gain a promised or implied reward. Based on a review of cases Gudjonsson[49] identified some concrete initiatives for this type of confession, such as not being allowed to sleep, eat, make a phone call, go home, or, in the case of drug addicts, the need to feed a drug habit. Like the classical forms of influence observed in psychological studies of conformity, compliance, and obedience to authority, this type of confession is an act of public capitulation and compliance and by a suspect who knows he or she is innocent but perceives that the short-term benefits of confession (for example, being left alone, fed, or released) outweighed the long-term costs (for example, a loss of reputation, conviction, and incarceration). This phenomenon was dramatically illustrated in the 1692 Salem witch trials, in which women confessed to witchcraft;[50] in *Brown* v. *Mississippi*, a classic case in which three black tenant farmers confessed to murder after they were whipped with a steel-studded leather belt; and in the infamous Central Park jogger case in 1989, in which five New York City teenagers confessed after lengthy interrogations, each claiming he expected to go home afterward. All the boys were convicted and sent to prison, only to be exonerated in 2002 when the real rapist gave a confession that was confirmed by DNA evidence.

COERCED-INTERNALIZED FALSE CONFESSIONS

Internalized false confessions are those in which innocent but vulnerable suspects confess and come to believe they committed the crime in question, a belief that is sometimes accompanied by false memories. Gudjonsson has argued that this kind of false confession results from "memory distrust syndrome," whereby people develop a profound distrust of their own memory that renders them vulnerable to manipulation from external cues.[51] Kassin likened this process of influence to the creation of false memories sometimes seen in psychotherapy patients. In both situations, an authority figure claims a privileged insight into the individual's past, the individual is isolated from others and in a heightened state of malleability, and the expert ultimately convinces the individual to accept a painful self-insight by invoking concepts like dissociation or repression. The case of 14-year-old Michael Crowe, whose sister was stabbed to death, illustrates this phenomenon. After lengthy interrogations, during which Michael was misled by lies into thinking there was substantial physical evidence of his guilt, he concluded he was a killer: "I'm not sure how I did it. All I know is I did it." Eventually, he was convinced he had a split personality—that "bad Michael" acted out of jealous rage while "good Michael" blocked the incident from his consciousness. The charges against Crowe were later dropped when a drifter from neighborhood was found with the victim's blood on his clothing.[52]

RECOMMENDATIONS TO REDUCE THE POSSIBILITY OF FALSE CONFESSIONS

Given that false confessions do occur, even if rarely, police administrators need to ensure their investigators are properly trained in interrogation techniques that elicit the most accurate and truthful information from suspects. The following recommendations will do much to reduce the possibility of a false confession.[53]

- *Use police skill teams.* The teams should consist of seasoned interview specialists who, through training and actual interview experiences, possess the skills necessary to conduct successful critical interviews.
- *Provide mandatory police training.* Investigators must be made aware of the circumstances under which false confessions may be obtained. These include:
  - The suspect's desire to eliminate friends, relatives, and close associates from the investigative process.
  - The suspect's attempt to distract police from identifying other motives and/or suspects through a false confession, which is usually fraught with inconsistencies.
  - Situations in which police officers provide too much information to the suspect, which the suspect may later repeat as part of a false confession. These include, among other things, the date and time of death, the location of the offense, the specific positioning of the body, wounds to the body, the instrumentation of death and so forth. Unless this kind of specific information has been released to the public by the media or

through some other source then only the police and the person(s) committing the crime should possess this kind of information.
- *Provide mandatory police training on special interview considerations in dealing with populations most vulnerable to false confessions.* These include juveniles, the mentally impaired, and individuals under the influence of alcohol and/or drugs.
- Police agencies that in the past have been involved in wrongful convictions based on false confessions should review existing policies and make the appropriate changes to eliminate the problem.
- Mandate that police conclude the interview by asking a series of questions that emphasize the voluntariness of the confession that is, no coercion was used and the suspect was not under the influence of alcohol and drugs. Interviews should be concluded with questions that firmly establish the fairness and professionalism of the interviewing investigators. A simple yet very effective way to achieve this result is by asking such questions as: "Why did you decide to talk to me?" and "Why did you decide to talk to me now?"

ADMISSIBILITY OF CONFESSIONS AND ADMISSIONS

Prior to 1936, the only test for the validity and admissibility of a confession or admission was its voluntariness. However, the determination as to whether it was given voluntarily by the suspect was subject to very loose interpretation. There were no rules restricting the method by which law enforcement obtained "voluntary" statements. Physical violence, psychological coercion, empty promises, and meaningless guarantees of rewards were not considered objectionable procedures.

THE FREE-AND-VOLUNTARY RULE

The first notable incidence of U.S. Supreme Court intervention into interrogation practices came about in *Brown* v. *Mississippi.*[54] In this 1936 case, the Supreme Court held that under no circumstances could a confession be considered freely and voluntarily given when it was obtained as a result of physical brutality and violence inflicted by law enforcement officials on the accused. The reaction to this decision by law enforcement was not unexpected. Many threw up their hands and claimed they could no longer function effectively because "handcuffs had been put on the police." However, as was true with many other decisions placing procedural restrictions on law enforcement agencies, the police found they were able to compensate by conducting thorough criminal investigations.

Subsequent to the *Brown* decision, the Supreme Court, in a succession of cases, has continued to reinforce its position that any kind of coercion, whether physical or psychological, would be grounds for making a confession inadmissible as being in violation of the **free-and-voluntary rule.** This includes such conduct as threatening bodily harm to the suspect or members of the suspect's family,[55] using psychological coercion,[56] engaging in trickery or deceit, or holding a suspect incommunicado. Investigators are also cautioned about making promises to the suspect that cannot be kept. All these practices were condemned in *Miranda* v. *Arizona* (discussed in much greater detail later in this chapter).[57] Despite the appearance that *Miranda* has eliminated all coercive techniques previously used in interrogations, this is not actually the case. What *Miranda* seeks is to abolish techniques that would prompt untrue incriminatory statements by a suspect. Thus, unlike physical coercion, psychological coercion, threats, duress, and some promises, the use of trickery, fraud, falsehood, and similar techniques are not absolutely forbidden. If such methods are not likely to cause an individual to make self-incriminating statements or to admit to falsehoods in order to avoid threatened harm, confessions or admissions so obtained are admissible.[58]

THE DELAY-IN-ARRAIGNMENT RULE

In 1943 the U.S. Supreme Court delivered another decision concerning the admissibility of confessions. Even though the free-and-voluntary rule was in effect in both the federal and state courts, another series of statutes seemed to have gone unheeded. Every state and the federal government had legal provisions requiring that after arrest a person must be taken before a committing magistrate "without unnecessary delay." Before 1943, if there was an unnecessary delay in producing the accused before a committing magistrate, the delay was merely one of a number of factors the courts were required to take into consideration in determining whether the confession was freely and voluntarily given.

The facts of *McNabb* v. *United States*[59] reveal that McNabb and several members of his family were involved in bootlegging. They were arrested after the murder of federal officers who were investigating their operation in Tennessee. McNabb was held incommunicado for several days before he was taken before a committing magistrate. He subsequently confessed, and the confession was admitted into evidence at his trial. He was convicted, but on appeal to the Supreme Court the conviction was reversed. The Court held that the failure of federal officers to take the prisoner before a committing officer without unnecessary delay automatically rendered his confession inadmissible. The significance of this case is that for the first time the Court indicated that failure to comply with this procedural requirement would render a confession inadmissible regardless of whether it was obtained freely and voluntarily. Thus, instead of examining the facts of the case to determine the voluntariness of the confession, the Court ruled, as a matter of law, that the procedural violation also rendered the confession inadmissible. The holding in the *McNabb* case was emphatically reaffirmed in 1957 by the Supreme Court in *Mallory* v. *United States*.[60]

As the mandate of the Supreme Court in the *McNabb* and *Mallory* cases had applicability only to federal prosecutions, the states were free to interpret their own statutes on unnecessary delay as they saw fit. Few chose to follow the *McNabb-Mallory* **delay-in-arraignment rule.** The majority have continued to require that there must be a connection between the failure of law enforcement to produce the accused before a committing magistrate without unnecessary delay and the securing of a confession.

INTERVIEWING AND INTERROGATION LEGAL REQUIREMENTS

PREINTERROGATION LEGAL REQUIREMENTS

Preinterrogation legal requirements became of critical concern during the 1960s. As a result, the Supreme Court handed down a landmark decision that dramatically affected the conditions under which interrogations take place. The issue revolved around the Fifth Amendment protection against self-incrimination and the Sixth Amendment guarantee of the right to counsel, both as made applicable to the states through the due process clause of the Fourteenth Amendment.

MIRANDA V. ARIZONA

In *Miranda* v. *Arizona*[61] the Supreme Court, in a five-to-four decision, spelled out the requirements and procedures to be followed by officers when conducting an in custody interrogation of a suspect.

In March 1963, Ernesto Miranda was arrested for kidnapping and rape. After being identified by the victim, he was questioned by police for several hours and signed a confession that included a statement indicating that the confession was given voluntarily. The confession was admitted into evidence over the objections of Miranda's defense counsel, and the jury found him guilty. The Supreme Court of Arizona affirmed the conviction and held that Miranda's constitutional rights had not been violated in obtaining the conviction because following the ruling from *Escobedo* v. *Illinois*[62] the year before, in which Escobedo's confession was ruled to have been improperly admitted because he asked to see his lawyer but was denied that right, Miranda had not specifically requested counsel. The U.S. Supreme Court, in reversing the decision, attempted to clarify its intent in the *Escobedo* case by spelling out specific guidelines to be followed by police before they interrogate persons in custody and attempt to use their statements as evidence. In clarifying the requirements of *Escobedo*, the Court felt compelled to include the Fifth Amendment requirements against self-incrimination in the decision. The guidelines require that after a person is taken into custody for an offense and before any questioning by law enforcement officers, if there is any intent to use a suspect's statements in court, the person must first be advised of certain rights (Figure 5-7.) These rights include:

THE EXPLANATION OF THE ADMONITION AND USE OR WAIVER OF YOUR RIGHTS	LA EXPLICACION DEL AVISO Y EL USO O NO DE TUS DERECHOS
1) You have the right to remain silent—you do not have to talk.	1) Tienes el derecho de quedar en silencio—no tienes que hablar.
2) What you say can be used, and shall be used against you in a court of law.	2) Lo que digas se puede usar y se usará en contra de ti en la corte de ley.
3) You have the right to talk with an attorney before you talk with us, and you have the right to have the attorney present during the time we are talking to you.	3) Tienes el derecho de hablar con un abogado antes de hablar con nosotros, y tienes el derecho de tener el abogado presente durante el tiempo que nosotros estamos hablando contigo.
4) If you do not have the funds to employ an attorney, one shall be appointed to represent you free of charge.	4) Si no tienes el dinero para emplear un abogado, uno sere fijado para que te represente, sin pagar.
5) Do you understand these rights as I have explained them to you, yes or no?	5) ¿Comprendes estos derechos como te los expliqué, si o no?
6) Do you want to talk to us about your case now, yes or no?	6) ¿Quieres hablar con nosotros de tu caso ahora, si o no?
7) Do you want an attorney present during the time we are talking to you, yes or no?	7) ¿Quieres un abogado presente durante el tiempo que estamos hablando contigo, si o no?

◀FIGURE 5-7
Warning-rights card in English and Spanish

(Courtesy Los Angeles County Sheriff's Department)

1. The right to remain silent.
2. The right to be told that anything said can and will be used in court.
3. The right to consult with an attorney before answering any questions and the right to have an attorney present during interrogation.
5. The right to counsel. If the suspect cannot afford an attorney, the court will appoint one.[63]

SUSPECT'S RESPONSE: WAIVER AND ALTERNATIVES

It is common practice for the officer to ask the suspect if he or she understands the rights as they have been explained. If the answer is yes, then the officer may ask if the subject wants to talk with the officer. At this point, four alternatives are open to the suspect:

1. *The suspect may choose to remain silent,* not wanting even to respond to the officer's question. The courts have held that choosing to remain silent does not imply consent to be interrogated and no questions should be asked.
2. *The suspect may request counsel.* At that point, the investigator must not undertake any questioning of the suspect, for anything said will not be admissible in court. In *Edwards* v. *Arizona* in 1981, the Supreme Court held that no police-initiated interrogation may lawfully take place once the suspect has invoked the right to counsel unless, and until, an attorney has been provided or unless the defendant voluntarily begins to talk with the officers.[64] In *Minnick v. Mississippi* in 1990, the U.S. Supreme Court held that once counsel is requested, interrogation must cease; officials may not reinitiate

interrogation without counsel being present, whether or not the accused has consulted with his or her attorney. The requirement that counsel be made available to the accused refers not to the opportunity to consult with a lawyer outside the interrogation room but to the right to have the attorney present during custodial interrogation. This rule is necessary to remove suspects from the coercive pressure of officials who may try to persuade them to waive their rights. The rule also provides a clear and unequivocal guideline to the law enforcement profession.[65]

The *Edwards* and *Minnick* lines of cases remained constant until the Supreme Court ruled in *Maryland v. Shatzer* in 2010. The facts involved an attempt by a detective to question Shatzer in 2003 about allegations that he had sexually abused his son. At the time Shatzer was in prison on an unrelated offense. Shatzer invoked his *Miranda* rights to have counsel present during the interrogation. The detective terminated the interview and the case was subsequently closed. Shatzer was returned to the general population. Another detective reopened the investigation 3 years later and attempted to interrogate Shatzer, who was still in prison. Shatzer waived his *Miranda* rights this time and, in 2006, made some inculpatory statements that were admitted at this trial for sexually abusing his son. Shatzer was convicted. After several appeals, which held the trial court was wrong to admit Shatzer's incriminating statements since he had previously asked for an attorney, the appeals courts held there was no exception once the request for an attorney had been made in accordance with the *Edwards* decision, since Shatzer was still being held in custody. The Supreme Court, however, agreed with the trial court, allowing the statements to be used against Shatzer. The Court reasoned that because Shatzer experienced a break in *Miranda* custody, lasting more than 2 weeks between the first and second attempts at interrogation, *Edwards* did not require suppression of his 2006 statements. The Court said that even though Shatzer was still in prison during the time between the 2003 and 2006 interrogations, he was in the general population, where he could have spoken with a lawyer during the 3-year break and was no longer in a police-dominated atmosphere on the sexual abuse case. Even though he was still in prison Shatzer resumed his "normal life."[66]

3. *The suspect may waive his or her rights and agree to talk with law enforcement without the benefit of counsel.* The waiver of rights is a sensitive topic for law enforcement,

as it is the responsibility of law enforcement and the prosecutor to prove in court the waiver was validly obtained. A valid waiver must be voluntarily, knowingly, and intelligently given by the suspect. The burden is on the prosecution to prove that the suspect was properly advised of his or her rights, that those rights were understood, and that the suspect voluntarily, knowingly, and intelligently waived those rights before the court will allow the introduction of any incriminating testimony in the form of a confession. The waiver cannot be presumed or inferred. It must be successfully proved by the prosecution. Therefore, it is preferable for the investigator who secures a waiver of rights from a suspect to attempt to get the waiver in writing with sufficient witnesses to substantiate its voluntariness. Figure 5-8 is a sample waiver form. Most law enforcement agencies also attempt to get

▶ **FIGURE 5-8   Rights waiver form**
(Courtesy Geauga County, Ohio, Sheriff's Department)

YOUR RIGHTS

Date_____

Time_____

WARNING

Before we ask you any questions, you must understand your rights.

You have the right to remain silent.

Anything you say can and will be used against you in court.

You have the right to talk to a lawyer for advice before we ask you any question and to have him with you during questioning.

If you cannot afford a lawyer, one will be appointed for you.

Geauga County has a Public Defender. Before answering any questions, you have a right to talk with the Public Defender.

If you decide to answer questions now, without a lawyer present, you will still have the right to stop answering at any time. You also have the right to stop answering at any time until you talk to a lawyer.

Do you understand these rights? _____

Signed: _____

Witnesses:

_____

_____

WAIVER OF RIGHTS

I have read this statement of my rights and I understand what my rights are. I am willing to make a statement and answer questions. I do not want a lawyer at this time. I understand and know what I am doing. No promises or threats have been made to me and no pressure or coercion of any kind has been used against me.

Signed: _____

Witnesses:

_____

_____

Date: _____

Time: _____

individuals in custody to sign a rights waiver form as one more step to show a good faith effort to comply with the requirements of the *Miranda* ruling.

However, a suspect who has waived his or her rights is free to withdraw that waiver at any time. If this occurs during questioning, the investigator is under a legal obligation to cease the interrogation at that point and either comply with the suspect's request for representation or simply cease the interrogation if the suspect refuses to talk.

4. *The suspect may indicate a desire not to talk with the investigators.* At this point, law enforcement has no choice other than to refrain from attempting to interrogate the suspect concerning the events of the crime for which he or she has been arrested. In this event, the case must be based on independent evidence, which may or may not be sufficient to warrant prosecution. The U.S. Supreme Court's emphatic position on terminating interrogation once a suspect has invoked the right to remain silent was announced in 1975 in the case of *Michigan* v. *Mosley.*[67]

Since the responsibility is on the prosecution, supported by evidence provided by the investigators, to substantiate the voluntariness of the waiver and the propriety of the warnings given to the suspect, many law enforcement agencies provide printed cards with the exact wording of the required warnings. They further recommend or require that when warnings are given they be read verbatim from the printed card. In this manner, the officer, when testifying in court, can positively state the exact words used in advising the suspect of his or her constitutional rights. Such a procedure avoids any confrontation with the defense as to the exact wording and contents of the *Miranda* requirements. But in 1989 in *Duckworth* v. *Eagen*, the Supreme Court held that it was not necessary that the warnings be given in the exact form described in the *Miranda* decision, provided the warnings as a whole fully informed the suspect of his or her rights.[68] This position was reaffirmed in a 2010 case *Florida* v. *Powell.*[69]

A person being subjected to **in-custody interrogation** often chooses not to answer any questions posed by law enforcement— or at least not until an attorney is present. When counsel is made available to the suspect before or during interrogation, it is almost universal practice for the attorney to advise the client not to say anything to the police. Therefore, the effect of the *Miranda* decision has been to reduce significantly the number of valid interrogations by law enforcement agencies in this country today. For the most part, however, confessions obtained in compliance with prescribed rules are of better quality and are more likely to be admissible in court.

It must be impressed on investigators that the failure to properly advise a suspect of the rights required by *Miranda* does not invalidate an otherwise valid arrest, nor does it necessarily mean a case cannot be successfully prosecuted. Even in light of the line of court decisions indicating that *Miranda* warnings may not be required in all interrogation situations, good practice or departmental policy may require that all suspects in custody be advised of their rights.

IN-CUSTODY INTERROGATION

For investigators to understand the proper application of the *Miranda* requirements, it is essential they understand the meaning of in-custody interrogation. The *Miranda* case involved simultaneous custody and interrogation. Subsequent police actions revealed that all cases were not so nicely defined and the meanings of "in custody" and "interrogation" required clarification. Although it may be difficult to separate the custody from the interrogation in certain factual situations, the two concepts must be considered separately.

Custody

Custody occurs when a person is deprived of his or her freedom in any significant way or is not free to leave the presence of law enforcement. Analyses of case decisions show there is not yet a universally accepted definition of custody. Rather, case-by-case analysis is used to determine the applicability of the *Miranda* requirements (Figure 5-9).

▲ **FIGURE 5-9**
Uniformed officer with handcuffed prisoner
In deciding when *Miranda* warnings are required, there is no universally accepted definition of "custody." In this, photograph, it is clear that this suspect is in custody between the officer leading him by the arm and the handcuffs; there is no doubt that the suspect is not free to leave. (©Cleve Bryant/ PhotoEdit)

MIRANDA AND MISDEMEANORS

The question of whether *Miranda* applies to misdemeanor arrests was the subject of controversy for many years. In 1984, the Supreme Court settled this issue. The Court ruled in *Berkemer* v. *McCarty* that *Miranda* applies to the interrogation of an arrested person regardless of whether the offense is a felony or a misdemeanor. The justices found that to make a distinction would cause confusion, because many times it is not certain whether the person taken into custody is to be charged with a felony or a misdemeanor.[70]

INTERROGATION AS DEFINED BY THE U.S. SUPREME COURT

For legal purposes, interrogation includes any express questioning or any verbal or nonverbal behavior by a law enforcement officer that is designed to elicit an incriminating statement or response from the suspect of a crime. For many years following the *Miranda* ruling, there was considerable confusion over what constituted questioning or interrogation. For example, in a 1977 case the Supreme Court found that an impermissible interrogation occurred when an investigator delivered what has been called the "Christian burial speech" to a man suspected of murdering a young girl. While the suspect was being transported between cities, the investigator told the suspect to think about how the weather was turning cold and snow was likely. He pointed out how difficult it would be to find the body later. The investigator went on to say that the girl's parents were entitled to have a Christian burial for the little girl, who had been taken from them on Christmas Eve and murdered. Subsequent to this little speech, the suspect led the investigators to the spot where he had disposed of the body. The Supreme Court held this to be an interrogation within the scope of *Miranda,* even though direct questions had not been asked of the suspect.[71]

The Supreme Court faced the question of what constitutes interrogation for the first time in the 1980 case of *Rhode Island* v. *Innis.* In that instance a robbery suspect was arrested after the victim had identified him from photographs. The prisoner was advised several times of his constitutional rights and was being transported by three officers who had been specifically ordered not to question the suspect. During the trip, two of the officers were having a conversation about the case, and one commented how terrible it would be if some unsuspecting child found the missing shotgun (used in the robbery) and got hurt. The conversation was not directed at the suspect, nor did the officers expect a response from the suspect. However, the suspect interrupted the conversation and, after again being advised of his rights, led the officers to the shotgun. The Supreme Court stated the rule regarding interrogation as follows:

> We conclude that *Miranda* safeguards come into play whenever a person in custody is subjected to either express questioning or its functional equivalent. That is to say, the term "interrogation" under *Miranda* refers not only to express

questioning, but also to any words or actions on the part of the police (other than those normally attendant to arrest and custody) that the police should know are reasonably likely to elicit an incriminating response from the suspect. The latter portion of this definition focuses primarily upon the perceptions of the suspect, rather than the intent of the police. This focus reflects the fact that the *Miranda* safeguards were designed to vest a suspect in custody with an added measure of protection against coercive police practices, without regard to objective proof of the underlying intent of the police.[72]

As a general rule, *Miranda* warnings need not precede routine booking questions that are asked in order to obtain personal-history data necessary to complete the booking process. As long as the questions are for that purpose and not a pretext to obtain incriminating information, *Miranda* warnings need not be given.[73]

RECENT U.S. SUPREME COURT DECISIONS ON THE RIGHT TO REMAIN SILENT

On June 1, 2010 the U.S. Supreme Court's decision in the area of **Berghuis v. Thompkins** was decided and shines new light on issues surrounding both the invocation and waiver of the *Miranda* right to remain silent.[74, 75]

In *Berghuis*, Van Chester Thompkins was arrested in Ohio for a shooting that occurred approximately 1 year earlier in Southfield, Michigan. While in custody, Thompkins was questioned by two detectives in a police interview room. At the beginning of the interrogation, the detectives presented Thompkins with a general set of *Miranda* warnings.[76]

To make sure Thompkins could understand English, one of the detectives asked Thompkins to read a portion of the warnings out loud, which he did. Thereafter, the detective read the rest of the warnings to Thompkins and asked him to sign the form, indicating that he understood his rights. Thompkins refused to sign the form, and the officers began interrogating Thompkins. "At no point during the interrogation did Thompkins say he wanted to remain silent, did not want to talk to the police, or wanted an attorney."[77]

With the exception of some minor verbal responses and limited eye contact, Thompkins remained silent for most of the 3-hour interview. Approximately 2 hours and 45 minutes into the interrogation, one of the detectives asked Thompkins if he believed in God. Thompkins said he did. The detective then followed up by asking Thompkins if he prayed to God. Thompkins said, "Yes." The detective then asked, "Do you pray to God to forgive you for shooting that boy down?" To which, Thompkins answered, "Yes." Thompkins refused to make a written statement, and the interrogation ended.[78]

COURT PROCEEDINGS

Thompkins filed a motion to suppress the statements he made during the interrogation and claimed his Fifth Amendment right to remain silent had been violated. The trial court denied the motion, and Thompkins' admission was used against him at trial. Thompkins was convicted of first-degree murder and sentenced to life in prison without parole.

Thompkins appealed.[79] The Michigan Court of Appeals rejected the *Miranda* claim, and the Michigan Supreme Court denied review. Thereafter, Thompkins filed a petition for a writ of habeas corpus in the U.S. District Court for the Eastern District of Michigan that was likewise denied. The U.S. Court of Appeals for the Sixth Circuit reversed the district court ruling in favor of Thompkins.[80] However, for the reasons set forth herein, the Supreme Court reversed the judgment of the Sixth Circuit Court of Appeals and found no *Miranda* violations.

RIGHT TO REMAIN SILENT—INVOCATION

In filing his motion to suppress the statements he made during the interrogation, Thompkins first argued he had invoked his right to remain silent by not saying anything for the first 2 hours and 45 minutes of the interrogation. If, in fact, he had invoked his right to remain silent, it is undisputed the officers would have been obligated to stop questioning.[81] However, Justice Kennedy, in writing the majority opinion, explained that Thompkins' mere silence in the face of questioning was not clear and unambiguous invocation of his right to remain silent.[82] The Court noted that, unlike its earlier ruling in *Davis* v. *United States* regarding the invocation of the *Miranda* right to counsel, it never had defined whether an invocation of the right to remain silent must be unambiguous. In *Davis*, the defendant initially waived his *Miranda* rights and was interrogated for 90 minutes before saying, "Maybe I should talk to a lawyer." The Court held that if a subject is unclear, ambiguous, or equivocal in requesting a lawyer, officers can ignore the reference and proceed with the interrogation.[83]

In *Berghuis*, the Court acknowledged "there is no principled reason to adopt different standards for determining when an accused has invoked the *Miranda* right to remain silent and the *Miranda* right to counsel at issue in *Davis*. . . . Both protect the privilege against compulsory self-incrimination . . . by requiring an interrogation to cease when either right is invoked." Moreover, the Court explained there are no practical reasons for requiring that an invocation of the right to silence be clear and unambiguous. Namely, "an unambiguous invocation of *Miranda* rights results in an objective inquiry that 'avoid[s] difficulties of proof and . . . provide[s] guidance to officers on how to proceed in the face of ambiguity.'"[84] Accordingly, *Berghuis* does for the invocation of the right to silence what *Davis* did for the invocation of the right to counsel—it mandates that an invocation of either *Miranda* right must be clear and unambiguous to be effective.

RIGHT TO REMAIN SILENT—WAIVER

Thompkins next argued that absent an invocation of his right to silence, his statements still should be suppressed because he never

adequately waived his right to silence. Two portions of the original *Miranda* decision seem to tilt the scale in Thompkins' favor on this issue. First, the *Miranda* Court said, "a valid waiver will not be presumed simply from the silence of the accused after warnings are given or simply from the fact that a confession was in fact eventually obtained."[85] Additionally, "a heavy burden rests on the government to demonstrate that the defendant knowingly and intelligently waived his privilege against self-incrimination. . . ."[86]

However, the Supreme Court has clarified its position with respect to the waiver since the *Miranda* decision. The impact has been to keep *Miranda* focused on the right to refrain from speaking and to consult an attorney. As the Court in *Berghuis* noted: "The main purpose of *Miranda* is to ensure that an accused is advised of and understands the right to remain silent and the right to counsel. . . ."[87] Thus, "if anything, our subsequent cases have reduced the impact of the *Miranda* rule on legitimate law enforcement while reaffirming the decision's core ruling that unwarned statements may not be used as evidence in the prosecution's case in chief."[88]

SALINAS V. TEXAS

In another landmark case, *Salinas v. Texas,* July 15, 2013, the Supreme Court addressed the following question as it relates to self-incrimination statements:

"Does the Fifth Amendment Self-Incrimination Clause protect a defendant's refusal to answer questions asked by law enforcement before he/she has been arrested or read their Miranda rights?"

Following are the facts of the case.

In 1992, Houston police officers found the bodies of two homicide victims. The investigation led officers to a person of interest, Genovevo Salinas. Salinas agreed to accompany the officers to the police station where he was questioned for about one hour. Salinas was not under arrest at the time and had not been read his Miranda rights. Salinas answered every question until an officer asked whether the shotgun shells found at the scene of the crime would match the gun found in Salinas' home. According to the officer, Salinas remained silent in response to the question but showed signs of deception. A ballistics analysis later matched Salinas' shotgun with shotgun shells found at the scene. Police also found a witness who said Salinas admitted killing the victims. In 1993, Salinas was charged with the murders, but could not be located.

Fifteen years later, Salinas was finally captured. The first trial ended in a mistrial. At the second trial, the prosecution attempted to introduce evidence of Salinas' silence about the gun casings. Salinas objected, arguing that he had the right to invoke his Fifth Amendment protection against self-incrimination whether he was in custody or not. The trial court admitted the evidence and Salinas was found guilty and sentenced to 20 years in prison and a $5,000 fine.

In a 5 to 4 majority decision the Court concluded that the Fifth Amendment's privilege against self-incrimination does not extend to defendants who simply decide to remain mute during questioning. Long-standing judicial precedent has held that any witness who desires protection against self-incrimination must explicitly claim that protection. This requirement ensures that the government is put on notice when a defendant intends to claim this privilege and allows the government to either argue that the testimony is not self-incriminating or offer immunity. The plurality of the justices reiterated two exceptions to this principle: 1) that a criminal defendant does not need to take the stand at trial in order to explicitly claim this privilege; and 2) that failure to claim this privilege must be excused when that failure was due to government coercion. The opinion declined to extend these exceptions to the situation in this case. Notwithstanding popular misconceptions, the Court held that the Fifth Amendment does not establish a complete right to remain silent but only guarantees that a criminal defendant may not be forced to testify against themselves. Therefore, so long as police do not deprive defendants of the opportunity to claim a Fifth Amendment privilege, there is no Constitutional violation.[89]

DETECTION OF DECEPTION

Identifying deceit is so difficult that repeated studies begun in the 1980s show that most people—including judges, attorneys, clinicians, police officers, FBI agents, politicians, teachers, mothers, fathers, and spouses—are no better than chance (fifty-fifty) when it comes to detecting deception.[90, 91] It is disturbing but true. Most people, including professionals, do no better than a coin toss at correctly perceiving dishonesty. Even those who are truly gifted at detecting deception (probably less than 1% of the general population) are seldom right more than 60% of the time. Consider the countless jurors who must determine honesty or dishonesty, guilt or innocence, based on what they think are deceptive behaviors. Unfortunately, those behaviors most often mistaken for dishonesty are primarily manifestations of stress, not deception.[92] There is simply no single behavior that is indicative of deception—not one.[93]

This does not mean we should abandon our efforts to study deception and observe for behaviors that, in context, are suggestive of it. But a realistic goal is to be able to read nonverbal behaviors with clarity and reliability.

THE CRITICAL ROLE OF THE COMFORT/DISCOMFORT EQUATION IN DETECTING DECEPTION

Those who are lying or are guilty and must carry the knowledge of their lies and/or crimes with them find it difficult to achieve comfort, and their tension and distress may be readily observed. Attempting to disguise their guilt or deception places a very distressing cognitive load on them as they struggle to fabricate answers to what would otherwise be simple questions.[94]

The more comfortable a person is when speaking with investigators, the easier it will be to detect the critical nonverbal discomfort associated with deception. The goal is to establish high comfort during the early part of any interaction or during the period of time characterized as "rapport building." This

helps to establish a baseline of behaviors during that period when the person, hopefully, does not feel threatened.

ESTABLISHING A COMFORT ZONE FOR DETECTING DECEPTION

In pursuing the detection of deception investigators must be aware of their impact on the actions of suspects being interrogated and recognize how their behavior will affect the other person's behavior.[95] How the investigator asks the question (accusingly), how the investigator sits (too close or not close enough), how the investigator looks upon the person (suspiciously), will either support or disrupt the suspect's comfort level. It is well established that if a person's personal space is violated, he or she will have a tendency to act nervous. In addition, if a person is questioned in a prosecutorial tone, this will very likely negatively intrude on the questioning process.

DEFINING SIGNS OF COMFORT

Comfort is readily apparent in conversations with family members and friends. It is easy to sense when people are having a good time and are comfortable. While seated at a table, people who are comfortable with each other will move objects aside so that nothing blocks their view, and over time, they may draw closer so they do not have to talk as loudly. Individuals who are comfortable display their bodies more openly, showing more of their torsos and the insides of their arms and legs (they allow ventral access or fronting). In the presence of strangers, comfort is more difficult to achieve, especially in stressful situations such as a formal interview or a deposition. This is why it is so important for the investigator to create a comfort zone from the very outset and to facilitate beneficial interaction with the person to be questioned.

When we are comfortable, there should be *synchrony* in our nonverbal behavior. The breathing rhythm of two comfortable people will be similar, as will the tone and pitch of their speech and their general demeanor. If a person is standing while talking to someone, leaning to the side with their hands in their pockets and feet crossed, most likely the person they are talking to will do the same. By **mirroring** (called isoparaxis) another person's behavior, they are subconsciously saying "I am comfortable with you" (Figure 5-10).

In an interview setting or any situation where a difficult topic is being discussed, the tone of each party should mirror the other's over time if there is synchrony.[96] If harmony does not exist between the people involved, synchrony will be missing, which will be discernible. They sit differently, talk in a manner or tone different from each other, or at the least their expressions will be at odds, if not totally disparate. Asynchrony is a barrier to effective communication and is a serious obstacle to a successful interview or discussion.

Obviously, displays of comfort are more common in people speaking the truth; because there is no stress to conceal, and no guilty knowledge to make them uncomfortable.[97] Thus, the investigator should still be looking for signs of discomfort—when they occur and in what context—to assess for possible deception.

▲ FIGURE 5-10 Isoparaxis (mirroring)
Here is an example of isoparaxis: both people are mirroring each other and leaning toward each other, showing signs of high comfort. (©Canva Pty Ltd/Alamy RF)

SIGNS OF DISCOMFORT IN AN INTERACTION

We all show signs of discomfort when we do not like what is happening to us, when we do not like what we are seeing or hearing, or when we are compelled to talk about things we would prefer to keep hidden. We display discomfort first in our physiology, due to arousal of the limbic brain.[98] Our heart rate quickens, we perspire more, and we breathe faster. Beyond the physiological responses, which are autonomic (automatic) and require no thinking on our part, our bodies manifest discomfort nonverbally. We tend to move our bodies in an attempt to block or distance ourselves from the source of our discomfort. We rearrange ourselves, jiggle our feet, fidget, twist at the hips, or drum our fingers when we are scared, nervous, or significantly uncomfortable.[99] We have all noticed such discomfort behaviors in others—whether at a job interview or being questioned about a serious matter. These actions do not automatically indicate

deception but do indicate that a person is uncomfortable in the current situation for any number of reasons.

When the investigator is attempting to observe discomfort as a potential indicator of deception, the best setting is one that has no objects (such as furniture, tables, desks, or chairs) between the person being observed and the investigator. Movements of the lower limbs are particularly revealing. Thus, if a person is behind a desk or table, the investigator should try to move it or get the individual to move away from it because such an obstacle will block the vast majority (nearly 80%) of the body surfaces that need to be observed. In fact, the investigator should watch for the deceptive individual using obstacles or objects to form a physical barrier between the investigator and himself or herself. The use of objects is a sign that an individual wants distance, separation, and partial concealment, because the subject is being less open—which goes hand in hand with being uncomfortable or even deceitful. When it comes to questioning someone, more nonverbal clues can be obtained from standing rather than sitting.

Other clear signs of discomfort seen in people during a difficult or troubling interview include rubbing the forehead; covering the throat; difficulty swallowing; clearing the throat; coughing; covering or twisting the mouth; biting or licking lips; yawning and sighs; itching and rubbing the nose, mustache, or beard; tugging at their ears or covering their ears; pulling their hair or grooming it; flushing of the skin or becoming extremely pale; squeezing their face; rubbing their neck; and stroking the back of their head with their hand. People may show their displeasure with the process by rolling their eyes in disrespect, picking lint off themselves (preening), or talking down to the person asking the questions—giving short answers, becoming resistant, hostile, or sarcastic, or even displaying microgestures with indecent connotations such as giving the finger.[100]

When making false statements, liars will rarely touch or engage in other physical contact with the investigator. Since touching is more often done by the truthful person for emphasis, this distancing helps to alleviate the level of anxiety a dishonest person is feeling. Any diminution of touching observed in a person engaged in conversation, especially while hearing to or answering critical questions, is more likely than not indicative of deception.[101]

When observing a person's face for signs of comfort or discomfort, investigators should look for subtle behaviors such as a grimace or a look of contempt.[102] Also, the person's face should be observed to see if their mouth is quivering. This is a clear indication of nervousness and discomfort. Any facial expression that lasts too long or lingers is not normal, whether a smile, a frown, or a surprised look. Such contrived behavior during an interview is intended to influence the investigator's opinion and lacks authenticity. Often when people are caught doing something wrong or lying, they will hold a smile for an unusual period of time. Rather than being an indication of comfort, this type of false smile is actually an indication of discomfort.

On occasion, when we do not like what we are hearing, whether a question or an answer, we often close our eyes as if to block it. The various forms of eye-blocking mechanisms are analogous to folding one's hands tightly across the chest or turning away from those with whom we disagree. These blocking displays are performed subconsciously and occur often, especially during a formal interview, and are usually related to a specific topic. Eyelid flutter is also observed at times when a particular subject causes distress.[103]

All of these eye manifestations are powerful clues as to how information is registering or what questions are problematic for the recipient. However, they are not necessarily direct indicators of deceit. Little or no eye contact is *not* indicative of deception.[104] As a matter of fact, predators and habitual liars actually engage in greater eye contract than most individuals and will lock eyes with the person they are communicating with. Research clearly shows that psychopaths, con artists, and habitual liars will actually increase eye contact and it is consciously employed by these individuals, because they are aware it is so commonly (but erroneously) believed by many that looking someone straight in the eye is a sign of truthfulness.

However, it is important to understand that there are cultural differences in eye contact and eye-gaze behavior that must be considered in any attempt to detect deception. For example, individuals belonging to many groups of people such as Latinos, Asians, and people from the Middle East are often taught to look down or away when being questioned by individuals in a position of authority. This is considered to be a gesture of respect and deference.[105]

Head movements can also be revealing. If a person's head begins to shake either in the affirmative or in the negative as they are speaking, and the movement occurs simultaneously with what they are saying, then the statement can typically be relied upon as being truthful. If, however, the head shake or head movement is delayed or occurs after the speech, then most likely the statement is contrived and not truthful. Although it may be very subtle, the delayed movement of the head is an attempt to further validate what has been stated and is not part of the natural flow of communication. In addition, honest head movements should be consistent with verbal denials or affirmations. If a head movement is inconsistent with or contrary to a person's statement, it may indicate deception. While typically involving more subtle rather than exaggerated head movement, this incongruity of verbal and nonverbal signals happens more often than we think. For example, someone may say, "I didn't do it," while slightly nodding his or her head in the affirmative.

During discomfort, the limbic brain takes over, and a person's face can conversely either flush or lighten in color. During difficult conversations, the investigator may also see increases in perspiration or breathing, an accelerated pulsation of the carotid artery, and the person noticeably wiping away sweat or trying to control his or her breathing in an effort to remain calm. Any trembling of the body, whether of the hands, fingers, or lips, or any attempt to hide or restrain the hands or lips (through disappearing or compressed lips), may be indicative of discomfort and/or deception, especially if it occurs after the period of normal nervousness should have been dissipated.

However, indications of nervousness do not necessarily mean deception. The following case illustrates this point.

In a Florida case several years ago a suspect whom the investigators accused of sexual assault and murder was interrogated for 16 hours and eventually confessed. The statement was later suppressed by the judge and the charges were dropped. The suspect had become a prime suspect because his face flushed and he appeared embarrassed during an initial interview, a reaction interpreted as a sign of deception. Investigators did not know the suspect was a recovering alcoholic with a social anxiety disorder that caused him to sweat profusely and blush in stressful social situations. These same characteristics that could have been interpreted as someone who is acting guilty in this case were a person responding to extreme stress.[106]

A person's voice may crack or may seem inconsistent when being deceptive; swallowing becomes difficult as the throat becomes dry from stress and the person begins to swallow hard. These can be evidenced by a sudden bob or jump of the Adam's apple and may be accompanied by the clearing or repeated clearing of the throat—all indicative of discomfort. These behaviors are indicators of distress, not guarantees of deception. For example, many honest people who testify in court display these behaviors simply because they are nervous and not because they are lying. Even after years of testifying, many law enforcement officers still acknowledge they get nervous on the witness stand. Thus it is important to remember that signs of tension and stress need to be deciphered within the context in which they are occurring.

PACIFYING BEHAVIORS

Although pacifiers, which are physical behaviors we use to calm ourselves, are not alone definitive proof of deception (since they can manifest in innocent people who are nervous), they do provide another piece of the puzzle in determining what a person may be truly thinking.

Reading Pacifying Nonverbal and Interpersonal Interactions

- *Expect some pacifying behaviors.* A certain level of pacifying behavior is normal in everyday nonverbal displays; people do this to calm themselves as they adapt to an ever-changing environment. Pacifying behaviors take many forms. When stressed we might soothe our necks with a gentle massage, stroke our faces, or play with our hair. This is done automatically. Our brains send out the message "please pacify me now," and our hands respond immediately, acting in a way that helps make us comfortable again. Sometimes we pacify by rubbing our necks or our lips from the inside with our tongue, or we exhale slowly with puffed cheeks to calm ourselves. If a stressed person is a smoker he or she will smoke more, if given the opportunity. If the person chews gum, he or she will chew faster. All these pacifying behaviors satisfy the same requirement of the brain, that is, the brain requires the body to do something that will stimulate nerve endings, releasing calming endorphins in the brain so that the brain can be soothed. As a general rule, men prefer to pacify by touching their face while women prefer to pacify by touching their clothing, jewelry, necklace, and neck.

- *Get a clear view.* Have nothing blocking the total view of the person to ensure that no pacifying behavior will be missed. If, for example, the person pacifies by wiping their hands on their lap, the investigator would want to see this. This is difficult to observe when there is a desk in the way.

- *Expect initial nervousness.* Initial nervousness in the questioning process by the police is normal. For example, if an innocent person is being told by the police that he or she is considered a suspect in a murder or rape investigation one would certainly expect a certain level of nervousness.

- *Get the person to relax first.* As questioning progresses, individuals should eventually calm down and become more comfortable. In fact, a good investigator will make sure this happens by allowing the person to relax before asking questions or exploring topics that might be stressful.

- *Establish a baseline.* Once a person's pacifying behaviors have decreased and stabilized to normal (for that person), the investigator can recognize that pacifying level as a baseline for assessing future behavior.

- *Look for increased use of pacifiers.* As the interview or conversation continues, it is normal for pacifying behaviors to increase (spike) in their frequency, particularly when they occur in response to a specific question or piece of information. For example, if a person is questioned about a crime and starts to ventilate his collar (a pacifier), that means that specific inquiry has caused a sufficient amount of stress to make the brain require pacification. This indicates the issue needs to be pursued further. The behavior does not necessarily mean that deception is involved but simply that the topic is causing the interviewee stress.

- *Ask, pause, and observe.* Good investigators, like good conversationalists, should not engage in staccato-fashion type questioning. Unfortunately, some false confessions (discussed earlier in this chapter) have been obtained because of sustained staccato-like questioning, which causes high stress and obfuscation and nonverbal cues. Innocent people have been known to confess to crimes and have even provided written statements in order to terminate a stressful interview when excessive or inappropriate pressure is applied.[107]

- *Keep the person being interviewed focused.* Investigators should keep in mind that many times when people are simply talking and telling their side of the story there will be fewer useful nonverbals performed than when the investigator controls the scope of the topic. Pointed questions elicit behavioral manifestations that are useful in assessing a person's honesty.

- *Chatter is not truth.* One mistake made by both novice and experienced investigators is the tendency to equate talking with truth. When the person being questioned is talking, there is a tendency for investigators to believe them. When the person is reserved, it is assumed they are lying. During conversation, people who provide an overwhelming amount of information and detail about an event or a situation may appear to be telling the truth; however, in reality they may be hoping it will obfuscate the facts or lead the conversation in another direction.

- *Stress coming in and going out.* A person with guilty knowledge will present two distinct behaviors in sequence. When asked a difficult question such as "Were you involved in the murder of your wife?" The first behavior will reflect the stress experienced when hearing the question. The person will subconsciously respond with various distancing behaviors including foot withdrawal (moving them away from the investigator) and may lean away or may tighten his jaw and lips. This behavior will be followed by the second set of related behaviors, pacifying responses to the stress that may include signals such as neck touching, nose stroking, or neck massaging as he ponders the question or answer.

- *Isolate the cause of the stress.* Two behavior patterns in series—the stress indicators followed by pacifying behaviors—have traditionally been erroneously associated with deception. This is unfortunate, because these manifestations need to be explained more simply as what they are—indicators of stress and stress relief—not necessarily dishonesty. No doubt someone who is lying may display these same behaviors, but individuals who are nervous also show them.

SPECIFIC BEHAVIORS TO CONSIDER IN DETECTING DECEPTION

Following are some specific behaviors to consider when attempting to determine if a subject is being deceptive.

- *Lack of emphasis in hand behaviors.* As noted social psychologist Aldert Vrij and others have reported, a lack of arm movement and a lack of emphasis are suggestive of deception.[108] Any sudden reduction in or change in movement reflects brain activity. When arms shift from being animated to being still, there is a reason, be it dejection or (possibly) deception.

    Deceptive individuals will tend to display less steepling of the fingers. The investigator should look for the white knuckles of the individual who grabs the chair armrest in a fixed manner as though in an "ejector seat." Many criminal investigators have found that when the

▲ FIGURE 5-11 Flash frozen
Sitting for long periods in a chair, as though flash frozen in an ejector seat, is evidence of high stress and discomfort. (©YAY Media AS/Alamy RF)

head, neck, arms, and legs are held in place with little movement and the hands and arms are clutching the armrest, such behavior is very much consistent with those who are about to deceive, but again, it is not definitive (Figure 5-11).

- *Swearing to the truthfulness of assertions.* Interestingly, as individuals make declarative statements that are false, they will avoid touching not only other people but also objects, such as a podium or table as well. It is almost unheard of for a person who is lying to yell affirmatively, "I didn't do it," while pounding his or her fist on a table. It is not at all unusual for individuals who are not being truthful to immediately invoke the name of God and say such things as "I swear to God," or perhaps even invoke their children by making statements such as "if I'm lying may my children die or lose their eyesight," or some other ridiculously desperate plea to convince the interrogator they are not lying. The same psychological motivation for swearing is involved in the use of such expressions as "I have a spotless record" and "I am a very religious man, I couldn't do anything like that." Expressions of this type are frequently used by guilty subjects in an effort to lend forcefulness or conviction to their

assertions of innocence. Also, what usually happens in this case is that there may be very weak, nonemphatic statements and gestures that are equally mild. People who are being deceptive lack commitment and confidence in what they are saying. Although their thinking brain (neocortex) will decide what to say in order to mislead, their emotive brain (the limbic system—the honest part of the brain) simply will not be committed to the ruse and therefore will not emphasize their statements using nonverbal behaviors (such as gestures). The sentiments of the limbic brain are hard to override.

- *The rogatory position.* When people place their outstretched arms in front of their bodies, with palms up, this is known as the *rogatory* (or "prayerful") display (Figure 5-12). Those who worship turn their palms up to God to ask for mercy. This behavior is also seen in individuals who say something that they want you to believe. When a person makes a declarative statement, note whether the hands are palms up or palms down. During regular conversation in which ideas are being discussed and neither party is vehemently committed to a particular point, the investigator can expect to see both palms-up and palms-down displays.

▲ FIGURE 5-12 The rogatory position (palms up)
The palms-up, or "rogatory," position usually indicates that the person wants to be believed or wants to be accepted. It is not a dominant, confident display. (©SolStock/iStock/Getty Images RF)

▲ **FIGURE 5-13   Palms-down position**
Statements made palms down are more emphatic and more confident than statements made with the palms up, in the rogatory position. (©Ned Frisk Photography/Getty Images RF)

However, when a person is making a passionate and assertive declaration such as "You have to believe me, I did not kill her," those hands should be face down (Figure 5-13). If the statement is made palms up, the individual is supplicating to be believed,

and such a statement should be highly suspect. Although this interpretation is not definitive, any declarative statement made with palms up should raise serious questions about the truthfulness of the statement being made. People who are telling the truth do not have to plead to be believed; they make a statement, and it stands.

USE OF TECHNOLOGICAL INSTRUMENTS TO DETECT DECEPTION

POLYGRAPH

The first workable polygraph is attributed to John Larson (1892–1983) in 1921. Its use spread relatively quickly in policing circles, and since then it has been improved upon a number of times, such as by adding the use of computer scoring (Figure 5-14). The primary purpose of a **polygraph** examination is to determine if victims, suspects, and informants are being truthful or untruthful about what they say. The polygraph is an adjunct to, but never a substitute for, other methods of investigation. Other common objectives for polygraph examinations are determining the reliability of informants, eliminating suspects, and narrowing the scope of an investigation. Research on the accuracy of the polygraph varies, roughly from 64% (laboratory studies) to 98% ("real world" use). Such differences may in part be attributable to laboratory protocols in which one group is told to lie about a mock crime scene or other event and the other group tells the truth. When people are not in real jeopardy for lying they may not have the same physiological responses as those who are lying to avoid criminal culpability for a felony.

Polygraphs record indicators of a person's cardiovascular pattern and fluctuations, respiratory patterns and fluctuations, and changes in skin resistance or sweat on the fingertips. The three

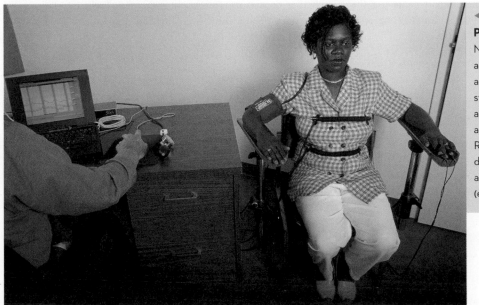

◄**FIGURE 5-14**
Polygraph examination
Note that a blood-pressure cuff is attached to the subject's right upper arm; two pneumograph tubes are stretched across the chest and abdomen; and metal plates are attached to the index and ring fingers. Readings from these sources are displayed on the examiner's screen at the left side of this photograph.
(©Anna Clopet/Getty Images)

most common findings by an examiner are no deception indicated, deception indicated, and inconclusive.

A supervisor's approval is required before an investigator can have a person examined by a polygraphist. The investigator is obliged to work with the examiner in a number of ways, such as:[109]

1. Providing the examiner with the information obtained in the investigation that supports and justifies the use of the polygraph.
2. Giving the polygraphist copies of incident, supplemental, and other relevant documents.
3. Calling attention to evidence that the subject does not yet know the police have.
4. Making available background information on the subject, including criminal history and possible motives.
5. Advising of statements made by the subject to victims and witnesses, as well as alibis provided.
6. Giving news articles and other general information about the case.
7. Helping the examiner arrange for a sign-language interpreter or translator, as necessary.
8. Not trying to plan the procedures to be used, which is the purview of the examiner.
9. Not interrogating the suspect just before the examination.
10. Ensuring that persons authorized to be with the subject are present (for example, attorneys, parents, or legal guardians).
11. Promptly advising the examiner if the subject is going to be late or has cancelled.

COMPUTER VOICE STRESS ANALYSIS

Computer Voice Stress Analysis (CVSA) was originally developed in 1988 by the National Institute for Truth Verification (NITV) and grew out of the Vietnam-era Psychological Stress Evaluator (PSE), which was used to differentiate between suspected Viet Cong and civilians. Around 1,600 police departments use the CVSA. The CVSA is small, easily portable, and, unlike the polygraph, does not require any attachments to the subject.

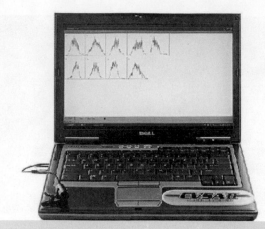

▲ **FIGURE 5-15**

Computerized voice stress analysis system (CVSA)

Newly developed and released second-generation computerized voice stress analysis system (CVSA II) displayed on a laptop computer. (©NITV Federal Services, LLC)

Basically, the CVSA notes microvariations in the audible and nonaudible portions of speech. As with the polygraph, reports of its accuracy have varied—for example, one laboratory study found that it was not significantly better than random chance, whereas NITV cited a number of studies showing much higher rates. Here, too, the earlier comments about the absence or presence of real jeopardy affecting the studies' outcomes apply.

The NITV spent many years and invested tremendous resources to develop an automated system to accurately quantify CVSA patterns with the goal of removing any subjectivity in evaluating CVSA charts. A new scoring algorithm has been developed and field tested in state and local law enforcement agencies across the country. The charts under this new CVSA II (Figure 5-15), which was released in January 2007, reflect whether deception is or is not indicated. Field evaluations are showing a 96% accuracy rate for the new system, with a false positive rate of less than 1%.[110]

KEY TERMS

admissions
Berghuis v. *Thompkins*
body language
Brown v. *Mississippi*
coerced-compliant
competency
computer Voice Stress
   Analysis (CVSA)
confession
delay-in-arraignment rule
detection of deception

eyewitness identification
free-and-voluntary rule
in-custody interrogation
interrogation
interviews
Maryland v. *Shatzer*
McNabb v. *United States*
Minnick v. *Mississippi*
Miranda v. *Arizona*
mirroring
pacifying behaviors

polygraph
proximity
rapport
Salinas v. *Texas*
special needs groups
suspect
victim
voluntary false confessions
witness
witness intimidation

1. What are the similarities and differences between interviews and interrogations?

2. What are the four commonly recognized objectives in the interrogation process?

3. What are the qualifications of interviewers and interrogators?

4. What should an interrogation room look like?

5. What steps should an investigator take in order to prepare for an interview or interrogation?

6. What are the major categories of people with disabilities that officers are most likely to encounter?

7. Why is eyewitness testimony so unreliable?

8. What are the forms that witness intimidation can take?

9. What can the police do to deter individuals who would be inclined to intimidate witnesses?

10. What are the advantages of using electronic recordings for interrogation?

11. There are two basic categories of people who tend to confess to crimes. Which two groups are these?

12. Three categories of false confessions were discussed. What are they?

13. What recommendations were made to reduce the possibility of false confessions?

14. What was the first notable incident of U.S. Supreme Court intervention into interrogation practices by nonfederal law enforcement officers?

15. What requirements are imposed on law enforcement personnel by *Miranda* v. *Arizona*?

16. What are the facts and the significance of the U.S. Supreme Court case involving *Maryland* v. *Shatzer* in 2010?

17. What is the significance of the U.S. Supreme Court decision in the case of *Berghuis* v. *Thompkins*?

18. What is the significance of the U.S. Supreme Court decision in the case of *Salinas* v. *Texas*?

19. In the discussion of detection of deception a number of body positions were discussed: namely; isoparaxis, flash frozen, rogatory position and the palms-down position. What is the significance of each of these positions as it relates to the detection of deception?

20. What types of measurements are employed by the polygraph and computer voice stress analysis to detect deception?

Much debate surrounds the fairness and effectiveness of eyewitness identification in police lineups. Go to *www.eyewitness.utep.edu/consult04A.html* and read the summary of the whitepaper regarding evaluating lineup fairness. What two aspects of lineup fairness should investigators consider? How similar to one another should the members of the lineup be?

▶ The tall woman is being interviewed by Los Angeles Officers. Earlier that day, a man shot and wounded a woman. Later that day, the man came to the apartment building where the tall woman's brother lived. Another shooting occurred, but the woman's brother was not the victim. Responding officers killed the shooter.

Assuming she is not a plainclothes officer or have some other valid role, should the woman wearing the sunglasses be allowed to hear the woman's statement?

(©Irfan Khan/Los Angeles Times/Getty Images)

6

FIELD NOTES AND REPORTING

CHAPTER OBJECTIVES

1. Define field notes.
2. State four examples of the importance of field notes.
3. Explain why NIBRS may be the future incident report form.
4. Define transgender and gender expression.
5. Explain why issuing a suspect BOLO must be done quickly.
6. State why short sentences should be used in incident reports.
7. Explain two problems caused by substandard reports.
8. Identify four things supervisors check when reviewing reports.
9. Identify a key difference in the disposition of handwritten and automated reports.
10. State the purpose of supplemental reports.
11. Explain why an incident report is unfounded.
12. Explain why an incident report would be assigned an inactive disposition.

Taking field notes, writing reports, and
conducting follow-up investigations are crucial skills for
law enforcement officers. Admittedly, these duties are
not ordinarily considered a pleasurable part of the job.
In addition to other reasons why taking field notes and
writing reports are important is that it is a way to develop a reputation as a conscientious
officer. Many other people, from those in your agency to judges, prosecutors, defense
attorneys, and members of the news media will have access to them and form an opinion
about your work. As a well-known saying goes: You don't get a second chance to make a
first impression. The following Chapter Outline reveals in detail the topics addressed in
this chapter.

It is a standard practice for investigators to gain as much information as possible when
arriving at the crime scene. The beginning of this process is taking a mental snapshot of
conditions at the scene. A key part of writing the report afterward is having made field
notes from which you can "paint the picture" for someone who wasn't at the scene. Even
facts and details that seem unnecessary at first may later prove to be highly valuable to an
investigation.

THE IMPORTANCE OF FIELD NOTES

Making field notes is a skill officers must master to produce
quality reports because they are the foundation on which much
of an incident report rests. This section uses three components
to provide a good understanding of field notes: (1) the importance of field notes, (2) basic investigative questions, and (3)
using information from body-worn cameras and audio recorders
to help write incident reports.

Field notes are the shorthand written record made by a police
officer from the time he or she arrives at the scene until the
assignment is completed (Figure 6-1). Field notes are more reliable than an officer's memory. It is probably easy to remember
what you had for breakfast this morning, but what about your
lunch five months ago?[1]

Detailed field notes compensate for the fact that crime
scenes can be chaotic: several people may be speaking to officers
at once, emotions of victims and witnesses may be running high,
combatants may have to be separated, protection of the crime
scene demands attention, emergency technicians may need
some direction, supervisors may arrive with questions. In short,
many things can simultaneously compete for our attention and
we don't have perfect memories. If officers consistently rely on
their memories, there is a serious risk that they will introduce

▲ **FIGURE 6-1**

**Homicide investigators sharing information from their
field notes**

These investigators have just finished interviewing neighbor
residents in an apartment building where a homicide
occurred. The investigators are discussing the information
gleaned from their interviews. One investigator is conferring
on a cell phone with a third colleague in an effort to join the
pieces of the event into a whole story. (©James D. DeCamp/
Columbus Dispatch)

CHAPTER OUTLINE

misinformation into the incident report. Among the ills that can result are false arrest suits and wasted investigative effort.

Moreover, there is some question about whether officers are getting all the relevant information from their notes into incident reports (see Box 6-1).

Field notes serve several important purposes:

1. They are *the foundation for writing the incident report* because field notes are its primary source of information. The terms "incident report" and "offense report" are often used synonymously. An **incident report** is the permanent record of what a police officer learns through his or her senses and does from the time of arrival to the time of departure from a scene that requires one to be initiated.

2. Officers may respond to several calls before they have time to write a report. *Even in a short period of time some important details may be forgotten.* However, detailed field notes are reliable and can help ensure that important details are not left out of a report.

   The first responding officer writes the incident report, relying to a significant degree on information in the field notes. Other officers who also respond to the same call may have done something that is also important to an investigation and will write **supplemental reports**, which add pertinent information to the incident report file. Whether writing incident or supplemental reports, well-written, detailed field notes are the wellspring of strong reports.

3. *Police field notes and reports are filled with hearsay evidence and would ordinarily not be admissible in court except for one of the exceptions to the hearsay rule:* they are business records that are regularly prepared in the course of doing police work.

4. *Officers can refer to field notes to refresh their recollection when testifying in court.*

5. *They establish that the elements of a specific crime occurred.*

6. *Strong field notes demonstrate that a thorough investigation was conducted.*

7. *They can document inconsistent statements made by those at the scene.*

8. *Field notes can be used to defend the accuracy and integrity of the incident report* by showing a link between the field notes and the content of the report.

9. *They contribute to the community perception that the department has well-trained officers.* Conversely, when officers' field notes and the corresponding incident reports fail to include facts that would exculpate or tend to prove a suspect in custody did not commit the crime, officers run a significant risk of impeachment, having their credibility discredited.

10. *Field notes can ensure that evidence will be admitted* because its presence at the scene is documented.

Additionally, field notes generate important investigative information, such as:

1. Establish the location of the event and an indication of when it occurred (Figure 6-2).

2. Document scene conditions answer questions such as: Where was the victim's body found? Is the blood wet/drying/hard/cracked? Was the victim tortured? Is the body decomposing or, if found outside, has it been subject to animal predation? Was the body staged in some way?

   Serial Killer, Danny Harold Rolling (the Gainesville Ripper) was 37 years old when he saw the movie the *Exorcist* in 1990. That same day he started murdering students. When it was over, four University of Florida students and one at nearby Santa Fe Community College were dead (Figure 6-3). Some victims were raped, at least one after she was dead; the bodies were mutilated; some body parts were removed; and at least one crime scene was staged. One of the victims was positioned as if sitting, but Rolling placed her severed head on a shelf across the room. In 2006, Rolling was executed by lethal injection in Florida.

   Other particulars of the scene are also important to note, for example, which lights were on; what odors were present; the appearance that a struggle occurred; and if

BOX 6-1 | GETTING INFORMATION FROM FIELD NOTES INTO INCIDENT REPORTS

A study with a small sample size examined officers' field notes from witness interviews with the information that appeared in their reports. They accurately transferred 94% of the information from their notes to their reports. However, they *failed to include* 40% of crime-relevant information. A replication study with a large, multijurisdictional sample size has not yet been done.[2]

◄**FIGURE 6-2**
A Syracuse (NY) patrol car responding to a call. Sometimes officers are assigned to ride in areas with which they are not familiar. These two officers appear to be trying to establish where the complainant is located.
(©S. Schild/Syracuse Newspapers/The Image Works)

◄**FIGURE 6-3**
Panel on Gainesville, Florida, wall in 2009 commemorating the five 1990 victims of serial killer, Danny Harold Rolling. (©Pat Canova/Alamy)

ransacked by an offender, whether the premises were searched in a systematic or disorganized manner. Although unusual, the suspect may have left a message, placed symbols or wrote on the victim's body, walls, or other surfaces.

There are notable examples of writing at crime scenes. For example, in 1969, followers of cult-leader Charles Manson brutally murdered actress Sharon Tate and three others in a Los Angeles home. Tate was to have given birth two weeks later. One of the killers wrote "Pigs" on the home's front door.

The next night, a group personally led by Manson murdered Leon and Rosemary LaBianca in their home. "War" was carved into Leon's stomach, "Death to Pigs" was inscribed on a wall in blood, and "Helter Skelter" was written on the refrigerator. Helter Skelter was Manson's

prophecy that a race war was coming during which blacks would eradicate all white people, except for Manson and his followers, who would repopulate the world. The murders were committed to help get the war started. The break in the case came when a biker gang member told police Manson had bragged to him about the murders, including details withheld from the news media. Perhaps the most compelling written message was left at a Chicago crime scene by a serial murderer in 1946 who was eventually arrested and convicted for his crimes (Figure 6-4).

3. Provide a chronology of what the responding officer did while present at the scene, for example, separated combatants, called for an ambulance, and requested a supervisor to authorize the presence of crime scene unit and detective at the scene.

▶ **FIGURE 6-4**
A 17-year-old University of Chicago student horrifically killed three people, including a 6-year old girl whose body was dismembered and parts of it left around the neighborhood. On one victim's wall he wrote the message in lipstick seen above "For heavens sake catch me before I kill more I cannot control myself." The so-called Lipstick Killer died in 2012 after 65 years in an Illinois prison. (©Jonathan Kirn/Corbis/Getty Images)

4. Identify victims, witnesses, persons of interest, and suspects at the scene.

5. Indicate whether persons left the scene, what period they were there, what did they do while there, what is their relationship to the suspect or victim, did they leave or remove anything, what did they do or say while there, and who they are.

6. Establish what people were doing when the first officer arrived.

7. Record dying declarations, spontaneous, and other statements made by persons at the scene that have evidentiary value.

8. Will eliminate the need for the officer writing the incident report to re-contact victims and witnesses. Sometimes, they get annoyed and even angry when re-contacted by an officer who didn't ask enough questions or take good field notes when he or she talked to them the first time and doesn't have enough information to complete the report. Such mistakes are uncommon, but one embarrassment quickly stimulates better performance. However, it can leave a bad impression of the officer and the department. Comments such as "Weren't you listening to me?" or "You couldn't be very interested in my case, or you would have asked about this when you talked to me the first time" can be avoided.

Follow-up investigators are often required by departmental policy to make at least one recontact of victims. Sometimes they have another reason to do so: shortcomings in the incident report.

GUIDELINES FOR NOTE-TAKING

Employing agencies often provide officers with forms on which to make field notes. If not, officers should use a loose-leaf notebook with sufficient blank pages. Entries should be made in black ink and never with a pencil. Notes from two different cases should never be on the same page, and dates/times/case identification data should be placed on each page of the notes. Each page of notes pertaining to a different case should be numbered starting with a notation of "1 of 5 pages" or "1x5pp" so you can be sure no pages are missing. If officers maintain their own notes, periodically they should be removed, placed in a larger envelope, sealed, and the range of dates and case numbers they cover.

Although notes are typically made with paper and pen, they can also be made on smartphones, tablets, small laptops, or recorded on audio or body-worn cameras (BWCs). However, some law enforcement agencies do not allow officers to view the BWC recordings before writing an incident report, a matter discussed later in this chapter. While smartphones can also be used to write incident reports, their smaller keypads will be a challenge for some officers. The advantage of using paper and pen to make notes is you can be sure there won't be any "technological glitches," such as "file corrupted" or "file not readable."

Regardless of how an officer makes notes, the following are important guidelines:

1. Separate witnesses from each other to avoid contamination of recall, and interview them individually.

2. Identify the emotional or other state of a person being interviewed. To illustrate, an estimated 7% of police contacts in jurisdictions of 100,000 or more people involve emotionally disturbed persons (Figure 6-5).[3] A three-city study revealed 92% of the officers had contact with a mentally disturbed person in the last month.[4] Contacts between the police and the mentally ill can be dangerous to both parties, and approximately 50% of the officers

◄FIGURE 6-5
Des Moines, Iowa, police officer talking to mentally ill man to determine what assistance he needs.
In 2014, nationally three officers were killed by mentally ill persons, and from all causes nationally, 9 assaults per 100 officers were committed by the mentally ill. (©Mikael Karlsson/Alamy)

involved in a study generally didn't feel comfortable dealing with the mentally ill.[5] Some law enforcement agencies have trained officers on duty to help with such encounters, and agencies usually have a protocol for dealing with these and related situations, including getting assistance.

3. Do not reveal your emotions, impatience, or disbelief when conducting an interview. These things have high potential to create a barrier between you and a victim and are likely to get in the way of you doing a good job. Victims may be angry because you weren't there sooner, and they may speak slowly because they are drunk, using drugs, confused, old, have reduced ability, are injured, in shock, or are trying to form a coherent response. Maintain your interest even if victims relate an incident that seems improbable or incredulous to you. Sometimes the incredulous is true, and at other times it will take some skillful questioning to ferret out what happened. Sometimes victims die before any productive questioning is possible. In Chapter 14, "Burglary," there is information about a high-rise burglar who committed over 100 burglaries. Police were baffled about how the burglaries were committed. Ultimately they discovered an incredulous truth: the burglar, without any equipment, free-climbed as many as 30 stories to commit the offenses.

QUICK FACTS

The Man in the Alley

An officer walking a skid row beat found a badly beaten man in an alley who was passing in and out of consciousness. Reeking of alcohol, the man moaned and said "the bastards" and gave incoherent or seemingly unrelated responses to the officer. The man didn't have a watch, wallet, or any money. Taken to a nearby emergency room he died a few hours later. He was quickly identified by fingerprints. Despite significant efforts to find where he had been before entering the alley, who he had been seen with, who he may have left a bar or other place with, who his associates were, and other details, the case was never cleared.

4. Use nonverbal cues to encourage the person to continue speaking. Cues, such as nodding, leaning slightly forward, and good eye contact lets the person know you are interested and "with them."

5. If a speaker loses focus or verbally is wandering, bring him or her back to the topic pleasantly by using such phrases as "Can we go back to when you met him?" or "Were you finished talking about when you found the body?"

6. Record exact words, phrases, or sentences whenever possible. To illustrate, the words spoken by rapists to a victim may be part of their modus operandi or method of operation. The perpetrator's language may also suggest a familiarity with an occupation, such as locksmith or military service.

7. Make sure you have all victim and witness locator information, and read it back and have them correct or verify it.

8. Develop a shorthand and use it consistently, for example, V: Husb V hr 2x mouth w fist 35 mins ago, imed left n hs car. A victim rarely has that much information in a single sentence. Instead, the details come out in bits and spurts, often as you ask questions. This means you have to assemble the story. The takeaway: Don't write the information into the incident report as though it were a single direct quote.

9. It is unsurprising that people lie to the police. As street experience accumulates it often becomes easier to detect those lies, and for many it is an accumulated skill. Some lies are betrayed by physical evidence or careful questioning.

10. Treat all people with dignity and respect regardless of their social status, race, religion, country of origin, immigration status, sexual orientation, skin color, life style, or other variable, including a crime such as a child molestation. If officers reveal their personal judgment about people's life styles, the crime committed, or other factors, they have lost the focus on the job at hand: getting as much information as is possible under the circumstances.

NOTE-TAKING AND INCIDENT REPORTS: BODY-WORN CAMERAS, AUDIO RECORDERS, AND PUBLIC ONLINE REPORTING SYSTEMS

Police officers wearing audio recorders is an accepted practice. Although there are many calls for officers to use body-worn cameras (BWCs) and solid reasons to do so, some controversy within police circles attends how such recordings can be used. Officers can listen to audio recorders to help write an incident report, but where BWCs are used, law enforcement policies are divided on whether the recordings from them can be used for the same purpose. This section addresses these and related issues, as well as recognizing the growing number of law enforcement agencies that allow the public to report certain crimes online.

BODY-WORN CAMERAS

In 2013, a national survey of local law enforcement agencies established that 32% of them used BWCs (Figure 6-6),[6] which provide both digital and audio recordings.

Beginning in 2014, there were a series of events that began in Ferguson, MO, that involved the deaths of African American men while in contact with police officers. Those events resulted in demonstrations, the Black Lives Matter movement gained momentum, there was significant national and international news media scrutiny of policing, and numerous recommendations were made for law enforcement agencies to use BWCs to establish greater accountability in use of force incidents.

A 2015 report showed that in large cities and counties only 19% had fully implemented BWC programs, although 77% indicated they were moving toward them.[7] However, nearly 70% of those respondents said their information technology infrastructure was presently inadequate to support BWC use.[8] There appears to be a long way to go before there is substantial use of BWCs.

Among the reasons to use BWCs are: (1) the "third eye" of the camera appears to encourage officers and members of the public to be more cordial toward each other; (2) frivolous complaints and suits against the police are reduced; (3) some recordings will provide important evidence. In 2016, a Milwaukee police officer's BWC recorded that the man the officer shot and killed was pointing a gun at officers. Both men were African

▲ **FIGURE 6-6 BWC**
A Rialto, CA, Police Department Sergeant wearing a BWC mounted on his sunglasses that records video and audio while he speaks with a felony suspect. BWCs are also commonly worn roughly chest high. (©Jonathan Alcorn/ZumaPress.com/Alamy)

Americans; (4) occasionally, the recordings will provide good material for training recruits; (5) officers who seriously misbehave can be separated from the service if BWC recordings may be used in administrative hearings; (6) police litigation costs are reduced because recordings can convince law enforcement agencies and their attorneys to accurately gauge whether a suit should be settled or brought to trial; and (7) public confidence in the police is stimulated.

As of mid-2016, at least 11 states have passed laws regulating some aspect of BWC use, for example, how data is stored, who has access to the data, and prohibiting the use of facial recognition software on the data collected.[9] However, most states have not yet enacted any BWC legislation. Where the concern is spoken to in law enforcement policies, the data recorded is not reviewed to identify misbehavior by police officers.

Releasing BWC recordings is consistent with calls to make the police more transparent. However, some law enforcement agencies and civil liberties advocates have resisted making such data readily available on several grounds: (1) the cost of responding to open records requests would be considerable; (2) the release of videos can result in events being deliberately or accidentally misinterpreted, with the accompanying potential for dangerous consequences; (3) there are concerns about the privacy rights of people being recorded, for example, assume a couple is arguing about infidelities when the police arrive at a domestic disturbance call. The couple would certainly not want that information to become public knowledge; and (4) such recordings may be part of an active investigation and releasing information could compromise it.

Usually by policy, law enforcement officers have guidance about when their BWCs may or must be turned on or off. "Off conditions" include during lineups, when recording would violate medical patient privacy rights, during conversations with confidential informants, personal/casual conversations, administrative

BOX 6-2 | INTERPRETATION OF BWC RECORDINGS

Sommers argues that despite the seeming objectivity of video recordings such footage remains susceptible to misinterpretation by biased observers. In a study of mock grand juries, which viewed actual police footage, Sommers concluded that the prior attitudes of observers toward police officers colored their interpretation of the events viewed. Study participants who identified strongly with the police were more confident in their decisions

after viewing the video. However, those who identified weakly with the police did not find the recordings so persuading. The study concluded that video evidence did not outperform the non-video evidence presented to participants. A key question remains unanswered: Would actual grand jury members behave consistent with the study results?[10]

---

meetings, and when taking statements from victims and witnesses. Officers are not to make narrations to explain what BWCs are recording. At the end of each shift, officers with BWCs transfer their data to a secure site, where it is treated as evidence. Police policies usually exempt plainclothes officers from using BWCs because it defeats the purpose of being out-of-uniform; they may be talking to confidential informants, people may be reluctant to speak if they are being recorded, and it may create discovery rights that would hamper investigative progress.

On the subject of whether to allow officers to access their own BWC videos, to make notes or before they write the corresponding reports, agencies fall into two groups:

1. The "no access" agencies believe viewing a video may taint an officer's recollection by reminding the officer of forgotten actions that can be "explained away" in a report and/or work to the disadvantage of a suspect. Police officers are concerned that the no-access policy could result in their being disciplined or terminated for flawed recollections.

2. The "access" departments recognize that (a) the human field of vision covers 180 degrees, (b) the human brain has a field of attention of 50–60 degrees, and (c) under conditions of stress this field narrows to one-half of a degree.[11] Stress also induces sound and time distortions that can prevent the brain from remembering all the stimuli in an event. Allowing an officer access to his or her videos increases the accuracy of notes and reports and reduces the likelihood that an officer's testimony and report will be discredited in court because of disparities with the actual recording of the situation. This protects both the officer's and the department's reputations.

Some issues, such as if officers can review their own recordings before writing reports and the grounds upon which any releases of recordings can be made, are still being struggled with by law enforcement agencies. Some of their own local legislative bodies and state assemblies have already weighed in on this matter, and it bears monitoring to see if there is a clear trend one way or another. In the interim, police executives would do well to make sure that their policy on BWCs gets significant attention to ensure that no rights are violated by their use, that the recordings are treated in a manner that would allow their

use in criminal trials, and the access/no access position is thoughtfully determined. Bakardjiev argues that weak BWC policies will result in more legal challenges to their uses.[12]

AUDIO RECORDERS

Digital audio recorders (DARs) using flash technology are at the cutting edge of this technology. For departments that don't presently make any type of recording, can't afford BWCs, and want to be responsive to calls for greater transparency, DARs may offer a good entry point to do so. Where DARs are used, police policies roughly parallel the use of BWC policies. It is estimated that roughly 25 percent of local law enforcement agencies use some type of belt-worn audio recorders.

Generally, police policies require uniformed officers to wear DARs, while their use by plainclothes personnel is optional. Any recordings made are downloaded and retained as evidence. Where enabled, the recordings are put on the officers' mobile computers and automatically transferred to a departmental server when the vehicle is within range. Retention of recordings may be subject both to records management policies and legal requirements. Unless otherwise required to maintain them, policies commonly allow the recordings to be purged after 6 months to 2 years.

Police policies commonly allow an officer to review DARs to prepare notes, write a report, or for other department-approved reasons, for example, refresh recollection before testifying. If multiple officers are involved in a recorded event, departmental polices may allow each one to listen to the other officers' DARs.

Some state laws prohibit the surreptitious recording of a conversation when any party to it has a reasonable belief it is private. In those states, officers must obtain the consent of all parties to the conversation before activating a DAR. Two usual exceptions to this are interrogations and when questioning a person suspected of a violation of law.

Public Online Reporting Systems

In December 2007, a Great Recession began, strangling tax revenues for local and state governments. This recession was declared over in June 2009, although many jurisdictions did not agree with that assessment. The Great Recession resulted in many law enforcement agencies selling off their assets, including fixed wing and rotary aircraft, harbor patrol boats, horses, and cars; civilians were hired for "inside jobs" because they were cheaper than using sworn personnel in them; volunteer programs were substantially expanded and volunteers often performed important tasks, for example, legal research and maintaining computer systems; staffing levels were cut, and officers who remained after the cuts often had to take one or more mandatory furloughs annually, often of a specified number of days, for example, 5–10 days. Some cities closed their police departments and contracted with another jurisdiction for law enforcement services, and other local government units simply went bankrupt. In Stockton, CA, police staffing was so low that during some hours of the day the department could only respond to crimes in progress.

Technology became an important means of coping with the deep staff cuts of the Great Recession. Although online incident reporting systems for citizens got attention from about 2002, their use was not widespread. However, during and after the Great Recession such systems proliferated because it was an important strategy of leveraging resources to create four important advantages: (1) the public could almost instantly report many types of crimes 7 days a week, 24 hours a day without waiting for an officer to respond, (2) the time of officers was preserved to provide other services, (3) community participation in policing would be enhanced, and (4) online reporting system are a cost-effective alternative to officers answering all calls for service while maintaining quality service to the public.

The online reporting systems normally employ a series of "qualifying questions" (Figure 6-7) for example, to make sure the crime was committed in the jurisdiction in which the citizen seeks to make a report. The reports can be made on a tablet, computer, or smartphone, and citizens can immediately make a copy of the report.

Although here and there portions of cuts in police staffing have been restored, technology will remain as an important driver of police productivity. In the wake of the cuts many citizens have said, "Can we really afford the police department we used to have?" In this regard, the recovery of policing from the Great Recession is not yet been fully written.

It is important to take only the notes pertaining to the case about which you are testifying into the courtroom. The defendant's attorney can inspect your notes. Bringing in your field notes book with multiple cases in it opens you to more questions. For example, the attorney may state, "You seem to have taken many more notes about my client's case than any other one. Are you prejudiced against her?"

BOX 6-3 | NEW JERSEY SUPREME COURT RULES ON FIELD NOTES

In 2013, New Jersey's Supreme Court ruled in *State* v. *Samander V. Dabas* that field notes cannot be destroyed and are subject to discovery by attorneys. In other states there may be legislative enactments that affect the disposition of field notes. Make sure you understand your department's policy on this subject.

▶ **FIGURE 6-7**

An online screening questionnaire for members of the public to use to determine if their case can be reported online. (Source: San Jose Police Department, 2016)

☐ Yes	☐ No	Is this an emergency? (If yes, please call 911 immediately)
☐ Yes	☐ No	Are you reporting a lost or stolen firearm?
☐ Yes	☐ No	Do you have in your possession, actual physical evidence of this crime such as video or digital evidence?
☐ Yes	☐ No	Do you believe you are the victim of a crime because of your race, religion, sexual orientation, handicap, ethnicity or national origin?
☐ Yes	☐ No	Did the incident occur on a State highway or freeway?

If you answered NO to all the questions in this section, please continue.

NOTE: Filing a false police report is a crime! Every person who knowingly makes a false report is guilty of a misdemeanor per 148.5 (a) of the California Penal Code.

☐ Yes	☐ No	Do you understand that filing a false police report is a crime?
☐ Yes	☐ No	Did the incident occur within the San Jose city limits?
☐ Yes	☐ No	Are you eighteen (18) years of age or older?
☐ Yes	☐ No	Are you the victim of the crime you are reporting?
☐ Yes	☐ No	Do you have an email address? (*A valid return email address is required in order to file an online report.*)

If you answered Yes to all the questions in this section, please click the Submit button below.

SIX BASIC INVESTIGATIVE QUESTIONS

To gather needed information, first-responding officers and follow-up investigators should phrase all questions beginning with the six interrogatories—who, what, where, when, how, and why. Although no single set of questions can meet the investigative needs in all types of crime, following this format should provide the needed information for the officer/investigator to understand the chronological order of events as they occurred and to enable the preparation of a well-written and thorough incident report. Here are some examples of typical questions:

1. **Who**
   —was the victim?
   —discovered the crime?
   —reported the crime?
   —took the victim to his or her present location?
   —does the suspect associate with?
   —was last seen with the victim?
   —last saw the victim?
   —may be with the suspect when he or she is arrested?
   —are the witnesses connected with or related to?
   —had a motive and the means of committing the crime?
   —completed the crime scene entry and other logs?
   —processed the scene?
   —took what evidence where?
   —else may have heard, smelled, touched, or seen anything of investigative value?

2. **What**
   —crime was committed?
   —actions did the suspect take?
   —methods did the suspect use?
   —do witnesses know about the crime?
   —evidence is there?
   —tools or weapons were used?
   —actions did you take?
   —further action is needed?
   —information may victims and witnesses be withholding?
   —does the victim claim was stolen?
   —parts of the victim's account of the event match that of any witnesses, the appearance of the scene, and the physical evidence?
   —information (and evidence of what types) do you need to clear the crime?
   —knowledge, skills, or strength was needed?
   —other units or agencies are involved or need to be notified?
   —is the case about?
   —are the potential charges?
   —information does the prosecutor need to file formal charges or seek a grand jury indictment?
   —are the elements of the offense?
   —does the prosecutor need to prove the case?

3. **Where**
   —was the crime discovered?
   —was the crime committed?
   —were any tools, evidence, or recovered property found?
   —was the victim when the crime was committed?
   —is the victim now?
   —were the witnesses?
   —did the suspect go?
   —does the suspect frequent, live, and work?
   —is the suspect now?
   —was the suspect arrested?
   —was the evidence marked?
   —is the evidence stored?
   —might other witnesses be located?

4. **When**
   —were you dispatched, and when did you arrive?
   —was the crime discovered?
   —was the crime committed?
   —was the victim last seen?
   —did help arrive, and what type was it?
   —was the suspect arrested?
   —did the suspect decide to commit the crime?

5. **How**
   —was the crime committed?
   —did the suspect get to and from the scene?
   —did the suspect get the information needed to commit the crime?
   —were tools and weapons obtained?
   —was the arrest made?
   —much injury was done to the victim?
   —much damage was there to any premises involved?
   —much money was taken, and what type of valuables?
   —difficult was it to carry off the property that was stolen?
   —is the suspect described by the victim and witnesses?
   —closely do the descriptions of victims and witnesses match and diverge?

6. **Why**
   —was the crime committed?
   —were particular tools or weapons used?
   —was the crime reported?
   —was there a delay in reporting the crime?
   —were the victim or witnesses reluctant to talk?
   —were the victim or witnesses so quick to identify the suspect?
   —am I uncomfortable with the victim's account and description of the suspect?

INCIDENT REPORTS

Despite the fact that **incident/offense reports** are a crucial source of investigative information, writing them is often not a popular duty. However, officers can contribute to the effectiveness of their agencies by consistently doing a good job writing incident reports. Moreover, it gives officers an opportunity to showcase their abilities. A variety of people inside and outside of an officer's department read the reports, and their impressions of reports becomes part of the reputation an officer may unknowingly be creating.

An incident report must tell a story. It must be written in such a manner that someone reading that report can understand what happened and can know the answers to the questions who, what, where, when, how, and why. Along with his or her memory, an officer/investigator must use the field notes taken to tell the story of the events. There are two indispensable elements of reports: (1) accuracy and (2) clear communication of the meaning that the writer intended.

More than a few excellent investigations have been wasted by an officer's failure to fully document what was done and not done. The case history that follows indicates the importance of recording all aspects of an investigation:

A burglary in progress was reported at a one-story doctor's office. As two officers moved to cover the building, a suspect was seen leaping from an office window carrying a small flight bag. The suspect ran from the scene, followed by one of the officers. He attempted to scale a fence. In the ensuing struggle, the suspect fell on the far side of the fence, breaking his arm. During treatment at a hospital, the suspect told the officer, in front of medical personnel, that he was going to claim his arm was broken by the officer when he questioned him. He further indicated this would be an attempt to discredit the police, as he had only recently been released from the state prison and feared that such an immediate second violation would cause the court to invoke a stringent sentence upon conviction. Because many arrested people state that they are going to claim the police violated their civil rights, the officer regarded it as little more than a commonplace occurrence. The suspect's remarks and the identity of the persons witnessing them were included in the report as a matter of thoroughness. Subsequently, when the FBI investigated the matter of a possible violation of the suspect's rights, the allegation was easily refuted by corroborating statements from the medical personnel identified in the officer's report.

A well-prepared incident report based on a thorough investigation of an offense can promote the rapid apprehension of the suspect, thus preventing further crimes and making the recovery of property more likely. The report also serves as the official memory of the department so that anyone who needs access to the file after the reporting officer or investigator is no longer available, can make sense of the report and the event.

Incident reports serve important operational and administrative purposes. When their data are combined, useful crime analysis reports can be produced, personnel assignments in the department can be properly aligned with the actual workloads, and geographic information system (GIS) data can produce informative maps showing, for example, where robberies with certain types of characteristics are being committed.

FORMATS FOR INCIDENT REPORTS

Although the exact layout for incident reports varies from one jurisdiction to another, all incident report forms have a "face" with blank spaces that must be filled and boxes that need to be checked in by the officer conducting the preliminary investigation. He or she enters basic case information in the blanks, such as information about the type of crime committed; the complainant, victim, witnesses, and offenders; and other details.

NIBRS

During the late 1920s, the International Association of Chiefs of Police (IACP) developed a system to collect crime statistics.[13] In 1930, the Congress authorized the U.S. Attorney General to collect crime data.[14] This task was assigned to the FBI and the IACP system became the foundation of the federal Uniform Crime Reporting (UCR) Program. In the fall of each year, the FBI releases crime data for the previous calendar year.

By the 1980s, agencies and researchers were asking for more detailed crime data. In response, during 1985, a FBI report provided the blueprint for a redesign of the UCR Program.[15] This led to the National Incident-Based Reporting System (NIBRS).[16] Presently, 33 states are certified to submit NIBRS data.[17] Seventeen states are making measurable progress towards NIBRS certification.[18] In 2015, more than 16,000 law enforcement agencies participated in the NIBRS program.[19] The goal is to have NIBRS fully implemented by January 1, 2021. If achieved, NIBRS will replace the Uniform Crime Reporting Program and be of great value to researchers and crime analysts.

GENERATING REPORTS

Some 93% of local police officers have computer access in their cars, giving them the capability to write incident reports in their cars (Figure 6-8).[20] Because the majority of police officers work in large departments, the data can be misinterpreted: It does not mean that 93% of all police departments have this capacity. Instead, it reveals that in some number of smaller departments there are still officers working without the advantages of a terminal/computer in their cars. Those without an in-car computer handwrite or use a typewriter or a dictation system.

QUICK FACTS

eCitations

A growing number of law enforcement agencies are using electronically generated citations or eCitations. When an officer stops a speeding car and the operator presents a driver's license, the officer's smart handheld device reads the barcode on the back, the device automatically fills in the appropriate spaces in the citation,

◄FIGURE 6-8
Mobile computer terminal in a law enforcement vehicle
The officer in this car has been dispatched to a domestic disturbance. She is in that 93% of officers who can write reports on a computer in their cars. (©The Washington Post/Getty Images)

the officer makes a few very short entries, and the citation with the court date can be printed in the officer's car or by the handheld device. Estimates for the time saved by using eCitations differ. Manufacturers' claim that preparing handwritten citations takes 18–20 minutes and eCitations can reduce that time to 4–5 minutes. Agencies using eCitations tend to estimate the reduction is from 16 minutes to 8 minutes. Any time saved is an efficiency gain that can be redirected for other purposes, such as random or directed patrol, traffic enforcement, working special assignments, monitoring hot spots, checking vacation watches, community policing meetings, gathering intelligence, and other activities.

Although the capabilities of an in-car computer vary, those advantages often include being able to check driver and criminal histories, outstanding warrants, vehicle registrations and stolen cars, and submit incident reports electronically to supervisors. Some agencies are conducting experiments to determine if iPhones, tablets or small laptops can replace existing larger and more expensive in-car computers (Figure 6-9). An often-quoted figure is that on average handwritten reports take 30–45 minutes depending on its complexity and computer-generated reports take roughly half of that.

COMMON ELEMENTS OF INCIDENT REPORTS

Incident-report contents vary, ranging from the essential data in a basic incident report to the more extensive information in an NIBRS-compliant report. However, certain elements are common to most reports. The importance of obtaining as much detailed and complete information as possible for inclusion in the incident report cannot be over emphasized.

Name

The full names of complainants, witnesses, and other parties must always be obtained. In the recording of proper names, the first time an individual is referred to in a report the sequence of names should be last, first, middle. When a person mentioned in the report is commonly known to acquaintances by some name other than the proper name or an apparent derivation, the nickname should also be provided. The full names and badge or identification numbers of other officers/investigators should be reported, including those from other agencies who participated in the investigation. The identity of a person and the spelling of his or her name should always be confirmed by a government-issued identity card with a picture.

▲ **FIGURE 6-9**
A Seattle police officer uses an iPhone for a report while working in a park in downtown Seattle, Wednesday, March 3. (©Elaine Thompson/AP Images)

Gender, Race/Ethnicity, and LGBT Persons

On incident reports, gender/sex is recorded as "M" (male) of "F" (female). While this remains true, the prominence of the lesbian, gay, bisexual, and transgender (LGBT) community has created the need for law enforcement agencies to create polices for interacting with such individuals to get to whether a "M" or "F" is going to be indicated on the report. Some groups have added a Q after LGBT, which stands for queer or questioning one's sexual identity (Figure 6-10).

Some members of minority populations have a negative opinion of the police. Regardless of which minority population harbors such opinions, officers must work to gain their trust because: (1) crimes within those populations are typically underreported; (2) the lack of trust reduces the flow of information to policing, and (3) unreported and unsolved crimes contribute to offenders going unprosecuted and having the opportunity to victimize more people.[21]

During their shifts, officers have contact with a range of people with varying outwardly manifested characteristics. Others have illnesses, occupations, life styles, and other variables, such as gender, that might not be so immediately apparent. In compiling field notes and completing incident reports, a record of the complainant's or victim's gender is made. However, in LGBT communities, with an estimated 9.5 million members,[22] genders may not be what they appear to be and victims may not wish to divulge their actual genders. Twenty-one percent of LGBT community members perceived a variety of police hostility toward them[23] and are victims of 18% of all reported, sexual orientation hate crimes.[24]

Transgender is an umbrella term for people whose *gender identity* (a person's internal sense of being male, female, or something else, which is not necessarily visible to others) and *gender expression* (how people represent or express their gender identity to others, often through behavior, clothing, hair styles, voice, or body characteristics) is inconsistent or different from the attributes typically associated with their assigned sex at birth. Such persons may be preoperation, postoperation, or elect not to have an operation. Broadly, members of the transgender community include gay, lesbian, bisexual, transgender, and intersex persons.

Often, transgender people will attempt to align their gender identity and expression. However, for some transgender people gender identity and expression may be more complex than the male–female dichotomy. Some people whose gender identity and expression fall outside that dichotomy may self-describe as "genderqueers," which should only be used after they have self-identified as such or given permission to be described as such. Some Native American tribes in North America recognize several genders. In the last 30 years, the use of "two-spirit" has been used by some Native Americans to describe or self-describe the combining of male and female qualities within a person and to avoid any of the labels associated with transgender people.

The following points are drawn from a nonscientific sampling of recently developed (2013–2016) police policies regarding interactions with LGBT people and recording gender in notes and reports:

1. As with members of other groups of people with whom officers have contact, professionalism and courtesy must be consistently displayed.
2. The first names of individuals with whom officers have field contact should not be used, unless invited. Instead the appropriate Mr., Mrs., Miss, or other form of respectful address should be used, for example, by using the appropriate pronoun, he or she.
3. Interact in a manner appropriate to peoples' gender or gender expression, as preferred by them.

▶ **FIGURE 6-10**

Members of the transgender community and their supporters march together in Northampton, MA. (©Custom Life Science Images/Alamy)

Transgender People, Lexicon, and Derogatory Terms

The terms "transgender" or "transgender people/persons" are not pejoratives, but "transgenders" and "transgendered" are. A transgender person may be offended by being called a "transsexual." "Cross-dressing" as a gender expression has replaced the use of "transvestite." Substitute "transition" for any reference to preop, postop, or sex-change surgery. Transition often occurs in stages and may not involve surgery. Likewise, use assigned/recorded/designated birth gender versus "born a man" or a kindred term, for example, biologically born a woman. Without exhausting other offensive labels and phrases, the following should not be used: queer, she-male, tranny, masquerading, and "pretending to be."

4. Use pronouns appropriate to an individual's preferred gender or gender expression. For those self-identifying as a female, "she, her, hers," and for those self-identifying as a male, "he, him, his".

5. Using demeaning references of any type to an individual's language, appearance, dress, behavior, or other factors is forbidden.

6. A LGBT individual may have an unofficial adopted name that is used for self-reference and may be known to others by that name. If requested, address the individual based on this adopted name, even if different from that on a government-issued identification.

7. Being or appearing to be a LGBT person is never in and of itself sufficient cause to stop, search, or arrest an individual or inquire about their sexuality.

8. On citations, arrest cards, reports, and other official departmental documentation, the individual's identity on their most recent government-issued identification shall be used and their proffered self-identification shall be included as "AKA" or "Also Known As." Some LGBT persons may have legally changed their names, and while there may be an inconsistency between an officer's perception of some aspect of how a person's gender expresses and the data on a valid government-issued identity card, that card should be relied upon.

9. If an individual's identity cannot otherwise be established and an arrest is required, then their adopted name should be used as an AKA until identity can be conclusively established. It doesn't take an identity to be arrested, but it takes one to get out of jail.

10. Arrested individuals, as is the case with other arrested persons, may be asked to remove jewelry, wigs, prosthetics, or cosmetic items.

11. Searches may not be made for the sole purpose of establishing gender nor may searches be more intrusive than for other persons.

Police Departments, such as Seattle and Philadelphia, have well-developed policies on searches, well beyond the limited comments made here. Those policies carefully spell out the appropriate steps that need to be taken when searching an arrested LGBT persons in the field. Officers should have a substantial understanding of all their department's policies to (a) follow established procedures, (b) avoid possible disciplinary action, and (c) ensure they do not create a liability for themselves or their agency.

12. Officers shall not unreasonably endanger themselves, other departmental personnel, or members of the public to comply with applicable departmental policy.

13. It is the jail's responsibility to make the decision about what the safe, humane, and

14. The jail is responsible for classifying all arrested persons and providing then with safe, legal, and humane housing.

When handwriting reports, the sequence for indicating race and sex is, for example, B/F (black female). On computerized reports there are separate race and gender/sex blocks for victims, witnesses, and suspects in which the codes or abbreviations are entered (see Table 6-1).

Age

On entries requiring only a person's age, it should be indicated as of the last birthday. However, the first reference to the individual in the narrative portion of the report should give the exact date of birth, if known. For certain parties, such as an unidentified deceased person or a suspect whose identity has not been established, age may be approximated or given in a narrow span of years—for example, "approximately 32 years" or "approximately 31–33 years."

Physical and Email Addresses

This information is essential because it allows investigators to reliably make contact with victims and witnesses for additional

TABLE 6-1	Race/Ethnicity Abbreviations
RACE/ETHNICITY	**NIBRS ABBREVIATION**
Native Hawaiian or Other Pacific Islander	P
Black or African American	B
Asian	A
American Indian or Alaska Native	I
Hispanic or Latino/Not Hispanic or Latino	H/N
White	W

Source: Drawn from the Federal Bureau of Investigation, Recent Changes to the NIBRS, Washington, D.C.: 2012, p. 2). Some police agencies use "U" for unknown. EEOC uses the category of "2 or more" races, but this seemingly has not found its way into wider abbreviations of race/ethnicity.

interviews, to view a lineup, or other purposes. Each residence and business address should show the street number and, when applicable, the apartment, suite, or room number. If this information is not immediately ascertainable, the general location should be described in sufficient detail to make its whereabouts known. When military personnel are involved, record their rank, and their location information should include unit designations, and ship or installation, if applicable. By 1974, all branches of the military ceased using their own unique service member numbers and instead now use each person's social security number for that purpose. Because the military used the full social security number on identification (ID) cards and many documents, identity theft became a problem for service members, for example, if they lost their ID card.

The practice now is to only place the last four digits of a social security number on ID cards and many documents, using the full numbers only for the most important purposes, such as the DD214, which is the Certificate of Release or Discharge from Active Duty and is a summary of a member's service. Examples of information on a DD214 include the dates a member entered and left the service, creditable service, decorations, medals, and badges, for example, the Silver Star, marksmanship medal, and the gold and black Ranger Tab. If a person is only visiting a location, both temporary and permanent addresses should be obtained. People often have work and personal email addresses, both of which need to be included in the report. If the person has multiple work and/or personal email addresses, all of them should be in the report and marked as to which type of address they are.

Telephone, Cell-Phone, and Pager Numbers

The telephone numbers of an individual should always be obtained, including area code, residence number, business number, and any extension number. Although transcended by the capabilities of cell phones, pagers are still being used. In 2012, Americans spent $7 million on pagers, roughly buying 10,000 of them. They are for people who want to stay in touch, but not be too reachable. A person calls a pager number and leaves a message, which is transmitted to a small belt-worn pager that "beeps" or vibrates when a message comes in. The message is time and date stamped. If a person has a pager, officers should get the associated telephone number and any code required to access the line.

Personal Description

If the victim or a witness can provide a description of the suspect, there is an imperative to get it and have a preliminary pickup order or BOLO broadcast as soon as possible because it may prevent an officer from unknowingly approaching a dangerous subject. As quickly as the first BOLO can be competently done, additional interviewing will ordinarily produce additional useful information that can also be broadcasted.

The following information should be disseminated as quickly as possible. If available, the following are descriptors

to include: name, street name, nick name, age, race, sex, height, weight, age, eye color, wore mask (describe), condition of teeth (white, stained, or missing), build (thin, slender, medium, heavy, obese, muscular), complexion [freckles, tone (light, medium, dark), pimples, acne, pock marked], glasses, scars, marks, tattoos, type and color of clothing, including any logos or wording seen, alcohol on breath, and deformities/amputations/physical defects (missing tip of right index finger or lame/limped).

It is also essential to initially get out any information about weapons carried, displayed, or used by the suspect, such as a baseball bat, knife, handgun, rifle, or shotgun, what threats were made by the suspect, for example, "I'll shoot your son if you don't ...", what violence was inflicted on the victim or witness; violent acts committed at the scene, such as shooting up coolers in a convenience store; and how the suspect left the scene and the direction traveled. The description of a car should be as detailed as possible, including the number of people in it. Under the "Property Description" section in this chapter, there is information about describing stolen cars. Those descriptors also apply to describing the "getaway" car.

Follow-up questioning could include a description of the voice (such as mumbled, loud, raspy, squeaky, soft, regional/foreign accent, use of poor grammar and/or profanity); exact words spoken to victim; unusual conditions of clothing (for example, left pants torn at knee, blue jeans very faded blue); jewelry worn; whether the suspect smoked or chewed gum/tobacco; and whether the suspect is left or right handed.

Where known, the height of a person is recorded in incident reports with three digits. For example, 5′9″ is entered as 509. If a height is given as a range, e.g., 5′4″–5′7″, it is recorded as 504–507.

Property Description

Elements useful in describing property are make, model, serial number, color, and type of material from which constructed. Other types of information may also be pertinent. Using the case of a stolen car as an example, the make; body type (for example, 4-door sedan, station wagon, or SUV); model year; color; vehicle identification number; license plate state and number; locations, shapes, sizes, colors, logos, and writing on window and bumper stickers; whether the windows are cracked or tinted; body damage; loud engine/muffler; articles hanging from the mirror; and other unique characteristics.

Occupation

The occupation of a person may be of some importance to an investigation. In the case of a suspect, it may establish familiarity with the use of certain types of equipment or procedures associated with a particular function, such as banking. It may also lend further credibility to the statement of a witness:

A man exited from a restaurant as two suspects ran about 15 feet from the bank they had just robbed, entered a vehicle, and rapidly drove around the corner. Despite being presented with only a brief view of the car, the witness was able to give the police a fairly detailed description of it. At the trial, the defense was unsuccessful in casting doubt on the accuracy of the description, since the witness operated an automobile repair service.

Occupation is also useful in suggesting times when a person might be successfully and conveniently contacted by the investigator. An unemployed individual's ordinary line of work is to be given along with the notation "currently unemployed." College students or homemakers should be so designated. If the individual is employed, the occupation given in a report should be as specific as possible—for example, "brick mason" as opposed to "manual laborer."

Value

The value of property stolen may determine whether the offense is a felony or misdemeanor. For articles subject to depreciation, the fair market value should be used, unless the property is new or almost new, in which case the replacement cost should be used. On goods stolen from retail establishments, the merchant's wholesale cost, which constitutes the actual dollar loss, is the proper value to use. The value placed on nonnegotiable instruments such as traveler's checks or money orders should be the cost of replacing them; negotiable instruments, including bonds payable to the bearer, are valued at the market price at the time of the theft.

When the stolen property is subject to appreciation from the time of its acquisition by the owner—for example, limited-edition prints—the current fair market value is to be indicated.

The value of recovered stolen property ordinarily equals the valuation placed on it at the time of theft unless damaged, in which case it is to be established by the fair market value. In cases where the value of the stolen article is not readily ascertainable, the conservative estimate of the owner may be used.

Date

Many dates are used in a report, but officers/investigators must know what dates are most critical. Often, important dates needed by prosecutors to file formal charges are hard to find or are missing from reports. For example: it is more critical to know what date a motor vehicle was stolen rather than recovered. It is important to know what date a bad check was presented for payment or to be cashed (uttered) rather than the date it was returned from the bank and reported to law enforcement. In any investigation, learn which dates are most important to include in the report. Dates are entered in the sequence of two digits for month, 01–12, two digits for day, 01–31, and four digits for year, 2018.

Time

For all official business, excluding general public and related information, most police agencies use the military system, or 24-hour clock, of hundred hours. Time runs from 0001 hours (12:01 A.M.) through 2400 hours (12 A.M.).

WRITING EFFECTIVE REPORTS: THE NARRATIVE

THE NARRATIVE

Almost always, there is more information to document than can fit on the face of an incident report. The additional information is entered in **narrative style** (Figure 6-11). There are a number of ways to organize the incident report to tell the story, but the narrative report generally makes the most sense if written in a chronological format beginning with the earliest thing that happened and progressing to the most recent fact or happening. The hardest part of writing a narrative is making sure that all the necessary information, including the smallest details, are transposed from the officer's/investigator's head and notes and recorded on paper. Doing a good job of report writing takes time, takes concentration, takes desire, and takes commitment. This sounds great on paper, but the realities of law enforcement often mean that an officer or investigator has calls backed up or a heavy caseload. Because very few cases ever go to trial, some officers believe writing short, direct reports is the sensible thing to do.

QUICK FACTS

Decide: Would You Fire the Officers for This Investigation?

In 2016, two officers were working the midnight shift in a medium-sized city. Around 4:00 A.M., they responded to a call from a home owner who lived across the street from a construction site. He reported hearing no yelling, just six quick gunshots, and then silence. The officers, each of whom had at least 4 years of service on that police department, walked over to the construction area, listened for a while, shined their flashlights around, and left. There was an 8-foot chain-link fence around the site. The chain on the entry gate was loose enough for a person to slip through, but the officer didn't enter the site.

Around 6:00 A.M., the same officers responded to a call at the construction site: an early-arriving worker found the night watchman's body on the ground, inside of the gate. He had been shot to death.

The officers maintained they had handled the call in a reasonable manner. The Chief examined the scene and felt if the officers had shined their flashlights through

We received a call to go to 207 W. Riddle Ave. reference a missing person. Circumstances as stated by dispatch was that a female adult was missing from the home. It was reported that the husband came home from work, found the door open, his wife's belongings such as purse, keys, and cell phone at the residence. It was also reported that a person was to take a test ride in a vehicle for sale this morning.

Based on information given by dispatch I asked Detective Francis to accompany myself and Ptl. Wilmington to the residence. Upon arrival we were met by Mr. Andrews who was in the front lawn talking on a cell phone. He appeared to be upset but not frantic.

Upon speaking to him he stated that his wife paged him at work around 9:00 am this morning and told him that a lady was coming by to take a look and test drive their jeep that was for sale. The Pr stated that they have the jeep listed in trading times and were trying to sell the car. He stated that he tried to call back around noon or so and could not get an answer. He stated that he told her not to go with anyone, just get their driver's license and let them take a drive. Pr stated that upon arriving home he found the front door wide open. He stated that his wife's purse, house keys, and cell phone were in the house but she was gone as was the jeep.

The Pr described his wife as being 8 1/2 months pregnant and not feeling well. He stated that she has to be helped in and out of bed and that she had not been feeling well. Pr stated he had checked the hospital and was trying to phone the doctor to see if something had happened with the baby. The jeep was described as all black 1999 with soft top and Ohio Reg. CAB4351 and is a Wrangler type.

Ptl. Wilmington, Det. Francis and myself checked the interior of the house as well as the yard and garage area. No one was located. The house appeared to be very tidy with no signs of foul play or struggle. I instructed dispatch to place a COPS teletype, administrative teletype, and radio broadcast with the information. I also advised dispatch to enter Mrs. Andrews as missing as well as the vehicle.

▲ FIGURE 6-11 Part of the narrative portion of an incident report

the gate they would have seen the watchman on the ground, who may not have been dead yet. Moreover, the Chief felt the officers were grossly negligent for not entering the site and searching for the watchman because they knew the site had a watchman, so he fired both officers.

As we continue to point out in this chapter, the reality is that no one can predict which cases may later develop into something significant, where the quality of a report is critical. The narrative portion of an incident report is written in the blank space on the reverse of the report's face or on a page referred to as "continuation," "investigative narrative," or "supplemental" (Figure 6-11, a case that started as a missing-person report and turned into a criminal homicide investigation). Furthermore, even cases that are plea bargained require certain information to pass muster with the local prosecutor's office. It is of utmost importance that first-responding officers and follow-up investigators learn the minimum amount of information required by the prosecutor to enable her/him to do the basic filing of

formal charges. It cannot be over emphasized that complaints by law enforcement officers that prosecutors don't do a very good job are too often based on ineffective reports submitted by officers.

The incident report must also contain as much detail about the suspect as is known, including descriptive data, clothing, hair, complexion, language or accent information, and weapons displayed. All information from witnesses or other people interviewed, including details of the information provided, along with name and contact information needed by follow-up investigators and prosecutors, must be obtained. The report must include a listing of all evidence seized or found, with details about where it was found, by whom, who has control of it, how it was marked and recorded, and any other information necessary to protect the chain of custody.

If incidents reports are to serve the many uses to which they can be put, they must meet certain standards. Among the standards most usually cited are proper classification; complete, accurate, concise, objective, and fair information; and timely submission. Keep the nine guidelines that follow in mind when you are preparing incident and supplemental reports. Supplemental reports are written when there is new pertinent information to be added to a incident report.

1. *Fill in all the blanks* on the incident report unless the information is not available or it is withheld, in which case this should be explained in the report. As discussed earlier, it is easier to get the necessary information at the scene than to try to recontact complainants and witnesses.

2. *Write the report in the first person,* using "I arrived at the scene at 1645 hours" as opposed to "Officer Morales arrived at the scene at 1645 hours." The reader of the report knows that Officer Morales wrote the report, and the officer's constant reference to himself/herself in the third person (Officer Morales) is awkward. Although some departments require the use of the third person in reports, the trend in report writing is not to use it.

3. *Avoid unnecessary technical or legalistic jargon* such as "hereinafter," "point of fact," or "thereof," because you may convey a meaning that you do not intend or do not fully understand. Such jargon is a means by which your credibility can be attacked. Avoid writing statements of your own whose meaning you cannot fully explain. Certainly, if a suspect tells you, "I was abducted by aliens who implanted a control box in my head and they sent me commands to rob the pharmacy," you must faithfully record the statement even if you can't explain it—but the words are not your own.

4. *Write short sentences,* because they are less likely to be confusing to (or misunderstood by) readers, such as the prosecutor. A concise, "punchy" presentation of the facts makes it easier for the reader to understand what you wrote and assign accurate meaning to what has been read.

5. *Use short paragraphs* for the same reasons as those for writing short sentences. Longer paragraphs often end up with too many ideas in them, which requires readers to use extra effort to grasp what has been written. This creates the prospect that some of the meanings you intended to communicate is misunderstood.

6. *Support any conclusions you express with details,* because others who read the report, such as the prosecutor, need to know what facts shaped your thinking. Also, when a trial begins weeks, months, or even years later, you will have forgotten many facts. If you included them in the report, you will be able to refresh your recollection and provide convincing testimony. Many police departments express a preference in their policies that officers do not express their opinion in incident reports.

7. *Don't repeat facts more than once,* unless doing so is required by your department's reporting format or policies. Duplication of entries wastes your time, and it creates the possibility that when you are distracted, tired, or in a hurry, your entries may conflict in some way with one another, calling your credibility into question.

8. *Check your spelling.* People who don't know you will form opinions of your capabilities on the basis of the reports you write and they read. Also, you are representing your department, so its reputation is on the line, because defense attorneys, judges, members of the news media, juries drawn from the community, and prosecutors read police reports. Misspelled words can change the meaning of a sentence or cause the meaning to be lost. Spellchecker software is an aid to accuracy, but it does not catch words that are spelled correctly but used inappropriately (for example, "E. Wazolewski took a write turn").

9. *Edit what you write.* Don't miss an opportunity to catch and correct your errors. Many people do this best when they read slowly and out loud, but you may find a system that works better for you.

Not infrequently a new investigator will, if only at the subconscious level, attempt to impress those who will be reading the incident report by writing in an elaborate manner in order to display mastery of the English language. However, persons reading the report will learn much, or perhaps all, they will ever know about the investigation from what has been written. Therefore, it is essential to write in a clear and uncluttered style; the report must be written not only so that it can be understood but, more important, so that it also cannot be misunderstood.

The report must be completely accurate. No detail should be added or deleted; the potential or actual consequences of such deviations, however innocent the motivation, are considerable. For example, at the scene of an armed robbery, an officer who had just completed his probationary period and was in the first week of riding solo, was conducting interviews necessary to prepare the original report. One of the questions he asked the victim was "Have you ever seen the perpetrator before this happened?" The response was "Yes, he works on the loading platform of the grocery on Sixth Avenue." Out of a desire to provide as much detail as possible, the investigator supplemented this statement with information from the telephone directory, writing a portion of the interview in the following manner:

The victim told the undersigned officer that the suspect works at Blake's Grocery Wholesale, located at 1425 Sixth Avenue, telephone number (813) 223-3291.

Later, the following exchange took place between the officer and the defense attorney in court:

Q Defense Attorney: *Officer, do you recognize this report?*
A Officer: *Yes, I do.*

Q Defense Attorney: *Did you prepare it?*
A Officer: *Yes, sir, I did.*

Q Defense Attorney: *Would it be fair to say that it represents your investigation?*
A Officer: *That is correct, sir.*

Although the detailed information about Blake's Grocery was accurate, the officer made a mistake by entering it in the report as part of the interview. The result was a flurry of questions as the defense attorney tried unsuccessfully to impeach the officer. However "innocent" mistakes might be, a single one could result in a person who might otherwise have been convicted going free and possibly committing additional crimes.

SUPERVISORY REVIEW AND DISPOSITION OF INCIDENT REPORTS

SUPERVISORY REVIEWS AS A QUALITY CONTROL MEASURE

Supervisory review of subordinates' incident reports is an essential component of quality control, but not the only one. As an example, in the Minneapolis, MN, Police Department (MPD), an officer who turns in five substandard reports in a 12-month period or a sergeant who approves three substandard reports in a 12-month period have committed an "A" violation. They would both receive attention in the form of counseling, coaching, training, or other nondisciplinary measures, all for the purpose of correcting their deficiencies. Another "A" violation during the next 12-month period rises to a "B" violation with disciplinary consequences.[25]

In the MPD system, substandard report allegations can come from a number of sources, including supervisors, the records unit, the assigned follow-up investigator, the city attorney, the district attorney, and city and county judges, all of whom have standard forms on which to register what they perceive as lacking and constituting a substandard report. Some incident report and records management software packages have a feature to track, count, and categorize serious deficiencies by officers, shifts, and units.

The MPD is not alone in instituting incident report quality control measures, and similar policies were reviewed. While there is apparently no national data available, impressionistically these measures appear more consistently in large jurisdictions and in some medium-sized ones. Substandard reports may cause a delay in victims getting a copy of the report and their insurance reimbursement, and such delays may deprive crime analysts of the data needed to inform operations commanders of fully current data. Finally, such standards clearly help communicate expectations across the department and implicitly give notice that mediocre job performance will not be tolerated.

SUPERVISORY REVIEW OF INCIDENT REPORTS

Supervisory reviews of incident reports are more alike than different across law enforcement agencies. Among the things

supervisors check for on reports are (1) grammar, spelling, and punctuation, (2) is the report consistent with departmental guidelines? (3) if handwritten, is it clearly legible? (4) does the report rest on facts, physical evidence, witness statements, and the law? (5) is the narrative of the report is not confusing and does it support the officer's classification of the crime? (6) is there missing information? (7) did the officer conduct a full preliminary investigation? and (8) are references correct,[26] for example, the geocoding (geocoding in an incident report is the geographic code number, for example, 18A, for the area in which the crime was committed)? Reports that need further attention are returned to the officer with specific direction to items that need further attention. This does not count as a substandard report.

Figure 6-12 shows the report approval and disposition process in a handwritten/nonautomated system. In such systems,

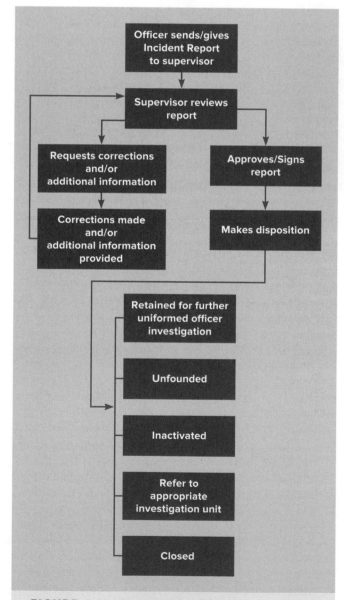

▲ FIGURE 6-12 Report approval and disposition process

supervisors will meet with their subordinates one to several times a day to collect reports for review. Reports that have a deficiency are immediately returned to the officer, the corrections are made, the supervisor reviews it again, and then the reports are taken to the records unit to be distributed according to the supervisor's disposition.

In an automated system there is a key difference in the reporting process. The officer initiating the incident report electronically may mark a disposition or the computer will select one based on a solvability model. One of these models is discussed more fully in Chapter 7, "The Follow-up Investigation and Investigative Resources." For present purpose, it is sufficient to note that the model includes variables that are associated with successful investigations; for example: Is there a detailed description of the suspect? Is there a vehicle description or tag number that would provide a lead? Was traceable property taken? Can a composite sketch of the suspect be prepared? When a case accumulates a certain number of variables, it is referred for follow-up investigation.

Officers electronically submit their reports to a report pending file in an automated system. The supervisor retrieves the report the same way. Supervisors can override any disposition made by the officer or the computer and sends accepted reports to the records unit for distribution. Reports that need additional information or has other deficiencies, are routed back to the officer for correction and then reviewed again by the supervisor.

Supervisors cannot change a factual narrative, and if they are a key figure in an event requiring an incident report, the watch/shift commander will designate another supervisor to do so.

SUPERVISORY DISPOSITION OF INCIDENT REPORTS

In both handwritten and electronic systems, supervisors may make any of the following **dispositions of incident reports:**

1. The case is retained for further investigation by uniformed officers.
2. The case is "unfounded," meaning the complaint is false.
3. The case is inactivated for a lack of leads and will not receive further investigation unless new information is received.
4. It may be referred for follow-up investigation by the Detective Division, the Criminal Investigation Bureau, or some similarly titled unit.

5. The case may be closed; for example, a misdemeanor arrest for family violence is made and the offender is in custody.

SUPPLEMENTAL REPORTS AND FOLLOW-UP INVESTIGATIONS

The purpose of a supplemental report is to augment the information contained in the incident report. Many, perhaps most, supplemental reports get written by follow-up investigators. However, patrol officers also write a number of them. As illustrations: (1) a victim may call to report she has discovered additional missing property from the burglary of her home, (2) a witness may have an additional recollection, and (3) a middle-school principal wants the police to have a copy of the official estimate of the damage done when the school was vandalized several days ago, which documents the damage as $6,000, more than estimated in the incident report.

Department policies vary as to when a follow-up investigator shall write a supplemental report, the purpose of which is to augment the incident report. Illustrations of this variation include these excerpts from actual policies: (1) supplemental reports shall be written as new information is discovered, (2) within 10 days of a newly assigned case, the investigator shall write a supplemental report, (3) supplemental reports shall be written every 30 days a case is actively investigated, (4) if no significant information is developed within 30 days, the detective supervisor, considering all applicable factors, may inactive a case, and (5) a supplemental shall be written when an investigative milestone occurs, including, composite sketch made, identification of a suspect, search/arrest warrants obtained/executed, and property recovered.

Policies often state that certain types of crimes must be reported to the appropriate investigation unit supervisor for his or her determination of whether a detective will be sent to the scene, for example, significant injuries to a child that are suspicious and occurred under suspicious circumstances, nonparental kidnappings, murders, and an assault that produces injuries likely to result in a death. When an investigator responds to a crime scene, the unit's supervisor is subsequently briefed and an initial supplemental is written fairly immediately.

Supplemental reports can be written for inactive cases, and a single important supplemental or several supplemental reports sometimes result in reactivation of cases. Much less frequently, this applies to cold cases, for example, when someone with key information finally decides to come forward, for revenge, to ease a troubled mind, or other reason.

KEY TERMS

disposition of incident reports
field notes
incident/offense reports

narrative style
NIBRS
supplemental reports

Uniform Crime Reporting (UCR)
Program

REVIEW QUESTIONS

1. What are the advantages of making field notes with pen and paper?
2. How often do officers have contact with emotionally disturbed persons?
3. What are three nonverbal cues to keep people talking?
4. Field notes important for what reasons?
5. What are the six main investigative questions?
6. There are five advantages to the use of body-worn cameras. What are they?
7. What are the two stances on whether officers should be able to review recordings from their body-worn cameras before writing an incident report? Which stance do you support?
8. Why are plainclothes officers usually exempt or can choose whether to wear a body camera?
9. There are four advantages to public online reporting systems. What are they?
10. What led to the development of NIBRS?
11. Officers should try to gain the confidence of the transgender community for what three reasons?
12. Why should you get a BOLO out with a suspect's description as quickly as possible?
13. There are nine guidelines for preparing an incident report. Which five do you think are most important?
14. Substandard reports create what problems?
15. Supervisors reviewing incident reports look for a number of things. If you were required to cut the list of things down to just five things, which five would you keep?

INTERNET ACTIVITIES

1. The policies of larger law enforcement agencies often include specific guidance on when it is mandatory for an officer to write an incident report. Search the Internet for U.S. police departments' policies on this subject, and develop a list of five mandatory circumstances for which officers must write a report.

2. Search the Internet to find articles on how to write an effective police report. Develop a list of seven suggestions you found in various articles.

Design Element: (crime scene tape): ©UpperCut Images/Getty Images RF

7

THE FOLLOW-UP INVESTIGATION AND INVESTIGATIVE RESOURCES

CHAPTER OBJECTIVES

1. Describe the use of solvability factors.
2. Explain the preparation of a case file.
3. Discuss reinterviewing victims and witnesses.
4. Describe the purpose and use of NamUs.
5. Summarize NCIC (National Crime Information Center) files and capabilities.
6. Explain LeadsOnLine.
7. Identify behaviors in which investigators should not engage with informants.
8. State the purposes of physical surveillance.
9. Describe how a photo lineup should be conducted.
10. Identify three potential indicators of a staged crime.
11. Describe the intelligence cycle.
12. Summarize the use of facial recognition software by law enforcement agencies.
13. Identify the ways crime analysts link crimes.
14. Explain the role of the scientific method in crime scene reconstruction.
15. Describe the four factors on which criminal profiling focuses.
16. Summarize geographic profiling.
17. Provide four examples of remote sensing.
18. Identify four ways investigators use the Internet.

Certain crimes, such as murder, rape, and child abuse, are always going to receive a follow-up investigation. To ensure that the use of investigative resources is warranted, other crimes are screened. Only those that have some promise for success receive a follow-up investigation. Investigators should be familiar with the numerous information sources and databases that are available to them. They should also have an understanding of special topics, such as conducting photo lineups and handling informants. These and related topics are covered in this chapter.

CHAPTER OUTLINE

THE DECISION TO INITIATE A FOLLOW-UP INVESTIGATION

The follow-up investigation is the period of police effort expended on a case from the time the incident report is completed until it is unfounded, determined that it did not happen as the complainant alleged, turned over for prosecution, or inactivated. In some unusual circumstances investigative effort is suspended because: (1) the agency lacks venue, which is rare; (2) the victim steadfastly refuses to assist in any way with the prosecution, which is not uncommon in domestic violence cases; or (3) it is determined that it is a civil matter. A prosecutor may still bring charges without the assistance of an uncooperative complainant, but even with substantial other evidence a conviction may be is difficult to obtain.

The decision to inactive a case or refer it for further investigation is often made through the use of a case screening model, which requires the presence of a sufficient number of solvability factors to exist before a case will be referred for follow-up investigation. **Solvability factors** are elements of information that have been demonstrated to correlate with higher probabilities of investigative success.[1]

In some models, each solvability factor may have a different mathematical weight attached to it. These weights must total a certain number of points for a case to be referred for follow-up. Common solvability factors include:

1. Is the suspect's identity known?
2. Can the suspect's identity be established even if unknown to the victim?
3. Did a security camera record the crime or capture an image of the suspects or their vehicle?

4. Is there an independent, reliable, creditable witness?
5. Can the suspect be described?
6. Can a likeness of the suspect be prepared?
7. Has the suspect previously been seen in the area?
8. Is the suspect's work or home location known?
9. Are the suspect's hangouts known?
10. Is there a unique description of the suspect's car?
11. Is part of the license number known?
12. Will the victim be able to identify the suspect?
13. Was traceable property taken?
14. Was important physical evidence recovered, for example, DNA or usable fingerprints?
15. Is a distinctive modus operandi (M.O.) involved?
16. Have threats been made against complainants or witnesses?
17. Does the crime suggest a potential imminent threat to the community?

On high profile cases, policies often provide tha the division commander be regularly informed through the chain of command. The division commander will keep more senior officials informed, as well as the public information officer (PIO).

THE FOLLOW-UP INVESTIGATION PROCESS

As a visual aid to follow-up investigators, some departments have checklists. Figure 7-1 is a "universal" checklist, meaning that it is not crime specific. The steps involved in a follow-up investigation do not necessarily occur in an exact order. The specifics of each case will dictate how those steps actually unfold. For example, if a suspect is already in custody, the attempt to interrogate him/her will come much earlier than if an arrest is made much later. Figure 7-1 provides a quick look at follow-up investigations. The balance of this section goes into greater depth. Although some points from Figure 7-1 are repeated, there is also substantial new content which amplifies them:

1. Departmental policies regarding follow-up investigation files vary but as a minimum require that a case file be prepared to organize the information that is immediately available—for example, the incident and supplemental reports. Over the course of an investigation the file will grow as lab reports, copies of checks, credit card charges, travel records, and other relevant data are acquired.

---

1. Review the preliminary investigation and any supplemental reports.
2. View physical evidence, and obtain permission to submit to laboratory as soon as practical.
3. Check departmental, regional, and national databases, for example, for criminal histories and outstanding warrants of known case figures. As additional figures emerge, do so for each one.
4. As early as can reliably be done, enter information into NCIC and other databases about missing persons, fugitives, and stolen property.
5. If in custody, interrogate suspects as soon as practical, but only after checking their criminal histories.
6. Determine if the crime was recorded by a store, homeowner, or other camera.
7. Determine if the modus operandi used in the current offense suggests possible suspects.
8. As needed, meet with officers who responded to the incident; for example, was there a field show-up at which the victim didn't make an identification, but which is not documented in the incident report?
9. Contact the victim and witnesses, and arrange for a meeting to verify report contents and collect any newly available information, for example, additional stolen property discovered.
10. If not already done, conduct a neighborhood canvas.
11. Interview the victim's relatives and friends as needed.
12. Check with informants as needed, but avoid the investigator's serious error of overworking informants.
13. As early as possible, determine what crime(s) were committed and whether a federal offense is also involved.
14. Disseminate case information to other agencies as appropriate.
15. Conduct lineups and photo arrays.
16. Treat victims with dignity and respect, and advise them of state and local ordinances conferring special rights on them as a crime victim.
17. Victims and witnesses may be hospitalized, such as gunshot, mugging, or rape victims, or otherwise be under medical care. The Federal Health Insurance Portability and Accountability Law (HIPPA) confers important rights about disclosing medical information. Investigators must be familiar with their department's policy on it and refrain from interviewing persons in the hospital without the permission of the attending physician.
18. If approved, make appeal for public assistance.
19. Evaluate lab reports.
20. Conduct surveillance as needed.
21. Arrange for polygraph or other deception examination.
22. Prepare search warrants, and seize any additional evidence; recovery stolen property.
23. Determine suspect's involvement in other crimes.
24. Obtain arrest warrant and take suspect(s) into custody.
25. Help prepare the prosecution's case.
26. Testify at trial.

◄ **FIGURE 7-1**
Universal follow-up investigation checklist
Many law enforcement agencies use a universal form, but a large number of other departments have specialized investigation checklists for some crimes, such as domestic violence and homicide. Less frequently, departments have original and follow-up investigation checklists for particular crimes, for example, when the victim is younger than 12 years old. Investigative checklist forms may have a small space to place a check mark when an activity is completed, while others have room for when they "Began/Completed" and for notes about each activity. Additionally, the victim's name, case number, investigator assigned, and other information also appears on the form. This example focuses just on the activities.

Some agencies require an **investigative plan (IP)** showing what lines of inquiry will be pursued and any special resources needed—for instance, the assistance of a surveillance unit. As the investigation progresses, many factors can cause IPs to be revised, such as a newly identified witness who names a suspect or can describe where unrecovered physical evidence—for example, a handgun—is located. A case log may also be required, which is a chronological listing of what the investigator has done and the results.

Local prosecutors may have an effect on the paperwork for a follow-up investigation. For example, they may require a sheet that specifies the specific statutory crime to be charged, a list of each element needed to prove the crime, and the evidence supporting each element.

2. Read the offense report and any supplemental reports and review visual documentation of the scene. If possible, visit the crime scene. As needed, contact or meet with the officer originating the report and those writing supplements to clarify information or resolve discrepancies. As a practical matter, this happens infrequently.

3. As early as possible, enter identifiable stolen property and arrest warrant information into appropriate databases.

4. Get the criminal histories of complainants, witnesses, and suspects. Consider the possibility that, although infrequent, the victim is in collusion with another person and making a false crime report, for example, insurance fraud.

5. Obtain, as appropriate, the credit histories of key figures in the investigation.

6. Review other incident reports that may be related.

7. Attempt to link suspects to other crimes by modus operandi (M.O.) analysis.

8. Examine the physical evidence (Figure 7-2) and review lab results as examinations are completed.

9. Contact victims and witnesses for in-depth interviews and search for other witnesses. Being a crime victim is often traumatic. Sometimes the victim will be able to recall something about the suspect that is helpful, such as a facial mole, a missing front upper tooth, or a tattoo.

10. Attempt to locate additional witnesses. If it has not already been done, conduct a neighborhood canvass (Figure 7-3).

11. Assess the credibility of witnesses and also people who are unusually helpful.

▶ **FIGURE 7-2**
Investigator examining evidence in the property room
(©R. Scott Freeman, Ph.D., Chief of Police, Athens-Clarke County (Georgia) Police Department)

▲ **FIGURE 7-3 Neighborhood canvass**
An Allentown, Pennsylvania Police Department Detective going door to door, canvassing residents in an effort to find witnesses to a shooting. If he develops information, he can immediately inform other investigators by using the departmental radio in his left hand. (©Dennis Wetherhold, Jr.)

12. Policies on death notifications are handled differently for current and retired civilian and sworn members of a law enforcement agency. For nonmembers, in some jurisdictions the county coroner or medical examiner's office handles them. Civilian deaths, such as from an industrial accident, may be assigned to a patrol officer. By policy if those officers cannot determine if there is a family pastor, one of the agency's chaplins and, if possible, someone close to the bereaved should accompany the officer. Delivering such a message requires compassion and sensitivity.

13. If not already done, arrange the preparation of a drawing/likeness of the suspect. Releasing the likeness and some general details about the crime to the news media may be necessary to solicit public assistance. A release may require the approval of the investigator's supervisor. Before any information is released, it should be carefully scrutinized to ensure that people are not endangered and that it does not hinder the investigative effort—for instance, by alluding to tactics or avenues of inquiry. The Crime Stoppers tip line may also be useful.

14. Reevaluate the case periodically, especially as new information is received, for example, could it be someone other than the suspect on whom you've been focusing?

15. Disseminate information about the crime and suspects within the agency as needed or secure the assistance of specialists—for example, profilers.

16. Coordinate with other jurisdictions which have crimes with substantially similar M.O.s If this leads to a serial offender, a joint jurisdiction task force may be established.

17. Explore lines of inquiry and pursue leads by using databases available through a variety of international, national, regional, private organizations, and your own department. (These databases are covered in more detail later in this chapter.)

18. Identify and interview former and current associates of the suspect who may have information.

19. Obtain any documentary evidence—for example, bank statements, credit card expenditures for hotels, gasoline, meals, and other purchases, as well as telephone records.

20. Use specialized investigative procedures if appropriate, such as physical and technical surveillance.

21. Prepare necessary affidavits, apply for and execute search and arrest warrants, and make the required returns to the court specifying what action was taken, such as property recovered.

22. Identify, locate, and apprehend the suspect, if he/she is not already in custody.

23. Arrange for a lie detection/truth verification examination if the suspect agrees to one.

24. Conduct a lineup or photographic array.

25. Conduct a custodial interrogation to have a documented confession, identify co-defendants, and evaluate the suspect as a potential informant.

26. Determine if the suspect's auto or other property is subject to seizure under federal or state laws. If so, refer to initiate seizure and condemnation procedures when appropriate.

27. File supplemental reports on the progress of the investigation as required by departmental policy (for instance, case status and the release of any property to the victim or his/her family).

28. Keep all records well organized.

29. Keep victim/victim's family informed on any changes in the status of the case.

30. Meet with the prosecuting attorney.[3]

REVIEWING THE INCIDENT AND SUPPLEMENTAL REPORTS

The incident and supplemental reports may answer many of the follow-up investigator's initial questions, such as: (1) how, when, and where the crime was committed, including a chronological description of the events; (2) the victim's identity and if appropriate, his/her medical condition and statement; (3) the number of suspects, if any are in custody, whether they are in the jail or a hospital, and their descriptions or identities; (4) whether composite sketches of suspects at large have been prepared and distributed; (5) the words spoken by suspects during the commission of the crime, spontaneous statements made by them following their arrest, and any post-Miranda statements made by them to the arresting officer; (6) the identities and statements of witnesses and any conditions noted, such any degree of drinking or appearance of having been using drugs; (7) the nature and value of the property stolen; (8) the types of physical evidence seized; and (9) a description of any vehicles involved or a copy of an impound report for vehicles seized.

THE JAIL BOOKING REPORT

The jail booking report is created when a subject is in-processed at a jail. This jail may be part of the investigator's agency, or it may be operated by another entity, such as the sheriff. The booking report is often computer generated and may have an incident report integrated into it, as well as a color photo; fingerprints; and description of the subject's health and medications; his/her mental state (for example, drunk or verbally or physically combative); medical treatment received while in custody; a full description of the subject, including scars, marks, and tattoos; criminal history; employment and home addresses; aliases used; and an inventory of the personal effects seized by jailers during the in-processing. In particular, the personal effects may provide useful information.

Among personal-possession items often found are matchbooks; Zig Zag paper; condoms; business cards for the subject (and from his/her associates or people he/she recently met); foreign currency; identity and credit cards in several different names; scraps of paper with telephone numbers on them; and various types of lists. Such items may suggest places the subject habituates or recently visited, suggest possible personal habits and associates, identify countries recently visited, or connect him/her to other crimes.

In one case, an investigator went to the jail to interview a subject arrested for stabbing a man in a bar. Among the subject's personal possessions was a real-estate card from a woman murdered several days previously. Although the man initially denied knowing the woman or being in the area where she was killed, he finally admitted to the crime after being confronted with the real-estate card.

THE VEHICLE IMPOUNDMENT REPORT

If a suspect is arrested while driving a vehicle, the vehicle is inventoried and towed to an impoundment lot. Articles that appear on the inventory list may or may not have a relationship to the case. Moreover, the impounding officer may not recognize their

significance, as can be the case with common tools that have been modified for use in burglaries. Thus, the impounding report should be carefully read. Under most circumstances, a follow-up investigator cannot search a car after it has been impounded without a search warrant issued on a showing of probable cause.

FIELD CONTACTS AND INTERVIEWS

Like other law enforcements agencies, the Tucson, Arizona Police Department (TPD) values and works at having a good working relationship with the community. Knowing the community and the residents is part of delivering quality service. For decades, police officers stopped people and made inquiries about them because they "didn't look right" or for some other thin reason. There were also inquiries made that would pass all of today's hurdles for doing so. Given this history, profiling, racism, harassment, and discrimination allegations claims are not without some foundation. Thus, in policing today, policies provide clear guidance about what many departments are calling: (1) consensual contacts and (2) stops. The TPD's guidance to its officers on these subjects is:

1. *Consensual contacts.* The police may make mutually voluntary **consensual contacts** at any time from wherever they can legally be. There is no need for an articulable police purpose in a consensual contact. To illustrate, an officer approaches someone getting out of a just-parked car and says, "Hi, I'm Officer Gonzales. As you pulled to the curb I noticed your left rear tire is nearly flat. It still looks pretty new. If you drive on it, you may ruin it. So you may want to get it fixed." In this consensual contact, the driver is free to depart without explanation at any time of his/her own choosing. There is not even a temporary seizure of the person in this instance.

2. *Stops.* In contrast to consensual contacts, when a law enforcement officer makes a **stop**, it rests on the use of police authority to limit a person's liberty of movement and is communicated in a manner that a reasonable person understands he/she is not free to go until the officer's business is completed. Examples of this is the officer asking the person, "Please turn your ignition off"; directing the person to go to, or stay in, a certain place ("Don't get out of your car"); or to perform some act ("Please show me your driver's license").

Consensual contacts can turn into stops or arrests when what started as a friendly meeting comes apart. A person approached by an officer in a friendly spirit may reply, "I've just been out of prison four hours and already you guys are on my ass." In that situation, the officer, after some brief questions, may use his/her smart phone to write a **Field Contact/Information Report (FCIR)** (Figure 7-4).

Cumulatively, the information on a FCIR provides a great deal of intelligence. You learn who is running with whom, where they frequent, and descriptions of cars they are driving. In a few

FRONT

SPRINGFIELD POLICE DEPARTMENT FIELD INFORMATION

Data: _____ Time: _____   FIR #: _____

Stopped/Seen at: _____ Beat: _____

Subject #1:

Name: _____ Address: _____

Sex: ____ Race: ____ Age: ____ DOB: ____ Hgt: ____ Wgt: ____ Hair: ____ Eyes: ____

Tattoos/Misc Description: _____

Subject #2:

Name: _____ Address: _____

Sex: ____ Race: ____ Age: ____ DOB: ____ Hgt: ____ Wgt: ____ Hair: ____ Eyes: ____

Tattoos/Misc Description: _____

Subject #3:

Name: _____ Address: _____

Sex: ____ Race: ____ Age: ____ DOB: ____ Hgt: ____ Wgt: ____ Hair: ____ Eyes: ____

Tattoos/Misc Description: _____

BACK

Vehicle Color (top/bottom): _____ Year: _____

Make: _____ Model: _____ Style: _____

License Number _____ License Year: _____ State: _____

Misc. Description: _____

Reason for stop: _____

List Suspicious Activity/Admitted or Known Criminal History/Gang Activity:

_____

_____

_____

_____

_____

_____

_____

_____

Officer/ DSN: _____ Supervisor: _____
                     Signature   Initial

◀ **FIGURE 7-4**
Field interview/information report (FIR) card
(Adapted from Springfield, Missouri, Police Department)

instances, FCIR cards have provided suspects with solid alibis and they have been excluded as suspects in other cases because when a robbery occurred, they were with a police officer.

On February 1, 2017, President Trump signed an executive order that affects over 300 cities, and counties, as well as four states, all of which are self-described as sanctuaries for people who illegally entered the United States. The order prohibits sanctuaries from receiving federal funds if they continue their policies of noncooperation with federal immigration agents. Many applaud this action, and others anticipate the courts will find it unconstitutional. A federal District Court Judge issued an injunction barring implementation, in anticipation of further legal action.

In some sanctuary jurisdictions, officers are given directions not to ask about the immigration status of those with whom they come into contact. Some chiefs and sheriffs approve of the sanctuary movement because to enforce immigration laws would create tensions in their communities and make it harder to solve crimes. There are an estimated 10,000,000 undocumented people living in the United States illegally, and the number grows by 700,000 annually. Some of these undocumented workers have been deported multiple times for the commission of serious crimes but have returned. Others who have returned multiple times were seeking to be reunited with their families.

The twin problems of a porous border and determining what is equitable for people who have lived here for decades are serious issues that deserve thoughtful responses. Those issues will not go away easily. Whether an officer is making a consensual contact or a stop, people deserve to be treated respectfully. Stops should not be made because of a person's manner of dress, their perceived sexuality, race, ethnicity, religion, appearance, or other factors that have no manifest relationship to policing. Such behavior is against the policies of many departments and may be illegal, as well. It also angers people and poisons the well of public support the police need.

TRAFFIC CITATIONS

As with FIR cards, traffic citations can link suspects to the vehicles they register and drive, as well as those to which they also have access. Access to the vehicles of others usually denotes a special relationship and may help identify girlfriends or boyfriends, criminal associates, relatives, or operators of particular kinds of businesses, such as used-car and scrap-metal firms. Traffic citations can also pinpoint where the operator was at a particular date and time. Occasionally, FIR cards are also written during traffic stops, so these two sources of information may provide useful investigative information.

EXAMINING PHYSICAL EVIDENCE

The physical evidence should be viewed early in the investigation, because it may soon be forwarded to the crime laboratory for analysis. Actually seeing the evidence adds a level of specific understanding about each item of evidence as to its appearance, color, weight, damage done to it in the commission of the crime, modifications to weapons, and other matters. These observations may help the investigator make connections when he sees or hears a comment at a later stage in the follow-up. As an example, assume the property entered into the evidence form reveals "One (1) men's size medium orange short sleeved shirt with blood on it, property of Joseph Jones." Later, when a witness says, "It was the fella in the orange shirt that started the whole thing. He punched the little guy in the mouth, pulled a knife, and cut him on his hand," you know who was wearing the orange shirt.

REINTERVIEWING VICTIMS AND WITNESSES

Victims or their families should be contacted very early in the process. They often have questions about the status of the case, their rights, whether they need protection, how a case gets processed through the criminal justice system, if they are eligible for victim's compensation for medical expenses or funerals, and, if they have been disabled by the crime, is there living assistance available to them. The investigator can answer some of these questions and then make sure the victims get linked to victim assistance entities, which may be state agencies. Some religious denominations also provide victims assistance on an ad hoc or other basis.

Recontacting victims and witnesses serves to confirm information in the incident or supplemental reports and to develop further information. Unfortunately, such contacts are sometimes met with questions such as "I already told the other cops everything I know. Why aren't you out looking for the guy that did this instead of bothering me with the same questions? Don't you cops talk to each other?" Experienced investigators let such frustrated comments politely roll off of their backs. "Look, I'm only trying to help you" has the potential to produce a downward spiral. It is better to "join" the victim or witness by using statements such as "I want to arrest the person that did this to you. In my experience sometimes victims or witnesses think of something else that is important, and rather than burden you with trying to find me, I thought it would be courteous for me to come to you." An often overlooked purpose of reinterviewing is to assess, if possible, the credibility of witnesses.

Before any reinterviewing is done, the investigators should carefully assess what a witness said he/she:

- saw—under what lighting conditions, at what distance, for how long, and was the witness wearing any needed glasses or contacts? A fair question to an 18-year-old witness would be "How do you know it was a '57 Chevy Impala?"
- heard—for example, "I heard him hitting her." What facts support that conclusion? Any auditory problems? Wearing a needed hearing aid?
- smelled—"The man who raped me was wearing Old Spice shaving lotion or cologne." A key question is "How do you know that odor?"
- touched—a blind person touches her mugger's face and reports it was unshaven with a short vertical scar above the left eye. The investigator might ask for other examples of her tactile sensitivity. If she reads Braille proficiently, it is likely to be very good. Blindfolded victims may also have useful tactile data: "I traced the letters GHS and the number 87 on a jacket while in the trunk of the car."
- tasted—for example, a hospitalized woman says that her last meal "tasted funny, like almonds," a sign of cyanide poisoning. How is she familiar with that taste?

LEADS

Some leads turn out to be "good," whereas others are simply "dry holes" and an unproductive use of time. The truth is that both kinds chew up resources and must be followed up, because often we can't accurately tell one from the other.

The fact that an incident report specifically names a suspect does not mean the person actually committed the offense or knows anything substantive about it. Victims can be mistaken about a person's name, report their suspicions as "fact," or attempt to cause problems for someone they don't like or have had difficulty with in the past. Or, their theory about how the crime was committed is simply wrong:

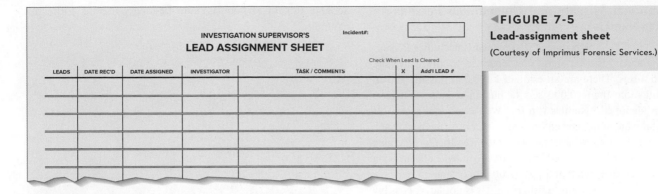

Two Promising Suspects

A burglary victim called an investigator to explain that she thought the offenders were two employees of a firm that the apartment complex had hired to do some work in her apartment. The described suspects, names unknown, had been given a key to her apartment in order to perform the necessary work. The burglary had been committed eight days later, and there had been no forced entry. The apartment manager, when contacted by the investigator, vouched for the men but had not directly supervised their work. The owner of the firm employing the men testified to their long-standing reliability and a lack of similar allegations in the past. A message was left for the suspects to contact the investigator. The suspects called back about a half-hour later and gave the investigator all the information requested and described the work done on the victim's apartment in detail. The investigator checked their backgrounds and concluded the men were not likely to have been the offenders and closed the investigation.

Major cases, such as the murder of a community leader or a robbery with a large "score," typically require the combined efforts of a number of investigators, who report to the supervisor responsible for the case. A key responsibility of the case supervisor is coordination of information, especially with respect to making sure that leads are prioritized and worked and that the results are disseminated to all team members. One way this can be done, by hand or on a computer, is by using a lead-assignment sheet log (Figure 7-5).

USING DATABASES

The use of databases allows investigators to rapidly close off some lines of inquiry, encourage the continuance of others, and suggest new ones. The available databases are international, national, multistate, state/regional/local, as well as private. The ones identified here are illustrative and not exhaustive, and other capabilities are mentioned within crime-specific chapters.

INTERNATIONAL

One of the most frequently used databases of the International Criminal Police Organization (Interpol) is SLTD, which determines whether passports, identity cards, and visas have been reported lost or stolen. Other examples of Interpol databases include piracy and radiological and nuclear materials.

NATIONAL

Bureau of Alcohol, Tobacco, and Firearms

The Bureau of Alcohol, Tobacco, Firearms and Explosives (ATF) has multiple capabilities. It trains firearms examiners and operates NIBIN, a ballistic intelligence database. When a law enforcement agency seizes a gun in a criminal investigation, a key question is, "Was this gun used in other crimes?" To get the answer, the agency up-loads evidence about the gun in question and submits it to ATF. It runs the data through NIBIN to see if there is a match. ATF also operates the U.S. Bomb Data Center with detailed files on over 400,000 bombing and arson related incidents. The National Tracing Center establishes the origin of guns recovered in law enforcement investigations to provide leads.

Drug Enforcement Administration: EPIC

In 1974, the Drug Enforcement Administration's (DEA) **El Paso Intelligence Center (EPIC)** became operational as a regional intelligence center to collect and disseminate information about aliens, drugs, weapons smuggling, and other activities. Around 2000, its mandate was expanded to provide tactical intelligence for federal, state, local, and tribal law enforcement agencies operating along the Mexican border. Following the 2001 terrorist attacks on New York and Washington, D.C., EPIC was tasked to help locate those who were responsible.

Today, EPIC is an all-threats intelligence center staffed by personnel from 20 different agencies. Despite some shifts in mission, the **National Drug Pointer Index (NDPI)**, which became operational in 1997, has remained a constant. The Index promotes agent safety and prevents duplication of effort. Although EPIC cannot access the database, permitted system users can make sure they are not running investigations on the same subjects and operations.

The National Missing and Unidentified Persons System (NamUs)

Launched in 2009, the **National Missing and Unidentified Persons System (NamUs)** is a database now operated by the University of North Texas. There are an estimated 100,000 missing person cases and more than 40,000 sets of human remains that have not been identified.[4] NamUs is a free Web-based tool accessible to everyone, including law enforcement, coroners/medical examiners, victim advocates, and families and friends. Considerable data remains to be uploaded into NamUS; only 2,800 missing people have been entered and just 6,200 sets of human remains. The number of cases resolved using NamUs is not large, possibly because it is a great untapped resource by investigators.

QUICK FACTS

NamUs Finds Missing Sister after 22 Years

Family members have resolved some cases using NamUS. A woman's sister had been missing for 22 years. The woman discovered that her sister had been murdered and dumped alongside a highway in another state. Authorities there were unable to identify the body, and the woman's sister was buried as a "Jane Doe" in a pauper's grave. However, subsequently the woman identified "Jane Doe" by the pictures of her murdered sibling's unique unicorn and rose tattoos.

Department of Homeland Security's (DHS's)

Among the Department of Homeland Security's (DHS's) programs is the **National Counter-Improvised Explosives Device Capabilities Analysis Database (NCCAD)**, which seeks ways to improve the capabilities, training, and equipment of those responsible for responding to IED threats. These improvements are aimed at: (1) the IED responders at the unit, local, state, regional, and national levels and (2) informing decision-makers on policy decisions, resource allocation, and crisis management.[5]

A second notable program is operated by DHS's Immigration and Customs Enforcement (ICE). ICE is responsible for admitting those who may do so lawfully, denying entry to those who do not qualify, and arresting persons who attempt to enter unlawfully. ICE has a key and difficult role in fighting terrorism by identifying those seeking entry into the country who would do us harm.[6]

Federal Bureau of Investigation

The FBI maintains the **National Crime Information Center (NCIC)**, which is the most comprehensive criminal justice data set in the country. Established in 1967, its structure has been periodically refined. NCIC has provided the information critical to solving high-profile cases, including the 1968 murder of Dr. Martin Luther King, Jr., which led to the arrest of James Earl Ray. NCIC was also instrumental in the arrest of Timothy McVeigh on the same day as the 1995 Oklahoma City bombing. The NCIC database consists of 21 files that are available continuously to those with approved access (see Box 7-1).

The impact of NCIC can be seen in the following examples:

1. An officer noticed a man, with a small child in the front passenger's seat, driving his car too rapidly and weaving through traffic, causing other drivers to slam on their brakes. The officer stopped the vehicle and did a NCIC check on the driver. The subject was a registered sexual offender, who should not have been with a young child, was on parole in another state, and should not have left it.[7]

2. A patrolling officer saw a pickup pulling a sailboat. The brake lights for the trailer were either not working or not hooked up. The officer stopped the truck with the intent of getting this deficiency corrected. The driver nervously handed over his license. The officer noticed a second driver's license on the dashboard of the pickup. Both photographs matched the driver, but there were different names and birth dates on them. An NCIC check revealed that both names were aliases used by the man. He had a criminal history and was wanted in connection with a series of boat thefts. In his patrol car, the officer received the suspect's real name, his mug shot, a photograph of his tattoo, and a photograph of, and other data on, the boat attached to the suspect's truck, which was stolen.[8]

The FBI also has other capabilities that support investigations. The purpose of the **National Center for the Analysis of Violent Crime** (NCAVC) is to provide behavioral-based analytical support to federal, state, local, and international law enforcement agencies. The **Violent Criminal Apprehension Program (ViCAP)** is part of NCAVC and provides advice and support for a range of cases, including child abductions, serial rapes and murders, and cybercrime. NCAVC and ViCAP are further discussed in Chapter 9, "Injury and Death Investigation."

Begun in 1999, the FBI's **Next Generation Identification (NGI) Program** is producing the world's largest set of biometric data to supplement its fingerprint records. "Biometric" simply means measuring living things, in this case people. NGI released its first enhancement, Advanced Fingerprint Identification Technology (**AFIT**) in 2011, which provided faster, more accurate fingerprint handling than its aging predecessor AFIS. Fingerprint identification increased from 92% to 99.6%. Another NGI program that is operational is **Rap Back**, which could ease the minds of parents. When people who hold positions of special trust, such as day care workers and school teachers, are under criminal investigation, criminal supervision, or have been arrested, their employers automatically receive a notification.[9]

BOX 7-1 | THE 21 FBI NCIC FILES

1. **Article File:** Records on stolen articles and lost public safety, homeland security, and critical infrastructure identification.
2. **Gun File:** Records on stolen, lost, and recovered weapons and weapons used in the commission of crimes that are designated to expel a projectile by air, carbon dioxide, or explosive action.
3. **Boat File:** Records on stolen boats.
4. **Securities File:** Records on serially numbered stolen, embezzled, used for ransom, or counterfeit securities.
5. **Vehicle File:** Records on stolen vehicles, vehicles involved in the commission of crimes, or vehicles that may be seized based on federally issued court order.
6. **Vehicle and Boat Parts File:** Records on serially numbered stolen vehicle or boat parts.
7. **License Plate File:** Records on stolen license plates.
8. **Missing Persons File:** Records on individuals, including children, who have been reported missing to law enforcement and there is a reasonable concern for their safety.
9. **Foreign Fugitive File:** Records on persons wanted by another country for a crime that would be a felony if it were committed in the United States.
10. **Identity Theft File:** Records containing descriptive and other information that law enforcement personnel can use to determine if an individual is a victim of identity theft of if the individual might be using a false identity.
11. **Immigration Violator File:** Records on criminal aliens whom immigration authorities have deported and aliens with outstanding administrative warrants of removal.
12. **Protection Order File:** Records on individuals against whom protection orders have been issued.
13. **Supervised Release File:** Records on individuals on probation, parole, or supervised release or released on their own recognizance or during pre-trial sentencing.
14. **Unidentified Persons File:** Records on unidentified deceased persons, living persons who are unable to verify their identities, unidentified victims of catastrophes, and recovered body parts. The file cross references unidentified bodies against records in the Missing Persons File.
15. **Protective Interest:** Records on individuals who might pose a threat to the physical safety of protectees or their immediate families. Expands on the U.S. Secret Service Protective File, originally created in 1983.
16. **Gang File:** Records on violent gangs and their members.
17. **Known or Appropriately Suspected Terrorist File:** Records on known or appropriately suspected terrorists in accordance with HSPD-6.
18. **Wanted Persons File:** Records on individuals (including juveniles who will be tried as adults) for whom a federal warrant or a felony or misdemeanor warrant is outstanding.
19. **National Sex Offender Registry File:** Records on individuals who are required to register in a jurisdiction's sex offender registry.
20. **National Instant Criminal Background Check System (NICS) Denied Transaction File:** Records on individuals who have been determined to be "prohibited persons" according to the Brady Handgun Violence Prevention Act and were denied as a result of a NICS background check. (As of August 2012, records include last six months of denied transactions; in the future, records will include all denials.)
21. **Violent Person File:** Once fully populated with data from our users, this file will contain records of persons with a violent criminal history and persons who have previously threatened law enforcement.[10]

Source: **https://www.fbi.gov/services/cjis/ncic**

REGIONAL INFORMATION SHARING SYSTEMS (RISS)

There are six multistate RISS centers (Figure 7-6). Each of the six centers, funded by the federal government, can tailor its services to the investigative and prosecutorial needs of its member agencies. The core services of all centers are information sharing, analytic services, loan of specialized investigative equipment, confidential funds, training conferences, and technical assistance. RISS communicates over its secure intranet, RISSNET. The RISS National Policy Group consists of the Director and Policy Board Chairperson of each of the six centers. Law enforcement agencies join their regional center based on its established application process.

Outside RISS, there are also a number of multistate databases, such as (1) the Alert-Emerging Threat Analysis Capability (ETAC), formed by a cooperative agreement between Missouri and Kansas law enforcement agencies and governed by a Board of Directors consisting of one representative from each participating agency, and (2) the Western Identification Network (WIN), with Alaska, Montana, Oregon, Washington, Idaho, Nevada, Utah, and Wyoming as members of the consortium, as well as some local law enforcement agencies in those states.[11] WIN was the first multistate Automated Fingerprint Identification System (AFIS) compact. AFIS, a capability pioneered by the FBI, uses high-speed computers to digitize, store, and compare fingerprint data and images. When possible matches are found, they are evaluated by expert examiners. The impetus for WIN came from (1) the recognition that people frequently moved among the member states and (2) smaller member states lacked the expertise and resources to create their own AFIS capability. In 2011, under NGI, the FBI's aging AFIS system was replaced by AFIT.

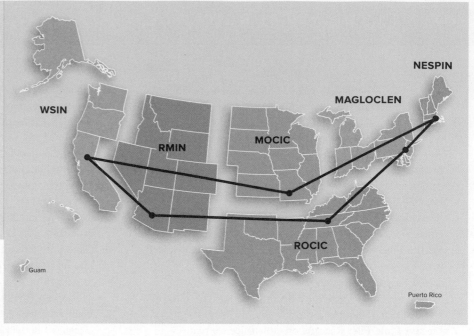

▶ FIGURE 7-6

RISS multistate centers

The members of RISS are the Western States Information Network (WSIN), the Rocky Mountain Information Network (RMIN), the Mid-States Organized Crime Center (MOCIC), the Regional Organized Crime Information Center (ROCIC), the Mid-Atlantic-Great Lakes Organized Crime Law Enforcement Network (MAGLOCLEN), and the New England State Police Information Network (NESPIN). **(Source: Based on data from RISS)**

STATE AND LOCAL SYSTEMS

State information systems are robust; they contain files on over 100 million offenders. State information systems include wanted, missing, and endangered persons; stolen property; driver's license and vehicle registration information; protective orders for juveniles and adults; state and local court information; Department of Corrections offender tracking; probation, parole, and supervised release data; prosecutorial information; and gang-related, juvenile justice, sexual-predator tracking, and other data-bases. Local systems serve a single jurisdiction, all the law enforcement/criminal-justice agencies in a county, or a multi-county area.

NONPROFIT AND PRIVATE SOURCES

The **Law Enforcement Intelligence Unit (LEIU)** was formed in 1956 by 29 local and state law enforcement agencies to exchange information about organized crime not available through normal police channels. LEIU originally excluded federal agencies, although that stance has been abandoned. In 2008, it changed its name to the Association of Law Enforcement Intelligence Units but kept its original acronym, LEIU. Its present focus is gathering, recording, and exchanging information about suspected or known criminal figures, groups, and businesses and terrorism.

Formed in 1966 as the Law Enforcement Teletype System (LETS) and incorporated as a not-for-profit in Delaware in 1973, LETS has morphed into the **National Law Enforcement Telecommunication System (NLETS)**. NLETS handles some 1.5 billion transactions daily for law enforcement and other criminal-justice agencies.[12] In addition to providing secure channels for members' communication, NLETS also is a conduit for information and alerts flowing from the U.S. Department of Homeland Security (DHS). NLETS provides access to files from other states,

such as those for wanted persons and concealed weapon permits; federal files, including the Federal Aviation Administration's (FAA's) aircraft registration data and tracking information; and the Canadian Police Information Centre (CPIC), which is similar to NCIC.

LeadsOnLine is a private subscription service used by more than 1,600 law enforcement agencies. It provides access to transactions from thousands of reporting businesses, including scrap metal processors, secondhand stores, Internet drop-off stores, pawnshops, and eBay:

QUICK FACTS

Diamond Ring for Sale

A husband listed a diamond ring for sale on Craigslist. A man made an appointment to come see the ring and along with several accomplices committed a home invasion robbery. While defending his son from violence the husband was killed. The invaders pawned the ring, which investigators located using LeadsOnLine, and the pawnshop records led them to the killers.[13]

Significant information about persons of interest is available for a fee from credit-reporting agencies such as Equifax, TransUnion, and Experian. **Accurint for Law Enforcement (ALE)** is an example of a group of high-end providers of information and information services that go beyond credit reports. Approximately 3,000 government entities use Accurint, which has access to 12 billion public records. It can quickly retrieve information about businesses and individuals, including current and former addresses, and links, such as to family members, neighbors, and associates. Among its capabilities is Person Alerts (PA); each time an individual who is a person of interest or fugitive appears in the database, the investigator is automatically notified. Intelligence units, discussed later in this chapter, make use of ALE and similar businesses.

Internet sites that can provide information about persons of interest are People Finder, Yahoo People Search, AnyWho, and BigFoot. The types of information vary somewhat from one site to another but include current and past addresses, possible relatives, birth dates, current telephone numbers, marriage and divorce information, litigation history, and e-mail addresses. WhoIs provides information about e-mail addresses both domestically and internationally.

Information about corporations can be obtained from each state's Secretary of State's Office. If a company uses a registered agent, some corporate information, such as officers, may not be available online, although some useful information about the corporation can be gleaned as a starting point. Dunn & Bradstreet can provide a Business Background Report, which provides summary coverage about the operations, history, and

background of a company and its senior management; its Supplier Evaluation Report indicates the likelihood that a firm will cease doing business without paying its obligations in full or will seek debt relief under applicable federal and state laws.

Social network sites (SNS) are a category of websites that contain personal profiles and that may offer dating or other such services—for example, Facebook, Instagram, Twitter, and LinkedIn. Legal restrictions apply to accessing some data, such as the names of people a victim was dating, but some useful information may still be gleaned from SNS files without a search warrant.

INFORMANTS

Informants provide information that is of investigative significance. They may expect to be paid or to receive consideration on charges pending against them or family members, or they cooperate for some other reasons. They may also be designated as confidential informants; some departments have adopted the term "cooperating individual" for them.

BOX 7-2 | CINCINNATI POLICE DEPARTMENT INFORMANT DEFINITIONS

Sources of Information (SOI). Persons or organizations not under the direction of a specific police officer. A source of information furnishes information without compensation and will not take an active part in an investigation. When a source of information seeks compensation or becomes an active part of an investigation, their status changes to confidential informant. SOIs do not require registration.

Confidential Informants (CI). Persons under the direction of a specific police officer giving information or other lawful assistance on criminal activity. Confidential informants take active parts in investigations and/or receive compensation. Register all CIs.

Confidential Defendant Informants (CDI). Confidential informants who are current defendants in pending court cases and expect compensation in the form of judicial or prosecutorial considerations. Register all CDIs.

Inactive Confidential Informant. Confidential informants not debriefed within a year or declared inactive by the control officer.

Debriefing. Initial and continued questioning of confidential informants. Intelligence gathering on backgrounds, motives, limitations, and other information they have on all types of criminal activity.

Compensation. Money or judicial/prosecutorial considerations.

Informant Control Officer (ICO). Officer controlling the confidential informant.

Informant Secondary Officer (ISO). Serves as a contact for the confidential informant when the control officer is unavailable and acts as a witness for the control officer.

Source: City of Cincinnati. (2015, Nov. 19). "Confidential Informant Management and Control." Retrieved from http://www.cincinnati-oh.gov /cityofcincinnati/

Law enforcement policies generally identify activities that investigators should refrain from with informants. These includes socializing with them, becoming romantically involved, paying them without confirmation of the information, entering into a business relationship with them, accepting gifts, gratuities, or money from them, and loaning them money or accepting a loan from them. Policies also restrict who may be used as informants and determine whether prior special approval is required before they are used. Typically, restrictions apply to persons under 18 years of age, those who have been previously used and were not reliable, former drug-dependent individuals, and those on federal or state probation or parole (whose use as informants may require the approval of a judicial official).

An informant file, to which there is restricted access, consists of a recent photo of the informant, a complete informant sheet providing detailed information about him/her, copies of warrants and NCIC, and other items, including a criminal history, copies of cases in which the informant is a defendant, and debriefing reports following each meeting with him/her.

As a practical matter, some investigators run their own low-level informants, paying them out of pocket for their information or otherwise helping them. On the one hand, this is practical and works. On the other hand, an officer could be lured into a trap, and if he/she is killed, the department has to work the case in ignorance of the existence of the informant.

Inexperienced investigators tend to contact informants too frequently or expect too much too quickly. To get inexperienced or lazy investigators "off their back," informants will "burn" them by knowingly giving them bad information. A more experienced investigator uses informants more judiciously:

QUICK FACTS

Quick Facts: Recruiting an Informant

A patrol officer passed a house in a rundown neighborhood near shipping docks. He heard screams and shouts through the screen door. Upon investigating he was told by a German seaman that "one of these whores stole my watch and wallet." Interviewing the woman alleged to be involved, the officer saw a small amount of marijuana on the bedside table. Several other "ladies" were also present in the house. The officer told the "mom" to have her "daughter" give the things back, which was done, and the seaman departed.

While talking to mom, the officer saw a picture of a boy on a table in the living room and asked about it. She proudly said it was her grandson, who lived with her and who was her "angel." The mom maintained a separate residence a few blocks away from her "office." The officer told the mom it would be regrettable if he had to arrest her, because the grandson would be placed in a foster home and be grown by the time she was released from prison. They reached an agreement.

Five months passed before the officer returned, seeking information about a local fugitive who had committed five burglaries of high-end jewelry stores. Three days later, based on mom's information, the suspect was arrested.

SURVEILLANCE

While some think of surveillance as "following," it actually means the continued observance of individuals, groups, locations, areas, and particular things. It is an important investigative tool, and at times may be the only way of obtaining factual information. Surveillance should only be used for legitimate law enforcement purposes and conducted in a manner that doesn't infringe on anyone's statutory or Constitutional rights.[14] Ordinarily, surveillance is covert, although there may be occasions when it is made obvious to spook a subject into making a mistake. The single most important element of a surveillance plan are 1) the safety of surveillance personnel, 2) a detailed briefing of everyone involved, including those responsible for providing security for the surveillance team and 4)making sure the right equipment is available and is checked out prior to the operation.

THE PURPOSES OF SURVEILLANCE

The purposes of surveillance include:

1. Determining whether suspected criminal activity exists.
2. Gathering intelligence on illegal activities by individuals, groups, and organizations.
3. Obtaining probable cause for a search warrant.
4. Apprehending suspects by warrant or as they commit a crime.
5. Identifying the associates of criminals, their vehicles, homes, and places/people they frequent.
6. Determining the reliability of informants.
7. Providing security for undercover officers.
8. Locating people, places, and things.
9. Gathering intelligence about targets and premises prior to serving warrants.
10. Preventing a crime by allowing suspects to become aware they are being closely watched.
11. Gathering information for an on-going investigation.

TYPES AND LEVELS OF SURVEILLANCE

Broadly, there are two types of surveillance: physical and technical/electronic. These are often done by two-person teams with an additional two-person security team to protect them.

Physical surveillance may be:

1. *Casual surveillance* includes taking note of cars present, persons seen, and so forth each time you happen to drive by the surveillance area, and it doesn't require any additional personnel and equipment. The chief disadvantage is that it takes a long time to accumulate intelligence.
2. *Formal surveillance* requires some planning and lasts from a few hours to a longer period. Careful planning is essential and physical surveillance ordinarily requires more personnel than technical/electronic surveillance.
3. *Long-term surveillance* is an ongoing, indefinite proposition whose end is often determined by the value of what raw intelligence is being collected. If, for example, for several weeks you are getting some really good stuff and then little or nothing, you've been made and it's time to shut it down.[15]

Technical/electronic surveillance may be accomplished by ongoing mechanical monitoring equipment (Figure 7-7), the use of which may require a court order. Many departments also require the approval of a senior police official before the department's attorney or prosecuting attorney drafts the application and any supporting documents. The use of any type of surveillance because of a target/person's religion, race, ethnicity, support for unpopular causes, or political affiliation is not permitted, unless they are manifestly violating the law by advocating violence. Equipment operators must maintain a log and be fully trained in the operation of equipment.

Small agencies should not allow a single person or only two persons to conduct surveillance without proper backup. A nearby larger agency with surveillance resources may engage in a cooperative investigation and provide the surveillance capability, as might the state police, state patrol, or state investigative agency.

PLANNING FOR SURVEILLANCE

The most important aspect of every surveillance plan is the safety of the officers. An essential part of that is to determine the following: Does the target have a history of violence? Is he/

BOX 7-3 | NEW APPLICATIONS OF TECHNOLOGY TO SURVEILLANCE

As technology continues to advance, a question becomes increasingly crucial to ask: How do we balance what we can do technologically with civil rights? Two recent developments illustrate this question.

"Stingray" is a cellphone-tracking device that 70 agencies in 23 states and the District of Columbia have.[16] Stingrays simulate being a cell site that mimics being a cell tower, tricking cell phones into sending their locations and identifying information. While a tremendous asset for tracking suspects and criminals, information about innocent bystanders is also gathered.

In 2015, Freddie Gray died of injuries, which apparently occurred while being transported in a Baltimore police van. In the days which followed, the city was racked by protests and riots. A Chicago company scanned social media sites, such as Facebook, Instagram, and Twitter, to gather information on what was being posted on them.[17] This information and the location of the postings, but not any identities, were provided to the police, which responded to situations as needed.[18] Arguably, the violence in Baltimore may have more extensive without the data. There is no relationship between of information and Freddie Gray's death . . .

The American Civil Liberties Union (ACLU) and civil libertarians see a darker, more intrusive side to scanning Twitter, Instagram, and Facebook to assist law enforcement agencies in the surveillance of protestors and civil activists. Facebook, Instagram, and Twitter have all cut off third party developers who mine the data and sell it to law enforcement agencies.[19] There are less controversial uses of this technology, e.g., the Federal Emergency Management Agency and kindred organizations can get real-time data when disasters strike.

▲ **FIGURE 7-7**

Automated digital video surveillance on New York City's Brooklyn Bridge. (©Neil Setchfield/Alamy)

she known to carry weapons? To have used them? Against police? Is the target a martial arts expert? A weightlifter? Working for an organization as an enforcer? Just as important, is the target a drug user, which might make him/her more impulsive or harder to restrain due to his/her violent impulses.

All surveillances should be based on a carefully conceived plan that includes a thoughtful selection of (1) what type of surveillance is involved, for example, a fixed location; (2) who the targets are; (3) the objectives, for example, to gather information to make arrests or to tail targets to lead them to other aspects of their operations and their associates; (4) what cars the targets drive; (5) the rough schedule the targets keep; and (6) the possibility of the targets operating anti-surveillance techniques and equipment.[20]

GUIDELINES FOR CONDUCTING SHOW-UPS, PHOTO ARRAYS/LINEUPS, AND LIVE LINEUPS

Eyewitnesses may be requested to see if they recognize anyone connected with the crime in one of three procedures: (1) a show-up, (2) a **photo array/lineup,** and (3) a "live" lineup.

THE SHOW-UP

A **show-up** allows the police to conduct an immediate eyewitness identification of someone they have temporarily detained. The practice permits the immediate clearing of a wrongfully suspected person, and detention is kept to a minimum. One witness at a time is brought to view the person temporarily detained. Even if the person detained is not in handcuffs in the back seat of a car, the process is patently suggestive because the person is clearly under police control. For that reason alone, show-ups should be avoided whenever possible. A photo array or a live lineup both offer better defensibility, more control, and better logistics. If a show-up must be used, the following procedures should be followed:

1. If not already done, separate the witnesses. Establish how long they have been allowed to talk together if that has occurred. Record the information as part of the Brady requirement.
2. Have each witness, separately, provide a detailed description of the person he/she is to view.
3. Refrain from using suggestive words, for example, "We have the suspect in custody," and refrain from conduct that indicates you are sure you have the suspect. Use more neutral language, such as "We have someone with us at another location and would like to know if you recognize him."
4. Whenever possible, present the suspect without handcuffs in a setting and under circumstances that tarnish the suspect the least.
5. Read the departmental form for show-ups to the witness. Figure 7-8 illustrates such a form. Make sure the witness

understands it, and have him/her complete the form which includes his/her statement.

6. Bring the witnesses to the suspect's location one at a time and do not allow them to have contact with the other witnesses afterward.
7. Preferably, all contact with a witness at a scene should be digitally videotaped with audio. At a minimum it should be audio recorded.[21]

CHOOSING BETWEEN THE PHOTO ARRAY AND A LIVE LINEUP

The assigned investigator determines whether a case requires the use of a photo array or live lineup and usually is responsible for all aspects of preparing them—for example, completion of a lineup creation form. The investigator also coordinates the process with witnesses, because they have some familiarity with him/her. The request to view any type of lineup should be kept factually neutral, such as "We'd like you to see a collection of photographs." Unless specifically asked by a witness, no mention of any suspect in custody should be made.[22] Several languages

▶ **FIGURE 7-8 Show-up form**
Source: Adapted from Garen Horst, Placer County California District Attorney's Office (2010 Version).

SHOW-UP FORM

Case No: _____   Place: _____

Date/Time: _____   Administrator: _____

Witness: _____

Others present: _____

ADMONITION

As a witness, you will be asked to look at a person or persons. You are not obligated to identify anyone. It is just as important to clear innocent persons from suspicion as it is to identify guilty parties. You should not conclude that the person or persons you see committed the crime simply because they are present. Please be advised that I cannot give you feedback on any identification you make. If you make identification, please do not discuss the case with the news media or other witnesses or indicate to them in any way that you have identified someone. Regardless of whether identification is made, law enforcement will continue to investigate the incident.

ACKNOWLEDGEMENT

I hereby acknowledge that I have read the foregoing admonition and understand it.
Witness: _____   Officer: _____

STATEMENTS/COMMENTS:

_____
_____
_____
_____

Investigator's note: If an identification is made, ask the witness to state, in his or her own words, how certain he or she is of any identification. Remember to record both positive identifications and non-identification results in writing, including the witness' own words how sure they are.

may be spoken in a community, and written witness instructions should be available in those languages. The investigator also needs to make sure that qualified language, including American Sign Language (ASL), interpreters or other necessary accommodations are available. Sometimes the fact situation dictates whether a photo lineup or live lineup should be used.

QUICK FACTS

Had to Be a Photo Array

A cab driver reported to the police that he had been robbed by one of his passengers. The cab driver made the report immediately after the suspect had fled on foot with the money. The driver reported that the suspect was a black male, approximately 25 years old, 6 feet 6 inches tall, 285 pounds, and armed with a large nickel-plated type semiautomatic pistol. The man was wearing an orange shirt, blue jeans, and a white cowboy hat. Exactly $52.12 in cash had been taken.

Approximately 30 minutes after the crime was reported, the suspect was observed walking in the vicinity of the robbery by the same two officers who had taken the original report. The suspect was arrested by the police officers. A search produced a nickel-plated .45-caliber semiautomatic pistol and $52.12.

The investigator assigned to the case immediately knew that his only option was a photo lineup, because finding enough people for a live lineup who approximated the suspect in size, race, age, attire, and so forth would be very difficult.

In 2009, the Innocence Project released *Reevaluating Lineups: Why Witnesses Make Mistakes*.[23] It identified numerous problems with existing photo and live lineup procedures and provided guidelines for using them in the future. Although these guidelines did not carry the weight of law by themselves, many states passed laws substantially mandating their use, and elsewhere many prosecutors and law enforcement agencies voluntarily adopted them. The processes described here are consistent with those guidelines.

To avoid investigators giving subtle, unintended cues to witnesses, a "double blind" method of conducting photo array and live lineups is now being widely used. The actual procedures are conducted by a trained lineup administrator who does not know who the suspect is or who the "fillers" are. In a photo lineup, fillers are photographs of people not involved in the crime. Administrators should be independent of the investigative unit—this is a good role for community volunteers and retired persons. The assigned investigator and anyone with knowledge of the suspect may not be in the same room as the procedure.

If several witnesses independently look at a lineup, the administrator could get some idea who the suspect is and unintentionally guide a witness to a particular identification, which is why such administrators require training. A better practice is to use a different administrator with every witness. In addition to leading witnesses through a lineup procedure, the administrator has

substantial recordkeeping responsibilities. These often include, whether documented by video, audio, or in writing: (1) all identification and nonidentification decisions signed by the witness (if a signature is refused, the administrator records this fact and signs his/her own name); (2) the names of all persons present at the lineup and their affiliations; (3) the date, time, and location of the lineup; (4) the exact words used by the witness to identify the suspect; (5) the number of photos or individuals in the lineup; (6) the sources of all photographs or individuals used; (7) all photographs from a photo lineup; and in a live lineup, a photo or other visual recording of the lineup that includes all persons who participated in the lineup.[24] The administrator returns all photos and reports the results to the assigned investigator. Depending on departmental policy and the results, the photos may be placed in the case file or the evidence room. After the lineup is completed, the investigator can be available to answer any of the witness' questions or to ask questions.

PHOTO ARRAY LINEUPS: STEP BY STEP

A photo array lineup (Commonly referred to as a photo lineup) is a procedure in which a series of usually six photographs, each in a separate folder, are shown sequentially to a witness for the purpose of determining if he/she can identify the perpetrator of a crime. One practice is that as each photo is shown to a witness, he/she must make a decision about whether the person is the suspect before viewing the next photo. The second practice is to allow them to view all photos sequentially, but not simultaneously, before any potential identification is made. There is some concern that allowing witnesses to see all photos sequentially before making a decision could contribute to some misidentifications, in mentally comparing photos a witness might point to the photo which *most appeared like the suspect*.

As a minimum, a photo lineup consists of six photographs—one of the suspect and at least five "fillers." Fillers are photographs of the same quality, size, shape, and type (black and white or color) of individuals who are similar in appearance—for example, sex, age, skin and hair color[25] Although software may be able to make the background and lightening of photos similar, the witness should be told not to attach any weight or significance to such peripheral differences. Figure 7-9 is a Photo Array Lineup Form with instructions for witnesses, who are given the information individually in a private setting.

The photos are placed in the same position—for instance, middle of the page, in separate identical file folders that are numbered on the back for record keeping purposes and shuffled. The files are also shuffled before each new witness looks at them. It is also recommended to have four blank files so the administrator doesn't even know that the next file to be opened has a photo.[26]

If there are several witnesses, each is led separately through the process by the administrator. If there are multiple suspects, a separate photo lineup must be prepared for each suspect using different fillers; only one suspect can be in any single lineup. If witnesses cannot be scheduled so they can be processed contemporaneously, without the opportunity for any personal contact with one another, a new photo lineup for each suspect must

▶ FIGURE 7-9
Photo lineup form
Source: Adapted from Garen Horst, Placer County California District Attorney's Office (2010 Version).

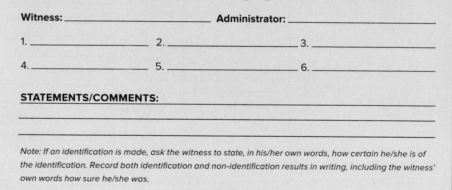

PHOTO LINEUP FORM

Case No:_____   Place:_____

Date/Time:_____   Assigned investigator:_____

Administrator:_____   Witness:_____

Others present:_____

ADMONITION

The lineup administrator will show you a collection of photographs. Look at all six photos before making any comment. You do not have to identify anyone. It is just as important to clear innocent persons from suspicion as it is to identify suspects. Individuals may not appear exactly as they did on the date of the incident. For example, head and facial hair are subject to change. Do not attach any significance to differences in the characteristics of photos. The person who committed the crime may or may not appear in these photos. If you recognize any person in the photos as the suspect, tell the lineup administrator and sign on the number below identifying the suspect. The lineup administrator cannot give you feedback on any identification you make. If you make an identification, please do not discuss the case with other witnesses or the media or indicate to them in any way that you have identified someone. Regardless of whether an identification is made, law enforcement will continue to investigate the incident.

ACKNOWLEDGEMENT

I hereby acknowledge that I have read the foregoing admonition and understand it.

Witness:_____   Administrator:_____

1._____   2._____   3._____

4._____   5._____   6._____

STATEMENTS/COMMENTS:_____
_____
_____

Note: If an identification is made, ask the witness to state, in his/her own words, how certain he/she is of the identification. Record both identification and non-identification results in writing, including the witness' own words how sure he/she was.

be prepared with different fillers for later witnesses. Even if a witness makes an identification, he/she should be guided to carefully consider any remaining photos. If a witness wants a second chance to view a photo lineup, wait at least 48 hours and then use another picture of the suspect wearing different clothes. If the posture of all the suspect and fillers is not standard, the suspect's picture should reflect him/her in a different posture. All new fillers must also be used.

Software is available to prepare a photo lineup and also produces the required recordkeeping documents. Because the computer selects the fillers, the investigator cannot be accused of selecting them in a manner that was intentionally biased against the suspect.[27]

LIVE LINEUPS

A **live lineup** is a process in which a series of "real people" are shown to an eyewitness to establish whether they can pick out the suspect (Figures 7-9 and 7-10). All members of a lineup usually appear simultaneously, although there is some interest in sequential appearances. A suspect should be allowed to pick the order in which he/she appears. Requests from any attending defense attorney should be carefully considered and the request and its disposition documented by the administrator.

The suspect and at least four fillers are used, with the fillers selected on the same criteria as those used in a photo lineup. Some agencies prefer to use five fillers to make their photo and live lineup procedures parallel. If there are multiple witnesses, each one views the live lineup alone. The position of the suspect is changed in the lineup before each new witness to the same offense views it. If the witness has previously viewed a lineup involving a suspect and is asked to view another lineup with a second or subsequent suspect potentially involved in the same offense, the fillers must be entirely new each time.

LIVE LINEUP FORM (Part 1)

Case No: _____ Date/Time: _____

Place: _____

Administrator: _____ Witness: _____

Others present: _____

ADMONITION

WHY WE'RE HERE: You were recently a crime victim or a witness to one. You will see a live lineup of five persons. There may be a person or persons in this lineup you recognize from the crime that brought you here today. The purpose of this form is to help you understand the lineup process and your role in it. Please carefully read all instructions. If you understand the instructions please sign at the bottom of this page. After you have seen the lineup, you will be asked to complete the other side of this form, which is about your experience in the lineup and sign it.

PERSONS PRESENT: An administrator will conduct the lineup. He/she is a "neutral" and doesn't know anything about the people in the lineup. The administrator cannot answer any questions related to them. Other people will be present who are not witnesses, however they are required to attend the lineup. If any of the other people present should ask you a question, you are not required to answer it.

WHAT YOU WILL SEE: You will be brought into a small, dimly lighted room (the lineup room). It has one-way glass separating it from the adjoining room. **While in the lineup room you cannot be heard or seen by anyone in the adjoining room no matter how close you get to the glass. You will be perfectly safe.** After you enter, the administrator will instruct you to look into the adjoining room. There will be five people who are similar in appearance and dress. They will be standing in a fully lighted room with their backs against a wall. There will be a number above each of them. Although you can see them, all they see is a mirror.

WHAT YOU SHOULD CONSIDER:

1. You are under no obligation to pick anybody from this lineup. Your only obligation is to be truthful. It is just as important to clear innocent persons from suspicion, as it is to identify suspects.

2. The **person** or **persons** involved in the crime **MIGHT or MIGHT NOT** be standing in the lineup.

3. Appearances can change over time (for example, head or facial hair may have grown or been cut, body weight may have been lost or gained, and height can be made to look different by slouching or standing very straight.

4. You might want to see the participants facing another direction. Please circle your choice below:

   Facing the wall   *Facing left*   *Facing right*

5. You might want to see the participants' gesture, walk, or make other movements. Please circle your choice below:

   Walk back and forth   *Step closer to glass window*   *Any other movement, such as bend over at the waist or kneel down,*

   please specify: _____

6. You might want the participants to repeat something you heard during the crime.
   Please write what you want them to say: _____

7. If you make an identification, neither the administrator nor others in the room can give you any feedback. Regardless of whether an identification is made, law enforcement will continue to investigate the incident.

TAKE YOUR TIME: Be sure to look carefully at each person and the number each is standing under. You may stand as close to the window or move back and forth as you want. **Remember, you cannot be seen or heard.** Again, if you want the lineup participants to do or say something, you only need to ask the administrator. When you are finished please inform the administrator and follow his/her instructions. If you have any questions or concerns, please talk with the administrator.

I hereby acknowledge and understand the foregoing admonition.

Signed: _____ Date: _____

▲ **FIGURE 7-10 Live lineup form (part 1)**

Source: Adapted from Garen Horst, Placer County California District Attorney's Office (2010 Version).

LIVE LINEUP FORM (Part 2)

Case No: _____   Place: _____

Administrator: _____   Witness: _____

Others present: _____

Instructions: Please complete this form to the best of your ability, remembering the instructions that you were given. If you are unclear or uncertain about how to complete this form the administrator cannot tell you what to write. He/she can clarify the use of the form.

On _____, 2010, I viewed a live lineup of five persons. They were numbered 1 through 5. There are three statements below. Each statement has a box next to it. I checked the one box that describes my thoughts about the lineup. I also personally filled out the information asked for in the statement I checked. If I am unable to identify anyone, I will write a few sentences explaining why. I understand this is not a shortcoming on my part, but a reflection of my best judgement.

☐ **I AM CERTAIN** that person number _____ was the person who (describe what he/she did during the crime):

_____

_____

_____

_____

_____

☐ **I AM NOT SURE,** but I think person number _____ was the person who (describe what he/she did during the crime):

_____

_____

_____

_____

_____

☐ **I DID NOT RECOGNIZE ANYONE** in the lineup as being a person who was involved in the crime, because:

_____

_____

_____

_____

_____

<u>YOUR LAST INSTRUCTION:</u>
DO NOT DISCUSS THIS LINEUP IN ANY WAY WITH THE NEWS MEDIA. DO NOT DISCUSS THIS LINEUP IN ANY WAY WITH OTHER POTENTIAL WITNESSES, NOW OR IN THE FUTURE.

Signed: _____   Date: _____

▲ **FIGURE 7-10** Live lineup form (part 2) (*concluded*)

The instructions to live lineup witnesses comport to those used in photo lineups, as does the need for the administrator to maintain strict neutrality. If any person in the live lineup is asked to perform a gesture, walk, or other movements, all others must individually do the same thing. The lineup administrator must be out of sight of the witness while conducting the lineup. The decision of the witness as to any identification must be conducted after the members of the lineup have left the room.

QUICK FACTS

Eyewitnesses and Accuracy

How important is it for investigators to make every effort to get the best possible eyewitness account of a crime? DNA exonerations of criminal convictions have indicated that mistaken eyewitness identification has been a factor in almost 75% of wrongful convictions.[28]

STAGED CRIME SCENES

Investigators should be open to the possibility that the offense they are investigating was staged. Staged crime scenes are not new. In the Bible, Joseph's brothers sold him into slavery and then dipped his robe in the blood of a goat they had killed to convince their father that Joseph had been devoured by a wild animal.[29] There are no official statistics on how often investigators encounter **staged crime** scenes, but there is some limited evidence that about 3% of all cases may involve some element of staging.[30]

One panel of experienced investigators concluded that the most common staged nonfatal crime was the false allegation of a sexual crime, followed by murder staged as a "burglary gone bad" or a robbery.[31] In part, the absence of statistics is due to the fact that when confronted with a staged crime scene, the police have simply unfounded the original report of a crime, reclassified it, or charged the person reporting it with filing a false report.

In recent years, some agencies have filed civil suits against the person falsely reporting a crime or staging a crime scene in order to recover costs of wasted investigative efforts. In addition to other charges that may apply to situations involving staged scenes, many states have laws dealing with fabricating false evidence and concealing, altering, or destroying evidence.

The essence of staging a crime scene is to misdirect investigators, usually away from the actual perpetrator. It may also be done for other reasons, such as protecting a family from embarrassment or financial hardship—for example, trying to make a suicide appear as an accident or a murder.[32] Most life insurance policies have a minimum waiting period, often two years, before suicides are covered. Assume that a man purchases a new life insurance policy, subsequently developed cancer, and commits suicide 23 months after the policy is issued. If his suicide is successfully staged as a murder, the family is financially protected.

Staging investigations focus on two questions: (1) what act is the staging intended to conceal, and (2) what was the motive for staging the crime, the determination of which usually leads to the perpetrator.[33] The staging motive is often one of self-preservation, to get away with the crime, or the previously mentioned avoidance of embarrassment or shame.[34]

Some staged crimes are so clumsy that they are immediately apparent. For example, a husband starts using meth and is secretly selling his wife's jewelry to buy it. To hide this fact, he breaks the window leading from the carport into the house to make it appear a burglary occurred. However, all the broken glass is on the carport—there is none on the inside of the house—meaning that the window was broken from the inside, not the outside. However, with so many crime investigation shows on television, people are learning more about police and laboratory capabilities and are becoming more sophisticated in staging scenes.

The first inklings of something being wrong may come from noticing that those who would seemingly be most affected by the crime, such as the murder of a spouse, display unusual behavior. Even allowing for the complexity of human behavior, when a surviving spouse treats the murder as an inconvenience, is only minimally distressed, or is even oddly undisturbed by it, investigators should be alerted. Stated somewhat differently, when there is an observable lack of congruence between the surviving spouse's affect and the murder, the cautious investigator wants to understand the reason for the gap.

Even when surviving spouses do not verbally express feelings of loss and despair to a significant degree, there are usually still nonverbal signs of distress—for instance, facial expressions, clutching their stomach, reaching for something to steady themselves or a chair to lower themselves into, moving their hands in circular motions as though they are trying to grasp the situation, and a mouth moving without the utterance of words suggest an inability to comprehend the loss.

In other staged situations, the investigator notes inconsistencies between the statements of the witness and the scene's physical evidence. These inconsistencies must be satisfactorily resolved, which may not be possible until the investigation gathers more information and receives the laboratory reports. Some staged crimes may be so successful that the case is closed and reopened only after the receipt of new information. For example, a new widow who came into a considerable amount of inheritance from the deceased is suddenly out partying continuously, immediately having an intense emotional relationship with someone, and cutting off contacts with the family's former friends and relatives, and rumors are surfacing about her previous affairs.

The best tool for identifying a staged crime is a thorough original and follow-up investigation. That documentation remains available and unchanging, needing only additional analysis.[35] Staged crime investigations profit from a logical process:[36]

1. Conduct a comprehensive and thorough review of the documented scene, which may be very time-consuming in violent crimes because of the abundance of evidence.

2. Carefully consider the victim's character, lifestyle, personal and professional associates, drug and alcohol use, normal hangouts, daily schedule and routines, physical condition, occupation, previous complaints to the police, and recent conversations with neighbors and friends. Is this information consistent with the scene and any behavior imputed to the victim; do any inconsistencies emerge that are significant?

3. Look at the incident from several perspectives. Does the reported sequence of events make sense—for example, why didn't the offender target the greatest threat first? Why did the greatest threat to the offender have the least amount of injuries? How did the husband escape a life-threatening injury or death while the assaults on his wife and children were fatal? Were the items taken from the scene valuable and easily removed, or did the offender take less valuable and odd items? Where were the stolen items before they were taken? How did the perpetrator know their location? Are the final positions of the bodies consistent with the location of postmortem lividity (livor mortis), which is the settling of the blood to the parts of the body closest to the ground?[37] (Lividity produces a visible discoloration that is ordinarily reddish purple.

4. Identify and document in detail all possible indicators of staging.

5. Identify and document possible motives for the original act and for the staging. The person staging the scene is not someone who happened by and gratuitously changed things; it is almost always someone who knew the victim and had some association or relationship with him/her.

6. Determine who benefits from the original act and the staging.

COLD CASE INVESTIGATION

A cold case is the most extreme form of a follow-up investigation because it is the reopening of an inactivated, unsolved case. The most common type of cold case investigation is a murder or serial murders, followed by rapes. In some agencies "cold" is a term that lacks precision, covering from months to many years. Other departments have their own definitions of what constitutes a cold case, and some states provide one. By statute in Arizona, a cold case is one that remains unsolved one year after it is reported and for which there are no viable and unexplored leads.

A cold case may have been inactivated because there were no more leads to pursue; applicable forensic examinations had been fully used; potential witnesses were reluctant to talk, hostile, disappeared, or murdered; and evidence degraded or was lost before it could be examined.

One of the reasons for the growth of cold case units is advances in forensic technology, such as Parabon NanoLab's SnapShot discussed in Chapter 1, "The Evolution of Criminal Investigation and Forensic Science." With the ability to get a probabilistic image of a suspect in a cold case, some cases may now be good candidates to be activated (Figure 7-11). Cases are also good candidates for reexamination when a witness finally comes forward or when the person who committed the crime has died and someone who was uninvolved, but knew or suspected the details wants to clear his/her conscious. The work is challenging but has the potential to help families reach a resolution. In some cases, a significant predator may be apprehended. However, sometimes loved ones oppose a cold case investigation because they have "moved on" with their lives and don't want to revisit their painful past.

In the past, a single officer might be assigned to work promising cold cases and then when the "low hanging fruit" was gone, reassigned back to regular duties because of the caseload.[40] Cold case investigation has become a specialty with policies identifying how cold cases will be selected, prioritized, and other details. From medium-sized to larger departments, the cold case unit may have its own space within Homicide Investigations and have multiple investigators assigned to it. In some instances, a cold case may be solved by making a new plea for public help (see Box 7-5).

BOX 7-4 | COLD CASES: HOMICIDE AND NON-NEGLIGENT MANSLAUGHTER

Murders and non-negligent homicides in the United States in the three-year period from 2014 to 2016 totaled 47,297 deaths. The average of the clearance rate for the three years was 61.8% or 29,229 cases. Roughly calculated, the remaining 18,068 deaths became cold cases.[38] In 2015, half of the homicides in Dallas were uncleared.[39]

BOX 7-5 | TWO 35-YEAR-OLD COLD CASES CLEARED AND SUSPECT CHARGED

In 1980, two women were murdered in separate crimes in Venture County, California. One was found in an orchard, and the other in a parking lot.

In a cold case investigation, the Ventura County Sheriff's Office decided to substantially republicize pictures and details about both women, including pictures of two tattoos a victim had on one arm.

The suspect was already serving a life sentence in state prison for kidnapping, robbing, and raping a woman and kidnapping and robbing another woman. He was tied to the cold cases by DNA evidence. The suspect was described by a law enforcement official as "a true monster."[41]

Many law enforcement agencies agree that investigators assigned to cold case units should have certain qualities and identify the following:

1. *Significant experience in homicide investigations.* One lieutenant went so far as to suggest that it is important to "put your most experienced detectives on the cold case squad."

Following a two-year interagency investigation involving the Montebello Police Department, ATF, the Los Angeles Sheriff's Office, and the California Department of Corrections, 40 gang members and their associates were arrested. In addition to other charges, six cold case murders resulted in arrests. (©Ted Soqui/Corbis/Getty Images)

2. *Trial and prosecution experience.* Investigators with this experience typically have better insight into the value of testimony and careful evidence collection.

3. *Self-motivation.* Investigators with the desire to work independently fit well into a cold case unit because the work often demands it.

4. *Compassion.* It is essential to be able to relate to the victim's family and friends.

5. *Knowledge of technology and forensics.* The ability to conduct research independently, locate information, and analyze it effectively is a crucial skill set.

6. *Communication skills.* Investigators must possess effective interviewing and interrogation skills. A key indicator of this is their ability to work effectively with a wide cross section of people.

7. *Patience and perseverance.* Those attributes "may be the two most important qualities for working cold cases," stressed one investigator. You can put a lot of effort into pursuing a lead and come up empty. You have to be able to shake it off, refocus, and get right back on it. The victim doesn't have any advocate, except you.[42]

Cold case units are often supported by motivated volunteers who cull through files seeking solvability factors, do some analysis, and pass along promising cases to investigators. The volunteers may be retired officers, higher-education faculty members, and retired research chemists. In some cases students have been used successfully.

FUSION CENTERS

Following 9/11, it was concluded that if the isolated parcels of information known about the terrorists and their activities before the attacks had been pooled and analyzed, the attacks may have been disrupted, mitigated, or prevented. As part of the overall response, fusion centers (FCs) were developed, staffed by multiple federal, state, tribal, and local agencies and private-sector entities (Figure 7-12). In 2015, 78 FCs were operational.[43] Fusion is defined as turning information and intelligence into actionable knowledge; it is the fundamental process by which homeland security and crime-related information and intelligence are shared. There are two types of fusion centers:

- *Primary fusion centers.* A **primary fusion center** typically provides information sharing and analysis for an entire state. These centers are the highest priority for the allocation of available federal resources, including the deployment of personnel and connectivity with federal data systems.

- *Recognized fusion centers.* A **recognized fusion center** typically provides information sharing and analysis for a major urban area. As the Federal Government respects the authority of state governments to designate fusion centers, any fusion center not designated as a primary fusion center is referred to as a recognized fusion center.[44]

The essence of FCs is the constant merging, analysis, and dissemination of information and data from many disparate sources, including hospitals and the epidemiological monitoring capabilities of the Centers for Disease Control; this information is used both tactically and strategically for homeland security and crime-fighting purposes.

FCs have resulted in a convergence of crime analysis and intelligence to produce real-time, immediately actionable information. The concentration of information in FCs has alarmed civil libertarians concerned about abuses, and at the state level there is some sentiment that the federal government's intelligence contributions need to be more timely and substantial. It is predictable that issues will arise in an effort of such magnitude, and those issues deserve serious consideration.

▶ **FIGURE 7-12 Fusion center**
(Courtesy of Kentucky Office of Homeland Security)

INTELLIGENCE ANALYSIS AND CRIME ANALYSIS

In the 1960s, few law enforcement agencies agencies had intelligence units. Typically, agencies accumulated vast amounts of information, such as incident reports, citations, field interview reports and simply filed them. As data accumulated, more and more filing cabinets were bought. The fact is that for a long time policing deluded itself in the belief that possessing reams of information was the same as having usable intelligence. Table 7-1 distinguishes between information and intelligence.

In the wake of riots that wracked the nation, protests against the Vietnam War, the recommendations of several presidential commission reports, and grants from the now-defunct Law Enforcement Assistance Administration, police intelligence was largely birthed during the late 1960-ws into the 1970s. Slowly, policing began to embrace the ability to turn its raw information into intelligence and crime analysis data that helped inform the decisions of chiefs and sheriff's.

Given the amount of information accumulated and a general lack of understanding about intelligence, it is unsurprising that crime analysis gained some degree of prominence in police agencies before intelligence did. At its simplest, crime analysis involves a set of analytical methods that converts raw data into

TABLE 7-1	Examples Distinguishing Between Information and Intelligence
INFORMATION	**INTELLIGENCE**
• Criminal history and driving records	• A report by an analyst that draws conclusions about a person's criminal liability based on an integrated analysis of diverse information collected by investigators and/or researchers
• Incident reports	
• Statements by informants, witnesses, and suspects	
• Registration information for motor vehicles, watercraft, and aircraft	• An analysis of crime or terrorism trends with conclusions drawn about characteristics of offenders, probable future crime, and optional methods for preventing future crime/ terrorism
• Licensing details about vehicle operators and professional licenses of all forms	
• Observations of behaviors and incidents by investigators, surveillance teams, or citizens	• A forecast drawn about potential victimization of crime or terrorism based on an assessment of limited information when an analysis uses past experience as context for the conclusion
• Details about banking, investments, credit reports, credit cards, and other financial matters	
• Descriptions of travel including the traveler(s) names, itinerary, methods of travel, date, time, and locations.	• An estimate of a person's income from a criminal enterprise based on a market and trafficking analysis of illegal commodities[45]
• Statements of ideologies, beliefs, and values.	

products aimed at informing police leaders on a timely basis about crime volume, patterns, and trends; victims; community characteristics; methods of criminal operation; and relationships between individual offenses and suspects. This is done to provide leaders with analyses for deploying resources for taking offenders into custody, recovering property, and preventing future offenses. Arguably, crime analysis operates more in the present and uses existing data sets more than intelligence does.

In contrast, intelligence analysis seeks to frame a predictive response that may include some use of existing data sets, but often requires the collection of new data from interviews, covert means, aerial surveillance, remotely operated videography, trash diving, and other methods. Intelligence analysis may be tasked to provide administrators with its best estimate of specific questions, such as, "What is the most vulnerable infrastructure target for terrorists in our community?" "Gangs will fight to gain control of the distribution of fentanyl because it is in high demand and extremely profitable. What is the best ways to protect our community from fentanyl?" Intelligence analysis often starts with its own questions, such as, "What do we know about this? What do we need to know? And, how are we going to get the information we need?"

Over roughly the past 12 years, many governments have seen revenues fall dramatically. Many city and county departments have experienced substantial cuts. Although the recovery from the Great Recession was pronounced to be under way several years ago, many areas still await better times. Some financially conservative citizen groups have openly been asking, "Can we really afford or do we need the police department we had?" In the past, in law enforcement agencies one or several people did both intelligence and crime analysis. It is likely that more of that is being done and raises the question of how well both can be done by just one or several professionals.

THE INTELLIGENCE/ANALYTICAL CYCLE

Intelligence is a five- or six-part cycle driven by the needs of the end user of what analysis produces. The five-part intelligence cycle is used by the CIA and the U.S. Departments of Justice and State, as well as numerous other agencies. Sometimes it is called the six-part intelligence cycle. The difference is whether the sixth element is numbered or just a labeled arrow (Figure 7-13).

Analysts must keep the needs of the end user firmly in mind or risk pursuing the answers to interesting, perhaps even important, questions that are of no utility to the end user's needs.

As part of their responsibilities, analysts must let commanders know what the possibilities and limitations of the techniques are. Four common categories of intelligence are:

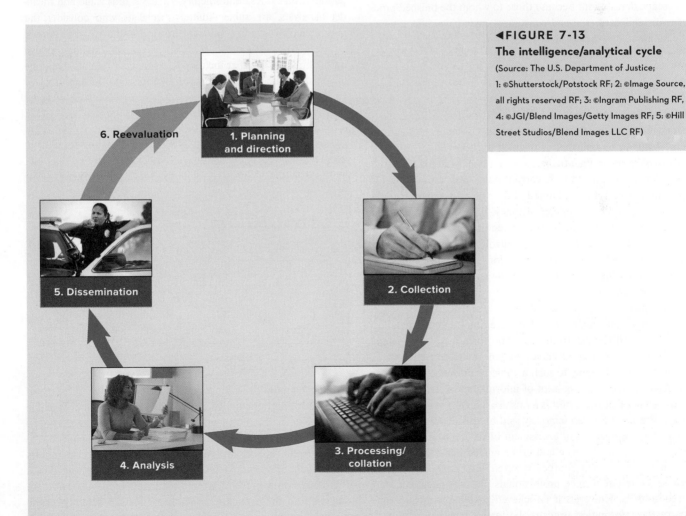

◀ FIGURE 7-13
The intelligence/analytical cycle
(Source: The U.S. Department of Justice; 1: ©Shutterstock/Potstock RF; 2: ©Image Source, all rights reserved RF; 3: ©Ingram Publishing RF, 4: ©JGI/Blend Images/Getty Images RF; 5: ©Hill Street Studios/Blend Images LLC RF)

6. Reevaluation

1. Planning and direction

2. Collection

3. Processing/ collation

4. Analysis

5. Dissemination

1. *Indicative intelligence*. Focuses on new and emerging criminal developments.
2. *Tactical intelligence*. Immediately actionable and often results in arrests.
3. *Strategic intelligence*. Gathered and analyzed over time and usually confirms newly discovered patterns of criminal activity.
4. *Evidential intelligence*. Factual, precise information that can be presented in court.[46]

Policing's understanding of intelligence has continued to expand beyond its own immediate needs, to apprehending other aspects of their communities as well, such as the suspicion unfairly heaped on people just because they are Muslims, Mexicans, refugees from the Syrian war, and sometimes people who are simply different from us.[47]

1. PLANNING AND DIRECTION

The intelligence analysis process is directed at two primary levels: (1) Police executives must recognize it as a tool of great importance and make sure that the tasks and questions assigned to it warrant encumbering its resources, and (2) the unit commander must instill a sense of esprit de corps in all members. Outstanding finished intelligence may determine to what degree a community can escape devastation. Because those to whom the finished product is disseminated (the end consumers) may have different specific interests, this should be factored into the work plan and may affect both data collection and the types of analysis used.

2. COLLECTION

The gathering and reporting of the raw information that is needed to produce finished intelligence is called collection. What needs to be collected is decided ahead of time, although there may be some unanticipated sources that are found as the due diligence of collection is carried out. This point illustrates that however carefully planned, the collection plan can be dynamic. The military version of this is no battle plan survives with certainty the first contact with the enemy.

Sources of information that are available to everyone are called **"open source intelligence"** (OSINT). More specifically, OSINT is publically available information that anyone can lawfully order, observe, or purchase.[48] Thus, examples of it include government records, scientific reports, periodicals, news media accounts, the many things that can be found on the Internet, and detailed reports on individuals from Accurint for Law Enforcement (APE). It may be a good choice to jump-start collection. Two thoughts seemingly apply to such a choice: (1) caveat emptor (let the buyer beware): Having a lot of information doesn't eliminate the possibility that some of it is a mistake, and (2) in dealing with Russia, President Reagan famously said he trusted them . . . with verification. Verification or assessment of reliability is one of the cornerstones of intelligence and crime analysis.

The value of open sources is often undervalued, possibly because some intelligence professionals put too much value on closed sources. However, it is believed that between 80% and 95% of the information used by the intelligence community is

OSINT.[49] The opposite view is there is so much OSINT that it's "hard to filter out the important signals (points) from all of the noise" (the volume of information).[50]

There are also closed sources of information. Law enforcement officers collect such information from various sources, including citizens who report crime, investigations that are conducted, informants, undercover agents, physical and electronic surveillance, and by reaching out to other agencies, for example, prison intelligence units.

3. PROCESSING/COLLATION

The goal of processing is to transform the data collected into forms that facilitate its examination by analysts. This may require translating and interpreting documents, decrypting messages, and interpretation of images and other techniques. The data transformed is stored on a computer from which it can be retrieved and worked with by analysts.

4. ANALYSIS AND PRODUCTION

This is the phase in which data are worked with to produce a finished intelligence product. It includes integrating, evaluating, and analyzing all available data, including that which is fragmentary and sometimes contradictory. Analysis adds value and meaning. Analysts, are subject-matter specialists who consider the information's reliability, validity, timeliness, and relevance. They integrate data into a coherent whole, giving it context, and produce finished intelligence that includes assessments of events and judgments about the implications of the information for end users.[51]

5. DISSEMINATION

The fifth element in the cycle is the dissemination of the finished intelligence report to the end-user who requested it.[52] The end user can then make decisions or take actions on the basis of the intelligence provided.

6. REEVALUATION

It is crucial that the end user provide feedback about the value of the intelligence so that there can be an ongoing cycle of improvement. Moreover, the finished intelligence report itself, the decisions made, and the actions taken all have the potential to create new questions that lead back to the first element, planning and direction, thus beginning a new intelligence/analytical cycle.[53]

CRIME ANALYSIS

A fuller definition of **crime analysis** is that it relies on a set of quantitative and qualitative techniques to analyze data valuable to police agencies and their communities. It includes the analysis of crime and criminals, crime victims, disorder, quality-of-life issues, traffic issues, and internal police operations, and its results support criminal investigation and prosecution, patrol activities, crime prevention and reduction strategies, problem solving, and the evaluation of police efforts.[54] Table 7-2 summarizes the three types of crime analysis.

TABLE 7-2   Types of Crime Analysis and Their Description

1. Tactical Crime Analysis

Tactical crime analysis deals with immediate criminal offenses, such as burglaries or robberies. The period of analysis may be weeks to years, depending on the fact situation. Source material for analysis comes largely from police documents, such as incident and supplemental investigative reports, Computer-Aided Dispatch (CAD) records, arrest reports, modus operandi (MO) summaries, intelligence sources, traffic citations, field stops, and pawnshop records. External sources which may be consulted include federal, state, and local law enforcement agencies, NCIC, Parole/Probation, departments of motor vehicles, and social media sites. When it is produced, tactical crime analysis is often the basis for a quick response by operational units. It is an important basis for operational decisions designed to deter, disrupt, or arrest criminal offenders and clear cases.

2. Strategic Crime Analysis

In contrast to the immediate orientation of tactical crime analysis, strategic crime analysis deals with entrenched crime problems and emerging crime/criminal trends. Entrenched crime problems include organized crime and "hot spots," concentrations of a high number of crimes in a relatively small area. The use of crystal meth, a form of methamphetamine, exploded in the early 1990s as a new trend, that brought with it soaring numbers of emergency room visits, admission to treatment facilities, and suicides and other deaths. Gangs turned even more violent as they fought over suppliers and control of territory. More recently, terrorism and state and local policing has become a strategic concern.

3. Administrative Crime Analysis

The primary purpose of administrative crime analysis is to inform relevant audiences with summary/aggregate information about crime conditions, including neighborhood/crime watch groups, the general public, the city/county manager, city councils/county commissions, the news media, and other law enforcement officials. The level of detail and disclosures often varies by the audience for which the analysis is intended, e.g., the need to have an easily understood document with charts, figures, photographs, and GIS maps and non-disclosure of sensitive information to some audiences. In general, the internet is an excellent way to reach many of these audiences. Other uses of administrative crime analysis include providing information for annual reports, meeting grant requirements, recalculating the deployment of the patrol force, cost-benefit analysis of police programs, and maintaining transparency. [55]

Within tactical crime analysis is the technique of linking crimes together. When this can be successfully accomplished, the information in multiple incident reports is combined and may form the basis for special police attention, e.g., hot spots and/or provide investigative leads. Commonly used methods to link crimes include:[56]

- *Trends.* **Trends** are general tendencies in the occurrence of crime across large geographic areas over extended periods of time. They arise when areas become more conducive or less conducive to a particular crime or crimes. Trends can be associated with shifts in demography; for example, as a neighborhood ages, its residents may be seen as soft targets for muggings and home-invasion robberies. Trends can also stem from the creation of new targets; for instance, the presence of a new shopping mall increases the opportunities for shoplifting and thefts from, and of, vehicles.

- *Patterns.* If the same crime is committed repeatedly over a short period of time, sometimes, but not always, by the same offender, it is a pattern. For example, outside a five-star restaurant, a number of female patrons who are leaving alone have their purses snatched.

- *Series.* In a **series,** the same type of crime is committed over a short period of time, probably by the same offender. For instance, in an affluent, gated residential community of 73 houses, six burglaries occur in nine days.

- **Sprees**. When the same type of offense is committed at almost the same time by the same offender(s), it is called a spree. An example is the vandalizing of cars by a group of kids who spray-paint license plates while walking through a neighborhood.

- *Hot spots.* A **hot spot** is a location where various crimes are committed on a regular basis, usually by different perpetrators. An example is a bar where underage drinkers are served, there are numerous fights, user-level drug sales take place, prostitution flourishes, and patrons are occasionally mugged, robbed, or carjacked in the parking lot (Figure 7-14).

- *Crimogens.* A **crimogen** is either an individually known offender who is responsible for a large number of crimes or one victim who reports a large number of crimes. Examples include a career criminal and a convenience-store operator who reports gas drive-offs, shoplifting, robberies, assaults, and even thefts of entire ATM machines.

Crime-analysis reports, depending on their intended use and sensitivity, may be distributed at staff meetings, shift briefings, the departmental intranet, or other method.

CRIME SCENE RECONSTRUCTION

Reconstruction of past events is routine in law enforcement. The first officer at a domestic violence call listens to the parties involved, examines any injuries, looks at the scene where the

Violent Crime/Drug Site

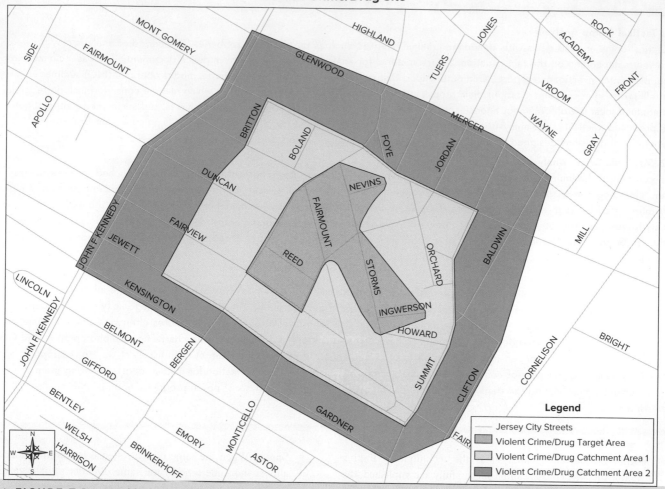

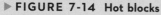

▶ **FIGURE 7-14 Hot blocks**

The pink, "T" shaped area defines a hot spot where violent crimes and drug activity were the targeted concerns for intensive police enforcement. Catchment Areas 1 and 2 were policed in the normal way to determine if hot spot policing simply displaced crime a few blocks away, into one of the catchment areas. There was no immediate crime displacement into the catchment areas. Instead, there was a diffusion of crime prevention benefits beyond the target area as a result of the intensive policing in the target area (David Weisburd, et. al., "Does Crime Just Move Around the Corner? A Study of Displacement and Diffusion in Jersey City, N. J. (Washington, D.C.: National Institute of Justice, U.S. Department of Justice, October 2005), pp. 3 and 18. (Source: David Weisburd, et al., "Does Crime Just Move Around the Corner? A Study of Displacement and Diffusion" in Jersey City, New Jersey, (Washington, D.C., U.S. Department of Justice, 2005, p. 3))

violence allegedly took place, evaluates the credibility of statements made by the parties involved and any witnesses, and in consideration of all the information available at that time makes a decision on the proper handling of it. Even the most basic crime scene construction efforts attempt to answer two key questions: (1) What happened at this scene? and (2) How, including the sequence, did it happen?

In contrast, to the first officer at a domestic violence call **crime scene reconstruction** (CSR) involves analysis of more complex scenes, integrates data from varied sources, and uses a more rigorous methodology to reach its conclusions. The scientific method is at the heart of CSR. The Association for Crime Scene Reconstruction (ACSR) defines CSR as "the use of scientific methods, physical evidence, deductive reasoning, and their interrelationship to gain explicit knowledge of the

series of events that surround the commission of a crime." There are different approaches to CSR, but they share common perspectives:

- Data defines the conclusion.
- The context in which evidence is found, as well as its analysis, provides objective data.
- Consider human testimony cautiously.
- Effective forensic examination produces more refined data.
- What happened is not the only question—its sequence is also important.
- Use "reverse engineering" to work backward from the evidence to develop an understanding of what happened.[57]

STEPS IN THE SCIENTIFIC METHOD	RECONSTRUCTION APPLICATION
1. State the problem	IQ: Was the victim approaching or going away from VMS when she was shot?
2. Gather the relevant data	Crime scene photographs and diagrams; medical examiner's report; lab reports: bloodstain pattern analysis, ballistics.
3. Form a hypothesis	Victim was going away from VMS.
4. Predict what the hypothesis would indicate if true	It would contradict VMS's account of incident: victim attacked him with a knife in her hand; he shot her with SW revolver in self-defense at a range of 18″; she turned around, staggered down the hallway and collapsed.
5. Test of hypothesis	1. Victim found 13 feet from VMS's alleged shooting position, near end of "L" shaped hallway. 2. No blood evidence at the point victim was allegedly shot. 3. No back spatter blood on revolver or VMS's person/clothing. 4. Bullet's entry point was the victim's back, through her nightgown. 5. High-velocity bloodstain pattern indicates victim was shot approximately 9′ from VMS's position. 6. Lab test concluded victim could not have been shot at distance claimed by VMS.
6. State the conclusion	Victim was shot moving away from VMS's position at a distance of approximately 9 feet.

◄**FIGURE 7-15**
The scientific method and CSR

The different CSR approaches also ask four basic questions as each item of evidence is being considered:

- What is it?
- What function does it serve?
- What does it tell about the timing and sequence of events?
- What interrelationships does it have with other items of evidence?[58]

The **scientific method** is at the heart of all approaches to CSR. The steps of the scientific method and their application to CSR are identified in Figure 7-15. This illustration addresses a single investigative question (IQ).

The six steps of the scientific method are easily followed in a controlled laboratory experiment where there can be a single test point of a hypothesis before a conclusion is reached. However, in investigation we develop multiple hypotheses, often at different times—such as the victim was seated when shot; the suspect gained entry through the victim's rear door; the first of three shots fired through the glass window came from the inside; and the suspect returned to the scene and mutilated the victim's body. These hypotheses are not collectively tested at a single point in time but intermittently throughout the investigation as the appropriate information—for example, autopsy reports, surveillance camera images, and lab reports—becomes available (Figure 7-16). The testing, as well as the addition of new information, causes us to refine some hypotheses, discard others, and formulate new ones to test.

The scientific method is somewhat circular, because after we test a hypothesis, it often leads to new questions that require answers; thus, the employment of the scientific method produces an ever-expanding and self-correcting body of knowledge related to the crime.[59] This expanding body of knowledge may also introduce thorny new problems that require entirely new hypotheses. Assume a man's body is found next to his car in the parking lot behind a bar. The car door is open, the keys are near the victim's hand, and the scene suggests he was about to enter or leave his car when he was shot once in the chest and head. One rear trouser pocket is semi-turned inside out, and there was no wallet. The investigator's initial impression was that a lone gunman killed the victim in a robbery gone bad. Later, the autopsy report arrived, and bullets from two different caliber handguns were recovered from the victim. Before reading any further, the investigator entertains several new possibilities: One shooter using two different weapons? Two shooters? One shooter scared off before taking anything, and quickly thereafter an

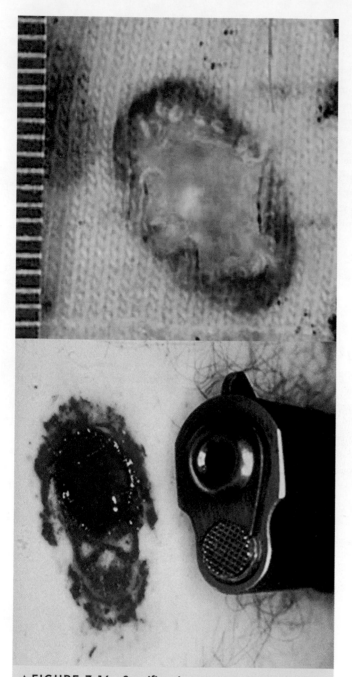

▲ FIGURE 7-16 Specific crime scene reconstruction
Suspect related he shot the victim from across the room. The victim's yellow sweater and skin reveal the shot was fired with the gun's muzzle in contact with the victim. There was also "blowback" evidence on the pistol, blood and tissue, from the victim. The physical evidence contradicts the suspect's story.
(Courtesy of Forensic Training and Consulting LLC)

process that rejects evidence and conclusions that lack sufficient proof; it does not allow, for example, assumptions to masquerade as facts.[61] Key skills associated with critical thinking include analyzing, synthesizing, and evaluating.

One approach to CSR is Event Analysis (EA) model of CSR. "*Incident*" is any situation a reconstructionist is asked to investigate; the term is neutral and avoids the implicit assumption that a crime has been committed. An incident includes all of the activity from its beginning to its end.[62] Incidents consist of macro components, "*events*"; these, in turn comprise a series of actions, "*event segments*," that are much like a series of time-phased photographs.[63] The primary focus of EA is to identify as many event segments as possible; each event segment is a miniconclusion based on the verifiable data associated with it[64] (Figure 7-17).

The scientific method is designed to eliminate other explanations and cannot establish a final, "absolute truth." Scientific methods and statements are open to re-examination, particularly in light of new data and new analytical techniques. An allied example is the number of people who were convicted by eyewitness testimony but freed years later by DNA analysis. What this means in investigation is that at the end of using the scientific method we have eliminated the impossible and implausible and what is left is a valid possibility. CSR does not deal with the "why" of crimes; that is the purview of criminal profiling, discussed next in this chapter.

CRIMINAL INVESTIGATIVE ANALYSIS

An early event on the road to criminal profiling involved New York City's "Mad Bomber," who from 1940 until 1956, with a "patriotic pause" during World War II, left over 30 bombs in public places. After reviewing the amassed evidence, psychiatrist James Brussels concluded:

> He is a male, middle-aged, meticulous, largely self-educated, Slavic, Roman Catholic, has an Oedipal Complex, lives in Connecticut, and worked for Consolidated Edison or one of its subsidiaries. The police would have to publicize the profile to draw the man out, and when apprehended he will be wearing a buttoned double-breasted suit.[65]

Drawn out by the publicity, George Metesky wrote letters to newspapers, which unintentionally contained clues that ultimately led to his arrest in 1957. Remarkably, he was wearing a buttoned double-breasted suit, and other aspects of the profile were also correct. Conversely, the profiles of the Washington D.C. snipers who terrorized that area in 2002 with their random murders were substantially off-target.

The FBI led the modern development of profiling beginning in the 1970s and assisted law enforcement agencies looking for an unknown subject in serious crimes by providing the subject's personality and behavioral traits based on what happened at the crime scene. However, over a period of decades, criticisms of profiling accumulated. Some critics see profiling as a pseudo-science. It was also characterized as never having been a scientific process and essentially based on commonsense intuitions and faulty theoretical assumptions that appear to be consistent with educated guesses and wishful thinking.[66] A more moderate

opportunistic criminal took the wallet and finished the possibly conscious victim off? Found wounded and killed by a spurned lover, who then staged a robbery by taking the wallet?

Despite such thorny problems, CSR goes forward using the discipline of the scientific method, blending empirical knowledge, gained from observation and deduction, and rationalism, inductive thought and reasoning,[60] particularly critical thinking. At its heart, critical thinking is an unremitting intellectual

Case Situation:

Officers responded to call where a husband (TJM) returning home alone parked his BMW in the garage, closed the garage door, and entered the house through the door opening into kitchen. Although his wife was on an out-of-state trip, he expected his 17-year-old stepdaughter to be home. She was the only other person who would be in the house. He discovered "lots of blood" in her first-floor bedroom located in the home's west wing. TJM immediately went just outside the front door and used his cell phone to call 911. He did not reenter the house until arriving officers cleared it without finding anyone. The first arriving officer remained continuously with TJM, first outside the front door and later in the living room. Crime scene technicians arrived and began processing the scene. Soon thereafter, investigators reached the scene and 35 minutes later took TJM from the living room to the station, where he gave the statement used to describe this case situation.

Data Elements:

1. TJM brought BMW to scene.
2. TJM parked in garage.
3. TJM closed garage door.
4. TJM arrived alone at house.
5. TJM found blood in his stepdaughter's bedroom.
6. TJM immediately went outside the front door and called police on his cell phone.
7. First arriving officer stayed continuously with TJM, first outside the front door and later in the living room.
8. Other arriving officers searched but did not find anyone else in house.
9. Blood recovered from stepdaughter's room.
10. Visible blood droplets found on floor of master bathroom in home's east wing.
11. Blood found on inside of shower in master bathroom.
12. Blood found on rear bumper of BMW.
13. Blood found in trunk of BMW.
14. Blood noted in 5 and 9–13 above consistent with stepdaughter's DNA.

Event Segment:

Subsequent to stepdaughter's bleeding, TJM transferred her blood to the master bathroom and the BMW's bumper and trunk.

For detailed information about Event Analysis see Ross M. Gardner and Tom Bevel, *Practical Crime Scene Analysis and Reconstruction* (Boca Raton, Florida: CRC Press, 2009).

◀**FIGURE 7-17**
Illustration of event segment analysis

criticism was raised in 2009, which called for a higher level of scientific validity.[67]

Because of such problems, the FBI quietly stopped using the term "criminal profiling" in favor of "criminal investigative analysis," which it also saw as a broadening of the services provided to law enforcement agencies, which now include the following:

- Indirect personality assessments
- Equivocal death analyses
- Investigative suggestions
- Interview strategies
- Linkage analyses
- Media strategies
- Threat assessments
- Search warrant affidavit assistance
- Trial strategies
- Expert testimony
- Geographic profiling
- Critical incident analyses[68]

Of these terms, equivocal death analyses requires a few comments. Coroners and medical examiners can classify deaths as homicide, suicide, natural, accidental, and undetermined. An equivocal death analysis is an intensive examination of the death in order to determine in which classification it belongs. Many families want or even need to know more about the death of a loved one when the manner of death was undetermined.

It remains to be seen how criminal investigative services plays out. Some of the data suggest the broader services are being very well received.

GEOGRAPHIC PROFILING

Geographic information system (GIS) software provides the capability to superimpose various types of data on a map. For example, a law enforcement administrator might want to see where traffic citations are being written versus where accidents frequently occur, which could lead to a refocusing of the enforcement effort. **Geographic profiling** is a specialty that rests on the premise that given a sufficient number of crimes, with adequate information suitable for analysis, a probabilistic map of the area in which the offender's residence is located can be calculated. A study of crimes committed by 92 prolific

▲ **FIGURE 7-18**

Geoprofiling for illegal entries into the United States that resulted in criminal dispositions. The land of Mexico is to the left of the river (blue line); to the right is the United States. Note that the yellow line turns purple near the top of the image, showing an increase in elevation. Higher vertical lines portray more crossings made at that point. (Courtesy Dr. Kim Rossmo, Center for Geospatial Intelligence and Investigation (GII), Texas State University, San Marco)

burglars revealed that 72% of the actual burglars lived in the top 5% of geographical areas predicted as where their residences were.[69] The size of the area depends on the amount and quality of data. Geoprofiling has also proven itself useful in locating insurgents responsible for planting improvised explosive devices and in border security (Figure 7-18).

Although others had worked on geographic profiling, the term was coined by Rossmo, a former Detective Inspector with the Vancouver (Canada) Police Department. While studying for his doctorate, he conceived of the idea of using geographic profiling to target the residence of offenders and was the central figure in developing the first software package to be able to do this. As in the case of other recently developed investigative technologies, geoprofiling is in a state of transition as refinements are developed. It is not a perfect tool, and its capabilities can be decreased if the number of cases in a series are roughly less than 5 or the crime linkage is inaccurate.[70]

REMOTE SENSING

Remote sensing is the process of collecting and analyzing information about areas, objects, or events without being in contact with the focus of analysis.[71] Aerial surveillance was the first type of remote sensing; during the Civil War (1861–1865), officers were sent aloft in balloons to observe the disposition of enemy forces and report on what they saw. Some photographs were taken and used by commanders.[72] Today, aerial/visual sensing is conducted by manned space craft, satellites, rotary and fixed-wing aircraft, unmanned aerial vehicles (UAVs), and public surveillance cameras.

Aerial remote sensing can be used by law enforcement personnel to detect illicit drug crops and clandestine labs, monitor airstrips, provide over-the-horizon (OTH) intelligence about drug smuggling boats and planes, quickly identify incipient forest fires, rescue lost hikers and mountain climbers, find airplane crash sites, locate fugitives and abducted persons, recover automobiles and other evidence from water systems, identify possible clandestine graves, as well as to provide investigative leads, the identification of suspects, and proof that the elements of a crime were committed.

Aerial surveillance platforms may be equipped with not only visual recording and transmitting capabilities but other sensor packages as well. Many police aircraft are equipped with Forward Looking Infrared Radar (FLIR), which is a significant asset in tracking fugitives on foot at night through their heat signatures.

There are also numerous other remote-sensing capabilities, including (1) the use of canines to detect contraband and cadavers (Figure 7-19) and (2) ground-penetrating radar to locate clandestine graves, which is a process that is nondestructive to physical evidence. (3) Potential burial sites can be worked from the surface to a depth of several feet using metal detectors to search for items such as shell cases, projectiles, belt buckles, jewelry, buttons, and zippers. Advanced metal detectors with screens can show the depth of an item and estimate the probability that it is one type of artifact or another. (4) Radar-based through-the-wall surveillance (TWS) provides 3-D color images, including static objects and moving people, from a distance through walls as thick as 8 inches of concrete. This capability substantially reduces the danger to officers making high-risk entries into buildings to free hostages or apprehend violent offenders. Booby traps can also be identified, the number and locations of suspects determined, and other important tactical information provided. (5) Aquatic acoustic sensors can track boats smuggling drugs or weapons; and (6) smaller gamma-ray-based density meters can identify variations in the density of dashboards, tires, walls, and other surfaces. Such variations allow hidden compartments containing contraband to be identified, and larger gamma ray units can scan cargo (Figure 7-20).

TIME-EVENT CHARTING AND LINK ANALYSIS

Follow-up investigations often result in the accumulation of significant amounts of data. As a result, financial transactions, relationships, the importance of places, events, telephone calls, and other data can be obscured and their importance overlooked, resulting in an unnecessarily protracted or unsuccessful investigation. Software has automated creating a variety of charts, saving investigative effort for other uses. Two commonly used investigative tools are **time-event charting** and link analysis.

A time-event chart is shown in Figure 7-21; it depicts the major events involving an offender paroled from the state prison. Time is shown as intervals between major events. The actual dates for events could be added to the chart. For seven months, he made his regularly scheduled meetings with his parole officer. Three months later, an informant described him

◀**FIGURE 7-19**
A police officer working a cadaver dog, specially trained to locate dead bodies.
In Arundel, Maine, a 63-year old man was discovered dead under suspicious circumstances. His wife, who suffered from dementia, was missing. A state law enforcement officer uses a cadaver dog to search for her. (©Shawn Patrick Ouellette/Portland Press Herald/Getty Images)

◀**FIGURE 7-20**
Truck-mounted gamma-ray scanning the contents of a tractor-trailer
(©Jean-Marc Bouju/AP Images)

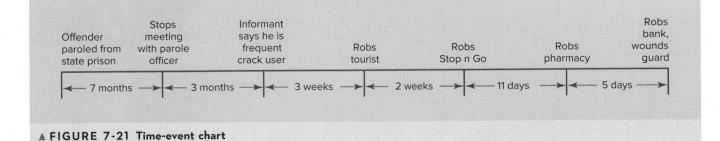

▲ **FIGURE 7-21 Time-event chart**

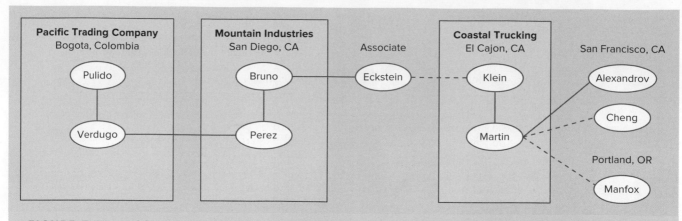

▲ FIGURE 7-22 Link/association diagram

Organizations are in boxes. Solid lines indicate confirmed relationships. Dotted lines are suspected relations.

as a frequent crack user. Three weeks after that, the parolee robbed a tourist. Over the next 30 days, he committed three more robberies, each time progressing upward to a more lucrative target. The choice of a pharmacy as a target gave him both money and drugs, which are the same as money on the streets. If he is selling drugs, informants may know of it. The interval between robberies is growing shorter, and the parolee has become violent. It is possible that he is pulling jobs while high, so the potential for further violence is great. Figure 7-22 is a link chart showing the relationships between individuals involved in importing drugs.

THE INTERNET

The possibilities of the Internet have not escaped law enforcement, which has been quick to use it for investigative, administrative, and public information purposes. For investigative purposes, the police use the Internet in many ways, such as:

1. Appealing to the public for information about specific crimes, often through "crime-stopper" programs.
2. Requesting information about missing children and adults.
3. Posting federal, state, and local most-wanted lists. These lists may be limited to the "top 10," or there may be separate most-wanted lists, such as a list for the most-wanted violent felons or burglars.
4. Soliciting information about individuals who are wanted as fugitives.
5. Alerting the public about jail and prison escapees and requesting information if they are sighted.
6. Requesting information about the identities of unknown subjects ("unsubs").
7. Showing photographs of recovered stolen property so that the owners can identify and claim it.
8. Providing crime-mapping capabilities so that investigators can approach their work with better information and citizens can be informed.

KEY TERMS

Accurint for Law Enforcement (ALE)
cold case
consensual contact
crime analysis
crimogen
crime scene reconstruction
El Paso Intelligence Center (EPIC)
Field Contact/Information Report
fusion center
hot spot
investigative plan (IP)
Law Enforcement Intelligence Unit (LEIU)
Link/Association Diagram

live lineup
National Drug Pointer Index
National Counter-Improvised Explosive Device Capabilities Analysis Database (NCCAD)
National Center for the Analysis of Violent Crime (NCAVC)
Next Generation Identification Program (NGI)
National Law Enforcement Telecommunication System (NLETS)
open source intelligence (OSINT)
photo array lineup
primary fusion center

recognized fusion center
series
scientific method
show-up
social network sites
solvability factors
sprees
staged crime scene
stop
surveillance
Time Event Charting
trends
Violent Criminal Apprehension Program (ViCAP)

REVIEW QUESTIONS

1. How are solvability factors used?
2. How do you prepare a case file?
3. Why are victims and witnesses reinterviewed?
4. NamUs provides what capabilities?
5. What is NCIC?
6. How can LeadsOnLine help an investigation?
7. What things should you not do with informants?
8. Why conduct physical surveillance?
9. How should a photo lineup be conducted?
10. What are three potential indicators of a staged crime?
11. What stages make up the intelligence cycle?
12. How is facial recognition software being used by law enforcement agencies?
13. How do crime analysts link crimes?
14. Why is the scientific method important to crime scene reconstruction?
15. Criminal profiling focuses on what four factors?
16. What is geographic profiling?
17. What are four examples of remote sensing?
18. In what ways can the Internet be used by investigators?

INTERNET ACTIVITIES

1. Officers initiate a number of contacts with people. We know the difference between consensual contacts and stops. Law enforcement agencies have policies titled "Field Contacts," "Field Interviews," "Field Contacts and Interrogations," "Field Contacts and Pat-Downs," or something similar to deal with citizens in the field.

   The police are also well aware of issues such as racial profiling and bias against gender identification and expression. Some agencies have specific policies on relating to members of the LGBT community.

   Pick six agencies in different geographic areas of the country. Do this randomly or because you expect the agency to have well-thought-out policies. However, do it one way or the other. Examine their policies on "field contacts." What differences and similarities, positive or negative, do you see? If you were Chief of Police, what changes would you have made in the policies you read?

2. Go to the Center for Geospatial Intelligence and Investigation, Texas State University to learn more about geoprofiling (*http://txstate.edu/gii*).

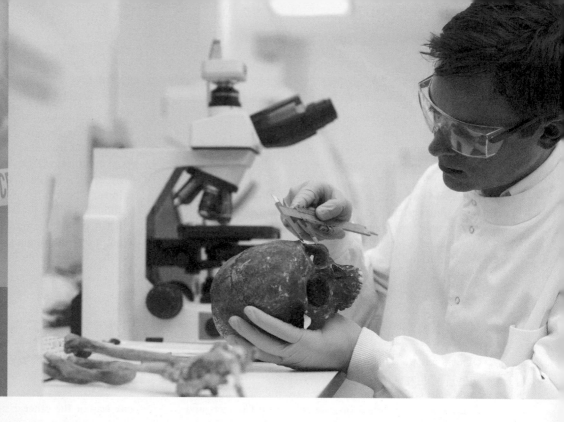

► The FBI crime laboratory is recognized as one of the most comprehensive and prestigious crime labs in the world. Since its inception in 1932, the FBI crime lab has provided invaluable services for law enforcement agencies at the state, county, and municipal level.
(©Adam Gault/age fotostock RF)

8

THE CRIME LABORATORY

A crime laboratory is a scientific organization with a dedicated mission of aiding the process of criminal justice. It provides this aid by answering, or helping to answer, the vital questions of whether a crime was committed, how and when it was committed, who committed it, and who could not have committed it. The criminal laboratory seeks answers to questions such as these through scientific analysis of material collected primarily from the scenes of crimes or from suspects.[1] Although there are hundreds of federal, state, and local crime laboratories throughout the United States, the range of services and personnel expertise within the laboratories varies among the organizations.

To understand the role of crime laboratories, one must understand their relationship to the scientific community and to the functions of the criminal justice system. There are two distinct activities involved in laboratory work. One is the gathering of evidence at the scene of a crime, which is done by evidence technicians or investigators. The second function is the scientific analysis of evidence, which occurs in the laboratory. The effectiveness of the second activity often depends on the efficiency with which the first operation is performed.

An important issue addressed in this chapter is an investigator's expectations regarding the function and responsibilities of a crime laboratory. Although the laboratory is one of the most valuable tools for a criminal investigator, he/she must be aware of its capabilities and limitations. It is not uncommon, for example, for an investigator to send evidence to a laboratory and delay the investigation until the laboratory results are received. Crime laboratories are not intended to replace field investigations. In addition, investigators are often not familiar with the types of evidence that are subject to laboratory analysis. Even the most minute and seemingly insignificant pieces of evidence may be subject to laboratory examination. If investigators are not aware of a laboratory's capabilities, critical pieces of evidence can go uncollected, unprocessed, and unused in substantiating guilt or innocence. Because the analysis of evidence is no better than the samples submitted, investigators play an important role in the success of scientific analysis.

The terms *forensic science* and *criminalistics* are often used interchangeably. **Forensic science** is that part of science applied to answering legal questions. It is the examination, evaluation, and explanation of physical evidence in law. Forensic science encompasses pathology, toxicology, physical anthropology, odontology (dental structure, development, and diseases), psychiatry, questioned documents, firearms, tool-mark comparison, and serology, among other fields. Recent technological advances have added molecular biology and genetics to this list.

One of the branches of forensic science, **criminalistics,** deals with the study of physical evidence related to a crime. From such a study, a crime may be reconstructed. Criminalistics is interdisciplinary, drawing on mathematics, physics, chemistry, biology, anthropology, and many other scientific endeavors. The late Paul L. Kirk, a leader in the criminalistics movement in the United States, once remarked: "Criminalistics is an occupation that has all of the responsibilities of medicine, the intricacy of the law, and the universality of science."[2]

CRIME LABORATORIES

According to the last census available, convened in 2009, there are more than 400 state, municipal, county, and federal **crime laboratories** operating in the United States. Our country's publicly funded forensic crime labs engage in a wide range of services, including DNA tests, controlled substance analyses, and latent fingerprint examinations—receiving a combined total of around 4 million requests for services within a year. It's worth noting that, at the end of that census period in 2009, publicly funded crime labs carried an estimated backlog of around 1.2 million requests for services.[3] The oldest crime laboratory in the United States was established in 1923. Fifty-five percent of the labs were established between 1968 and 1978, just after Supreme Court decisions limited police interrogations and while funds were available from the now defunct Law Enforcement Assistance Administration. Seventy-nine percent of the laboratories are within public safety and law enforcement agencies; the remainder is distributed among medical examiners' offices, prosecutors' offices, scientific and health agencies, and other private and public institutions.[4]

Most crime laboratories have developed in response to a particular need in a community or region. The areas of scientific concentration in particular laboratories are based on those needs and also on the interests and skills of the people available. Not all crime laboratories have the same capabilities, owing to the availability of resources and the fact that some laboratories tend to emphasize and build up expertise in particular areas. The manner of collection of some types of physical evidence varies according to the type of test procedures the laboratory applies. Therefore, police investigators

must familiarize themselves with the capabilities of the crime laboratories supporting their jurisdictions, as well as with the requirements of the national forensic science laboratories.[5]

As can be expected, almost all laboratories originated or were expanded to examine drugs (and, more recently, DNA), but the percentage of crime laboratories with the capability to examine other categories of physical evidence varies from 5% to 81%. In an effort to overcome some of the problems caused by varying specializations and concerns, and because of the absence of agreement on what should be the purpose, function, and services of crime laboratories, the **American Society of Crime Laboratory Directors (ASCLD)** was formed (Figure 8-1). This organization is a nonprofit professional society of more than 400 crime laboratory directors, managers, and supervisors from the United States and 17 other countries who have backgrounds as biologists, chemists, document examiners, physicists, toxicologists, and law enforcement officers. The ASCLD is devoted to the improvement of crime laboratory operations through sound management practices. Its purpose is to foster common professional interests, management practices, information, and communication among its members and to promote, encourage, and maintain the highest standards of practice for crime laboratories. To carry out its purpose, ASCLD has established two additional entities.[6]

ASCLD/LAB, the crime laboratory accreditation program, is a voluntary program in which any crime laboratory may participate to demonstrate that its management, operations, personnel, procedures, instruments, physical plant, security, and personnel safety procedures meet certain standards. At the federal level, the ATF laboratory system was the first to be accredited, and, the FBI laboratory, perhaps the most comprehensive crime laboratory in the world, received its accreditation in the late 1990s. This is not to imply that a laboratory is inadequate or untrustworthy if it chooses not to undertake this voluntary accreditation process.[7] Accreditation can be very time-consuming and expensive.

The National Forensic Science Technology Center (NFSTC) was established by ASCLD in 1995 and began operating in 1996. Its two primary functions are to help crime laboratories prepare for accreditation, especially laboratories whose primary focus is on DNA analysis, and to offer continuing education programs for crime laboratory personnel, including the support of college and university degree programs.[8]

THE MORGUE

One type of crime lab often forgotten is the morgue. A **morgue** is not just a place that houses the bodies of deceased persons; it is the critical element of the forensic process as the place where cause of death is determined. Experienced forensic

▶ **FIGURE 8-1 ASCLD**
The ASCLD/LAB is an independent organization originally established from ASCLD dedicated to providing excellence in forensic science analysis through leadership in the management of crime laboratories; see *www.ascld.org*. (Source: American Society of Crime Laboratory Directors)

AMERICAN SOCIETY OF
CRIME LABORATORY DIRECTORS

"Excellence Through Leadership in
Forensic Science Management"

pathologists conduct autopsies and analyze body fluids, tissues, and organs to produce information useful in an investigation when cause of death is questionable or when death has been caused by something other than a known disease.

DIGITAL CRIME LABS

As our society has become increasingly reliant on computers and the exchange of digital information, police have addressed the collection of the digital evidence through specialized crime laboratories staffed with highly trained technicians. Although many of the digital crime labs servicing the needs of local law enforcement have been federally operated by the FBI or the U.S. Secret Service, today most large police agencies also have digital forensics laboratories to help recover deleted or damaged files, restore hard drives, and collect digital information from almost any type of electronic device (for example, personal computers, laptops, cell phones, digital cameras and camcorders. There are also 15 FBI-operated Regional Computer Forensic Labs (RCFL) and one national program office in the United States that attempt to combine federal and local law enforcement efforts in a more efficient and uniform manner in finding, extracting, and storing digital evidence and presenting it in court.[9]

There are three primary purposes for digital crime labs:

1. Examine and collect relevant digital evidence that may exist on personal computers in support of a crime. This activity is often associated with organized crime investigations involving vice, gambling, and drug trafficking. For instance, some of the most notorious vice cases involving U.S. Congressmen have developed from examining seized computers in the brothels of high-paid madams. In a similar manner, narcotics officers have long used digital crime labs to discover patterns of contacts in large racketeering cases derived from email sent from one courier to the next, supported by illegal payments and purchases involving off-shore accounts. More recently, police investigators have started seizing personal computers at the scenes of more traditional crimes. The following case study provides an insight into this methodology:

disturbing to parents was the finding that Highman had been photographing his basketball players shirtless and storing the files in his home. As a result of the work by these digital laboratories, Highman pleaded guilty and was sentenced to over 11 years in jail and 10 years of supervised release thereafter. Highman will have to register as a sex offender for the rest of his life. The ability of the digital forensics lab to find, extract, and preserve the evidence in this case ensured that Highman's network of child pornography can count no further victims.

2. Digital crime labs are also instrumental in securing evidence that directly involve computer crimes such as money laundering, possessing child pornography, embezzlement, fraud, and identity theft. In these cases, the computer and other devices become instruments of the crime, and police technicians and investigators work closely to analyze digital information as evidence of crime (Figure 8-2). (For more information relating to the computer as an instrument of the crime, refer to Chapter 17, "Cyber Crime.")

3. Police crime labs have also been instrumental in preventing and investigating terrorist attacks in the United States. In fact, the USA PATRIOT Act (2001) was instrumental in developing federal and local efforts in establishing digital crime labs to investigate suspected terrorist activities on our homeland. The threat of terrorist attacks on the Internet aimed at destroying the critical infrastructure of our country poses a significant risk. Digital crime labs are often involved in potential or real "cyber terrorism" attacks that include everything from defacing governmental websites and spreading malicious viruses to thwarting attempts to take over air traffic control systems and damage major energy and telecommunication systems. (Again, refer to Chapter 17 for a more detailed description of crimes involving computers.)

Ohio's Miami Valley Regional Computer Forensics Lab assisted the FBI Columbus Cybercrimes Task Force in the investigation of Michael Highman, 43, a middle-school teacher and boys' basketball coach at an area school. Highman was identified by the FBI as a user of a peer-to-peer sharing program through which pictures and videos could be downloaded on the Internet by other users. A search warrant was issued for Highman's home, and during their search investigators found a number of hidden computer storage devices. A hard drive was even concealed in his basement ceiling. The RCFL combed through Highman's electronic files and discovered nearly 200,000 images and videos of teenage boys engaged in various sexual acts. Most of the victims were between the ages of 14 and 17 and were depicted in sexual poses or engaging in sexual acts with other teenagers or older men. Highman's peer-to-peer capabilities allowed him to share his files and download additional pictures 24 hours a day. Particularly

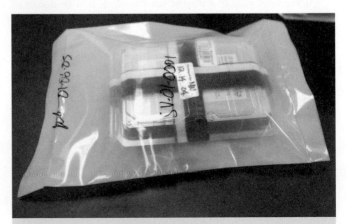

▲ **FIGURE 8-2 Digital crime lab**

A computer hard drive can provide vital evidence in some criminal cases. Computer crime technicians analyze digital evidence that may support everything from a murder case to a terrorist attack. (©Kim Kulish/Getty Images)

EXPECTATIONS

It is not unusual to find situations in which investigators not acquainted with the services of the crime laboratory expect too much from scientific analysis. Popular culture has become a burden to bear for crime labs that are expected to run DNA tests or match ballistics evidence on a moment's notice, as their television counterparts on *CSI* do. Investigators may also expect the crime laboratory to provide a solution in every criminal case for this or other reasons. When investigators do not receive answers to the questions they pose through the submission of physical evidence, they are not only disappointed but more than occasionally also reluctant to use the technical assistance of the laboratory again.

To some extent, investigators must be selective in collecting and preserving evidence that they believe can be profitably submitted for scientific analysis to a crime laboratory. Always keep in mind that the laboratory was never intended to replace a complete field investigation. The function of the laboratory is to support the investigator and the primary line units of the police agency. The laboratory is sometimes capable of lightening the burden of the investigator, but it can never completely assume that burden. Too often, personnel collect evidence at the scene, send it to the laboratory, and then allow the investigation to stall until the laboratory report is received, expecting the laboratory to come up with some magical solution. This is an unrealistic expectation and largely results because the investigator does not understand what is and is not evidence subject to laboratory examination. The analysis of evidence can be no better than the samples submitted. The investigator therefore has a vital role to play in the success of laboratory examinations. James Osterburg, another criminalistics leader, summarizes why there is underutilization or total neglect of crime laboratories. What he said in 1968 is still largely true:

1. Lack of knowledge about how the laboratory can aid the criminal investigator.
2. Unfamiliarity with the more esoteric varieties of clue material, resulting in evidence not being preserved for examination.
3. Failure to collect physical evidence. This may be caused by a fear of cross-examination on some technical, legal, or scientific requirement that may be overlooked. It may be due to inadequate training or experience or to the overcautiousness of field investigators and the fear of destroying evidence.
4. Overrepresentation of laboratory capabilities.
5. Inconvenience to the investigator when there is no local laboratory available or backlogs are so great as to prohibit timely reports of laboratory results.[10]

This list is accurate and complete. The second and fourth points are especially important. If investigators do not know how the most minute or insignificant looking item can be processed at a properly equipped laboratory, critical pieces of material go uncollected, unprocessed, and unused in substantiating guilt or innocence. In addition, if the capabilities of a crime laboratory are overrepresented so that investigators, uniformed officers, prosecutors, and judges all believe it can produce results that it, in fact, cannot produce, these people eventually will underuse the laboratory. Too often scientists fail to keep justice personnel informed of the state of the art in forensic work.[11]

The laboratory can be an extremely valuable investigative tool if the field investigator uses it intelligently and understands its capabilities and limitations. The investigator must also assume responsibility for providing the laboratory with evidence that is properly collected, marked, and preserved so that laboratory analysis, to the effective limits of present technology, can be successful.[12]

MEASURES OF CRIME LABORATORY EFFECTIVENESS

After two years of listening to sworn testimony, independent research and investigative work, the Committee on Identifying the Needs of the Forensic Sciences Community at the National Academy of Sciences (NAS) issued a report (February 18, 2009) entitled, "Strengthening Forensic Science in the United States: A Path Forward."[13] The congressionally mandated report found that serious deficiencies in the nation's forensic science system existed. It called for significant reforms and new research focusing on the *effectiveness* of crime laboratories. Among the findings and recommendations discussed in the report were these:

- Rigorous and mandatory certification programs for forensic scientist are currently lacking, as are strong standards and protocols for analyzing and reporting on evidence.
- There is an absence of uniform, mandatory accreditation programs for crime laboratories and a gross shortage of adequate training and continuing education for laboratory practitioners; hence, some are accredited as with the ASCLD certification (previously mentioned), but others are not. The NAS report recommends that all crime laboratories should be *mandated* to seek accreditation which includes defined and documented levels of training and education for scientists and forensic specialists.
- There is a lack of autonomy and independence of crime laboratories; as a result, crime laboratories and police agencies should be fiscally and administratively separated. Crime labs should have strong and independent leadership away from any criminal justice agency.
- Many forensic science and crime laboratories are seriously underfunded, understaffed, and have no effective oversight; hence, special funding at both the state and federal level should ensure professional standards for personnel working within crime labs and enhance independent and evidence-based approaches to forensic science findings.
- The broader research community generally is not engaged in conducting research relevant to advancing the forensic science disciplines; thus, resulting court testimony from the forensic sciences is often flawed and unclear admitted through a case-by-case basis. Court testimony should be grounded in science. The committee concluded that two criteria should guide the admission of forensic evidence and testimony in court: the extent to which the forensic science discipline is founded on a reliable scientific methodology that lets it accurately analyze evidence and report findings (such as noted in fingerprinting and DNA analysis) and the extent to which the discipline relies on human interpretation that could be tainted by error, bias, or the absence of sound procedures and performance standards.

In addition to the findings and recommendations listed above, the NAS report found that there was no unified strategy for developing a forensic science research plan across agencies. In other words, state and federal agencies often had their own crime lab that not only duplicated effort and work but also produced relatively shoddy and untimely findings. The NAS report has had a significant and far-reaching ramification impacting the measures of crime lab effectiveness, including the traditional criteria of quality, proximity and timeliness as reflected in the following discussion.[14]

QUALITY

Quality is judged largely on the technical capabilities of the laboratory and the abilities of the personnel who staff the laboratory.

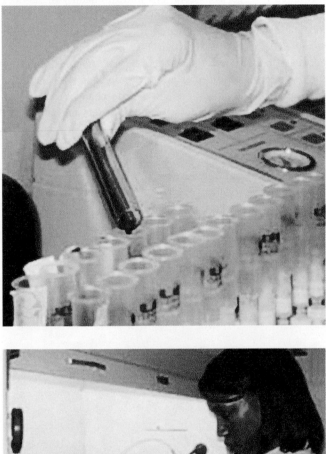

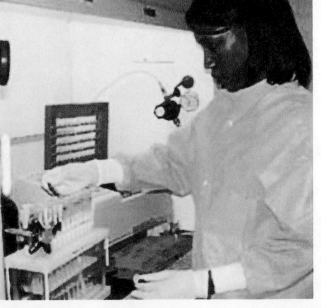

The technical capabilities of the scientific community affect how fully laboratories answer the questions posed by investigators. Although technical advances are developing rapidly, there are still limits on what science can do in analyzing and individualizing evidence. Unfortunately, because of these inherent technological limitations, crime laboratories may not receive the needed resources to expand or even deliver basic services.

Budget considerations largely determine the level of services that a crime laboratory can deliver. A lack of understanding of the extent to which efficient crime laboratory programs can contribute to the effectiveness of a law enforcement agency has led many administrators to channel financial resources into more traditional kinds of law enforcement operations.

"The most important resource in any crime laboratory is the scientific staff. Without an adequately trained, competent staff, the best organized and equipped laboratory will not be efficient."[15] Historically, there has been a shortage of qualified personnel with scientific backgrounds interested in working in a criminalistics laboratory. Many who are qualified shun police laboratory work, particularly on a local level, because private industry can offer much more attractive salaries.[16]

PROXIMITY

It is understood, if not accepted, that most law enforcement agencies cannot afford to staff and maintain a crime laboratory (Figure 8-3). In light of this fact, however, police agencies that

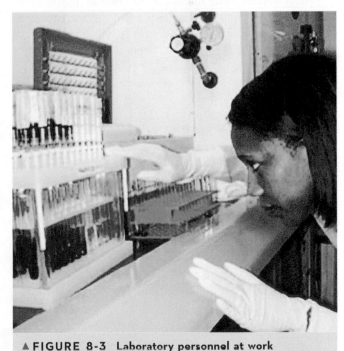

▲ **FIGURE 8-3 Laboratory personnel at work**
Modern police crime labs are typically equipped to scientifically examine a wide range of evidence submitted by investigators. The scientists working in these labs usually have college degrees in chemistry, biology, or the physical sciences and are often called on to testify in criminal trials regarding the evidence they examined. Here, a lab scientist separates biological evidence for comparative purposes. (©Georgia Bureau of Investigation, Toxicology Section)

desire and will use the facilities of a crime laboratory should not be denied the opportunity to have such services at their disposal. Experience indicates that police investigators rarely seek laboratory assistance when the facility is inconvenient. There are areas where the technician or investigator must travel an unreasonable distance to obtain laboratory services. Studies have shown that evidence submission decreased sharply as the distance from the crime scene to the laboratory increased.[17] The solution to this dilemma lies in adequate planning on the state level to provide needed laboratory services.

Studies have indicated that a unified state system can best serve the needs of the law enforcement community by providing a parent, or core, laboratory on the state level capable of delivering most laboratory services and strategically located regional laboratories that respond to immediate, less sophisticated analytical needs and funnel evidence when more sophisticated analysis is required. Texas, for example, has its headquarters laboratory located under the auspices of the Texas Department of Public Safety in Austin, with 13 regional laboratories spread throughout the state. The division of Consolidated Laboratory Services in Richmond, Virginia, serves as a parent laboratory with regional facilities located in Norfolk, Roanoke, and Fairfax. Other states adopting the regionalized concept include Alabama, California, Florida, Georgia, and Illinois. Figure 8-4 shows the location of Florida's regional crime laboratories and state-subsidized local laboratories joined into a regional network.

Several studies have addressed the issue of proximity of crime labs. One recommended that a regional crime laboratory should be established to serve each population group of 500,000 to 1,000,000 in an area where at least 5,000 Part I crimes are committed each year. (Part I crimes are serious offenses categorized by the FBI's *Uniform Crime Reports* into the following eight categories: murder, forcible rape, robbery, aggravated assault, burglary, larceny, arson, and vehicle theft.) Another study recommended that regional laboratories be located within a 20-mile radius of 90% of the law enforcement agencies' sworn personnel who would use the facilities. A third recommendation is that a regional laboratory be located within 50 miles of any agency that it routinely serves.[18] Local laboratories, such as those serving large cities or counties, continue to provide the level of services within their capabilities and also serve as regional laboratories for surrounding agencies.

Even in law enforcement agencies that have a crime laboratory, the organization of the lab and its placement within the organizational structure may reveal much about the importance the criminalistics function carries within the agency, which in turn affects budget considerations and the quality of services provided. It is highly unlikely that an administrator who has fought for and was instrumental in establishing a crime lab would give it anything other than high priority and provide for adequate funding. But what about the next administrator? Or the one after that? Priorities in a law enforcement agency, just as in any other organization, can and do change.

If the crime lab or forensic science program has any importance to the chief executive, that function will not be buried within the organization; rather, it will be accessible to the operation functions and "within sight" of the administration in case assistance is needed. The committed chief executive will ensure that the supervisory chain of command understands and appreciates the scientific roles and responsibilities of the laboratory. In fact, it is in the agency's and the laboratory's best interests for

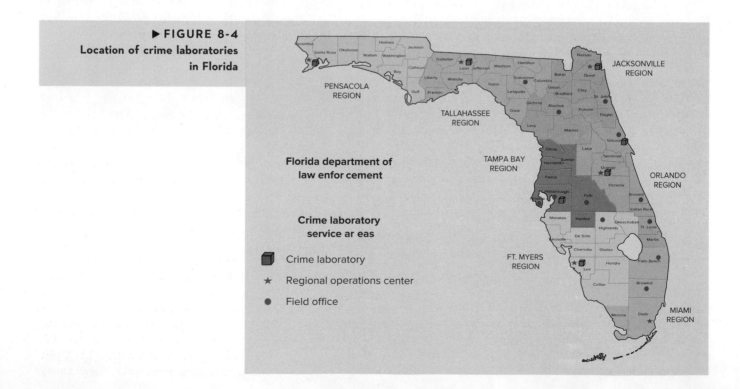

▶ **FIGURE 8-4**
Location of crime laboratories in Florida

the entire supervising and command staff of the laboratory to be scientists who happen to have supervisory or command capabilities. In this manner, when resource allocation and criticality-of-function issues arise in the agency, the people representing the laboratory are knowledgeable about the scientific mission.

TIMELINESS

Timeliness, also extremely important to the investigator, is the third measure of effectiveness of a crime laboratory. A major portion of the caseload of most laboratories today results from investigators' requests for analysis of suspected or known samples of narcotics or dangerous drugs[19] and DNA evidence. Regarding narcotics and dangerous drugs, even in areas where officers carry and are trained to use presumptive test kits that are available on the commercial market, the results of laboratory analysis provide conclusive evidence necessary to the success of cases. Unlike the case with many other articles or items submitted to a laboratory for examination, which only corroborate evidence possessed by the investigator, the analysis of suspected narcotics or dangerous drugs can be the key to a successful prosecution. Their identification can significantly affect early stages of the judicial proceedings, such as the probable cause hearing; and very often this is an essential piece of corpus delicti evidence. Hence, it is necessary that the results of laboratory examinations be made available to the investigator as quickly as possible. Such a prompt turnaround requires an appropriate allocation of money and personnel to the process by those who control the purse strings and make the decisions.

Unfortunately, crime lab turnaround is increasingly and notoriously slow in many instances. The most recent information available shows that crime labs are increasingly overwhelmed by requests for DNA, latent prints, and controlled substance verifications. One study showed that for every four requests cleared by a crime lab, one request went unworked by the end of a year's time.[20] Issues with funding, particularly in a struggling economy have left many labs understaffed, much to the chagrin of investigators and private citizens. Low staffing ratios, combined with the length of time it takes for processing or examining evidence, certainly affects timeliness. In one case, a DNA match in Montgomery County, Maryland, gave prosecutors the evidence that they needed to clear a violent rape from 1993. However, the laboratory was so backlogged that they were unable to process the detailed analysis of the match in time for trial. The suspect walked free as the state was forced to drop their case.[21] Notably, in 2010, a large proportion of the grant awards given by the National Institute of Justice were earmarked for "forensics, DNA, backlog reduction."

RESPONDING TO THE NATIONAL ACADEMIES OF SCIENCE (NAS) REPORT

The NAS report was sponsored by the National Institute of Justice at the request of Congress. It was authored by some of the nation's foremost scientists with expertise in physics, chemistry, biology, engineering, statistics, medicine, law and forensics, and was profoundly critical of forensic science and crime labs across the country. In the aftermath of the report, a number of initiatives were undertaken to address some of the shortcomings identified. The White House established the Subcommittee on Forensic Science (SoFS) under the National Science and Technology Council (NSTC) to coordinate the response to the report recommendations; both of these operated until 2012. During its tenure, SoFS conducted broad research, performed cost analyses, and made policy recommendations that serve as an important foundation for continued work and implementation related to lab proficiency and accreditation.

Furthermore, the Department of Justice and the NSTC collaborated to create the National Commission on Forensic Science (NCFS) in 2013. The Commission is made up of a selection of federal, state and local forensic science service providers, plus research scientists and academics; law enforcement officials; prosecutors, defense attorneys and judges; and other stakeholders. Its stated goal is to "enhance the practice and improve the reliability of forensic science [and] promote scientific validity, reduce fragmentation, and improve federal coordination of forensic science." Generally, the NCFS will develop recommendations and advice to the DOJ on forensic sciences, medico-legal death investigations, and digital evidence.

The SoFS also established 21 scientific working groups that looked at specific areas of forensics, such as fiber analysis, firearms and toolmarks, and fire debris and explosives, specifically to guide quality assurance protocols. It also established the Organization of Scientific Area Committees (OSAC), charged with developing a registry of standards and guidelines for forensic science practice.

The report also spurred increased federal funding for research in forensic science. In the six-year period from 2009 to 2014, the National Institute of Justice's Office of Investigative and Forensic Sciences awarded more than 250 research grants totaling $125 million. A renewed focus on research has also been encouraged through the development of a Forensic Science Center of Excellence led by Iowa State University, and through the funding of workshops and other educational opportunities for forensic scientists.

ADMISSIBILITY OF EXAMINATION RESULTS

In 1923, a federal court rendered a decision in the case of *Frye v. United States* that ruled inadmissible the results of a "deception test," an early version of the polygraph. The decision established a standard which provided that, for the results of a scientific technique to be admissible, the technique must be sufficiently established to have gained general acceptance in its particular field.[22]

Half a century later, the federal **rules of evidence** were adopted, which provide that if scientific, technical, or other specialized knowledge will help the trier of fact understand the evidence or determine a fact in issue, such evidence is admissible. The federal rules of evidence do not apply to the states, and several circuits continued to follow *Frye* rather than the federal rules. In 1993 the U.S. Supreme Court decided the case of *Daubert v. Merrell Dow Pharmaceuticals, Inc.* In that case, the Court said that the "general-acceptance" test of *Frye* is not part of the federal rules and, in fact, was superseded by the rules' adoption. The Court went on to say that the trial judge must make a preliminary assessment of whether the testimony of an expert provides an underlying reasoning or methodology that is scientifically valid and can properly be applied to the facts of the case. Many considerations will bear on the inquiry, including whether the theory or technique in question can be (and has been) tested, whether it has been subjected to peer review and publication, its known or potential error rate, the existence and maintenance of standards controlling its operation, and whether it has attracted widespread acceptance within a relevant scientific community. The Court went on to say that the inquiry is a flexible one and that its focus must be solely on principles and methodology, not on conclusions that they generate.[23]

Although *Daubert* applies only to cases in federal courts, a number of states have adopted the *Daubert* standard. Consequently, the application of *Daubert,* and its aftermath, has presented a challenge to crime laboratories to ensure that the standards imposed by the Court are followed in forensic examinations so that expert testimony and the results of examinations by crime laboratory personnel will be admissible, in both state and federal courts. In the most recent test of the *Daubert* standard, the 3rd Circuit Court of Appeals held in *United States* v. *Mitchell* that testimony be rigorously tested and excluded if compliance with requirements for ensuring accuracy in its application cannot be demonstrated.[24] (This case is discussed again later in this chapter.)

BOX 8-1 | FINGERPRINTS AND THE LAW: PASSING THE *DAUBERT* TEST

The scientific history of forensic analysis has maintained that no two people have the same pattern of swirls and ridges on their fingertips; a unique pattern we call "fingerprints." This assumption has provided the basis for irrefutable testimony in courtrooms, and fingerprint analysts have been linking latent prints found at crime scenes to suspects for the last century of criminal trials in America. All of that may now change. In 2002, federal Judge Louis H. Pollak became the first legal authority to question these assumptions. At issue was not whether a fingerprint is a unique identity marker (that assumption is still intact), but whether a fingerprint examiner working in a governmental lab is capable of using scientifically sound techniques in identifying a suspect from a partial smudge of a fingerprint found at a crime scene.[25] Ruling that fingerprint evidence does not meet the standards of scientific scrutiny established by the U.S. Supreme Court, Judge Pollak set ablaze a new controversy surrounding the veracity of forensic analysts working in the crime lab. Essentially, Pollak found that fingerprint "matching" failed the Daubert test, meeting only one of the criteria, that of general acceptance.[26] Although Judge Pollak reversed his findings three months later, the initial ruling set a precedent revealing ever-increasing challenges on the techniques used for scientific comparisons and the qualifications and expertise of individual fingerprint analysts and the labs in which they work.

Despite nearly 100 years of routine use by police and prosecutors, there has been woefully little empirical evidence to verify or test the accuracy of testimony presented by fingerprint examiners in court. Leading scientists argue that fingerprints many not be the gold standard in court, as once considered. Consider the following criticisms since Judge Pollak's original ruling in 2002:

- Fingerprint examiners lack objective standards for evaluating whether two prints actually "match." There simply is no uniform approach to deciding what counts as a match. Many use a process call "point-counting" that involves counting the number of similar ridge character-

istics on the prints ... but there is no agreement about how many points are necessary to determine a positive match ... six points, nine, twelve?

- The potential error rate for fingerprint identification in actual practice has virtually no systematic study. In other words, there is no quality control relating to the examiners themselves. In some tests of proficiency, 34% of FBI fingerprint examiners failed the test.
- Fingerprint examiners are compelled in court to testify with "absolute certainty" about a match. However, in actuality, they are only providing a probability of the match since they do not have access to all fingerprints worldwide and do not have a body of empirical evidence in which to justify "absolute certainty."
- The reliability of fingerprints is surprisingly untested; and until such pursuit of knowledge and reliability is completed, reliance on fingerprint identification should be treated with higher skepticism.[27]

The Scientific Working Group on Friction Ridge Analysis, Study and Technology (SWGFAST) was commissioned by the National Institute of Justice and developed *The Fingerprint Sourcebook* in 2011, aimed specifically to address many of these issues and set forth guidelines for fingerprint examiners. The group posited "that forensic friction ridge impression examination (fingerprint examination) is an applied science based upon the foundation for biological uniqueness, permanence, and empirical validation through observation."[28] They also argued that fingerprint examination was technical. Hence, the testimony of fingerprint examiners fell squarely under that of a scientific expert, applying directly to Federal Rules of Evidence (FRE) 702, opening analysts and examiners to the scrutiny of opposing attorneys, and allowing challenges under Daubert. Fingerprint evidence is no longer accepted in the court without the testimony of an examiner that can pass the rigors of Daubert as a scientific expert.[29]

TECHNOLOGIES

The speed at which technological advances with forensic applications are developing, expanding, and evolving makes their description immediately obsolete. Computerization has increased speed and reliability of many of the processes formerly manually performed (Figure 8-5). Computer software is available to identify and track serial killers; produce aging progression, facial imaging, and other data to aid in the search for missing children; analyze hair to improve the detection of drug abuse, particularly after a long period of time has elapsed since the use of specified drugs; highlight fingerprints that were previously unrecognizable or undetectable on smooth surfaces with the use of laser technology; and digitally enhance photographs. Other new and exciting technologies that are revolutionizing crime labs include:

- Forensic techniques that can detect the source of impurities within chemicals.
- Mathematical analysis of blood spatter that allows scientists to plot how blood droplets will fall from a ceiling or wall.
- Advancements in ballistics technology using 3D imaging that can help determine where a weapon was fired based on shells and cartridges.
- A software program that takes DNA information and translates it into possible physical traits of suspected criminals.

DNA ANALYSIS

Advances in technology have helped DNA testing to become an established part of criminal justice procedure. Despite early con-

▲ **FIGURE 8-5**

Computer technology and forensic science

New technologies that combine computer software with sophisticated scientific equipment have become powerful tools for analyzing evidence. (©BSIP/UIG/Getty Images)

troversies and challenges by defense attorneys, the admissibility of DNA test results in the courtroom has become routine. In 2005, the last year that data was available as of this writing, crime laboratories in the United States received DNA samples from about 39,000 known- or unknown-subject cases. All 50 states, plus the District of Columbia, required that offenders convicted of certain crimes submit DNA samples. Most required that all felons submit samples.[30] In a 2007 survey, nearly 70% of prosecutors in jurisdictions with populations of more than 500,000 indicated that they used DNA evidence in felony cases. DNA was primarily used in cases involving sexual offenses, followed by a lesser number of murder and manslaughter cases, as well as aggravated assaults.[31]

Questions about the validity and reliability of forensic DNA test methods have been addressed, and for the most part validity and reliability are established. As a result of DNA testing, traditional blood testing and saliva testing have been rendered obsolete, because DNA is found in these substances and, in fact, is found in all body tissues and fluids.

Deoxyribonucleic acid (DNA) consists of molecules that carry the body's genetic information and establish each person as separate and distinct. Until recently, DNA was found primarily within the nuclei of cells in the chromosomes. DNA can now be extracted and processed from blood, tissue, spermatozoa, bone marrow, hair roots, saliva, skin cells, urine, feces, and a host of other biological specimens, all of which may be found at crime scenes. DNA has been recovered from fingerprints, cigarette butts, drinking cups, and hatbands and other articles of clothing.

DNA is generally found in cells that have a nucleus, hence the name **nuclear DNA.** However, some biological cells do not have nuclei, such as those forming fingernails, hair shafts, and teeth. What those cells do have is a more primitive form of genetic coding called **mitochondrial DNA (mtDNA),** found in the mitochondria, which are in the body of the cell. When a sperm and an egg join at conception, the new individual gets half of his or her nuclear genetic information from each parent. Conversely, mitochondrial DNA is inherited only from the mother. At conception, all of the new person's mitochondria come from the mother. Since mitochondrial DNA is passed directly through maternal relatives, it serves as a perfect identity marker for those relatives.[32] Indeed, the mitochondrial-DNA sequencing technique was originally developed by anthropologists to help trace human ancestors.

Identifying and Collecting DNA at a Crime Scene

DNA evidence may be found and collected from virtually everywhere at a crime scene, and only a few cells can be sufficient to obtain useful DNA information. DNA does more than just identify the source of the sample; it can place a specific person at a crime scene, refute a claim of self-defense, disprove a claimed alibi, and put a weapon in a suspect's hand. Consequently, the more an investigator knows about how DNA can be used, the more powerful a tool it becomes.[33]

Because samples of DNA are easily contaminated, extreme care should be taken while collecting samples. Several precautions are offered to maintain the integrity of the sample and the analysis:

- As discussed in Chapter 4 "Physical Evidence", collecting biological DNA evidence in the field requires special considerations. The standard recommendation for collecting biological evidence is not to remove the stain from an object but rather to collect the object with the stain, provided that the stain can be adequately protected from contamination. If the entire object cannot be collected, then the next best way to gather such evidence is to remove the stain by cutting it out (for example, from a piece of carpet or clothing). On occasions when it is impossible to collect a stain by cutting it from the object, the two preferred methods of collection are (1) to use a dampened cotton swab (with distilled water) to collect the stain or (2) to use a clean instrument such as a razor blade to scrape the stain into a clean paper bindle. In both cases, the samples should be placed in a clean paper bag and allowed to air dry.[34]
- Wear gloves and change them often.
- If the sample is not completely air dried, it can be dried in the laboratory using a drying hood. Make sure the evidence is properly marked and the table below the drying hood is clean from contamination.
- Use disposable instruments, or clean instruments thoroughly before and after handling each sample.
- Use enough sample to optimize the chance of getting a clear result; however, consideration must be given to leaving a sufficient amount of sample so that a second test can be conducted by the defense. Avoid touching any area where it is believed DNA may exist.
- Avoid touching areas where the sample may exist or be placed. Avoid talking, sneezing, or coughing over evidence. Use physical face barrier protections whenever possible. Avoid touching your face, nose, and mouth when handling evidence and conducting analysis.
- Return evidence to new paper bags or envelopes. Label and store in the evidence room. Do not use plastic bags, and do not use staples to seal bags or envelopes.[35]
- For long-term storage, keep biological evidence in the freezer.[36]

DNA Technologies

In 1985 Alec Jeffreys and his colleagues in England first used DNA in a criminal case. Shortly thereafter, DNA evidence began making appearances in trials in the United States. Initially, DNA analysis required a fairly large sample, and the manual processing technique, called Restriction Fragment Length Polymorphism (RFLP), took up to 14 weeks, on average, to produce results. The RFLP system is slow but produces good results. Technological advancements have led to

a polymerase chain reaction (PCR), which takes small samples of DNA and reproduces as many copies as are needed for adequate analysis. Short tandem repeats (STRs), which are even smaller pieces of the DNA helix (ladder), can be reproduced using PCR to generate multiple copies in an instrument called a *thermocycle*. With the PCR-STR process, it takes about 24 hours to extract DNA from an evidentiary sample and only 2 to 3 hours to type the DNA using automation. It works well on degraded samples and on analysis of old cases.[37]

Contamination

Just as contamination is an issue in the collection and packaging of evidence containing DNA, it is a very big issue in the handling of DNA during extraction and examination. It is also an issue that can affect the admissibility of, and credibility given to, DNA evidence in court. Coughing or sneezing while handling DNA evidence can cause contamination.

Population-Genetics Statistics

The effectiveness of DNA evidence in court depends on the ability of a witness to explain the probability that no other person, except an identical twin, has the same DNA type as that discovered on a crime scene sample that identically matches the DNA type of the defendant. Thus, the question is this: is it possible to individualize the identity of a person on the basis of an analysis of his or her DNA? The answer is yes and maybe. Although there are a number of ways geneticists can calculate the probability that no other person has the same genetic chart or "footprint" as the defendant, the question often arises as to what database of individuals is being used to calculate the probability (Figure 8-6). For example, if a Hispanic person is the defendant, would the probability that there would be another person with the same DNA sequence be any greater if the database used to compare DNA consisted of only Hispanics? Is this the fair way to determine probability? This is a simplified example of some of the issues being examined. In the end, the statistical probability derived by any method of calculation is an estimate.

Data Banking and CODIS

Today, all U.S. jurisdictions have legislation requiring the data banking of DNA evidence of convicted offenders. In some jurisdictions, DNA can be collected only from offenders convicted of sex-related crimes and homicides. In others, legislation has been expanded to allow for the collection of DNA specimens from all convicted offenders. This development has dramatically increased the workload of laboratories that are processing the material to establish the data banks.

In addition to individual-jurisdiction data banking, there is a national investigation support database, developed by the FBI, called the Combined DNA Index System (CODIS). CODIS is used in the national, state, and local index-system networks to link typing results from unresolved crimes with cases in multiple jurisdictions or persons convicted of offenses

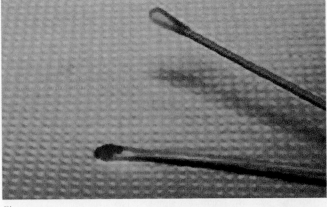

(1)

(2)

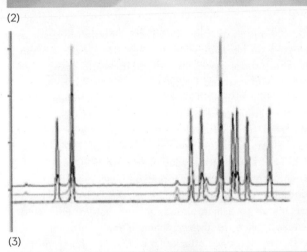

(3)

▲ **FIGURE 8-6 From blood sample to DNA "footprint"**
Human biological evidence such as saliva, urine, semen or blood is collected at the scene on cotton swabs. Those same swabs can be presumptively tested to indicate blood (pink color on lower swab). (2) If a blood reference sample from a suspect or victim is submitted, it will be spotted on blotter paper and preserved. (3) DNA instrumentation can reveal the forensic profile of the suspect and compare it to the crime scene sample or be entered into a database for future comparisons. (Courtesy of the Utah Department of Public Safety/ Bureau of Forensic Services)

specified in the data-banking laws passed by the jurisdictions. By alerting investigators to similarities among unsolved crimes, CODIS can aid in apprehending perpetrators who commit a series of crimes. As of May 2016, The National DNA Index (NDIS) (which is one part of CODIS, which contains the DNA profiles contributed by federal, state, and local participating forensic laboratories) holds over 12,348,009 offender 1 profiles, 2,361,870 arrestee profiles, and 708,416 forensic profiles. CODIS has produced over 332,348 hits and has assisted in more than 318,824 investigations.[38]

Today, DNA analysis is used for a variety of forensic purposes, from identifying victims of mass disasters (such as 9/11 and Hurricane Katrina) to tracing a person's ancestry. Each state collects a DNA sample and fingerprints from serious offenders such as persons convicted of rape and murder, but a few states have extended this practice to all arrestees, not just those successfully prosecuted for violent crimes. California, Florida, Louisiana, Texas, and Virginia are the five states with such legislative provision, and there are others focusing more on child predators and offenders associated with crimes against children.[39]

Standards, Testing, Research, and Developments

Laboratory accreditation by the ASCLD's accreditation board in all areas of forensic science requires that quality-assurance measures be in place at the laboratory. Quality-assurance standards have been developed for DNA analysis by the FBI's DNA Advisory Board. The National Institute of Standards and Technology has tested these performance standards for the various analysis techniques discussed earlier. The National Institute of Justice supported the development of criteria for external DNA proficiency training.

The NIJ also supports ongoing research and development related to DNA evidence in the following areas:

- Alternative Genetic Markers
- Compromised DNA Evidence
- Human DNA Quantitation
- General DNA Tools and Information
- Miniaturization and Automation
- Mitochondrial DNA
- Non-Human DNA
- Sperm Detection and Separation
- Y-Chromosome

New developments in DNA technologies now allow forensic scientists to produce genetic profiles from a few cells worth of genetic material. New "high-sensitivity" labs are now able to use DNA testing to solve crimes heretofore reserved for violent crimes such as homicide, rape, and assault where significant amounts of biological-evidence (for example, blood, hair, semen, saliva) were present. These labs can solve routine property crimes such as burglary, auto theft, and larceny. The concept behind "high-sensitivity" labs focuses on **low copy number DNA samples** (or samples that have fewer than 150 cells of genetic material) that result from minutia evidence (for instance, skin cells left on a smudged fingerprint, saliva traces on a cigarette butt, or perspiration droplets left on a window). The first use of such evidence came in 1999, when low-number DNA samples found on a weapon and other objects handled by a suspect helped solve a murder case being investigated by the Royal Canadian Mounted Police. Of course, the practice has become controversial, because no national standard for tests on such a small sample exists. Further, the admissibility in court of low copy number DNA analysis has not been tested. Yet, the potential for solving a wide range of crimes exists with this new technology, if not as the primary evidence against a suspect but perhaps even as a supporting part of the prosecutor's case.[40]

Familial or Kinship DNA Searches

As technology advances, so does the use of DNA. More recently, forensic investigators have begun using a practice called **"familial DNA searches,"** or **"DNA kinship searches,"** in investigating crimes. A familial DNA search is conducted when a DNA sample collected from a crime does not match any of the samples in the database. If this occurs, scientists can expand the search to see if the database contains any samples with similar patterns to the sample collected from the crime. Although each person's DNA is individually unique to that individual, family members will have similar DNA profiles. By expanding the search, forensic scientists are hoping that a relative to the potential suspect is in the system. The odds of finding a relative are high considering there are over three million DNA samples in U.S. state and federal databases and that a survey conducted by the U.S. Department of Justice found that 46% of jail inmates reported that they have at least one close relative who has been incarcerated.[41]

The use of familial DNA searches could have a huge impact on the justice system. If there are no known suspects for an offense, investigators will run any DNA samples collected from the scene through CODIS in hopes that the potential suspect is not in the system. Matches found this way are commonly called "cold hits." To date, there have been 30,000 cold hits using CODIS. If kinship DNA searches were used, the number of cold hits would surely increase. Forensic scientists claim that in a familial DNA search a parent/child relationship would be identified at the first lead 62% of the time, and 99% of the time the hit would be in the first 100 leads.[42]

Not everyone supports the use of familial DNA searches. Opponents believe DNA kinship searches cast suspicion on innocent family members who happen to be related to someone in the system.[43] Plus there is the concern of misuse by law enforcement officials. A familial DNA search often results in multiple hits, and forensic scientists state that it is the responsibility of the investigators to follow the leads with the highest degree of shared DNA makeup (those more likely to be a close relationship to the potential suspect). Others are concerned that the success of kinship DNA searches could lead to the creation of a universal or national database containing every citizen's DNA and fingerprints.[44]

Case Studies in Familial DNA

In 2000 Welsh police reopened the murder case of Lynette White. White had been fatally stabbed in 1988, and the case had gone unsolved for 15 years. In 2000 the police caught a break after reexamining the crime scene and finding blood spots on a skirting board that had been missed in the 1988 investigation. No exact matches were made when the DNA sample taken from the blood spots was run through the national database, but the system did find a similar DNA profile in the system. Both the sample from the crime scene and the sample in the system contained a rare form of a gene. The sample belonged to a 14-year-old boy who obviously could not be a suspect, considering that the crime took place six years before he was born. What police did have was a lead. There was a good possibility that the offender was related to the young man. After interviewing and taking DNA samples from the boy's family, police were able to make an exact DNA match to the boy's paternal uncle, Jeffrey Gafoor, who later confessed to killing White.[45]

On the morning of August 10, 1984, Deborah Sykes was abducted on her way to work. The 25-year-old woman was raped, sodomized, and stabbed to death. Police later arrested and charged Darryl Hunt, then 19, with Sykes's murder. Hunt claimed he was innocent, but he was sentenced to life in prison. Later, in 1990 and in 1994, DNA tests from semen found on the victim's body did not match Hunt's DNA (at the time of his trial, these more reliable tests were not available). In both 1990 and 1994, law enforcement officials ignored these new findings. Eventually, further investigations of the DNA did find a close match to a man already in the system. Following this lead, police discovered that this man's brother, Willard Brown, had once attacked a woman not far from the place where Sykes had been killed. In December of 2003, when confronted with the DNA evidence, Willard confessed to murdering Sykes. That February, Darryl Hunt was released from prison after spending close to two decades incarcerated for a crime he did not commit.[46]

Successes

Even though DNA may be collected from a crime scene, it may not be submitted to a laboratory for a variety of reasons. Something may prevent further investigation on the case, or the DNA may not be needed to resolve the case. The backlogs and slow turnaround times previously discussed may also hinder investigations, but despite this, DNA evidence has proved to be a huge boon to the justice system by identifying and confirming a suspect, and by clearing or excluding others who may have been suspects.

For instance, a woman informed the FBI that she had overheard a man talking on a pay phone. The man said that he had killed a woman and buried her in the woods of a local park reserve. The local police were notified, and they located the badly decomposed skeletal remains of a person but could not find the victim's teeth. Since the medical examiner could not visually identify the person or use dental records for identification, she sent the remains to the FBI laboratory, where examiners removed DNA from the victim's bones and performed mitochondrial-DNA analysis. The results were compared to the DNA of missing persons in a national database. Law enforcement authorities were able to identify the victim and later convicted her killer—the man on the pay phone.[47] Another example involved a threatening letter that was sent to a newspaper editor. The FBI swabbed the envelope flap and recovered some saliva cells, which were then typed using a DNA marker. The result was compared to a known suspect and was found to match.[48]

DNA can be extracted and analyzed from specimens that may be years or even decades old. In a case involving Kirk Bloodworth, who was found guilty of sexually assaulting and murdering a young girl, the verdict was based on an anonymous tip, identification from a police artist's sketch, eyewitness statements, and other evidence. He was later retried and again found guilty. But in 1993, more than eight years after his arrest, prosecutors compared DNA evidence from the victim's clothing to Bloodworth's DNA and found that the two did not match. He was subsequently released and then pardoned.[49]

QUICK FACT

The Future: Protein-Based Identification in the Hair

Researchers at Lawrence Livermore National Laboratory are in the early stages of using genetic mutations in the protein of cells to match evidence with a specific person. "Proteomics," or the study of proteins that genes produce, is at the same stage as DNA identification and profiling was in the early days of its development during the late 1990s. While initial work is focused on the mutations found in the protein in hair cells, the hope is that the process will be viable for all human cell structures such as those found in not only hair, but also in blood, sweat, tears, skin, semen, and the like.

Sources: Lawrence Livermore National Laboratory News. See: www.llnl.gov/news/llnl/team-develops-forensic-method-identify-people-using-human-hair-proteins
Spencer S. Hsu, "Has DNA Met Its Match as a Forensic Tool?" *The Washington Post* (September 9, 2016).

THE INNOCENCE PROJECT

The Innocence Project, founded in 1992, is a nonprofit legal organization founded for the purpose of exonerating wrongfully convicted people through DNA testing. The use of DNA testing has forever changed the criminal justice system.[50] Before the use of DNA, forensic evidence relied on the comparison of hairs, particles, fibers, and blood types. As discussed in Chapter 4, blood types were determined from collected bodily fluids at a crime scene and compared with a potential suspect. Samples that were the same blood type suggested that the suspect *might be* the offender; however, conclusive statements indicating that the suspect *definitely* was the offender were not possible. As one would think, the practice of comparative blood typing is now considered outdated and has been replaced with DNA analysis. In the past five years, significant problems have arisen with the microscopic examination and comparison of hairs, fibers, and other microscopic evidence primarily because of the lack of sufficient reliability and the frequency of erroneous results.[51] The Innocence Project is especially interested in cases in which the defendant was convicted using what they consider "unreliable methods" and in cases in which the evidence was misrepresented or could have been subject to DNA analysis.

In recent years, the federal and some state governments have begun to allow incarcerated individuals who claim they are innocent to have access to DNA testing. In 2004 the federal Justice for All Act was created, which grants federal inmates access to DNA testing, and provides funding to similar state programs. By the end of 2010, 48 states had enacted legislation that permits inmates access to DNA testing. There are only two states that do not have legislation focusing on retesting of DNA evidence: Oklahoma and Massachusetts.[52]

Despite these improvements in legislative action and DNA technological access, there are still significant flaws in the process:

- Some courts will not consider newly discovered evidence *after* trial.
- Most of the new legislation fails to include adequate safeguards for the preservation of DNA evidence in the future.
- Several states do not allow individuals to appeal denied petitions for testing; therefore, the decision to retest is left to the appellate judges.
- A number of states fail to require full, fair, and prompt proceedings once a DNA testing petition has been filed, allowing the potentially innocent to languish interminably in prison.[53]

QUICK FACT

The Innocence Project: Statistics Speak Volumes

The Innocence Project was founded in 1992 by Barry Scheck and Peter Neufeld, two nationally known attorneys dedicated to exonerating wrongfully convicted individuals through DNA testing. The mission of the Innocence Project is to free innocent people who remain incarcerated and to bring reform to the criminal justice system that is responsible for their unjust imprisonment. Since its inception through July 2016, the Innocence Project has exonerated 342 cases by DNA analysis; over 100 of these cases were death sentence cases. Many of these cases are compelling, pointing to breaches in investigative protocol by police officers and detectives, coerced interrogations and compelled and/or false confessions, misconduct (e.g., fabricating evidence, bias and prejudice, bribery) on the part of prosecuting attorneys, and the unreliability of eyewitness testimony.

The following chart shows DNA exonerations from 1989 to 2012:

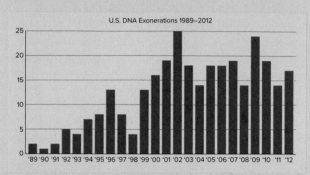

U.S. DNA Exonerations 1989–2012

Visit the Innocence Project website and read some of the latest case histories at: www.innocenceproject.org

Sources: CNN, "Exonerated: Cases by the Numbers" (December 4, 2013) at: http://www.cnn.com/2013/12/04/justice/prisoner-exonerations-facts-innocence-project/
The Innocence Project: www.innocenceproject.org
Emily M. West, *Court Findings of Prosecutorial Misconduct Claims in Post-Conviction Appeals and Civil Suits Among the First 255 DNA Exoneration Cases* (New York: The Innocence Project, August 2010).

A Postconviction DNA Case

In the early morning hours of July 25, 1985, in Garland, Texas, a woman woke up to see a man standing over her bed with a knife. He then raped her and left. As he was leaving, the woman followed him to the patio door and believed she had gotten a good look at her attacker. She described her assailant as a young, white male, around 5′8″, 140 pounds, blond, slim, very tan, and wearing beige pants and no shirt. The police suspected David Pope, but the victim was unable to identify him in a photographic line up. She did, however, pick him in a live lineup a month later. She also identified Pope in court as the man who raped her.

Evidence used against Pope in court included a knife found in the defendant's vehicle that resembled a knife stolen from the victim's house and a "voice print analysis" that matched Pope's voice to messages the attacker had left on the victim's answering machine in the weeks following the attack (voice print analysis is no longer used by the courts, because of reliability issues). Pope represented himself during the punishment phase of his trial and proclaimed his innocence. He stated that he had lived in the same apartment complex as the victim until the month before the attack, when he had been evicted. In the month of the attack, he had been living in his car on the apartment

complex's property. He was convicted in 1986 for aggravated sexual assault and was sentenced to 45 years in prison.

In January 1999, an anonymous call to the Dallas County District Attorney's Office supported Pope's claim of innocence. The case was reopened, and the rape kit was submitted for DNA testing. The results not only proved that Pope was innocent, but the sample matched another person already convicted and serving time for rape. Pope was granted a pardon on February 2, 2001, *after* he had served 15 years.

Exonerated from Death Row

In 2007 Curtis Edward McCarty was exonerated after spending 21 years on death row in Oklahoma (Figure 8-7). He had been convicted of murdering and raping a woman in 1985. District Court Judge Twyla Mason Gray dismissed the charges after ruling that the evidence used to convict McCarty had been tainted by the questionable testimony of former police chemist Joyce Gilchrist. In her original notes, Gilchrist stated that the hairs and other biological evidence did not match McCarty; later she changed her notes, and in two trials Gilchrist testified that McCarty could have been the killer. In both trials he was found guilty and sentenced to death. The defense requested that the hairs be retested, but subsequently the hairs were lost. A judge has said that Gilchrist either destroyed or "lost" the evidence intentionally. In recent years, DNA has also proven that another person had raped the victim, not McCarty. McCarty is the 124th person to be exonerated from death row in the United States.[54]

Biometrics and Next Generation Identification (NGI)

In the mid-1970s in San Francisco, Miriam Slamovich, a concentration camp survivor, was shot point-blank in the face. She died a month later. On the bedroom window, her killer left a full, perfect fingerprint that became the object of thousands of hours

▲ **FIGURE 8-7 DNA errors**
Ex-police chemist Joyce Gilchrist stated that she always based her opinion on scientific findings and that she felt comfortable with her conclusions and testimony given to the court. Unfortunately, internal documents indicated otherwise.
(*Left:* ©Steve Gooch/The Daily Oklahoman/AP Images;
right: ©Martial Trezzini/Keystone/AP Images)

of manual fingerprint comparisons over a 10-year period. When San Francisco installed an **Automated Fingerprint Identification System (AFIS),** the latent print from the Slamovich case was the first search made, and a hit was recorded in less than 6 minutes. (Figure 8-8). The killer was in custody the same day.[55]

AFIS, which is a term still used out of habit and legacy, later morphed into **IAFIS,** or **Integrated Automated Fingerprint Identification System,** which included both the fingerprint records and criminal history database with identification and response capabilities. In NGI, data on fingerprints is now held within the **Advanced Fingerprint Identification Technology (AFIT)** system. AFIT offers enhanced fingerprint and latent processing services as well as a new fingerprint-matching algorithm that improves the matching ability of 92% obtainedwith the old AFIS to better than 96.2% within IAFIS. AFIT also offers faster response times, fewer rejections, increased frequency of matches, and other functional improvements.[56]

AFIT allows law enforcement agencies to conduct comparisons of applicant and suspect fingerprints with literally thousands or millions of file prints in a matter of minutes. A manual search of this nature would take hundreds of hours with little hope of success. The heart of the technology is the ability of the computer equipment to scan and digitize fingerprints by reading spacing and ridge patterns and translating them into the appropriate computer language coding. The computer is capable of making extremely fine distinctions among prints, lending greater accuracy and reliability to the system. Today, IAFIS and AFIT are part of the overall Next Generation Identification project being developed by the FBI as discussed earlier. See Figure 8-9 and Box 8-2.

```
AFIS*          CANDIDATE DATA & IMAGE SCREEN (DPCV-T)      04/11/90 13:46
 JOB NO.    : 11-0-0059-4-0      JOB INITIATED: 04/11/90       PRTY:3
 OPERATOR ID: CATES              TERMINAL ID : F000
                                                        SEARCH-PRINT
                                                        <           >
                                                        SEX  :M
                                                        YOB/R:??/?
                                                        PAT. :RLRWR-LRLLI
                                                        REF. :     - A
                                                        QUAL.:ABBBB-BABCI
                                                        RDB-T:1
                                                        LOC. :005

                                                        CANDIDATE-PRINT
                                                        RANK :001 / 005
                                                        <01-02-00100709>
                                                        SCORE:04354
                                                        PAT. :RLRWR-LALLI
                                                        QUAL.:BBBBB-ABBBI
                                                        SEX  :M
                                                        YOB/R:51/?
                                                        RDB-T:1,6
     SEARCH-PRINT IMAGE      CANDIDATE-PRINT IMAGE      MEMO :0075-0630
     FINGER NO.: 01          FINGER NO.: 01                  1 2 3 4 5
                                                             6 7 8 9 0
                                                             ZOOM (X2)
                                                             ZOOM (X4)
                                                             L  R
                                                             U  D
                                                            *CHARTING
                                                             ERASE
```

◀ **FIGURE 8-8**
AFIS fingerprint comparison
This is an actual AFIS print. On the left is a file print several years old. On the right is a latent print left at the scene of a burglary. Even though a new scar is seen on the fingerprint on the right, AFIS was still able to match the prints.
(Courtesy of Dallas Police Department)

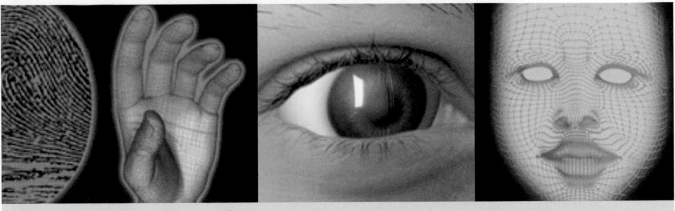

▲ **FIGURE 8-9   Next Generation Identification (NGI) program**
The FBI's new program that incorporates a variety of biometric data (other than just fingerprints) on known suspects, including palm prints, voice data, iris measurements, and facial structure. (For more information, *visit www.fbi.gov/about-us/cjis/fingerprints_biometrics /ngi/ngi2.*) (Source: Federal Bureau of Investigation)

BOX 8-2 | NEXT GENERATION IDENTIFICATION (NGI) FLYER

U.S. Department of Justice
Federal Bureau of Investigation
Criminal Justice Information Services Division

NEXT GENERATION IDENTIFICATION

IMPLEMENTING THE FUTURE OF IDENTIFICATION & INVESTIGATIVE SERVICES

The Federal Bureau of Investigation's (FBI's) Criminal Justice Information Services (CJIS) Division operated and maintained the Integrated Automated Fingerprint Identification System (IAFIS), which became the world's largest person-centric biometric database when it was implemented in July 1999. Since then, advancements in technology and the changing business needs of IAFIS's customers necessitated the next generation of identification services. To further advance biometric identification services, the CJIS Division, with guidance from the user community, established the vision for the Next Generation Identification (NGI).

The NGI system was developed over multiple years, and it is an incremental replacement of the IAFIS that provides new functionality and improves existing capabilities. This technological upgrade accommodates increased information processing and sharing demands from local, state, tribal, federal, and international agencies. The NGI system offers state-of-the-art biometric identification services and compiles core capabilities that serve as the platform for multimodal functionality.

U.S. Department of Justice
Federal Bureau of Investigation
Criminal Justice Information Services Division
1000 Custer Hollow Road, Clarksburg, WV 26306
(304) 625-3437

NGI Website: www.fbi.gov/hq/cjisd/ngi.htm

Source: Federal Bureau of Investigation. See: https://www.fbi.gov/services/cjis/fingerprints-and-other-biometrics/ngi

Technicians can computer-enhance fingerprints when preparing them for a search. This process enables an experienced technician to fill in missing or blurred portions of print fragments or to correct for breaks in patterns or ridges caused by burns or scars.

As noted, the computer translates patterns into mathematical computer codes. Thus, the computer is not comparing images of a suspect's prints against images of known prints; rather, it is conducting a mathematical search that can compare a subject print against file prints. Search time varies depending on such factors as preparation time, demographic data that are entered to limit the prints required to be searched, the size of the file, and the number of key factors, or matchers, being used to seek a match.

The system itself never makes a final decision on identity. The system produces a list of possibles, called a *candidate list*. It is from this list that further determinations are made by a qualified fingerprint examiner.

Another facet of NGI is the Repository for Individuals of Special Concern (RISC). This mobile fingerprint device offers a 10-second response to on-scene inquiries and thus provides nearly instantaneous access to a national repository of warrants related to immigration violations, sex offense registries, and terrorism watch lists. NGI also offers latent prints searched against criminal, civil, and unsolved crimes and access to search and upload palm prints.

Also included in NGI is Rap Back, a service that gives authorized agencies the ability to be notified if someone in a position of trust or someone under criminal justice supervision has a status change in his or her criminal history. In other words, if someone is hired for a job requiring a security clearance, Rap Back would notify that person's employing agency months or even years after the person's initial background check if his or her fingerprints were entered into the national database due to a subsequent arrest or conviction.

NGI also employs the Interstate Photo System (IPS) to search millions of photos via facial recognition software, algorithms that offer enhanced searches for cold cases, and a pilot program for a repository of photos of the irises of criminals.[57] The irises of an individual's eyes are complex, random, and unique—and the fact that they remain stable over a lifetime makes them a viable biometric measure. In September 2013, the FBI initiated an Iris Pilot (IP), which evaluates available technology and the challenges of developing a system capable of performing iris image recognition services. While still under development, the project shows significant promise.[58]

The primary purpose of the NGI program is to reduce error in the identification of suspects and individuals, as well as quickly and securely identify known suspects that may pose special risks.

NATIONAL INTEGRATED BALLISTIC INFORMATION NETWORK PROGRAM

A joint program of the Bureau of Alcohol, Tobacco, Firearms, and Explosives (ATF) and the FBI, the **National Integrated Ballistic Information Network (NIBIN)** integrates all the elements of Ceasefire and Brasscatcher (both former ATF programs) and Drugfire (an FBI program) (Figure 8-10).

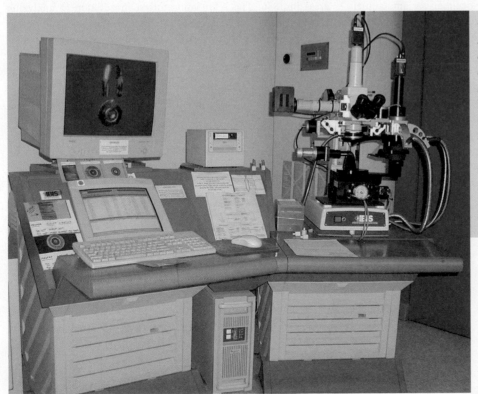

◄**FIGURE 8-10 NIBIN system**
Just as individual fingerprints differ, each firearm leaves different, unique characteristics on expended ammunition. The national integrated ballistic information system network, developed by ATF and the FBI, compares images of ballistic evidence obtained at crime scenes to recovered firearms. Matches or "hits" are confirmed by a firearms examiner in the lab. (Source: Bureau of Alcohol, Tobacco, Firearms and Explosives)

Just as each fingerprint is different, so a firearm leaves unique identifiable characteristics on expended ammunition. NIBIN compares images of ballistic evidence, both projectiles and casings, obtained from crime scenes and recovered firearms. As new images are entered, the system searches the existing database for possible matches. Hits are confirmed by a firearm examiner.

The system has amassed a large ballistic-image database filled with crime gun data submitted by local, state, and federal agencies throughout the country, and the intelligence information is available to all law enforcement agencies. Since the inception of the program in 1999, NIBIN partner agencies have captured approximately 2.8 million images of ballistic evidence and confirmed more than 74,000 hits.[59]

HANDLING EVIDENCE IN THE LABORATORY

HUMAN FACTORS

In handling evidentiary materials, laboratory personnel— scientists and technicians alike—have always been cautious not to disturb or ruin the viability of the materials for any possible examination that would later prove to be useful. Today, because of concerns over the transmission of hepatitis and the AIDS virus, the handling of evidence is of even greater concern.

Although a few laboratories may autoclave specimens, such sterilization with heat may tend to decrease the usefulness of the specimen for analysis purposes. Most laboratories, including the FBI, are merely extra careful in handling evidence involving tissue or body fluids. The procedure followed normally is to ask the agency sending the specimen for any factual information available on the subject so that a determination can be made as to whether the evidence was obtained from a person who may have been infected. In addition, scientists and technicians are instructed to keep their work areas clean, to clean those areas between conducting examinations, and to change and clean lab coats and gloves frequently.

INSTRUMENTAL ANALYSIS

The kinds of evidence subject to laboratory examinations are many and varied. For laboratory purposes, examinations generally fall into the following categories: chemical examinations, biological examinations, physical examinations, personal identification, firearm identification, documentary examinations, and photography.

In a textbook of this nature it is not practical to present a detailed discussion of the technical intricacies of various scientific instruments. However, it is appropriate to acquaint readers with some of the capabilities of instruments used in the scientific analysis of evidence. Table 8-1 presents some of the more sophisticated equipment currently being used in full-service crime laboratories. It excludes the more obvious or technical examination methods, such as many chemical analyses, fingerprint identification, firearm identification, physical and chemical documentary examinations, photographic techniques and equipment, microscopy, and DNA analysis; some of these methods were discussed earlier (Figure 8-11).

ATF FORENSIC SCIENCE LABORATORIES

The Bureau of Alcohol, Tobacco, and Firearms (ATF) of the U.S. Department of the Justice maintains five forensic science laboratories. The ATF National Laboratory was created by Congress in 1886. The ATF laboratories, in addition to analyzing alcohol and tobacco samples, conduct forensic examinations in support of the bureau's explosives, bombing and arson, and illegal-firearm-trafficking investigations, along with major case

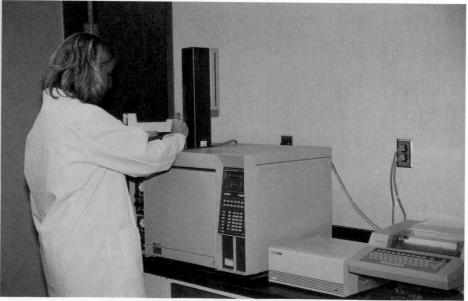

▶ **FIGURE 8-11**
Gas chromatograph
The gas chromatograph is used to separate and identify gases and fluids from complex mixtures and solutions. In criminal investigations, it is often used to analyze organic materials such as narcotics, explosives, and paints.
(Courtesy of Evansville Regional Laboratory, Indiana State Police)

TABLE 8-1	Instrumental Analysis in the Crime Lab	
NAME OF INSTRUMENT	**PRIMARY USE**	**ADVANTAGES & WEAKNESSES**
Light Microscopy	Stereomicroscopes, polarizing microscopes, and comparison microscopes are widely used in trace evidence analysis.	Provides search and comparison of samples under magnification.
SEM—Scanning Electron Microscope	Based on principles similar to a light microscope; however, uses a stream of electrons to search for and view minute elements or samples.	Provides a detailed 3D black & white image of the sample viewed; expensive.
Emission Spectrograph	Identification of metals and elements (e.g., sodium, tin, iron, copper) from the light emitted when each element is burned. Hence, rapid analysis from unknown substances can be developed; detection of traces of metallic impurities in residues such as oils and glasses.	Complete analysis of an unknown substance through one operation; requires only a relatively small sample for analysis.
Mass Spectrometer	Identifies unknown samples by creating profiles of the individual compounds and molecules of a substance.	Often used in expediting DNA analysis; sample is destroyed during analysis.
Visible Spectrophotometer	Compares dyes and coloring agents in materials such as hair, cloth, paint, and glass. Records the percentages of each color in a substance or sample.	Eliminates personal error in color comparisons; requires only a relatively small sample with a rapid analysis.
Infrared Spectrophotometer	Primarily identifies and compares inorganic materials such as plastics, rubber, paint, and and other chemical substances through the analysis of infrared energy passing through a substance.	Detects slight differences in the composition molecular arrangement of minute amounts of material.
Atomic Absorption Spectrophotometer	Determines quantitative and proportional concentrations of specific elements in materials through the analysis of a vaporized sample.	Very accurate and sensitive method of determining elemental concentration; relatively economical and rapid procedure.
Gas Chromatograph	(Figure 8-11) Separates and identifies gases or liquids from complex mixtures and solutions; often used to analyze narcotics, paints, plastics, inks, and petroleum-based products such as gas, oil, explosives, and accelerants. Often used in conjunction with the mass spectrometer.	Used in a wide variety of tasks through the analysis of volatile solids, high-boiling point liquids, and gases; sample is destroyed during analysis.
X-Ray Diffraction Spectrophotometer	Identifies and compares unknown crystalline substances through the diffraction of X rays.	Requires only a small amount of sample, and the sample is not consumed in the technique.

investigations of state and local authorities. In 2015, ATF laboratories completed forensic analysis for 1,975 cases.[60]

The laboratories hold the distinction of being the first federal laboratory system accredited by the ASCLD.[61] The majority of the examinations conducted by the laboratories involve chemical and physical examinations of explosives, firearms, and arson evidence, as well as the document, tool-mark, and latent-fingerprint examinations associated with those investigations.

Employees at the labs include chemists, physical scientists, document analysts, latent-print specialists, and firearm and tool-mark examiners. The remainder are evidence technicians and clerical personnel.

Evidence collected at crime scenes of suspected arsons is examined to identify accelerants, incendiaries, and incendiary-device components. Evidence collected at explosion scenes is examined to identify explosives used, blasting caps, leg wires, fuses, timing mechanisms, energy sources, containers, wires, tapes, and various other component parts used to make the bomb. The laboratory system maintains liaisons with explosive manufacturers, who provide exemplars of new explosives products on the market.

Comparative trace-evidence examinations are conducted on materials including tapes, wires, glass, metals, soil, hair, paint, fibers, ink, paper, and wood to determine whether the materials could have a common origin and thereby associate a suspect with a crime.

Questioned-document examinations are conducted to identify handwriting on firearm transaction forms. In addition, examinations are performed to identify typewriters, copy machines, and cigarette tax stamps. Attempts are also made to decipher indented and obliterated writings.

The laboratories also perform a full range of fingerprint, firearm, and tool-mark examinations in support of agency investigations.

Firearm examinations involve primarily serial-number restoration, determination of the operability of weapons, comparison of metals in sawed-off barrels, and determination of the possible common origin of silencers seized from different suspects or locations (Figure 8-12). Gunshot-residue tests are conducted in

▲ **FIGURE 8-12**

Forensic examiner conducting firearm examination

In serious violent crimes such as armed robbery and homicide where a handgun is used, the crime lab firearms examiner often plays a major role. Frequently, he/she will be called on to examine recovered firearms in an effort to link suspects or their handguns to a particular crime. (Courtesy of Evansville Regional Laboratory, Indiana State Police)

shootings that involve law enforcement officers. In addition, special tests to evaluate the performance of ammunition and weapons are occasionally done.

Tool-mark examinations generally involve evidence associated with bombings and arson. This includes examination of cut wires, torn tapes, drill holes, pipe wrench marks, saw marks on wood and metal, and numerous other marks made by tools.

The bureau has four National Response Teams that respond to major bombings and arson disasters, nationally and internationally. The teams consist of highly trained investigators, forensic chemists, and explosives technology experts. The teams respond within 24 hours, collect evidence, and complete most laboratory examinations before leaving the crime scene.[62]

THE FBI CRIME LABORATORY

The **FBI Crime Laboratory** is one of the largest and most comprehensive forensic laboratories and is the only full-service forensic laboratory. It was established in 1932. Of importance to the investigator is the fact that the facilities of the FBI laboratory are available without charge to all state, county, and municipal law enforcement agencies in the United States.[63] There are, however, some provisos concerning the submission of evidence for examination to the laboratory. The laboratory will not make examinations if any evidence in the case has been or will be subjected to the same type of technical examination by another laboratory or other experts. This policy is designed to eliminate duplication of effort and to ensure that evidence is received in its original condition, thereby allowing laboratory personnel to interpret their findings properly and ensure meaningful testimony and presentation of evidence in subsequent court cases.

To more effectively and efficiently use its current resources, the FBI laboratory has a policy not to accept cases from other crime laboratories that have the capability of conducting the requested examination. If such cases are submitted by other crime laboratories and there are no special circumstances to warrant the submissions, the cases will be returned unopened and unexamined. This policy should not be construed as lessening the FBI laboratory's continuing commitment to the scientific training of state and local crime laboratory personnel, and it does not limit the laboratory's acceptance of cases from other crime laboratories when special circumstances prevail.

Also, the FBI laboratory no longer accepts evidence from state and local law enforcement agencies regarding property crime investigations unless the cases involve personal injury or the offenses were designed to cause personal injury.

In addition to doing analysis, the FBI furnishes the experts necessary to testify in connection with the results of its examination in either state or federal courts. Again, there is no charge to local law enforcement agencies for this service.

The laboratory provides a comprehensive array of forensic services. Laboratory personnel conduct microscopic examinations of hair and fiber, fabric, tape, rope, and wool (Figure 8-13). Chemical examinations are conducted on many substances, often to supplement examinations conducted by other sections.

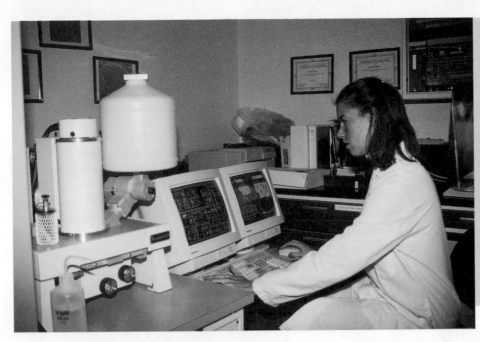

◀**FIGURE 8-13**

Forensic examiner conducting examination with a scanning electron microscope

One of the standard instruments in today's crime labs is the electron microscope. Typically, evidence such as hair, fiber, fabric, and rope undergoes microscopic examination in the crime lab. Many criminal investigations have been solved by lab personnel, with the help of an electron microscope, matching these types of physical evidence to materials found in the possession of a suspect.

(Courtesy of Evansville Regional Laboratory, Indiana State Police)

Examinations are conducted on poisons (toxicology), paint, ink, tear gas, dyes, and flash and water-soluble paper, among others.

Mineralogy examinations are conducted on soils and combinations of mineral substances such as safe insulation, concrete, plaster, mortar, glass, ore, abrasives, gems, industrial dusts, and building materials.

Firearm examiners may be asked to determine if firearms are operating properly or to conduct gunpowder shot-pattern tests. Using the same basic principles of firearm examination, the identification of telltale marks left at crime scenes by punches, hammers, axes, pliers, screwdrivers, chisels, wrenches, and other objects can be made. The explosives specialist can analyze fragments of explosives to determine their original composition and possible sources of raw materials.

The metallurgy unit is called on to restore obliterated or altered numbers on such things as firearms, sewing machines, watches, outboard motors, slot machines, automobiles, tools, and other metallic items. Tests can show whether two or more pieces of metal are related, the possible cause of metal separation, and whether production specifications for metals have been met.

Handwriting examiners agree that no two individuals write exactly alike. Even though there may be superficial resemblances in the writing of two or more persons as a result of similar training, the complexity of writing is such that individual peculiarities and characteristics appear. These characteristics can be detected by a document expert, who then can arrive at a scientific opinion.

The FBI laboratory has also developed the ability to conduct forensic examinations on chemical, biological, and nuclear hazards. In 1996 the Hazardous Materials Response Unit was established in response to the threat of terrorism involving chemical, biological, and nuclear weapons (weapons of mass destruction—WMD), and to an expanding caseload of environmental crimes. After the horrific events of September 11, 2001, and the "anthrax

cases" that closely followed, the FBI Lab greatly expanded its role in determining biological, chemical, and nuclear agents that may be used by terrorists. The laboratory works closely with the Centers for Disease Control in developing standardized protocols for handling and analyzing suspected WMD materials. As mentioned earlier, the laboratory has also developed the Computer Analysis and Response Team (CART) program, capable of conducting examinations in which information is extracted from magnetic, optical, and similar storage media and converted into a form usable to investigators or prosecutors. The CART team also has an integral role in preventing and investigating acts of sabotage and terrorism against American infrastructure (for example, telecommunications, computer, and transportation systems). Finally, the FBI's laboratory is leading the research and development efforts to improve and expedite DNA analysis methods and is one of the few laboratories conducting mitochondrial-DNA testing.

QUICK FACT

Flaw in the FBI Hair Analysis Unit Marks Largest Forensic Scandal in History

The investigative world was rocked by statements from the U.S. Department of Justice and the FBI in 2015 acknowledging "that nearly every examiner in an elite FBI forensic unit gave flawed testimony in almost all trials in which they offered evidence against criminal defendants over more than a two-decade period before 2000." Of the 28 examiners within the FBI Laboratory's microscopic hair comparison unit, 26 overstated forensic matches in favor of the prosecution in more than 95% of the 268 trials reviewed to date. The cases included 32 defendants sentenced to death, of which 14 have already been executed or died in prison. The admissions marked a watershed in the largest forensic scandal in history surrounding bogus scientific information and confirmed that subjective, pattern-based forensic techniques—like hair and bite-mark comparisons—have contributed to wrongful convictions of innocent people since 1989. As a result, the FBI has identified roughly 2,500 cases for review.

Source: Spencer S. Hsu, "FBI Admits Flaws in Hair Analysis over Decades," *The Washington Post,* April 18, 2015.

REFERENCE FILES

To aid examiners in their work, the FBI laboratory in 1932 established what is now one of the largest reference collections for helping solve cases. These files are of two types: standard reference files and collections, which contain known samples of items, generally of manufactured products, and reference files of questioned materials, which are composed of items actually arising from cases worked and which may form the basis for subsequent identification of individuals or their method of operation (MO). Many of these collections and reference files have been computerized to provide better and faster analyses and comparisons.

The Standard Ammunition File contains over 15,000 specimens of domestic and foreign manufacturers' samples. The Firearms Reference Collection contains over 3,500 handguns and 2,000 shoulder weapons and is used for identifying gun parts and locating serial numbers. The Reference Fired Specimen File contains test bullets and cartridge cases from weapons that have been in the laboratory.

The National Automobile Altered Numbers File is composed of selected specimens, including replica plastic impressions of altered vehicle identification numbers (VINs) found on stolen cars, trucks, and heavy equipment. The file helps investigators identify recovered stolen cars and link them with commercialized theft rings nationwide or other FBI-investigated cases. The National Vehicle Identification Number Standard File maintains standards of VIN plates from each factory of the major manufacturers of American automobiles. The file enables laboratory personnel to determine if a submitted VIN plate is authentic. In the event that bogus VIN plates are being prepared in an automobile factory, the factory as well as the particular machine used can be identified.

The Typewriter Standards File consists of original samples of typewriting from numerous styles of type made in this country as well as in foreign countries. The file permits classification of questioned typewriting on the basis of make and model. The Watermark Standards File is an index of watermarks and brands used by paper manufacturers and aids in tracing the source or origin of paper. Original samples of safety paper used for checks are the contents of the Safety Paper Standards File. These can be used to determine manufacturers. The Checkwriter Standards File is a collection of original checkwriter impressions and permits classification of questioned checkwriter impressions as to make and model. As an aid in determining the manufacturers of office copying machines (either photocopy or duplicator), the laboratory maintains the Office Copier Standards File.

The Shoe Print File contains photographs of designs used in soles and heels made by major U.S. manufacturers. The Tire Tread File, including wheelbase and tire-stance information, is now in a database against which comparisons can be made. This replaces the blueprints, drawings, and photographs of tire-tread patterns, furnished by tire manufacturers, that used to form the basis of the reference file.

The National Motor Vehicle Certificate of Title File consists of original state motor vehicle certificates of title, manufacturers' certificates of origin, and vehicle-emission stickers. This file also contains photographic copies of fraudulent titles, statements, and stickers. The National Fraudulent Check File contains over 100,000 samples of checks, writings, and other documents. More than half of all checks examined are identified with other material in this file. The Anonymous Letter File consists of photographic copies of kidnap notes and extortion and threatening letters. The Bank Robbery Note File contains photocopies of writings of known bank robbers and holdup notes. The Pornographic Materials File includes pornographic materials submitted to the laboratory; it assists in determining the production and distribution sources of the materials. The Explosive Reference Files contain technical data, known standards of explosive items, and bomb components of commercial and military explosives and improvised explosive devices or homemade bombs.

Other files maintained by the FBI are the Automotive Paint File (which can identify makes and models involved in hit-and-run cases), the Hair and Fiber File, the National Stolen Coin File, Blood Serum Files, Safe Insulation Files, and the National Stolen Art File.

PROBLEMS IN CRIME LABORATORIES

Forensic technology such as DNA analysis offers a great deal of hope to crime victims and law enforcement. And when used and interpreted correctly, it has truly revolutionized the way we prosecute cases, examine cold cases, and even exonerate wrongfully convicted inmates. Significant legal limitations still apply to the use of DNA as part of a criminal investigation. Further, major concerns relate to the ethics and the training of the individuals who collect, process, and present DNA evidence in court. Human error is unpreventable, but negligence and the falsification of results is unacceptable and undermines the integrity of criminal justice discipline.

A number of forensic labs have fallen under investigation in recent years.

- An analysis of the FBI's elite microscopic hair comparison unit revealed that 26 of 28 examiners overstated forensic matches, overwhelmingly in favor of the prosecution. 14 of those convicted during involved trials have since been executed or died in prison.[64]
- In Massachusetts, a chemist was sentenced to a prison term after admitting that she fabricated results from thousands of drug cases that resulted in imprisonment for the accused.

- In St. Paul, Minnesota, the crime lab was subjected to an independent review that found, among other things, that lab employees actually used Wikipedia as a technical reference in at least one drug case. Overall, the review found that there were major errors in almost all facets of the lab's work.

These errors, and many others, have contributed to something of a reckoning in modern forensic science. Hair comparison has come squarely under scrutiny as a result of the FBI problems mentioned above—and bite-mark analysis, once widely used, is now considered almost entirely unreliable. A new emphasis, as discussed earlier in the chapter, has focused on increasing accreditation and training standards. But still, science and technology—as much as it's changed the landscape of criminal investigations—is only as good as the manner in which we use it.

Many of the problems found in crime labs can be traced to two causes: not enough funding and too close a relationship with the police. Underfunding is problematic because across the country many crime labs are backlogged with evidence that needs to be analyzed. The processing of backlogged evidence is sometimes rushed, resulting in human errors or blatant misconduct. The Massachusetts State Crime Lab reported that in mid-2007 it had more than 16,000 cases that needed to be retested and that some of the evidence was from cases as far back as the early 1980s. Even more alarming is the fact that the statute of limitations may have run out on a number of those cases. Having overly close ties to the police can potentially be a drawback, because the analysis of evidence must be objective and impartial. The job of lab technicians is to analyze evidence and present the findings, not necessarily to strengthen the prosecution's case. When the line between the two functions becomes blurred, the result can be an environment conducive to misconduct.

Human and analytical errors made in these laboratories often mean the difference between freedom for the guilty and incarceration of those who are innocent. Therefore, all people concerned must understand the extent of the existing problems within local, state, and federal crime laboratories.

LACK OF TRAINING

Continuing professional development is necessary for forensic scientists to remain current and to advance to an elevated level of expertise and responsibility. They are obligated to remain up to date in their field through specific and continued education and other developmental activities.[65] Unfortunately, few universities present degrees in forensic science, and even fewer provide certification for the operation of specific analytical instruments. Most chemists, biologists, geologists, and physicists prepare themselves for careers in forensic science by training under a person who is an experienced examiner and by studying independently.[66] Few defined or organized programs exist for the profession of forensic science. There are few minimum course requirements in terms of structured courses or core curriculum, since most educational requirements are determined by individual laboratories. In fact, in the last decade the number of forensic science academic programs has declined, and the ones that do exist have such low enrollment that support from

universities is limited.[67] This situation is particularly surprising given the public interest in the subject created by the myriad popular crime-scene and forensics-oriented movies and television shows (for example, *Silence of the Lambs, CSI, The Profiler, Cold Case, Forensic Files*). This problem is further compounded by the fact that laboratory analysis and forensics require a rigorous background in the sciences (for instance, biology and chemistry) and not the social or behavioral sciences, where criminology and criminal justice students often study. As a result, many students who are interested in the wider subject matter simply do not have the technical and scientific background to enter the field. For those who are prepared properly, salary and benefits often do not match those in the scientific community, and so well-qualified individuals often choose to enter similar work in the medical or health fields.

Finally, although the formal education that scientists receive provides a foundation for learning and understanding the techniques of forensic science, for the most part, courts rely on additional training and years of experience in order to measure the actual knowledge and ability of the expert. The advancements in technology and sophisticated software used in crime laboratories across the country have created a gap between the skills of scientists and their ability to perform their tasks properly.[68] Many are not updated and trained to know how to use the new equipment appropriately, and as a result, many cases become flawed owing to the lack of training and contemporary knowledge.

LACK OF ACCREDITATION

Crime labs must identify a system for establishing its credentials as a forensic laboratory. As mentioned earlier, the primary credentialing organization is the American Society of Crime Laboratory Directors (ASCLD). Whenever a lab applies for accreditation, it has to meet certain requirements, which include the development and publication of a quality-control manual, a quality-assurance manual, a lab-testing protocol, and a program for proficiency testing. *Quality control* refers to the way a product, such as a DNA-typing result, is measured to make certain the product meets a specific standard of quality. *Quality assurance* refers to the actions taken by the laboratory to monitor and document the quality of work being performed. A *lab-testing protocol* is a technical manual that includes validation studies performed by the lab itself. Such a protocol sets forth standardized methodologies for performing routine tests in the laboratory. Last, *proficiency testing* monitors lab workers individually, as well as the laboratories as institutions. These tests determine whether or not lab workers are performing up to the specified standards of the institution.[69] Yet the fundamental problem with forensic science in crime labs is that, unlike clinical labs, forensic labs are unregulated by the government, allowing them to set their own standards. Forensic scientists do not have to establish competence by obtaining a license or certification. Therefore, a majority of crime labs do not seek accreditation (with the exception of New York, Texas, and Oklahoma, primarily reacting to a series of scandals within major crime labs within their states). In addition, accreditation rates are low for practicing forensic scientists, even though certification boards for all the major fields of forensics have been in existence for more than a decade.[70] According to ASCLD, of the 455 larger crime labs conducting forensic work, only 255 are accredited. Accreditation can cost a few thousand dollars for small operations and as much as $70,000 for the larger, multilaboratory operations. This price tag does not include the more significant costs associated with implementing new training programs and the equipment needed to meet current standards.[71]

Furthermore, most forensic scientists are not independent experts. About 80% of forensic scientists in North America are affiliated with prosecution or police agencies. Indeed, most forensic scientists work in police laboratories, and many are themselves law enforcement officers, as are their superiors. This association has been known to create a sense of bias within the courtroom between forensic testimony and prosecution. Since the FBI, the police, and the crime lab have similar missions (to arrest, prosecute, and convict), the chance that forensic scientists' courtroom testimony will be unbiased by any other considerations becomes more unlikely.[72] Hence, accreditation alone does not ensure accurate, unbiased, and/or objective laboratory results. For instance in Oklahoma City, Oklahoma, a police chemist (Ms. Joyce Gilchrist, Figure 8-7) appears to have falsified evidence dating back as far as 1982. An internal police report detailed "compelling circumstantial evidence" that Ms. Gilchrist "either intentionally lost or destroyed" evidence from crime scenes. The most significant misconduct involved the case of a convicted man, sentenced to death for the murder of a police officer's teenage daughter in 1982. As a result, the Oklahoma State Bureau of Investigation and the FBI launched a review of nearly 2,000 cases—focusing first on 12 pending death row convictions and 11 cases in which death sentences had already been carried out. At least three current convictions, including the 1982 murder conviction, were reversed after DNA testing proved that the defendants were not guilty. In overturning the convictions, the Oklahoma Court of Criminal Appeals noted that even though Ms. Gilchrist was a highly educated and well-trained technician, her testimony was "terribly misleading, if not false."[73]

DNA CONTAMINATION

DNA technology can do astonishing things. Not only can DNA be used to identify criminals with amazing accuracy when biological evidence exists, but it can also be used to clear suspects and exonerate persons who have been mistakenly accused or convicted of crimes. However, the current federal, state, and local DNA collection and analysis system needs improvement. Numerous cases have emerged revealing faulty practices of forensic crime lab experts who mishandled DNA tests causing them to become contaminated and unable to be used.

Contamination is a concern for proper preservation of evidence. As we learned in Chapter 4, DNA evidence must be collected and packaged separately in individual containers, and each piece of evidence must be segregated from other evidence.[74] Unfortunately, some forensic scientists have tainted tests with their own DNA, in addition to throwing out evidence swabs,

misreading results, fingerprinting the wrong suspect, and even cross contaminating different cases.

Washington's State Patrol crime lab was investigated in 2004 after wrongly accusing and sentencing a man for committing the rape of a 10-year-old girl. The forensic scientist working on the case simply botched the test, accidentally contaminating the child's clothing with DNA from another case he had previously been working on. The investigation revealed that forensic scientists contaminated tests or made other mistakes while handling DNA evidence in at least 23 cases which involved major crimes over the previous three years in that department. They were found to have tainted tests with their own DNA in 8 of the 23 cases and made mistakes in 6 other cases by discarding important evidence and by misreading results.[75] This is not the only such incident. Similar contamination was discovered in a December 2002 audit of the Houston Police Department Crime Lab, which noted analysts' lack of training, insufficient documentation of evidence, and evidence contamination. As a result, the Harris County District Attorney's Office has reviewed over 400 cases involving DNA evidence, and the Houston PD Crime Lab has remained closed.[76]

In 1997 U.S. Department of Justice documents obtained by the National Association of Criminal Defense Lawyers identified several examples of questionable practices in the DNA Unit of the FBI laboratory. These practices included the use of plastic pipettes used to extract DNA that had been dissolved in chloroform. However, chloroform also dissolves plastic pipettes, which could have contaminated the sample. Also, examiners commonly overexposed autoradiographs so that DNA bands appeared as football-shaped rather than as a line. This makes it difficult for an examiner to accurately locate the center of a band in order to analyze it. Some examiners would then move a band by hand for analysis, which could also have resulted in a contaminated misreading.[77]

SENTENCING MISTAKES AND POOR TRAINING

Josiah Sutton was tried and convicted in 1999 for rape. Although prosecutors had little to build the case on, since the victim was the only eyewitness and her recollection was faulty, they were able to get him convicted. Technicians from the Houston police crime laboratory had the rapist's DNA and told the jury that his was a solid match. They sent Sutton to prison to serve a 25-year term. After serving four years, new testing by the Houston crime laboratory showed that the DNA did not match Sutton's. He was released after spending four years of his life behind bars because of a mistake made by forensic examiners in a crime lab. The only reason his DNA was retested stemmed from a state audit and review conducted at the Houston crime laboratory. The audit found that technicians had misinterpreted data, were poorly trained, and kept poor records that did not meet specified levels of acceptance within the laboratory. They found that in most cases, they used up all available evidence, barring defense experts from refuting or verifying their results. They also discovered a leaky roof that had dripped so profusely that dozens of DNA samples of evidence had become contaminated with water.[78] Such mistakes not only harm the validity of evidence in cases, but they also cause citizens to lose confidence in law enforcement and the experts who work in the crime laboratories in their communities.

BACKLOG OF CASES

As previously discussed, public crime laboratories are overwhelmed by backlogs of unanalyzed DNA samples. As a result, these labs may become ill-equipped to handle the increasing arrivals of new DNA evidence and have no space to store the samples. The problems that emerge from the backlogs result in considerable delays in the administration of criminal justice.

Providing exact numbers for the number of backlogged cases in laboratories nationwide is a challenge, mostly because there is no universal definition of a backlog. The National Institute of Justice (NIJ) considers anything more than 30 days old to be backlogged, and by that definition nearly 75% of cases in crime labs would qualify.[79] Crime labs have two types of backlogs: case backlogs, in which DNA or other biological evidence is collected as potential evidence of a crime, and offender/arrestee backlogs, when samples are taken from convicted offenders and arrestees for review and uploaded to the FBI's CODIS system. Evidence that is stored in law enforcement custody awaiting submission to a laboratory is not considered by NIJ as backlog.

Backlogs in crime labs are a simple function of supply and demand. Labs are simply unable to meet the increased demand for DNA analysis created by the following five factors:[80]

- *Increasing awareness:* Knowledge of the potential of DNA evidence to solve cases has grown exponentially among criminal justice practitioners and the general public alike
- *Property crimes:* The number of DNA submissions for property crimes has skyrocketed, and these types of crime are much more commonplace than violent crimes.
- *Scientific advances:* Advances that make it possible for tiny, trace amounts of DNA samples to be analyzed has led to more requests for DNA testing of guns and steering wheels to determine who may have last handled the object.
- *Cold cases:* Older and unsolved cases from the pre-DNA era are being opened and their samples submitted for testing in the hopes that usable information can be recovered.
- *Post-conviction testing:* Older, pre-DNA cases resulting in a conviction have been reopened so DNA testing can be done. The Innocence Project is a perfect example of this type of demand for testing.

Backlogs at crime laboratories are primarily the result of growing demand and limited resources. Crime laboratory analysts often have to work overtime and on weekends to complete analysis of backlogged cases, especially when the case is considered high profile. The time that it takes to process DNA cases in crime laboratories poses significant delays in many jurisdictions. State crime laboratories take an average of 23.9 weeks to

process an unnamed suspect rape kit, and local laboratories average 30.0 weeks to process such tests. The cost to test these rape kits is estimated to be $1,100 per case, not accounting for additional overhead costs.[81]

In addition to problems with backlogging, both state and local labs reported that their main concern for their DNA programs was the lack of personnel. They expressed a need for supplemental funding for additional DNA staff and to increase current salaries to avoid the loss of skilled personnel within their laboratories to other potential employers willing to pay more money. Most labs also reported that although federal funding has played an important role in assisting with backlogged DNA cases, the amount of their overall budget funded through federal sources is minimal. Only 20.5% of state crime laboratories receive 50% or more of their funding from federal sources. Local laboratories receive only 4.5% from federal funding.[82]

Furthermore, postconviction DNA testing resulting in exoneration has caused many state legislatures to impose requirements for the indefinite storage of evidence used in crime convictions, although such requirements frequently become unfunded mandates passed down to local jurisdictions. Indeed, there have been reports of large metropolitan law enforcement agencies who discarded potential DNA evidence in an attempt to create additional storage space for new evidence.[83] Therefore, evidence that could have possibly helped a victim is now gone forever and useless to future crime investigations.

SCANDALS AND MISTAKES WITHIN THE FBI CRIME LAB: THE MADRID BOMBING CASE

Another widely publicized incident relating to problems within crime labs involves the allegations made in 1995 by Frederic Whitehurst, a former FBI laboratory supervisory special agent who had worked for the lab since 1986. He alleged that over the course of several years, laboratory examiners had improperly testified outside their expertise, presented unacceptable evidence, perjured themselves, fabricated evidence, and failed to follow the appropriate procedures of the laboratory. He also said that he believed that FBI management retaliated against him for making those accusations.[84] Yet changes have been made within the FBI laboratory since Whitehurst blew the whistle on his coworkers. After intense investigation into his accusations, the FBI lab implemented a formal quality assurance plan and has since been accredited by the ASCLD.[85]

However, the most significant blunder to date in any crime lab within the United States occurred in March 2004 with the arrest of Portland, Oregon attorney, Brandon Mayfield. On March 17, 2004, the Spanish National Police provided the FBI with digital, electronically transmitted photographic images of latent fingerprints that were recovered from the plastic bag containing the detonator in the March 11 bombings in Madrid that killed 191 people and injured 2,000 others[86] (Figure 8-14). The FBI Lab in Quantico, Virginia, used the Automated Fingerprint Identification System (AFIS) to search for possible matches to

▲ **FIGURE 8-14   The Madrid Bombing Case**

The FBI Laboratory error in matching the latent print (*left*) as that of Mr. Brandon Mayfield has cast doubt on the integrity of fingerprint evidence. Noting that the error print (*right*) was not rotated and cropped to match the corresponding latent print was a serious mistake that embarrassed the FBI as well as complicated the entire Madrid bombing investigation. (For more information on the technical aspects of this case, see *www.onin.com*.) (*Left:* ©Don Ryan/AP Images; *Right:* Source: Federal Bureau of Investigation)

the fingerprints. Mayfield's fingerprints were one of 20 candidates suggested for comparison by the system.[87] At least three FBI fingerprint specialists, including a supervisory agent with over 30 years of experience verified the identification of Mayfield as the suspect from the latent print on the plastic bag. One examiner testified that the latent print was "the left index finger of Mr. Mayfield."[88] It is not known whether the identification process was influenced by information pertaining to Mayfield's conversion to Islam or his activities as a lawyer in defending recent "terrorist" suspects before the match was officially declared.[89] However, what is known is that at some point in March or April, the FBI began "sneak and peak" and electronic surveillance of Mayfield under the Foreign Intelligence Surveillance Act (FISA) and the U.S. PATRIOT Act.[90] According to court documents, FBI agents began their surveillance of Mayfield two weeks after the attacks in Madrid, and, under a provision of the U.S. PATRIOT Act, they entered his home without his knowledge—but aroused suspicion by bolting the wrong lock on their way out and leaving a footprint on a rug inside the house. During a later raid based on the fingerprint identification, the FBI seized computers, modems, safe deposit boxes, assorted papers, and copies of the Quran.[91]

On May 20, the Spanish National Police reported that they had identified the latent print in question as that of a different individual . . . an Algerian national living in Spain. As the information became conflicted between the two agencies, the FBI sent agents to Spain in order to recover the original latent print. To their surprise, the print had been destroyed.

Four FBI examiners with a combined total of 93 years of experience in latent print science reexamined and reanalyzed the latent print. The examiners concurred that the latent print had multiple separations (that is, it was divided by many lines of demarcation possibly caused by creases in the underlying material, multiple touches by one or more fingers, or both).[92] On the morning of May 24, 2004, utilizing information from this new evaluation by the four examiners, the FBI *reversed* its position on Mayfield and indicated that the print had no value for identification purposes, and Mayfield was subsequently released.

The ensuing investigation revealed that the FBI had originally sent examiners to Spain but that the investigators did not speak Spanish. Further, they never asked to see the original latent print. More problematic, if the print indeed had "no value for identification purposes," how could such a positive and previous identification to Mayfield be developed in the first place? After all, this was an international event with over 190 persons killed that focused on suspected terrorist links to al-Qaeda. It appears that the FBI violated one of the most basic rules of investigation: failing to maintain objectivity during scientific analysis and failing to compare the best evidence to samples found at the scene. Essentially, FBI fingerprint analysts drew much of their attention to Mayfield's past and relied on improper methodology to confirm the identification of a latent print to a suspect. As one expert indicated: "There were many discrepancies . . . and a competent (fingerprint) expert should have seen all the discrepancies."[93] The FBI's contention that the misidentification occurred as a result of problems with the quality of the digital image is in itself an indictment of the poor procedures followed by analysts. If the image was corrupted, then a positive identification should have never been made. Worst of all, this case has far-reaching implications concerning the scientific integrity of fingerprint identification, the acceptance of fingerprint evidence in court, and the scrutiny of crime laboratory personnel.

BOX 8-3 | REFORMING CRIME LABS

Aside from recommendations and reforms to accreditation, funding, and training suggested by the federal government, justice scholars have suggested additional reforms to prevent the kinds of problems described in this chapter. These reforms highlight the role that bias can play in forensic analysis—whether intentional or not. Roger Koppl, the director of the Institute of Forensic Science Administration, and Radley Balko, an investigative journalist for justice issues at *The Washington Post*, published a list of potential reforms as part of a series on forensic lab missteps:[94]

- *Forensic counsel for the indigent:* The complexity of and technological basis for analyzing forensic evidence requires means that there are few experts able to correctly interpret it . . . and those experts are generally very expensive. As such, the only forensic experts testifying in most trials are there for the prosecution, which completely goes against the adversarial nature of our criminal justice system. Indigent defendants should have access to their own experts, qualified to review forensic analysis and any conclusions made by prosecutorial experts.
- *Expert independence:* Simply put, crime labs and medical examiners should not be a part of the same agency or bureaucracy that houses district attorney's offices or law enforcement agencies. This creates an obvious conflict of interest.
- *Statistical analysis:* Forensic lab results should be subjected to examination for statistical anomalies. Match rates that routinely exceed what is expected on a national average should be flagged, triggering further examination.
- *Removal of evidentiary context:* Lab analysts should not know the context of the evidence that they are examining, where possible. Police or prosecutors should not be permitted to describe elements of the case, as these can introduce bias unconsciously or even consciously. A heart-wrenching murder case, for example, involving a small child might drive an analyst—even a professional and well-intentioned one—to disregard important protocols in their quest to find a match.

Although crime labs represent amazing leaps in technology and amazing potential for criminal investigations and justice, the stories of errors and wrongful convictions make clear that the power that the crime lab holds must be carefully reviewed, monitored, and researched. If criminalistics includes the responsibilities of medicine, the intricacies of law, and the universalities of science, it stands to reason that it should be held to the highest standards of each discipline in order that justice be achieved.

In a recent case, *United States* v. *Mitchell*,[95] the court concluded that latent fingerprint identification evidence, as produced by the FBI's procedures, met the requirements for admissibility established by *Daubert* v. *Merrell Dow Pharmaceuticals, Inc.* However, the FBI latent print unit's performance in Mayfield's case suggests that, notwithstanding *Mitchell*'s recognition of a valid scientific basis for fingerprint identification, the potential for error in the making of an identification requires that identification testimony be rigorously tested and excluded if compliance with requirements for ensuring accuracy in its application cannot be demonstrated.[96]

CODE OF ETHICS

The findings of forensic scientists are often the critical element in determining the guilt or innocence of an individual. The examination, which is the basis of the findings, must be conducted in accordance with the principles necessary to achieve an unfailing conclusion. Scientists must examine the subject matter as a whole, and their conclusions must be delivered under conditions that support their comprehension and use.

Different codes of ethics for forensic science have been adopted over the years. The American Society of Crime Laboratory Directors, the American Board of Criminalistics, and the Council for the Registration of Forensic Practitioners are all examples of organizations that have incorporated a specific code of ethics for forensic science.[97] An example of a code of ethics for forensic science can be found under the Preamble of the SAFS Ethics Committee, a pharmaceutical research group. It states that there is a requirement for forensic scientists to possess a comprehensible knowledge in the subject matter in which they are investigating. This requires them to have the necessary skills, background knowledge, and forensic science judgment that can be directly applicable to issues at hand. Also, it is required that scientists conduct examinations in accordance with the principles of the scientific method by using state-of-the-art methodology. In addition, it is required that scientists employ enough safeguards necessary to assure control of the quality of the examination. These safeguards include the preservation of adequate materials to allow for reexamination if necessary and ample documentation to permit a reasonable evaluation of the protocol employed and a confirmation of the accuracy of the findings. Last, it is required that forensic scientists present their comprehensive presentation, whether verbal or written, in language that is understandable to counsel for the client, the court, and the jury.[98]

These ethics codes require competence, quality, training, and integrity on the part of forensic experts and managers working in every crime laboratory across the country. Forensic experts must be competent to take on tasks that are required in the assignments they receive. They are expected to perform their tasks to the best of their abilities, conducting themselves in a trustworthy and honest manner, especially when facing obstacles that may hinder their performance.

Unfortunately, scandal has become commonplace in a realm where science and integrity must be the hallmarks of competency. For example, a publicized report in Washington revealed how a crime lab chemist was caught snorting heroin on the job for months, stealing the drug from evidence he was testing. In addition, a review of two dozen crime lab disciplinary records in the state raised questions about the professionalism of some scientists on the payroll. It was discovered that in the past five years, a lab supervisor was caught viewing pornography on his office computer; another lab manager was fired because he sexually harassed female coworkers; and a DNA analyst was found sleeping on the job.[99] Another example of a lack of ethics focuses on the issue of proficiency tests. Crime lab workers must pass one test every year in each specialty to satisfy voluntary rules set by the American Society of Crime Laboratory Directors' Laboratory Accreditation Board. For instance, a Tacoma lab forensic scientist took a routine proficiency exam in September of 1998, in which his ability to interpret footprint evidence was tested. When accreditation inspectors visited the lab a year later, they could not find any record of the exam. They discovered that the scientist's supervisor had never reviewed the test or realized that the scientist had actually failed to correctly match all the footprints with the correct shoe.[100]

Unfortunately, stories such as these have become commonplace. A number of forensic crime lab examiners have failed to conduct themselves in an ethical manner, and it has become increasingly apparent that these mistakes can lead to even more detrimental problems over time. It is also apparent that justice cannot be served fairly under such circumstances.

KEY TERMS

Advanced Fingerprint Identification Technology (AFIT)

American Society of Crime Laboratory Directors (ASCLD)

Automated Fingerprint Identification System (AFIS)

crime laboratory

criminalistics

Daubert v. Merrell Dow Pharmaceuticals, Inc.

deoxyribonucleic acid (DNA)

familial DNA search (DNA kinship search)

FBI Crime Laboratory

forensic science

Frye v. United States

Integrated Automated Fingerprint Identification System (IAFIS)

kinship DNA searches

low copy number DNA sample

mitochondrial DNA (mtDNA)

morgue

National Integrated Ballistic Information Network (NIBIN)

nuclear DNA

rules of evidence

REVIEW QUESTIONS

1. Define *forensic science*. What distinguishes it from criminalistics?

2. What difficulties are caused by an investigator not understanding the capabilities and limitations of crime laboratories?

3. What is the measure of effectiveness of crime laboratories and how do they relate to the 2009 National Academy of Science (NAS) report on forensic science in the United States?

4. What is the most important resource in a crime laboratory?

5. How important is DNA analysis in a criminal investigation?

6. What are AFIS, NIBIN, IAFIS, and CODIS?

7. What are the main areas of responsibility of the ATF laboratories?

8. What limitations are placed on the submission of evidence to the FBI laboratory?

9. What are the primary DNA analysis techniques that have been used since 1985?

10. Distinguish the *Frye* test from the *Daubert* test regarding the admissibility of scientific evidence. What is the importance of these two cases?

11. What are some of the major problems confronting police crime labs?

12. Discuss suggestions for the reform of crime labs.

1. Visit the FBI website at *www.fbi.gov* and search for the crime laboratory. What services are provided to law enforcement by the lab? What are the primary missions of the FBI, and how does the crime lab support those missions? What are CART and CIRG? What are the primary forensic examinations performed by the lab? Finally, what is LEO, and how is it employed in reference to sharing forensic information among law enforcement agencies?

2. Go to *www.crimelynx.com* and search for information about postconviction DNA cases under "Crime Policy Links." What is the most recent estimate of the number of convicted offenders who have been exonerated owing to DNA testing? Under what conditions can an offender request DNA testing? Who pays for the testing? What occurs if the DNA tests are inconclusive? In your opinion, will the increasing popularity of postconviction DNA testing affect the nature of criminal investigations? Now go to *www.innocenceproject.com* and compare your information with that found on this website. Is there a difference?

3. Visit the National Institute of Justice website at *http://www.nij.gov/topics/forensics/pages/welcome.aspx#randd* and explore the NIJ Forensic Science Research and Development Portfolio. What types of projects does the NIJ fund? What are its research priorities? How do the projects help the underlying deficiencies identified by the 2009 report by the National Academies of Science?

▶ The investigation of deaths, whether by accidental or felonious cause, can often be aided by modern technology. For example, the underwater search for missing bodies can be facilitated by sonar tracking devices such as the one shown in this photo from Hennepin County, Minnesota, where deputies are using a side-scan sonar unit to locate a body.

(©Steve Kohls/BrainerdDaily Dispatch/AP Images)

9

INJURY AND DEATH INVESTIGATIONS

CHAPTER OBJECTIVES

1. Understand the various legal definitions related to felony assaults and homicides.

2. Discuss the various stages of the medico-legal examination, including the autopsy.

3. Describe the various postmortem changes occurring at the time of death.

4. Recognize the potential evidentiary value of gunshot wounds, incised and stab wounds, lacerations, and defensive wounds.

5. Discuss the role of the forensic entomologist in determining time of death.

6. Identify the characteristics of strangulation wounds.

7. Describe wounds inflicted with a blunt object as opposed to those inflicted with a sharp-edged instrument.

8. Discuss information used by investigators to distinguish between homicides and suicides.

9. Be familiar with the methods and evidence involved in suicides.

10. Distinguish the differences between the characteristics of various poisons and their associated manifestations.

11. Outline facts that need to be determined in the investigation of fire deaths.

12. Understand the differences between spree killings and mass murders.

13. Discuss serial murderers, their profiles, myths and misconceptions.

14. Understand the role of the National Center of the Analysis of Violent Crime (NCAVC) and the Violent Criminal Apprehension Program (ViCAP) in serial murder investigations.

The investigation of felonious injuries and criminal homicides can be the most important, yet difficult, responsibility assigned to a police investigator. First, these crimes are viewed as being among the most serious offenses committed in our society. The seriousness is reflected in all state statutes, which impose severe penalties for acts resulting in the grave bodily injury or death of a human being. Second, in the beginning stages of some criminal homicide investigations, the inability to identify the decedent greatly complicates the investigative process and prevents it from moving forward. In all criminal homicides, questions such as "Who were the victim's enemies?" and "Who would benefit most from the victim's death?" must be answered before any significant progress can be made in the investigation. Estimating the time of death also needs to be done early in the investigation. Third, criminal homicides, in particular, can generate a lot of media attention and public scrutiny for the department. Pressure to solve the crime from both inside and outside the police agency creates added strain on the criminal investigator.

For these cases, in particular, investigators may need to call on the assistance of experts in the scientific and medical fields. Investigators should create working relationships with specialists such as forensic dentists, forensic pathologists, toxicologists, serologists, entomologists, and botanists, who can all provide useful assistance to the case. There are also steps law enforcement executives can take to positively impact homicide investigations.

QUICK FACTS

10 Things Law Enforcement Executives Can Do to Positively Impact Criminal Homicide Investigation Outcomes

1. Invest in the relationship with the homicide unit investigators (this includes determining who they are, what their needs are, how they work, and what resources they need to succeed at their work).

2. Have a system in place for standardized and structured management of investigations (this includes the proper training for investigators, supervision of investigators, and a set of standard protocols to follow).

3. Mandate information sharing (this includes patrol, all other investigative units, school resource officers, and multi-jurisdictional task forces).

4. Support investigations with appropriate resources (this includes the use of crime scene specialists, as well as encouraging investigators to identify emerging trends and practices that can foster their success).

5. Assess the current response to victims/survivors (this includes, among other things, evaluating the next-of-kin notification protocol and making certain the agency is maximizing opportunities to strengthen relationships).

6. Build up and reinforce partnerships with other agencies (this includes prosecutors, probation, crime labs, crime scene specialists, researchers, schools, public health, local emergency rooms, and federal agencies).

7. Build community outreach programs and give them options (this includes monitoring text messages from citizens 24 hours a day, analyzing tips, and passing them on to the appropriate unit or division for follow-up).

8. Manage political and public expectations of homicide investigations (this includes developing and improving protocols about how information is distributed or addressed by the agency to the media, the public, and others).

9. Know your criminal homicide numbers (this includes the rate of occurrence, location, and solvability factors).

10. Measure closure and beyond (this includes outcome success [identification, prosecution, and conviction of factually guilty offenders], procedural success [quality of the investigative process and systems implemented], community impact reduction success [increasing community reassurance and public confidence], and preventive success [prediction, prevention, and pre-emption of future criminal homicides]).[1]

THE LAW

The various state statutes contain different names for **felonious assault**—such as aggravated assault, assault with intent to commit murder, and felonious battery—but all have one common legal element, namely, that the assault was committed for the purpose of inflicting severe bodily harm or death. In most such assaults, a deadly weapon is employed.

Police officials and members of the public often use the terms "homicide" and "murder" interchangeably. In fact, murder is only a part of the broad category of homicide, and homicide is divided into two broad classifications: nonfelonious homicide and felonious homicide. **Nonfelonious homicides** may be justifiable or excusable. **Justifiable homicide** is the necessary killing of another person in performance of a legal duty or the exercise of a legal right when the slayer was not at fault.

Excusable homicide differs from justifiable homicide in that one who commits an excusable homicide is to some degree at fault but the degree of fault is not enough to constitute a criminal homicide. There are two fundamental types of excusable homicide. The first involves death that results from misadventure. This is similar to what may be termed "accidental" death at the hands of another. Misadventure is death occurring during the commission of a lawful or an unlawful act when the slayer has no intent to hurt and there is not criminal negligence. An example of misadventure is the death of a person who runs in front of a moving automobile whose driver is unable to avoid the collision.

The second type of excusable homicide involves death that results from self-defense when the slayer is not totally without fault, such as someone who gets in a sudden brawl and has to kill to preserve his or her life.[2]

Felonious homicides are treated and punished as crimes and typically fall into two categories: murder and manslaughter.

Murder is defined in common law as the killing of any human being by another with malice aforethought. Most states now provide for varying degrees of murder. **Manslaughter** is a criminal homicide that is committed under circumstances not severe enough to constitute murder but that cannot be classified as either justifiable or excusable homicide.[3]

THE MEDICO-LEGAL EXAMINATION

The **medico-legal examination** brings medical skill to bear on injury and death investigations. The medical specialist frequently called on to assist in such cases is the forensic pathologist. **Forensic pathology,** a subspecialty of pathology, is the study of how and why people die. To become a forensic pathologist, a physician first attends an approved pathology residency program and then attends three years in a strictly anatomic program or five years in a combined anatomic and clinical program. One or two additional years are devoted to studying the pathology of sudden, unexpected, natural death, as well as violent death, in an approved forensic fellowship training program (there are approximately 30 throughout the country). Most programs are centered in major cities that have a large number of deaths from various causes. The most important area of study for a forensic pathologist is death investigation, but some forensic pathology programs also include examination of the living to determine physical and sexual abuse. Physicians specializing in forensic pathology are ordinarily employed by some unit of government and are not in private practice.[4]

THE AUTOPSY

All violent and suspicious deaths require an **autopsy** to determine the time and precise cause of death.[5] The autopsy may also answer the following questions:

- What type of weapon was employed?
- If multiple wounds were inflicted, which wound was fatal?
- How long did the victim live after the injury?
- What position was the victim in at the time of the assault?
- From what direction was the force applied?
- Is there any evidence of a struggle or self-defense?
- Is there any evidence of rape or other sex-related acts?
- Was the deceased under the influence of alcohol or any type of drug?[6] (The actual analysis will be done by the toxicologist discussed later in this chapter.)

Answers to all or even some of these questions increase the possibility of bringing the death investigation to a successful conclusion.

DEAD BODY EVIDENCE CHECKLIST

The following dead body evidence checklist will assist both the investigator and the medical examiner in systematically following all the steps necessary to be certain no physical evidence is overlooked:

- Thoroughly photograph everything before moving or touching it.
- Collect fragile evidence on the body.
- Obtain samples of hair, fingernails and other trace evidence. Use toothpicks to collect evidence that might be under the fingernails if they are short. Place the items in waxed paper, bundle them, and place them in envelopes.
- Brush the head hair and the pubic region (if the body is unclothed). Hold butcher paper under the area being brushed.
- Remove trace evidence from the entire body's skin and clothing, including the face, hands, feet, legs, torso, pubic area, and neck, with Scotch tape or lint rollers. Use only frosted tape.
- Collect samples of pooled blood.
  - Use hemasticks to confirm it is actually blood.
  - Collect control samples (as close to the injured area as possible).
  - Use a cotton swab with one drop of distilled water on it. Place the swab in wax paper loosely, and then place it in an envelope.
- Collect exemplars from the following areas:
  - Environment (vegetation, soil, maggots, other).
  - Residence (carpet fibers, paint, misc. fibers, other).
  - Vehicle (carpet fibers, seat fibers, roll the tires, VIN number, wheel base).
  - Animals (hairs, bedding).
- Collect blood samples from the victim.
- Swab the bite mark areas.
- Swab the oral cavity.
- Collect exemplar hairs.
- The victim should be fingerprinted even if there is positive proof of identification.
- If circumstances dictate, palm prints and footprints should also be obtained. They may prove useful in matching prints that are later found in the suspect's home, business, car, or other location.
- Collection of the victim's clothing.
  - If the clothing is damaged, the investigator should determine whether the damage is related to the assault or was caused by hospital or emergency personnel giving emergency treatment. When a determination is made of the cause of the damage, it should be recorded in the investigation report.[7]

POSTMORTEM CHANGES AND TIME OF DEATH

A recurring problem in forensic medicine is the need to fix the time of death within the limits of probability. The longer the interval of time between death and the examination of the body, the wider will be the limits of probability. The longer the postmortem interval, the more likely it is that associated or environmental evidence will furnish more reliable data on which to estimate the time of death than will anatomical changes.[8]

It is necessary to be alert to the possibility that the postmortem interval (the time elapsed from death until discovery and medical examination of the body) may be preceded by a significant survival period (the time from injury or onset of the terminal illness or death). The survival interval is best established by evaluating the types, severity, and number of injuries present and the deceased's response to them, taking into account preexisting natural disease.

Establishing the times of an assault and death has a direct bearing on the legal questions of alibi and opportunity. If the suspect is able to prove that he or she was at some other location when the fatal injury was inflicted then the suspect has an alibi and innocence is implicit. Conversely, if the time of a lethal assault coincides with the time when the suspect was known to be in the vicinity of the victim, then the suspect clearly had an opportunity to commit the crime.

ESTIMATING TIME OF DEATH

Many physico-chemical changes begin to take place in the body immediately or shortly after death and progress in a fairly orderly fashion until the body is fully decomposed. Each change has its own time factor or rate. The rates of development of postmortem changes are strongly influenced by unpredictable changes within the body and environmental factors. Consequently, the longer the postmortem interval, the wider is the range of estimate as to when the death probably occurred. In other words, the longer the postmortem interval, the less precise is the estimate of the time of death.[9]

ALGOR MORTIS (BODY COOLING)

After death, the body cools from its normal internal temperature of 98.6°F to the surrounding environmental temperature. Many studies have examined this decrease in body temperature, called **algor mortis,** to determine formulas that could predict its consistency. Unfortunately, because of numerous variables, body cooling is an inaccurate method of determining the postmortem interval. In general, however, evaluating a decrease in body temperature is most helpful within the first 10 hours after death. During this time, with a normal body temperature and at an ideal environmental temperature of 70° to 75°F, the body cools at approximately 1.5°F per hour, however the problem with using the 1.5°F-per-hour calculation is based on the assumption that the internal temperature is 98.6°F and the environmental temperature remains at a constant 70° to 75°F. If a decedent's body temperature is higher than normal at the time of death because of an infection resulting in a fever then the body temperature of 98.6°F cannot be used. Furthermore, the outside environment is rarely in the 70° to 75°F range, and a body may actually gain heat if an individual expires outdoors during the summer, when temperatures may be greater than 100°F. Conversely, if a person expires in a 25°F environment, rapid cooling takes place.

Nonetheless, if body temperature is measured at a scene, it should be taken by the attending physician on at least two separate occasions before the body is moved. A rectal or liver temperature is the most accurate measurement. The environmental temperature should also be recorded. If these relatively simple procedures are followed, a very crude estimate of the postmortem interval can be made.[10]

Other factors that will affect the rate of cooling include:

- *The size of the body.* The heavier the physique and the greater the obesity of the body, the slower the heat loss.[11]
- *Clothing and coverings.* These insulate the body from the environment and therefore cooling is slower. It has been estimated that cooling of a naked body is half again as fast as when clothed.[12]
- *Movement and humidity of the air.* Air movement accelerates cooling by promoting convection and even the slightest sustained air movement is significant. Cooling is said to be more rapid in a humid rather than a dry atmosphere, because moist air is a better conductor of heat.
- *Immersion in water.* A cadaver cools more rapidly in water than in air, because water is a far better conductor of heat. For a given environmental temperature, cooling in still water is about twice as fast as in air and in flowing water about three times as fast.[13]

OCULAR CHANGES

In **ocular change,** the cornea becomes cloudy within 2 hours or less if the deceased dies with eyes open. If closed it will be 12 to 24 hours. On the third postmortem day, the corneas become opaque. When gases begin to collect in the body, the eyes may bulge out of the eye socket, but when advanced decomposition sets in, the eyes become endopthalmic, or retracted into the socket.[14]

STOMACH CONTENTS

After a light meal, food will leave the stomach in 1 to 2 hours, a medium meal 3 to 4 hours, and a very heavy meal, 4 to 6 hours. Examination of the stomach contents may provide information not only about the time of death but also about what the person had eaten just before dying.[15]

RIGOR MORTIS

After death, the muscles of the body initially become flaccid. Within 1 to 3 hours they become increasingly rigid, and the joints freeze—a condition called **rigor mortis** (or postmortem rigidity or rigor) (Figure 9-1).

Rigor mortis is affected by body temperature and metabolic rate: the higher the body temperature, the more lactic acid produced and the quicker rigor occurs. For example, a person dying with pneumonia and a fever will develop rigor sooner than a person with normal body temperature. Similarly, if a person's muscles were involved in strenuous physical activity just before death, rigor develops much more quickly. The process is also retarded in cooler environmental temperatures and accelerated in warmer ones.

All muscles of the body begin to stiffen at the same time after death. However, muscle groups may appear to stiffen at different rates because of their different sizes. For example, stiffness is apparent sooner in the jaw than in the knees. Thus, an examiner must check to see if joints are movable in the jaws, arms, and legs.

A body is said to be in complete rigor when the jaw, elbow, and knee joints are immovable. This takes approximately 10 to 15 hours at an environmental temperature of 70° to 75°F. A body remains rigid for 24 to 36 hours before the muscles begin to relax, apparently in the same order they stiffened.

A body remains rigid until rigor passes or until a joint is physically moved and rigor is broken. Consequently, in addition to

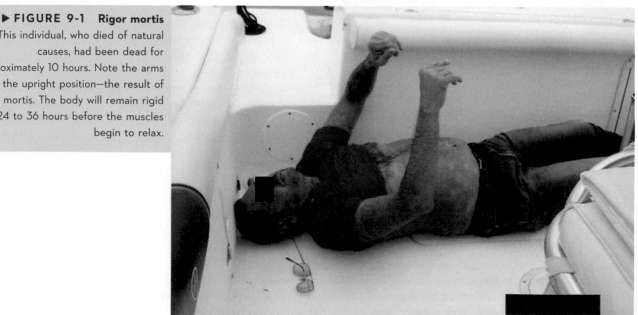

▶ **FIGURE 9-1 Rigor mortis**
This individual, who died of natural causes, had been dead for approximately 10 hours. Note the arms in the upright position—the result of rigor mortis. The body will remain rigid for 24 to 36 hours before the muscles begin to relax.

indicating an approximate time of death, body position in full rigor can indicate whether or not a body has been moved after death.[16]

LIVOR MORTIS

Livor mortis (lividity, postmortem hypostasis) is a reddish purple coloration in dependent areas of the body due to accumulation of blood in the small vessels of the dependent areas secondary to gravity (Figure 9-2). Postmortem lividity is occasionally misinterpreted as bruising by people unfamiliar with this phenomenon.

Dependent areas resting against a firm surface will appear pale in contrast to the surrounding livor mortis, owing to compression of the vessels in this area, which prevents the accumulation of blood. Thus, areas supporting the weight of the body, for example, the shoulder blades, buttocks, and calves in individuals lying on their backs, show no livor mortis but appear as pale or blanched areas. Tight clothing, for example, such as a brassiere, corset, or belt, which compresses soft tissues, may collapse the vessels, also producing pale areas.

Livor mortis is usually evident within 30 minutes to 2 hours after death. In individuals dying a slow, lingering death with terminal cardiac failure, livor mortis may actually appear antemortem (prior to death). Livor mortis develops gradually, usually reaching its maximum coloration at 8 to 12 hours. At about this time, it is said to become "fixed." Before becoming fixed, livor mortis will shift if the body is moved. Thus, if an individual dies lying on his or her back, livor mortis develops posteriorly (i.e., on the back). If one turns the body on its face, blood will drain to the anterior surface of the body, now the dependent aspect. Livor mortis becomes "fixed" when shifting or drainage of blood no longer occurs, or when blood leaks out of the vessels into the surrounding soft tissue owing to hemolysis and breakdown of the vessels. Fixation can occur before 8 to 12 hours if decomposition is accelerated, or at 24 to 36 hours if it is delayed by cool temperatures. Thus, the statement that livor mortis becomes fixed at 8 to 12 hours is really just a vague generalization. That livor mortis is not fixed can be demonstrated by applying pressure to a dependent discolored area and noting the subsequent blanching at the point of pressure.

Although livor mortis may be confused with bruising, bruising is rarely confused with livor mortis. Application of pressure to an area of bruising will not cause blanching. An incision into an area of contusion or bruising shows diffuse hemorrhage into the soft tissue. In contrast, an incision into an area of livor mortis reveals the blood to be confined to vessels, without blood in the soft tissue. Livor mortis is extremely important for three reasons:

1. When considered with other factors, it may help estimate the time of death.
2. It may indicate that the body has been moved after death. For example, if a body is found face down with lividity on the back, this would indicate the body has been moved. For this reason, the exact measurements, sketches, and photographs must be made at the scene before and while the body is being recovered.
3. The coloration of the skin may indicate the cause of death, as in the case of carbon monoxide poisoning, certain forms of cyanide poisoning, or extreme cold, when the color of the lividity is not purplish but cherry-red color.[17]

CADAVERIC SPASM

Cadaveric spasm refers to a kind of instant rigor mortis discussed earlier in this chapter. The same physiological changes occur except at a more accelerated rate. Cadaveric spasm is also commonly called "a death grip." It typically involves a decedent's hand tightly clutching a weapon, usually a gun, a knife, or a razor at the moment of death[18] (Figure 9-3).

DECOMPOSITION

In general, as rigor passes, skin first turns green at the abdomen. As discoloration spreads to the rest of the trunk, the body begins to swell because of bacterial methane-gas formation. The bacteria are normal inhabitants of the body. They proliferate after death, and their overgrowth is promoted in warm weather and retarded in cold weather.

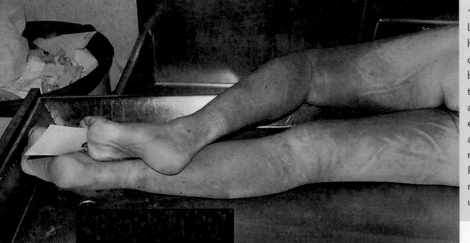

◄**FIGURE 9-2 Livor mortis**
Livor mortis (lividity, postmortem hypostasis) is a reddish purple coloration in dependent areas of the body due to accumulation of blood in the small vessels of the dependent areas secondary to gravity. It is usually evident within 30 minutes to 2 hours after death, typically reaching its maximum coloration at 8 to 12 hours. Postmortem lividity is occasionally misinterpreted as bruising by people unfamiliar with this phenomenon.

▶ **FIGURE 9-3 Cadaveric spasm**
Cadaveric spasm is a term used to describe the instantaneous tightening of a hand or other body part at the time of death. Note the weapon clutched tightly in the left hand of this victim of a self-inflicted gunshot wound to the head.

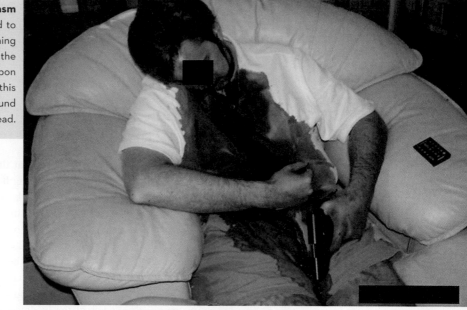

▶ **FIGURE 9-4**
Advanced stages of decomposition
The individual shown here had been dead approximately two weeks in an unheated, unventilated room. Note the extreme discoloration and swelling of the facial area as well as the abdomen.

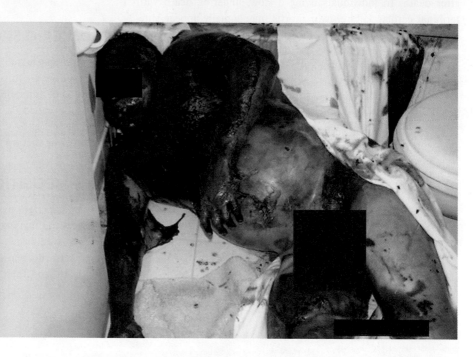

The different rates and types of decomposition a body undergoes depend on the environment (Figure 9-4). Bodies buried in earth, submerged in water, left in the hot sun, or placed in a cool basement appear different after the same postmortem interval. When a body is bloated, epidermal sloughing and hemoglobin degradation begin. Moreover, as bloating continues, air is forced from the skin. The increased internal pressure, caused by bacterial gas production, forces decomposed blood and body fluids out of body orifices by a process called *purging*. As the body undergoes skeletonization, the rate of tissue deterioration is dependent on environmental temperature. For example, a body exposed to a 100°F environmental temperature may completely decompose to a skeleton within a few weeks. In contrast, a body in a temperature of 65°F may not skeletonize for many months. In general, a body decomposing above ground for a week looks similar to a body that has been under water for two weeks or has been buried for six weeks. This generalization should serve as a reminder that an uncovered or naked body decomposes more rapidly than a covered or clothed one.

After a body is found, it is usually refrigerated until an autopsy is performed or a final disposition is made. Decomposition slows down or ceases if a body is refrigerated. When the body is exposed to room temperature, decomposition occurs rapidly. Recognition of this accelerated decomposition is particularly important if a person dies in a cold environment and is then moved to a warmer one.

Decomposition may not occur evenly throughout the body. For example, decomposition occurs more rapidly in injured areas. If a person is struck on the head and bleeding occurs only in that area, decomposition may be much more advanced on the head than on the remainder of the body. Fly larvae proliferate during summer, spring, and fall in warm, moist areas of the body such as the eyes, nose, and mouth. Larvae are attracted to injured areas, where they feed on exposed blood proteins and cause accelerated decomposition. Owing to the uneven decomposition, it is common to see skeletonization in only part of the body.[19]

FORENSIC ENTOMOLOGY

Entomology is the study of insects, and forensic entomology is the study of the insects associated with a dead body, which is used to determine the elapsed time since death. An analysis of the insects found on a homicide victim by a qualified **forensic entomologist** can also tell the investigators whether the body has been moved from one site to another, if it was disturbed after death, or the position and presence of wound sites, long after they are no longer visible as such to the naked eye. Insects can also be used in drug identification and the determination of the length of time of neglect.[20]

Insects are invariably the first witnesses to a crime, arriving within minutes or even seconds after death. There are two ways to use insects to determine time since death. The first method involves using dipteran (blow fly) larval development, and the second involves using insect succession over time (Figures 9-5 and 9-6).

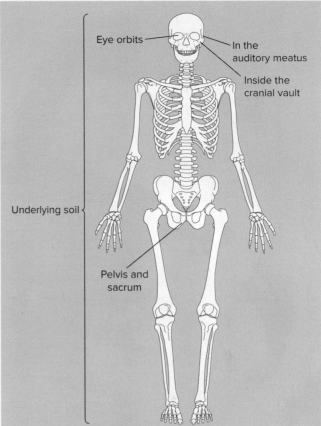

▲ **FIGURE 9-6**
Areas of skeleton most likely to harbor insects

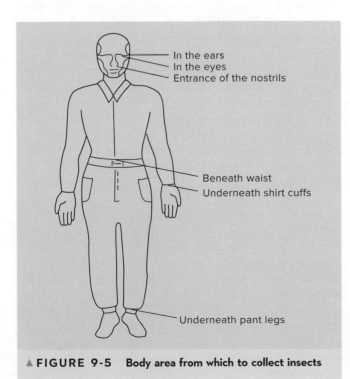

▲ **FIGURE 9-5   Body area from which to collect insects**

The first method is used in the first hours, days, or weeks after death and can determine the time of death accurate to a day or less, or a range of days. The insects used in this method are those that arrive first on the corpse, that is, the calliphoridae or blow flies (diptera). These flies are attracted to a corpse very soon after death. They lay their eggs on the corpse, usually in a wound, if present, or in any of the body's natural orifices (Figure 9-7). Their development follows a set, predictable cycle, and each of these developmental stages takes a set, known time. This time period is based on the availability of food and the temperature. In the case of a human corpse, food availability is not usually a limiting factor. Insects are "cold blooded," so their development is extremely temperature-dependent. Their metabolic rate increases with increased temperature, which results in a faster rate of development, so that the duration of development decreases in a linear manner with increased temperature, and vice versa.

An analysis of the oldest stage of insect on the corpse and the temperature of the region in which the body was discovered allows an entomologist to determine the day or the range of days in which the first insects oviposited, or laid eggs, on the corpse. This determination, in turn, leads to a day or a range of days during which death occurred. For example, if

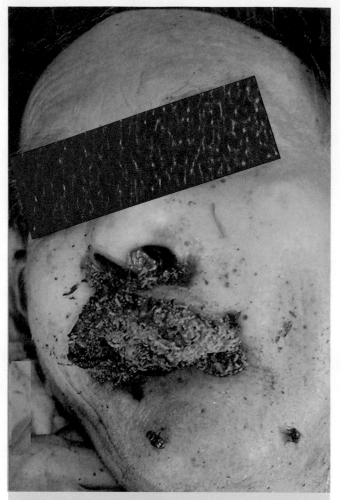

▲ FIGURE 9-7 Fly larvae
This individual had been dead for approximately four days. His body was found in the backyard by neighbors. During this period of time, temperatures had reached into the 90s. Note the fly larvae (maggots) in his nose and mouth.

oldest insect stage, together with data from the local weather station, indicated they had died more than 11 days before discovery. Reluctant eyewitnesses were later brought forward during the police investigation and confirmed the date of death. The eyewitnesses were also able to identify the killer. However, as the eyewitnesses had not come forward earlier, it was possible the jury might doubt their word. This situation became more probable when two other people came forward saying that they had seen the victims alive and well and shopping in the mall only eight days before their bodies were discovered. This conflicted with the date of death identified by the two eyewitnesses and meant that the jury would have to make a subjective decision on who was lying and who was telling the truth. However, in this case, there was also the scientific, entomological evidence, which clearly indicated that the victims had died more than 11 days before discovery. This evidence refuted the testimony of the two shoppers and supported that of the two eyewitnesses. Therefore, the jury believed the earlier eyewitnesses, who were able to identify the killer. He was convicted of two counts of first-degree murder.

the oldest insects are seven days old, then the decedent has been dead for at least seven days. This method can be used until the first adults begin to emerge, after which it is not possible to determine which generation is present. Therefore, after a single blow fly generation has been completed, the time of death is determined using the second method, that of insect succession.

The second method of using insects to determine time since death is based on the fact that a human corpse, or any

The highly decomposed and maggot-infested remains of two women were found in a bushy area. Two species of blow fly were collected, and an analysis of the

kind of carrion, supports a rapidly changing ecosystem. The body decomposes from the fresh state to dry bones in a matter of weeks or months depending on the geographic region. As the body decomposes, it goes through a predictable sequence of biological, chemical, and physical changes. Each of these changes is attractive to a different group of insects. Some insects, such as the blow flies, prefer to feed on the fresh body. Others prefer the remains a few days after death, while still others prefer the remains when they are dry. Some insects are not attracted to the body itself, but arrive to feed on other insects at the scene. Many species are involved at each decompositional stage, and each group of insects somewhat overlaps the ones adjacent to it. The insects that colonize a body are primarily species of flies (diptera) and beetles (coleoptera).

Therefore, with knowledge of the regional insect fauna and times of carrion colonization, the investigator can analyze the insect assemblage associated with the remains to determine a window of time in which death took place. This method is used when the decedent has been dead from a few weeks up to a year, or in some cases several years after death, with the estimated window of time broadening as time since death increases. It can also be used to indicate the season of death (i.e., early summer). A knowledge of insect succession, together with regional, seasonal, habitat, and meteorological variations, is required for this method to be successful.

The partially skeletonized remains of a man were found in a wooded area close to a freeway in early spring. A large number of empty blow fly puparia were discovered with the remains, along with several groups of insects that are commonly later colonizers, including piophilidae and fanniidae, as well as a number of beetle adults and larvae. To analyze sequential insect evidence, the entomologist must have local data for the geographical region, habitat, and season, because there can be a great deal of difference between insect arrival and tenure in one region versus another. The species of insects present in this case indicated a minimum elapsed time since death of two months. However, since the body was found in very early spring, death must have occurred earlier than this. Large numbers of empty blow fly puparia indicated the earlier presence of many blow fly larvae, which would have been present only in warm weather. This fact indicated that death must have occurred before the previous fall, when numerous blow flies would have colonized the remains and gone through an entire life cycle, as evidenced by the empty puparia. It would also have allowed for the later colonizers to arrive by March. The onset of cold weather would have prevented further blow fly colonization in winter, allowing some flesh to remain uneaten, which explained why the remains were only partially skeletonized. If the remains had not been discovered in early spring, blow flies from the upcoming summer would have completed the skeletonization process. Also, if the deceased had died earlier in the previous year, the body would have been entirely skeletonized before discovery. The insects, therefore, indicated that death had occurred in late summer of the previous year.

| THINKING OUTSIDE OF THE FORENSIC ENTOMOLOGY BOX

Thus far we have dealt primarily with the two most common ways that forensic entomologists can assist investigators in determining the time of death. However, one creative detective along with assistance from a forensic entomologist took it a step further. The following case illustrates how forensic entomology can go even beyond determining the approximate time of death.

A woman, her three children, and mother were found shot to death execution-style in their home in Bakersfield, California. In addition to being shot, the victim had multiple stab wounds. There was no sign of forcible entry into the home and nothing of value was taken. In processing the crime scene there were no unexplained fingerprints. Also there were no hairs and fibers that would be of any value in the investigation. During the course of the investigation detectives did determine that the woman and her husband had been estranged for several months after she learned about his apparent infidelity.[21]

At first the investigation indicated that at the time of the murders the victim's husband was 2,200 miles away in Columbus, Ohio. The initial telephone contact between the lead detective in this case, Detective Jeff Watts, and the husband did not raise any suspicions because he was able to verify through receipts from a local store that he had used his credit card in Columbus, Ohio on the date of the murders. Thus he appeared to have a solid alibi and was not at that time considered a suspect.

Because the follow-up investigation did not provide any significant leads the husband was once again contacted to see if he could provide any additional information or be of assistance. However, during the follow-up contact the husband no longer seemed to be the grieving father and in fact completely stonewalled the inquiries by the detective raising the level of his suspicion, thus now making him a suspect.

Detective Watts decided to take a closer look at the husband's alibi. Receipts from his credit cards indicate that he flew from Bakersfield, California to Columbus, Ohio on July 2, four days before the murders. When he arrived in Columbus he rented a Dodge Neon and claimed he only used it to operate in the Columbus area. However, when Detective Watts studied the rental car records he found that the automobile the suspect had rented had 5,424 miles on it. When he questioned him about how he had accumulated such a high number of miles if he had not left the Columbus area the suspect had no explanation.

The high miles on the odometer indicated that the vehicle could have been driven from Columbus to Bakersfield and back, which meant it was possible for the suspect to have driven to Bakersfield, killed his family, then driven back to Columbus. However Detective Watts still had some obstacles in his way. The first was the paper trail that put the suspect in Columbus during the murders. Second, was the lack of any physical evidence connecting him to the actual crime. Although his fingerprints and stray hairs were all over the murder scene, this was not unexpected since he had previously lived in the house.

Detective Watts flew to Ohio to inspect the rented Dodge Neon. He was able to track the rental car from the first day it was ever rented and put into service and was thereby able to determine who the first four drivers were. All four of these drivers reported that they never left the Columbus, Ohio area. Detective Watts examined the car but could find nothing in the interior to connect it back to the murders. However, the one thing Detective

Continued

Watts did find was insects in the radiator. Even though the rental car had been washed, the radiator was still packed with insects.

Because of his knowledge that many bugs are indigenous to some areas but not to others, he considered the possibility that these dead insects could disprove the suspect's alibi. Thus, he made a decision to seek the assistance of forensic entomologist Dr. Lynn S. Kimsey in the Department of Entomology at the University of California, Davis to assist him in trying to determine the geographical location where these bugs would be found.

The radiator and air filter were removed and delivered to Dr. Kimsey who in turn removed every piece of insect she could find. The sheer number of possible insects she was dealing with was staggering. In the United States there are close to 200,000 known species of insects. California alone contains 100,000 different kinds of insects. In order to keep track of all these insects, entomologists rely upon collections like the Smithsonian Institution's National Insect collection, which is one of the largest in the world. They house over 35,000,000 known specimens in more than 130,000 drawers, 33,000 jars or vials, and 23,000 slides. The collection helps scientists compare insects to known species and prove critical information about their geographical distribution.

Dr. Kimsey found pieces of at least 100 different insects on the radiator and a few on the air filter. She also found a number of house flies, which are common and found all across the United States, along with some honey bees, one of the most widespread insects in the entire world. However she did find something that stood out, namely a portion of a grasshopper. Although grasshoppers look similar from across the country, this one had bright red legs. It is called the red shanked grasshopper, and its coloration is very distinctive and is not native to Ohio. In fact, it is usually found to the west in regions like Oklahoma and north Texas, and as a result she determined that the car had likely traveled through these other states. The suspect continued to claim he never drove the Dodge Neon out of the state. But the little grasshopper proved the vehicle had certainly been driven out of the state.

The problem was that the grasshopper evidence was contradicted by the credit card receipts the suspect had provided indicating he was in Ohio at the time of the murders. Detective Watts pursued this alibi a little further and seized surveillance tapes of a Walmart and other stores where the suspect had allegedly been shopping. The video clearly showed that the individual using the credit card was not the suspect but rather was his brother. Thus his alibi was proven to be a false one. However

further evidence would be needed to prove that the suspect was in California at the time of the murders.

Detective Watts once again contacted Dr. Kimsey and asked if she could find any information that would indicate the insects found in the radiator and filter could have been a species that was indigenous to an area west of the Rockies or to California. Dr. Kimsey continued to inspect her inventory of insect parts and found even more evidence that the car had been outside Columbus, Ohio. She found three other insects that actually provided evidence the vehicle had been further west than New Mexico, Colorado, or Utah. As each species was discovered, Dr. Kimsey was able to map out their distribution. She even found a bug that seemed to indicate the car was driven at night. She found insects called Antlions which fly around only at night and are normally associated more with arid regions. Antlions are abundant in the dry areas of the southwest, further evidence that the car was driven outside of Ohio. Dr. Kimsey made another promising discovery of two additional bugs in a large category of insects called true bugs, which includes more than 50,000 species. They all have tubular mouth parts like a soda straw. They do not have jaws so they feed by piercing things, like aphids which pierce when they suck. But these species of true bugs are not very common, so Dr. Kimsey checked with experts at the Smithsonian Institution to help confirm the identification. They were able to identify two species of insects, namely, the pesemid and the logia. The pesemid has a distribution that is specific to Utah, Arizona, and the border of California, and the logia's distribution extends even a little further into California. The true bugs definitely showed that the radiator at least had been west of the Rockies. But the true bugs' distribution is only partially in California. To really make their case that the suspect had driven all the way to Bakersfield, they needed to do better than that. After identifying close to 50 species, Dr. Kimsey went back to the radiator and found a bug that changed everything, namely a paper wasp, which was the only insect found very abundantly in California. The paper wasp gets its name from the papery material it produces to build its nest, and while there are several kinds of paper wasps, the one found on the grille of the suspect's rental car is found only in the extreme southwest, especially in California. It was this evidence that Detective Watts had been hoping for.

Authorities arrested and charged the suspect, who was subsequently convicted of five counts of murder and sentenced to death.

EVIDENCE FROM WOUNDS

A basic knowledge of wounds is of great assistance to officers who are responsible for injury and death investigations. It helps them reach preliminary conclusions. The five most common types of wounds encountered by police officers in injury and death investigations are firearm wounds, incised wounds, stab wounds, puncture wounds, and lacerations.

FIREARM WOUNDS

When a bullet strikes a body, the skin is first pushed in and then perforated while in the stretched state. After the bullet has passed, the skin partially returns to its original position, and the entry opening is drawn together and is thus smaller than the diameter of the bullet. The slower the bullet speed, the smaller the entry opening. The bullet passing through the stretched skin forms a so-called contusion ring around the entrance opening as the bullet

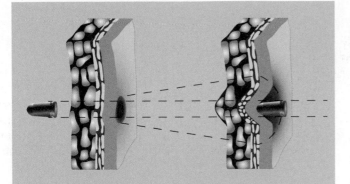

▲ **FIGURE 9-8   A bullet penetrating the skin**

The skin is pressed inward, stretched, and perforated in the stretched condition, after which it returns to its original position. The entry opening is smaller than the diameter of the bullet. Immediately around the opening is a contusion ring, because the bullet rubs against this part of the skin and scrapes the external layer of epithelial cells.

Source: Nucleus Medical Art Illustration. (2007). www.nucleusinc.com, as depicted in Vernon J. Geberth's *Practical Homicide Investigation*.

slips against the skin that is pressed inward and scrapes the external epithelial layers (Figure 9-8). The skin in the contusion ring becomes conspicuous by drying after some hours. In a favorable case, rifling marks on the bullet leave such a distinct mark in the contusion ring that the number of grooves in the rifling can be counted. The combined section of the contusion ring and entrance opening corresponds to the caliber of the bullet or exceeds it slightly. When a bullet strikes the body squarely, the contusion ring is round; when a bullet strikes at an angle, the ring is oval.

Along with the contusion ring, there is another black-colored ring, the "smudge ring," which often entirely covers the contusion ring (Figure 9-8). It does not contain any powder residues or contamination from the bore of the firearm but consists wholly of small particles originating from the surface of the bullet. The smudge ring may be absent in the case of clean-jacketed bullets or a bullet that has passed through clothing.

A bullet passing through the body forms a track that is usually straight but can also be bent at an angle in an unpredictable manner if the bullet meets or passes through a bone. Thus it is not possible to determine with certainty, from observation of the entrance and exit openings, in which direction the weapon was pointed when the shot was fired. The direction must be calculated by the pathologist from the results of the autopsy. The velocity of the bullet has a great influence on the appearance of the track: straight tracks indicate a high velocity, and bent or angular ones indicate a low velocity.

In gunshot injuries in soft parts of the body, especially in the brain, the bullet can produce a considerable explosive effect, which is greatest with unjacketed or soft-nosed bullets from large-caliber firearms. Such a bullet may split into several parts, each of which forms its own track, and thus there may be several exit wounds. When such a bullet strikes the head, large parts of the cranium can be blown away and the brain scattered around. A soft-nosed bullet that, before hitting the body, is split by

striking against a hard object such as a tree branch can produce a number of irregularly shaped entrance holes.

A shot through the head is not always fatal. To be immediately fatal, the bullet must either produce a bursting effect or injure an artery of the brain or a vital brain center. A shot through the brain that is not immediately fatal does not always produce unconsciousness. Even when the heart has been perforated by a bullet, it occasionally happens that the injured person lives for several hours, retaining some capacity of movement.

It is often difficult to distinguish the exit wound from the entrance wound, especially from a shot at long range with a metal-jacketed bullet, assuming, of course, that the bullet passes through the body intact. In a favorable case, the exit wound may have a ragged appearance with flaps directed outward. To determine the direction of the shot with certainty in such a case, an autopsy is necessary. If the bullet was damaged by its passage through the body or if there was a bursting effect, it is generally easy to determine the exit wound, which is then considerably larger than the entrance wound and shows a star-shaped, ragged character, with flaps directed outward. Note, however, that in contact shots the entrance wound may be ragged and star-shaped. A bullet that ricochets may strike with its side, or obliquely, and produce a large and characteristic entrance wound.

Close and Distant Shots

It is very important to be able to estimate the distance from which a shot was fired. In many cases this fact is the only evidence available that can distinguish among suicide, a self-defense killing, manslaughter, or murder.

In practice, a distinction is made among *contact, close,* and *distant* shots. A **contact bullet wound** is made when the muzzle of the weapon is pressed against the body when the shot is fired. In a close shot, the distance of the muzzle is less than about 18 inches from the body (Figures 9-9 and 9-10), whereas a distant

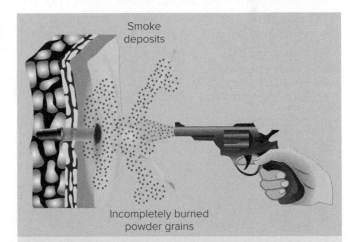

▲ **FIGURE 9-9   Firearm discharge at close range**

Close shot, short distance. The diagram shows both incompletely burned powder grains and smoke deposits in the zone of blackening. The powder grains are concentrated immediately around the entrance hole.

Source: Nucleus Medical Art Illustration. (2007). www.nucleusinc.com, as depicted in Vernon J. Geberth's *Practical Homicide Investigation*.

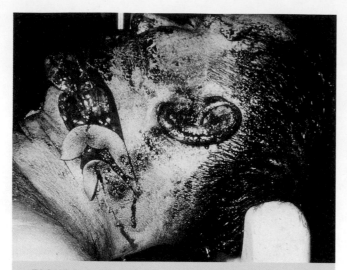

▲ **FIGURE 9-10** **Close range gunshot wound**
This victim was first assaulted with a knife and then shot numerous times in the left side of the head. Note the blackened area around the multiple bullet wounds on the left side of his head indicating direct contact or very close contact with the skin.

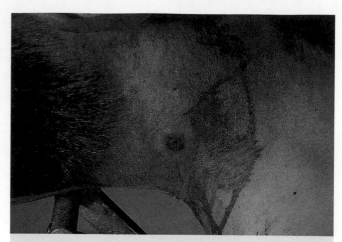

▲ **FIGURE 9-12** **Distant shot**
When a bullet strikes a body from a distance, the skin is first pushed and then perforated while in the stretched state. After the bullet has passed, the skin partially returns to the original position, and the entry opening is drawn together and is thus smaller than the diameter of the bullet. The bullet passing into the stretched skin forms what is called a *contusion ring* around the entrance as the bullet slips against the skin that is pressed inward and scrapes the external epithelial layers.

shot is one fired at a distance greater than 18 inches[22] (Figures 9-11 and 9-12).

In the case of a contact shot against an exposed part of the body, soot, metallic particles, and powder residues are driven into the body and can be found there during the autopsy. Blackening, caused by soot and powder, around the entry opening is often absent. A contact shot against a part of the body protected by clothing often produces a powder zone on the skin or in the clothes, and soot, powder residue, and fragments of clothing are driven into the track. In a contact discharge, the entrance wound differs considerably from an entrance wound in a close shot or a distant shot. When a contact shot is fired, the gases of the explosion are driven into the track but are forced out again and produce

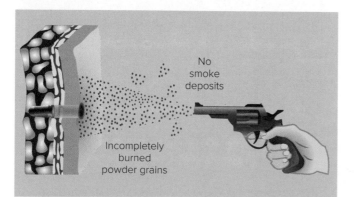

▲ **FIGURE 9-11** **Firearm discharged from a distance**
Close shot, greater distance than in Figure 9-9. The diagram shows unburned powder grains, but no smoke deposits in the zone of blackening.
Source: Nucleus Medical Art Illustration. (2007). www.nucleusinc.com, as depicted in Vernon J. Geberth's *Practical Homicide Investigation.*

a bursting effect on the skin and clothes. The entrance wound is often star-shaped with flaps directed outward (Figure 9-13).

A close shot produces a zone of blackening around the entrance wound of the track, either on the skin or on the clothes. Sometimes the flame from the muzzle causes a singeing action around this opening, with hair and textile fibers curled up. The zone of blackening is formed of substances carried along with the explosion gases. When a cartridge is fired, the bullet is forced through the barrel of the weapon by the explosion gases. Only a small amount of the gas passes in front of the bullet. The combustion of the powder is never complete, even with smokeless powder and still less with black powder, and the explosion gases therefore carry with them incompletely burned powder residues, the amount of which decreases as the distance increases. Thus, in a close shot, a considerable amount of incompletely burned powder residue is found on the target. In addition to carrying this residue, the gases also carry impurities from the inside of the barrel, consisting of rust (iron), oil, and particles rubbed off the bullet. Metallic residues from the percussion cap and cartridge case also occur in the gases of the explosion. If the shot is fired at a right angle to the body, the zone of blackening is practically circular; if it is fired obliquely, the zone is oval. The extent of the zone of blackening is often difficult to determine by direct observation, and it is often better to photograph it, using infrared-sensitive material, which intensifies the zone of blackening so its extent is more easily determined. The zone of blackening gives valuable information for determining the distance from which a shot was fired, which may be an important factor in deciding between murder and suicide. It is important that

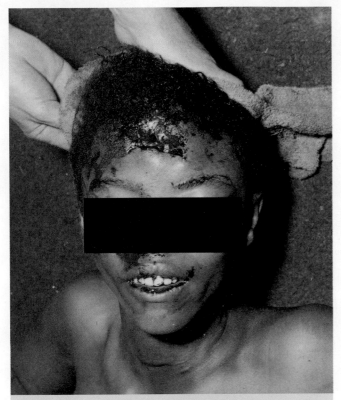

▲ FIGURE 9-13   Contact bullet wound
Homicidal contact bullet wound to the forehead. Note the charring of the edges and the irregularly shaped tears of the skin owing to the undermining of the scalp. This contact bullet wound was made from a .38-caliber bullet against an exposed part of the body (in this case, the head). Soot, metallic particles, and powder residue are driven into the body and can be found during the autopsy.

comparative test shots be fired with the same weapon and same type of ammunition as those used in the actual crime.

Close shots with black powder show marks of burning up to a distance of 4 to 6 inches and a distinct deposit of powder smoke up to 10 to 12 inches. Dispersed grains of powder embedded in the target may be detected even at a distance of 3 feet. In distant shots, none of the characteristics of a close shot can be detected.

Powder residues occur on the object fired at in the form of incompletely and completely burned particles. A careful microscopic examination should precede any chemical examination, as it is often possible to establish in this way the shape and color of unburned powder particles and to distinguish many kinds of powder.

Black powder, which consists of potassium nitrate, sulfur, and charcoal, is identified by the presence of potassium and nitrate in the entrance wound. Smokeless powder consists chiefly of nitrocellulose or of nitrocellulose with nitroglycerine and is identified by the presence of nitrite, which can be detected by various microreactions. The grains of smokeless powder are generally coated with graphite and occur in many forms (for example, round or angular discs, pellets, and cylinders).[23]

High-Velocity Rifle Wounds

The difference in the size of the wounds and damage done between handgun bullets and rifle bullets, especially those of a large caliber, can be considerable. For example, Figure 9-14 depicts an individual who was shot in the head one time by a police swat team member. The officer was armed with a .308 Remington 700 rifle. The subject had barricaded himself in a motel room while holding a hostage. He was shot in the head after he made the fatal mistake of slightly opening the door to the motel room and pointing his rifle in the direction of a police SWAT team member. The rifle the decedent was holding is depicted on the left side of his body.

◄ FIGURE 9-14
High-velocity rifle wound
This individual was shot in the head one time by a police swat team member. The officer was armed with a .308 Remington 700 rifle. The subject had barricaded himself in a motel room while holding a hostage. He was shot in the head and made the fatal mistake of slightly opening the door to the motel room and pointing his rifle in the direction of a SWAT team member.

Shotgun Wounds

A shotgun is a smooth-bore, shoulder-fired firearm and is typically used to fire multiple pellets, rather than a single slug. The most common gauges with their corresponding bore diameters are as follows:[24]

- The pellets fired range in size from 0.08 inch for a No. 9 shot to 0.33 inch for 00 Buck.
- A "wad," which may be either paper or plastic, lies between the shot pellets and the powder. Most modern shotgun shells use plastic wads.
- A shotgun shell can contain anywhere from a couple of hundred pellets to nine for 00 Buck, as well as one large lead slug.

Shotgun Entrance Wounds. From contact to 12 inches, there is a single round entrance 0.75 to 1 inch in diameter. The edge of the wound shows an abrasion ring. As the distance between muzzle and skin increases, powder tattooing appears. Powder blackening is most prominent at less than 12 inches. Powder tattooing is considerably less dense than it is in pistol wounds.

When pellets are discharged at between 3 and 6 feet of range, the single entrance wound widens to 1.5 to 2 inches in diameter and shows "scalloping" of the edges. At about 6 feet, the pellets begin to separate from the main mass of pellets. Beyond 10 to 12 feet, there is great variation in the spread of the pellets (Figure 9-15).

The Wad. At close ranges, the wad will be propelled into the body through the large single entrance wound. Beyond 10 to 15 feet, the wad will have separated from the pellets and will not enter. However, it may mark the body. The gauge of the shotgun and the size of the pellets can be determined from the wad and pellets, respectively. On occasion, a plastic wad may be marked by the choke or irregularities at the end of the barrel, making ballistic comparison possible.

Range Determination. Range determinations can be made later if the size of the shotgun pattern was described at autopsy and duplicated on paper. The same weapon with the same type of ammunition must be used in duplication of the pattern if accurate results are desired. Range formulas do not work.

X-ray patterns of the shot in the body are useless for range determinations, as are patterns on the body in which the shot first struck the target.

The size of the shot pattern on the body depends primarily on the choke of the gun. The type of ammunition and barrel length are secondary factors. The size of the pellet pattern is independent of the gauge of the shotgun, and an increase in gauge just increases the density of the pattern.

Exit Wounds. Shotgun pellets rarely exit except when used as instruments of suicide in the region of the head.

Firearm Residues

Detecting firearm residues on the hands of an individual may be of great importance in evaluating deaths caused by gunshot wounds. Detection of such residues on the hands of a deceased individual is often confirmatory evidence of a suspected suicide.[25]

One of the earliest methods of determining whether an individual discharged a weapon, the paraffin test or dermal nitrate test, was based on the detection of nitrates on the surfaces of the hands. Paraffin was employed for the removal of powder residues from the hands. Diphenylamine was the reagent used to detect the nitrates picked up by the paraffin. This test is no longer considered valid, because no distinction can be made between nitrates of gunpowder origin and those from other sources, which are quite commonly encountered in day-to-day living.

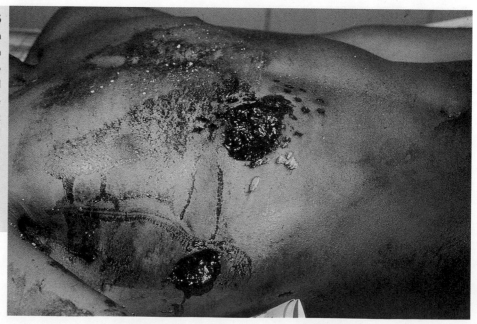

▶ **FIGURE 9-15**
Close-range wound from a 12-gauge shotgun
In shotgun entrance wounds, the characteristics of the wound vary based on the distance between the muzzle and the skin. For example, from contact to 12 inches, the edge of the wound shows an abrasion ring. As the distance increases, powder tattooing appears. This photo shows that powder tattooing is considerably less dense than it is in pistol wounds.

Several years ago, a series of chemical spot tests for detection of metallic components of firearm discharge residues was developed. Such metallic substances originate mainly from the primer, although they can also come from the bullet or cartridge case. Spot tests were developed for the presence of antimony, barium, and lead substances found in most primers. These tests are inconclusive because they are essentially qualitative rather than quantitative.[26]

The concept of detecting metallic primer components led to more sophisticated approaches now in general use. As mentioned, compounds of antimony, barium, and lead are used in modern noncorrosive primers. When a handgun is discharged, discrete particulate matter containing these elements is deposited on the thumb, forefinger, and connecting web (the back of the hand holding the weapon). The metallic compounds are removed from the hand, either with paraffin or, more commonly, with cotton swabs saturated with a dilute solution of acid. This material is then submitted for analysis.

Removal of Gunshot Residue Whatever system of analysis a pathologist uses, the procedures for removal of firearm discharge residues from the hand are the same. The solution most commonly used is of dilute acid. Four cotton swabs are used to remove the firearm discharge residues from the hands. Two swabs are used on each hand; one for the palm, the other for the "back" of the hand. The swabs of the nonfiring hand and the palm of the hand suspected of discharging the weapon act as controls. A control swab dipped in the acid also should be submitted as a blank. Cotton swabs with plastic shafts should be used. Those with wood shafts should not be used because the wood may be contaminated with metallic elements and wood also shows great variation in the concentration of such elements.

If a person has discharged a handgun, firearm discharge residues should appear only on the back of the hand that fired the weapon, not on the palm, and normally not the other hand, unless the shooter was holding the handgun with both hands as police officers are typically trained to do in combat shooting situations. Some people, because of their occupations, may have high levels of barium, antimony, or lead on their hands. Thus if the back of the hand were the only area submitted for examination, a misleadingly positive report would come back. If analysis reveals firearm discharge residues only on the palms, it strongly suggests that the individual's hands were around the weapon at the time of the discharge or were trying to ward off the weapon. However, in suicide, high levels of residue often show up on the nonfiring palm when that hand is used to steady the weapon by grasping the barrel, thus receiving the muzzle or cylinder discharge.

It must be realized that determining whether an individual fired a gun cannot be based on absolute quantities of primer residue on the hands. Rather, it is based on contrast of the levels of these compounds from right to left and from palm to back.

INCISED AND STAB WOUNDS

The **incised wound**—more commonly referred to as a "cutting wound"—is inflicted with a sharp-edged instrument such as a knife or a razor. The weapon typically employed in inflicting both incised and stab wounds is a pocketknife, although kitchen knives are also

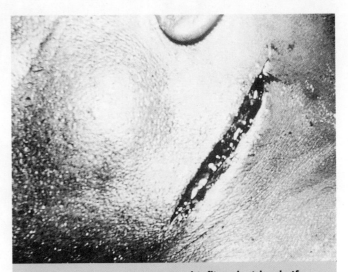

▲ **FIGURE 9-16   Incise wound inflicted with a knife**
The wound is narrow at the edge and gaping at the middle. Such wounds typically bleed a lot. Incise wounds are often inflicted with a sharp-edged instrument such as a knife or a razor. The wounds are sometimes found on the arms, face, and legs.

common. In comparison with shootings, fewer cutting assaults result in death, largely because the perpetrator's intention was to injure or disfigure rather than kill the victim. Cutting wounds are often found on the arms, face, and legs. Even in these "friendly" cuttings, as they are sometimes referred to, death may occur. When the victim does die from a cutting wound, it generally is found around the throat. The severity of most incised wounds is directly related to the shape and sharpness of the weapon, the part of the body being cut, and the amount of force used in striking the victim. The incised wound is typically narrow at the edges and gaping at the center, with considerable bleeding (Figure 9-16). The inexperienced investigator may conclude that a gaping incised wound was inflicted by a large cutting instrument. However, a small knife with a honed blade is capable of causing very severe wounds.

Most frequently, death is caused after a stab results in severe damage to a vital organ, internal bleeding, shock, or secondary infections that develop several days after the attack. Any of these factors may itself be fatal; they often occur in combination. The shape, size, and keenness of the blade all determine a wound's shape and depth, as does the manner in which the knife is thrust into and pulled out of the body. One noticeable aspect of multiple stab wounds is their different shapes when made with the same knife. The proximity of the wounds in a multiple-stabbing assault may be helpful in determining the actions of the victim before death. If the wounds are concentrated within a small region of the body, then there is a good possibility that the victim was immobilized at the time of the assault, that is, held down, asleep, or intoxicated (Figure 9-17).

PUNCTURE WOUNDS

At one time the weapon most frequently used in assaults resulting in **puncture wounds** was the ice pick. However, its use and ready

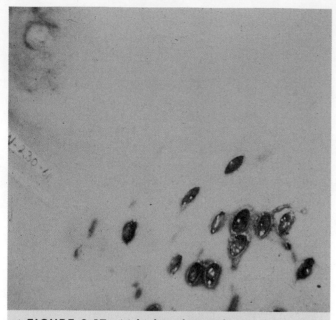

▲ FIGURE 9-17　Multiple stab wounds
Death from stab wounds generally results from severe damage to a vital organ, internal bleeding, shock, or secondary infection that may develop several days after the attack. The close proximity of these wounds indicates that the victim was unable to struggle to any sufficient degree. Even wounds inflicted with the same knife as depicted in this figure can be quite different in size and shape.

LACERATIONS

When used in an assault, clubs, pipes, pistols, or other such blunt objects can produce open, irregularly shaped wounds called **lacerations.** Such wounds bleed freely and characteristically are accompanied by bruising around the edges. There is no necessarily a relationship between the shape of the wound and that of the weapon employed. Occasionally, such force will be used in an attack that an impression of the weapon is left on the victim's skin. Most frequently, when death results from an assault in which lacerations were inflicted, the cause is severe head injuries. Laceration wounds may be inflicted accidentally, as in the case of an intoxicated person who falls and strikes his or her head against a curb or step. In some instances, circumstances may appear more suspicious:

Checking the back doors of businesses at about 9:30 P.M., an officer found the proprietor of a jewelry store dead at the open rear entrance to his store. He had sustained a large laceration on his forehead and had bled considerably. At first, it appeared that a murder had taken place during a robbery or burglary. Careful processing of the scene yielded traces of blood and one small skin fragment from the brick wall near the rear entrance.

Nothing was missing from the business. The medical examiner found the cause of death to be a heart attack. The head laceration contained minute traces of brick. Thus a reconstruction of events showed that as the owner was closing his business, he suffered a heart attack and convulsions, striking his head against the brick wall. The lacerations he suffered made it look as though he had suffered a fatal head wound.

availability are not as common today as it once was. Leather punches and screwdrivers also are capable of producing puncture wounds, which are normally small and have little or no bleeding. Such wounds can be easily overlooked, particularly if they are in hairy parts of the body. Infliction of a puncture wound produces death in the same way as do stab wounds (Figure 9-18).

▶ FIGURE 9-18　Puncture wound
This victim received multiple ice-pick stab wounds. Leather punches and screwdrivers are all capable of producing puncture wounds. Because there is often little bleeding, a single wound can easily be overlooked, particularly if it is on a hairy part of the body.

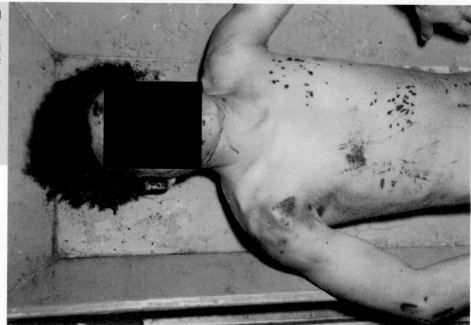

The severity, extent, and appearance of injuries due to blunt trauma depend on the amount of force delivered to the body, the amount of time over which the force is delivered, the region struck, the amount (extent) of body surface over which the force is delivered, and the nature of the weapon. If a weapon deforms and/or breaks on hitting the body, less energy is delivered to the body to produce injury, since some of the energy is used to deform and/or break the weapon. Thus, the resultant injury is less severe than would have been the case if the weapon did not deform and/or break. If the body moves with the blow, this increases the period of time over which the energy is delivered and decreases the severity of the injury.[27]

For any given amount of force, the greater the area over which it is delivered, the less severe the wound, because the force is dissipated. The size of the area affected by a blow depends on the nature of the weapon and the region of the body. For a weapon with a flat surface, such as a board, there is a diffusion of the energy and a less severe injury than that due to a narrow object—for example, a steel rod, delivered with the same amount of energy. If an object projects from the surface of the weapon, then all the force will be delivered to the end of the projection and a much more severe wound will be produced. If a blow is delivered to a rounded portion of the body, such as the top of the head (Figure 9-19), the wound will be much more severe than would be the case if the same force is delivered to a flat portion of the body, such as the back, where there will be a greater area of contact and more dispersion of force.[28]

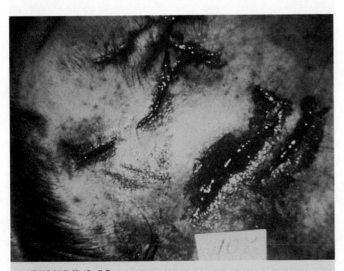

▲ FIGURE 9-19
Lacerations resulting from a pistol whipping
This victim was pistol whipped to death by an armed robber. This assault resulted in numerous lacerations to the head. Such wounds bleed freely and characteristically are accompanied by bruising around the edges. There is not necessarily a relationship between the shape of the wound and that of the weapon employed.

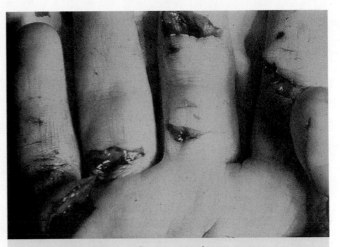

▲ FIGURE 9-20   Defense wounds
This victim received severe defense knife wounds on the hands while trying to stop his assailant from stabbing him to death.

DEFENSE WOUNDS

Defense wounds are suffered by victims attempting to protect themselves from an assault, often by a knife or club. These wounds are commonly found on the palms of the hands, the fingers, and the forearms (Figure 9-20). In the most aggravated form defense wounds resulting from a knife may even result in one or more fingers being severed.

STRANGULATION WOUNDS

Ligature Strangulation

In **ligature strangulation,** the pressure on the neck is applied by a constricting band that is tightened by a force other than the body weight. Virtually all cases of ligature strangulation are criminal homicides. Females predominate as victims. Suicides and accidents are rare. The mechanism of death is the same as in hanging, namely, occlusion of the vessels that supply blood and thus oxygen to the brain. Consciousness is lost in 10–15 seconds.[29]

Ligatures used range from electric cords (Figure 9-21), neckties, ropes, and telephone cords to sheets, hose, and undergarments. The appearance of a ligature mark on the neck is subject to considerable variation, depending on the nature of the ligature, the amount of resistance offered by the victim, and the amount of force used by the assailant. The ligature mark may be faint, barely visible, or absent in young children or incapacitated adults, especially if the ligature is soft (e.g., a towel) and removed immediately after death. If a thin ligature is used, there will be a very prominent deep mark encircling the neck. Initially, it has a yellow parchment-like appearance that later turns dark brown.

In ligature strangulation, in contrast to hangings, the ligature mark usually encircles the neck in a horizontal plane often overlying the larynx or upper trachea. When a wire or cord is used, it usually completely encircles the neck. There may be a break in the furrow, however, usually at the back of the neck, where a hand has grasped the ligature and tightened it at that point.

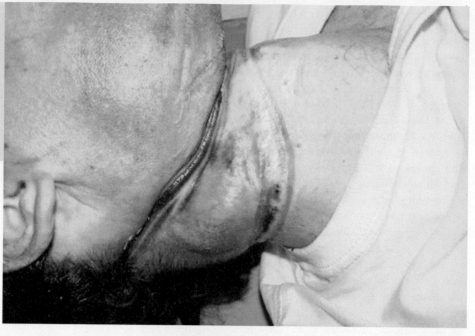

▶ FIGURE 9-21
Ligature strangulation
The pressure on the neck is applied by a constricting band that is tightened by a force other than the body weight. Virtually all cases of ligature strangulation are homicides. The victim in this photo died as a result of strangulation by use of an electric cord.

Aside from the ligature mark, abrasions and contusions of the skin of the neck are usually not present. They may occur, however, if the assailant places his or her hands beneath and around the ligature and twists it, tightening it around the neck, or if the victim claws at the neck in an attempt to remove the ligature or relieve the pressure. If there is more than one loop of the ligature around the neck, there may be bruising of the skin if the ligature pinches the skin between two loops.

Manual Strangulation

Manual strangulation is produced by pressure of the hand, forearm, or other limb against the neck, compressing the internal structures of the neck. The mechanism of death is occlusion of the blood vessels that supply blood to the brain. Occlusion of the airway probably plays a minor role in causing death, if any at all.

Virtually all manual strangulations are criminal homicides. One cannot commit suicide by manual strangulation, since as soon as consciousness is lost, pressure is released and consciousness is regained.

In most cases of manual strangulation, the assailant uses more force than is necessary to subdue and kill the victim. Hence, marks of violence are frequently present on the skin of the neck. Usually, there are abrasions, contusions, and fingernail marks on the skin (Figure 9-22).

While in most manual strangulations, there is evidence of both external and internal injury to the neck, in some cases there is no injury, either externally or internally. For example, one medical examiner reported seeing three women in a three-month period who had been manually strangled. The first woman showed absolutely no evidence either externally or internally; the second showed congestion of the face with fine petechiae of the conjunctivae and skin of the face, but no evidence of injury to the neck, either externally or internally; and the third victim showed the classic evidence of injury: abrasions and scratches of the skin with extensive hemorrhaging into the muscles of the neck. All three women were killed by the same

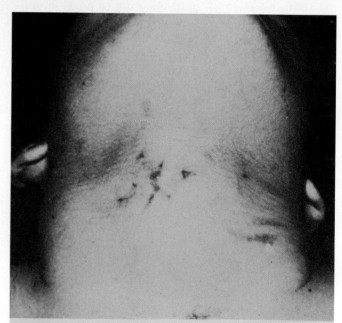

▲ FIGURE 9-22 **Death by manual strangulation**
This victim died as a result of manual strangulation. Note the crescent-shaped fingernail marks on the center of the throat along with bruising on the sides of the neck, indicating that the assailant attacked from behind.

individual. All three had blood alcohol levels above 0.30. The modus operandi of the perpetrator was to meet a woman in a bar, buy her liquor until she was extremely intoxicated, and then go off with her and have intercourse. He would then strangle her. At the time he strangled them, the women were unconscious due to acute alcohol intoxication, so a very minimal amount of pressure was necessary. He would place his hand over their necks and push downward, compressing the vessels of the neck. In the last case, the individual regained consciousness and struggled, with the resultant injuries. The perpetrator admitted having killed a number of other women in the same way over previous years in a number of states.

In manual strangulation, the victims are usually female. When they are male, they are often highly intoxicated. It is suggested that in all manual strangulation cases a complete toxicological screen should be performed.

SUICIDE

For the investigator, a major concern in an apparent suicide case is to make certain that the death was self-induced and not the result of a criminal homicide. In some cases, the investigator finds overwhelming evidence to this effect at the scene. In other cases, important information about the victim's behavior before death can be obtained from relatives, friends, coworkers, and employers. Suicide is often committed for the following reasons:

- Ill health or considerable pain.
- Severe marital strife.
- A recent emotionally damaging experience, such as an unhappy love affair, separation, or divorce.
- Financial difficulties, including the threat of a much lower standard of living or failure to meet some significant and past-due financial commitments.
- Perceived or actual humiliation.
- Remorse over the death of a loved one.
- Guilt for an act of one's own doing for which he or she cannot forgive themselves.
- Revenge, frequently by adolescents who have serious difficulties with parents or spurned lovers and want to punish them and make them feel guilty about whatever difficulty preceded their death.[30]

These factors are far from all inclusive, but the investigator will find a significant number of suicides associated with them. Conversely, if there is an apparent suicide and thorough scrutiny fails to produce a solid motive, then the investigator's suspicion should be aroused. Thus, in all apparent suicides the possibility of a criminal homicide should never be lightly discarded.

QUICK FACTS

Suicide Rate at a Glance Factors Related to the Suicide Rate

- Suicide was the tenth leading cause of death for all ages in 2013.[31]
- There were 41,149 suicides in 2013 in the United States—a rate of 12.6 per 100,000 is equal to 113 suicides each day or every 13 minutes.[32]
- Based on data about suicides in 16 National Violent Death Reporting System states in 16 National Violent Death Reporting System states in 2010, 33.4% of suicide decedents tested positive for alcohol, 23.8% for antidepressants, and 20.0% for opiates, including heroin and prescription pain killers.[33]
- Suicide results in an estimated $51 billion in combined medical and work loss costs.[34]

METHODS AND EVIDENCE OF SUICIDE

Nine methods are most commonly employed in suicides: shooting, hanging, ingesting sleeping pills and other pharmaceuticals, drowning, cutting and piercing, ingesting of poisons, inhaling gases, jumping from high places, and intentionally crashing an automobile.[35]

Although all of these can be simulated in the commission of murders, there are important differences in physical evidence that distinguish suicides from murders.

Gunshot Wounds

It is sometimes difficult to determine whether a gunshot wound was self-inflicted or resulted from the actions of an assailant. However, there are certain indicators that may be helpful in reaching a conclusion. One of these is the location of the wound and the trajectory of the projectile on entering the body. The most common method of committing suicide with a firearm involves the victim placing a handgun to the temple and firing a shot. If there is no exit wound it will be difficult for the investigator to determine the precise angle at which the projectile entered. This information will eventually be obtained during the autopsy, but it may be several days before one is performed. However, in the meantime, the investigator must make some preliminary determinations. The following case illustrates some of the points discussed thus far.

A man telephoned the police hysterically, reporting that his wife had just shot and killed herself. When the police and an ambulance arrived, the victim was dead of a bullet wound in her upper left temple. The husband was holding the gun with which he alleged his wife had shot herself. He stated that he had arrived home from work just before the incident but that neither his wife nor their three preschool-age children had been there. His wife had arrived home a short while later, and she had been drinking heavily. When he questioned her about the whereabouts of their three children, she told him they were at his mother's home. A heated argument then followed about her neglect of their children, her drinking, and her seeing other men. According to the husband, his wife then slapped him in his face, and he slapped her back. At that point, she walked over to a nearby desk drawer, where he kept a revolver. She removed the revolver from the desk drawer, placed the barrel against her head, fired a single shot, and fell to the floor. No one else was home at the time this incident occurred.

The following set of facts was revealed by the medical examiner's autopsy report:

- The bullet entered the upper left portion of the head, traveled downward through the brain, and continued downward through the victim's body, coming to rest in her chest.
- There were no powder burns present around the gunshot wound.

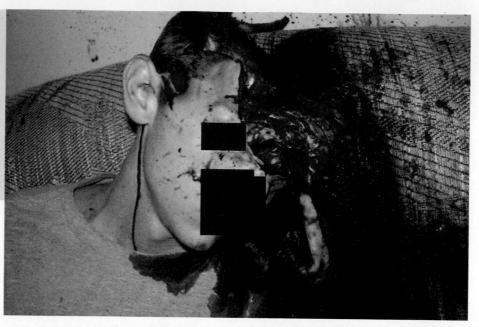

► FIGURE 9-23
Suicide by shotgun
This individual placed a 12-gauge shotgun against his right temple and pulled the trigger. As can be noted, there are scorch marks around the entry wound near the right ear. Shotgun wounds to the head, especially those involving large-gauge shotguns, generally result in enormous damage to the head.

- Death occurred immediately.
- Based upon the findings of the autopsy the only way the wound could have been self-inflicted is if the victim was holding the weapon in her left hand at least two feet from her head and using her thumb to pull the trigger (*not a likely scenario*).

The relatives of both the victim and her husband provided the police with the following information:

- To their knowledge, the victim had not been despondent, nor had she ever previously attempted or discussed suicide.
- The victim and her husband had been having serious domestic difficulties, because she was seeing other men, spending the house money on liquor, and not properly caring for their three young children.
- Both parties were known to have assaulted each other in domestic disputes in the past.
- The victim was right-handed.

These facts tended to indicate the victim's death was not a suicide but a criminal homicide. An interrogation of the husband established what the facts suggested. The husband related he had been truthful about the events leading up to the argument but after his wife slapped him he became angry and knocked her to the floor. He then got a revolver from a nearby desk drawer, walked over to his wife and while standing over her fired a single shot into her head. After shooting her he became frightened and fabricated the story about his wife's suicide.

This case demonstrates the importance of two factors in the investigation of an alleged suicide. The first is the importance of the location of the wound on the body and its trajectory on entering the body. Second is the presence or absence of evidence indicating that the victim was predisposed to committing suicide.

Suicide by Use of a Shotgun

The use of a shotgun to commit suicide can result in enormous physical damage, especially if the gun is discharged into the head (Figure 9-23).

Hanging

Certain misconceptions associated with suicidal hangings can lead to erroneous conclusions. The first is that the victim's neck gets broken and second, that the feet are suspended from the floor. Although both of these conditions may occur, they are exceptions rather than the rule. The first misconception is related to the circumstances of legal executions by hanging. In legal executions, the procedures involved in inflicting death are intended to result in the neck being broken. This is accomplished by the use of a specific type of noose and a gallows with a trap door through which the person will drop some distance before being abruptly stopped. However, in a suicidal hanging, even when the feet are suspended, the neck is rarely broken, because the fall is not long enough to cause the severe jolt necessary to break the neck (Figure 9-24).

It is also fairly common in suicidal hangings for the victim's feet or even the knees to be touching the ground. Occasionally, the victim is found in a sitting position. Finding victims in these positions often creates suspicion, because it is difficult for inexperienced investigators to understand how anyone could remain in these positions while slowly choking to death. They might improperly conclude the victim first was rendered unconscious or was killed and placed in the hanging position. It is more likely, however, the victim did not slowly choke to death but rather first tied the rope around some supporting device and then around his or her neck. Pressure was then applied by the victim either by crouching down, if in a standing position, or leaning forward, if in a sitting position. This initial pressure painlessly cuts off the flow of blood to the brain, which results

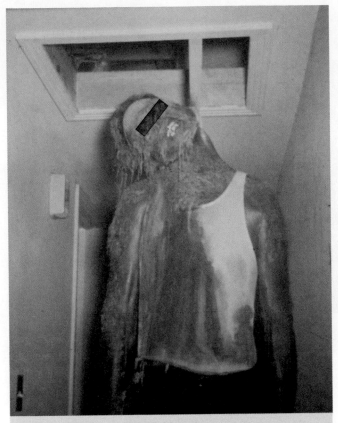

▲ FIGURE 9-24 Suicidal hanging
This suicide victim has been in this hanging position for approximately three weeks. The body is in an advanced stage of decomposition; the mosslike substance on the body is dried body fluids. The victim has used a ligature-type device wrapped around a beam in the attic to suspend his body.

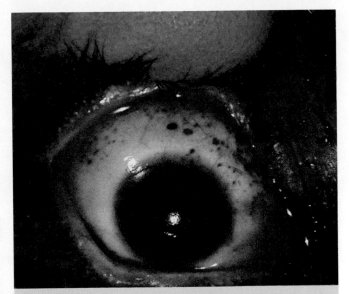

▲ FIGURE 9-25 Petechial hemorrhaging in the eye
The victim of a suicidal hanging. In suicidal hangings, investigators often find what is referred to as a petechial hemorrhaging in the eyes of the deceased. This is a result of the small vessels in the eye bleeding because of an increase in blood pressure caused by the compression around the neck.

in unconsciousness. When unconsciousness does occur, the full weight of the body is then applied to the noose, whereupon all oxygen is cut off to the brain and death follows. There is very little physical pain associated with suicides of this type. If one considers that many suicidal hangings occur in victims' homes, then it is logical to expect the feet not to be suspended above the floor, because few household objects are strong enough to hold the weight of a fully suspended body or one that has fallen several feet from a chair or table.

Livor mortis is most pronounced in the lower portion of the arms and legs and around the face, lips, and jaw. There may be some variations in the location of the discoloration, depending on the position of the body. When death occurs in this manner, one frequently finds petechial hemorrhaging in the eyes, caused when small blood vessels in the eye bleed because blood pressure increases in response to compression around the neck (Figure 9-25).

Occasionally, hangings are accidental, not suicidal. The individual may have himself in a modified hanging position while masturbating and accidentally fall, slip, and knock over the object on which he is standing, resulting in an accidental death, known as autoerotic death or sexual asphyxia; the intent is sexual rather than suicidal. In these cases, the genitals are exposed, and semen may be present. (Chapter 10, "Sex-Related Offenses," provides an in-depth explanation of autoerotic death.) The presence of feces and urine is common because of the total relaxation of the bladder and bowel muscles at the time of death.

Sleeping Pills and Other Pharmaceuticals

Sleeping pills and other pharmaceuticals have for many years been a common means of committing suicide. However, some deaths resulting from the ingestion of sleeping pills or tranquilizing drugs may be accidental, not suicidal. The investigator has an obligation to determine whether the death was accidental or suicidal. Certain types of medication, such as barbiturates, when mixed with alcohol have a synergistic effect, which increases the potency of the drug beyond its normal strength. One should not be too quick to decide that the death is a suicide until the investigation is completed and some evidence is available to support this conclusion. In such cases, the investigator should seize as evidence any remaining medication and its container. Frequently, the container identifies the medication, the drugstore dispensing it, and the physician prescribing it. There is always the possibility that the medication was purchased or obtained illegally, thus complicating the investigative process. As in all apparent suicides, the investigator should conduct interviews of relatives, friends, and neighbors who may be able to provide background information about the victim.

Drowning

The majority of drowning incidents are either accidental or suicidal, but some are homicidal. Three questions must be answered in apparent drowning cases before any final conclusions can be

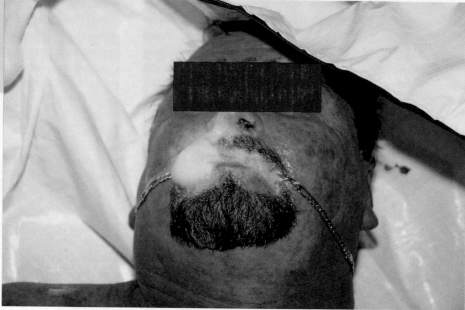

▶ FIGURE 9-26 **Drowning victim**
This individual died from an accidental drowning. Note the pink foam extruding from his nose and open mouth.

reached: Was the cause of death drowning, or was the victim first killed and then placed in the water? If the cause of death was drowning, did it take place in the water where the body was recovered, or was the victim drowned elsewhere and then placed in the water where found? Was the victim conscious when placed in the water? Answers to these questions can be obtained by external examination of the body by the investigator and an internal investigation of the body by a physician. External signs to indicate that the victim was alive and conscious when entering the water include:

- Objects clutched in the hand, such as grass or bottom soil commonly found in water.
- Fingernail marks on the palms of the hands.
- White, pink, or red foam extruding from the nose and open mouth (Figure 9-26).
- Livor mortis most marked in the head and neck, because the body settled with these parts in a dependent position.[36]

An internal examination by a physician serves to establish whether death occurred by drowning. The following evidence may be found in drowning cases:

- The chest cavity and the lungs are distended and soggy, with fine foam in the trachea and bronchi.
- The heart is flabby, with its right side dilated and filled with dark red fluid. The blood is unclotted and usually hemolyzed owing to the absorption of the drowning fluid into the system.
- The mastoid cells of the ear have hemorrhaged.
- Air embolisms may have formed in the blood in deep-water drowning.
- There may be water in the stomach and duodenum.
- Algae and other marine particles may be found in the stomach and adhering to the sides of the air passages.

In removing the body from the water, the investigator may notice considerable damage to portions of the victim's body, especially around the head and face. This should not cause the investigator to conclude prematurely that the victim was the object of foul play. Some bodies of water contain many rocks and shells; a free-floating body that is subject to strong currents can be repeatedly slammed into and dragged across such objects, causing severe damage, especially to the forehead, knees, tops of the feet, and backs of the hands. In addition, if the water is rich with fish, crabs, and other marine life, these too can cause damage. It is not unusual for the lips, ears, and nose to be at least partially eaten away. The extent of damage from objects or marine life in the water varies; understanding what can result from their presence minimizes the possibility of premature conclusions. But the investigator must also not prematurely conclude that all damage resulted after the body was placed in the water. The medical examiner can help draw conclusions about the actual nature of wounds (Figure 9-27).

Cutting and Piercing Instruments

The instruments ordinarily employed in suicides by cutting are razor blades, knives (Figure 9-28), and occasionally glass. One of the common characteristics of suicides inflicted by these instruments is the presence of hesitation marks. Hesitation marks are a series of lesser wounds inflicted by the victim in the general region of the fatal wound, often the wrists, forearms, or throat. In certain throat cuttings, it may be possible to reach a conclusion about whether the injury was self-inflicted or resulted from an assault. If a wound is self-inflicted, it tends to be deep at the point of entry and to shallow out at its terminus, which is near, or slightly past, the midline of the throat. In homicidal throat cutting, the wound appears deep from the start to the terminus. It is not unusual for a victim to inflict a series of severe cuts on different parts of the body to ensure death. The reasons vary, sometimes involving the influence of alcohol

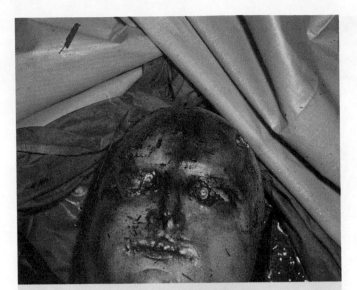

▲ FIGURE 9-27
Decomposition and marine life damage to an immersed body
Damage sustained by the victim in this photograph occurred while the victim was immersed in water. Note that the ears and eyelids are completely missing, and there is extensive damage to the nostrils and lips. These areas are among the first parts of the body to be attacked by marine life.

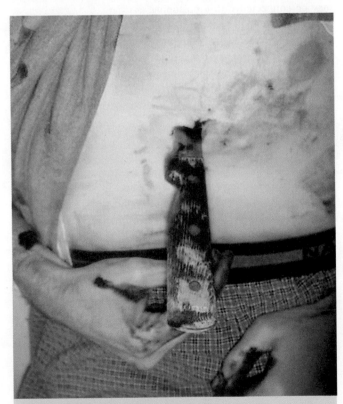

▲ FIGURE 9-28   Suicide by knife
This photo depicts an individual who took his life by stabbing himself in the abdomen with a knife.

or hallucinogenic drugs. The ingestion of drugs may have been a planned prelude to the act of self-destruction. Self-inflicted wounds can be surprisingly brutal and tend to make people disbelieve they were self-imposed. This is particularly true when mutilation of the sexual parts is involved. In one case, a 28-year-old man used a single-edged razor blade to cut off his penis. When questioned by paramedics, the man said: "It's just been eating away at me for so long, and when I thought about it, I heard voices saying 'Do it, do it.' I was just angry at myself. I had it all planned out and I did it."[37]

Poisons

The ingestion of liquid **poisons** is sometimes clear from outward signs on the body. Powerful caustic lyes or acids may produce vomiting once the liquid reaches the digestive tract. There is considerable damage to lips, tongue, and mouth, and there may be blood in the vomitus, along with pieces of the esophagus and stomach. Usually, death does not occur rapidly, and victims may employ another means of suicide to stop the excruciating pain (Figure 9-29).

Cases of suspected poisoning frequently pose very difficult problems to the police investigator and to the medical examiner. Many poisons produce symptoms similar to those of certain diseases, a fact that can complicate determination of whether a crime has been committed. However, if there is any reason to suspect poisoning, the investigation must proceed along the lines of a possible criminal homicide, suicide, or accidental death until death due to natural causes is established.[38] To compound the problem, suicides and accidental deaths by poisoning are sometimes very difficult to distinguish from criminal homicide. Alcohol, when consumed with certain medications, may result in an accidental (possibly suicidal) death by respiratory failure. An example is the combination of barbiturates and alcohol. When the alcohol level in the blood reaches about half the lethal dose, most individuals lose consciousness and thus stop breathing. But with the addition of a stimulant, such as an amphetamine, this effect may not occur, and individuals may drink a lethal dose of alcohol before they fall into a coma.

Actually, poisoning is now rarely used in homicides, because modern laboratory techniques can readily detect most poisons, thus unmasking an intended criminal homicide. But when it is the method, a wide variety of poisons may be used (Table 9-1).

Characteristics of "Ideal" Poisons. There are certain elements that characterize an "ideal" poison, including:

- Being odorless, tasteless, and colorless, which allows for the administration of the poison to the intended victim, while providing no warning signs that the victim can detect by the normal bodily senses of smell, taste, and sight.
- Being readily soluble, preferably in water, which allows for easy administration in normal foods and drinks that the victims might eat or drink.
- Having a delayed onset of action which allows for a time period in which the poisoner can attempt to create an alibi.

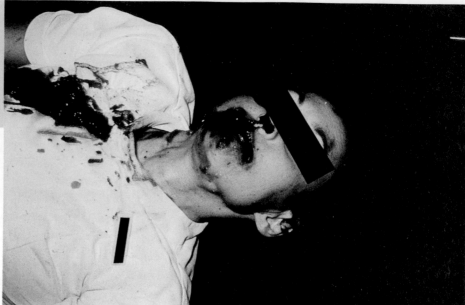

▶ FIGURE 9-29
Ingestion of a caustic drain cleaner
This victim committed suicide by ingesting a strong caustic drain cleaner. On ingestion, vomiting was induced, thereby causing severe burns to the nose, chin, and chest area.

- Being undetectable, and certainly the more exotic the poison the more likely it will not be detected in more routine toxicological analyses.
- Having a low-dose lethality, which means less of the toxic material needs to be administered. It is much easier to distribute a pinch of a substance than to distribute a pound.
- Being easily obtained, but not traceable, so it will leave no investigative trail that would lead to the poisoner.
- Being chemically stable, which makes it easy to store without loss of potency.[39]

Role of the Crime Scene Investigator in Suspected Deaths by Poisoning Cases. Even though the crime scene investigators seldom can identify the chemical compound that caused the death, they should be alert to the general range of possibilities and the potentially hazardous environmental factors that may be connected with a poisoning.

Regardless of the nature of the incident—criminal homicide, suicide, or accident—the symptoms of death by poison are the same. The field investigator should attempt to determine if the victim had any of the symptoms—vomiting, convulsions, diarrhea, paralysis, rapid or slow breathing, contracted or dilated

TABLE 9-1	Poisons and Associated Physical Manifestations
TYPE OF POISON	**SYMPTOM OR EVIDENCE**
Caustic poison (lye)	Characteristic burns around lips and mouth of victim
Carbon monoxide	Victim's skin takes on an abnormally bright cherry-red color
Sulfuric acid	Black vomit
Hydrochloric acid	Greenish-brown vomit
Nitric acid	Yellow vomit
Silver salts	White vomit turning black in daylight
Copper sulfate	Blue-green vomit
Phosphorus	Coffee-brown vomit with an onion or a garlic odor
Cyanide	Burnt almond odor in air, cherry-red lividity color
Ammonia, vinegar, Lysol, etc.	Characteristic odors
Arsenic, mercury, lead salts	Pronounced diarrhea
Methyl (wood) alcohol, isopropyl (rubbing) alcohol	Nausea and vomiting, unconsciousness, possibly blindness

Source: Richard H. Fox and Carl L. Cunningham, *Crime Scene Search and Physical Evidence Handbook* (Washington, DC Government Printing Office, 1985), p. 126.

pupils, changes in skin color, or difficulty in swallowing—just before death. These symptoms are general manifestations of systemic poisoning. They do not provide proof of poisoning but can be meaningful in relation to other evidence. Someone who observed the victim just before death provides the best source of information concerning his or her symptoms. If no witness is available, the investigator must rely all the more on physical evidence from the crime scene. Table 9-1 lists common poisons and their associated physical manifestations.

The investigator should collect all available information concerning the activities of the victim during the last three days of life. Information on what types of medication were taken, when the last meal was eaten, and where it was eaten can be very important in determining the type of poison involved. Medical history may indicate that death was due to natural causes.

A **toxicologist** is a scientist trained in the identification and recognition of poisons, along with their physiological effects on humans and animals, and their antidotes. Crime laboratories usually provide some toxicological support but vary considerably in the amount and type that they can furnish. However, full toxicological support is always available through a combination of hospital, medical examiner's, coroner's, and criminalistics laboratories. Crime laboratories can direct police to local facilities.

If the investigator suspects that poison was ingested, a diligent search should be conducted for the container. In suicides and accidental poisonings, the container frequently is close at hand. Even though a container appears empty, it should be processed for fingerprints, packaged, marked, and forwarded to the laboratory for examination. Additionally, any other object that could reasonably relate to the poisoning should be collected, such as unwashed dishes and glasses, wastebasket contents, envelopes, and medicine containers.

Opiate-Overdoses

Drugs are classified into different groups based on their origins and effects on the human body. The opiate class of narcotics, which includes morphine, heroin, and oxycodone, are commonly referred to as downers because of their sedative-like effects. With the exception of alcohol, opiates account for the largest portion of drug-related hospital admissions.[40]

Police agencies often identify fatal drug overdoses as accidental deaths, but being aware of and alert to the indicators of a drug overdose before entering a crime scene enables investigators to more effectively conduct their investigation.

Victims of an opiate overdose often exhibit specific characteristics. For example, victims may have a "foam cone," tinged orange or red with blood, around their nostrils and mouth, which is the most common characteristic of such an overdose. Opiates act as a central nervous system depressant, causing a decrease in heart rate and breathing. This slowing causes fluids to gather in the lungs, inhibiting the life sustaining exchange of oxygen and carbon dioxide. Essentially, victims drown in their own pulmonary fluids. As the fluids gather, victims may expel these fluids, mixed with gas bubbles, which then forms the foam cone. Autopsies of opiate overdose victims often reveal that death resulted from pulmonary edema, a swelling of the lungs with a pooling of fluids inside them.[41]

Because of this lack of oxygen, extremities, as well as the lips and tongue, frequently turn blue. Pupils may be constricted to a pinpoint. Many heroin users inject the drug into their body with a needle, a practice known as mainstreaming. Consequently, they also may have needle or track marks, generally found on their arms. Chronic users often damage the blood vessels in their arms to such a degree that they resort to injecting the heroin into their legs, eyelids, or between their toes. Others also attempt to mask the needle marks by injecting into a tattoo.[42] Although only an autopsy can determine the exact cause of death, investigators and first responders can use these characteristics to initially determine that the death likely resulted from an opiate overdose.

Gases

The gas most frequently involved in medico-legal investigations is carbon monoxide. When a death does result from this gas, it is generally accidental or suicidal. Carbon monoxide is found in automobile exhaust fumes and improperly ventilated space heaters in homes. In a suicide death caused by auto emissions, the individual may have started the engine of the vehicle in the garage after closing the garage door or may have extended a flexible hose from the exhaust pipe into the vehicle and then closed the windows.

When death occurs from carbon monoxide poisoning, the victim's skin takes on an abnormally bright cherry-red color because of the reaction of the red blood cells to the gas. The red blood cells have a very high affinity for carbon monoxide molecules (approximately 250 times greater than for oxygen), absorbing them rapidly, thereby making the red blood cells incapable of absorbing oxygen and rendering them dysfunctional in the life-sustaining process. Death generally occurs when the red blood cells have reached a saturation level usually above 40%, although this varies; the level sometimes goes higher before death results if the victim is asleep, owing to the body's reduced oxygen needs (Figure 9-30).

Jumping from High Places

The major question to be answered in death resulting from jumping is whether the victim voluntarily leaped or was thrown or pushed. Often, there are suicide notes, witnesses who can provide this information, or background information that indicates previous suicide attempts or a predisposition toward suicide.

The Suicide Note

Research indicates that suicide notes are not left in most suicides. One study revealed certain facts about persons who do and do not leave notes. Generally, there are no differences between the two groups in age, race, sex, employment, marital status, history of mental illness, place of suicide, reported causes or unusual circumstances preceding the act, medical care and supervision, or history of previous suicide attempts or threats. However, the note writers differed from the non-note writers in the methods used to kill themselves. The note writers used

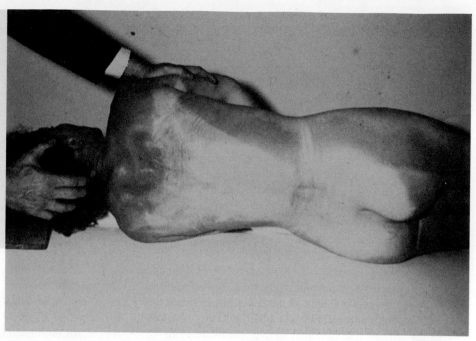

▶ **FIGURE 9-30**
Carbon monoxide death
This victim died accidentally from carbon monoxide poisoning resulting from an improperly ventilated space heater. Note the abnormally bright cherry-red color resulting from the reaction of the red blood cells to the gas and the pale area in the back region. This results because this area was resting against a firm surface and compressing the vessels in this area, which prevents the accumulation of blood.

poisons, firearms, and hanging more often as a means of death than did the non-note-writers.[43]

GENDER DIFFERENCES IN SUICIDAL BEHAVIOR

Studies of suicide in the United States indicate that the suicide rate is higher for men than for women, whereas the attempted suicide rate is higher for women than men. Some evidence suggests that there are differences between men and women in the methods employed to commit suicide: women prefer barbiturates and poisons; if women do use a firearm, the fatal wound is frequently in the body rather than the head. It has been suggested that these methods are used because they are not disfiguring and because women are often more concerned about their appearance after death than are men. It is not unheard of for a woman to leave a note to her female friends or relatives specifying in detail the clothing and jewelry she wants to wear in her open casket and at her funeral, along with details relating to facial cosmetics.[44]

In contrast, some males kill themselves where their bodies will not be discovered by family members, such as in the woods or some other isolated area. These types of suicides can create investigative problems, especially if a note is not written. For example, if a passerby should come upon the body and steal the gun used in a suicide as well as valuables from the suicide victim, the police may initially believe the death was a murder and robbery rather than suicide.

FIRE DEATHS

Frequently, human remains are found at the scene of a fire. Properly examined, these remains may provide important data to the investigator about the facts surrounding the

fire and the cause of death. Investigators should ask these questions:

- Was the decedent accidentally killed by the fire (whether or not the fire was caused by arson)?
- Was the decedent deliberately killed by the fire?
- Was the decedent already dead when the fire occurred?

To answer these questions, investigators should determine certain facts. These facts are outlined in the remainder of this section.[45]

COORDINATION AND COOPERATION

Coordination of, and cooperation between, police and fire investigators are of paramount importance in the successful investigation of any questioned fire. As with other forms of physical evidence at a fire scene, a body should never be moved until fully examined at the scene, unless there is some possibility that the person is still alive or there is danger of further destruction of the body if it remains where it is. Also, because a dead human being is probably the most complex and rapidly changing type of physical evidence at a crime scene, cooperation between medical personnel (preferably forensic pathologists) and investigators is essential. This coordination should extend from the scene of the fire to the medical facility where the postmortem examination is conducted.

DEGREES OF BURNING

Burns are medically classified into four types. The extent of burns may provide information about the proximity of the body to the point of origin of the fire, the length of time the body was exposed to the fire, and the intensity of the fire.

First-degree burns are superficial and limited to the outer layers of skin. Although the burned area is red and swollen,

◀**FIGURE 9-31**
Third-degree burns
This individual was driving a truck when it caught on fire. He leaped from the truck, but the burn injuries he had sustained would eventually prove fatal. The area of his face, hands, and abdomen are classified as third-degree burns. The cause of his death was listed as thermal injuries.

blisters do not form and peeling may follow. Second-degree burns involve blistering and the destruction of the upper layers of skin. They occasionally cause scarring in living victims. With third-degree burns, the entire thickness of the skin (epidermis and dermis) is destroyed. In living victims with third-degree burns, pain is initially usually absent as nerve endings are destroyed; scarring results, and skin grafting is usually necessary (Figure 9-31). Fourth-degree burns completely destroy (char) the skin and underlying tissue.

IDENTIFICATION OF REMAINS

Because fire destroys human tissue, identification of the remains may be especially difficult. Yet because identification of a decedent is a key factor in any questioned death investigation, an orderly, sequential approach must be used in the identification process. The six means that follow should be considered in sequence, from the "best" identification tools to the "worst":

- Fingerprints
- Dentition
- DNA printing
- Scars, marks, or tattoos on the exterior of the body
- Anatomical abnormalities or artificial appliances used to replace hips or knees inside the body
- Identification, jewelry, and clothing on the body

SCENE CONSIDERATIONS

As with any physical evidence, burned bodies must be sketched, measured, and photographed in place and in relation to other evidence at the scene of the fire. The actual location of the body may be crucial to the investigation. Determination as to whether the decedent was a smoker is important for establishing what caused the fire and whether he or she was alive at the time of the fire.

EXAMINATION OF THE EXTERNAL BODY

The body of the deceased should be examined in detail both at the scene and again at the morgue. Significant areas for examination include those discussed next.

SIGNS OF TRAUMA

Any sign of injury to the external body should be carefully noted, sketched, and photographed. The use of a five-power magnifying glass (as a minimum) is required, because fire obscures signs of injury.

Skull Fracture

Another factor that may be misconstrued is the discovery that the victim's skull is fractured. Care must be taken to determine whether the fracture is implosive or explosive. An implosive fracture may have been caused by a fall, may be evidence of a previous felonious assault or criminal homicide, or may result from a collapsed structural member. The exact cause will be determined at autopsy and evaluated during the follow-up investigation. An explosive fracture, however, is usually a natural consequence of fire. The extreme heat may cause the fluids in and around the brain to boil and expand. The resulting steam produces pressure sufficient to cause an explosive (pressure-release) reaction. The fracture(s) that result usually follow the natural suture lines of the skull. In extreme cases, the cranium may burst, causing the expelled brain and skull matter to form a circular pattern around the head. This is more common in children than in adults: the fontanel, or membrane-covered opening between the uncompleted parietal bones, is the weakest point in a fetal or young skull. The resulting circular pattern (0 to 12 inches from the skull) is significant when compared with the type of splattering that might result from a shotgun blast or high-order explosion.[46]

Blistering and Splitting Skin

The inexperienced investigator may be somewhat apprehensive in attempting to evaluate the effects of heat and flame on the skin of the victim. The medical investigator is in the best position to render a judgment in this area.

The formation of blisters (vesicles) is part of the body's natural defense system. The exact distinction between antemortem and postmortem blistering can be made only at autopsy. There are, however, certain signs that a medical investigator can use in developing a hypothesis. Postmortem blisters are generally limited in size and may contain only air or air mixed with a small amount of body fluid. Antemortem blisters are larger in size and contain a complex mix of body fluids. The precise determination of the fluids requires microscopic analysis. A blister surrounded by a pink or red ring can be considered to have occurred before death; the reddish ring is the result of an antemortem inflammatory reaction.

In some instances, temperatures may not have been sufficiently high to produce blistering. Likewise, if the skin is burned off or otherwise heavily damaged, blistering will not be evident.

The heat and flames of the fire also cause the skin to shrink or tighten and ultimately split. The splitting or lesions may be seen on the arms, legs, and torso. At first glance, one could misinterpret this condition, coupled with a pugilistic attitude, this could be misinterpreted as indicating defense wounds.

In some cases, a seriously burned person survives the fire and is removed to a burn center. In an effort to save the person, the medical staff at the center may attempt to duplicate the natural splitting of the skin with a surgical technique known as an escharotomy. This technique is used to help foster circulation and to prevent the onset of gangrene. Should the burn victim die some time after the fire, these splits should not be misinterpreted as fire induced.[47]

Noncranial Fractures

If enough heat is applied, bones shrink, warp, and fracture. Determining whether fractures were caused by a trauma or heat requires painstaking examination.

Pugilistic Attitude

The so-called pugilistic attitude of the body is a natural result of the dehydrating effect caused by the heat from the fire and is not related to the cause or manner of death. The arms and legs will be drawn into a posture resembling that of a boxer (Figure 9-32).

More often than not in fire deaths, a forensic pathologist who is an expert on burned bodies may have to be summoned.

EXAMINATION OF THE INTERNAL BODY

After the body has been closely examined, sketched, and photographed, an internal examination of it should be conducted by a forensic pathologist. Investigators should attend this procedure to get information about the facts, to correct discrepancies in data (such as measurements), and to recover evidence from the body. Significant areas for examination are as follows.

Soot, Other Debris, or Burning in the Air Passages

These findings may indicate that the decedent was breathing while the fire was burning.

Pulmonary Edema

A frothy substance in the lungs may result from irritants breathed in during a fire.

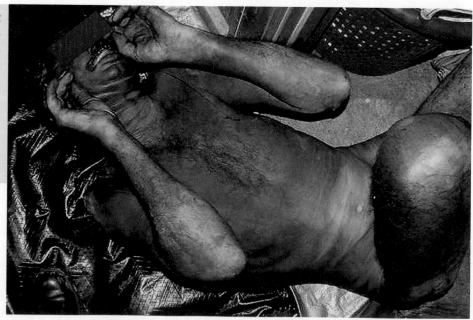

▶ **FIGURE 9-32**
Pugilistic attitude
The heat of a fire can result in the arms and legs of the body being drawn up into a posture resembling that of a boxer. That is precisely what happened to this individual, who died in an accidental house fire. The cause of his death was determined to be inhalation of smoke and soot.

Epidural Hemorrhages

Hemorrhages above the tough membrane covering the brain (the dura mater) and under the skull may occur at the rear of the head due to heat. These hemorrhages should not be mistaken for the hemorrhages associated with blunt-force injuries.[48]

Internal Injuries

All internal injuries should be closely examined, measured, and photographed, with samples taken by the pathologist for later microscopic examination.

Foreign Objects

Any foreign objects found in the body, such as bullets, should be recovered as evidence by the investigator. Because these objects are frequently small and difficult to locate, X-ray examination of the body before internal examination is recommended.

Toxicologic Examination

The pathologist should take samples for later examination by a toxicologist. Toxicologic results may be of extreme importance to the investigation.

Alcohol

Alcohol in blood indicates whether the decedent was incapacitated at the time of the fire and thus unable to escape. A finding of high levels of alcohol raises questions for the investigator about the decedent's habits.

Other Drugs

Indications of other possibly incapacitating drugs may provide new leads. The possibility of drug interactions—barbiturates with alcohol, for example—should also be considered.

Carboxyhemoglobin

Carbon monoxide (CO) is an odorless, colorless gas present at hazardous levels in all structural fires. Carbon monoxide asphyxiation (usually above 40% saturation) is probably the most common cause of death in fires. As previously discussed, CO causes the cherry-red color of postmortem lividity (as well as that of internal organs and muscle tissue).

Presence of Other Chemicals

Chemicals given off by burning materials may indicate the accelerant of the fire, as well as offer evidence that the decedent was breathing them in at the time of the fire.

MOTIVES IN FIRE DEATHS

In fire deaths, the following motives should be kept in mind by investigators:

- Destruction or mutilation of the body to conceal the identity of the decedent.
- Destruction or mutilation of the body to conceal the true cause or manner of death.
- Incineration of the body with criminal homicide intent.
- Incineration of the body to collect on an insurance policy. For example, a decedent may have committed suicide but have an insurance policy prohibiting collection after death by suicide. Beneficiaries may burn the body to indicate accidental death by fire.
- Suicide with an accelerant.
- An attempt by a suicide victim to hide the cause of death.
- A victim trapped in a building burned by an arsonist or by accident.

SPREE KILLINGS

The **spree killer** is an individual who embarks on a murderous rampage. His killing takes place within a given period of time, generally hours or days, with an interval, or time break, between the killings. The killer appears to be under pressure, poorly organized, and hunting for humans. The killer is in the grip of strong emotions and attacks people indiscriminately. Therefore, there is no similarity among his victims, who may be of different sexes, ages, or races. The crime may take place at different locations. Spree killing has some similarities to running amok, a Malay word that means "out of control" and often equates with suicide. The person who runs amok is usually a man, desperate and weary of his life. It can be opined that the Western spree killer is also basically a desperate suicidal person.[49]

Typical spree killers were Mark James Robert Essex, who in 1972 kept the city of New Orleans under siege, eventually killing eight people, and, more recently, Andrew Cunanan who, in 1997, killed the Italian fashion designer Gianni Versace in Florida after a killing spree across the United States that left four other people dead. Occasionally, it is difficult to differentiate the spree killer from the mass murderer.

Andrew Phillip Cunanan had led a flamboyant life style in San Diego, CA. He was soft-spoken, unassuming, and friendly. Openly homosexual, he craved attention, especially from older, wealthy gay men. At the time of his killings, he led authorities on a massive manhunt throughout the United States. His spree killing was preceded by a personality change, a depressed mood disorder, after he allegedly lost the financial support of his older friends. The rejection apparently caused him to snap. Indeed, in Minneapolis, MN he killed two former lovers, bashing in the head of one and shooting the other in the head. In his frantic destructive rampage, he killed an older real estate man in Chicago, IL, unknown to him, with pruning shears and a saw blade. Later, he shot a New Jersey cemetery worker and, after stealing the victim's car, drove to Miami, FL. In Miami, he shot and killed Versace at the gate of his home as he was returning from buying the morning newspaper. A few days later, Cunanan shot himself to death while hiding on a houseboat in Miami.

The above case portrays well the killing spree of a young person who was unable to contain his anger and his feelings of rejection, lashing out at the world with destructive force, careless of the consequences.

MASS MURDERS

Mass murder consists of the intentional killing of a group of people (four or more). Except for the family annihilators, it frequently occurs in a public place, such as a restaurant, post office, school, or anywhere people are assembled together.[50] For example, one of the more recent mass murders occurred in a shooting in Sutherland Springs, Texas. The shooter was armed with a semi-automatic rifle and had in his possession several additional fully-loaded magazines. He entered the church and killed 26 people and in the process wounded 20 additional parishioners whose ages ranged from 18 months to 72 years old. It was eventually determined the shooter was motivated by anger towards his mother-in-law who he thought would be in the church. She was not. A neighbor in close proximity to the church heard the gunshots, responded to the scene with his own rifle and shot the shooter twice, wounding him. The shooter then got into his vehicle, an SUV, and fled. The civilian with the rifle flagged down a man in a pick-up truck and they started pursuing the shooter. After driving a short distance the shooter pulled his vehicle off the road and shot himself in the head.

Contrary to random killings, drive-by shootings, and serial murders in which the victims, although numerous, are killed one at a time usually by a single individual, mass murder involves the killing of several innocent people at an unknown, unexpected moment and at or about the same time. "Mass murders occur more often in cities, as do, for that matter, homicides in general," asserted Levin and Fox, adding that "some massacres . . . apparently occur when the killer breaks under the strain of urban life." This type of crime attracts public attention because of its suddenness and the usually large number of victims. Because mass homicides evoke a great deal of publicity, it can be argued that the perpetrator of such crimes suffers from a celebrity mania.

Mass killers can be divided into three major types, family annihilators, pseudocommandos, and hit-and-run killers. Motivations vary between altruistic feelings, anger, revenge, and "pay back" time. Mass murderers often experienced impaired childhood attachments and traumatic experiences during their development. They harbor distorted thoughts and fantasies, become isolated, preoccupied, and disregard socially accepted constraints on behavior.

However, on rare occasions the motivation is not clear. An example of this was the recent mass shooting in Las Vegas, Nevada at a music concert. The shooter was firing randomly into a crowd of thousands from his position in a room on the 32nd floor of a nearby high rise hotel. This shooting was done with a semi-automatic assault weapon which had been by modified to be fully automatic by the use of a "Bump Stock." He shot and killed 59 people and wounded 124 others.

With an average age range that varies from 15 to 60, almost all mass murderers are males with a racial composition that closely approximates that of the general population. They are impulsive in their killing and unconcerned about being captured or killed during their offense. The killer is not concerned with leaving evidence that may lead to his arrest. Occasionally, the mass murderer has periods of obsessive rumination about an undefined destructive act. That gives the impression that the crime is somewhat premeditated. However, although the idea of wanting to kill people, massacre them, may be ruminative in character, the place where the act will take place is not usually preestablished. Frequently, the killer possesses an arsenal of guns—handguns, rifles, and/or semiautomatic weapons. The killer has at times displayed moody, antagonistic, rebellious, frustrated, and violent behavior and has occasionally been under the care of mental health personnel.

Notes, when found, and statements, when given, bespeak deep frustration with perceived wrongs by employers, authority figures, and/or the social system at large. The offense is usually locally limited and non-repetitive. Alcohol use or the use of illicit drugs may be present in the life history of the mass murderer. Because of his sudden acting-out, people at large think of him as having committed a "crazy" act or at least to have been an individual with a shaky inner self, unable to withstand stress and prone to explosive behavior. The mass murder often ends in suicide, but the dynamics in these cases are not like those in the ordinary murder-suicide or in the extended suicide or of misguided altruism as, for example, when parents kill their children to "protect" them from real or imagined dangers.

In the recent past, younger white males, aged 11–17, achieved sudden notoriety as mass killers in and around school in the United States. The two groups, adults and adolescents, differ not only in age but in the apparent motivational dynamics of their crimes and in the finale of their actions. The adults frequently commit suicide at the site of the mass homicide or are killed or taken into custody by the law enforcement officials. Few of the younger age group has so far been reported to have committed suicide at the site of the crime. Thus far, no study, however, has attempted to analyze any difference in the propensity of adult and juvenile mass murderers to commit suicide after the act.

The young killers, like their adult counterparts, seem to be unable to contain their destructive hostility. Their actions appear to be fueled by fantasies and, as in the adults, their emotions are not well rationalized. Often, the juveniles are reported to be shy, submissive, or aloof, with unconventional behavior, and to have resented parental and authority figures. They are not only angry but in need of self-assertion. Their actions are regarded as unconscionable and are certainly inconsistent and incongruous with their status as young adolescents. Their killing seems to have had strong ludic characteristics. Although the characteristics of both adult and juvenile offenders may show similarities in the homicidal act itself, the juveniles are obviously emotionally immature, although at times apparently bright and cognitively intact. They are reported to have been obsessed with the violent pop culture, music, films, and video games. They gave ample warning signs at home and at school not only with their behavior but through their writings, poems, and, in the case of at least one juvenile killer, a simple last will.

Personality-wise, both adolescent and adult killers range from immature to inadequate (as are many adolescents) with a plethora of neurotic feelings to a frank paranoid personality (usually in the adults, mixed with depressive states). Some may suffer from a borderline type of personality, with sudden shifts in mood or panic states and a strong and long-standing antisocial pattern of behavior. Generally, the acting-out is "the culmination of a continuum of experiences, perceptions, beliefs, frustrations, disappointments, hostile fantasies and (perhaps) pathology." The above may have been present for some time prior to the offense. There is certainly planning in the politically motivated pseudocommando type of mass murder, and planning is also present in some family altruistic mass murder.

Sensationalism is common to the pseudocommando type of mass killers and to some family annihilators. However, this destructive sensationalism reaches its worst in the mass murder typical of terrorism. Suicide bombings and the September 11, 2001 terrorist attack on the World Trade Center Complex in New York City testify to the sadistic intentions of the perpetrators of this modern form of programmed political mass murder.

In summary, despair, revenge, and notoriety seem to be common to all mass murders. The idea of "pay back" time occurs in many cases. These killers, through the vicissitudes of life, often came to perceive society and/or some of its members as responsible for their personal suffering. However, their life history points out their personal psychopathology. They are reported as people who harbored intense destructive hostility which, at a certain moment, they were no longer able to contain.

SERIAL MURDER

In the past thirty years, multiple definitions of **serial murder** have been used by law enforcement, clinicians, academicians, and researchers. Previous definitions of serial murder specified a certain number of murders, varying from two to ten victims.[51]

This quantitative requirement distinguished a serial murder from other categories of murder (i.e., single, double, or triple murder).

Most of the definitions also required a period of time between the murders. This break-in-time was necessary to distinguish between a mass murder and a serial murder. Serial murder required a temporal separation between the different murders, which was described as: separate occasions, cooling-off period, and emotional cooling-off period.

DEFINING SERIAL MURDER

There has been at least one attempt to formalize a definition of serial murder through legislation. In 1998 a federal law was passed by the United States Congress, titled: Protection for Children from Sexual Predator Act of 1998. This law includes the following definition of serial killings.

The term "serial killings" means a series of three or more killings, not less than one of which was committed within the United States, having common characteristics such as to suggest the reasonable possibility that the crimes were committed by the same actor or actors.

Although the federal law provides a definition of a serial murder, it is limited in its application. The purpose of this definition was to set forth criteria establishing when the FBI could assist local law enforcement agencies with their investigation of serial murder cases. It is not intended to be a generic definition for serial murder.

Serial murder is a relatively rare event, estimated to constitute less than one percent of all murders committed in any given year. However, there is a macabre interest in the topic that far exceeds its scope and has generated countless articles, books, and movies. This broad-based public fascination began in the late 1880s, after a series of unsolved prostitute murders occurred in the Whitechapel area of London. These murders were committed by an unknown individual who named himself "Jack the Ripper" and sent letters to the police claiming to be the killer.

These murders and the *nom de guerre* "Jack the Ripper" have become synonymous with serial murder. This case spawned many legends concerning serial murder and the killers who commit it. In the 1970s and 1980s, serial murder cases such as the Green River Killer, Theodore Robert (Ted) Bundy (Figure 9-33), and BTK sparked a renewed public interest in serial murder, which blossomed in the 1990s after the release of films such as *Silence of the Lambs.*

MYTHS AND MISCONCEPTIONS ABOUT SERIAL KILLERS

The relative rarity of serial murder combined with inaccurate, anecdotal information and fictional portrayals of serial killers has resulted in the following common myths and misconceptions regarding serial murder:

Serial Killers Are All Dysfunctional Loners

The majority of serial killers are not reclusive, nor social misfits who live alone. They are not monsters and may not appear strange. Many serial killers hide in plain sight within their communities. Serial murderers often have families and homes, are gainfully employed, and appear to be normal members of the community. Because many serial murderers can blend in so effortlessly, they are often times overlooked by law enforcement and the public as indicated in the following cases.

- *Robert Yates* killed 17 prostitutes in the Spokane, Washington area, during the 1990s. He was married with five children, lived in a middle-class neighborhood, and was a decorated U.S. Army National Guard helicopter pilot. During the time period of the murders, Yates routinely patronized prostitutes, and several of

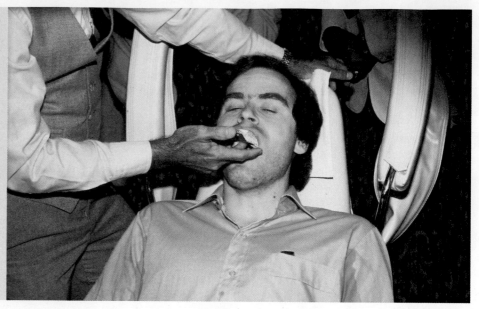

▶ FIGURE 9-33
**Serial killer Theodore Robert
(Ted) Bundy**
This photo depicts a forensic dentist
obtaining dental impressions from serial
killer Theodore Robert (Ted) Bundy in
conjunction with the murder of two
Florida State University female
students. Bundy's dental impressions
were compared with bite marks left on
the body of one of the victims. The
marks were positively identified as his.
Bundy, who was suspected of killing as
many as 100 women, was subsequently
executed in the state of Florida.
©Leon County Sheriff's Office, Tallahassee,
Florida, Courtesy of W. Ken Katsaris

his victims knew each other. Yates buried one of the
victims in his yard, beneath his bedroom window. Yates
was eventually arrested and pled guilty to thirteen of
the murders.

- *The Green River Killer, Gary Ridgeway*, confessed to killing
48 women over a twenty year time period in the Seattle,
Washington area. He had been married three times and
was still married at the time of his arrest. He had been
employed as a truck painter for thirty-two years. He
attended church regularly, read the Bible at home and at
work, and talked about religion with co-workers. Ridgeway
also frequently picked up prostitutes and had sex with
them throughout the time period in which he was killing.

- *The BTK* (Bind, Torture, and Kill) *killer, Dennis Rader*,
killed ten victims in and around Wichita, Kansas. He
sent sixteen written communications to the news media
over a thirty-year period, taunting the police and the
public. He was married with two children, was a Boy
Scout leader, served honorably in the U.S. Air Force,
was employed as a local government official, and was
president of his church.

Serial Killers Are All White Males

Contrary to popular belief, serial killers span all racial groups.
There are white, African-American, Hispanic, and Asian serial
killers. The racial diversification of serial killers generally mirrors that of the overall U.S. population. For example:

- *Charles Ng*, a native of Hong Kong, China, killed numerous victims in Northern California, in concert with
Robert Lake.

- *Derrick Todd Lee*, an African-American, killed at least six
women in Baton Rouge, Louisiana.

- *Coral Eugene Watts*, an African-American, killed five victims in Michigan, fled the state to avoid detection, and
murdered another twelve victims in Texas, before being
apprehended.

- *Rafael Resendez-Ramirez*, a native of Mexico, murdered
nine people in Kentucky, Texas, and Illinois, before
turning himself in.

- *Rory Conde*, a Columbian native, was responsible for
killing six prostitutes in the Miami, Florida area.

Serial Killers Are Only Motivated by Sex

All serial murders are not sexually motivated. There are many
other motivations for serial murders including anger, thrill,
financial gain, and attention seeking. For example:

- In the Washington, D.C. area serial sniper case, *John
Allen Muhammad*, a former U.S. Army Staff Sergeant,
and *Lee Boyd Malvo* killed primarily for anger and
thrill motivations. They were able to terrorize the
greater Washington, D.C. metro area for three weeks,
shooting thirteen victims, killing ten of them. They
communicated with the police by leaving notes, and
they attempted to extort money to stop the shootings.
They are suspected in a number of other shootings in
seven other states.

- *Dr. Michael Swango*, a former U.S. Marine, ambulance
worker, and physician, was a health care employee.
Although he was convicted of only four murders in
New York and Ohio, he is suspected of having poisoned and killed 35 to 50 people throughout the
United States and on the continent of Africa. Swango's motivation for the killings was intrinsic and never
fully identified. Increasingly, Swango kept a scrapbook
filled with newspaper and magazine clippings
about natural disasters, in which many people were
killed.

- *Paul Reid* killed at least seven people during fast food
restaurant robberies in Tennessee. After gaining control
of the victims, he either stabbed or shot them. The
motivation for the murders was primarily witness elimination. Reid's purpose in committing the robberies was

financial gain, and some of the ill-gotten gains were used to purchase a car.

All Serial Murderers Travel and Operate Interstate

Most serial killers have very defined geographic areas of operation. They conduct their killings with comfort zones that are often defined by an anchor point (e.g., place of residence, employment, or residence of a relative). Serial murderers will, at times, expand their activities outside their comfort zone, when their confidence has grown through experience or to avoid detection. Very few serial murderers travel interstate to kill.

The few serial killers who do travel interstate to kill fall into a few categories including:

- Itinerant individuals who move from place to place.
- Homeless individuals who are transients.
- Individuals whose employment lends itself to interstate or transnational travel, such as long distance truck drivers or those in military service.

The difference between these types of offenders and other serial murderers is the nature of their traveling lifestyle, which provides them with *many* zones of comfort in which to operate.

Serial Killers Cannot Stop Killing

It has been widely believed that once serial killers start killing, they cannot stop. There are, however, some serial killers who stop murdering before being caught. In these instances, there are events or circumstances in the offenders' lives that inhibit them from pursuing more victims. These include increased participation in family activities, sexual substitution, and other diversions. For example:

- *BTK killer, Dennis Rader,* murdered ten victims from 1974 to 1991. He did not kill any other victims prior to being captured in 2005. During interviews conducted by law enforcement, Rader admitted to engaging in auto-erotic activities as a substitute for his killings.
- *Jeffrey Gorton* killed his first victim in 1986 and his next victim in 1991. He did not kill another victim and was captured in 2002. Gorton engaged in cross-dressing and masturbatory activities, as well as consensual sex with his wife in the interim.

All Serial Killers Are Insane or Are Evil Geniuses

Another myth that exists is that serial killers have either a debilitating mental condition, or they are extremely clever and intelligent.

As a group, serial killers suffer from a variety of personality disorders, including psychopathy, anti-social personality, and others. Most, however, are not adjudicated as insane under the law.

The media has created a number of fictional serial killer "geniuses" who outsmart law enforcement at every turn. Like other populations, however, serial killers range in intelligence from borderline to above average levels.

Serial Killers Want to Be Caught

Offenders committing a crime for the first time are inexperienced. They gain experience and confidence with each new offense, eventually succeeding with few mistakes or problems.

While most serial killers plan their offenses more thoroughly than other criminals do, the learning curve is still very steep. They must select, target, approach, control and dispose of their victims. The logistics involved in committing a murder and disposing of the body can become very complex, especially when there are multiple sites involved.

As serial killers continue to offend without being captured, they can become empowered, feeling they will never be identified. As they continue to commit murders, the killers may begin to take shortcuts when committing their crimes. This often causes the killers to take more chances, leading to identification by law enforcement. It is not that serial killers *want* to get caught; they feel they *can't* get caught.

CAUSALITY AND THE SERIAL MURDERER

Following the arrest of a serial killer, the question is always asked: How did this person become a serial killer?[52] The answer lies in the development of the individual from birth to adulthood. Specifically, the behavior a person displays is influenced by life experiences, as well as certain biological factors. Serial murderers, like all human beings, are the product of their heredity, their upbringing, and the choices they make through development.

Causality can be defined as a complex process based on biological, social, and environmental factors. In addition to these factors, individuals have the ability to *choose* to engage in certain behaviors. The collective outcome of all of these influences separates individual behavior from generic human behavior. Since it is not possible to identify all the factors that influence normal human behavior, it is not possible to identify all the factors that influence an individual to become a serial murderer.

Human beings are in a constant state of development from the moment of conception until death. Behavior is affected by stimulation received and processed by the central nervous system. Neurobiologists believe that our nervous systems are environmentally sensitive, thereby allowing individual nervous systems to be shaped throughout a lifetime.

The development of social coping mechanisms begin early in life and continues to progress as children learn to interact, negotiate, and compromise with their peers. In some individuals, the failure to develop adequate coping mechanisms results in violent behavior.

Neglect and abuse in childhood have been shown to contribute to an increased risk of future violence. Substance abuse can and does lead to increased aggression and violence. There are documented cases of people who suffered severe head injuries and ultimately became violent, even when there was no prior history of violence.

It is generally agreed that *there is no single identifiable cause or factor that leads to the development of a serial killer. Rather, there are a multitude of factors that contribute to such development. The most significant factor is the serial killer's personal decision in choosing to pursue his/her crimes.*

However, the following observations have been made by social scientists who study this particular type of criminal:

- Predisposition to serial killing, much like other violent offenses, is biological, social, and psychological in nature and is not limited to any specific characteristic or trait.
- The development of a serial killer involves a combination of these factors, which co-exist in a rare confluence in certain individuals. They have the appropriate biological predisposition, molded by their psychological makeup, which is present at a critical time in their social development.
- There are no specific combinations of traits or characteristics shown to differentiate serial killers from other violent offenders.
- There is no genetic template for a serial killer.
- Serial killers are driven by their own unique motives or reasons.
- Serial killers are not limited to any specific demographic group, such as sex, age, race, or religion.
- For the majority of serial killers who are sexually motivated by erotized violence during their development, violence and sexual gratification are inexplicably intertwined in their psyche.
- More research is needed to identify specific pathways of development that produce serial killers.

SERIAL MURDER AND THE NCAVC

If a serial murderer confines his or her activities to a single community or a small region, local police are in a good position to see emerging patterns. But because many serial murderers cover many miles in a short period of time, the FBI has developed the **National Center for the Analysis of Violent Crime (NCAVC).** It is designed to form a partnership among federal, state, and local law enforcement agencies in the investigation of potentially related, unsolved violent crimes. NCAVC combines law enforcement techniques, behavioral science principles, and data processing to help any law enforcement agency confronted with unusual, bizarre, particularly vicious, or repetitive crimes.

Following are the types of offenses and incidents reported to NCAVC for analysis:

- Sexually oriented murder or assault by mutilation or torture, dismemberment, violent sexual trauma, or asphyxiation.
- Spree murder (a series of indiscriminate murders or assaults, all committed within hours or days—e.g., a series of sniper murders).
- Mass murder (four or more murders in a single incident).
- Robbery murder and nonfatal robbery with extreme violence.
- Murder committed during the commission of another felony.

- Kidnapping: fatal, with injury, or for ransom.
- Murder of a hostage.
- Murder for hire, contract murder, syndicate execution.
- Murder of a law enforcement officer.
- Political or other assassination.
- Terrorist or nationalistic murder.
- Drug-related murder.
- Gang murder.
- Missing person with evidence of foul play.
- Unidentified dead body when the manner of death is classified as a homicide.[53]

NCAVC can analyze every unsolved murder in the United States, identify the existence of serial patterns, and link cases together. It then notifies the individual local agencies that have similar murders, and they in turn may establish investigative contact among themselves. NCAVC emphasizes that the primary responsibility for investigating cases lies with the state and local authorities.

NCAVC also conducts research on violent crimes and trains local officers in analytic techniques. It is located at the FBI Academy in Quantico, Virginia, where it is administered by the Behavioral Science Unit. The FBI Academy was chosen as the site because it is a national law enforcement training center with vast resources for research and many capabilities for providing investigative support.

VICAP CRIME REPORT

When a violent crime remains unsolved for a period of time, the local law enforcement agency provides details about it on a special **Violent Criminal Apprehension Program (ViCAP)** reporting form.[54] This form is submitted to the nearest FBI field office, which reviews it and forwards it to NCAVC. Following are examples of several murder cases solved with the assistance of ViCAP.

In 2001, a ViCAP crime analyst reviewed a state police publication that mentioned a bag of human bones found by hunters in a seaboard forest of an eastern state. The victim was a white male, about 40 to 60 years old, and between 5 feet, 7 inches and 5 feet, 9 inches in height. His cause of death was blunt-force trauma to the head. Recovered with the remains was a 14-carat gold ring with engraved letters. Authorities had no leads for identification of the remains.

The ViCAP crime analyst searched the database using the physical description of the victim and made an additional search, thinking that the letters engraved in the ring might be the initials of a name. A possible match was made with a July 1998 case in which three people were reported missing from a mid-western state. The report was made by a fourth member of the family, a son who waited a week before reporting his mother, father, and sibling as missing persons. Law enforcement personnel had exhausted all investigative leads.

Authorities in the eastern and mid-western states contacted each other. In January 2001, ViCAP learned that forensic odontology had identified the bones in the bag as those of the father missing from the mid-western state. The letters in the recovered ring represented the maiden name of the missing mother and the name of the missing father.

ViCAP learned that a suspect who was identified and charged with the murder turned out to be the older son who made the report in the Midwest. The remains of his mother and sibling have not been located.[55]

In 1999 a series of homicides occurred in Texas. Early in the series, the cases were presented as murders in the victims' homes. Female victims were sexually assaulted, blunt force trauma was the cause of death,[56] and items of value were stolen from the homes.[57] The murder scenes were close to railroad tracks, sometimes only a few feet away.

In May 1999, personnel from the command post in Texas called ViCAP with information about three of the murders. One of the ViCAP crime analysts remembered a case from Kentucky in which railroad tracks were prominently mentioned. The analyst searched the database and quickly found the case in Kentucky: a male was killed along a pair of railroad tracks. The cause of death was blunt force trauma.[58] His male companion was sexually assaulted and left for dead. ViCAP relayed information concerning the Kentucky rape/homicide to the command post in Texas. Subsequent DNA examinations linked the Texas cases with the Kentucky case.

An itinerant freight train rider was identified as the suspect in the series of cases.[59] He was apprehended by authorities on July 13, 1999, when he surrendered at the border in El Paso, Texas. Charged with nine murders; two in Illinois, one in Kentucky, and six in Texas,[60] the subject was tried, convicted, and sentenced to death. In July 2000, he confessed to the 1997 murders of two teenagers on a railroad track near Oxford, Florida.[61] The male victim's body was found on March 23, 1997; the female victim's body was not found until July 2000, when authorities, following the killer's directions, found her skeletal remains wrapped in a blanket and jacket.[62]

While confessing to the two murders in Florida, the subject said he once killed a woman in a southeastern state, somewhere along railroad tracks. She was an old woman, hanging her wash on the line, and he killed her inside her house. He did not provide more details.

LONG DISTANCE DRIVERS ON INTERSTATE HIGHWAYS

As suggested earlier, the category of long distance truck drivers who travel the interstate highways has received some attention recently from ViCAP. For example, several years ago the senior criminal analyst with the Oklahoma Bureau of Investigation (OBI) was working on a string of slayings along I-40 in which truck-stop prostitutes had been killed and left at roadside locations. The OBI analyst's inquiry was given to an analyst with the FBI's Violent Criminal Apprehension Program, which maintains the agency's crime database. The analyst found that the database contained more than 250 cases of roadside female crime victims, many of them bearing enough similarities to suggest patterns in the violence. Subsequent searches and Internet research bumped the number to 350. As a result, bureau officials created a separate computer database to track such crimes and assigned an analyst to work full time on the serial killer program.

Later that year, Turner's suspected killer was identified as John Robert Williams, a 28-year-old trucker.

Williams and his girlfriend had kidnapped a woman from a casino in Mississippi, killed her, and dumped her body along a rural county road, authorities said. Concerned that they'd been seen leaving the casino with the victim, William's girlfriend panicked and called police, telling them that she and Williams had found the body. Their story quickly unraveled, and the pair were arrested for murder.

During subsequent interrogations, police said Williams confessed to more than a dozen slayings—including many of the cases Turner had been investigating. He had detailed knowledge of how the crimes had been committed, such as whether the women were killed by manual strangulation or with the use of a ligature, according to authorities. He explained how some had been sexually assaulted, in some cases after they were dead, they said.

Williams knew, for example, that one victim, Buffie Rae Brawley, had the word "Ebony" tattooed on her right thigh, investigators said. And he knew that the truck-stop prostitute had deep lacerations on her head, which he said she suffered when he struck her with a "tire thumper," a trucker's tool used to bounce off truck tires to gauge their pressure.

Police said Williams told them that Brawley solicited him for sex at a truck stop in Indianapolis.

"The second she tapped on my window, she was a dead woman," one investigator quoted the trucker as saying.[63]

KEY TERMS

algor mortis
autopsy
cadaveric spasm
contact bullet wound
defense wounds
excusable homicides
felonious assault
felonious homicides
forensic entomologist
forensic pathology
incised wound

justifiable homicide
lacerations
ligature strangulation
livor mortis
manslaughter
manual strangulation
mass murder
medico-legal examination
murder
National Center for the Analysis
    of Violent Crime (NCAVC)

nonfelonious homicide
ocular changes
puncture wound
rigor mortis
serial murder
spree killer
toxicologist
Violent Criminal Apprehension
    Program (ViCAP)

REVIEW QUESTIONS

1. What are the various categories of felony assaults and homicides?
2. What are the purposes of an autopsy?
3. What is algor mortis, and how does it help to determine the time of death?
4. Livor mortis is important for three reasons. What are they?
5. What is cadaveric spasm?
6. Briefly describe the typical entrance and exit gunshot wound.
7. Describe an incised wound, stab wound, and laceration.
8. What are defense wounds, and where are they most commonly found?
9. How is death produced by manual strangulation?
10. What are the most common reasons for committing suicide?

11. Which misconceptions are associated with suicidal hangings?
12. Why are poisons rarely used in homicides?
13. Discuss the differences in the suicidal behavior of men and women.
14. In regard to human remains at the site of a fire, what three broad questions should investigators keep in mind?
15. What are the common motives in fire deaths?
16. What does the profile look like for a spree killer?
17. What does the profile look like for mass murderers?
18. What are the myths and misconceptions about serial killers?
19. What role does the National Center for the Analysis of Violent Crime play in assisting local law enforcement officers in apprehending serial killers?

INTERNET ACTIVITIES

1. A special forensic entomology website at *www .forensicentomology.com* has been created to assist in the education of crime scene technicians, homicide investigators, coroners, medical examiners, and others involved in the death-investigation process. This site assists in answering these questions: What do the insects of forensic importance look like? What are the proper methods of their collection? How can communications between the police and the forensic entomologist be enhanced?

2. As the twentieth century progressed, so did technology and the scientific sophistication of toxicology. Thus, the use of poison as a weapon also needed to evolve in order to remain covert and evade detection. The website *www. porfolio.mvm.ed.ac.uk/studentwebs/session2/group12/20th.htm* helps address these questions: What historical changes have occurred in the use of poisons to commit homicide? Which older types of poison are still popular? What new types are being used? How have advances in technology helped make poison more detectable in the body?

◀ At just 10 years old, Tanya Kach was abducted by her school's security guard and kept as a sex slave for over 10 years in this room in McKeesport, Pennsylvania. Her abductor, Thomas Hose was convicted and sentenced to 15 years in prison.

(©Laurentiu Garofeanu/Barcroft USA/Barcoft Media/Getty Images)

10

SEX-RELATED OFFENSES

CHAPTER OBJECTIVES

1. Discuss interview procedures and investigative questions for sexual-assault cases.

2. Discuss victim-centered and trauma-informed sexual assault response.

3. Explain how investigators can be sensitive to the needs of transgender assault victims.

4. List some of the unique elements of interviewing a deaf victim of sexual assault.

5. Identify the signs and symptoms of sexual abuse of elders.

6. Explain why women do not report rape/sexual battery to the police.

7. Outline the types of physical evidence collected in rape and sexual-assault cases.

8. Discuss the importance of condom trace evidence.

9. Describe different types of electronic evidence that can be considered in sexual assault cases.

10. Identify the use and effects of Rohypnol and gamma hydroxybutyrate (GHB) in rape/sexual battery cases.

11. Assess investigative and evidence collection techniques for drug-facilitated sexual assaults.

12. Recognize the common characteristics of autoerotic death (sexual asphyxia) and how they occur.

13. Describe the reason for and elements of a psychological autopsy.

This chapter discusses how to best interview sexual-assault victims, which can be a most delicate and challenging task for the criminal investigator. The investigator must obtain all the necessary information, yet do so with respect and concern for the victim. It is absolutely imperative that the investigator does not in any way pass judgment on the victim, which would result in revictimization. In this chapter we focus primarily on sexual assaults that are typically directed toward postpubescent adult females and discuss the considerable amount of physical evidence that is often available when sex crimes are committed. We also discuss several other categories of victims that need special attention, such as transgender persons, deaf survivors of sexual assault, and the elderly. All categories of victims present some unique interview challenges to investigators. In addition, we will consider some elements of sexual motivations that may be considered by homicide investigators. This chapter concludes with a discussion of autoerotic death (sexual asphyxia) and the value of conducting psychological autopsies in such cases.

THE LAW

The term **sex-related offenses** covers a broad category of specific acts against adults, children, males, and females. **Rape** or **sexual battery** is legally defined as the crime of a person having sexual relations with another person under the following circumstances: (1) against a person's consent; (2) while the person is unconscious; (3) while the person is under the influence of alcohol or drugs; (4) if the person is feeble-minded or insane; (5) if the person is a child who is under the age of consent as fixed by statute.

SEX-RELATED INVESTIGATIONS

Statistics show the incidence of sexual violence in the United States is alarmingly prevalent: at some point in their lives, one in five women and one in 71 men will experience rape.[1] Rape is an issue that disproportionately affects women, but can certainly affect victims of any age, gender, or sexual identity. In general, society places a great stigma on victims of sexual assault: fear and shame prevent a great many victims—both male and female—from reporting their experience. While there is some conflict amid research reports, it is estimated that most sexual assaults (63%) are not reported to the police. This low number of reported crimes is supported by the most recent U.S. Department of Justice study that states that only 16% of all rape

cases are actually reported to the police.[2] As such, when a sexual assault is reported to law enforcement, investigators must treat victims with respect, compassion, and sensitivity. If a victim of sexual assault is treated well, they are much more likely to cooperate with the investigation, ensuring justice not only for the victim, but for the community at large.[3]

Despite the gender or sexual identity of the victim, when police and medical examiners are confronted with a dead body, they are obviously not able to interview the deceased victim to obtain an explanation for what has occurred. Investigators must rely on their initial impression of the scene, such as the state of the victim's clothing, positioning of the body, items found, and the presence or absence of injuries related to sexual activity (for example, bite marks, hickeys, direct genital or oral injury), in deciding whether sexual activity or attempted sexual activity was related to the cause of death. The investigator must be mindful, however, in weighing the significance of the presence of sexual evidence. Although the victim may have engaged in sexual activity with another person before death, the intercourse might not be related to the cause of death.

In the case of criminal homicide involving a female victim, investigators often question whether a rape has taken place. However, the possibility of rape must also be raised when the homicide victim is male; this is especially true when a male child is involved. Currently, the U.S. Department of Justice estimates that about one out of every ten rape victims over the age of 12 is male and that fully half of all underage sexual-abuse victims are male.[4] Sex is a major motivator and modifier of human behavior. Therefore, a determination of sexual activity may be of great value not only in a rape-murder case but also in natural, suicidal, and accidental deaths. Careful observation of the scene and the body may indicate a need for a rape investigation. Even if sexual intercourse does not seem to have any direct bearing on the cause of death, it may explain motives or the timing of death or simply provide a check on the veracity of a suspect or witness. The following cases illustrate these points:

A 53-year-old businessman was found dead in a motel room. There was no evidence of foul play. The bed was in slight disarray, with one of the pillows on the floor. The bed covers were bunched in an unusual position. The body on the floor was dressed in a shirt, loosened tie, trousers, underclothes, and socks. Shoes were neatly laid out next to a chair, and a jacket was on the back of a chair. Examination of the contents of the deceased's trouser pockets revealed the usual items, except for a pair of female panties. The autopsy revealed that the decedent had a massive heart attack; also, no vaginal cells were found on the penis. A logical reconstruction of the events preceding death suggested sexual foreplay with a female, in the course of which a wrestling match ensued during which the man took the woman's panties and then suffered a heart attack.

Although establishing the absence of sexual intercourse in this case did not significantly add to the medical solution of the problem, it did explain why the victim was found at a motel when he was supposedly having lunch.

A furnace repairman was found dead, slumped over the front seat of his van. There was no evidence of foul play, and the medical examiner was not called to the scene. Observation at the morgue revealed that there were peculiar parallel linear abrasions over the victim's knees, tearing of the overalls at the same region, and no underwear. His boots were reversed and loosely laced. Penile washings were positive for vaginal cells. Further investigation disclosed that he had visited a woman at 7 in the morning under the pretext of cleaning her furnace and had been stricken by a heart attack during intercourse. The woman hastily dressed him and dragged him across the back alley to his truck, not realizing that his underwear was neatly tucked under her bed.

A 15-year-old girl's body was found in a vacant lot. The absence of clothing on the lower body suggested sexual intercourse immediately before or at the time of death. Faint abrasions were present on the back of the neck, and marked hemorrhages were present in the eye. The medical examiner believed that this was a case of rape-murder. The autopsy confirmed recent sexual intercourse. The scratch on the back of the neck, however, proved to be superficial, and there were no deeper injuries. Reconstruction of the events immediately preceding death confirmed that the girl had had sexual intercourse with her boyfriend (who lived nearby), in the course of which (according to the boyfriend's testimony) the girl started making choking noises. She reported pain in her chest but said that it was going away. The boyfriend resumed intercourse. The girl started making even more violent noises. He assumed these to be related to her having an orgasm. After intercourse, he noticed the girl was motionless and unresponsive. After a few minutes, he decided she was dead and became very scared. He escaped from the scene and told investigators he had not seen his girlfriend on the night of her death.

VICTIM-CENTERED AND TRAUMA-INFORMED RESPONSE

There was a time in this country when sexual-assault victims were questioned extensively about their sexual histories or were not taken seriously due to societal bias against women; even today, sex workers and transgender women struggle to have their reports of sexual assault taken seriously. And though there is much work to be done to improve law enforcement response to sexual assault, there has been a shift over the past few decades to a victim-centered and trauma-informed response model. **Victim-centered response** is, simply, a law enforcement investigation that focuses on the actions and choices of the offender—not the actions or inactions of the victim. Secondarily, but importantly, a **trauma-informed response** seeks to reduce the physical and psychological trauma to the victim of sexual violence by responding in a compassionate, sensitive, and non-judgmental manner.[5]

Police officers should be trained to understand issues surrounding sexual assault and victim response to trauma. First and foremost, they should realize that there is no textbook response to trauma: victims can react to sexual violence in a variety of ways, exhibiting extreme distress on one end of the spectrum or laughing and joking with first responders on the other end. Secondly, police should recognize that trauma affects a victim's ability to give details or relay the chronology of the assault. Trauma survivors may remember information over a period of time, as details are triggered and as relationships are established with investigators. It is very important that police do not base a victim's credibility on their demeanor or ability to recall details about the assault.

And finally, police officers should remember that perpetrators of sexual violence often choose their victims based on what they see as a lack of credibility. For example, sex workers have historically been seen as non-credible victims of sexual assault. Conventional wisdom held that a person who performed sex acts for a living couldn't be sexually assaulted, creating opportunities for sexual predators to attack women that didn't report the violence because police didn't take them seriously. The result of this type of mistrust is evident in a number of terrible crimes in our nation's history: Texas Monthly crime writer Skip Hollandsworth details one such instance in Houston. Police responded to a report of a body to find a murdered sex worker in a field: the detectives in that case eventually uncovered three separate offenders—one a violent felon, one a serial rapist, the other a serial killer—all working separately to rape and or/murder prostitutes in the area. The key takeaway from the article for police officers is the following line, from a sex worker who was interviewed by a detective working the case:

> "Why you here askin' what's happenin' to us,
>   Miss *Poh-leece*?" one of them said.
> "We know you ain't gonna do shit."[6]

In this case, sexual predators chose prostitutes because they knew that their cases were rarely reported and rarely taken seriously. Other populations vulnerable to predators due to this perception of non-credibility include drug addicts, the alcohol-impaired, transgender individuals, undocumented immigrants, the homeless, and other special populations. Officers and investigators should learn to identify and address their own biases against such populations in order to effectively conduct a victim-centered investigation. By being sensitive to these considerations, law enforcement officials can avoid perpetuating a cycle of mistrust and can avoid intensifying emotional distress on the part of the victim.

Interview Procedures and Investigative Questions

Today, best practices for sexual-assault investigations make clear that there should be a preliminary victim interview as part of the initial law enforcement response and a subsequent in-depth interview in the investigative phase. The preliminary interview, also known as a **minimal fact interview**, is intended to be brief and non-intrusive, establishing basic facts of the assault and general elements of the crime. After the victim has recovered from the initial trauma and their memory has started to consolidate, an investigator should follow up for a more detailed interview.

Though the interview should be conducted in a private location, if the victim wishes to have a support person with them then that should be accommodated if appropriate and if that person is available. Close friends, family members, or advocates from the local rape crisis center may often lend physical or moral support to a reporting victim. If a translator is necessary, officers should make every effort to find someone who is *not* a friend or family member of the survivor, as this can inhibit responses or cause additional distress to the victim or his/her family.[7]

The minimal fact interview should not be used as a test for victim credibility; nor is it a time to ask a victim if she/he wishes to pursue prosecution of the offender. At this stage in their trauma, many victims are simply unable to consider all the factors involved and make such a decision. Officers should collect evidence in a thorough and professional manner that will aid a prosecution if and when it is pursued.

Minimal fact interviews should obviously collect contact information for both the victim and any persons or family members who can consistently and reliably contact the victim during the course of the investigation. Interviewers should ask open-ended questions such as "help me understand what you can remember about your experience," being careful not to interrupt, and avoiding questions like "how many times did he do that?" or "how long were you there?" that quantify the assault. The interviewer should attempt to find out information about the suspect's identity, such as physical description or distinctive features; locations of the assault; weapons used; injuries to both victim and suspect; and use of drugs and alcohol by the victim.[8] The location or existence of additional evidence should be determined, and the victim should be prompted to remember whether there are any text messages, voicemails, photographs, or social media posts related to the offense or suspect.

There is some question about whether the investigator interviewing the victim should be male or female. Some argue that a female victim feels more at ease in discussing the details of the assault with another woman. Others argue that an understanding male may help the victim to overcome a possibly aversive reaction to men, especially if the victim is relatively young or sexually inexperienced. The major criterion, regardless of whether the investigator is male or female, is that the person has the ability to elicit trust and confidence from the victim while possessing considerable investigative ability. Many police departments have moved toward male-female teams in rape investigation.[9]

In interviewing the victim, the investigator may find that the victim uses slang terms to describe the sex act or parts of the body. This is likely done because the victim does not know the proper terminology. At some point the investigator may find it necessary to use slang terms to interview the victim; however, in today's world, investigators must protect themselves from allegations of insensitivity or professional misconduct. Delicately employed proper terms can be used immediately after a victim's slang usage. This in no way demeans the victim's intellect; rather it conveys an image of professionalism to which most victims respond positively.

At the conclusion of the minimal fact interview, the officer should explain next steps to the victim, provide contact information for the appropriate investigator, and review steps to ensure the victim's immediate safety. Once it is appropriate to re-interview the victim, a trauma-informed approach should be used.

THE FOLLOW-UP INTERVIEW

Much like the minimal fact interview, the follow-up should be conducted using open-ended questions and avoiding interruption. The investigator should treat the victim professionally, with compassion, and give assurances that their case is important and will be investigated fully. The purpose of the interview should be explained, contact information should be fully updated, and the interviewer should acknowledge the victim's feelings and emotions. Once the free narrative is complete, the investigator can delve into details, clarifying and asking for additional information. This is not an interrogation, however; inconsistencies should be clarified with follow-up questions but not presented as a challenge. The follow-up should explore issues of consent, corroboration, and identity in detail. Additional inquiries into the following areas may also be explored.

TYPE AND SEQUENCE OF SEXUAL ACTS DURING AN ASSAULT

To determine the motivation behind a rape, the investigator must ascertain the type and sequence of sexual acts during the assault.[10] This task may be made difficult because of the victim's reluctance to discuss certain aspects of the crime out of fear, shame, or humiliation. Often, however, investigators can overcome a victim's reluctance with a professional and empathic approach. It has been found that although interviewers are likely to ask about vaginal, oral, and anal acts, they often do not ask about kissing, fondling, use of foreign objects, digital manipulation of the vagina or anus, fetishism, voyeurism, or exhibitionism by the offender.[11] In a sample of 115 adult, teenage, and child rape victims, researchers reported vaginal sex as the most

frequent act, but they also reported 18 other sexual acts. Repetition and sequence of acts are infrequently reported. Most reports state that the victim was "raped," "vaginally assaulted," or "raped repeatedly."

By analyzing the sequence of acts during the assault, the investigator may determine whether the offender was acting out a fantasy, experimenting, or committing the sexual acts to punish or degrade the victim. For example, if anal sex was followed by **fellatio** (oral sex—mouth to penis), the motivation to punish and degrade would be strongly suggested. In acting out a fantasy, the offender normally engages in kissing, fondling, or cunnilingus (oral sex—mouth to female genitals). If fellatio occurs, it generally precedes anal sex. If a rapist is experimenting sexually, he is moderately forceful and verbally profane and derogatory. Fellatio may precede or follow anal sex.[12]

Verbal Activity of Rapist

A rapist reveals a good deal about himself/herself and the motivation behind the assault through what the rapist says to the victim. For this reason, the investigator must elicit from the victim everything the rapist said and the tone and attitude in which the rapist said it.

A study of 115 rape victims revealed several themes in rapists' conversations, including "threats, orders, confidence lines, personal inquiries of the victim, personal revelations by the rapist, obscene names and racial epithets, inquiries about the victim's sexual 'enjoyment,' soft-sell departures, sexual put-downs, and taking property from another male who was with the victim at the time of the rape."[13]

Preciseness is important. For example, a rapist who states "I'm going to hurt you if you don't do what I say" has threatened the victim, whereas the rapist who says "Do what I say, and I won't hurt you" may be trying to reassure the victim in order to gain compliance without force. A rapist who states "I want to make love to you" has used a passive and affectionate phrase and may not want to harm the victim physically. But a statement such as "I'm going to fuck you" is much more aggressive, hostile, and angry. Compliments to the victim, politeness, expressions of concern, apologies, and discussions of the offender's personal life, whether fact or fiction, indicate low self-esteem in the offender. In contrast, derogatory, profane, threatening, or abusive language suggests anger and the use of sex to punish or degrade the victim.

When analyzing a rape victim's statement, the interviewer is advised to write down an adjective that accurately describes each of the offender's statements. For example, the interviewer might record "You're a beautiful person" (complimentary); "Shut up, bitch" (hostility); "Am I hurting you?" (concern). The interviewer then has better insight into the offender's motivation and personality.

Verbal Activity of the Victim

The rapist may make the victim say certain words or phrases that enhance the rape for him. By determining what, if anything, the victim was forced to say, the interviewer learns about the rapist's motivation and about what gratifies him. For example, a rapist who demands such phrases as "I love you," "Make love to me," or "You're better than my husband" suggests the need for affection or ego-building. One who demands that the victim plead or scream suggests sadism and a need for total domination. If the victim is forced to say things that are demeaning, the offender may be motivated by anger and hostility.

Sudden Change in Rapist's Attitude During Attack

The victim should be specifically asked whether any changes were observed in the attitude of the rapist during the time they were together. The victim should be asked whether the rapist became angry, contrite, physically abusive, or apologetic and whether this was a departure from his previous attitude. If the victim reports such a change, she should be asked to recall what immediately preceded the change. A sudden behavioral change may reflect weakness or fear. Factors that may cause such sudden behavioral changes include a rapist's sexual dysfunction, external disruptions (a phone ringing, noise, or a knock on the door), the victim's resistance or lack of fear, ridicule or scorn, or even completion of the rape. An attitudinal change may be signaled verbally, physically, or sexually. Because the rape can be stressful for the rapist, how he reacts to stress may become important in future interrogations, and knowing what caused the change can be a valuable psychological tool for the investigator.

In attempting to determine the experience of the rapist, the investigator should ask the victim what actions the offender took to protect his identity, to remove physical or trace evidence, or to facilitate his escape. It may be possible to conclude from the offender's actions whether he is a novice or an experienced offender who may have been arrested previously for rape or similar offenses. Most rapists take some action, such as wearing a mask or telling the victim not to look at them, to protect their identity. But some go to great lengths to protect themselves from future prosecution. As with any criminal act, the more rapes a person commits, the more proficient he becomes in eluding detection. If a person has previously been arrested because of a mistake and later repeats the crime, he/she is not likely to repeat the same costly mistake.

The offender's experience level can sometimes be determined from the protective actions he takes. Novice rapists are not familiar with modern medical or police technology and take minimal actions to protect their identity. Some wear a ski mask and gloves, change their voice, affect an accent, or blindfold and bind their victims. The experienced rapist's modus operandi can indicate a more than common knowledge of police and medical developments. The rapist may walk through the victim's residence or prepare an escape route before the sexual assault, disable the victim's telephone, order the victim to shower or douche, bring bindings or gags rather than using those available at the scene, wear surgical gloves during the assault, or take or force the victim to wash items the rapist touched or ejaculated on, such as bedding and the victim's clothing.

Theft During Rape

Almost without exception, police record the theft of items from rape victims. All too often, however, investigators fail to probe the matter unless it involves articles of value. But knowing about the items stolen may provide information about the criminal and aid in the investigative process. In some cases, the victim initially may not realize that something has been taken. For this reason, the victim should be asked to inventory items.

Missing items fall into one of three categories: evidentiary, valuables, and personal. The rapist who takes evidentiary items—those he has touched or ejaculated on—suggests previous rape experience or an arrest history. One who takes items of value may be unemployed or working at a job providing little income. The type of missing items may also provide a clue as to the age of the rapist. Younger rapists have been noted to steal such items as stereos or televisions; older rapists tend to take jewelry or items more easily concealed and transported. Personal items taken sometimes include photographs of the victim, lingerie, driver's licenses, and the like. These items have no intrinsic value but remind the rapist of the rape and the victim. A final factor to consider is whether the offender later returns the items to the victim, and if so, why. Some do so to maintain power over the victim by intimidation. Others want to convince the victim that they meant her no harm and want to convince themselves that they are not bad people.

Rapists often target their victims beforehand. A series of rapes involving victims who were either alone or in the company of small children—who would not be able to defend them or effectively intervene—is a strong indication that the offenders had engaged in peeping or surveillance. They may have entered the residence or communicated with the victims earlier. For this reason, the investigator should determine whether the victims or their neighbors, before the rape, experienced:

1. Calls, texts, or notes from unidentified persons;
2. Residential or automobile break-ins;
3. Prowlers or peeping toms incidents;
4. Feelings of being watched or followed.

Frequently, rapists who target their victims have prior arrests for breaking and entering, prowling, peeping, or theft of women's clothing.

Delayed Reporting

If the victim has delayed making a complaint, the investigator should establish the reason. It may be that the victim was frightened, confused, or apprehensive. However, delays of several weeks or months reduce the likelihood of apprehending the suspect and tend to weaken the state's case should a trial be held. Nevertheless, such a complaint must be investigated in the same way as all other similar complaints, until or unless it is substantiated or considered unfounded. When a case is determined to be unfounded, that generally means either the crime was not committed or the case lacked the necessary legal elements for the specific crime. In some cases, the prosecutor will decide not to seek prosecution because of a lack of medical evidence, intoxication of the victim, a previous relationship between the victim and the suspect, or because the victim is too embarrassed or too upset to cooperate.[14]

TRANSGENDER VICTIMS OF SEXUAL ASSAULT

A transgender person is one who experiences incongruence between the sex that they were assigned at birth and their internal gender identity, or who experiences binary gender as restrictive or inaccurate.[15] Culturally, it's widely accepted that gender is a binary concept: most people identify as either male or female. For transgendered persons, identifying as one or the other may be a struggle. Some don't feel they fit neatly into either category, while others have a clear preference that just doesn't match their anatomy. And while some transgender individuals choose to transition medically or legally into their gender identity, many do not.

The transgender community is subject to much stereotyping, bias, and to high rates of sexual abuse and assault. Half of all transgender individuals can expect to experience sexual abuse or assault in their lifetime, with some subpopulations experiencing even higher rates. Transgendered persons who are of color, are incarcerated, homeless, disabled, young, or who are sex workers can experience victimization rates at a much higher level.[16]

Complicating their experiences of victimization is the fact their sexual identity may have motivated the attack. It is not uncommon for transgendered people to be physically and/or sexually assaulted when potential sexual partners discover their biologically assigned gender, and investigators may have to determine if elements of a hate crime are present during their course of their investigation. See Chapter 21 on Terrorism, relating to hate crimes.

Transgender individuals must be dealt with using the same victim-centered and trauma-informed response as all other victims, which may be challenging for many police officers and investigators who are not familiar with the "trans" community or who may hold conscious or unconscious biases against that community. The Internet provides a number of informative resources about the transgender community for police agencies. Further the local Lesbian, Gay, Bisexual, and Transgender (LGBT) groups may offer training to help engage officers and increase their understanding of special challenges facing transgender victims of sexual offenses.

Addressing such biases and providing culturally competent and professional services to the transgender community is important because many transgender individuals report that they are afraid that law enforcement professionals will be ignorant of transgender issues and worse, that they will experience further harassment or hostility from police. It's estimated that only 9% of sexual assaults against transgender people are reported.[17]

When interviewing transgender victims of sexual assault, investigators should be careful to address the victim with their preferred name and using preferred pronouns. Continuing to refer to a transgender woman as "he" or insisting on calling them by a legal name that they no longer use creates an atmosphere of distrust and can serve to further traumatize the victim. If a victim's appearance and stated name are clearly feminine, the investigator should use the appropriate pronouns. If the investigator is confused, it is best to ask. Such questions may feel uncomfortable, but they acknowledge the victim's identity and establish that police intend to treat the victim respectfully. It is especially important when working with transgender victims that police focus only on the information they need to conduct a quality investigation: questions or comments about appearance or gender identity that are not related to the assault are inappropriate and further traumatizing.

Police should not interpret a transgender person's reticence to cooperate with police in sexual-assault investigations as defensiveness or as an indication of deception; frequently, transgender persons perceive that law enforcement will blame them, harass them, or wrongfully arrest them and will attempt to minimize their contact with police. As such, providing transgender victims with sensitive and respectful care can facilitate cooperation.

To maximize cooperation and minimize further trauma, investigators should document the assault using consistent and appropriate gender pronouns; allow the victim to describe the assault using words that are most comfortable to them; and ensure that if you talk to a victim's family, you are not disclosing information about their gender identity that they are uncomfortable with. Investigators should also be able to identify resources for the victim that are sensitive to their needs as a transgender victim, such as a rape crisis center or transgender support group.

QUICK FACTS

Police Sexual Violence (PSV)

Police sexual violence (PSV) is an egregious form of sexual misconduct that involves sexual harassment and violence, including rape and other sexual assault perpetrated by police officers. Unfortunately, it has emerged as a critical issue for law enforcement agencies. The PSV issue has surfaced within the context of recent high-profile cases that clearly demonstrate the problem. The city of San Diego (CA) for example recently (2015) paid $5.9 million to settle a civil lawsuit involving a former San Diego Police Department officer who groped a woman in a public restroom while on-duty. The officer was found guilty of 12 different sex-related charges perpetrated against five different women during a previous criminal trial. Other cases in Los Angeles (CA), Eugene (OR), Nassau County (NY), Houston (TX), Milwaukee (WN), Oklahoma City (OK), and Chicago (IL) have also raised the specter of PSV.

Police work affords ample opportunities to rogue police officers to perpetrate acts of sexual deviance and violence. Opportunities for sex-related misconduct derive from the context of the job. Police commonly patrol alone and largely free from any direct supervision. Police commonly encounter citizens who are vulnerable and compromised, usually because they are victims or criminal suspects. Police-citizen interactions often occur in the late-night hours that provide low public visibility and ample opportunities to those officers who are able and willing to take advantage of them to commit acts of sexual deviance and to perpetrate sex crimes. In almost all cases, police sexual violence is casually dismissed by responding officers who dismiss the allegations of compromised victims. It is not until the suspect officer has been implicated in multiple offenses or by a non-compromised victim that investigation unravels large numbers of victims and embarrassment to the agency.

A 2014 national-scale study identified 548 arrests of police officers across the United States for sex-related crimes from 2005–2007. The most serious offense charged in over 20% of these cases was forcible rape (n = 117). There were also 107 cases of forcible fondling, 59 cases involving statutory rape, 54 cases involving forcible sodomy, and 39 cases involving child pornography. Most compelling is that the study demonstrates that the most egregious forms of police sexual violence are not isolated events, but abound across the United States.

Source: Phillip Matthew Stinson, Sr., John C. Liederbach, Steven L. Brewer, and Brooke E Mathna, "Police Sexual Misconduct: A National-Scale Study of Arrested Officers," *Criminal Justice Policy Review*, April 2014. Published On-Line DOI 10.1177/0887403414526231.

DEAF VICTIMS OF SEXUAL ASSAULT

Sexual-assault victims who are deaf face unique issues not encountered by the hearing.[18] Thus investigators distinguish these people's experiences as sexual-assault victims from other sexual-assault victims. For example, when a deaf woman reports a sexual assault, she will often encounter stereotypes about being both a sexual-assault victim as well as being deaf. Also, like other rape victims she often has feelings of guilt and embarrassment because of the social stigma frequently attached to rape. These feelings can be compounded owing to the small

and generally close-knit nature of the deaf community, which can contribute to a hesitancy to report a sexual assault. In addition, the closeness of the deaf community can compromise a victim's anonymity and erode privacy. Many deaf victims of sexual assault perceive a lack of support within the deaf community, particularly if the perpetrator is also deaf. Consequently, deaf victims can experience a profound sense of isolation.[19]

Another impediment to deaf victims seeking help is the lack of awareness about deafness and deaf culture among hearing people. Many view deafness from a medical perspective, focusing on hearing deficits rather than viewing deaf people as members of a linguistic and cultural community. In fact, many deaf women do not view themselves as disabled but rather as having a culture and a way of communicating not recognized by the dominant hearing culture.

RELUCTANCE TO REACH OUT

Many deaf victims may be reluctant to reach out to agencies that serve sexual-assault victims because most of the providers are hearing and do not have systems for effectively communicating with deaf people. For example, deaf sexual-assault victims cannot count on service agencies having access to a TTY (teletypewriter), much less a staff member who knows how to operate it. Even if a social service or law enforcement agency has an interpreter, deaf victims, like hearing victims, may be reluctant to divulge intimate details to yet another stranger.

Some deaf victims of sexual assault also believe they cannot rely on interpreters to accurately represent their words and experiences. Service agencies that do not have qualified interpreters on site often use the victim's family or friends to assist in interviews, which can further inhibit a sexual-assault victim's candor.

IMPROVING POLICE RESPONSE

Deaf victims who were interviewed in a study conducted in Minneapolis, Minnesota, several years ago had varied opinions on how helpful police could be after a sexual assault. Although most said they regarded law enforcement as a resource, few had actually called the police after they were victimized. Many related frustrating experiences when dealing with the police department, including 911 call-takers who could not operate a TTY machine and police officers who mislabeled a deaf person as drunk or mentally ill or who misread body language as aggressive when a deaf person was simply moving closer to lip-read.

Service providers and deaf community members agreed that law enforcement must improve its methods for communicating with the deaf community, whether they are victims, witnesses, or suspects. They also suggested that police officers need training, interpreters, and more clearly defined agency policies. For example, in a research project involving the Minneapolis Police Department it was found that the department had policies for locating interpreters, but its officers knew very little about determining if a person was deaf or how to communicate with him or her in the field.

Despite these challenges, the Minneapolis Police Department is considered a model for other jurisdictions when it comes to serving the deaf community.

ELDER SEXUAL ABUSE

As an increasing percentage of our population grows older, we are beginning to see an increase in the number of **elder sexual abuse**. In some cases, sexual assaults are being inflicted by intruders who make unauthorized entry into nursing homes or assisted-living facilities, and in other cases these abuses are being inflicted by home providers, nursing-home staff, and in some cases nursing-home residents.[20]

SIGNS AND SYMPTOMS OF SEXUAL ABUSE

Emotional symptoms of anxiety and depression with accompanying feelings of fear and confusion are not uncommon complaints of the elderly. The cause of the distress may not be known, but the elder is treated for the symptoms. Unless a thorough inquiry is made, a sexual assault, either acute or chronic, may be missed.

Also, because there are often delays in the reporting of the abuse, elder victims of sexual assault are less likely to have a complete sexual-assault examination.

ASSISTED-LIVING FACILITIES

Assisted-living facilities generally provide different shifts of staff, check on residents over a 24-hour period, and meals and cleaning services are often provided. It is generally believed that an elder living in an assisted-living facility is in a protected environment and has safety features in place; however, this is not always the case. Unfortunately, sometimes access into the facility is not tightly controlled, thereby allowing sexual predators easy access to the patients. The following case illustrates this.

A 41-year-old man entered the unsecured door of an assisted-living facility and raped an 83-year-old woman in her room. The woman reported she was awakened to the man being in her room and that he stated, "Don't scream or I am going to kill you." She further stated that he held her down and assaulted her, taunting her and ordering her to use profanity. She refused. After the assault, the man ran into a facility employee and asked her to help him find a friend who he said worked at the facility. He then put his hand over her mouth and wrestled her to the ground, grabbing her checkbook. He escaped, and the employee called 911. The police arrived at 2:45 A.M. and found the perpetrator a few blocks away. When shown videos of himself at the facility, he admitted he entered the premises to sexually assault someone. The victim's son reported that his mother's personality changed after the attack. She moved out of the facility to be closer to him but became withdrawn and reclusive, which was exactly the opposite of her pre-assault personality characteristics.

NURSING HOMES

Three common nursing-home sexual-abuse victim profiles include these: (1) physically disabled older resident; (2) cognitively impaired resident; and (3) physically impaired younger resident. The physically disabled older resident has no cognitive or mental impairment but requires assistance with mobility. The assistance may be short term, such as needing rehabilitation following surgery, or long term, as for residents with complications from a stroke. The cognitively impaired resident has a primary diagnosis of Alzheimer's disease or other dementia, and the physically impaired younger resident may have a physical impairment owing to a chronic neuromuscular disorder, such as multiple sclerosis or amyotrophic lateral sclerosis (ALS, or Lou Gehrig's disease), or an impairment as a result of trauma from a motor vehicle accident or other severe head injury.

Nursing homes are, for the residents, precisely that—a home in which the staff functions as the residents' caregivers (in both a literal and figurative sense). The nursing home and its staff are perceived as "safe," and violations represent a more profound betrayal of trust than do violations committed outside the sanctity of the nursing home.

The sexual victimization of older adults in nursing homes is under-recognized and under-reported. Even when an incident is identified as earlier suggested, reporting is delayed and treatment and postrape services are often inadequate.[21] Furthermore, prosecution of these crimes is fraught with problems related to poor-quality evidence because of delays in reporting. Older adults residing in nursing homes often require assistance with basic activities of daily living such as bathing, dressing, and feeding because of physical and cognitive impairments. These disabilities make an individual dependent on others and as a result make the older person an easy target for a sexual predator.[22]

Resident-on-Resident Sexual Abuse

The issue of elder sexual activity is sometimes addressed in policy manuals of nursing homes with a section on the sexual rights of the elderly. Unfortunately, in some nursing homes, nursing home staff are said to ignore the pleas for help by resident females. The cases in this category generally involve elderly women who have tried to reject the sexual advances of elderly males who, in most cases, preyed on many elderly victims. In such cases, there is no history of a developing relationship but rather of a male being predatory.

EARLY RECOGNITION AND DETECTION

Early recognition and detection of abuse and reporting of cases means knowing the physical and behavioral indicators of sexual abuse in the elderly, being able to ask the right questions of the elder, and to report all suspected cases to the proper agency (for example, law enforcement, protective services, and/or hospital for forensic services). There are two major barriers that mitigate the need to report elder sexual abuse. The first barrier is the victim's reluctance to report the incident, which may occur because she is too frightened or embarrassed. In other cases, the offender may be a domestic partner, a situation often noted in domestic violence cases. In such situations, the elder may fear being sent to a nursing home and losing his or her independence and/or financial base from the partner. Thus, a plan needs to be worked out with the elder that will not jeopardize her/his financial security. This can be done by identifying the resources and social support available to help the elder remain in the home. This may require talking with law enforcement and/or the prosecutor regarding charges that can be brought against the offending partner.

The second barrier in reporting elder sexual abuse is that of disbelief. Caregivers, staff, and family may believe the elder is fantasizing, in a cognitive disorganized state, or making up a story. As with all ages of victims, staff need to take seriously all reports of sexual abuse. It will be up to experts in the area of elder sexual abuse to determine the credibility of the allegation and up to the prosecutor as to the viability of the case in the criminal justice system. Even if the prosecutor does not find adequate evidence to make the case, the elder should be respected and receive therapy services.

INTERVIEWING ELDER VICTIMS OF SEXUAL ABUSE

The following therapeutic tasks are important to develop trust with the elder in order to do an accurate assessment of the complaint of sexual abuse.

- Tell the senior what to expect. Talk slowly and clearly. Advise victims they will be going to a hospital for an examination and for collection of evidence.
- Assess the victim's sensory abilities. Can the victim hear and see people? A quiet and well-lighted area should be used, and the investigator's/staff person's face should be well in line of vision of the elder. If there are sensory problems, learn how the elder adjusts to the deficit by asking him/her or the family or caregivers.
- Observe the victim's demeanor. Is the victim quiet, crying, angry, or in distress? Ask how the victim is feeling and if he/she has any questions about what is going to happen. Allow adequate time for the elder to express his/her emotions.

SIGNS OF PHYSICAL TRAUMA

- *Signs of physical trauma* include observable objective evidence of injury such as bruises, abrasions, lacerations, and/or bleeding. The elder and accompanying family members need to be told that a comprehensive physical assessment will be conducted by the forensic examiner observing injury to the elder's general body condition, and a separate genital examination will be conducted. Evidence of intentional injury is sought by asking the question as to how the injury occurred. Accidental injury needs to be ruled out. For example, nursing-home staff have described genital bleeding as the result of "rough peri-care" (which involves cleaning of urinary and/or rectal orifices). This may or may not be accidental, and such assertions need medical verification.
- *Symptoms of physical trauma* include an indication of trauma provided by the elder. For example, the elder may say she was slapped or held by her throat, but no observable injury can be noted. This, too, should be noted as part of the forensic record.
- *Signs of emotional trauma* include observable signs such as crying, rocking, hands shaking, flushed appearance, signs of perspiration. Elders may try to hide their feelings by being very quiet, guarded, or controlled in their demeanor.

WHY WOMEN DO NOT REPORT RAPE TO THE POLICE

Studies have shown that many women are reluctant to report rape to their local police. The reasons most often given include:

- Lack of belief in the ability of the police to apprehend the suspect.
- Worries about unsympathetic treatment from police and discomforting procedures.
- Belief that they were somehow at fault for the rape.
- Embarrassment about publicity, however limited.
- Fear of reprisal by the rapist.[23]
- Apprehension, as a result of television programs or newspaper reports, of being further victimized by court proceedings.

Unfortunately, some complaints about the criminal justice system's treatment of rape victims are justified. In many jurisdictions, efforts are being made to correct deficiencies. Many corrections have come about through legislative changes.[24] In other instances, women's groups have worked with local police departments to educate the public, especially women, about the crime of rape and to correct much of the misinformation that may be transmitted via television programs and other news media.

The failure of victims to report rapes has serious implications, because without such information, the effectiveness of the police in protecting other women is considerably diminished. A case in point occurred a few years ago in San Francisco:

A young woman who was raped turned first to her friends for help and comfort, then sought aid from a local Women Against Rape group. No one encouraged her to make a police report; she was indecisive and did nothing. Several days later, she read a news account describing a rape similar to her own. She immediately notified the police and learned the rapist had attacked three other women. With the additional information she provided, the police located and arrested the rapist by the end of the day.[25]

QUICK FACTS

Tips for Responding to Victims of Sexual Assault

The National Office for Victims of Crime (OVC) within the U.S. Department of Justice offers several tips for responding to victims of sexual assault. None are more important than this first directive:

Be prepared for virtually any type of emotional reaction by victims. Be unconditionally supportive and permit victims to express their emotions, which may include crying, angry outbursts, and screaming. Avoid interpreting the victim's calmness or composure as evidence that a sexual assault did or did not occur. The victim could be in shock. (Note: False accusations of sexual assault are estimated to occur at the low rate of 2%—similar to the rate of false accusations for other violent crimes.)

Source: See VC Archive, https://www.ncjrs.gov/ovc_archives/reports/firstrep/vicsexaslt.html

BOX 10-1 | DATE RAPE AND SEXUAL ASSAULT ON U.S. COLLEGE AND UNIVERSITY CAMPUSES

The number of forcible rapes on U.S. college and university campuses has more than doubled in the last ten years! More shocking, reports of sex crimes increased by nearly 1,000 incidents from 2012 to 2013 alone, and the problem appears to be growing as high-profile media cases continue to dot the front pages of American newspapers. Several recent government studies relating to unwanted sexual contacts experienced by female students support the rising campus sexual assault crisis.

The first such study was released in December 2014 by the U.S. Department of Justice, Bureau of Justice Statistics focusing on nearly 20 years of data related to rape and sexual assault among women aged 18 to 24 years, comparing student versus nonstudent populations.[26] Highlights from the report using National Crime Victimization Survey (NCVS) data revealed that the rate of rape and sexual assault was 1.2 times higher for nonstudents (7.6 per 1,000) than for students (6.1 per 1,000). However, most importantly, for both college students and nonstudents, the offender was known to the victim in about 80% of all rape and sexual-assault victimizations. In other words, the victims knew their offenders. . . and in most cases knew them well, since over 50% of the incidents occurred during a leisure time with the offender.[27] Combined with other studies, the survey dispelled a number of myths about rape, particularly on campus, reporting that nearly 20% of all undergraduate women reported experiencing completed or attempted sexual assault since entering college.[28]

Supported by these and other studies, specifically those conducted by the Centers for Disease Control and Prevention, The National Intimate Partner and Sexual Violence Survey, revealing that 92% of female rape victims were assaulted by someone they knew and that just 12% of all college sexual-assault victims ever reported the crime to law enforcement, President Barack Obama commissioned the White House Task Force to Protect Students from Sexual Assault in 2014.[29] Their first report in April 2014, shocked American colleges and universities stating that one in five college students experienced sexual assault during their college career. Further the ACLU estimated that 95% of the U.S. campus rapes go unreported.[30]

The college rape crisis continues to grow fueled by several incidents involving high-profile, university athletes. Many of these stories involved alleged rape by football players at various campuses and none are more compelling than the Florida State University case involving Heisman Trophy-winning quarterback, Jameis Winston. In 2012, Winston was accused by a fellow FSU student (Erica Kinsman) of rape, and Florida State University was subsequently sued by the victim, alleging that the Tallahassee Police took steps to ensure that Winston's alleged rape of the plaintiff would not be investigated either by the university or law enforcement. She further accused FSU of failing to respond when she became a target of hostility and was forced to leave the university because of the mental and emotional trauma she suffered as result of the incident. In 2013, after a botched investigation by police detectives and presentation to the State's Attorney's Office in Tallahassee, no criminal charges were ever brought forth against Jameis Winston. Instead, Winston was a celebrated athlete that led the FSU Seminoles to a national championship in football and won the Heisman Trophy. However in early 2016, Florida State University reached a $950,000 settlement with Ms. Kinsman and her attorneys.

As a result of this case, as well as others at various universities across the country, two important documentaries have garnered several national awards and attention. First, *The Hunting Ground*, a collaborative documentary film between Radius and CNN Films, directed by Kirby Dick and produced by Amy Ziering was released in late 2015, and chronicles the high incidence of sexual assaults on campuses in the United States. More importantly, the film suggests that many of these cases are covered-up and/or dismissed by university administrators in order to safeguard the institution's or high-profile athlete's reputation. The second work, by bestselling author Jon Krakauer is entitled, *Missoula: Rape and the Justice System in a College Town* (New York: Penguin Random House, 2015), is a powerful book focused on a series of sexual assaults at the University of Montana, described as a typical university in a typical college town across America. Both works were well-researched and document the crisis confronting American colleges and universities. More importantly, they stand as a "call to action" for colleges and universities to confront this issue in an immediate effort to safeguard victims from sexual assault.

As of July 1, 2016, the three States of Connecticut, New York, and California have enacted affirmative consent laws that govern sex on campuses. The state laws outline "affirmative consent" as a knowing, voluntary, and mutual decision among all participants to engage in sexual activity. Further, the state laws emphasize that affirmative consent may be revoked at any time during the sexual activity by any person engaged in the sexual activity. Without such affirmative consent, rape ensues. Many other states have similar legislation in process and the *2016 Campus Accountability and Safety Act* requiring all colleges and universities to have an affirmative consent policy is under Senatorial review at the federal level.

It is also fair to say that several high-profile rape cases over the past few years have served to further marginalize sexual-assault victim experiences. In 2016, Stanford University student Brock Turner was sentenced to six months in a county jail and probation after he was found guilty of three counts of sexual assault for raping a woman behind a dumpster in 2015. The judge, during sentencing, asserted that he felt a longer sentence would hurt Turner's future: he had been a champion swimmer and had hoped to attend medical school.[31] The fallout from that case included assertions from the man's father that Allen had already "paid a steep price for 20 minutes of action," and dialogue about how Allen's privilege and class led the judge to value the rapist's experience over that of the victim's.

In turn, the Palo Alto district attorney's office released a victim impact statement from the victim that perfectly sums up many of the reasons why victims do not report their assaults:

I was pummeled with narrowed, pointed questions that dissected my personal life, love life, past life, family life, inane questions, accumulating trivial details to try and find an excuse for this guy who didn't even take the time to ask me for my name, who had me naked a handful of minutes after seeing me. After a physical assault, I was assaulted with questions designed to attack me, to say see, her facts don't line up, she's out of her mind, she's practically an alcoholic, she probably wanted to hook up, he's like an athlete right, they were both drunk, whatever, the hospital stuff she remembers is after the fact, why take it into account, Brock has a lot at stake so he's having a really hard time right now.[32]

Additionally, a number of cases on college campuses have highlighted that when cases involve athletes in high-value athletic programs, charges were not taken seriously. At Baylor University in Waco, Texas, allegations of rape perpetrated over a period of years by several football players were not investigated by the university; furthermore, victims were denied security, medical care, or counseling resources. It wasn't until an investigation by journalists uncovered multiple levels of inaction and cover-up at the institution that details of the assaults were made public. The university quickly fired multiple administrators in response and vowed to be more sensitive to victims of sexual assault in the future.[33] See Box 10-1 relating to rape and athletes on U.S. college and university campuses.

Ultimately, each of these cases highlight why sexual-assault victims are reticent to report to police: their experiences were not valued by the justice system or by other societal institutions. The perpetrators of the assault were assigned diminished responsibility secondary to alcohol consumption or their value as athletes. Such high-profile cases do nothing to inspire confidence in the criminal justice system's ability to ease a victim's trauma and punish an offender.

To make matters worse, a major U.S. Department of Justice Investigation[34] analyzing police bias in Baltimore, Maryland revealed that the police culture in that city was deeply dismissive of sexual-assault victims and hostile toward prostitutes and transgender people.[35] The report characterized the response of the Baltimore Police Department as "grossly inadequate" and found that officers often humiliated women who tried to report sexual assault, often failed to gather evidence and conduct a proper investigation, and in some cases, disregarded complaints filed by prostitutes.[36] Some of the officers blamed victims and/or discouraged them from reporting such crimes, suggesting a pattern and practice within police departments across the nation that may arise to gender bias in the reporting of sexual assault.

FALSE RAPE ALLEGATIONS

False rape allegations are a difficult subject for law enforcement. Ultimately, law enforcement officers have a responsibility to ensure that no one is falsely accused of sexual assault: the stakes are very high. However, it is a myth that false accusations are commonplace. The prevalence of false reporting is somewhere between 2% and 8%: one study of over 2,000 cases found a 7.1% rate of false reports, while another case that examined 812 reports found a 2.1% rate.[37]

Best practices in law enforcement suggest that investigators approach each case using victim-centered response. Officers should begin by believing, until facts begin to prove otherwise. If elements of the case are inconsistent, if there is a lack of evidence, or if the victim exhibits obvious credibility issues (such as a past history of false allegations), then those elements should be further explored by investigators.

Although there is a small chance that a rape investigation is false, the investigator must remember that, according to the FBI's *Uniform Crime Report,* in 47% of all forcible-rape cases, sufficient evidence is present to make an arrest.[38] There are a large number of cases where a rape has clearly occurred, but no specific offender can be determined from the evidence. Furthermore, there are cases in which police investigators simply find no evidence that a crime has taken place. Even in these cases (which police often dismiss), it is still possible that a rape has occurred. The following story illustrates this point.

On arriving home late one evening and before going to bed, a 30-year-old woman living alone checked all the windows and doors to be certain they were locked. After checking them, she went to bed. Shortly thereafter she was awakened by a man in her bed; he held a knife to her throat and warned her not to make any noise or attempt to resist or he would kill her. The man then proceeded to rape the woman. After raping her, he ordered her to go to the bathroom and to douche. After douching, she was instructed to flush the toilet. The suspect then fled by the front door. When the police arrived, they could find no signs of forced entry into the home. When the woman was examined at the hospital, there was no evidence of sexual intercourse or the presence of semen. The police thought the woman had fabricated the incident because of the absence of forcible entry into the home or any physical evidence of sexual intercourse. The case was classified as unfounded. Two months later the man was arrested for another rape in the same general area where the first rape had occurred. The police found in his possession a number of keys; with the cooperation of his family members, it was determined that one of the keys was for a home the family had been renting several months before. This was the same home in which the first victim had been raped. The owner of the home had failed to rekey the lock after the family moved out and the new tenant moved in. The rapist merely retained the key and used it to enter through the front door and commit the rape.

THE VICTIM AND PHYSICAL EVIDENCE

Rape investigations usually begin when the victim either places a call to report the rape or takes herself to a hospital. The report may be filed moments after the incident occurred, or it may be days or weeks later. In either case, the investigator must remember that the victim is a walking crime scene. Certain investigative procedures must be followed to ensure that physical evidence on the victim's person is not lost or accidentally destroyed.[39]

For example, when the victim is deceased and it is not practical or possible to process the victim's hands and fingernails at the crime scene, it is best to bag the hands (Figure 10-1). After the body is transported to the medical examiner's office, the hands and fingernails can be processed for physical evidence.

INSTRUCTIONS TO THE VICTIM

The officer responding to a reported sexual assault should make a great effort to ensure that any evidence that may be on the victim is secure. Once evidence is destroyed, it cannot be retrieved. Attending to the victim's well-being is unquestionably the primary concern; if she is in immediate need of medical attention,

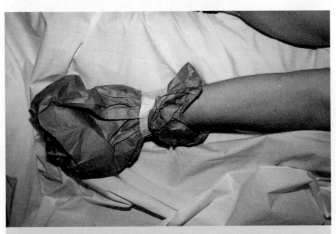

▲ **FIGURE 10-1 Bagged hands**
This victim of rape and murder had her hands bagged at the crime scene in order to avoid loss of any possible physical evidence on her hands or under her fingernails.

attending to that need is the officer's first responsibility. However, a well-trained officer will tactfully find a way to meet the victim's physical and psychological needs while preserving potentially useful and incriminating evidence. For instance, the officer should encourage the victim not to shower or douche (assuming she has not already done so) and should urge her not to change clothes. These actions cause the loss of hair and body fluids such as blood and semen that could be analyzed at the crime lab and used to corroborate the victim's testimony as well as lead to the identification, prosecution, and conviction of the perpetrator.

The victim should also be advised not to alter the scene of the crime. Even the location of body fluids and hairs can be telling, and such routine actions as flushing the toilet may mean a loss of crucial evidence (for example, in cases where the perpetrator used a condom and dropped it into the toilet).[40]

SEMEN AND HAIR AS EVIDENCE

As was discussed in considerable detail in Chapter 4, "Physical Evidence," semen that contains sperm and hair that has the root attached can now be identified through DNA typing as coming from a specific individual. Thus, it is absolutely essential that appropriate samples be collected and preserved from the victim and the suspect. Note that the presence of semen is not evidence that a rape occurred, nor does its absence mean a rape did not occur. For example, because rapists sometimes experience sexual dysfunction, the examining physician may find no semen during the pelvic examination. In interviews of 133 convicted rapists, 50 (37%) admitted some sexual dysfunction. Of the rapists, 23 stated that they were unable to achieve an orgasm during the sex act; 22 experienced difficulty in achieving and sustaining an erection; and five experienced premature ejaculation.[41]

Note that the terms "semen" and "sperm" are not synonymous. **Semen** is a grayish-white fluid, produced in the male reproductive organs, that is ejaculated during orgasm. In liquid form, it has a chlorinelike odor; when dried, it has a starchlike consistency. **Sperm** are the tadpolelike organisms that are contained in, and travel through, semen to fertilize the female egg. This distinction is important, because the laboratory examinations and tests employed to search for each are quite different. Thus, if a rape was committed by a male who is sterile (having no sperm in his ejaculate), then semen but not sperm may be present. Note that DNA typing is conducted on the sperm, not the semen. The physician examining the victim for sperm in the vagina therefore aspirates the vagina—removes fluids with a suction device—and microscopically examines them for sperm. The motility of sperm in the vagina is short, measured in hours rather than days; motility decreases to zero in about 3 hours. Menstruation may prolong motility to 4 hours. If large numbers of highly motile sperm are aspirated from the vagina, one may conclude that sexual intercourse had occurred 1 to 2 hours before the examination. If a few motile sperm remain, one may conclude that sexual intercourse occurred within 3 hours of the examination. Nonmotile sperm may be found in a living female in small numbers up to 48 hours after sexual intercourse. Nonmotile sperm have been found in dead bodies for up to several hours after death.[42]

When sperm cannot be found, a second test may be employed to identify the presence of acid phosphatase. Acid phosphatase, an enzyme, is a component of the liquid portion of semen. The test should be conducted by experienced crime laboratory personnel and interpreted with care. Routine hospital laboratory techniques are not applicable to this type of examination and may be erroneously interpreted as significant. Only strong reactions should be considered evidence of semen, because mild positive reactions have been noted with vegetable matter, feces, and many other types of organic substances. Experiments have been conducted to determine the persistence of a significantly positive reaction to the acid phosphatase test over variable lengths of time following sexual intercourse. In the living, acid phosphatase may be lost from the vagina after 12 to 40 hours.

BOX 10-2 | DALLAS POLICE DEPARTMENT TACKLES RAPE KIT BACKLOG

By Jennifer Davis-Lamm

In 2009, an assistant prosecutor in Detroit, Kym Worthy, brought to light that over 11,000 rape kits collected from victims of sexual assault had been untested in that jurisdiction. Her work to bring attention to this issue set off a national revolution in sexual-assault investigation and prosecution; a number of advocacy organizations took notice and began to raise funds to end that backlog and others across the nation. As a result of the increased attention in Dallas, Texas, a grant was made through the Texas Department of Public Safety to fund the Dallas Police Department's efforts to test a backlog of over 4,000 kits—at approximately $500 a piece. The grant would allow testing back to 1996. The department submitted 2,356 kits for laboratory testing between August, 2014 and September, 2015. This represents a significant dent in the caseload logjam for DNA analysis within rape kits.

Those 4,000 plus kits represent much more than the evidence inside them: they represent lives in limbo. Assembling them requires re-traumatizing sexual-assault victims, who have to undergo an intensive examination by a nurse certified in evidence retrieval. Once medically stabilized, victims spend somewhere in the neighborhood of an hour under harsh lights being probed and swabbed and plucked and photographed in a process that is demeaning and painful. Dallas detective sergeant Amy Mills is adamant that this process should never be in vain. "If you endure that invasive exam when all you want to do is take a shower, brush your teeth—take a drink of water, even . . . then we owe it to you . . . the victim . . . to process that evidence, to be an advocate for you, and to let you have some sense of closure."

Mills makes it clear that the backlogged kits didn't stay untested due to negligence or lack of regard toward crime victims. In fact, DPD is one of the few departments that keeps evidence past the statute of limitations—the property room actually has rape kits that date back 30 years, well beyond the 1996 limit set by the grant. But for a variety of reasons, too large a number remained untouched. Sometimes, the survivors weren't willing or able to participate in investigations. Funding and personnel limitations were often a factor. And, Mills says, investigators have only recently begun to understand the full evidentiary value of the kits. Sexual-assault perpetrators are rarely one-time offenders. Mills details burglary cases, domestic assaults, sex offenses, even murders that were solved by evidence obtained from a single rape kit. "We're finding out how intertwined these crimes are," she says, "It's amazing how one victim's evidence can link us to so many other investigative leads."

The work and analysis conducted on these kits in Dallas are having a tangible effect. The tests are coming back from the lab; DNA profiles have been entered in CODIS (the FBI's national database); and so far over 30% have resulted in a match. When those matches occur, Sergeant Mills triages the cases: some are just confirmations of a case that's already been adjudicated, so no action is required. Others identify a known suspect who is capable of committing further assaults: Mills puts one of her seven detectives on those cases immediately. She's confident that re-testing that mountain of cases results in prevention of further assaults, particularly when she's able to affect an arrest. And she also loves being able to call a survivor and tell them that it's over— that she or he can have peace of mind knowing their assailant won't do this again.

Processing these rape kits has the potential to change the dialogue about sexual assault and the perception of how rape victims are treated in the United States. As Sergeant Mills describes it:

> *People understand that they are not forgotten; that they didn't endure this for nothing. Ultimately, I think this means that more people will report these types of crimes because they know that we believe them. They know now that we want to give them peace of mind and to do everything we can. Hopefully that means they trust us to help them. I'm just sorry it took so long to get to this point.*

©Jennifer Davis Lamm

INFORMATION FOR THE EXAMINING PHYSICIAN/SEXUAL-ASSAULT NURSE EXAMINER

The medical personnel responsible for examining the victim should be provided with all the available facts before the physical examination.

Usually, certain hospitals in a community are designated as the ones to which rape victims are taken for a physical examination. These hospitals frequently have both specially trained staffs and the necessary technical facilities. Under no circumstances should a male investigator be present in the hospital room when a female victim is being physically examined. If a male investigator believes that some physical evidence may be adhering to the victim's body, he should instruct the examining physician to collect such evidence and turn it over to him. The collection of physical evidence in this manner must conform to all guidelines for preserving the chain of custody.

COLLECTION OF THE VICTIM'S CLOTHING

The victim's clothing should be collected as soon as possible. If she is still wearing the clothes worn during the incident, she should undress over a clean cloth or large paper mat so that any evidence that may be dislodged from her clothes is not lost. Even if the victim was forced to disrobe before the sexual attack, it is possible that hair, semen, or fibers from the suspect's clothing have been deposited on her clothing. Each article of clothing should be placed in a separate container, properly labeled, and stored for later analysis. The victim may then be photographed before redressing to document any evidence of physical abuse.[43] Underpants should not be the only item of a victim's clothing recovered, because they often offer only limited physical evidence and are likely to be contaminated with other stains, such as vaginal secretions or urine, that interfere with the laboratory examination. Other garments, such as the dress, slip, or coat, may be of greater value in providing physical evidence. The evidence most frequently obtained from the victim's clothing consists of fibers from a suspect's clothing and loose pubic hairs. If the assault occurred in a wooded or grassy area, there will often be soil, seeds, weeds, and other vegetation adhering to the victim's clothing.[44]

The following actual case, which occurred before the advent of DNA typing, illustrates the importance of a careful search for physical evidence:

The partly dressed body of a 16-year-old female was discovered by two young boys traveling through a wooded area. The victim's slacks and underpants were pulled down around her ankles, and her brassiere was pulled up around her head. A check of the missing-persons file revealed that a female fitting her description had been reported missing by her parents 18 hours earlier. The body was later identified as the missing female.

The victim's body was removed from the scene in a clean white sheet and transported to a local hospital. The medical examination of the victim revealed that she had died from a fatal brain injury after being struck repeatedly with a blunt object. In addition, she had a large bruise on her right cheek, also caused by a blow from a blunt object, possibly a fist. The examination of the deceased's person and clothing yielded the following:

- Her clothing.
- Pubic-hair samples.
- Blood samples for typing.
- Grease stains on the inside of her thighs. The grease was initially deposited on the suspect's hands after he used an automobile master cylinder that had been on the floorboard of his car to batter the victim unconscious.
- A single human hair clutched in her hand, mixed with considerable dirt, leaves, twigs, and so forth.
- No semen was found either in or on her body, clothing, or in the immediate area.

Physical evidence also was obtained from the crime scene:

- Tire impressions.
- Samples of soil, leaves, weeds, and other vegetation.

A suspect who had been the last person seen with the victim and who also had an arrest record for a similar offense was taken into custody, and his vehicle was impounded. The vehicle's entire interior, including steering wheel, dashboard, door panels, seats, floor mats, and visor, was removed, as were all four wheels. These items were transported to the crime laboratory along with all the evidence collected from the victim and the crime scene. A pair of blood-stained trousers and hair samples were obtained from the suspect. The results of the laboratory examination revealed:

- The victim's brassiere had several fibers caught in the hooks, which were identical to those of the terrycloth seat covers in the suspect's car.
- The grease stain on the victim's thighs was compared with the grease found under the dashboard and near the ignition switch in the suspect's vehicle and found to be identical. An examination of the ignition switch revealed that the car could be started only if someone reached under the dash and crossed the ignition wires; thus, when the suspect tried to start his car, he deposited grease from the master cylinder onto the ignition switch.
- The single hair found in the victim's hand was similar in all characteristics to that of the suspect.
- Samples collected from the victim's hair at the morgue were similar to those recovered from the floorboard of the suspect's vehicle.
- Fibers from the victim's underpants were identical to fibers recovered from the suspect's vehicle.
- A tire impression at the scene matched a tire on the suspect's vehicle.
- Debris collected from the scene matched debris recovered from the interior of the suspect's car and dirt extracted from the rims of the wheels of the suspect's car.
- Human blood was found on the steering wheel of the suspect's car, but the presence of various contaminants prevented the blood from being typed accurately.
- Because the suspect had soaked his trousers in cold water overnight, blood typing was impossible.

The suspect confessed to murdering the victim after meeting her at a nearby teenage dance and convincing her to get in his car. He then drove her to an isolated, wooded area where upon he killed her for rejecting his sexual advances. Although his confession was not needed in view of the physical evidence. As previously indicated, he identified the murder weapon as an automobile master cylinder, which he had disposed of after the crime. It was never located.

Examination of most hair, fiber, debris, and tire or shoe prints at the scene can narrow the field. Analysis of these materials, however, will most often yield evidence characteristic of class (discussed in considerable detail in Chapter 4, "Physical Evidence"), not individualized results. However, the preponderance of class-characteristic evidence, coupled with the particulars of the case, made a compelling argument against the suspect.

THE ROLE OF THE INVESTIGATOR IN SECURING THE RAPE SCENE

It is the criminal investigator's job to collect, catalog, and store physical evidence for later analysis in the laboratory. As soon as possible, the investigative unit should take photographs of the scene of the crime, including the specific area where the rape is believed to have occurred, the area around the rape, and the areas around the entrances, exits, and general perimeter of the facility where the rape occurred (if it occurred indoors). After this is done, various methods may be used to gather evidence for laboratory testing. Evidence recovery methods may include naked-eye searches, the use of oblique light to spot hair and fiber on the surface of furniture or other surfaces, the use of ultraviolet light to illuminate fibers, careful vacuuming of selected small areas, adhesive lifts, combing or brushing, scraping under the fingernails and certain other surfaces, the use of blue light to detect semen, and the use of lasers.[45]

INCIDENCE OF ERRORS IN THE COLLECTION OF EVIDENCE

Physical evidence in a case is often the decisive factor in determining guilt or innocence. Developments in DNA technology over the last 25 years have added a new dimension to rape investigation. Currently, DNA analysis combined with careful hair and fiber analysis can "describe the clothes worn by the criminal, give an idea of his stature, age, hair color, or similar information" and thereby significantly limit the officers' search for a suspect.[46] With the exception of identical twins, no two persons have the same DNA structure. A good DNA sample can now be analyzed to identify with forensic and legal certainty any individual whose DNA structure is known.[47]

However, DNA testing is only as good as the investigative techniques used to gather the evidence. As items are collected, the investigator must carefully label the items and store them in such a way that they are preserved intact and uncompromised for later laboratory analysis. Current laboratory technology is accurate to such a degree that defense lawyers have little to challenge other than the chain of custody of the evidence and any possible contamination. Keeping careful records of the chain of custody of the evidence and protecting the evidence from contamination are crucial both for preserving the sample itself so that it can be analyzed and for ensuring that conclusions drawn from the analysis of the sample cannot be challenged in court.[48]

COLLECTING SAMPLES FOR DNA ANALYSIS FROM SUSPECTS

In 2013, the U.S. Supreme Court ruled that a police officer has the right to take DNA samples from a suspect arrested for a serious crime.[49] Most states authorize law enforcement officers to take cheek swabs from suspects, similar to taking fingerprints. More importantly, all 50 states have laws requiring the collection of DNA from defendants convicted of felonies.

Police officers use a **buccal swab**, also referred to as a buccal smear or a cheek swab, as the easiest and most efficient way to collect DNA from a suspect. Most departments have buccal swab collection kits that are used by officers and detectives during the DNA collection process. These buccal swab kits usually contain a number of commonly found first aid items and material used to collect and transport DNA samples. These include:

- Two sterile swabs with cotton, foam, or flocked tips (medical swabs generally come in packages of two sealed in a paper wrapper)

- Two pairs of sterile gloves (latex or nitrile)
- One protective or surgical mask
- Dry test tubes with covers or sterile collection envelopes
- Consent forms (if required by specific jurisdictions)
- Swabbing instructions

Collecting a buccal swab sample from a suspect is best described in a series of steps:

1. If required by your jurisdiction, have the suspect read and sign a consent form.
2. Place the protective/surgical mask over your mouth and nose in order to reduce the chances of contamination of the sample with your DNA.
3. Wash your hands and then place the sterile gloves on your hands.
4. Make sure the suspect's mouth is empty. Ask the suspect to open their mouth, and visually inspect and insure that the suspect's mouth is indeed empty.
5. Carefully remove a swab from the kit or package, avoiding any direct contact with the surface of the swab and anything else.
6. Ask the subject to open his or her mouth and immediately swab the inside of the cheek. It does not matter which side of the cheek is chosen.
7. Gently rub and rotate the swab along the inside of the cheek for 5 to 10 seconds, ensuring that the entire swab-tip has made contact with the cheek.
8. Immediately remove the swab, being careful not to contact the teeth, lips or any other surface of the suspect's face.
9. Place the entire swab into the dry test tube or transport tube, or into the sterile collection envelope.
10. Seal the swab in the tube or envelope with evidence tape.
11. Label the tube or envelope with the name of the suspect, date and time the sample was taken, case number, and your name as the collecting officer for verification of chain of custody.
12. Transport and store the swab at room temperature for testing and analysis per your department's procedure for processing evidence through the forensics laboratory.
13. Document the entire process in your report.

Of course, the above procedure necessarily requires a cooperating suspect. For those individuals that do not consent and/or will not cooperate with the above procedure, a court order or search warrant must be obtained. Investigators should work with their jurisdiction's prosecuting offices in order to comply with the necessary legal procedures to procure a warrant or court order for the suspect's DNA from a magistrate.

SEXUAL-BATTERY EXAMINATION

Most hospitals or crisis centers responsible for the collection of evidence from sex-offense victims have developed sexual-battery examination kits. (See Figures 10-2 and 10-3 for a detailed description of the contents of these kits.)

▶ FIGURE 10-2
Sexual-assault victim exam kit contents

Sexual-assault victim exam kit contents

1. Collection vial—for urine.

2. Collection vial—for blood.

3. Pubic hair combings specimen envelope—used in the collection of possible foreign material in the pubic hair of the victim.

4. Head hair combings specimen envelope—used in the same way as pubic hair combings, but for hair on the head of the victim.

5. Vaginal smear slides—used in the collection of semen fluid for DNA evidence deposited by the assailant in the vagina of the victim. One slide is used for the vaginal area and the other is used for the specimen taken from the cervix of the victim.

6. Smear slides—used to collect DNA (seminal fluid) from other areas where the perpetrator's DNA may be found on the victim such as those resulting from the anal or oral penetration of victim.

7. Swabs—used in the collection of seminal fluid for DNA evidence that the perpetrator may have left on the victim (anal, oral, or other areas).

8. Vaginal swabs (4)—used to collect seminal fluid for DNA evidence of the perpetrator.

9. Cervical swabs (2)—used to collect seminal fluid from the cervix for DNA evidence of the perpetrator.

10. Saliva standard swabs—used to collect DNA evidence of the perpetrator from the victim's mouth.

11. Buccal swab—used to collect the victim's DNA.

12. Extra swabs—to collect possible semen from the perpetrator wherever it may be found on the victim.

13. Extra swabs—used to collect saliva left by the perpetrator from areas that may have been bitten, licked, or kissed.

14. Underwear specimen bag.

15. Genoprobe—used to screen for chlamydia and gonorrhea. This is taken at the time of evidence collection.

The same kit is used to collect evidence with male victims, but the differences are in the genoprobe that is used in the physical areas of the body from where the evidence is collected. Instead of vaginal swabs, penile swabs are used as well as anal or penile cultures for gonorrhea.

Source: Florida Department of Law Enforcement.

CONDOM TRACE EVIDENCE

Manufacturers produce condoms using a variety of materials, both natural and synthetic. Each manufacturer has its own formula, which may vary even among its different brands.[50] Some condoms are made from lamb membranes, and one manufacturer recently introduced a model made from polyurethane plastic. Still, latex rubber condoms have, by far, the largest share of the market, perhaps because they cost considerably less. In addition to the basic materials they use to produce condoms, manufacturers also add other substances, known as **exchangeable traces** that comprise particulates, lubricants, and spermicide.

EXCHANGEABLE TRACES

Particulates

Condom manufacturers add finely powdered particulates to prevent a rolled-up latex condom from sticking to itself. Particulates found in different brands include cornstarch, potato starch, and lycopodium (a powder found in plants), as well as amorphous silica, talc, and other minerals. In the laboratory, forensic scientists use several different techniques to characterize these particles and compare them with those obtained from other condom brands.

Lubricants

Sexual assailants prefer lubricated condoms, probably for the same reason they use petroleum jelly—that is, to help facilitate their crimes.[51] Many condom brands contain a liquid lubricant, which may be classified as either "wet" or "dry." Both types of condom lubricant have an oillike consistency, but wet lubricants are water-based and/or water-soluble, whereas dry lubricants are not. Although many different manufacturers use the same dry lubricant, the viscosity grades sometimes differ. The forensic laboratory can recover these silicone oils easily from items of evidence and possibly associate them with a condom manufacturer. Wet lubricants may contain either

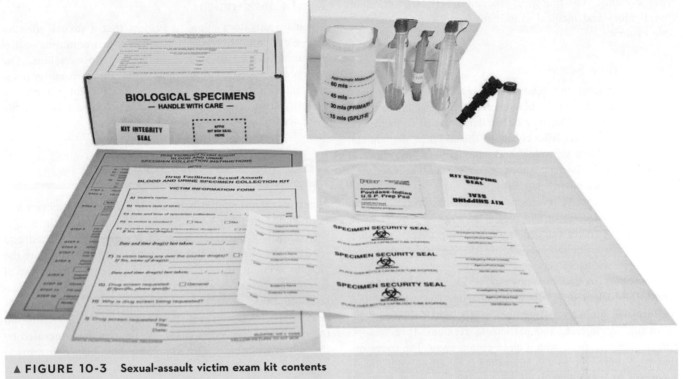

▲ **FIGURE 10-3   Sexual-assault victim exam kit contents**
(Courtesy of North Carolina Lab Test)

polyethylene glycol or a gel made from a combination of ingredients similar to those found in vaginal lubricants. Forensic examination can associate specific formulations with particular condom brands, despite their similarities to other products on the market.

Spermicide

Both wet- and dry-lubricated condoms also may contain the spermicide nonoxynol-9. Its recovery and detection, along with lubricant ingredients and particulates, can help show condom use and indicate the specific brand.

THE VALUE OF CONDOM TRACE EVIDENCE

Condom trace evidence can assist investigators in several ways. It can help prove corpus delicti, provide evidence of penetration, produce associative evidence, and link the acts of serial rapists.

In Proving Corpus Delicti

Traces associated with condoms can help prove **corpus delicti,** the fact that a crime has occurred. This evidence can support the claims of either the victim or the accused. For example, the U.S. military can prosecute personnel diagnosed as HIV-positive for aggravated assault if they engage in unprotected sex, even if it is consensual. If servicemen accused of aggravated assault claim that they did in fact wear a condom but it broke or slipped off, condom trace evidence can support that claim.

In Providing Evidence of Penetration

Condom traces found inside a victim can provide evidence of penetration. In many jurisdictions, this evidence raises the charge to a higher degree of sexual assault.

In Producing Associative Evidence

Recovered condom traces may correspond to those found in a certain brand or used by a particular manufacturer. An empty packet of this particular brand found near the crime scene, especially if it bears the suspect's fingerprints, provides a strong association between the suspect and the crime. Unopened condom packages of the same brand found on the suspect, in his car, or at his residence also would help tie the suspect to the crime.

In Linking the Acts of Serial Rapists

People tend to be creatures of habit, and sexual criminals are no exception. A serial rapist likely will use the same brand of condom to commit repeated acts. Moreover, repeat offenders whose DNA profiles have been stored in a computer data bank may be likely to use a condom when committing subsequent crimes. Along with other aspects of his modus operandi, traces from the same condom brand or manufacturer found during several different investigations can help connect a suspect to an entire series of assaults.

GUIDELINES FOR EVIDENCE COLLECTION

Investigators need not make any drastic changes in their usual procedures in order to include the possibility of condom trace evidence. The following guidelines will assist criminal investigators and medical examiners in collecting this valuable evidence.[52]

At the Crime Scene

First and foremost, investigators must wear powder-free gloves to protect themselves from blood-borne pathogens and to avoid leaving particulates that may be similar to those contained in some condom brands. After collecting the evidence, they should package the gloves separately and submit them with the evidence so that the forensic laboratory can verify that the gloves did not leave behind any particulates.

At the crime scene, investigators should make every effort to locate any used condom and its foil package. If a condom is recovered, the traces from the victim on the outside and the seminal fluids from the assailant on the inside will have the greatest evidentiary value.

If investigators find an empty packet, they first should try to recover any latent prints from the outside. The inside of the package will probably not contain prints, but it may contain lubricant, spermicide, and particulate residues. Investigators should wipe the inside with a clean cotton swab. The traces on this swab will serve as a standard for comparison with traces recovered from the victim and the suspect.

With the Victim

In addition to providing general information about the crime, victims may be able to supply valuable details about the condom and its wrapper. They may recall the brand itself or other important details, including the condom's color, shape, texture, odor, taste, and lubrication.

After obtaining facts about the condom, investigators should ask victims about their sexual and hygienic habits, which might account for traces not attributable to the crime. A comprehensive interview would include the following questions:

- Has the victim recently engaged in consensual sex?
- If so, was a condom used? A vaginal lubricant? What brand?
- Does the victim use any external or internal vaginal products (anti-itch medications, deodorants, douches, suppositories, and so on)?
- If so, what brands?

These questions assume an adult female victim. Investigators must modify the interview to accommodate male or child sexual-assault victims.

With the Suspect(s)

Investigators also should question the suspect about the condom. A cooperative suspect will reveal the brand, tell where he purchased it, and describe how and where he disposed of both the condom and the empty packet. An uncooperative or deceitful suspect may claim he does not know or cannot remember, or he may name a popular brand but be unable to describe the condom or the packet in detail.

Legal Considerations

When investigators know or suspect that a sexual offender used a condom, they must remember to list condoms on the warrant obtained to search the suspect's possessions. The search of a suspect's home may reveal intact condom packets, but if investigators have not listed condoms on the search warrant, they will not be able to seize this valuable evidence.

RECORD OF INJURIES

A careful record should be made of the victim's injuries and be included in the report. Photographs of the victim's injuries serve two purposes. First, if a suspect is arrested and tried for the offense, the photographs tend to corroborate the victim's account of the attack. Second, the injuries may be of an unusual nature—bite marks, scratches, or burns from cigarettes—and may provide data valuable for developing the suspect's MO. In some cases, the injuries are readily visible to the investigator. In other cases, the injuries are concealed by the victim's clothing. The examining physician can provide details of injuries not readily noticeable. Color photographs should be taken if the victim has sustained visible severe injuries. If the injuries are in a location that requires the victim to disrobe partially or completely to be photographed, it is essential that a female police officer (not a male officer) or some other female officially associated with the police department or the hospital be present. If possible, a female police photographer should photograph the victim's injuries.

ELECTRONIC EVIDENCE

There are a number of electronic resources germane to sexual-assault investigators. Police should examine security cameras that may have captured the assault, or that might document the pre- or post-assault behavior of the victim and/or the perpetrator. Sources of video may include ATM cameras, neighborhood security cameras, nightclubs, retail locations, parking structures, and police surveillance systems.

Social media can also be a source of evidence. Footage from a number of assaults have found their way onto apps such as Snapchat or Periscope, sometimes giving law enforcement an opportunity to retrieve data from the service provider through proper means, often followed up by a warrant. Social media messaging and interaction between victims and offenders may also offer evidence of chronology or circumstances surrounding the assault. Law enforcement can use screen shots of publicly available portions of social media interactions, or can enlist the victim's cooperation to retrieve private data[53].

Cell-phones often have useful applications in sexual assault investigations: GPS and usage data available from the provider may corroborate the location of the suspect, victim, witnesses, or the assault. Text messaging, apps, and call logs may also contain useful information. Investigators should consult with their forensic units and/or prosecuting attorneys to secure search warrants to examine such devices.

DRUG- AND ALCOHOL-FACILITATED SEXUAL ASSAULT

A drug- or alcohol-facilitated sexual assault is one that occurs when a person is made vulnerable or is incapacitated by the ingestion of drugs or alcohol. That ingestion can be voluntary, or can occur without the victim's knowledge. Alcohol is the most common substance in such cases.

Assaults that are drug- and alcohol-facilitated are complicated. Despite the fact that voluntarily ingesting a substance is immaterial to an offender's choices and actions, victims who are drunk or high during their assault are often blamed for their own choices, unable to recall details of the assault, and are left feeling responsible for the actions of another person. Perpetrators may have specifically targeted a person who is intoxicated in hopes that their substance use will lessen the chance that others will believe the victim—or the perpetrator may have been intoxicated themselves, to the point where they disregarded the victim's lack of consent. Either way, it's important for investigators to focus on the actions of the perpetrators.

Adding to the challenge of such an investigation is the fact that victims may be confused about what has happened. They may think that they might have been assaulted, but aren't sure—reporting that their clothes seem rearranged, that they are experiencing unexplained soreness in their genital area, or experiencing a level of intoxication that doesn't match their level of consumption.

As a result, additional questions may be required to determine elements of the assault. Investigators should determine the following from follow-up interviews related to alcohol- or drug-facilitated sexual assault:

- Prescription or over-the-counter medications used by the victim.
- Recreational substances taken voluntarily.
- Victim's experience with alcohol or drugs to assess tolerance and expected levels of intoxication.
- Black-outs or missing periods of time related to intoxication or consumption.
- Amounts of drugs or alcohol consumed.
- Sensory experiences after consumption.[54]

The U.S. Department of Justice has estimated that over 430,000 people in this country are victimized by sexual assault each year and that three out of four victims are acquainted with their attackers. Many of the women who report being raped by an acquaintance also report unusual symptoms such as blacking out and having hazy or no memories about the attack. Sexual offenders' increasing use of **date-rape drugs,** such as Rohypnol and gamma hydroxybutyrate, as tools of submission accounts for much of the complexity surrounding these cases.

Congress has responded to the growing use of date-rape drugs by passing the Drug-Induced Rape Prevention and Punishment Act of 1996, an amendment of the Controlled Substance Act. The law imposes a prison term of up to 20 years on anyone convicted of giving any controlled substance to another person without his or her knowledge, with the intention of committing a sexual assault.

Law enforcement personnel can contribute to the successful prosecution of drug-facilitated sexual-assault cases by recognizing the symptoms of drugging, the availability and toxicology of widely used substances, and the range of delivery methods.[55]

DRUGS OF CHOICE

As already indicated, the two drugs that are most commonly used by sex offenders to facilitate their crimes are Rohypnol and gamma hydroxybutyrate.

Rohypnol

Rohypnol, also known as flunitrazepam, belongs to a class of drugs called benzodiazepines. It produces a spectrum of effects similar to those of diazepam (Valium), including skeletal muscle relaxation, sedation, and a reduction in anxiety. Of these effects, the sedative and hypnotic effects are the most important. Flunitrazepam is considered to be approximately 8 to 10 times more potent than Valium. The effect or "high" may last from 7 to 12 hours or longer after the dose. With pills or "hits" readily available for prices ranging from $2 to 5, Rohypnol is extremely sought-after. Street names include "roofies," "R-2s," "roach-2s," "trip and fall," and "mind erasers."

This fast-acting drug can be ground into a powder and easily slipped into food or drink. It can take effect within 30 minutes, and symptoms may persist for up to 8 hours.[56] Symptoms of Rohypnol intoxication include sedation, dizziness, visual disturbances, memory impairment, and loss of consciousness and motor coordination.[57] These effects may be compounded, and made potentially lethal, by alcohol. It is traceable in a person's urine for 48 to 96 hours after ingestion and in blood for only 12 hours.

The drug is easily obtained on the black market, through the Internet, and in other countries. A significant amount of Rohypnol makes its way to the United States from Mexico and Colombia. The recent notoriety of Rohypnol as a date-rape drug has prompted manufacturers to create a tablet that is more difficult to dissolve in liquid and that will turn a drink blue. Unfortunately, the original colorless, dissolvable tablets are still widely available (Figure 10-4).

Many victims of drug-induced sexual assault are targeted at parties, clubs, and bars. Members of the high school- and college-age populations are especially vulnerable to perpetrators of drug-induced sexual assault. The following case, which occurred in Prince William County, Virginia, illustrates this point.

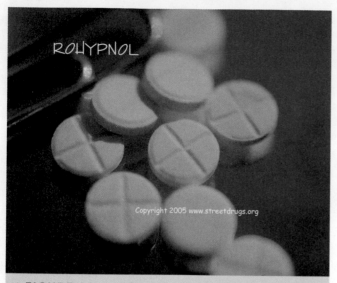

▲ FIGURE 10-4 Rohypnol

The drug Rohypnol is commonly used by sex offenders to facilitate their crime. It produces effects such as skeletal muscle relaxation, sedation, and a reduction in anxiety. The drug can be easily slipped into food or drink and can take effect within 30 minutes. It is often present in cases of date rape. (©streetdrugs.org)

Two 15-year-old girls were forcibly raped after unknowingly ingesting Rohypnol. During the trial, prosecutors dubbed this drug the "new stealth weapon" on the basis of its odorless and tasteless properties. Commonly known as the "date-rape drug," it dissolves rapidly when placed in a carbonated drink, making it virtually impossible for unsuspecting victims to detect. Once in the victim's system, it quickly produces physical as well as mental incapacitation. Approximately 8–10 times stronger than Valium, Rohypnol's sedative effect occurs within 30 minutes after ingestion. The main side effect is amnesia, but it also produces an intoxicated appearance, impaired judgment, impaired motor skills, drowsiness, dizziness, and confusion.

Prince William County's investigation revealed that in the late afternoon, the two young girls were taken willingly to an adult's apartment, having been reassured that they would be returned home after they saw the apartment. Once at the apartment, they were offered a soft drink. They both drank a Mountain Dew and started to feel "weird," as one victim put it, within about 30 minutes. Neither victim could remember what occurred over the next 9 hours.

The first victim woke up, disoriented, on the couch in the early morning hours. She went to the bathroom and noticed "hickeys" on her neck that had not been present the day before. She could not remember having sexual contact with anyone. She then went to look for the second victim, whom she found asleep on a pull-out bed. Once awakened, she, too, was disoriented. The second victim noticed a "hickey" on her inner thigh but did not remember engaging in any sexual contact. During the subsequent interviews, the men present in the apartment admitted having sexual intercourse with the victims but said it was consensual.

Three white tablets, marked "RH" were recovered from one of the men. These tested positive for Rohypnol. Both victims were seen by a sexual-assault nurse examiner. The internal genital findings were consistent with nonconsensual sexual assault.

After a jury trial, the defendant was found guilty of rape, distribution of a Schedule IV drug to a minor, and contributing to the delinquency of a minor. The co-defendant was found guilty of contributing to the delinquency of a minor.[58]

Gamma Hydroxybutyrate

Gamma hydroxybutyrate (GHB) (also known as "Grievous Bodily Harm," "gamma-OH," "liquid ecstasy," "georgia home boy," and "goop"), is another central nervous system depressant that is used to perpetrate sexual assaults. It is a clear liquid, slightly thicker than water, and can easily be mixed into food or drinks. As with Rohypnol, ingestion of GHB can lead to a variety of symptoms, such as an intense feeling of relaxation, seizures, loss of consciousness, coma, and even death.[59] The effects can be felt within 10 to 20 minutes after ingestion. A coma can occur within 30 to 40 minutes. The drug is traceable in a person's blood for only 4 to 8 hours and in urine for 12 to 15 hours (Figure 10-5).

It is often marketed as an antidepressant and a bodybuilding and weight-control supplement. In addition, the Internet abounds with recipes for homemade GHB. The drug's intoxicating effects have led to its increasing popularity at parties and nightclubs,[60] where in some cases it becomes the tool of sexual offenders. The following case illustrates this point:

Over a two-year period several years ago, two men had been drugging women with GHB at "raves" and nightclubs. After the Los Angeles Sheriff's Department received complaints and had sufficient evidence to obtain a search warrant, officers uncovered more than 2,000 photographs of unconscious, naked women being assaulted and in sexually explicit poses. Many of the victims were unaware they had been violated until they identified themselves in the photographs, and many of the women in the photographs have yet to be identified. The men were convicted of over 50 counts of rape and sexual assault. One of the men received a 77-year sentence; the other was sentenced to 19 years.

▲ FIGURE 10-5 Gamma hydroxybutyrate (GHB)
This drug is a central nervous system depressant that produces a euphoric and hallucinatory state. Generally ingested orally after being mixed in a liquid, reaction to the drug is usually rapid, and an overdose results in unconsciousness that can occur within 20 minutes, and a coma within 30 to 40 minutes. GHB can be tasteless, colorless, and odorless, which makes it easy to add unobtrusively to beverages by individuals who want to intoxicate or sedate others. (©streetdrugs.org)

MALES AS RAPE VICTIMS

People tend to think that only females are the victims of date rape or stranger rape. However, that is an incorrect assumption. For example, several years ago, a man was arrested and charged in Tampa, Florida, with raping seven men. The suspect is alleged to have given the men GHB in their drinks. According to the affidavit filed by the Drug Enforcement Administration, the suspect is accused of having purchased the date-rape drug on the Internet from Canada. Most of the victims were picked up in local bars, but in one case the victim and rapist met on an American online chat room.

OTHER DATE-RAPE DRUGS

Rohypnol and GHB are only two substances used to facilitate rape. A host of other depressants and benzodiazapines can debilitate sexual-assault victims. Valium, Ambien, temazepam, Flexeril, Xanax, and Benadryl are all drugs that may be legitimately obtained but then appropriated for illicit purposes. Five teenage girls who were raped at a party went to the authorities with strong suspicions that they had been drugged. Each victim tested positive for Valium. Two men were later convicted on five counts of rape in connection with the incident.[61]

EVIDENCE COLLECTION AND PROCESSING

Because victims may be unaware, or may only suspect, that an assault has occurred, law enforcement personnel have the critical task of gathering as much physical evidence as they can as quickly as possible.

Investigators should be trying to look for specific types of evidence that have been present in other cases. Drug-related evidence may be found in the glasses from which the victim drank, containers used to mix drinks, and trash cans where these items were discarded. In one case, traces of GHB were found in the box of salt that was used to make margaritas. GHB is often carried in small bottles, such as eyedropper bottles, and is frequently administered in sweet drinks, such as fruit nectars and liquors, to mask its salty taste.

Recipes for making GHB have been found on an offender's computer. In several cases, rapists who use drugs to incapacitate their victims also photograph or videotape them. These pictures led to the identification of additional victims of the same offenders.[62]

Dispatchers or call takers should be trained to recognize the signs and symptoms of drug-facilitated rapes. Call takers should be prepared to handle calls in which victims are confused, incoherent, or unclear about what may have happened, and they should keep victims on the phone until an officer arrives. In addition to the standard instruction that the victim should not bathe or discard the clothes she was wearing, it is imperative to advise the victim not to urinate until she has been transported to a medical facility for an examination and there has been a proper collection of her urine. Because many drugs exit the system within hours, a urine sample should be the first order of business as soon as a sexual assault is suspected. Treating all sexual assaults as possibly drug-induced ensures consistent evidence collection of urine in every case. However, it is important to get a victim's consent before drug screening is conducted.

Many laboratories are not equipped to do proper screening for the types of drugs used in sexual assaults. For an adequate drug screen, the laboratory test should include a screen for benzodiazapines, muscle relaxants, sleep aids, antihistamines, cocaine, marijuana, ketamine, opiates, and other substances that can depress the central nervous system. However, even though a laboratory might have the capacity to test for all these substances, its tests may not be sensitive enough to detect the minute amounts that can trigger criminal prosecution. For instance, most laboratories can detect 50 to 200 nanograms of Rohypnol per milliliter of urine, but even 10 nanograms per milliliter is sufficient for the purposes of an investigation, and it is recommended that GHB should be detected as low as 1 microgram per milliliter.[63]

THE INVESTIGATION

Law enforcement officers cannot rely on forensic toxicology reports alone, because the drugs may already have left the victim's system by the time evidence collection is initiated. The victim may delay contacting police because of embarrassment, guilt, or lack of knowledge regarding the incident. In many cases, it may take a victim time to piece together the events that led to the blackout period. The investigator should remain objective and open-minded when interviewing the victim. A victim's inability to offer a clear and detailed account of the assault may be quite frustrating for the investigating officer, but he/she should always remember that the "not knowing" is even more frustrating and traumatic for the victim. It is quite normal for a victim of drug-induced sexual assault to have significant gaps in her memory and incomplete facts regarding the incident.

Accounts from any people at the scene of the suspected drugging can be very valuable for corroborating any unusual behavior or identifying possible suspects. These witnesses may also be useful in determining who escorted the victim from that location and what statements the suspect made about the victim. They may also provide leads to more evidence.

Inquiring about the victim's level of alcohol consumption before the incident and ascertaining the victim's typical reactions to alcohol may help clarify whether the symptoms resulted from drugging or from "normal" intoxication. Parents, roommates, or other persons residing with the victim can assist in establishing the victim's state of mind and behavior after the incident and in piecing together a time line of events.

EVIDENCE

When the investigation reaches the point at which a search warrant can be obtained for a suspect's residence, car, or place of work, the following items should be included in the search warrant:

- Packages of Rohypnol and other drugs;
- Bubble envelopes and other types of packaging that indicate receipt of a drug shipment;
- Cooking utensils;
- Precursors and reagents;
- Prescriptions (from the United States and other countries), especially for sleeping aids, muscle relaxants, and sedatives;
- Liquor bottles, mixers, and punch bowls (in which drugs may have been mixed with liquor);
- Glasses, soda cans, bottles, and any other containers that might contain drug residue;
- Video and photo camera equipment;
- Photographs or videotapes of the victim;
- Pornographic literature;
- Internet information on Rohypnol and GHB recipes;
- Computers and computer disks.

SEXUAL MOTIVATIONS IN HOMICIDE INVESTIGATION

Male homosexual homicides involving interpersonal violence often present patterns of injuries that can best be described as overkill. These injuries are usually directed to the throat, chest, and abdomen of the victims. It has been suggested, but not empirically proven, that the assaults to the throat take place because of the sexual significance of the mouth and throat in male homosexual sex acts. There may also be certain **psychosexual wounds** present in homosexual and heterosexual

homicides. For example, this may include the cutting of the throat, stabbing wounds to the throat and chest, the slashing of the abdomen, and attacks to the genitalia. These types of injuries are indications of a sexual motive. The psychological significance in an attack to the throat in male homosexual homicides could possibly manifest the destruction of this **substitute sex organ** that engulfs the penis. Anal intercourse is often thought to be the most prevalent sexual behavior between homosexual men. However, one study found that fellatio (mouth to penis oral sex) was the most common mode of sexual expression.[64]

Although most of these interpersonal violence-oriented scenarios involve male participants, there are similar cases of extreme sexual violence involving female victims engaged in a lesbian relationship. One particularly vicious case involved the brutal sexual torture and mutilation murder of a 12-year-old girl in Indiana. The victim, whose first name was Shanda, was killed because she had begun a lesbian relationship with a young girl who had previously dated another lesbian named Melinda. Melinda talked three other teenage girls into helping her kill Shanda. Shanda was taken to a remote location where she was stripped then physically and sexually assaulted. The pathologist later reported findings which indicated numerous multiple insertions had been made into the victim's anus. She was strangled, stabbed, and hit in the head with a tire iron. Her tormentors then poured gasoline on her and set her on fire while she was still alive. All four assailants were convicted and are currently serving long sentences in the Indiana Women's Prison in Indianapolis.

Interpersonal violence-oriented scenarios can also include instances in which a homosexual male solicits or is solicited by another male to engage in fellatio. Young heterosexual male subjects and others, who are described as **hustlers (male prostitutes)**, participate in this conduct as long as the nature of the sexual activities allows them to set the "ground rules." The homosexual male (customer) is allowed to perform fellatio on the subject with the expectation that the subject will not have to reciprocate. When these ground gules are broken, homicide sometimes results. These cases usually involve the homicide of an older homosexual male involved in sexual liaisons with younger males or hustlers. The older male may attempt to carry the activities beyond performing fellatio or demand the younger male reciprocate. The younger male, who usually denies being a homosexual, suddenly has his masculinity threatened and responds with violence and viciously attacks the victim. The injuries inflicted on the victim usually indicate extreme rage and sexual violence. In any event, if presented with the death of a male in a crime scene that suggests sexual activity and in which the throat has been stabbed, cut, or slashed, the investigator should consider the possibility of a homosexually oriented interpersonal violence motivation.

MURDERS INVOLVING FORCED ANAL SEX AND/OR SODOMY

Sodomy is noncoital sex—usually anal or oral sex. Homosexual homicides involving forced anal and/or oral sex are to some extent analogous to rape-homicide among the heterosexual population. These can be extremely brutal homicides, and death occurs as a result of the amount of force used to overcome the victim's resistance, or the victim is killed to prevent identification.

There is some evidence to suggest that when a belt, strap, or ligature is observed around the neck of a male victim, there is a good possibility that forced anal sodomy has occurred. This method of controlling the victim by choking off the air is sometimes employed in prisons by more aggressive male inmates in order to intimidate and sexually dominate other, weaker males.

EXTREME SEXUAL SELF-MUTILATION

Law enforcement officers should be aware of the degree to which individuals are capable of **sexual self-mutilation.** When responding to a crime scene where extreme sexual mutilation is involved, law enforcement officers might assume incorrectly that someone would not or could not do this to him-/herself. If the person is dead, it is more likely than not that an assumption will be made that a criminal homicide has been committed and that a criminal investigation will be initiated. This point, however, is made not to suggest that such an inquiry should not be made—but it is important for investigators to keep an open mind and at least consider the possibility, in the absence of other evidence, that self-mutilation may be involved.

LUST, MURDERS, AND OTHER ACTS OF SEXUAL PERVERSION

In sadomasochistic sex, one partner is the "master," the other is the "slave." The master, who usually has a sadistic personality, obtains sexual pleasure in tying up the slave, whom he then beats or whips. The slave, who is usually a masochist, is sexually aroused from being treated this way. Some sexually-motivated homicides involve bizarre and sadistic methodologies such as **sado-masochism (S&M)** or **bondage and discipline (B&D)** scenarios. A male might be chained to a rack to be whipped by a master, who is dressed in a special leather suit, while the slave might wear a leather discipline mask in a display of submission. In some scenarios, in these B&D sex games, the slave is forcibly raped (anally sodomized) by the master or other dominant participant. In some cases, the slave is urinated or defecated on by others.

AUTOEROTIC DEATHS/SEXUAL ASPHYXIA

Autoerotic deaths/sexual asphyxia occasionally occur as a result of the masochistic activities of the deceased. Typically, this form of death involves a white male who is found partially suspended and sometimes dressed in women's clothing (Figure 10-6). In other cases, the individual may be found completely nude (Figure 10-7). This type of death involves a ligature around the victim's neck, which is suspended from a fixed point usually within easy reach of the decedent. In such cases, there is no indication of suicidal intent, and the death often surprises friends, relatives, and associates. Usually the decedent has no history of mental or sexual disorder.

Individuals who regularly engage in this practice (but, obviously, do not die) report that the pressure from the ligature around their neck reduces oxygen to the brain and thereby heightens the sense of pleasure they receive from the orgasm.

◄FIGURE 10-6

Autoerotic death (sexual asphyxia)
Deaths from accidental asphyxia (asphyxiation) occasionally occur as a result of the voluntary activities of the deceased. The manner of death is described as autoerotic death or sexual asphyxia. The victim, most often a white male, is sometimes dressed in female clothing, as is the case in this photograph. The individual may bind his hands behind his back in such a way so that the binding mechanism can easily be released. Unfortunately, the person sometimes waits too long to release the binding mechanism, lapses into unconsciousness, and dies.

▶ **FIGURE 10-7**
Autoerotic death (sexual asphyxia)
The victim in this photograph was found completely nude. Before death he was viewing pornography and very likely masturbating. Unfortunately, before he had the opportunity to reduce the pressure from the collar around his neck, he lapsed into unconsciousness and died.

Death is attributable to asphyxia. The most common method is neck compression; more exotic forms involve chest compression, airway obstruction, and oxygen exclusion with gas or chemical replacement. Neck compression is illustrated in the first case that follows, and chest compression in the second.

A 33-year-old government employee was found in a rented motel room. He was in an upright position, and his feet were resting on the floor. A T-shirt around his neck suspended him from a room divider. He was attired in a skirt, sweater, brassiere padded with socks, panties, panty hose, and high heels. In the room were two suitcases. One contained men's trousers, shirts, socks, and undergarments. The second contained a knit sweater, skirt, slip, panties, bra, panty hose, and high heels. Investigators determined that he was married, had two pre-school children, had recently been promoted in his job, and was well thought of by his associates.[65]

The victim was a 40-year-old commercial airline pilot who was married and the father of two small children. On his day off, he left home, telling his wife that he was going to target practice. A fisherman discovered him a short time later, crushed against the left rear fender of his 1968 Volkswagen in a large turnaround area at the end of a secluded road. The left door was open and the motor was running. The steering wheel was tied with a rope in an extreme left-turn position and the automatic transmission was in low gear. The tire tracks indicated

that the automobile had been moving in concentric circles. The body was held against the car by a heavy link chain and was totally nude except for a chain harness. The harness had a moderately tight loop around the neck and was bolted in front. The chain passed down the sternum and abdomen and around the waist to form a second loop. From the waist loop, strands of chain passed on each side of the testicles and into the gluteal fold and were secured to the waist loop in the small of the back. A 10-feet length of chain was attached from the waist loop to the rear bumper and had become wound around the rear axle five times. It is not known whether he jogged behind the car or was dragged; however, when he tired of the exercise, he approached the car intending to turn off the motor. In doing so, the chain became slack and the back tire rolled over it, causing the chain to become wound onto the rear axle. The trunk of the car contained his clothing and a zippered bag holding locks, bolts, chains, and wrenches. A lock and key were on the ground beside the body, and another lock was found 20 feet from the body.[66]

Airway obstruction is illustrated in the following case:

The victim, a middle-aged male, was discovered dead in his apartment. He was totally nude and held to a pole that had been fitted into his apartment floor. Several black leather belts had been permanently affixed to the pole. These belts supported the victim from the neck, waist, and legs. Leg irons connected his ankles, handcuffs dangled from one wrist, and a gag was over his mouth. The belt around his neck was so tightly buckled that it lacerated his neck. On removal of the gag, it was found that he had placed so much paper in his mouth that he had been asphyxiated. Evidence of masturbation was also present.

The following is a case of oxygen exclusion with gas replacement:

A 50-year-old dentist was discovered dead in his office by an assistant. He was lying on his stomach, and over his face was a mask that he used to administer nitrous oxide to his patients. The mask was connected to a nitrous oxide container and was operational. His pants were unzipped, and he was thought to have been fondling himself while inhaling the gas.

Each of these cases was ruled accidental, and each occurred while the victim was involved in autoerotic activities. Although the motivation for such activity is not completely understood, asphyxia appears to be the cardinal feature of the act: "A disruption of the arterial blood supply resulting in a diminished oxygenation of the brain . . . will heighten sensations through diminished ego controls that will be subjectively perceived as giddiness, light-headedness, and exhilaration. This reinforces masturbatory sensations."[67] In autoerotic deaths, there does not appear to be a conscious intent to die, although the danger of death may well play a role. The masochistic aspect of this activity is evidenced by the elaborate **bondage** employed. Another masochistic practice associated with sexual asphyxia is the practice of infibulation, or masochism involving the genitals. The fantasies of the individuals who engage in sexual asphyxiation are heavily masochistic, involving such thoughts as one's own "penis being skewered with pins; being tied up in an initiation rite; being the leader of an imperiled group; and being raped by cowboys."[68] Evidence of the fantasy involvement may be found in the form of diaries, erotic literature, pornography, films or photographs of the individual's activities, or other such paraphernalia.

It appears that this phenomenon is quite rare among females, but the following case illustrates that it does occur.[69]

This case involved a 17 year-old girl who was originally thought to have committed suicide but in fact was an autoerotic asphyxiation. Her body was found in the basement of a single-family home occupied by her family. The victim was home alone at the time of the incident. The area the victim selected was secluded from the rest of the home. There was no evidence of any break-in or entry. The victim's brother found her

hanging from a wire noose, which had been affixed to a rusty metal clothes rod. There was a white towel wrapped around the victim's neck, which would have formed a padding between the wire and her neck. She was nude from the waist up and was wearing a pair of black sweat pants. A wet T-shirt was observed approximately 6 feet away and appeared to have been discarded by the deceased. A white 5-gallon bucket was observed lying on its side near the area where the deceased was found. Forensic examination of the bucket revealed latent prints, which were later identified as belonging to the right foot of the deceased, the material on the deceased's hands turned out to be rust from the metal pipe to which the wire had been affixed (Figure 10-8).

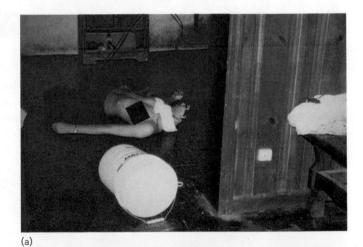

(a)

(b)

▲ **FIGURE 10-8 Female victim of autoerotic death**
(a) This victim reported as a suicide was actually an autoerotic fatality. She had been standing on a plastic bucket, which slipped out from under her feet. She was found hanging from an electrical wire fastened into a noose. (b) Close-up showing padding. The presence of the padding was a crucial factor in the analysis of this case.

THE PSYCHOLOGICAL AUTOPSY

Occasionally the medical examiner or police investigator is confronted with a death and must determine if it is the result of autoerotic or suicidal intent. For resolving questions about the death, there is a technique employed called the **psychological autopsy**, described as follows.

Resolution of unexplained death has long been of concern within law enforcement agencies and for the past quarter century, an object of inquiry within the mental health specialties. The term "autopsy" is usually associated with postmortem examination of human remains to determine the cause of death. The psychological autopsy is an analytical statement prepared by a mental health professional based on the deceased's thoughts, feelings, and behavior.

Its specific purpose, therefore, is to form a logical understanding of death from tangible physical evidence, documented life events, and intangible, often illusive, emotional factors. To accomplish its purpose, the psychological autopsy is structured to address three questions: What was the deceased like? What occurred in his/her life that could have been stressful? For example: marital or relationship problems; business failures; problems with parents; school problems; drug or alcohol addiction, and so on. What were his/her reactions to those stresses? To accomplish this understanding, structured interviews are conducted with friends, relatives, teachers, and business associates of the deceased in the hope of developing psychological motivation for the death and pinpointing patterns of life-threatening behavior.[70]

KEY TERMS

autoerotic death
bondage
bondage and discipline
   (B&D)
corpus delecti
date-rape drugs
elder sexual abuse
exchangeable traces
fellatio
gamma hydroxybutyrate
   (GHB)

hustlers
male prostitutes
minimal fact interview
police sexual violence (PSV)
psychological autopsy
psychosexual wounds
rape
Rohypnol
sado-masochism (S&M)
semen
sexual asphyxiation

sexual battery
sexual self-mutilation
sex-related offenses
sodomy
sperm
substitute sex organ
transgender
trauma-informed response
victim-centered response

REVIEW QUESTIONS

1. Briefly discuss the major factors that should be considered in interviewing rape victims.
2. What is a victim-centered approach to sexual-assault investigation?
3. Describe how an investigator should approach a preliminary interview of a sexual-assault victim.
4. Describe special considerations involved with transgendered victims of rape.
5. Why is it important to understand the differences between deaf victims of sexual assault and hearing victims?
6. What are the therapeutic tasks that must be developed with elders in order to do an accurate assessment of their complaint of sexual abuse?
7. What are some of the major reasons that women do not report rape?
8. Describe the frequency of false sexual-assault reports.
9. Why is the discovery of semen, sperm, and hair valuable in rape investigations?
10. Why is the absence of semen fairly common in rape cases?

11. What items are needed to complete a buccal swab?
12. What items can be surreptitiously collected in an effort to obtain DNA from suspects during questioning?
13. What are condom exchangeable traces composed of?
14. How can condom trace evidence be of value in linking acts of serial rapists?
15. Describe types of electronic evidence that might be collected in a sexual-assault case.
16. What are the effects of Rohypnol and gamma hydroxybutyrate?
17. When laboratories conduct drug screening tests in order to identify drugs that might have been used in sexual assaults, which types of drugs should they screen for?
18. In the investigation of a possible drug-facilitated sexual assault, what kinds of evidence should be collected?
19. What factors should indicate to the investigator that a death may have resulted from accidental sexual asphyxiation?
20. What is a psychological autopsy?

1. Visit the Rape Victim Advocates Web site at www.
   rapevictimadvocates.org. This site provides a discussion on
   the phases and concerns experienced by victims of rape
   trauma syndrome. In addition, it presents an overview of
   males as rape survivors—a topic not frequently addressed.

2. Read the full text of the Stanford rape victim's victim
   impact statement at http://www.paloaltoonline.com
   /news/2016/06/03/stanford-sex-assault-victim-you-took-away
   -my-worth. What are the implications of this type of
   sentencing on sexual-assault investigations?

► Ariel Castro was sentenced to life without parole plus 1000 years for abducting and sexually assaulting three young girls in Cleveland, Ohio between 2002 and 2004. The women finally escaped from Castro in May 2013.

(©Angelo Merendino/Getty Images)

11

CRIMES AGAINST CHILDREN*

CHAPTER OBJECTIVES

1. Recognize types and patterns of burn injuries found in child abuse.

2. Define and discuss shaken-baby syndrome.

3. Explain Munchausen Syndrome by Proxy.

4. Identify types of child molesters, and explain investigative and interview techniques for cases of child molestation.

5. Discuss the differences between coup and contre-coup injuries relevant to traumatic brain injuries.

6. Understand the relationship between child pornography and sex tourism.

7. Outline the types of child pornography.

8. Discuss the use of the computer and the Internet in child pornography.

9. Discuss additional ways that the Internet is used to exploit children.

10. Be able to differentiate between sudden death syndrome and physical abuse.

11. Understand what sudden infant death syndrome (SIDS) is and its misconceptions.

12. Discuss the prevailing theories in SIDS research.

13. Understand criminal homicide as a possibility in SIDS deaths.

14. Describe the profile of the infant abductor.

15. Outline the assessments and investigative procedures used to determine whether a child has run away or has been abducted.

16. Discuss sex-offender registration and community notification laws.

17. Describe the personality traits and behaviors of individuals inclined to commit school crime.

18. Understand the role of law enforcement in school crime.

*Robert W. Taylor and Jennifer Davis-Lamm updated and revised this chapter for this edition.

Probably no other crimes are more emotionally laden than those involving children as victims. Police officers and investigators often speak of the intense emotion associated with viewing innocent children as victims of crime. Unfortunately, incidents of crime against children have increased dramatically during the past decade. Today, their prevalence seems to have reached epidemic proportions. It takes little effort to find reports of child abuse and assault in newspapers, on television, and from other media sources. As a result, increasing numbers of police departments have investigators who are assigned exclusively to the investigation of crimes against children. For this reason, this chapter focuses on issues of child abuse and assault, including some of the techniques and problems associated with investigating these crimes.

Crimes perpetrated against children occur in many forms and contexts. Children may experience abuse, for example, that results in burn injuries; yet deliberate burning often goes unrecognized. It is especially important in such cases that investigators establish good rapport with hospital workers and, particularly, emergency medical technicians, who probably are the first persons to see the child's injuries. After discussing burn injuries, the chapter explains shaken-baby syndrome and Munchausen Syndrome by Proxy, two crimes that have recently received much media attention. Next, the chapter addresses the investigation of sexual crimes against children, such as molestation. This type of investigation is one of the saddest experiences in any officer's career, and few officers are able to complete one without some feeling of anger and remorse, particularly since in many cases these crimes are committed against children by their own parents or guardians.

Also discussed in this chapter are sex tourism, and child pornography, crimes that are rapidly increasing owing to facilitation by the Internet. Other types of Internet exploitation are also covered. Next, infant abduction is defined and analyzed. In regard to older missing children, strategies are provided for use by investigators in determining whether a child has been abducted or has run away. The chapter concludes with sections on sex-offender registration and on crimes in schools, including overviews on threat assessments and on personality traits and behaviors of troubled children who commit crimes in schools.

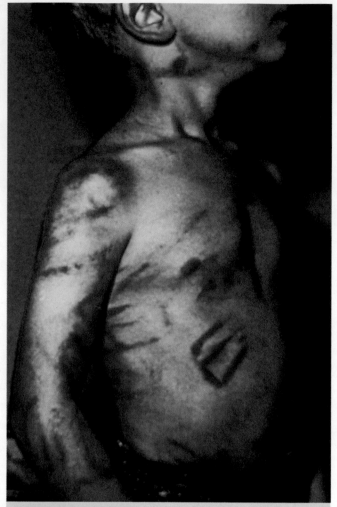

▲ **FIGURE 11-1**

Boy beaten with the buckle end of a belt

One of the most common instruments used to physically abuse children is the belt. While the leather portion of a belt can inflict significant pain, the buckle end can cause serious injuries to young children, as is depicted in this photo.

ASSAULTS AGAINST CHILDREN

The most common cause of child deaths is physical abuse, often perpetrated by the parents. The clinical term commonly used to describe physically abused children is the **battered-child syndrome.** Abuse of children takes various forms, from minor assaults to flagrant physical torture. Many times these injuries cannot or will not be explained by the parents, or the story seems inconsistent with the injuries received. For example, bruises in various stages of healing generally vary in color. Thus, one should be suspicious of an explanation of such injuries as being caused by a fall from a bike. Intentional injuries tend to occur most frequently on the face, back, ribs, buttocks, genitals, palms, or soles of the feet. Although abusers use a wide variety of instruments, the two most common are belt and electric cord (Figure 11-1).

The possibility of abuse should be considered for any child exhibiting evidence of bone fracture, subdermal hematoma, soft-tissue swelling, or skin bruising; for any child who dies suddenly; or for any child when the degree and the type of injury are at variance with the history given regarding the occurrence of the trauma.[1] Bruises, in particular, are the most common signs of physical abuse. In a systematic review of studies comparing the patterns of bruising among normal and abused children, Maguire and associates[2] identified a number of patterns distinguishing accidental bruises from nonaccidental bruises. Primarily, they found that bruises indicative of physical abuse were not located on bony prominences, such as knees and elbows, but rather on the head, chest, abdomen, and hands. Moreover, the bruises among physically abused children were more likely to be clustered, greater in size, observable during all seasons as opposed to warm months, and documented among children less than 3 years of age. Note, however, that bruising may also be a manifestation of an underlying medical condition (for example,

leukemia);[3] therefore, investigators should consider bruises in a broader context to include the child's medical history and environmental factors.

BURN INJURIES AND CHILD ABUSE

Although general awareness of the magnitude of child abuse is increasing, deliberate injury by burning is often unrecognized. Burn injuries make up about 10% of all child-abuse cases, and about 10% of hospital admissions of children to burn units are the result of child abuse. In comparison with accidentally burned children, abused children are significantly younger and

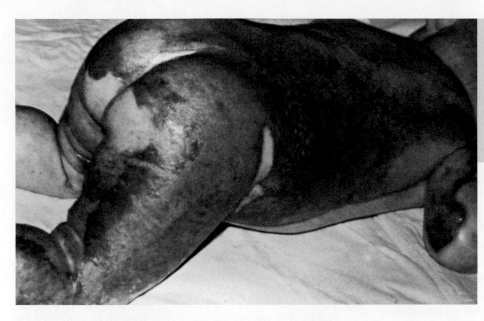

◄FIGURE 11-2
Infant scalded with hot water
This infant was scalded with hot water by his mother as punishment for not responding to toilet training. Such unreasonable and absurd expectations are not uncommon for certain types of abusive parents.

have longer hospital stays and higher mortality rates. Child burn victims are almost always under the age of 10, with the majority under the age of 2.[4]

Children are burned for different reasons. Immersion burns may occur during toilet training, with the perpetrator immersing the child in scalding water for cleaning or as punishment (Figure 11-2). Hands may be immersed in a pot of scalding hot water as punishment for playing near the stove, or a person may place a child in a hot oven as punishment or with homicidal intentions.

Inflicted burns often leave characteristic patterns of injury that fortunately cannot be concealed. Along with the history of the burn incident, these patterns are primary indicators of inflicted burns versus accidental ones. Findings in response to the following questions can raise or lower the index of suspicion, as well as help to determine whether a burn was deliberately inflicted:

- Is the explanation of what happened consistent with the injury? Are there contradictory or varying accounts of the method or time of the "accident" or other discrepancies in the witnesses' descriptions of what happened?
- Does the injury have a clean line of demarcation, parts within or immediately around the injured area that are not burned; a burn pattern inconsistent with the injury account; or any other typical characteristics of an inflicted burn? Are the burns located on the buttocks, the area between the child's legs, or the ankles, wrists, palms, or soles?
- Are other injuries present, such as fractures, healed burns, or bruises?
- Are the child's age and level of development compatible with the caretaker's and witnesses' account of the injury?
- Was there a delay in seeking medical attention? (Less serious burns may have been treated at home.)
- Does the caretaker insist there were no witnesses to the injury incident, including the caretaker?

- Do those who were present seem to be angry or resentful toward the child or each other?
- A detailed history, including previous trauma, presence of recent illnesses, immunization status, and the status of routine medical care, is critical, as is careful documentation of the scene of the injury, including photographs and drawings. To investigate a burn injury, the investigator should do the following:
  - Stay focused on the facts, and proceed slowly and methodically.
  - Ask questions, be objective, and reenact the incident.
  - Treat each case individually.

The incidence of further injury and death is so high in deliberate burn cases that it is critical for all concerned persons to be aware of the indicators of this form of child abuse.

TYPOLOGIES OF BURNS

Children may incur various types of burn injuries. A burn may be classified by how severe, or "deep," it is or by how the injury occurred. It is essential to have an understanding of the different grades of burn severity and to recognize the cause of a burn by observing the patterns that are evident when a child's skin comes into direct contact with hot objects or liquid. An informed analysis of burn cause and severity is fundamental in ascertaining whether a child's injury is deliberate or accidental.

MEDICAL CLASSIFICATION OF BURN SEVERITY

Physicians primarily categorize burns as having either partial thickness or full thickness (Table 11-1). Only an experienced medical practitioner can determine how deeply a burn has penetrated the skin, but there are some features of partial- and full-thickness burns that can be observed immediately after the incident:

TABLE 11-1	Classification of Burns
CLASSIFICATION	**CHARACTERISTICS**
First degree	*Partial-thickness burns:* • Erythema (localized redness) • Sunburn-like • Not included when calculating burn size • Usually heal by themselves
Second degree	*Partial-thickness burns:* • Part of skin damaged • Have blisters containing clear fluid • Pink underlying tissue • Often heal by themselves
Third degree	*Full-thickness burns:* • Full skin destroyed • Deep red tissue underlying blister • Presence of bloody blister fluid • Muscle and bone possibly destroyed • Require professional treatment
Fourth degree	*Full-thickness burns:* • Penetrate deep tissue to fat, muscle, bone • Require immediate professional treatment

- Patches of reddened skin that blanch with fingertip pressure and then refill are shallow partial-thickness burns. Blisters usually indicate deeper partial thickness burning, especially if the blisters increase in size just after the burn occurs.
- A leathery or dry surface with a color of white, tan, brown, red, or black indicates a full-thickness burn. The child feels no pain, because the nerve endings have been destroyed. Small blisters may be present but will not increase in size.

Investigators must develop good rapport with medical personnel, including both the hospital staff workers involved with the case and emergency medical technicians (EMTs). The EMTs, especially, can provide a wealth of information owing to the fact that they were probably the first persons to see the child's injuries. Also, an experienced social service investigator can provide valuable information regarding family history and any observed patterns of abuse.

Several factors affect the severity of a burn. A child's age plays a part in how severely the child is injured by a particular incident. For example, an adult will experience a significant injury of the skin after 1 minute of exposure to water at 127°F, 30 seconds of exposure at 130°F, and 2 seconds of exposure at 150°F. A child, however, will suffer a more severe burn in less time than an adult will, because children have thinner skin. As such, a young child's skin will be severely harmed even more rapidly and by less heat than will an older child's skin.

Furthermore, certain parts of the body have thinner skin, including the front of the trunk, inner thighs, bottom of forearms, and inner-arm area. Thicker-skinned areas include the palms, soles, back, scalp, and back of the neck. Given the same cause, burns incurred in thinner-skin areas tend to be more severe than burns incurred in areas protected by thicker skin.

CAUSES OF BURN INJURIES

The severity of a burn is also directly influenced by the circumstances that caused the burn:

- Scald burns occur when the child comes into contact with hot liquid.
- Contact burns occur when the child encounters a hot solid object or flame.

Scald Burns

Scald burns are the most common type of burn injury to a child. They are caused by hot liquids—hot tap water, boiling water, hot drinks such as tea or coffee, and thicker liquids such as soup or grease. Scald burns may occur in the form of spill/splash injuries or as immersion burns. Most deliberate burns are scald burns caused by immersion in hot tap water (Figure 11-2).

Spill/Splash Injuries. **Spill/splash injuries** occur when a hot liquid falls from a height onto the victim. The burn pattern is characterized by irregular margins and nonuniform depth. Ascertaining the area of the skin where the scalding liquid first struck the victim is the key to determining whether a burn is accidental or nonaccidental. Water travels downward and cools as it moves away from the initial contact point. When a pan of water is spilled or thrown on a person's chest, the initial contact point shows a splash pattern. The area below this point tapers, creating what is called an "arrow-down" pattern. This pattern is more commonly seen in assaults on adults than in assaults on children.

If the child was wearing clothing at the time of injury, the pattern may be altered. This is why it is important to determine whether clothing was worn and, if possible, to retain the clothing. Depending on the material, the water may have been against the skin longer, which would result in a deeper injury and pattern. A fleece sleeper, for instance, will change the course of the water and hold the temperature longer in one area as opposed to a thin, cotton T-shirt.

Questions to ask in a scalding-injury investigation include these:

- Where were the caretakers at the time of the accident?
- How many persons were home at the time?
- How tall is the child? How far can he or she reach?
- Can the child walk, and are the child's coordination and development consistent with his or her age?
- How much water was in the pan, and how much does it weigh?

- What is the height to the handle of the pan when the pan is on the stove (or counter or table)?
- Was the oven on at the time (thus making it unlikely that the child could have climbed onto the stove)?
- Does the child habitually play in the kitchen or near the stove? Does the child usually climb on the cabinets or table?
- Has the child been scolded for playing in the kitchen? For touching the stove?

It is unusual for a child to incur an accidental scald burn on his or her back, but it has happened. As in all burn investigations, factors other than location of the burn must be considered before concluding that the injury was nonaccidental. Deliberate burning by throwing a hot liquid on a child is usually done either as punishment for playing near a hot object or in anger. However, the child may have been caught in the crossfire between two fighting adults and then been accused of having spilled the liquid accidentally.

Immersion Burns. When a child falls or is placed into a tub or other container of hot liquid, **immersion burns** result (Figure 11-3). In a deliberate immersion burn, the depth of the burn is uniform. The wound borders are very distinct, sharply defined "waterlines" with little tapering of depth at the edges, and there is little evidence that the child thrashed about during the immersion, indicating that the child was held in place. Occasionally, there may be bruising in the area of the soft tissue where the child was being forcibly held.

Only children with deliberate immersion burns sustain deep burns of the buttocks and/or the area between the anus and the genitals. The motivation for this type of injury generally involves punishment for failing to toilet train or for soiling of clothing. Dirty diapers or soiled clothing may be found in the bathroom. The water in the bathtub may be deeper than what is normal for bathing an infant or child and may be so hot that the first responding adult at the scene is unable to immerse his/her own hand in it.

Several key variables must be observed in investigating immersion burns:

- *The temperature of the water:* Variables that must be taken into account include the temperature of the water heater, the ease with which it can be reset, and recent usage of water.
- *The time of exposure:* This is an unknown that can sometimes be estimated from the burn pattern and its depth.
- *The depth of the burn:* Several days may need to pass before the true depth of the burn can be determined.
- *The occurrence of "sparing":* There may be areas within or immediately around the burn site that were not burned.

When a child's hand is forced into hot water, the child will make a fist, thus "sparing" the palm and discounting the statement that the child reached into the pan of hot water for something. A child whose body is immersed in hot water will attempt to fold up, and sparing will show as creases in the abdomen. Curling up the toes when the foot is forced into a hot liquid

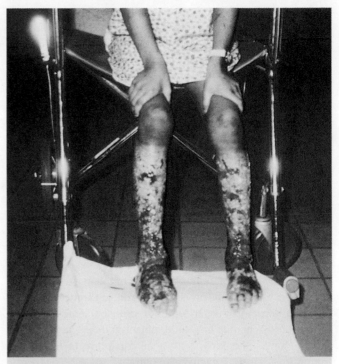

▲ **FIGURE 11-3   Immersion burn**
This child was forcibly immersed in a tub full of hot water by her mother. Note the end of the immersion line near the knees. In this case, the child's legs were placed in water hot enough to cause significant blistering. The mother who was in the process of divorcing the child's father became angry with her when she caught the child talking to the father on the phone.

will spare part of the soles of the feet or the area between the toes. The area where the child was held by the perpetrator will also be spared. These flexing actions prevent burning within the body's creases, causing a striped configuration of burned and unburned zones, or a "zebra" pattern.

Deliberate immersion burns can often be recognized by one of the following characteristic patterns:

- *Doughnut pattern in the buttocks:* When a child falls or steps into a hot liquid, the immediate reaction is to thrash about, try to get out, and jump up and down. When a child is held in scalding hot bathwater, the buttocks are pressed against the bottom of the tub so forcibly that the water will not come into contact with the center of the buttocks, sparing this part of the buttocks and causing the burn injury to have a doughnut pattern.
- *Sparing the soles of the feet:* Another instance of sparing occurs in a child whose buttocks and feet are burned but whose soles have been spared. If a caretaker's account is that the child was left in the bathroom and told not to get into the tub, and that the caretaker then heard screaming and returned to find the child jumping up and down in the water, the absence of burns on the soles of

the child's feet is evidence that the account is not true. A child cannot jump up and down in hot water without burning the bottoms of the feet.

- *Stocking- or glove-pattern burns:* Stocking and glove patterns are seen when feet or hands are held in the water. The line of demarcation is possible evidence that the injury was not accidental.
- *Waterlines:* A sharp line on the lower back, or in some cases the legs, indicates that the child was held still in the water. A child falling into the water would show splash and irregular-line patterns. The waterline on a child's torso, for example, indicates how deep the water was at the time of the incident.

Contact Burns

Contact burns occur when a child's skin comes into contact with a flame or a hot solid object. A contact-burn injury may be caused by a curling iron, steam iron, cigarette or lighter, fireplace, stovetop burner, outdoor grill, or some other hot implement. When a hot solid object touches a child, the child's skin is "branded" with a mirror image of the object. Flame burns are a much less common cause of deliberate injury. When they do occur, they are characterized by extreme depth and are relatively well-defined as compared with accidental flame burns.

When a child accidentally touches a hot object or the object falls on the child, there is usually a lack of pattern in the burn injury, since the child quickly moves away from the object. However, even brief accidental contact, such as falling against a hot radiator or grate, can cause a second-degree-burn imprint of the pattern of the object.

Distinguishing Nonaccidental from Accidental Contact Burns.

Nonaccidental burns caused by a hot solid object are the most difficult to distinguish from accidental injuries. Cigarette and electric steam iron burns are the most frequent types of these injuries. Cigarette burns, especially multiple burns on the child's feet, back, or buttocks, are unlikely to have been caused by an accident; therefore, they are more suspect than individual burns in the area of the child's face and eyes, which can occur accidentally if the child walks or runs into an adult's lit cigarette held at waist height. Accidental burns are usually more shallow, irregular, and less well defined than are deliberate burns.

Purposely inflicted "branding" injuries usually mirror the objects that caused the burn (such as cigarette lighters and curling irons) and are much deeper than the superficial and random burns caused by accidentally touching these objects. Most accidental injuries with hot steam or curling irons occur when the hot item is grasped or falls. These are usually second-degree injuries that are randomly placed, as might be the case when a hot electric steam iron strikes the skin in multiple places as it falls. It is important to know where the iron was—for example, was it on an ironing board or a coffee table at the child's height?

Another source of accidental burns is contact with items that have been exposed for prolonged periods to hot sun. Pavement in hot sun, which can reach a temperature of 176°F, can burn a child's bare feet; however, such burns are not likely to be deep. A child placed in a car seat that has been in a car in the sun can receive second- and even third-degree burns. Full-thickness burns have also resulted from contact with a hot seat-belt buckle.

The following key questions will help in determining whether contact burns are accidental or nonaccidental:

- Where is the burn injury, and could the child reach the area unassisted?
- Does the child normally have access to the item (such as a cigarette lighter) that caused the injury?
- How heavy is the item, and how strong is the child? For instance, is the electric steam iron a compact, travel-size one that a small child could lift or a full-size home model that might be too heavy to lift?
- Is there any sparing that would be significant to the injury?
- How was the item heated, and how long did it take for the item to become hot enough to cause the injury?
- Is the injury clean and crisp, with the distinctive pattern of the object, or is it shallow or irregular, as from a glancing blow? Several cleanly defined injuries, especially on an older child, could indicate that the child was held motionless by a second perpetrator while the first perpetrator carefully branded the child.
- Are there multiple burns or other healed burns?
- Has the child been punished before for playing with or being too close to the hot object?

UNEXPLAINED CHILD FATALITIES

For those who work in law enforcement, there are few incidents that will affect them more than responding to the death of a child. Officers are trained to deal with mass shootings, decomposing bodies, and gruesome vehicle accidents, and yet many law enforcement officers find any one of those incidents far preferable than showing up on the scene where a child has died. Unfortunately, child death is a reality that most officers will have to face at some point in their career. These types of calls are certainly traumatic for all involved, and are often less straightforward than other types of homicides or unexplained deaths. Because of the emotion and confusion involved in child death cases, law enforcement officers—even well-meaning and well-educated ones—often make mistakes that can affect the outcome of an investigation.

Not all child fatalities that police come across are homicides, obviously. More often than not, a child fatality is easily identified as accidental—such as a drowning or a pedestrian-vehicle incident—whereas others will be quickly attributed to natural causes. But other times, it's either not obvious why or how a child dies—or it is all too clear that they have suffered either acute or chronic maltreatment at the hands of an adult. Nonetheless, law enforcement officers must understand that

ALL sudden and unexplained child deaths must be investigated thoroughly, because the consequences of improperly investigating such an incident mean that subtle clues can be missed or evidence can be misread, and a case that should have been treated as a homicide might be overlooked. Or, in other cases, a conclusion of homicide may be unwarranted. And finally, as we saw in the JonBenet Ramsey case, investigative focus may be attributed to parties that were not responsible for the death of the child, wasting valuable time that could be spent tracking the individual or individuals truly responsible. Any one of these scenarios is, of course, objectionable to law enforcement, and it is up to first responders to set the investigation on a course that will avoid any of these outcomes.

Sudden and unexplained child deaths are, according to the Office of Juvenile Justice and Delinquency Prevention, any death that involves a child who was not under the care of a physician for a known illness or disease. The death can be from either natural or unnatural causes, including: natural diseases such as flu or cancer; unsafe sleeping environments; trauma; accidental poisoning; homicide; and Sudden Infant Death Syndrome, or SIDS.[5]

SUDDEN INFANT DEATH SYNDROME

Although **sudden infant death syndrome (SIDS)** is a medical phenomenon, not a crime, a lack of knowledge about its elements can cause individuals involved in its investigation to erroneously conclude they have a criminal homicide.

Health professionals in the past had limited contact with SIDS families, because SIDS rarely occurs outside the home. A few babies have died of SIDS while hospitalized, but the usual case involves a baby who is brought to the hospital emergency room and is pronounced dead on arrival. As a result, many physicians and nurses have had little knowledge of SIDS.[6]

What Is Sudden Infant Death Syndrome?

Simply defined, SIDS (also often referred to as *crib death*) is the sudden and unexpected death of an apparently healthy infant that remains unexplained after the performance of a complete autopsy. On the average, two of every 1,000 infants born alive succumb to SIDS, and it is the leading cause of death among infants 1 week to 1 year of age.

In the majority of instances, the baby is apparently in good health prior to death and feeds without difficulty. Although there may be evidence of a slight cold or stuffy nose, there is usually no history of serious upper respiratory infection. In most cases, the infant is placed in a crib to sleep and is found dead several hours later.

Most SIDS deaths occur between November and March. Sudden changes in temperature may trigger SIDS. The risk of SIDS appears to be highest in crowded dwellings; in infants of young mothers; in males; in nonwhites regardless of socioeconomic status; in families of lower socioeconomic status regardless of race; and in premature infants. Twins have an increased risk of

SIDS, which is likely a consequence of their low birth weight and premature birth. SIDS occurs in both breast-fed and bottle-fed babies. Most victims are between the ages of 1 and 6 months, with the highest frequency of occurrence between 2 and 4 months.

Characteristics of SIDS Victims' Appearance

- Usually normal state of nutrition and hydration
- Blood-tinged, frothy fluids around mouth and nostrils, indicative of pulmonary edema
- Vomitus on the face
- Diaper wet and full of stool
- Bruiselike marks on head or body limbs (postmortem pooling or settling of blood in dependent body parts)

Autopsy Findings

- Some congestion and edema of the lungs
- Petechial hemorrhages in thymus, heart, and lungs
- Minor evidence of respiratory tract inflammation

Misconceptions about SIDS

- *Aspiration, choking:* The babies do not inhale or choke on their feeding.
- *Unsuspected illness:* Particularly if the baby had a cold, the parents may feel guilty about not having taken the child to the doctor. If the baby was checked by the doctor, the parents (and the doctor) may wonder what the doctor missed. In any case, neither is at fault.
- *Freezing:* Although the body may be cold when discovered, this is a postmortem change.
- *Accidental injury, neglect, or abuse:* Law enforcement officers should not jump to the wrong conclusions because of the appearance of the infant. The results of accusations of wrongdoing have been tragic. A few innocent and grief-stricken parents have been accused of murdering their babies and put in jail. Appearances can be deceiving.

SIDS Research—Prevailing Theories

There are a number of theories about the causes of SIDS. One of the theories about the mechanism of SIDS is that it results from spontaneous, protracted apnea, or cessation of breathing. Considerable progress in understanding SIDS has been made by the SIDS Institute at the University of Maryland. In comprehensive tests of 1,000 babies, it was found that fully 10% stopped breathing for periods longer than 15 to 20 seconds or their heart rate dropped below 80 beats per minute. Detected in time, such infants are considered at risk for SIDS and are monitored with an electronic device that sets off an alarm if the child's breathing or heart rate drops below a certain level.

The most significant research supporting the apnea theory has been done by Dr. Richard Naeye of the Pennsylvania State University College of Medicine. Dr. Naeye began to look for structural changes in the infant's body during the autopsy that would indicate chronic lack of oxygen, attributable to repeated and relatively long periods of apnea.

He found the following changes in a large group of SIDS victims:

- The walls of the small arteries in the lungs were thicker than normal.
- The wall of the right ventricle of the heart was thicker than normal.
- The relative retention of brown fat around the adrenal gland was greater than normal.
- There was abnormal retention of fetal capacity for the production of red blood cells in the liver.

In a study conducted several years ago and reported in the *New England Journal of Medicine,* it was found that infants who usually slept in the face-down position had a significantly higher risk of SIDS than those who slept on their back.[7] Respiratory obstruction in relation to the position of infants has also been studied.[8] It was concluded that the air passage of an infant is impaired when the body is placed face down on any type of mattress or pillow. And in a 2006 study, researchers at Children's Hospital Boston and Harvard Medical School revealed that infants that die of SIDS often have abnormalities in the brainstem, particularly in those areas controlling breathing, blood pressure, temperature, and heart rate. This finding is the strongest evidence to date that suggests physiological brain differences may place some infants with an increased risk of SIDS.[9]

THE POLICE OFFICER'S ROLE

The law enforcement officer serves a key role in the SIDS case and is often the first person to encounter the shock, grief, and guilt experienced by the parents. It may be an experience such as this: The officer responds to a call, entering a house where an infant has just died. The mother is hysterical, incoherent, and unable to clarify what happened. The father is dazed yet tearless; he is confused and responding evasively. As the officer proceeds, the mother continues to sob, blaming herself. The infant is in the cradle, its head covered with a blanket. When the blanket is removed, the officer notes a small amount of blood-tinged fluid in and around the mouth and nose and bruiselike marks on the body where the blood settled after death.

Was the death a result of illness, abuse, neglect, or unexplained causes? The officer will make a preliminary assessment based on the information obtained at the scene. If the circumstances are unclear, an autopsy may establish the need for criminal investigation.

Information to Be Obtained by the Police Investigator at the Scene

Obtaining answers to the following questions are of considerable value to both law enforcement officers and medical personnel in determining the cause of death.

- Age, date of birth, birth weight (if known), race, and sex.
- Who was the last person to see the infant alive (date and time)?
- Who discovered the dead infant (date and time)?
- What was the place of death (the child's crib or bed, the parent's bed, or elsewhere)?
- What was the position of the infant when found dead?
- Was the infant's original position changed (why and by whom)?
- If resuscitation was attempted, note the method employed and the name of the person who attempted the resuscitation.
- Had the infant been sick recently? Have a cold or sniffles? Any other minor illnesses?
- Was a physician consulted about the recent illness? If so, who was the physician?
- What treatment was prescribed?
- Was the child on any medication? If so, what type?
- When was the child last seen by a physician? If so, why and by whom?
- Was the infant exposed to any illnesses recently?
- Had there been any illnesses in the family recently?
- When was the time of the last feeding? What was the child fed?
- Had there been a difference in the appearance or behavior of the child within the last few days?
- Have there been any other SIDS deaths in the family?
- If someone other than the parent was caring for the child, have any other children died in his or her custody?[10]

CRIMINAL HOMICIDE AS A POSSIBILITY

In spite of the findings just discussed, the police must be sensitive to the possibility of criminal homicide. Some studies raise the specter that in recent years there may have been cases in which children had actually been murdered but the deaths were incorrectly classified as SIDS.

Probably the most commonly missed method of criminal homicide in infants and young children is smothering. Smothering is, after impulse homicides, the second most common type of homicide in infants. In infants, smothering is very easily accomplished. One closes off the child's nose with two fingers, at the same time pushing up on the lower jaw with the palm to occlude the airway. Other methods have involved placing a pillow or towel over the child's face, and pressing down; pushing the face down into bed clothing; or just covering the nose and mouth with one's hand. These descriptions are based on either confessions or witnessed homicides. In a few cases, attempted homicides have been videotaped.[11]

For example:

- Dr. David Southall of City General Hospital in Stoke-on-Trent, England, set up video cameras in the hospital rooms of children brought in after parents reported that the children had stopped breathing and nearly died. The cameras captured 39 instances of mothers trying to smother their babies. Fully one-third of these "near-miss-SIDS" cases, it is estimated, are actually cases of Munchausen Syndrome by Proxy. Overall, Dr. Southall concludes that 5 to 10% of SIDS deaths are in fact infanticides.[12]

- In an unpublished study, Dr. Thomas Truman concluded that as many as one-third of the repeated near-SIDS cases at what may be the most prestigious SIDS center in the United States may be cases of Munchausen Syndrome by Proxy. While serving a fellowship at Massachusetts General Hospital from 1993 to 1996, Truman analyzed the medical records of 155 children treated at the hospital. In 56 of these cases, the child's chart contained circumstantial evidence of possible abuse. One baby suffered repeated breathing crises at home, turning blue and limp, but only when the mother (and no one else) was present. Another one had no breathing problems during the six months he spent in a local hospital, but the day he went home alone with his mother he had a life-threatening breathing emergency. The authorities were alerted to the possibility of the case, but no action was taken. The child died one year after being sent home.[13]

It should be noted that if death has been induced by intentional suffocation, there may be petechial hemorrhaging of the eyes and surrounding areas. (See Chapter 9, "Injury and Death Investigation," for a more detailed discussion of this condition.)

TRAUMATIC BRAIN INJURIES AND DEATH

In the minority of cases, children are killed by someone outside of their immediate family and are generally murdered outside of their homes. Statistically, these cases are relatively rare, with only about 16% of child fatalities attributed to strangers. Children that are victims of these types of homicides may not have any known history of neglect or abuse by their parents or families but can show obvious signs of trauma and sexual assault at death. These children tend to be between the ages of 6 and 11, far older than the usual victims of child abuse, burn injuries, or SIDS, as previously discussed.

Most child deaths are directly related to injuries that are a result of a specific act of hitting, striking, or physically abusing the victim. Prime examples of such crimes occur as the result of an adult caregiver or parent striking the child in the head. Often the child (especially if the child is younger or is an infant), is taken unconsciously to the hospital emergency room under the ruse of "falling out of the bed" or "falling down the stairs." Such is the case of little, 14-month old Angela who was taken to the emergency room of an urban hospital in a semiconscious state. According to her mother and accompanying boyfriend, Angela had fallen out of her crib and was found lying "lifeless" on the floor. After a courageous effort, doctors in the emergency room were unable to revive Angela, and she died within hours from **blunt-force trauma** to the head; that is, injuries derived from forces transmitted by objects that have relatively broad surfaces, with thick or round surfaces. These types of injuries often cause significant injury to the brain if the trauma is directed to the head. Under such suspicious circumstances, the police were called to investigate and were quickly confronted by a child death as a result a massive brain **hemorrhage** (a significant injury causing extensive bleeding into the surrounding tissue). The question, however, was "what" caused the hemorrhage? Was Angela's death a tragic accident resulting from a fall from her crib as reported by her mother and boyfriend, or was she intentionally struck in the head by someone causing her death?

"COUP-CONTRECOUP" INJURIES

From the French word for head, "coup" injuries are observed at the direct site of the impact of the head and a moving object. For instance, a person hit on the side of the head with a rock will usually have significant bruising and laceration at the point of contact with the rock. In serious cases, the brain will be involved on one side—the side in which force was transmitted. A "contrecoup" injury occurs inside the skull on the opposite side of the area of impact. In these cases, a moving head is abruptly stopped and inertia keeps the brain moving within the skull. While the exact mechanism of the injury is the subject of much debate—the brain either "tears" from the opposite side of the skull when the head is stopped or "bounces" back from the inside of the head and collides with the opposite side of the skull—the result is exactly the same: a significant internal injury or hemorrhage to the brain observable on the opposite side of the head (inside the skull) in which contact with a fixed object occurred. To reemphasize, contrecoup injuries are internal to the skull and can only be observed through a CT (Computed Tomography) scan, MRI (Magnetic Resonance Imaging), or during autopsy (Figure 11-4).

Although these types of injuries are not observed only in children, and are often seen as a result of fights or altercations between adults, "coup-contrecoup" injuries occur only to the brain and head and are often the key evidence refuting suspicious statements by suspects. In many child fatalities there are no witnesses to the death. The child's death took place in the privacy of the home, witnessed only by his/her assailant. With a small child, family members are often the only ones who know the child's whereabouts and schedules, and it is difficult to corroborate accounts. Trace evidence is also hard to come by in child fatality investigations. If a child dies of maltreatment in his or her home, the fingerprints of his/her caretakers will obviously be everywhere throughout the house, making it impossible to link them directly to the crime itself. And interestingly, most child deaths are not the result of the use of a traditional weapon (such as a firearm or knife). Indeed, most are the result of blunt-force trauma to the head or to another body organ and are rarely observable to the naked eye.

Returning to our illustrative case of 14-month old Angela, an autopsy clearly revealed that the injury to her brain was the result of a large coup injury only—meaning her head was *not* moving, and she did not accidentally fall from her crib. In Figure 11-5, note the extensive hemorrhaging or bleeding from the left (not right) side of her brain and the absence of any "contrecoup"

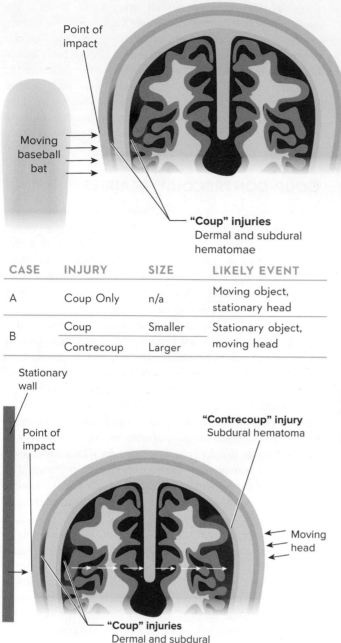

CASE	INJURY	SIZE	LIKELY EVENT
A	Coup Only	n/a	Moving object, stationary head
B	Coup	Smaller	Stationary object, moving head
	Contrecoup	Larger	

▲ **FIGURE 11-4** **Coup-Contrecoup injuries**
Coup-contrecoup injuries are particularly unique to the head and skull. A careful and important determination of these wounds can assist investigators in determining if the injury occurred while the head was in motion or stationary at the time of the trauma contact. (Source: Dr. Zug Standing Bear, 2010)

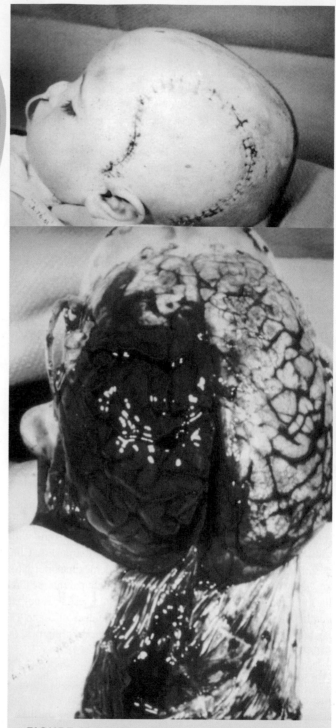

▲ **FIGURE 11-5** **Coup-Contrecoup injuries at autopsy**
Note that in the top picture, "Angela" appears with a repaired and stitched skull as a result of the valiant efforts of emergency room doctors to save her life. However, the autopsy clearly shows massive coup hemorrhage on the left side of the brain with no countercoup injuries on the right side. Angela's head was stationary at the time of trauma contact, physical evidence that conflicted with statements indicating that she fell from her crib.

injuring on the right (not left) side of the brain. Confronted with this evidence, the boyfriend to the mother of Angela confessed to having "kicked" the child in the head while wearing steel-toed work boots. According to the suspect, he just wanted to stop the child from "crying and being fussy." Unfortunately, attempting to stop a child from crying often acts as the trigger to much more violent and abusive behavior toward the child.

SHAKEN-BABY SYNDROME

The phrase "shaken-baby syndrome" was coined to explain instances in which severe intracranial trauma occurs in the absence of signs of external head trauma. **Shaken-baby syndrome (SBS)** is the severe intentional application of violent force (shaking), in one or more episodes, that results in intracranial injuries to the child. Physical abuse of children by shaking usually is not an isolated event. Many shaken infants show evidence of previous trauma. Frequently, the shaking has been preceded by other types of abuse.[14]

Those who inflict SBS on children are often caretakers who shook the child violently in response to some kind of trigger. Often, that trigger is incessant crying that causes an inappropriate frustration response in the caretaker. In SBS cases, children show a cluster of injuries upon autopsy, including brain swelling from direct brain damage, retinal hemorrhages or other eye damage, and bleeding under the membrane that covers and protects the brain (Figure 11-6). However, what makes these cases difficult for police is that the child will often show no outward signs of injury when first responders arrive.[15] Many caretakers take SBS victims to the hospital after the child begins to show signs of injury, such as unresponsiveness. Often, there may be hours or even days between the SBS incident and the physical manifestation of symptoms, making investigation particularly challenging.

SBS cases are notoriously difficult for police and prosecutors to investigate. In one case that garnered national attention, 19-month-old Freya Garden's babysitter was charged in her death after the infant died in a Seattle emergency room in 2005. The 13-year-old sitter admitted (in conflicting statements) to becoming frustrated with the infant's crying and fussiness and shaking her once or twice. However, the autopsy revealed extensive brain damage consistent with SBS, as well as blunt head trauma. Blunt trauma injuries are often found in conjunction with SBS, often as a result of throwing or impact injuries. However, the charges against the babysitter were ultimately thrown out because of doubts over exactly when the injuries to the child could have occurred and mishandling of the babysitter's confession by police.

Mechanism of Injury

The mechanism of injury in SBS is thought to result from a combination of physical factors, including the proportionately large size of the adult relative to the child. Shaking by admitted assailants has produced remarkably similar injury patterns (Figure 11-6):

- The infant is held by the chest, facing the assailant, and is shaken violently back and forth.
- The shaking causes the infant's head to whip forward and backward from the chest to the back.
- The infant's chest is compressed, and the arms and legs move about with a whiplash action.
- At the completion of the assault, the infant may be limp and either not breathing or breathing shallowly.
- During the assault, the infant's head may strike a solid object.

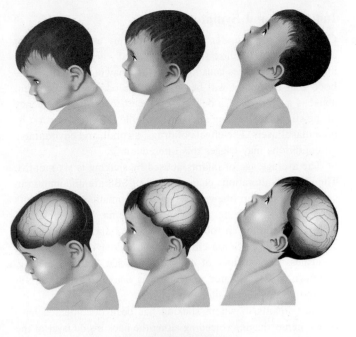

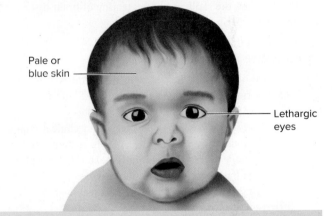

Pale or blue skin

Lethargic eyes

▲ FIGURE 11-6   Shaken-baby syndrome
The top diagram shows the external mechanism of shaking a baby; The middle diagram clearly reveals the internal injuries resulting from SBS; The bottom diagram shows outward signs of victimization from SBS. (Source: Top diagram from www.medscape.com. Middle diagram from www.aurorahealthcare.org. Bottom diagram from http://health.allrefer.com/health/shaken-baby-syndrome-shaken-baby-symptoms.html.)

- After the shaking, the infant may be dropped, thrown, or slammed onto a solid surface.

The last two events likely explain the many cases of blunt injury, including skull fractures, found in shaken infants. However, although blunt injury may be seen at autopsy in shaken infants, research data suggest that shaking in and of itself is often sufficient to cause serious intracranial injury or death.

Indicators and Symptoms

Crying has come under increasing scrutiny as a stimulus for abusive activity. Because shaking is generally a response to crying, a previous illness causing irritability may increase the likelihood that the infant will be shaken. The occurrence of infant abuse is a product of a delicate balance between the frequency of the stimulus of crying and the threshold for violent action by potential abusers. The effects of drugs, alcohol, and environmental conditions may trigger this interaction.

The average age of infants abused by shaking is six months. The physical alterations characteristic of SBS are uncommon in children older than one year. Many symptomatic shaken infants have seizures, are lethargic, or are in a coma. Many are resuscitated at home or en route to the hospital and arrive there in serious condition. Some children have milder changes in consciousness or a history of choking, vomiting, or poor feeding. Although gross evidence of trauma is usually absent, careful inspection may reveal sites of bruising.

Most infants in whom shaking has been documented have retinal hemorrhaging (bleeding along the back inside layer of the eyeball). Other intracranial injuries ascribed to shaking trauma are fluid between the skull and brain, tearing of brain tissue, and swelling of the brain.

Investigative Guidelines

- The use of MRI has helped detect old and new intracranial injuries and has aided recognition of subtle instances of repetitive shaking.
- Repetitive abuse has important legal and clinical implications. If abuse is repetitive, the child is at high risk for further injury unless legal action is taken. Establishing that there has been a pattern of abuse can also help in identifying potential perpetrators and may lead to increased legal penalties.
- The fact that shaken children, and possibly their siblings, often have been previously abused should dispel the notion that shaking is an isolated and somewhat "unintentional" event.
- From the perspective of the protection of the child or the criminal prosecution of the abuser, it is not as important to distinguish the precise mechanism of injury as it is to be certain that the event was nonaccidental.
- Pediatricians should not be deterred from testifying when the cause of the nonaccidental injury is not entirely clear.
- Shaking a child creates an imminent risk for an acute injury.
- Injuries that appear to be caused by shaking create a high index of suspicion of child abuse and should be followed by intensive efforts (for example, skeletal survey, CT scan, and MRI) to identify concurrent and previous abuse of the patient and any siblings.
- If an infant's injuries are fatal, an autopsy should be performed by a forensic pathologist. Autopsies of all infants who die of causes other than known natural illness should include thorough skeletal imaging.

MUNCHAUSEN SYNDROME BY PROXY

Munchausen syndrome is a psychological disorder in which the person fabricates the symptoms of disease or injury in order to undergo medical tests, hospitalization, or even medical or surgical treatment. To command medical attention, individuals with Munchausen syndrome may intentionally injure themselves or induce illness in themselves. In cases of **Munchausen Syndrome by Proxy (MSBP),** a parent or caretaker suffering from Munchausen syndrome attempts to elicit medical attention for him-/herself by injuring or inducing illness in a child. The parent then may try to resuscitate the child or to have paramedics or hospital personnel save the child.[16] The following actual cases are examples of MSBP.

M. A., a 9-month-old boy, had been admitted repeatedly to Children's Hospital because of recurrent life-threatening apnea (cessation of breathing). At 7 weeks of age, he experienced his first apneic event, and his mother administered mouth-to-mouth ventilation. Spontaneous respiration returned, and M. A. was hospitalized, treated, and discharged with a home monitor.

During the next 9 months, M. A. experienced 10 similar events and seven more hospitalizations. Eight of the events required mouth-to-mouth ventilation. All these episodes occurred while mother and child were alone, so only M. A.'s mother witnessed the actual events. Two episodes occurred in the hospital.

Unfortunately, despite many tests and surgical procedures, M. A.'s apnea persisted and his growth slowed. Because of his persistent apnea and failure to thrive, M. A. received home nursing care. During these home visits, several nurses observed that M. A. would refuse to eat in his mother's presence. If she left the room, however, he would eat.

In time, both medical and nursing staffs became increasingly suspicious that Mrs. A. was somehow responsible for her child's apnea. To better observe mother-child interaction, M. A. was moved to a hospital room equipped for covert audiovisual surveillance.

On the sixth day, the video clearly recorded Mrs. A. bringing on the apnea by forcing the child against her chest, which caused him to lose consciousness. M. A. became limp and experienced a falling heart rate. Mrs. A. then placed the baby back on the bed, called for help, and began mouth-to-mouth resuscitation.

The hospital immediately informed child protection services and police authorities, who reviewed the recording. Shortly thereafter, a team consisting of a physician, nurse, social worker, and police officer confronted her. At first, Mrs. A. expressed disbelief at the suggestion that she had smothered M. A., but when she was informed of the video, she made no comment. She was then arrested.

Mrs. A. was a 36-year-old occupational therapist and the mother of three boys. Late into her pregnancy with M. A., she worked in an early intervention program for developmentally delayed children. During many of M. A.'s hospitalizations, she appeared caring and concerned but emotionally distant. Clearly, Mrs. A. was the dominant parent, who made all decisions regarding medical treatment.

Mrs. A. subsequently pled guilty to felonious, third-degree assault. At the time, she stated: "The only time I ever caused M. A. to stop breathing was in the hospital." She received three years' probation, during which she was to receive psychotherapy. If she successfully completed psychotherapy, the felony charge would be reduced to a misdemeanor. She also had to live apart from her children and could visit them only in the presence of two other adults.

M. A. had no further apnea, and at 24 months of age he appeared vigorous, healthy, and normal. Eventually, the family was reunited.

C. B., a 10-month-old girl, was admitted to a hospital because of recurrent life-threatening apnea. C. B. had been born in another state and had been sexually assaulted at the age of 3 months by an acquaintance of her father. After the assault, local child protection services closely monitored the family.

At 6 months of age, C. B. experienced her first apneic episode. Her father shook her vigorously, and then administered mouth-to-mouth ventilation. She was subsequently admitted to a local hospital. After examination and treatment, she was discharged with a home monitor. During the next two months, C. B. experienced six apneic events and three hospitalizations. The family then moved to Minnesota.

During her first month in Minnesota, C. B. experienced four apneic episodes and three more hospitalizations. All required vigorous stimulations to restore spontaneous breathing. Other family members observed the child immediately after the events. However, only C. B.'s father had witnessed all the actual events. C. B. was eventually referred to Children's Hospital.

While in the hospital, C. B. had no clinical apnea or monitor alarms. Most of the time, she appeared happy and playful. However, when anyone attempted to touch her face, she became hysterical and combative. Over time, both the medical and nursing staffs began to suspect that C. B.'s parents were responsible for her apnea. Local police and child protection services were notified, and C. B. was placed in a room with covert audiovisual surveillance. On the third day of monitoring, the video recording clearly showed C. B.'s father producing an apneic event by smothering her. Mr. B. was seen picking up the sleeping child, placing her prone on the bed, and forcing her face into the mattress. C. B. awoke and struggled to escape, wildly kicking her legs. Mr. B. continued until C. B.'s struggling stopped and she appeared limp and unconscious. Then he repositioned her on the bed and called for help. A nurse entered the room, stimulated her, and administered supplemental oxygen.

C. B.'s parents were confronted by a physician, nurse, and police officer. Mr. B. adamantly denied smothering C. B. He was subsequently arrested and removed from the hospital.

Mr. B. was a 27-year-old, unemployed, semiliterate laborer in good health. He was actively involved in C. B.'s day-to-day medical care and was clearly the dominant parent. He also became very knowledgeable about the mechanics of the various county and hospital welfare systems. Officials described him as "demanding and manipulative." During C. B.'s hospitalizations, the family lived in a hotel adjacent to the hospital with room, board, and radio pagers provided by the hospital. Throughout C. B.'s hospitalization, Mrs. B. was passive and deferred all medical decisions to her husband.

When they first arrived in Minnesota, the family had received emergency financial assistance and was closely monitored by local social service agencies. Four years earlier, Mrs. B. had allegedly been assaulted and raped. Two months prior to C. B.'s monitored episode, Mrs. B. was evaluated at a local emergency room for a "hysterical conversion reaction."

Following the incident at Children's Hospital, Mr. B. was taken to the county jail, and upon viewing the video, he admitted smothering C. B. He was charged with felonious, third-degree assault. The judge ordered a psychiatric examination. Mr. B. received a 10-month sentence in a local workhouse and 5 years' probation. Also, he was to have no contact with his daughter and no unsupervised contact with any child in the future.[17]

INVESTIGATIVE GUIDELINES

- Consult with all experts possible, including psychologists.
- Exhaust every possible explanation of the cause of the child's illness or death.
- Find out who had exclusive control over the child when the symptoms of the illness began or at the time of the child's death.
- Find out if there is a history of abusive conduct toward the child.
- Find out if the nature of the child's illness or injury allows medical professionals to express an opinion that the child's illness or death was neither accidental nor the result of a natural cause or disease.

- In cases of hospitalization, use covert video surveillance to monitor the suspect.
- Determine whether the caretaker had any medical training or a history of seeking medical treatment needlessly. MSBP is often a multigenerational condition.

THE ROLE OF THE PHYSICIAN IN CHILD-ABUSE CASES

The problem the investigator often encounters is that the victim is either too young to explain what has occurred or too intimidated to cooperate. In injuries or deaths of young children, investigators find radiologists (physicians who specialize in the interpretation of X rays) especially helpful. It is common for abused children to be brought to the hospital emergency room by their parents or relatives, who tell hospital personnel that the child was injured in a fall or some other accident. When there is a discrepancy between the characteristics of the injury and the explanation, X rays can be useful in determining whether the injuries were accidental. X rays of the entire body reveal not only the presence of fractures and other injuries to joints and bones but also the existence of older injuries in various stages of healing.

Careful questioning of the persons bringing the child to the hospital may be sufficient to confirm the need for a complete investigation. The following facts about child abuse are helpful in such questioning:

- In many cases, only one of a number of children in the family is chosen as the target of abuse, and frequently that child was conceived or born extramaritally or premaritally.
- The marital partner tends to protect the abusive parent through denial of the facts.
- Occasionally, an abusing father also assaults his wife, but more frequently he restricts the gross abuse to a child.
- In over half the cases in which child abuse results in hospitalization, there was a preceding incident of abuse of equal severity.
- Not infrequently the battered child is taken to a different hospital after each abuse in order to conceal the recurrence of injuries.[18] However, with the mandatory reporting of all suspicious child abuse injuries to the proper authorities and the computerized storage of previously reported events, it has become increasingly difficult for this ploy to work.

The families of battered children range across the entire socioeconomic spectrum. The investigator cannot assume that an injured child who comes from what appears to be a "good home" is not the victim of child abuse.

In cases where medical examination is inconclusive but abuse is strongly suspected, interviewing becomes even more significant. The rule is to leave no source unexamined. To fail to do so places the abused child back into a defenseless position in which further injury or death could occur. The interviewing of baby sitters, neighbors, teachers, and others must be conducted sensibly and sensitively. The aim is not to "get the person who did it," because there may not in fact have been an abuse incident; instead, the primary objective is to get the information so that if there has been abuse, the child can be protected.

CHILD SEXUAL EXPLOITATION

The sexual exploitation of children is a particularly heinous offense in our society. The primary areas of child sexual abuse include child molestation, child pornography, and sex tourism. Sex tourism often involves visiting foreign countries for the purposes of acquiring sexual activities with children, but there is recent evidence that as many as 600,000 children may be involved in child prostitution in the United States.[19] (Chapter 12 focuses on human trafficking and child sex slavery and provides greater insight into this growing problem.)

CHILD MOLESTATION

For purposes of discussion, Kenneth V. Lanning, supervisory special agent of the Federal Bureau of Investigation, divides child molesters into two categories—namely, situational and preferential.[20]

Situational Child Molesters

The **situational child molester** does not have a true sexual preference for children but engages in sex with children for varied and sometimes complex reasons. For such a child molester, sex with children may range from a once-in-a-lifetime act to a long-term pattern of behavior. The more long term the pattern is, the harder it is to distinguish from preferential molesting. The situational child molester usually has fewer numbers of different child victims. Other vulnerable individuals, such as the elderly, sick, or disabled, may also be at risk of sexual victimization by him or her. For example, the situational child molester who sexually abuses children in a daycare center might leave that job and begin to sexually abuse elderly people in a nursing home. The number of situational child molesters is larger and increasing faster than that of preferential child molesters. Members of lower socioeconomic groups tend to be overrepresented among situational child molesters. Within this category, the following four major patterns of behavior emerge: regressed, morally indiscriminate, sexually indiscriminate, and inadequate (Table 11-2).

Morally Indiscriminate. The morally indiscriminate pattern characterizes an increasing number of child molesters. For such an individual, the sexual abuse of children is simply part of a general pattern of abuse in his life. He is a user and an abuser of people. He abuses his wife, friends, and coworkers. He lies, cheats, or steals whenever he thinks he can get away with it. His primary victim criteria are vulnerability and opportunity. He has the urge, a child is there, and so he acts. He typically uses force, lures, or manipulation to obtain his victims. He may violently or nonviolently abduct his victims. Although his victims frequently

| TABLE 11-2 | Situational Child Molesters | | | |

	REGRESSED	MORALLY INDISCRIMINATE	SEXUALLY INDISCRIMINATE	INADEQUATE
Basic Characteristics	Poor coping skills	User of people	Sexual experimentation	Social misfit
Motivation	Substitution	Why not?	Boredom	Insecurity and curiosity
Victim Criteria	Availability	Vulnerability and opportunity	New and different	Nonthreatening
Method of Operation	Coercion	Lure, force, or manipulation	Involve in existing activity	Exploits size, advantage
Pornography Collection	Possible	Sadomasochistic; detective magazines	Highly likely; varied nature	Likely

Kenneth V. Lanning, *Child Molesters: A Behavioral Analysis for Law Enforcement Officers Investigating Cases of Child Sexual Exploitation*, 3rd ed. (Arlington, VA: National Center for Missing and Exploited Children, 1992), p. 10. Reprinted with permission of the National Center for Missing and Exploited Children (NCMEC). Copyright 1986, 1987, and 1992, NCMEC. All rights reserved.

are strangers or acquaintances, they can also be his own children. The incestuous father (or mother) might be a morally indiscriminate offender. He frequently collects detective magazines or adult pornography of a sadomasochistic nature. He may collect some child pornography, especially that which depicts pubescent children. Because he is an impulsive person who lacks conscience, there is an especially high risk that he will molest pubescent children.

Regressed. A regressed offender usually has low self-esteem and poor coping skills; he turns to children as a sexual substitute for the preferred peer sex partner. Precipitating stress may play a bigger role in his molesting behavior. His main victim criterion seems to be availability, which is why many such offenders molest their own children. His principal method of operation is to coerce the child into having sex. This type of situational child molester may or may not collect child or adult pornography. If he does have child pornography, it will usually be the best kind of evidence from an investigative point of view and will often include homemade photographs or videos of the child he is molesting.

Sexually Indiscriminate. The sexually indiscriminate pattern of behavior is the most difficult to define. Although the previously described morally indiscriminate offender often is a sexual experimenter, the sexually indiscriminate individual differs in that he appears to be discriminating in his behavior except when it comes to sex. He is the "try-sexual"—willing to try anything sexual. Much of his behavior is similar to, and most often confused with, that of the preferential child molester. While he may have clearly defined sexual preferences—such as bondage or sadomasochism, he has no real sexual preference for children. His basic motivation is sexual experimentation, and he appears to have sex with children out of boredom. His main criteria for his victims are that they be new and different, and he involves children in previously existing sexual activity. Again, one must realize that these children may be his own. Although much of his sexual activity with adults may not be criminal,

such an individual may also provide his children to other adults as part of group sex, spouse-swapping activity, or even some bizarre ritual. Of all situational child molesters, he is by far the most likely to have multiple victims, be from a higher socioeconomic background, and collect pornography and erotica. Child pornography will be only a small portion of his potentially large and varied collection, however.

Inadequate. The inadequate pattern of behavior includes persons suffering from psychoses, eccentric personality disorders, mental retardation, and senility. In layperson's terms, the inadequate individual is the social misfit, the withdrawn, the unusual. He might be the shy teenager who has no friends of his own age or the eccentric loner who still lives with his parents. Although most loners are harmless, some can be child molesters and, in a few cases, even child killers (Figure 11-7). This offender seems to become sexually involved with children out of insecurity or curiosity. He finds children to be nonthreatening objects with whom he can explore his sexual fantasies. The child victim could be someone he knows or could be a random stranger. In some cases, the victim might be a specific "stranger" selected as a substitute for a specific adult (possibly a relative of the child) whom the offender is afraid of approaching directly. Often his sexual activity with children is the result of built-up impulses. Some of these individuals find it difficult to express anger and hostility, which then builds until it explodes—possibly against their child victims. Because of mental or emotional problems, some might take out their frustration in cruel sexual torture. The inadequate molester's victims, however, could be elderly persons as well as children—anyone who appears helpless at first sight. He might collect pornography, but it will most likely be of adults.

Preferential Child Molesters

Preferential child molesters have a definite sexual preference for children. Their sexual fantasies and erotic imagery focus on children. They have sex with children not because of some situational

▲ FIGURE 11-7

Donald James Smith was a registered sex offender in Florida with a lengthy criminal record including attempted kidnapping, selling obscene materials, and child abuse. In 2015, he was charged with abducting and killing 8-year-old Cherish Perrywinkle in Duval County, Florida. (©Will Dickey/The Florida Times-Union/AP Images)

stress or insecurity but because they are sexually attracted to and prefer children. Although they can possess a wide variety of character traits, they engage in highly predictable sexual behavior. Their sexual behavior patterns are called *sexual rituals* and are frequently engaged in even when they are counterproductive to getting away with the criminal activity. Although preferential offenders may be fewer in number than situational child molesters, they have the potential to molest large numbers of victims. For many of them, their problem is not only the nature of the sex drive (attraction to children) but also the quantity (need for frequent and repeated sex with children). They usually have age and gender preferences for their victims. Members of higher socioeconomic groups tend to be overrepresented among preferential child molesters. More preferential child molesters seem to prefer boys rather than girls. Within this category, at least three major patterns of behavior emerge: seduction, introverted, and sadistic (Table 11-3).

Seduction. The seduction pattern characterizes the offender who engages children in sexual activity by "seducing" them—courting them with attention, affection, and gifts. Just as one adult courts another, the pedophile seduces children over a period of time by gradually lowering their sexual inhibitions. Frequently his victims arrive at the point where they are willing to trade sex for the attention, affection, and other benefits they receive from the offender. Many seduction offenders are simultaneously involved with multiple victims, operating what has come to be called a child sex ring. This may include a group of children in the same class at school, in the same scout troop, or in the same neighborhood. The characteristic that seems to make the seduction molester a master seducer of children is his ability to identify with them. He knows how to talk to children—but, more important, he knows how to listen to them. His adult status and authority are also an important part of the seduction process. In addition, he frequently selects as targets children who are victims of emotional or physical neglect. The biggest problem for this child molester is not how to obtain child victims but how to get them to leave after they are too old. This must be done without the disclosure of the "secret." Victim disclosure often occurs when the offender is attempting to terminate the relationship. This child molester is most likely to use threats and physical violence to avoid

	SEDUCTION	INTRODUCED	SADISTIC
| TABLE 11-3 Preferential Child Molester			
Common Characteristics	Sexual preference for children; child pornography or erotica	Sexual preference for children; child pornography or erotica	Sexual preference for children; child pornography or erotica
Motivation	Identification	Fear of communication	Need to inflict pain
Victim Criteria	Age and gender preferences	Strangers or very young	Age and gender preferences
Method of Operation	Seduction process	Nonverbal sexual contact	Lure or force

Kenneth V. Lanning, *Child Molesters: A Behavioral Analysis for Law Enforcement Officers Investigating Cases of Child Sexual Exploitation*, 3rd ed. (Arlington, VA: National Center for Missing and Exploited Children, 1992), p. 10. Reprinted with permission of the National Center for Missing and Exploited Children (NCMEC). Copyright 1986, 1987, and 1992, NCMEC. All rights reserved.

identification and disclosure or to prevent a victim from leaving before he is ready to "dump" the victim.

Introverted. The introverted pattern of behavior characterizes the offender who has a preference for children but lacks the interpersonal skills necessary to seduce them. Therefore, he typically engages in a minimal amount of verbal communication with his victims and usually molests strangers or very young children. He is like the old stereotype of the child molester in that he is more likely to hang around playgrounds and other areas where children congregate, watching them or engaging them in brief sexual encounters. He may expose himself to children or make obscene phone calls to them. He may use the services of a child prostitute. Unable to figure out any other way to gain access to a child, he might even marry a woman and have his own children, very likely molesting them from the time they are infants. He is similar to the inadequate situational child molester, except that he has a definite sexual preference for children and his selection of only children as victims is more predictable.

Sadistic. The sadistic pattern of behavior characterizes the offender who has a sexual preference for children but who, in order to be aroused or gratified, must inflict psychological or physical pain or suffering on the child victim. He is aroused by his victim's response to the infliction of pain or suffering. Sadistic molesters typically use lures or force to gain access to their victims. They are more likely than other preferential child molesters to abduct and even murder their victims. There have been some cases where seduction molesters have become sadistic molesters. It is not known whether the need to perform sadistic acts developed late or was always there and surfaced late for some reason. In any case, it is fortunate that sadistic child molesters do not appear to be large in number.[21]

Interviewing Molested Children

Common sense and formal research agree that children are not merely miniature adults. We know, for example, that children develop in stages during which they acquire capacities for new functions and understanding. Adults, for the most part, attempt to speak to and treat children in accordance with their capabilities. We do not ordinarily expect children to understand or function on a par with adults.[22]

When children become victims or witnesses of violence or sexual abuse, however, they are thrust into an adult system that traditionally does not differentiate between children and adults. As one attorney has said:

> Child victims of crime are specially handicapped. First, the criminal justice system distrusts them and puts special barriers in the path of prosecuting their claims to justice. Second, the criminal justice system seems indifferent to the legitimate special needs that arise from their participation.[23]

What are some of the reasons for the problems that arise when children are called to participate in criminal proceedings? The first reason is the children's immaturity with regard to physical, cognitive, and emotional development. The second reason involves unique attributes of the offense of child sexual abuse, particularly when the perpetrator is a parent, parent substitute, or other adult having a trusting or loving relationship with the child. The third reason is our limited understanding of children's capabilities as witnesses. These three factors affect children's ability to comply with the expectations of our judicial system and inform our entire discussion of interviewing molested children.

Developmental Issues. Three developmental issues are important when allegations of sexual abuse arise.[24] First is the child's developmental level relative to other children in his or her age group. Knowing this information will dictate the nature of questioning to which the child can reasonably be expected to respond. It will also help place the child's observable reactions to victimization in an appropriate context.

Second is the child's developmental level with regard to sexuality. Normal preschoolers, for example, express curiosity about the origin of babies and mild interest in physical differences between the sexes. While it is not unusual for young children to engage in self-stimulatory behavior or exhibitionism, intercourse or other adult sexual behaviors are quite rare.[25]

Third is the child's ability to respond adequately to interviews and to testify in court. Those who work with young children should be aware of the following principles:

- Children think in concrete terms.
- Children do not organize their thoughts logically. They often include extraneous information, and they have trouble generalizing to new situations.
- Children have limited understanding of space, distance, and time. A child may not be able to say at "what time" or in "what month" something occurred but may be able to say whether it was before or after school, what was on television, or whether there was snow on the ground.
- Children have a complex understanding of truth and lying.
- Children see the world egocentrically. Because they believe that adults are omniscient, they may expect to be understood even when they have answered questions only partially.[26]
- Children have a limited attention span.
- Children may have varying degrees of comfort with strangers.

These kinds of cognitive limitations are common among young children. Older children tend to exhibit different, yet equally challenging, developmental patterns.[27] For example, although preadolescents have fairly sophisticated language capabilities, they may use words or phrases they do not fully understand. The emergence of sexuality and concern with sexual identities during preadolescence make these youngsters particularly vulnerable to disruption when they are sexually abused. As they enter adolescence, they tend to become very self-centered and have strong needs for privacy and secrecy. It is common for preteens and teenagers to express their feelings through the arts or physical activity or by acting out in inappropriate or socially unacceptable ways.

Some researchers have specifically explored the developmental aspects of children's understanding of the legal system.[28] Not surprisingly, they have found that older children have more accurate and complete knowledge of legal terminology (for example, court, lawyer, jury, judge, and witness) as well as a better grasp of certain basic concepts of American justice. The researchers caution that children's understanding of the legal system is not only limited but sometimes faulty, so child witnesses may behave in ways that appear counterintuitive or inappropriate to the context.

For example, an interview with a child may begin by requesting identifying information: name, age, school, grade, home address. But young children may misinterpret these initial questions as meaning they are under suspicion or arrest.[29] Also, because they do not understand the different roles and obligations of all the people who interview them, children do not understand why they must tell their stories repeatedly to the police, social workers, doctors, prosecutors, and, ultimately, the court. While this repetition may be simply exasperating for some children, others may relive the traumatic event each time, and still others may assume the story is already known and omit important details in subsequent interviews. Some children may feel protected by the presence of the judge, but others may be intimidated.

To correct these problems, researchers recommend that attorneys, judges, and investigators choose their words with care when questioning child witnesses.[30] Some believe that targeted instruction for children who may serve as witnesses, possibly in the form of a "court school," would be helpful as well.[31] Many

prosecutors and victim advocates take children for a tour of the courtroom and introduce them to some of the key players before their scheduled court date. Critics contend, however, that such precautions may induce unnecessary apprehension for children who ultimately are not called to testify. At a minimum, interviewers would be wise to explain thoroughly the nature and purpose of each interview or court appearance before the child is questioned.

An additional problem in interviewing children who may be victims of sexual molestation centers on the delicate issue of body parts and techniques for achieving accurate communication. One of the most common methods involves the use of anatomically detailed dolls.

Anatomically Detailed Dolls. When anatomically detailed dolls (male and female dolls with all body parts, including genitals; Figure 11-8) were first introduced in the late 1970s,[32] they were widely hailed and almost universally adopted by child-serving professionals as an important advance in techniques for communicating with troubled children. Congress (in the Victims of Child Abuse Act of 1990) and eight states[33] have enacted legislation expressly permitting the use of anatomically detailed dolls as demonstrative aids when children testify in court, and many appellate courts have upheld the use of such dolls.[34] The use of dolls at trial appears limited, however: courtroom observations of child sexual-abuse trials in eight jurisdictions revealed only one use of dolls per jurisdiction over the course of a year, with one exception where dolls were used in three of the four cases observed.[35]

Yet even as the dolls' value as demonstrative aids in court has gained widespread acceptance, their use in investigative interviews to arrive at a finding of sexual abuse that is later presented in court as expert opinion has been sharply criticized.

▶ FIGURE 11-8
Anatomically detailed dolls
Interviewing children who either have been sexually abused or have witnessed sexual abuse creates challenges for investigators. One tool that often assists investigators is the use of an anatomically detailed doll with all body parts, including genitals, present. Although there is some disagreement among experts as to the overall usefulness of these dolls, many law enforcement agencies still use them. (Courtesy of Teach-a-Bodies)

At the core of the controversy is the extent to which anatomically detailed dolls may suggest sexual behaviors even among children with no history of abuse. Improper use of the dolls, and unsupported inferences about children's behavior with them, can imperil the search for truth.

Proponents of anatomically detailed dolls maintain that, when properly used, the dolls can facilitate and enhance interviews with children.[36] Dolls can help in the following ways:

- They can help establish rapport with the interviewer and reduce stress. Most children relate well to dolls. The dolls can have a calming effect and make the interview room appear less formal and more child-oriented.
- They can reduce vocabulary problems. Interviewers can use the dolls to learn a child's sexual vocabulary before questioning the child about the alleged abuse.
- They allow the child to show what may be difficult or embarrassing to say. Anatomically detailed dolls can be an invaluable aid to children who are unable or unwilling to verbalize what happened to them.
- They can enhance the quality of information. Dolls may help interviewers gather information without resorting to leading or protracted questioning to overcome children's reluctance to describe sexual acts.
- They can establish competency. Interviewers can use the dolls in a general way to demonstrate the child's mental capacity and ability to communicate.

Many critics fear, however, that anatomically detailed dolls could have adverse effects, whether by provoking horror or alarm at the sight of genitalia or by eliciting apparently sexualized responses, even among children who have not been sexually abused. Even some appellate courts have raised the issue that interviewing children with anatomically detailed dolls may contaminate their memory.[37] Research offers little support for these contentions, however. For example, one study of "nonreferred" children (that is, children with no history or current allegation of sexual abuse) found that although they did play more with undressed dolls than with dressed dolls, the children's primary activity was, in fact, dressing the dolls.[38] Others report that nonreferred children do examine the genitalia and orifices of anatomically detailed dolls, but only rarely do they enact sexual behaviors.[39] Of course, some proportion of nonreferred children may have experienced some form of undetected sexual abuse.

Related to this controversy is the fact that professionals in this field have yet to reach consensus on "proper" use of anatomically detailed dolls. A number of questions remain unanswered:[40]

- How "correct" in their appearance must the dolls be? Some respondents to a survey by Boat and Everson[41] revealed using Barbie dolls, Cabbage Patch dolls, and homemade stuffed dolls with varying degrees of accuracy in their representation of genitalia. Does the presence or absence of certain details influence children's behavior with the dolls? Must the dolls also be matched by age and racial features to the child and alleged perpetrator?
- When and how should the dolls be used to assist an investigation? Should the dolls be available to children at the start of the interview, or should they be introduced only after the child falters in responding to traditional questioning? Who should undress the dolls, and how should this activity be incorporated into the interview?
- How many sessions with a child are necessary before drawing conclusions about the child's behavior with the dolls?
- Should other adults be present during the interview?
- How many dolls should be available?

The answers to these questions vary with the professional orientations of the people who are asked. Clinicians' responses are more likely to reflect concerns for the children's well-being; legal professionals, on the other hand, express concern for the potential effects of certain practices when revealed in court. From the courts' perspective, it is probably least objectionable to:

- Introduce the dolls only after the child has verbally disclosed some abuse, or as a last resort to assist reluctant children.[42]
- Allow children to choose from a variety of dolls (rather than present only two to represent child and perpetrator).[43]
- Offer the child minimal or no instruction in use of the dolls.
- Incorporate information gathered from doll interviews with other data to provide a complete assessment.[44]

Similar recommendations would apply to use of other props, such as puppets or artwork.

Asking Leading Questions. Professionals who interview children who are suspected of having been sexually abused are caught in a perilous dilemma. In the words of two well-known clinicians:

> In the best of all possible worlds, it would be advisable not to ask children leading questions. . . . But in the best of all possible worlds, children are not sexually assaulted in secrecy and then bribed, threatened, or intimidated not to talk about it. In the real world, where such things do happen, leading questions may sometimes be necessary.[45]

As with the anatomical dolls, leading questions are widely used as a courtroom technique to assist child witnesses,[46] but they are seriously challenged when used in investigative interviews. There is, however, a grain of truth to the argument that children can be led, coached, or even "brainwashed" by the interview process, and interviewers would be wise to reexamine their methods in light of our growing experience in the courts.

Briefly, the defense argument rests on the social psychological theory of social influence. In essence, as it applies to child sexual-abuse cases, this theory holds that children's responses to questioning are heavily influenced by the perceived authority or power of the adult interviewers. When they are praised or otherwise "rewarded" for disclosing elements of abuse, children learn what the interviewers want to hear. In other words, children answer to please adults.[47]

Furthermore, to continue this argument, the effect of social influence is magnified in child sexual-abuse cases, because the children are typically interviewed repeatedly by several different adults, each of whom contributes to the child's expanding story by infusing—and reinforcing—new information. Ultimately, according to one of the leading defense experts:

> In situations where a child will eventually testify, the memory will consist of a combination of recall and reconstruction influenced by all of the interrogations, conversations, and sexual abuse therapy that have occurred during the delay. The longer the delay, the greater the possibility of social influence and the more the memory may consist of reconstruction rather than recall.[48]

Challenges based on this theory have successfully undermined prosecution of several highly publicized cases, including the well-known McMartin Preschool case.

In one study, 72 children age 5 to 7 underwent physical examinations. Half received external examinations of their genital and anal areas; the other half were examined for scoliosis (curvature of the spine). Within one month of the exam, the children were interviewed about the event using open-ended questions, anatomically detailed dolls, and specific and misleading questions. The results of this study were both illuminating and provocative. Specifically:

- The majority of children who experienced genital and anal touching did not report it, either in response to open-ended questions or when asked to demonstrate with the dolls.
- All but five (of 36) disclosed touching in response to specific questions (for example, "Did the doctor touch you here?").
- Only three (of 36) girls who received scoliosis examinations incorrectly reported genital or anal touching; only one of those provided additional (incorrect) details.

In sum, based on the total number of questions asked: "When all of the chances to reveal genital/anal contact were considered, children failed to disclose it 64% of the time, whereas the chance of obtaining a false report of genital/anal touching was only 8%, even when leading questions were asked."[49]

Children's Reactions to Victimization

There are few in our society who would argue that child sexual abuse does not cause serious problems for its victims. The burgeoning research on this subject suggests that the effects of victimization on children can be far-reaching, negative, and complex. In one study that compared 369 sexually abused children to 318 nonabused children, a number of factors emerged to distinguish the two groups.[50] The sexually abused children were significantly more likely to demonstrate:

- poor self-esteem;
- aggressive behaviors;
- fearfulness;
- concentration problems;
- withdrawal;
- acting out;
- need to please others.

Another study compared sexually abused children to two groups of nonabused children: one from a psychiatric outpatient clinic and the other from a well-child clinic. The researchers found that the sexually abused children were more similar to the psychiatric outpatients than to the normal children.[51] Sexually abused children displayed significantly more behavior problems (particularly sexual behaviors) and fewer social competencies than did normal children.

Sexually Abused Child Syndrome. Early attempts to describe a "sexually abused child syndrome" were quickly discarded as lacking a foundation in empirical research. Today, however, some of the leading researchers and clinicians in this field are moving toward consensus on behavioral indicators of child sexual abuse. The results of a nationwide survey of professionals experienced in evaluating suspected child sexual abuse revealed high levels of agreement concerning the following factors:[52]

- The child possesses age-inappropriate sexual knowledge.
- The child engages in sexualized play.
- The child displays precocious behavior.
- The child engages in excessive masturbation.
- The child is preoccupied with his or her genitals.
- There are indications that pressure or coercion was exerted on the child.
- The child's story remains consistent over time.
- The child's report indicates an escalating progression of sexual abuse over time.
- The child describes idiosyncratic details of the abuse.
- There is physical evidence of abuse.

Note, however, that these indicators represent a broad constellation of behaviors that are frequently seen among sexually abused children as a group. Owing to the many forms sexual abuse may take and the variations in individual coping methods and personalities, every child will exhibit a different set of behaviors subsequent to abuse. Thus, a child who experienced a single abusive incident may well be consistent with his or her story over time. Conversely, a child who experienced several years of abuse by a close relative may seem to contradict his or her story over time, depending on the attitudes expressed by family members or the manner in which he or she is questioned. In other words, there is no single array of behavioral indicators that definitively identify a sexually abused child.

The Risk of False Allegations

A recent spate of highly publicized sexual-abuse allegations has caused the public to recoil and question the limits of credulity. These allegations tend to fall into two categories: alleged sexual abuse of preschool children in day-care facilities, sometimes including bizarre and ritualistic elements; and sexual abuse allegations arising in the context of divorce and custody or visitation disputes. Such cases have caused many observers to question the veracity of child-sexual-abuse reports.[53]

Researchers have attempted to determine the percentage of unsubstantiated cases that can actually be attributed to false reports. The most comprehensive of these studies analyzed all reports of suspected sexual abuse filed with the Denver Department of Social Services (DSS) several years ago. All 576 reports had been investigated by the DSS Sexual Abuse Team and designated either "founded" (53%) or "unfounded" (47%). With the assistance of DSS caseworkers, the researchers applied clinical judgments to the case files and reclassified these reports, using the following categories:

- *Founded cases:*
  Reliable accounts
  Recantations of reliable accounts
- *Unfounded cases:*
  Unsubstantiated suspicions
  Insufficient information
  Fictitious reports by adults
  Fictitious reports by children

The last two categories, "fictitious reports by adults" and "fictitious reports by children," included deliberate falsifications, misperceptions, confused interpretations of nonsexual events, and children who had been coached by adults. On reclassification by the researchers, 6% of the total cases (34 allegations) were found to be fictitious. Of those, only eight allegations had been made by five children, four of whom had been substantiated victims of abuse in the past.[54]

In a second phase of this study, the researchers examined 21 fictitious cases that had been referred to a sexual-abuse clinic for evaluation over a 5-year period. Of these allegations, five had been initiated by the child and nine by an adult; in seven cases the researchers could not determine who had initiated the charge. Custody or visitation disputes were ongoing in 15 of these cases: in one child-initiated case, in seven adult-initiated cases, and in all the "mixed" cases.[55]

Another study examined 162 consecutive sexual-abuse cases seen at a children's hospital over a 10-month period. Twenty-five of those cases involved allegations against a parent, and seven of those (28%) involved a custody or visitation dispute. The disputed cases were less likely to be substantiated than cases without such conflict, but they were nevertheless substantiated more than half the time.[56]

Other studies have approached the relationship between custody disputes and false allegations from a different perspective, beginning with cases that are referred to clinicians for custody evaluations (rather than sexual-abuse diagnosis). These studies have found that a relatively high proportion of custody disputes involve false sexual-abuse allegations.[57] Note, however, that these studies depend on clinical populations (that is, troublesome cases that had been referred to a specialist for evaluation or diagnosis). Findings are based on a small number of cases, and, furthermore, the decision to label a report "fictitious" is based on clinical judgment: there is no objective, definitive measure of "truth." Because of these limitations, such studies cannot generalize to a conclusion that sexual-abuse allegations associated with custody disputes are necessarily false.[58]

In fact, sexual-abuse allegations arising from divorce and custody disputes appear to be quite rare. One study that attempted to quantify this phenomenon found that in most courts, about 2 to 10% of all family court cases involving custody and/or visitation disputes also involved a charge of sexual abuse. As an alternative way of framing the magnitude of this problem, sexual-abuse allegations occurred in the range of approximately 2 to 15 per 1,000 divorce filings among the courts that were studied. Based on data from seven jurisdictions, 105 of 6,100 cases (or less than 2%) of custody or visitation disputes involved sexual-abuse allegations.[59]

Research also suggests that sexual abuse in day care is no more common than it is within families. Extrapolating from 270 substantiated cases in 35 states over a three-year period, researchers estimated that 500 to 550 actual cases occurred in that period, involving more than 2,500 children. On the basis of the total of 7 million children attending day-care facilities nationwide, the researchers calculated that 5.5 of every 10,000 children enrolled in day care are sexually abused. This compares to an estimated 8.9 of every 10,000 children who are sexually abused in their homes. The conclusion: the apparently large number of sexual-abuse cases reported in day care "is simply a reflection of the large number of children in day care and the relatively high risk of sexual abuse to children everywhere."[60]

Emotional Reaction to the Pedophile

Because many investigators are parents, they react strongly to the pedophile. However, for legal and pragmatic reasons, such feelings must never be translated into physical or verbal abuse. Physical abuse by police is unlawful and should result in criminal and civil charges. Verbal abuse or open expressions of revulsion minimize the possibility of obtaining the suspect's cooperation and, perhaps, of obtaining a much-needed voluntary statement. The following case illustrates this point.

A 5-year-old girl told her mother that the man next door had taken her into his home, removed her underpants, placed his penis between her legs, and rubbed her vagina with it. After putting her underpants back on, he had sent her home. The mother called the police, but when they arrived the child was very hesitant to repeat the story.

Careful handling of the interview by the officer provided enough information to justify probable cause for an arrest, although the suspect denied the offense. Supplementing the child's statements were those of neighbors who had seen the man taking the child into his house, where she had remained for about 10 minutes.

The child was taken to the hospital and given an examination. The examining physician could find no injuries, semen, or pubic hair. The victim's clothing was normal in appearance. The situation at this juncture was a shy young child who probably would not be a good witness, an absence of physical evidence, a suspect who denied the charges, and witnesses who saw the child enter the suspect's house but saw no molestation. A voluntary statement was imperative if a successful prosecution was to result.

The suspect was interrogated and at first denied the charges. But when confronted with the child's and the neighbors' statements, he admitted molesting the child in the manner she described. He said that he had been drinking heavily at the time and attributed his actions to intoxication. The suspect agreed to give a full statement under oath to the state prosecutor.

Before the suspect was sworn in, the prosecutor was advised by the investigator, outside the presence of the suspect, the facts in the case. The prosecutor requested that the suspect be brought into his office. In an angry voice, he told the suspect, "If that had been my little girl, you son of a bitch, I would have broken your goddamned neck." The prosecutor then asked the suspect if he would like to make a statement. The suspect replied, "I have nothing to say to you." Subsequently, the suspect pleaded guilty to contributing to the delinquency of a minor, a misdemeanor.

The reason for this misdemeanor rather than the felony charge was insufficient evidence. The prosecutor was not new to this job, and he had an excellent reputation. Unfortunately, what he had done was identify the victim with his own daughter, who was about the same age as the molested child.

▲ FIGURE 11-9
Accused pedophile awaits the start of trial
Eric Franklin Rosser, who had been on the FBI's 10-most-wanted list, is shown here after his arrest. He is being prosecuted for his alleged involvement in child prostitution and pedophilia. He was arrested in Bangkok, Thailand.
(©Reuters/Alamy)

CHILD PORNOGRAPHY

Kenneth V. Lanning, supervisory special agent of the Federal Bureau of Investigation, divides what the pedophile collects into two categories: child pornography and child erotica.[61] **Child pornography** can be behaviorally (not legally) defined as the sexually explicit reproduction of a child's image and includes sexually explicit photographs, negatives, slides, magazines, movies, videotapes, and computer disks. In essence, it is the permanent record of the sexual abuse or exploitation of an actual child. To legally be child pornography, it must be a visual depiction (not the written word) of a minor (as defined by statute) that is sexually explicit (not necessarily obscene, unless required by state law). Child pornography can be divided into two subcategories: commercial and homemade.

Child erotica is a broader and more encompassing term than child pornography. It can be defined as any material, relating to children, that serves a sexual purpose for a given individual. Some of the more common types of child erotica include toys, games, drawings, fantasy writings, diaries, souvenirs, sexual aids, manuals, letters, books about children, psychological books on pedophilia, and ordinary photographs of children. Child erotica might also be referred to as pedophile paraphernalia. Generally, possession and distribution of these items does not constitute a violation of the law.

For investigative purposes, child erotica can be divided into the categories shown next.

Published Material Relating to Children

Examples of this include books, magazines, articles, or videotapes dealing with any of these areas:

- child development;
- sex education;
- child photography;
- sexual abuse of children;
- sexual disorders;

- pedophilia;
- man-boy love;
- personal ads;
- incest;
- child prostitution;
- missing children;
- investigative techniques;
- legal aspects;
- access to children;
- detective magazines;
- "men's" magazines;
- nudism;
- erotic novels;
- catalogs;
- brochures.

Listing of foreign sex tours, guides to nude beaches, and material on sponsoring orphans or needy children provide investigators with information about access to children. Detective magazines saved by pedophiles usually contain stories about crimes against children. The "men's" magazines collected may have articles about sexual abuse of children. The use of adult pornography to lower inhibitions is discussed elsewhere in this book. Although the possession of information on missing children should be carefully investigated to determine possible involvement in abduction, most pedophiles collect this material to help rationalize their behavior as child "lovers," not abductors. Personal ads include those in "swinger" magazines, video magazines, and newspapers, and may mention "family fun," "family activity," "European material," "youth training," "unusual and bizarre," "better life," and so on. Erotic novels may contain stories about sex with children but without sexually explicit photographs. They may contain sketches or drawings. Materials concerning current or proposed laws dealing with sex abuse; arrested, convicted, or acquitted child molesters; or investigative techniques used by law enforcement are common.

Unpublished Material Relating to Children

Examples include items such as these:

- personal letters;
- audiotapes;
- diaries;
- fantasy writings;
- manuscripts;
- telephone and address books;
- pedophile manuals;
- newsletters and bulletins;
- directories;
- adult pornography;
- financial records.

Commercial Child Pornography

Commercial child pornography is pornography that is produced and intended for commercial sale. Because of strict federal and state laws today, there is no place in the United States where commercial "child" pornography is knowingly openly sold. In the United States, it is primarily a cottage industry run by pedophiles and child molesters. The commercial child pornography still being distributed in the United States is smuggled in from foreign countries—primarily by pedophiles. The risks are usually too high for the strictly commercial dealer. Because of their sexual and personal interests, however, pedophiles are more willing to take those risks. Their motive goes beyond just profit. Commercial child pornography is still assembled and is much more readily available in foreign countries. United States citizens, however, seem to be the main customers for this material. Some offenders collect their commercial child pornography in ways that make it appear to be homemade child pornography (for example, by taking photographs of pictures in magazines; cutting up pictures and mounting them in photo albums, with names and descriptive information written below; or putting homemade labels on commercial videotapes). If necessary, highly experienced investigators and forensic laboratories can be of assistance in making distinctions between homemade and commercially produced child pornography.

Homemade Child Pornography

Contrary to what its name implies, homemade child pornography can be as "good" as, if not better than, the quality of any commercial pornography. The pedophile has a personal interest in the product. "Homemade" simply means it was not originally produced primarily for commercial sale. Although commercial child pornography is not openly sold anywhere in this country, homemade child pornography is continually produced, swapped, and traded in almost every community in the United States. While rarely found in "adult" bookstores, child pornography is frequently found in the homes and offices of doctors, lawyers, teachers, ministers, and other apparent pillars of the community. There is, however, a connection between commercial and homemade child pornography. Sometimes homemade child pornography is sold or winds up in commercial child pornography magazines, movies, or videos. The same pictures are reproduced and circulated again and again. With rapidly increasing frequency, more and more of both commercial and homemade child pornography is in video format. This actually increases the odds of finding child pornography in any investigation.

The law enforcement investigator must realize that most of the children in prepubescent child pornography were not abducted into sexual slavery. They were seduced into posing for these pictures or videos by a pedophile they probably know. They were never missing children. The children in child pornography are frequently smiling or have neutral expressions on their faces, because they have been seduced into the activity after having had their inhibitions lowered by clever offenders. In some cases, their own parents took the pictures or made them available for others to take the pictures. Children in pubescent or technical child pornography, however, are more likely to be missing children—especially runaways—being exploited by morally indiscriminate pimps or profiteers. In contrast to adult pornography, but consistent with the gender preference of most preferential child molesters, there are more boys than girls in child pornography.

In understanding the nature of child pornography, the law enforcement officer must recognize the distinction between technical and simulated child pornography. The Child Protection Act of 1984 defines a *child* as anyone under the age of 18. Therefore, a sexually explicit photograph of a 15-, 16-, or 17-year-old girl or boy is *technical child pornography*. Technical child pornography does not look like child pornography, but it is. The production, distribution, and, in some cases, possession of this type of child pornography could and should be investigated under appropriate child pornography statutes. Technical child pornography is an exception to much of what we say about child pornography. It often is produced, distributed, and consumed by individuals who are not child molesters or pedophiles; it is openly sold around the United States; and it more often portrays females than males. Because it looks like adult pornography, it is more like adult pornography.

However, sexually explicit photographs of 18-year-old or older males or females are not legally child pornography. But if the person portrayed in such material is young looking, dressed youthfully, or made up to look young, the material could be of interest to pedophiles. This is *simulated child pornography*. Simulated child pornography looks like child pornography, but it is not. It is designed to appeal to the pedophile but it is not legally child pornography because the individuals portrayed are over 18. This illustrates the importance, and sometimes the difficulty, in proving the age of the child in the photographs or videotapes.

Uses of Child Pornography Collections

Although the reasons why pedophiles collect child pornography and erotica are conjecture, we can be more certain as to how this material is used. Studies and police investigations have identified certain criminal uses of the material.

Child pornography and child erotica are used for the sexual arousal and gratification of pedophiles. They use child pornography the same way other people use adult pornography—to feed sexual fantasies. Some pedophiles only collect and fantasize about the material without acting out the fantasies, but in most cases the arousal and fantasy fueled by the pornography is only a prelude to actual sexual activity with children.

A second use of child pornography and erotica is to lower children's inhibitions. A child who is reluctant to engage in sexual activity with an adult or to pose for sexually explicit photos can sometimes be convinced by viewing other children having "fun" participating in the activity. Peer pressure can have a tremendous effect on children; if other children are involved, the child might be led to believe that the activity is acceptable. When the pornography is used to lower inhibitions, the children portrayed will usually *appear* to be having a good time.

Books on human sexuality and sex education, as well as sex manuals are also used to lower inhibitions. Children accept what they see in books, and many pedophiles have used sex education books to prove to children that such sexual behavior is acceptable. Adult pornography is also used, particularly with adolescent boy victims, to arouse them or to lower inhibitions.

A third major use of child pornography collections is blackmail. If a pedophile already has a relationship with a child, seducing the child into sexual activity is only part of the plan. The pedophile must also ensure that the child keeps the secret. Children are most afraid of pictures being shown to their friends. As such, pedophiles use photographs taken of the child as blackmail. If the child threatens to tell his or her parents or the authorities, the existence of sexually explicit photographs can be an effective silencer.

A fourth use of child pornography and erotica is as a medium of exchange. Some pedophiles exchange photographs of children for access to, or phone numbers of, other children. The quality and the theme of the material determine its value as an exchange medium. Rather than paying cash for access to a child, the pedophile may exchange a small part (usually duplicates) of his collection. The younger the child and the more bizarre the acts, the greater the value of the pornography.

A fifth use of the collected material is profit. Some people involved in the sale and distribution of child pornography are not pedophiles, they are profiteers. In contrast, most pedophiles seem to collect child erotica and pornography for reasons other than profit. Some pedophiles may begin nonprofit trading, which they pursue until they accumulate certain amounts or types of photographs, which are then sold to commercial dealers for reproduction in commercial child pornography magazines. Others combine their pedophiliac interest with their profit motive. Some collectors even have their own photographic reproduction equipment. Thus, the photograph of a child taken with or without parental knowledge by a neighborhood pedophile in any U.S. community can wind up in a commercial child pornography magazine with worldwide distribution.

Child Pornography, the Internet and the Law

Over the past decade, several important laws have been proposed and adopted to deal with the issue of child sexual exploitation on the Internet. For example, the *Child Protection and Sexual Predator Punishment Act of 1998* specifically addressed the issues of online sexual victimization of children. The law prohibits the transfer of sexually explicit material to minors, and increases penalties for offenses against children. Furthermore, the act amends the *Child Abuse Act of 1990* by requiring online service providers to report evidence of child pornography offenses to law enforcement agencies. In 1998 Congress enacted the *Protection of Children from Sexual Predators Act*, which established three new criminal offense areas:

1. use of interstate facilities to transmit information about a minor;
2. transfer of obscene materials to or from minors;
3. definition of sexual activity to include the production of child pornography.

This important and landmark legislation also helped establish the Morgan P. Hardiman Child Abduction and Serial Murder Investigative Resource Center (CASMIRC), tasked with improving the coordination of major violent crimes involving children. CASMIRC also provides on-site consultation and advice for state and local agencies as well as operational support to any law enforcement agency confronted with a child abduction, mysterious disappearance of a child, child homicide, serial murder, or expansive child pornography case. There are numerous state laws that also prohibit the possession, manufacturing, distribution, and sale of child pornography. In almost all instances, simple possession is a felony. Federal law on possession of child pornography also outlines the sexual exploitation of children prohibiting people from using children in the production of any sexually explicit material. Emphasis on the prosecution of child pornography has become a priority for federal authorities presumably because of the explosion of such activity via the Internet.[62] In the last decade, federal prosecutions for child pornography possession nearly tripled nationwide, and in some states, more child porn cases were filed than traditional federal crimes such as mail and wire fraud and bank robbery.

QUICK FACTS

The Problem of Child Pornography by the Numbers

The problem of child pornography is enormous, according to the National Center for Missing and Exploited Children (NCMEC). Here are some of the numbers:

  147 million images and videos of child pornography reviewed by the NCMEC

  Over 1 million child porn images/videos reported on the NCMEC Cyber TipLine per year

  Over 10,000 FBI arrests for possession of child pornography since 1996

  Over 5,000 cases investigated by the FBI's Crime Against Children Unit (CACU) per year

  2,315 suspects indicted on child pornography charges in 2010 alone

  2,500 percent rate of increase of child pornography arrests, since 1996

Sources:

- See Child Exploitation and Obscenity Section (CEOS) website at: https://www.justice.gov/criminal-ceos
- Associated Press, "Child Porn Prosecutions Soaring in the U.S." February 5, 2011
- See "Today's FBI: Investigative Programs" website at: https://www2.fbi.gov/facts_and_figures/investigative_programs.htm

CHILD SEX TOURISM

Child pornography is closely tied to another form of child sexual exploitation—that of **child sex tourism**. Child sex tourism, which is also a by-product of sex trafficking, is defined by the United Nations as "tourism organized with the primary purpose of facilitating the effecting of a commercial-sexual relationship with a child."[63] Nearly half of child sex tourism cases were closely connected to child pornography.[64]

Child sex tourism allows pedophiles, mostly men,[65] to either arrange a trip through a travel agency that specializes in sex tours, or arrange travel themselves to an area known for child prostitution and child sex trafficking. Some of these travel agencies are virtual, or Internet based, and can be found among networks of child pornographers. Others hide behind the front of commercial travel agents. For example, Big Apple Oriental Tours, located in New York City, was discovered to have taken clients to nightclubs in the Philippines, Thailand, and Cambodia, where tour guides actually negotiated fees and sexual acts on behalf of their clients.[66] However, many pedophiles simply travel to areas known for lax law enforcement and bustling child sex industries to pick and choose for themselves.

Locations recognized for being sex tourism destinations generally are poverty-stricken nations with unstable economies and political structures.[67] In Thailand, for example, the government estimates that 10,000 children are involved in the commercial sex industry; however, nongovernmental agencies believe that the number is as high as 800,000. Growth in the demand for young boys in the area is attributed almost entirely to the sex tour industry.[68] Thailand is hardly the only destination for sex tourists, however. Other countries with abundant opportunities for child sex tourists include Mexico, India, Indonesia, Nepal, the Philippines, Cambodia, China, and Colombia.[69] Surprising to many people, the United States is also a popular destination for sex tourists seeking children, with Las Vegas and New Orleans serving as hot spots for affluent pedophiles.[70]

Approximately 24 to 25% of the world's sex tourists are American, thus constituting the largest concentration from any one country.[71] Some individuals travel with the singular intent of abusing children, whereas many are situational abuses and engage in the practice opportunistically while on business trips or family vacations.[72] Regardless of the intent, American law specifically forbids the practice of child sex tourism. Federal statutes under Chapter 18, Sections 23 and 24 of the U.S. Code prohibit traveling across state lines or into the United States for the purpose of engaging in any illicit sexual conduct (which includes any commercial sex act with a person under 18). These statutes also prohibit an American citizen or national from engaging in illicit sexual conduct outside the United States. A violation of this law can result in a 30-year maximum sentence. The law does not require that the citizen have traveled outside the country with the intent of engaging in illicit sexual conduct in a foreign country. In 2003 the Protect Act, signed into law by President George W. Bush, reinforced these provisions.[73] The Department of Homeland Security has also developed the "Operation Predator" initiative to combat child exploitation, child pornography, and child sex tourism, with Immigrations and Customs Enforcement acting as the primary investigative agency. The United States has also funded global programs that conduct major public awareness and deterrence campaigns aimed at sex tourists, including Internet messages, pamphlets at international airports and public service announcements.[74]

Nevertheless, child sex tourism is a difficult crime to investigate, prosecute, and prevent. The actions of foreign governments can implicitly encourage the industry[75] by directly targeting sex tourists or refusing to assist in the investigations of such crimes.[76] Owing to the nature and location of sex tourist crimes, federal investigators generally assume jurisdiction over these types of cases rather than local law enforcement.

USE OF THE COMPUTER AND THE INTERNET IN CHILD PORNOGRAPHY

Computers have become a pervasive part of daily life. Unfortunately, the ubiquity of the computer, and by extension the Internet, is an asset to the child pornographer (Figure 11-10). Child pornographers use personal computers to create, distribute, and catalog pornographic depictions of children and to widen their net of victimization.

Many child pornographers are compulsive record keepers, and for them the computer as a cataloging tool is electronic gold. While most people might use computers to track a bank balance or store family vacation photos, law enforcement investigations have determined that child pornographers use computers to organize and store photographs and movies that graphically depict scenes of sexual exploitation of children.

Child pornographers can acquire additional material through instant contact with other pedophiles. Chat rooms, bulletin boards, newsgroups, instant messaging, and e-mail are just some of the means child pornographers currently use to communicate with other pedophiles. Once he has made contact with willing cohorts, a pedophile can electronically exchange photographs, movies, and other depictions of child pornography. In a matter of seconds, a child pornographer may send or receive child pornography to or from almost anywhere in the world. Web cams have even made it possible to broadcast and receive live, real-time images of child molestation and pornography.

In addition, the home computer provides tools that make it easy to store and retrieve names and addresses of accessible

▶ **FIGURE 11-10**
Child pornography
The Internet provides an easy pathway to share and distribute child pornography, often involving criminality on a global scale. Here, computers are seized from two fake call center businesses located in Manilla, The Philippines that sold child pornography online to clients in the United States. (©Noel Celis/AFP/Getty Images)

victims. This library of victims can be developed with great ease and efficiency by way of referral from the pedophile's perverse network of colleagues.

Also, pedophiles can use computers to directly establish a rapport with children. Adolescent boys who spend a great amount of their time online are at particularly high risk of this type of contact. Again, using chat rooms, e-mail, and instant messaging, the pedophile may pose as an adolescent to gain the trust of the child. He may then indirectly victimize the child by sharing with him or her sexually explicit information or material. He may further attempt to obtain the child's phone number or whereabouts in order to engage in face-to-face contact and direct sexual victimization.

Desktop publishing holds unique possibilities for child pornographers. Like any other small publisher, pedophiles that use child pornography as a profit-making business can produce high-quality prints with relative ease. They can collect, record, "publish," and distribute pornographic material either as hard copy or as an electronic file. They can also create false or doctored graphic images of children in pornographic positions. The question then arises: are such false images punishable by law?

In the United States, Title 18, Section 2252, of the U.S. Code, commonly known as the Child Pornography Prevention Act (CPPA), deals with this aspect of child pornography and the Internet. The CPPA makes it a crime to sell, possess with intent to sell, download, or produce child pornography or any visual depiction that is intended to *represent or resemble* child pornography. This includes material "transported, by any means, including by computer, if (i) the producing of such visual depiction involves the use of a minor engaging in sexually explicit conduct; and (ii) such *visual depiction* is of such conduct."[77]

We must reiterate that there does not have to be an actual child involved in the making of such pornography for it to be legally punishable; there must be merely the presence of the "visual depiction" of a child. This stipulation assumes that there are harmful secondary effects associated with virtual child pornography—namely, as mentioned earlier, that pedophiles may use graphic depictions of child pornography to seduce children to join in the "fun."[78]

The movie *Traffic* contains a scene in which an underage character enacts having sex with a drug dealer. Under the CPPA, this scene would, in legal terms, be viewed as child pornography. For this reason, the Free Speech Coalition, an adult trade organization, has challenged the CPPA claiming that it is overly vague and violates First Amendment free speech rights.[79] A federal district court ruled against the Free Speech Coalition in 1997, but the 9th Circuit reversed that decision in late 2001, and the reversal was upheld by the Supreme Court in Spring 2002.[80]

Unfortunately, owing to the anonymous nature of the Internet and the sheer volume of Internet activity, transactions involving child pornography are often difficult for government agencies to track. As discussed in Chapter 17, "Computer Crime," however, some investigators are taking advantage of the anonymity of the Net by posing as minors in order to identify pedophiles. Once a pedophile has been discovered, his records of his computer activities can frequently be used as incriminating evidence.

Furthermore, under strictly regulated circumstances, investigators may be able to track the Internet activity of pedophiles through various watchdog programs.[81]

Child pornography is often found in computer files on hard drives. Whenever such a condition may exist, it is important to remember the special techniques of investigating technologically based crime and retrieving digital images as evidence. (For a more thorough discussion of digital forensics and the investigation of child pornography involving computers, refer to Chapter 17, "Cyber Crime.")

Currently, 50% of Internet child pornography cases call for investigation abroad.[82] The recent upsurge in worldwide child pornography prevention and detention agencies lends credence to the notion that child pornography on the Internet cannot be tackled by one country alone but has to be dealt with globally.[83]

INTERNET CRIMES AGAINST CHILDREN

With the popularity of the Internet in homes and schools, and particularly with the advent of social networking sites such as Snapchat and Facebook, child pornography is no longer the only threat to children on the Internet. Cyberenticement through social sites, instant messaging, e-mail communications, and gaming connections can lure an unsuspecting child into sexual contact with a pedophile. In addition, online advertisers, such as Craigslist, are also presenting opportunities for child prostitution and solicitation. Although only a small percentage of the nation's youth (around 13 percent) experience online solicitation, the prospect is a frightening one for parents and law enforcement officers[84] (See Box 11-1).

Most of the youth exposed to online solicitations were girls between the ages of 14 and 17. Profiles of those soliciting children sexually show that they tend to be men more than 70% of the time, and about 43% of these men are over the age of 18.[85] About 75% of the time, the person soliciting the child asked to meet them in person.[86]

As a result of the over 45 million children[87] on the Internet today, parents, law enforcement officials, and even website managers are taking steps to ensure that online solicitations do not result in a criminal act against a child. The Internet Crimes Against Children (ICAC) Task Force Program was developed in response to these issues and provides resources to local and state law enforcement agencies to "enhance their investigative response to offenders who use the Internet, online communication systems, or other computer technology to sexually exploit children."[88] Investigations of online predators by law enforcement using undercover techniques appears to be making an impact. In a study examining arrests of online predators, researchers found that 87% of arrests of online predators in 2006 involved undercover investigators posing as youth. However, it should also be noted that arrests of online predators accounted for only 1% of all arrests for sex crimes against children in 2006.[89] This particular statistic seems to

BOX 11-1 | ONLINE SOLICITATION

Parents and law enforcement already concerned about the potentially harmful online contacts that children encountered on social media apps got a whole new headache when Snapchat launched in late 2011. The messaging app contained a number of familiar functionalities, namely networking capabilities, imaging, and chats, but offered a whole new wrinkle to spontaneous electronic communication. Snapchat messages, videos, and photos disappear between one and ten seconds after they have been read—from the server, from the inbox of the recipient, and from the outbox of the sender.

This feature was added by the developers ostensibly to encourage a multi-media experience that's quick, fun, and ephemeral. Unfortunately, it leads young people to believe that compromising photos they might send are fleeting—when they can, in fact, be screen-shot. It also allows child predators to send inappropriate photos and messages to teenagers in a way that's undetectable to even social media-savvy parents.

Combined with the anonymity that the Internet allows, Snapchat (as with basically any other social media service) can allow predators to post under pseudonyms or fake profiles. But surprisingly, such predators don't always misrepresent their ages, openly stating that they are adults when soliciting inappropriate photos or conversations. Often, teens feel flattered by the attention.

Ultimately, though, conversations with predators may not be the biggest threat presented by Snapchat: it's the overconfidence that sexually explicit or suggestive photos that teens share with each other will disappear. For instance, in Newtown, Connecticut, in 2015, three high school students were charged with selling the sexually explicit photos and videos that some of their

©Valentin Wolf/imageBROKER/age fotostock

classmates had sent them. They had used a combination of screen shots and photographs taken by a secondary phone, trained on the initial phone used for the messaging. Unfortunately, the photos—once sold—could have been transmitted to anyone, for any purpose, making the issue exponentially horrifying to the students in the photos and their parents.

Experts recommend that preventing such incidents starts with conversations between parents and children about the consequences of photo sharing, of messaging people they've never met in person, and about general Internet safety principles. It is important to remember that regardless of the specific technology, social media will always pose a risk to children . . . and cause worry for their parents.

suggest that though the threat of online predators is real, and should be addressed with children using the Internet, it is not as commonplace as the media would suggest.

Nonetheless, social media apps such as Facebook have built-in safeguards against child predators. In Facebook's case, the company has banned convicted sex offenders from their site; they also employ algorithms[90] and scanning functions that alert site administrators when people with loose connections and vastly different age groups message each other. Facebook relied on archives of chats that preceded sexual assaults to identify patterns and develop their algorithms. They also scan postings and chats for inappropriate conversations with minors, a process that they employ only based on specific red flags.

Investigators also have several tools at their disposal to help investigate Internet crimes against children. Facebook, for instance, will preserve an account involved in a criminal investigation for 90 days with formal legal process; they also have emergency procedures and a special online request system for

law enforcement if an investigation uncovers that a child is in imminent danger.[91] Generally, subpoenas, search warrants, and/or court orders will be required for any disclosure of account records from a social media application.

In some cases, forensic analysis of cell phones used by victims or perpetrators of Internet crimes against children may uncover what the site cannot: data, messages, and photos within the phone itself may contain information that isn't available on the app or website. Agency crime labs, area task forces, or federal agencies may have resources to assist investigators in this process.

Finally, the apps themselves may hold the key to investigations via undercover operations involving "catch a predator" style operations. However, law enforcement officials should be careful to follow terms of services or other special procedures required by the app.

The Internet—although providing limitless educational and entertainment possibilities to children—is clearly a means for predators to exploit children in a variety of ways. Internet crimes against children can include child pornography, communications involving sex trafficking and tourism, and even harassment among peers. Although law enforcement officers can pose as children in Internet chat rooms in an effort to lure sex offenders, the process is time-consuming. The best tool to protect children from Internet crime is parental education and involvement. The more a child is supervised while on the Internet, the less likely he or she is to be a victim of exploitation.[92]

BULLYING AND CYBERBULLYING

For generations, bullying has been seen as an ugly rite of passage for children and teenagers. In schools across the country, students were forced to endure daily abuse that included name calling, social exclusion, taunts, intimidation, pranks, and even physical violence. Teachers and parents were either unaware of the problem or simply unable to stop the bullying from occurring. However, what was once seen as fact of life is now considered to be a crime in many jurisdictions. Law enforcement is increasingly becoming involved in investigations of bullies and cyberbullies as the result of high profile bullying cases that have changed the way we think about this behavior.

Bullying is defined as "aggressive behavior or intentional harm by an individual or group repeated over time that involves an imbalance of power."[93] It can be verbal, physical or even psychological in nature and can have devastating effects on its victims. Studies show that male victims of bullying are more than five times more likely to be moderately to severely depressed and four times more likely to be suicidal, whereas bullied girls are more than three time more likely to be moderately to severely depressed and eight times more likely to be suicidal.[94] In 2009 an 11-year-old Massachusetts boy named Carl Hoover committed suicide after being extensively bullied; the following year, 15-year-old

Phoebe Prince killed herself after being tormented by female classmates jealous over her relationship with a school football player. And 2010 was also marked by a spate of suicides by young men who were mercilessly taunted for either being gay or being perceived by their peers as being homosexual. The result of these heartbreaking incidents was increased legislation related to bullying; most states now have anti-bullying legislation on the book.[95]

Of the 50 states, 23 have included specific references to "cyberbullying," while 48 address electronic harassment.[96] **Cyberbullying** is defined as using the Internet, cellular phone, or other technology to harass another person. Facebook has become a popular venue for cyberbullying, allowing bullies to spread rumors and post unflattering photographs of victims as well as use chat and messaging features to send hurtful communications. Other types of cyberbullying include posting private videos on YouTube or other video hosting sites in an effort to humiliate the subject and using telephone text messaging to send photos or disparaging messages.

Police involvement in bullying cases is still fairly limited. For the most part, legislation addressing bullying or cyberbullying requires schools to adopt policies to address the issue and mentions nothing about law enforcement intervention. But obviously if the bullying is physical in nature, police may be involved as they would in a simple assault. Furthermore, many states have separate laws regarding using electronic means to harass another person. For example, Wisconsin's statute 947.0125 prohibits unlawful use of computerized communication systems, which therefore classifies cyberbullying as a Class B misdemeanor and punishes it with a fine up to $1,000, or imprisonment for up to 90 days, or both. Though this issue is still evolving, the best thing that law enforcement officers can do to help victims is be aware of the statutes within their state, and understand the seriousness of the effects of bullies on their victims.

BOX 11-2 | THE PROBLEMS OF CYBERBULLYING AND SEXTING

According to recent research by the Pew Research Center[97] and the Cyberbullying Research Center[98], the proliferation of social media sites on the Internet has caused dramatic increases in the number of these unique crimes, often targeting children and teenagers:

Cyberbullying: Defined as the use of the Internet, cell phones, or other devices to send or post texts or images intended to harass, hurt, and/or embarrass another person.[99] In many cases, these activities are repeated over and over again in an effort to inflict further pain on the victim. Over one-third of all teens who use the Internet report being targeted or victimized by this crime. Adolescent girls aged 14 to 17 are most often the victims, with a greater number of those in student populations now using Instagram and Facebook as compared to Twitter or Ask.fm. Most of the

©Jennifer Blankenship

documented cyberbullying attacks have involved explicit and/or sexually related photos or videos, often referred to as "sexting" events.

Sexting: Defined as sending by cell phone or posting sexually explicit photos, images, or videos, now a common part of many romantic relationships. However, when these images become viewable by the public, or when there is a threat to publicly humiliate another person through the release of these images, a new form of harassment often arises. The crime can quickly escalate. If the image reveals a person under the age of 16, child pornography charges can be instigated. In unique cases, even an individual that texts or sends an image of themselves in a revealing and explicit way can be guilty of sending child pornography. However, the most egregious of these cases have often involved **sextortion,** or threats to expose a sexual image in order to make a person do something (most often pay money) or for other reasons, such as revenge or humiliation.[100] In these cases, the victim most often knew the perpetrator, and indeed was often a past romantic partner, giving way to the more slang-oriented term of "revenge porn" to describe the entire incident. These cases

rise to criminal events and should be investigated by the police, however, the formal reporting of such crimes has been almost non-existent.

Advice aimed specifically at teenagers to help in preventing these types of digital crimes, but also good for the general public, can be found on the Cyberbullying Center website. Tips include:

- Delete any explicit image of yourself or others that you have taken or that you have on your cell phone.
- Do not distribute explicit images.
- Reject any request from others for inappropriate images.
- Resist sexting; it is not a necessary part of a healthy, functional romantic relationship. Send images that are suggestive, but not explicit.
- If you receive (or someone shows you) an explicit image of someone else, contact that person to tell them that their images are being circulated.
- Inform a teacher or counselor, or call the police if explicit threats are made that require inappropriate action or the payment of money, or if multiple texts appear that are designed to harass or humiliate another person.[101]

CHILD ABDUCTION

Although high-profile news stories might perpetuate the notion that child abductions are often perpetrated by strangers, research indicates that most abductions are perpetrated by family members; in fact it is estimated that stranger abductions associated with a high risk of victim mortality account for only a small number of cases annually (for example, between 200 and 300 cases). This is in stark contrast to the presumably hundreds of thousands of cases involving family members. Moreover, when a child goes missing, it is often the case that the child has run away or been abducted by a non-custodial parent.[102]

THE PARENTAL INTERVIEW

Parents must be interviewed separately from each other and from other family members and reporting parties. Responding officers may feel reluctant to conduct separate interviews of the parents because of their emotionally escalated state. Conversely, if the parents do not appear particularly concerned about the child's absence, the officers may not view separate interviews as necessary. While they cannot determine what a parent's "normal" reaction to a missing child would be, officers must remain objective and realize that a family member may later become a suspect if the child has been abducted. They must balance this objectivity with empathy and support if the parents are in a state of emotional crisis. Most importantly, officers must ensure that they interview parents individually, preserve potential evidence, and document each parent's demeanor and attitude throughout the interview.

During the parental interview, officers should quickly compile accurate physical characteristics of the child, such as his or her appearance, age, and clothing, and should obtain recent photographs and videotapes. Officers should attempt to include full criminal- and psychiatric-history checks of all family members who had access to the child, as well as acquire a local agency history of any prior abuse or neglect calls to the home. In separate interviews of family members, responding officers should question whether the child's absence shows a significant deviation from established patterns of behavior.[103] However, further exploration into the victimology of the missing child can answer this question.

VICTIMOLOGY OF THE MISSING CHILD

To understand whether the child's absence is consistent with established patterns of behavior, officers first must understand the child's normal actions before the disappearance. Officers should use the following guidelines for assessing the personality of the missing child.[104]

- Develop and verify a detailed time-line of the child's last known activities up to the time the child was last seen or reported missing.
- Determine habits, hobbies, interests, and favorite activities.
- Identify normal activity patterns, and determine the victim's known comfort zone. Officers should assess the child's survival skills, ability to adapt to new or strange circumstances, and intellectual maturity. Did the child frequently travel alone? Did the child have a routine where independent travel occurred on a regular basis

(for example, riding a bike to school)? What fears and phobias did the child exhibit? For example, if the child was afraid of the dark, the probability of leaving voluntarily at night is low. Similarly, if the missing child was afraid to travel without a favorite item, such as a toy or security blanket, and the item remains in the house after the disappearance, the child may not have left voluntarily.

- Note any recent changes in behavior or activity patterns and any unusual events and stressors. Officers should explore any motivations for leaving. How does the child normally deal with stressful situations? Have any recent traumatic or stressful events caused such a prompt departure? Have any abuses occurred within the residence or family? Officers also should determine whether there were any recent changes in sleeping and eating patterns that would indicate stress.
- Identify and separately interview family members, close friends, schoolmates, teachers, coworkers, and other significant individuals. The FBI's National Center for the Analysis of Violent Crime has created a general assessment form for distribution to family members and associates that can assist in police officers' efforts to understand the child's personality.[105]
- Determine any history of alcohol and other drug use. Does the child have any particular medical conditions or allergies? If so, are the child's medications for the existing conditions still in the house? The presence of medications that the child needs may indicate an involuntary departure.
- Identify and interview boyfriends and/or girlfriends; determine normal dating patterns, including sexual activity. If the missing child is a postpubescent female, are there pregnancy and abortion issues? If so, officers should consider contacting local pregnancy, health, and abortion clinics. Also, officers should familiarize themselves with department policy and legal issues concerning confidentiality if they find the missing child at such a clinic. Obtain and review any personal writings, diaries, drawings, and schoolwork, including any entries into a personal computer or interaction with online systems or services. A critical item often overlooked in the missing-child call is the presence or absence of journals or diaries. Besides the obvious insights that diaries may provide into the child's state of mind, the presence or absence of any written communication can prove relevant. A child who consistently and regularly has expressed thoughts and feelings in writing might not depart voluntarily without leaving some form of written communication for people left behind.[106] Similarly, calendars or schedules indicating planned events may provide insight into the child's possible motivation for staying or leaving.
- Determine any history of running away, discontent with home life, or ideas of suicide. Has the child disappeared voluntarily on prior occasions? If so, officers should note the last time the child ran away and the length of time missing. Did the child go to friends, other family members, or a runaway shelter? Officers should determine what enabled the child to run away successfully or, conversely, what prevented the child from sustaining a long-term absence. What happened that prompted the child's departure in previous absences? Officers should determine whether the child exhibited any runaway tendencies (for example, staying out all night), threats to leave, or other behaviors that violated clear directives from parents or caregivers. Officers also should determine the existence of any prior suicide attempts or gestures by the child and consider the possibility that the child has disappeared as a result of a self-inflicted injury.

These observations will assist officers in crafting the child's victimology, which will indicate whether the child had the motivation and capability of leaving voluntarily. If the victim assessment suggests that these two factors do not exist, officers must consider the possibility that an abduction has occurred.

Similarly, abductions of toddlers also occur primarily for emotion-based reasons. These cases typically lack planning, are impulsive, and frequently involve the mother's boyfriend or ex-boyfriend as the perpetrator.[107] Because toddlers typically are in the constant care of a caregiver, there is little opportunity for strangers to access them. Additionally, sexually motivated abductions are infrequent among this age group, possibly because of their increased mobility and independence which make them difficult to control.[108]

ABDUCTION PATTERNS

Experts in the field have noted patterns in familial and non-familial perpetrated abductions within victim-specific age groups. For example, newborn and **infant abductions** (that is, the taking of a child less than 1-year-old) occur, by definition, for reasons not typically associated with kidnappings, such as a desire for money, sex, revenge, or custody, which are considered traditional motives in kidnapping cases.[109] Although little research exists on the topic of infant abductors' motivation, it is suggested that these crimes are either emotion-based or motivated by maternal desires.[110] By way of general background, infant abductors usually are women, who account for 141 of the 145 cases analyzed. Offenders whose ages were verified ranged from 14- to 48-years-old, with an average age of 28. Race was determined in 142 cases: 63 offenders were white, 54 were black, and 25 were Hispanic. To gain further insight into infant abductors and the crimes they commit, members of the FBI's National Center for the Analysis of Violent Crime (NCAVC) interviewed 16 abductors; 105 offenders in this analysis had abducted infants in 10 different states. Nine of the abductors targeted hospitals directly: five approached the infant's residence: and two chose other locations. Although none had committed a violent crime before, four killed the infant's mother before stealing her baby.

Although emotion-based abductions also occur among pre-school-aged children, this age group is at an increased risk of sexually motivated and profit-based abductions compared to infants and toddlers. Owing to their physical and emotional development, caregivers generally allow them greater autonomy which can increase their accessibility to strangers and acquaintances. In this age group, sexually motivated offenders are typically male, an acquaintance of the victim, and have access to the child's yard or neighborhood. Acquaintances also are associated with profit-based abductions which generally occur in the context of crimes against older, related victims, such as a parent.[111]

Child abductions most commonly are observed among elementary and middle school children where the victimization rates nearly triple.[112] Motives for abductions within this age group shift from emotion-based, as seen among younger age groups, to sexually driven crimes. Generally, the perpetrators are male, acquaintances or strangers, and target female victims. Younger children in this category tend to be abducted near their home, whereas older children often are abducted from more distant locations.[113]

The risk of sexually motivated abductions decrease as children become of high school age. In this case, emotion- and profit-based crimes are more prevalent. This may be due to the fact that high school-aged children have money and other valuable possessions and are exposed to high-risk activities, such as drug use and abusive relationships. Emotion-based abductions typically resemble adult domestic violence cases, often times involving a female victim and the boyfriend as the perpetrator. In contrast, profit-based abductions frequently pertain to drugs: victims tend to be male, and offenders are generally strangers and acquaintances.[114]

CHECKLIST FOR LAW ENFORCEMENT

The following checklist describes the most important steps that law enforcement can take as the investigation begins. The order of the steps is likely to vary depending on individual circumstances.

- Issue a BOLO (Be On the Look Out) bulletin to be broadcast to local law enforcement agencies alerting them to the missing child, and send a teletype locally or regionally.
- Implement the **AMBER Plan,** which is a voluntary partnership between law enforcement and broadcasters to activate the bulletins in the most serious child abduction cases. (This plan is discussed in greater detail shortly.)
- Immediately enter the child's name into the National Crime Information Center (NCIC) registry of missing persons. There is no waiting period for entry into NCIC for children under age 18.
- Request the National Center for Missing and Exploited Children (NCMEC) fax the child's picture to law enforcement agencies throughout the country.
- Inform the **FBI Child Abduction and Serial Murder Investigative Resource Center (CASMIRC)** of the case or ask for assistance if there is a chance the abduction was predatory.

- Notify the local FBI field office in case additional services and support are needed.
- Notify the state missing children's bureau and request additional services if needed.
- Secure the crime scene—for instance, the location outside a home where the child might have been abducted—and the child's bedroom. The officers who respond initially to the call must evaluate the contents and appearance of the child's room and retrieve the child's used bedding, clothing, and shoes and place them in clean bags to be used as scent articles. Also retrieve the child's toothbrush, hairbrush, and other items that might contain DNA evidence. Protect footprints in dust, mud, or snow to preserve the scent. Determine if personal items are missing, and interview the last persons known to have seen the child.
- Request tracking dogs or a helicopter equipped with an infrared or a heat-sensitive device (to detect heat emitted from the body) if needed after the residence, yard, and surrounding areas have been searched unsuccessfully.
- Advise airlines, airports, bus and taxicab companies, subways, ferries, and ports of the disappearance as necessary and distribute posters of the missing child.
- Revisit various "hot spots" or checkpoints at the same time of day and/or same day of the week following the disappearance to see if any eyewitnesses can be uncovered.
- Contact the neighborhood watch to see if anything suspicious was reported.
- Check the daily log of parking and traffic tickets and traffic stops to see if anything relates to the child's disappearance.
- Check the convicted sex offender registry to find out if a potential suspect lived or was ever stopped by the police in the area.
- Collect and review local newspapers in hopes of possible clues or leads to aid in the search. Check out local regional events and activities—such as carnivals, county fairs, festivals, sports events, and music concerts—and want ads for hired help in search of leads regarding the predator and/or any witnesses to the disappearance.
- Establish a procedure for handling extortion attempts, if needed.
- Contact neighboring jurisdictions to find out if incidents of a similar nature have occurred there.[115]

AMBER ALERT PLAN

The AMBER Alert program is a voluntary partnership between law enforcement agencies, state transportation officials and radio, television and Internet broadcasters to activate an urgent news bulletin in child abduction cases (Figure 11-11). Broadcasters use the Emergency Alert System, formerly known as the Emergency Broadcast System, to air a description of the missing child, the suspected abductor, and any vehicles involved in the abduction. The program was first introduced after the kidnap and murder of 9-year old Amber Hagerman of the Dallas-Fort Worth area and is now established in all 50 states.

▲ FIGURE 11-11   AMBER alert

An AMBER alert is displayed on a highway messaging sign increasing the opportunity for a member of the public to find the missing/kidnapped child. (©Nati Harnik/AP Images)

TIME FRAME	RUNAWAYS RETURNED
Within 7 days	50%
7–14 days	30%
14–30 days	17%
More than 30 days	3%

These statistics indicate that the majority of runaway children cannot sustain an absence of more than two weeks from home. In general, the longer the absence, the greater the likelihood that an individual has abducted the child or that the child has fallen victim to a violent crime. If the child has a history of running away, officers should determine the length of time the child remained missing during previous absences. If the time length of the current absence grossly exceeds that of previous absences, officers should consider the current disappearance a deviation from normal behavior patterns.

Responding officers should note the amount of time that transpired between when the child was last seen and when the parents or guardian alerted authorities. While 24 hours or more may indicate apathy or neglect, this time frame also may reflect the common misconception that an individual must be missing for 24 hours before law enforcement can respond. The responding officers should construct a time line identifying the parents' activities during this interval. The time line highlights family dynamics and clarifies the parents' potential role in the child's disappearance.[117]

How Does the AMBER Alert Work?

Once law enforcement is notified of an abducted child, they must determine whether the case meets the criteria set forth in the AMBER alert plan. The national AMBER Alert Coordinator, affiliated with the U.S. Department of Justice Office of Justice Programs, has recommended the following criteria:

- There is reasonable belief by law enforcement that an abduction has occurred.
- The law enforcement agency believes that the child is in imminent danger of serious bodily injury or death.
- There is enough descriptive information about the victim and the abduction for law enforcement to issue an AMBER alert to assist in the recovery of a child.
- The abduction is of a child 17 years old or younger.
- The child's name and other critical data elements, including the Child Abduction Flag, have been entered into the National Crime Information Center system (NCIC).

If these criteria are met, alert information is put together and faxed to radio stations designated as primary stations under EAS. These stations then send the same information to area radio, television, and cable systems where it is broadcast to millions of listeners. Radio stations interrupt programming to announce the alert, and television and cable stations run a "crawl" on the screen with a picture of the missing child.[116]

Time Factors

How long does a runaway child typically stay away from home, and how does the passage of time influence the classification of a missing-child case? The California Department of Justice's Missing/Unidentified Persons Unit has reported the following trends in runaway returns:

SEX OFFENDER REGISTRATION AND NOTIFICATION

In 1994 Congress passed the **Jacob Wetterling Crimes Against Children and Sexually Violent Offender Registration Act.**[118] The act required that states create sex-offender registries within three years or lose 10% of their funding under the Edward Byrne Memorial program.[119] Offenders who commit a criminal sexual act against a minor or commit any sexually violent offense must register for a period of 10 years from the date of their release from custody or supervision. All 50 states have sex-offender registration.[120]

Although sex-offender registration requirements vary according to state laws, some common features exist in registries throughout the country. In most states, the state criminal justice agency or board (for example, the state police or state bureau of investigation) maintains the state's registry. Sex offenders, both juveniles and adults, register at local law enforcement or corrections agencies, which then forward the information to the state's central registry. Registry information typically includes the offender's name, address, date of birth, Social Security number, and physical description, as well as fingerprints and a photograph. In addition, Iowa requires information about the sex-offense conviction that triggered the registration, and at least eight states collect samples for DNA identification.[121]

Most state laws require that offenders register only if their convictions occurred after the law's effective date, although some states, such as Minnesota, require that offenders register after they are charged with a sexual offense.[122] Offenders receive notice of the registration requirement from the court or registry agency. In Iowa, offenders can contest the registration requirement by filing an application for determination with the State Department of Public Safety.

In essence, the Jacob Wetterling Act gave states the option of releasing information about registered sex offenders to the public but did not require that they do so. This changed in 1996 when Congress amended the act to require that states disclose information about registered sex offenders for public safety purposes. This legislation became known as **Megan's Law,** in memory of Megan Kanka.[123]

U.S. Department of Justice guidelines allow states considerable discretion in determining the extent and manner of notification when warning the public about sex offenders living in the community. All states now have community notification laws.[124]

The most basic form of notification, sometimes referred to as *passive notification,* allows citizens to access registry information at their local law enforcement agencies. In Iowa, citizens must complete a request form at their local police or sheriff's department and provide the name of the person being checked and one of three identifiers: address, date of birth, or Social Security number. If the agency finds the person's name on the registry, it can release certain information about the offender; however, federal guidelines prohibit states from releasing the identities of victims. Employers also may check potential employees.

In addition to allowing passive notification, a number of states permit government agencies to disseminate information about registered sex offenders to vulnerable individuals and organizations. Using this process, known as *active notification,* officials may choose to notify prior victims, landlords, neighbors, public and private schools, child-care facilities, religious and youth organizations, and other relevant individuals or agencies. Most officials reserve community-wide notification for only the most dangerous sex offenders. Community-wide notification usually involves using the media and public forums such as neighborhood associations and other community meetings.

The Pam Lychner Sexual Offender Tracking and Identification Act of 1996[125] established a national sex-offender database, which the FBI maintains.[126] This national tracking system gives law enforcement authorities access to sex-offender registration data from all participating states. The Lychner Act also requires that the FBI register, and verify the addresses of, sex offenders in states that have not met the minimum compliance standards set forth by the Jacob Wetterling Act, although this may change.[127]

CRIME IN SCHOOLS

Sixty-five years ago, surveys of public school teachers indicated that the most pressing classroom problems were tardiness, talkative students, and gum chewing.[128] Far more serious complaints are currently heard from teachers, administrators, and students— about the presence of drugs, gangs, and weapons on campus and the threat of assault, robbery, theft, vandalism, and rape.[129]

According to the popular media, such as *Time* magazine and *U.S. News and World Report,* the problems in our nation's schools may be paralyzing the system.[130] In an effort to develop a systematic procedure for threat assessment and intervention in school violence cases, the FBI's National Center for the Analysis of Violent Crime (NCAVC) conducted an in-depth review of 18 school shootings. Because of confidentiality issues, the shooting cases studied were not identified. The study analyzed the shootings from a behavioral perspective and resulted in the development of the threat assessment intervention model. The model outlines a procedure for evaluating a threat and the person making the threat so that an accurate assessment can be made of the likelihood that the threat will be carried out.

QUICK FACTS

An Analysis of School Shootings

There were 188 shootings on school campuses in the United States between the Sandy Hook Elementary School shooting in Newtown, Connecticut on December 14, 2012 and July 1, 2016 . . . an average of nearly one per week. In all, these incidents have resulted in 59 deaths and 124 non-fatal gunshot wounds. Eighty-four of the shootings were in K-12 schools (53%) and 76 were on college or university campuses (47%). Twenty-four of the shootings occurred after a confrontation or verbal argument intensified. Many of the students who perpetrated these shootings had easy access to guns at home. Indeed, over 79% of those suspects that were involved in school-associated homicide or suicide obtained the gun from the shooter's home or that of a friend or relative.

Source: Everytown for Gun Safety Website: https://everytownresearch.org/reports/analysis-of-school-shootings/

THREAT ASSESSMENT

A threat is an expression of the intent to do harm or act out violently against someone or something. A threat can be spoken, written, or symbolic—for example, motioning with one's hands as though shooting at another person.

Threat assessment rests on two critical principles: (1) that all threats and all threateners are not equal and (2) that most threateners are unlikely to carry out their threats. However, all threats must be taken seriously and evaluated.

In NCAVC's experience, most threats are made anonymously or under a false name. Because threat assessment relies heavily on evaluating the threatener's background, personality, lifestyle, and resources, identifying the threatener is necessary so that an informed assessment can be made—and so that charges can be brought if the threat is serious enough to warrant prosecution. If the threatener's identity cannot be determined, the evaluation will have to be based on the threat alone. That assessment may change if the threatener is eventually identified: a threat that

was considered low risk may be rated as more serious if new information suggests the threatener is dangerous; conversely, an assessment of high risk may be scaled down if the threatener is identified and found not to have the intent, ability, means, or motive to carry out the threat (Figure 11-12).

Motivation

Threats are made for a variety of reasons. A threat may be a warning signal, a reaction to fear of punishment or some other anxiety, or a demand for attention. It may be intended to taunt; to intimidate; to assert power or control; to punish; to manipulate or coerce; to frighten; to terrorize; to compel someone to do something; to strike back for an injury, injustice, or insult; to disrupt someone's or some institution's life; to test authority, or to protect oneself. The emotions that underlie a threat can be love, hate, fear, rage, or desire for attention, revenge, excitement, or recognition.

Motivation can never be known with complete certainty, but understanding motive to the extent possible is a key element in evaluating a threat. A threat reflects the threatener's mental and emotional state at the time the threat is made, but it is important to remember that a state of mind can be temporarily but strongly influenced by alcohol or drugs or by a precipitating factor such as a romantic breakup, failing grades, or conflict with a parent. After a person has absorbed an emotional setback and calmed down, or when the effects of alcohol or drugs have worn off, his or her motivation to act on a violent threat may also diminish.

Signposts

In general, people do not switch instantly from nonviolence to violence. Nonviolent people do not "snap" or decide on the spur of the moment to meet a problem by using violence. Instead, the path toward violence is an evolutionary one, with signposts along the way. A threat is one observable behavior; another may be brooding about frustration or disappointment or fantasizing about destruction or revenge in conversations, writings, drawings, and the like.

Factors in Threat Assessment

Specific, plausible details are a critical factor in evaluating a threat. Details can include the identity of the victim or victims; the reason for making the threat; the means, weapon, and method by which it is to be carried out; the date, time, and place that the threatened act will occur; and concrete information about plans or preparations that have already been made.

Specific details can indicate that substantial thought, planning, and preparatory steps have already been taken, suggesting a higher risk that the threatener will follow through on the threat. Similarly, a lack of detail suggests that the threatener may not have thought through all the contingencies, has not actually taken steps to carry out the threat, and may not seriously intend violence. He or she may merely be "blowing off steam" over some frustration or be trying to frighten or intimidate a particular victim or disrupt a school's events or routine.

Details that are specific but not logical or plausible may indicate a less serious threat. For example, a high school student writes that he intends to detonate hundreds of pounds of plutonium in the school's auditorium the following day at lunchtime. The threat is detailed, stating a specific time, place, and weapon, but the details are unpersuasive. Plutonium is almost impossible to obtain, legally or on the black market. It is expensive, hard to transport, and very dangerous to handle, and a complex high-explosive detonation is required to set off a nuclear reaction. No high-school student is likely to have any plutonium at all, much less hundreds of pounds, nor would a student have the knowledge or complex equipment required to detonate it. A threat this unrealistic is obviously unlikely to be carried out.

The emotional content of a threat can be an important clue to the threatener's mental state. Emotions are conveyed by melodramatic words and unusual punctuation—"I hate you!!!!!" "You have ruined my life!!!!" "May God have mercy on your soul!!!!"—or in excited, incoherent passages that may refer to God or other religious beings or may deliver an ultimatum.

Though emotionally charged threats can tell the assessor something about the temperament of the threatener, they are not a measure of danger. They may sound frightening, but no correlation has been established between the emotional intensity in a threat and the risk that it will be carried out.

Precipitating stressors are incidents, circumstances, reactions, or situations that can trigger a threat. The precipitating event may seem insignificant and have no direct relevance to the threat, but nonetheless it becomes a catalyst. For example, a student has a fight with his mother before going to school. The argument may be a minor one over an issue that has nothing to do with school, but it sets off an emotional chain reaction that leads the student to threaten another student at school that day—possibly something he has thought about doing in the past.

The effect of a precipitating event obviously depends on predisposing factors: underlying personality traits, characteristics, and temperament that predispose an adolescent to fantasize about violence or act violently. Accordingly, information about a temporary "trigger" must be considered together with broader information about underlying factors, such as a student's vulnerability to loss and depression.

Personality Traits and Behavior

- *Leakage:* "Leakage" occurs when a student intentionally or unintentionally reveals clues to feelings, thoughts, fantasies, attitudes, or intentions that may signal an impending violent act. These clues can take the form of subtle threats, boasts, innuendos, predictions, or ultimatums. They may be spoken or conveyed in stories, diary entries, essays, poems, letters, songs, drawings, doodles, tattoos, or videos.[131] Leakage can also occur when a student tries, at times deceptively, to get unwitting friends or classmates to help with preparations for a violent act (for example, the student asks a friend to obtain ammunition for her because she is "going hunting").
- *Low tolerance for frustration:* The student is easily psychologically bruised, insulted, angered, and hurt by real or perceived injustices done to him or her by others and has great difficulty tolerating frustration.
- *Poor coping skills:* The student has little, if any, ability to deal with frustration, criticism, disappointment, failure, rejection, or humiliation. His or her response is typically inappropriate, exaggerated, immature, or disproportionate.
- *Lack of resiliency:* The student lacks resiliency and is unable to bounce back even when some time has elapsed since a frustrating or disappointing experience, a setback, or a put-down.
- *Failed love relationship:* The student may feel rejected or humiliated after the end of a love relationship and cannot accept or come to terms with the rejection.
- *"Injustice collector":* The student nurses resentment over real or perceived injustices. No matter how much time

has passed, the "injustice collector" neither forgets nor forgives the wrongs the people he or she believes are responsible. The student may keep a hit list with the names of people who have wronged him or her.
- *Signs of depression:* The student shows symptoms of depression such as lethargy, physical fatigue, a morose or dark outlook on life, a sense of malaise, and loss of interest in activities that he or she once enjoyed.
- *Narcissism:* The student is self-centered, lacks insight into others' needs and/or feelings, and blames others for failures and disappointments. The narcissistic student may embrace the role of a victim to elicit sympathy and to feel temporarily superior to others. He or she displays signs of paranoia and assumes an attitude of self-importance or grandiosity that masks feelings of unworthiness.[132] A narcissistic student may be either very thin-skinned or very thick-skinned in responding to criticism.
- *Alienation:* The student consistently behaves as though he feels different or estranged from others. This sense of separateness reflects more than in just being a loner. It can involve feelings of isolation, sadness, loneliness, not belonging, and not fitting in.
- *Dehumanization of others:* The student consistently fails to see others as fellow humans. He or she characteristically views other people as "nonpersons" or objects to be thwarted. This attitude may appear in the student's writings and artwork, in interactions with others, or in comments during conversation.
- *Lack of empathy:* The student shows an inability to understand the feelings of others and seems unconcerned about anyone else's feelings. When others show emotion, the student may ridicule them as being weak or stupid.
- *Exaggerated sense of entitlement:* The student constantly expects special treatment and consideration and reacts negatively if he or she doesn't get that treatment.
- *Attitude of superiority:* The student has a sense of being superior and presents himself or herself as smarter, more creative, more talented, more experienced, and more worldly than others.
- *Exaggerated need for attention:* The student shows an exaggerated, even pathological, need for attention, whether positive or negative, no matter what the circumstances.
- *Externalization of blame:* The student consistently refuses to take responsibility for his or her own actions and typically faults other people, events, or situations for any failings or shortcomings. In placing blame, the student frequently seems impervious to rational argument and common sense.
- *Masking of low self-esteem:* Although the student may display an arrogant, self-glorifying attitude, his or her conduct often seems to veil underlying low self-esteem. The student avoids high visibility or involvement in school activities, and other students may consider him or her a nonentity.

- *Anger-management problems:* Rather than expressing anger in appropriate ways and circumstances, the student consistently tends to burst out in temper tantrums or melodramatic displays or to brood in sulky, seething silence. The anger may be noticeably out of proportion to the cause or may be redirected toward people who had nothing to do with the original incident. The anger may come in unpredictable and uncontrollable outbursts, and it may be accompanied by expressions of unfounded prejudice, dislike, or even hatred toward individuals or groups.

- *Intolerance:* The student often expresses racial or religious prejudice or intolerant attitudes toward minorities or displays slogans or symbols of intolerance through such means as tattoos, jewelry, clothing, bumper stickers, or book covers.

- *Inappropriate humor:* The student's humor is consistently inappropriate. Jokes or humorous comments tend to be macabre, insulting, belittling, or mean.

- *Manipulation of others:* The student consistently attempts to con and manipulate others and win their trust so that they will rationalize any signs of his or her aberrant or threatening behavior.

- *Lack of trust:* The student is untrusting and chronically suspicious of others' motives and intentions. This lack of trust may approach a clinically paranoid state. The student may express the belief that society has no trustworthy institution or mechanism for achieving justice or resolving conflict and that if something bothersome occurs, he or she has to settle it in his or her own way.

- *Closed social group:* The student appears introverted. He or she has acquaintances rather than friends or associates only with a single small group that seems to exclude everyone else. Students who threaten or carry out violent acts are not necessarily loners in the classic sense, and the composition and qualities of peer groups can be important pieces of information in assessing the danger that a threat will be acted on.

- *Change of behavior:* The student's behavior changes dramatically. His or her academic performance may decline, or the student may show a reckless disregard for school rules, schedules, dress codes, and other regulations.

- *Rigid and opinionated outlook:* The student appears rigid, judgmental, and cynical, voices strong opinions on subjects about which he or she has little knowledge, and disregards facts, logic, and reasoning that might challenge these opinions.

- *Unusual interest in sensational violence:* The student demonstrates an unusual interest in school shootings and other heavily publicized acts of violence. He or she may declare his admiration for those who committed the acts or may criticize them for "incompetence" or failing to kill enough people. The student may explicitly express a desire to carry out a similar act in his or her own school, possibly as an act of "justice."

- *Fascination with violence-filled entertainment:* The student has an unusual fascination with movies, TV shows, computer games, music videos, or printed materials that focus intensely on themes of violence, hatred, control, power, death, and destruction. He or she may repeatedly watch one movie or read one book with violent content, perhaps involving school violence. Themes of hatred, violence, weapons, and mass destruction recur in virtually all the student's activities, hobbies, and pastimes. The student spends inordinate amounts of time playing video games with violent themes and seems more interested in the violent images than in the game itself. On the Internet, the student regularly searches for websites involving violence, weapons, and other disturbing subjects. There is evidence that the student has downloaded and kept material from these sites.

- *Negative role models:* The student may be drawn to negative, inappropriate role models such as Hitler, Satan, or others associated with violence and destruction.

- *Behavior relevant to carrying out a threat:* The student appears to be increasingly occupied with activities that could be related to carrying out a threat (for example, spending unusual amounts of time practicing with firearms or visiting violent websites). The time spent on these activities has noticeably begun to exclude normal everyday pursuits such as doing homework, attending classes, going to work, and spending time with friends.

CLASSIFICATION OF THREATS

Types of Threats

Threats can be classified into four categories:

1. A direct threat identifies a specific act against a specific target and is delivered in a straightforward, clear, and explicit manner: "I am going to place a bomb in the school's gym."

2. An indirect threat tends to be vague, unclear, and ambiguous. The plan, the intended victim, the motivation, and other aspects of the threat are masked or equivocal: "If I wanted to, I could kill everyone at this school!" While violence is implied, the threat is phrased tentatively—"If I wanted to"—and suggests that a violent act *could* occur, not that it *will* occur.

3. A veiled threat is one that strongly implies but does not explicitly threaten violence: "We would be better off without you around anymore." Such a statement clearly hints at a possible violent act but leaves it to the potential victim to interpret the message and give a definite meaning to the threat.

4. A conditional threat warns that a violent act will happen unless certain demands or terms are met: "If you don't pay me one million dollars, I will place a bomb in the school." This type of threat is often used in extortion cases.

▶ **FIGURE 11-13**
Weapon detection program
A firearm discovered in a student's locker as a result of a successful, but labor-intensive, weapon detection program at a New York City high school. Given the frequency with which handguns and other weapons have been discovered on school grounds, some school districts have gone to considerable expense to install metal detectors at entry points. In addition, security officers must be present at these sites to further review suspicious circumstances. (©Dwayne Newton/PhotoEdit)

THE ROLE OF LAW ENFORCEMENT

In the vast majority of cases, whether to involve law enforcement hinges on the seriousness of the threat: low, medium, or high.[133]

- *Low level:* A threat that has been evaluated as low level poses little danger to public safety and in most cases would not necessitate law enforcement investigation for a possible criminal offense. (However, law enforcement agencies may be asked for information in connection with a threat of any level.) Appropriate intervention in a low-level case would involve, at a minimum, interviews with the student and his/her parents. If the threat was aimed at a specific person, that person should be asked about his/her relationship with the threatener and the circumstances that led up to the threat. The response—disciplinary action and perhaps a referral for counseling or some other form of intervention—should be determined according to school policies and the judgment of the responsible school administrators.
- *Medium level:* When a threat is rated as medium level, the response should in most cases include contacting the appropriate law enforcement agency, as well as other sources, to obtain additional information (and possibly reclassify the threat into the high or low category). A medium-level threat will sometimes, though not necessarily, warrant investigation as a possible criminal offense.
- *High level:* Almost always, if a threat is evaluated as high level, the school should immediately inform the appropriate law enforcement agency. A response plan, which should have been designed ahead of time and rehearsed by both school and law enforcement personnel, should be implemented, and law enforcement should be informed and involved in whatever subsequent actions

are taken in response to the threat. A high-level threat is highly likely to result in criminal prosecution (Figure 11-13).

INVESTIGATING SCHOOL VIOLENCE

When investigating threats of violence in schools, listen carefully to witnesses in order to correctly identify the level of the threat and subsequently take appropriate action. Key questions include:

- Who made the threat?
- To whom was the threat made?
- Under what circumstances was the threat made?
- Exactly what words were said?
- How often were threats made?[134]

On some occasions, undercover juvenile informants can be used by police to gain insight in a school where threats have been received or plots of violence are suspected.[135] However, this practice is usually discouraged, since it places juveniles in a very precarious and potentially dangerous position. Some jurisdictions forbid the practice; others have developed very sophisticated guidelines regulating the use of a confidential informant who is under 16 years of age.

Ascertaining who made the threat or committed the act is often the least difficult part of the investigation due to the fact that juvenile perpetrators frequently use their crimes as a way of getting attention. Also, a young criminal often lacks the experience, sophistication, and self-control needed to adequately avoid detection (Figure 11-14).

Clearly, most of the police effort is on prevention, focusing on the development of programs that emphasize "team" efforts among school administrators, the police, and the community at large. When an incident does occur, specially trained teams of police intervention officers lead the investigation in an attempt

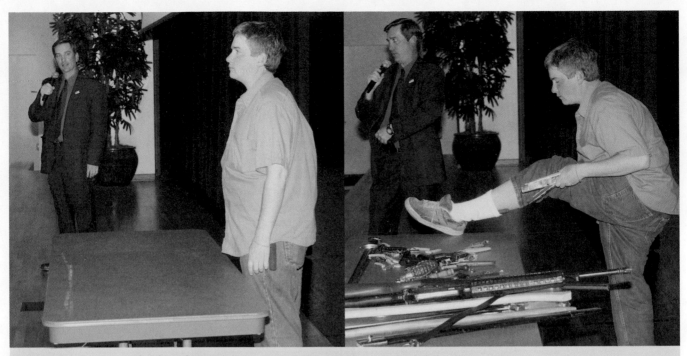

▲ **FIGURE 11-14 Schools and weapons**

Chris Dorn joins his father, national school safety expert, Michael Dorn, in a presentation of concealed weapons. Chris Dorn pulls out one of 138 weapons from grenades to a submachine gun concealed in his clothing. Easy-to-hide items, such as box cutters, are also used in most school attacks involving weapons. (©Chris Dorn, Safe Havens International)

to not only apprehend the suspect but also quell growing fear that might arise from recent high-profile incidents of school violence. Some departments are now using **rapid response deployment** or **quick action deployment (QUAD)**. This approach focuses on training patrol officers in the principles and tactics of rapid deployment for responding to critical incidents, especially incidents of school violence. In theory, the concept has merit: immediately responding officers are able to enter buildings where life-threatening situations are in progress or where loss of victims' lives is imminent. Proponents of the concept argue that such intervention cannot wait until the SWAT team responds and therefore that police action must be taken immediately. While there is no doubt that such a condition has presented itself, the vast majority of incidents (including school shootings) are deescalated by time. It's suggested that the best approach for patrol officers responding to a critical and violent incident at a school, especially one involving potential hostages, is to take action only when appropriate and that their primary mission is to control and contain the scene. They should let specially trained hostage negotiation and critical-incident teams handle any protracted incident of school violence. Once the scene has been secured, investigators should then treat the crime as they would any other homicide, assault, or threat.

Home Searches: For Weapons

A number of planned school shootings and bombings around the nation have been successfully averted by the use of home searches. Some years ago, officers of the Bibb County Board of Education Campus Police Department in Georgia began regu-

larly conducting searches of students' homes for firearms, explosives, and other items. The practice has now become widely used around the nation.

Home searches are conducted when a gun or components of an explosive device are recovered from a student on campus or when investigating reports show that someone has made a threat to commit a weapons assault at a school. Home searches can be conducted with the consent of the parents in most states or with a search warrant if sufficient probable cause exists.

The Georgia Emergency Management Agency (GEMA) has shared the concept with thousands of educators and law enforcement officials from across the country in seminars, articles and training videos. This technique has been used to prevent several dozen planned school shootings and bombings.

After attending home search training, a School Resource Officer in Oklahoma conducted a home search and prevented a planned school bombing on the first day of school last year. A plot by a Georgia student to kill hundreds of his classmates was foiled with a home search. The student planned to place a bomb in a field near his school and call in a bomb threat. Local law enforcement officials found the plans and bomb-making components in the student's bedroom during a home search.

The home search should be included in every community's inventory of prevention measures. Although this technique has become standard practice in many regions, there are still missed opportunities for its application.

Home searches should be conducted only by armed law enforcement officers. In some cases, it is desirable for campus administrators or mental health staff to assist officers in the search, because they may notice danger signs in a student's bed-room that could be missed by officers. Campus officials should enter the residence only when officers feel it is safe to do so.

Parental Consent. In many cases, officers will be able to obtain consent from parents or guardians (in the case of K–12 students). In some cases, officers may have to agree not to pursue criminal charges for gun or drug possession in order to obtain consent. This option should first be discussed with the local prosecutor before using it. Officers should clearly advise that other offenses, such as possession of a stolen gun or evidence pertaining to an assault with the weapon, may still be prosecuted. If probable cause to obtain a search warrant does not exist, it may be more important to recover the weapon than to prosecute.

Search Warrant. In other cases, a search warrant may be required. If possible, officers should be certain that the warrant specifically lists such associated items as ammunition and paper-work of the offender that may show a direct link between the offender and the weapon; how the items were illegally trafficked; and plans to commit criminal acts with the weapon(s). An effort should be made to include computer-based records in the warrant as well.

Multiple Weapons. When one weapon is found, the possibility that other weapons may be present should be considered.

Avoid Publicity. The use of the home search to find concealed weapons should not be publicized in order to avoid losing the element of surprise and thus providing the student with the opportunity to use alternative places of concealment in the home.

The use of the home search technique has prevented much potential bloodshed on our nation's campuses, but unfortunately, several mass school shootings have occurred when officials failed to utilize this simple technique. Those who need to use it must be familiar with the technique. It could mean the difference between life and death.[136]

KEY TERMS

AMBER Plan
battered-child syndrome
blunt-force trauma
bullying
child pornography
contact burns
cyberbullying
FBI Child Abduction and Serial Murder
    Investigative Resource Center
    (CASMIRC)
hemorrhage

immersion burns
infant abduction
Jacob Wetterling Crimes Against
    Children and Sexually Violent
    Offender Registration Act
Megan's Law
Munchausen Syndrome by Proxy (MSBP)
preferential child molester
rapid response deployment or quick
    action deployment (QUAD)
scald burns

sex tourism
Sexting
Sextortion
shaken-baby syndrome (SBS)
situational child molester
spill/splash injuries
sudden infant death syndrome
    (SIDS)
threat assessment

REVIEW QUESTIONS

1. What are the two most common instruments used in child abuse?
2. What are some of the ways that intentional immersion burns are distinguished from accidental immersion burns?
3. Why was the phrase "shaken-baby syndrome" coined?
4. What is the mechanism of injuries in shaken-baby syndrome?
5. What role does the physician play in child-abuse cases?
6. What is Munchausen Syndrome by Proxy (MSBP)?
7. What are some of the major behavioral characteristics of situational and preferential child molesters?
8. Identify the three developmental issues that are important when allegations of sexual abuse arise.
9. What are some of the benefits of using an anatomically detailed doll in interviewing children?
10. How is child pornography behaviorally defined?

11. Describe the appearance of a SIDS victim.
12. What motivations are typically *not* involved in infant abduction?
13. What appears to be the major motivating factor that drives female offenders to abduct infants?
14. A parental checklist to assist police in locating a missing child should include what instructions?
15. What is the AMBER Plan?
16. What resources must a runaway child have to success-fully sustain a voluntary long-term absence?
17. What are the major features of the Jacob Wetterling Crimes Against Children and the Sexually Violent Offender Registration Act?
18. Threats in school violence can be classified into four categories; what are they?

| INTERNET ACTIVITIES

1. The National Sudden and Unexpected Infant/Child Death Pregnancy Loss Resource Center (*www.sidscenter.org*) provides information services and technical assistance on sudden infant death syndrome (SIDS) and related topics. The material put out by this group and found on their website at *www.sidscenter.org* can answer the following questions. What is the relationship between sudden infant death syndrome and prenatal maternal smoking? Is mother/infant cosleeping a factor? What factors influence the use of home cardiorespiratory monitors for infants? Are repeated sudden unexpected and unexplained infant deaths natural or unnatural? Does a sudden infant death syndrome gene exist?

2. For a comprehensive discussion of shaken-baby syndrome, visit the National Center on Shaken Baby Syndrome and Abusive Head Trauma (*www.dontshake.org*). The site puts readers in touch with the most current medical and investigative information on SBS.

► This 17-year-old girl in hand-cuffs was arrested by this vice squad police officer. She was subsequently charged with soliciting with the intent to commit prostitution.

(©Robert Nickelsberg/Getty Images)

12

HUMAN TRAFFICKING

CHAPTER OBJECTIVES

1. Discuss the major legal provisions of the Mann Act and the Travel Act.

2. Be familiar with the Trafficking Victims Protection Act 2000, Trafficking Victims Protection Reauthorization Acts of 2003, 2005, 2008, and the Racketeer Influenced and Corrupt Organizations Act (RICO).

3. Discuss the precipitating factors that contribute to children becoming involved in prostitution.

4. Understand the psychological and emotional difficulties sex-trafficking victims suffer.

5. Discuss why the Stockholm syndrome sometimes occurs and how it can inhibit victim cooperation.

6. Identify the major symptoms of sex-trafficking victims who are suffering from post-traumatic stress disorder (PTSD).

7. Understand the ways in which foreign women are sex trafficked, transported, delivered, marketed, and exploited in the United States.

8. Identify those locations where sex-trafficked women are most likely to be found.

9. Develop an interview protocol for interviewing sex-trafficking victims.

10. Explain how reverse stings and sting operations work.

11. Discuss how the Internet is used in the transactions of commercial sex and how the police can use it to track down sexual predators.

12. Understand the importance of the multi-agency task force in combating sex trafficking.

Human **trafficking** has emerged as the second largest money maker for criminals in the world today, exceeded only by drug sales. Not too many years ago it was in third place behind arms sales. The reason human trafficking is so lucrative is that unlike the sale of drugs, which are sold then used once, a human being can be sold over and over again thus generating enormous profits with very little investment.[1]

However, it is important to understand that human trafficking can take a number of forms. These include sex trafficking, forced labor, involuntary servitude, peonage,[2] and the illegal trafficking of human organs.[3] In this chapter we will be focusing primarily on the criminal investigation of sex trafficking since it is this aspect of human trafficking that local law enforcement agencies tend to direct their major enforcement efforts. This however is in no way meant to diminish the tragic consequences associated with the other forms of human trafficking.

We will first start by discussing some of the most important federal laws in sex trafficking that law enforcement officers have available to them to combat sex trafficking, along with a brief discussion of existing state laws on human trafficking. We will then proceed to discuss the investigation of two different categories of sex trafficking victims, namely, American children, who are trafficked in the United States and foreign women and children who are trafficked into the United States. The investigative techniques employed in these two categories of victims are in many respects quite different and these differences will be discussed in considerable detail. We will also examine the ways in which American law enforcement officers are working to reduce the size of the commercial sex market by focusing on the customers (**johns**). Lastly, we will discuss the use of **multi-agency task forces** to combat sex trafficking and why they are absolutely essential to maximize effectiveness in dealing with the crime of sex trafficking.

QUICK FACTS

Profits Derived from Human Trafficking Internationally

Recently, The International Labour Organization released a groundbreaking report estimating that victims of this crime generate a staggering $150 billion in profits per year for the private global economy: $99 billion in the sex industry and $51 billion in other sectors.

UNITED STATES LAWS ON SEX TRAFFICKING

THE MANN ACT

The Mann Act, passed on June 25, 1910 (also known as the White Slave Traffic Act), was named after Representative James Robert Mann (R-IL) and is one of the oldest U.S. laws relating to sex-trafficking prohibitions (Figure 12.1). This law prohibits the transportation of individuals across state lines for purposes of engaging in prostitution or other criminal sexual activity.[4,5]

The Mann Act has separate provisions relating to adult and minor "transportees."

These are distinguished as follows:

Adults

Whoever knowingly transports any individual in interstate or foreign commerce, or in any Territory or Possession of the United States, with intent that such individual engage in prostitution, or in any sexual activity for which any person can be charged with a criminal offense, or attempts to do so, shall be fined under this title or imprisoned not more than ten years.[6]

CHAPTER OUTLINE

▲ **FIGURE 12-1**
The Mann Act, or White-Slave Traffic Act
Named after Representative James Robert Mann (R-IL) became law on June 25, 1910. It created the federal law against "prostitution or debauchery, or for any other immoral purpose." It dealt with forced prostitution, harboring immigrant prostitutes, and the transportation across state lines. As of April 1912 the white slave investigations overshadowed the entire balance of the Bureau's [the future Federal Bureau of Investigation (FBI)] work. The Mann Act was passed into law at a time when the prostitution debate and the white-slave trade were high-profile issues. (**Source:** Prints & Photographs Division, Library of Congress, LC-B2-3818-2)

Minors

A person who knowingly transports an individual who has not attained the age of eighteen years in interstate or foreign commerce, or in any commonwealth, territory or possession of the United States, with intent that the individual engage in prostitution, or in any sexual activity for which any person can be charged with a criminal offense, shall be fined under this title and imprisoned not less than ten years or life.[7]

THE TRAVEL ACT

The "Travel Act," federalizes the crime of operating prostitution businesses.[8] It prohibits, in part, the following activities:

Traveling in interstate or foreign commerce or using the mail or any facility in interstate or foreign commerce, with intent to . . . promote, manage, establish, carry on, or facilitate the promotion, management, establishment, or carrying on, of any unlawful activity, [including] any business enterprise involving . . . prostitution offenses in violation of the laws of the State in which they are committed or of the United States.[9]

The Travel Act, passed in 1952, is similar to the Mann Act in that it does not require a showing of compelled prostitution. It does require a showing of a "business enterprise" that was involved in prostitution, which has been interpreted to mean "a continuous course of conduct" as opposed to "isolated, casual, or sporadic activity."[10] The Travel Act, in contrast to the Mann Act, also requires the actual carrying on of the prostitution business as opposed to the mere intent to do so. Like the Mann Act, there is no statutorily mandated minimum sentence where adult transportees or victims are involved. The maximum sentence under the Travel Act is only five years for each count (unless death results), as compared to not less than 10 years or life under the Mann Act if it involves a minor.

TRAFFICKING VICTIMS PROTECTION ACT 2000

In 2000, the Government of the United States of America enacted the **Trafficking Victims Protection Act (TVPA)**, which makes human trafficking a federal crime, establishes resources to combat human trafficking, and issues measures for the protection of victims, thus squarely targeting human trafficking for federal criminal prosecution.[11]

CREATION OF SPECIAL STATUS VISAS

An important part of the 2000 *Trafficking Victims Protection Act* was the creation of two special status visas, namely the U visa and the T visa. These visas are intended to assist these trafficking victims to stay in the United States as long as certain stipulations are met.

THE U VISA

It is important to understand that the rescued victim's fear of deportation has created a class of silent victims which undermines law enforcement's attempts to arrest and eventually prosecute the traffickers. In order to help victims overcome their fear of deportation Congress has created the **U visa**.[12] The U-visa is available to immigrants who are victims of a wide range of serious crimes and provides victims with a means to stabilize their legal status. The U visa encourages them to report the crimes. It helps to curtail criminal activity, protects the innocent, and encourages victims to "fully participate in proceedings that will aid in bringing perpetrators to justice."[13] The U visa also can promote contact with law enforcement officers within isolated communities, which provides valuable assistance to individuals at heightened risk of victimization.

The U visa provides an avenue to legal status for immigrant crime victims who:

- Have suffered substantial physical or mental abuse as a result of victimization;
- Possess information regarding the activity;

- Offer a source of help in the investigation or prosecution.[14]

THE T VISA

The **T visa** on the other hand is available for victims who self-petition to stay in the U.S. for up to four years if they can show the following:

- They have been a victim of a severe form of trafficking;
- They have complied with reasonable requests to assist in the investigation or prosecution of their case (or are not yet 18 years of age);
- They are physically present in the U.S. on account of trafficking; and
- They would suffer severe hardship if repatriated.

People whose T visa applications have met the specific qualifications can receive benefits through the Health and Human Services certification process even before their visa petition has been finalized. It should be noted, however, that processing for the T visa takes time, and there is no guarantee the victim will be approved to receive one.

TRAFFICKING VICTIMS PROTECTION REAUTHORIZATION ACT 2003

The **Trafficking Victims Protection Reauthorization Act 2003** was passed by Congress in order to meet the increasing challenges posed by the deficiencies of the TVPA 2000 and included new legal resources against trafficking such as allowing victims to bring civil law suits against traffickers.

TRAFFICKING VICTIMS PROTECTION REAUTHORIZATION ACT 2005

The **Trafficking Victims Protection Reauthorization Act 2005** gave jurisdiction to US courts over government employees who become involved in human trafficking abroad. The amendment also provides new antitrafficking measures such as developing grant programs directed towards aiding state and local enforcement of antitrafficking activities and expanding assistance programs to aid victims who are US citizens or resident aliens.

WILLIAM WILBERFORCE TRAFFICKING VICTIMS PROTECTION REAUTHORIZATION ACT OF 2008

The **William Wilberforce Trafficking Victims Protection Reauthorization Act of 2008** authorizes the appropriations for 2008 through 2011 for the TVPA and establishes a system to monitor and evaluate all assistance under the act. The act requires the establishment of an integrated data base to be used by US government departments and agencies to collect and analyze data on trafficking in persons (Figure 12.2).

FEDERAL LAWS RELATED TO DOMESTIC MINOR SEX TRAFFICKING

Table 12.1 summarizes federal laws and penalties that are most commonly used in the prosecution of domestic minor sex trafficking.

RACKETEER INFLUENCED AND CORRUPT ORGANIZATIONS ACT (RICO)

Congress enacted the **Racketeer Influenced and Corrupt Organizations Act (RICO)** in 1970 to "seek the eradication of organized crime."[15,16] Originally formed in response to the increasing problem of organized crime's penetration into lawful business operations,[17] "[a]s finally enacted, RICO authorized the imposition of enhanced criminal penalties and new civil sanctions to provide new legal remedies for all types of organized criminal behavior."[18] As a result of its liberal construction clause imposed by Congress, RICO has been successfully expanded to prosecute large criminal syndicates involved in narcotics, arms dealing, gambling, prostitution, and sex trafficking.

HARSHER PENALTIES UNDER RICO

A criminal RICO violation allows for a 21-year prison sentence, or more if the underlying offense has a greater penalty.[19,20] Because a defendant can be charged both with a RICO violation and with conspiracy to violate RICO, the potential for a 40-year sentence exists. Additionally, a defendant can receive consecutive sentences for a RICO violation and a predicate offense, or participants in an enterprise can be convicted of racketeering conspiracy without being convicted of an underlying predicate offense.[21]

An additional lure for prosecutors is the portion of the law that requires asset forfeiture of any interest or property gained as a

▲ **FIGURE 12-2 William Wilberforce**
William Wilberforce was a deeply religious nineteenth century member of the British Parliament and social reformer who was very influential in the abolition of the slave trade and eventually slavery itself in the British Empire. (©Everett Collection Historical/Alamy)

result of RICO violation.[22] Congress included the criminal forfeiture provision in RICO to "break the economic power of organized crime as well as to punish and deter offenders."[23] The provision mandates the forfeiture of a defendant's entire interest in the enterprise, possibly including the enterprise itself, regardless of whether some parts are engaged in legitimate business.[24] The law also specifies forfeiture of "property or contractual rights[s] of any kind affording a source on influence over" the enterprise.[25]

STATE LAWS ON HUMAN TRAFFICKING

All 50 states prohibit the prostitution of children under state and local laws that predate the enactment of the TVPA. **The Innocence Lost Initiative** is a collaboration of federal and state law enforcement authorities and victim-assistance providers focused on combating the prostitution of children. The U.S. Department of Justice's (DOJ) Child Exploitation and Obscenity Section and U.S. Attorneys' Offices also prosecute child sex trafficking cases outside the Innocence Lost Initiative. In more recent operations, however, federal law enforcement disseminated guidance, screen-

TABLE 12-1	Federal Laws Related to Domestic Minor Sex Trafficking	
FEDERAL	**MINIMUM SENTENCE**	**MAXIMUM SENTENCE**
18 U.S.C. §2423 (a) – Transportation of a minor with intent for minor to engage in criminal sexual activity)	10 years	Life
18 U.S.C. §2422 – Coercion and enticement (transportation for prostitution or other criminal sexual activity)	10 years	Life
TVPA 18 U.S.C. §1591 – Sex trafficking of children or by force, fraud, or coercion	15 years (child is under 14)	Life (child under 14 or under 18 with force, fraud, or coercion)
	10 years (between 14–17)	Life (child between 14–17 and no force, fraud, or coercion used)
18 U.S.C. §2251 – Sex exploitation of children	15 years	30 years (first offense)
	25 years	50 years (one prior conviction)
	35 years	Life (two or more prior convictions)
	30 years	Life (if caused the death of the victim in the course of the crime) or sentence of death
18 U.S.C. §2251 – Selling or buying of children	30 years	Life
18 U.S.C. §2252 – Certain activities related to material involving the sexual exploitation of minors	5 years	20 years
	15 years	40 years (if prior conviction)
	None	10 years (possession of pornography)
	10 years	20 years (if prior convictions)
18 U.S.C. §2252A – Certain activities related to material constituting or containing child pornography	5 years	20 years
	15 years	40 years (if prior conviction)
	None	10 years (possession of pornography)
	10 years	20 years (if prior conviction)
18 U.S.C. §1466A – Obscene visual representations of sexual abuse of children	None	10 years
	10 years	20 years (if prior conviction)

Smith, Linda A., Vardaman, Samantha Healy, Snow, Melissa A., "The National Report on Domestic Minor Trafficking America's Prostituted Children," May 2009, p. 14. Copyright © 2009 by Shared Hope International. All rights reserved. Used with permission.

ing instruments, and cross-referral and coordination protocols to investigative agents and prosecutors nationwide to enhance capacity to identify and assist adult sex-trafficking victims and to investigate and prosecute this form of trafficking. Traffickers were also prosecuted under a myriad of state laws.

WHERE TO PROSECUTE: FEDERAL OR STATE COURTS

In the final analysis, law enforcement officers will always be guided by the advice and recommendations of federal or state prosecutors as to which law(s) can best be applied in a specific case in order to maximize the possibility of a successful prosecution.[26] However there appears to be considerable consensus, at least at this time, that sex trafficking prosecutions are best handled at the federal level, due to their having greater financial resources, enhanced expertise of federal law enforcement agents, and more stringent penalties under the federal statutes.

Additionally, when human trafficking cases are prosecuted at the federal level, victims qualify for additional benefits that aide their recovery in the form of restitution from the traffickers based on the **Mandatory Restitution Act** of 1996. This act provides for the monetary repayment of victims by defendants in an amount commensurate with the servitude into which they were forced.[27]

SEX TRAFFICKING OF AMERICAN CHILDREN

NATURE AND SCOPE OF THE PROBLEM

In trying to understand the scope of the problem of youth who engage in prostitution, it is important to recognize that the often hidden population of homeless and runaway youth—from which many prostituted children are drawn—is difficult to study.[28] Data from service providers may reflect only a small segment of homeless youth, and the small sample sizes of some studies cannot be generalized to a larger population.[29] In addition, no reliable estimates of the number of children engaging in prostitution in the United States exist because no one has defined the concept in measurable terms.[30] Nevertheless, while caution regarding some statistics may be warranted, they provide an indication of the extent of the problem that is helpful to a basic understanding of the current situation.

THE DEMOGRAPHICS OF SEXUALLY EXPLOITED CHILDREN

According to one U.S. Department of Health and Human Services report, up to 300,000 prostituted children may live on the streets in the United States.[31] Many are only 11 or 12 years old, and some are as young as nine.[32] The average age at which they enter prostitution is reported as 14,[33] and the median age of involved youth is 15.5 years.[34] These children come from inner cities, suburbs, and small towns,[35] and there appears to be an increase in recruitment of middle-class youth from schools and shopping malls in the suburbs.[36]

The vast majority of youth involved in prostitution are girls;[37] although, some service providers, which give food, shelter, etc., report an increase in the number of boys. Some attribute this reported increase to a greater willingness by the boys to disclose their sexual activities.[38] Larger cities are more likely to have a higher proportion of boys involved in prostitution; however, even service providers in smaller cities report seeing an increase in prostitution activity by boys. This possibly suggests a migration to smaller urban areas, an increase in visibility due to heightened awareness, or the greater willingness of boys to use the services of these various service providers[39] (Figure 12.3).

▲ **FIGURE 12-3**
Boy prostitute waiting for a client. (©ullstein bild/Getty Images)

PRECIPITATING FACTORS AFFECTING WHY CHILDREN BECOME INVOLVED IN PROSTITUTION

Children may encounter numerous difficulties in their lives that make them more vulnerable to sexual exploitation through prostitution. Homelessness, poverty, and intolerance of their sexual orientation may all affect children who either are or have been prostituted.[40] General psychological and emotional problems,[41] housing instability,[42] substance abuse, educational and vocational failure,[43] and major problems at home[44] have also been cited as common precipitating factors in the lives of prostituted children.

VARIOUS FACTORS THAT LEAVE YOUTH VULNERABLE TO TRAFFICKERS

The primary factor of vulnerability is the child's age. Pre-teen or adolescent girls are more susceptible to the calculated advances, deception, and manipulation tactics used by trafficker/pimps—and no youth is exempt from falling prey to these tactics, which will be discussed in greater detail later in this chapter.

Any child can become a trafficking victim, and domestically trafficked minors are diverse in terms of ethnicity, age, socioeconomic status, sexual orientation, and gender. However, traffickers are particularly able to take advantage of certain life-characteristics that leave holes in a child's social and emotional safety net. Youth who come from dysfunctional families in which there is abuse or trauma are particularly vulnerable to a trafficker's/pimp's method of recruitment and control.[45]

RUNNING AWAY FROM HOME

According to statistics from the National Runaway Switchboard, between 1.6 and 2.8 million children run away from home each year. Traffickers, as well as buyers, strategically prey upon runaway children because of their mental, physical, and financial vulnerability (inability to secure jobs due to their transient nature and age). Traffickers often find their best opportunities to locate unsupervised children at local shopping malls, and even though many children who do run away from home hitchhike to another location, some also use buses to relocate. Thus, bus stops can also be places that traffickers target for opportunities to entrap children. It has been determined that one in three runaway children will be approached within 48 hours of being on the street for the purpose of being sexually exploited.[46]

These children are much more likely to have histories of drug and alcohol abuse or to have had contact with the juvenile-justice system.[47] Many children, who are prostituted, are socially isolated and unsuccessful in school and with peers, and this often leads them to drop out of school.[48] They also experience more frequent school expulsions and discipline, resulting in lower levels of completed education.[49] Associated problems include parental harassment and fighting,[50] as well as parental drug and alcohol abuse.[51] This dysfunctional family life, combined with an unstructured and unsupervised childhood,[52] characterizes many of the lives of prostituted children and provides greater incentive for them to leave home.

SURVIVAL SEX

Among runaway and homeless youth, up to one-third report engaging in street prostitution as a form of **survival sex** in order to achieve the basic necessities of life such as food, shelter, or money.[53] Among prostitution-involved youth, up to 77% report running away from home at least once.[54] Surprisingly, one study showed that more than half of the interviewed prostitution-involved youth were living with their parents or families at the time of their most recent experience, and about 30% were living on the streets or in a shelter.[55] Others were staying with friends or in another unspecified arrangement. Other studies, however, show that prostitution-involved youth were less likely to live in a relative's home or shelter. If they were not on the streets, they were more likely to live with unrelated roommates, including other prostituted children or their **pimps**, who often demanded sexual favors in lieu of rent.[56]

EARLY CHILDHOOD ABUSE AND NEGLECT

The homes children run away from are often marked by emotional, physical, or sexual abuse, neglect, and regular violence between the parents. Sexual abuse has a significant impact on the probability that a runaway will become involved with prostitution. Early childhood abuse or neglect is a strong predictor of prostitution for girls; although, it does not seem to have the same impact on boys. Sex abuse appears to indirectly increase the chance of prostitution by increasing the risk of running away—"It is not so much that sexual abuse leads to prostitution as it is that running away leads to prostitution."[57]

While a majority of girls who enter prostitution appear to have suffered prior childhood sexual abuse, not every child who suffers such abuse will become a runaway or prostituted child. But the sexual exploitation of children, combined with other family tensions or emotional deficiencies, increases the probability that an adolescent runaway will engage in prostitution.

FAMILIAL TRAFFICKING

Connected to the issue of physical and sexual abuse is the problem of familial trafficking—when a family member trades or rents their child for sexual use by another in exchange for money, food, or drugs. Familial trafficking happens at alarming rates in the United States. In fact, the trafficking of children by family members was noted frequently in the assessments done by Shared Hope International, which is one of the best known and best administered non-governmental organizations (NGOs) providing services to sexually exploited children. Due to a lack of training and understanding of child sex trafficking by state child protection service agencies, and even many law enforcement officers, this crime is often misclassified as child sexual abuse. This mislabeling results in the commercial component of the crime being lost. WestCare Nevada, a non-governmental organization in Las Vegas, has determined that an estimated 30% of domestically trafficked minors who receive services at their shelter, were first trafficked by a family member.[58] Staff at WestCare Nevada

is quick to point out, however, that victims rarely disclose family involvement at the beginning of treatment, but typically disclose this much later in the restoration process.[59]

DRUG-ADDICTED PARENTS

Another common element found among sex-trafficked minors is the existence of a drug-addicted parent. It is not uncommon in these cases for an in-kind commercial exchange to occur with the parent selling sex with their child in exchange for drugs.[60] Having a drug-addicted parent creates several areas of danger— the parents themselves, congregation of other drug-addicted persons with access to the child, faulty parental supervision, and the introduction of drug use to the child. An example occurred in a domestic minor sex trafficking case in Monroe, Louisiana where the mother of a 14-year-old girl sold her child to her crack dealer in order to pay for drugs. Though the mother was arrested and charged with cruelty to a juvenile, the child remained in the custody of the drug dealer (a registered sex offender) who supplied the minor with drugs and continued to sexually abuse her. The drug dealer then prostituted the minor in partnership with another man.[61]

PSYCHOLOGICAL AND EMOTIONAL DIFFICULTIES

Whether caused by problems in the home or some other contributing factor, both boys and girls have often experienced psychological and emotional difficulties before they enter prostitution. Many children who are later prostituted are socially isolated and become entangled in a delinquent lifestyle.[62] On the streets, these children seek the emotional attachments they could not find at home, making them vulnerable to those who would exploit them. In addition, fear of familial rejection or ostracism based on sexual orientation, especially in the case of boys, may increase the likelihood that a teenager will run away, thus increasing the likelihood the child will engage in prostitution.[63]

Given all of these potential difficulties, it is not surprising that the vast majority of children who enter prostitution have low self-esteem and negative feelings about themselves prior to doing so.[64] In an attempt to escape circumstances they consider unbearable, many youth, once on the street, land in situations that may equal or exceed the physical and psychological traumas they experienced in their homes.

MENTAL HEALTH SYMPTOMS

Depression, anxiety, hostility, irritability, recurring nightmares, memories of abuse, difficulties concentrating and sleeping, and feelings of apathy or emotional detachment, are all symptoms frequently found among torture victims and victims of other traumatic events, and are also identified as prominent psychological reactions to sex trafficking victims.[65]

▶ FIGURE 12.4
Badly traumatized young sex-trafficking victims, who were forced into prostitution before being rescued, are depicted here in a therapy room where they are encouraged to release suppressed feelings by physically acting out. (©Preda Foundation, www.preda.org)

For example, in one study of trafficked women, it was determined, not surprisingly, that the levels of poor mental health they experienced were much higher than those in the general female population. However, while in the care of NGOs, victims' symptom levels did decrease, but this decrease happened very slowly and not very often. Even after three months of care, victims' reported depression levels that were still at the level of the top 10% of the most depressed women in an average population. Anxiety and hostility levels were not quite as high but still well above the average. This is likely to inhibit trafficking victims from re-engaging in normal daily activities, such as caring for family, employment, or education.[66]

In fact it is not at all uncommon for a victim to be "annoyed, easily irritated by everything," and have "temper outbursts."[67] In some forms of therapy of sex trafficking, victims are encouraged to release suppressed feelings by physically acting out in a controlled and safe environment (Figure 12.4).

POST-TRAUMATIC STRESS DISORDER AND SEX-TRAFFICKING VICTIMS

Post-traumatic stress disorder (PTSD) is a term that describes a mental health disorder caused, in part, by exposure to one or more traumatic events. This disorder manifests in a number of severe psychological symptoms experienced by those who have been exposed to a life-threatening experience that has had a traumatic effect on them.

SYMPTOMS OF POST-TRAUMATIC STRESS DISORDER (PTSD)

Studies of sex-trafficking victims have found that they display many PTSD symptoms, the most common of which are:

- Headaches.
- Stomach upset.
- Nausea.
- Weakness and fatigue.
- Muscle tension and twitches.
- Changes in appetite and sexual functioning.
- Sleep impairment, with frequent awakenings and often nightmares.
- Intrusive imagery and flashbacks may occur.
- Distorted memories.
- Anxiety and depression.
- Panic attacks.
- Unusual and disorienting feelings of helplessness, fearfulness.
- Self-second-guessing and guilt feelings.

THE STOCKHOLM SYNDROME (SURVIVAL IDENTIFICATION SYNDROME/TRAUMA BONDING)

Investigators are sometimes mystified by the reaction of women and children, who they rescue in sex-trafficking operations because in some cases the rescued victims not only refuse to cooperate but appear to be protective of the sex traffickers and/or pimps. In fact, the reaction from the sex-trafficking victim may be a result of their suffering from what is characterized as the "**Stockholm Syndrome**," which is a group of psychological symptoms that occur in some persons in a captive or hostage situation. The term takes its name from a bank robbery that occurred in Stockholm, Sweden, in August 1973. The robbers took four employees of the bank (three women and one man) into the vault with them and kept them hostage for 131 hours. After the employees were finally released, they appeared to have formed a paradoxical emotional bond with their captors; they told reporters that they saw the police as their enemy rather than the bank robbers, and that they had positive feelings toward the criminals. The syndrome was first named by Nils Bejerot

(1921–1988), a medical professor who specialized in addiction research and served as a psychiatric consultant to the Swedish police during the standoff at the bank. The Stockholm syndrome is also known as **Survival Identification Syndrome or trauma bonding.**[68] (Figure 12.5).

CENTRAL CHARACTERISTICS OF THE STOCKHOLM SYNDROME

Most experts agree that the Stockholm syndrome has three central characteristics:

- The hostages have negative feelings about the police or other authorities.
- The hostages have positive feelings toward their captor(s).
- The captors develop positive feelings toward the hostages.

The Stockholm syndrome does not affect the vast majority of hostages or persons in comparable situations. In fact, a Federal Bureau of Investigation (FBI) study of over 1200 hostage-taking incidents found that 92% of the hostages did *not* develop the Stockholm syndrome. FBI researchers then interviewed flight attendants who had been taken hostage during airplane hijackings, and concluded that three factors are necessary for the syndrome to develop:

- The crisis situation lasts for several days or longer.
- The hostage takers remain in contact with the hostages; that is, the hostages are not placed in a separate room.
- The hostage takers show some kindness toward the hostages or at least refrain from harming them.

However, hostages who are abused by their captors typically feel anger toward them and do not usually develop the syndrome.

RECRUITMENT AND PIMP CONTROL

A pimp's process of recruitment and control are sophisticated. There is a calculated method to preying on youth, and the pimps share tactics with each other, assist one another, and craft their techniques together. Experts and survivors refer to these methods as "brainwashing." One survivor expert noted commonalities between the tactics pimps use and those utilized by cult leaders.[69]

Pimps make it their business to understand the psychology of youth and to practice and hone their tactics of manipulation. The pimp's goal is to exploit and create vulnerabilities and remove the minor's credibility in the eyes of their families, the public, and law enforcement. Their ultimate goal is profit.

THE INITIAL APPROACH BY THE PIMP

The pimp's initial approach may be to just gather information about the girl's circumstances.

The pimp will befriend her, sweet-talk her, and provide companionship and intimacy.[70] He may try to impress her with promises of money and a comfortable lifestyle. Runaways with problems at home are especially vulnerable to these tactics because all they really want is to belong.[71] The pimp makes the girl feel special and important, lavishing attention on her, buying her clothes and jewelry, and creating a facade of friendship and romance.[72] He may promise to marry her or make a lifetime commitment.[73]

The pimp may then initiate a sexual relationship with the girl, continuing to become the primary person in her life. This pretense of love lulls the girl into thinking theirs is a mutually developing relationship, making her emotionally and psychologically dependent on the pimp as a substitute for the family that abused her or turned her away.[74]

At this point the pimp may demand that she have sex with someone else, often a "friend" of the pimp, to prove her love for him. Next, she must have sex with a stranger for money.[75] Soon she finds herself prostituted as a condition of her love for him. The young girl, however, continues to think of the pimp as her boyfriend, and this perception of the relationship sustains the control and abuse. After creating this dependency, the pimp begins to dominate, control, and become an integral part of her life.[76]

SEASONING TECHNIQUES AND TACTICS OF POWER AND CONTROL

Before a girl has been "**turned out**," the pimp may "season" her for life as a prostitute with physical and verbal abuse.[77] **Seasoning** is meant to break her will and separate her from her previous life so that she does not know where to turn for help.[78] He may change her identity and move her around because constant mobility breaks any personal ties she may have developed and ensures new ties are only temporary.[79] The demoralizing and dehumanizing experience of prostitution confirms the child's poor self-image and provides another tool for manipulation by the pimp.[80] Some traffickers and pimps have even resorted to tattooing their victims in order to show that the girls are their personal possession (Figure 12.6)

The pimp may withhold love and affection or use verbal abuse, fear, and violence to control her.[81] By that time, the girl is completely under his control. As one victim explains

> "I was so much in love with him it really didn't matter as long as he was there. . . .
> When he told me he loved me I believed everything would work out all right. I had been alone for so long and he'd told me I'd be with him for the rest of my life."[82]

The pimp's relationship to the young girl closely parallels the dynamics of a battering relationship.[83] The pimp first isolates the girl from family and friends and minimizes the exploitative nature of prostitution.[84] He then uses threats and intimidation

▲ **FIGURE 12-6**
In order to show physical possession of the girls who work for them pimps will occasionally tattoo the girls. In this case the pimp whose name was King Koby tattooed his name on her neck. (©Anthony DelMundo/NY Daily News/Getty Images)

to control her. Such tactics invariably involve emotional, sexual, and physical abuse. He may beat her up or threaten to leave her.[85] The pimp creates an environment of total emotional deprivation. And most like a batterer, he uses random acts of violence to establish power.[86]

Physical abuse occurs in over half of pimp-prostitute relationships.[87] When violence is no longer effective in controlling the girl, the pimp may use drugs or threats against her family or friends.[88]

The prostituted child is expected to turn over all of her earnings to the pimp and is punished if she fails to do so.[89] Because the child becomes financially dependent on the pimp,[90] she must rely on him for all necessities, and this places her even more in his "debt."[91]

THE USE OF PORNOGRAPHY AS A MEANS OF CONTROL

Forcing performance in pornography is another means by which pimps achieve control over the girls they prostitute. For example, they may take photographs or videos of the girl in the act of engaging in sexual relations.[92] Then after learning about the girl's family and friends, and getting her home address and other personal information,[93] the pimp blackmails her by threatening to send the photos or videos to her family and friends. Pimps also use the pornography to control and humiliate the girl and break her resistance.[94] Pornography is also often used to normalize the practice of prostitution during the "seasoning" process by weakening the child's resistance.[95]

Pimps may also show pornographic pictures to advertise their girls, while customers often want to take pictures for their later gratification. Customers may also use pornography to describe the sexual act they want and to rationalize their behavior and their demands of the child.[96]

◄ FIGURE 12-7
The Asian women depicted in this photo were trafficked into the United States and were engaging in prostitution in a massage parlor in San Francisco when they were arrested. Law enforcement officers guarding the women can be seen reflected in the mirrors. (©Lt. George Koder, Clearwater Police Department)

SEX FOR DRUGS

Given the high rate of substance abuse among runaway and homeless youth, the "sex for drugs" phenomenon is not surprising, but the devastation it causes is considerable.

In some cases the victims have already been drug-addicted when they established a relationship with the pimp. However, in many cases the pimps provide the girls with drugs so they become addicted. After becoming drug dependent the girls will willingly exchange sex for drugs and have to look to their pimps for the drugs necessary to feed their habit. At this point these girls become little more than indentured servants, if not outright slaves just so they can feed their drug addiction.[97]

SEX TRAFFICKING OF FOREIGN WOMEN AND CHILDREN INTO AMERICA

It is indisputable that sex trafficking has reached epidemic proportions worldwide and the United States is no exception.

QUICK FACT

It has been estimated by the U.S. State Department that between 700,000 and 2,000,000 people are trafficked each year worldwide and 80% of them are being exploited as sexual slaves. Of this number, it is estimated that 14,500 to 17,500 are trafficked into the United States every year. The majority of sex-trafficking victims are being taken from economically depressed locations in Southeast Asia, the former Soviet Union, Central and South America, and other less developed areas. They are then trafficked to the more developed areas of the Middle East, Western Europe, Asia, and North America[98] (Figure 12.7).

THE DIFFERENCES BETWEEN TRAFFICKING AND SMUGGLING

As it relates to the sex trafficking of foreign women and children it is important to understand the differences between trafficking and smuggling. **Smuggling** occurs when someone is paid to assist another in the illegal crossing of borders. This relationship typically ends after the border has been crossed and the individual has paid the smuggler a fee for assistance. If the smuggler sells or "brokers" the smuggled individual into a condition of servitude, or if the smuggled individual cannot pay the smuggler and is then forced to work that debt off (called **debt bondage**), the crime has now turned from smuggling into human trafficking. The key distinction between trafficking and smuggling lies in the individual's freedom of choice. A person may choose and arrange to be smuggled into a country, but when a person is forced into a situation of exploitation whereby their freedom is taken away, he/she is then a victim of human trafficking. Central to the distinction is the denial of the victim's liberty (Table 12.2).

| TABLE 12-2 | Differences between Trafficking and Smuggling |

TRAFFICKING	SMUGGLING
• Is not voluntary; one cannot consent to being trafficked or enslaved	• Is voluntary; an individual typically contracts to be taken across border
• Entails forced exploitation of a person for labor or services	• Ends after the border crossing
• Need not entail the physical movement of a person	• Fees are usually paid in advance or upon arrival
• Can occur domestically, where citizens are held captive in their own country	• Is always international in nature
• Is a crime against the right of each person to be free from involuntary servitude	• Is a crime against the nation's sovereignty

Source: *The Crime of Human Trafficking: A Law Enforcement Guide to Identification and Investigation,* International Association of Chiefs of Police (2006), p. 4.

STAGES OF INTERNATIONAL SEX TRAFFICKING

There are essentially four stages of the trafficking of international women into the United States namely: recruitment; transportation; delivery/marketing; and exploitation.[99]

RECRUITMENT

Recruiters, traffickers, and pimps who engage in trafficking foreign women for the purpose of sexual exploitation have developed common methods of recruitment. One method is through advertisements in newspapers offering lucrative job opportunities in foreign countries for low skilled jobs, such as waitresses and nannies. Some advertisements promise good salaries to young, attractive women who will work as nannies, models, actresses, dancers, and hostesses. Women, especially from Eastern European countries, are recruited through social events and auditions, such as photo sessions. The process is usually complex, with detailed deception calculated to reassure the women that the employment opportunity is genuine.[100] It is estimated that 20% of trafficked women are recruited through media advertisements.

Another method of recruitment is through "marriage agencies," sometimes called mail-order-bride agencies or international introduction services. According to the International Organization for Migration, all mail-order-bride agencies with women from the republics of the former Soviet Union (discussed later in this chapter) are under the control of organized crime networks.[101] Many of these agencies operate on the Internet.[102] Recruiters use "marriage agencies" as a way to contact women who are eager to travel or emigrate. This route into the sex industry can take several forms. The recruiters may be traffickers or work directly with traffickers. The woman may meet with a man who promises marriage at a later date. The man may use the woman himself for a short period of time, then coerce her into making pornography and later sell her to the

sex traffickers in the sex industry, or he may directly deliver the woman to a **brothel**. There are, however, strict U.S. laws intended to regulate the marriage broker industry.

Some traffickers use the woman's legal documents and tourist visas to legally enter the destination countries. The women may be put on a circuit by pimps in which they are moved from country to country on legal tourist visas or entertainers' visas. Other times, the woman is given false documents. In this case, the woman is even more vulnerable after she arrives in the destination country because she is there illegally.

METHODS OF TRANSPORTATION

The main means of trafficking women from Eastern Europe and Asia into the United States is by air.[103] Most often, these women are trafficked according to a previously planned route, often using the services of a tourist agency that may or may not be linked to trafficking. Trafficked women may be transported across borders with or without legitimate documentation. The use of forged or stolen passports and visas and the use of tourist visas are common.[104] Again, the interplay between smuggling and trafficking is evident at this stage of the process.

In some locations, especially those states along the U.S.-Mexican border (Arizona, Texas, New Mexico, and California) where the borders are porous or stretch across inhospitable or isolated territory, smugglers and traffickers, also known as coyotes, or polleros, may offer safe passage across established or known routes. Smuggling along these routes is accomplished either on foot or by loading a multitude of immigrants into vehicles such as trucks or vans and then surreptitiously crossing the border into the United States. However, women and children who are transported to the United States from Mexico by traffickers face not only the risks inherent in being trafficked, but also the serious risks of the journey.[105] Each year, between 400 and 500 people are known to die while attempting to cross the border between Mexico and the United States. The National Foundation for American Policy reported that the US Border

Patrol identified 477 deaths along the U.S.-Mexico border in 2013, the most recent year for which statistics are available.[106] The numbers are probably higher. These are only the cases discovered or reported in the United States; the numbers of those who die while still in Mexico are not known. Also not known is the number of victims who have been swallowed up by the deserts and unforgiving conditions of the American Southwest, never to be discovered.[107]

Young girls often unwittingly become trafficking victims when they are singled out by their smugglers during the journey north. They are told they can travel at no cost, if they will agree to work later to pay off their debts. These smugglers/traffickers deceive and dupe the girls through false promises of jobs and other economic opportunities waiting for them in the United States. During their journeys, the girls are shown favoritism, and even given clothes, makeup, and gifts. Upon arriving at their destinations, however, they are informed that they owe a debt to their smugglers and they will have to pay it off by working in the sex industry. In the United States, these girls are often held in slavery-like conditions and forced into prostitution. They are terrorized emotionally, forced to take drugs, moved frequently, locked up, raped, beaten, deprived of sleep, and starved. The smugglers knew from the start that exploitation would be the cost of the "travel now, pay later" deal (Figure 12.8).

DELIVERY/MARKETING

Both before and after a woman has reached the United States, the availability for her sexual services can be marketed through standard outlets, such as advertising in personal columns, but by far the most effective marketing is via Internet chat rooms, bulletin boards, and the many web sites that offer matchmaking services for men and women.[108] Where a prior arrangement has been reached to traffic a woman for prostitution, she is handed over to her intended employer upon arrival at her destination. In cases where there is no delivery to a specific person or organization, the woman is technically not trafficked, but smuggled. In this case, if she is young, without family, and without the ability to speak English, she may end up in the sex trade, and her trafficked status will be difficult to determine by local police.

EXPLOITATION

Trafficked women are extremely vulnerable for three reasons. First, as undocumented aliens, many women do not know they have rights and therefore are fearful of seeking assistance from police or other service agencies. Second, women and their families are often in debt to the traffickers. This debt is characterized as a debt bondage and occurs when a person provides a loan to another who uses his or her labor or services to repay the debt. When the value of the work, as reasonably assessed, does not apply towards the liquidation of the debt, the situation becomes a debt bondage.[109] Third, should a woman's situation, such as working in the sex trade become known back home, her family's honor may be damaged. As a result, those who "employ" trafficked women have enormous control over them. In effect, conditions of employment become conditions of slavery.[110] However, the definition of exploitation is difficult because trafficked persons—and even legal immigrants—often consent to exploitation in the hope that they can improve their circumstances by doing so.[111] This creates a serious problem for local police because victims may refuse to cooperate and may even resist attempts to improve their circumstances.

FACTORS CONTRIBUTING TO THE EXPLOITATION OF TRAFFICKED WOMEN

Globalization, along with dramatic shifts in the politics and economies of some countries, has facilitated the movement of

▲ FIGURE 12-9
These two tearful Eastern European women, who were forced into prostitution, comfort each other after being rescued by law enforcement officers. (©Philippe Lopez/AFP/Getty Images)

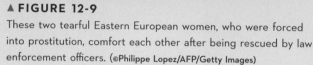

▲ FIGURE 12-10
This is the door to a bedroom where a sex-trafficking victim was forced to have sex with customers ("johns"). At night the door was padlocked to keep her imprisoned. (Courtesy of Leonard Territo and Florida Department of Law Enforcement, Tallahassee, FL)

women for the sex trade from one country to another. This is especially true for women from four Eastern European countries that were part of the former Soviet Union (Figure 12.9). These countries are Ukraine, Russia, Belarus, and Latvia. In 1991, the Soviet Union collapsed politically and economically, thus resulting in many countries that had been part of the former Soviet Union becoming independent states. As independent states emerged from the former Soviet Union, they lacked organized efficient regulatory agencies to hinder the growth and activities of crime networks.[112] When the state system was no longer able to pay the salaries of many employees, they joined the criminal networks.[113] For example, in Ukraine, people who were no longer able to support themselves with one salary or were not being paid for long periods of time, sought additional work. The only jobs available were in the newly emerging privatized or criminal businesses. The result was the criminalization of the economy in general and expansion of organized criminal networks.

Transnational trafficking of women became a new type of crime in the republics of the former Soviet Union. This activity first started during perestroika in 1986[114]; this was a program of economic, political, and social restructuring that also resulted, in part, on the restrictions on international travel being eased. It also opened borders for travel, migration, and privatized trade, all of which facilitated the operations of criminal networks. Sex industries in receiving countries created demand for women that transnational crime networks from the newly independent states organized to fill with relatively low risk and high profit for the networks. Trafficking exists to meet the demand for women, who are then used in brothels, massage parlors, bars, and stretches of streets and highways, where women are sold to men in prostitution. Ukraine, especially, has become a major source of young women for the international sex markets, including the United States.[115]

INDICATORS OF SEX TRAFFICKING VENUES

Indicators of a venue where sex trafficking may be found include:

- Buildings with heavy on-premises security, such as barred windows, barbed wire fences, especially those with the barbed wire facing inward indicating that it is intended to keep people in rather than to keep people out, electronic surveillance, and external and internal locked doors (Figure 12.10).
- There is excessive taxi traffic at the residence or place of business.
- The neighbors observe heavy traffic and rarely see the occupants.
- Sexual service menus are available.
- There are hidden passages and/or trap doors.[116]
- Buildings in which women both live and work.
- Brothels that advertise only in foreign language newspapers or that restrict services to members only.
- Advertisements for escorts or other sexual services.
- Internet web sites and chat rooms with a strong sexual orientation.

Other possible sources of information to verify sex trafficking:

- Hospital emergency rooms and health and abortion clinics.
- Ethnic healthcare providers.
- Immigrant support groups.
- HIV/AIDS community groups.
- Money wire transfer receipts.
- Phone records, especially to overseas locations.

- Legal or fraudulent identification, immigration documents.
- Weapons.

Items at the scene that can be used to verify or strongly suggest a sex-trafficking operation:

- Personal lubricants.
- Empty condom wrappers, hand towels, alcohol, rubbing oil, and cash (Figure 12.11).
- Overcrowded and inadequate living and working conditions.[117]
- Travel photographs.
- Business cards (Figure 12.12).
- Handwritten maps to the brothel.
- Locations with large numbers of transient males, such as military bases, sports venues, conventions, and tourist attractions.
- Nail salons, bars, and strip clubs can also serve as fronts for sex-trafficking operations.

◀ **FIGURE 12-12**
This business card was distributed to Mexican-American stores in the United States by a Colombian drug trafficker. The pimp placed his name and phone number on the back of the card. In this operation the women would be delivered to the locations where men had requested they be delivered for the purposes of prostitution.

If there are no visible signs of the sex trade in an area, the investigators should look into the informal networks that exist in all localities. Word of mouth, whether from a bartender or a taxi driver, is a typical way of finding out about the underground sex trade. The purveyors of sex must advertise their services; if customers can learn about these services, so can the police.

TYPES OF CALLS OR CONTACTS THAT MAY INDICATE HUMAN TRAFFICKING

- Sexual assault.
- Aggravated assaults/battery.
- Domestic violence.
- Kidnapping/false imprisonment.
- Lost/found reports (child/adult).
- Traffic stops.
- Casual contact.
- Prostitution complaint/citizen complaint.
- Labor dispute.
- Thefts/robbery.
- Suspected narcotic activity that turns out to be human trafficking.
- Any other type of call.[118]

SUGGESTED INTERVIEW PROTOCOL FOR SEX-TRAFFICKING VICTIMS

Over the years, experienced sex-trafficking investigators have gained valuable experience in identifying those protocols that result in the most successful interviews. The following list has a series of suggestions that less-experienced sex-trafficking investigators may find useful.

- Be aware that traffickers might not be easy to distinguish from victims.
- Educate yourself on trauma, its impact and effects on the sex-trafficking victim and consider collaborating with a trauma specialist to assist with the interviews.
- Adopt a compassionate and non-judgmental manner.
- If possible, conduct interviews with victims/witnesses while in plain clothes and keep attire informal.
- Do not display weapons or badges during the interview process.
- When an interpreter is needed, select one that is in no way connected to the traffickers. While a good interpreter is essential, the interviewer must use the vocabulary the victim understands. Briefing and debriefing an interpreter can ensure that the victim will understand the language used in the interview. An interpreter trained in sex-trafficking issues can also help eliminate confusion regarding language nuances, such as differences in dialect and other culturally sensitive issues.
- Do not ask "Are you a trafficking victim?"
- Allow the interviewees to describe what happened to their counterparts before focusing on their own suffering; it is often easier for them to initially talk about what happened to other people.
- Only persons absolutely essential to the interview should be present during the interview.
- Provide victims the opportunity to tell their story; it may help for them to be able to do so.[119] Investigators should avoid repeatedly interviewing the victim because the process can be physically and psychologically exhausting and may result in re-traumatizing the victim who will be reliving her experience every time she has to talk about it.
- Do not use interrogation methods. Investigators must remember, this is an interview.
- It is best to use a conversational approach rather than a rapid series of questions in order to obtain preliminary information.
- Open-ended questions will elicit more information from victims than those answerable with a yes or no response.[120]
- It can be very helpful to have trusted victim service providers conduct a parallel interview as they can assist in reducing the victim's fear of law enforcement. They will not be gathering the facts of the crime, but instead will be assessing practical needs of the victim.
- Be sure the victim has some control in the situation (breaks, water, seating placement).
- Allow the victim to set the length and pace of the interview.
- Do not make promises you may not be able to keep.
- Do not videotape or audiotape the initial conversations. This is suggested because it is quite likely that the rescued victim will still be somewhat traumatized with her first encounter with American law enforcement. As a matter of fact, she might even be under the influence of

drugs and or alcohol during the initial interview. This is not the kind of interview prosecutors want to have recorded and then be required to show to a jury. It tends to exacerbate the problem of inconsistencies should the victim later change her testimony when she is sober and/or has developed a level of trust with the investigator.

DEMAND-REDUCTION AS A PRIMARY PREVENTION: THE JOHN FACTOR

In any discussion of sex trafficking it is important to understand the role played by the customers (**johns**). There are a number of things that can and are being done address this component of the sex-trafficking problem.[121] These include the use of police tactics known as "stings" or "reverse stings"; the use of the Internet and the use of surveillance cameras.[122]

The total elimination of commercial sex markets is unrealistic as a short-term goal, but there is no reason to assume that markets cannot be significantly reduced if the root causes are addressed, thereby resulting in fewer victims. This is the hallmark of primary prevention and is the only method that has been empirically demonstrated to substantially reduce the size of the commercial sex market.[123]

REVERSE STINGS

The most commonly used tactic to address demand for commercial sex is usually referred to as the "**reverse sting.**" These police special operations feature one or more female police officers serving as a decoy (or decoys), by posing as prostitutes to await being approached by those attempting to purchase sex[124] (Figure 12.13).

Areas of the city known to be active for street prostitution are selected, and a tactical plan is either discussed or written and submitted for a supervisor's approval. Usually, five or more officers are used in a street reverse sting. In addition to the female officer or officers, there are usually several additional undercover police in supporting roles. The operations often consist of one or two male plainclothes officers on foot, posing as pedestrians, at least one unmarked car carrying plainclothes officers, and at least one police patrol car with officers that may be in uniform. There are usually other officers who support the operations by processing arrestees and their vehicles. In some cases, police use a van serving as a mobile booking or screening station, and in other instances processing occurs in nearby police stations or substations. In the latter circumstance, the operations require more on-site officers so that there is less "down time" between arrests. At least two officers are usually required to transport each arrestee away from the site of the arrest: at least one escorting the arrestee, and the other driving the arrestee's vehicle (when applicable).

A supervising Sergeant is usually in charge of the reverse stings. Decoys are escorted to drop-off locations near where the operations will occur. An unmarked police van serving as a mobile screening or booking station is usually parked nearby, but

out of sight of the street operation. In some locations, police stations or substations are nearby, so a mobile unit is not necessary. The decoy officer usually has a hidden recording device and a cell-phone (the first to collect evidence, the latter for safety, in case she is abducted). Some police departments videotape the reverse stings surreptitiously from an unmarked police car.

The decoy always tries to remain in visual contact with the other officers. When potential "clients" speak with the decoy, the supporting officers track her until she makes a pre-arranged signal indicating a "good case," which is when the man has made an offer of money in exchange for sex and has committed an "act in furtherance" of that offer. An act in furtherance is any overt behavior that can be construed reasonably as progress toward consummating the act of prostitution being negotiated by the John and female police officer. Such acts, in addition to the verbal exchange, complete the legal requirements for making an arrest. Acts in furtherance can include reaching for a wallet, pointing to money on a bed or a car seat, driving around the block to the area where the sex act was arranged to take place, or opening a car or hotel door so that the decoy can enter.

When the signal for a "good case" is given, the officers on foot or in unmarked cars converge and make the arrest. At this point, the decoy officer enters the police car as quickly as possible and leaves the scene, while the man is arrested and driven to a point where he will be processed. Sometimes he is driven in his own car by a plainclothes officer, and other times they are driven in a police car while another officer drives the offender's car. Arrestees who are on foot are driven to the van or police station in a patrol car.

THE USE OF THE INTERNET TO PROMOTE COMMERCIAL SEX

The Internet has been used with increasing frequency to transact commercial sex. Ads are posted on websites devoted to commercial sex (eroticreview.com, worldsexguide.com, myredbook.com) or on websites serving as a venue for a broader spectrum of transactions, such as BackPage.com, Yellow Pages, Craigslist.com, and periodicals such as the Phoenix New Times or SF Weekly. It is widely observed that the solicitation of commercial sex throughout the United States has shifted from the streets to online.

ONLINE REVERSE STINGS

Many police departments throughout the United States have used online ads for commercial sex to their advantage. Approximately one-third of all police departments that conduct street-level reverse stings have also implemented web-based reverse stings. Online reverse stings are easy for police to initiate. The typical procedure is to post a decoy ad, and when potential johns respond with a phone call or an email, the officers pose as prostituted persons or pimps and arrange for a meeting—usually at a hotel that has been prepared for a reverse sting. At the hotel, a female officer poses as a prostituted person, and once the john is face-to-face with the officer, the operation is essentially the same as that used in conventional reverse stings.

THE USE OF SURVEILLANCE CAMERAS AS A DETERRENT TO SOLICITING PROSTITUTION

While cameras are very widely used for general surveillance purposes, and the growth in their use began decades ago, their use specifically to target men who are (or may be) buying sex has not been widely adopted. Some applications are covert, with hidden cameras used to produce visual evidence that can be used by police and prosecutors. Other uses are overt and designed for deterrence rather than punishment[125] (Figure 12.14).

▲ **FIGURE 12-14**

Vallejo, CA uses 28 cameras to control prostitution. City Council approved expanding the cameras from 6 to 22 because of the success of these cameras in controlling prostitution. (©Clive Gee/PA Wire/AP Images)

THE MULTI-AGENCY TASK FORCE

A multi-agency task force is necessary because it is impossible for any single agency or organization to respond comprehensively to the problem of human trafficking (Figure 12.15). Traffickers range from opportunistic individuals to sophisticated criminal organizations with multijurisdictional activity. The response to human trafficking is therefore most effective through multidisciplinary and collaborative problem-solving efforts and also increases the likelihood of the crime being discovered, the victims being rescued, and prosecutorial efforts being successful.[126]

THE CORE TEAM MODEL

Similar to most organizational startups, Task Force development begins with a small core team building upon a vision for a successful collaborative effort in combating the problem. A core team is needed to create and execute an effective plan for the development of the Task Force.

While Task Forces can be successful without such a team, Task Forces just starting up will benefit greatly from the shared experiences and information provided by the core team as they strategically determine how the Task Force will operate, the group structure for long-term sustainability, the establishment of strong leadership to manage the operations, and how to foster commitment and a clear purpose for the group.[127]

The most important credential of the core team and members of the Task Force is a commitment to developing an effective community response to human trafficking. Many Task Forces, for instance, have been formed out of local or regional interest without external funding because they believe in the necessity of a coordinated Task Force response (Figures 12.16).[128]

▶ **FIGURE 12-15**
A multi-agency task force preparing to conduct a raid. FBI agents and other law enforcement officers gather to get briefed before conducting raids on a number of brothels involved in sex-trafficking operations. (Source: Federal Bureau of Investigation, New York)

WHAT TO LOOK FOR...

Constantly accompanied by a controlling person or boss, not speaking on their own behalf.

Lack of control over personal schedule, money, identification or travel documents.

Transported to and from work, lives and works in the same place.

Debt owed to employer/crew leader, unable to leave job.

Bruises, depression, fear, overly submissive.

WHAT TO DO...

If you think you have come in contact with a victim of human trafficking in the Pinellas, Pasco or Hillsborough County area, call the CATF Hotline at **(727) 562-4917**; other areas can contact the national Trafficking Information and Referral Hotline at **1-888-373-7888**.

These hotlines will help you determine if you have encountered victims of human trafficking, will identify local resources available in your community to help victims and will help you coordinate with local social service organizations to help protect and serve victims so they can begin the process of restoring their lives. For more information, visit *www.catfht.org*.

WHAT IS HUMAN TRAFFICKING?

Trafficking in women and girls for the purpose of sexual exploitation in the form of prostitution, pornography and escorts is a growing phenomenon in the US and throughout the world. These women become prey to traffickers who promise such work as dancing or hostessing. Instead, these women end up living in slave-like conditions, under the control of the trafficker.

Human trafficking is the exploitation by force, fraud or coercion of vulnerable people – often immigrants – for forced labor, domestic servitude or commercial sex operations. Human trafficking has become a multi-billion dollar global crime impacting nations – and neighborhoods – around the world. **Florida is one of the highest destination states for women and children trafficked into the United States.** In the past five years, law enforcement and social service providers have identified multiple cases of human trafficking in the Tampa Bay area.

In October 2006, the Clearwater, Florida Police Department was awarded a Department of Justice grant to fund the creation of the Clearwater/Tampa Bay Area Task Force on Human Trafficking (CATFHT). The mission of the task force is to identify and rescue victims, create a coordinated law enforcement system to investigate and prosecute these crimes, and to deliver social, legal and immigration services to human trafficking victims in the Clearwater and Tampa Bay area.

Human trafficking also includes children and adults who are forced into unpaid labor in sweatshops, commercial agriculture, domestic servitude, construction, restaurant, housekeeping and other service industries in the US and abroad.

THE TASK FORCE CONSISTS OF THE FOLLOWING AGENCIES

Clearwater Police Department
The US Attorney's Office for the Middle District of Florida
World Relief
The Regional Community Policing Institute
Hispanic Outreach Center of Clearwater
Religious Community Services
Pinellas County Sheriff's Office
Pasco County Sheriff's Office
Hillsborough County Sheriff's Office
Gulfcoast Legal Services, Inc.
The Florida Department of Law Enforcement
The Salvation Army

The Largo Police Department
The Social Security Administration
Immigration and Customs Enforcement (ICE)
The Pinellas Park Police Department
The St. Petersburg Police Department
The Federal Bureau of Investigation.
Florida State University *Center for the Advancement of Human Rights*
U.S. Border Patrol
The Florida Department of Health
The State Attorney for the 6th Judicial Circuit
Directions for Mental Health, Inc.

▲ **FIGURE 12-16 Human Trafficking**

This is an example of a brochure prepared by the Clearwater Area Task Force on Human Trafficking in an effort to solicit the assistance of citizens in identifying cases of human trafficking in the area. (Courtesy of The City of Clearwater Police Department)

| KEY TERMS

brothel
debt bondage
johns
Mandatory Restitution Act
multi-agency task forces
pimps
post-traumatic stress disorder (PTSD)
Racketeer Influenced and Corrupt Organizations Act (RICO)
reverse sting

seasoning
smuggling
Stockholm Syndrome
Survival Identification Syndrome
survival sex
The Innocence Lost Initiative
trauma bonding
T visa
The Mann Act
The Travel Act

Trafficking
Trafficking Victims Protection Act 2000
Trafficking Victims Protection Reauthorization Act 2003
Trafficking Victims Protection Reauthorization Act 2005
turned out
U visa
William Wilberforce Trafficking Victims Protection Reauthorization Act 2008

REVIEW QUESTIONS

1. What is a "reverse sting"?
2. What was the Mann Act also known as when it was passed in 1910?
3. What does the Mann Act prohibit?
4. What did the Travel Act do?
5. What kind of public service benefits is a T visa applicant entitled to?
6. What must an immigrant to do qualify for U visa status?
7. What was the purpose of passing the Trafficking Victims Protection Act (TVPA) 2000?
8. What is a coyote or *pollero*?
9. What caused the dramatic increase in the sex trafficking of women from Russia, Ukraine, Belarus, and Latvia?
10. What are the indications of women possibly being involved in sex trafficking?
11. What was recommended, as it relates to the officer's attire, when conducting an interview with a sex trafficking victim?
12. What is a "reverse sting"?
13. How can surveillance cameras be used to deter men who are soliciting prostitutes?
14. Why is a multi-agency necessary to effectively combat sex trafficking operations?

INTERNET ACTIVITIES

1. Most law enforcement agencies that are having human trafficking problems in their area have increasingly created multi-agency task forces to deal with the problem. There are certain organizational and administrative steps that need to be taken to be certain that these entities are organized and created properly. To be more familiar with various elements to achieve these goals go to Anti-trafficking Task Force Strategy and Operations e-Guide Bureau of Justice Assistance (U.S. Department of Justice, 2011), *http://www.umt.edu/mansfield/events /conference/2014-archive/workshop/resources/task-force -guide.pdf*

2. One of the most important aspects in the investigation of human trafficking is the role of the prosecutor. These cases are highly complex and require experienced and dedicated prosecutors. For a more detailed discussion of what is involved to successfully prosecute a case go to: Laura Hersh, "Sex Trafficking Investigations and Prosecutions," in Jill Laurie Goodman and Dorchen A. Leidholdt, eds., Lawyer's Manual on Human Trafficking (Supreme Court of the State of New York, Appellate Division, First Department New York State Judicial Committee on Women Courts), pp. 256–257. Online at *https://www. nycourts.gov/ ip/womeninthecourts/pdfs/LMHT.pdf*

◄ Use of surveillance cameras to prevent robberies. A Paterson, New Jersey, police officer is monitoring simultaneously 18 high-crime areas by the use of surveillance cameras. Each camera pans on a time sequence, produces high-quality video, and also allows the monitoring officer to zoom in on a particular location. The cameras can be moved to a new location within two hours.

(©Paterson New Jersey Police Department)

13

ROBBERY

CHAPTER OBJECTIVES

1. Identify and explain the elements of a robbery.
2. Describe the three styles of robberies based on the amount of planning involved.
3. List the various types of robberies.
4. Discuss the three explanations provided for the increase in carjackings.
5. Define and give examples of robbery prevention measures.
6. Understand the most effective and safest way to respond to the robbery scene.
7. Describe action, physical, and situational stereotyping.
8. Be familiar with follow-up robbery investigation procedures.

The importance of robbery resides in its economics, its frequency, its resistance to investigative efforts, the fear it creates, and the potential for violence that accompanies it. Robbery can occur in several contexts, including visible street robberies, carjackings, home invasions, truck hijackings, bank robberies, and automatic-teller-machine (ATM) robberies. Further, taxicab drivers and convenience-store personnel in particular are easy targets for robbery, because they often work alone at all hours of the day and night, with minimal or no protection from robbers, and a large part of the business they conduct is on a cash basis. Similar to their variation by place, robberies also vary in terms of the amount of time spent on their planning: Some robberies occur without any planning; others involve considerable premeditation.

Because of the face-to-face confrontation between perpetrator and victim, the potential for violence is always present in a robbery. When violence does occur, it may range from minor injury to loss of life. Due to its personal and often violent nature, robbery is one of the crimes most feared by the public, a fear that may be heightened by perceptions of police inability to deal effectively with robberies. However, witnesses are often upset and may have seen the perpetrator only briefly—factors that sometimes limit how much they can assist the investigative process. These factors, coupled with the fact that most offenders operate alone, can make robbery investigations extremely difficult. Mitigating the investigative challenge are recent identification technologies that make it possible to quickly generate and distribute a likeness of a suspect. When security cameras are present and operating, they can also be of major assistance in providing leads.

In coping with a heightened sense of fear and alarm, robbery victims often seek guidance and advice to help prevent repeat victimization. Along with arresting suspects and recovering the victim's property, investigators and their departments can serve in a crime prevention role. Providing the public with tips on what to do before, during, and after a robbery not only helps prevent robberies but also helps lessen the chance of repeat victimizations.

ELEMENTS OF THE CRIME

A **robbery** consists of these elements: the (1) taking and (2) carrying away of (3) personal property of (4) another, with (5) the intent to deprive the victim permanently, by (6) the use of force, fear, or threat of force.

TAKING

The property taken in a robbery must be taken illegally by the robber. Someone who has the right to take such property cannot properly be convicted of robbery. This illegal taking is called **trespassory.** The property must be taken from the custody, control, or possession of the victim and, as will be seen later, from the victim's presence. This element of the crime is satisfied once the robber has possession of the property; until possession has occurred, only an attempt has taken place.

CARRYING AWAY

Once the element of taking has been satisfied, the robber must then carry away the property. This element can be satisfied simply by showing that the accused totally removed the article from the position that it formerly occupied. It is not necessary to show that any great distance was involved in the carrying away.

PERSONAL PROPERTY

The object of the robbery must be personal property as opposed to real estate or things attached to the land. Again, as in larceny (discussed in greater detail in Chapter 15 "Larceny/Theft and White-Collar Crime"), any tangible property and some forms of intangible property represented by tangible items, such as stocks and bonds, gas, electricity, minerals, and other such commodities, can be objects of robbery.

ANOTHER

The property taken must belong to another, not to the accused. This again relates to the first element of taking. If the taking is trespassory—illegal—then the property must be the rightful property of someone other than the robber.

INTENT TO DEPRIVE PERMANENTLY

Robbery is a crime of specific intent and requires that the prosecution establish, in court, that the defendant, at the time of taking the property by force or threat of force from the victim or the victim's presence, did, in fact, intend to deprive the victim of the use and enjoyment of that property permanently. In most cases, this fact can be concluded from the facts and the circumstances surrounding the case, but in specific-intent crime cases, juries are not permitted to assume

this particular fact. Thus, the police officer's investigation must be geared to establishing this as an essential element of the crime. The fact that force or the threat of force was used to secure the property from the victim is often enough to convince a jury of the accused's intent to deprive permanently.

USE OF FORCE, FEAR, OR THREAT OF FORCE

This element of the crime requires that the force or threat of force be directed against the physical safety of the victim rather than his or her social well-being. For example, threats to expose the victim as an embezzler do not satisfy this element of the crime. Proof that force was used or, at the very least, that threats were made such that the victim feared imminent bodily harm, is essential for successful prosecutions of robbery cases. However, the force used to separate the victim from his or her property in robbery need not be great.

When the victim of a robbery is seriously injured, there is usually little difficulty in convincing the investigator or the jury that force was used. However, difficulties may arise in the case of a victim who claims to have been robbed under the threat of force when no actual injury occurred. In this case, the skill of the investigator in determining the facts of the case becomes crucial to successful prosecution.

There are also more subtle situations in which the investigator must know legal requirements as well as investigative techniques. The typical purse-snatching case is an illustration. Often, the force element of the crime of robbery can be satisfied only by determining whether the victim attempted to resist the force used and, if so, the extent of that resistance. It is generally accepted by courts that a woman who puts her purse next to her on the seat of a bus without keeping her hand on it or loosely holds it in her hand is not the victim of robbery if someone quickly grabs the purse and runs. In these cases, the woman has not resisted. However, if she were clutching the bag tightly and someone managed to grab it from her after even a slight struggle, sufficient force and resistance would have occurred to constitute robbery. A good rule for the investigator to follow in cases of uncertainty is that the removal of an article without more force than is absolutely necessary to remove it from its original resting place constitutes larceny. If any additional force, no matter how slight, is used, it is then robbery, provided the object is taken from the presence or person of the victim. The property does not have to be held by the victim physically or be on his or her person. It merely has to be under the victim's control. "Control" in this sense means the right or privilege to use the property as the victim sees fit. Neither is it necessary or essential that the property be visible to the victim when the crime is committed.

When force is not used but a threat to the physical well-being of the victim is made, it is not necessary that the victim actually be frightened to the point of panic. It is enough that the victim is reasonably apprehensive and aware of the potential for injury.

OVERVIEW: THE OFFENSE, THE VICTIM, AND THE OFFENDER

In terms of weapons used, a firearm is used in 40% of the incidents, a knife or other cutting instrument in 8% of the cases, and "some other weapon" in another 10% of reported robberies; the remaining 42% of the incidents are robberies **strong-armed,** meaning no weapon was used.[1] An illustration of the use of "some other weapon" is the robbery of a convenience store by a man using a hypodermic needle filled with what he claims is AIDS-contaminated blood.

Together, these data reveals that approximately 6 of every 10 robberies are armed, and the balance are strong-armed. Armed robbers often carry two or more weapons. Because of this, officers must continue to exercise great caution when approaching a suspect who has thrown a weapon down.

About one-third of all robberies result in a physical injury to the victim.[2] Females are about 10% more likely to be injured than are males; Caucasians and African-Americans face nearly the same prospects for being injured.[3] Robbery is basically a stranger-to-stranger crime: 71% of the time the robber and the victim do not know each other.[4] About 60% of all robberies are committed by a single offender.[5] This factor tends to make robbery investigations more difficult: if the sole offender can keep his or her mouth shut, does not attract attention to him-/herself or run with other criminals, and does not get a bad break, the offender can be hard to catch. Although a small number of victims fight back in some way, in 82% of robberies it is the offender who initiates violence.[6]

The objective of the confrontation between robber and victim is to get the victim's immediate compliance. In most situations, the mere showing of a gun will accomplish this. One offender reports: "Sometimes I don't even touch them; I just point the gun right in front of their face. I don't even have to say nothing half the time. When they see that pistol, they know what time it is."[7] A victim who hesitates or is seen as uncooperative may or may not get a warning.

Other robbers are less "tolerant" and when faced with uncooperative victims, they may shoot them in the leg or the foot. However, for some offenders, injuring the victim is part of the thrill, the "kick" of "pulling a job." What type of violence is used and when it is used may form part of an identifiable modus operandi (MO). Such an MO can tie together several robberies, and the combined information from various investigations often produces significant investigative leads.

There is no question that being under the influence and committing robberies are intimately related. Victims believe that 28% of those robbing them are high on drugs and/or alcohol.[8] Some offenders use alcohol to lessen their apprehension about getting caught. Robbery is basically an intraracial crime; in one study, blacks said that they were robbed by blacks 80% of the time, and whites said that they were robbed by whites 75% of the time.[9] Nationally, among those apprehended for robbery, 90% are males, 54% are blacks, and 19% are under the age of 25.[10]

Although no robbery is routine to victims, many cases are fairly straightforward to investigators. Some robberies, however, stand out because of unusual circumstances, as the following incidents illustrate:

A lone robber held up a bank and made off with $600. As police were chasing him, the robber crashed the stolen Chevrolet Suburban he was driving. It burst into flames, and the money burned up. Now being pursued on foot by a police officer, the robber tossed off his plaid jacket and escaped. The police found a napkin with a name and a telephone number in the jacket. With the bank's surveillance photos in hand, the police confronted the man identified on the napkin. In turn, he identified the robber as someone whom he had been letting sleep on his couch. An arrest was subsequently made in the case.[11]

Two thugs were cruising in a residential area looking for someone to rob. They spotted two men playing pool in an open garage. Blissfully unaware that the two men were off-duty police officers, the thugs approached them and placed a gun to one officer's head, and the officer began to struggle. The second officer pulled a weapon and shot both offenders.[12]

A teenage boy robbed a convenience store at knifepoint around 1:30 in the morning, taking money and merchandise and fleeing on foot. The police solved the case by following the offender's shoeprints in the freshly fallen snow straight to his home.[13]

Despite such variations, three styles of robberies—the ambush, the selective raid, and the planned operation—can be classified according to the amount of planning conducted by the perpetrators. The **ambush** involves virtually no planning and depends almost entirely on the element of surprise. A prime example is robberies in which victims are physically overpowered by sudden, crude force and in which "scores" are generally small.[14] The lack of planning does not mean, however, that there is no premeditation.

The **selective raid** is characterized by a minimal amount of casual planning. Sites are tentatively selected and very briefly cased, and possible routes of approach and flight are formulated. Scores vary from low to moderate, and several robberies may be committed in rapid succession.

The **planned operation** is characterized by larger "scores," no planned use of force, less likelihood of apprehension, and careful planning.

TYPOLOGY OF ROBBERIES

In addition to knowing the broad profile of the offense, the investigator must also be familiar with various types of robberies, such as the following.

VISIBLE STREET ROBBERIES

Approximately 5 of every 10 robberies happen on the street.[15] In 93% of the cases, the victim is alone[16] and typically on the way to or from a leisure activity within five miles of his or her home,[17] such as patronizing a nightclub or restaurant:[18]

> I'd watch people in bars and follow them. One time, I followed this guy and grabbed his tie and swung it down to the ground. And, uh, he hit his head, and that's when I took the money and ran.[19]

The victim is three times more likely to be confronted by a single perpetrator than by multiple perpetrators.[20] Youthful robbers are particularly likely to commit strong-armed robberies—also referred to as **muggings**—in which no weapons are involved and in which they suddenly physically attack and beat the victim, taking cash, jewelry, wallets, purses, and other valuables. Purse snatching may or may not be a robbery. If a woman is carrying a purse loosely on her open fingers and someone grabs it and runs and she then experiences fear, robbery is not an appropriate charge because the fear did not precede the taking. But if the same woman sees or hears someone running toward her and in fear clutches her purse, which is then ripped from her by the perpetrator, a robbery has occurred. If apprehended, the suspect would likely be charged with some degree of larceny, depending on the value of the object(s) being stolen. The penalty for larceny is generally much lower than that for the crime of robbery, and in many states if a firearm is used during the commission of a robbery the penalty is often even more severe than for unarmed robbery.

Street robberies usually involve little or no planning by the perpetrators, who may have been waiting in one place for a potential victim to appear or walking around looking for someone to rob on the spur of the moment.

Because street robberies happen so quickly and often occur at night in areas that are not well lighted, victims often have difficulty providing anything more than a basic physical description. The description may be even more limited if the victim is injured either by a weapon or by a beating in a sudden, overpowering mugging.

Spontaneous street robbers may "graduate" to jobs that involve a certain amount of planning. For example, they may stake out ATMs or banks (discussed in greater detail later in this chapter). In the case of ATMs, they may have decided that they are going to rob the first "soft-looking" person who is alone and driving an expensive car. In the case of banks, they may rob someone on the street whom they have watched long enough to know that the person is going to the bank to make a cash deposit or to use the night depository. Although people sometimes commit robberies for excitement or to be "one of the guys," for the most part they do it to get the money, which often goes to pay for drugs.

USE OF SURVEILLANCE CAMERAS TO PREVENT STREET ROBBERIES

The use of surveillance cameras to monitor the streets to prevent robberies and other crimes is becoming increasingly common. For example the Paterson, New Jersey, Police Department makes extensive use of surveillance cameras in their city. Currently they are using 18 surveillance cameras installed in high-crime areas throughout the city. The cameras can be moved to other locations within two hours as needed. They are also monitored around the clock by a police officer.

The monitoring officer can zoom in on a particular image as needed. These images are also recorded, so in the event something is missed officers can go back and replay the video for a closer examination. The cameras have captured several robberies in progress as well as drug transactions. The police department also reports observing drugs and weapons being discarded as police officers approach the suspects. The officers monitoring the surveillance cameras can inform officers at the scene what they have observed and direct them to areas where any contraband may have been discarded. The cameras have been characterized by one high-ranking police official as having one officer walking multiple beats.[21]

CARJACKINGS

During the 1960s, many cars were stolen as temporary transportation by youthful offenders who used them for "joyriding" and then abandoned them. In many states, the criminal statutes recognized both a felony auto theft and a misdemeanor joyriding charge. Around 1970, there was a shift to stealing cars for their parts and an increase in stealing cars for resale here and abroad, after they had been "repapered," meaning that the vehicles were given new, false identities.

QUICK FACTS

Derivation of the term "Carjacking"

In conventional auto thefts, the car is removed surreptitiously, and there is no contact between the thief and the vehicle's owner. Before 1990, if an offender used a weapon to confront an owner and steal the person's car, the crime was simply classified as a robbery. But in 1990, with the number of such incidents increasing, the term **carjacking** was coined in Detroit to describe the growing numbers of this potentially violent type of confrontation between offender and victim.[22]

One explanation for the increase in carjackings is that such crimes are the result of too much success in the antitheft-device market, including tracking devices such as Lojack, the Club, computer chips in ignition keys, and motion sensors. A second explanation is that there is a widespread supply of potential victims, no skill is required, no inside information is needed, and the need for planning is minimal.

In terms of location, the most common places for carjackings to occur are at the victim's home, gas stations, ATMs, car washes, parking decks, shopping-center parking lots, convenience stores, restaurants, bars, offices, train stations, apartments, public transportation parking lots and at traffic control signs and signals.

Carjackers tend to operate in small groups of two to five perpetrators. The modus operandi used is to quickly separate the person from the car. In some instances, doing so may be as quick and violent as using a brick to shatter the driver-side window of an occupied car and manhandling the occupant out of the vehicle. Mothers with children are particularly vulnerable when confronted by offenders who threaten to harm the children if the keys to the car are not given up immediately. One method of carjacking involves accidentally bumping the victim's car from the rear; when the driver gets out to investigate, one perpetrator pulls a gun, takes control of the victim's car, and flees, followed by his or her accomplices in the "bumper car." Another tactic is to use several cars to "box in" the target vehicle and then slow down gradually until it is stopped and the victim can be dealt with. Some carjackers target victims who drive into high-crime areas to buy drugs; some watch expensive cars in parking lots and then carjack them because they believe the victims are more likely to have jewelry and cash that can also be taken.

According to the FBI, the primary motives for carjacking are to acquire transportation away from the crime scene after robbing the driver, to get to and from another crime, such as another robbery or a drive-by shooting, to sell the car for cash, to trade it for drugs,[23] and to acquire temporary transportation. Whenever a carjacking takes place, the potential for a more serious crime exists.

Carjacking may also be a tool used by perpetrators to execute other crimes, which can lead to murder. For example, in one case a woman was carjacked and then forced into another car by the offenders. She was taken to a different location and raped. Later, she was forced to make several ATM withdrawals. Over the next several days, she was further abused and then executed by being slowly strangled with a coat hanger by one of the perpetrators while the others taunted her and cheered the executioner.

HOME-INVASION ROBBERIES

Home-invasion robberies (HIRs) typically target the person, rather than the residence, often selecting women and senior citizens.[24] Invaders often follow potential targets from shopping centers to their homes. They may enter the residence through an unlocked door or window, talk an unsuspecting victim into opening the door, or simply force the door open.

In some cases, the targets are "fingered," or identified, by others who pass information on to the invaders for drugs or money. Such offenders will also use deceit to gain entry into a residence. Home invaders may pose as police officers, water department employees, florists delivering bouquets, motorists who have "just struck your parked car," natural gas and electric company representatives, and "supervisors checking on your newspaper delivery service," to name just a few. The following case describes one such incident:

> Two men knocked on the door of a home and asked to use the telephone. After gaining entry by this ruse and casing the place, they decided the home was worth robbing. They returned that afternoon, forced their way in, severely beat the couple—who were in their late seventies—and left with valuables and the victims' pickup truck.[25]

SMARTPHONE ROBBERIES

The risk associated with smartphone robberies is increasing for consumers as the reward for criminals is growing.[26,27] Law enforcement is finding that during the course of many robberies, criminals were passing up on other valuables and instead robbing only the phone.[28] People are not just having their cell phones taken; often, assaults occur in conjunction with the robbery.[29]

The top ten cities for smartphone theft and loss (determined by the number of reported stolen smartphone cases per capita) are:[30]

1. Philadelphia
2. Seattle
3. Oakland
4. Long Beach
5. Newark
6. Detroit
7. Cleveland
8. Baltimore
9. New York
10. Boston

A stolen iPhone equates to cash for thieves. In the United States, used iPhones can sell for $50 to $400,[31] and overseas, a stolen iPhone can be sold for as much as $2,000.[32]

While many of these thefts may be common criminal activity, in some cases, they may be much more. Recently, the FBI arrested suspected members of the terrorist group Hezbollah in Philadelphia, Pennsylvania, who purchased stolen electronics (including smartphones) for resale in foreign countries in an effort to finance weapons purchases.[33]

Reselling used smartphones is becoming more convenient and creating opportunities for stolen smartphones to be exchanged for cash or, in some cases, store credit. Retail stores such as Best Buy and Apple have exchange programs where used smartphones can be returned for credit towards an upgraded phone or in-store credit. These programs require the owner to provide personal information, including a fingerprint, when participating. Other third-party resellers use kiosks or mail-in programs to provide a convenient location to sell a used cell phone or smartphone for cash. These resellers ask the owner to volunteer personal information in accordance with state and local laws. Some local communities, such as Prince George's County, Maryland, require a secondhand dealer or pawn dealer's license in order for these types of third-party resellers to operate.[34]

Initiatives and Practices to Prevent Smart Phone Robberies

Several agencies are implementing measures to combat this growing criminal enterprise, such as:

- Law enforcement agencies have been successful in apprehending "Apple pickers" by using decoy officers on mass transit routes or bait cars with Apple products in plain sight.[35]
- The FCC entered into a public-private partnership to develop a tool for consumers that provides smartphone users with security steps customized by a mobile operating system. The smartphone Security Checker is available at http://fcc.gov/smartphone-security.[36]
- In Washington, DC, the Metropolitan Police Department has started a campaign for victims of stolen smartphones to "brick it." A "bricked" phone is one that has been reported stolen by the victim to the wireless carrier, which then remotely renders the phone inactive, deleting all information on the device and blacklisting the electronic serial number (ESN).[37]
- In San Francisco, California, police launched a transit ad campaign called "Be Smart With Your Smartphone."[38]
- Since early 2012, the New York City Police Department has been training officers on how to use the "Find My iPhone" application to locate stolen phones and possibly apprehend thieves.[39]
- CTIA-The Wireless Association provides consumer information through its "Before You Lose It" education campaign to help users deter smartphone thefts and protect their personal information.[40]
- The Baltimore, Maryland Police Department developed *Ten Core Concepts for Successful Wireless Investigations*[41] on which to structure an investigative technology team.

In 1999, Ronald V. Clark developed the idea of "hot products" to describe the consumer goods that are most attractive to thieves. Clark introduced the acronym CRAVED to define the attributes of hot products. The acronym stands for: *Concealable*—easily hidden in pockets, purses, knapsacks; *Removable*—moved and carried away with ease; *Available*—they are ubiquitous; *Valuable*—vast local and international market for "used" items; *Enjoyable*—they are cool; for many, possessions denotes status; and *Disposable*—easily converted to cash. Agencies can incorporate the hot products and CRAVED[42] concepts to tailor prevention, apprehension, and market-reduction programs when developing strategies to address cell phone and smartphone thefts.

Longer-term federal initiatives include persuading the cell phone industry to install an option for customers to require a password to disable their mobile device permanently.

Theft Prevention Tips for the Public

In addition to these agency initiatives, security experts are encouraging smartphone owners to do their part to secure devices and the data stored on their smartphones, including:[43]

- Enable auto lock.
- Have a mobile tracking app installed (i.e., Find My iPhone). In instances of theft or robbery, the Baltimore Police Department recommends that this function should not be activated by the victim alone but by law enforcement officers, who will accompany the victim to the location reported by the device.
- Erase your personal data remotely.
- Lock sensitive applications.
- Back up your smartphone's data.

Additional safety measures include the following:[44]

- Keep expensive items hidden.
- Be alert to your surroundings when out in public.
- Buy specific electronic device insurance.

QUICK FACTS

The Implementation of State Statutes to Combat Smartphone Thefts

Recently California passed a law which requires all phones sold to include some sort of technology allowing consumers to identify their devices as stolen and prevent them from being reactivated. The cellphone industry has voluntary agreed to implement the protections nationwide, with Apple, BlackBerry, Google, HTC, Huawei, LG, Motorola, Microsoft, Samsung and ZTE all on board, as well as the major cellular carriers. Many other states and territories are in the process of considering legislation. Any differences, even minor, in such legislation could result in the requirement that a different model of a smartphone be manufactured for sale in that state for compliance with local laws. The states and territories that plan on implementing such laws include: Puerto Rico; Michigan; Virginia; New Jersey; Rhode Island; New York; Illinois; New Mexico; and Nevada.

ROBBERY AT AUTOMATED TELLER MACHINES

Automated teller machines (ATMs) were introduced in the early 1970s, and their use has grown at a staggering rate since then. Automated teller machines (ATMs) were introduced in the early 1970s and their use has grown at a staggering rate since then. It is estimated by the ATM Industry Association that there are approximately 3 million ATMs in the world.[45] Robbery at ATMs is only one of several related problems the police must address related to ATMs. Other related crimes include:

- robbery of couriers who fill ATMs with cash
- theft of personal identification numbers (PINs) including theft by "shoulder surfing"
- theft by electronic data interception
- theft by fraudulent electronic transactions
- theft of money from ATMs by bank/ATM service employees
- burglary of ATMs (including theft of entire ATMs)
- presence of homeless people sleeping in ATM vestibules
- vandalism of ATMs
- fraudulent use of ATM cards obtained from customers through dummy ATMs that keep their cards.[46]

PREVENTING AND REDUCING ROBBERIES AT AUTOMATED TELLER MACHINES

Law enforcement officers should make the following recommendations to the banks within their jurisdictions in order to prevent and reduce robberies at their ATMs (Figure 13-1).

Ensure Adequate Lighting at and Around ATMs

This allows users to see any suspicious people near the ATM, and allows potential witnesses, including police, to see a crime in progress and get a good look at the offender.

Ensure the Landscaping Around ATMs Allows for Good Visibility

Trees and shrubbery should be trimmed routinely to remove potential hiding places for offenders and ensure the ATM is visible to individuals who are passing by.

Install Mirrors on ATMs

Rearview mirrors on ATMs and adjacent building corners allow ATM users to detect suspicious people and behavior.

Install ATMs Where There Is a Lot of Natural Surveillance and Surrounding Lighting

ATMs should be placed in areas where there is a lot of routine vehicle and pedestrian traffic.[47] (See Figure 13-1.) The potential for witnesses deters offenders, and heavy traffic increases the probability of victim assistance when a robbery occurs.

Install ATMs in Police Stations

Some jurisdictions have installed publicly accessible ATMs in police stations to attract ATM users to a safe place to conduct their business.[48]

Relocate, Close, or Limit the Hours of Operation of ATMs at High-Risk Sites

ATMs should not be placed in areas known for drug trafficking and sites near abandoned property or crime-prone liquor establishments.[49]

Install and Monitor Surveillance Cameras at and Around ATMs

These serve two main purposes – to deter robbery and fraud, and to facilitate offender identification.

Install Devices to Allow Victims to Summon Police During a Robbery

There are several mechanisms by which ATM users can summon police quickly. These include:

- Panic buttons installed on the ATM.[50]
- Telephones next to the ATM.

▶ **FIGURE 13-1**
Automatic teller machines: A natural target for robberies
Automatic teller machines are very popular today as a means of obtaining on-the-spot cash. At one point, robberies at these locations were so frequent that critics referred to ATMs as "magnets for crime." Placing ATMs in highly visible areas and improving surrounding lighting has led to a decrease in this form of robbery over the last few years. (©David Lassman/ Syracuse Newspapers/The Image Works)

- Live microphones in the ATMs with a security company monitoring the microphones.

Profile of the Typical Victim

The ATM robbery victim is typically a lone woman who is using the machine between 8 P.M. and midnight.[51] To minimize the time spent with the victim and to avoid having to pressure the victim to make a withdrawal, many offenders simply wait until the transaction is completed before they pounce. Others confront the victim before the transaction, forcing her or him to make large withdrawals. Many victims report that they never saw the robber coming.

Offenders are most likely to work alone and are typically armed. They are usually about 25 years of age and tend to position themselves near an ATM, waiting for a likely victim to appear.[52] In addition to taking the cash and any valuables the victim has, offenders may carjack the victim's vehicle to flee the scene.

Set Daily Cash-Withdrawal Limits

Bank regulations that limit the amount of cash a customer may withdraw each day from an ATM reduces the potential financial loss from a robbery, and potentially discourages some robbers who decide the benefits of the robbery are not worth the risk of apprehension.[53] However, most street robbers do not expect much cash from a robbery, while concluding it is worth the risk.[54]

TARGETING OFFENDERS

Control Street Drug Markets

High rates of street robbery usually coincide with high levels of street drug trafficking. Addicts have frequent and immediate cravings for drugs; street robbery, especially around ATMs, is one of the fastest ways for them to get cash to buy drugs.

Target Repeat Offenders

Where it can be established that a few offenders are likely responsible for many local ATM robberies, the offenders should be targeted by repeat offender programs.[55] Detectives and patrol officers should cultivate informants to identify and apprehend active offenders.[56] Offering rewards for information is also good practice. Interviewing offenders after they have been convicted is useful both for clearing other cases and for improving intelligence about the rate of ATM robbery committed by a few repeat offenders.[57]

Prohibit Loitering and Panhandling Near ATMs

Laws that prohibit loitering and panhandling near ATMs give police authority to keep opportunistic offenders away from potential victims.[58]

ROBBERIES IN CRAIGSLIST SALES

As more people buy and sell valuables online, people are becoming victims of violent robberies that sometimes end in death. As a result, police departments are increasingly setting up video-monitored locations in close proximity to their police station in what they characterize as a "Safe Zone." (See Figure 13-2.)

Safety tips recommended for consumers to consider:

- Meet during the day in a well-lit area.
- Meet in a public place and do not invite strangers into your home.

Police stations are a good option (although it's best to call in advance to make sure it's OK) as are banks, which allow you to go inside to withdraw and deposit cash rather than carrying it on you.

◄**FIGURE 13-2**
Safe zone for conducting business
This area set up by the Flower Mound, Texas Police Department has been located in close proximity to their police station. It is also under 24-hour video surveillance.
[Image source from an article in the *Dallas Morning News*, May 21, 2015, http://www.dallasnews.com/news /community-news/lewisville-flower -mound/headlines/20150521-flower -mound-police-department-creates -zone-for-online-transactions.ece]
(©Kaylin Clement, Town of Flower Mound, TX)

- Some police agencies will do spot checks to make sure the item you are buying is not stolen, such as running VIN numbers from cars.
- Avoid carrying large amounts of cash for extended periods. Deposit and withdraw money as soon as possible to limit the window of time when you could be a tempting target for criminals.
- Don't go alone. Your friend will not be as distracted by the haggling and product inspection, so he or she is more likely to notice if something seems out of place.
- Tell someone where you are going.
- Take your cell phone with you in case you need to make an emergency call.
- Trust your instincts. If something seems unusual, leave.[59]

TAXICAB ROBBERIES

Taxi drivers have a higher homicide victimization rate than any other occupation in the United States and are also at great risk for robbery.[60] This is due to a combination of factors related to the nature of their job, including:

- Having contact with a large number of strangers or people they do not know well.
- Often working in high-crime areas.
- Usually carrying cash with them in an unsecured manner and handling money as payment.
- Usually working alone.
- Often going to, or through, isolated locations.
- Often working late at night or early in the morning.

These risk factors, among others, have been mentioned in a number of studies of workplace homicide and violence in general.[61]

The Following Are Some Important Crime-Prevention Strategies to Prevent Robbery of Taxi Drivers

Although the cab companies or individual drivers must be the ones to implement the crime prevention strategies suggested below, crime prevention specialists in the police department can be proactive and work with cab companies to assist in operationalizing some of these recommendations.

- *Provide physical barriers to separate drivers from passengers*—Bullet resistant screens or partitions should be installed, because they make it more difficult for robbers to carry out the robbery.
- *Record activity with security cameras in the cab*—Police and prosecutors can use the images to help identify and catch offenders and increase the evidence available for prosecution and conviction.
- *Use of an alarm to call for help*—Can be used to signal someone at a central location (taxi company or police station) if they are having trouble or they can be a "trouble light" on the vehicle itself that cannot be seen by the passengers. Alarms must be designed so that they can be triggered easily through the pressing of a toggle switch at the driver's foot, on the steering wheel, or on the radio itself.
- *Keep track of vehicle locations with automatic vehicle location (AVL) systems*—With global positioning satellite (GPS) systems, all that is required is the triggering of an alarm and the monitoring of that alarm signal by someone who can send help.
- *Put trunk latches on the inside of vehicle trunks as well as near drivers*—This feature is designed to reduce the potential harm to drivers who may be locked in the trunk following the robbery incident. Trunk latches also permit drivers to open trunks without getting out of the cab, which may prove useful late at night if the driver does not think it is safe to exit the cab.
- *Eliminate cash payments*—Drivers should be encouraged to use payment systems that are cashless. These include:
  —Credit or debit cards.
  —Accounts accessible though mobile phones.
  —Accounts for regular customers, such as those used by restaurants, hospitals, and social services. (Authorized passengers merely sign the bill.)
- *Drop money off*—Drivers should be encouraged to drop off cash during their shifts. They can drop the cash at home, at cash machines, or at dispatching offices where the money can be secured until their shift is concluded. However, dispatching offices holding drivers' cash must be made secure against robbery as well.
- *Keep money locked up or out of sight*—Drivers can put money in a locked safe in the cab (Figure 13-3). If a safe is used it should be advertised on both the exterior and the interior of the cab. In addition, drop-off routines must be varied to prevent robbers from staking out drop-off locations and carrying out hold-ups as drivers leave their cabs.
- *Control who gets in*—Drivers can use a number of techniques to control who gets into their cabs by:
  —Keeping doors locked while drivers are waiting for the next fare.
  —Keeping windows rolled up enough to prevent someone from reaching in.
  —Limiting the number of passengers.
- *Find out the destination before moving*—One rule of thumb cited repeatedly is to determine passenger's destination "up front." It is seen as a sign of potential trouble if the passenger refuses to give a destination at the beginning of the trip or changes destinations while en route.
- *Share destination information with others*—Drivers should keep as many people informed of their whereabouts as possible, especially where cameras or GPS systems are not used.
- *Limiting where the cab will make a drop off*—Drivers should be wary of making a passenger drop off in a dark, isolated, or out-of-the-way location, because these do not permit surveillance by others or allow the driver to see if someone is lurking at the destination.

◀**FIGURE 13-3**
Robbery prevention sign on taxicab
The photo on the left depicts the typical location of a robbery prevention sign on a cab. The photo on the right provides a close-up of what the potential would-be robber would see upon approaching or entering the cab. The safety deposit box referred to in the photo is actually a heavy-gauge steel box bolted to the cab floor with a slot on top into which bills can be inserted. The box can be opened only by a key kept at the taxicab garage.
(Courtesy of Elena Territo)

- *Limit injury when a robbery occurs*—Taxi drivers are frequently advised to cooperate with those trying to rob them by handing over their money and not fighting back. Similarly, drivers should keep an extra key in a pocket to allow them to use their cab if the robbers have taken their keys. This is particularly important if they have been abandoned in a remote location and have no way of contacting the police or their dispatcher.

CONVENIENCE-STORE ROBBERIES

Convenience stores account for about 6% of all reported robberies. These stores do a great deal of business in cash, are often open 24 hours a day, have numerous locations, and typically offer little or no protection from robbers. Thus, it is not surprising that convenience-store workers are among the occupational groups having the highest risk for workplace violence.[62]

Specific Actions That Can be Taken by Retailers to Reduce Convenience Store Robberies

- *Maximize natural surveillance*—Employees should have an optimal view of the entrance and interior of the store.
- *Have multiple employees on duty during high-risk periods*—Businesses that remain open between 11 P.M. and 5 A.M. should use at least one of the following crime-reduction measures: two or more employees, bullet-resistant safety enclosures, a security guard, or a pass-through window to conduct business.[63]
- *Control access*—A consistent finding of studies involving the interview of convenience store robbers is that escape routes are a key factor to their target selection. Eliminating or at least limiting potential escape routes by using fences or landscaping is highly recommended.
- *Establish territoriality*—Stores in high-crime areas should discourage loitering as well as maximizing the existing lighting and design of their parking areas.

- *Train employees*—Training should include how to behave during a robbery and how to avoid violence.
- *Use cash-control procedure*—One 10-year study of convenience store robbers found that "80 percent of potential robbers can be deterred if a convenience store limits the amount of money kept in its cash register and this fact is conspicuously posted on the front door of the business."[64]
- *Install cameras and alarms*—The presence of CCTV monitors, clearly visible near cash registers, as well as signs that state surveillance equipment is in use, have been found to have some deterrent effect by increasing the robber's risk of identification.[65]

Police Robbery Prevention Recommendations for Convenience Stores

- *Provide robbery prevention and awareness training*—Police are in a prime position to guide businesses in crime prevention. They are typically the first point of contact after a robbery and can be particularly helpful to small businesses that may have limited access to other programs and must therefore rely more heavily on police to guide them in developing robbery prevention strategies.
- *Inspect convenience stores for compliance with robbery prevention measures*—Police might assume responsibility for regularly inspecting convenience stores to determine whether they have adopted either mandatory or voluntary robbery prevention measures.
- *Enforce prohibitions on loitering outside convenience stores*—Police should enforce loitering or trespassing statutes or ordinances that prohibit loitering (and panhandling) in order to keep opportunistic offenders away from potential victims.[66]
- *Conduct robbery stakeouts*—Police departments need considerable resources to be able to sustain the number

of officers needed to await possible robberies in various locations over a long time. Unless there is specific information that a robbery is likely to occur, a stakeout will not be set up. However, if a stakeout is set up police officers must work with store employees to carefully plan out the tactics that will be employed if a robbery should occur. This is so because in the event a police officer does confront an armed suspect there is the potential for a shooting to occur. Therefore the clerk on duty must be carefully informed about what course of action to take in the event a robbery occurs.

- *Increase police patrols*—Because it takes a relatively short time to complete a convenience store robbery, the chances of thwarting one by increased patrols is not highly likely. However, if the decision is made to increase patrol, it must be based on a careful analysis of the patterns of convenience store robberies in a particular jurisdiction. On occasion, clear patterns do develop where a particular segment of a community is targeted. In such cases the police may decide to saturate the area with marked patrol units in the hope of dissuading individuals to commit the robbery. This in turn raises the possibility that the robbers will decide to move to another geographical area or even another police jurisdiction to commit robberies. In other cases the police may decide to assign additional unmarked units to a particular geographical area that can respond very quickly if a robbery alert is activated in their area.

PHARMACY ROBBERIES

In recent years there has been a dramatic increase in the number of drug-related robberies being committed against pharmacies. The robbers are not necessarily looking for cash but rather for the highly addictive oxycodone painkillers like OxyContin and hydrocodone-laced products such as Vicodin. These drugs may either be used by the robbers who themselves are addicted or be sold for exorbitant profits on the street.

The Drug Enforcement Administration (DEA) has set forth the following guidelines as being the best course of action for pharmacists and citizens to take should they find themselves in the middle a robbery. These recommendations should be conveyed by local law enforcement agencies to the pharmacies within their jurisdiction.

- **Avoid taking any action that may provoke violence:** Robbers are usually armed. They are usually in a state of heightened excitement. It is important to remain as calm as possible, and to keep other people on the premises as calm as possible.
- **Give the robber what he asks for, but do not offer him more than he requests.**
- **Carefully observe the robber for identity characteristics, including:** clothing, height, weight, race, hair, eyes, nose, scars, tattoos, accent, etc. If there is more than one robber focus your attention primarily on one. Trying to identify too much may only result in confusion.
- **Watch carefully for any object that the robber touches.** Do not disturb or touch any area that the robber has touched. These areas may provide fingerprint identification and this information should be provided to the responding law enforcement officer(s).
- **Focus on the weapon** for later description to police.
- **Focus on what is taken, where it is put, and how it is carried.**
- **Do not prolong the stay through stalling.** The quicker the robber leaves, the less chance for violence to erupt.
- **Remember the method of escape.** If the robber enters a vehicle, get a full description, including the license plate number, if possible.
- **Notify the police immediately.** If a panic button/central station alarm is present, activate it while the robbery is still in progress, if this can be done safely.
- **While waiting for police, write down as many identifying details as possible.** If other people were present, have them do the same, but do not attempt to get a consensus of opinion. Each witness's individual opinion of what happened will be of more value to the police and should not be colored by the observations of the other witnesses.
- **Comply with all directions of the police** regarding the crime scene and the compiling of lists of stolen controlled substances.
- **When advised by the police that the crime scene is no longer required to be safeguarded, notify the nearest DEA office.**[67]

TRUCK-HIJACKING ROBBERIES/ CARGO THEFT

Truck hijacking is committed by experienced armed robbers acting on inside information. Because transporting goods by truck generates a substantial written record, there are many points at which insiders can learn the nature of a cargo and when it will be moved. Many truck hijackings happen in or near large cities because it is easy to dispose of the goods there. If there is a seaport, the goods taken may also be quickly on their way to a foreign country within hours. The contents of some hijacked trucks are off-loaded to another truck or several smaller trucks and may be in several other states by the time the investigation is getting started. Hijackers take what is valuable, with a preference for cargoes that are easy to dispose of and hard to trace. Examples include loads of clothing and high-tech equipment components.[68]

A number of truck hijackings involve collusion on the part of the driver with those committing this specialized form of robbery. The driver may be bribed or given some portion of the cargo for his or her personal use. In a variation of this, hijackers give drugs to drivers and provide them with women and then coerce the drivers into cooperating by threatening to cut off their supply of drugs and women, to give a spouse photographs of the driver's liaisons with other women, or to expose the driver's use of drugs to employers.

Drivers of rigs may be confronted at roadblocks, or "detours," set up by hijackers. They may be forced from the road or accosted by the hijackers as they enter or leave truck rest stops. Some drivers have been tricked into stopping to help a "disabled" motorist. In more brazen moves, hijackers may invade truck parks, seize or kill security personnel, and take the trucks that they have targeted.[69]

BANK ROBBERY

Although this portion of the chapter focuses primarily on bank robberies, many of the investigative and crime prevention suggestions set forth herein (some of which have already been discussed) can also be applied to large retail businesses, small convenience stores, jewelry stores, appliance stores, and so forth. This includes methods of escape, escape routes, target selection, and robbery prevention.[70]

Distinguishing Professional and Amateur Bank Robbers

Bank robberies and, for that matter, most robberies do not appear to be well-planned offenses committed by professional criminals; instead, increasing evidence suggests that many bank robberies are spontaneous and opportunistic crimes that are often acts of desperation.[71-78]

Because most bank robberies are committed by solitary, unarmed, and undisguised offenders, they can be considered the work of amateurs rather than professionals. In contrast, it is the less common armed bank robberies that more often involve multiple offenders and the use of disguises.[79-81] Distinguishing bank robberies as the work of amateur or professional robbers provides important insight about the risks or robbery in selecting crime prevention strategies most likely to be effective.

To a great extent, bank robbers can be classified as amateur or professional based on known characteristics of the robbery—the number of offenders, use of weapons and disguises, efforts to defeat security, timing of the robbery, target selection, and means of getaway (Table 13-1).

Method of Escape

The method of escape further distinguishes amateur from professional robbers. Cars are not the sole means of escape; many offenders escape on foot or even by bicycle, at least initially.

Getaway vehicles are more prevalent when there are two or more offenders: 72% of robbery teams use vehicles, which reflects some degrees of planning.[82] In contrast, 58% of solitary robbers escape on foot. Two factors discourage solitary robbers from using vehicles: without an accomplice to drive the vehicle, it must be parked and quickly accessible to the robber; further, solitary robbers typically select targets that are convenient, such as those close to their residence making a car unnecessary. In contrast, professional bank robbers appear willing to travel farther than other robbers, perhaps because there are fewer banks than other types of commercial targets or because banks tend to be clustered geographically and are open for fewer hours.[83,84]

Escape Routes in Target Selection

Because many bank robberies are the work of amateurs, it may appear that robbers randomly select targets. They do not. Instead, robbers select targets primarily based on their concern with getting away from the robbery quickly.

Although much effort to reduce bank robbery has focused on bank interiors and security measures, most bank robbers do not feel they are at risk of apprehension during the commission of the crime. Instead, robbers assume there will be easy access to cash and that the robbery will be completed

TABLE 13-1	Distinguishing Professional and Amateur Bank Robbers	
	PROFESSIONAL	**AMATEUR**
Offenders	• Multiple offenders with division of labor • Shows evidence of planning • May be older • Prior bank robbery convictions • Travels further to rob banks	• Solitary offender • Drug or alcohol use likely • No prior bank crime • Lives near bank target
Violence	• Aggressive takeover, with loud verbal commands • Visible weapons, especially guns • Intimidation, physical or verbal threats	• Note passed to teller or simple verbal demand • Waits in line • No weapon
Defeat Security	• Uses a disguise • Disables or obscures surveillance cameras • Demands that dye packs be left out, alarms not be activated, or police not be called	
Robbery Success	• Hits multiple teller windows • Larger amounts stolen • Lower percentage of money recovered • More successful robberies • Fewer cases directly cleared • Longer time from offense to case clearance	• Single teller window victimized • Lesser amounts stolen • Higher percentage of money recovered • More failed robberies • Shorter time from offense to case clearance, including same-day arrests • Direct case clearance more likely
Robbery Timing	• Targets banks when few customers are present, such as at opening time • Targets banks early in the week	• Targets banks when numerous customers are present, such as around midday • Targets banks near closing or on Friday
Target Selection	• Previous robbery • Busy road near intersection • Multidirectional traffic • Corner locations, multiple vehicle exits	• Previous robbery • Heavy pedestrian traffic or adjacent to dense multifamily residences • Parcels without barrier • Parcels with egress obscured
Getaway	• Via car	• On foot or bicycle

Source: Deborah Lamm Weisel, *Bank Robbery*, U.S. Department of Justice, Office of Community Policing Services, 2007.

quickly. Thus, robbers for the most part are relatively unconcerned about alarms and cameras, neither of which will slow their escape.

A robber's choice of target is shaped by two escape features: the type of transportation available and the ease and number of escape routes.[85-89] Because offenders prefer choices during flight, they tend to select targets that have more than one escape path.

Solitary offenders typically cannot escape in a vehicle because of the logistics of parking and retrieving a vehicle. Thus, solitary offenders typically escape on foot.

In contrast, multiple offenders typically escape in a vehicle—often stolen just before the robbery to reduce the likelihood that the vehicle has been reported stolen by the owner.

BANK ROBBERY PREVENTION

Following are some of the actions banks can take to reduce the likelihood of robberies and minimize their losses.

- *Limiting cash access:* Cash in banks is available at teller windows—the most frequent target of robbers—and safes. Most banks have cash management policies, such as removing cash from the teller drawers when it reaches a predetermined amount, a fairly common practice among convenience stores as well. Some banks use vacuum systems to quickly and efficiently remove cash from teller drawers.

- *Using dye packs:* Exploding **dye packs** are widely used by banks to prevent stolen money from being used. Dye packs stain both the robber and the cash, preventing use of the money and aiding in the detection of the robber. Many dye packs are supplemented by tear gas, which is triggered by an electromagnetic field near the bank exit door. When the tear gas explodes, the robber is effectively immobilized (Figure 13-4).

- *Slowing the robbery:* Because bank robbers want the crime to proceed quickly, some banks have adopted

▲ FIGURE 13-4   Exploding dye packs

Exploding dye packs are widely used by banks to prevent stolen money from being used. When they explode, the dye packs stain both the robber and the cash, thereby preventing use of the money and aiding in the detection of the robber. Many dye packs are supplemented by tear gas that is triggered by an electromagnetic field near the bank exit door. When the tear gas explodes, the robber will be effectively immobilized.

(©3SI Security Systems)

strategies that are intended to slow the pace of the robbery. A slow robbery may increase the suspect's perception of risk and will sometimes cause the robber to abandon the crime.[90,91] For example, interior obstacles such as revolving doors and customer service counters can slow the robber's escape; timed safes and withdrawal limits on cash dispensing machines can further extend the duration of the robbery.

- *Employing greeters:* Bank employees known as greeters welcome customers and reduce the anonymity of a would-be robber; this face-to-face interaction may discourage a robbery before it occurs. Greeters should be trained to be alert to suspicious behavior. They are more likely to discourage amateur robbers than professional robbers.
- *Use of security guards:* There is disagreement regarding the effectiveness of bank security guards.[91-93] Guards are expensive, and they may also create an environment that makes customers fearful. Some research suggests that

guards reduce the risk of bank robbery.[95-97] However, some studies also suggest that the presence of the armed guards increases the risks of violence during a robbery.[98-100]

- *Warning likely offenders:* Bank robbers tend to overestimate the amount of money they will get from a robbery, to underestimate the likelihood of arrest, and to be unaware of the sentences they face if convicted. Thus, some banks and trade associations have developed publicity campaigns designed to educate would-be offenders about the low take, high capture rate, and other perils of a career in bank robbery.[101]
- *Using tracking devices:* Some banks conceal electronic **tracking devices** with the robbery money, thus aiding police in locating offenders. Tracking devices use low-voltage transmitting microchips with transponders. However, since tracking devices are intended to increase the chance of apprehending offenders, they are not likely to prevent robberies from occurring.
- *Using bait money:* **Bait money** is cash with sequential serial numbers that are recorded by the bank. When the money reenters circulation, police track its use in hopes of locating the suspect. Bait money is already widely used by banks.
- *Offering rewards:* Some banks actively publicize "most wanted" bank robbers, displaying their surveillance photos and offering rewards for information leading to their capture. Banks use websites, local silent witness programs, and tip lines to publicize crimes and to seek out offenders. There are also national tip organizations that coordinate information about highly mobile robbers.
- *Upgrading electronic surveillance:* Bank surveillance cameras are in widespread use: 98% of robbed banks have interior surveillance cameras. However, cameras do not appear to reduce robberies. Many bank robbers are not deterred, because they simply do not believe they will be caught. Others believe that cameras can be thwarted with a disguise or by covert behavior or that cameras can be disabled, such as with spray paint; or they simply do not think about cameras at all.[102-104] However, sometimes electronic surveillance can have unanticipated benefits. For example, one alert employee in a Texas bank noticed a man hanging around the bank lobby and thought she recognized him from a photograph she had been shown several days before by law enforcement officials. The picture of the individual, who had held up other banks, was being shown to bank employees in the general area. The individual did not stay in the bank very long, but when he left the alert bank employee contacted the police who then started to surveil the bank parking lot. Several hours later the man returned to the bank. His partner remained in the car while he walked inside the bank to commit the robbery. Once again, his image was captured by the surveillance camera. The police were not able to prevent the robbery, but

▶**FIGURE 13-5 Bandit barriers**
Bandit barriers may discourage some bank robbers and also increase the safety of bank employees. Such devices are also becoming fairly common in convenience stores, especially those that operate 24 hours a day and are located in high-crime areas.
(©Clear Security Systems, www.clearsecuritysystems.com)

once the man exited the bank and entered the getaway car, police officers were able to converge in their vehicles and to place both men under arrest. Thus, one possible strategy for bank robbery prevention could be to obtain bank surveillance photographs of individuals who committed bank robberies and show them to bank employees in the same general area in order to alert them to what the potential robbers look like. As it turned out, the individual and his partner confessed to robbing seven other banks in a half dozen nearby towns.

- *Rapidly activating alarms:* Although alarms lead to the arrest of bank robbers in only about 6% of crimes, there is evidence that prompt activation increases apprehension rates. Some bank employees do not activate alarms until after the robber has left the premises. This is so because of safety concerns about the employees and customers in case the police trapped the robber inside the bank thus creating a potential hostage situation and violence. In other cases, the delay might be due to panic or to comply with instructions made by the robber.

- *Installing bandit barriers:* The FBI recommends that banks install bullet-resistant glass **bandit barriers** between tellers and customers. Such devices are also becoming fairly common in convenience stores, especially those that operate 24-hours a day and are in high-crime areas (Figure 13-5).[105] Although most of these are permanent installations, some bandit barriers "pop up" when activated by tellers or when an object crosses the counter.

- *Installing access control vestibules:* Access control vestibules—also known as man-catcher vestibules or man-traps—are a specialized form of access control device. These devices can be used to scan potential customers for weapons before they access the bank interior; others are designed to be manually activated by tellers.

- *Hardening targets:* Banks have employed a wide variety of target-hardening strategies that are designed to make the bank interior appear inhospitable to would-be robbers. These include revolving doors, increased distance between entrances and teller stations, higher teller counters, queuing and other physical barriers, and single-door entrances and exits.[106–108]

- *Consider the possibility of an inside job:* When a bank robbery does occur, investigators should consider the possibility of the robber having received assistance from someone inside the bank. One interesting case occurred recently in the Atlanta, Georgia, area. A Bank of America was held up by two young women identified as the "Barbie Bandits." These two young women, who would eventually be identified as Heather Johnston and Ashley Miller, both 19, were photographed by a bank security camera and subsequently identified by people who recognized them when their pictures were shown on local television (Figure 13-6). Their arrest and the subsequent investigation led to the arrest of two additional accomplices—namely, a convicted drug dealer, Michael Darrell Chastang, 27, and a Bank of America teller, Benny Allen III, 22. The four had conspired to commit the theft and divided the money after the crime was committed.

◄FIGURE 13-6 Bank robbery: Inside job
This photo depicts two young women, Ashley Miller (*left*) and Heather Johnston (*right*) both 19, dubbed by the media "the Barbie Bandits." Their images were captured on a bank surveillance camera wearing sunglasses and reportedly giggling throughout the robbery. The bank robbery occurred in the Atlanta, Georgia, area. The video camera images were broadcast on local television and the two young women were identified by viewers who knew them. As it turned out the robbery was actually an inside job in which the two women conspired with a convicted drug dealer and a bank teller who worked in the bank they robbed. (©Cobb County Police Dept/AP Images)

RESPONDING TO THE SCENE

In route to the scene of a robbery call, the officer must ensure that all information available from the dispatcher has been obtained, including the answers to the following questions: What is the exact location of the offense, including the type of business? Is the offense in progress? How many suspects are involved? What type of and how many weapons were displayed? What description of the suspect is available? By what method and in what direction did the suspect flee? What is the description of the means of transportation used by the suspect?

In approaching the scene, the officer must be alert for several possibilities:

- The dispatcher may provide information on the suspects' escape, such as their direction in fleeing from the scene and whether they were on foot or in a vehicle.
- Information about the target, MO, suspects, vehicles, weapons used, and other factors in recent robberies may help the responding officer recognize the suspects if they are moving away from the scene on the street along which the officer approaches, even if the dispatcher cannot supply any specific information other than the nature of the crime.
- The fleeing suspects may, as the officer approaches them on the way to the scene, abruptly turn off, fire at the officer, or otherwise suddenly reveal themselves.

The primary tactical objectives of officers responding to a robbery call are public safety, officer protection, and tactical control of the scene. Secondary objectives include conducting the preliminary investigation, apprehending perpetrators, and recovering property. Arriving at the scene unobserved by the suspects facilitates the achievement of both primary and secondary objectives. It also allows tactical control and the element of surprise to pass from the robbers to the police. Units assigned to a robbery call should plan and coordinate the actions to be taken at the scene. Because the perpetrators may have police scanners, care should be taken with respect to radio transmissions. Arriving officers should not give away their exact positions and should refer to buildings by prearranged letter designations (e.g., "the A building").[109] They can never assume that the robber(s) have left the scene; for example, robbers have been known to hide near or at the scene, seeking to escape detection. Responding units should approach separately on streets parallel to that on which the robbery occurred or is occurring, using emergency lights but not sirens. The use of emergency lights permits more rapid progress through traffic. The reason for not using a siren is that the sound may panic suspects near or at the scene, triggering violence or hostage taking. It is believed that 9 out of 10 hostage situations that develop out of robberies occur because of a too visible first-responding officer.[110]

However, remember that most states require a police vehicle responding in an emergency mode to have both its emergency lights and siren activated. Thus, when the tactically correct decision is made to deactivate the siren, the officer's driving must be adjusted accordingly, because now the motoring public no longer has the benefit of "hearing" the approaching police vehicle and being able to yield to it.

At a distance of three to five blocks from the scene in an urban area and much farther in rural settings,[111] the emergency lights should be turned off to avoid possible detection by a lookout. The police officer should begin to smoothly decelerate, thus avoiding engine noise, squealing tires, or "emergency" stops that could give away the police car's arrival.

The first officer on the scene must quickly "size up" the area to gather any possible intelligence, including location of the robbers, lookouts, and escape vehicles. The locations of the perpetrators are particularly important given the fact that such criminals may have automatic and other weapons—which they are willing to use. Actually identifying the lookouts may be difficult; two officers in New York City, for instance, were killed by a lookout disguised as a nun.[112] The officer should leave his or her car quietly and move—

unobserved—to a protected position to watch, where possible, two sides (e.g., north and east) of the building. One of these sides should be the exit most likely to be used by the robbers. Moving unobserved does not necessarily imply moving quickly. Running into position may invite passersby to "rubberneck," giving away the officer's location.[113] Before moving to any position, the officer should make sure the background of that position, when viewed from the perpetrators' positions, does not silhouette him or her.[114]

The officer in the second unit should take the same precautions as the first in moving into position. The second officer's responsibility is to cover the two remaining sides (e.g., the south and the west). Both officers should keep their vehicles and portable radios at low volume to avoid being detected. The primary and backup officers should be sure that their positions in the lines of fire do not endanger each other.

It is also of particular importance when moving into their respective unobserved positions, officers must not get inside of, that is, between, any possible lookouts and the robbery scene. Such a position would leave them vulnerable to fire from several sides.

Both in approaching the scene and at the scene, officers should avoid action, physical, or situational stereotyping.[115]

ACTION STEREOTYPING

Action stereotyping occurs when the officers' expectations are set to see one thing and this closes their minds to other eventualities. For example, the responding officer may expect the suspect to come rushing out of the store, hop into a car, and speed away. Although this may be the case, there are also other possible behaviors:

> Two robbers who confessed to over 20 "quick mart" robberies had been apprehended during a police surveillance. While being interrogated, the pair revealed that they had come close to being caught on several occasions when responding units arrived at the scene very quickly. They said they had escaped apprehension at those times by simply walking away in a normal manner. This proved to be an embarrassment for one officer who remembered the pair walking past his car. This officer said that they just appeared to be "normal" citizens and that there was nothing extraordinary about them.[116]

PHYSICAL STEREOTYPING

Physical stereotyping is an officer's expectations that the robber will be of a particular description. Such stereotypes may allow the suspect to escape or be fatal to officers:

> An officer entered a convenience store in response to an alarm; his gun was drawn, but he started to put it away when he didn't see anything out of the ordinary. As he approached the two clerks behind the counter, the younger one yelled a warning: the other "clerk" was an armed robber whose appearance—he was 60 years old—did not fit with the officer's stereotype of a robber.[117]

Another aspect of physical stereotyping is that investigators may have difficulty believing witnesses' descriptions. For example, we expect bank robbers to be relatively young adults and vigorous. However, in northern Colorado nearly a decade ago, an 82-year-old man known as the "salt-and-pepper bandit" was arrested for a string of bank robberies; in another case, a 105-pound 70-year-old woman donned a black plastic bag as a disguise and robbed a bank, declaring, "There's a bomb here; give me the money, no bells, no sirens."[118]

SITUATIONAL STEREOTYPING

In **situational stereotyping,** the officers' previous experience with, and knowledge of, a particular location increases their vulnerability:

> A silent alarm went off at a bar; the call was dispatched, and as the assigned unit drove toward the bar, the two partners joked about the inability of the owner to set the alarm properly, since he was continuously tripping it accidentally, creating frequent false alarms. The officer operating the police car parked it in front of the bar, and as the two officers began to saunter casually up to the front door of the bar, two suspects burst out with guns in hand and began shooting. Miraculously, neither officer was hit. One of the suspects was wounded and arrested at the scene; the other one escaped and was not apprehended until several weeks later.

Returning to some earlier points, although the suspects may be observed fleeing the scene or may reveal themselves in some manner to the officer assigned to respond to the call, such encounters do not take place with any regularity. In addition, deviating from the assignment to become engaged in a "pursuit," instead of proceeding directly to the call, is often unproductive. In such instances the "suspect," especially one driving an automobile, may merely be acting in a suspicious manner because he or she may have committed some minor traffic violation and is fearful that the officer is going to write a traffic citation. The officer actually assigned to the robbery call should not normally deviate from the assignment without significant reason; the officer's responsibility is to get to the scene and to get accurate, detailed information for the preliminary pickup order or BOLO as rapidly as possible. When the officer does this, more resources are then brought to bear on the offense, and the likelihood is reduced that other officers may unknowingly stop armed suspects for what they think is only a traffic violation.

If not assigned to the call as the primary or backup unit, other officers should not respond to the scene. Instead, they should patrol along a likely escape route such as entrances to expressways. They should avoid transmitting routine messages, because the primary unit will need to transmit temporary pickup orders or BOLOs concerning the offense.

If available, helicopters have the potential of being helpful in robbery investigations when a good description of the vehicle in which the robbers fled is included in the BOLO. Helicopters can cover territory rapidly. Flying at 500 feet, a helicopter provides observers accompanying the pilot with an excellent observation platform. Approximately 75% of all pursuits aided by a helicopter are successful.[119]

FOLLOW-UP ROBBERY INVESTIGATIVE PROCEDURES

To standardize the ways in which robberies are investigated, departments should have a standard operating procedure (SOP) that deals specifically with this crime. It is also extremely important that both the responding officer(s) and follow-up investigator are thoroughly familiar with this procedure. The specifics of the Robbery SOP naturally vary from jurisdiction to jurisdiction because of the sizes of communities and the number of investigative specialists that are available. However, we have attempted herein to provide a broad model from which an investigative procedure can be developed by an agency irrespective of its size or the number of investigative specialists it has.[120]

INITIAL INVESTIGATION

Although it may not always be possible, it is advisable to have an on-duty investigator (preferably one who works robberies) to respond to the scene of all reported robberies. If, however, a police department does not normally have investigators respond to the scenes of all robberies, then certain criteria must be set forth to determine when they should respond:

- When requested by a uniform supervisor.
- A victim or witness has been seriously injured.
- A suspect has been apprehended.
- A suspect has been identified.
- Victim(s) have been tied up or incapacitated for an extended period of time.
- Large sums of money or property have been taken.
- The robbery occurs inside a residence.
- Carjacking has occurred.

- When leads with a high solvability factor are present and will be lost by a delayed response.

Specific Responsibilities for the Robbery Investigator

- Assume responsibility for the investigation.
- Ensure that proper preliminary investigative action has been taken by uniformed personnel, and take additional steps as necessary.
- Interview victim(s) and witness(es) in detail.
- Collect physical evidence.
- Canvass the area and document the names and addresses of all persons interviewed and include a summary of their observations.
- Determine if identifiable property has been taken (serial number, bait money, etc.), and ensure that this information is entered into the National Crime Information Center (NCIC).
- Determine if a cell phone has been taken, and identify the cellular number, subscriber, and carrier information.
- Display photographs of known offenders and suspects to the victim(s) and witness(es). Request that they respond to the Robbery Bureau to view photographic files if necessary. If identification is made: have the victim(s) and witness(es) sign and date all photographs identified. Number and initial those photographs shown with the identified photograph(s) and preserve them as evidence for court presentation by placing them in an envelope sealed with evidence tape in the case file.
- Obtain notarized identification statements from individuals who are visitors or when the investigator believes that such a statement will enhance the possibility of prosecution.
- Follow up all available leads to a proper conclusion before terminating the initial investigation.
- When the investigation leads to the identification of a suspect, make record checks before obtaining an arrest warrant. It must be determined that the suspect was not incarcerated at the time of the offense.
- If verification of custody or detention dates is made, make a computer printout part of the case file. In instances where confusion exists concerning the subject's confinement, verification must be obtained from the appropriate governmental agency. When received, this information will be documented in the investigator's report.
- Discuss the case with the state's prosecutor and obtain an arrest warrant(s) in a timely manner.
- When applicable, consult appropriate federal law enforcement agencies (e.g., FBI, ATF, etc.) regarding the potential for filing federal charges against the suspect(s).
- If the subject is at large, and an arrest warrant has been issued, conspicuously display all relevant information along with a photograph at key locations within police

headquarters. Also distribute wanted fliers to uniform patrol officers as well as other investigators.

- Upon notification that a wanted subject has been taken into custody outside the police jurisdiction, the applicable supervisor shall evaluate the case and, if appropriate, request that Robbery Bureau personnel be utilized for the extradition. If Robbery Bureau personnel are not used, the lead investigator shall coordinate any investigative activity that is necessary immediately upon return of the subject and before the subject is booked into the jail.
- Review and analyze all reports prepared in the preliminary phase.
- Reinterview victim(s) and witness(es) if it appears there may be information that was not obtained owing to incomplete questioning or insufficient recall of the event. Occasionally, witnesses will remember some detail and not go to the "trouble" of looking for the police department's listing. Therefore, the investigator should leave a card with his/her name and departmental phone number.
- Return to the crime scene at exactly the same time of day the offense was committed and attempt to locate additional witnesses; at the same time, reconduct the neighborhood check. When conducting a neighborhood check, officers must be certain to record the names of all witnesses interviewed in order to avoid any type of duplication with other investigators who may be assisting on the case. In the event that possible witnesses are not at home, this, too should be recorded to be certain that they are recontacted later. It is imperative that every person who was in a position to have possibly witnessed the crime be contacted and interviewed.
- Make an attempt to tie the offense to other robberies, because the combined information from several offense reports may result in sufficient detail to identify the perpetrator.
- Review any pertinent departmental records, reports, or database.
- Seek additional information from other sources (e.g., uniformed officers, informants, other investigators, other agency investigations, or informational/intelligence bulletins).
- Review the results of laboratory examinations.
- Determine the involvement of subject(s) in other crimes.
- Prepare the case for presentation to the Prosecutor's Office.
- Assist in the prosecution as required.

False Robbery Report

A file check should be made of the victim's name to determine if the person has a history of making crime reports. For instance, certain types of businesses—such as economy gasoline stations and convenience grocery stores—may not conduct even a minimal background investigation of employees. Given the availability of cash and long periods of isolation during the night hours, an untrustworthy employee will occasionally pocket cash for personal gain and cover its absence by claiming a robbery was committed. A file check on the complaining witness may suggest such a pattern. For example, one of the authors, who was a robbery investigator, routinely checked the police records of robbery

victims. In one instance, he found that a clerk employed at a convenience store, who regularly changed jobs, had allegedly been the victim of an armed robbery three times at three different convenience stores during an 18-month period, and in each case the suspect reportedly had the same identical physical description, said the same exact words when demanding the cash, and carried the same type of firearm. Naturally, this caused considerable suspicion, and when the victim was confronted with this string of "coincidences" he was unable to explain how it occurred and adamantly denied he was stealing the money. He was asked to take a polygraph examination to verify the authenticity of these robberies but refused. His employer was notified of the pattern of previous robberies as well as his reluctance to cooperate, and he was subsequently dismissed from his job.

The following represent two additional examples of false robbery reports.

Two teenage clerks were shot in a robbery at a Quick Mart convenience store. Despite the clerk's wounds, investigators were suspicious about the incident. After further questioning by the police, both "victims" admitted they made up the story about being robbed to conceal their theft of $400 and shot each other to make it look more convincing.[121]

A woman told officers that a laughing man put a gun against her 2-year-old daughter's head and robbed her at an ATM. The victim also reported that no one else was around the ATM when the incident happened at 7:52 A.M. Investigators initially thought it was highly unlikely that nobody else was at the ATM around the time of the alleged robbery. They checked the transactions at the ATM and found that a man had used the ATM just 4 minutes before the robbery and did not see anyone matching the robber's description. Moreover, the man did not immediately leave the ATM after he had finished his transaction. Based on this evidence, it was established that the woman had made up the story because she wanted some attention.[122]

GENERATING A LIKENESS OF A SUSPECT

The likeness of a suspect should be created and distributed as rapidly as possible. There are a number of methods available to create a likeness. One of them is through the use of a police artist (Figure 13-7). There are several software programs can be used to generate suspect likenesses, including Sirchie's ComPhotoFit Plus Color[123] (Figure 13-8).

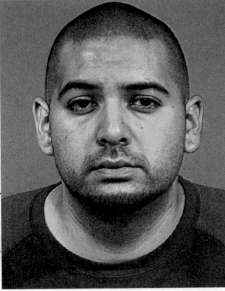

◄**FIGURE 13-7**

Facial likeness of a robbery suspect created by a forensic artist along with a police mug shot showing the resemblance
The photo on the left depicts a facial reconstruction completed by Police Artist Gil Zamora, working with a robbery victim. The photo on the right depicts the police mug shot of the robbery suspect at the time he was arrested. As can be seen, the similarities are remarkable. (Left: ©Gil Zamora, San Jose California Police Department; Right: Source: Lt. Rick Martinez, San Jose California Police Department)

◄**FIGURE 13-8**

Sirchie's ComPhotoFit Plus Color
The composite facial reconstruction photo on the left is a computer-generated composite sketch of a robbery suspect. The photo on the right, which is remarkably similar, depicts the photo of the suspect at the time he was booked into the county jail. The facial reconstruction was made with Sirchie's ComPhotoFit Plus Color. (Left: ©Laurie Joiner, Crime Scene Administrator, Polk County Sheriff's Office, Bartow, Florida; Right: ©Sheriff Grady C. Judd, Jr., Polk County Sheriff's Office, Bartow, Florida)

| KEY TERMS

action stereotyping	dye packs	robbery
ambush	home-invasion robbery (HIR)	situational stereotyping
bait money	muggings	strong-armed robbery
bandit barriers	physical stereotyping	tracking devices
carjacking	planned operation	trespassory

REVIEW QUESTIONS

1. What are the elements of the crime of robbery?
2. Give a profile of visible street robberies.
3. When is purse snatching a robbery?
4. Give three explanations for the increase in carjackings.
5. Discuss how home invaders operate.
6. What measures have been implemented by law enforcement agencies to combat the growing problem of Smartphone robberies?
7. What are the two occupations in which a person has the greatest danger of being the victim of a violent crime on the job?
8. What safety tips have been recommended for people who buy and sell items online?
9. Discuss the characteristics that distinguish professional from amateur bank robbers.
10. Discuss the multiple techniques that can be employed in bank robbery prevention.
11. Explain action, physical, and situational stereotyping.
12. Why is it important to have a standard operating procedure for robbery investigations?
13. Why should a file check be made of the victim in a robbery case?

INTERNET ACTIVITIES

1. Most large police agencies in the United States have robbery investigation units. Find several such agencies in your region. What is the total number of officers assigned to these units? What are the units' functions and responsibilities? Is there information concerning the numbers of robberies that are investigated and/or cleared? Is any robbery prevention information provided? Websites such as *www.officer.com* provide information to both local and international police agencies.

2. Go to the website *www.forensicartist.com* and learn more about how forensic artists generate the likenesses of people through age composition, composite drawing, and facial reconstruction.

CRIME SCENE DO NOT CROSS

14

BURGLARY

CHAPTER OBJECTIVES

1. Identify and briefly describe the elements of burglary.

2. Explain why "intent" and "possession" are important terms to consider when considering a charge of possession of burglary tools.

3. State the four most important deterrents to offending for burglars.

4. Name three purposes for which burglars can use drones.

5. Describe how seemingly innocent postings on Facebook help burglars select residential burglary targets.

6. Contrast the traditional burglar categories of amateur and professional.

7. Identify and briefly characterize the Fox Team's four burglary profiles.

8. Briefly explain why burglaries may be lower in winter months and higher during the summer months.

9. Describe how burglars search a home and what they expect/hope will be in different rooms.

10. State five different circumstances that might explain a theft being reported at a home, but for which there is no identifiable point of entry into the home.

11. Explain what covert and surreptitious lock picking are.

12. Describe how key bumping is done.

13. List three indicators of bad faith in buying property that is later discovered to have been stolen.

The two most striking aspects of burglary are its frequency and economic impact. If they were equally distributed in time, burglaries would average being committed once every 18 seconds.[1] In a single year, an estimated 1,729,806 burglaries were committed, which resulted in total losses of $3.9 billion.[2] The average loss per burglary was $2,251.[3] Despite the large number of burglaries committed, only 187,474 people were arrested.[4] These statistics establish burglary as a crime of major dimensions. Because items such as credit cards, checks, identity documents, and firearms are taken in burglaries, the offense may be associated with subsequent or secondary crimes, such as frauds, forgeries, identity theft, gun trafficking, and receiving stolen property. Investigating these secondary crimes can sometimes lead to the identities of burglars. Burglaries also have the potential to turn into violent crimes (Box 14.1 and Figure 14.1).

Many homes and businesses have alarms, but the alarms may be affected by improper installation, faulty equipment, bad weather, monitoring center mistakes (Figure 14.2), and user errors. Unfamiliarity with the system or not allowing for the size of roaming pets may produce as much as an estimated 10–25% of all automatic alarm calls being false ones.[5] In some cities false alarms run as high as 98%. Many jurisdictions have responded to this situation by allowing one free false alarm and then charging the owner for subsequent false alarms on a flat-fee or escalating-the-charge basis for each subsequent false alarm. Some cities have adopted the controversial policy of not responding to a burglary alarm unless it is confirmed by a private armed guard service. Sometimes there are exceptions to such policies, e.g., alarms at gun stores, retail stores, and businesses, and in at least one jurisdiction the homes of prominent politicians. In some jurisdictions confirmation can also be established when a perimeter burglar alarm is triggered, which in turn automatically triggers video surveillance of the inside of the premises and an offender can be seen.

BOX 14-1 | HOUSEHOLD BURGLARY AND VIOLENCE: THE HOT PROWL

In 28% of household burglaries a member of the household is present. In those situations, Eight percent of those cases result in the person at home becoming a victim of a violent crime.[6] A burglary with people on the premises is sometimes called a **hot prowl**. Some of those encounters are unanticipated by the offender. For example, a child may be sick and staying at home instead of going to school. In other burglaries, the breaking and entering may only be a prelude to the primary crime they came to commit: e.g., sexual assault or murder of a competitor or a witness.

▲ **FIGURE 14-1**

A maid found this offender asleep/passed out in the master bedroom of the home he was burglarizing. The plastic bag near him on the bed holds jewelry he had seized to take with him when he left. However, Sheriff's deputies arrived, took this picture, woke the man, and arrested him for burglary of an occupied dwelling. (©Sarasota County Sheriff Office/Rex Features/AP Images)

State burglary statutes cover many types of structures, e.g., stables, barns, outhouses, garages, storage facilities, hotel rooms, public laundries, and even tents. Likewise, state statutes also often address burglaries of means of transportation, e.g., cars, airplanes, motor homes, railroad cars, shipping containers, and freight trailers. Boats are also covered, although some states require there must be sleeping quarters to warrant a burglary charge.

◀ **FIGURE 14-2**
Security Alarm Monitoring Station.
(©Monty Rakusen/Alamy RF)

Various states also have a burglary statute for coin and currency operated vending machines, including parking meters and parking ticket dispensing machines.[7] Unlike other types of burglaries, this offense is often a misdemeanor for the first such act, but subsequent acts covered by that statute are often felonies.

In some states, the law protecting offenses involving vending machines is a larceny/theft charge. Whether the offense is a misdemeanor or a felony depends on the value of the coins/currency and goods stolen. This value is the dividing line between misdemeanor and a felony is established by state statutes and therefore varies, but often it is a felony when a loss of $1,000 or more is involved. Parenthetically, a number of states also have levels of larceny/theft based on the value involved. In Ohio, Aggravated Larceny in the First Degree is the charge used when the loss involves $1.5 million. Ohio has five levels of felony larceny/theft charges which carry progressively longer sentences for thefts of greater amounts. Second and subsequent burglary convictions carry more severe sanctions in many states.

Various aspects of burglary are summarized in Table 14.1. Most burglaries are through a door rather than a window, In general, commercial establishments are attacked at the rear at night, whereas homes are mostly victimized during the day at the front door. There is some evidence that, as the geographical distance between burglaries shortens, the likelihood of a serial offender increases. This is true for both residential (e.g., individual homes, apartments, time-shares, and condominiums) and non-residential burglaries (e.g., offices, churches, restaurants, finance companies and government buildings).[8] Statutorily, Maryland uses "non-habitation" synonymously with non-residential.

When the same home or business is burglarized shortly after the initial offense, roughly 30-days, it may be the same offender(s) seeking to steal items left behind during the first offense. For example, a large screen television may have been too big to take initially and the burglar(s) had to find a fence before returning for it or perhaps he/she/they came back to steal items the resident bought as replacements (for example, televisions) for losses in the first burglary.[9] **Serial burglars** can be thought of in two ways: (1) episodic victimization of the same premises (See Box 14.2) and (2) a series of burglaries committed at various locations by the same offender, small group, or large burglary crew.

TABLE 14-1	Burglary Facts

Type of Premises Attacked

Residential	71.6%
Non-residential	28.4%

Types of Attacks

Forcible Entry (e.g., used pry bar to break glass and enter)	57.9%
Unlawful Entry (e.g., through open door or window)	35.5%
Forcible Attempt	6.6%

Time of Attacks	Residential	Non-residential
Day	37.5%	10.0%
Night	20.7	11.9
Unknown	13.4	6.5

Offender Demographics for Arrested Offenders (12.7%)

Race	Gender	Age	
White 68.1%	M 81.1%	Under 15	5.4%
Black 29.5	F 18.9	Under 18	17.7
All Other	All Other 1.4	18 & over	76.9

Source: Federal Bureau of Investigation, Uniform Crime Reports 2015, Tables 1, 23, 36, 42, 43, and 47 (Washington, D.C.: Federal Bureau of Investigation, 2016), https://ucr.fbi.gov/crime-in-the-u.s/2015/crime-in-the-u.s.-2015/offenses-known-to-law enforcement/burglary, accessed October 3, 2016. The data may not add to 100 percent because of rounding or other data handling procedures.

BOX 14-2 | THE ULTIMATE SERIAL BURGLAR?

In 2016, Albuquerque (NM) Police Department investigators arrested a 35-year-old man who may be the ultimate serial burglar. He is accused of breaking into the same home four times in three months. The major break in the case came when the home's surveillance cameras showed a hooded man smoking a cigarette approaching the home. Apparently aware of the cameras, the man tried to hide his face while burglarizing the home. A cigarette butt was found in the yard, which provided a DNA sample that matched a known offender.[10]

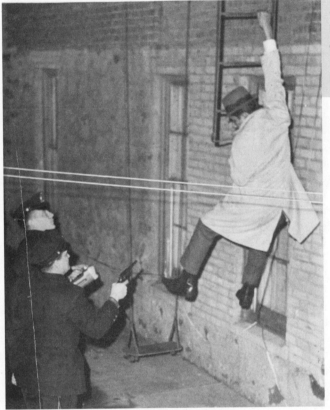

◀ **FIGURE 14-3   Police Nab Fire Escape Burglar**
In the 1960s, New York City Police Officers in the Bronx arrest a fire escape burglar as he nears the ground. Note that the revolver in the nearest Officer's right hand is trained on the suspect. (©Al Aaronson/NY Daily News Archive/Getty Images)

1. Presently, homes are primarily heated by natural gas and electricity. Only 0.01% of all homes in the United States are still heated by coal.[11] When coal was king, homes had double-doored chutes at the ground level. When coal was delivered, the double-doors were opened and coal ran down a wooden chute into the basement to be near the furnace in which it was burned. Burglaries through coal chutes are substantially a thing of the past.

2. Although some burglaries are still being committed by entering an apartment from an exterior fire escape, it is a dying practice (Figure 14-3). Apartment dwellers learned decades ago to put bars over windows which could be easily accessed from an outside fire escape. In response, burglars stepped-over the fire escape and onto any existing ledge. With their back flat against the building, they carefully inch along the ledge to get to an unprotected window, committing the so-called "step over" burglary. Legislative requirements for interior fire escape stairwells for new construction have reduced, but not eliminated attacks from exterior fire escapes. Likewise, enclosed exterior stairwells and specially constructed and powered evacuation elevators in high-rise buildings have also reduced step-overs.

BURGLARY METHODS CHANGE OVER TIME

From humans' earliest times, thieves existed and committed what we recognize as burglaries. To illustrate, despite security measures, the riches-filled tombs of the Egyptian pharaohs were often plundered by thieves of that period. While the nature of burglary remains fundamentally the same, changes in technology, architectural design, and legislative enactments have changed how burglaries are committed. To illustrate how committing burglaries has changed, two examples are provided: the demise of coal as a home heating source and dwindling exterior fire escape "step-over break-ins.

THE OFFENSES OF BURGLARY AND POSSESSION OF BURGLARY TOOLS

By the middle of the fifteenth century in England, burglary was legally differentiated from other crimes in which it had been embedded and in the United States by the early nineteenth century a few possession of burglary tool laws were developed. This section is a brief overview of these two topics and not a substitute for a more complete examination of these topics.

BURGLARY LAWS

Traditionally, burglary is the criminal offense of breaking and entering into a building or occupied structure illegally with the intent of committing a crime therein. Recall from earlier in this chapter the wide variety of structures that may fall within a state's definition of "structure." Elements of the traditional crime of burglary are:

1. *Trespass:* The entry is made into a premises without the permission of the victim or without the authority of the person entering (an officer serving a search warrant would have authority to enter without permission). If an offender gains entry to a premises by misidentification, ruse, or trick, for example, tells the victim he/she is from the gas company and is checking for leaks, the element of trespass is satisfied because there is no genuine consent.

2. *Breaking:* While an opening must be made to gain entry into the building, statutorily "breaking" has a different meaning than in our common language. The use of great force is not required. The mere opening of an unlocked screen door or sliding an unlocked window up to gain entry satisfies this element. Even if the door or window is partially open, but the opening is made somewhat wider to allow the offender to enter, this element is satisfied by enlarging the opening. The person need not actually enter the premises. If a window is raised just slightly to allow the offender's hand to be inserted to remove a valuable object a breaking has occurred. When the trespass is committed by misidentification, ruse, or trick, it is a constitutes *constructive breaking* and therefore also satisfies the breaking element.

3. *Intent to Commit a Crime Within:* the crime is usually theft, although any other crime, such as assault or vandalism, satisfies this element. When the intent to commit a crime is formed may be important in the charging decision. Assume two teenagers break into a neighbor's home on a dare/for a thrill with no thought of doing anything else and leave without committing any crime within. In some states the charge would be criminal trespass. If the intent is formed after the breaking and entering has been accomplished and any crime within is minor, a lower degree of burglary with less severe sanctions may be charged in some states. However, if the intent was formed before the breaking and entering, the burglary charge may be accompanied by a more severe sanction. State statutes commonly have degrees of burglaries with sanctions ranging from less to more severe. More severe sanctions are often attached to burglaries if: (1) committed at night of an occupied dwelling; (2) the offender arms him/herself with something found within; (3) committed while the offender is carrying explosives, firearms, or deadly weapons; (4) the perpetrator intentionally or recklessly attempts to, or causes, injury to another person; (5) it

involves the threatened or actual use of dangerous weapon; (6) while fleeing the scene, the perpetrator injures another; (8) the intent is to commit a felony; and (9) committed while a declared state of emergency exists.

A few states have misdemeanor charges of burglary. Maryland's charge of Burglary in the Fourth Degree illustrates this. Oklahoma distinguishes between felony and misdemeanor burglary charges by referring to the former as "Burglary" and the latter as "Breaking and Entering." A number of states have burglary statutes that do not include the traditional element of breaking. For example, Florida Statute 810.02 has a core definition of burglary as: entering or remaining in a dwelling, a structure, or a conveyance with the intent to commit an offense therein, unless the premises are at the time open to the public or the defendant is licensed or invited to enter or remain.

POSSESSION OF BURGLARY TOOLS

Not all states have a possession of burglary tools or similarly purposed law. For those that do, the sanction for violating it may be a felony or misdemeanor. "Possession" statutes can be a major asset for combating burglaries. Depending on the applicable state statute and the fact situation, they may allow an arrest to be made in situations where there is not sufficient cause to even charge an attempted burglary and therein lies a recurring difficulty with enforcing possession statutes. Such laws must be written broadly enough to allow officers discretion in enforcing them, but short of criminalizing tools commonly found in homes and used in occupations (Figures 14-4a and 14-4b). Using good judgement, officers must often conclude from the context and facts of the situation whether an arrest should be made. A careful analysis of whether the legal requirement of *intent* to use such tools to attempt or commit a burglary exists and whether *possession* of the tools actually exists.

A Mississippi man was arrested for possession of burglary tools when common tools were found in his car. Subsequently, that state's Supreme Court reversed his conviction in *Henley v. State of Mississippi (2014)* because none of the tools seized were "peculiarly adapted" for burglary and the *intent* to use them for that purpose was not established beyond a reasonable doubt. In Philadelphia County, Pennsylvania, at 5:00 a.m., police found a man standing near the outside door of a law firm which was recessed. When asked what he was doing, Gendrachi replied he was urinating and made no attempt to flee, did not have his hands on the door, and did not give evasive or incorrect answers. The police seized a flashlight and lock picks from his person and charged him with possessing an instrument of crime. In *Commonwealth v. Gendrachi (1978)*, the court struck the conviction, noting the plaintiff's truthfulness, the fact he was a certified locksmith, and no *intent* to commit a crime was established. In the *People of Colorado v. Lewis Burton Ridgeway (2013)*, a court also held that the *intent* to commit a crime was not demonstrated.

In West Palm Beach, Florida, Carbone approached a residential front door and tried to open it using a hand wrapped in a handkerchief. The homeowner scared Carbone away, but he was soon stopped by the police and arrested for attempted burglary. When the police searched the car he was driving they discovered

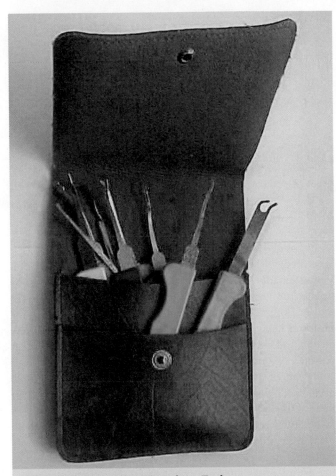

▲ **FIGURE 14-4a   Lock Picking Tools**
An inexpensive lock picking set. Such sets are available on the internet from around $25 and up, while more complete sets will cost $500 or more. Some people are lock picking hobbyists and there are local organizations to support lock sport communities, such as the Longhorn Lock Picking Club in Austin, Texas. There are also local, regional, national, and international contests for hobbyists and professional locksmiths. Forty-one states do not criminalize the mere possession of lock picks and the usual situation is that for a possession of burglary tools charge, criminal intent must be shown. (Courtesy of the Savannah-Chatham Metropolitan Police Department)

▲ **FIGURE 14-4b   Snip-EZ**
A battery operated Snip-EZ scissors with the shears removed and made into a lock picking device. Electrical toothbrushes and similar items can also be used to make electrical lock picks, also known as "snap guns" and they are commonly available on the internet for roughly $50. Some locksmiths use them when very rapid opening of a lock needs to be made. Typically, possession of such devices is not illegal and intent to commit a criminal act must be shown. Investigators should be very familiar of their state's possession of burglary tools statute and applicable court decisions. (Courtesy of the Savannah-Chatham Metropolitan Police Department)

items resulting in a possession of burglary tools charge. In *Carbone v Florida (2012)*, an Appeal Court upheld the attempted burglary conviction. However, it overturned the one for possession of burglary tools. When Carbone tried to open the door his tools were in his car.

State statutes may not identify any items that are "burglary tools." In others, any number of things that are enumerated, including devices, machines, explosives, thermal lances, screw drivers, hammers, drills and bits, center hole punch, lock picks, ski masks, dark clothing, bolt cutters, nippers, steel wedges, plier, and

BOX 14-3 | EXAMPLE OF POSSESSION OF BURGLARY TOOLS STATUTE

Wisconsin 943.12: Whoever has in personal possession any device or instrumentality intended, designed or adapted for use in breaking into any depository designed for the safekeeping of any valuables or into any building or room, with intent to use such device or instrumentality to break into a depository, building or room, and to steal therefrom, is guilty of a Class I felony.

homemade keys to remove coins from parking meters. Ceramic spark plugs and shards or pieces of them are specifically included in some possession statutes because when swung or thrown at windows they immediately shatter them with little sound. Some burglars carry them on a string around their neck. In a few states clothing is included among "tools," as are gloves, masks and ski masks, and dark clothing. There is a concern that statutes may criminalize the possession of tools commonly found in homes or needed in various occupations, such as construction jobs, steel workers, and farriers. Finally, possession statutes may also criminalize making, mending, or allowing the use of burglary tools.

Investigators considering charging someone with possession of burglary tools should be aware that over the past 15 years lock picking has grown into a substantial hobbyist movement. Locksport International is a global organization and there are also groups at the local level, such as the Longhorn Lockpicking Club, a University of Texas student organization chartered in 2006.[12] It provides training and competition opportunities. There is greater interest in lock picking in the Northeast versus the rest of the country. Seeing large quantities of lockpicking tools in plain view on the backseat of a car stopped for a traffic charge cannot be taken as evidence of nefarious intent.

Investigators thinking about making an arrest for possession of **burglar tools** should consider that "locksport" refers to hobbyists who possess a variety of lock picking equipment, some expertise, and practice to develop and refine their lock picking skills. There are local organizations, such as the Longhorn Lock Picking Club, a University of Texas student organization, to foster interest in lock picking, as well as local, state, national, and international conferences and competitions for hobbyist lock pickers. Failure to give sufficient weight to these facts and making an ill-advised arrest could result in a civil suit.

BURGLARY MOTIVATIONS, DETERRENTS, AND PERCEIVED RISK OF APPREHENSION

Burglars report different motivations for offending, for example, a bill needs to be paid, seeking a thrill, responding to dares, a sudden impulse, or an immediate opportunity presents itself. The quick facts box below has statements from active burglars that illustrate some of these motivations.

QUICK FACTS

Bills, Thrills, Dope, and Opportunity

Usually when I do a burglary or several of them, it's to get me over a rough spot and get straightened out . . . the only time I do burglary is if I need the money at that point in time . . . it would be strictly to pay a light bill, gas bill, or rent . . . Then I go with the flow until I hit another rough spot where I need money again.[13]

Burglary is exciting . . . it's just a thrill to go in undetected and walking out with all of their shit . . . like going on a treasure hunt.[14]

I might find somebody with some good crack . . . while I'm high I say damn! I want some more of that good shit. Go knock some place off, make some money, go buy some more dope.[15]

Usually when I get in my car and drive around I'm thinking I don't have any money, so what's my means for getting some? All of a sudden I'll just take a glance and say, there it is, there's the house . . . Then I get the feeling that very moment I'm moving in . . .[16]

A study of burglars empirically established that the top two motivations for committing burglaries are to get: (1) drugs by finding prescription or illegal substances (Figure 14-5) or (2) money. Any items stolen can be quickly sold to provide the means of buying drugs. About 90% of those studied also drank alcohol.[17] The drugs of choice were marijuana, crack, powder cocaine, or heroin.[18] Surprisingly, methamphetamine use was "only" about 34%, roughly only in the middle of the preferred drugs list.[19] Some 64% of offenders reported drugs were their most frequent expenditure of income derived from burglaries.[20] Drugs and alcohol are an important motivator and in many cases they are the direct cause for men and women committing burglaries. Seventy-three percent of offenders admit to the use of drugs and/or alcohol when they committed some burglaries.[21]

▲ FIGURE 14-5

The Burglar Who Stole Prescription Medicine
This man knocked on the front door of a Rutherford, N.J., home. When no one answered, he made an entry at the house's rear. The owners came home and found him stealing prescription medicine. He fled and was being sought by the police. (Courtesy of the Rutherford New Jersey Police Department)

| TABLE 14-2 | Burglars' Perception of the Most Effective Deterrents |

DETERRENT	PERCENT OF BURGLARS AVOIDING A TARGET WITH THE DETERRENT
1. Steel bars	25
2. Dog inside	33
3. Car in driveway	34
4. People walking nearby	34
5. Limited escape route	35
6. Traffic nearby	36
7. Cameras/Surveillance	41
8. Seeing Neighbors	44
9. Alarm System	45
10. Noise inside	47
11. Officer nearby	54
12. People inside	60

Source: Blevins, Kuhns, and Lee, "Understanding Decisions to Burglarize from the Offender's Perspective," (Charlotte, N.C.: Department of Criminal Justice and Criminology, University of North Carolina at Charlotte, December 2012), p. 33.

| TABLE 14-3 | Burglars and Planning |

AMOUNT OF PLANNING	PERCENTAGE
None to less than 24 hours	59.1
1–3 days	19.4
4–7 days	6.6
Around two weeks	3.1
1 month or more	3.4
Missing data	8.4

Source: Blevins, Kuhns, and Lee, "Understanding Decisions to Burglarize From the Offender's Perspective," (Charlotte, N.C.: Department of Criminal Justice and Criminology, University of North Carolina at Charlotte, December 2012), extracted from data in Table 4, p. 38.

Going on jobs while impaired is dangerous for burglars, any persons on the premises burglarized, and the general public as the offenders drive to and from the crime scene. In assessing whether to commit a break-in burglars are deterred to different degrees by both some security measures and situational variables, such as a car in the driveway, no weak point of entry, a close bus stop, and people walking nearby (See Table 14-2).

Less effective deterrents include neighborhood watch signs, outside lights, and beware of dog signs. As offending experience accumulates without being arrested, it reinforces a belief that apprehension is a low risk proposition.

BURGLARS: PLANNING, INFORMATION, AND GENDER DIFFERENCES

Burglars vary in the amount of planning they do, how much information they gather using different methods, and there are also gender differences. These variables are explored in this section.

PLANNING AND INFORMATION

The research team of Blevins, Kuhns, and Lee studied 422 incarcerated burglars and established that many burglaries involve some degree of planning[22] (See Table 14-3). The data shows that a remarkable number of burglars do zero to skimpy planning (less than 24 hours). The fact that 3.4% do one month or more of planning suggests that those offenders are picking targets with multiple security features, for example, perimeter alarms, surveillance cameras inside and outside, roving security patrols, and controlled access to the target area.

Burglars use four major low-technology methods to gather information about targets. They:

1. Personally have some initial knowledge of the victims' and their lifestyle. For example, they may have seen them driving newer cars, furniture being delivered, know that children and pets are not present in the home, see parcels on the porch, can see "goods" inside, for example, a wide-screen television or a pile of presents under the lighted Christmas tree as they drive past, nice grills left outside, or live in the same neighborhood or nearby. Burglars may also have occupations that allow them to personally gather information. Examples include servicing vending machines, driving delivery trucks to malls, auto repair, and liquor stores, working on loading docks, installer of cable television, real estate agents, or they may be restaurant health or fire inspectors, code enforcement personnel, plumbers, insurance adjusters, or school social workers.

2. May have contact with "tipsters" who can provide vital information. Tipsters are also referred to as "spotters," "fingers," and "setups." Maids may be familiar with guest lists for social events their employers are hosting. Thus, they know who will be away from their homes to attend; lawn maintenance workers have ample opportunity to learn a great deal about households for which they work; medical personnel know which patients are coming when for appointments and roughly how long they will be tied up; some delivery personnel go inside of many houses and can see what is available; vacation booking personnel can provide the names, dates of travel, and other data; and pet sitters have the opportunity to see a great deal.

BOX 14-4 | BURGLARIES: DRONES AND GOOGLE INSTANT STREET VIEW

Drones are believed to have been used to case home burglaries in England, Ireland, and New Zealand. They are thought to have been deployed to take photographs, identify alarm systems and other security features, plan escape routes, and surveillance of the police while the burglaries are in progress.[23] In New York and New Jersey a criminal crew dubbed the Tub Gang has used

them to plan their burglaries.[24] Using Google's **Instant Street View**, burglars can enter a home address on the first screen and study photographs of a home and those around it. The images may be several years old. However, with a little surveillance of your home, they can identify your living patterns and other information, such as the presence of alarms.

Insurance agents know who has added insurance to their home owner policies ("riders") to cover the potential loss of jewelry, silverware, statues, paintings, antiques, as well as and stamp, comic book, baseball card, rare book, fossil, guitar, and other collections.

　　Business employees also have valuable insider information. They know which coworkers are going on vacation and how long they will be gone, the type of alarm system, when valuable goods have just been added to the inventory, on what day the most cash is on hand, when bank deposits are made, and other details. Business employees may sell information to burglars. They may also believe they have been unjustly disciplined, wrongly passed over for a promotion, recently demoted or terminated, or are the odd-person out in a workplace love triangle and want revenge. Whether for revenge or profit, employees may cautiously tip a burglar they know, such as a family member or close friend.

3. Personally observe ("case" or "workup") potential residential or business targets for their likely valuables. Burglars may walk their dog or be "looking for it" in neighborhoods in which they have an interest, taking note of stickers on cars. National Rifle Association/ NRA and hunting stickers spells "guns inside" and Dive stickers suggests scuba gear. Burglars may pose as a

handyman, painter, or gutter cleaner seeking work, drive in congested traffic through a business district so they can "eyeball" potential targets, and patronize restaurants, bars, convenience stores, coffee shops to assess their potential.

4. Monitor informational sources to identify potential opportunities. An older method of doing so is reading local newspapers to learn who is getting married when and where they will honeymoon, who just had a big birthday party, the obituaries to discover what household may be empty because of a funeral, and other tidbits. In addition to burglars, many other entities are aware of the older method. In response, religious, social, and neighborhood groups sometimes offer to provide volunteer "house sitters." People will also hire a security guard, or take other precautions around these types of events. The new informational sources are technology based (Boxes 14-4 and 14-5).

GENDER DIFFERENCES

Gender differences in burglaries exist: (1) female burglars generally spend less time planning a break-in than their male counterparts;[25] (2) females are 9% more likely to burglarize homes than males and prefer to do so in the afternoon (Figure 14-6).[26] However, males have a 14% preference for burglarizing businesses

---

▶ **FIGURE 14-6**

The pregnant female in her 20s went to the home's front door and knocked while an accomplice waited in a car. When nobody came to the door, the female broke a front window, entered the home, took property, and left with the accomplice. "Knock-Knock" burglars usually go to the side or rear of the house to break in when no one comes to the door. She may be inexperienced, the home may be isolated so there is no concern about neighbors seeing the break-in, or some other factor is at work. Homes that are attacked at the front often have recessed front doors, limiting what neighbors can see.

(**Source:** King County Sheriff's Office)

BOX 14-5 | SOCIAL NETWORKING SITES AND CRAIG'S LIST PROVIDE RESIDENTIAL BURGLARY LEADS

Roughly 75% of convicted burglar offenders believe other burglars use **social networking sites** for targeting.[27] Some people using social networking sites unknowingly sow the seeds of the burglaries of their own homes. Devotees of networking sites derive pleasure from sharing their lives with family and friends. They post messages on Twitter, Facebook, and other sites that they are at the airport waiting to fly to Ireland, just reached their fabulous hotel in Honolulu, or their ship is pulling out of Miami for an exciting 7-day Caribbean cruise. Such posts and periodic updates let burglars identify a home as a potential target.

In addition to social networking posts, the photographs people upload, for example, "selfies," can also be problematic. Smartphones and modern cameras embed Exchangeable Image File Format (EXIF) data in a digital photograph's file, which gives the exact location where it was taken. Although many or

most networking sites now strip out the EXIF data in photographs, not all do. There are inexpensive means of reading EXIF files, which can be used to the advantage of burglars, stalkers, and other offenders.

Phone settings that allow GPS tracking should be carefully monitored and limited by users. The more businesses and other entities that know a person's location, the greater the person's exposure to unnecessary risk. Relatedly, posting ads on Craigslist has resulted in some home invasion robberies and burglaries. For burglars, the wording of ads let offenders know what valuable property is available and occasionally when someone might not be at home, for example, "Call after 7:00 p.m."[28] Some law enforcement agencies provide a portion of their buildings or their camera monitored parking lot to be used to conduct Craigslist deals.

---

in the late evenings;[29] (3) significantly more females report offending with their spouse/significant other, whereas men report doing so with friends;[30] (4) females are 12% more likely to seek out prescription drugs to steal;[31] (5) women spend more of their money on both legal and illegally obtained prescription drugs while men buy illegal drugs;[32] (6) females have a broader exposure to substance use experiences;[33] (7) women think being involved in substance abuse and religious/faith-based prison programs would help them resist re-offending while males believe educational programs would do the same for them;[34] (8) more males than women commit multiple within a single day or night;[35] (9) males who plan burglaries are more likely than women to attempt disabling an alarm;[36] (10) men are more likely to carry tools, perhaps because they prefer non-residential targets more than women do;[37] and (11) more men reported walking or riding a bike to a possible target, but both sexes are equally to use a car.[38]

BURGLAR OFFENDING RECORDS

Earlier in this chapter, Table 14-1, "Burglary Facts," provided national information about burglary offenders and offenses. The Blevins Study provide another important set of data from a random sample of incarcerated male and female burglary offenders in North Carolina, Kentucky, and Ohio. The purpose of the Blevins Study was to identify burglars' motives and how they committed their offenses.[39] These offenders committed from one to more than 100 burglaries in their lifetime. Those studied varied in age, gender, and offending experience.

QUICK FACTS

Understanding the Blevins Study Data

The Blevins Study was conducted with the support of the Alarm Industry Research and Educational Foundation. The protocol used in reporting data was to calculate results based on the total sample size of 422 offenders. Because some number of offenders did not respond to various questions, percentages describing a finding may not total 100%.

Offenders in the Blivens Study committed their first burglary as early as age 6 and as old as 50 with a mean of 21.8 years of age.[40] The age of their first arrest was from 9 to 50 years old with an average of 23.6.[41] Burglary was the most serious crime committed by 54% of the sample, although 12% and 8%, respectively, had also been charged with robberies and homicides. Those studied were broadly involved in criminal activities. However, the offenders were consistently burglars.[42]

BURGLARS AND BURGLARIES

This section includes a **typology** of burglars and a **taxonomy** of burglaries. Typology and taxonomy are often used synonymously, perhaps because their core feature is a classification system and both are information management tools. However, there is an important distinction between them. A typology is a classification system that creates groups into which similar things are respectively placed. While a taxonomy is also a classification system, its categories are formed by empirically studying observable and measurable characteristics. Reduced to its simplest, classification groups in typology rest on the thinking of the person creating them while groups in a taxonomy are data driven.

The traditional distinction between **professional** and **amateur burglars** is the typology used in this section. These professional and amateur burglars should not be thought of as a dichotomous choice, that is, the burglar is one or the other. Instead, they are polar opposite categories with an undeveloped continuum connecting them. The research team of Fox, Farrington, Chitwood, and James collaborated with law enforcement personnel to determine if different burglary offense styles could be identified.[44] Over a two-year period, the team analyzed 405 randomly selected and solved burglary cases in Volusia County, Florida. Additionally, they examined the criminal histories of

each offender for further insight. Much like an experienced investigator being able to recognize patterns in burglaries, the statistical analysis revealed there are four burglary profiles, which are empirically linked to a taxonomy of offenders: (1) organized; (2) disorganized; (3) opportunistic; and (4) interpersonal offenses. Following the discussion of professional and amateur burglars, the four burglar profiles developed are covered.

The Fox team's organized burglaries are akin to the traditional category of professional burglars, while elements of the traditional amateur burglar are seen in both the team's disorganized and opportunistic styles. Each the of the Fox Team's four burglary profiles represent offenders with a unique set of traits/crime scene behaviors and criminal histories. (These are discussed in detail later in this chapter.)

THE TRADITIONAL TYPOLOGY: PROFESSIONAL AND AMATEUR BURGLARS

There are two traditional types of burglars: (1) professional and (2) amateurs. Investigators widely believe that planning produces bigger "scores" and leads to evading arrest for longer periods of time, which are factors associated with professional burglars. Such offenders may be able to quickly sell what they take because of access to stolen goods markets with deep pockets. At the other end of the continuum, amateur burglars tend to be youthful, impulsive, exercise poor judgement, and lack expertise. As a result, they typically have lower gains from their crimes as compared to professionals, although occasionally they have a "big hit." Amateurs may offend four or more times a week if there have a substance abuse problem or need cash for their lifestyle. They may also have longer arrest records because they take imprudent risks and are careless and leave some forensic evidence (Figure 14-7). The forensic evidence may not initially lead to their identification, but if later arrested it may tie them to multiple offenses.

▶ **FIGURE 14.7**

Alleged Amateur Burglar

There are rare amateur burglars who offend frequently, but are not caught for long periods of time. In Rome, Maine, investigators load up evidence from the camp of a person known as the North Pond Hermit. He was arrested for stealing food. When investigators searched his camp, they found evidence he may have committed over 1,000 burglaries during his decades in the woods. (©Robert F. Bukaty/ AP Images)

Professional Burglars See More Things to Steal

A study allowed incarcerated professional burglars to break into a virtual residence and find items to steal. The value of their haul was compared to that of a control group of law-abiding students. The professionals averaged finding $1,560 more in things to steal per burglary, for example, designer clothes and checking coat pockets for cash, wallets, and credit cards. The two groups also differed in that the professionals had different search routines, but followed a cognitive roadmap while members of the control group did not.[45]

Like other types of offenders, professional burglars may operate alone or with others in "crews." They often work in multiple cities and the connection of their crimes may not be made for longer periods of time. They may commit fewer burglaries annually than amateurs due to their larger "scores," but that is not iron clad and perhaps only true for the highest echelon of professionals. Many burglars have legitimate jobs. Examples of professional burglars include:

1. In 1976, a Norman Rockwell painting, "Taking a Break" was stolen from a New Jersey home during a burglary. Valued at $1,000,000, it was on the cover of Saturday Evening Post in September 1919. The offender was never arrested. Despite the successes of the FBI's Art Crime Team, which has recovered over 2,650 works of art valued at over $150 million, "Taking a Break" was still missing in late 2016.[46]

2. In Chicago, a long-time burglar, with reported mob connections, operated his "crew" for 30 years. When the leader was arrested, more than $2,000,000 in jewelry and stolen property was found in his home. A member of the crew virtually signed his presence at burglaries by always taking expensive Lladro porcelain figurines and adding them to his personal collection. Part of the "formula" used so successfully by the gang for decades was that after spotting a potential victim, they would begin to accumulate information before making their move. The gang was also successful in identifying restaurant owners who skimmed money from their businesses and accumulated large sums of cash in home safes.[47]

Unusually Active Burglary Ring

In 2016, a 53-member crew, believed to be East Side Crips gang members, operating across five Southern California counties racked up more than 5,000 home burglaries during a roughly three-year period before many of them were arrested. Crew members would set out with specific goals for the day, such as get $5,000 in cash/sale of goods and a gun. Law enforcement authorities estimate each crew member may have participated in 125 to 150 burglaries.[48]

Because they have accumulated experience, acquired special skills, and carefully planned their attack, professionals have a reasonably good expectation of what is within it (Figure 14-8). Additionally, experience has taught them where the most valuable items should be looked for first. Professionals tend not to wildly ransack premises and occasionally one or more items they take may not be missed until well afterwards. Police were unable to solve 132 burglaries of high-rise apartments that resulted in losses of $6 million. Finally, "Spiderman," was apprehended. Working alone, he free climbed, that is, without any equipment, the outside of the high-rise buildings, reaching as far up as 30-stories to burglarize the apartments. Initially, investigators had difficulty in even considering Spiderman's method of operation, which demonstrates experience, acquired special skill, and planning. At trial, Spiderman was sentenced to a total of 53 years before he was eligible for parole.

▲ **FIGURE 14-8 The Spiderman burglar**
This offender's method operation was to free-climb the outside of tall buildings to commit burglaries. (©Wilfredo Lee/AP Images)

BOX 14-6 | BURGLARY TURNS DEADLY

A well-known cardiologist was shot to death when he walked into the burglary of his home in a fashionable section of Washington, D.C. The police arrested a man who was alleged to be a "Super Thief." Upon searching the suspect's swank suburban home, the police found some $4 million worth of stolen property. It took the police 472 man-hours and 400 legal-size pages to count, tag, and describe the property. The 18-foot truck in which the seized property was transported away contained 51 large boxes and two smelters that were believed to have been used to melt down precious metals.[49]

Professional burglars plan to enter a premises and leave without being detected. However, for them and for amateurs there is always the possibility of a surprise encounter with someone, that can lead to secondary crimes, including murder (See Box 14-6). Investigators need to determine as quickly as possible whether a burglar committed a violent crime as an outgrowth of an accidental meeting or if it occurred by design. The latter is motive driven and will require investigative effort to identify it, which could lead to the perpetrator. Assume investigators establish a 27-year-old woman was sexually assaulted in her apartment and murdered by 87 pre- and postmortem knife wounds. She was discovered under a sheet covering her whole body. To investigators, those few facts suggest: (1) there is some type of personal connection between the killer and the victim; (2) the 87 wounds s indicates a rage toward the victim; and (3) covering the body suggests a remorsefulness or anguish about the murder and an attempt by the killer to separate himself from it. These conclusions would lead investigators to quickly interview family members, any current and past boyfriends, coworkers, as well as other standard practices, for example, conducting a neighborhood canvas and examining the victim's telephone and computer records.

Professionals are of substantial interest to investigators because their crimes are taken as a challenge. Moreover, their crimes are often publicized by the news media. Sometimes this creates adverse publicity for police departments and there may be political pressure to make arrests. Moreover, professionals have wide knowledge of stolen goods markets and may be able to identify other active professional burglars.

When apprehended, most professionals are likely to initially claim their *Miranda* rights. Their sense of self or desire not to be labeled a "snitch" may require they never allow themselves to be interrogated. However, some professionals under the advice of their attorney, or driven by self-interest, will talk with the police. To gain some measure of leniency, they may "cut a deal" with the police by identifying other burglaries they have committed, which helps the police by increasing their burglary clearance statistics.

Unethical investigators will simply ask "Did you do the safe at Jones Auto Repair?" If the professional nods, the case is cleared. The proper way to clear the case is to have the burglar tell them the details of the offense. If those details match the incident report file, the case can be cleared. Sometimes, it may be necessary to put a handcuffed burglar in an unmarked car with two investigators and have him/her direct you to where they have broken-in because they may not remember details without having a visual clue.

When professionals are being interrogated, the police will also want to know the names of some active burglar(s) and the "jobs" they pulled. They will also be pressured by the police to reveal the names of fences, which the police will then target because it helps reduce the number of places burglars can sell the things they steal. If they do talk, professionals will try to "give up" the fewest people they can without disturbing their core "business partners."

Amateur burglars tend to work not only in a single city, but a small area within it. Sometimes they borrow the family car or one from a friend. About 23% of apprehended burglars are under 18 years of age.[50] Some of these don't yet have a driver's license because they aren't old enough, others can't afford a car and insurance so they don't drive, and members of a third group have had their licenses suspended. The result is that that many amateur burglars commit their crimes in local areas that are familiar to them from walking, skateboarding, or bicycling from here to there. Moreover, some jurisdictions may be so large that even if they have a car, they know their local "territory" much better and feel more comfortable in it as compared to offending at locations that are greater distances away in unfamiliar surroundings.

Amateurs often commit burglaries impulsively/opportunistically on little or no information. They may notice a couple driving out of the neighborhood to go to work. They see a partially raised window. Both of these signal opportunity. The amateurs' general lack of planning and lack of experience results in premises being searched with abandon instead of systematically. As a result, they often don't find, or don't recognize, as much "good stuff" as professionals do and the premises is left in a shambles (Figure 14-9). The amateurs lack of experience also is revealed when they steal costume jewelry in the mistaken belief the pieces are valuable.

THE FOX TEAM: FOUR BURGLARY PROFILES

The Fox Team's four burglary profiles, are briefly summarized on the following pages.[51] Additionally, information about the results that law enforcement agencies experienced with actually using these profiles is discussed. Presently, the application of the research

◄ FIGURE 14-9
"Tossed" home office
A heavily "tossed" home office. The chaotic scene suggests amateur burglars and, more particularly, juvenile perpetrators who became frustrated looking for things they could easily carry away. More seasoned offenders, for example, would have methodically searched the filing cabinet at the left of the picture from top to bottom or bottom to top. The open drawer in the middle of the cabinet suggests a more random approach and may imply a shorter juvenile offender. (Courtesy of Dwayne Orrick and Cordele, Georgia Police Department)

team's findings is very promising as a tool to solve burglaries and to reduce investigative expenditures, as well as the hidden costs of burglary to a community, such as public defender, trial, probation, and jail or prison expenditures.

Organized Burglaries

Organized burglaries are characterized by being very professionally executed. They also show signs of premeditation to reduce the burglar's risks and increase his/her gains (Figure 14-10). Organized burglary crime scenes usually have no forensic evidence and are left in a relatively unaltered state.

The motivation for these crimes is financial gain. Items commonly taken include jewelry, cash, and laptops. Organized burglars will selectively take pieces from a jewelry box, but will take care to make it appear that no one went into it. Most burglaries generally occur at homes unoccupied during the daytime, when many families are at work or school. While there are rarely any eyewitnesses to these crimes, the victim may have been visited by the offender prior to the offense. Organized burglars often use a ruse or other activity to gain intelligence on the victim, the target, and the contents of the home or business prior to the crime.

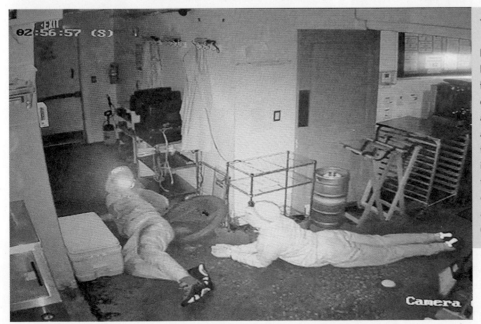

◄ FIGURE 14-10
Professional Burglars
Rare image of professional burglars in Houston, Texas crawling close to the floor to avoid tripping a motion-detected alarm system. Note burglars are wearing coveralls, apparently to avoid leaving any evidence and their faces are covered to prevent identification. If investigators recover the coveralls, there may be individual evidence recovered from their insides and class evidence from their outsides. (Courtesy of BB's Café)

Organized offenders are experienced offenders. They often accumulate several arrests for theft or burglary between adolescence and mid-adulthood. However, for organized offenders, burglary is usually not their only source of income. Organized burglars often have a legitimate job in a hands-on, flexible hours vocation such as tree trimming, delivery, or construction. They may have a girlfriend, wife, or family, own a car, and be very knowledgeable about police investigations, for example, how to conceal evidence, and avoid detection.

Disorganized Burglaries

Unlike the organized burglaries, **disorganized burglaries** often result in a crime scene that is left in a state of disarray. These offenders may carelessly smash windows to force entry into the premises, and ransack the home while searching for goods, drugs, or cash. The disorganized burglar may dump out a jewelry box, often taking its entire contents. However, in many disorganized burglaries no items are stolen, suggesting the offender did not find an item of interest, had no way to sell large desirable items they found and left them behind, the motivation for the crime was not property based, they panicked, or their crime was interrupted and they fled. Like their offenses, disorganized burglars display a recklessness, impulsiveness, and little consideration for the consequences of their own behavior. They may have difficulties holding a job, maintaining relationships, graduating from school, and may have issues with alcohol and/or drugs. Most disorganized offenders do not own a car, therefore they generally live within walking, skateboarding, or bicycling distance from their targets.

Opportunistic Burglaries

Opportunistic burglaries occur when offenders select a target and quickly strike because they perceived that some type of immediate opportunity exists. In almost all opportunistic burglaries there is no forced entry because the offender "takes the easy path" and enters through a window or door which is unlocked or easily defeated. Often, the premises is an unoccupied residence. It is unlikely that high value items are stolen. Instead, the items offenders take are often\random and for personal use as opposed to resale. In their haste to get in and then quickly flee, opportunistic burglars may not make it to a jewelry box, limiting what they steal from common areas of the home, such as the kitchen and living room (Figure 14-11). Opportunistic burglars do not bring burglary-specific tools with them and are easily scared away, sometimes before they can take anything from the home.

This type of burglar is young, impulsive, and the offense is usually a type of social activity committed by several teenagers after school. Females may be included in the group and play a supporting role, such as look-out. Opportunistic offenders generally target premises near their schools, home, or the homes of their friends. This type of offender may have a record for committing other opportunity-based crimes, such as shoplifting.

Interpersonal Burglaries

Unlike the other types of burglaries, **interpersonal burglaries** are deliberately committed when some particular person is present. The target of the crime is not property, but the victim. This act

▶ **FIGURE 14.11**
Although it appears to be daylight outside, it is actually outside lighting. The surveillance video shows that at around 3:44 a.m., a male suspect smashed the front glass door and once the door was breached, a total of four suspects entered the business and stole multiple electronics before fleeing the scene. The police arrested five juvenile suspects.
(Photo courtesy of PhoneAxiom)

BOX 14-7 | POTENTIAL IMPACT OF USING THE BURGLARY PROFILES

A scientific evaluation of the burglar profiles was conducted in Florida. A number of major police departments in Florida were matched by factors such as crime rate, number of sworn officers, location, and population.[52] One department received training in applying the four profiles, while the others conducted their burglar investigations in their usual way. Nationally, the burglary clearance rate stays around 12% in any given year. The police department that received profile training cleared over four times as many burglaries as compared to those which had not. The odds of making an arrest was also three times higher in the trained department versus those which did not receive that training.

implies that the actual purpose of the burglary is to instill fear in the victim and to display the offender's power over them. If anything is taken it holds personal meaning to the offender such as the victim's underwear, their cell phone, or their driver's license. These items can also be interpreted to be a trophy or memento, kept as a reminder of the burglar's power. If an interpersonal burglar takes jewelry, it is limited to a piece(s) that has sentimental value to the victim or for which there is a dispute between the offender and the victim about ownership, for example, an engagement ring.

Although most interpersonal burglars do not have a record, it does not mean they have not committed crimes, for example, they were not reported to the police or reported, but not cleared. If the offender has a criminal record it will most likely involve domestic violence, stalking, voyeurism, or rape. Interpersonal burglars are almost always adults and have some connection to the victim. While the other three types of burglary offenders will go to great lengths to avoid confrontation with occupants, interpersonal offenders will choose the victim to whom they want access. Victims are often female and may have been in a relationship with the offender at some point. While organized burglars have the most financial impact on victims, interpersonal offenders could be the most dangerous because their confrontations could escalate to the more serious violent offenses, such as rape and murder.

The cost to investigate a single burglary has been estimated to cost $7,000 to more than $22,000. Burglars commit between two and 38 burglaries annually, with an average of four. Proper use of the profiles has the potential to increase burglary arrest to a record-setting 50%. Daytona Beach, Florida has 1,800 burglaries annually. If every burglary arrest prevents one subsequent burglary, then a 50% arrest would eliminate the Daytona Beach Police Department's (DBPD) need to investigate 900 subsequent burglaries. Even using the lower cost of $7,000 to investigate a burglary, substantial savings in the DBPD's budget could be achieved (900 fewer burglaries times $7,000 = $6.3 million).[53]

Similarly, there are community costs for each burglary for factors such as damage to the premises, the theft of items not covered by insurance, the insurance reimbursement for items may be less than their actual replacement value, increased cost of insurance, the victim's pain, injury, and suffering, medical care costs, and loss of earnings, criminal justice system expenditures, such as pre-trial incarceration, legal representation, and adjudication, probation, incarceration, and parole following conviction. Although the community costs vary by location, they are substantial and often unconsidered because they are invisible to most of the public.

RESIDENTIAL AND NON-RESIDENTIAL BURGLARIES

RESIDENTIAL BURGLARY

Single family detached housing is a frequent burglary target (Figure 14-12). The rewards potentially can be greater than with other types of housing and there may be more than one attractive point at which to make an entry.[54] Some opportunistic/impulsive burglars use a rule of thumb for how long they will try to make an entry into a home: "One (minute) or I'm done." Time at a target is a risky proposition.

Burglars also want to make a "clean getaway" following their break-ins. To increase their chances of doing so, offenders "get in, get stuff, and get out." It is estimated that residential burglars complete their offenses within eight to 12 minutes.[55] The flip side is that professional burglars willingly take more than one minute when they are attacking harder, more lucrative targets.

Burglaries increase during the summer, when school is out. If they weren't able to get a job, young persons have time on their hands and a few become offenders. More importantly, summers also mean many people outside walking, jogging, and pushing baby carriages. In the midst of such movement, burglars may more easily go unnoticed as they surveille and move to their targets. Additionally, families may be vacationing and if their homes are identified they become prime potential targets. Conversely, during cold winters, the weather and a steep reduction in favorable situational conditions contributes to a decline in burglaries. Still, some burglars are not deterred by such factors.

In Evanston, Illinois, a witness said he saw three men running away from a residence carrying a television. Police followed

▲ **FIGURE 14-12   Forced entry of residential front door**
The burglary of this residence was accomplished by prying the front door open. The burglar first made an unsuccessful attempt to remove the deadbolt lock. When this failed, he simply pried the door open, as evidenced by the marks along the door's right edge. (Courtesy of Police Department of Columbus, Georgia)

their shoe prints in the freshly fallen snow to another residence (Figure 14-13). The officers circled that home and found no tracks leading away from it. After being admitted to the residence, the police heard noises in the attic, and found the three burglars hiding there with the television. Two of the offenders were 18 years old and the third one was a 16-year-old juvenile.

Houses on cul-de-sacs are less likely to be burglarized except when there are farms or wooded land at their rear, which increases the homes vulnerability. Such terrain allows offenders to surveille homes and approach them with a reduced risk of being discovered.[56] Homeowners on cul-de-sacs can see their neighbors' front doors, where about one-third of all residential break-ins occur. Because cul-de-sac residents are usually familiar with their neighbors' vehicles and their comings and goings, they recognize cars which "don't belong here" and monitor them.

Homes close to bus or other transit stops or near more heavily traveled streets are at a greater risk of being burglarized. More pedestrian and other traffic make it harder to detect suspicious activity. In socially disadvantaged and disorganized neighborhoods, the homes are at a greater risk of being burglarized, perhaps because residents do not have the resources to protect them.[57] Households living in mobile homes and rental properties experience high rates of burglary victimization. In violent encounter burglaries, the offender is known to the victim 65% of the time.[58]

Residential burglars usually do not carry tools because many homes are lightly protected and make "**soft targets**." In Mesquite, Texas, a burglary suspect kicked in French doors leading from the patio into the home. The doors were protected with only one lock at their middle and were quickly compromised. Many offenders have learned if they install a flashlight app on their smart phone, they eliminate the need to carry a flashlight. Although, burglary statutes often have increased sanctions for using tools to commit a burglary, some offenders continue to favor using particular tools or actually need them to force an entry into hardened targets (Figure 14-14).

▶ **FIGURE 14.13**
Teenage burglars, one a juvenile, stole a television. Police followed their shoe impressions in the snow directly to where they were hiding. (©Christopher Furlong/Getty Images)

▲ FIGURE 14-14

Crude force entry by burglar in Tacoma, Washington

All the burglar needed to force an entry into a Coin and Collectibles business in Tacoma, Washington was probably an axe and a rope ladder previously fabricated for the job. A crude hole was chopped in the roof and the burglar came down the rope. Leaving the rope may have been accidental or the burglar was in a panic to leave. The rounded intervals on the rope may have contained touch DNA. (©Janet Jensen/The News Tribune/AP Images)

Households burglarized when no one is home experience greater losses than those when a member is present; 30% of the former had losses of $1,000 or more while the latter had losses of less than $250.[59] Even small items can create large losses. To some extent, what is stolen is a function of what can be carried away covertly and used personally, given as gift, or for which there is a buyer/fence. Any officer seeing a skateboarder rolling along with a 55" television will want to know more, while a burglar who has loaded stolen goods in the trunk of his /her car will not be so noticeable.

Assuming a savvy burglar or two and a more expensive home, the master bedroom will be the first place searched because it is often "the jackpot." Even the bedrooms of houses in lower income areas will be the first stop for many offenders.[60] Bedrooms are places where people feel safe and comfortable. It

is predictable they would want to keep some valuables there and nearby in their bathroom and closet. Nightstands, chests, and under the mattress may yield guns, watches, and cash. Few guns stolen in residential burglaries are recovered. It's only a few steps from the bedroom to the master bathroom to check for perfumes, cosmetics, and prescription drugs. Having pills to sell on the street is like an ATM for burglars: quick cash. If the homeowners are thought to be traveling, unusual, unconventional places will be checked because at the last minute homeowners sometimes go into a "hiding frenzy" before leaving. The hamper will be tossed and between and behind stacks of clean towels will be checked. The back of the toilet may be removed to look for illegal drugs in watertight bags.

Closets in more expensive homes are often fertile places for finding valuables, including cash, collectables, high-end handbags, such as Gucci and Birkin, clothing, including shoes, scarfs, furs, and leather coats and luggage with designer labels. A Texas couple forgot to set their security alarm before going out to dinner. When they returned hours later, their 3,000 square foot closet had been plundered by a lone burglar. In just 40 minutes, the offender seized between $500,000 and $1,000,000 in valuables from just the closet. Adding insult to injury, the perpetrator used the couple's Louis Vuitton luggage to carry the valuables away[61] (Figure 14-15).

Few homes will have such finery, but they will still have some valuable items. Boxes on closet shelves, regardless of their labels, for example, "Fluffy's Vet Records," will also be rapidly examined. Burglars will feel the inside pockets of suitcoats because experience has taught them people sometimes absently-minded leave or hide things there, sometimes from their spouses. Clothes left hanging from doors suggest they may have been freshly worn and could contain credit cards and cash. Before Christmas there may be the bonus of gifts in the closets.

Safes may be found in bedrooms, closets, home offices, and sometimes garages. Some of these "safes" are smaller, handheld devices properly called fire chests and they offer little or no burglary protection (Figure 14-16). Likewise, some small, more traditionally appearing safes are only rated to be fire resistant, but not for burglary. Because they may weigh less than 100 pounds, they can be carried off to be opened elsewhere or forced open in place, sometimes with common handheld tools from the homeowner's garage. Such safes may be installed in a wall or bolted to a floor. If it takes too long to rip them loose, they are forced open where found. Beyond entry level fire resistant safes, there are those rated for both fire and burglary protection. Safes are discussed in detail later in this chapter.

Even a basic home office may yield both electronics and business machines. Desk computers are intrinsically valuable, made all the more so when account names and passwords are on them. The refrigerator, stove, and microwave may also hold valuables. Some soda cans in the refrigerator may be ones built to conceal small valuables, such as rings. If they are manufactured by a respected company and in good shape, expresso machines, food processors, microwaves, and convection-powered toaster ovens have values that add up quickly. Pantries may hold liquor and wine collections. The living area will be examined for DVDs, electronics, video game consoles, digital cameras,

▶ **FIGURE 14-15**
A portion of the atypical 3,000 square foot closet. (©James Nielsen/Houston Chronicle/AP Images)

▲ **FIGURE 14-16**
A Sentry Waterproof Fire-Resistant Chest
This $80 Sentry chest is classified to protect documents and other contents from temperatures of 1,700°F for one hour and from flood or other water. (©2017 Master Lock Company LLC)

collectables, and works of art. Hiding valuables in fake and behind actual books is a ruse with which burglars are familiar.

If a vehicle is in the garage or driveway and the keys are found in the home, it may be stolen. If bikes, grills, golf clubs, basketballs, power tools, and lawn mowers are in the garage the best of them may be taken. The burglar can leave the scene in the just-stolen car, walking, or biking, with whatever can be easily concealed, valuable, and not appear suspicious. If a vehicle is stolen in a burglary, it may be quickly abandoned, but left running somewhere in the hope it will be stolen and misdirect the investigation, sold to a chop shop, or set on fire to eliminate the possibility of the police finding physical evidence in it.

NON-RESIDENTIAL BURGLARIES

Non-residential burglaries account for approximately 28% of all burglary offenses.[62] As a reminder, "non-residential" includes a rich variety of structures, including churches, schools, retail businesses, service providers, such as plumbers, travel agencies, and pest control companies, hospitals, doctors' offices, and pharmacies, as well as fast food and "sit down" restaurants, banks, and non-profits.

Among those who have committed both residential and non-residential burglaries, 31% prefer to do the latter.[63] This is likely due to the belief or personal experience that "commercial" targets offer greater rewards. It is estimated that commercial buildings have an average burglary loss that is 20% higher than for homes.[64] Another reason for the preference may be that it is easier to predict when businesses are unoccupied. Although residential burglaries clearly outnumber non-residential burglaries, the victimization rate of the latter is proportionally greater because there are fewer targets. Some commercial targets are at greater risk to be burglarized because of their location, weak security, the desirable goods they offer for sale, and the offenders have previously had a successful burglary there.[65]

As with home burglaries, businesses attacked once are candidates to be victimized again, usually within 30 days. The likelihood of **repeat victimization** is estimated at 17%, although for houses some estimates reach as high as 40%.[66] Because of the prevalence of home burglaries, they have been more closely studied, while studying commercial burglaries is at an earlier stage. The bulk of commercial burglaries occur during the hours of darkness, although daylight burglaries of closed business also occur.[67]

In most cases, the burglars enter through a door or a window. However, in strip malls, one business may be broken into and then adjourning businesses are attacked through side walls. Businesses continue to suffer from the use of "crash and grab"

◄ **FIGURE 14-17**
Not all commercial burglars have huge "scores." A burglar in New Jersey was active for 20 years with an apparent shoe fetish. The boxes and plastic bins contained thousands of new shoes accumulated through his burglaries, which filled three truckloads getting them to the evidence room. A small portion of burglaries are not about money. Instead, the motive is taking trophies or satisfying a fetish. (©CB2/ZOB/WENN.com/Newscom)

attacks, which appear to be increasingly prevalent. Commercial burglars are largely motivated by economic gain, although some report the thrill of committing offenses is also an attraction.[68] In some areas of the country around 20% of the perpetrators may be responsible for as much as 75% of the commercial burglaries.[69] On the whole, commercial burglars tend to be somewhat older and more experienced as compared to the profile for residential offenders. Commercial offenders are often professionals and take a thoughtful approach to their work.[70] They will conduct surveillances of targets, try to get insider information from employees, plan the route they will drive to make a quick sale of the property stolen to fences, and communicate with pre-paid mobile phones.[71] Commercial burglars also steal things in greater volume or of greater value and may operate with a fence on a "steal to order basis.[72] (Figure 14-17).

The Jewelers Security Alliance's (JSA) reported its members in 41 states lost $18.7 million to burglaries.[73] The JSA calls "crash and grab" offenses "3-minute burglaries" (**B3M**) because that is the approximate time it takes for offenders to break the glass door or window of a jewelry retail store, break glass cabinets, grab whatever is available, and flee with an average of $23,000 in merchandise.[74] Repair and/or replacement of property damage and business interruption creates another loss. B3Ms account for 48% of jewelry store burglaries.[75] B3Ms peak on Mondays and the months of August, September, and October while conventional burglaries are typically on Sundays and the high months are February, March, and April.[76]

Roof top burglaries produced jewelry stores' largest losses.[77] That type of entry is a more advanced technique used by professionals, mostly against high value business targets. Moreover, a roof job implies the offenders plan to spend more time inside the premises, as opposed to a lightening quick smash and grab (Figure 14-18). Therefore, the higher losses from roof jobs are

not surprising. In some instances, officers responding to jewelry store perimeter alarms were unable to detect a break-in during a perimeter check and because they are also unable to do an inside sweep, left without checking the roof.[78] Any number of law enforcement agencies have an agreement with the fire department to send a ladder truck to help do roof checks and a few police departments are using drones for the same purpose. Overnight in 2016, professional burglars used a blowtorch to cut a hole in the roof of a New York City branch bank. To conceal their work, the offenders brought along sheets of plywood and a tarp and built a small structure over the area where they wanted to cut a hole in the roof. When the hole was completed, a ladder the perpetrators had also brought to the scene was used to climb directly into the vault.[79]

Based on the same M.O. being used, the offenders who entered the branch bank through the hole in the roof (Figure 14-19) are thought to have also committed a previous branch bank burglary. The combined losses for those two bank burglaries totaled approximately $5,000,000 in cash and valuables.[80]

Roof vents and skylights are also used as entry points into commercial buildings because these points may not be protected or only weakly so. Burglaries of banks, credit unions, saving and loans association, and similar enterprises are relatively unusual. There were just 53 of them in 2015, while there were 3,543 robberies of such financial institutions.[81]

Burglaries of hotel rooms are an understudied area. Hotels claim not to keep statistics for crimes on their premises, which anecdotally appear to be centered on guest rooms. National hotel associations maintain compiling such statistics is the responsibility of law enforcement agencies. Occasionally, hotel guests visiting major venues, such as Las Vegas, are victimized by burglaries or other crimes. Hotels maintain their security

▶ **FIGURE 14-18**
"Smash and Grab"
Chicago police officer processing a vehicle for evidence. It was used in a smash and grab at a Neiman Marcus. (©Michael Tercha/Chicago Tribune/TNS/Getty Images)

▲ **FIGURE 14-19**
A roof job at a New York City branch bank which allowed the burglars access to the bank's safety deposit vault. (**Source:** United States Attorney Office)

staffs are well-trained and such incidents are isolated. In contrast, in one week there were six robberies, 17 burglaries, and four thefts in Las Vegas hotels.[82] Initially, the report seems like more than just "isolated incidents." However, assuming the data are evenly distributed across time, with 813,696 people visiting Las Vegas weekly the risk of being a hotel burglary victim in any given week is 0.000021%.[83]

Some Las Vegas visitors who were burglary victims feel their hotel did little to help them, although it is unclear just what and how reasonable their expectations were. Common items stolen in casino hotel burglaries include cell-phones, wallets, cash, chips, sunglasses, and tablets. Similar complaints are also raised by victims to other cities.

An unknown number of hotel burglaries are precipitated by the guests themselves, who leave sliding glass doors to their balconies open or unlocked, creating an easy path into their room from a neighboring balcony. Occasionally, burglars will be discovered in a hotel room by the unexpected return of a guest and will wave a false set of credentials and badge around, purporting to be a security officer who discovered the door open.

ENTRIES BY UNKNOWN MEANS AND LOCK PICKING

Occasionally, a burglary investigation cannot immediately identify a point of entry. The absence of a forced entry point occurs in 11% of reported commercial burglaries and 36% of home burglaries.[84] About 13% of burglars participating in a multi-state study reported they picked locks or used a key they had acquired to make any entry.[85]

With no identifiable entry point, perhaps no clear evidence of an intruder, and property being reported stolen, investigators must deal with two key questions: (1) Is this actually a burglary?

and (2) If so, how did it happen? Like medical diagnosis, investigation of a reported burglary sometimes make progress by excluding other possibilities, such as:

1. An open/unlocked window or door was used to gain entry;
2. Insurance fraud;
3. An authorized key holder, e.g., a family member, household worker, or employee committed the burglary;
4. Collusion between an authorized key holder and an offender;
5. The emergency "outside key" was discovered;
6. An impression of an authorized key was used to make a key;
7. A key was stolen from a key bank; or
8. A lock was picked.

There are three major categories of lock picking: destructive, covert, and surreptitious. A destructive lock picking entry is apparent by immediately visible damage to the lock. The other two types of lock picking, covert and surreptitious, require elaboration.

Although "covert" and "surreptitious" are used synonymously, there is an important forensic difference. While covert picking leaves no apparent external marks on a lock, a forensic laboratory examiner will be able to locate marks on the internal lock mechanism. From the depth of gouges and other marks on a picked lock, the examiner may be able to make some statements about the skill of the burglar and sometimes perhaps which company made the tools used. If tools are seized from a suspect, the comparison of marks made on the lock during the burglary with test marks made with the seized tools may be able to connect the tools to the scene. An additional forensic possibility is when a portion of a suspect's pick has broken off in the lock, creating the potential for a fracture match if the remainder of the pick is still in the suspect's possession. Although unusual, examiners have found hairs and blood inside of locks submitted for examination, which creates the potential for individual identification.

In theory, true **surreptitious entries** leave no forensic evidence. However, examiners may find subtle indicators to be able to make a probabilistic statement about whether a surreptitious entry could have occurred. Even softer, anti-forensic lock pick tools can leave slight markings. Although unusual, examiners have found hairs and blood inside of locks submitted for examination, which creates the potential for individual identification.

Perhaps the three most common methods of lock picking are:

1. A lock pick or **snap gun**;
2. The lock is "loided." **Loiding** is the act of using a credit card or a similar plastic item to slip open or shim a spring-bolt lock that does not have an anti-shim device. Technically, a spring bolt without an anti-shim device should be considered a privacy, rather than a security, device. Spring-bolt locks are commonly found on the interior doors of a home, although some exterior doors also use them; or

3. The lock is **Key bumped** or a **bump key gun** is used. Both are lock picking techniques adopted by a growing number of burglars. Both methods require lower skill levels and can be effective against pin tumbler locks, which are commonly installed in many homes and businesses. Key bumping is a manual approach and the bump key gun is battery automated.

From a bump key set, a key is selected and inserted into the lock. It can only move forward a short way before being blocked. The head of the key is lightly struck or "bumped," moving the key slightly forward. The key is turned to compromise the associated tumblers. This process is repeated until the lock is compromised. The bump key gun is a variant on the manual procedure. Sets of bump keys and bump key guns are commonly available on the internet for approximately $20 to $120, respectively. Snap guns and bump key guns are differentiated because snap guns insert what is called a "needle" into the lock. In contrast, the bump key gun inserts a key.

BURGLARY SYMBOLS

America's Great Depression (1929–1939) cost millions of peoples their jobs, homes and farms. Many people were forced into wretched shacks they made from cardboard boxes. These cardboard settlements were derisively called "Hoovervilles" after President Herbert Hoover, who many blamed for the failed economy. Some 2,000,000 people were penniless, homeless "hoboes," some of whom illegally "hopped" on trains ("rode the rails") seeking food and work. Many were willing to work to earn their meal or an overnight in a barn. The hoboes left coded symbols for those who came behind them to indicate such things as "kind lady lives here" or "bad dogs."

In a criminal context, marking houses, their walls, and nearby light poles has been resurrected in England to give other burglars secret information about the households (Figure 14-20).[86] Investigators should be alert such a practice could emerge in the United States and get that information to intelligence, crime prevention, and neighborhood associations to disseminate the information so homeowners can quickly remove the symbols.

SAFE BURGLARIES

Safe burglaries have been declining for several decades, but have certainly not disappeared. As an example, in the first half of 2013, there were 165 burglarized safes reported in Dallas, Texas or roughly one every 1.1 days. Those burglaries represented losses totaling $500,000 and damages to property of $380,000. Because safe attacks were also an issue in neighboring jurisdictions, a joint Safe Burglary Task Force was formed.[87]

In part, the decline in safe burglaries is due to the prevalence of cashless transactions, for example, debit and credit cards, as well as target-hardening measures taken by home owners and businesses with respect to their premises. That the decline has

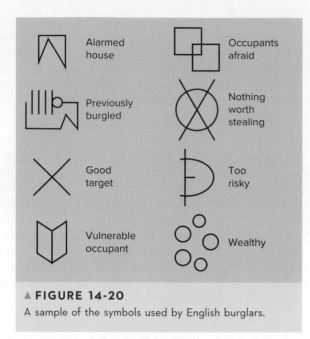

▲ FIGURE 14-20
A sample of the symbols used by English burglars.

not been steeper may be due to the growing popularity of home safes. Investigators need to have a basic understanding of safes and the types of evidence that may be found when they are attacked.

Underwriters Laboratories (UL) and Intertek test and set performance standards for different types of safes. Some safe manufacturers hire a private testing laboratory to establish the performance ratings on a label inside of the safe and do not rely on the UL standards. "Safe" is a term with two major protection categories: fire and burglary. There are also **dual safes** to simultaneously provide both fire and burglary protection at different levels of performance. Fire safes are used in some homes and many businesses. Homeowners buy them to protect birth certificates, marriage licenses, cash, titles to vehicles, insurance policies, investment reports, tax returns, and similarly important document.

Likewise, businesses use fire safes to prevent the loss of documents and records important to their enterprise. A UL Class 350-One Hour rating of a fire safe denotes that when exposed to an external temperature of 1,700°F the inside heat level will not reach 350°F for one-hour. Class 350 safes have fire protection ratings from 1 to 4 hours (Figure 14-21).

The ratings for burglary safes also identify specific burglary resistant performance capabilities. A TL-15 rating indicates that for 15 minutes the burglary safe will resist attacks using common hand-held tools, for example, hammers, crowbars, drills, and pressure applying devices, such as repeatedly tightening logging chains around the safe until it is forced open or the attack abandoned. The 15-minute time period includes only the actual time the tools are being actively used on the safe.

Low-cost home dual purpose safes will often have a reasonable degree of fire protection, but the burglary protection may be the **Residential Security Container (RSC)** rating. The RSC rating offers burglary protection analogous to a TL-5 rating. The RSC designation gives protection from an attack by one person using common hand-held tools, no powered tools, no hammer with a head weight more than three pounds, or tool longer than 18" Some gun safes use the RSC standard.

Knowledge of the protection capabilities of a safe coupled with surveillance images can provide important information to investigators. If a burglar spends 45 minutes unsuccessfully trying to get into a TL-15 safe versus spending 8 minutes successfully

▶ FIGURE 14-21
Example of a UL safe classification label.
(Courtesy of Dr. Charles Swanson)

attacking it gives a clear indication of the perpetrator's skill. Knowledge of the behavior of a suspect's actions while he/she was on the scene may provide an M.O.

Occasionally, safe burglary scenes are found with things carefully laid out, suggesting an experienced perpetrator was teaching someone about safe cracking. Which can then be compared during tests made in the laboratory using the suspect's equipment.

Drilling is noisy, so safe crackers may make special sound-deadening boxes in which to place their drills. The materials used to make the baffle boxes can potentially can be matched with left over materials in the suspect's possession. Bolt cutters recovered from the suspect can be tested in the laboratory to determine whether the striae made match those on chains, padlock hasps, or fences at the burglary site. Slag seized at the scene of a burning job can be analyzed for consistency with portions of it inadvertently transferred back to the floor mats in the suspects' car, embedded in the bottom of their shoes, on stolen property, and on their tools.

Some safe manufacturing companies use proprietary insulation which is unique to their line. Whenever safe insulation is exposed at a safe job, samples of it should also be collected. A search should be made for safe insulation in the same places slag may be found, but additionally, safe insulation should be looked for under the fingernails of offenders and in the inside of their shoes.

In a few cases, safe insulation was found in the nail holes of shoe heels several weeks after the commission of the offense. If safe insulation recovered at the scene and from the suspect is consistent, it is class, but not individual, evidence that the suspect could have been at the scene.

Opportunities to locate DNA evidence also exist: offenders may have left hats with hair or perspiration in the sweatbands, cut themselves accidentally when using equipment, leaving blood, left their saliva on cigarette butts or water bottles, or used the bathroom, but forgot to flush. Suspects may have removed their gloves and raised the toilet seat to urinate, leaving fingerprint evidence or left shoe impressions in exposed safe insulation.

CAR, RV, AND TRAILER BURGLARIES

Breaking into cars, recreational vehicles (RVs), and trailers constitutes a burglary. Car burglars tend to be juveniles, teenagers, and young adult offenders. Many entries by these offenders are done by simply opening unlocked car doors or involve breaking a window to reach inside and take whatever is available. Unlocked trunk releases are pulled and items in the trunk stolen. Some street-wise perpetrators carry a sparkplug or a porcelain chip from one with them to break a window on a locked vehicle. If "tools" are used, they may be tire irons, slim jims, or pry-bar type instruments, small hammers, or door lock punches. The more usual case is improvising with whatever is handy, such as portable signs, trash lids/cans, and brick/rocks.

Typical items taken include visible change, wallets left in the center console and purses left on the floor board, car electronics, CDs, speed detectors, laptops, cameras, and cellular phones.

Juveniles and teenagers often do more damage than is necessary in removing dashboard electronics. When valuable, but larger items, such as golf clubs, are left behind, due the lack of a vehicle to transport them out of the area and/or the inability to sell them quickly also suggests youthful offenders.

Many items taken from vehicles are quickly converted to cash. Like the profile of other types of burglars, a portion of vehicle burglars are drug dependent or drug involved and that group of offenders may have to commit offenses with more regularity. Wherever cars are parked, they can become a target. Apartment complexes, sorority and fraternity houses, and mall, mass transit, campus, and employee parking lots offer plenty of targets that allow offenders to quickly commit a series of car burglaries. Cars that are burglarized on railroad cars and new car sales lots tend to be more experienced car burglars. In many jurisdictions, car burglaries spike around Christmas time, because some shoppers leave packages in plain view in their vehicles.

The price of a basic pop-up campers starts around $5,000, while more elaborate ones are in the $20,000 range. The average cost of an RV is approximately $120,000 while the extravagant, fireplace-equipped ELeMMent Palazzo is $3,000,000. Not all RVs emphasize great comfort. For around $500,000 a tough RV with armor, solar panels, a water purification system, and a 2,000 mile gas tank will take owners over terrain that normal RVs cannot. Burglars at RV dealerships tend to steal electronics, and often the damage to the RVs is greater than the amount of the property stolen. Over several months, an RV dealership in Oregon suffered substantial losses as burglars broke into RVs for sale and stole flat screen TVs. At one stretch, the dealership was burglarized 20 times in three days. Police arrested a man who had broken in and was leaving with a 36" television. Other burglars are also believed to be involved.[88]

Many RV burglaries occur at RV storage sites and along interstate and major state highways, because those routes are typically used by travelers. Pop-ups are often attacked in state or national parks when the owners are away hiking, photographing, hunting, or fishing. High-end RVs often have safes and have been the target of home invasion style robberies. In addition to arrests by patrolling officers viewing crimes in progress, car, RV, and trailer burglaries are foiled by the unexpected presence of owners and parking lot attendants. Law enforcement employs a variety of strategies, including "bait cars," targeting repeat offenders, and automated surveillance of parking areas. Offenders may bring themselves down by openly bragging about their exploits and jubilantly flashing stolen goods on Facebook.

APPROACHING THE SCENE AND INITIAL ACTIONS

Many law enforcement agencies have at least some vehicles equipped with digital cameras. Some of those departments require that the cameras be turned on as officers get closer to a crime scene. Later, when the recordings are reviewed, images with investigative significance may be found, for example, a known burglar driving away from the general direction of the burglary-in-progress call to which the officer is responding.

When responding to a burglary-in-progress call, some law enforcement policies allow officers the discretion to just use their emergency lights without activating their siren, sometimes called "running silent." If they hear a siren, the sound may give perpetrators just enough time to flee the scene. However, if officers run silent they lose the immunities provided by their state's emergency vehicle operation law, including speeding in a prudent and reasonable manner. Such statutes commonly require that both emergency lights and an audible signal (siren or other device) must be in operation.

The last several blocks to the scene should be driven at lower speeds to enable officers sufficient time to make observations, for example, "Is that really a couple parking in this industrial park at midnight as though it's a lover's lane or are they lookouts for a burglary?

Some burglars prefer to drive big cars, like older Cadillacs and Lincolns in good condition for two reasons; They: (1) can load a lot of stolen property in them and (2) hope that officers may be a little less suspicious of people in such cars because the car suggests the driver has a degree of social status. When more urgent demands of the call are handled, officers should check cars parked near or within several blocks of the scene. Rapidly arriving police units may force burglars to flee the scene, but they might not have had enough time to get to get to their car.

Ordinarily, a burglary in progress requires the dispatch of at least two patrol cars. More than two units may be required if the building is very large, for example, a warehouse. In many departments, a supervisor is also dispatched to all felony-in-progress calls. Officers who are assigned to the call should attempt to coordinate their arrivals. This will enable the rapid formation of a perimeter around the building involved. One arriving unit can be assigned to watch the north and east sides of the building involved and another unit the south and west sides. If a two-officer unit is dispatched to a burglary-in-progress, the operator of the vehicle can get the same coverage described above by dropping his/her partner off in a position to view two sides of the building and positioning the vehicle to cover the remaining two sides. This value of this approach is obviously lessened when a larger, irregularly-shaped business is ringed by a 10' fence and heavy tree and bush growths.

Some policies direct that if the first arriving unit at a burglary in progress scene is an officer riding alone, he/she should park the car somewhat away from the scene, approach it unseen on foot to a stand-off position, check for lookouts, cars that don't seem to belong, persons acting suspiciously, and known criminals as well as monitoring the building involved for light changes, movements, and sounds and passing that along to other responding units. A policy exception to this approach is when a person lawfully in the building is in immediate danger of being physically harmed by an offender.

If there is any reasonable suspicion one or more suspects are still in the building, the Canine Unit should be requested, which ordinarily requires the approval of a supervisor. While waiting for the canine team to arrive officers should not hang around entry points to the building or walk inside even a short way. The mix of new scents may confuse the dog. The canine officer and dog takes the lead in searching for offenders, while other officers provide cover. Once the general location of the burglar is established, the cover officers take the lead. All clearing of a burglary site must be conducted with the thought the offender is still on the premises. While clearing a building, caution must be exercised to avoid the accidental destruction of physical evidence or property. However, that need is always subordinated to the need to protect the lives of officers.

INVESTIGATIVE CONSIDERATIONS AT THE SCENE

If gross physical force has been used in gaining entry, the point of attack is easily established. However, one cannot assume that it is also the point of exit. Often burglars will break into a building at one point and then leave by another. When gross physical force is used, the point of attack is of particular importance because examination of it may yield the types of physical evidence discussed in Chapter 4, "Physical Evidence." In combination, the determination of the points of attack and exit will suggest the avenues of approach and flight traveled by the perpetrator, which also must be explored for the possible presence of physical evidence.

Officers must be attentive for unusual signs that may be of investigative value. Juvenile burglars commonly commit destructive acts of vandalism and age and burglary experience may be suggested by what property that is taken versus what was left behind. The weight or dimensions of property taken in a burglary may suggest, if only roughly, the number of people involved in the offense, for example, absence the use of a dolly, a lone burglar is unlikely to carry off a 1,200 pound gun safe and its contents. Articles or tools left behind, may be useful in identifying an M.O. and may also can be good tracing evidence. To illustrate, assume a new slow speed cold cut saw is found abandoned at a safe burglary scene. The saw's identification number could lead to the buyer, who may be or know who the burglar is. If gross physical force has been used in gaining entry, the point of attack is easily established. However, one cannot assume that it is also the point of exit. Often burglars will break into a building at one point and then leave by another. When gross physical force is used, the point of attack is of particular importance because examination of it may yield the types of physical evidence discussed in Chapter 4, "Physical Evidence."

STOLEN GOODS MARKETS

Not all stolen property is traded or sold by burglars. Some of it may be kept to use as gifts or for personal use, or sold by the offender at flea markets or by other means. One way or another, a portion of stolen property also ends up overseas. "Fences" discretely buy goods from burglars and other thieves in what is largely an underground/invisible economy. In turn, the fences resell the stolen goods for a profit.

Buyers of stolen property may specialize because they have places where they can readily sell certain types of goods and/or they have a special expertise, such as works of art (See Box 14-8).[89] Fences may also serve in roughly a

BOX 14-8 | BURGLARS AND THEIR FENCES

"I've got different people all over the place that I'll take different types of items to. Like electrical goods may go one place, power tools or whatever goes to another place, to whichever person buys that type of thing. And I do my deal with him and he does his deal with whoever he deals with."[90]

mentoring role, teaching burglars how to recognize valuable items, fingering jobs for them, and having them steal items for which there is a great demand. However, stealing to order is not common.

The existence of stolen goods markets encourages property thefts, including those accomplished by burglary. Fences eliminate the risk to offenders for personally selling the goods and provides quick cash. Perpetrators want to "unload" their stolen goods as quickly as possible. Estimates of how quickly range from as little as 30-minutes to not more than 2 hours.[91] In addition to amateur, occasional fences, there are six types of stolen goods markets:[92]

1. *Commercial fence supplies:* Burglars and other thieves sell stolen goods to commercial fences operating out of their businesses, such as jewelry stores, pawnshops, and secondhand stores. The property is then resold to another entity that may resell it or offer it for sale in their own business, such as an auction.

   Pawnshops are heavily regulated. Just at the Federal level there are 15 laws and other provisions pertaining to pawnbrokers and transactions, for example, redemption periods and recordkeeping.

Pawnshops are collateralized lenders. The loan is based on the value of the property left with the pawn shop. Borrowers typically have 30 days, plus a 30-day grace period, to repay the loan and interest and redeem their property. Some states permit various types of extensions of the original redemption period to claim a pawned article. To escape usury laws, which prohibit exorbitant interest rates, pawnbrokers use "finance charges," which equate to 2 to 3% interest monthly.

While pawnshops are sometimes thought of as "seedy," some cater to the wealthy who are "in a pinch." Illustratively, in New York City, Borro and Suttons & Robertson both serve a clientele usually thought of as not having a need to pawn their property. (Figure 14-22).

2. *Commercial Sales:* Commercial fences usually pose as legitimate businesses, while secretly buying directly from offenders in order to sell the items to their regular, unsuspecting customers. More rarely, the commercial fence will sell items to someone who in turn will use it or resell it again.

3. *Residential fence supplies:* The stolen items are sold to fences which usually operate out of their own homes. In turn, the fence resells the property, for example, to the end user or to a business.

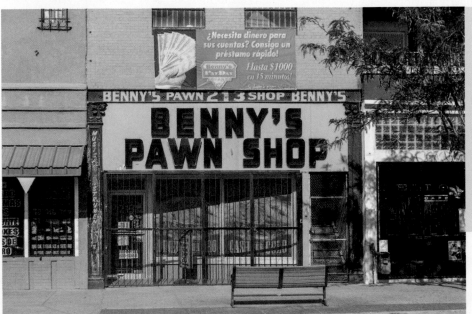

◀ **FIGURE 14-22**
Benny's Pawn Shop in El Paso, Texas
There are 10,000 pawnshops in the United States, 85% of which are locally owned. The primary revenue stream for many pawnshops is melting down unredeemed gold jewelry and selling the bars. A very small number of pawnshops are also fences. To conceal the origin of gold jewelry they buy, the gemstones are removed and the rest is melted into bars and sold.
(©Ian Dagnall/Alamy)

4. *Network sales*: Offenders sell the stolen goods, and the property is passed on to another buyer, who adds some profit and resells it again. This process is repeated several times until the final consumer receives the property. Networks may be ad hoc or based on friendship, kinship, or start with a residential fence.

5. *Hawking*: Offenders sell directly to "consumers," sometimes to people they have just met in a bar or other setting. The advantage to the burglar is they cut out the fence and therefore make a larger profit. For offenders there are three major disadvantages to hawking. They: (a) don't immediately get their cash all at once; (b) bear the risk of having stolen goods in their possession for a longer time; and (c) are at risk selling to strangers whose identity, occupation, and sense of civic duty are all unknown. For these reasons, hawking is generally the least preferred strategy for selling stolen goods.

6. *"e-Selling:"* Burglars may sell stolen goods through private websites such as Craigslist or through online auction sites such as eBay. This gives thieves access to buyers they would not otherwise reach. Alternatively, some fences will buy stolen goods from offenders and dispose of at least some of them by e-selling. Thieves and fences know the police check these internet sites so they usually will not offer items for sale if they have serial numbers on them.

The National Retailing Federation's refers to e-selling as e-fencing. Its 2016 report found an important shift in the percentage of business who reported making stolen property recovers from physical sites and e-fencing (See Table 14-4). Although the losses occurred as a result of retail thefts and not burglaries, it does suggest the possibility of a shift in fencing preferences.

The evidence of drug dealers acting as fences is mixed. Some authorities do not believe it is a widespread practice, while others acknowledge it as a more common practice. Both views are correct. Where it exists, drug dealers may pay cash for property or trade drugs for it. Even drug dealers who ordinarily don't get involved with stolen property may occasionally acquire fine pieces of jewelry. Drug dealers are also known to trade drugs for Electronic Benefit Transfer Cards (EBT, AKA "food stamps").

Implicitly part of the dealing between fences and burglars is that offenders must discount the goods. What a burglar gets paid for property brought to a fence is not a fixed rate. Deals may represent from as little as 20% of the value of the property up to roughly 50%. Deals are effected by variables such as the relationship of the fence and the burglar and how desirable an item is to the fence. Room for a certain amount of haggling exists. The burglar argues, "This Rolex is in nice condition . . . you got to come up with more." The fence may counter with, "I hear you, but it's so hot I won't be able to sell it right away. It has to sit on a shelf for a while and I can't have more of my money tied up like that." Neither side wants to be so rigid in bargaining as to lose the relationship with the other. It is more than the loss of a business partner: If arrested, a person who harbors hard feelings may "rat" on the other one if they get in trouble. The burglar needs buyers and the buyer needs goods; it is a symbiosis or exchange that benefits both parties. If unsatisfied with what is being offered, street-wise burglars may take their stolen property elsewhere, but the seller and the fence want this to happen without rancor so they can do business in the future. While the deal didn't work, the relationship is intact.

Sting operations are an effective means of combating fences, identifying active criminals, penetrating criminal organizations, and recovering property. In a typical sting, undercover officers set up a legitimate-appearing "front" business in which they slowly develop a reputation as being fences. All transactions are covertly digitally recorded and a great deal of intelligence is gathered that can be used in their current investigation or in collateral ones. Alternatively, officers may do business from a dilapidated warehouse that doesn't even have a name on it.

From a policy viewpoint, the police know the more the receiver markets can be disrupted or eliminated, the greater the likelihood there will be some reduction in burglary and other offenses, for example, shoplifting, whose profits depend on the availability of these illicit markets. Plainclothes officers quietly visit swap meets, flea markets, and other likely outlets, looking for known burglars or their associates offering merchandise for trade or sale. Such locations may be good candidates for the use of facial recognition software to identify sellers with criminal records who may be selling stolen goods. Plainclothes officers also examine merchandise for possible signs of being stolen, such as missing or newly attached serial numbers. Perhaps the leading software for tracking illegal transactions of property is LeadsOnline.

Once a potential fence is detected, officers work the case, investigating to confirm or exclude such an operation. If confirmed, officers attempt to broaden the case and arrest more than just the offenders in front of them. This often entails both physical and electronic surveillance to identify the places fences work, frequent, and their associates. An undercover officer may then be assigned to begin frequenting these places, covertly gathering additional information and/or attempting to develop a relationship with the fence and his/her associates (Figure 14-23). This method is also used when active burglars are targeted for arrest and surveillance is initiated. At some point, arrest and search warrants will be issued. When multiple locations and perpetrators are involved, simultaneous raids executing the warrants are conducted simultaneously to prevent offenders from slipping away.

Officers occasionally have to determine whether someone who bought what turned out to be stolen property did so in good or bad faith. A determination that it was in bad faith will

TABLE 14-4	Stolen Property Recovers by Retail Businesses[93]	
Recovery Source	2011	2016
A Physical Location	75%	63%
E-Fencing	28%	39%

◄ **FIGURE 14-23**
The police raided an inner-city fencing operation, which recovered a great deal of stolen property, some of which the police are shown inventorying. The goods were paid for with cash, drugs, and access to prostitutes. (Courtesy of the Savannah-Chatham Metropolitan Police Department)

often lead to being charges with possession of stolen property. Among the indicators of bad faith are:

1. Serial numbers are obliterated, missing, or clumsily attached to the merchandise;
2. Paying a price below that of a good bargain;
3. Buying from a person they don't know how to re-contact;
4. Accepting items without getting a bona fide receipt;
5. Buying items with unusual property control numbers on them, for example, indicating the owner is a state agency; and
6. Have a past history of receiving stolen property.

THE INVESTIGATOR'S ROLE IN BURGLARY PREVENTION

Before leaving the scene of a burglary, investigators should share some rudimentary precautions with victims to decrease the likelihood of their being "hit" again. Ideally, this would occur after investigators have gained the confidence of victims. The last contact with the victim before leaving the scene is often a good time for investigators to go over the precautions.

Some victims will adopt some to all of the precautions suggested, but others may not have the money needed to adopt any of them or don't want to spend it. Less frequently, victims will tell investigators "If the police had done their job, we wouldn't be having this conversation" or something similar. While the statement is directed at the police, victims may actually be annoyed at themselves for not being more proactive about protecting their property.

The "Residential Crime Prevention" section provides many free and moderate-cost precautions, some that are equally applicable to both home and business owners. There is a separate non-residential crime prevention portion of this chapter and some residential suggestions are repeated in it.

RESIDENTIAL CRIME PREVENTION

Products mentioned are not an endorsement, but simply an illustration. Consider different systems/products/capabilities to get the best match for your needs. These suggestions identified are not exhaustive. You must determine what may be helpful. Neither the publisher nor the authors assume any liability for any of the decisions you make regarding these suggestions.

1. When traveling, stop delivery of mail and newspapers, or arrange for a reliable family member, neighbor, or pet sitter to pick them up, as well as any packages left on the porch. Whoever handles these precautions should be shown a place to put them inside of the house that cannot be seen from the exterior of the home;
2. Arrange for a special watch on the premises by patrol officers when you are vacationing; let them know who has permission to be in your home while you are gone and what their relationship is to you. Many law enforcement agencies provide a free security analysis;
3. Use traditional timers to turn lights, radios, and televisions on/off/on at various times to make a home appear it is occupied. Automated lighting systems, for example, OSRAM ® have a smart hub that allows smartphone/pad/laptop users to schedule and modify lighting from nearly anywhere. Many automated lighting systems can also be remotely controlled through smart thermostats, including Ecobee 3 and Nest. Motion activated lights should be used to protect entry points preferred by burglars: the front door, first floor windows, and the rear of the house. Only 2% of burglaries have an entry point above the first floor.[94]

Ask the neighborhood watch association and neighbors to quickly call the police if there is any suspicious activity. report any suspicious activity. One example of a suspicious activity is when a car with three to four occupants is driving too slowly though your neighborhood looking/"rubber necking" a little too closely/long at homes, which may be a burglary crew looking for potential targets. Another example is someone who walks up to a front door, knocks, and when no one answers, walks to the rear of the house. A burglary crew sometimes sends their least imposing/threatening member, a woman, younger man, or juvenile to go house to house door knocking on residential doors/pressing the doorbells to determine where no one is at home. This practice is sometimes a prelude to what is called a "knock-knock" burglary;

4. Ask a trusted neighbor to come over occasionally while you are gone and change the position of drapes, blinds, the position of a car in the driveway, and other things;

5. Put a water bowl on your porch and post "Beware of Dog" signs even if you don't have one;

6. Exercise good key control. Don't make it easy for burglars to steal your vehicles. Install a key rack in a hidden location. Never leave a key outside in case you lose yours or for household workers to use. Do not put your name or your business's name on a set of keys. If lost, they may be returned to you, but a burglar could find them too;

7. If occasionally your car is parked in the driveway or on the street, always remove your garage door opener from it. Burglars steal the openers, raise the garage doors, lower them, select items to steal, open the garage doors again, and exit, being careful to lower the garage door. Relatedly, don't leave your garage door open unnecessarily, it's the functional equivalent of inviting burglars to have a preview of things you have. For the same reason, never put silverware sets and other valuables in plain view through a picture window;

Burglars don't want to be heard or seen. It makes them feel vulnerable. They will sometimes pass by good targets because of it. Trim your overgrown bushes so burglars can't stay out of sight while they break into your home and plant thorny bushes at potential points of entry for burglars. Don't let tree limbs grow to overhang second story windows and porches. It creates another means of attacking a home. A security system and a high resolution digital surveillance camera are strong deterrents; post signs that they are being used. Data suggests that homes without a security system are 2.7 times more likely to be targeted by a burglar.[95] A smart door lock may offer protection from knock-knock burglaries. Depending on the model, smart door lock features include sound and day/night motion detection across a 180 degree of sight, one-way video, two-way audio, and automatic/stored recording. Using their smart phones, users can see and talk to someone at their door as if they were home while they are actually on a beach.

Harden your physical security; use heavy duty deadbolt locks with at least 1' bolts, solid core doors, and high security locks and impact resistant glass on first-floor windows. As a minimum, place curtains in garage and basement windows. You can place grilles or grates on basement windows, but make sure that they can be opened from the inside in case of fire;

8. If snow is on the ground, back in and out of your driveway several times and back and forth from doors to traveled sidewalks so burglars can't tell if someone is home;

9. Don't leave notes on doors for family and friends saying "Be back at 1:30";

10. Don't leave tools in unsecured out-buildings and don't store ladders along the rear wall of the home;

11. Because you may be victimized, put identification numbers, marks, or symbols on items as may be appropriate. Record where they are on each item with a photograph. Take photographs of all valuables and include at least one additional image of them that has a ruler in it. Narrating a video for the same purpose is also a good measure. Safely store original receipts for valuable items and take photographs of them. Encrypt all photographs and store them on iCloud. These measures may help recover what is stolen and in the alternative, these records will make working with the insurance company much easier; and

12. Your home address number should be immediately visible to first responders.[96]

NON-RESIDENTIAL CRIME PREVENTION

1. Install bright exterior all night or motion detection lighting. Remove signs from windows that block inward views. Likewise, remove attractive merchandise from the window to avoid a small-scale smash and grab. Illuminate the inside areas visible from the street so patrolling officers can check the premises. Your safe should be in one of these visible areas for the same reason. Protect the exterior lighting with wire glass covers or other measures and routinely check bulbs and replace them quickly if they are not functioning. Depending on lighting from nearby businesses is not recommended.

2. Place shielded locks with a stainless steel body and at least a 9/32" inch thick case-hardened shackle on circuit breaker boxes that cannot be defeated with bolt-cutters or related means. Most padlocks are defeated by cutting the shackle. Combination locks are not a good substitute for a shielded padlock.

Strong locks don't make things burglar proof; they just make it harder. Layers of security measures will discourage many burglars. If burglars are making too much noise trying to gain entry they are likely to leave because of the risk of being detected. However, when attacking a feed store in an isolated area, noise may not be as much of a factor. Install a good quality alarm system which has one or more of the following components: magnetic contacts on windows and doors; photocell or pressure sensors with annunciators at unlocked windows and doors, heat or motion detectors in the interior, glass break detectors, keypads with the capability to check status of the system, and audible alarms. Many burglars think if you cut the telephone land line that sends the alarm signal to a security monitoring center, it makes the alarm system inoperable. Modern alarm systems commonly use cell lines for this purpose. Moreover, alarms that rely on land lines often have been enabled to automatically send a breach signal if the line is cut. A wireless alarm system should be explored before making a purchasing decision.

3. Install and protect the usefulness of high resolution digital surveillance cameras by siting them so they will be tamper-resistant. Cover the parking lot, entry points, and key places inside. The resolution should be high enough to establish individual identities. Consider analytic software on the security system that can provide an alert when suspicious activity occurs, for example, Viseum Intelligent Video Analytics. Post conspicuous signs at multiple places about using an alarm system and surveillance cameras. Dummy cameras are not a good alternative because criminals visiting your business on a reconnaissance may be able to recognize them as such and actually be encouraged to break in.

4. Along with using a digital surveillance camera, post signs requesting customers to remove hoodies, hats, and sunglasses when entering your business can be a robbery deterrent. It puts offenders on a robbery or burglary reconnaissance on notice that you take security seriously;

5. Consider buying equipment that is Underwriters Laboratory (UL) certified. All systems should be monitored. Make sure the monitoring center has backup power. The cost of acquiring and installing alarms and surveillance cameras should be partially offset by insurance reduction costs.

6. Key/card control is essential. Maintain a key/card control register so you know whose keys can open what areas. Mark all keys "Do Not Duplicate." Re-key locks every time people leave your employment even if their keys/cards are returned. Keep extra office keys/cards in anchored, burglary-resistant steel key cabinets with high quality locks. Business vehicle keys should be treated in the same manner. Lock vehicle keys up at the end of work days.

7. Before closing for the day, empty the cash register and make sure all valuables are secured under lock and key. Make a note of the serial numbers of large bills taken in after last daily bank deposit or armored car pickup.

8. Keep inventories as low as practical by implementing a "just-in-time" purchasing program.

9. Use metal doors or solid wood doors at least 1¾" thick. Consider reinforcing wooden doors with 16-gauge sheet metal. Door hinges should be on the inside or have non-removable pins.

10. Use double-cylinder deadbolt locks on all outside doors and those that lead to/from storage, garage, or similar places. Consider door edge guards installed with screws 3" to 4" long, and latch guards.

11. In addition to a double cylinder lock in the middle, French doors should also be secured with top and bottom flush bolts with at least a 1" throw.

12. Your address should be on the exterior of the business in numbers at least 12" high and lighted at night.

13. Form an informal mutual aid compact or, more formally, start a Business Watch Program with nearby business to watch for suspicious activity.

14. Exterior "roll-up" doors should be made of steel and secured from the inside by locking cane bolts.

15. Replace louvre windows with laminated glass to achieve a high level of security. Secure sliding glass windows by the same means used to secure sliding glass doors.

16. Determine if roll-down interior shutters are cost-effective for your business. They are noisy and it takes time to defeat them.

17. Target harden small ground level windows with laminate glass or bars.

18. Ensure air conditioners cannot be easily removed: it provides an entry point and they may also be stolen.

19. Use chain link fencing to protect your exterior work and employee parking area to allow visibility of your premises. The fence bottoms should be embedded in concrete or by another means to prevent people from being able to enter under them. Shielded padlocks should secure gates and fences.

20. Make sure the safe is closed at the end of business transactions and keep cash on hand to a minimum. Several employees should be authorized and trained to make bank deposits. The people used and the times deposits are made should not establish any time, route, car used, or other pattern. If deposits are made during banking hours and there are suspicious people around, the employee should call 911, if warranted, and return to the business. After hours use of a depository follows these same rules. Consider the use of an armored car service to make deposits. If used, always have the pickup ready.

21. Consider parking company cars or equipment in front of garage and other doors to thwart break-ins.

22. Train employees on your security precautions and protocols. In large cities, guard dog services are available on an hourly or other basis. Dogs are often deployed in pairs. They are dropped off after all employees have left the premises and picked up before the business opens the next day. They are effective in patrolling open, fenced business areas, large line-of-sight buildings, for example, warehouses, construction sites, where threats have been made, and similar situations.

23. Because you may be victimized, put identification numbers or marks on equipment that lacks them. Record where they are on each item with a photograph. Take complete photographs of all equipment. Also, narrating a video for the same purpose is a good measure. Safely

store original receipts for equipment and take photo-graphs of them. Encrypt all photographs and store them on iCloud. These measures may help recover what is stolen and in the alternative, these records will make working with the insurance company easier.

24. Consider private security patrols to supplement police patrolling. These patrols should have access to areas in which guard dogs are used.

25. Trim your overgrown bushes so burglars can't stay out of sight while they try to break into your business and plant thick, thorny bushes at potential points of entry for burglars.

26. Don't leave tools in unsecured vehicles or out-buildings. Lock ladders onto company trucks. Never leave ladders unsecured in the employee parking lot.[97]

KEY TERMS

B3M	Instant Street View	snap gun
bumping	interpersonal burglaries	social networking sites
burglar tools	key bumping	soft targets
disorganized burglaries	loiding	sting operation
drones	opportunistic burglaries	surreptitious entry
dual safes	organized burglaries	traditional amateur burglar
e-selling	repeat victimization	traditional professional burglar
hawking	Residential Security Container (RSC)	taxonomy
hot prowl	serial burglar	typology

REVIEW QUESTIONS

1. What are the most striking aspects of burglary?
2. There are two ways to think about "serial burglars." What are they?
3. When enforcing burglary tool laws, "intent" and "posses-sion" are key concepts. What are they and why are they key?
4. What are the top two motivators for committing burglary?
5. Why do burglars, compared to non-burglars, find more things to steal?
6. Burglary statutes vary in the sanctions applied based on the fact situation, e.g., a burglary committed while armed will result in a longer sentence. What are four other fact situations that will result in longer sentences?
7. Assume a lone burglar is inside of an unoccupied home. Of what value is "cognitive roadmap?" to him/her?

8. What are three methods burglars use to gather informa-tion about their targets?
9. What do burglars perceive as the least and most effective deterrents?
10. How quickly do offenders complete a home burglary?
11. Many residential burglars don't carry tools. Why?
12. Why do burglars think of the "jackpot" room in residen-tial burglary as the master bedroom?
13. What is the "carry off?"
14. You are investigating a residential burglar where a home safe has been compromised. If it has a UL Class 350-1 safe, label, what does that tell you?
15. An RSC rating approximates what TL rating?
16. Why are roof top burglaries associated with larger losses?

INTERNET ACTIVITIES

1. Name five law enforcement agencies that don't respond immediately to burglary security alarms.
2. The most famous burglary in American history had one name: Watergate. What was that about and what was the ultimate result?

3. In 1980, our national burglary rate was 1,684 per 100,000 people. By 2015, that rate dropped to 491. Why?

Design Element: (crime scene tape) ©UpperCut Images/Getty Images RF

◄ **Theft from retail merchant.** This teenage shoplifter takes one last look around before concealing merchandise in her backpack.

(©Steven Puetzer/Getty Images)

CRIME SCENE DO NOT CROSS

15

LARCENY/THEFT AND WHITE-COLLAR CRIME

CHAPTER OBJECTIVES

1. Distinguish between tangible and intangible property.
2. Understand the difference between petit/petty larceny and grand larceny.
3. Define, from two different perspectives, white-collar crime.
4. Discuss the most common deterrents to organized retail crime.
5. Identify the five basic categories of shoplifting.
6. List the tips for employees to follow to deter shoplifting.
7. Discuss the typical motives of bicycle thieves.
8. List different types of frauds, scams, and cons.
9. Define and describe methods of money laundering.
10. Describe security and investment frauds.
11. Identify and summarize telephone scams.
12. Outline common telemarketing and postal frauds.

This chapter deals with two groups of crimes: larceny/theft and white-collar crime. The traditional definition of larceny/theft is the unlawful taking and carrying away of the tangible personal property of another with the intent to permanently deprive that person of his interest in the property. **Tangible personal property** means things that have both a physical existence that can be touched and intrinsic value—such as jewelry, lawn mowers, cameras, laptop computers, televisions, furniture and clothing, and collectibles such as old rare coins.

In contrast, **intangible property** has value, but it is more abstract—such as stocks, bonds, checking and saving accounts, and other types of financial instruments, as well as patents and copyrights. State statutes have historically addressed the theft of intangibles through specific statutes, which supplemented the existing larceny statutes.

Larceny essentially incorporates the elements of the crime of robbery, except the element of the use of force, threat, or fear is not included (see Chapter 13, "Robbery"). Additionally, although robbery is a face-to-face crime, the law does not require that the victim of a larceny be present at the time of a crime. However, the victim may be present as illustrated by purse snatching, pickpocketing, and an owner driving home from work in time to see a stranger pick up his daughter's bicycle from the lawn of his home, toss it in the back of a SUV, and drive away.

Larceny/theft is often divided into **grand larceny** and **petit or petty larceny**; because states establish their own laws, they vary from one state to another. Some state statutes establish a single dollar figure to distinguish between a misdemeanor (often called petit larceny) and a felony (often referred to as grand larceny). For example, in Virginia, it's a misdemeanor if the value of the property illegally taken is less than $200 whereas above $200 a felony has been committed. Other states have several levels of larceny offenses. In Texas those levels are:

"Class C" misdemeanor: $50 or less

"Class B" misdemeanor: $50 or more, but less than $500

"Class A" misdemeanor: $500 or more, but less than $1,500

State jail felony: $1,500 or more, but less than $20,000

Third degree felony: $20,000 or more, but less than $100,000

Second degree felony: $100,000 or more, but less than $200,000

First-degree felony: $200,000 or more.

Many states have also enacted specifically titled larceny/theft statutes that reflect special aspects of their economy, such as "timber theft or fraud," or special problems, for example, "transit fare evasion, identity theft" or "organized retail theft" to distinguish between prosecutions that are aimed at rings of professional shoplifters causing significant losses and that have more serious penalties versus those directed at the teenager who "lifts or boosts" a CD, tube of lipstick, or shirt and is charged with "theft from retail merchants," a lesser **shoplifting** offense.

The term *white-collar crime* was coined in 1939 by sociologist E. H. Sutherland. His white-collar criminals were characterized by respectability and higher social status, which they used to commit more complex offenses such as **fraud** and **embezzlement,** as opposed to street crimes. Now, almost 70 years later, the U.S. Department of Justice defines **white-collar crime** as nonviolent, illegal activities that rely on deceit, deception, concealment, manipulation, breach of trust, subterfuge, or illegal circumvention. Note that Sutherland's definition was based on the characteristics of the offender versus the present orientation of white-collar crime being the characteristics of the actions taken by the offender.[1] There is no set of laws titled "white-collar crime." It is a construct, useful for how we think about such crimes, but offenders are often charged with larceny/theft crimes, such as theft by fraud. Many of these crimes are investigated and prosecuted at the federal level. For instance, the FBI investigates theft crimes that involve the transportation of stolen property across state lines, the U.S. Postal Inspectors investigate mail and wire fraud, and the U.S. Secret Service investigates fraudulent credit cards and checks drawn upon payment and financial systems of the United States. In addition, the Secret Service is charged with the enforcement of counterfeiting and fraud statutes aimed at preserving the integrity of United States currency, coin, and financial obligations.

ELEMENTS OF THE CRIME OF LARCENY

Although the traditional definition of larceny is still operative in some states, others have eliminated the distinction between the theft of tangibles and intangibles and created more comprehensive larceny/theft statutes to cover both types of losses. Such statutes drop the former "tangible personal property of another"

and use "property of another," to cover the loss of a wide range of things, such as stocks and bonds, services—such as electricity, natural gas, television cable, high-speed Internet access, tickets to the symphony and sporting events, lawn mowers, paintings, hotel rooms and rental cars, computer software and information files, cash and jewelry. To illustrate, in some states the failure to return a rental car within 72 hours of the agreed-on time in the lease is evidence of intent to commit larceny/theft.

The person from whom the property is taken in a larceny/theft need not own it and may simply be the custodian of it. Although he/she is the victim of the crime for reporting purposes, if the property is recovered it is returned to the owner. If there is no recovery, the owner receives the fair market value from his/her insurance company, assuming that the property was insured.

The broader larceny/theft laws recognize that the taking may be accomplished in a variety of ways, such as:

1. **theft by trick,** such as con games and swindles;
2. theft by receiving stolen property, meaning knowingly receiving and disposing of property he/she should have known or knew was stolen;
3. **theft by deception,** for example, the removal of a price sticker from one item for sale and replacing it with a less expensive sticker;[2]
4. **theft by fraud,** illustrated by the unauthorized use of another's credit card, using someone else's medical insurance card or Social Security number to get benefits, and "pump and dump" stock schemes, whereby a stock is heavily promoted—after the stock runs up in price, its promoters dump it;
5. **theft of services,** covering such things as "skipping out" on hotel, restaurant, and bar bills, or illegally connecting or reconnecting an electrical meter.

In states with comprehensive larceny/theft laws, the crime of embezzlement has often disappeared, because the language of the larceny/theft law usually provides a means to bring charges for that conduct, often by a crime titled **theft by conversion.** Where it remains, the elements of embezzlement are the same as the traditional larceny charge, with the addition that a person who has been entrusted with something valuable converts it to their own purpose or use in contravention of his/her legal obligation.

SHOPLIFTING

The national scope of the problem of shoplifting does not normally get the same level of attention in the media as more serious crimes. But it is nevertheless a very costly crime.

QUICK FACT

The Economic Impact of Shoplifting

In 2017 the FBI Uniform Crime Reports indicate there were 1,038, 574 shoplifting cases reported with an average value of $250 for each crime. Thus, the total exceeds $255 million per year.

There are many different categories of shoplifting with each requiring different investigative and prevention strategies which will now be discussed.

ORGANIZED RETAIL CRIME

Organized retail crime (ORC) refers to the problem of significant losses to retailers caused by crews or rings of often mobile professional shoplifters. ORC has emerged as a broader term and includes not only professional shoplifters but also other associated problems such as thefts from merchandise distribution centers, truck hijacking, credit card fraud, counterfeit goods, and the fences and other outlets for stolen merchandise.

DETERRENTS TO ORGANIZED RETAIL CRIME

Establishing early warning systems. Merchants in some areas have found it useful to establish a same-day early warning system whereby they notify one another about the presence of mobile gangs of organized shoplifters, but there have been no formal evaluations of this practice. Although local police are mainly alerted to organized shoplifting incidents through retail investigations, they can also identify suspicious activities, for example, by the discovery of large quantities of retail merchandise during routine calls or traffic stops.[3]

Forming task forces with other law enforcement agencies. Organized-theft groups rarely operate within one jurisdiction, and it is important that local police forge partnerships with state and federal law enforcement agencies. Several such partnerships have proven effective in dismantling some of the largest professional shoplifting groups in the country. Operation Greenquest established by the U.S. Customs Service targeted thieves who financed Al Qaeda and other terrorist groups.[4] Operation Blackbird, mounted by a task force comprising investigators from local, state, and federal agencies formed by the Pasadena (California) Police Department, uncovered some large organized crime shoplifting operations.[5]

Forming partnerships and working with retailers and manufacturers. Many partnerships have been established among law enforcement agencies, retailers, retail associations, and manufacturers. Successful partnerships of these kinds with local stores have been undertaken by the police in Charlotte-Mecklenburg, North Carolina;[6] Mesa, Arizona; Colorado Springs, Colorado;[7] Portsmouth, England;[8] and Boise, Idaho.[9] In Boise, for example, a growing organized shoplifting problem was addressed by the establishment of the Organized Crime Interdiction Team. This took a number of preventive initiatives that included updating stakeholders on recent trends through

regular monthly meetings, using email and text messaging to maintain an efficient intelligence flow between retailers and police, and responding immediately to in-progress incidents. These actions quickly led to a significant reduction in organized shoplifting incidents.

Notable partnerships that encompass wider areas and a larger number of entries include the following:

- The Law Enforcement Retail Partnership Network (LERPnet) was established in 2007 by the National Retail Federation in partnership with the FBI, the Food Marketing Institute, and the Retail Industry Leaders Association. LERPnet is a web-based repository that allows retailers to share information with each other and with police about shoplifting incidents.[10]
- The ORC Pilot Program was launched by U.S. Immigration and Customs Enforcement in four cities with known organized retail crime activity: Houston, Los Angeles, Miami, and New York City. The program developed a database with retail industry contacts and a threat assessment to help determine the extent of organized retail crime. It also explored how organized shoplifting groups exploit vulnerabilities in the banking system to launder profits. The pilot program resulted in multiple arrests and convictions, leading to the seizure of nearly $4.9 million in cash, property, and money instruments. It has now been expanded into an ongoing national initiative known as SEARCH (Seizing Earnings and Assets from Retail Crime Heists).
- Several years ago eBay launched the PROACT (Partnership with Retailers Offensively to Attack Crime and Theft) program aimed to combat stolen goods sales on its web site. Based on information received from regulatory and law enforcement agencies, the site created filters to search for prohibited goods for auction. eBay also cooperated with police in monitoring and reporting suspicious activity on its web site. Other web sites that are also potential outlets for stolen merchandise, such as Amazon.com, Overstock.com, and Craigslist, might usefully be drawn into such partnerships.[11]

Monitoring stores' goods suppliers. Retailers might individually buy goods that have been stolen by organized shoplifters unless they carefully monitor their suppliers.[12] Some store buyers might also be bribed by these suppliers to buy stolen goods. To reduce these risks, the retailer's loss prevention team can conduct unannounced visits to the suppliers' warehouse(s) to look for clues suggesting that the goods may be illegitimate. These include the products' condition and the overall warehouse condition, as well as the presence of:

- cleaning stations and chemicals
- security tags and labels on the floors or in the trash cans
- repackaging stations.

Talking to other retailers who obtain their goods from the same suppliers might also prove useful. In addition, buyers should be trained to identify and report possible suspicious transactions and they should be encouraged to report to police when a deal is "too good to be true."

Using social networking sites to gather information about shoplifting incidents. A recent survey of retailers found that about 70% of them use Facebook, Twitter, LinkedIn, Craigslist, Myspace, Google, Foursquare, Pipl, Carnivore Lite, YouTube, and Flickr to gather information about shoplifting from their stores. Using these networking sites they identify perpetrators, investigate connections between perpetrators and company employees, and identify premises where the stolen goods may be stored or sold. Retailers report "huge success" using Facebook to gather intelligence about past events and planned activities.[13] When "view only" is selected, no direct contact is made with the subjects, thereby allowing the investigators to gather information without their knowledge. Police, therefore, can use these social networking sites to gather similar information.

FACTORS CONTRIBUTING TO SHOPLIFTING

Understanding the factors that contribute to the problem of shoplifting will help frame the local analysis questions, determine good measures of effectiveness, recognize key points of intervention, and select an appropriate set of responses. Many of the following factors contribute to a heightened risk of shoplifting.[14]

GOODS SOLD

One of the main factors determining a store's shoplifting rate is the type of goods sold. For obvious reasons, furniture stores have much lower shoplifting rates than, say, convenience or drug stores. Numerous surveys have shown that the most common items stolen from retail stores in the United States include tobacco products (particularly cigarettes), health and related products such as over-the-counter analgesics and decongestants,[15] birth control products such as condoms, recorded music and videos, and apparel ranging from athletic shoes to children's clothing, with an emphasis on designer labels. One item that is especially popular among professional shoplifters at present is infant formula, presumably because it is expensive and easily sold.

Some items might be constantly stolen, while thefts of others may reflect the popularity of new product releases, such as movies, video games, and music titles. Also, the popularity for theft can be highly brand-dependent, so that, for example, only certain brands are stolen of razor blades, cigarettes, designer clothes or even, according to recent media reports, laundry detergent.[16]

The acronym CRAVED captures the essential attributes of these "hot products" which are Concealable, Removable, Available, Valuable, Enjoyable, and Disposable.[17, 18] The last of these attributes—disposability—may be the most important in determining the volume of goods shoplifted. Those shoplifting for profit must be able to sell or barter what they steal.

The most vulnerable parts of the store to shoplifting are those that carry hot products. One study in a large store found that the highest theft rates were in the sections carrying rock and pop recordings (nowadays, it would probably be rap or hip-hop). Equally expensive recordings in the classical music department were rarely stolen.[19]

DEMOGRAPHICS AND SEASONAL VARIATIONS FOR SHOPLIFTING

Slightly more men (55%) than women (45%) shoplift, although women take higher-value items, and juveniles account for roughly 33% of all cases.[20] Shoplifting is most likely to occur on Saturdays (18%) and Fridays (15%), and 60% of all cases occur between noon and 6:00 P.M.[21] There are also seasonal variations in shoplifting, with spikes in activity just before students go back to school in August, before Christmas, Easter, and when schools are letting out for the summer.

CATEGORIES OF SHOPLIFTERS

Shoplifters fall into five basic categories. These include:

- **Professionals:** This group represents a rather small percentage of shoplifters, but they proportionately can account for significant losses. Due to the fact that they operate in a very smooth manner, they are the most difficult to detect. Professionals usually steal merchandise in order to return it for cash, or sell to a "fence."
- **Amateurs:** This group represents the majority of shoplifters. Typically, they are more opportunistic in nature, not as skilled as professionals, and generally nervous and self-conscious.
- **Drug Users/Addicts:** This group steals to fund their drug habit. They will either resell the stolen merchandise to a fence, or attempt a cash refund. Their methods are crude and usually not well planned. They can become frantic, or even violent, when apprehended.
- **Kleptomaniac:** Very few shoplifters fall into this category. This type of individual has a psychological compulsion to steal. They will commit a theft whenever the urge hits. Normally they are nervous and shy.
- **Vagrant:** These individuals generally take food items, alcoholic beverages, or clothing needed for personal use. A vagrant often steals to exist and may be under the influence of alcohol.

METHODS USED BY SHOPLIFTERS

Following are some of the more common methods used by shoplifters to steal merchandise.

- **Palming:** This method consists of simply concealing the item in the palm of the hand and later hiding the item.
- **Booster Devices:** This can include a variety of devices. A booster coat will have large pockets sewn inside, as will booster pants or skirts. They are generally large and baggy to conceal the hidden merchandise. Booster boxes may appear as a gift wrapped box but with a hinged, false door on the bottom.
- **Wearing Items Out:** A customer will try on clothing in a dressing room, taking several items with him/her. Once in the dressing room they will layer the stolen clothing under their regular clothing or roll the items up and secret them between their legs, a method known as "Crotching."
- **Shields:** Involving multiple participants, one or more will shield or block the thief from view. The thief will then pocket or crotch the items. A variation of this method is to use a distraction to divert store employees from the thief.
- **Buggy/Stroller:** The shoplifter may come into the store pushing a buggy or stroller and attempt to conceal stolen merchandise in the stroller. When confronted, if there is a child in the buggy old enough to have reached out and grabbed the merchandise, the person may blame the child for having put the item in the stroller. Under these circumstances there may be insufficient information to make an arrest but at least the merchandise will be recovered.

TIPS FOR EMPLOYEES TO DETER SHOPLIFTING

- Acknowledge customers as they enter the store or department. Fast efficient services will deter most shoplifters. Shoplifters want minimum contact with sales help, thus a friendly, helpful, observant salesclerk is a good deterrence to theft.
- Know the sales area. A knowledgeable salesclerk is in a much better position to spot items that have been moved or are missing.
- Watch the nervous customer who does not want assistance.
- Be careful of persons walking with merchandise in hand. Ask them "May I help you? Would you like me to put that by the register until you are ready?"
- Watch the customer's hands.
- Keep an eye peeled for unauthorized people in the stock room or shipping and receiving area. They may be looking for items to steal, or they may be purposely there to distract you while their partner hits the sales floor.

- Watch customers with open packages, shopping bags, oversized handbags and purses.
- Place expensive items in locked cases.
- Never put out more than one expensive item at a time on a counter top (especially jewelry) for a customer to look at. If they should decide to grab the merchandise and run from the store at least the theft will be limited to that single item.[22]

SHOPLIFTING RISK FACTORS RELATED TO SPECIFIC LOCATIONS

Research does not provide a clear indication of the risk factors related to a store's location but shoplifting rates tend to be higher for stores with the following features:

- In city centers and other busy places, with a large number of casual customers
- Fronting on the open street
- Close to highways that provide easy escape routes
- Near schools, with many juvenile customers
- In economically deprived areas, with large concentrations of impoverished or addicted residents

RETAIL POLICIES, STAFFING, AND STOCK CONTROL

Retail policies, staffing, and stock control are store management's responsibility, but these are heavily influenced by how competitive, profit-driven, and technology-dependent is the broader retail environment. For example, stock control is usually deficient because the effort needed to keep proper track of stock has rarely been justified by any reductions in theft and other forms of shrinkage. Similarly, it would be impossibly expensive for stores to abandon self-service and rely instead on armies of helpful, attentive sales clerks, even though this would substantially reduce shoplifting.[23] The savings in reduced theft would be greatly outweighed by increased staff wages and, possibly, by sales lost as a result of shoppers being unable to inspect goods at their leisure. Such marketing considerations might also limit the scope for tightening up return policies, which, if too liberal, can encourage theft of goods to be returned for cash refunds. For example, some clothing stores do not have changing rooms because the staff costs of monitoring them to prevent shoplifting may be too great. These stores have to allow the return of clothes that do not fit.

However, increased competition is continually eroding retail profit margins, and thus the incentive to reduce shrinkage is increasing. At the same time, the sales environment is constantly changing in the search for increased profits. One current example is the increasing use of self-scan checkouts that reduce staff costs and perceived wait times for customers. However, self-scan presents new opportunities for shoplifting, despite security features that include cameras to monitor the transactions, and software systems to detect irregularities.[24] Theft methods include scanning one item and including more of the same items without paying for them, using wrong item codes that are cheaper and putting unchecked items in strollers. With increasing use of self-scan, stores might find ways of closing these security loopholes.

STORE LAYOUT AND DISPLAYS

Research provides little guidance, but common sense suggests certain store layout and display features contribute to shoplifting.[25] Most of these relate to the staff's ability to supervise shoppers, and stores at greater risk include large ones which make it easier for organized groups to hide among ordinary shoppers. Also vulnerable are stores with the following features:

- Many exits, particularly where they are accessible without passing through the checkout
- Passageways, blind corners, and hidden alcoves
- Restrooms or changing rooms
- High displays that conceal shoppers (and shoplifters) from view
- Crowded areas around displays of high-risk items
- Aisles that staff cannot easily survey from one end

Goods on the ground floor especially near entrances are at greater risk because this is often where the newest products are displayed, because these areas receive least employee attention, and because shoplifters can dart in and out quickly. Other risk factors include the store's security measures, such as closed-circuit television (CCTV) surveillance, security tagging, access control, employees' location, mirrors, and how well the hot products are secured.[26]

STOLEN GOODS AND THE INTERNET

It was calculated in one study that approximately 18% of all stolen goods were sold on the Internet.[27,28] In some cases, goods are stolen from stores by organized theft groups.[29] The profit on e-fence merchandise (approximately 70% of retail) is much higher than merchandise sold through a traditional fence.[30]

TIPS FOR THEFT PREVENTION INVESTIGATORS

Retail establishments can also combat shoplifting by a combination of prevention strategies, such as:

- posting signs about prosecuting shoplifters
- placing expensive items in locked cases
- putting on display only one of a pair of items
- keeping aisles uncluttered to facilitate observation
- having roving employees and uniformed security officers

In recent years, "clamshell blisters" have gained popularity. This type of packaging seals a product in a clear plastic container, which allows 360-degree visibility of the product and is difficult to open. Retailers also use a strategy of apprehension that involves the use of observable, real surveillance cameras, "spy cameras" (for example, inside of clocks, smoke detector sprinklers, and heads of mannequins), observation ports, and the use of store security to work the floor. *Source tagging* is used widely—merchants place a small insert between the pages of a book or in a package of tools; the tag emits a narrow-band radio frequency that triggers an alarm if the item has not been scanned.

Investigators working a shoplift detail should be alert for customers in a retail establishment who:

- avoid contact with sales personnel;
- pick up a small item and wander about the store until they have the opportunity to palm it or conceal it on their person;
- "have their heads on swivels" to assess their opportunity to steal;
- wear baggy clothing or coats in weather not requiring it;
- distract sales personnel or serve as shields so their partner can take and conceal items;
- make repeated trips to the fitting rooms, sometimes to wear store merchandise out under the clothes they wear;
- carry large handbags or push strollers in which items can quickly be concealed.

LOCAL POLICE RESPONDING TO SHOPLIFTING ARRESTS

The typical scenario which brings the police into contact with a shoplifter occurs when a business calls the police department to report that they have arrested someone in their store for shoplifting and are willing to press charges. Some agencies have imposed pre-conditions on when they will and will not respond to such calls. For example, in order to eliminate any ambiguity on the part of the police or merchants the Dallas, Texas Police Department has formulated instructions for shoplifting case filing.

BICYCLE THEFT

Bicycle thefts are often not reported to the police. This is largely due to the victim's belief that the police are not interested in bicycle theft and will therefore do little or nothing to catch the offender and return their stolen bicycle.[31,32]

A further reason for an underrepresentation of this type of theft is that police departments record bicycle thefts in different ways, thus inadvertently concealing the full scope of the problem. For example, police may record a bicycle theft as a burglary if it occurs in conjunction with a residential property.

CLEARANCE RATES FOR BICYCLE THEFT

Clearance rates for bicycle theft remain consistently low. In the United States, 23% of incidents of larceny-theft were cleared by arrest,[33] but this figure (which includes all categories of larceny) is likely to be a gross overestimate of the arrest rate for bicycle theft. One reason for this is that there typically exists little relationship between the victim and the offender, and hence it is difficult to identify suspects.[34] Bicycle theft is also largely a crime of opportunity and stealth and one which often goes unnoticed or unchallenged.[35] A further problem is proof of ownership. Even when crimes are reported to and recorded by the police, the majority of bicycle owners cannot supply sufficient details to assist in an investigation. As a consequence, even when an offender is detained for bicycle theft, if the owner cannot provide proof of ownership for the retrieved cycle, the suspect may be released without being charged and may even be given the stolen bike upon release. Addressing the proof-of-ownership problem is important to alleviate storage costs for recovered bikes and improve the process of bicycle identification, recovery, and reunification with legitimate owners.

QUICK FACT

Typical Motives of Bicycle Thieves

The typical motivations for bicycle thefts can be categorized as follows:[36]

- To joyride—those who steal any type of bicycle for transportation and/or enjoyment. These offenders generally abandon the stolen bicycle after use. Younger offenders (16 and under) typically fit this group.[37]
- To trade for cash—those who exploit easy opportunities to steal any type of bicycle and trade it for cash or goods (such as drugs).
- To fill a request—those who steal specific types of expensive bicycles to order.

TECHNIQUES EMPLOYED BY PERPETRATORS TO STEAL BICYCLES

Offenders use a number of techniques to steal bicycles. The technique an offender uses will often be directly linked to the cyclist's locking practices (i.e., the type of lock the cyclist uses and the way he or she applies it). When the bike is unlocked or poorly secured, little skill is required. Some common perpetrator techniques used to steal locked bikes include the following.

Lifting. Thieves lift the bike and lock over the top of the post to which the bike is secured. If it is a signpost, then the thieves may remove the sign to lift the bicycle clear. Sometimes the post itself is not anchored securely and can be lifted clear of the bike and lock (Figure 15-1).

Levering. Thieves will use the gap between the stand and the bike left by a loosely fitted lock to insert tools such as jacks or bars to lever the lock apart. Thieves will even use the bike frame itself as a lever by rotating it against the stand or other stationary object to which is it locked. Either the bike or the lock will break. The thief does not mind because—after all, it's not his or her bike! (Figure 15-2).

Striking. If a cyclist locks a bicycle leaving the chain or lock touching the ground, thieves may use a hammer and chisel to split the securing chain or lock (Figure 15-3).

Unbolting. Thieves know how to undo bolts and quick-release mechanisms. If a cyclist locks a bike by the wheel alone, then it may be all that is left when the cyclist returns. If a cyclist locks only the frame, then the thief may remove the wheel or wheels. In this case, if a cyclist leaves a wheel-less bike with the intent of picking it up later, then the thief may return before the cyclist returns and remove the rest of the bike (Figure 15-4).

▶ **FIGURE 15-1 Lifting technique**
Source: Shane D. Johnson, Aiden Sidebottom, and Adam Thorpe, "Bicycle Theft," *Problem-Oriented Guides for Police Problem-Specific Guides Series,* No. 52, U.S. Department of Justice, Office of Community Oriented Policing Services, June 2008, p. 11.

▶ **FIGURE 15-2 Levering technique**
Source: Shane D. Johnson, Aiden Sidebottom, and Adam Thorpe, "Bicycle Theft," *Problem-Oriented Guides for Police Problem-Specific Guides Series,* No. 52, U.S. Department of Justice, Office of Community Oriented Policing Services, June 2008, p. 11.

▶ **FIGURE 15-3 Striking technique**
Source: Shane D. Johnson, Aiden Sidebottom, and Adam Thorpe, "Bicycle Theft," *Problem-Oriented Guides for Police Problem-Specific Guides Series,* No. 52, U.S. Department of Justice, Office of Community Oriented Policing Services, June 2008, p. 11.

▶ **FIGURE 15-4 Unbolting technique**
Source: Shane D. Johnson, Aiden Sidebottom, and Adam Thorpe, "Bicycle Theft," *Problem-Oriented Guides for Police Problem-Specific Guides Series,* No. 52, U.S. Department of Justice, Office of Community Oriented Policing Services, June 2008, p. 11.

► **FIGURE 15-5 Cutting technique**
Source: Shane D. Johnson, Aiden Sidebottom, and Adam Thorpe, "Bicycle Theft," *Problem-Oriented Guides for Police Problem-Specific Guides Series,* No. 52, U.S. Department of Justice, Office of Community Oriented Policing Services, June 2008, p. 11.

► **FIGURE 15-6 Picking technique**
Source: Shane D. Johnson, Aiden Sidebottom, and Adam Thorpe, "Bicycle Theft," *Problem-Oriented Guides for Police Problem-Specific Guides Series,* No. 52, U.S. Department of Justice, Office of Community Oriented Policing Services, June 2008, p. 11.

Cutting. Thieves are known to use tin snips, bolt cutters, hacksaws, and angle grinders to cut their way through the locks and chains to steal bicycles (Figure 15-5).

Picking. For locks requiring keys, thieves can insert tools into the keyhole itself and pick the lock open (Figure 15-6).

A consistent finding is that most stolen bicycles, regardless of theft location, are either not locked at all or are secured using a lock that requires little force to break or remove.

ASKING THE RIGHT QUESTIONS

The following are some critical questions that law enforcement agencies should be asking when analyzing a community's bicycle theft problem, even if the answers are not always readily available. The answers to these other questions will help define the local problem and choose the most appropriate responses to either prevent the theft of bicycles or facilitate the recovery of bicycles and apprehension of the perpetrator.

Questions Related to the Theft Pattern of Bicycles

- Are bicycle theft data recorded in a way that aids analysis of the local problem?
- What was the type and quality of lock being used when the theft occurred?
- Have bicycles been locked when stolen? If so, how?
- Do locking practice vary by location (e.g., at home and public spaces)?
- To what objects were bicycles locked when stolen?
- When bicycles are stolen from residential locations are they secured to anything?
- What happens to bicycles once they are stolen? Are they sold illegally? If so, who is buying them? Are they stripped for parts? Are they abandoned?
- What perpetrator techniques are common? Do they differ across locations?
- What current preventive measures seem to be most effective or for that matter least effective?
- How soon are recovered bicycles found?

- How damaged are recovered bicycles?
- How concerned is the local community about stolen bicycles?
- What types of bicycles are thieves stealing?[38]

LOCATIONS AND TIMES OF BICYCLE THEFTS

Questions Relating to Locations and Times of Bicycle Thefts

- Where do most of the local bicycle thefts occur? At victims' homes? Workplaces? Certain streets? On-street versus off-street parking? Risky facilities? General hot spots (such as downtown areas)?
- When hot spots are identified, why are these locations at high risk of bicycle theft? For example, is it the lack of secure parking, high levels of flyparking, a lack of capable guardians informed and empowered to act?
- Which areas are particularly risky? For example, if on a university campus, is it at the gym, library, dormitories, or particular classroom buildings?
- What types of houses or apartment buildings do thieves target for bicycle theft? Large or small apartment buildings? (Visual surveys of victimized houses and apartments will help answer these and other questions.)
- Do theft rates vary across cycle-parking facilities? If so, how, and what factors might contribute?
- Which groups are the principal users of the facilities? For example, workers, shoppers, young people, or students?
- Is the lack of natural surveillance (guardianship) a factor?
- Where are recovered bicycles found?
- When do bicycle thefts mainly occur (time of day, day of week, month)?
- Are there local seasonal variations of bicycle thefts?

BICYCLE THEFT OFFENDERS

Questions Related to the Bicycle Theft Offenders

- What kinds of offenders are involved? For example, joyriders, acquisitive, drug addicts, or professionals?
- What do you know about the offenders? Are they local?
- Do offenders tend to work alone? Does this differ by offender category?
- Do bike thieves know their victims?
- Do bike thieves operate in the same location?
- Are stolen bicycles being sold in the local area?

BICYCLE THEFT VICTIMS

Questions Related to Bicycle Theft Victims

- Whom does bicycle theft harm (e.g., cyclists, business owners)?
- What is known about bicycle theft victims (e.g., their routine activities, demographics, cycle use, prior victimization)?

- Does victimization change a victim's cycle-related behavior? Locking practice? Parking location?
- Do cyclists see publicity regarding secure cycle practice? If so, where? Do they think current publicity is useful?
- Under what circumstances do thefts occur? Is victim behavior a contributory factor, such as leaving bicycles unsecured and visible/accessible?

IDENTITY THEFT AND FOLLOW-ON CRIMES

Identity theft, which began to emerge as a problem in the 1990s, has been called the "crime of the new millennium."[39] The normal daily activities of consumers include purchasing tickets and merchandise online, cashing checks, using credit and debit cards, and renting videos—all of which result in information being shared. At all points where personal data is collected, processed, or stored, there are opportunities for identity theft.[40] Identity theft may be the fastest growing crime of any kind in our society. The person whose identity is stolen is one victim, however, the businesses that suffered losses owing to the criminal use of the stolen identity represent another group of victims. Estimates of the cost to individual victims to clear their names vary, but sources maintain that it requires as few as 24 to as much as 600 hours of effort and from $80 to $1,500 worth of lost earnings to correct credit and other related problems. Over 1,300 victims have been the subjects of criminal investigations, arrests, or wrongful convictions.[41]

Identity crimes involve two types of criminal acts: (1) identity theft and (2) the **follow-on crimes** that occur, such as credit card and check fraud.

HOW IDENTITY THEFT OCCURS

Abundant opportunities exist for identity thieves to get the personal information of people they victimize. Among methods used to obtain data are these:

- Stealing wallets and purses containing identification, bank, credit, membership, and other types of cards.
- Stealing mail, which provides bank and credit statements, preapproved credit offers, Social Security numbers, and other personal data. Some thieves follow mail carriers at a distance and then steal from mailboxes that appear to have just had a large stack of mail delivered. Alternatively, they might cruise affluent neighborhoods looking for raised red flags on mailboxes and stealing outgoing correspondence.
- Going to the Post Office and completing a change of address form to divert mail to another location.
- Rummaging through the victims' trash, or the trash of businesses, to "mine" for personal data—a practice described as **dumpster diving.**

- Fraudulently obtaining the victim's credit report by posing as a potential landlord or employer.
- Stealing personal identification from the victim's home.
- Opportunistically using information from lost wallets and purses.
- Family members, relatives, roommates and acquaintances misappropriating information.
- Stealing personal data assistants (PDAs) and smartphones, such as Blackberries and iPhones, and laptops and tablets; this area may become more significant in the future, because more than one spyware virus for PDAs and smartphones are known to exist.
- Obtaining personal information by hacking into home and business computers or by such tactics as downloading spyware programs. (Identity thieves posing as a legitimate business duped an Atlanta-area company out of personal information for perhaps as many as 400,000 people nationally.[42])
- Stealing information from employers, medical and insurance offices, student records, and other locations or bribing corrupt employees to provide the victims' personal data.
- Scamming victims out of personal information on the Internet is done by a technique known as **phishing.**[43] Two common phishing scams are sending an e-mail to potential victims that appears to be from a legitimate source, such as eBay, AOL, Yahoo, Best Buy, Wells Fargo, a credit card company, or a bank, and asking that they update their account information data. The second method involves using an e-mail to notify victims they have won a prize, such as the Canadian or Netherlands Lottery, but need to pay a processing fee to receive it, thereby tricking the victims into completing an accompanying credit form.[44]

There are numerous variations on these two methods. One is an e-mail promising a free credit report subject to the recipient completing a personal information form. A second method is an e-mail from the U.S. Internal Revenue Service offering an $80 credit if they will participate in an online satisfaction survey, Form IR-2007-148, which also requires the disclosure of personal information.

Any time a possible victim reports an unsolicited e-mail contact from the IRS it is a phishing attack, because the IRS neither initiates unsolicited contacts that way nor does it ask for passwords and other related information. Other bogus forms falsely attributed to the IRS include IR-2007- ending in 49, 75, 104, 109, or 116. Victims should be directed not to open attachments associated with such e-mails and to report the attack to *phishing@irs.gov.* Since this mailbox was established in 2006, more than 30,000 taxpayers have reported 400 separate phishing incidents.

- **Shoulder surfing,** or watching and listening from a nearby location as victims identify themselves and use credit cards or write checks or are punching in their long-distance calling-card numbers.[45]

- Using technology, such as skimmers, to obtain personal data. **Skimmers** are pager-sized data collection devices that cost roughly $300. These are attached to the telephone line running between a business's legitimate card swipe and a telephone jack. During what appears to be a normal transaction, the skimmer reads and stores the data, which is retrieved later by the user. There are also portable skimmers through which waiters and clerks can run victims' cards while they are in the back of the restaurant. More difficult to detect is "skimmer bug" software that can be inserted into point-of-sale terminals. These bugs store the data read in the terminals' circuitry, and then the modem is used to send the data to the thieves' computers. Some banks have found dispensers filled with bank pamphlets attached to the side of their ATMs. What they discovered is that these thief-placed dispensers actually contain miniature cameras that record the names, debit card numbers, and codes of ATM users[46] (Figure 15-7).
- Employing *card trappers*. One example of this involves attaching a false card slot to the front of the ATM. As legitimate users enter their codes, shoulder surfers wait nearby or use binoculars or a camera with a telephoto lens to get the accounts' access codes. Unable to retrieve their cards, customers leave the ATM, and the thieves have both the access codes and the ATM cards.[47]
- Picking up discarded computers. From these, thieves recover sensitive files between 33% and 50% of the time.[48]
- Sending a fraudulent letter and IRS-like form to nonresident aliens who have earned income in the United States. The form is an altered version of IRS Form W-8BEN, "Certificate of Foreign Status of Beneficial Owner for United States Tax Withholding." This form asks for many types of personal information and account numbers and passwords. United States citizens receive a similar phony IRS Form, W-9095, the intent of which is also identity theft.
- An innovative and novel twist on sending a letter from the IRS, is the new scam-letter from the FBI that informs the recipient that they have been the "victim" of a fraud and that the FBI is investigating their case. The unsuspecting individual is then asked for important personal information on which further fraud and theft scams can be conducted. These letters can be received via e-mail or the postal mail and can be quite elaborate.
- Calling a home and telling the person that because he or she failed to come to court as required by "the jury duty summons sent to their residence" that the judge is going to

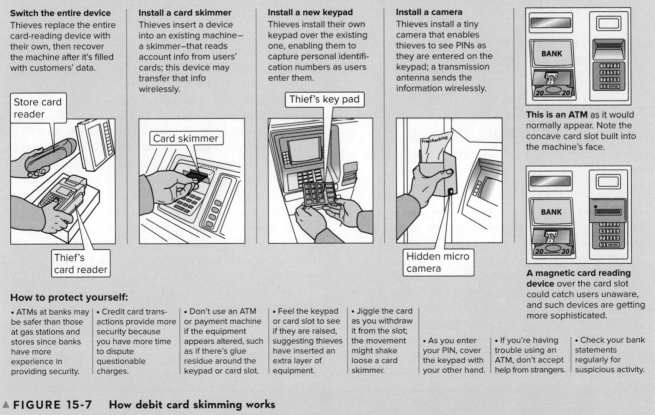

▲ FIGURE 15-7   How debit card skimming works
Source: (Identitytheft911, Wells Fargo Bank, Los Altos [Calif.] Police Department, *San Jose Mercury News; Dallas Morning News,* October 20, 2010, p.21a.)

issue a bench warrant for his/her arrest. When the panicked recipient of the calls insists no such summons was sent, the "Clerk of the Court" says "perhaps there has been a mistake, let's verify some information" and gets enough personal information to commit identity theft.

- Offering "debt consolidation" services by phone, promising the unwary that by working with the holders of their credit cards, they can immediately get up to 50% of their debt immediately forgiven, and the one remaining monthly payment "will be less than 20% of the total you are paying now; all I need to get you started right now is your credit card numbers."

- In yet another scheme, scammers are stealing Social Security numbers assigned to children who do not have bank accounts. The stolen Social Security numbers are then used to develop phony credit profiles, credit cards, bank accounts, and identification. Thieves run up huge debts that will never be paid off. These schemes unfortunately are quite successful and go undetected for long periods of time, until the rightful owner of the Social Security number applies for credit; if that person is a child, it may be years before the scheme is ever detected.

The U.S. Department of Education's (USDOE) Office of Inspector General reports that some students are receiving calls from people falsely claiming that they represent USDOE and offering them scholarships or grants. This financial assistance can be immediately obtained for a $249 processing fee that the student can pay with their credit card number. The USDOE does not charge a processing fee for financial assistance.[49]

FOLLOW-ON CRIMES

Once armed with enough stolen personal identification data, the process of identity theft is executed and follow-on crimes are committed by:

- Calling credit card companies, asking them to change the address "your" bill is mailed to and quickly running up charges on accounts. The victim may be unaware of any problems for a month or more. This practice is called **account takeover.**
- Opening up new, fraudulent, credit card accounts using the victim's name, banking information, Social Security information, and other data. The first hint of trouble for a victim may be when a card company or collection agency calls because the "account" is in serious arrears.
- Establishing new accounts for wireless telephone service, which go unpaid.
- Opening bank accounts on which they write worthless checks.
- Using counterfeit checks and debit cards to drain victims' banking accounts.

- Purchasing cars by taking out loans using the victim's name, defaulting on payments and then fleeing with what is now a stolen vehicle.
- Using the victim's identity if involved in an automobile accident, stopped for a traffic violation, or arrested by the police. If released by the police or bonded out of jail following an arrest, they don't show up for any required court appearance and an arrest warrant is issued in the victim's name.[50]
- Fraudulently obtaining other types of identification, including passports, drivers' licenses, Department of Defense cards, and Social Security numbers.
- Committing mail, investment, telemarketing, and Social Security frauds.

INVESTIGATION OF IDENTITY THEFT AND FOLLOW-ON CASES

From an investigatory view, the co-entwining of identity theft and follow-on crimes almost invariably means investigating multiple crimes, with a number of victims. Additionally, these crimes may be committed in many different jurisdictions, requiring careful case coordination and information sharing among the investigative agencies involved. All states and the District of Columbia have specific identity theft statutes;[51] Federal jurisdiction comes from United States Code, Title 18, Section 1028, The Identity Theft and Assumption Deterrence Act of 1998. This means there is often joint jurisdiction in identity theft cases. Depending on the nature and the specifics of the case, federal agencies with which state and local investigators may work include the FBI, the Secret Service, the Social Security Administration, the Post Office, and Homeland Security. In deciding whether there will be federal or state jurisdiction, one consideration will be the level of seriousness and extent of harm, with the most flagrant cases often becoming the responsibility of the jurisdiction with the most substantial criminal penalties.

The "big three methods" of obtaining personal information from victims are: 1) lost/stolen wallet, checkbook or credit card; 2) friends/acquaintances/relatives with access; and 3) corrupt employees with access to the information. Unless the available information dictates otherwise, the big three may initially provide fruitful avenues for the investigation. Eighty-five percent of victims report that their first realization about the theft comes from a negative contact[52] (for example, a credit card company soliciting payment of past due amounts) or a collection agency. This means investigators are responding to calls where victims are angry, confused, and worried about their financial futures and personal reputations. Another immediate difficulty for the investigator is that most identity thefts and the follow-up crimes come to light only one to six months after they began,[53] meaning that victims' recollections about how and when the identity theft occurred may not be very helpful and that documentary evidence is of vital importance in working the case.

Figure 15-8 is an identity theft and follow-on crimes checklist, with emphasis on the unique types of determinations which need to be made.

Completed	Task	Completed	Task
	How did victim become aware of identity theft?	_____	Opening utility/phone accounts in victim's name?
_____	Fraudulent charges on credit card bill(s)	_____	Unauthorized withdrawals from victim's bank accounts?
_____	Received bills for accounts not opened		
_____	Found irregularities in credit report	_____	Loans taken out in victim's name?
_____	Contacted by creditor demanding payment	_____	Access to/withdrawals from securities/investments accounts?
_____	Denied a loan		
_____	Sued for debt victim did not incur	_____	Obtaining government benefits in victim's name?
_____	Not receiving bills from legitimate accounts	_____	Obtaining employment in victim's name?
_____	Received legal filing, such as bankruptcy	_____	Obtaining medical services or insurance in victim's name?
_____	Denied employment		
_____	Driver's license suspended for violations not committed	_____	Committing crimes attributed to victim?
		_____	Check fraud?
_____	Incident report completed naming victim as suspect	_____	Passport/Visa fraud?
		_____	Other (specify).
_____	Victim advised of warrant or arrested		
_____	Other (specify): _____		*To assist in pinpointing when and by whom ID was stolen or compromised, determine whether in the last 6 months if:*
_____	What date did victim become aware of ID theft?		
_____	When reported? Explain any gaps.	_____	Victim carried social security daily.
_____	When did the first fraudulent activity begin?	_____	Kept PINs and passwords in wallet or purse.
_____	What is the presently known chronology of fraudulent activities?	_____	Had mail stolen. What? When? Get any reports.
		_____	While away, mail kept at Post Office/collected by someone else.
_____	Assign victim the responsibility for describing in as much detail as possible activities associated with all fraudulent activities.		
		_____	Traveled on business or pleasure outside of home vicinity. When? Where?
_____	What is the full name, address, birth date, and other identifying information that the fraudulent activities were committed under?	_____	Mail diverted by forwarding request to Post Office or in a way unknown to the victim.
		_____	Expected new credit card which did not arrive. Get particulars. Issuer contacted by victim? Report made?
_____	What documents and identifying information were stolen or compromised? If known, when?		
_____	Credit card: list banks, contact information, and account numbers.	_____	Garbage was stolen or gone through.
		_____	Left stamped payment bills in unlocked mailbox.
_____	ATM card: contact information and account numbers.	_____	Service providers (maids, delivery, electricians, etc.) in home.
_____	Get voided check or checking account number, bank info, and contact information.	_____	Placed documents with personal information in garbage without shredding—e.g., envelopes with victim's name on them, bank statements, payroll stubs.
_____	Brokerage and/or stock account numbers: who holds accounts, contact information.		
_____	Passport: obtain all relevant information, including country issuing.	_____	Placed pre-approved credit cards and "convenience" checks in garbage without shredding.
_____	Driver's license or license number ; state issuing.		
_____	State identity card: number, state issuing.	_____	Threw ATM and credit card receipts away without shredding.
_____	Social Security card or number, get number.	_____	Shared PIN and password information with someone else.
_____	Birth certificate (identify state and locality issuing), number.	_____	Home/office/car burglarized? When? Reported? If not, why?
_____	Resident alien green card or other documents, get all particulars.		
_____	Bank and other account password/secret word, such as mother's maiden name.	_____	Checkbook, wallet, purse stolen.
		_____	Provided personal information to service providers—e.g., blood collection agency, financial adviser, took out auto/health/life insurance. Identify, get details.
_____	Other (specify).		
_____	Unknown.		
	To the best of the victim's knowledge, what crimes have been committed?	_____	Copy of credit report issued to someone claiming a legitimate business interest or using victim's name.
_____	Use of victim's actual credit cards or numbers without authorization?		
_____	Opening new credit card accounts in victim's name?		

continued

▲ **FIGURE 15-8**   **Identity theft/follow-on crimes checklist**

Completed	Task	Completed	Task
_____	Victim authorized a business to obtain credit report information. Which? When?	_____	What information does the victim have about the suspects?
_____	Some personal information was available on the Net—e.g., genealogy or school reunion site.	_____	Run records checks on suspects identified by victim.
_____	Gave personal information to telephone solicitor, telemarketer, "government worker" working door-to-door, charitable organization, entered contest, or to claim prize supposedly won.	_____	Have the victim list all banks which have legitimate accounts, identify accounts which have fraudulent activities.
_____	Made legitimate purchase, but clerk was out of sight with card during transaction.	_____	Have the victim list all legitimate credit card companies and banks which have issued credit cards, identify those with fraudulent activities.
_____	A new credit card account was just opened by the victim.	_____	Have victim specify all legitimate utility company accounts, identify those with fraudulent activities.
_____	Victim's home/property was refinanced.		
_____	Victim provided information to obtain lease.	_____	Have victim identify all legitimate loans, leases, and mortgages, list those with fraudulent activities.
_____	Victim opened new utility account(s).		
_____	Victim applied for occupational or other license or permit.	_____	Have victim list all merchants with whom he/she has a store credit account—e.g., pharmacies and department stores. List all fraudulent activities.
_____	Victim took out new loan or finished paying one.		
_____	Victim applied for government benefits.	_____	Have victim list all financial institutions where fraudulent accounts were opened.
_____	Victim was featured in local paper, industry publications, on Internet, school site.	_____	Victim should list all fraudulent documents obtained in his/her name.
_____	Online purchases were made using victim's credit card.	_____	Provide assistance to the victim by suggesting he/she contact the three major credit reporting companies, Equifax, TransUnion, and Experian, as well as financial institutions, the Department of Motor Vehicles, Social Security, and other entities. Victim should do this immediately by phone and follow up within 48 hours with letters, asking for return receipts.
_____	Released information to family member/friend.		
_____	Over the past 6 months, what purchases did the victim make from which sites, when, and for what merchandise?		
_____	Have the victim list all persons, businesses, nonprofits, or others to which he/she provided Social Security number.		
_____	Does the victim have his/her Social Security number imprinted on checks?	_____	Provide any agency ID Theft Victim Assistant packages available. This information should include web addresses, such as the one at the Federal Trade Commission, which provides detailed guidance and sample forms and letters to use. Advise victim to log and carefully file all correspondence and return receipts from the Post Office.
_____	Get a list of all places such checks were tendered.		
_____	Has victim or others written his/her Social Security and driver's license numbers on checks tendered?		
_____	List all such instances.		
_____	Are identity crimes affecting the victim's business?		
_____	Whom does the victim identify as possible suspects? For what reasons?		

(**Source:** This information was adapted from content on an undated "Identity Theft" compact disk prepared by the Secret Service, United States Postal Inspection Service, and the International Association of Chiefs of Police.)

▲ **FIGURE 15-8** **Identity theft/follow-on crimes checklist (concluded)**

CREDIT CARD FRAUD

The link between identity theft and credit card fraud was established earlier in this chapter. However, there are also other types of credit card frauds. Altogether these frauds create losses of $2 billion globally according to the Federal Trade Commission. Credit card fraud is particularly prevalent in this country because Americans hold 71% of all credit cards issued worldwide.[54] Credit card fraud has become so lucrative that some organized crime rings and drug dealers have shifted their "careers" to engage in it because it is simple to execute and quickly profitable.[55]

The quickest exact growing sector of credit card fraud may be the counterfeiting of credit cards; the continuing availability of new technologies has helped counterfeiters produce exact replicas of bona-fide cards, including the so-called "hidden" security features, such as holograms, used by legitimate credit card issuers.[56] One source of the necessary equipment is the Far East; another is corrupt vendors. A Canadian vendor was arrested for supplying equipment to thieves and terrorist organizations as part of a multimillion dollar credit and debit card ring.[57] In the advanced payment scheme, the accounts created by credit cards that were obtained through yet-to-be detected thefts, identity theft, or counterfeiting are overpaid by the "card holder," with a bad check. The money is then quickly withdrawn by a cash advance before the check clears the bank. There are also other scams associated with credit cards. In the advanced fee scheme, a person with poor credit pays in advance to have their record "repaired." Other variants of advanced fee schemes involve victims paying by credit card to have a company find them new jobs, work-at-home employment (such as stuffing envelopes), scholarships, and low-cost car or other loans. These offers may appear in newspaper ads, be delivered by the postal service, or appear in the victim's e-mail inbox. Once victims have been taken in by a credit card or other type of fraud, criminals compile lists with their names to sell to other defrauders, including those who contact the victims with an offer to recover their lost assets.

CHECK FRAUD

Check fraud (Figure 15-9) is the forgery, alteration, counterfeiting, or knowing issuance of a check on an account that is closed or has insufficient funds to cover the amount for which the check is written.[58] People may innocently "bounce" a check because of nonsufficient funds owing to a math error in their checkbook or mistiming a deposit. Investigation and prosecution rarely happen, because the check is made good, and the necessary fees are paid.

Others write checks they know are no good and cannot cover; people leaving one state for another may write a bad check because they think there is no consequence; and others write checks on accounts they or others have closed. **Check kiters** open accounts at several banks, knowingly, issuing a check that overdraws their account at Bank 1 and then depositing a check in that account from their Bank 2 account to cover the first worthless check. This process is repeated with ever-increasing amounts until the scheme falls apart because it cannot be continued indefinitely. An employee with the standing authority to issue checks may sign unauthorized checks or forge the manager's or owner's signature.

EMPLOYEE CHECK-BASED CRIMES

Among the signs that an employee in a position of trust such as bookkeeper or business manager may be or is committing check based crimes are these:

- checks made payable to the business or to cash by customers are deposited in an account the employee controls;
- replacement checks to the employee are issued when there is no need to do so, for example, the original check was not lost;
- payroll advances to the employee are not subtracted from the next paycheck;
- there is no documentation explaining why checks are made payable to "Cash" or what happened to them;
- the employee is reimbursed for unexplained expenses;
- the employee keeps promising to show the business owner the bank statements, but it never seems to happen;
- vendors and suppliers are complaining about slow and late payments.

Altogether, check fraud produces losses of some $24 billion annually,[59] and in addition to the practices previously described, others involve more sophisticated techniques. In one, an individual

◄ FIGURE 15-9
NSF (Not sufficient funds) stamped check
For one reason or another, 40% of all Americans are without a credit card and are totally dependent on paying bills with a written check. With an estimated 30 billion checks written annually, it is remarkable that only an estimated 1.2 million checks were not honored owing to "not sufficient funds" (NSF). NSF checks that are not made good are often sold to collection agencies for 80% or more of their face value. NSF checks are "bad checks," and the issuer may be subject to criminal charges, which may be a misdemeanor or a felony, depending on the amount for which the check was written. The amount separating these charges varies from one state to another. (©Tony Freeman/PhotoEdit)

learns that he/she has gotten a job applied for online, which offers "signing bonuses" of $2,500 or more to "new hires." The "new employer" advises the "employee" that by mistake a larger amount in the $19,000 to $50,000 range has been sent to the employee, who is instructed to keep the signing bonus but wire the remaining funds to the employer, often at a European location. Of course, the job doesn't really exist, and the check sent by "mistake" is fraudulent. Because the "new employee" deposited the check originally, it is his/her responsibility to make it good. A wrinkle on this technique is when someone shows up to buy a car or other large-ticket item with a counterfeit cashier's check from a bank or a credit union that was "made out for too much," and the unsuspecting seller not only gives the buyer a check for the difference but also allows the suspect to drive off with the car, which may be quickly sold, creating an additional profit for the suspect. Very good counterfeit checks can be produced by using around $10,000 to purchase a computer system and software. It is estimated that counterfeit checks account for about $1 billion in annual losses.

Checks can be altered by washing them in commonly available chemicals and then dried with little damage to the checks. This process removes ink from the check. The checks can then be scanned into a computer, many copies can quickly be printed, and the checks cashed for the amounts desired by the "payees," who are in on the scheme and may be using identification obtained through identity theft.

Listed below are some of the indicators that a check has been altered or counterfeited:

- There is no perforated edge; most checks should have perforation on one edge.
- The routing and fractional routing numbers are inconsistent and/or do not match the location of the bank listed on the check.
- The check contains spots or stains.
- The word "VOID" appears.

COUNTERFEITING

Although we most often associate counterfeiting with currency, there is a vast range of other types of counterfeiting, including stamps, checks, bonds, and securities, as well as ski lift, sporting event, rodeo, and concert tickets. None of these are just-emerging crimes; the 1966 Beatles concert in Cleveland was plagued with this problem.

Gangs counterfeiting Universal Product Codes (UPC) have been operating a number of years. UPC codes help with inventory control and proper pricing at the point of sale where cashiers scan in the price. In particular Wal-Mart, Lowe's, and Home Depot have been hard-hit, with Wal-Mart's losses reaching $1.5 million.[60] The modus operandi was to counterfeit UPCs in large numbers at print shops or by using personal computers, enter the stores and affix these UPCs over real ones, thereby lowering the price of the item that would be scanned in at the point of sale:

A kitchen faucet worth $169 would suddenly wear a UPC code indicating the price to be $39 or a lighting fixture's price would shift from $249 to $55.[61] Later the same day at a different location for the same retailer, another person would show up—with the phony UPC removed—and get a refund for the actual amount; doing this several times per day easily netted $1,000 to $1,500 daily. False identifications were presented at the refund counter, including English or Irish passports.[62]

FRAUDS, SCAMS, AND CONS

The economic turndown and resulting recession since 2008 has heralded a new wave of frauds, scams, and cons. While the largest of these frauds involved investment and "Ponzi" schemes (discussed later in this chapter), a notable rise in not only the individual number but also the financial losses associated with fraud has been reported.[63] Losses ranged from a few hundred dollars attributed to classic charity cons to over $150 million dollars associated with the largest Medicare fraud in history.

VENDOR FRAUD

Virtually every unit of government and business are dependent on outside vendors who supply such things as office supplies, equipment, vehicles, merchandise for retail, and consulting services. Vendor fraud costs businesses more than $400 billion in losses annually. Among the fraudulent practices used by vendors are these:

- Bidders colluding to set bids at a higher than warranted price per unit and bidders concealing they are insolvent or have a record of defaulting on their bids.
- Providing employees in the procurement office with cash and other types of bribes, such as trips in exchange for being the winning bidder.
- Substituting lower-costing or counterfeit goods to fulfill the terms of a bid.
- Consultants or contractors overstating the number of days worked or the amount of materials required to do the job.
- Submitting bogus invoices for office supplies or other goods in the hope they will be paid.
- Bogus Yellow Page advertising. In the minds of most people the "Yellow Pages" are legitimate ads in the local telephone directory; however, because the phrase was never copyrighted or registered others can use it. Fraudsters may offer "yellow page" advertising and either produce just a few one-page copies for the subscribers or simply abscond with the money.

In large corporations, these crimes may be investigated internally and the information turned over to the police, or the police may be invited in at an earlier stage. In units of government, the agency having jurisdiction will investigate instances of criminal fraud by bidders.

CHARITY AND DISASTER FRAUDS

There are some 70,000 charities. Unfortunately, a very small number are frauds and create two types of problems: (1) people are scammed out of their money and do not get a tax deduction, and (2) public confidence in charities is undermined, making it harder for legitimate charities to raise funds for important causes. Sham charities are skillful at their pitches, using words that suggest good causes; included are terms such as veterans, hunger, children, and orphans. They also often use names that are similar to those of legitimate charities and religious organizations. These pitches are made in person at homes, with buckets at intersections, through the mail, and Internet solicitations.

INSURANCE FRAUD

Insurance frauds can be **hard fraud** or **soft fraud**.[64] Hard fraud is when someone deliberately fakes an injury, accident, theft, arson, or other loss to illegally collect from insurance companies.

Virgil made a car collision insurance claim, stating that he had been trying to avoid a deer and crashed into a wall. The insurer deemed the car a total loss, and the claim was paid. Later, the insurance company learned that Virgil's son Brian was driving the car even though he was not covered by the policy. Both were arrested on one felony count of insurance fraud.[65]

In contrast, soft fraud, also called opportunity fraud, involves normally honest people who tell "little white lies" and collect reimbursements to which they are not entitled, as in the case when the value of the items reported stolen in burglary is overstated. Too, insurance companies have been known to scam insurers by charging them more than is warranted or declaring bankruptcy and going out of business when faced with a flood of claims they cannot pay following a natural disaster. Other types of insurance frauds are discussed next.

Arson Fraud

Chapter 19, "Arson and Explosives Investigations," addresses in much greater detail arson fraud. However, the following case is offered because it illustrates the point that such frauds can go tragically wrong.

Helen hired two local teenagers to "torch" her Tampa restaurant, Gram's County Kitchen, so she could collect insurance money. However, fumes from the gasoline the teenagers poured in the restaurant accidentally ignited, causing an explosion. One died and the other was permanently scarred.[66]

Automobile Fraud

One source of automobile fraud is staged accidents, which include the **swoop and squat,** the **drive down,** and the **paper accident.** In the swoop and squat, a car quickly cuts in front of a legitimate motorist, hits the brakes, and creates a rear-end collision for which repair and fake medical claims can be made (Figure 15-10). The drive down involves waving to another

◀ **FIGURE 15-10**

The classic "swoop and squat" auto accident fraud occurs when the perpetrator rapidly pulls in front of a car and then hits the brakes. The victim vehicle then rear-ends the other car, after which significant medical and auto damages are claimed. The victims of these types of crimes often drive more expensive makes, such as Mercedes-Benz, BMW, Porsche, Cadillac, and the like.

(©Christof R. Schmidt/Getty Images)

driver to go ahead and make a turn in the intersection or elsewhere and then driving into the car, making it appear that the struck vehicle is at fault. Paper accidents are exactly that: no accident has taken place. Collusion is required by a body shop operator, who may even provide a wrecked car for the adjuster to inspect. By only filing for the cost of repairs, which are not done, the amount paid by the insurance is not out of line and therefore not scrutinized closely. Naturally, the insured and the body shop owner split the money for the repairs. Owners who cannot make their car payments, which often involve luxury cars, arrange to have them stolen, and the insurance pays for the car. Then the car is sent to a chop shop. The owner protects his/her credit record and receives some money from the chop shop profit. To make false claims of injuries in accidents believable, the collusion of a doctor is necessary. In one very aggressive case, a chiropractor had "runners" out scouting for accidents and recruiting people to his practice, where false treatment bills were submitted to insurers and false medical records were created to submit to insurance companies.

HEALTH-CARE AND MEDICARE FRAUD

Annual health-care costs are estimated to be $2.2 trillion; the magnitude of spending is a magnet for fraud.[67] Estimates of the dollar loss attributable to fraud range from 3% to 14% of annual expenditures.[68] The most commonly affected agencies in health-care fraud are two federal programs: (1) Medicare, which provides comprehensive care for the disabled and people 65 or older, and (2) Medicaid, a provider of services for low-income people.[69]

Perhaps the most common health-care fraud scheme is billing for services never provided. This is done by making claims for services, equipment, and tests not actually rendered, by filing claims for tests on patients who had, but did not show up, for appointments or by using patient information to file entirely fictitious claims.[70] Other fraud methods used by medical providers:

- Filing duplicate claims.
- "Upcoding" or using billing codes for more expensive tests or longer office visits than actually occurred.
- "Unbundling charges," which is the practice of charging separately for each component of service. This produces a greater claim than if the service was properly billed as one single charge.
- Misrepresenting the diagnosis in order to get paid for services not covered by the health plan or to charge for costly tests not actually provided.
- Performing unnecessary tests;[71] a Massachusetts orthopedic surgeon routinely gave patients potentially harmful X rays and steroid injections they didn't need so he could falsely bill Medicaid. In less than 3 years, one patient was X rayed 74 times and given steroid injections on 112 occasions.[72]

- Billing using the names of people who are deceased.
- Charging for home health aide visits which were not made.

Others involved in health-care fraud are employers and employees. Employers may enroll employees who are actually not eligible in plans or change the dates of employment or termination to expand the dates of coverage. Members enrolled in health plans may alter the documents they submit in order to get a greater reimbursement than they are entitled to or to let someone else use their plan identification to obtain services.[73] An often overlooked effect for many types of medical fraud is that a person may end up with a false medical history, which may affect their ability to get life insurance or alter how they are subsequently treated medically.

Schemes to defraud the Medicare system are not limited to unscrupulous employees and medical providers. Recently, federal investigators uncovered over 2,000 cases of healthcare-related fraud[74]—with a portion of these perpetrated by organized criminal enterprises. In addition federal investigators have also recently exposed a massive fraudulent billing scheme perpetrated by an Armenian-American organized crime ring known as the Mirzoyan-Terdjanian Organization. The scam, dubbed "Diagnosis Dollars," involved more than 73 individuals working in conjunction across the United States to defraud the system out of $163 million dollars. The group not only opened over 120 fake clinics, they also stole the identities of Medicare beneficiaries and healthcare providers, frequently opening bank accounts in the names of the doctors whose identities were stolen.[75] To date, it was the largest Medicare fraud scheme ever perpetrated by a single criminal enterprise and represents the vulnerability of not only Medicare, but other American financial systems (for example, Social Security, State welfare programs, food stamp programs, unemployment systems) that may be compromised from an organized attack (Figure 15-11).

The Mirzoyan-Terdjanian Organization represented a very sophisticated and select group of high-level criminals from the former Soviet Union. The primary leader, Armen Kazarian was identified as a leading member of the "Vory v Zakone," a term that means "thief-in-law" and refers to members of the Russian organized crime cartel composed of former members of the secret police and intelligence agency (KGB) of the Soviet Union, popularized by the 2007 hit movie, *Eastern Promises*.

The Food and Drug Administration (FDA) identifies another type of health-care fraud: "It is the deceptive promotion, advertising, distribution, or sale of articles represented as being effective to diagnose, prevent, cure, treat, or mitigate an illness or condition, or provide a beneficial effect on health, but has not been scientifically proven safe and effective for such purposes."[76] Products identified as such by the FDA may also cause serious health problems. Some of these products are counterfeit drugs with no therapeutic value; others claim they can produce rapid weight loss, or cure skin cancer, Alzheimer's disease, rheumatism, hardening of the arteries, diabetes, improve virility, and eliminate gangrene and prostate problems.

WORKERS COMPENSATION FRAUD

The most common worker compensation fraudulent claim is when people falsely claim that they were injured on the job. They may have actually been injured while away from the job, faked the injury while working, or have an actual injury about which they report exaggerated symptoms. In New York, 18 people, including several teachers and a chiropractor, were arrested for defrauding the workers compensation system out of $550,000, because they were seen working other jobs while receiving benefits.[77] In addition to state workers compensation agencies being defrauded, cases may also involve insurance companies providing disability coverage.

MORTGAGE FRAUD

An array of fraudulent practices related to the real estate and mortgage industry have also been recently exposed. According to the Federal Bureau of Investigation, mortgage fraud schemes typically involve misrepresentations, false statements, or exclusions related to the property or the prospective buyer. These often take form as inflated appraisals, false loan applications, kickbacks, and straw buyers which are manifested in reverse mortgage and foreclosure rescue schemes, illegal property flipping, builder bailout scams, and air loans.[78]

Investigators are often made aware of these schemes through Suspicious Activity Reports (SAR) provided by federally funded banks and other financial institutions. The information in SARs can supply officials with leads to direct their investigations.[79] Additionally, the Federal Bureau of Investigation created the Financial Intelligence Center (FIC) to boost investigations of alleged mortgage fraud. Through the use of various technologies and data exploitations tactics, the FIC provides analyses of intelligence and financial databases.[80] Task forces comprised of federal, state, and local law enforcement agencies also exist in "high-threat" locations and are utilized in the effort to combat mortgage fraud schemes.[81]

HOME IMPROVEMENT AND REPAIR FRAUDS

Common home improvement and repair scams include unneeded roofing, gutter, plumbing, chimney, or other repairs or replacements; paving driveways with a thin surface that quickly cracks; using materials and methods that do not meet local building codes; substituting cheap paint for higher-quality paint; not replacing rotted or missing decking when roofing; charging for more expensive shingles or for more bundles of shingles than were actually used, or not replacing valley gutters and shingles in places that are hard for the owner to see; using whitewash instead of paint; and "free" home, furnace, or other inspections that turn up "serious problems." Often, the "inspector" causes the damage that needs to then be repaired. These scams are usually worked going door-to-door using high-pressure sales and scare tactics, particularly with older people. Mention may be made that they just finished a job "nearby" and have leftover materials so "I can make you a good deal." Representations will be made that "we are having a sale and I can knock 20% off of the bottom line," although the actual price is never specified.

The "vendor" usually refuses to provide a written estimate or contract and evades giving information about the location of his business. Natural disasters, including tornados, hurricanes, floods, and mud slides often bring out packs of repair scammers who prey on people desperate to get their lives back in order.

These scam artists often ask for a down payment or the whole amount and are never seen again; do the work in a substandard manner or not at all; or urge the victim to make temporary repairs that are poorly done when more substantial work is needed, only worsening a problem.

The Federal Trade Commission recommends dealing only with licensed and insured contractors, checking references and consumer affairs agencies for complaints about the vendor, getting recommendations from family, friends, and coworkers who have used contractors, not doing business with door-to-door solicitors, obtaining several bids from reputable contractors, and not using homes as financing collateral because owners may end up losing them.

INTERNET FRAUDS AND SCAMS

The fastest growing area of theft and larceny involves the myriad of frauds and scam on the Internet. These range from the common, unsolicited Nigerian 419 scams and "lottery winner" e-mails that almost everyone who has ever used the Internet has received, to the more sophisticated auction frauds that now threaten legitimate corporations such as eBay, PayPal, and Western Union. The Internet Crime Complaint Center (IC3) is a unique partnership between the FBI, the National White Collar Crime Center (NW3C), and the Bureau of Justice. Its primary purpose is to serve as a vehicle to receive, develop, and refer criminal complaints regarding the rapidly growing area of cybercrime.[82] Cybercrime is specifically addressed in Chapter 17; however, this section discusses the various larceny and fraud crimes stemming from Internet use.

IC3 reports that **auction fraud** (including nondelivery of merchandise and/or payment) was by far the most reported Internet offense, accounting for over 58% of referred complaints. Auction fraud involves the misrepresentations of a product advertised for sale through an Internet auction site or the nondelivery of products purchased through an Internet auction site.[83] These types of crimes commonly fall within three broad categories:

- **Overpayment fraud** targets the seller. A seller advertises a high-value item—such as a car or a computer—on the Internet. A scammer contacts the seller to purchase the item, then sends the seller a counterfeit check or money order for an amount greater than the price of the item. The purchaser asks the seller to deposit the payment, deduct the actual sale price, and then return the difference to the purchaser.
- **Wire-transfer schemes** start with fraudulent and misleading ads for the sale of high-value items being posted on well-known online auction sites. When buyers take the bait, they are directed to wire money to the crooks using a money transfer company. Once the money changes hands, the buyer never hears from them again.
- Second-chance schemes involve scammers who offer losing bidders of legitimate auctions the opportunity to buy the item(s) they wanted at reduced prices. They usually require that victims send payment through money transfer companies, but then don't follow through on delivery.[84]

Many of these auction frauds are committed by perpetrators living in a foreign country, such as South Africa or Romania.

Consumers should exercise extreme caution when the seller posts the auction as if he resides in the United States, but then responds to the victim outside the United States. The perpetrators almost always request that funds be wired directly to him or her via Western Union, MoneyGram, or bank-to-bank wire transfer to addresses outside the United States. These services have virtually no recoverable recourse and sadly, provide dead-end leads for local police investigators. Finally, consumers should be wary if the deal "sounds too good to be true." Unfortunately, it usually is! Local police investigators should make sure that the victim files a complaint with the IC3, as well as provides security alerts to eBay or PayPal, if those sites were involved. Each provides a strong security alert and fraud prevention program as well as a list of "tips" for would-be buyers.[85] A common auction fraud reported by one victim is as follows:

I was sold a stolen vehicle on eBay. The seller indicated that he had recently moved to South Africa to start a new business and that he "had to sell his relatively new Beemer" for $10,000. I thought it was a great deal, so I wired the money to the seller (in South Africa) after checking him out on the Internet. He indeed had a number of businesses listed worldwide and a new one on his website in South Africa. I sent the money via Western Union, because I did not want to pay the state sales tax and I figured that the deal would go through, since the car was being shipped from Houston and I lived in Dallas, not even two hundred miles away. When I received the "bill of sale" on the vehicle, it was from one of the seller's businesses and not in his personal name. The problem was . . . of course . . . when the vehicle arrived, so did the police who informed me that the BMW was stolen and had to be impounded. I guess the deal was too good to be true![86]

Internet Gambling and Lottery Scams

While the Unlawful Internet Gambling Enforcement Act was passed in 2006 by Congress, essentially making all forms of gambling via the Internet illegal, a number of underground Internet sites still exist. The sites are "off-shore," meaning that they are hosted in foreign countries, making enforcement very difficult. Further, the extent to which some of these sites are honest also appears to be an open question, as so many are beyond the reach of gaming regulatory agencies and American law enforcement.

Most Internet frauds involving gambling are usually based on phony letters announcing you as a winner (Figure 15-12). In these types of scams, the victim is notified of his/her "winnings" and is requested to provide confidential information on which false identifications are developed and/or more sophisticated identification theft schemes are placed into motion.

From: POWERBALL NOTIFICATION <pabet4us@yahoo.co.uk>
Date: October 23, 2010 12:57:16 PM EDT
To: undisclosed recipients
Subject: Check Your E-mail

FROM THE DESK OF THE PROMOTIONS MANAGER
POWERBALL LOTTERY E-GAMES PROMOTIONS,
Accredited Claim Agent-
29 Colmore Row,
Birmingham, B3 2EW
United Kingdom
www.powerball.com

23th October, 2010.

Attn: Lucky Winner,

RE: AWARD WINNING EMAIL NOTIFICATION!!!

We wish to notify and congratulate you on the selection of your email ID as the jackpot winning entry in the
Powerball E-Games Promotions, being the inaugural edition of our new e-lottery program. Your email ID
identified with winning No. 10, 17, 18, 26, 43, 47 and was selected among the winning email ID's in the draws held
today using the latest version of the Computer Random Selection System (CRSS) from the 50,000 promotional
entries submitted by our international software support/affiliate companies.

You have been awarded with the jackpot promotional cash prize of $1,000,000.00 (One Million United States
Dollars Only) credited to Reference Numbers PB/EGP/60961/OV. You will join the other two winners from
Nigeria, Your payment will be made through our Nigerian payment center, since we have two winners already
from Nigeria. Your winning cash prize has been transferred into an ATM VISA CARD to curtail the risk of carrying
huge amount of money around. You shall receive your winning cash prize as an international ATM VISA Card
which you shall cash in your country. To immediately process the claims of your prize award, please contact
your assigned claims agent:

Name: Mohammed Hakim Ali
E-mail: mohammedhakim1949@hotmail.com
TEL: +2348060850444

To facilitate the claims of your winnings, you are advised to provide the claims officer assigned to you with the
following details for processing the payment of your winnings:

Name:
Address:
Telephone Number:
Email Address:
Occupation:
Nationality:
Social Security Number:
Bank Name:
Bank Address:
Account Number:
VISA or MASTERCARD Bank:
Account Number:
Reference Number:
Award Prize Amount:

Once again, congratulations from all our staff on your promotional prize winning

Patricia Riley (Mrs.)
Coordinator; Powerball E-Games Promotion.

▲ FIGURE 15-12   Internet "winners" notification
Note the important and confidential information requested from this unsolicited e-mail.

Nigerian 419 and Black Money/ Wash-Wash Schemes

The Nigerian advanced fee scam begins with a potential victim getting an unsolicited fax, e-mail, or letter that purports to be from a current or former Nigerian governmental official or a relative of such. The recipient is told that a "confidential source has recommended the contact." The con takes its name from Chapter 42, Section 419, of the Laws of the Federation of Nigeria and Lagos, which deals with advanced fee frauds. Millions of U.S. dollars are available through an over-invoiced deal with the Nigerian National Petroleum Corporation, the recovery of unclaimed insurance money, money from a dead or defeated former government official, or other such spin. The letter writer wants the victim's help in investing in the United States and will pay handsomely for it, up to 30% of the "total." Another 10% to 15% of the money will be set aside to pay for miscellaneous expenses in getting the money transferred. The victim provides personal information, including bank account numbers to facilitate the movement of funds from Nigeria to this country. The personal information is not immediately abused; later it may be sold or employed in another type of fraud. The victim is pressured into sending money to cover unanticipated costs, which continues as long as the victim sends money. The money requests to the victim are accompanied by official-looking government and bank documents with embossed seals and verification stamps, all of which are counterfeit or phony.

"Wash-wash" (Figure 15-13) is what Nigerian cons call the black money scheme, also an advanced fee scam. It may be run in conjunction with a 419 or as a stand-alone con. The con reports that the dollars he is trying to get into this country have been treated with a chemical that turned them black,

disguising their true value; in order to be able to wash the $100 bills clean so they can be used, special, expensive chemicals must be bought, and the victim must pay for them. A meeting is set up outside the United States, to avoid the higher risk of arrest. The victim flies there to actually see the money that will be "cleaned and divided." The meeting is conducted in a hotel room or other location. The con has a specially treated bill that is black, and he uses the "small amount of special cleaning chemicals he has left" to demonstrate the process, and the bill is partially cleaned. This process is actually very cheap and on the order of a sleight-of-hand trick. The victim advances several thousand dollars to buy the chemicals; but then, the vial is "accidentally left in a cab or broken." So, the victim advances more money. This is repeated as many times as the victim pays up and then the fraudsters disappear, allegedly to get the chemicals themselves.[87]

OTHER FRAUDS: PIGEON DROP AND BANK EXAMINERS CONS

Confidence games are practiced by individuals who understand human nature, gain the mark's trust by being good listeners, and through smooth talking, set the hook, and run the scam. As many as 70% of con games may be run against the elderly, who are often very trusting. Among the most enduring con games are the pigeon drop scheme and the bank examiner scheme.

The **pigeon drop** is run in many variations; commonly, two cons operate it. The first one strikes up a conversation with the mark on a street filled with shops or at a mall. The job of the first con is to make a "quick connection" with the mark and gain his/her confidence; they talk about the mark's family

▶ **FIGURE 15-13**
Partially cleaned $100s in the Nigerian "wash-wash" advanced fee scheme
(©Eduardo Munoz/Reuters)

or whatever is comfortable. The second con approaches with a story of having just found an envelope filled with a lot of money and asks them if it belongs to them. When the envelope is opened, there will be some paperwork suggesting that it came from drug sales or other illegal activity. After asking the first con and the mark what should be done with the money, the mark is lead to the conclusion that all three should share it. Because there is no identification in the envelope, the money cannot be returned, and there is no real harm because the person who lost the money is dishonest. The two cons, quickly joined by the mark, talk about all the things they could do with the money. One of the cons calls his/her employer, who is an "attorney." The attorney advises that the money be put in "his firm's" trust account while a due diligence search is made to find the owner of the lost money. Additionally, the mark and the two cons are to provide a sum of money, as a show of good faith until the found money can be distributed, which will also be placed in the mythical trust account. After the mark withdraws his good faith money, the lawyer may take the group to lunch and take control of all of the money. The victim—the pigeon—has thus lost all the money he withdrew from the bank.

The **bank examiner con** often begins with a call to the mark's home in which the caller identifies himself as a bank examiner who relates there is some apparent wrongdoing at the bank, and the assistance of the mark is solicited in finding out who it is. The mark is asked to withdraw some money from his/her account and then to meet the examiner at a nearby location. The bank examiner may be accompanied by "Sgt. Jones," who flashes a badge and praises the mark for his help. The bank examiner gives the mark a counterfeit cashier's check to replace the funds withdrawn but asks him/her not to deposit it for the week it takes to complete the investigation. By then,

the scam has been run several times in that community, and the con men are long gone before the mark finds out that the check is bogus.[88]

Pigeon-drop and bank examiner frauds are often started via the Internet. Unsolicited e-mails and other communications are transacted between the victim and the con through e-mail as well as the telephone. Clearly, the ubiquitous nature of the Internet has aided in new and various forms of scams that will undoubtedly continue to evolve over the years. Table 15-1 reveals recent variations of scams via the Internet.

VICTIMS OF FRAUD: SENIOR CITIZENS

Senior citizens are particularly susceptible to being the victims of a variety of fraud schemes, including Medicare fraud, telemarketing and funeral scams, counterfeit prescription drugs, Internet scams and cons, and phony reverse mortgages. For instance, many senior citizens are new to the Internet and unaware of the potential for fraud and scams associated within its use. They often come from a social genre that "trusted" their neighbor and believe that the government "protects" them from criminal predators. They often believe that scams and cons are relatively rare and that most people are honest in their business dealings. These are characteristics of the "greatest generation," who fought in World War II and who believe that most people are basically honest and technology is well-regulated . . . criminals are often viewed as street thugs that involve themselves in relatively minor crimes like shoplifting and other thefts. Most senior citizens polled continue to believe that violent crime is relatively rare in our communities and that the police can prevent most crime.[89]

From the perspective of a scammer, senior citizens are ideal victims for a number of reasons. First, they generally have good

TABLE 15-1	Examples of Internet Scams	
SCAM	TYPE OF SCAM	DESCRIPTION
"Hitman Scam"	E-mail extortion	An e-mailer claims to have been sent to assassinate a victim, but the victim would be spared if he/she wires money overseas.
Astrological reading scam	Spam or pop-up message	A victim receives a free reading but is enticed into paying for a full reading to learn about something favorable about to happen.
Economic stimulus scam	Telephone call and online	A recorded phone message that sounds like President Barack Obama directs victims to websites requiring online applications and $28 in fees to receive a large sum of stimulus money.
Job site scam	Online	Victims are persuaded to provide personal information or copies of payroll checks only to find their bank account drained.
Fake pop-ups for antivirus software	Online	Victims click on fake pop-up ads warning them about threatening viruses on their computers and end up downloading malicious computer codes or viruses.

Source: *2009 Internet Crime Report* (Washington, DC U.S. Department of Justice, 2010) and "Dallas Summit Target Cyber Crime," *The Dallas Morning News*, May 2, 2010, p. 18A.

▶ **FIGURE 15-14**
Senior citizens are often the victim of scams and cons
Federal and local police are trying to better educate senior citizens through individual workshops, Senior Citizen Police Academies, and general e-mails and postal mailings focused on fraud prevention. (©Tom Carter/PhotoEdit)

credit and a sizable savings. Second, elderly victims are not as likely to report being a victim of fraud because they may not realize they were conned; if they do acknowledge their victimization, they may not report it, owing to embarrassment or shame. Third, even if they were to report the crime, some senior citizens can be poor witnesses, based on their limited ability to recall information. Moreover, a significant time lapse between the scam and discovery of the crime makes details of the event more difficult to remember.[90] Senior citizens account for a large amount of the victims to frauds and cons—so much so, that the FBI has focused considerable attention on educating senior citizens in an attempt to lower their victimization (Figure 15-14).

MONEY LAUNDERING

Criminals want to launder money to avoid prosecution, increase their profits, avoid seizure of their accumulated wealth, evade paying taxes whenever possible, and appear legitimate.[91] In laundering cases prosecuted, 60% of the money came from embezzlement or fraud, 17% involved drug trafficking, and 7% involved racketeering or customs charges.[92] **Money laundering** is the illegal practice of filtering "dirty" money or ill-gotten gains through a series of transactions until the money is "clean," appearing to be proceeds from legal activities. The United States Criminal Code defines money laundering as the concealment of the source and/or the destination of money, which has usually been gained through illegal activities.[93] Worldwide money laundering activity is estimated to be $1 trillion each year.[94] Money launderers have access to all the speed and ease of modern electronic

finance to move funds globally. Thus, substantial cooperation and information sharing among law enforcement agencies are essential to identify the sources of illegal proceeds, trace the funds to specific criminal activities, and confiscate criminals' financial assets.[95]

At the risk of oversimplifying a complex subject, money laundering involves three distinct steps: (1) **placement,** (2) **layering,** and (3) integration (Figure 15-15).[96]

PLACEMENT

Placement is the process of placing unlawful proceeds into legitimate financial institutions or systems. Transactions are kept to $10,000 or less to avoid triggering the requirements of the federal Bank Secrecy Act (BSA, 1970). The BSA obligates institutions to report single transactions exceeding $10,000 to the U.S. Department of Treasury's Financial Crimes Enforcement Network (FinCen). FinCen is one of the Treasury's primary agencies to establish, oversee, and implement policies to prevent and detect money laundering. It also provides intelligence and analytical support to law enforcement. With FinCen's leadership, a meeting of financial intelligence units (FIUs) was held in 1995 in Brussels. An outgrowth of this meeting was the formation of the Egmont Group, which is an international network of FIUs dedicated to information sharing and coordination.

The BSA also requires a report when one entity makes multiple deposits exceeding $10,000 in a single day. In 1996, under regulatory authority granted by the Annunzio-Wylie Money Laundering Act (1992), the U.S. Treasury adopted a rule requiring banks and other depository institutions to report to FinCen any *suspicious* activities involving $5,000 or more.

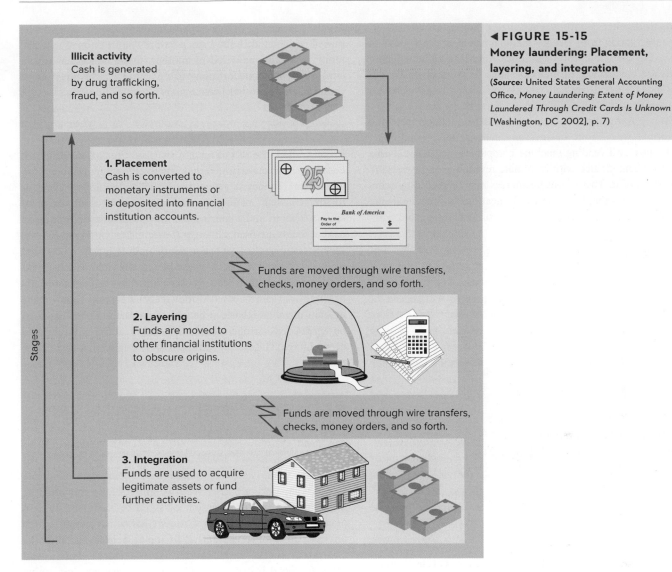

◀ **FIGURE 15-15**

Money laundering: Placement, layering, and integration
(*Source:* United States General Accounting Office, *Money Laundering: Extent of Money Laundered Through Credit Cards Is Unknown* [Washington, DC 2002], p. 7)

Illicit activity
Cash is generated by drug trafficking, fraud, and so forth.

1. Placement
Cash is converted to monetary instruments or is deposited into financial institution accounts.

Funds are moved through wire transfers, checks, money orders, and so forth.

2. Layering
Funds are moved to other financial institutions to obscure origins.

Funds are moved through wire transfers, checks, money orders, and so forth.

3. Integration
Funds are used to acquire legitimate assets or fund further activities.

Stages

Placement is often done by **smurfing,** or making multiple deposits of cash or buying multiple bank drafts, which are checks issued by one bank against funds deposited in that bank that authorize a second bank to make payment to the entity named in the draft. One or more individuals conduct these transactions, often at multiple financial institutions. Other methods include buying money orders or travelers' checks at one institution, depositing them at another and using cash to buy chips at a casino, participating in gambling activities, and then cashing in the chips for a casino check. As a general matter, casinos withhold federal income tax at a 25% rate on winnings above $5,000. Placement has also been facilitated by bribing bank officials to ignore FinCen reporting requirements (which is increasingly difficult) by purchasing entire banks and operating them as part of a criminal enterprise and using "safe haven" **off-shore accounts** in some 60 nations that advertise "untraceable" financial services. These nations include the Cook Islands, Egypt, Guatemala, and Ukraine. In these jurisdictions, launder-

ers may buy a "shelf company" that has been registered for years and open accounts into which illegal funds are deposited. Laws in the Seychelles Islands provide immunity to depositors from all outside criminal charges, even if it is known the money came from criminal acts. The only government requirement is that investors not engage in illegal activities in the Seychelles Island chain.[97]

Another method of placement is the Colombian **black market peso exchange (BMPE).**[98] Colombian drug dealers export drugs to North America and Western Europe. Sales of drugs produce vast amounts of money in the currency of the countries in which the drugs are sold. The drug cartel contacts a peso broker, who will give it pesos for the currency held in foreign countries for roughly 80 cents on the "dollar." The cartel thus has its money, and the BMPE must now pick up the money and get it placed into the banking systems of the respective countries. In the final phase, the broker advertises to Columbian importers that they have foreign funds available to buy goods from other countries. On behalf of importers, the BMPE purchases goods from foreign manufacturers whose goods are shipped to the Caribbean or a South American country. These goods are then smuggled into Colombia to avoid expensive tariffs. Once the goods are sold, the broker is paid in pesos, which are then deposited into a legitimate banking system.

Money from illegal sources also still gets laundered in the traditional way. Front businesses—such as bars, restaurants, night clubs, and vending machine companies—and illicit source funds are commingled with legitimate revenue, with taxes being paid on all of it. These front businesses may be owned by criminals or be ones that they control. Indications of accounts being used for money laundering are summarized in Table 15-2.

LAYERING

Layering involves converting the funds placed into other assets or moving them to other financial institutions, the purpose of

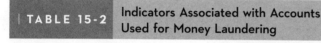

TABLE 15-2	Indicators Associated with Accounts Used for Money Laundering

1. Smurfing

2. Unusual underlying business plan

3. Account holder's wealth atypical for his/her profile

4. Unusually high rates of return for low-risk business activity

5. Reactivation of dormant account, often with increasingly large deposits

6. Questionable, unrealistic, or conflicting explanation of business plan or account activity; account holder has lack of knowledge about the field his/her business is in

7. Unnecessarily complex transactions

8. Disbursement of funds by several checks when one would do

9. Account holder has criminal record or suspicious associates

10. Account holder has defensive stance when asked about account activity

11. True beneficiary of account is deliberately concealed

12. Last-minute changes in fund transfer instructions

13. Account holder is discovered to use false/stolen identification

14. Account revenue is atypical for size and nature of business

15. Funds transferred to personal or relative's accounts

16. Account behavior changes without explanation

17. "Tidy" or rounded sums used to pay for commodities

18. Business lacks normal documentation

Source: No author, *FIUs (Financial Intelligence Units) in Action: 100 Sanitized Cases* (London: Egmont Group, 2000), drawn from a 170-page document.

which is to further distance the funds from their illegal source; these assets include bonds, stocks, works of art and jewelry. The money may also be wired to another institution to pay into a controlled account for non-existent goods or simply move through multiple other accounts anyplace in the world.[99]

INTEGRATION

In **integration**, the illegal funds that have been placed and layered are now clean and are virtually indistinguishable from wholly legal money. They are then used to buy luxury items or to invest in legitimate business ventures, real estate, or other sectors.[100] Both in the layering and integration phases some credit card accounts are used, although the actual extent is not known. In this country, the practice appears limited, but it is practiced through off-shore banks.[101] These banks offer anonymous ATM and credit cards that bear no user name, just an account number, and that can be used worldwide; there is no limit on the amount of money that can be withdrawn daily. The cards must be "preloaded" or deposits made to cover 200% of anticipated expenditures. The money not spent is held in a trust account by the bank.

SECURITY AND INVESTMENT FRAUDS

Securities fraud is any manipulation or deception that affects the purchase or sale of a security and usually includes the misrepresentation or omission of significant information. In general, a security is an investment instrument from which an investor expects to derive financial benefit through the efforts of others.[102] Illustrations include stocks, bonds, and other financial instruments. The two primary laws governing the securities industry and protecting investors are the Securities Act of 1933 and the Securities Exchange Act of 1934, both of which have been amended through the years.[103] In addition to these federal laws, each state has statutes and regulations pertaining to securities transactions, and the various stock and commodity exchanges also have regulatory requirements.[104]

In the 1987 movie *Wall Street,* the character Gordon Gekko soothingly intones at a stockholders' meeting, "Greed is good," which seemed to become the order of the day for some individuals and corporations. In 1990 Michael Milken, the "junk bond king," pled guilty to securities fraud and related charges and paid a fine of $600 million, thereby avoiding the more serious charges of racketeering and insider trading.

Formed by a merger of two companies in 1985, energy trading company Enron quickly soared owing to the deregulated energy markets, becoming the seventh largest corporation in this country. By 2000, Enron had filed for bankruptcy, brought down by some 5 years of using accounting methods that concealed massive losses, leading to a downward estimate of its net value by $1.1 billion. The scandal caused thousands of employees to lose their retirement savings and resulted in

▲ **FIGURE 15-16 Bernie Madoff**
Madoff pled guilty to a federal indictment alleging that the former securities broker dealer carried out one of the largest Ponzi schemes, defrauding his clients out of an estimated $64 billion. He pled guilty in June 2009 and was sentenced to 150 years in prison. (©Kathy Willens/AP Images)

massive losses to investors. Its activities led to the conviction of some Merrill Lynch and Arthur Anderson officials, prison terms for some Enron officials, one of whom pled guilty to conspiracy to commit money laundering and conspiracy to commit wire fraud. The Board of Directors paid a $168 million fine to settle charges that they failed to adequately protect investors.

In 2008 federal officials investigated and arrested former NASDAQ chairman, Bernie Madoff, on charges of securities fraud (Figure 15-16). Madoff operated an asset management firm that, for decades, used the funds from new clients to pay profits and redemptions to existing clients. Often using his social networks to attract new investors, Madoff eventually defrauded his clients out of $64 billion, representing the largest investment fraud in history, and incredibly equaled the monetary losses for all conventional property crimes against U.S. citizens for the previous 3 years.[105] There has been some retribution and repayment of loss since 2008. Madoff pled guilty and was sentenced to 150 years in prison, and in December 2010 federal authorities revealed that many Madoff's victimized clients may regain about half of their losses as a result of seized property and assets by the federal government.[106] There has been some retribution and repayment of loss since 2008. Madoff pled guilty and was sentenced to 150 years in prison, and in December 2010 federal authorities revealed that

many Madoff's victimized clients may regain about half of their losses as a result of seized property and assets by the federal government.[107]

Bernie Madoff's investment fraud was brought to light the same year that was fictional character, Gordon Gekko reappears in the sequel, *Wall Street: Money Never Sleeps;* in this movie, Gekko hawks his new book entitled, "Greed is Good!" The cynical nature and devastation of monetary loss from Bernie Madoff's investment fraud provide the backdrop to the movie, which highlights one of the oldest and most successful cons: the Ponzi Scheme.

PONZI/PYRAMID SCHEMES

Carlos "Charles" Ponzi formed the Security Exchange Company in Boston in 1919 and promised to double people's investments in the company within 90 days (Figure 15-17). For early investors, this actually happened, because he used the deposits of

▲ **FIGURE 15-17 Ponzi schemes**
Carlo Ponzi (1882–1949) immigrated to the United States, where he swindled thousands of investors out of millions of dollars. He was deported to his native Italy in 1934 and at one point worked for the dictator Mussolini. In 1949 he died penniless in Brazil. The scam he developed is timeless.
(©Bettmann/Getty Images)

subsequent investors to pay for the money doubling of previous investors. Eventually the scheme collapsed, because recruitment of new investors could not be sustained. Ponzi was arrested, convicted, and imprisoned for various crimes. This type of investment fraud is still practiced today and is referred to as a **Ponzi scheme, pyramid scheme,** or endless chain scheme. The ruse is based on "greed" and attempts to lure would-be investors into a program that promises or guarantees extraordinarily high returns. As in the initial Ponzi fraud, the scheme actually appears to be working in the beginning, as investors receive monetary "returns on investment," however; these returns are not based on profits from a working corporation or stock fund, but rather from new investors entering the program. The entire scheme fails when additional investors cannot be enticed into the scheme. It is usually at this time that the fraud becomes apparent as the perpetrator suddenly vanishes, taking all of the remaining investment money. Sudden stock market downturns and a slowing economy also quickly reveal Ponzi schemes as investors withdraw their money from the program, causing a rapid acceleration of payout and revealing the fraudulent nature of the scheme. This is precisely why so many Ponzi and pyramid schemes came to light in the past few years, as the U.S. stock market dipped to its lowest point in decades. Table 15-3 lists some of the more infamous cases within the last few years. To would-be investors, the best adage may again well be, "if it sounds too good to be true, it usually is!"

As with most frauds, there are numerous variations in the Ponzi and pyramid routines. For example, these schemes may be run as "gifting clubs" or "women empowering women" programs. Eight new participants, called *givers*, are recruited, and each "gifts" the "receiver," who is the person at the head of the pyramid, with $2,000. When the receiver has $16,000 in hand, the pyramid splits, and the eight new participants move upward in the pyramid, each hoping eventually to become the receiver; to do so requires each of them to recruit new entry-level givers.

New participants in pyramid schemes are often required to sign confidentiality agreements requiring them not to discuss the specifics or the names of participants and attesting that they were not promised anything for participating in the program (although each is led to believe that they all will become receivers). As the following sections indicate, Ponzis can be run in many different ways.

PUMP AND DUMP SCHEMES

The U.S. Securities and Exchange Commission describes **pump and dump** schemes, which are also called "hype and dump manipulation," as involving the touting of a company's stock through false and misleading statements to the market place often by using the Internet.[108] After distributing favorable, but false, information to drive up the price of the stock (the pump), the price of the stock rallies by its being bought. The pump or hype may include urging potential investors to "buy now before it is too late," suggestions that the recommendation is based on "inside" knowledge, or that an "infallible" economic model identified the stock.[109]

The pump is often done with microcap stocks, issued by the smallest companies, over half of which have capitalizations of less than $1.25 million.[110] Thus, "microcap" means companies that have micro capitalizations. Microcap stocks are traded in the over-the-counter (OTC) market, which has no listing standards. This is in sharp contrast to the great amount of information on companies whose stocks are traded on the major exchanges. Therefore, detailed, accurate information about the company is usually not available for victims who need such data in the face of a pump hustle.

AFFINITY FRAUD

Affinity fraud is run on groups of people who share some affinity to one another, such as religious, ethnic, and professional groups and groups whose members have a high sense of friendship and trust in one another.[111] The scammers often recruit the most respected members of the group to help promote the program, which offers "guaranteed returns." The use of such members makes it easier to recruit victims, and when it is apparent that the group has been defrauded, it may choose not to report the victimization to spare the respected member and the group embarrassment. The investment fraud can be run as a Ponzi scheme or as one of many other iterations:

African-American groups were approached by a company that was portrayed as being successful and having more than $36 million in assets, when in fact it had a negative net worth of more than $27 million. The company promised to insure all investments made, and make a 30% tax-free return. Eventually, groups were conned out of $52 million before the company was stopped; the defendant later pleaded guilty to conspiracy to commit securities fraud.[112]

ONE-YEAR CALLABLE CERTIFICATES OF DEPOSIT

The stock market has been volatile in recent years, and many older investors have fled it looking for more stable investments, such as certificates of deposit (CDs). CDs issued by local banks insured by the Federal Deposit Insurance Corporation (FDIC) have long been a trusted investment, because they are covered for losses up to $100,000. In purchasing a CD, the buyer agrees to invest a fixed amount for a fixed time. In return, the issuing entity agrees to pay the purchaser interest at regular intervals.[113] In addition to banks, CDs are now sold by national and regional brokerage firms and independent sales people or "deposit brokers." These brokers can sometimes negotiate a higher interest rate for their customers on the promise of bringing a certain sum of money to the bank.[114]

The stock market plunge in September and October, 2008, revealed a number of Ponzi and Pyramid type frauds; some of the more infamous frauds and schemes are listed here.

	R. ALLEN STANFORD	SHAWN MERRIMAN	NICHOLAS COSMO	ARTHUR NADEL	STEPHEN WALSH, PAUL GREENWOOD	WEIZHEN TANG	RAY M. WHITE	MARVIN RAY COOPER
Age	58	46	37	76	62, 64	50	50	32
Location	Texas and Antigua, West Indies	Aurora, CO	Hauppauge, Lake Grove and Queens, NY	Sarasota, FL	Sands Point, NY, North Salem, N.C.	Toronto	Mansfield, TX	Honolulu, HI
Company or companies	Stanford Financial Group, Stanford International Bank and others	Market Street Advisors	Agape World, Agape Merchant Advance	Scoop Management, Scoop Capital and others	Westridge Capital Management, WG Trading Investors and others	Oversea Chinese Fund, WiWin Capital Management and others	CRW Management	Billion Coupons, Billion Coupons Investment
Alleged length	At least 1999–09	1994–09	2004–09	1996–09	2006–09	2009–09	2007–09	2007–09
Amount raised from investors/clients	More than $8 billion	$17 million–$20 million	$370 million	$60 million	At least $553 million	$50 million–$75 million	At least $10.9 million	More than $4.4 million
Number of investors/clients	About 50,000	At least 38	More than 1,500	More than 100	Universities, public pension and retirement plans	More than 200	More than 250	At least 125 (many members of the deaf community)
Personal expenses	At least $1.6 billion in personal loans	Masterpieces by Rembrandt, Rubens, and other artists	Jewelry, hotel and limousine bills, youth baseball league	More than $1 million in wire transfers to private accounts	Homes, horse farm, collectible Steiff teddy bears	NA	Real estate and car-racing activities	Flying lessons, $1 million home, computer equipment

Source: Court filings by federal prosecutors and records from the Securities and Exchange Commission, Commodity Futures Trading Commission, FBI and U.S. Postal Inspection Service. Web Bryant, "Economic Troubles Reveal Plague," *USA Today*, April 17, 2009, p. B-1.

Unscrupulous sellers of CDs often trumpet the higher rates of interest to be paid but do not explain to investors about the terms used, thus misleading them. For example, a **one-year callable CD** has a "one-year call provision," meaning that the entity issuing the instrument can choose to call (terminate it by redeeming) a CD before its maturity date. The option to call a CD is with the bank and not with the investor. However, investors typically may not understand this language or are misled about its meaning, thinking that after a year of earning interest they can terminate their investment and use the money any way they want. Not only can they not do so, penalties for early withdrawal may amount to 25% or more. There are numerous cases across the country of investors in their 90s being sold CDs by unscrupulous entities that do not mature for 20 to 30 years. In addition to selling people unsuitable investments, these "brokers" may not be working with an FDIC institution but acting as the agent for other investors, or the investor is not told that they own only a portion, and not all, of the CD. Moreover, some CD programs are operated as pyramid schemes, with the early investors receiving "Ponzi payments."

PROMISSORY NOTES

A **promissory note** is essentially a short-term written I.O.U. that promises to pay its holder, the investor, the fixed amount invested plus a fixed amount of interest at some specified date in the future.[115] Although promissory notes can be legitimate investments, those that are mass-marketed, sold door-to-door, or promoted on the Internet or through telemarketing are often scams, which amount to some $300 million annually. Most promissory notes have to be registered as securities with the Securities Exchange Commission and in the states where they are to be sold, but notes with maturities of nine months or less may be exempt from being registered. Therefore, when notes are not registered and mature in nine months or less, it is another sign that a scam may be in the offering instead of a great investment opportunity. Legitimate corporate promissory notes are not usually sold to the general public, but to sophisticated buyers who conduct a due diligence search before investing.[116]

The fraudsters recruit a sales staff with lucrative commissions ranging from 20% to 30%; frequently, life insurance agents known and trusted in the community are recruited for this role.[117] These agents do not have a license to sell securities and rely solely on the information their employer provides, which later turns out to be false or misleading.[118] Enticed by promises of a 15% or 20% return on an "insured, guaranteed, no risk investment" and dealing with someone who is familiar to them, few victims ask any tough questions.[119] The pitch may include statements that reinforce the notion that this is a no risk investment, there is substantial collateral, and the investment is insured against loss. The money raised by the promissory notes may be needed to "open oil wells that were capped years ago because they were

unprofitable to operate then, but new technology now makes it profitable to bring them on line." The notes may also be associated with activities such as "bringing out new products, funding a new television show, helping a real estate company acquire prime land for development, modernizing a Mexican gold, Colombian emerald, or South African diamond mine, or financing an e-commerce venture."

The fraudsters may simply take the money and run, leaving their unwitting sales agents to face charges, or operate the investment fraud as yet another variation on a Ponzi scheme. Promissory note fraud is also run as a type of affinity fraud.

PRIME BANK NOTES

International defrauders invented the prime bank note investment scam, which promises extremely high yields in a relatively short period of time.[120] They claim to have special access to investments that are usually "limited to only the very wealthy." The yields promised range from 5% per month to hundreds of percent annually. Victims are told that their money will be pooled to trade in prime bank notes, prime bank guarantees, prime bank debentures, letters of credit, bank purchase orders, zero coupon bonds, or other official sounding instruments.[121] Victims believe that such instruments can be purchased for a steep discount and then quickly resold for a substantial profit. They may also be advised that the profits are so vast that the International Money Fraud or the Federal Reserve Bank requires that a certain percentage of it be spent for charitable relief in third-world countries or elsewhere, which adds respectability to the pitch. The funds are actually sent to overseas banks in Geneva, London, or elsewhere. From there, they are transferred to off-shore institutions, where they are laundered, and the victims' money disappears. As is frequently the case in many types of frauds, this one can also be operated as a Ponzi scheme. Although individual investors are frequently victims, units of government are sometimes reeled in by the scheme—for example, the city of Clovis, New Mexico, lost $3.5 million in a prime note investment fraud.

VIATICAL SETTLEMENTS

Viatical settlements were developed during the 1980s, in part to help dying AIDS patients pay their bills; their life insurance policies were bought by investors for less than the face value of the policy, and the investors had their money returned and a profit made upon the death of the insured.[122] Later, the practice was extended to others, especially the elderly. Because some people live longer than their medical diagnosis suggests is possible, and because new treatments are constantly developed that extend the life of the insured, this is a risky venture even when operated legitimately.[123]

Viatical settlement frauds are conducted in many guises—for example:

The National Medical Funding Company placed ads in gay publications soliciting terminally ill patients to sell their life insurance policies. The company never bought the policies; instead, they used the information from applicants to fabricate phony viatical contracts, which were then sold to Arizona investors as fully insured 12- to 16-month investments that paid 14% or more. As investors started complaining about bounced checks and payments that never arrived, the fraud was identified, with investors losing $13 million.[124]

TELEPHONE SCAMS

Unrelated to telemarketing fraud are three scams related to telephone billing, such as: (1) 1-900 and foreign exchange numbers, (2) the Mexican collect call scam, and (3) cramming.

1-900 AND FOREIGN EXCHANGE NUMBERS

Scammers will leave a telephone message or send an e-mail from someone offering to engage in phone sex, telling the recipient they have won a prize (which may end up being only a few dollars), telling them that a family member is sick, or some other bogus message. The return number may be a 1-900 (pay for service calls, some of which may be legitimate), 809 (Dominican Republic), 284 (British Virgin Islands), 876 (Jamaica), or some other three-digit code.[125] While international calls normally require a "011" prefix, calls to the just-identified countries, Canada, and some other Caribbean countries do not. The recipients think they are making a domestic long-distance call, but they are actually being connected to a number outside the United States and are billed at international call rates. Return callers often have to wade through automated menus and hear "dentist office" music to keep them on the line. These scams average $35 per call or more, which appears on the victims' telephone bills. Victims' vulnerability can be greatly reduced if they determine what country the three-digit prefix designates.

MEXICAN COLLECT CALL SCHEME

The Mexican collect call scam originated in that country, preys upon Hispanic consumers, and is basically a reverse of the scheme just described. The telephone rings and a voice, using the correct names of family members, says this is an emergency collect call, and the caller accepts the charges only to discover a stranger is on the line talking about something entirely different.

CRAMMING

It is entirely legal for phone companies to bill consumers for certain types of services as part of their regular telephone bill.

Cramming is the practice of placing unauthorized, misleading, inaccurate, or deceptive charges on the victims' telephone bills, which may be accidental but is often intentional. Categories of cramming include voice-mail, long-distance service, paging, Internet access, memberships, and pornography. Worldwide, pornography is a $97 billion industry, $13 billion of which is earned in the United States; a full 25% of all search engine requests involve pornography.[126] It did not, however, become a major industry simply by providing "free pornography." One source of its revenue is cramming—for example, visitors to some porn sites read that they can "download" movies for free; but the next month there is a charge on their telephone bill. Similarly, another common "cram" used in the porn industry is to request age verification through a VISA or MasterCard number. However the following month, there is a charge on their card for access to the porn website. There is virtually no recourse, since many of these sites are hosted in foreign countries. Much worse, the billing continues on a month-to-month basis until the victim contacts their credit card company. Yet in other cases, the "good" credit card numbers are sold to others and the fraud continues. The victim is forced to close their account and in the most vicious of cases, the victim's credit history is diminished for nonpayment of services.

TELEMARKETING AND POSTAL FRAUDS

Many of the types of frauds discussed earlier in this chapter can be run as telemarketing and postal frauds. These two mediums of communication are a means of reaching massive numbers of potential victims quickly. Table 15-4 identifies the top 10 telemarketing frauds, a number of which were discussed earlier in this chapter. Note that many of these top 10 telemarketing schemes are variations on advance fee frauds. It is estimated that consumers lose $40 billion to telemarketing annually, and one out of six consumers is cheated each year.

In the postal or mail fraud content that follows, some scams not already covered are described. Remember that these can also be run by other means, such as telemarketing. Included in postal scams are real estate, franchise scams, unsolicited merchandise, fees for normally free services, and phony inheritance cons. The top five postal frauds are (1) free prize schemes, (2) foreign lotteries, (3) pyramids scams, (4) investment frauds, and (5) work-at-home cons.[127]

LAND FRAUD

Offerings to sell parcels of land arrive in the mailboxes of potential victims, describing wonderful land on which to build vacation cabins or retirement homes or even just to hold as a "prime investment." The letters and brochures are slick and the language is glowing. Potential buyers should check with other brokers in the area or see if there are complaints against the person or company making the offer. This may simply be a version of

TABLE 15-4	Top 10 Telemarketing Scams		
NUMBER	SCAM	PERCENTAGE OF ALL COMPLAINTS	AVERAGE LOSS
1	**Fake Check Scams** Consumers paid with phony checks for work or items sold, instructed to wire money back. These have been the #1 telemarketing scam reported 2 years running.	58%	$3,854.78
2	**Prizes/Sweepstakes** Requests for payment to claim prizes that never materialize.	14%	$6,601.40
3	**Advance Fee Loans** False promises of business or personal loans, even if credit is bad, for a fee upfront.	5%	$1,583.02
4	**Lotteries/Lottery Clubs** Requests for payment to claim lottery winnings or get help to win, often foreign lotteries.	3%	$8,417.61
5	**Phishing** Calls or e-mails pretending to be from a well-known source, asking to confirm personal information.	2%	$149
6	**Magazine Sales** Con artists misrepresent cost of subscriptions or pretend to be the publisher offering renewals.	1.5%	$118.79
7	**Credit Card Offers** False promises of credit cards, for a fee, even if credit is bad.	1.5%	$292.58
8	**Scholarships/Grants** Scammers falsely promise to help get scholarships or government educational grants, for a fee.	1.4%	$532.28
9	**Buyers Clubs (not travel or lottery)** Charges for memberships in discount buying clubs consumers never agreed to join. This is the first time Buyers Clubs have appeared in the top 10 telemarketing list since 2004.	1%	$99.35
10	**Nigerian Money Offers** False promises of riches if consumers pay upfront to transfer money to their bank accounts. This once popular scam has not made an appearance in our top 10 telemarketing list since 2002.	1%	$1,687.50

Source: National Fraud Information Center, 2010.

an advanced fee scheme, or the land is worth very little because it is far from utility connections or cannot be built on without enormous costs because it is on the side of a steep ridge or mountain. Once they purchase the land, victims cannot resell it for even a fraction of what they paid for it.[128]

FRANCHISE CONS

Franchise offers arrive in the mail touting fast food or quick printing business opportunities that require a substantial investment. These offers mention brand names, such as FedEx Office or McDonald's, which are familiar to people or "soon to be very big in this area of the country." Using the cover of appearing to be a legitimate business opportunity, con men drain money from victims for application and other fees and then disappear.[129]

UNSOLICITED MERCHANDISE

People may receive gifts in the mail they didn't request, such as key chains, return address labels, and pens. Accompanying the

gift is a postcard that suggests the sender's affiliation, such as recording for the blind, scholarships for students, and after-school programs. Money may not be directly solicited by the postcard, but many people send a check, thinking of it as payment for the gift or a small donation. Recipients of unsolicited merchandise have several alternatives: (1) if unopened, they can return it to the sender, which the Post Office does for free; (2) if opened and the contents are unattractive, throw them away, and (3) if opened and the merchandise is attractive, keep it without any obligation.[130] If recipients elect either of the last two options, they may get a high-pressure call or even a visit. In both cases, they should hang up, or not talk to the visitor or allow him/her inside the home. They are under no obligation to pay for unsolicited merchandise.

FEES CHARGED FOR NORMALLY FREE SERVICES

Many services are available for free from the government or other legitimate organizations. A mail come-on hopes that you are unaware of these services and offers to provide them for a fee. Victimization schemes include child-support collection, unclaimed income tax refunds, and filing for property tax exemptions, all of which are run as advanced fee frauds.[131]

MISSING RELATIVES

One of the cruelest frauds is the **missing person fraud,** which plays on victims' hopes of locating a missing loved one. The con men read the newspapers and visit official police sites where there are Internet postings soliciting information about missing persons, including personal information and the circumstances surrounding the disappearance. The fraudsters send a letter in which they pose as "people recovery specialists," offer phony credentials as former FBI, CIA, or other governmental agents, tout their national and international contacts, provide false accounts of successes, including recovering people from cults, and mention their access to special databases.

Once the offer is accepted, preliminary information is gathered by telephone, an advance fee is required, a face-to-face meeting is scheduled, and the fraudsters are never heard from again. Alternatively, they may come back with some vague information, which to follow up on involves some costs that require an additional sum of money.

PHONY INHERITANCE SCHEMES

Everybody fantasizes about winning the lottery or inheriting some money from a distant relative. Con men know this and fuel our fantasy with letters delivered to our mailboxes from **"estate locators"** or "research specialists," which purport to be efforts "to locate the heirs of a substantial sum of money." These letters are, like other mail frauds, sent out in the thousands to unwary recipients who are asked to pay $30 or more for an "estate assessment."[132] This scam may also ask for personal information as the first step in an identity theft.

| KEY TERMS

account takeover
affinity fraud
auction fraud
bank examiner con
black market peso exchange
   (BMPE)
check kiters
cramming
drive down
dumpster diving
embezzlement
estate locators
follow-on crime
franchise offers
grand larceny
hard fraud
identity theft

intangible property
layering
missing person fraud
money laundering
off-shore accounts
one-year callable
organized retail theft
overpayment fraud
paper accident
petit or petty larceny
phishing
pigeon drop
placement
Ponzi scheme
promissory note
pump and dump
pyramid scheme

shoplifting
shoulder surfing
skimmers
smurfing
soft fraud
swoop and squat
tangible personal property
theft by conversion
theft by deception
theft by fraud
theft of services
theft by trick
viatical settlement
white-collar crime
wire-transfer scheme

| REVIEW QUESTIONS

1. How is grand larceny and petit or petty larceny differentiated?
2. What evidence is there to support the assertion that shoplifting is a very expensive crime?
3. What types of deterrent acts were suggested to fight organized and retail crime?
4. What are the five basic categories of shoplifters?
5. What are the most common methods used by shoplifters to steal merchandise?

6. What suggestions were made to assist theft prevention investigators?
7. What were the typical motives for bicycle thieves?
8. What are the critical questions law enforcement should be asking when analyzing a bicycle theft problem in their communities?
9. List eight ways identity thieves can identify victims' personal information.
10. What types of follow-on crime can be committed once an identity theft has occurred?

11. What are the "big three" that account for 50% of the cases of identity theft?

12. What are the signs that an employee in a position of trust, such as a bookkeeper or business manager, may be committing check-based crimes?

13. What is the difference between insurance frauds characterized as hard fraud or soft fraud?

14. How is money laundering defined and what are its three distinctive steps?

15. Who was Bernie Madoff?

16. What is a Ponzi/pyramid scheme?

17. What are pump and dump schemes?

18. How are promissory note frauds operated?

19. How does the missing person fraud work?

INTERNET ACTIVITIES

1. Visit the website for the National Association of Shoplifting Prevention (NASP) at *www.shopliftingprevention.org/main.asp*. Search through the website and learn about "shoplifting addiction." Discuss the addictive qualities of committing petty crimes, including shoplifting. What can be done to stop this vicious cycle?

2. Visit the website of the Federal Trade Commission at *www.ftc.gov* and click on the link entitled "Identity Theft." Discuss the steps that you can take to "deter, detect, and defend" against identity theft. List at least three other Internet sites that provide detailed information about what to do if you become a victim of identity theft.

CRIME SCENE DO NOT CROSS

16

VEHICLE THEFTS AND RELATED OFFENSES

CHAPTER OBJECTIVES

1. Identify types of motor vehicle theft.

2. List techniques for disposing of stolen motor vehicles.

3. Describe challenges associated with the theft. investigation of heavy equipment and farm equipment.

4. Identify major investigative resources.

5. Discuss methods for assisting in the identification of a recovered vehicle.

6. Describe vehicle fire-investigation methods.

7. Explain vehicle and equipment theft-prevention approaches.

8. Assess title and registration issues related to marine theft.

9. Discuss aircraft and avionics theft and relevant identification and investigative techniques.

In 2014, there was one motor vehicle theft about every 46 seconds.[1] While this is still a somewhat alarming number, it does actually reflect a downward trend; such thefts have dropped 58% from their peak in 1991.[2] As a result, most Americans don't actively worry about their cars being stolen. Efforts of law enforcement, anti-theft and prevention programs, and technology that deters or prevents theft have all contributed to lower numbers of motor vehicle theft and "peace of mind for vehicle owners" across the country.

And while that's certainly good news, that doesn't mean that it's been easy sailing for vehicle theft investigators: while numbers of cases have decreased, the complexity of the crimes has increased. An evolution in the ways that thieves access vehicles presents new challenges for law enforcement—as does an increase in the number of these crimes that involve some sort of fraud. Investigation of such crimes require resources and contacts in the private sector, broad knowledge of technology, and a keen eye for thefts or frauds that are actually part of a bigger criminal enterprise.

When investigating vehicle theft, officers must consider the reason for the theft. Vehicles may be stolen temporarily, for example, for use in the commission of other crimes such as robberies or drive-by shootings, after which the vehicles are abandoned. Often, the stolen vehicle is not reported as such, because it is considered secondary or incidental to the robbery or drive-by shooting. Other reasons for theft can include joyriding, professional theft, and fraudulent schemes.

Professional thieves use a variety of means such as chop shops, stripping, salvage switches, and export to other countries to dispose of stolen vehicles. Once a vehicle has been chopped or stripped, trying to identify particular stolen vehicles and/or parts can be extremely difficult. However, this seemingly formidable task has been made easier in part by the creation of standardized vehicle identification number systems. Finally, investigators are often faced with situations where the perpetrators are not strangers or professional thieves but the owners themselves.

Given limited law enforcement resources and an economically difficult time, vehicle theft may not be considered a top priority. Nonetheless, investigators have many major resources and organizations at their disposal. This chapter provides an overview of several of these resources, such as the National Insurance Crime Bureau and the American Association of Motor Vehicle Administrators, as well as the information they can provide. Although motor vehicle theft is the main topic of this chapter, also addressed is the theft of other high-value items, such as heavy equipment; commercial vehicles and cargo; marine vehicles; and aircraft and avionic equipment. We also discuss prevention programs that can help minimize the theft of motor vehicles and other items.

MOTOR VEHICLE THEFT

The number of motor vehicle thefts in the United States for 2014, as reported by the FBI, was 689,527, representing a loss of $4.5 billion dollars. Of those thefts, 74.5% were automobiles.[3] While the average rate of recovery for a stolen vehicle is around 50%, that number varies wildly by location with some states seeing a recovery rate of 71% (Washington) and others only 19% (Michigan).[4] Regardless of whether or not the car is ever recovered, the fact remains that very few vehicle thefts are ever cleared by arrest: in 2014, only 12.8% of motor vehicle thefts were cleared by arrest of the suspect(s) by law enforcement agencies.[5]

While motor vehicle thefts overall have trended downward, perhaps due to a combination of technology, prevention awareness, and law enforcement efforts, motorcycle thefts have shown a slight bump in the last few years: in 2014, there was a 6% increase in such crimes, though it's worth noting that overall, motorcycle theft has decreased nearly 32% from a peak in 2006.[6] Motorcycles have grown increasingly expensive, with many models exceeding $20,000—making their illegal resell as well as the stripping of each motorcycle for parts a very lucrative business. Motorcycle parts—down to the bare frame are very easy to alter, having no individual serial number and making it almost impossible to recover once the vehicle is actually stripped. Only 25% of motorcycle parts are ever recovered after the initial theft.[7]

Heavy equipment theft, which includes things like riding lawn mowers, loaders, and tractors, has also seen a slight bump in occurrence, up a little over 1% in 2014. This crime is costly for home and business owners, as only 20% of these items are ever recovered.[8]

Thefts of 18-wheelers or "big rig" thefts are also a growing concern for law enforcement, with thieves targeting the cargo onboard these large vehicles as well as the vehicle itself. While the rates of these types of thefts have remained relatively constant, or even decreased slightly, over the past few years, the value of the loss in such incidents is dramatically increasing, primarily because of the expensive cargo that is also taken in these types of vehicle thefts. Many times the cargo includes high value items like electronics (for example, computers, small engines, boat motors, computer chips and/or parts, TVs, and telephones), or expensive liquid material that can be easily sold on the open market or to independent outlets, manufacturers, or refineries (for example, airplane/jet fuel, automotive gas, crude oil, diesel, or chemicals used in manufacturing processes).[9]

QUICK FACTS

In 2015, the most stolen vehicles in the United States were:

1. 1996 Honda Accord
2. 1998 Honda Civic
3. 2006 Ford Pickup (Full Size)
4. 2004 Chevrolet Pickup (Full Size)
5. 2014 Toyota Camry
6. 2001 Dodge Pickup (Full Size)
7. 2014 Toyota Corolla
8. 2015 Nissan Altima
9. 2002 Dodge Caravan
10. 2008 Chevrolet Impala

Source: National Insurance Crime Bureau. "NICB's Hot Wheels: America's Most Stolen Vehicles." (August 1, 2016). See: https://www.nicb.org/newsroom/nicb_campaigns/hot%E2%80%93wheels.

TYPES OF THEFT

Motor vehicle thefts generally fall into one of four categories: temporary theft, joyriding, professional theft, or fraud.

Temporary Theft

The term **temporary theft** is not used to imply that the crime is not serious but to distinguish joyriding from something more ominous. Of growing concern are the thefts of vehicles specifically for use in the commission of other crimes such as robberies or drive-by shootings, after which the vehicles are abandoned. These thefts are on the increase and, when reported, are often recorded only as the underlying crime rather than also as a motor vehicle theft, thereby skewing the actual theft figures.

Joyriding

Joyriding is most often engaged in by teenagers—15 to 19 years old—who steal a car simply to drive it around before abandoning it. Among the reasons teenage joyriders cite for the thefts are that joyriding makes them feel important, powerful, and accepted among their peers; it's fun and exciting; they did it on a dare; it relieves boredom and gives an adrenaline rush; they don't feel like walking; they want to impress girls; to make money by stripping cars and selling the parts; to get even with parents, or to escape family problems; and it was done as part of a gang membership or initiation. Since many youngsters are not professionals, they frequently target vehicles that are easy to steal and generally lack any antitheft devices. The large number of apprehensions in this age category may be due to the arrests of joyriders.

▲ **FIGURE 16-1 Thief breaks car window**

The professional car thief is motivated by high profits and relatively low risk of apprehension. These thieves use a variety of means for entering locked cars, including breaking windows to open locked doors. The professional thief can break into a car, start it, and drive away in as little as 20 seconds.

(©KatarzynaBialasiewicz/Getty Images RF)

Professional Theft

In **professional theft** (Figure 16-1), the car thief is motivated by very high profits and generally low risk. The profits to be gained are second only to those from drugs. Anyone who has ever purchased a replacement part for a car is aware that the cost of replacing all the parts of a vehicle is much higher than the original cost of the entire vehicle. The professional can often sell the parts of a stolen car for up to five times the original assembled value. Considering what the thief "paid" for the vehicle, the profit margin is substantial.

However, professionals do have costs in operating their "businesses." It is not infrequent for professional thieves to employ and train youths to steal cars. Often a youth is paid a set amount, several hundred to several thousand dollars, for each theft. The amount varies depending on the make, model, and year of the vehicle. There are even "training schools" in some areas of the country where juveniles and young adults are taught how to steal cars, trucks, motorcycles, and other vehicles. The professional thief, for example, can break into a locked, high-priced car, start it, and drive it away in as little as 20 seconds.

Fraud

Although certain types of theft involve fraud perpetrated on innocent purchasers, the major category of **vehicle fraud** as described here does not actually involve the theft of vehicles by professionals or even strangers. The various types of vehicle fraud are generally committed by the owner or someone acting on behalf of the owner, with the underlying purpose of profiting at the expense of an insurance company.

The Natiional Insurance Crime Bureau (NICB) estimates that anywhere from 15% to 25% of all reported vehicle thefts involve some type of fraud and that a vast majority of them involve fraudulent insurance claims. Insurance crime is an enormous problem, and its true magnitude is almost impossible to pinpoint. The associated crimes of identity theft and credit card fraud, both of which have reached epidemic proportions, make the fraud problem even more complex.

In addition, some insurance experts estimate that between 16 and 35 cents of every dollar in premiums paid by the public for motor vehicle insurance is used to pay fraudulent claims or to fight fraud. The NICB says that if the amount of insurance claim fraud and vehicle theft occurring in the United States represented a corporation, it would rank in the top 25 of the Fortune 500 and be called a growth industry. In addition, insurance fraud is on the rise, because it is an easy crime to successfully commit. Insurance companies, even those with highly qualified special investigation units whose function is to investigate suspected cases of fraud, must be concerned about potential liability resulting from lawsuits if someone is wrongly accused or a claim is wrongly denied. The fact that insurance companies are believed to have a great deal of money—deep pockets—makes these companies even more susceptible to civil suits and potential liability and, in turn, even more cautious.

METHODS OF OPERATION— THE PROFESSIONAL

To turn a profit, professional thieves use a variety of means to dispose of stolen motor vehicles. Among the most common are chop shops, quick strip, salvage switch, export, and cloning.

Chop Shops

Very simply, a **chop shop** is a place where stolen vehicles are disassembled for resale of their parts (Figure 16-2). The operators and employees of chop shops cut stolen motor vehicles

▲ **FIGURE 16-2 Interior of a chop shop**

A chop shop such as the one pictured here is a place where stolen vehicles are disassembled for resale of their parts. Stolen vehicles are cut apart in as little as 8 minutes in these chop shops. Parts are then sold to repair shops or salvage yards. Sometimes the repair shop operator is in collusion with the thief or the chop shop. (©National Insurance Crime Bureau)

BOX 16-1 | AUTO COMPONENT AND ACCESSORY THEFT

While technology has made stealing entire vehicles less attractive to thieves, it's made the theft of vehicle components more lucrative. Airbag theft constitutes a $50 million loss to insurers and vehicle owners; they are the third most stolen auto part today, behind stereos and wheels. Stolen airbags can fetch between $150 and $1000 each, sold to unscrupulous auto body shops that then replace deployed bags with the stolen ones. Once the bag is replaced, the shop can claim that they used a new air bag system in the repair, charging insurance companies or consumers upward of $3000 each—and profiting hugely.

Xenon headlights, common in luxury cars, are also prone to theft; there's been speculation that the lights can be easily adapted to grow marijuana, but such cases are largely anecdotal. More likely, the lights simply have a good black market value, making them attractive to thieves—especially since they're relatively easy to steal—and illegally install. Catalytic converters are also highly sought after by thieves. The presence of small amounts of platinum and palladium, precious metals whose value has risen with the use of catalytic converters and the growth in popularity of platinum jewelry, makes them an easy sell for thieves.

Technology has also brought a host of accessories to our automobiles, some installed as vehicle components and some merely left out of habit by drivers and passengers. Items such as BluRay players, GPS systems, tablets, and cell-phones have become such a regular part of the driving experience that many drivers don't think twice about leaving them visible to potential thieves. These items are rarely recovered from vehicle burglaries, and in many cases, are not reported to police.[10]

---

apart with torches, power saws, and other tools, sometimes in as little as 8 to 9 minutes. They alter or dispose of the parts that are potentially traceable and sell the untraceable parts to repair shops or salvage yards. Sometimes the parts buyers are unsuspecting. Often, the salvage yard or repair shop operator is in collusion with the thief or the chop shop. In fact, a chop shop may well direct the theft of a specific type of motor vehicle in order to "fill an order" for a specific part needed by a repair shop or salvage yard. See Box 16-1.

A modification of the typical chop-shop operation is as follows:

Thieves steal a car, disassemble it carefully so that the parts are not damaged, have the remainder conveniently recovered and disposed of through a salvage sale, buy the salvage, reassemble the vehicle with all its original parts, and sell the vehicle, which has already been classed as a recovered theft and is no longer considered stolen.

Quick Strip

In a **quick strip,** a vehicle is stolen and stripped mainly for valuable accessories such as seats, stereos, car phones, and tires. These items are attractive to thieves because they normally do not contain any identifying numbers, thus making them difficult to identify and easy to dispose of.

Salvage Switch

Generally, a **salvage vehicle** is one that has been damaged or wrecked to such an extent that the cost of repairing it is beyond its fair market value. Thus, its primary value in the legitimate market comes from the sale of its undamaged parts. To the criminal, however, the value of a salvaged vehicle is far greater than its parts. The real profit is made after the criminal buys the salvage, provided it is accompanied by the certificate of title and the vehicle identification number (VIN) plate. Often the offender does not even want the vehicle and leaves it at the salvage yard from which it is purchased or disposes of it elsewhere. The thief then steals a vehicle identical to the wreck, changes the VIN plate, and sells the stolen vehicle, with a matching title, to an innocent purchaser or to a purchaser who is offered such a "good" price that no questions are asked. Through the **salvage switch,** the thief is able to disguise and dispose of stolen vehicles in the legitimate market.

Export

Vehicles manufactured in the United States are extremely popular in other countries. The sale of American-manufactured vehicles can also be highly profitable. Vehicles manufactured in other countries for sale in the United States are also stolen for export. Buyers in foreign nations often pay double the purchase price for quality cars, some of which is due to high tariffs. Mexico and Central and South American countries are among the most popular but certainly not the exclusive destinations for stolen U.S.-manufactured vehicles. There are no reliable statistics for vehicle thefts for export in the United States: these thefts are generally going to be categorized as unrecovered vehicles.[11] However, crime analysts have found that vehicle thefts are overrepresented in border states, particularly California. In fact, in the southern portion of San Diego County, which borders Mexico, the vehicle theft rate has been measured at four times the national average. Similar findings have been found in parts of Arizona and South Texas. This suggests that many of those vehicles may be finding their way across the border into Mexico.[12]

The ten most popular metropolitan statistical areas (MSAs) for car theft are often located relatively close to the border with Mexico, or have easy access to large seaports servicing Mexico and/or Asian countries. Few stolen cars are transported to Europe primarily because of much more stringent law enforcement efforts and duty inspections on arrival in European ports versus other areas of the world.

1. Modesto, California
2. Albuquerque, New Mexico
3. Bakersfield, California
4. Salinas, California
5. San Francisco-Oakland-Hayward, California
6. Stockton-Lodi, California
7. Pueblo, Colorado
8. Merced, California
9. Riverside-San Bernardino-Ontario, California
10. Vallejo-Fairfield, California

Source: National Insurance Crime Bureau. "Hot Spots 2015." (June 2016). See: https://www.nicb.org/newsroom/nicb_campaigns/hot_spots.

Contributing to this problem are the limited, although effective, controls exercised by Mexican customs and the few effective controls exercised by the United States over southbound traffic entering Mexico. The volume of traffic going into Mexico makes it almost impossible to inspect and investigate all vehicles. Additionally, there's a substantial legal trade of used cars between the U.S. and Mexico. The top two items exported to Mexico from the U.S. are vehicle parts and vehicles, making it difficult to differentiate illegitimate exports from legitimate business. Further, border controls are more focused on arrivals from Mexico—not departures from the United States. Port cities also experience a large number of auto thefts and exports, possibly lending to inflated statistics in California.[13]

With the collapse of communism and the opening of free market economies in eastern Europe, auto theft has grown to become an enormous international problem. According to Interpol, auto theft has become the second largest source of terrorist funding.[14]

Cloning

Vehicle cloning is a crime in which stolen vehicles receive the identity of nonstolen, legally owned vehicles of the same make and model. This is accomplished by counterfeiting labels, stickers, VIN plates, and titles to make the stolen car look legitimate. Illicit profits from vehicle cloning in the United States are estimated by the NICB to be in excess of $12 million each year. Many high-priced, luxury vehicles are objects of cloning.[15]

Cloning is not confined to the United States. Many offenses have occurred in Mexico, Canada, and the United Kingdom. Exportation of legitimate vehicles is also used by professional thieves to clone vehicles. Once exported, the VIN number and other counterfeit indicia appear on stolen, cloned vehicles

titled and registered in one or more states. These vehicles are referred to as being "reborn." Often, multiple copies of the counterfeit indicia will appear on stolen vehicles and, unless the vehicles are thoroughly inspected by trained investigators, these stolen vehicles are almost impossible to identify as being fraudulent. Many of the stolen, cloned vehicles are then exported to such popular destinations as Eastern Europe, Russia, the Caribbean, the Dominican Republic, Central and South America, and the Far East.[16] The NICB says that cloned vehicles are also used to facilitate drug trafficking, money laundering, and for transportation to and from crime scenes by organized crime.[17]

Many of the fraudulent theft schemes described in the next section apply equally to the cloning of a vehicle.

FRAUDULENT THEFT SCHEMES

Fraudulent auto-theft claim schemes fall into three major categories: false-vehicle schemes, in which no vehicle exists or the vehicle is not owned by the criminal; false-theft schemes; and inflated-loss-theft schemes.

False-Vehicle Schemes

False-vehicle schemes are particularly prevalent where insurance companies are lax or have ineffective programs to verify the existence of a vehicle before issuing an insurance policy. As a general rule, this type of fraud is planned well in advance of obtaining insurance coverage. The criminal purchases a policy that has a provision covering loss by theft. In fact, the vehicle does not exist except on paper, has already been salvaged, or does not belong to the person who buys the insurance. Most often, the vehicle insured is a recent model. Some time later (generally within three months, to hold down the cost of the insurance coverage purchase) a theft report is filed with a law enforcement agency, and a claim is made to the insurance company.

Several modifications of the salvage switch, described earlier, are illustrative of false-vehicle schemes. Once a salvaged vehicle is purchased, insurance coverage is obtained. After a short time, a theft-loss claim is filed for the vehicle, which, of course, was in "excellent condition."

In some jurisdictions, a **salvage title** may be issued. This does not necessarily prevent false-theft claims on salvage; it merely channels the process in a different direction. One way the criminal avoids the problems associated with the issuance of salvage titles is by **washing,** or laundering, the title. This is done by fabricating the sale of the vehicle and transferring the title to an alleged purchaser in another state that does not issue salvage titles or does not carry forward a "brand" on the title issued by another state. The "buyer" then obtains a clean title in that state and transfers it back to the insured either directly or through several other people or businesses to make it appear to be a legitimate transaction. Then, with a clean title, the insured files a theft claim.

In another technique, the salvage buyer falsifies the necessary support documentation so that it shows the salvage vehicle as being completely rebuilt or restored and thereby obtains a "clean," or regular, title. The thief may not even bother to get a clean title; upon filing a claim for the alleged theft, he/she may simply contend that the vehicle was rebuilt or restored but was stolen before the insured could file the necessary paperwork to obtain a nonsalvage title.

In still another version of the salvage switch, the VIN plate may be attached to a rented or borrowed car of the same make and model and, along with the certificate of title, may be presented to and inspected by an agent of the company from which coverage is sought. After the policy is issued, the salvage vehicle VIN plate is removed and the vehicle is returned to the person or company from which it was borrowed or rented.

Presenting a counterfeit or stolen certificate of title or manufacturer's certificate of origin (MCO) as the basis for having a policy issued on a **"paper vehicle"** or on a stolen vehicle with a concealed identity is another technique for defrauding insurance companies through the filing of false-vehicle claims. A manufacturer's certificate of origin is the original identification document issued by a vehicle's manufacturer, somewhat like a birth certificate. It accompanies the vehicle through its delivery to a new car dealer until it is first sold to a retail purchaser, after which the MCO is surrendered to the jurisdiction issuing the first certificate of title in the name of the retail purchaser.

A variation on the counterfeit- or blank-title scheme is the altered title, whereby the criminal manages to conceal the existence of a lienholder who may have already repossessed the vehicle because of missed payments. A theft report is then filed along with the fraudulent insurance claim.

It is not uncommon to find the following scenario in a fraudulent claim on a false vehicle:

Henry Johnson owns a late-model full-size car. The vehicle is paid for and Johnson has the title in his possession. Johnson decides to sell the car. After he has it advertised for a few days, he receives a satisfactory offer from a person who pays cash and takes the car to another state to have it titled and registered. Johnson signs the title over to the buyer, who takes possession of the vehicle and drives it to his own state of residence. The next day, Johnson, claiming he can't find his car title, applies for a duplicate title in his own state. The title is issued and is branded with the word "duplicate." Although it may take several weeks to receive the duplicate title, the process may still be faster than it takes for the buyer's home state to issue a new title to the buyer and send the original of Johnson's title back to his state for official cancellation. Upon obtaining the duplicate title, Johnson files a theft claim with his insurance company and surrenders the duplicate title to the company in exchange for the theft-loss payment. After learning of the scam, the insurance company goes looking for Johnson and finds that all the information he provided was false, and he has disappeared not only with the insurance money but also with the money he made from selling the vehicle. Normally, the issuance of a duplicate title renders the original or any previously issued duplicate void, but this fact was unknown to the buyer of Johnson's car or to the buyer's home state, where he applied for a title in his own name.

False-Theft Schemes

As opposed to the many different fraudulent schemes in which no vehicle exists, in a **false-theft scheme,** the vehicle does exist and is in fact owned by the person who has obtained the insurance policy. The primary reason why an owner would file a phony theft-loss is generally either to avoid liability for some conduct that resulted from the use of the vehicle or to reduce or avoid some financial loss. The specific motivation leading to the filing of the fraudulent claim may exist at the time the policy coverage is obtained or may result from circumstances that develop later.

Among the vast number of motivations—and there are as many motivations as there are false claims—for filing false theft-loss claims are these:

- To cover or avoid personal responsibility for a hit-and-run accident. The owner reports the car stolen (before the police come to question him or her) and subsequently files an insurance claim.
- To replace an old vehicle that just doesn't look good or drive smoothly any longer.
- To replace a "lemon" that can't be sold for a decent price.
- To obtain money for another vehicle that is in need of repair or replacement.
- To avoid loss of the vehicle without receiving any financial gain—for example, through repossession caused by a default of payments or in response to a court order to transfer the title to a former spouse after a divorce.
- To end costly car payments or repair bills.
- To avoid the hassle of selling.
- To obtain a more favorable interest rate on a car loan.
- To break a restricting car lease.

As noted at the outset of this chapter, fraud may be committed by the insured acting alone or with another person or persons. When a vehicle owner conspires with others, the fraud is often referred to as an "owner give-up." Examples of both solo and give-up false-theft schemes include these:

- The vehicle is abandoned and later reported stolen (Figure 16-3).
- The vehicle, which may have been previously damaged or had some major mechanical defects, is reported stolen. Shortly afterward, it is recovered, and the insured claims that the damage or defects were caused by the theft.
- The vehicle is sold to an out-of-state buyer, and then a duplicate certificate of title is applied for and used to file the claim—just as in the Johnson scenario, reported earlier.

▲ FIGURE 16-3

Vehicle abandoned in false-theft scheme

Vehicle owners have been known to file false theft reports on their cars, often to avoid liability for some conduct associated with the vehicle or to reduce or avoid financial loss. The owner typically attempts to abandon the vehicle in a location beyond the scope of a general search conducted by the police.

(©Ron Bailey/Getty Images RF)

wooded edge of the airport. After his attempts to sell the car met with no success, the insured, who worked as a landscaper at the airport, decided to use a backhoe to dig a pit and bury his car inside. He then reported the car stolen in order to collect an insurance settlement.[18]

- Vehicle arson is another form of fraud that is planned beforehand and is motivated by a desire to collect on an insurance policy either to make a profit or to solve a financial problem. (Vehicle arson will be covered in more detail later.)

Inflated-Theft-Loss Schemes

In contrast to the preceding schemes, in the **inflated-theft-loss scheme** the vehicle actually exists, actually belongs to the insured, and actually is stolen. The fraud occurs when the insured makes a false claim concerning the physical or mechanical condition of the vehicle when it was stolen; actually causes some damage or removes some parts on recovery of the vehicle but before it is inspected by the insurance company; claims there were expensive parts on or improvements made to the vehicle before it was stolen; or, if no follow-up inspection is conducted by the insurer, claims certain damage occurred that actually did not happen.

One frequently used scam has the insured enter into a conspiracy with a repair shop, after a stolen vehicle is recovered, to allege that damages were caused during the theft. The damages do not exist. The vehicle is immediately "repaired" before the insurance appraiser has the opportunity to inspect the vehicle, and the repair shop insists that the insurer accept the repair bill, possibly using a photo of a wrecked vehicle of the same make and condition as the vehicle "before repair." A spinoff of this basic scenario has the repair shop show the appraiser an actual wrecked vehicle in its possession of the same make and model as the insured's car.

The inflated-theft-loss claim also extends to vehicle contents. The claimant alleges the vehicle contained valuable clothes, cameras, golf clubs, and other "new" items of considerable value when it was stolen.

Defrauding the Owner and the Insurer

Sometimes the owner is not involved in the fraud, and both the owner and the insurer become victims, as illustrated in the following example:

An individual leases a vehicle from a rental company and, during the rental period, reports the vehicle stolen to both the police and the rental company. Shortly after, the renter again calls the police and reports that the vehicle was recovered, using some excuse such as his coworker took it to the store or he forgot where he parked it the night before because he had had too much to drink. Consequently, the police never enter the "stolen" report into the National Crime Information Center (NCIC).

- The vehicle is not stolen but is hidden before the theft report and before the claim being filed. After the loss is paid, the vehicle can be returned to use, stripped, sold, chopped for parts, taken out of state, or otherwise disposed of.
- The vehicle is dumped in water, a method of causing damage that is increasing in use. This is often referred to as car dunking or vehicle dumping. Such vehicles generally cannot be repaired economically even if recovered.
- Vehicle burying is another way that owners dispose of unwanted vehicles—for example, an employee at the Charlotte/Douglas International Airport in North Carolina was charged with insurance fraud after police unearthed his car from the ground at a remote,

Conveniently, the renter fails to notify the rental company, which assumes that the law enforcement agency entered the theft into NCIC. The thief may have several days' or longer use of the vehicle before the victims can put the whole story together.

Some vehicles are exported by owners for the purpose of filing and collecting on fraudulent theft claims.

Another type of export fraud occurs when a vehicle owner makes multiple copies of proof-of-ownership documents to present to the Bureau of Customs Enforcement officials and exports his or her vehicle. After the vehicle arrives at its foreign destination, the VIN plate is removed and mailed back to the owner, who steals a car of the same make and model, switches the VIN plate, and, using the additional copies of ownership documents, exports the stolen vehicle. This is another variation of cloning.

As illustrated by the preceding examples, people who engage in insurance fraud are limited only by their imaginations. They are able to change tactics as quickly as law enforcement agencies and the insurance industry devise methods for combating current fraud schemes.

THEFT OF HEAVY CONSTRUCTION EQUIPMENT

The National Crime Information Center (NCIC) captured 11,625 heavy equipment theft reports in 2014, with annual loss estimates varying between $300 million to $1 billion—not including losses from business interruption as a result of the theft.

Equipment theft levels are relative to the amount of heavy equipment in a given area. In other words, in places where there is a lot of construction or agricultural work, there will be more equipment thefts. It's no surprise that Texas, then, tops the list for equipment thefts; followed by North Carolina, Florida, South Carolina, Georgia, California, Tennessee, Oklahoma, Arkansas, and Indiana.[19]

Off-road equipment is stolen for the following reasons: its high value, a demand for the equipment, low security, low risk, and high rewards.[20] Thieves may steal on order, for stripping, or for export. One offender was caught with a notebook filled with photographs he had taken of machinery on various farms. When interrogated, he stated he had roamed the countryside obtaining the photographs in the notebook. The notebook was then used as a "sales catalog" when meeting with prospective

buyers and as a means of instructing thieves working with him as to exactly what equipment from a particular location was to be taken. This arrangement made it possible for the equipment to be consigned or sold before it was even stolen, minimizing the amount of time that the equipment was in the thieves' hands and therefore their risk.

The theft of off-road equipment and the investigation of the thefts cause numerous problems for owners, manufacturers, and law enforcement agencies. Title or registration generally is not required for such equipment, and owners have traditionally resisted such requirements for several reasons. They fear that the title and registration records could be used to levy taxes on expensive items of property and that such a financial burden would have to be passed on to their consumers. Further, they believe that registration requirements would impede their ability to move the equipment rapidly and freely around the country.

Owners are also victimized by the problem of inventory control. Construction equipment is often spread over several miles of job site or over several job sites and may be left idle for days or weeks at a time in isolated areas. Thus, when the professional thief is overcome by the irresistible temptation, it is often days before the theft is noticed and reported to the police.

Another issue that compounded the construction equipment theft problem until recently was the fact that off-road equipment, unlike conventional motor vehicles, had no standard, permanently affixed identification number. Historically, each manufacturer had its own system of identification, and the numbering systems could vary from 4 to as many as 15 alphanumeric digits. On January 1, 2000, the 237 manufacturers of heavy equipment throughout the world (including the big four U.S. manufacturers—Case, Caterpillar, Deere, and Ford) began using a standardized 17-character **product identification number (PIN)** on all new equipment models[21] (Figure 16-4). The definition of "new model" will not necessarily change by calendar year. Consequently, it will take a few years before the standardized 17-character PIN becomes uniformly applied.

In at least one instance, the PIN is now more difficult to counterfeit than has been the case in the past. The new PIN plate on Caterpillar equipment is laser-engraved on black anodized aluminum and has a bar code and a microprinted security feature—the PIN number.[22]

Heavy equipment is also easily stolen; a single key may be used to start all models produced by a particular manufacturer, and where key locks are in place, the machinery can be jumped by placing a pocket knife or screwdriver across the electrical posts on the starter. Although manufacturers offer antitheft devices, they are costly items that add substantially to the base price of the equipment.

The unfamiliarity of most law enforcement officers with the nature, identity, and terminology of construction and farm equipment is among the principal problems faced by law enforcement. Few agencies have anyone with the expertise to identify specific machines or to locate and interpret identification numbers (Figure 16-5).

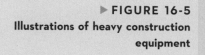

▶FIGURE 16-4
Product identification removed from stolen piece of construction equipment
The Product Identification Number (PIN) had been removed from this piece of construction equipment and, following its recovery, an NICB special agent was able to identify the unit by other partial numbers so it could be returned to its rightful owner.
(©National Insurance Crime Bureau)

▶FIGURE 16-5
Illustrations of heavy construction equipment

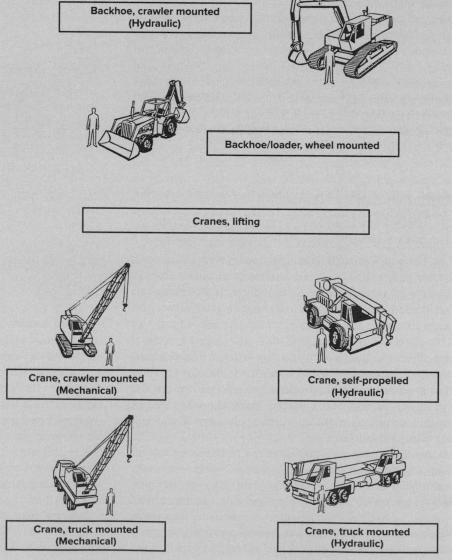

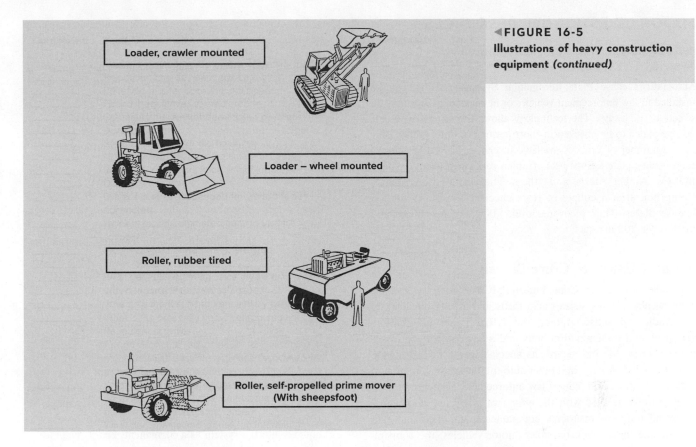

◄FIGURE 16-5
Illustrations of heavy construction equipment *(continued)*

COMMERCIAL-VEHICLE AND CARGO THEFT

The insurance industry pays out about $18 million every year because of **commercial-vehicle theft.** It is difficult to convert this figure to the number of vehicles stolen, because commercial-vehicle theft data is incorporated into the overall motor vehicle theft statistics. Suffice it to say, the number is significant and rising. Additionally, it is estimated that the actual number of cargo thefts is 20% more than reported.

The theft of cargo from, or in, commercial vehicles—is a rapidly growing criminal enterprise. Although not a separate crime in itself, **cargo theft,** in the United States, is estimated as accounting for as much as $25 billion in direct merchandise losses each year.[23] As an aside, cargo theft is just one aspect of a larger problem called *cargo crime,* which also includes smuggling, counterfeiting, and product piracy. Total direct merchandise losses from all cargo crime are estimated as approaching $60 billion per year.[24] The products most vulnerable to cargo crime, in general, and cargo theft, in particular, are assembled computers, computer components and software, electronic products, cigarettes, and fashion apparel, packaged foods, appliances, and seafood.

In January 2010 the FBI announced that a cargo-theft data element was adopted in the national uniform crime reports program. This means state and local agencies need to begin capturing and reporting this date to the FBI. The new program called

Cargo Net provides that state UCR programs will have 18 to 24 months to implement needed software changes to begin collecting the data on the state level.[25]

INVESTIGATIVE TOOLS AND TECHNIQUES

Vehicle theft investigation is a fairly technical and sophisticated specialty. An effective investigator needs experience and expertise. Despite the fact that vehicle theft may not be among the offenses receiving the highest priority for the allocation of limited resources by a law enforcement agency, there are thousands of specialists in the United States and elsewhere whose expertise is available to any investigator or street officer needing assistance. Often, these resources are just a telephone call away.

In any specialized investigative field, one is not born an expert and cannot become an expert without extensive training and experience. So it is with vehicle thefts and related crimes. Individuals who possess the expertise, such as highly skilled investigators, cannot assume that uniformed officers with general policing responsibilities have any knowledge about the field beyond their limited exposure in an academy setting. Thus, if investigators are anxious for patrol officers to perform some initial investigative tasks, the investigators should offer to teach those officers how to perform the desired tasks.

MAJOR INVESTIGATIVE RESOURCES

Automatic License Plate Recognition Systems (ALPR)

Automatic License Plate Recognition Systems (ALPR) can be installed in law enforcement vehicles or at permanent locations on streets or highways. The technology allows thousands of vehicle license plates to be checked in short periods of time, limited only by the number of vehicles available to check. The ALPR checks each license plate against lists of stolen cars (with license plates), BOLOs, Amber Alerts, and others. The City of Long Beach, California, after a couple of years checked almost 7.5 million license plates. They recovered over 1,000 stolen vehicles and made over 200 arrests.[26]

National Insurance Crime Bureau

The **National Insurance Crime Bureau (NICB)** is not a law enforcement agency that investigates auto thefts and arrests offenders in the traditional sense. Rather, the NICB is an information-gathering and dissemination body and a law enforcement assistance agency. In this regard, its special agents do investigate professional theft rings and other auto-theft cases in conjunction with local, state, and federal law enforcement agencies.

Beginning in 1912 with the efforts of a few individuals representing different insurance companies that joined forces to disseminate information on stolen motor vehicles, the cooperation gradually spread and evolved into several independent regionalized and, later, national groups. This growth limited communication and interaction. Duplication of efforts and costs, along with the creation of considerable confusion among law enforcement officials in deciding whom to contact for information, led to the initial consolidation of all existing auto-theft information agencies and organizations into the National Automobile Theft Bureau (NATB) in 1912. In 1965 the NATB was completely nationalized and centralized.

Late in 1991 a merger took place between the NATB and the Insurance Crime Prevention Institute (ICPI), and on January 1, 1992, the National Insurance Crime Bureau was formed. The NICB now has approximately 150 investigative field agents working with another 800 fraud investigators who work for individual insurance companies.

The NICB is not a government organization. It is a not-for-profit organization operated by, funded by, affiliated with, and serving approximately 1,000 associated insurance companies nationwide. It supports engineering, research, and experiments aimed at reducing vehicle theft and fraud and is a recognized national voice for law enforcement and the insurance industry on legislative matters.

The NICB assists in the identification of vehicles and helps educate law enforcement officers in investigative techniques of vehicle identification, fraud, and theft. Online Insurance Crime Training for Law Enforcement, including material on vehicle theft fraud, can be found at *www.nicbtraining.org*.

In addition to the expertise of its field personnel, the computerized records developed and established by the NICB, and now maintained and administered by the Insurance Service Office, Inc. (ISO), a private company, are invaluable investigative aids. These database services include:

- *Insurance theft file:* More than 1,000 insurance companies report stolen vehicles. Theft records from the Canadian Automobile Theft Bureau (CATB) and most European countries are also maintained and include all types of vehicles, off-road machinery, boats, parts, and accessories. The records contain full ownership and insurance information.

- *Salvage file:* Salvage vehicle reports are received from insurance companies on vehicles for which there has been a loss settlement and the company has taken the title. These vehicles are generally sold through salvage pools or to salvage buyers. The file contains information on both sellers and buyers of salvage.

- *Export file:* The U.S. Customs Service and others send copies of export declarations for entry into the system. The information aids in the detection of illegal exports and of fraudulent theft reports on exported vehicles in cases where a subsequent stolen vehicle report is filed.

- *NCIC mirror image and purge file:* All active and inactive theft records on vehicles and boats housed in NCIC are also contained in the mirror image file. In addition, vehicle theft records purged from NCIC since 1972 for a variety of reasons are provided to NICB on a daily basis and are entered into the system as a permanent record. The file is an important and time-saving tool for law enforcement.

- *Information-wanted file:* When a purchaser skips out on payments to a finance company that has purchased physical-damage insurance on the vehicle from one of the NICB sponsoring member companies, the information is made available to law enforcement agencies investigating the vehicle as a suspected stolen unit.

- *Inquiry file:* When a law enforcement agency makes an inquiry on a vehicle for an investigation, any subsequent information received or any inquiry on the same vehicle from another person or agency will be passed on to the original inquirer.

- *Shipping and assembly file:* This file holds the shipping and assembly records for most automobiles; light-, medium-, and heavy-duty trucks; semitrailers; motorcycles; and snowmobiles produced for sale in the United States and Canada.

- *Impound file:* An increasing number of states are now collecting and reporting impound records to NICB for entry into this file. The file helps clear many stolen records and is a valuable investigative tool.

- *VINASSIST:* This NICB program, provided to law enforcement agencies at no cost, defines, edits, evaluates, and corrects vehicle identification numbers, a process that greatly aids law enforcement in positively identifying specific recovered motor vehicles.

- *All-claims database:* With this database, claims filed against participating member insurance companies can be compared to detect possible fraudulent claims, including auto theft–related insurance fraud.

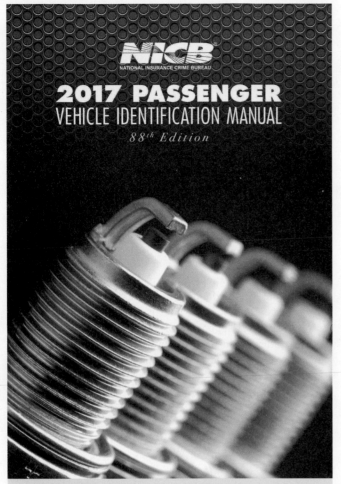

▲ **FIGURE 16-6**

The passenger vehicle identification manual

One of the most important investigative tools used in vehicle theft cases is the Passenger Vehicle Identification Manual. Published by the National Insurance Crime Bureau, this booklet contains useful information, including an explanation of vehicle identification numbers, the federal motor vehicle theft prevention standards, and VIN plate attachment and location.

(©National Insurance Crime Bureau)

The NICB is organized into nine geographic areas, with its headquarters in the Chicago suburb of Palos Hills, Illinois, serving as the Area 1 office. The other offices serving major metropolitan and surrounding locales are in Seattle; Los Angeles; Dallas; Tampa; Washington, D.C.; New York; Columbus, Ohio; Hartford, Connecticut; and Chula Vista, California.[27]

Since 1919 the NICB or its predecessor, the NATB, has annually published the *Passenger Vehicle Identification Manual* (Figure 16-6), which contains the following information:

- Federal motor vehicle theft prevention standards;
- Explanation of vehicle identification numbers;
- VIN plate attachment and location;
- Federal safety standards certification stickers;
- Passenger vehicle and light-duty truck VIN structure;

- Motorcycles and all-terrain vehicle VIN structure;
- General information on snowmobiles and boats;
- Vehicle shipping and assembly record information.[28]

Every 5 years, the NICB also publishes the *Commercial Vehicle Identification Manual,* which contains the following information:

- World manufacturer identification codes;
- Model year identifier;
- Truck-tractor identification;
- Commercial-trailer identification;
- Off-road equipment identification.[29]

Insurance Bureau Canada (IBC)

Known formerly as the Canadian Insurance Crime Prevention Bureau, the Insurance Bureau Canada has been functioning since 1923 but became an independent division within the Insurance Council of Canada on January 1, 1998. It is to Canada what NICB is to the United States. IBC is supported by over 90% of private-property and casualty insurers. Within the organizational structure of IBC are found the Canadian Automobile Theft Bureau (CATB) and the Canadian Police Information System, the sister organization of NCIC. IBC is headquartered in Toronto, Ontario. It has four regional offices, located in Innisfall, Alberta; Toronto; Montreal, Quebec; and Halifax, Nova Scotia.[30]

International Association of Auto Theft Investigators

Another resource available to the investigator is the International Association of Auto Theft Investigators (IAATI) and its regional affiliated chapters, which are located in many parts of the world, including Europe and Australia. With a current membership of 3,604 representing more than 35 countries, IAATI was formed in 1952 for the purpose of formulating new methods to attack and control vehicle theft and fraud. Its members represent law enforcement agencies, state registration and titling agencies, insurance companies, car rental companies, the automobile manufacturing industry, and other interested groups. International and regional training seminars are held throughout the year. As with many such organizations, it is a great network of specialists all willing to assist any investigator or officer who requests help.

State Organizations

Many states have organizations consisting of auto-theft investigators who meet regularly to exchange intelligence information and learn new methods of combating the problems of theft and fraud.

National Crime Information Center

Another valuable resource for the investigator is the FBI's National Crime Information Center (NCIC). Online inquiries can be made to NCIC's vehicle or license plate files to check on records for stolen vehicles, vehicles wanted in conjunction with felonies, stolen component parts, and stolen license plates. In addition, a request can be made for an off-line search, which is a tool designed to assist an investigator by providing lead information. For example, an investigator attempting to track a stolen vehicle that is known to be traveling across the country can request an off-line search to see if any stolen inquiries had been made within a specific time frame on that vehicle. A hit would identify the time and location from which the inquiry was made, thus providing a lead to locating the vehicle.

The original NCIC system held more than 40 million records in its 17 databases and processed more than 2 million transactions a day, but it was more than 30 years old. An updated, new-generation system, NCIC 2000, was implemented in July 1999. It has all the advantages of the old system plus impressive new capabilities such as image processing, whereby mug shots, other photographs, signatures, and identifying marks can be electronically submitted; single-finger fingerprint matching, including storing and searching for right-index fingerprints; a linkage field, whereby multiple records concerning the same criminal or the same crime can be automatically associated; and several new databases, including the Convicted Persons on Supervised Release Database, the Convicted Sexual Offender Registry, and the SENTRY file of persons incarcerated in federal prisons. These can all be accessed through NCIC 2000.[31]

The NCIC databases can be used for many different purposes. For instance, through the linkage function, an inquiry on a gun can also identify a wanted person or a stolen car. Since vehicle information can be included in the Convicted Sexual Offender Registry, a traffic stop with an inquiry on the license plate may identify an individual as a registered sexual offender.[32]

Special Investigative Units

In the mid-1970s Kemper Insurance Company created the first special investigative unit (SIU) for insurance companies. Its primary purpose was to investigate potentially fraudulent auto-theft claims. There are more than 800 SIU investigators employed in the insurance industry working fraud claims. Approximately 80% of the insurance companies now have SIUs. The agents and units work with and train insurance adjusters to detect oddities and "red flags" indicating potential fraud. The SIUs also work closely with law enforcement by lending assistance in investigations—providing computer information, claims histories, and statements of insureds made under oath.

AAMVA AND NMVTIS

The **American Association of Motor Vehicle Administrators (AAMVA)** is the system operator for the **National Motor Vehicle Title Information System (NMVTIS)**. The NMVTIS was initially developed in 1992 as part of the Anti Car Theft Act passed that year; since that time, it has evolved into Department of Justice program that works to prevent consumers from vehicle fraud. It's a fee for service program where consumers use data providers to access a complete and up-to-the-minute history of a vehicle, including whether it was reported stolen, salvaged, or exported or is otherwise incapable of being the subject of a new transfer. In addition to inquiry capability, the system prevents the laundering of titles between states for the purpose of removing brands such as those that appear on sal-

vage, flood-damaged, rebuilt, or unrepairable vehicles. Currently, with the exception of Illinois, all states are either fully operational, partially online, or providing data by batch.[33] The ultimate goal of the developers is to provide a system whereby a potential purchaser of a used vehicle will be able to inquire about the status of the vehicle before making a final commitment to purchase.

Government Agencies

In virtually all state governments, organizations or entities exist that possess information of value to investigators. Specifically, motor vehicle and driver's license offices, insurance fraud investigative units, and fire and arson investigative units may provide valuable information or assistance.

Manufacturers

Manufacturers are one of the most important resources an investigator can cultivate and turn to for assistance, particularly as they relate to the content and location of numbers on vehicles or parts. Domestic and foreign automobile manufacturers are generally most supportive of an investigator's inquiries, as are the Harley-Davidson Motorcycle Company and the John Deere, Case, and Caterpillar companies, which manufacture construction and farm equipment. This list is not meant to be exhaustive. Help will generally be given by any manufacturer when requested.

North American Export Committee

In an effort to stem the tide of stolen vehicles being exported from the country, the NICB, U.S. and Canadian Customs, Royal Canadian Mounted Police, Insurance Bureau Canada, and Miami-Dade Police Department in Florida, along with other law enforcement agencies, the insurance industry, and other interested parties, established the North American Export Committee in 1995. The committee investigates ways in which the exporting of stolen vehicles could be slowed without impeding commerce at port facilities.

Shipments of vehicles occur in two ways—some vehicles are rolled on and then rolled off a ship, and some are shipped in containers. These are quite different concepts requiring entirely different approaches. U.S. Customs is charged with the responsibility of checking the paperwork on vehicles to be exported, and the paperwork must be received by Customs three days before a vehicle can be shipped. Only limited resources are devoted to this responsibility, however, because Customs is more concerned about property coming into the country and about commodities, other than vehicles being exported. Customs' role has become even more limited after 9/11. It was moved from the Treasury Department to the Department of Homeland Security and was reorganized. Customs inspectors are now part of the Bureau of Customs and Border Protection (CBP), whereas the law enforcement agents are part of the Bureau of Immigration and Customs Enforcement (ICE). Either Customs or local law enforcement checks the paperwork, physically examines as many of the vehicles as possible, and enters the VINs into a computer that transmits all those checked to databases with NICB, NCIC, OCRA (Mexican law enforcement database), a

◄ FIGURE 16-7
Stolen vehicle recovered through gamma-ray scan
This stolen vehicle was located when the container in which it was found passed through a gamma-ray scan at the Port of Miami. The container's manifest reported its contents as household goods. (Courtesy of Miami-Dade Auto Theft Task Force)

rental car database, and a motor vehicle liens database. Overnight, the list is run against the export, stolen, salvage, and VIN verification files of NICB and the other databases. The next morning, an exceptions report is available to the submitting agencies so that the "trouble messages" (problems) can be checked out before the vehicles are shipped. At the Port of Miami, trouble messages occur on approximately 20% of the exports. Such electronic reporting is now used at 80 ports in the United States.[34]

Containerized vehicles present a different set of problems. There are over 8 million containers exported from the United States in a year. No manifest is going to acknowledge that a container has one or more stolen vehicles. Checking a container, even if it meets a predetermined set of conditions called a profile, is hot, sweaty work—the unloading and reloading take hours—and it interferes with commerce. Stolen vehicles are usually found in the front or middle of a container, with goods packed all around them. To make enforcement more productive,

an efficient, effective, and economic method of looking inside containers had to be found.

Science Applications International Corporation developed a device that examines and photographs the contents of a container as it is passing through a gamma ray. In mid-1998, the corporation, in cooperation with the Miami-Dade County Multi-Agency Auto Theft Task Force and on behalf of the North American Export Committee, tested this equipment for a 90-day period at the Port of Miami in what was called the **Stolen Auto Recovery (STAR) System** (Figure 16-7). Before the 90 days were up, more than 7,700 containers were scanned in less than 6 seconds each, while it continued to move. A total of 630 vehicles were identified, and six stolen vehicles were recovered, valued at $217,000. There were no false identifications, and the flow of commerce was not impeded. The units cost around $270,000, are very transportable, are easily installed in one day, and the gamma-ray scan preserves a video image of the contents of the container (Figure 16-8).

▲ **FIGURE 16-8 Gamma-ray scan showing two utility vehicles**
Advances in technology have assisted in the discovery of stolen vehicles being exported from the United States aboard ships. Science Applications International Corporation has developed a device that examines and photographs the contents of a container as it is passed through a gamma-ray scan. These units cost around $270,000, are very transportable, and are easily installed in one day's time. (Courtesy of Miami-Dade Auto Theft Task Force)

Because of the success of the STAR System, Florida committed to installing a total of 10 systems across the state (at least three additional ports on Florida's east coast have been equipped).[35] Unfortunately, Miami-Dade reorganized its port facility and changed four lanes into 16 lanes of ingress onto the port. The money was not available to continue the gamma-ray scan technology at that location.

There are other technologies available. The use of X-ray equipment has been made safe. Portels is an X-ray system that scans from both the front and back of a container and gives an even higher definition picture than does the gamma-ray system. It is manufactured by AS&E and uses what is called "Backscatter" technology to allow X rays from both the front and rear portion of a container going through the system. The company also manufactures a mobile system that can be mounted on a van with the equipment inside. The van can pull up to a stack of containers at a port and within seconds see sufficient contents to determine if vehicles or other items that may be contraband are inside. The equipment can "inspect" containers stacked three high.[36] VACIS is another system using X-ray technology. Customs and Border Protection has 40 of these units installed at U.S. ports and Canada; Mexico and Arizona have these units at border crossings.[37]

Canada has developed a task-force operation at the port in Vancouver, British Columbia, using this technology, with data transfer to the Canadian Insurance Crime Prevention Bureau. Early results were the recovery of 12 vehicles, all stolen from the province of Ontario.[38] The North American Export Committee also committed to the further development and implementation of the National Motor Vehicle Title Information System (NMVTIS).

National Equipment Register

The scope of the theft of heavy construction equipment has led manufacturers, dealers, and insurers to support the development of a national database of stolen equipment and provide the services of law enforcement specialists in the recovery of stolen equipment. The National Equipment Register (NER) facilitates the identification of lost and stolen equipment and the return of such equipment to owners and insurers and promotes due diligence in the purchase of used equipment, thereby deterring the trade in stolen equipment. The NER owner database has over 20 million records, and its databases are connected to the databases of the Insurance Services Office, Inc. (ISO), the organization that provides all the computer services for the National Insurance Crime Bureau (NICB). In February 2008 NER, ISO, and NICB formed an alliance to strengthen the ability of the insurance industry to recover stolen heavy equipment.[39] The NER is available to law enforcement for advice on where to locate product information numbers, check on the status of stolen equipment, and identify and locate owners of recovered equipment. If requested, NER can provide on-site assistance to law enforcement. The organization provides training seminars (for example, equipment recovery) for law enforcement and theft-prevention sessions for equipment owners.[40] (NER can be reached at 866-663-7872 or online at www.ner.net.)

Indicators of Theft and Fraud

NICB publishes lists and pocket guides for law enforcement officials on the suspicious conduct of people or the status of vehicles that should cause the officer/investigator to make a closer inquiry to determine if a vehicle is stolen or if fraudulent conduct is afoot. Similarly, NER has recommendations about suspicious conduct of people or circumstances that should lead to further inquiry about possible heavy-equipment theft.

LOCATING AND HANDLING VEHICLES

In recent years some investigators have gotten seriously ill while performing their jobs. Locating and handling the recovery of vehicles and parts can be very dangerous. Often, an investigator will climb or crawl around, through, and over wrecks, in a remote area of a salvage yard in order to locate or identify a vehicle part. Not only is the physical work dangerous, but, unknowingly, the investigator may be exposed to toxic waste, which can cause permanent physical damage. Gloves should be worn at all times, along with protective clothing and a mask or breathing device, when encountering the unknown. Similarly, when investigating a vehicle fire, investigators must take precautions, because toxic chemicals may be around that can cause serious long-term illness owing to exposure.

QUICK FACTS

The National Insurance Crime Bureau offers a free service where potential car buyers can check a VIN number against their database to determine if the vehicle has been reported stolen and not recovered, or if the vehicle matches a salvage report. For more information, visit their website at: https://www.nicb.org/theft_and_fraud_awareness/vincheck.

VEHICLE IDENTIFICATION

Often the most difficult and time-consuming task facing an investigator is the identification of a recovered vehicle. Although there are a number of ways by which motor vehicles can be identified, including a description by year, make and model, or license number, these items are easily generalized or alterable. For the investigator, identification is made by numbers affixed to, or inscribed on, the vehicle.

Since 1954 American automobile manufacturers have used a **vehicle identification number (VIN)** instead of an engine number as the primary means of identification. However, before 1968 VINs, although usually inscribed on metal plates, were not uniformly located on vehicles, nor was there any standard method for attaching a **VIN plate** to a vehicle (Figure 16-9). On varying makes and models, VIN plates were affixed with screws or rivets or were spot-welded on doors, doorposts, or dashes. Since 1968 VIN plates on almost all domestic and foreign cars have been attached to the left side of the dash on the instrument panel in such a fashion as to be visible through the windshield. Corvettes, before 1984, had the VIN plate attached to the left-side windshield post. Tractor and semitrailer manufacturers still lack consistency in the placement of VIN plates, as do construction and farm equipment manufacturers in the placement of product identification numbers (PINs).

VIN plates still are attached by a variety of methods. Several foreign manufacturers use a round-head "pop" rivet made of aluminum, stainless steel, or some plastic material. A six-petal "rosette" rivet made of aluminum or stainless steel has been used on General Motors products since 1966, on Chrysler-manufactured vehicles since 1968, and on Ford units since 1970. Sheet-metal screws are still occasionally used on some imports (Figure 16-9).

The use of a public VIN is designed to provide a positive, individualized means of identifying a motor vehicle. The 1981 adoption of a standardized 17-character VIN for all cars manufactured in or sold in the United States was certainly a forceful step in that direction. Previously, General Motors used a 13-digit VIN, Ford and Chrysler each used 11 characters, and imports used a host of other lengths. The standardized 17-character configuration is required of all imports manufactured for sale in the United States. The first 11 characters of the standardized VIN identify the country of origin, manufacturer, make, restraint system, model, body style, engine type, year, assembly plant, and a mathematically computed check digit that is used to verify all the other characters in the VIN. The last six characters are the sequential production number of the vehicle (Figures 16-10 and 16-11). The letters "I," "O," "Q," "U," and "Z" are not used so as to avoid confusion with similar-looking numbers.

Under the standardized 17-character system, the check digit is always the ninth character in the VIN and is calculated using the formula process illustrated on the worksheet depicted in Figure 16-12. By assigning specified numerical values to each letter and number, and then multiplying and dividing, the appropriate check digit can be determined and matched with the check digit on the VIN in question to ascertain whether there are any flaws in the construction of the VIN such as altered or transposed characters.

The tenth character of the VIN represents the year of manufacture or vehicle model year. The letter A was used to designate 1980, B for 1981, and so on. Without the letters "I," "O," "Q," "U," and "Z," the remaining 20 letters, followed by the use of numbers one to nine, establish a 30-year cycle before the possibility of an exactly duplicated VIN could result from the normal manufacturing process (Figure 16-13).

On some newer vehicles, VIN plates also have a bar code that contains all the information represented by the alphanumeric characters of the VIN (Figure 16-14). The Federal Safety Standards Certification Sticker found on the door post of most vehicles, has been required since 1970, and now includes the full VIN and bar code (Figure 16-15).

Gray-Market Vehicles

When the U.S. dollar is strong overseas, it becomes economically feasible for individuals to purchase motor vehicles in other countries and have them shipped to the United States for sale, resale, or personal use. This effort can be profitable even though it may cost up to several thousand dollars apiece to "legalize" the vehicles for use in the United States. Since such vehicles are not manufactured for sale in this country, they are not constructed to meet U.S. emission control or safety standards, nor do they have a 17-character standardized VIN. If **gray-market vehicles** are brought into this country legally, a bond for each must be posted with Customs and Border Protection (CBP) until such time as the appropriate modifications have been made to bring the vehicle into compliance with the U.S. Environmental Protection Agency (EPA) emission control requirements and the safety standards promulgated by the U.S. Department of Transportation (DOT). When these steps have been accomplished and the modifications approved, the federal government will issue a replacement VIN plate that conforms with the 17-character standard.

**Round-head "pop" rivet
aluminum, stainless steel, or plastic**

Used on early General Motors vehicles prior to 1965 after departure from "spot weld" method of attaching VIN plates. Still used by most foreign manufacturers.

**"Rosette"-type rivet
6 petals, aluminum, or stainless steel**

Used by General Motors Corp. since 1965, Chrysler Corp. since 1966, and Ford Motor Co. since 1970. There have been instances when round-head rivets were used at some assembly plants but only on very rare occasions.

**"Rosette"-type rivet
5 petals, aluminum**

Used by Toyota since 1985, except for the 1985 Corolla front-wheel drive, diesel, and 1989 and 1990 Cressida models, which have round aluminum rivets.

Sheet-metal screws

Screws are occasionally used to attach VIN plates on some imported vehicles.

Note: From 1974 to the present, some manufacturers have used VIN plates with both concealed and exposed rivets.

▲ **FIGURE 16-9 Various methods of attaching VIN plates**

(Source: National Insurance Crime Bureau, 2001 Passenger Vehicle Identification Manual [Palos Hills, IL: NICB, 2001], p. 46.)

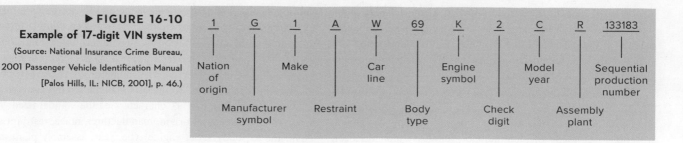

► FIGURE 16-10
Example of 17-digit VIN system
(Source: National Insurance Crime Bureau,
2001 Passenger Vehicle Identification Manual
[Palos Hills, IL: NICB, 2001], p. 46.)

► FIGURE 16-11
World manufacturer identification codes
(*Source:* NICB, Palos Hills, Illinois)

Code	Manufacturer	Code	Manufacturer
JH4	ACURA	1LN	LINCOLN
ZAR	ALFA ROMEO	SCC	LOTUS
1AM	AMERICAN MOTORS	ZAM	MASERATI
SCF	ASTON MARTIN	JM1	MAZDA
WAU	AUDI	WDB	MERCEDES BENZ
12A	AVANTI	1ME	MERCURY
ZBB	BERTONE	WF1	MERKUR
WBA	BMW	JA3	MITSUBISHI
1G4	BUICK	JN1	NISSAN
1G6	CADILLAC	1G3	OLDSMOBILE
1G1	CHEVROLET	VF3	PEUGEOT
1C3	CHRYSLER	ZFR	PININFARINA
2E3	EAGLE PREMIER	1P3	PLYMOUTH
JE3	EAGLE SUMMIT	1G2	PONTIAC
VF1	EAGLE MEDALLION	WPO	PORSCHE
SCE	DELOREAN	VF1	RENAULT
1B3	DODGE	SCA	ROLLS ROYCE
ZFF	FERRARI	YS3	SAAB
ZFA	FIAT	SAX	STERLING
1FA	FORD	JF1	SUBARU
KMH	HYUNDAI	JS3	SUZUKI
JHM	HONDA	JT2	TOYOTA
JAB	ISUZU	WVW	VOLKSWAGEN
SAJ	JAGUAR	YV1	VOLVO
1JC	JEEP		

Many vehicles are found operating on the streets and highways of this nation before, or without conforming to, the legal conversion requirements for gray-market vehicles. The operation of these vehicles is unlawful, and they are subject to seizure by CBP. The frequency of such seizures and the ability to ensure compliance with the EPA and DOT regulations are, of course, a direct function of the resources devoted to the programs and the priorities established. Not unlike state and local agencies, federal law enforcement programs also suffer from limited resources. In some years, the number of gray-market imports has approached 100,000 vehicles.

The nonconforming VIN on a gray-market vehicle is sometimes nothing more than a Dymotape label stuck on the left-side dash and visible through the windshield. Often such a VIN is on a plate riveted in the appropriate place, but its construction does not satisfy the accepted format requirements. Learning the proper appearance and configuration of the accepted VIN format will aid investigators not only in identifying gray-market vehicles but also in detecting altered VINs.

Attempts to Conceal the Identity of Vehicles

Salvage switches, cloning, defacing, or altering numbers are among the many ways of concealing the identity of a vehicle, thus making it difficult for even a trained investigator to accurately identify a vehicle.

	1	2	3	4	5	6	7	8	9	10	11	12	13	14	15	16	17
A																	
B																	
C	8	7	6	5	4	3	2	10	0	9	8	7	6	5	4	3	2
D																	

= ___
Final
sum

On line A, enter the 17-digit VIN.

On line B, enter the assigned value of each character of the VIN, utilizing table B, shown below.

*Multiply the numbers in line B with the numbers in line C, for each of the 17 digits in the VIN. Record the product of each of these separate computations in the appropriate box in line D.

11 | _____

*Divide together all of the numbers recorded in line D and enter the final sum in the place provided.

*Divide the final sum by the number 11. The remainder of this division is the "check digit" (the ninth character of the 17-digit VIN). If the remainder of this division is a single-digit number, then it should match the check digit in the VIN exactly; if the remainder is the number 10, then the check digit is the letter X.

Table B

A-1	J-1	T-3	1-1	6-6	Assign to each number in the VIN its actual value
B-2	K-2	U-4	2-2	7-7	and record that value in the appropriate box in line B.
C-3	L-3	V-5	3-3	8-8	
D-4	M-4	W-6	4-4	9-9	
E-5	N-5	X-7	5-5	0-0	The letters I, O and Q are never used in
F-6	P-7	Y-8			the new 17-digit VIN's.
G-7	R-9	Z-9			
H-8	S-2				

To determine the year of manufacture from the 17-digit VIN (character 10 of the VIN) use the listed table.

1980-A   1981-B   1982-C   1983-D   1984-E   1985-F   1986-G   1987-H

The decoding chart, shown above, may be photocopied to provide multiple blank work sheets for computing the check digits of the new 17-digit VIN's.

Example: 1981 Ford Mustang 1FABP12A4BR101093, final sum = 246

$$\begin{array}{r} 22 \\ 11\overline{)246} \\ \underline{22} \\ 26 \\ \underline{22} \\ 4 \end{array}$$

Check digit

▲ **FIGURE 16-12 Check-digit calculation formula**
(Courtesy of National Insurance Crime Bureau)

Why is concealing a vehicle's identity so important? Simply put, if a vehicle cannot be positively identified, it cannot be proven that the vehicle was stolen, when it was stolen, or from whom it was stolen. Thus, one who is in possession of such a vehicle cannot be prosecuted as a thief. Even the most careful thief has extreme difficulty totally concealing the identity of a stolen vehicle.

Although it does happen, total inability to identify a vehicle is rare if the investigator doesn't hesitate to call on his/her own or others' knowledge, training, and experience. Knowing how and when to call on outside resources is important to the successful investigation. NICB special agents and other highly qualified law enforcement officers know how and where to look for clues to a vehicle's identity.

1980	A	1995	S	2010	A
1981	B	1996	T	2011	B
1982	C	1997	V	2012	C
1983	D	1998	W		
1984	E	1999	X		
1985	F	2000	Y		
1986	G	2001	1		
1987	H	2002	2		
1988	J	2003	3		
1989	K	2004	4		
1990	L	2005	5		
1991	M	2006	6		
1992	N	2007	7		
1993	P	2008	8		
1994	R	2009	9		

▲ **FIGURE 16-13 Vehicle model year**
(*Source:* National Insurance Crime Bureau)

▲ **FIGURE 16-14**
General motors VIN plate with bar code
(IAATI-SE newsletter, 1997)

▲ **FIGURE 16-15**
Federal safety standards certification sticker with bar code
(IAATI-SE newsletter, 1997)

The public VIN on the dash is not the only number that identifies a specific vehicle. The VIN may be stamped in several different places on the vehicle's body, frame, or component parts. The location of some of these secondary numbers is not a big secret, but others, referred to as **confidential VINs,** are stamped into frames or bodies in places supposedly known only to the manufacturer and to law enforcement agencies and officers who are specialists in vehicle identification and auto-theft

investigation, such as NICB special agents. Various other parts such as engines and transmissions will be given an identification number when manufactured, but, because they are distinct component parts, often manufactured in different locales from the final assembly plant, the numbers may be totally different from the VIN. However, documents created and maintained by the manufacturer, and provided to NICB, can be checked to determine the VIN of the vehicle in which the part was installed.

Other parts or components of a vehicle manufactured or subassembled elsewhere may be designed to fit a specific vehicle. In such cases, the part may have a serial number that is related to, but not identical to, the VIN. It may have a number that is a derivative of the VIN or that's formed from parts of the VIN, the same way a T-top may need to be matched to a vehicle of a specific body type denoted by the sixth and seventh characters of the VIN and the six-digit sequential number. Numerous combinations are possible and plausible; again, this is where the manufacturer's records become indispensable (Figure 16-16).

The numbers often used to match parts so as to foster accurate assembly of a vehicle may be written on components with pen, pencil, chalk, marking pen, or crayon. It does not matter what they are written with, as long as there are numbers that can lead an investigator to the end result of positively identifying a vehicle. Frequently, the various components subassembled elsewhere in the same plant or shipped from other plants will be accompanied by production order forms or written orders containing the VIN or a derivative number, which matches the parts for assembly. After the parts are matched and assembled, the production form has no use and may be left in some nook, cranny, or crevice of the assembly. If the investigator knows where to look, such a document may often be found and thus lead to vehicle identification.

Federal Safety Standards Certification Sticker

All cars distributed in the United States since 1970 must have a **federal safety standards certification sticker.** This sticker, in addition to the required certification statements, also contains the vehicle's VIN. If the sticker is removed, it leaves behind a "footprint" that often shows the word "void." Obviously, if the correct sticker is in place and the correct public VIN shows through the windshield, the VINs should match.

The shape and size of the labels, as well as the materials from which they are constructed, vary among manufacturers. More common among domestic manufacturers is a paper label covered with a clear Mylar-type plastic.

The label is bonded to the vehicle with a mastic compound. Construction is such that the label should be destroyed if removal is attempted. Some foreign manufacturers construct the certifying label out of thin metal and attach it with rivets. In either case, security against removal and replacement is not absolute. However, investigators are encouraged not to use the VIN on the safety certification label as absolute proof of vehicle identification. The federal safety sticker will be located on the driver's door or on the doorpost and, in recent years, also includes a description of the vehicle and VIN on a barcode.

Federal Legislation

In an effort to reduce auto theft by easing the process of vehicle identification, Congress enacted the **Motor Vehicle Theft Law Enforcement Act** of 1984. Title I of the law requires that manufacturers place additional permanent identification numbers on up to 14 major parts of certain car lines. The car lines are selected every year for each manufacturer by the National Highway Traffic Safety Administration (NHTSA), the federal agency charged with setting the standards for the administration of the law. The car lines chosen each year for **parts marking** are those designated as high-theft lines. The parts requiring the additional identification are the major parts that are normally most sought after in a chopshop operation and include: the engine; transmission; both front fenders; hood; both front doors; front and rear bumpers; both rear quarter panels; decklid, tailgate, or hatchback (whichever is applicable); and both rear doors (if present) (Figure 16-17).

The numbers must either be inscribed on the designated parts or be printed on labels attached to the parts. Labels must tear into pieces if removed; if completely removed, they must leave a "footprint," which becomes visible through certain investigative techniques such as using an ultraviolet light. The standards apply to the major parts of the designated new car lines and to replacement parts for the same car lines. The new-part labels must have the manufacturer's logo or other identifier printed on them and must use the full 17-character VIN for identification (Figure 16-18); if, however, a VIN derivative of at least 8 characters was being used to identify the engine and transmission on a particular covered line on the effective date of the law, that practice may continue. The identifier on covered replacement parts must carry the manufacturer's trademark, logo, or other distinguishing symbol, the letter "R" to reflect replacement, and the letters "DOT" (Figure 16-18). The labels are to be affixed to the part on a surface that is not normally exposed to damage when the part is installed, adjusted, removed, or damaged in an accident. When the part is removed from the vehicle, the label or inscription must be visible without disassembling the part.

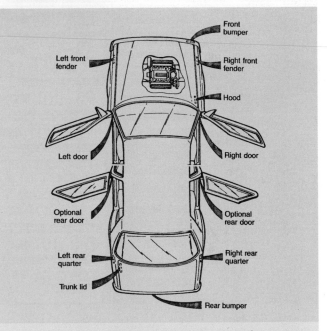

▲ **FIGURE 16-17 Components requiring marking**
(**Source:** 3M Corporation)

The law limits the application of the requirements to no more than 14 production car lines for any one manufacturer, and the costs to the manufacturer for compliance cannot exceed $15 per vehicle, excluding the costs of marking the engine and transmission.

There is an exemption in the law, called a "black-box" exemption, which allows NHTSA to exempt from compliance with the standards up to two car lines per year for any single manufacturer if the vehicle line is equipped by the manufacturer with a standard equipment antitheft device determined by NHTSA to be as effective in deterring and reducing vehicle theft as would

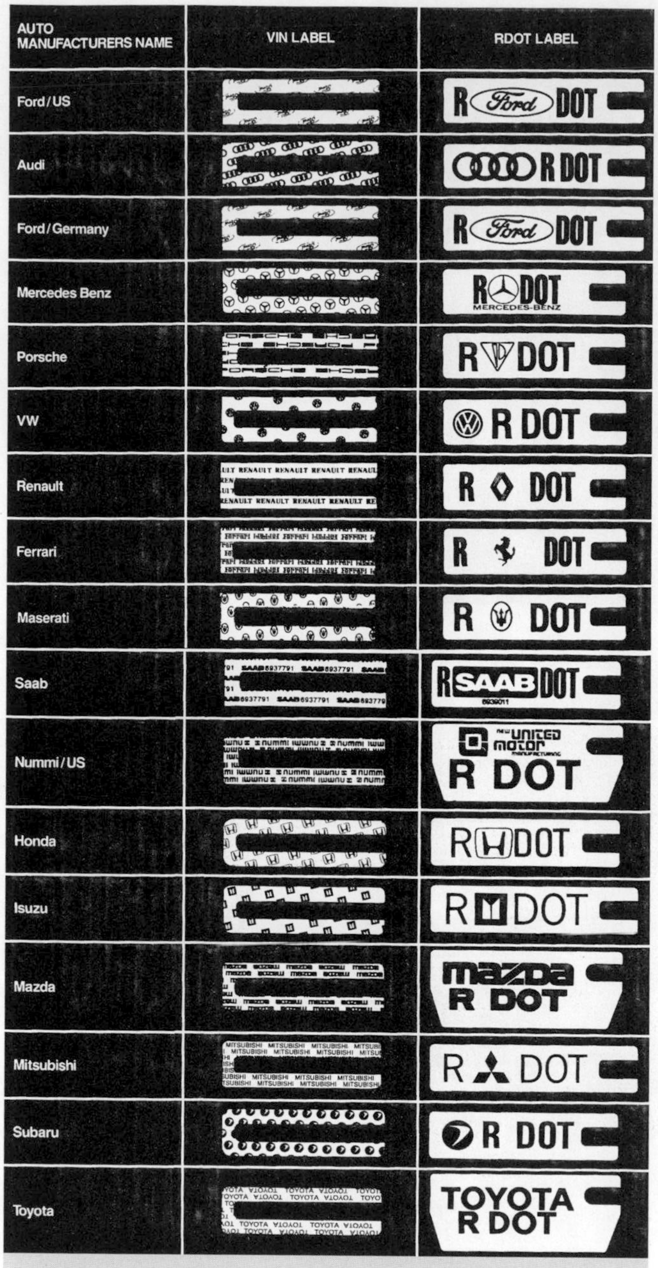

AUTO MANUFACTURERS NAME	VIN LABEL	RDOT LABEL
Ford/US		R Ford DOT
Audi		OOOO R DOT
Ford/Germany		R Ford DOT
Mercedes Benz		R DOT MERCEDES-BENZ
Porsche		R DOT
VW		VW R DOT
Renault		R DOT
Ferrari		R DOT
Maserati		R DOT
Saab		R SAAB DOT
Nummi/US		NEW UNITED MOTOR MANUFACTURING R DOT
Honda		R H DOT
Isuzu		R DOT
Mazda		mazda R DOT
Mitsubishi		R DOT
Subaru		R DOT
Toyota		TOYOTA R DOT

▲ **FIGURE 16-18**
Original- and replacement-part labels for selected manufacturers
(*Source:* 3M Corporation)

be compliance with the parts-marking requirements of the theft prevention standard.

The intent underlying the passage of the law, the promulgation of standards, and the marking of original and replacement parts was to reduce auto theft by ostensibly making it more difficult for the thief to conceal the identity of major parts, by providing fewer significant parts that would be untraceable, and by making it easier for law enforcement investigators to identify stolen parts.

Having determined that the parts-marking program initiated in 1984 was effective, Congress passed the Anti-Car Theft Act

of 1992, which continued and extended the program. The 1992 legislation also called for the U.S. Attorney General to conduct an initial evaluation, in 1997, of the effectiveness of the program in inhibiting chop-shop operations and deterring motor vehicle theft, with the objective of extending the parts-marking program to all lines (makes and models) by the end of 1997. The study recommended continuance of the program. The act required a long-range review of the program in 1999. In addition to evaluating whether chop-shop operations were affected and theft had been deterred, the study was to determine whether the black-box exemptions were an effective substitute for parts marking in substantially reducing motor vehicle theft.

The act also required repair shops to check the VIN on all parts against a national file. Previously, this was the NCIC stolen-vehicle file, but the FBI, by direction of the act, established the National Stolen Parts Motor Vehicle Information System (NSPMVIS). Other provisions of the law made armed carjacking a federal crime; doubled the maximum penalty for importing, exporting, transporting, selling, or receiving a stolen vehicle; and directed U.S. Customs to spot-check vehicles and containers leaving the country.

To carry out the study mandate of the 1992 legislation, the Attorney General directed the National Institute of Justice to commission a study on the effectiveness of the parts-marking program. The report, released in 2000, concluded that the available evidence warrants application of the parts-marking standard to all motor vehicle lines. The decision was, in large measure, based on estimates and the absence of negative information. The study estimated that parts marking costs manufacturers about $5 per vehicle.[41] The study also concluded that 33 to 158 fewer cars are stolen per 100,000 marked cars because of parts marking.[42] The research was unable to establish whether antitheft devices installed in vehicles were an effective alternative to parts marking.[43]

Manufacturers urged the Attorney General not to expand the program, but the Attorney General listened to law enforcement investigators who identified four ways that parts marking provides assistance. First, thieves often remove, alter, or obliterate the VIN plate and other numbers, but as long as one part number remains intact, the vehicle can be identified; this enables the owner to be identified and facilitates proving that the vehicle was stolen and securing an arrest. Second, auto-theft investigators in many jurisdictions have been given authority to seize parts or vehicles when markings have been removed or destroyed. Third, the absence of markings causes investigators to inquire further, and such investigations often lead to larger stolen-vehicle cases. Fourth, in jurisdictions requiring inspections of rebuilt vehicles before issuing a new certificate of title, a determination can be made as to whether stolen parts are being used in the rebuilding process.[44]

VIN Editing and Reconstruction

In any investigation, even when it appears that the VIN has not been altered or defaced, the investigator must check the validity of the identifying numbers. Using the worksheet in Figure 16-12 will verify the correctness of the check digit only as compared with, and calculated from, the other 16 characters. A VIN edit

computer program available at many law enforcement agencies and state motor vehicle regulatory offices can readily determine if the entered VIN is "good." If the VIN is invalid, computer programs can analyze the available information and at least narrow the valid possibilities of a correct VIN. Such programs replace what formerly was a long drawn-out manual process accomplished by checking manufacturers' records.

VIN Restoration

The restoration of manufacturers' serial numbers altered or obliterated from metal is a process that can be performed by an investigator with the proper material at hand (Figure 16-19). There is no mystery involved in number restoration as long as the investigator is willing to do the necessary preparation and has the patience to await results that are often slow in developing.

When a die is struck on metal, the molecules beneath the die are compressed, and it is on these compressed molecules that the restoration mediums are applied. The type of metal surface dictates which of the three primary methods of restoration—heat, acid, or acid and electricity—should be used. In the heat process, an oxygen-acetylene torch is used on cast iron only. An electrolytic process in which five to six volts of electricity at two to three amps are used in conjunction with a solution of hydrochloric acid is generally used on steel. For the etching of aluminum, one solution of potassium hydroxide and a second of hydrochloric acid and mercuric chloride are applied using a cotton or fiberglass swab.

Regardless of which type of surface is involved and which restoration process is used, the surface must be painstakingly prepared. All paint, oil, grease, or other foreign matter must first be removed by using any solution that will work, including paint remover and acetone (Figure 16-20). The surface is not to be scraped with a wire brush, knife, or any other tool, since one major purpose of preparation is to eliminate scratches and grind

marks. Depending on how badly the surface is defaced, it may need to be polished with emery paper, a mill file, or a high-speed sanding or polishing disk to remove scratches or gouges. Polishing the surface to a mirror-like finish is desirable. Sometimes careful preparation of the surface will make all or some of the numbers visible.

Documenting the surface before beginning the restoration process is advisable. This can be done by photographing the area to be restored, dulling the shine with the use of fingerprint powder or carbon paper, and then taking a tape lift of the area (similar to lifting a fingerprint from a metal surface) and/or making a large-scale drawing of the area. It is always advisable to check with the manufacturer to ascertain the structure of the numbers used on a factory identification number if it is not already known. For example, the investigator should ask whether Os are rounded or squared and if 3s have rounded or flat tops. Such information can assist the investigator in determining whether visible numbers are valid.

If the heat process is to be used on cast iron, the ignited torch should be slowly moved back and forth over the area to be processed and gradually brought closer to the surface in a manner that will not crack the block. When the top of the blue cone of the flame is being moved back and forth about half an inch above the surface, the surface will soon reach a cherry-red color. When that happens, the torch should gradually be drawn away from the surface until it is about six inches away, all the while being slowly moved back and forth. After the surface has cooled, it should be very lightly polished with emery paper to remove the carbon deposits. The restored numbers should show up as a lighter color than the surrounding metal. If no numbers appear, either too much of the metal was removed and restoration will not produce results or the surface was not heated to a high-enough temperature, in which case the process should be repeated.

In the electrolytic process of restoring numbers on steel, two pieces of number 12 or 14 braided wire, 18 to 24 inches in length with alligator clips attached to the ends, along with a 6- or 12-volt battery, are needed. Direct current may be used if a battery is not convenient. One wire should be connected to the positive pole, with the other end grounded somewhere near the area to be restored. The other wire, connected to the negative pole, should have a swab dipped in acid solution attached to the other end; the swab should be moved one way only over the surface until any numbers are restored. The acid, speeded by the electricity, eats the surrounding metal surface until the numbers (if not totally destroyed) are revealed. In this and all acid-processing techniques, drawings or sketches should be made as individual numbers or letters are revealed because they may fade before more heavily ground characters are restored. Once the process is completed, the surface should be neutralized with water, dried, and coated with oil to prevent rust. In using any acid, good ventilation is imperative.

Good ventilation is also necessary in the acid process of restoring numbers on aluminum. Using potassium hydroxide solution and a swab, the surface area should be brushed in one direction for about 1 minute. The surface should then be dried and brushed with a solution of hydrochloric acid and mercuric chloride in the same direction for 2 minutes. The surface should be dried again. This process constitutes one application. Often, results will appear after two to four applications, but repeated applications may be made as often as necessary.[45]

INVESTIGATION OF VEHICLE FIRES

Along with the general increase in crimes in the United States has come an increase in automobile fires. Many of the criminal fires occur when stolen vehicles have been stripped of valuable parts and the rest is burnt to destroy the evidence. However, as in other fire investigations, the investigator first must eliminate natural and accidental causes of fire.

Before beginning the physical investigation of a vehicle fire scene, the investigator must understand that the crime scene examination includes both the vehicle and the area in which it was burned. Hence, the investigation must follow established principles by first recording the scene. Photographs should be taken immediately, before there is any disturbance of the crime scene (Figure 16-21). Measurements must be taken to establish the exact location of the vehicle in relationship to fixed objects, crossroads, houses, and so on. A description should be noted regarding the terrain, nearby roadways, and weather conditions (including prevailing wind directions).

A thorough search should be made of the area for tire-tread marks, footprints, cans, bottles, other containers, unusual residue or materials, old tires, matches, or any other item that may be related to the case. Samples should be taken of soil, which may contain evidence of flammable liquids. When found, each item should be photographed before being moved, and then it should be properly packaged and marked as evidence.

An inspection of the salvage must be completed for information on the origin and possible motive for the fire. Generally, investigators inspect the burnt automobile before contacting the owner, and the inspection is made as soon after the fire as possible. The inspection starts where the fire apparently originated. In accidental fires, this will normally be the part of the vehicle that is the most badly damaged from the intensity of the heat. Accidental fires usually spread in diminishing degrees from the point of origin according to prevailing conditions. Conditions include direction and velocity of wind and/or materials on which flames feed, such as gasoline in the tank, woodwork, or other similarly flammable parts of the vehicle. When there are significant variations in these patterns, arson emerges as a possibility. Arson fires started with flammable materials usually show intense heat

◄ FIGURE 16-21
Photographing and documenting burned vehicle
A fire investigator photographs and documents the burned vehicle as part of his investigation. This process is essential in preparing for any subsequent prosecution of the arsonist.
(©Geoff Crimmins/Daily News/AP Images)

in more than one place. The investigator should carefully note the extent of the fire and its path. This information may prove valuable in the later questioning of the owner or witnesses.

The car also should be inspected for the removal of equipment such as stereo, heater, air horns, fog lights, and so forth. Notice should also be made of other irregularities such as old tires on new cars or missing spare tires.

Inspection of the Fuel System

The investigator should determine whether the cap to the gas tank was in place at the time of the fire. Sometimes gasoline to start the fire is siphoned from the tank, and the cap is carelessly left off. If the cap is blown off, it will show effects of an explosion. The drain plug in the bottom of the tank should be checked. In addition, if it was removed or loosened before the fire, there might be evidence of fresh tool marks, especially pliers' marks, on it.

The gas lines should be examined for breaks between the tank and the fuel pump. Breaks should be examined for tool marks. Some arsonists disconnect the line below the tank to obtain gasoline to start the fire and fail to replace the line.

Gasoline to start the fire is sometimes obtained by disconnecting the line from the fuel pump and running the starter. If the fuel pump is melted, there should be evidence of fire on the sidepans. If the fuel pump was disconnected to allow the gasoline to run out and then be set on fire, there may be carbon deposits inside the gas line at the fuel pump.

The investigator should establish whether parts of the fuel pump are missing. If key parts of the fuel system are missing, and the owner says that the vehicle was running at the time of the fire, then there is strong reason to suspect arson. This is true regardless of whether the vehicle is equipped with a mechanical pump in a low-pressure carbureted system or an electric pump in a high-pressure fuel-injected system.

Inspection of the Electrical System

A short circuit in the electric wiring is the most common excuse offered for automobile fires. The chances of a modern automobile's burning up from a short in the wiring are negligible. Engineers have virtually eliminated this hazard. If a fire in fact did start from malfunctions in the electrical system, there generally is enough evidence to substantiate it.

The wires near where the fire started should be inspected. If the wires are not melted completely, a short can be located. A short melts the strands of wire apart and causes small beads of melted wire to form on the ends. Wires that are burned in two have sharp points. If the fire started in an electrical system, the system must be close to a flammable substance for the fire to spread. If a fire started from a short while the motor was running, the distributor points will be stuck or fused.

Inspection of the Motor, Radiator, and Parts Under and Near the Hood

The only possible place for an accidental fire to start at this location is around the fuel pump or carburetor and at the wiring. Any evidence of a fire on the front lower part of the motor not attributable to these parts indicates the use of flammables. If lead is melted from any lower or outside seams of the radiator, this is strong evidence of flammables. The fan belt does not usually burn in an accidental fire.

Gasoline on the motor sometimes causes the rubber cushions for the front of the motor to show evidence of fire. This evidence does not occur in accidental fires.

The radiator should also be checked. A badly burned lower right corner indicates that the gas line from the fuel pump to the carburetor was disconnected, the starter was run to pump out gasoline through the fuel pump, and then the gasoline was set on fire.

Inspection of the Body

The body of the car is usually so badly burned as to afford little evidence. However, signs of the intensity of heat sometimes point to the use of an inflammable. An excessive amount of flammable material may run through the floor of the car and burn underneath, causing oil or gasoline soot to form on the underside of the car. An examination should be made for this soot. If the hood was raised during the fire, the paint on the top panels may be blistered but not be burned off where the two panels touched. If the wind was blowing from the rear of the car to the front, the paint should be burned for almost the length of the hood. The radiator core will be burned, but there will not have been enough fire at the rear of the car to do much damage to the gasoline tank. If the paint on the hood is burned only an inch or so from the rear toward the front, this would indicate that the wind was blowing from the front of the car toward the rear, in which case the gasoline tank may be badly damaged but the radiator will be intact.

CONTACT WITH THE OWNER

An investigation must be made of the car owner for evidence of intent, motive, and opportunity, and the owner must be questioned to establish his or her knowledge of the fire and to verify information. Before interviewing the owner, the investigator should learn as much as possible about him/her. This information may prove quite useful during the interview. The importance of preplanning the interview cannot be overemphasized. The more facts the investigator has available, the greater the probability of a successful clearance or later conviction.

Information should be obtained from the owner about the details of the purchase, such as date, cost, trade-in, down payment, amount of mortgage due, payments past due, name of salesperson, and so forth. The investigator should also inquire about the general condition of the car at the time of the fire and ask about defects, mileage, presence or absence of unusual equipment, and recent repairs.[46]

PREVENTION PROGRAMS

Each year new and innovative approaches to the prevention and the detection of crime and the apprehension of offenders are developed. Some of these are related to investigative techniques, whereas others are high-tech equipment developments that are designed to reduce the vehicle theft problem or assist law enforcement officers in their efforts. Other strategies are available to reduce the incidence of fraud.

AUTO THEFT

Law enforcement officers and agencies in a number of jurisdictions now rely on integrated communications and computer networks of the FBI, state, and local police to identify and locate stolen vehicles. If a car thief today wants to physically steal a car, they should probably lower their expectations. Most cars stolen are older cars, around the 8-year-old mark, according to the NICB. The reason? Technology built into today's models has made it much more difficult to steal a car. Gone are the days of inserting a screwdriver into a steering column, forcing the lock ignition device, starting the car, and taking off; most cars manufactured today utilize an immobilizer system. Immobilizers were first introduced in the 1980s in luxury cars, but today the technology that requires that the automobile's computer recognizes the key before the engine can start is standard.

Other new technology includes sensors that set off alarms if a jack is used on an automobile, or window sensors that alert the car owner if a window is smashed. Some high-end models feature internal motion detectors, connected to electronic notification systems or even smart-phone apps. See Box 16-2.

LoJack pioneered the concept of stolen car tracking in the 1980s; they attached radio transmitters within automobiles that can be activated by police upon theft, and then tracked to a specific location. Over 90% of LoJack equipped cars are recovered. While this isn't technically a prevention system so much as a recovery system, it should be noted that the deterrent nature of LoJack is real: car thefts fell 50% in Boston, 20% in Los Angeles, and 35% in Newark after the system was introduced in those cities.[47]

Theft deterrent devices are of two types—passive or active. With a **passive system,** the driver does not need to do anything to activate the system, though he or she may be required to do something to deactivate the system. An **active system** requires that the operator do something every time the vehicle is driven or parked. The following are examples of each:

- Audible alarm systems may be either passive or active and may be effective if anyone pays attention when an alarm is activated. Because some systems activate easily when someone passes the vehicle, a strong wind blows, or lightning strikes half a mile away, many people pay little attention, beyond a passing glance, to a vehicle with an alarm blaring. Escape from the vicinity of the noise is more important than determining if a theft is occurring. The alarms are treated more as an annoyance than as a theft deterrent.
- A boot is an active device installed under a front tire that prevents the vehicle from being moved until the boot is removed. Other active devices can key lock the transmission or the brakes.
- Many communities have instituted decal "alert" programs that provide decals for vehicles registered with the local law enforcement agency and authorize any law enforcement officer to stop the vehicle and question the driver if the vehicle is observed on the streets during certain hours (such as 2 A.M. to 6 A.M.).
- A fuel shut-off device, which blocks the fuel line, may be activated by removal of the ignition key or by the throwing of a switch.

General Motors' OnStar system uses GPS to track vehicles whose drivers need assistance. OnStar can now slow down a stolen vehicle. The Stolen Vehicle Slowdown (SVS) service is an enhancement to the normal stolen vehicle assistance

BOX 16-2 | CYBERSECURITY AND CARS: A NEW FRONTIER

Late model cars have become extremely difficult to steal, employing a series of ignition controls and software security enhancements that have rendered screwdrivers and popped steering columns obsolete. But the problem with the computer-based security in today's automobiles is that the number of sophisticated "hackers" continues to rise. Refer to Chapter 17: "Cybercrime" for more details on computer hackers. For instance, in 2016, the Houston Police Department investigated the theft of a 2010 Jeep where the perpetrators hooked a laptop up to the car's computer to enable a new key fob. Further, so-called "smart keys" (which use radio waves) can be easily exploited; transmitter devices can trick cars into believing that radio waves are coming from the original key fob, when indeed, the signals emanate from a forged device.

Beyond merely accessing a car for the purposes of theft, tech-heavy cars like Teslas, Mercedes-Benz, Lexus, and some luxury GM and Ford models, can also be easily accessed by hackers for malicious mischief. In 2015, Fiat Chrysler had to recall 1.4 million vehicles after hackers accessed a 2014 Jeep and controlled its air conditioner, engine and windshield wipers remotely. Obviously, this type of criminal mischief creates not only a security problem, but also a significant and potential threat to public safety as the driver of the vehicle no longer is in control of the vehicle being operated. In response, carmakers and tech companies have begun to work on a number of patches and applications to prevent hacking and other acts of technological tampering. Computer apps that detect hacking attempts immediately and shut down the ignition system as well as alert owners have been developed. Further, car manufacturers have developed best practices and multi-layer cybersecurity protections for drivers, including increased cryptography that utilizes next generation technology such as fingerprints and iris detection. This is an emerging and interesting new field that marries technology and auto-theft prevention in a whole new direction for the future.[48]

program offered by OnStar. When an OnStar equipped vehicle is stolen, OnStar can provide the vehicle's exact GPS location to law enforcement. They would also notify law enforcement if the slowdown service is available. When law enforcement has sight of the stolen vehicle, the OnStar operator can flash the lights of the car to verify that law enforcement has the correct vehicle. If necessary, law enforcement can request a slowdown. OnStar will then send a signal to the vehicle that causes the throttle input to be ignored. As a result, the vehicle will start slowing down to idle speed. All other systems of the vehicle continue to act normally.[49]

A steel or an alloy post, rod, or collar may attach to the steering wheel, which can be extended and locked in place. The device prevents the steering wheel from making full rotations. This type of active device can be an effective deterrent to theft if used properly, but it is obviously ineffective if the operator of the vehicle forgets or considers it an inconvenience to install it each time the vehicle is left unattended.

VIN etching is a process that helps identify vehicles recovered by the police after a theft has occurred. As noted earlier, thieves often attempt to conceal the identity of stolen vehicles by grinding numbers. When the VIN is permanently etched, using acid, on all the vehicle's windows, the identifying numbers are often overlooked by the thief or require that the thief remove all the window glass to prevent identification, a major task a thief may not be willing to undertake.

Some programs focus on the responsibilities of vehicle owners to do their part in preventing vehicle theft. The Michigan affiliate of the American Automobile Association implemented a law providing that if a car is stolen and the keys are anywhere in the passenger compartment, the owner, in addition to absorbing his or her insurance deductible, also absorbs an extra $500 plus 10% of the value of the vehicle. The total amount is deducted from the amount of the insurance payment made on the theft loss claim. The responsibilities of owners are also reflected in a survey initiated by the NICB that consists of scoring answers to some questions and taking necessary preventive actions on the basis of the total score. This is called a *layered approach to theft deterrence* (Figure 16-22).

Some other prevention techniques include these:

- Putting phone chargers, adapters, and other cables out of sight. Thieves look for such accessories in hopes that there may be something attached, like a cell-phone, laptop computer, or tablet.
- Always lock the vehicle and remove the keys.
- Lock valuables in the trunk. Do not leave personal identification or credit cards in the vehicle.
- Do not leave a vehicle running while unattended.
- Photocopy registration and insurance papers and carry them on your person, not in the glove compartment.
- Park in a garage or in a well-lighted, heavily traveled area.
- When parking at a curb, turn the wheels toward the curb and use the emergency brake. This makes the vehicle harder to steal.
- Do not hide spare keys in or on the vehicle.
- Write the name of the owner and the VIN in crayon under the hood and in the trunk.

Theft of vehicles from new- and used-car dealers is not a new phenomenon. Sometimes the dealership knows a vehicle is missing, such as when a vehicle taken on a test drive is not returned. Other times, if an inventory is large, a vehicle may be

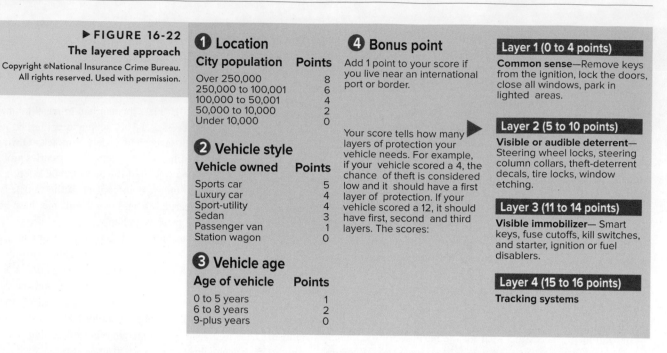

▶ FIGURE 16-22
The layered approach
Copyright ©National Insurance Crime Bureau. All rights reserved. Used with permission.

① Location

City population	Points
Over 250,000	8
250,000 to 100,001	6
100,000 to 50,001	4
50,000 to 10,000	2
Under 10,000	0

② Vehicle style

Vehicle owned	Points
Sports car	5
Luxury car	4
Sport-utility	4
Sedan	3
Passenger van	1
Station wagon	0

③ Vehicle age

Age of vehicle	Points
0 to 5 years	1
6 to 8 years	2
9-plus years	0

④ Bonus point

Add 1 point to your score if you live near an international port or border.

Your score tells how many layers of protection your vehicle needs. For example, if your vehicle scored a 4, the chance of theft is considered low and it should have a first layer of protection. If your vehicle scored a 12, it should have first, second and third layers. The scores:

Layer 1 (0 to 4 points)
Common sense—Remove keys from the ignition, lock the doors, close all windows, park in lighted areas.

Layer 2 (5 to 10 points)
Visible or audible deterrent— Steering wheel locks, steering column collars, theft-deterrent decals, tire locks, window etching.

Layer 3 (11 to 14 points)
Visible immobilizer— Smart keys, fuse cutoffs, kill switches, and starter, ignition or fuel disablers.

Layer 4 (15 to 16 points)
Tracking systems

stolen overnight and not missed for several days. Employee theft is also a problem. Key control is an essential crime prevention practice for a dealership. Keys should be kept in a locked cabinet with only a few people having access. Keys that are out for demonstration or sales purposes must be monitored. Controls should be so tight that no one can take a key and get a duplicate made. Customers should never be allowed to test-drive a vehicle without a salesperson going along. Display lots should be well lighted, and barriers should be erected that permit access and good observation from outside but are sufficient to deter theft at night and when the dealership is closed. Officers who are familiar with the concepts of crime prevention through environmental design should be consulted.

CAR RENTALS

Car rental companies are generally knowledgeable about motor vehicle theft and techniques of prevention, but an investigator would be wise to understand some basics. In daily rental, the company is handing over the keys of a car to a person no one in the company has seen before or knows anything about. The rental agreement should be completely filled out, and the picture and information on the renter's driver's license should be carefully checked to make sure it matches the description of the person to whom the vehicle is being rented.

Rental companies generally require a credit card even for a cash rental. This not only serves as a good indication that the customer is a responsible person but also helps ensure that the contract will be paid. The employee of the rental company should make sure the credit card is current and check it against the driver's license to make sure the same name is on both documents.

Theft of rental vehicles generally occurs when a vehicle is not returned after it has been rented. However, one new car theft technique targets rental agencies. Frequently, when cars are rented, drivers are given two keys. In this type of theft, the criminals remove one of the keys, replace it with a "dummy" key or fob that looks like the true key/fob, and simply return later to steal the car with the other good, or workable key/fob.

Stolen vehicles from rental agencies are often used in other crimes like burglary, robbery, kidnapping, drug and human trafficking, and in at least one known terrorist bombing. See Box 16-3.

HEAVY EQUIPMENT

Tiny transponders that act as identification devices are now available. The device can be glued anywhere on the vehicle. Some agencies are experimenting with injecting the transponder into tires of construction equipment. If attempts are made to completely conceal or alter a stolen vehicle's identity, a receiver can accurately distinguish the vehicle from all others.

Owners of construction equipment are also encouraged to take the following actions:

- Use security devices such as ignition locks, stabilizer arm locks, and fuel shut-off valves.
- Record all product identification numbers, and participate in equipment identification programs.
- Photograph all equipment, paying particular attention to unique features such as dents, decals, and scratches, to aid in later identification.
- Leave equipment in well-lighted and fenced areas at job sites and equipment yards.
- Know the location of all construction equipment at all times.
- Keep law enforcement informed about where equipment is located and how long it will be maintained in a particular location.
- Take extra precautions on weekends. Most equipment thefts occur between 6 P.M. on Friday and 6 A.M. on Monday.

BOX 16-3 | SCRAP OF METAL WITH 'VIN' LEADS TO TERRORIST INVOLVED IN THE FIRST WORLD TRADE CENTER BOMBING

On February 26, 1993, a group of terrorists including Ramzi Yousef, Mahmud Abouhalima, Nidal A. Ayyad, and Mohammed A. Salemeh carried out the first bomb attack on the World Trade Center in New York City. A rented yellow Ryder truck was loaded with nearly 1,500 pounds of urea nitrate fertilizer and detonated using a nitroglycerin and smokeless black powder fuse in the garage basement of the North Tower of the WTC. The resulting explosion was huge, ripping a 30-foot hole in the side of the building, killing six people and wounding more than a thousand others.

During the ensuing investigation, nearly 300 federal agents and bomb technicians were dispatched to the scene to comb the debris area for clues. A small, twisted scrap of metal believed to be from the axle of the suspect vehicle revealed a legible Vehicle Identification Number (VIN). The VIN led investigators to a Ryder truck rental outlet in Jersey City, New Jersey. The VIN matched the model and size of the one used in the bombing and had been rented during the previous week by Mohammed A. Salameh, a cousin of Ramzi Yousef, a known operative on the Terrorist Watch List. Salameh had reported the van stolen. When Salameh returned to the outlet in order to retrieve his deposit, agents and police arrested him.

Subsequent interrogation of Salameh led to the arrest of six other suspects and the recovering of other documents and bomb-making materials in the apartment of Ramzi Yousef.[50] The bombing was carried out by a group of terrorists linked to al-Qaeda and masterminded by Khaled Sheikh Mohammed and

Source: Federal Bureau of Investigation

Sheikh Omar Abdel Rahman, a radical blind Muslim cleric living in Newark, New Jersey. Both were subsequently arrested and convicted, and continue to serve long prison sentences imposed by the United States.[51]

The terrorists' original plan was that the explosion would destroy the base of the North Tower resulting in its collapse into the South Tower causing both towers to crumble. However, the North Tower did not fall and many lives were spared in 1993; 8 years later the ultimate goal was finally achieved, again by al-Qaeda terrorists as a result of the attacks on the World Trade Center on September 11, 2001. Both towers were destroyed and nearly 2,800 people were killed.

- Do not leave keys in any equipment that uses keys, and lock all machines that can be locked when not in use.
- Immediately report suspicious activity (such as a stranger taking photographs of equipment) to law enforcement officials.

Other methods of reducing or preventing theft of off-road equipment are available. Programs are available through private enterprise whereby heavy equipment can be registered, with each piece being assigned its own identification number. The equipment is "decaled" with its own number welded on at several locations. Should a law enforcement officer become suspicious, the dispatcher can call a toll-free number and remain on the line as the company calls the owner to verify the location of the equipment.

FRAUD

The prevention of fraud can best be accomplished by knowing some things about both the insured and the vehicle. "Know your insured" is always sound advice for an insurance agent. Getting

good identification on the person, learning why the person selected a particular agent or agency, and finding out how the insured learned of the agent or agency can all be useful in helping to determine whether the act of insuring is legitimate. Knowing about the insured vehicle is equally important in the fight against fraud.

Perhaps the most profound fraud prevention effort ever initiated is the preinsurance inspection program, particularly when photographs are required. Deceptively simple in concept and application, it is amazing that fewer than half a dozen states have even considered, much less adopted, mandatory legislation. The concept requires that before a vehicle can be insured, it must be physically inspected by a representative or an agent acting on behalf of the insurer.

A simple inspection requirement can immediately eliminate or substantially reduce two of the most prolific tactics in committing insurance fraud. First, it virtually eliminates the false-vehicle theft, which is normally based on insuring a "paper," or "phantom," car—in other words, a vehicle that does not exist—and subsequently reporting it stolen in order to file against and recover on an insurance policy. Second, a well-written preinsurance report can substantially reduce fraudulent claims about theft of expensive equipment on a vehicle or claims that damage actually present before issuance of the policy occurred when the substandard vehicle either was involved in a reported accident or was stolen.

Photographs or digital images supporting an inspection report make the program particularly effective, and color photographs are even more revealing. Photographs can show the exact condition of a vehicle at the time a policy was issued so as to dispel fraudulent damage claims filed later. It is recommended that at least two photographs be taken from diagonal corners so that one picture shows the front and one side of the vehicle and the other photo shows the rear and other side. These two photos will eliminate false damage claims, but there remains the question of proving that the photos are of the insured vehicle and not simply one of the same year, make, and model. To resolve this concern, a few of the jurisdictions having inspection programs require that a third photograph be taken of the federal motor vehicle safety certification label (often called the EPA label), which is usually found on the left door. This label contains, among other information, the vehicle identification number, which, as noted earlier, is the specific identifier for that vehicle as distinguished from all other vehicles. This reverifies the number contained in the written report, thus avoiding or explaining inadvertent omissions or the accidental transposition of numbers.

In 1977 New York became the first state to enact legislation mandating photographic inspection before the issuance of insurance policies. The program initially required that two photographs be taken from a 180-degree angle, but the law was amended in 1986 to require the third photo of the federal motor vehicle safety certification label. Massachusetts was the next state to adopt a preinsurance inspection program. Legislation followed thereafter in New Jersey and Florida, although not all these states have equally effective legislatively mandated programs. In addition to these states, two insurance companies have their own photographic inspection programs. Neither GEICO nor State Farm will insure a noninspected vehicle.

Is the program effective? Although it is difficult to measure how much crime (insurance fraud) is deterred by a photo inspection program, it has been estimated that in the state of New York, reduction in costs and in insurance fraud claims has saved well over $100 million, and these savings have been passed on to insurance buyers through premium reductions. Although insurance premiums have not actually been reduced in New York, the overall increase in premiums in that state has amounted to less than half the national average.[52]

ODOMETER FRAUD

While you might think that the old days of cranking back odometer dials is over, thanks to digital odometers, that's not the case. In fact, digital odometers are susceptible to manipulation through computer software that's easily available to criminals. To make matters worse, it's harder to tell if digital odometers have been tampered with, as there are no visible moving parts

to the system. Regardless, **odometer fraud** remains one of the most costly consumer frauds of modern times.

The most susceptible vehicles to odometer tampering are those that are relatively new with exceptionally high mileage. Of the total number of passenger cars sold in the United States each year, approximately half are sold to car rental or leasing companies or to others for business use. Each year, at least 4 million of these late-model high-mileage cars are replaced. Those that are taken off lease or are no longer used for business purposes find their way into the used-car market.

The reason for odometer rollbacks is to increase the value of used vehicles on the market. Obviously, a car with fewer miles should bring a higher price than one with high mileage. It has been conservatively estimated that on a small or intermediate-size car, the sales value increases $50 for each 1,000 miles that the odometer is set back; in larger vehicles, the value increases to around $65 per 1,000 miles the odometer reading is reduced. Thus, a late-model car that is clocked from 70,000 miles to 30,000 miles can increase its value to the seller by $2,000 to $2,600. This amounts to a nice additional profit for persons inclined to indulge in such deceitful conduct.

Besides the obvious profits to the seller of clocked vehicles, the costs to the purchaser can be even greater in the form of potential unanticipated safety problems and increased repair costs. Since cars are generally the largest purchase made by people after the cost of a home, the condition of a car and the anticipated costs for repair and maintenance figure prominently in the decision of whether to buy a particular car. But when the odometer has been clipped, mileage is not a dependable guide for estimating potential maintenance costs, since such a vehicle will be more costly to maintain and more likely to need expensive repairs. If the purchaser-owner is unable to afford the higher costs, the quality of maintenance and repairs may suffer, along with the safety and roadworthiness of the vehicle.

Because of the proliferation of this fraud, most states have created some type of investigative unit to deal with odometer tampering by accepting complaints from citizens and determining if there is any basis for enforcement action. In addition, there are national and federal agencies and organizations actively engaged in enforcing laws and trying to prevent odometer and title fraud. NHTSA has an odometer fraud investigation arm. They work on multiple state large-volume cases. The Department of Justice attorneys prosecute the cases investigated by NHTSA. The National Odometer and Title Fraud Enforcement Association comprises investigators from the member states, NHTSA investigators, federal prosecutors, and interested auctions and dealers. State investigators can be most helpful in local investigations.

CarFax or other title histories should be considered critically; look for discrepancies or a history that would belie the numbers on the dashboard. Furthermore, when examining a late-model low-mileage vehicle that is suspected of being clocked, the investigator should check for extensive wear on the brake pedal, the driver's seat, and the seals around the trunk. Does the extent of wear conform to the claimed mileage? A check should be made for service stickers on the door, on the doorpost, and under the hood. If present, a date and odometer reading may be present; missing stickers may suggest tampering. Any of these conditions may be indicative of a rollback and warrant further inquiry. The investigator should order a vehicle history file through the state's motor vehicle titling agency and then check with each successive owner (including individuals, dealers, and auctioneers), obtain all odometer disclosure statements, piece together an odometer history, and attempt to determine if there has been a rollback. If a rollback seems likely, the investigator should determine the possessor of the vehicle when it was clocked. Standard investigative techniques should then be applied.

Title fraud is as big a part of the odometer rollback problem as is the act of clocking. Title alteration, discarding of title reassignment forms to complicate the tracing of ownership, manufacturing of false reassignments, and title laundering are criminal acts that violators often engage in to support and cover up odometer rollbacks.

To mandate better record keeping, reduce the opportunity for odometer tampering, and assist law enforcement in the investigation of cases, Congress enacted the **Truth in Mileage Act** in 1986. This act, along with amendments made in several subsequent years, attempts to improve the paper trail of odometer readings by requiring more tightly controlled documentation and recording of odometer readings each time that ownership of a vehicle changes. The law attempts to close loopholes that permit the inception of fraudulent title schemes and to reduce the incidence of title washing between jurisdictions by requiring all states to adhere to strict record-keeping criteria, thus avoiding schemes to create confusing paper trails that intentionally avoid jurisdictional boundaries of courts and law enforcement agencies.

MARINE THEFT

Marine theft is an expensive problem for the boating community (Figure 16-23). It includes the theft of boats, boat trailers, outboard motors, jet skis, and all equipment associated with boating or water activities. Marine theft is a "shadow crime." It is real but difficult to define because of the lack of accurate statistical information. The main reporting mechanism, the *Uniform Crime Report* (UCR), compiled and reported annually by the Federal Bureau of Investigation, enters the theft of an outboard motor in the burglary index, the theft of a boat trailer in the vehicle file, and other related thefts in different categories. As a result, the magnitude of the marine theft problem is hidden in other crime indexes. Marine insurance theft data are similarly disjointed because there are many types of policies—home owners', business, inland marine, yacht—that provide coverage for marine equipment.

The majority of thefts occur from homes, businesses, or dry storage facilities. A boat and outboard motor on a boat trailer can be stolen in a matter of seconds by a thief who simply backs up to the trailer, hooks up, and drives away. Although locking mechanisms are available for boat trailers and may deter the amateur thief, such devices are easily overcome by the professional.

Theft by water is accomplished simply by towing the boat away with another boat or by starting the motor and driving away. Boats powered by outboard motors, under 25 horsepower, usually do not have keyed ignition switches. However, even on larger boats, a dozen master keys will start virtually any marine motor, whether outboard or inboard.

Most watercrafts stolen fall under the "water ski" or "inboard motor" categories. Law enforcement experts agree that most thefts are not investigated thoroughly (if at all) because of the difficulty investigators experience understanding marine equipment identification numbers and the lack of available ownership information.

Because of the absence of accurate statistical data, law enforcement is somewhat hampered in its efforts to address the problem. Consequently, there is a general lack of knowledge about marine theft and a resulting lack of commitment of resources to address the problems. In many agencies, marine theft reports are assigned to the auto theft or burglary unit and are treated as low-priority items.

◄ **FIGURE 16-23**
Marine police on lookout
Marine theft, which includes theft of boats, trailers, and all associated equipment, is a serious problem in the boating community. In communities that have extensive waterways, local police often have a marine patrol unit that provides routine patrol and investigates theft of marine equipment.
(©James Kirkikis/123RF)

Why are boats stolen? The number-one reason is profit. Marine theft is a high-profit, low-risk crime. Most often, a boat, motor, and trailer are stolen and sold as a package at a fair market value. To reduce the possibility of identification, some organized theft rings operate a chop shop, switching stolen motors, trailers, and boats or selling them separately.

There is also a lucrative market for the exportation of stolen outboard motors. In Central and South America, a used outboard motor will sell for more than a new motor in the United States. In addition, as in auto theft, insurance fraud may be involved in 25% or more of the reported marine thefts.

The increase in marine theft has often been linked by the media to drug trafficking. Experts tend to disagree. If, in fact, 87% of the boats stolen are under 20 feet in length, it is unlikely that these are being used for drug trafficking. Boats 30 feet and longer could very well be involved in drug trafficking, but such thefts constitute only 3% of the problem. Of course, larger boats are also targets for professional thieves because of their high value. However, there may be some legitimate linkage between the theft of outboard motors and the drug problem. A 300-horsepower outboard motor, which retails for over $15,000, can be sold without any ownership documents.

Most small boats are stolen not by professionals but for the personal use of the thief or, occasionally, for joyrides. This is particularly true in the theft of personal watercraft. Approximately 20% of all boat thefts involve personal watercraft stolen by juveniles for their own use. Only occasionally are boats stolen to be used as transportation in other crimes, such as burglary of a waterfront home or business.

HULL IDENTIFICATION

Effective November 1, 1972, the Federal Boating Safety Act of 1971 required boats to have a 12-character **hull identification number (HIN)**. Before this, boat manufacturers assigned whatever numbers were needed for their own production records. The HIN was subsequently codified by federal regulation. The promotion of boating safety was the original purpose for the HIN. It enabled the U.S. Coast Guard to identify "batches" of boats produced by a manufacturer that failed to meet certain production standards. This consumer protection function soon became secondary after titling and registering authorities began using the HIN assigned to a boat to identify ownership in much the same manner as the VIN is used for a motor vehicle.

Although manufacturers are required to affix each HIN to the outside of the boat's transom in a "permanent manner" so that any alteration or removal will be evident, in reality this is rarely enforced. Many manufacturers attach the HIN using a plastic plate pop-riveted to the transom. This can be easily removed and replaced with a false HIN. Some manufacturers of fiberglass boats place the HIN on the outer layer of the gelcoat using a "Dymo label"–type device during the molding process. However, this can easily be scraped or gouged out by a thief with a screwdriver or knife. A professional thief will replace the removed HIN with automotive body filler that often matches the color of the gelcoat. Then, by stamping a false HIN into

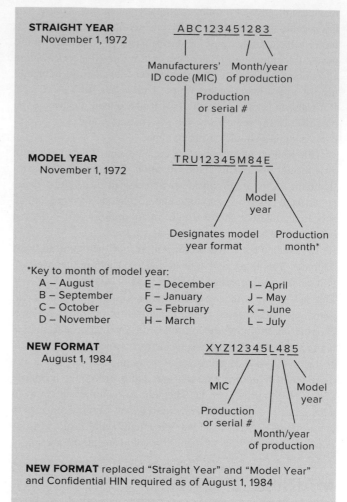

STRAIGHT YEAR November 1, 1972

ABC123451283

Manufacturers' ID code (MIC)   Month/year of production

Production or serial #

MODEL YEAR November 1, 1972

TRU12345M84E

Model year

Designates model year format   Production month*

*Key to month of model year:
A – August
B – September
C – October
D – November
E – December
F – January
G – February
H – March
I – April
J – May
K – June
L – July

NEW FORMAT August 1, 1984

XYZ12345L485

MIC   Model year

Production or serial #

Month/year of production

NEW FORMAT replaced "Straight Year" and "Model Year" and Confidential HIN required as of August 1, 1984

*Key to month of production of new format:
A – January
B – February
C – March
D – April
E – May
F – June
G – July
H – August
I – September
J – October
K – November
L – December

▲ **FIGURE 16-24**
Hull identification number (HIN) formats

the body filler, it appears that the HIN was affixed by the manufacturer and the alteration often goes undetected. An additional problem occurs when the Coast Guard allows a manufacturer to alter a HIN on any boat that remains in inventory by changing the production dates or model year to reflect a newer model year. Even for an experienced marine investigator, it is difficult to recognize whether a HIN was altered to cover a theft or modified by a manufacturer to reflect a newer model year.

Figure 16-24 shows the three different HIN formats approved by the Coast Guard. The straight-year and model-year formats were used from November 1, 1972, until August 1, 1984, when a new format replaced them. The only differences between the three formats are the last four characters. In the straight-year format, the last four characters reflect the calendar month and year of production. In the model-year format, the ninth character is always the letter "M" followed by the model year and a letter indicating the month of production. The newer format, optional starting January 1, 1984, and mandatory as of August 1, 1984, uses the ninth and tenth characters to reflect the calendar month and year of production and the eleventh and twelfth characters to represent the model year.

The first three characters of the HIN are the manufacturer's identification code (MIC), assigned to each manufacturer by the Coast Guard. Since 1972, over 16,000 MICs have been assigned. Many codes have been reassigned after the original company went out of business. Because of this, it is very difficult even for the most experienced marine investigator to remain familiar with all the manufacturer's codes. In addition, large conglomerates such as Mercury Marine and Outboard Motor Corporation have purchased many boat manufacturers and used manufacturer's identification codes assigned to the parent corporation for multiple boat lines.

The middle five characters of the HIN are used as production numbers or serial numbers assigned by the manufacturer. Although the letters "I," "O," and "Q" cannot be used, any other letter can be used in combination with numbers. These "production" numbers can and often are repeated on a monthly basis for an entire year. Whereas the automobile VIN has a 30-year uniqueness and a check digit to avoid unintentional or deliberate omission of numbers and intentional or unintentional transposition of numbers, the HIN does not yet have these features.

TITLE AND REGISTRATION ISSUES

There are approximately 12 million pleasure boats in the United States. Roughly 225,000 of these are federally registered by the Coast Guard and are referred to as "documented." Ownership and financial disputes over **documented vessels** can be resolved in the federal courts. The remainder of the pleasure boats are registered and/or titled by each state, except Alaska, in which registration issues are regulated by the Coast Guard.

Most states require that boats be titled, but only a few states require the titling of outboard motors. Even in titling states, many boats are exempted by being less than a specified length or powered by less than a specified horsepower of motor. More than half the titling programs are administered by wildlife or natural resource agencies. The remainder are operated by motor vehicle agencies.

Many jurisdictions that title boats do not have computerized ownership records or do not retain the information for more than 1 year. The boat registration or title files in only a few states can be accessed using the National Law Enforcement Telecommunications System (NLETS). The inability of an investigator to obtain ownership information in a timely and efficient manner makes boat theft investigation very difficult.

NCIC BOAT FILE

The Boat File, one of the 17 NCIC 2,000 files, records information on stolen boats, boat trailers, and boat parts. Information in the file is retrievable on an online basis by entering the registration or document number, the hull identification number, or the assigned NCIC number. Unless otherwise removed or located, information in the Boat File is maintained for the balance of the year of entry, plus 4 years. The exception to this is records that have no boat hull identification number or other number assigned by the owner that can be used for identification purposes. These remain in the file for only 90 days after entry.

The boat theft problem may be much greater than what the NCIC statistics display. There is no mandate requiring that boat thefts be entered into NCIC and, because of the difficulty of reporting, many thefts are not entered. According to marine theft experts, new edits installed in the NCIC Boat File in late 1993 contained errors, causing valid entries to be rejected and further discouraging the entry of stolen boat information by law enforcement agencies. Another major flaw in the system is that NCIC does not enter all the Coast Guard–assigned manufacturer's identification codes and, in some cases, has assigned codes that are not those recognized by the Coast Guard.

INVESTIGATIVE RESOURCES

Marine theft investigations are often complex and time-consuming. With the difficulty in obtaining ownership information, the tens of thousands of boat manufacturers, and the lack of computerized theft information, the success of an investigation is often predicated not on what the investigator knows but on whom he or she knows to contact for assistance. A major resource is the International Association of Marine Investigators. This organization has over 2,000 members who network with other law enforcement officers and agencies and insurance investigators throughout the United States, Canada, Europe, the Caribbean, and Central and South America. The organization holds an annual training seminar on marine theft issues.

PREVENTIVE MEASURES

There are several ways a boat owner can lessen the possibility of marine theft. For example, one individual who used to make his living by stealing boats and reselling them recommended that any boat with an electric starter should have a toggle switch that shuts off the electrical system when in the off position. The switch can be located under the dash or behind a panel. Typically, when a thief attempts to start the boat and cannot, the thief assumes that it is malfunctioning and gives up the effort to steal it.

To discourage theft, a boat owner may want to remove a vital engine part when the boat is left unattended. Trailered boats are more easily stolen than boats in the water. The best way to protect boats on trailers is to keep them out of the sight of thieves. They should be parked behind a house or behind or inside a garage where they cannot be seen from the street.

Owners should never leave boats where they will tempt a potential thief. If a boat appears difficult to steal, the thief will seek an easier victim. The owner should never leave the keys or the registration on board when the vessel is not attended. Outboard motors should be bolted through the hull and secured with clamping locks. If the owner is to be away from the place where the boat is stored for an extended period of time, the engine should be disabled or one or more wheels should be removed from the trailer.

AIRCRAFT AND AVIONICS THEFT

The theft of aircraft electronic equipment, or **avionics,** can be a highly lucrative enterprise for thieves. Avionics include all the electronic radio and navigation equipment on board an aircraft—easily valued at over $10,000 in even the smallest aircraft (Figure 16-25). Many pieces of avionics look similar and can be accurately identified only by referring to the model number and/or name. Part of the difficulty encountered by many law enforcement officers is their unfamiliarity with such pieces of equipment.

There are many reasons for equipment burglaries. One of the prime reasons is the lack of security at airports and the indifference on the part of many sales outlets regarding the identification and sources of used equipment. In addition, although most avionics contain stickers and plates identifying the manufacturer, model number, part number, and even the serial number, these are often easily removed and in some cases are just stick-on labels.

Most modern avionics are designed to be easily removed from the aircraft panel to facilitate frequent repair and maintenance of the equipment. Stolen avionics are often resold through the used-parts market or to persons who need the items and are willing to overlook the source of such reasonably priced equipment.

Much of the stolen avionics equipment is exported to other countries. Some is resold using counterfeited VIN labels and VIN plates. Other equipment is switched so that the stolen equipment is never discovered, as illustrated by the following example: A thief will identify the type of equipment desired in a specific aircraft at a specific airport. The thief or thieves will then locate the same type of equipment in another aircraft at another airport. At the time of theft, the electronic equipment will be removed from the first aircraft and placed in the second aircraft after the second aircraft's equipment has been removed. The equipment from the second aircraft is then sold on the market; normally, the owner of the second aircraft doesn't even know the equipment is missing because the same material, stolen from the first aircraft, has been installed in his or her craft. The theft of equipment from the first aircraft is reported, but it is never recovered because it is already comfortably installed in aircraft number two.

RESOURCES

An investigator who is unfamiliar with aircraft and aircraft thefts should not hesitate to obtain assistance from those who have the necessary expertise. It is advised that before undertaking a significant investigation, an investigator should visit a local airport, contact airport management, aircraft companies, flight schools, and so forth, to learn basic information about aircraft, avionics, and the theft of both. The Aviation and Crime Prevention Institute located in Hagerstown, Maryland, is an excellent source of assistance and support for law enforcement officers involved in the investigation of aviation theft.[53] The mission of the institute is to reduce aviation-related crime through information gathering, communication with law enforcement and the public, and education programs in theft prevention and security awareness.

▶ **FIGURE 16-25**
Stolen aircraft crashes into bank building
The theft of aircraft in the United States is a relatively rare event. However, breaking into an aircraft to steal electronic parts is relatively simple, since both door locks and ignition locks on many private planes can easily be picked. Thefts of aircraft are most likely to occur at airports that are poorly lit and unattended at night. The aircraft in the picture was stolen by a juvenile from a small airfield and ultimately crashed into a downtown bank building. (©Chuck Sutnick/Tampa Fire Rescue/Getty Images)

THEFT TECHNIQUES

The techniques thieves use to steal aircraft and burglarize aircraft for the avionics equipment are not that much different from, and most frequently parallel to, those used for stealing automobiles. Of course, if theft of the aircraft is the objective, it is unlikely that the thief will gain access by smashing a window. Indeed, smashing a window is generally not necessary. Perhaps the weakest security point of any aircraft is its locks. Most aircraft manufacturers use a limited number of key combinations, and a single key may open many aircraft of the same make. Occasionally, one manufacturer's key will open an aircraft of a different manufacturer.

Both door locks and ignition locks can easily be picked, and generally there are no antitheft devices on aircraft. Many of the more expensive aircraft don't even use ignition keys, so the only requirement for the thief is to enter the cabin.

Many of the techniques used to cover the theft of aircraft are similar to the processes used to conceal the theft of motor vehicles. The following illustrates a salvage switch involving aircraft: A thief decides on the type of aircraft desired and then purchases a total wreck of a similar aircraft from a junkyard. Rather than the certificate of title and VIN plate that come with a motor vehicle, the wrecked aircraft comes with its VIN plate and log book (a document required by the Federal Aviation Administration [FAA] that records the aircraft's history and repair record). The thief then steals (or has stolen) an aircraft of the same year, make, and model; switches the VIN plate; and installs the log book. After the thief adapts the registration markings and ensures that colors match the wrecked aircraft, the salvage switch is complete.

Thefts of aircraft are most likely to occur at airports that have poor lighting and are unattended at night, especially if they have little or no security, have no control tower, and perhaps are not even fenced.

AIRCRAFT IDENTIFICATION

Aircraft have the same basic identification information as do motor vehicles. The major difference is that aircraft are regulated under a federal licensing system, whereas motor vehicles are regulated under state licensing systems. All aircraft are identified by a registration number, which is similar to a license plate number; a VIN; and make and model. The U.S. registration numbering system is part of a worldwide system under which each country has a letter and/or number code. In the United States, the code begins with the letter "N." Consequently, all U.S.-registered aircraft display an N number.

Most registered aircraft receive their N numbers when they are manufactured. It is possible for the purchaser of a used aircraft or of an aircraft currently being built to request a special N number. Such requests are processed by the FAA.

The N number is found on each side of the aircraft or on the vertical tail in large or small letter and numeral combinations. In some cases, such as on older aircraft, the N number may be displayed on the underside of one wing and the topside of the opposite wing. Helicopters have the N number displayed under the nose or undercarriage.

Most aircraft have a small plate on the instrument panel with the plane's N number on it. An investigator can look at the plate and determine whether the plate number matches the N number displayed on the exterior of the aircraft. If the plate is missing, further investigation is warranted.

Although each aircraft has a VIN, manufacturers design their own numbering systems, and the location of a VIN plate varies depending on the make. For example, on Cessna aircraft the VIN plate is found on the doorjamb; the door must be open to see the plate. The VIN plate on most single-engine and small twin-engine Beechcraft planes can be found on the right side above the wing flap; large Beechcraft planes have the VIN plate inside the main-cabin entry door frame. On Piper aircraft the VIN plate is usually found on the lower side of the tail on the aircraft's body.

As in any attempt to identify a vehicle, a vessel, or aircraft, the investigator should understand the construction process well enough to know whether and where to look for identifiers. When aircraft are built, many of the parts are subassembled elsewhere in the plant, and such subassemblies are marked with the VIN number in Magic Marker or pencil so that the aircraft can later come together at the main assembly point. If the plate is missing, the investigator should look under seats, under carpeted areas, in inspection panels, and elsewhere for ID numbers relating to the VIN.

When trying to locate a VIN plate in aircraft other than those previously mentioned, the investigator should look in some of the most common locations, such as on the doorjamb on either side of the plane, on the lower tail section on either side of the plane, on the body where the main wing is attached, near the nose wheel, or on the lower body. In other words, when in doubt, the dedicated investigator will look over the entire aircraft in an attempt to find the attached plate, which will provide make, model, and VIN information.

THEFT PREVENTION TECHNIQUES

Following are a few examples of the theft-deterrent devices available and the actions an aircraft owner can take, some without cost, to reduce the chance of theft of the aircraft or the avionics.

- There are a number of alarm systems on the market, and some even have a pain generator, a second piercing alarm inside the cockpit that is most aggravating to the human ear.
- Ignition kills, which require entry of a security code into the control panel in the cockpit, are available. If the pilot fails to get the code right after a specific number of tries, the engine-starting circuits are disabled and, in some cases, a siren will sound.
- There should be a prearranged password known only to crew members and the airport operator. Thus, a person who calls and directs that the plane be prepared for flight

must know the password in order to get the plane readied. This technique has prevented the theft of many aircraft.

- A wheel-locking device, or "boot," prevents the plane from being towed or from moving under its own power.
- More secure locks can be installed.
- Airplanes should be parked at night at airports that are well lighted, fenced, and otherwise provided with security. Window covers should be used to conceal avionics.
- Avionics equipment should be checked to ensure that it is the manufacturer-installed equipment. Each piece should then be marked with a dot, paint, engraving, or

scratch, and a detailed inventory should be made and recorded.

- Propeller chains and locks are available.
- Instrument panels can be equipped with a locking bar or locking cover.
- Flight operations personnel at airports should be given a list that identifies each crew member and other persons permitted to be around the plane or to authorize service over the phone.
- Airport authorities should have a central point of contact available 24 hours a day.
- Vital aircraft records should not be kept in the aircraft.

KEY TERMS

active system (theft deterrent)
American Association of Motor Vehicle
    Administrators (AAMVA)
Automatic License Plate Recognition
    System (ALPR)
avionics
cargo theft
chop shop
commercial-vehicle theft
confidential VIN
documented vessel
false-theft scheme
false-vehicle scheme
federal safety standards certification
    sticker
gray-market vehicle

heavy equipment
hull identification number (HIN)
inflated-theft-loss scheme
joyriding
marine theft
Motor Vehicle Theft Law Enforcement
    Act (1984)
National Insurance Crime Bureau
    (NICB)
National Motor Vehicle Title Information
    System (NMVTIS)
odometer fraud
off-road equipment
"paper vehicle"
parts marking
passive system (theft deterrent)

product identification number (PIN)
professional theft (of vehicle)
quick strip (of vehicle)
salvage switch
salvage title
salvage vehicle
Stolen Auto Recovery (STAR) System
temporary theft (of vehicle)
title fraud
Truth in Mileage Act (1986)
vehicle fraud
vehicle identification number (VIN)
VIN plate
washing (of title)

REVIEW QUESTIONS

1. Describe a chop-shop operation.
2. How does a salvage switch work?
3. Distinguish false-vehicle, false-theft, and inflated theft-loss schemes.
4. What is a "paper" vehicle?
5. How is a certificate of title "washed"?
6. What are some of the factors contributing to the theft of off-road equipment?
7. What is the National Insurance Crime Bureau, and what functions does it perform for law enforcement?
8. Why is vehicle identification the most difficult and time-consuming task faced by an investigator in an auto theft case?
9. Why do vehicles have a standardized identification numbering system?

10. What was the purpose behind passage of the Motor Vehicle Theft Law Enforcement Act of 1984?
11. Describe the three basic methods for restoring vehicle identification numbers.
12. Describe some of the principal investigative steps in determining whether a vehicle fire is an accident or arson.
13. Describe the workings and benefits of a photographic preinsurance inspection program.
14. What is odometer fraud, and why is it a significant offense?
15. Discuss the nature and seriousness of marine theft.
16. What are avionics, and why is avionics theft prevalent?

1. Check the web to see if your state has law enforcement and/or insurance organizations that specialize in the investigation of motor vehicle and other related thefts. What types of investigative services do they provide? Are auto theft statistics available for your state? Does the site have auto theft prevention information? If you were a criminal investigator, what other information do you think should be available on the site?

2. Learn more about the export of stolen motor vehicles and other items by logging on to the U.S. Customs site at *www.cbp.gov* and the North American Export Committee site at *www.naexportcommittee.org*. The latter website also has several related links to insurance fraud and vehicle theft prevention.

Design Element: (crime scene tape): ©UpperCut Images/Getty Images RF

▶ Cyber criminals have many advantages. They can strike anyplace in the world without face-to-face contact with their victims.

(©Yuri Arcurs/Getty Images RF)

17

CYBERCRIME

CHAPTER OBJECTIVES

1. Distinguish between computer-assisted crimes and cybercrimes.

2. Identify the two prerequisites for the emergence of cybercrime.

3. State six advantages cybercriminals have over traditional criminals.

4. Define malware.

5. Differentiate between black hatters, gray hatters, and white hatters.

6. Describe the operation of botnets.

7. Describe the typical methodologies associated with attacks by outsiders.

8. State the purpose of DoS/DDoS attacks.

9. Explain the threat posed by the Chinese PLA in APT1.

10. Describe the use of scareware.

11. Contrast polymorphic and metamorphic viruses.

12. Explain the use of ransomware and a rogue program called "CryptoLocker."

13. Describe how keylogger attacks are accomplished.

14. Summarize the general rules for consent searches in the computer crime context.

15. Identify the major main points for securing and evaluating a computer crime scene.

16. Describe the Silk Road, the deep web, and the Tor Network.

17. Briefly describe the process of digital forensics relating to a seized storage device.

Computer-assisted crime, such as identity theft, is discussed in Chapter 15, Larceny/Theft and White-Collar Crime. In the crime of identity theft the computer is a tool used to assist in the commission of the offense. However, **cybercrime** differs from computer-assisted crime in that the computer itself is the target.

This chapter explores the conditions that had to exist before cybercrime could emerge; offenders and offenses; the differences between traditional crime and cybercrime; cybercrime tools and services; the types of computer intrusions that make cybercrime possible; and other related topics.

CYBERCRIME: AN OVERVIEW

In 2015, worldwide costs to consumers and businesses exceeded $1.8 trillion, expecting to crest $2 trillion by 2019.[1] Further, the year witnessed some of the most sophisticated of online crimes, accompanied by huge losses. The Carbanak case involving two malware gangs (Carberp and Anunak) that targeted banks worldwide by defeating internal systems and operational control programs, resulting in a total of nearly $1 billion in loss, with an average loss of $8 million per bank. Many of these banks were in the United States.[2] The year also witnessed a new form of malware that targets both human and technical weaknesses in a business—ransomware—that resulted in losses over $1.6 million in

2015.[3] (Ransomware will be discussed in much detail later in the chapter). The average total cost of a data breach (per case) increased from $3.52 million in 2014 to $3.79 million in 2015; and projections for 2016 and beyond run rampant.[4] The FBI reported nearly 290,000 complaints/incidents of cybercrime in 2015, up 6% from 2014, and an average of 300,000 such complaints over the last 5 years.[5] However, the most disturbing factor may be that these complaint numbers only represent a fraction of the actual cases of cybercrime that occur each year in the United States, as an estimated 85% of Internet-based, financial fraud cases go unreported.[6]

There were two prerequisites for the emergence of cybercrime: (1) computers had to be commonplace, and (2) they had to be linked in a network. The first electronic computer was built in 1942, and the first personal computer (PC) was the Kenbak-1, introduced in 1971, although fewer than 50 were ever built. Radio Shack began selling the TRS-80 in the late 1970s; IBM jumped into the PC market in 1981; and the Apple Macintosh appeared 3 years later. Joseph Licklider, in 1962, conceived of what is now called the Internet, with his idea of a "Galactic Network." A rudimentary form of the Internet, ARPANET, was publically demonstrated in 1972, the same year Ray Tomlinson developed e-mail. In those early years the Internet was largely used only by the government and universities. However, the rapid development of the PC market and the commercialization of the net in the early 1990s quickly led to a worldwide network; the first online service provider for consumers was Delphi (1992). Presently, there are over 7,000 Tweets sent, over 55,000 Google searches performed, over 2,500,000 emails transmitted, and over 36,000 GB of other Internet traffic conducted every second of every hour, every day—a monumentally huge number from such a sparse beginning little over 20 years ago.[7]

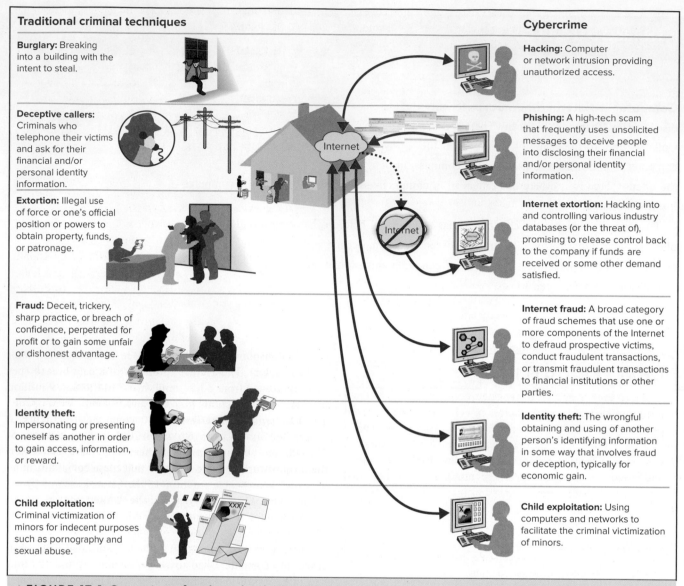

▲ FIGURE 17-1 Comparison of traditional and cybercrime techniques
Source: No author, *Cybercrime: Public and Private Entities Face Challenges in Addressing Cyber Threats* (Washington, DC: General Accountability Office, June 2007), p. 6

The satisfaction of the two prerequisites set the stage for a new breed of criminals who (1) didn't have to leave the comfort of their homes to commit crimes; (2) were invisible/anonymous, avoiding the dangers of personal contact with their victims; (3) could strike anywhere in the world; (4) were enabled to approach thousands of potential victims simultaneously; (5) executed crimes that victims might never detect or be too embarrassed to report; (6) committed crimes that might be discovered only much later, hampering investigations; (7) stood to reap profits far beyond those associated with conventional crimes; and (8) didn't have to worry about fencing tangible stolen property—for example, televisions and cars—because what they stole was intangible property—for instance, they looted checking, savings, and casino accounts.[8] Figure 17-1 illustrates some of the differences between traditional and cybercrime techniques.

THE EVOLUTION OF CYBERCRIME: FROM TEENAGE HACKERS AND SCRIPT KIDDIES TO SOPHISTICATED CRIMINAL ORGANIZATIONS, INTERNATIONAL ESPIONAGE, AND CYBER TERRORISM

Cybercrime is an evolved state of traditional crime; it continues to mature in complexity as well as sophistication.[9] In the early years (1970s through 1990s), cybercriminals would direct their attacks at consumer computers or corporate networks, conducting a myriad of unsophisticated outsider attacks. For example, early teen hackers often entered secure databases associated with government or corporate organizations simply for the ability to cause havoc and malicious mischief. Creating their own teenage delinquent subculture, teen hackers and script kiddies (individuals that used existing computer codes, tools, and/or scripts rather than write their own to exploit vulnerabilities in early computer and Internet systems) boasted openly about their computer attacks. They even wrote about their exploits on now-archaic bulletin board systems for others to follow.[10] As time went on, schemes directed at stealing money became much more commonplace, like "Salami Slicing" (shaving pennies from little used accounts) as in the New York Dime Saving Bank case, resulting in $1.5 million in loss or the First National Bank of Chicago, which suffered $70 million loss through fraudulent wire transfers and authorizations (late 1980s), or Kevin Mitnick's famous attack on phone systems beginning in the late 1980s and progressing through the 1990s.[11] One of the first cases of international espionage was the theft of classified information from the U.S. military by Dark Dante (Kevin Poulsen) in 1995.[12] These attacks took advantage of the lack of security controls protecting computer networks, systems, data, and processes that were easily compromised. The inventors of such technology typically focused their early efforts on the functionality and stability of the network or system, rather that the security and process control requirements necessary to protect it from being breached. As a result, cybercrime was able to evolve with little resistance during the period from late the 1970s through the 1990s. Hackers and relatively unsophisticated criminals were able to understand the inherent weaknesses of computer systems and networks, making for an easy classroom for helping burgeoning cybercriminals learn how to mature their new tradecraft. Today, most computer systems and networks have the technological tools, software controls, and protocols necessary to protect against these types of low- and medium- level attacks from external intruders.[13]

However, sophisticated high-level attacks that are often coordinated by multiple actors are another story. These types of cases almost always include large scale insider fraud schemes, organized criminal conspiracies, sabotage, and/or espionage. In some cases, the suspects are state actors working in specialized groups targeting industry and government in the United States for intelligence purposes. See Box 17-1.

Organized Crime Groups

Organized crime is defined by the FBI as "any group having some manner of a formalized structure and whose primary objective is to obtain money though illegal activities. Further, such groups maintain their position through the use of actual or threatened violence, corrupt public officials, graft, or extortion, and generally have a significant impact on their locales, region, or the country as a whole."[14] These organizations often attempt to hide their cybercrimes by involving multiple resources with knowledge of organizational processes and controls, working in different locations, branches, or departments. These resources are either selling information to the organized crime group or they are employed by them, and often act as "insiders" to the targeted specific business.

These types of "insider" attacks were found to occur during normal working hours while on-site and using authorized physical and logical access. Attack methods and examples included the following:[15]

- **Social Engineering**—The process of deceiving people into giving away access or confidential information.[16] For example, a sales representative arrives early for an appointment with a corporate manager in order to become friendly with his or her secretary or assistant. After several minutes of casual conversation, the sales representative meets with the executive. Later in the week, the sales representative calls the executive at a time when he knows the executive is out of the office and talks with the secretary/assistant. The sales representative convinces the secretary/assistant to provide secure information so that he may follow-up with the executive. The type of information may include everything from detailed information about the executive's family, travel plans, personal emails and resident addresses, and hobbies. The sales rep then uses this information to further ingratiate himself with the executive. The ultimate goal is to gain the trust of the executive in order to infiltrate the computer system or network.

- **Authorized use of an organization's systems**—Insiders using the access already provided by the organization to conduct their attacks. For example, call center representatives, with access to customer credit reports, were colluding to sell customer data to an outside organized crime organization for the purposes of identity theft and the creation of fraudulent (disposable) cell phone accounts.

- **Bypassing security and control processes**—Again, an activity usually by an insider that is aware of the organization's safeguards, auditing practices and frequencies, thresholds for approval and alerts, and/or regulatory controls. The suspect(s) can conduct their crimes under the radar and/or without the additional involvement of organization personnel. For example, an organization's check issuance process required the involvement of two employees as a fraud control, however both employees in this case were insiders from the same criminal enterprise and would issue fraudulent checks to their co-conspirators.

- **Compromised accounts**—Obtaining the user ID and passwords of organization personnel to conceal criminal activity and/or obtain the necessary access for conducting a specific crime. For example, an individual used passwords stolen from co-workers to conceal the changes he made to credit reporting data in exchange for money, and in support of his co-conspirator's identity theft activities.

In 2012, the FBI presented an exhaustive study of organized crime groups, cartels, and associations active in the cybercrime arena.[17] Organized crime groups infiltrate and impact legitimate businesses and industries like construction and trash hauling, they manipulate and monopolize financial markets, and they infiltrate traditional institutions like labor unions. They introduce and supply drugs to cities and increase the level of violence in our communities through the corruption of government and elected officials, and use extortion, intimidation, and murder

BOX 17-1 | MANDIANT REPORT ON APT1

Sophisticated attacks against U.S. commercial and governmental entities are not only the prevue of organized crime cartels and groups, but also foreign countries and even terrorists. For instance, China has established a separated entity within the People's Liberation Army (PLA) referred to as PLA Unit 61398, or Advanced Persistent Threat 1, or APT1. Since 2004, APT1's activities have been directly attributed to cyber-attacks on western governments, high-tech firms, oil companies, military and research organizations, along with various other entities across every sector of critical infrastructure within the United States.

Mandiant is a security research organization that has been researching advanced persistent threat (APT) operations since 2004. In early 2013, Mandiant collected enough evidence to substantiate a position that the APT attacks at 141 victim organizations over the last 7 years were likely conducted by a Chinese military unit, and had authorization from the Chinese government. The report continues to provide details related to the origins, locations, and structure of the APT1 group. In addition, the report provided insight in various activities and behaviors, including:

- Once APT1 established access to the victim network, they would periodically revisit the network over several months or years to steal data, including intellectual property, contact lists, and emails. This access was maintained, on average, for 356 days without being noticed. The longest period of access was 1,764 days (4 years, 10 months).

- APT1's slow and methodical attack allowed them to steal over 6.5 terabytes of data from one organization during a consistent 10 month period.
- In January 2011, APT1 was able to compromise 17 new victim networks located in 10 different industries.
- The vast majority of APT1 activity occurred during the hours of 8am and 5pm local China – Shanghai time. APT1 headquarters is in Shanghai, China.
- 832 different network IP addresses were identified as the source of APT1 connections. 817 of those IP addresses resolved back to China.
- The purpose of APT1 appeared to be focused on information collection and reconnaissance.
- Victim organizations were compromised by malware that was likely delivered in rogue emails. The malware either provide access to the network via a reverse shell, allowing APT1 to gain a foothold, or by harvesting credentials from the infected user, which APT1 later used to authenticate to the victim network.

In an unprecedented move to thwart APT1, the U.S. Department of Justice issued warrants for individuals associated with the Chinese military unit in May 2014. Charges against the individuals focused on economic espionage, sabotage, and trade secret theft. As of July 2016, no arrests have been made against APT1 members.

Conspiring to Commit Computer Fraud; Accessing a Computer Without Authorization for the Purpose of Commercial Advantage and Private Financial Gain; Damaging Computers Through the Transmission of Code and Commands; Aggravated Identity Theft; Economic Espionage; Theft of Trade Secrets

Huang Zhenyu   Wen Xinyu   Sun Kailiang   Gu Chunhui   Wang Dong

Source: Federal Bureau of Investigation

Sources:
1. Mandiant, *APT1: Exposing One of China's Cyber Espionage Units*, February 18, 2013.
2. Edward Wong, "Wide-Ranging Motives for Chinese State Hackers," *New York Times,* May 23, 2014.
3. John Quigg, "Strike Back at Chinese for OPM Hack; Build a Cyber Strategy," *Breaking Defense,* June 9, 2015. See: http://breakingdefense.com/2015/06/strike-back-at-chinese-for-opm-hack-build-a-cyber-strategy/

when needed to maintain their operations. In addition, prostitution, gambling, child pornography, and human trafficking and the various frauds and financial scams they perpetrate are impacting global economies. These crimes are facilitated by the Internet, providing criminals global reach to suppliers, customers, and conspiracies in a faster and more secure (less risky) manner than the face-to-face and telephone communications of the past.

Traditional groups like the Mexican and Columbian drug cartels, the Chinese Triads, the Japanese Yakuza, La Cosa Nostra, and Russian mafias, as well as nontraditional groups like the Russian Business Network, the Shadowcrew, and the Nigerian Cashing Crew, have actively targeted individual businesses for specific scams, while still being heavily involved in drug trafficking and money laundering. Over the last decade, they have become increasingly involved in high-tech, cybercrime operations including large scale theft of services, monetary and product counterfeiting, and online fencing of goods, as well as various types of fraud including mass marketing fraud, advanced fee fraud, insurance fraud, online identity theft, and sophisticated credit card fraud.[18]

Along the Silk Road with the Deep Web or TOR Network

Historically, the Silk Road was a great East to West trade route originating in China around the second century BC, and flowed across the fabled Himalaya Mountains to the countries of India, and the Near and Middle East. The road was fraught with dangers and intrigue as merchants crossed the great expanse with goods and services for sale.

More contemporarily, the **Silk Road** was an underground website that, again, traded in goods and services. The difference: Most everything on the sprawling network was illegal, from the sale of drugs, weapons, forged documents, exploit kits in which to attack computer networks, and even body parts, to the services of prostitutes, computer hackers, money launderers, and hit men. Silk Road was euphemistically referred to as the "e-Bay" of drugs and illegal contraband. However, on October 1, 2013, activities on the Silk Road came to a screeching halt as the FBI arrested Ross Ulbricht, a 29 year-old former nanotechnology student, in a computer lab at a public university in San Francisco. At the time of his arrest, Ulbricht was using the Internet identity pseudonym "Dread Pirate Roberts" or "DPR," the same pseudonym as the operator and mastermind of the underground network, Silk Road.

The network was ingenious, and operated as part of the **deep web**, a vast uncharted part of the world wide web, not accessible through regular Internet browsing or search engines. Most of the information in the deep web is hidden and encrypted with a unique application called Tor. Tor links participating servers, websites, and Internet services together while also encrypting all of the communications between each piece. Because users of the deep web use Tor, another synonym for the deep web is the Tor net or **Tor Network**. This secretive online world remains mostly untraceable and difficult to access for regular Internet users and even traditional law enforcement, which unfortunately permits a large criminal domain to exist and thrive today. This underground world is the Internet's secret black market where criminals, rogue agents, and even terrorists can conduct criminal and illegal activities. In this dark world of secret web sites and illicit opportunities, there are real-time, illegal transactions, drug deals, weapons sales, human trafficking coordination, murder for hire contracts, solicitations for hacker services, and the planning of terrorist events—all taking place with relative anonymity, and mostly untraceable. (Figure 17-2). Rarely do law enforcement officers and/or agents breach the deep web, making the arrest of Ulbricht and the closure of the Silk Road all that much more important.

The Silk Road operated for over 3 years. In that time, nearly 1.5 million transactions were conducted involving several thousand seller accounts and more than 100,000 buyer accounts. It was virtually a "blueprint" for a new way to use the Internet to undermine law and facilitate criminal enterprise. Ross Ulbricht was sentenced to life in prison in 2015 and interestingly, within 48 hours of closure of the Silk Road, another Silk Road was reportedly opened, again encrypted by the anonymity of the Tor Network.[19]

Cyber Terrorism

The evolution of technology is also a factor that is driving terrorists to use the Internet and its connected systems. **Cyber terrorism** or **digital terrorism** are two terms often used interchangeably and can be defined as the premeditated, politically or ideologically motivated attack against information systems, networks, programs, and/or data that can result in violence against a civilian target.[20] Often, it encompasses the use of the Internet and/or any electronic communication technology intended to effect traditional terrorist outcomes. Cyber terrorism uses technology for a wide range of purposes, including recruitment, funding, providing training, planning acts of terrorism, incitement to commit and/or the execution of acts of terrorism, and the execution of cyber-attacks.[21]

- **Recruitment**—Terrorists are using technology as a means to publish their extremist propaganda (e.g. text, video, audio, posters, etc.) and build relationships with those interested in their cause. Their message is being published on social media sites, including Instagram, Facebook, Twitter, chat groups, and YouTube; and the deep web, where uncensored content and discussions can occur. Some of these sites require login credentials provided by the recruiter. The use of the Internet greatly expands the reach of recruitment geographically and the ability to market the terrorist message through various social media outlets such as YouTube, Twitter, Facebook, chat rooms, and the like.[22]
- **Financing / Funding**—Terrorist groups often engage in cybercrimes as a means of funding their activities. There are four general categories for Internet-based funding operations: (1) direct solicitation via email and website locations; (2) e-commerce, including the online sale of goods to include books and recordings that support the cause; (3) exploitation of online payment tools, such as PayPal; and (4) charitable donations requested through direct email and website

► **FIGURE 17-2**
Screenshot from the Tor Network for the "Black Market Reloaded" site (Drugs, Weapons, Data, and Other Illegal Services)

locations. As an example, the Islamic State (ISIS or ISIL) provides a variety of websites to solicit donations, as well as maintains a presence on the Tor Network for more clandestine funding operations. (Figure 17-3).

Training—Terrorist groups utilize the Internet to disseminate training materials that have traditionally only been provided to attendees of a training event, which could be costly and more conspicuous. Training materials disseminated through the Internet include training videos, training manuals, and audio guides. With a virtual training platform, terrorists can train geographically dispersed groups or individuals in attack methods, and the construction of explosives, and also solicit feedback through interactive video conferencing (e.g. Skype) sessions. In addition, there are a number of YouTube videos widely available on the web that discuss bomb construction, and even the development of suicide bomb vests.

Planning—Terrorists use the Internet to communicate with individuals involved with a particular terrorist operation, to coordinate events and responsibilities, share intelligence information, and provide logistical support. For instance, in 2008, the Global Islamic Media Front released a new set of encryption tools, called Mujahedeen Secrets, for terrorist groups to use to encrypt their communications while operating online.[23] According to a 2012 United Nations report on the use of the Internet for terrorist purposes, many criminal justice practitioners indicated that almost every case of terrorism, that was prosecuted involved the use of the Internet.[24]

Execution—Terrorists often use the Internet to execute a specific attack or act. Activities that might be conducted through the Internet include signals for executing an attack, coordination and logistics, executing commands that remotely trigger a device or activity via the Internet, and the use of the Internet to communicate violent threats intended to induce fear.

Cyber-Attacks—With respect to cyber terrorism, cyber-attacks are the use of technology and hacking and/or techniques to exercise the deliberate exploitation of computer systems or networks, as a means of launching an attack intended to compromise, disrupt, and/or damage target computer systems or technology. Furthermore, the cyber-attacks can be used to instill fear, cause kinetic damages, and result in direct harm to humans. Types of cyber-attacks that have been identified for the express purpose of causing harm to human life include:

- *Electronic airport, civil and military air traffic, and airspace control systems*—possibility of remote controlling or disabling a system and effectively putting aircraft in dangerous positions or a collision course.
- *Electronic controls systems on civil and military aircraft*—causing problems for aircraft during takeoff or landing, or falling out of the sky in mid-flight.
- *Electronic systems of companies which design and develop the hardware and software used in airports, in air traffic control, and in the construction of aircraft, both civil and military*—corrupting software during the design and manufacturing phases.
- *Electronic national defense systems*—causing a "non-willed" attack on a specific nation.
- *Fully automated subway control systems*—compromising the security of the train systems leading to collisions, derailment, or crash through the end of the line.
- *Water supply and controls systems*—depriving an area of drinking water, or providing contaminated drinking water.
- *Gas and petroleum pipeline control systems*—manipulating the control systems to cause instability in high pressure / flammable pipelines that run through metropolitan areas.
- *Hospital electronic systems*—manipulation of patient records, drug dosing, surgery requests, etc.

Fund The Islamic Struggle Without Leaving a Trace.

السلام عليكم ورحمة الله وبركاته

abumustafa@tormail.org

13Pcmh4dKJE8Aqrhq4ZZwnM1shKFcMQEEV

- *Electronic emergency management systems (911)*–making the service unavailable, rendering those in need without support services.
- *Electricity grid management systems*–collapse of a localized grid, disabling safeguards and overpowering transformers, generators, and substations.
- *Railway electronic systems*–similar to subway systems, though railways carry heavier and often dangerous cargo. Manipulating train management could result in a large area event, especially if the train is hauling dangerous chemicals.
- *Electronic traffic light systems*–manipulation or disabling traffic signals across a large area would result in widespread traffic jams and accidents.[25]

Radical Islamic groups such as al-Qaeda, Boko Harem, and the Islamic State, as well as domestic groups like the Black Panthers, Earth Liberation Front, and Black Blocs, plus hate groups such as the Neo-Nazis and Ku Klux Klan, have long used social media such as Twitter, Facebook, and Wickr to express their ideological views and propaganda. However, an attack on the U.S. Central Command (Centcom) Twitter account in January 2015, delivering pro-Islamic State messages, revealed that specialized Internet teams and units within many groups are now emerging.[26] (Figure 17-4). While not reaching a high sophistication level yet, it is clear that some groups are now cultivating and recruiting specialized computer programmers aimed at developing specialized units to carry out cyber-attacks.

CYBERCRIME TOOLS AND SERVICES RELATED TO THEFT AND FRAUD

Cybercrime tools and services are being mass marketed on the Internet. They are found on publicly accessible web forums, such as Internet Relay Chat (IRC) as well as on the Deep Web; the major vendors are principally located in Russia, Eastern Europe, and Malaysia.[27] Sellers and buyers also communicate by ICQ software (pronounced "I seek you"). Table 17-1 summarizes three major categories of cybercrime tools and services related to theft and fraud.

Buying malicious tools and services on the Internet from anonymous vendors in foreign countries has resulted in many would-be cybercriminals being scammed and left empty handed. These "wannabes" are in no position to complain to anyone about their losses, and "honest" malicious tools and services vendors, referred to as "verified sellers,"[28] stand to lose potential sales if their industry is generally seen as fraudulent. As a result, independent "guarantors" often act as the middlemen in the sales process for 3 to 5% of the selling cost, ensuring that the exact terms of the contract are met.[29] Guarantors hold the buyer's money, verify that the software works as advertised, and then transmit the money to the vendor and the product to the buyer.

OFFENDERS

As described above, most computer enthusiasts of the 1970s hacked into computers out of curiosity or for excitement. Most of them were armed with cheap, low-powered, and relatively inefficient home-based computers like the old Commodore 64, Atari-8, or TRS 80 computers by Tandy/Radio Shack. Today, the overwhelming motive is for financial gain. Hackers/crackers who use their skills to illegally make money are called "**black hatters**"; those who use them for good—for example, for identifying security risks in computer systems and networks and then notify corporations of their vulnerability—are called "**white hatters.**" Other computer hackers or computer security experts who may violate the law or at least violate ethical business standards, but who do not have the malicious or criminal intent of a black hatter, are often called "**gray hatters.**" These individuals often have exceptional skills and when they find vulnerability in a system, rather than exploit it directly for their own financial gain, or sell it to others for financial gain, they may attempt to fix it for a fee.[30]

In cases for which perpetrator data is available, 76% of cybercriminals are male, and most range in age from 14 to 30 years. Hackers are often described as "antisocial loners," which is not very useful for investigators. More helpful is Table 17-2, a taxonomy or classification scheme that categorizes cybercriminals by type, characteristics, motivation, and skill. This table is not a fixed hierarchy of offenders, but it does provide a framework for thinking about the capabilities and threats posed by different cybercriminals. To a degree, Table 17-2 is limited in that it represents "pure" categories, when in fact cyber-offenders may be active in several different categories. Table 17-3 summarizes data about cybercrime perpetrators and complainants. It suggests that offenders have a preference not to victimize people living in the offenders' own state.

TABLE 17-1 Cybercrime Tools and Services		
TOOLS/SERVICES	**DESCRIPTION**	**PERCENTAGE OF MARKET SHARE**
Malicious Software	Ready to run crimeware is often purchased on the Internet—e.g., viruses, worms, and spyware. Cost ranges from less than $10 for a simple virus to over $5,000 for advanced capability programs. The Trojan horse is the most commonly sold malicious software at approximately $750 per copy. (Malicious software is discussed later in this chapter.) Some sites offer free downloads of older versions of malicious software that may be useable or that places a virus on the downloader's computer.	39
Cybercrime Services	Examples include distribution of spam and pop-up messages, and denial of service attacks to shut down websites.	34
Stolen Data	Includes bank, savings, checking, credit card, PayPal, iTunes, and casino account numbers; user names and passwords; identity documents—for example, data from scanned passports—are also available to assume new identities or engage in fraud. Offenders may use or sell data "harvested."	27

Source: Bill Chu, Thomas J. Holt, and Gail Joon Ahn, *Examining the Creation, Distribution, and Function of Malware On-Line* (Washington, DC: U.S. Department of Justice, March 2010), pp. 7–8, with some changes and additions.

TABLE 17-2	Taxonomy of Cybercriminals		
TYPE	**CHARACTERISTICS**	**MOTIVATION**	**SKILL LEVEL**
1. Novice	• Limited computer/programming skills • Use software ("tool kits") written by others, e.g., SpyEye, IcePack, XRumer, and KanBe, which cost from $700 to several thousand dollars • Referred to as "script kiddies" or "script bunnies" • Commit simple cybercrimes, e.g., virus attack	• Thrill seeking • Ego enhancement • Prove themselves to others • Collect "trophies"	Low
2. Cyberpunks	• Higher skills than novices • Can write some of their own programs • Better understanding of systems they attack • Deface web pages, send spam • Many engage in account data thefts, cyberfraud	• Media attention • Financial gain	Moderate
3. Internals/ Insiders	• Often information technology (IT) professionals • Represent greatest risk because in position of trust • Historically have triggered great losses • Inflated sense of their importance/value • Have strong sense of entitlement	• Typically revenge • Feel slighted, e.g., not promoted • Disgruntled, seek to "right" a "wrong" done to them	High
4. Petty Crooks	• Some are making transition from novice or street to cybercrimes • Not interested in notoriety/attention, keep low profile • May work to obtain requisite skills, e.g., attend technical school • May show a progression in skill or interest over time, such as moving to professional criminals category	• Greed, financial gain • In small number of cases may act out of revenge, e.g., former employer, ex-girl/boyfriend	Moderate
5. Virus Writers	• Often in transition to some other category • Age of VWs varies • Stop or shift to another category during mid- to late-20s	• Mixed motives • Motives may be similar to novices and petty criminals	Very high
6. Old Guard Hackers	• Generally have no criminal intent • However, disregard for others' property may cause operational interruption or other losses • Enjoy technical challenge of hacking • Write but generally do not use tool kits they sell to novices	• Curiosity • Need for challenges	Very high
7. Professional Criminals	• Some number are well trained former intelligence operatives—Russia, Eastern Block European countries and some Asian gangs • Crime is their career field • Seldom arrested; convicted even less often • Choose lucrative targets, e.g., banks, casinos, intellectual property (e.g., games, movies, recipes) • Fully exploit the potential of the Internet as a crime tool • Apolitical, will commit national security espionage for profit, even against their own governments • "Guns for hire," if the price for accepting a "project" is right • High tolerance for risk	• Money and financial gain • Life-style attractive	Very high

CONTINUED

| TABLE 17-2 | CONTINUED |

TYPE	CHARACTERISTICS	MOTIVATION	SKILL LEVEL
8. Information/ Espionage Warfare	• Targets are defense industry corporations to nations • Disrupt, destabilize, corrupt, exploit, or otherwise compromise operational capabilities, e.g., production schedules, satellites, military unit communications, and data integrity/reliability • Theft of national security information, e.g., stealth capabilities of aircraft and submarines, weapons in development • May be conducted, or sponsored by corporate competitors, a national government, or contracted with professional criminal gangs	• Highly trained, skilled, and experienced, • May be very patriotic • Profit motivation may be primary	Highest
9. Cyber Terrorism	• Targets are random; however past attacks have been on government and military sites • Disrupt, destabilize and/or compromise operational capabilities. • Plan and implement attack scenarios using clandestine communication and control techniques • Promote propaganda and recruit new actors to their groups or organizations • Solicit funding for support	• Fairly skilled, however vastly improving • Trying to recruit highly skilled individuals to work in international teams • Looking to perform cyber-attacks causing direct harm to humans	Moderate; Improving to Very High

Source: Markus Rogers, "A Two-Dimensional Circumplex Approach to the Development of a Hacker Taxonomy," *Digital Investigation*, Vol. 3, Issue 2, 2006, pp. 98–100, with some changes and additions by Robert W. Taylor (2016).

| TABLE 17-3 | Cybercrime Perpetrators and Complainants per 100,000 People |

RANK	STATE	PERPETRATORS PER 100,000 PEOPLE	RANK	STATE	COMPLAINANTS PER 100,000 PEOPLE
1	District of Columbia	116.00	1	Alaska	485.91
2	Nevada	106.73	2	New Jersey	166.74
3	Washington	81.33	3	Colorado	143.21
4	Montana	68.20	4	Nevada	135.75
5	Utah	60.22	5	District of Columbia	131.90
6	Florida	57.28	6	Oregon	124.18
7	Georgia	56.99	7	Maryland	121.67
8	Wyoming	56.40	8	Arizona	121.01
9	North Dakota	51.01	9	Washington	120.56
10	New York	48.10	10	Florida	116.25

Source: No author, *2009 Internet Crime Report* (Washington, D.C.: Internet Crime Complaint Center, the National White Collar Crime Center and the Bureau of Justice Assistance, 2010), pp. 7 and 9.

COMPUTER INTRUSIONS

Computer intrusions are accomplished by the use of malware, a term derived from combining *mal*icious and soft*ware*. **Malware** is intended to (1) deny use of computers; (2) covertly gain control over computers, for example, through the use of a Remote Administrator Tool (RAT); (3) secretly access or intercept computer data; and (4) subvert the operation of computers for personal profit. Many of the techniques discussed in this section are being adapted for attacks on smartphones.

Although malware is often for a single purpose, the clear trend of cybercriminals is to use multipurpose or **"blended threat" malware** —for example, the ABC Virus, which includes spyware, control from remote sites, and data theft capabilities. Malware may be transmitted with downloaded images, a "spoofing" e-mail, which appears to come from a legitimate source, such as a bank; Valentine's Day and Christmas cards; files saved on CDs and flash drives that are shared with other users; fake free security software offers; "You have won an instant $100" messages; bogus news, storm, or sports reports; or by other means discussed in this chapter, such as drive-bys. This section addresses common malware intrusions; there is some inherent overlap in these categories—for instance, an infostealer Trojan horse can also be categorized as spyware.

1. *Botnets:* A **"herder"** (**"botmaster"**) uses malware to hijack hundreds to tens of thousands of computers and is able to remotely control them all, including the ability to update the malware and to introduce other programs such as spyware. Hijacked computers are called **zombies** (robots, or **bots**). The malware creating the bot "lies low," waiting for commands from the herder and thus is difficult for security software to detect.

   A **botnet** is a network of zombies or bots (Figure 17-5). The Georgia Institute of Technology estimates that globally 15% of all computers may be zombies.[31] The herder makes money from repeatedly selling clandestine botnet access to others to use for pop-up advertising or other purposes, at an average cost of 37 cents per week for each zombie.[32] A herder with 10 weekly clients for a botnet with 10,000 zombies could gross $1.9 million annually.

   Computers are often hijacked by what appear to be legitimate e-mail messages. A growing method is **"drive-bys,"** which occurs as a user-unintended side-effect of visiting a website; Drive-bys are made possible by exploiting web browser vulnerabilities. For example, a person on Facebook sees a video on YouTube that friends might be interested in and sends the link to them. When the friends click on the link, the malware is surreptitiously installed. A variation of this involves seemingly innocent celebrity websites that are actually malicious; click on one, and a drive-by occurs. In the past, Jessica Biel, Cameron Diaz, Rihanna, Lady Gaga, Jennifer Anniston, Justin Bieber, and Miley Cyrus have all been on the "most dangerous sites to visit" list; visits to these celebrity websites created a 10% chance of being a drive-by victim. For instance, a reported sex tape of Miley Cyrus in 2014 on Facebook acted as a bait to lure

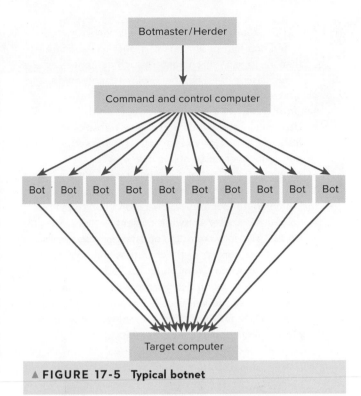

▲ FIGURE 17-5 Typical botnet

would-be victims to a specific site that downloaded an exploit to the victim's Facebook page, giving suspects not only access to the victim's identity and personal information, but also that of the victim's friends.[33]

2. *Viruses:* At any one time there may be as many as 16,000 viruses floating around. The *primary purpose* of a **virus** is to replicate as many times as possible and to cause as much mischief or damage as possible. A number of programs provide a good level of security from infection, including Norton, AntiVirus, McAfee, Intego, and Kaspersky.

   A virus is an unauthorized software program that is surreptitiously inserted into an executable program on a single computer.[34] When a user launches the infected program, the virus looks for other executable programs in which to place a copy of its malicious code. Thus, the typical virus requires human intervention to spread itself. The user may spread the virus to other computers—for example, if it has attached itself to outgoing e-mail. Infected computers may run slower and slower as more programs are infected. The viruses can also reformat a hard drive, causing the loss of all data, or odd/taunting messages may appear on the screen.

QUICK FACTS

Protect Yourself on the Web

How to keep your personal information safe.

- Never share your personal information over email, social media sites, or instant messaging.
  - Personal information can include your last name, home address, banking information, social security number, school name, and telephone number.

- Make sure that your passwords are strong.
  - When creating passwords it is best to use more than 7–16 varying characters such as upper and lower case letters, numbers, punctuation marks, and special characters for instance: %, $, *, or &.
  - Don't share your username or password.
  - Use unique passwords across the websites you frequent. If one of your accounts is hacked, it could put your other accounts at risk.
- Whenever it is an option use "two-factor authentication" for accessing websites.
- Install computer security software on your computer.
- Keep your computer software current.
  - Update your software as the updates are made available.
    - Updates consist of patches that will help prevent your computer from being hacked.
- When shopping online use secure websites only.
  - A secure website will usually have a symbol such as a lock which indicates that it employs software to protect your personal information.
- Beware of phishing scams.
  - Never connect to link within an email.
    - Instead to confirm that a website is legitimate, open a new window and access the website typing the address into the new window's address bar.
    - Attachments and programs may contain viruses.
- Be careful when you play games over the internet.
  - Confirm that your security software works for that particular game.
- Be aware that people can pretend to be anyone they want using the anonymity of the internet. Not everything you read online is true, and others may lie in order to gain your trust.
- Be aware of your children's online computer use.
  - Use parental controls.
  - Make sure sites and games are rated for the age of the children accessing the site.
- Be careful about what you post online.
  - Watch what you post about yourself or others. Photos or videos featuring embarrassing or possibly illegal activities can be stored forever by service providers or copied and spread by other users.
  - Be aware that tagging places you're associated with makes it easier for others to know your location and schedule.
- Always use a password protected secure network at home and trusted secure networks when using public wifi.

Sources: Davis, Gary, "McAfee, 10 Tips To Stay Safe Online," *McAfee,* July 7, 2017. https://securingtomorrow.mcafee.com/consumer/consumer-threat-notices/10-tips-stay-safe-online/; McAfee, "Online Safety Tips," *McAfee Online Security Center,* 2003–2017, http://mc.umt.edu/cyber/Documents/Online%20protection%20tips.pdf; Bruce, Debra, "Teen Internet Safety Tips," *WebMD,* n.d., http://teens.webmd.com/features/teen-internet-safety-tips#1; Ilube, Tom, "Share Take Care," *BBC,* February 1, 2013, http://www.bbc.co.uk/webwise/0/21259413; Chen, Brian, Jonah Engel Bromwich, and Ron Lieber, "How to Protect Your Information Online," *New York Times,* September 7, 2017, https://www.nytimes.com/interactive/2017/technology/how-to-protect-data-online.html; Bronwich, Jonah Engel, "Protecting Your Digital Life in 9 Easy Steps," *New York Times,* November 16, 2016, https://www.nytimes.com/2016/11/17/technology/personaltech/encryption-privacy.html; Profis, Sharon, "The Guide to Password Security and Why You Should Care," *CNet,* January, 1, 2016, https://www.cnet.com/how-to/the-guide-to-password-security-and-why-you-should-care/

Polymorphic and metamorphic viruses are similar in that they each make changes to their replicants to hide from security software, but they do so differently. A **polymorphic virus,** such as Virut, encrypts its replicant into an alternate form, but it must then decrypt itself back into its original form to execute. In contrast, a **metamorphic virus** completely rewrites itself each time it reproduces. No metamorphic replicant or "child" looks like its parent.

Worms are considered a variant or subclass of viruses and therefore are substantially similar to them. The key difference between the two is once inserted into a computer, a worm can distribute itself across the Internet without any action by the computer user because it is self-contained and does not have to be part of another software program.

One of the most famous worms was the e-mail that appeared in 2000 with the tag line of "I Love You." When recipients clicked on its "love letter" attachment, the virus was installed. Originating in the Philippines, this worm affected 10% of all Internet users in nine days by sending itself automatically to everyone on each infected computer's contact list. It is estimated that this virus created losses of $15 billion.[35]

The software security firm Sophos estimates that an unprotected computer connected for the first time to the Internet has a 40% chance of getting a worm within 10 minutes; that risk reaches 94% after an hour.[36]

In 2010, just 2 years after it was discovered, the Conficker worm had infected 7 million computers. Its encryption code is so sophisticated that only a small number of people would have the skill to write it; moreover, Conficker is adept at reappearing even after some antivirus packages have eliminated it.[37]

3. *Time, logic, and e-mail bombs:* A **time bomb** is programmed to "go off" at a particular time or date, such as April Fool's Day, Halloween, or Friday the 13th. A **logic bomb** is "detonated" when a specific event occurs—for example, all personnel records are erased when an electronic notation is made that a particular person was fired. **E-mail bombs** are intended to overwhelm a person's e-mail account by surreptitiously subscribing it to dozens or even hundreds of mailing lists. Alternatively, 10 knowledgeable people might be able to collectively send 650,000 e-mail messages in an hour to a single user's account. In such circumstances, the Internet service provider usually suspends the use of the e-mail account, disrupting the ability of the victim to use it. Such a circumstance is called a **denial of service (DoS)** attack.

On a larger scale, a botnet herder can use all of his/her zombies to overwhelm even the largest servers, in a **distributed** (across the botnet) **denial of service (DDoS)** attack.

DDoSers are also referred to as **flooders,** and their known corporate victims include Yahoo!, Amazon, and CNN. In 2007 Tallinn, Estonia, decided to relocate a Soviet-era monument from the center of the city to the suburbs. Two days of rioting by ethnic Russians was followed by DDoS attacks against Estonian agencies. Many believe that the attacks were conducted by or on behalf of the Russian government.

DDoS threats can also be used for extortion. Russian gangs successfully extorted millions of dollars from 50 online casinos and betting businesses in 30 different countries by threatening such attacks; the profitability from remaining online 24 hours a day was greater than the extortion paid by the victims.[38]

QUICK FACTS

CryptoLocker

One of the fastest growing and most pernicious malware programs in 2016 is CryptoLocker, a form of Trojan horse ransomware that targets computers running Microsoft Windows. It uses a variety of methods to spread itself, such as emails, infected thumb drives, compromised WiFi systems, or any mounted storage connection. CryptoLocker is a program that encrypts files; and while the program itself is easy to remove, the files remain encrypted. The only way to unlock the files is to pay a ransom by a specific deadline. If the deadline is not met, the ransom will increase significantly or files will begin to be deleted. The ransom usually amounts to $400 cash payment. CryptoLocker infected an estimated 500,000 computers in 2015, with the number of those who paid the ransom approximately 1.3%, amounting to about $3 million.

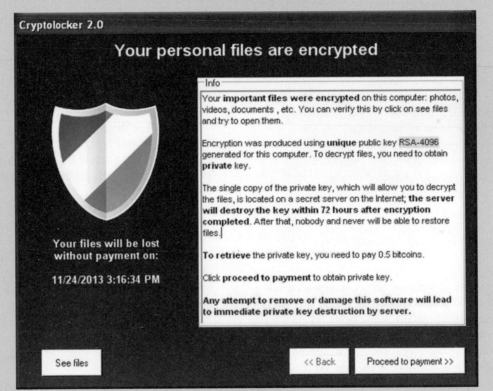

Source: Azwan Jamaluddin, "10 Most Destructive Computer Viruses," Hongkiat (July 19, 2016) See: http://www.hongkiat.com/blog/famous-malicious-computer-viruses/

4. *Ransomware:* Also known as a cryptovirus, **ransomeware** holds the data on a computer or the use of the computer hostage until a payment is made. Ransomware encrypts the target's files—for example, through a Cry-Zip Trojan—and the attacker tells the victim to make a payment of a specified amount to an E-Gold, a Yandex, or a WebMoney account to receive the decryption key.[39] Alternatively, the attacker requires the victim to prepay for a certain value of goods with a specific business in a foreign country. The goods are used or traded by the attacker, or the "business" may simply exist on paper and the attacker receives the ransom from the sale of it.

Ransomware encryption methods are too sophisticated to be easily cracked, and pressure is placed on the victim by the notification "For every 30 minutes that goes by without full payment, one file will be deleted."[40] Although ransomware attacks have been aimed primarily at businesses, individual personal computer users have also been victimized with the demanded payment in the $200–$300 range.

Movieland, also known as Moviepass.tv and Popcorn. net, allegedly puts displays or plays music on a computer that cannot be closed or turned off. Movieland's creators claimed the "users" did not pay the required $29.95 for the program after the trial period, and users state that their systems were being held hostage Ransomware attacks represented the fastest growing type of computer attack in 2015.[41]

5. *Dead drop:* To avoid personal contact, intelligence agents use a location called a **dead drop** or drop zone to leave and pick up messages. Similarly, some cybercriminals prefer to distance themselves from incriminating files; they use another computer or server, a virtual dead drop, sometimes called an egg drop or drop zone, on which to store the data they have stolen.[42] The attackers sell the data or use it to commit cybercrimes themselves.

6. *Trojan horse:* There are numerous platforms for delivering **Trojan horses.** One way is to offer what appears to be legitimate software program with a title that mimics a well-known package that many users may try, such as a free download of a "Web Accelerator." The Trojan horse piggybacks on the Web Accelerator download. In another version, a pop-up appears on the screen with "Yes" and "No" buttons to answer the question "Do You Want to Optimize Your Internet Access?" No matter which button is pushed, the Trojan horse is downloaded. Another pop-up that functions in the same manner is a window that offers some type of a browser plugin.

Symantec, a leading antivirus company, recognizes three categories of Trojans: (1) backdoor, with a primary purpose of establishing the opportunity for remote access at some later time; (2) downloader, with the main goal of facilitating the downloading of some other type of software, most usually additional malware; and (3) infostealer, with an objective of stealing information, such as account names, numbers, and passwords.[43]

7. *Spyware:* **Spyware** is a broad term that sometimes is used to mean the same thing as malware but more narrowly is thought of as a surveillance tool, such as the infostealer form of a Trojan horse. Webroot, an antivirus software company, audited 19,480 businesses in 71 countries and found an average of 19 pieces of spyware.[44] Crimes involving stolen passwords result in losses of $2.75 billion annually.[45]

A keystroke logger, referred to as a keylogger, may be the most common form of spyware. As shown in Figure 17-6, a **keylogger** secretly "harvests" every keystroke that a computer user makes and thus steals sensitive data for profit.

Keyloggers may be hardware or software. KeyGhost makes a hardware version that is roughly the size of a small thumb and is easily installed. The keyboard cord is plugged into the keylogger, which in turn is inserted into the back of the computer. There are two families of keylogger software: (1) ZeuS, Zbot, and Wsnpoem, whose attack channel is spam e-mails that trick users into opening them, and (2) Limbo2 and Nethel, which are downloaded as a drive-by when users visit a malicious website.[46] There are over 200 unique programs designed to steal passwords via keylogging.[47]

Some spyware is relatively benign, learning what sites a user visits on the Internet to shape marketing strategies. However, an accumulation of benign spyware slows down a computer's speed.

8. *Rootkits:* In many computer operating systems (OSs), the "root" is a "superuser" account for system administration. A "kit" is the malware introduced into the computer. A **rootkit** gives an attacker "super powers" over computers—for example, the ability to steal sensitive personal information, or engage in cyber warfare or cyber espionage. See Box 17-2.

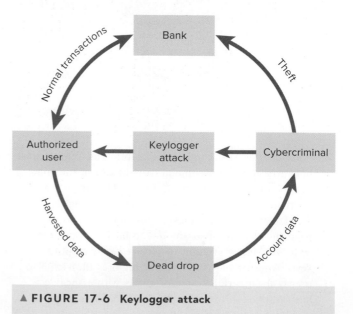

▲ **FIGURE 17-6   Keylogger attack**

BOX 17-2 | OF WORMS, SCADAS, STUXNETS, AND FLAMES

"Stuxnet" is a malicious worm program developed by the United States and Israel (under the Obama Administration) to sabotage Iran's nuclear program in 2012. The program was jointly developed under the code name "Operation Olympic Games."[48] The purpose of the Stuxnet worm was to infect the supervisory control and data acquisition (SCADA) systems of very specific devices—the Siemens industrial control systems, the primary devices found within the pumps and gas centrifuges used in the Natanz nuclear enrichment facilities in Iran. See the diagram below. Stuxnet reportedly ruined almost 25% of Iran's nuclear centrifuges, seriously setting their entire nuclear program back several years and costing hundreds of millions of dollars in repair.[49] Stuxnet has three important modules bundled within one program: a worm that executes all routines related to the main attack; a link that automatically executes the propagated copies of the worm to the SCADA; and a rootkit component that hides all malicious files and processes, preventing detection, and hence elimination of the program.[50]

Later in 2012, another highly destructive and sophisticated malware program called "Flame" was observed in various countries throughout the Middle East, including Iran. Unlike Stuxnet, which was designed to sabotage or destroy a specific SCADA device, Flame was a large program written primarily for espionage and intelligence gathering. The program allowed an attacker to seek and secure a variety of documents stored within a computer or computer network, again, with the vast amount of these targets in Iran. Similar to Stuxnet, Flame was almost impossible to detect, even after an attack had been made. In other words, host computers had no record of the theft of their documents even after the attack was completed.

Stuxnet and Flame represent some of the most complex and advanced cyber-attack programs every developed.[51] And, because they specifically attack SCADA devices and/or are extremely difficult to either detect and/or remove, they are not just another common malware development. They were designed specifically to target industrial systems often used in critical infrastructure. The problem is that both Stuxnet and Flame appear to have migrated into the realm of the cybercrime arena. Similar malware programs, such as Conficker, Taidoor APT Backdoor, Zbot and Sality, and other new variants, including ones that attack the Microsoft Windows operating system (Enfal), are now plaguing U.S. corporations.[52] Even though fixes and patches for the systems are available, international countries are leery of companies like Microsoft, knowing well that their primary operating system has been exploited by such sophisticated and well-concealed worm programs.

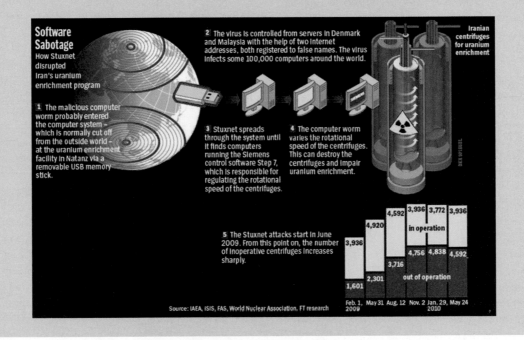

Software Sabotage
How Stuxnet disrupted Iran's uranium enrichment program

1 The malicious computer worm probably entered the computer system – which is normally cut off from the outside world – at the uranium enrichment facility in Natanz via a removable USB memory stick.

2 The virus is controlled from servers in Denmark and Malaysia with the help of two Internet addresses, both registered to false names. The virus infects some 100,000 computers around the world.

3 Stuxnet spreads through the system until it finds computers running the Siemens control software Step 7, which is responsible for regulating the rotational speed of the centrifuges.

4 The computer worm varies the rotational speed of the centrifuges. This can destroy the centrifuges and impair uranium enrichment.

Iranian centrifuges for uranium enrichment

5 The Stuxnet attacks start in June 2009. From this point on, the number of inoperative centrifuges increases sharply.

in operation: 3,936 / 4,920 / 4,592 / 3,936 / 3,772 / 3,936
out of operation: 1,601 / 2,301 / 3,716 / 4,756 / 4,838 / 4,592

Feb. 1, 2009   May 31   Aug. 12   Nov. 2   Jan. 29, 2010   May 24

Source: IAEA, ISIS, FAS, World Nuclear Association, FT research

Rootkits—for instance, TDSS—are considered the most sophisticated type of malware and are quickly emerging as the largest intrusion threat to computers.[53] There are at least five different "flavors" of rootkits. A common one, after being introduced into a computer, alters the OS so that it can remain hidden indefinitely.

Rootkits do not replicate or ordinarily do not cause damage to files.

9. *Scareware:* A **scareware** attack often starts with a pop-up message on your screen, "Virus Activity Detected!" claiming that your computer has a virus—and for $19.95 you can download antivirus software to fix the problem

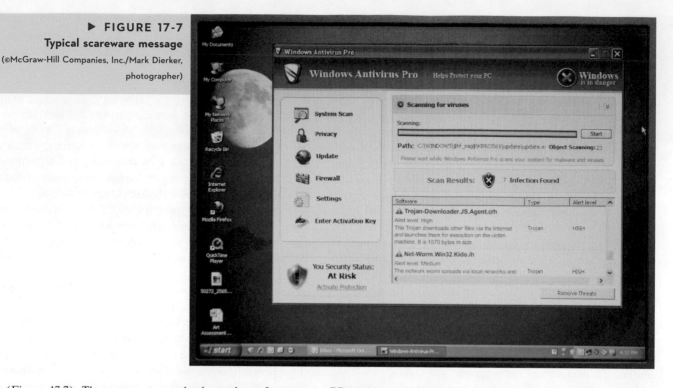

▶ FIGURE 17-7
Typical scareware message
(©McGraw-Hill Companies, Inc./Mark Dierker, photographer)

(Figure 17-7). The unwary user who buys the software thinks the problem is resolved, but the software is really useless and delivers malware, and the vendor sells the user's credit card number. In 2010 a new method of delivering scareware, using a bogus update to the Firefox web browser, was discovered in England.

MOBILE DEVICES

A **mobile device** is a term use to describe any small, computer device, typically small enough to be held in the hand. In earlier years, these pieces of computer equipment were often called PDAs (personal device assistants), or tablet computers. However, today's mobile devices include media players, notebook computers, and computer tablets, such as those manufactured by Samsung, Sony, HTC, LG, Motorola, ASUS, and Apple. For most mobile devices, the equipment is powered with a stable battery power such as a lithium battery. Mobile devices also include "smartphones"—cell phones that have a computer processing capability as well as a telephone function built into the unit (Figure 17-8).

There are several different operating systems within the smartphone, personal computer, and/or computer tablet market, to include Nokia's Symbian, Motion's Blackberry OS, Palm OS,

▶ FIGURE 17-8
Examples of mobile devices
(©Georgejmclittle/Shutterstock RF)

Hewlett-Packard's Open Web OS, Firefox OS, Microsoft Phone OS. However the largest number of devices in the United States use one of the following two major operating systems:

1. **Google Android:** This is the most popular mobile operating system in the world by sales and was created and developed by Google. It is based on the Linux software core and is designed primarily for a variety of touch-screen mobile devices such as computer tablets and smartphones.

2. **Apple iOS:** This is the mobile operating system created and developed by Apple, Inc. and is distributed exclusively for Apple products, such as the iPhone, iPad, iPod, and iPod Touch.

Mobile devices may be the "weakest link" in any secure system (See Box 17-3). Indeed, they are very difficult to control from a physical security perspective, because everyone has a cell phone or tablet and they can be easily concealed. More importantly, cell phones and tablets do not share the same "fear" as personal computers do as potential gateways to more sophisticated systems. When stopped at a physical security checkpoint, cell phone holders rarely stop and think that their cell phone attaches to the same Internet that spreads harmful viruses and malware, much less a more advanced and/or directed attack from an outsider. Mobile devices just do not have the same level of security awareness among the public as more traditional computer devices. In fact, most users of mobile devices do not even use basic software security such as virus/malware protection software, or personal identification numbers (PINs) to secure entry into their device. Much of the public is naïve to the potential victimization resulting from loss or theft of their cell phone.

Then too, there are a variety of rogue mobile apps that can infect a mobile device; some record the information that users type into a device (i.e., passwords, bank account numbers, PINs) and are used later to attack an unsuspecting victim. Some apps even have the ability to take over email, text message, and social media apps and use them as a host in which to search for other needed information to perform a theft, fraud, or other financial crime; or act as a "zombie computer" that sends out thousands of "bot" programs or "bot" emails to the victim's friends or email contacts. The goal may be so innocuous as to only gain enough information to assist in further "social engineering" of the victim. A phone call may even be surreptitiously recorded and then transmitted to cyber criminals, including those in foreign countries, who further exploit the unsuspecting victim.[54]

The risk from mobile device infection is compounded in the workplace through WiFi networks and systems that link directly to cell phones and tablets. Malware and viruses easily transcend basic WiFi protection protocols and software, as the system is compromised once the "infected" mobile device is accepted into the existing system. The problem is compounded when the device malware focuses on the communication software between devices or "things" like cell phones, TVs, tablets, thermostats, personal computers, security systems, remote keyless entry systems, and the like; as well as unsuspecting WiFi systems.[55]

Sadly, the problem is expected to get much worse in the future, as malware attacks and viruses have skyrocketed in the past 5 years,

BOX 17-3 | FIVE NEW THREATS TO MOBILE DEVICES

Mobile devices, and especially cell phones, are being used by cyber criminals as new points of attack. Indeed, mobile devices may be the new "weak link" in the chain of advanced technology. Here are five new threats identified for mobile devices:

1. **Mobile Phishing and Ransomware:** Just like their counterpart in PC scams, suspects use social engineering through mobile apps and SMS text messaging to gain trust, access data and infiltrate secure systems. Malware then ends up on the victim's PC via the mobile device.

2. **Using an Infected Mobile Device to Infiltrate Nearby Devices:** An infected mobile device (such as a cell phone) can easily breach an organization's physical perimeter security, and directly attack devices via the internal WiFi instead of having to break-in some other way. Any computer or device using WiFi is vulnerable to any infected mobile device sharing that network.

3. **Cross-Platform Banking Attacks:** Suspect apps are downloaded to the mobile device which then spies on the user as they access their banking website or surf various stock brokerage houses. Dubbed the "man in the browser"

attack, these programs intercept banking credentials and/or brokerage login information before they get encrypted.

4. **Cryto-Currency Mining Attacks:** Malware that infiltrates mobile devices in search of digital currencies, such as Bitcoin, Litecoin, and Dogecoin. While not all individuals have such accounts, those that do often suffer enormous financial losses.

5. **The Enemy May Be Us:** Despite the fact that ongoing public announcements, corporate training, and constant awareness programs inundate our lives, it does not appear to be having a positive impact in altering user behavior. In other words, we still do not use even simple security solutions, even when they are widely available for all devices—mobile or stationary. Indeed, nearly 60% of mobile device users were unaware that security solutions even existed for mobile devices, according to a 2014 survey!

Source: Stacy Collett, "Five New Threats to Your Mobile Device Security," CSO—Computer Security Online, May 21, 2014. See: http://www.csoonline.com/article/2157785/data-protection/five-new-threats-to-your-mobile-device-security.html

aimed specifically at mobile devices. In part, this increase follows the huge increase in cellphone (smartphone) usage. The number of smartphones is expected to breach 2.1 billion worldwide in 2016.[56] Mobile devices may be the weakest link for cybercriminals to slip through to more sophisticated systems or in which to exploit innocent victims; this has led one computer security analyst to state, "Taking steps to secure one's mobile device is the twenty-first century equivalent of locking your door at night."[57]

INVESTIGATION OF CYBERCRIMES

FEDERAL EFFORTS

The FBI and the United States Secret Service (USSS) play prominent roles in investigating computer assisted and cyber-crimes. The FBI has a four-fold mission in this area: (1) to stop those behind the most serious computer intrusions and the spread of malware; (2) to identify and thwart online sexual predators who use the Internet to meet and exploit children and those who produce, possess, or share child pornography; (3) to counteract operations that target U.S. intellectual property, endanger national security or competitiveness; and (4) to dismantle national and transnational organized criminal enterprises engaging in Internet fraud.

The FBI Operational Technology Division (OTD) provides a number of tools that are used to analyze digital data and computer systems in large-scale hacking and cybercrime cases. These same tools can be used to address cyber-espionage cases, and include cell phone tracking systems, video analysis software, facial and iris recognition tools, wiretap operational tools, and a variety of intelligence gathering software tools able to hack suspect networks and/or mimic cellphone towers to elicit signals from cellphones in a specific area. These tools have not gone without controversy relating to encryption as well as illegal eavesdropping.[58] See Box 17-4.

The US Secret Service has broad jurisdiction to investigate computer crimes, including unauthorized access to protected computers, identity theft, DDoS attacks involving disruption of e-commerce or extortion, and distribution of malware. The USSS has established Electronic Crimes Task Forces (ECTFs) in approximately 39 cities across the country, bringing together the expertise of federal, state, and local agencies and representatives from industry and the academic community. The mission of ECTFs is the prevention, detection, mitigation, and aggressive investigation of attacks on the United States' financial institutions and critical infrastructures.

Many federal agencies participate on ECTFs and lead or serve on other investigative task forces (TFs) spread across the country. Among the federal agencies participating in these efforts are United States Attorney's Offices, the FBI, United States Postal Inspection Service (USPIS), and the U.S. Immigration and

BOX 17-4 | THE ENCRYPTION ISSUE

In 2013, a classified intelligence leak from former defense contractor Edward Snowden revealed the collection of *all* phone-tracing data from all Verizon digital telephone communications under the USA PATRIOT Act. The revelation from Snowden's leak made it clear that at least some (intelligence) agencies had overstepped their power. Telephone companies and Internet Service Providers (ISPs) like AOL, Verizon, AT&T were spending countless hours and dollars every day trying to fulfill the requests made by police and security agencies under the PATRIOT Act.

In November 2014, in the wake of the Snowden leaks, a civil suit was filed by Twitter, requiring agencies to publish a full transparency report on their surveillance activities. The suit was joined by other entities such as Apple and Google. In early 2015, the Senate failed to block agencies from continuing to collect individual phone records and other data from social media and ISPs. In response, Apple and Google, as well as other companies began offering encryption programs to secure private data and text messages on mobile devices (especially smartphones). The encryption program renders a locked mobile device (smart phone) impervious to external intrusion without a key, held only by the owner of the phone. The issue came to a head in December 2015 with the shootings in San Bernardino, California; the FBI had recovered an Apple iPhone 5C from terrorist suspect Syed Farook, and

the FBI needed Apple assistance to "unlock" the phone. The U.S. Department of Justice file a court order in February 2016, in an effort to require Apple to help the FBI access the contents of the phone, however that court order was vacated by the courts a month later in March 2016. Former FBI Director James Comey has continually warned that such encryption (by Apple and Google) will cost American lives as agencies will not be able to use a variety of tools to track criminals and victims alike, as well as gain valuable intelligence information from terrorist phones. The issue is certainly not over as the U.S. faces a larger predicament on how to balance the need for intelligence to prevent future terrorist attacks, collect evidence in which to prosecute criminals, and secure our nation from today's threats posed by cyber criminals and cyber spies with individual and Constitutionally guaranteed rights of privacy, trust, and security.

Sources: Marjorie Cohn, "The Surveillance State: NSA Telephony Metadata Collection: Fourth Amendment Violation." (January 16, 2014) See: http://jurist.org/forum/2014/01/marjorie-cohn-nsa-metadata.php

National Public Radio, The Morning Edition, "Encryption, Privacy Are Larger Issues than Fighting Terrorism," March 14, 2016 See: http://www.npr.org/2016/03/14/470347719/encryption-and-privacy-are-larger-issues-than-fighting-terrorism-clarke-says

Customs Enforcement (ICE). The Social Security Administration (SSA) participates in approximately 100 such TFs. Many of these TFs are aimed at specific computer assisted crimes, such as identity theft, advance fee schemes, and exploitation of children.

STATE AND LOCAL EFFORTS

Computer/cyber/high-technology/electronic crime units are commonly found in all larger municipal and county agencies, although their mission, expertise, and capabilities vary widely. As departmental size decreases, so does the probability that such units exist. These "poor cousins" and larger agencies both face barriers to establishing and growing an effective computer-, cyber-, or electronic-crimes unit, because: (1) the needs for, and benefits of, an electronic crimes unit are not well understood; (2) many local agencies cannot alone afford to provide adequate office space, purchase the necessary hardware and software, or dedicate and train the staff required; (3) administrators are reluctant to engage in the hard and uncertain work of recruiting qualified information technology partners from industry and the academic community; (4) support for such units is often nonexistent or low, especially for administrators who are trying to meet more basic service delivery needs; (5) the inability to fully staff such units means that where they do exist, their mission may be restricted to a few crimes—for example, identity theft, child pornography, online child predators, cyberbullying and stalking, and non-delivery of merchandise ordered online—because the "unit" consists of a single officer; (6) it is difficult to retain trained and experienced officers; (7) existing laws may be inadequate; and (8) prosecutorial expertise may be lacking.[59]

Of necessity, many local agencies depend on the computer-crime expertise of their state investigative agency, state police, or state patrol. These state agencies are often staffed with a combination of officers trained in computer-crime investigation and civilian information technology specialists. In addition to a staff located at headquarters, qualified personnel are usually located within troop commands or other geographical districts. These agencies also operate TFs, as do State Attorney Generals and local prosecutors. A number of local agencies have also cooperated in founding their own units, the services of which are shared.

LEGAL CONSIDERATIONS

Federal laws pertaining to computer-assisted and cybercrimes are comprehensive, although the corresponding state statutes vary in their sophistication and breadth. As with other types of crime, investigators must be thoroughly familiar with the applicable federal and state laws. In particular, knowledge of the federal Electronic Communications Privacy Act (ECPA) of 1986 and its subsequent amendments is essential. ECPA violations may result in criminal charges being brought against officers, personal civil liability, and the suppression of evidence. Therefore, investigators should be guided by their department's policies and those of the local prosecuting authority.

CONSENT SEARCHES

Search and seizure were discussed in Chapter 2, "Legal Aspects of Investigation." Consent searches are revisited here within the personal computer-crime context, because unlike warrant applications there is no judicial official screening to guide investigators' actions when a consent search is sought in the field.[60]

Whenever reasonably possible, investigators' should seek a warrant. However, many times a request to search on the basis of consent may be a sound, even prudent, course of action, because a consent search does not require probable cause. To avoid conflicting accounts that may arise later, the party granting consent should execute a written consent form (Figure 17-9) prepared by the local prosecuting authority. When the examination of a computer system is contemplated, the consent form should specify in broad terms that computer and other electronic evidence may be searched. Computer case law continues to evolve, and the discussion here is for general information and is not a guide to authoritative practice.

The general rules for **consent searches** is that the police can rely on a person's *actual authority* to consent to a search or the *apparent authority* of such other parties they reasonably believe can grant a search of the premises—for example, an adult guest who has "the run of the household" while the owners are absent.[61]

The consent must be freely and voluntary given; police threats such as "Let us look at your computer files or we'll arrest your girlfriend and take away your children" will nullify the consent.[62] Different fact situations determine whether investigators can conduct a consent search:

1. If the persons with actual or apparent authority to consent are not native English speakers and appear to lack meaningful comprehension, the burden is heavier on the government to show the consent was voluntary.[63] It must be demonstrated *before* the search that such persons comprehended the situation well enough to understand the action to which they consented.
2. The extent of a consent search is limited by the subject and scope of the consent—for example, consent to "search the computer in my son's room" does not extend to household computers located elsewhere.

In *United States v. Stierhoff* (549 F.3d 19, 2008) a defendant suspected of stalking signed a broadly worded consent form for the Rhode Island State Police to search the room he rented as a residence and in which his computer was located. Over $140,000 in cash and financial records in the room suggested the possibility of a separate tax evasion case. When investigators began examining his computer, Stierhoff verbally narrowed his consent to the

CONSENT TO SEARCH FORM

I, _____, presently residing at _____ have been informed of my right to refuse to consent to a search. I have not been promised anything nor have I been threatened in any manner. My consent is given freely and voluntarily. I have been advised that I can modify or withdraw my consent at any time.

I authorize and consent to a search of the _____ located at _____ by _____ and such other personnel as he/she shall designate, including any containers of each and every kind.

The officer(s) are authorized by me to seize and take custody of any notes, letters, pages, papers, records, materials or other property, including computers, together with all of their components, related processing and internal and external storage devices, scanners, routers, printers, display monitors, modems, and any and all accessories and property the officers believe to be pertinent to their investigation.

The officer(s) are authorized by me to search for and seize electronic data within the authority, consent, and scope given above. The officer(s) may use any means to search any or all files, including deleted, encrypted, and password protected files.

I also authorize the officer(s) to remove to another place(s) they deem appropriate any property, equipment, or other material related to their investigation, to sort out, read, examine, analyze, evaluate, test, and reproduce it. I also authorize these actions by those the officer(s) may designate to perform them.

Date: _____   Time: _____

Signature of Consenting Party: _____

Witness Signature: _____

Witness Signature: _____

◄ **FIGURE 17-9**

Consent to search form oriented toward personal computers

Source: Priscilla Adams, *Consent Searches* (Oxford, Mississippi: National Center for Justice and the Rule of Law, University of Mississippi Law School, 2010), p. 6 with modifications

files containing his "love poems." However, the police also opened a file labeled "Offshore," which deepened their suspicions about tax evasion. Later that night, investigators, with a separate consent form from Stierhoff, searched the defendant's storage unit and found more evidence of tax evasion. The Internal Revenue Service was notified. Stierhoff was later convicted at separate trials of stalking and failure to pay taxes on over $1 million during a 4-year period. His lone "victory" was that both the tax evasion trial and appeal courts agreed that the evidence from the "Offshore" file was not admissible. This case illustrates that consent may be modified or withdrawn at any time.

United States v. Wong (334 F.3d 831, 2003) shows the importance of being patient and using a warrant when possible. The investigation of a murder led to the seizure of a computer under warrant. The investigator later obtained a search warrant to have it forensically examined for graphic files pertaining to the case. Child pornography was found, which the court held was a plain view exception to the Fourth Amendment.

3. When a person is asked for permission to search personal computers in a home, his/her mere silence does not rise to consent. If investigators falsely tell a person "we have a warrant to search your computer" the fruits of the search are not admissible.

4. Consent to enter a home does not constitute authority to conduct a search. A nonverbal gesture to "come in" is sufficient to enter the premises. Although mere entry does not authorize a search, investigators can act on plain view offenses—for example, child pornography pictures or drugs lying on a table.

5. Among those who cannot give law enforcement officers consent to search private living areas for computers or other purposes are landlords and apartment managers. Under some rental agreements they may be able to enter and inspect for an agreement violation—for instance, if a nonpermissible pet is on the premises, if the tenant is given reasonable notice, if the manager does so at a reasonable time and conforms to other related provisions of the agreement. If evidence of a crime is observed—for instance, credit-card-making machines or computers being used to produce counterfeit currency—the manager's information can form the basis of probable cause for a search warrant. However, if the manager's intention is actually to "get the goods" on tenants and is essentially

acting as a law enforcement officer, the evidence will be inadmissible.

Dormitory, sorority, and fraternity managers, and usually medical and administrative staff with respect to a patient's room, cannot give consent when there is a reasonable expectation of privacy.[64] Hospital security personnel responsible for protecting a patient's possessions, such as a laptop, do not appear to have a right to surrender them to investigators. Hotel managers cannot normally give consent to search private rooms, although they can if tenants have terminated their occupancy or eviction proceedings have been completed.

6. Spousal and domestic partner search consents for domiciles may be valid depending on the circumstances. If a spouse or partner is absent, consent by the other is usually approved by the courts. Even so, the courts have imposed restrictions; in *Trulock* v. *Freeh* (275 F.3d 391, 2002) a housemate consented to a search of the computer she shared jointly with her boyfriend; both accounts on the computer were password protected. The police found incriminating evidence in the boyfriend's account, but the court refused to admit the evidence on the basis that the use of a password created a reasonable expectation of privacy by him.

If, however, the password is on a "sticky note" attached in plain view to the computer or has been shared with others, the courts may not be deferential to a claim of privacy. Encrypted files might create a privilege similar to password protected files. Short of password protection, defendants may claim an expectation of privacy based on instructions such as "no one is to use my computer except me" or keeping it locked up when not in use.

If both spouses or partners are present and one affirmatively objects and the other consents, any search is unconstitutional (*Georgia* v. *Randolph* 547 U.S. 103, 2006). Under Randolph, the nonconsenting party must be physically present and immediately challenge any qualified co-occupant who consents.[65]

In *U.S.* v. *Groves* (530 F. 3d 506, 2008) the question arose whether police could strategically plan to avoid the presence of a potentially nonconsenting cotenant. Groves was a convicted felon who did not consent to a search of his residence, shared with a live-in girlfriend. Three weeks later, knowing Groves was at work, the police revisited the Groves domicile and were granted entry by the girlfriend. The court held the search was constitutional because Grove was not "objecting at the door," and the police had no role in removing him from it.

7. Parents ordinarily have unlimited authority to consent to searches over the dissent of their children who are under 18 years old and living at home, because there is a recognized hierarchy in the family. However, if juveniles have created "private space," such as footlockers to which only they have a key, a right to privacy claim might be raised. If their children are older than 18 years, a parent may in some circumstances be able to give consent. However, if children are older than 18, pay rent, and have asserted their right to deny access to their room, the courts have held that parents' consent to search that private space is not valid.

8. Montana appears to be the only jurisdiction that has clear guidance as to whether a minor child can consent to a search of their parent's home; a child there who is 16 years or older may be able to authorize a search in the absence of both parents. Elsewhere, the fact situation will guide whether children can do so. As the Supreme Court noted, no one "would reasonably expect an 8-year-old to be in a position to authorize anyone to rummage through his parents' bedroom."[66] The authority of minors to consent to a search of their parents' home and computers has no "bright line" test.

A search warrant is a better option than relying on the uncertain authority of a child. Nonetheless, *before* acting on a child's consent, investigators' should pursue a rigorous line of inquiry to determine if it is *reasonable* to believe such authority is valid. The courts will closely scrutinize the basis on which the police acted on the consent of children, including their, age, maturity, physical and mental state, intelligence, education, and the instructions their parents gave them—for example, "don't let anyone in the house unless it's an emergency."

9. The courts have held differently on whether a computer-repair person may allow the police access to a computer being repaired that has evidence on it. Some states have laws requiring computer-repair services to report crimes they detect—for example, credit card fraud.

In *United States* v. *Grimes* (244 F.3d 375, 2001), the defendant's wife brought her husband's computer to a repair shop with the complaint that it wouldn't boot up. Subsequently, the repairman called the wife and reported that there were a lot of image files, and he recommended deleting some of them, which the wife authorized. In the process of determining which files might be deleted, 17 pornographic images were discovered and reported to a local detective, who looked only at the 17 images and did not request that the repairman examine the remaining image files. The 17 files were copied on a floppy and given to an FBI agent, who patiently obtained a warrant to seize the computer, which was held to be lawful by the court.

10. Those on parole or probation may have their releases based on conditions creating diminished Fourth Amendment rights that approximate consent. In *United States* v. *Herndon* (501 F.3d 683, 692, 2007) a warrantless search of a probationer's computer was upheld, based on reasonable suspicion that he had violated the terms of his probation. Herndon's release prohibited him from using the Internet, and he was required to allow his probation officer to search his computer at any time for such use. After Herndon told his probationer officer he was using the Internet to look for a job, the officer drove to his residence and searched an external hard drive, finding child pornography. The court upheld the search, noting that Herndon's privacy rights were "dramatically reduced" by the terms of his release and the government's legitimate interest in preventing his recidivism.

11.   *Routine* searches at border crossings or other points of entry into or departure from this country do not require a warrant, probable cause, reasonable suspicion, or consent. In *United States* v. *Arnold* ((523 F.3d 941, 946, 2008) the court ruled that reasonable suspicion was not required to search a laptop or other personal electronic devices, because it was a non-destructive intrusion akin to searching luggage. This decision did not address border searches involving password protected or encrypted files.

    More intrusive *nonroutine* searches of people that involve their dignity and privacy—for example, strip and body-cavity searches—require a degree of reasonable suspicion; destructive searches—for instance, cutting open panels in a car to look for drugs—fall into this category also.[67]

12.   Although outside the scope of consent searches, it is noted that inventory searches that discover evidence of a crime are admissible if the searches are conducted pursuant to a departmental policy that is uniformly followed in similar cases and the inventory has a legitimate non-investigatory intent—for example, protection of the property of an arrestee. However, because the intent is to protect tangible personal property, it is unlikely that the examination of the files on a computer inventoried from the trunk of an impounded vehicle would pass judicial scrutiny.

THE CRIME SCENE

COMPUTER AND PERIPHERAL EVIDENCE

Evidence related to computer-assisted and cybercrimes is subject to the same fundamentals of crime processing that were discussed earlier. Important evidence may be associated with many items, including tablets, computer notebooks and laptops, desktops, rack systems, and main frames, as well as external hard drives, printers, scanners, compact disks, flash drives, memory card readers, web cameras, and wireless access points and network servers. The existence of a wireless network should alert investigators to the possibility that evidence may also be located on devices located away from the primary crime scene, such as in another room or a garage.

Search warrants may be issued to cover both the seizure of the targeted computers and peripherals and the actual digital forensic examination of them, or separate search warrants may be used.

CRIME SCENE PROCESSING

If the resources are available, trained and experienced computer investigators are the best choice for processing a cybercrime scene. In many jurisdictions this option may not exist, and so the first responding officer will have that responsibility. In all instances, investigators must be sure of their legal authority to search and any applicable limits.

This section is not a definitive guide to processing computer crime scenes, which is properly covered by in-service training covering a full range of situations, such as searching corporate computers that may hold trade secrets and other confidential information. It does provide a perspective on common situations, but a department's policy is the definitive source for action.

Securing and Evaluating the Scene

1.   Remove and exclude all persons from the area where evidence is to be collected.[68] Do not accept advice or assistance from "volunteers" whose actual motive may be to destroy evidence or misdirect the investigation.

2.   If a wireless system is involved, direct non-investigative personnel to stay in a particular room until the possibility of potential evidence in rooms beyond where the computer is located is determined. If several persons of interest and/or suspects are present, they should be placed in separate rooms.

3.   If a computer and other devices are off, leave them off. If they are on, do not move them, press any keys, check for DVDs, or click the mouse, because changes or damage to evidence may be triggered. If the computer is on but the screen is blank, *very slightly* move the mouse to see what information is displayed.

4.   If the computer's power state cannot be immediately determined, look and listen for indications that it is on— for example, fans running, drives spinning, and light-emitting diodes (LEDs), and observe the monitor to see if the machine is on, off, or in a sleep mode.

5.   If the computer is on, check the display for signs that files are being deleted or overwritten, such as the words *delete, format, remove, destroy, copy, move*, or *wipe*. Also check the monitor for signs that the computer is being remotely controlled. In all these cases, the immediate disconnection of power is recommended.

6.   If the destruction of evidence is not a concern, the immediate disconnection of power is not recommended, because information, data, and images of apparent evidentiary value may be seen on the screen and photographed—for instance, financial documents, child pornography, identities of coconspirators/other suspects, text documents, chat rooms used. In such cases, assistance from investigators qualified to capture volatile data is essential.

7.   If no destructive processes are running and if there is no information of evidentiary value on the screen, remove the power cord from the back of the computer.

8.   Do not attempt to examine the computer's contents. This is highly technical and specialized work that should be undertaken only by qualified personnel.

Preliminary Interviews

In addition to other information, the following should be established:

1.   Who owns the computers? For example, the homeowner, a renter, or a business?

2.   Who uses the computer and its related devices? What are their login names, user account names, and instant messaging screen names?

3. What are the passwords for any password-protected accounts, and are any files encrypted? Whose accounts are these?

4. What e-mail, personal web, or social networking websites, such as MySpace and Facebook, accounts exist, whose are they, and what passwords are used?

5. What data-access restrictions, destructive devices or software, or automated applications are in use?

6. For wireless networks, where is all accessible equipment located?

7. Who provides the Internet service?

8. Whose name is on the Internet bill, and who actually pays the bill?

9. How is the Internet accessed? For example, cable, modem, Digital Subscriber Line (DSL), Wi-Fi, or T-1 leased service, which normally involves 20 or more people online simultaneously.

Documenting the Scene

1. Both in the report and by video and photography identify the location, type of devices, their condition, and power status. Get views of all sides, including the backs, where cables are attached.

2. Record all activity and processes visible on the monitor.

3. Note all devices physically connected to the computer as well as the same for wireless components. Record their serial numbers, the content of "sticky notes" attached to them, and related written information.

4. Note the condition and power status of the computer's network access.

5. Document, photograph, and sketch all wires, cables, and devices connected to, or inserted in, the computer.

6. Tag every cable as to where each end was attached.

7. Document and photograph every wireless device in the locations at which they were found.

8. Document and photograph the locations of related evidence, such as printed pages of Internet addresses, financial records, images, and computer code, GPSs/maps/directions, electronic money transfers, books on hacking, software packages, lists of computers accessed and dead drops, credit card information, reproductions of signatures, checks and money orders, diaries and calendars, mail in victims' names, cash, fictitious identification, passwords and information on encryption and steganography. ("Steg" or "Stego" has been used for thousands of years. Historically, steg means writing in a cipher or code so that only the sender and the recipient know what the message means. In the context of computers, steg means hiding a file in a larger file so that others are not aware of its presence or meaning.)

Collecting and Transporting Evidence

The following steps should be followed when collecting and transporting computers and related devices:

1. Remove batteries from laptops and place tape over the power switch on all computers and associated devices. Disk-drive trays should also be taped closed.

2. Place all digital evidence in **antistatic packaging;** do not use regular plastic bags or other containers that can produce static electricity and condensation, both of which can damage or destroy evidence. Antistatic bags and packaging is often colored—for example, pink or light blue—to distinguish them from regular evidence bags, and they may have bubble wrap built into them to protect evidence. If antistatic bags or packaging are not available, wrap the evidence in sturdy manila/kraft paper.

3. Each computer and peripheral should be placed in a separate container to avoid cross-contamination. In some investigations, examining them for DNA evidence may become an important possibility.

4. Carefully pack all evidence to prevent it from being damaged from shock and vibration while being transported.

5. Keep digital evidence away from magnetic fields—for instance, those produced by radio transmitters and magnetically mounted emergency lights. Other transportation hazards include prolonged exposure to heated seats, hot car interiors and trunks, and static electricity produced by shuffling feet on carpets. Prolonged exposure to cold and humidity are also threats.

6. Regular procedures for handling other types of evidence, such as maintaining the chain of custody, should be carefully followed.

Digital Forensics

The area of digital forensics is highly technical and should be left only to those individuals trained and qualified in this specific area. Failure to follow this guideline will result in the discovery and analysis of digital evidence being *excluded* from the court.

Most data in criminal cases is derived from **storage forensics,** that is, data and information retrieved from physical media connected to a computer. The vast majority of all digital forensics involves retrieving and analyzing data on storage devices such as seized hard drives (inside the computer), flash drives, thumb drives, external hard drives, and/or compact discs (CDs) often found outside the computer itself. When data and information is stored on a physical medium, it is said to be "static" or not moving, distinguishing itself from data that is moving along a network or the Internet. There is a significant difference between static data versus "live" data found on a network or the Internet in terms of the law; however, the collection and the collection procedures are virtually identical from a forensic perspective.

As with any other forensic operation, maintaining the continuity of evidence from the source to the final analysis product is the most important task of the examiner.[69] The following is a brief description of the basic process of storage forensics as conducted by various data forensic software, like Encase, SANS Investigative Forensics Toolkit—SIFT, Mandiant Redline, X-Ways Forensics, Computer Online Forensic Evidence Extractor—COFEE, and others. These steps require technical knowledge and training on the specific software, hence the need for a specialist in this area. The following steps make significant use of **hash values,** which act as electronic fingerprints of the hard drive used during analysis (also called the bench drive). A hash value is a numeric value that ensures data integrity by use of a fixed length that uniquely identifies data on a specific drive.[70] A program implementing the Message Digest 5 (MD5) marker is the most commonly used method of creating a hash. This program is almost always found within the digital forensic software package enabled for the analysis. This process is easier to understand if one keeps in mind the need to verify that the drive analyzed has *not* been contaminated or altered since it was seized from the suspect (called the evidence drive):

- Step 1 is to verify mathematically the contents of the evidence drive. This value will prove that any future copies match the evidence (or suspect) drive exactly. This process is performed by the forensic software using MD5 hashing algorithms, and documenting the results.
- Step 2 is to create an exact "image," or bit stream copy, of the evidence drive, again, performed by the forensic software package.
- Step 3 is to verify that the image of the evidence drive is indeed, a true copy (archival copy) of the evidence drive. This can be accomplished by noting the hash value produced in Step 1 is the same as the hash value from the evidence drive. Again, document the results.
- Step 4 is to wipe the bench drive completely. The bench drive is the drive to be used in analyzing the archival image, or the image created in Step 2. Again, document the process by noting the comparison value for the blank hard drive to be used in this analysis after the wipe.
- Step 5 is to create a hash of the clean bench drive and compare the value to the value of the drive when it was last known to be blank. It is important to document the hash value produced (#0) is the same as the hash from the blank bench drive. In this manner, the analyst (and court) can be assured that no data from a previous forensic analysis contaminates the current bench drive.
- Step 6 is to restore the archival copy from Step 3 of the evidence drive to a blank bench drive from Step 5. This is performed by the data forensic software.
- Step 7 is to authenticate the restored image by calculating an MD5 hash and comparing the hash value to the hash of the evidence drive, noting that the hash value produced (#1) is the same as the hash from the evidence drive (#1).

- Step 8 is to conduct analysis on the bench drive using a variety of software tools within the forensic package.

In any given investigation, the variety of possible analyses is as broad as the evidence sought. Essentially, the forensic analyst attempts to find information that is in itself incriminating (e.g., child pornography, records of past drug sales, gambling records); or that help establish the elements of a crime (e.g., paper trail for a financial fraud, social media posts that show the stalking of a specific victim, an email that is threatening in a murder case, maps relating to a terrorist bombing). *Electronic Crime Scene Investigation: An On-the-Scene Reference for First Responders*, published by the U.S. Department of Justice, National Institute of Justice (NIJ), is intended to assist state and local law enforcement and other first responders who may be responsible for preserving an electronic crime scene and for recognizing, collecting, and safeguarding digital evidence. Box 17-5 uses information in the guide to list the best sources of digital evidence for crimes that range from child abuse and exploitation to international terrorism.

Digital Forensics and Mobile Devices

The above process details the forensic analysis of storage devices, most commonly hard drives taken from a suspect. In the last 5 years, several "triage" programs have been developed to assist the investigator at the scene, particularly involving mobile devices (computer tablets and/or smart phones). XRY is a mobile forensic tool developed by Micro Systemation and is used to analyze and recover crucial information from mobile devices. Cellebrite's UFED solutions present a unified workflow to allow examiners, investigators, and first responders to collect, protect, and act on mobile data with the speed and accuracy a situation demands—without ever compromising one for the other. The UFED program is designed for forensic examiners and investigators who require comprehensive, up-to-date mobile data extraction and decoding support to identify various new data sources. Most importantly, UFED Platform documents workflows between the field (at the crime scene) and the digital forensics lab, making it possible to view, access, and share mobile data via in-car workstations, laptops, tablets, or a secure location at a station.[71]

BOX 17-5 | COMMON EVIDENCE OF SELECTED CRIME TYPES

Child Abuse and/or Exploitation

- Calendars and Journals
- Video and still photo cameras and media
- Digital camera software
- Internet activity records
- Notes or records of chat sessions
- Video/web cameras and tapes, CDs, and other physical media

- Voice over Internet Protocol (VoIP) phones

Computer Intrusion

- Network devices, routers, switches, and/or antennas
- Handheld mobile devices
- Web camera(s)
- Lists or records of computer intrusion software;
- Lists of IP addresses

- Notes or records of Internet activity; or books and references on hacking

Counterfeiting

- Checks and money orders; credit card information
- Database printouts
- Magnetic strip readers
- Online banking software
- Scanners, copiers, laminators
- Reproductions of signatures

Domestic Violence, Threats, and Extortion

- Mobile communication devices
- External data storage devices
- User names and accounts
- Address books, personal writing, and or diaries
- Printed email, notes, and letters
- Caller ID units
- Telephone records and telephone bills/invoices

Email Threats, Harassment, and/or Stalking

- Caller ID records
- Financial and legal documents
- Maps, directions, and GPS equipment
- Personal web sites, writings, and/or diaries
- Telephone records

Gambling

- Electronic money transfers and all financial records
- Online banking software and/or accounting software
- Sports betting statistics; references to odds and/or lines
- Customer information or credit card data
- References and lists to online gambling sites

Identity Theft and Fraud

- Financial asset records and/or accounting software
- Laminators and/or high quality printers
- Copies and/or reproduction of signatures
- Check cashing cards and/or credit card information
- Online banking software
- Web site transaction records

Narcotics

- Handheld mobile devices, radios, police scanners and/or walkie-talkies
- Mobile devices, address books, and contact information
- GPS devices, maps, and beacons
- Blank prescription forms
- Forged identification
- Drug receipts and/or unfilled prescriptions

Prostitution and Human Trafficking

- Printed as well as digital photos of young boys or girls and/or foreign passports
- Appointment logs and client lists
- Credit card information and electronic money transfers
- Financial software and records
- Medical records
- Online banking software

Software Piracy

- CD and DVD burners and labelers
- Credit card information and/or electronic money transfers
- Financial records
- Forged documents and/or materials
- Software activation codes and/or software duplication equipment

Terrorism

- Cash and credit card information
- Electronic money transfers
- Fictitious identifications and/or passports
- GPS equipment, maps, and/or photos of important locations
- Stolen phones and/or single use "burner" phones
- VoIP phones and/or records of telephone calls (foreign and domestic)
- International communications and/or emails
- Records of suspicious website visitations (bomb-making websites, ideologically oriented websites, foreign websites)

Source: U.S. Department of Justice, National Institute of Justice, *Electronic Crime Scene Investigation: A On-the-Scene Reference for First Responders* (Washington, DC: Office of Justice Programs, 2009). See: https://www.ncjrs.gov/pdffiles1/nij/227050.pdf

KEY TERMS

antistatic packaging	consent search	e-mail bomb
black hatters	cybercrime cyber terrorism	flooder
blended threat malware	dead drop	gray hatters
bot	deep web	hash values
botmaster	denial of service (DoS) attack	herder
botnet	distributed denial of service (DDoS) attack	keylogger
carder	drive-by	logic bomb
computer-assisted crime		malware

metamorphic virus

mobile device

polymorphic virus

ransomware

rootkits

scareware

script kiddies

Silk Road

spyware

storage forensics

time bomb

Tor Network

Trojan horse

virus

white hatters

WiFi

worms

zombies

REVIEW QUESTIONS

1. How are computer-assisted and cybercrimes contrasted?
2. What two prerequisites were fulfilled before cybercrime could emerge?
3. What six advantages do cybercriminals have over traditional criminals?
4. What is malware?
5. How do black hatters, gray hatters, and white hatters differ?
6. What is a botnet?
7. What is the primary purpose of a virus?
8. What is APT1?
9. How are DoS/DDos attacks carried out?
10. What are the Silk Road and the deep web?
11. How are scareware attacks executed?
12. What is ransomware? What is CryptoLocker?
13. What are the basic components of a keylogger attack?
14. What are the general rules for a consent search?
15. What are the steps in the process of digital forensics relating to a storage device?
16. What are the major points of securing a computer crime scene?

◄ One of the greatest potential threats to U.S. agriculture is from acts of agroterrorism, which is defined as the deliberate act of a plant disease or an animal disease such as foot and mouth disease for the purpose of generating fear, causing economic losses, or undermining social stability. This photo depicts a cow infected with foot and mouth disease, which causes slobbering or drooling. Ulcers may also form on the mouth and on the tongue, which will often break and cause raw patches, thus making it impossible for the cow to eat or drink. The disease also results in the hooves being ulcerated. Diseased animals must be euthanized to prevent other animals from becoming infected.

(©Zuma Press, Inc./Alamy)

18

Agricultural, Wildlife, and Environmental Crimes

OBJECTIVES

1. Discuss the economic impact of agricultural, wildlife, and environmental crimes on the economy of the United States.

2. Discuss the prevalence of timber theft.

3. List the major categories of wildfires.

4. Explain how horses and cattle rustlers operate.

5. List and describe the major methods of marking horses and cattle for identification.

6. Understand the most effective method to prevent rural and agricultural crime.

7. Discuss the major aspects of agroterrorism.

8. Identify the four major threats to wildlife.

9. Distinguish between situational and professional poachers.

10. List and describe the characteristics of hazardous waste.

Conventional wisdom says that crime is fundamentally a big-city problem and in fact crimes related to agricultural, wildlife, and environmental crimes rarely make the types of headlines one sees on the evening news every night. However, these three categories of crime cost U.S. taxpayers billions of dollars a year and result in countless deaths. In this chapter we will provide specific investigative guidelines to those law enforcement officers responsible for investigating crimes falling into these three categories. In addition, we will also provide specific crime prevention suggestions for these three categories of crimes.

THE ECONOMIC IMPACT OF AGRICULTURAL, WILDLIFE, AND ENVIRONMENTAL CRIMES

Ranchers, farmers, and others living in rural places are often the victims of thefts, including thefts of livestock, tack, pesticides, tractors, dirt bikes, all-terrain vehicles, drip lines, stock trailers, plants and timber, tools, hay, grains and citrus, irrigation pipes, and sprinkler heads. Some variation in what is stolen is accounted for by fluctuations in the economy. For example, when freezes kill oranges and grapefruit or droughts kill avocados, prices rise and in the process thieves looking for an easy way to make money will seize upon the opportunity to steal and sell them.[1] Annual losses owing to avocado theft amount to $12 to $15 million.[2] Lone **"night pickers"** may opportunistically steal from orchards and groves after dark, farm hands may throw a few sacks in the trunk of their cars to "supplement their wages," or entire crops may be picked clean in a single night by a well-organized ring. One grower reported that a tour bus stopped so people could pick fruit from his trees.

Recently in one case in Florida two thieves stole 11 truckloads of tangerines and sold them to a local farmer's market. The individuals were arrested after a Polk County Sheriff's Office helicopter saw them. The Sheriff's Office report said the thieves had picked about 2,000 tangerines (in one truck load) which was worth $338.[3] A van loaded with stolen grapes creates a loss of $3,000 or more to a vineyard.[4] One almond grower reported two trucks loaded with 88,000 pounds of almonds valued at $260,000 were stolen by "nutnappers" the night before the nuts were to be driven to market.[5] In Florida, state and county parks are being plundered of palmetto berries, which are offered by herbal companies for baldness and enlarged prostates. The thieves, often illegal immigrants from Mexico and Guatemala, are organized; they are dropped off by a truck and picked up later in the day.[6] The "pickers" are paid a dollar a pound for the berries and may be able to collect up to 150 pounds a day.[7]

Reported losses due to livestock theft are $19.7 million annually[8]; this crime is believed to be at least 50% underreported, so losses may actually be in the $40 to $50 million range. Horse rustling may amount to 40,000 to 55,000 head annually. Beef and calf production is a $49.5 billion industry, yet there are no definitive numbers of heads of cattle stolen each year.[9] Special Rangers for the Southwestern Cattle Raisers Association investigate approximately 1,000 agricultural crime cases a year and recover an average of $5 million in stolen cattle, horses, saddles, and trailers.

There are also less common thefts associated with livestock. In Maryland, burglars entered an out building and took $75,000 worth of bull semen that had previously been collected from about 50 bulls and kept frozen in individual 5-inch straws with the bulls' names on them.[10] A barn was burglarized in California to take $30,000 worth of the genetically engineered rBST hormone in filled syringes, which is used to increase milk production in dairy cows; investigators believed the syringes would be sold on the black market to unscrupulous dairy farmers.[11]

Private and public lands are being invaded by stealthy fossil hunters, who are also described as **bone rustlers.** Depending on the type, a complete dinosaur skeleton may command $500,000 or more. In South Dakota, thieves dug up the graveyard

Although ginseng roots are cultivated, it is the wild variety growing in hardwood forests that command substantial prices. The roots are used in Asian medicine and also sold domestically with the reputed effect of reducing cholesterol and blood sugar levels, enhancing memory, and fighting colds and other conditions. Kentucky gathers more wild ginseng than any other state, a crop worth $8 million; about 50% of it is poached.[14] The prices paid pickers in good years may reach $365 to $800 per pound; it is sold to overseas brokers for as much as $2,000 per pound.[15] The theft of saguaro cacti (Figure 18-1) for landscaping purposes in the southwest is episodically a problem. There are also occasional thefts of quaking aspen trees from the western mountains; but recently the red-flowered ocotillo plant (Figure 18-2) has been in greater favor with thieves, because many more can be stolen with less risk of detection. Depending on their size, ocotillo plants retail for $150 to $5,000.

▲ **FIGURE 18-1 Saguaro cacti**
The theft of saguaro cacti from national lands in the West is a continuing problem. Saguaros grow very slowly; after 10 years they may be only 4 to 6 inches tall. They reach maturity in about 150 years and may live another 50 years beyond that, reaching a height of about 45 feet. Consequently, saguaro thefts amount to stealing part of our national heritage. (©Paula Patel RF)

of rhinoceros-like mammals called *Titanotheres* and made off with 18 skulls, each worth $5,000.[12] In one national forest, park rangers marked fossils at several different sites with chemicals invisible to the unassisted eye. By inventorying these areas over a six-week period, they learned that 32,000 pounds of fossils had been stolen. One of the most successful fossil-poaching investigations was a joint local, state, and federal effort dubbed "Operation Rockfish," named after a fossil common in southwest Wyoming. A Lincoln County Sheriff's Department pilot noticed new holes in the ground in and around Fossil Butte National Monument. First suspecting that toxic chemicals were being dumped, he invited several federal agents to fly with him. On-the-ground investigation revealed that fossils were being stolen and sold both in the open and on black markets, some for prices in excess of $10,000. Nationally, Operation Rockfish resulted in the recovery of $7 million worth of stolen fossils. Although petrified wood can be obtained legally from some sources, because of its great beauty it is being stolen from federal lands to make countertops and furniture.[13]

Our national and state lands are also victimized by plant poachers, whose targets vary as market conditions shift. Several years ago matsutake mushrooms, which grow in the northwest, reached $30 per pound. However a few years later when the prices had fallen to $3 to $5 per pound it reduced much of the incentive for wholesale poaching.

▲ FIGURE 18-2 Ocotillo plant
Like the saguaros, these plants are prized for landscaping and thrive in loose to stony soil in open areas that are well drained. They occur naturally in the southwest and Mexico in desert areas below 5,000 feet. Their blood-red blooms appear in March and April. Ocotillos ordinarily grow to 15 to 20 feet in height with a corresponding width of roughly 10 to 15 feet.
(©Jordana Meilleur/Alamy)

QUICK FACTS

Theft Prevention of Saguaro Cactus

Several years ago in an effort to combat the theft of saguaro cacti, park rangers in Saguaro National Park started using technology to deter cactus theft. The device used is a passive integrated transponder (PIT) tag which inserts tiny microchips into cacti to allow positive identification of saguaro cacti when stolen from the park (Figure 18-1). This program makes the cacti less attractive for thieves since it is easy to verify that a tagged cactus is stolen goods. The small electronic "tags" have also been used in recent years to help monitor and identify many kinds of animals ranging from pets and valuable race horses to wild mammals, birds and even fish.

TIMBER THEFT

Forest economists believe that thieves are stealing trees worth $1 billion annually and that one in every 10 trees is cut down illegally.[16] Large areas don't have to be cut down to create serious losses (Figure 18-3). In Pennsylvania, a prime black cherry tree, valued for making furniture, can bring $6,000.[17] Because of its beautiful swirl grain, curly maple trees in Washington are being poached to make guitars and other musical instruments.[18] On a larger scale, two Wyoming men were charged with stealing 8,439 trees valued at $100,000 from Medicine Bow National Forest; the clear-cutting operation could result in fines of $500,000.[19] Unlike thieves who must sell what they steal to fences for pennies on the dollars, thieves involved in **timber theft** get full value. In some urban areas, particularly along parkways and expressways in the month leading up to the Christmas holiday, Christmas-type trees "disappear" as motorists cut them down and cart the trees home to decorate. To combat such thefts, some cities chemical-coat trees that are likely targets, causing them to smell "awful." Another coating has an unnoticeable odor until it starts to heat up, and then it "smells worse than cat urine."

Investigations into the illegal cutting of timber involve a full range of investigative techniques (Figure 18-4). Examination of crime scenes continues to result in the discovery of evidence of paint transfers and tool marks on wood debris left behind by suspects. These marks and paint transfers result from the use of axes, wedges, and splitting mauls and serve to tie a suspect to a crime. Examination of tool marks on wood is based on established principles: it is possible to identify a suspect tool with the mark it leaves on a surface (see Chapter 4, "Physical Evidence" for a more detailed discussion of tool mark identification). In several cases, containers left at the scene of a timber theft have been processed and fingerprints developed. These fingerprints have been useful in identifying and placing suspects at the scene. In addition, casts of both shoe and tire impressions that were later identified as belonging to particular suspects and vehicles have been found at some crime scenes.[20] Increasingly, DNA (discussed in much greater detail later in this chapter) is proving important as key evidence in many of the types of crimes, including plant and tree thefts, livestock rustling, and fish and wildlife poaching.

Although the crime scene examinations at the site of timber thefts are important, they are supplemented by the long process of interviewing potential witnesses to the crime, conducting investigations to develop witnesses, and checking possible outlets where forest products might be processed or sold. To conduct investigations concerning timber sales, law enforcement officers must become familiar with the variety of terms and techniques pertaining to a timber sale, from its inception to the eventual purchase.

WILDFIRE INVESTIGATIONS

Every year many people die and are severely injured in wildfires (especially firefighters) and they also result in billions of dollars in property damage. However, because there are multiple

◄ **FIGURE 18-3**
Illegal cutting of trees
A Federal Bureau of Land Management Ranger discovered that 17 old-growth juniper trees had been illegally cut and removed from the Badlands Wilderness Study Area (WSA) in Oregon. Such trees grow so slowly that they are considered a nonrenewable resource: a juniper tree with a 3-feet diameter takes 1,000 years to reach that size. The juniper stumps with the yellow evidence cone at the right were part of the multiple crime scenes involved with the thefts. (Source: Federal Bureau of Land Management)

◄ **FIGURE 18-4**
Timber theft crime scene
A Mason County Deputy Sheriff examines the work of maple tree thieves. In their haste to turn their contraband into cash, tree thieves may abandon tools and other important physical evidence. (©Mark Harrison/MCT/Newscom)

possible causes for wildfires, it is absolutely essential that investigators be thoroughly familiar with the various potential causes of such fires as well as the investigative factors that need to be taken into consideration in order to conduct a thorough and successful investigation.[21]

FIRE CAUSE CATEGORIES

Following are some of the most common categories used to describe the various causes of wildfires.[22]

- Arson/Incendiary
- Children
- Lightning
- Campfires
- Smoking
- Debris Burning
- Equipment Use
- Railroad
- Power lines
- Fireworks
- Cutting, welding, and grinding
- Firearms use
- Blasting.

ARSON/INCENDIARY

Arson/incendiary wildfires are defined as those fires that are deliberately and/or maliciously set with the intent to damage or defraud.

Cause Indicators and Other Investigative Factors to Consider

- These fires are often set in more than one location and in areas that are frequently traveled.
- They are set in locations where detection is limited and they may be set after hours of darkness. Their origins will most often be near roads and trails.
- Matches, cigarette lighters, fireworks, and other ignition devices may be found in the area of origin.
- The fire-setter may use a time-delay ignition device. Items to look for include cigarettes, matches, rope, rubber bands, candles, and wire.
- Arson ignition sources:
  - Direct—hand carried and placed.
  - Remote—those which can be thrown or projected to another location (for example, fireworks, Molotov cocktail).
  - Hot set—those which involve and open flame source and start a fire immediately.
  - Time delay—those which incorporate a timer or delay mechanism before being triggered (for example, candle, slow match, etc.)

CHILDREN

Wildfires started by children are defined as those fires started by persons 12 years of age or younger. The child may be motivated by normal curiosity and use fire in experimental or play fashion. Matches or lighters are the most frequent ignition source. These types of fires often involve multiple children.

CAUSE INDICATORS AND OTHER INVESTIGATIVE FACTORS TO CONSIDER

- Fires located near play areas, footpaths, or homes.
- Multiple matches, fireworks, etc. found around the origin.
- The time of the start of the fire indicates it was started after school or on school breaks.

- A fort and/or toys found in the area where a fire started.
- Children's footprints or bicycle tracks at or near the scene.

LIGHTNING

A lightning fire is defined as any wildland fire started as a result of lighting activity. Lighting occurrence maps are a significant tool to be utilized in suspected lightning-caused fires.

Cause Indicators and Other Investigative Factors to Consider

- Lightning or other damage to objects such as trees, shrubs or brush, posts, poles, or other structures (Figure 18-5).
- Blow holes in the ground and possible presence of fulgurites which are natural tubes or crusts of glass formed by the fusion of silica (quartz) sand or rock from a lightning strike. Their shape mimics the path of the lightning bolt as it disperses into the ground.
- The fire may smolder undetected for as long as several days/or weeks after a lightning strike before transitioning to an active wildfire.

CAMPFIRES

A campfire is defined as any fire kindled for warmth, cooking, light, religious, or ceremonial purpose. Campfires may occur at any location. Responsible parties may be hunters, campers, fisherman, or hikers.

Cause Indicators and Other Indicative Factors to Consider

- Circles of rocks or pits with a large amount of ash and coals, or a pile of wood are good indicators of a campfire (Figure 18-6).
- Signs of recent camping activity, including discarded food containers, metal tent stakes, or metal grommets from a tent indicating the possibility of a campfire.
- Wet ash and/or ash being mixed with soil in a failed effort to extinguish the fire.

▶ **FIGURE 18-5 Lightning scar**
(Courtesy of National Wildfire Coordinating Group)

◀ **FIGURE 18-6**

Escaped campfire (on page 4 of attachment).

Sierra National Forest (California) officials say this escaped campfire was a source of a fire which resulted in the destruction of 12,827 acres of the forest and cost close to $8 million to fight. (Source: USDA Forest Service)

SMOKING

A smoking-caused fire is defined as any fire that results from smoking activities or accoutrements and includes those started by matches, cigarettes, cigars, pipes, etc. (Figure 18-7.)

Cause Indicators and Other Investigative Factors to Consider

- Cigarettes, under normal conditions, generally do not start wildland fires unless the relative humidity (RH) is under 22%, it is windy, and a continuous, cured, and a finely-particulated fuel-bed exists. Exceptions to this basic rule are expected; let the strength of the evidence support the cause.
- The average full-length cigarette burns for approximately 13 to 15 minutes (1" in 4 minutes).
- Most people discard cigarettes almost totally burned, therefore, it is generally exposed to the fuel bed for approximately 62 to 122 seconds.

- The following circumstances must usually occur in order for a cigarette to start a wildfire:
  - The RH is less than 22%
  - 30% of the glowing tip is exposed to extremely fine fuel.
  - There is a favorable tip orientation with the wind (wind will assist ignition).
  - A cigarette comes to rest in fuels at an angle when lit and its end is facing down.
- Other physical evidence at the crime scene may include:
  - Burned match heads, a cigarette butt, as well as a cigarette ash column found within a few feet of the exact point of origin which may suggest malicious or willful intent.
  - Evidence of human activity in area.

DEBRIS BURNING

Debris burning-caused wildfires are defined as fires started for purposes of burning slash, garbage, stubble, right-of-way, or other controlled burning.

Cigarette Caused Fires

THE PROBABILITY OF IGNITION BASED ON RELATIVE HUMIDITY (RH)

Fuel conditions critically dry:

The RH is less than 22% and the fine dead fuel moisture is less than 14%

Start Likely	Start Possible	Start Unlikely	No Start
0% RH	10% RH	18% RH	22% RH

◀ **FIGURE 18-7**

(Source: Wildfire Origin & Cause Determination Handbook, NWCG Handbook 1 PMS 412-1, Boise, ID: Great Basin Cache, National Interagency Fire Center, May 2005, p. 70.)

Cause Indicators and Other Investigative Factors to Consider

- Fires that occur at dumpsites, as well as at residences from garbage and other debris set on fire. Often a fire or sparks from these operations spreads to the neighboring vegetation.
- The presence of burn barrels or incinerators may be a consideration as a fire cause. In windy conditions, hot ash and debris can be transported aerially and start a fire some distance away, especially if corrugated cardboard is being burned.
- The interview of witnesses is often the best way to confirm whether or not debris burning was the cause of the fire.

EQUIPMENT USE

Equipment use fires are defined as wildland fires which result from the operation of mechanical equipment that range from heavy construction equipment to small portable engines.

Cause Indicators and Other Investigative Factors to Consider

- The presence of the actual equipment or signs of any types of equipment used such as construction, logging, land clearing, harvesting, mowing, grading, etc.
- Ignition mechanisms include exhaust systems particles, friction, fuel, lubricant, fluids, mechanical breakdown or other malfunction, rock strike, vegetation buildup on hot surfaces, and radiant or conductive heat transfer.
- Charred material on the exhaust or other hot surfaces.

RAILROAD

Railroad fires are defined as those wildfires caused by any railroad operations, personnel or rolling stock and can include track and right-of-way maintenance.

Cause Indicators and Other Investigative Factors to Consider

- It will be located along active railroad lines and could have multiple starts.
- A special arrangement will need to be made to obtain the records from the locomotive data recorder ("black box") and samples from the locomotive (oil and soot from the exhaust system).
- A witness(es) may have seen the train pass recently.
- The investigator should look for signs of recent track maintenance, including welding and grinding.

POWER LINES

Power line fires are those defined as fires that result from a conductor failure or faulting, insulator failure, hardware failure, birds, small animals, and Mylar balloons, which are helium-filled balloons typically used for special occasions, such as "Happy Birthday," "Happy Anniversary," "Happy Valentine's Day," etc.

Cause Indicators and Other Investigative Factors to Consider

- Power lines located in or near the area of origin.
- Downed power lines.
- Trees or other vegetation or contact with power lines.
- A recently downed tree limb located on the ground under or near lines and area of origin.
- Discoloration of a power line and/or signs of arcing or other equipment failure.
- Circuit breakers in the open position.
- Blown fuses.
- A recently found dead bird in the area of origin.
- High winds and/or high temperatures prior to the start of the fire.
- Recent power outages or brownouts.
- Pole damage or a vehicle accident in which the pole was struck.

FIREWORKS

Fires caused by fireworks are defined as wildfires caused by ground-based, handheld, or aerial explosives.

Cause Indicators and Other Investigative Factors to Consider

- Location of the fire start.
- Presence of spent fireworks remains at the point of origin.
- The fire occurrence was near a holiday period (in the United States this would typically be around the 4th of July and New Year's Eve).

CUTTING, WELDING, AND GRINDING

Cutting, welding, and grinding-caused wildfires are defined as those caused by an industrial or agricultural operation, but may also result from an individual or residential activity.

Cause Indicators and Other Investigative Factors to Consider

- Locations in relations to equipment or an equipment use area.
- The presence of slag, welding rod, metal fragments, or grinder disks.
- Welding cart wheel impressions or fire extinguisher residue.

FIREARMS

Black powder discharge, tracer, incendiary, and steel core ammunition are capable of causing wildfires (Figure 18-8).

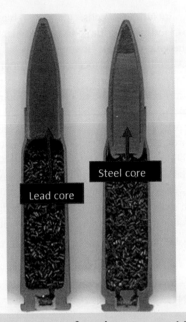

▲ FIGURE 18-8 X-ray of steel-core ammunition.
(Courtesy of National Wildfire Coordinating Group)

Lead core

Steel core

Cause Indicators and Other Investigative Factors to Consider

- Areas used for target shooting.
- Evidence consisting of targets, spent shell cases, and ammo boxes.
- Strike marks on rock or other hard objects in the origin area.

BLASTING

Blasting fires are defined as wildfires started by flaming debris associated with blasting activities.

THEFT OF AGRICHEMICALS

Agrichemical is a broad term whose meaning encompasses a variety of products used on farms, including pesticides, fertilizers, and herbicides. As a rule of thumb, fertilizers are not a target of theft because of their bulk and relatively low cost. In contrast, pesticides and herbicides can be costly; even a truckload may be worth thousands of dollars. The exact type of agrichemical taken varies by geographic region, depending on what the predominant crop is. Currently, anhydrous ammonia, is the agrichemical of choice for thieves. Agrichemical theft from farmers may have crested in recent years, owing to operators buying only the quantities they could immediately use and employing more stringent security measures when they are even briefly stored.

Because the theft of agrichemicals may take the form of any of several different criminally chargeable acts, it would be pos-

sible for investigators in different parts of the same agency to be working on various activities by the same ring without knowing it. For example, the hijacking of a truck might be worked on by robbery investigators, the burglary of a dealership by the property section or burglary investigators, while personnel assigned to the ranch and grove unit might be working on the theft of pesticides from a local farmer. Although one ring might not exhibit a wide range of criminally chargeable behaviors, these behaviors may be sufficiently different to cause the fragmentation of investigative information.

To be effective in the investigation of agrichemical thefts, the investigator must become familiar with the legal supply channels and the principal agrichemicals that are used in his or her region. In particular, note that the same basic chemical or formulation may be sold by several different manufacturers under different product names. For example, atrazine is manufactured and sold by Ciba-Geigy as AAtrex for use as a corn herbicide. Imagine the difficulty created for an investigation if a victim reports the theft of "50 gallons of atrazine," and the information is entered into police records that way—but the victim was using "atrazine" as a synonym for "AAtrex."

Finally, a few farmers steal agrichemicals or buy them at "bargain prices" from thieves. Once the agrichemicals have been used, the manufacturers' containers are burned, thereby making the detection of the criminal receiving the stolen property very difficult. One method of identifying farmers who are possible illegal receivers of agrichemicals is to determine whose purchasing patterns through legal supply channels are inconsistent with their crop needs.

LIVESTOCK AND TACK THEFT

Although new and often sophisticated methods of rustling are now used, the reason for the theft of livestock and tack remains the same, as do the motivations: profit and food.

Livestock refers to cattle, horses, sheep, goats, hogs, mules, donkey, and other such species. **Tack** refers to saddles, bridles, harnesses, horse blankets and related equipment. Certain generalizations can be made with respect to live-stock and tack thefts:

- Most livestock thefts are committed by persons who have been or are currently employed in some aspect of a livestock business. One significant exception to this broad observation is that in economically hard times, rural areas adjacent to urban centers experience more thefts; thus the physical evidence suggests that the motivation was food rather than profit. Such so-called **freezer crimes** typically involve the theft of only one or a few head of cattle, and when they are butchered at the scene, it is often in a manner that reflects only a crude understanding of the process.[23]
- It is common for livestock to be stolen, transported, and disposed of before the theft is discovered. Whereas the theft of horses may be discovered in a day to two weeks, theft of range cattle may go undetected for months.

- Except for small roadside slaughters committed as freezer crimes, livestock is stolen to be sold for economic gain. The excellent interstate systems that cross the country lend themselves—like the famous trails of frontier days—to transporting the stolen livestock rapidly for sale in states other than the one in which the theft took place.
- Because horse owners are typically very attached to their animals, thefts are often very emotional for them.
- Horse thieves also tend to be tack thieves.

Many law enforcement agencies, particularly sheriffs' departments, have created specialized investigative units or designated a particular individual as the agency's specialist in such matters.[24] Regardless of whether the investigator works as part of a specialized unit or as the sole specialist, he/she must have or develop an expertise in the various aspects of livestock identification, including breeds, markings, blemishes, scars, marks, tattoos, and brands. In short, to be effective, the investigator must be able to speak "livestock."

The heaviest burden in livestock investigation often falls on the uniformed officer who takes the original offense report, because such officers may have no knowledge, or only rudimentary knowledge, of livestock and the applicable special laws.[25] Police agencies can help compensate for this by adopting forms similar to those shown in Figures 18-9 and 18-10 and by providing training in their use. When such forms are not used, a good guide to follow is that an animal is property and can be described as any other type of property can, although the language may be unfamiliar to the investigator. In such situations, the frank acknowledgment of a lack of familiarity or expertise can elicit a systematic and detailed description from the owner. Subsequent to the taking of the

▶ FIGURE 18-9
Cattle identification form
(Source: Los Angeles County, California, Sheriff's Department)

CATTLE IDENTIFICATION FORM

Officer Reporting	Agency	Date

Classification Lost ( ) Found ( ) Theft ( ) Other ( )
File No._____

Date & Time_____ Location_____

Victim ( )
Informant ( )

	Address	City	Phone

Suspect_____

	Name	Address	City	Phone

DBO_____ Sex_____ Race_____ Age_____ Hair_____ Eyes_____ Ht.____ Wt.____

Vehicle Year_____ Make_____ Body_____ Color_____ Lic._____

Trailer_____ Stock Rig_____ Make_____ Color_____ # Axles_____ Gooseneck

In the space below, please indicate whether the cow has any identifiable characteristics, including but not limited to branding, unique spots, ear marks, unique facial pattern, injuries, horns, docked tail, dewlap, wattle markings, etc. Note any non-symmetrical characteristics, such as more coloring on one side.

_____
_____
_____

Bull ( ) Cow ( ) Steer ( ) Calf ( ) Heifer ( )	Type of Brand.	Method of Operation Check all that apply
Breed	Chemical_____ ( )	Barn ( ) Corral ( ) Dairy ( ) Driven ( )
Age____Wt_____Color____	Freeze_____ ( )	Feed, Auction or Sale Yard ( )
Polled_____Horned_____	Hair Brand_____ ( )	Pasture ( ) Range ( ) Residential ( )
Ear Tag ( ) No.____Color___	Horn Brand_____ ( ) Hot Iron_____ ( )	Trailered ( ) Other ( )

Please fill in the following section if applicable.

Field Slaughter
Items used   Gun ( ) Knife ( ) Axe ( ) Rope ( ) Hoist ( ) Chainsaw ( ) Other ( )

Carcass
Removed entire Carcass ( ) Hind Quarters ( ) Other ( )

Left at Scene   Feet ( ) Head ( ) Hide ( ) Waste ( ) Other ( )

To move Animal   Used Horses ( ) On Foot ( ) Dogs ( ) Motorcycle ( ) Lead ( ) Other ( )

Additional comments._____

Please attach a photograph (if possible) of the cow.

HORSE IDENTIFICATION FORM

Officer Reporting	Agency	Date

Suspect_____

Name   Address   City   Phone

DBO_____Sex_____Race_____Age_____Hair_____Eyes_____Ht._____Wt._____

Vehicle Year_____Make_____Body_____Color_____Lic._____

Trailer_____Stock Rig_____Make_____Color_____# Axles_____Gooseneck_____

In the space below, please indicate whether the horse has any identifiable characteristics, including but not limited to branding, lip tattoo, unique spots, ear marks, unique facial, main, or tail pattern, injuries, white or black outlines, etc. Note any non-symmetrical characteristics, such as more coloring on one side.

_____

_____

_____

Breed_____Sex_____

Color_____Ht.___Wt._____Age_____

Brands_____Tattoo_____

Scars & Marks_____

Other I.D. Info_____

(Use Reverse for Saddles)

Owner_____
(name)   (address)

_____
(city)   (phone)

Date & Time Stolen_____Reported To_____
(agency)

Date Reported_____File No._____

Method: Barn ( ) Corral ( ) Lead Away ( ) Pasture ( )
Ride Away ( ) Stall ( ) Trailer ( ) Other ( )

Please attach a photograph (if possible) of the horse.

▲ **FIGURE 18-10 Horse identification form**
(Source: Kern County, California, Sheriff's Department)

original offense report, the progress of an investigation often hinges on the mutual assistance, cooperation, and free exchange of information given by ranchers, feedlot operators, stock auctions, farmers, sale yards, livestock associations, and other entities.

CATTLE RUSTLING

The majority of cattle-rustling thefts are committed by one or two people who take the animal for their own use.[26] The usual method of operation is to drive to an isolated area, locate an animal, shoot it, and either butcher it there or load the carcass into a vehicle and butcher it at home. Butchering the animal at the scene means the thieves must spend more time there, but it avoids the problem of having to dispose of unused remains later. There have been cases recently reported of horses being stolen and butchered for their meat. In 2015, a champion jumping horse was found near Parrish, Florida, butchered. Records show that dozens of horses have been stolen and butchered in Miami-Dade County, Florida annually.[27] Sometimes the thieves shoot the animal and then drive to a place where they can watch to see if anyone comes to investigate. If no one comes, they return to butcher the animal. Since the rustlers often work at night, they can see the headlights of

approaching vehicles for some distance, giving them ample time to depart the area. Freezer-crime rustlers are difficult to apprehend, because they must be caught when they are committing the act or while they are transporting the carcass or meat. Surveillance methods that work well in urban areas are usually difficult to execute in rural areas. Given this, rural surveillance success depends on:

- The topography of the area;
- The availability of cover for concealment;
- The number and position of access roads;
- The size of the area containing the cattle.

One method for successful surveillances is for investigators to select an area that is attractive to thieves and well suited for surveillance.[28] Ranchers should be requested to move cattle into the area selected by the investigator. The rancher must not allow employees or other persons to learn that an operation is being set up. If other people are involved in moving the cattle to the area selected, they should be given a fictitious but plausible reason for the move—for example, a change of pasture is needed, a tally must be taken, there is going to be a veterinary inspection, or brands must be checked.

Vehicles coming out of isolated areas should routinely be visually inspected for signs of blood on the rear bumper or trunk areas.[29] Because rustlers are invariably armed with some type of firearm, extreme caution must be used when approaching suspicious vehicles. Panicky suspects, who might not otherwise think of assaulting a peace officer, may do so impulsively. In addition to having firearms, this type of rustler will also often be carrying butcher knives and ropes.

In contrast to the modest equipment usually employed by the freezer thief, professional rustlers use more sophisticated means to commit their crimes, such as light planes or helicopters to spot vulnerable herds and watch for patrolling officers. The thieves coordinate their movements with walkie-talkies, and "dirt-bike cowboys" herd the cattle to where they will be killed and butchered, often by the use of chain saws. Refrigerated trucks with meat-processing equipment inside quickly transform the rough-butchered cattle into salable products.[30] Professionals may also have a full array of forged documents, such as a bill of sale and counterfeit U.S. Department of Agriculture inspection stamps. The professional rustling operation can be very profitable. Thirty head of cattle can be taken from the range, loaded onto a truck, and butchered in the truck; the waste is dumped off the road, and the 60 sides of beef are illegally stamped and delivered. The dressed or hanging weight in the meat cooler is roughly 300 pounds per side. This means that 60 sides of stolen beef can be sold to an unwary or unscrupulous butcher for a profit of roughly $15,000 to $17,000 for a night's work.

As a general matter, peace officers have a right to stop any conveyance transporting livestock on any public thoroughfare and the right to impound any animal, carcass, hide, or portion of a carcass in the possession of any person whom they have reasonable cause to believe is not the legal owner or is not entitled to possession.[31] To transport cattle legally, certain written documents may be required, such as:

- Bill of sale;
- Certificate of consignment;
- Brand inspector's certificate;
- Shipping or transportation permit.[32]

Because these provisions vary by state, every investigator must know:

- What documentation is required for lawful transportation (for example, a "horse-hauling permit");
- What the investigator's precise authority is in such matters;
- How to handle violations of law.[33]

Equipped with such knowledge, the investigator is better prepared to deal with issues related to transportation violation or a possible theft. Although the applicable state law may permit the officer to impound livestock or meat, there are several less drastic alternatives. Under unusual conditions or when only slight suspicion exists, investigators may elect to get a full description and identifying information of the driver and the rig and its contents. Other information essential for a useful follow-up inquiry is the origin and destination of the trip. If suspicion is more pronounced, specialists may be requested to come to the scene of the stop. Such specialists may come from the investigator's own agency, another local department, the state police or state investigative agency, or the Marks and Brands Unit of the state's department of agriculture. If the investigator is sufficiently confident that a shipping violation or theft exists, he/she can make the arrest and impound the load. Live animals can be delivered to the nearest feedlot or sales yard, and meat can be placed in refrigeration storage. Such situations require that officers in the field have a basic working knowledge of the applicable laws and exercise sound judgment. They are not required to be experts in such matters, and their general investigative experience is a substantial asset in making an evaluation of the situation.

HORSE RUSTLING

There is not a great deal of variation in how horse rustlers operate (Figure 18-11). If the horse is in a corral, the thief will park

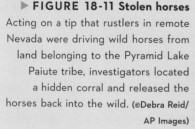

▶ **FIGURE 18-11 Stolen horses**
Acting on a tip that rustlers in remote Nevada were driving wild horses from land belonging to the Pyramid Lake Paiute tribe, investigators located a hidden corral and released the horses back into the wild. (©Debra Reid/ AP Images)

a vehicle and trailer nearby, walk up and take the horse, load it in the trailer, and drive off.[34] Because such thefts usually occur during the hours of darkness, the rustler can be several hundred miles away before the theft is discovered. When horses are in a pasture, the task of stealing them is only slightly more difficult. The thief walks into the pasture with a bucket of grain. One or more of the horses will usually approach him, and because they are herd animals, if one approaches, others are also likely to follow along. The theft then proceeds in the same fashion as a corral theft.

One tactic commonly used by horse rustlers is to knock down the corral or pasture fence after loading up the trailer with horses and chase any remaining horses down the road. The owner will think that the horses got out on their own, and it may be several days before he/she realizes that some horses were stolen. Thus, even if there is no clear evidence of a theft, the investigator should not assume that the horse just strayed off; at least, a lost report should be initiated. If the horse is later discovered to have been stolen, the incident can be reclassified.

TACK THEFT

Tack is equipment that is used with horses; the most common items are saddles, bridles, harnesses and horse blankets.[35] Of all stolen tack, approximately 80% is saddles—which often have base prices in excess of $2,000 each. Unfortunately, tack is not always marked for identification, making tracing a very difficult proposition. A specialized reporting form (Figure 18-12) is a very useful investigative aid. Some owners have injected microchips, which are about the size of a grain of uncooked rice, in their saddles to facilitate recovery if they are stolen.

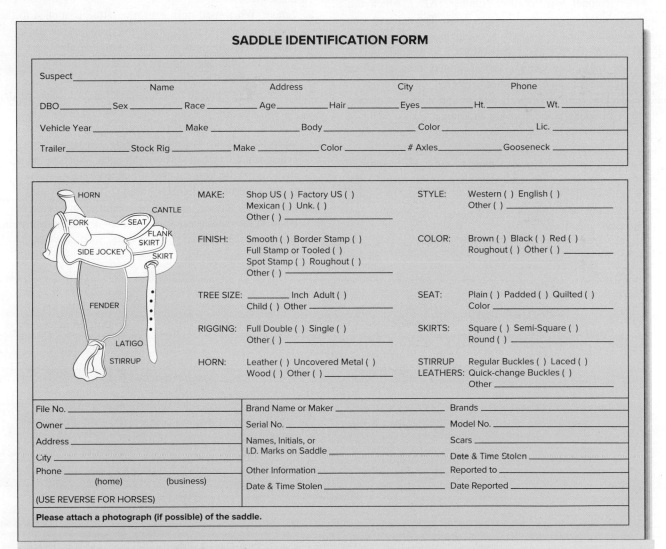

▲ **FIGURE 18-12 Saddle identification form**

(Source: Los Angeles County, California, Sheriff's Department)

LIVESTOCK IDENTIFICATION

The purpose of **livestock identification** is to establish that a particular animal is the property of a specific owner. Methods of livestock identification continue to change. In times long past, some ranchers would supplement their brands with wattles. They were formed by pinching skin on the animals' neck or jaw, and cutting most, but not all of it off; the hanging portion was the wattle. In more recent years, ear cropping has largely fallen away, because it is expensive to do and not easy to read by the uninitiated. In the wake of the 9/11 attacks, concern about agroterrorism (discussed in much greater detail later in this chapter) was directed towards livestock and crops and was the driving force in the formation of the **U.S. Department of Agriculture's National Animal Identification System (NAIS),** the framework for which was announced in 2004.

Presently, NAIS participation is voluntary from a federal perspective. Under NAIS, all agricultural animals would receive a 15-digit Animal Identification Number (AIN), which ultimately could track them from birth to death. The national security and public health interest is compelling; every time an animal is sold, its AIN and owner information become part of a database that could quickly and accurately pinpoint where disease outbreaks occur, whether triggered by terrorists or nature, such as foot and mouth disease and mad cow disease. Although program guidelines are unfolding, AINs could be established by bar-coded ear tags or microchips implanted under the skin.

In general, people are more willing to use a wider range of identification methods on cattle than they are on their horses. Cattle are commonly branded, and there are a lot of brands: over 26,000 different ones in Utah alone, some of which date back to 1847.[36]

Brands are combinations of numbers, letters, marks, and shapes that establish a unique identification and must be registered with the state before they can be used. The state agencies approving a brand application are often located with the department of agriculture and have a name such as "Brands and Inspections." In some states, brands must be in a specific location on the animal, whereas in others there is some flexibility. As shown in Figure 18-13, there are three ways to read brands. Treated as a separate category are picture brands, which simply mean what they represent (Figure 18-14).

There are five major methods of marking horses and cattle for identification:[37]

1. *Hot-iron.* Hot-iron branding is a method of identification that has been used in this country for nearly 400 years. It is simple to use; an "iron" is heated in a fire and then the end bearing the brand is impressed on the upper hip of the animal, producing a permanent, hair-free shape in the hide that duplicates the face of the branding iron.

2. *Tattoos.* When used on horses, the tattoo is applied to the inside of the top lip; on cattle, the inside of the ear is tattooed near the mid-vein. Tattoos should always be placed in either the right ear or the left ear, or in both ears, but should be consistent for an entire herd.

3. *Freeze Brands.* Freeze branding uses liquid nitrogen or dry ice and alcohol to supercool the hide and when it is applied it kills cells that produce hair pigments, thus when the hair grows back it is white. On light-colored cattle, white hair cannot be easily seen. When branding such cattle, the iron should be applied longer, which leaves a permanent hairless brand.

4. *Ear tags.* Plastic ear tags can be bought prenumbered or blank so the rancher can use his/her own numbering system.

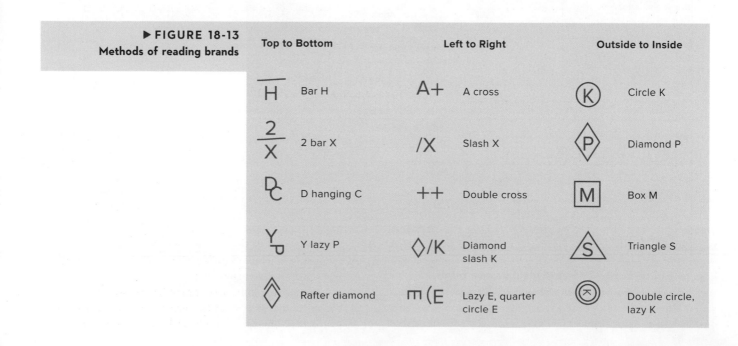

▶ **FIGURE 18-13**
Methods of reading brands

Top to Bottom		Left to Right		Outside to Inside	
H̄	Bar H	A+	A cross	Ⓚ	Circle K
2/X	2 bar X	/X	Slash X	◇P	Diamond P
D⌐C	D hanging C	++	Double cross	☐M	Box M
Y⌐P	Y lazy P	◇/K	Diamond slash K	△S	Triangle S
◇̂	Rafter diamond	⊓(E	Lazy E, quarter circle E	⊚	Double circle, lazy K

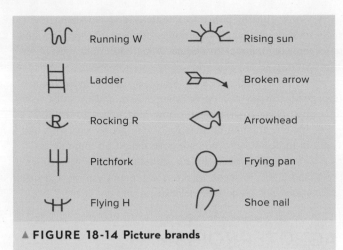

W	Running W		Rising sun
	Ladder		Broken arrow
R	Rocking R		Arrowhead
	Pitchfork		Frying pan
	Flying H		Shoe nail

▲ **FIGURE 18-14 Picture brands**

Different colors and sizes of tags are available, and they can be read at a distance. The tags are placed through the ear of cattle at a point between the ear's second and third cartilage rib, to prevent them from being easily ripped out. But because these tags can be pulled out, many experts recommend that a second method of identification also be used. A non-electronic ear tag is the means selected by most ranchers and farmers to identify cattle.

5. *Electronic.* A microchip equipped with a radio transponder has Radio Frequency Identification (RFID) capabilities.[38] These chips may be injected, worn as part of ear tags, or embedded in neck collars. The information on the microchip can be read using a handheld RFID reader. If RFID-enabled ear tags are properly placed on cattle, they can be read with great accuracy as cattle move through properly positioned gates with readers.

DNA profiles of expensive horses and bulls are common as a theft deterrent and, some breed associations as well as insurance companies mandate that DNA profiles of expensive horses and bulls are required. This is done in part to prevent insurance scams. For example, an owner may kill a less-expensive horse but a claim is made for an expensive horse, which has already been sold, thus creating an additional source of "profit" for the owner. DNA can easily be obtained from animals by means of nasal swabs or mane or tail hair with the root attached.

PHYSICAL EVIDENCE

The processing of a crime scene where an agriculture-related theft has occurred is in many respects no different from the processing of any other crime scene. For example, when cattle rustling occurs, the perpetrators frequently cut the barbed wire or locks that secure a grazing area. The cut wire and lock will have tool marks on them from the cutting tool. In addition, if the suspect's clothing came into contact with any of the barbed wire at the scene, pieces of fiber may adhere to the barbs. Shoe or tire impressions found at the crime scene may later be linked

to a specific suspect and vehicle. Soil samples collected at the crime scene may also prove to be valuable, linking evidence to a suspect with similar soil on his/her shoes or clothes or on the vehicle used to transport the cattle. DNA evidence is also playing an increasing role in livestock theft cases (for a more detailed discussion of both soil samples and DNA as evidence see Chapter 4, "Physical Evidence").

CRIME PREVENTION METHODS

Information about how to prevent rural and agricultural crimes can be obtained from a variety of sources, including sheriff's departments, county police, state investigative agencies, state departments of agriculture, county extension agents, and various associations. Although some techniques developed in urban areas can be readily applied to the farm, there are others that are unique to farms. The suggestions that follow are target-specific.

FARM EQUIPMENT THEFT

- Participate in identification programs and keep photos of equipment.
- Do not leave unattended equipment in remote fields for hours at a time or overnight. If it is necessary to do so, disable the engine by taking a vital part, and use logging chains to secure other equipment. Even if such precautions are taken, equipment in remote areas should be hidden from view from roadways.
- Equipment is best protected, in descending order of preference, by positioning it as follows: secured in a locked building near the main house or an inhabited house; secured in a gated area that is kept locked and is close to the main or an inhabited house; secured in one or more ways and not visible from commonly traveled roads.
- Immediately report all suspicious activity, such as strangers taking photographs of equipment, to local enforcement officials.

TIMBER THEFT

- Post the property.
- Document its condition with date-stamped photographs.
- Check periodically to determine if any timber has been cut.
- Promptly report all losses.
- Take aerial photos of land.

AGRICHEMICAL THEFT

- End-users, whenever feasible, should buy only in quantities that they can readily use.
- If large-quantity purchases cannot be avoided, they should be stored in a locked, lighted building very close to the main house or an inhabited house. If possible,

place a few geese or guinea hens inside as watch animals. They can be quite noisy when startled or if they feel threatened in any way.

- Rural dealers should employ security personnel during the months when they have large inventories.
- Be suspicious of people offering unusually good buys on agrichemicals; the absence of a market helps deter thefts.

LIVESTOCK AND TACK THEFT

- Mark all livestock for identification; maximum deterrence is obtained when marks are readily visible.[39]
- Take a regular tally or count.
- Do not follow a set routine, such as going to the movies every Friday night, which would give a thief an advantage.
- Enter into cooperative arrangements with trusted neighbors to help watch one another's places.
- When possible, avoid leaving animals in remote pastures or on faraway ranges.
- Mark tack and keep it in a room that lends itself to security measures.
- Do not use "set guns" or "booby traps." They are often illegal and frequently injure innocent people or animals; surviving thieves have won damage suits because of such injuries.
- Keep photographic records of livestock and tack.

OTHER CRIME PREVENTION SUGGESTIONS FOR FARMERS

- Develop and maintain good relations with your neighbors. Let your neighbor know when you will be away from the farm and leave a contact telephone number, email, etc. Ask them to keep an eye out for strangers and strange vehicles entering your property and ask them to contact you if any problems arise.
- Install security lighting and closed circuit television. They can help ensure the security of important and valuable property, such as your home, the sheds where you store your vehicles and equipment, and fuel holding tanks.
- Maintain gates and ensure they have sturdy locks and hinges.
- Maintain good networks within the local farming and rural communities, and encourage the community to commit to, or establish, Neighborhood Watch and Rural Watch programs.
- Report all crimes to the police. This will help them to build up a profile of local farm crime and to target their prevention enforcement efforts to those areas with the greatest need.
- Encourage the police to visit farms in order to regularly build up a sense of community and to help reduce the feeling of isolation that some farmers may experience.

- Work with the police to initiate a local newsletter to provide regular information to farmers and the surrounding communities to discuss crime and crime prevention strategies.
- Help the local police by volunteering to provide them with regular training on general farm and livestock issues that relate to crime and crime prevention strategies.[40]
- Explore training options for young people on farms and in local industry, through government or community training programs—this could help reduce youth crime and unemployment, enhance community spirit, and help young people develop self-esteem and confidence.

AGROTERRORISM

The United States enjoys a safe, plentiful, and inexpensive food supply.[41] Americans spend only 11% of their income on food compared with the global average of 20% to 30%.[42] Also the nation's agricultural industry has an estimated value of $1 billion which in turn helps drive our economic prosperity. It is estimated that one of six jobs are linked to agriculture. In addition, agriculture-related products comprise nearly 10% of all U.S. exports, amounting to nearly $145 billion annually.[43] Thus it is very clear that a healthy agricultural system is essential for the good health and well-being of its citizens as well as for its economy.

Terrorists are well aware of this and thus consider America's agriculture and food production tempting targets. They know that its food supply is among the most vulnerable and least protected of all potential targets of attack. When American and allied forces overran al-Qaeda sanctuaries in the caves of eastern Afghanistan in 2002, among the thousands of documents they discovered were U.S. agricultural documents and al-Qaeda training manuals targeting agriculture.

A subset of bioterrorism, agroterrorism is defined as "the deliberate introduction of an animal or plant disease for the purpose of generating fear, causing economic losses, or undermining social stability."[44] It represents a tactic to attack the economic stability of the United States. Killing livestock and plants or contaminating food can help terrorists cause economic crises in the agriculture and food industries. Secondary goals include social unrest and loss of confidence in the government.

QUICK FACTS

Quick Facts: Four Categories of Agroterrorists

The first category, and the foremost threat, is posed by transnational groups, like al-Qaeda—widely believed to present the most probable threat of inflicting economic harm on the United States.

The second category is comprised of economic opportunists tempted to manipulate markets. Such groups understand that, for example, an outbreak of foot and mouth disease (FMD) would have a dramatic impact on markets. By introducing this virus, they could exploit the markets for personal economic gain.

The third category includes domestic terrorists who may view the introduction of FMD as a blow against the federal government. As an outlier of this category, the unbalanced individual or disgruntled employee may perpetrate an attack for a variety of idiosyncratic or narcissistic motivations.

The fourth category is militant animal rights groups or environmental activists who are opposed to any industry involved in the production of animals for food. This includes such groups as the Animal Liberation Front and its sister organization the Earth Liberation Front. Attacks upon these types of industries are viewed as positive events by these activist groups.[45]

THREAT ENVIRONMENT

Because it lacks drama and the spectacle of more common terrorist violence, such as bombings and murders, agroterrorism has remained a secondary consideration, and no documented attacks in the homeland have occurred since 9/11. However, the threat environment has changed dramatically. Because America has had so many recent successes against the al-Qaeda leadership it has forced the group to reformat itself in both structure and tactics. The increasingly dangerous environment it now must operate in has prevented it from mounting catastrophic terrorist attacks on the scale of 9/11. Now, al-Qaeda places its emphasis on smaller, independent attacks following a "death by a thousand cuts" strategy to exhaust, overwhelm, and distract U.S. Department of Homeland Security forces. The group seeks to flood America's already information overloaded intelligence systems with myriad threats and "background noise."[46] Agroterrorism also may serve as a way to magnify the social upheaval caused by smaller, independent attacks, like bombings.

ECONOMIC DISRUPTION OF AGRICULTURE AT THREE LEVELS

Terrorists know that a successful agroterrorism incident threatens America's economic welfare and standing as a leading exporter of agricultural exports. A successful attack would have a ripple effect in the United States' and global economies. This economic disruption would occur on three levels.

The first involves direct losses due to containment measures, such as stop-movement orders (SMOs) or quarantines of suspected stock. Additional costs would arise from the culling and destruction of disease-ridden livestock.[47] Second, indirect multiplier effects, such as compensation to farmers for destruction of agricultural of agricultural commodities and losses suffered by directly and indirectly related industries would arise.[48] Third, international costs would result from protective trade embargoes. Less measurable consequences would include the undermining of confidence in and support of government, creation of social panic, and threat to public health on the national and global levels.

Given its ease of execution and low cost of high benefit ratio, argoterrorism fits the evolving strategy of al-Qaeda that focuses on inexpensive but highly disruptive attacks in lieu of monumental ones. Agroterrorism could exacerbate the social upheaval caused by random bombings. The ability to employ cheap unsophisticated means to undermine America's economic base, combined with the added payoff to potentially overwhelm its counterterrorism resources, makes livestock- and food-related attacks increasingly attractive.[49]

FOOT AND MOUTH DISEASE (FMD)—THE MOST OMINOUS THREAT

Attacks directed against the cattle, swine, or poultry industries or via the food chain pose the most serious danger for latent, ongoing effects and general socioeconomic and political disruption. Experts agree that FMD presents the most ominous threat.[50] Eradicated in the United States in 1929, FMD remains endemic in South America, Africa, and Asia.[51] An especially contagious virus 20 times more infectious than small pox, FMD causes painful blisters on the tongues, hooves, and teats of cloven-hoofed animals, goats, and deer, rendering them unable to walk, give milk, eat, or drink. Although people generally cannot contract the disease, they can carry the virus in their lungs for up to 48 hours and transmit it to animals. The animal-to-animal airborne transmission range is 50 miles.[52] An infected animal can shed the virus in large quantities from its upper respiratory tract via drooling, coughing, and discharging mucus, FMD can survive in straw or clothing for one month and spread up to 100 kilometers via the wind. Because herds exist as highly crowded populations bred and reared in extremely close proximity to one another, a significant risk exists that such pathogenic agents as FMD will spread well beyond the locus of a specific outbreak before health officials become aware of a problem. An FMD outbreak could spread to as many as 25 states in as little as five days simply through the regulated movement of animals from farm to market.

TERRORIST THREATS IN THE PAST

Interestingly, one of the first known attempts to intentionally introduce diseases into American livestock by foreign agents occurred in 1915 while World War I was raging in Europe. The United States had not yet entered the war and would not do so until 1917 but was shipping thousands of horses and mules to the British and French fighting the Germans. Both horses and mules were still a major means by which men and material were being moved in battle. The German high command made a decision that the transportation of these valuable animals to their enemies from the U.S. had to be stopped. As a result German agents were sent to the United States for the purpose of introducing into the stocks of horses and mules two diseases, namely anthrax[53] and glanders[54] each capable of killing these animals. These two different types of bacteria were introduced by German agents in a variety of ways including hypodermically injecting the animals as well as dumping bacteria-laden liquid into their food and water troughs. In the end their efforts were not very successful and had very little impact on the ability of the United States to continue transporting hundreds of thousands of horses and mules to Europe for the British and their allies.[55] However, if it had been successful it could have had a devastating effect on the war effort by the allies as well as the real possibility that the disease-infected animals could have infected others of the equine stock not necessarily intended for shipment overseas. As a matter of fact, one American workman who was cleaning out the stables of these animals contracted the highly contagious glanders and died shortly thereafter. However, at the time of his death the cause was undiagnosed and would not be determined until 9 years later. It was also the intention of these German agents to introduce these two diseases, especially anthrax, into the American population via the New York City subway system.

LAW ENFORCEMENT PREPAREDNESS

Farms, ranches, and feed lots in America are dispersed, open, and generally unprotected. The majority of state and local law enforcement agencies face financial and strategic challenges when responding to agroterrorism, yet the laws of many states treat agroterrorism as a crime, thus giving local law enforcement agencies primary responsibility.

An outbreak of FMD would exhaust law enforcement resources quickly. After recognition of the disease by state agriculture authorities, subsequent steps in the emergency response involve containment and eradication, often involving multiple herds and a large quarantine area that may encompass multiple countries. State agriculture with the U.S. Department of Agriculture's Animal and Plant Health Inspection Service have responsibility and authority for animal disease.[56] Specially trained animal health officials make decisions on disease control, such as livestock quarantine and the timing and method of livestock depopulation—culling, destroying, and disposing of diseased animals from infected herds by burning or burial.

BIOSECURITY MEASURES AND PREVENTION

Following strict biosecurity measures can prevent the spread of disease. Local and state law enforcement would play a pivotal role in this effort by adhering to three primary responsibilities.

First, police officials would enforce quarantine orders given by state agricultural authorities. This involves isolating and containing infected stock to prevent the spread of disease. A quarantine area would comprise a 6-mile radius, approximately 113 square miles, surrounding the point of origin; (Figure 18-15) numerous roadblocks would prevent vehicles, equipment, or persons from entering or leaving without detailed decontamination measures and authorization.[57] Inside the quarantine area, officials would establish an "exposed zone" in which all cloven-hoofed animals should be destroyed. For effectiveness, quarantine of infected premises and SMOs would have to remain in effect for a minimum of 30 days.[58]

The second responsibility occurs in conjunction with quarantine. Officers would enforce SMOs issued by the state governor to prevent the spread of the disease.[59] Initial biosecurity efforts could require placement of all animals under an SMO. Law enforcement may be empowered to restrict human and animal movement in and out of the quarantine zone. This authority would include all animals in transit within a wide geographic area until the investigation clarified the extent of the infection and determined which animals can move safely. Although FMD affects only cloven-hoofed animals, humans, horses, and other animals may carry the virus.

Enforcing an SMO would require care and shelter for animals in transit that must be temporarily unloaded and housed at local sites providing feed and water.[60] During the SMO, law enforcement would interview drivers to determine points of origin and destinations of animals. Research indicates that officers

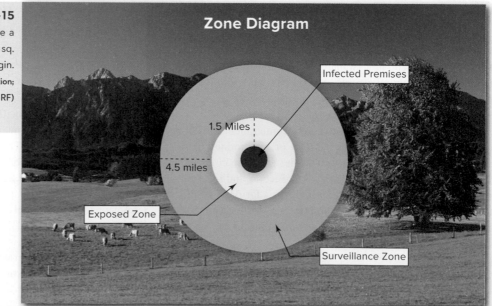

▶ **FIGURE 18-15**
A quarantine area would comprise a 6-mile radius of approximately 113 sq. miles surrounding the point of origin.
(Source: Federal Bureau of Investigation; (rural scene): ©Ingram Publishing RF)

Zone Diagram

Infected Premises
1.5 Miles
4.5 miles
Exposed Zone
Surveillance Zone

would stop and evaluate an average of nearly 50 vehicles per hour in the first day of an SMO.

Third, the criminal investigation of the outbreak further would tax already strained law enforcement resources. The investigation would focus on identifying the source of the virus and the mechanism used to infect susceptible animals. The danger of additional infections by the perpetrators would make the criminal investigation time sensitive.

Many law enforcement agencies lack the sufficient resources and procedures to simultaneously cope with quarantines, SMOs, and criminal investigations while also staffing widely dispersed checkpoints around the clock for the duration of the emergency. When combined with the need also to deliver routine law enforcement services, most agencies would struggle to meet these demands, especially during the protracted nature of an FMD outbreak.

WILDLIFE CRIMES

Wildlife officers require many of the same types of knowledge and skills as do other peace officers, including knowledge of the laws of arrest, search, and seizure, and skills such as interviewing people, crime scene processing, and interrogating suspects. In addition, wildlife investigators need to know specialized laws pertaining to their field and to be able to recognize the species and gender of wildlife. They also must be able to master unusual skills, such as interpreting tracks and being able to follow a trail (Figure 18-16). Because many poaching incidents come to light only long after the event, when the remains of the animal are discovered, wildlife officers must be familiar with methods of cold case investigation. Such discoveries may come months later when the snow melts to reveal the remains of game or predatory animals dig up remains that were buried by poachers to conceal their crime.

Because wildlife investigators often patrol alone in the wild, they encounter individuals and small groups of people who may be difficult or even deadly to deal with, including survivalists, fugitives, radical environmentalists, paramilitary units, drug smugglers, and persons engaged in illegal activities on public lands, such as growing marijuana and operating clandestine drug labs.

MAJOR THREATS TO WILDLIFE

There are a number of major threats to our wildlife. Urban sprawl destroys animal habitats, as does the accidental or illegal release of chemicals, land erosion, and oil spills. Wildlife **poaching** is also a major threat; it is defined as the illegal taking or possession of game, fish, and other wildlife. Because poaching is a secretive crime committed in the wild, it is believed that wildlife investigators find only 1% to 5% of all poached animals.[61]

Poaching makes it more difficult to reestablish game populations, as some states are trying to do with elk and bighorn sheep, threatens endangered species, reduces our enjoyment of being outdoors, and hampers the development of tourism. We

▲ **FIGURE 18-16 Evidence of deer poaching**
In the course of a major poaching investigation, wildlife investigators seized these boots, whose soles had been carved to resemble cattle hooves. This was done in part by the poachers to eliminate the possibility of investigators retrieving any boot prints. Also, by using them, the poacher tried to lay down a false trail and mislead investigators. (©Earl Nottingham/ Texas Parks & Wildlife Department)

do not know what poaching and the illegal trade in animals and animal parts cost annually, but it is believed to be in the billions of dollars annually worldwide.

Poachers and Poaching

Poachers can be categorized into two types: **situational poachers** and **professional poachers.** Most poachers are situational, some being motivated by opportunity and others by circumstance. A driver sees an elk on the road, frozen by the car's headlights. Impulsively, or after short deliberation, he opportunistically shoots the elk out of season. Some situational poachers kill to feed their families because of economic hardship. A few opportunistic poachers kill simply for the thrill of it (Figure 18-17).[62] Although fewer in numbers, professional poachers take much more game than do situational poachers, because they kill for profit.

There is almost a fixation on possessing world-class game trophies (Figure 18-18).[63] The dark side of this fixation results in very organized poaching and often involves unlicensed guides taking trophy seekers into areas closed for hunting, hunting out of season on public lands or on private lands for

▶ **FIGURE 18-17 Wolf killed**
Faced with this scene, a wildlife investigator is quickly led to two competing theories: this is a thrill kill, or a rancher shot the wolf to stop predatory attacks on his/her herd. A detailed examination of the scene, knowledge of local events and people, and the follow-up investigation established this as a thrill kill. Although infrequent, claims are sometimes made that an animal was killed in self-defense; this usually involves grizzly bears. If such a claim is reported promptly, an examination of the scene, particularly with an eye toward the distance between the person and the bear, is one key to making a determination of the claim's legitimacy. (Courtesy of New Mexico Department of Game and Fish)

▶ **FIGURE 18-18 Poached trophy**
The investigation into this poaching of a bighorn sheep resulted in the recovery of the trophy part of the kill and the arrest of one subject. (Source: Colorado Parks and Wildlife)

a fee, or using illegal hunting methods. Over a 3-year period in Canada, rich "hunters," many of who were millionaires, rode in a helicopter until a moose was spotted. The chopper would touch down and a hunter would disembark. Once airborne again, the pilot would force the moose to run back toward the waiting hunter.[64] The use of aircraft for such purposes is periodically uncovered; 20 years ago an Alaskan admitted that all 37 Boone and Crockett Club's record book

grizzlies that he had helped hunters bag were illegally herded to them using an airplane.[65]

Some of the impetus to poach comes from the fact that there are only a very limited number of big game tags available each year, which are usually distributed by a statewide lottery. For example, recently the state of New Mexico awarded through a lottery only 12 out of 7,382 hunters who had applied for tags to hunt big horn sheep. Also, in Montana, a hunter

◄ FIGURE 18-19
Poaching investigation
A Nevada Department of Wildlife game warden photographs a boot impression in the snow; note the ruler laid beside the impression to establish the scale. The boot impressions were thought to be made by "hunters" poaching chukars, a medium-sized game bird in the pheasant family. (©Brad Horn/The New York Times/Redux)

who gets a bighorn sheep tag has to wait 7 years before becoming eligible for the lottery again. In New Mexico, two bighorn sheep tags a year are auctioned off to help manage that population. One of them alone brought in $177,500; the reason for the price is simple: most animals taken are Boone and Crockett record book class, and 1 year the biggest Rocky Mountain bighorn sheep taken in North America was in that state.[66]

There is a substantial Asian market for body parts from poached wild black and grizzly bears. Across the United States and Canada, the mutilated carcasses of bears are found with their gall bladders cut out and their paws chopped off. The gall bladders are thought to have special curative powers in traditional oriental medicine, and a single one may be sold for as much as $3,400 in South Korea, making it by weight more valuable than narcotics.[67] The sale of wild-bear bladders is illegal and there are domestic bear "bile milking" farms. However, because wild-bear products are thought to be more potent, a lucrative black market flourishes for people willing to pay top dollar. Wild-bear-paw soup is a great delicacy and a single bowl costs as much as $1,000.[68] At the end of their bile-producing days, farmed bears in China are slaughtered, but the soup from their paws is much less expensive.[69]

INVESTIGATIONS

Wildlife officers generally spend only about 20% of their time engaged in law enforcement activities (Figure 18-19). The balance is spent teaching hunting, boating, and snowmobile safety courses to the public, staffing exhibits at fairs or other functions, participating in disaster/emergency preparedness training, and conducting surveys and censuses.

Information

Information is an essential commodity in combating poachers and in increasing investigators' rate of success. In some states, 80% of all poacher arrests come from leads from citizens. To assist wildlife officers in getting information, a number of states have established special programs, such as Citizens Against Poachers (CAP) and Turn in a Poacher (TIP).

Uniformed Patrol

Uniformed wildlife officers patrol in boats and cars to see if game is being taken out of season or by illegal means; they visit various sites to observe, to check licenses, and to examine the daily take. In addition to patrolling by car, they use airplanes during the day to locate hunters, trappers, and camps in remote areas. At night, aircraft can also be useful in pinpointing places where it appears that artificial light is being used by poachers to take game, a tactic known as **jacklighting.** In both day and night uses of aircraft, the pilot or spotter relays information to ground units so that they can take appropriate action. In some instances, aircraft keep poachers from leaving an area under surveillance and direct wildlife officers in cars to intercept the poachers.

Intensive Hunting Patrols

Wildlife officers also employ intensive hunting patrols, especially during the opening weekends for various types of game such as pheasant, wild turkey, waterfowl, grouse, and deer. Intensive patrols tend to be concentrated in areas of high public use, especially those with a history of excessive violations.

Vehicle Check Stops

Vehicle check stops are strategically set up on carefully selected roads to check vehicles for bag limits, unplugged shotguns, and

▶ **FIGURE 18-20**
Fishing violation arrest
Violation for catching undersized crabs Fisherman Larry Rogash, of Fort Bragg, Calif., waits aboard his boat the 'Kay Bee' as Department of Fish & Game warden Ian Bearry, left, writes him a citation for catching undersize crabs Thursday, Jan. 12, 2012 near the Montara State Marine Reserve, Calif. California began enforcing a vast network of new marine protected areas on Jan. 1, which means game wardens are now issuing tickets and in some cases, arresting fishermen, for illegal fishing in these newly protected areas. (©Ben Margot/AP Images)

licenses and to determine whether necessary special stamps (for example, duck hunting) have been acquired.

Fishing Patrols

Fishing patrols (Figure 18-20) check to see that no protected or endangered fish, eels, crabs, lobsters, or other aquatic life-forms are being taken, that aquatic species are taken only by legal means during the proper seasons and times of day, that legal limits are being respected, and that the proper licenses have been obtained. Wildlife investigators are also vigilant in determining the taking of sport and game fish by commercial fishing methods, such as through the use of seines and trot-lines.

Resident License Verification

Despite the availability of a variety of databases, some out-of-state hunters attempt to pass themselves off as residents, primarily for two reasons: (1) the allocation of tags for residents for bears, antelope, elk, and other species requiring tags is greater than for nonresidents; and (2) they can save a great deal of money: in Idaho recently, a combined hunting and fishing license and an elk tag cost a resident $66.75 versus $472.25 for the nonresident. It is a matter of false economy; the chances of "getting away with it" are low, detection appears to be fairly high, and penalties are stiff.

Covert Investigations

Covert investigations vary in their complexity. At the simplest, a wildlife officer who could not approach an area without being plainly visible for some distance may dress as a trout fisher and work his way along a stream watching for violations. Wildlife investigators also employ sophisticated sting operations. In Texas, some ranchers learned that their well-managed trophy deer herds were targets for poachers (Figure 18-21). The ranchers normally charge $2,500 to $10,000 for the right to hunt their property legally. Undercover investigators

▲ **FIGURE 18-21 Organized poaching ring**
Texas investigators arrest members of a highly organized poaching ring that operated at night. The group was apprehended on a private hunting preserve that specialized in having trophy deer to hunt for a substantial fee. The poachers' equipment included weapons with silencers, night-vision goggles, and GPS systems. (©Earl Nottingham/Texas Parks & Wildlife Department)

agreed to take poachers out at night or to hunt from roads on the ranches. They received as little as $125 and a bag of marijuana from one "client." The sting operation netted dozens of arrests and broke the back of poaching for a number of ranchers.

THE ROLE OF OUTFITTERS, GUIDES, AND LANDOWNERS IN TROPHY POACHING

Trophy poaching offenders include both residents and nonresidents with each playing different yet complimentary roles in poaching activities. The residents who are familiar with the poaching area will provide their services to nonresidents in exchange for money, thus taking on the role of outfitters or guides.[70] Individuals will work with local landowners who will for a fee provide access to private land which would otherwise be inaccessible to offenders. **Outfitters** and **guides** are recreation specialists who provide guiding services to hunters for a fee, and they often lease private property for their hunting activities. Nonresident offenders are willing to pay large sums of money for the opportunity to pursue trophy wildlife in these areas.[71]

Outfitters contribute extensively to trophy poaching because, as already suggested, it can result in enormous profits for outfitters. The outfitter's assistance to trophy poachers can take place during legal hunting seasons, or outside of legal hunting seasons. Nonresident hunters pay large sums of money to hire the services of outfitters as well as to purchase nonresident hunting licenses. With so much money invested, some of these hunters expect to see and harvest trophy class animals, and this pressure sometimes leads outfitters to bend the rules in order to please and satisfy their clients. Outfitters will break the law to get the extra edge for the hunter." The following comments from some highly experienced wardens describe methods and tactics used by outfitters to help poachers obtain trophy wildlife illegally:

Big game outfitters are more prone to break the law. Seventy percent of big game outfitters will bend the rules to help clients get game. For example, using powdered salt to attract critters, or guides who will shoot game for clients.

[Outfitters] provide licenses (illegally) to those willing to pay a high price. They educate hunters to loop holes in laws. Provide technology (airplanes, 4-wheelers, horses, etc.) to get where normal hunters cannot and limited law enforcement will not be.

Transfer tags, sell "extra" hunts, guide unlicensed hunts, provide 'locked gate' hunts, etc.

Outfitters will let them hunt without the proper licenses and find a tag to cover [the] animal.

Some outfitters also have exclusive access to leased properties where they can take individuals to poach trophy animals. Their knowledge of the landscape and ability to pattern movements of game animals allow outfitters to provide valuable assistance to nonresident trophy poachers:

"Willing. . .outfitters. . .take them to secluded ranches or land where there are good animals. They. . .know the trophies in their respective areas, and the lay of the land. They also use local poachers for knowledge."

"Mainly they provide exclusive access to the animals through land leasing, not by their guiding skills."

"Provide access to prime locations and pattern the target animals for the clients."[72]

In some states outfitters are required to be licensed in order to operate legally. Those who provide illegal (unlicensed) outfitting services are known as "rouge outfitters." These illegal outfitters are able to avoid insurance and other fees imposed on licensed outfitters, and are thereby able to provide their illegal services at a cheaper rate and take away clients from legitimate outfitters.

THE ROLE OF TAXIDERMISTS IN TROPHY POACHING

After poachers illegally kill trophy wildlife, they will find it necessary to obtain the services of a taxidermist in order to preserve their trophy specimens. **Taxidermists** are the individuals who mount the heads and antlers of game animals for hunters. Describing the need for taxidermists, one warden stated "They give poachers an outlet to preserve their kills for display, because poaching is no fun if you can't show off the trophies." Although most taxidermists are honest and will comply with the laws, some will participate in trophy poaching by accepting and mounting illegally taken wildlife from poachers.[73]

In some cases states require taxidermists to keep a record of the animals they accept for mounting. However some taxidermists who operate illegally will keep inaccurate or incomplete records of the animals they accept in their shops, and deliberately falsify their record books. By doing this, they are able to "launder" heads and antlers of illegally taken animals. Just as organized crime groups launder their illegal earnings through legitimate business enterprises to make it appear "clean," taxidermists can help poachers make their illegally taken animals look legitimate.

Taxidermists may become involved in trophy poaching in ways other than mounting illegally taken animals. Given the nature of their occupation, taxidermists interact with numerous hunters every year. When combined with their connections to members of the local community including outfitters and landowners, taxidermists sometimes find themselves in a position to facilitate poaching activities. Wardens noted that some taxidermists participated in trophy poaching by functioning as an intermediary between poachers and outfitters or landowners and providing a brokering service for arranging illegal hunts between these individuals.[74]

U.S. FISH AND WILDLIFE SERVICE FORENSIC LABORATORY: A TOOL TO FIGHT POACHING

In order to prosecute an individual for a violation of law, the criminal justice system requires that the individual's guilt be established "beyond a reasonable doubt." Two ways that prosecutors can link the suspect to the victim and to the crime (and thereby meet the 'beyond a reasonable doubt' requirement) are to present to the court:

1. Eye-Witness Testimony.
2. Physical Evidence.

However, because the reliability of eye-witness testimony is often considered questionable at best (often dependent upon the circumstances of the observation, as well as the reputation and perceived self-interest of the witness), prosecutors often insist that investigators obtain linking physical evidence and relevant expert witness testimony before they are willing to take a case to court.

Prior to 1988, wildlife law enforcement officers at the federal and state levels were at a distinct disadvantage in taking their cases to a prosecutor because they had little or no access to wildlife-related forensics services. However, after 1988 all this started to change, with the creation of the U.S. Fish and Wildlife Service Forensic Laboratory. Investigators now had available to them individuals who possess the analytical techniques to evaluate the physical evidence and also serve as expert witnesses in court on their behalf. This resulted in a dramatic increase in the successful investigation, prosecution, and conviction for violations of wildlife laws.

The Primary Mission of the Laboratory

- Identify the species or subspecies of pieces, parts, or products of an animal.
- Determine the cause-of-death of an animal.
- Help wildlife officers determine if a violation of law has occurred.
- Identify and compare physical evidence in an attempt to link suspect, victim, and crime scene.

In order to accomplish their assigned mission, and to meet the forensic needs of wildlife law enforcement officers at the federal, state, and international levels, the lab's forensic specialists conduct crime scene investigations, examine submitted items of evidence, and provide expert witness testimony in court. They do so much like their counterparts in conventional police crime laboratories.

In performing their mission they support federal law enforcement efforts of our 200+ Special Agents and Wildlife Inspectors throughout the United States, all 50 State Fish & Game Commissions, and approximately 150 foreign countries who have signed the United Nation's Convention on International Trade in Endangered Species (CITES) Treaty.[75,76]

ENVIRONMENTAL CRIMES

This planet—which our children and their children have to live in—suffers from what we do to it. Rainforests are being chopped down for timber. The entry of raw (untreated) sewage into water systems threatens fish populations. Worldwide, smokestack industries pour carbon dioxide into the air, polluting it and counteracting our efforts to combat the greenhouse effect and rising temperatures. Nuclear accidents render portions of countries uninhabitable. Swamps and marshes are disappearing at an alarming rate, along with their rich ecosystems. And toxins are dumped illegally. In fact, Native-American tribal lands in this country regard illegal dumping as one of the major problems facing them; for example, the Torres-Martinez Reservation outside Los Angeles identified 26 illegal dump sites across its 24,000 acres.

Although not all these events constitute environmental crimes, they do suggest that our planet is in distress. Therefore, we must enforce environmental laws.

THE LEGAL AND ENFORCEMENT FRAMEWORK

There are roughly 18 major federal environmental laws that form the basis for Environmental Protection Agency (EPA) programs. These laws deal with a number of issues, including chemical safety and site security, clean air and water, oil pollution, toxic-substance control, emergency planning, and environmental cleanup. Many states have substantially similar laws on some of these issues, and a number of local jurisdictions have enacted their own laws to combat environmental crimes. From this maze of laws, three patterns of enforcement emerge, regarding:

- Acts over which only the federal government has jurisdiction;
- Acts for which there is concurrent federal and state jurisdiction;
- Acts for which there is unique state and/or local jurisdiction.

Individuals and businesses may be subject to criminal and civil fines for violating laws and consent decrees. Other sanctions that can be applied include the revocation of licenses and permits and the imposition of freezes on eligibility to receive federal grants.

The federal Resource Conservation and Recovery Act (RCRA) of 1976 and its subsequent amendments give the Environmental Protection Agency authority over hazardous waste from "its cradle to its grave." **Hazardous waste** may be solids, liquids, sludges, or byproducts of manufacturing processes. They may also be commercial products such as battery acid and household cleaning supplies. A waste is hazardous if it has one or more of the following characteristics (Figure 18-22):

- *Ignitability:* Wastes that can create fires, those that can readily catch fire, and friction-sensitive substances (for example, paints, degreasers, linseed oil, and gasoline).
- *Corrosiveness:* Wastes that are acidic and those capable of corroding metal objects such as drums and tanks (for instance, cleaning fluids, battery acids, and rust removers).
- *Reactivity:* Substances that are unstable under normal conditions and that can create explosions and/or toxic

▲ FIGURE 18-22 Characteristics of hazardous waste

(Source: Environmental Protection Agency)

Ignitability Corrosivity Reactivity Toxicity

fumes, gases, and vapors when mixed with water (for example, sulphur-bearing wastes and cyanides).

- *Toxicity:* Substances that are harmful or fatal when ingested or absorbed and that, when improperly disposed of on land, may eventually pollute groundwater (for instance, mercury, certain pesticides, and lead).

PROVISIONS OF STATE RCRA LAWS

Many states have enacted laws that are very similar to the federal RCRA. Among the common provisions of these laws are these:

- Identification and listing of hazardous wastes.
- Establishment of permit and license systems regarding various types of hazardous waste, including their treatment, storage, and disposal (T/S/D).
- A manifest or shipping-paper system that tracks hazardous waste from "its cradle to its grave."
- Identification of the responsibilities of the generators and the transporters of hazardous waste.
- Requirements for hazardous-waste management facilities, such as proof of financial reliability.
- Designation of enforcement authority and criminal penalties.

In a typical case, hazardous-waste crime charges are brought against one or more individuals and/or corporations involved in any combination of the three major components of the waste cycle:

- *Generating:* Among the companies engaging in activities that involve hazardous waste are chemical companies, which produce it as a byproduct of their legal activity; furniture and wood manufacturing companies working with various solvents and ignitable wastes, which must periodically be disposed of; and vehicle maintenance operations, which involve lead-acid batteries, solvents, and heavy metal and inorganic wastes.

- *Transportation:* This component involves the hauling away of hazardous waste from industrial sites. False manifests may be prepared to make the loads look less harmful, thereby allowing for inexpensive disposal of the waste. Tankers in poor condition may leak hazardous waste as they are driven along highways, and illegal disposal of hazardous waste also occurs when tankers deliberately discharge the waste in small amounts onto the road.

- *Treatment, storage, and disposal(T/S/D):* **T/S/D crimes** are committed by companies that treat hazardous waste without a permit or treat it inadequately; store it without a permit to do so; improperly identify the nature of the waste or store it under inadequate conditions discharge it into sewers, simply abandon it, mix it with regular waste for cheaper disposal, or store incompatible chemicals or amounts of chemicals above their permitted amount or concentration (Figure 18-23).

Hazardous-waste generators vary in the level of regulatory requirements that they are required to meet (Table 18-1). Regardless of generator status, all generators must comply with basic RCRA requirements, including the use of manifests to track waste shipments. Conditionally exempt small-quantity generators must obtain an EPA permit once they generate more than 100 kilograms of hazardous waste per month. In all cases, waste must be properly stored and labeled. The EPA's *universal waste* list identifies items thrown out in large numbers, including batteries, some lamps, obsolete pesticides, and thermostats. The T/S/D requirements for universal waste are less stringent and do not count against a generator's status.

The most frequent violators of hazardous-waste regulations and laws are the small to midsize generating firms. Companies in this group violate hazardous-waste laws to maintain their profitability by avoiding the cost of legal disposal. However, large companies (or their employees) that have violated state RCRAs or various federal environmental laws include such well-known businesses as Texaco, Ocean Spray Cranberries, Fleischmann's, Ashland Oil, B. F. Goodrich, and Kaiser Steel.

Investigators must be alert to the fact that traditional crimes are also involved in acts that constitute **environmental crimes.** Examples of these include falsification of records and forgery—typically involving manifests and T/S/D records—and bribery of public officials, such as regulation inspectors and landfill operators, who accept money to certify that the hazardous waste was properly disposed of when it actually ended up being illegally dumped or abandoned.

INVESTIGATIVE METHODS

Patrolling officers should be alert for signs that indicate the possibility or presence of **illegal dumping of hazardous waste.** Some of these signs are similar to the signs of a mass chemical attack, but in illegal-dumping cases the scale is smaller. Among the signs to watch for:

- Suspicious discharges into waterways;
- Discolored and dying vegetation that is unusual for the season;

▶ FIGURE 18-23
Storage of hazardous waste under inadequate conditions
Properly identified hazardous waste improperly stored in deteriorated drums. The federal government and many states have enacted laws to protect against hazardous-waste violations that threaten both people and the environment. Treatment, storage, and disposal (T/S/D) violations are committed by companies that fail to follow specific guidelines, including those that identify proper conditions for storage of hazardous materials. (Courtesy Illinois Environmental Protection Agency)

TABLE 18-1 EPA Hazardous-Waste Generator Status			
GENERATOR CATEGORY	**MONTHLY GENERATION RATE**	**MAXIMUM QUANTITY ACCUMULATION LIMIT**	**MAXIMUM TIME ACCUMULATION LIMIT**
Conditionally exempt small-quantity generator (CESQG)	Less than 100 kg	1,000 kg	None
Small-quantity generator (SQG)	100 to 1,000 kg	6,000 kg	180 days
Large-quantity generator (LQG)	More than 1,000 kg	No storage limit	90 days

Source: Environmental Protection Agency

- Unusual number of dead animals, fish, and/or birds;
- Unusual and persistent odors;
- Odors that are accompanied by uncomfortable sensations (for example, burning) affecting skin, eyes, and respiratory system;
- New activity by trucks at closed businesses or abandoned buildings or on secondary roads;
- Tankers visiting waterways in which they might illegally dump their cargoes.

Officers should approach suspected hazardous-waste spills and toxic-waste sites with the wind at their backs and from the highest ground reasonably available. They should use binoculars to assess the scene in a standoff mode and notify their communications center as quickly as possible.

Leads on illegal hazardous-waste sites may be offered by disgruntled or former employees, occasionally by a current employee (who may have reservations about doing so because of the possibility of losing his/her job should the employer shut down); by home owners in the area of such sites; and by local pilots, boaters and fishers, competitors, building inspectors, and others. As in other types of investigation, the most immediate concerns are determining the reliability and the motive of the person bringing the information forward and assessing the public safety and health risks.

Surveillance is an excellent tool for gathering information, because it can establish illegal practices and the persons involved with them. Night-photography equipment is essential, and thermal imaging and nightscopes are very useful in investigating "midnight dumping." Satellite and aerial photographs of known hazardous-waste dumping areas can assist in locating the sites of additional illegal dumps and are useful in determining whether generators and disposal facilities are exceeding their legal or permit capacities.

For most environmental crimes, it is necessary to form a team to conduct the investigation. Access to an attorney or inclusion of one on the team is a must because of multiple, complex laws, consent decrees, and regulatory guidance. An attorney can be helpful in drafting or reviewing requests for search warrants, arrest warrants, and other legal documents.

◀ FIGURE 18-24 Unusual hazard
An investigator from the Illinois Environmental Protection Agency uses a blade of grass to point at an artillery projectile found at a closed military instillation. (Courtesy Illinois Environmental Protection Agency)

The team should also include people whose skills match the needs of the investigation, such as backhoe operators or hydrologists. Because of the dangers associated with hazardous-waste sites, investigators must wear PPE to protect themselves. Even when properly equipped, investigators can encounter unusual or unanticipated hazards (Figure 18-24). Specialized investigators from federal and state agencies are often available to assist with complex investigations. The EPA's National Enforcement Investigations Center (NEIC) has multi-disciplinary teams for conducting investigations, one of the leading forensic environmental chemistry laboratories, and an extensive library, all of which are available to federal, state, and local agencies.

KEY TERMS

agrichemicals
agroterrorism
anthrax
bone rustlers
brands
copper theft
environmental crimes
foot and mouth disease
freezer crimes
glanders
guides

hazardous waste
illegal dumping of hazardous waste
jacklighting
livestock
livestock identification
night picker
outfitters
poaching
professional poachers
situational poachers
tack

taxidermists
timber theft
treatment/storage and disposal
    (T/S/D) crimes
trophy poaching
US Department of Agriculture National
    Criminal Identification System
    (NAIS)
wildlife crimes

REVIEW QUESTIONS

1. Some variations in what is stolen from farms and ranches are caused by fluctuations in the economy. Why is this happening, and how does this reflect fluctuations in the economy?

2. If you were going to make a public presentation on the subject of timber theft, what major points would you make?

3. What are the common categories used to describe the various causes of wildfires?

4. Compare how horse and cattle rustlers operate. What are the differences and similarities?

5. There are five major methods of marking horses and cattle for identification. If you used your horse casually, just for recreational enjoyment, which method would you use to identify your horse? Why?

6. What biosecurity measures and prevention can local and state law enforcement officers take to deal with potential acts of agroterrorism?

7. What role is played by outfitters, guides, and landowners in trophy poaching?
8. What is the primary mission of the U.S. Fish & Wildlife Service Forensic Laboratory?
9. Identify and describe the four characteristics of hazardous waste.
10. What are three examples of treatment, storage, and disposal (T/S/D) crimes?
11. What are six signs of illegal dumping of waste?

INTERNET ACTIVITIES

1. You have become increasingly concerned about the potential of livestock agroterrorism in your area and want to educate yourself about its many dimensions. In order to do so you should visit the following websites: U.S. Department of Agriculture, Animal and Health Inspection Service, *USDA-APHIS Publications* Factsheets on: Foot-and-Mouth Disease, Emergency Response: Foot-and-Mouth Disease and Other Foreign Animal Diseases, and Protecting America From Foot-and-Mouth Disease and Other High-Consequence Livestock Diseases, https://www.aphis.usda.gov/publications/aphis_pubs.php, accessed February 28, 2016. Agroterrorism: Preparedness and Response Challenges for the Departments of Defense and the Army, http://www.aepi.army.mil/publications/sustainability /docs/agroterror-prep-resp.pdf, accessed February 28, 2016. After you review this material develop an agroterroism prevention plan that would be most appropriate for the potential targets in your area.

2. You have been called upon to develop a comprehensive agricultural crime prevention program to address the crimes of tractor theft, large equipment theft, livestock/poultry theft, chemical/fuel theft, grain/feed/seed/fruit and vegetable theft, burglary of farm buildings, and vandalism. There exists a large body of theory that can assist you in developing a multidimensional agricultural crime prevention program, specifically information as it relates to opportunity theory and deterrence theory. To assist you in accomplishing this objective you should access the following: The Policy Brief, "Policy, Theory, and Research Lessons from an Evaluation of an Agricultural Crime Prevention Program," Urban Institute, Justice Policy Center, Florida State University College of Criminology and Criminal Justice, http://www.urban.org/research /publication/policy-theory-and-research-lessons-evaluation -agricultural-crime-prevention-program, accessed February 28, 2016. After you review this material you are to develop a crime prevention program that will focus primarily on preventing the theft of farm equipment.

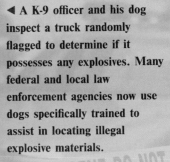

◄ A K-9 officer and his dog inspect a truck randomly flagged to determine if it possesses any explosives. Many federal and local law enforcement agencies now use dogs specifically trained to assist in locating illegal explosive materials.

(©Albin Lohr-Jones/Pacific Press/LightRocket/Getty Images)

19

ARSON AND EXPLOSIVES INVESTIGATIONS

CHAPTER OBJECTIVES

1. Discuss the steps in the preliminary investigation of arson.

2. Be familiar with various types of burn indicators.

3. Describe ignition devices that may be used in arson.

4. Assess several common motivations of arsonists for setting fires.

5. Explain the scientific methods used in arson investigation.

6. List several groups of people whom an arson investigator should interview.

7. List questions that investigators should ask in interviews and interrogations.

8. Understand how legal entry can be made into a fire scene and how evidence may be legally obtained.

9. Discuss the two types of major explosions, namely, mechanical and chemical.

10. Understand how improvised explosive devices (IEDs) work.

11. Outline the procedures for handling and investigating bomb threats.

12. Understand how to collect and preserve evidence at the bomb scene.

Arson is an inherently difficult crime to detect and prosecute, in part because the motivations for and methods of committing arson vary widely. Some arsonists may be troubled juveniles who start fires with matches or cigarettes; others are professional arsonists, who frequently use timing devices and accelerants. Arson investigation also falls between police responsibility and fire department responsibility, an area that is too often not effectively covered. Both the police and the fire services can legitimately claim authority in arson cases, but each also may rationalize that the responsibility belongs to the other. Unfortunately, in most jurisdictions, neither is prepared to devote the resources needed to achieve identification, arrest, and conviction rates commensurate with other crimes. Arson investigators need more cooperation and better training. Administrative officials need to help, but in order to help they need to give the problem a greater share of their attention. Probably the most urgent step in controlling arson rates is for top fire and police officials and local, state, and national governments to recognize the magnitude of the problem and then provide the necessary resources to combat it.[1]

QUICK FACTS

National Dollar Cost of Arson

Arsonists set fires that destroyed $729 million worth of property in 2014, up 10% from $663 million in 2013, according to the National Fire Protection Association (NFPA). The $729 million loss in 2014 included $116 million from vehicle fires and $613 million from fires in structures.[2] Untold thousands of jobs are also lost when factories and other types of businesses are burned for profit. Likewise, thousands of homes are destroyed by arsonists each year, forcing home owners and tenants to relocate and often incur higher house and rent payments.[3] In addition, hundreds of firefighters and citizens are also injured or killed as a result of arson.

In the second half of this chapter, we discuss explosive investigations, which are in many respects quite different from arson investigations. We will provide a detailed discussion of the different types of explosives used, and the techniques employed to detonate them. We will also be discussing improvised explosive devices (IEDs)—their contents, components, and the most common types of IEDs that have been employed or attempted to be employed in the United States and around the world. We will also be discussing serial bombers and the ways in which they leave specific "signatures" which can assist law enforcement in linking bombings.

PRELIMINARY INVESTIGATION

Arson investigations entail several exceptions to fire-service training. For example, the fire service has taught firefighters that fire loss is less and public relations are better if they clean premises of debris, water, and so forth. However, if arson is suspected, firefighters should not disarrange the premises, especially at the point of origin. Moving debris, even window glass, may destroy valuable physical evidence.[4]

In nearly all cases, there is little additional loss if the area encompassing the point of origin is not cleaned out, because this area is usually the most heavily damaged by the fire, with little salvage possible. Often it is necessary during overhauling to move large quantities of acoustical tile, plasterboard, canned goods, cartons, and other items. If this material is beyond salvage, it is natural to throw it into the worst-burned area of the building. But this is probably the area the investigator will want to examine carefully, and such discards will have to be moved again. In the confusion, the fire's cause is likely to remain in doubt.

One effective way to determine fire causes is to determine the point of origin. For instance, a point of origin in the middle of a bare concrete basement floor typically eliminates defective heating appliances or wiring. Points of origin sometimes are

established by reconstructing furniture and walls, and replacing loose boards and doors. Neighbors and occupants can help describe how things were before the fire. The direction of heat flow then can be followed by checks for the deepest charring, indications of highest temperature, and the duration of heat. Temperatures are indicated by the condition of metal, glass, wood, plastics, and other materials. Because heat rises, a general rule is to look for the lowest point of deep char as the point of origin. This rule, however, has many exceptions.

After the area of origin has been established, the investigator should check for the level of origin by examining the bottoms of shelves, ledges, moldings, and furniture and all sides of the legs, arms, and framework of reconstructed furniture. The investigator also should clean the floor carefully at the point of origin, examining and moving all objects to one side. After this is done, the floor or rugs should be swept as clean as possible for examination of burn patterns (Figure 19-1).

The floor and lower areas of the room produce the most clues to the cause of the fire, because they are the living area. Most equipment and contents are near floor level, actions of occupants are conducted near floor level, and most materials drop there during a fire.

WHERE AND HOW DID THE FIRE START?

Once the fire is out, the primary task is to begin examining what is left of the building for physical evidence that may indicate how the fire began.

The point of origin can be a clue to possible arson. For example, if two or more distinct points of origin are found, two or more separate fires probably were deliberately set. Also, if the fires started in the middle of a large room or in a closet, then the index of suspicion should go up sharply.[5]

TWO FACTORS NEEDED TO CAUSE A FIRE

During the investigation, it should be borne in mind that a fire always has two causes: a source of heat and material ignited. In checking for the fire cause at the point of origin, it is usually an advantage to use the **layer-checking technique.** Before any material is moved or shoveled out, the investigator should make notes and carefully examine the strata while working through to the floor. These layers often contain wood ash, plaster, melted aluminum, window glass, charred drapery fabric, and charred newspapers. They may give a picture of the sequence of burning. If, for example, charred newspapers were found beneath charred drapery fabric, this could indicate a set fire, particularly if papers would not usually be in the area or if they were of different types of dates. Aluminum and similar alloys melt fairly early in a fire (at about 1,150°F), often splash or run over other material near floor level, solidify, and protect the material from further damage. Draperies and heavy curtains may burn free and drop on flammable liquid, preventing it from being completely consumed, especially if the liquid is heavy or not particularly volatile.[6]

▶ **FIGURE 19-1**
Arson Investigators at Work
A team of arson investigators search the scene of a suspected arson. Arson investigators receive hours of specialized training to effectively conduct this type of investigation. They must be careful not to destroy potential evidence while sifting through soot and debris. (*Source: Pinellas County, Florida Sheriff's Office*)

ACCIDENTAL FIRES

Once the point of origin has been discovered, the next step is to determine how the fire started. Even though arson may be suspected, the investigator must first investigate and rule out all possible accidental or natural causes. Many courts have held that this elimination of accidental causes is a firm basis for an arson charge. Also, if the investigator is put on the witness stand, it is likely that a question will be raised about the possibility of accidental causes. A failure to eliminate accidental causes could substantially weaken the prosecution's case.

Some of the more common accidental or natural causes of fire fall into the following categories:

- *The electric system:* Fuses in which pennies have been inserted; broken or rotted insulation; overloaded circuits; defective switches; and improperly installed wiring.
- *Electrical appliances and equipment:* Defective electrical units with short circuits; overheated irons; and light bulbs covered by paper shades.
- *Gas:* Leaks in gas pipes; defective stoves and heating units.
- *Heating units:* Overheated stoves or steam pipes; clothing being dried too close to fireplaces or open flames; faulty chimneys; explosions from kerosene stoves; and overturned space heaters.
- *Sunlight:* The concentration of sun rays on bubbles in glasses, windowpanes, or convex shaving mirrors placed near combustible materials such as paper or rags.
- *Matches:* Children playing with matches, especially in enclosed areas such as closets or utility rooms.

- *Smoking:* The careless disposal of cigars, cigarettes, pipe ashes, and other lighted devices into trash cans in the home; individuals who fall asleep while smoking in bed or in a chair.

Indications of cigarettes in furniture or mattresses are heavy charring of the unit and the floor; a char pattern on furniture frames, heaviest on the inside; heavy staining and blackening of mirrors and window glass in the area, indicating a long, slow fire; a burning time of 1 to 4 hours; collapsing of part or all of the core springs. Lying flat on a padded surface, cigarettes usually char a small hole and burn out. If the cigarette is partially covered at the sides or bottom, a fire usually results in an hour or so. Cigarettes ignite foam rubber padding to about the same degree as other padding. With foam rubber padding, fire occurs a little faster, because smoldering rubber reaches an ignition temperature faster and burns with greater intensity.[7]

SPONTANEOUS HEATING AND IGNITION

There are a few fundamental causes of spontaneous heating, but the conditions under which these factors may operate are numerous. Nearly all organic materials and many metals are subject to oxidation, fermentation, or both and therefore have some potential for spontaneous heating.

Spontaneous heating is produced in three major ways: chemical action, fermentation, and oxidation (the most common way). For example, chemical-action heating occurs when unslaked lime and water or sodium and water are combined. Fermentation heating is caused by bacterial action. Here, moisture is a prime factor. The most dangerous materials are those subject to combinations, such as fermentation and oxidation with drying. Fresh sawdust over 10 feet deep is subject to fermentation heating but rarely reaches ignition temperature. In oxidation heating, rapid oxidation must take place in the presence of a good insulating factor and an oxygen supply. Oxidation takes place in oils containing carbon, hydrogen, and oxygen. This combination is mostly found in vegetable and fish oils and, to some extent, in animal oils.

The susceptibility to spontaneous heating is usually determined by drying time. Unadulterated hydrocarbons, such as mineral and petroleum oils, are not considered subject to spontaneous ignition.

Spontaneous ignition is rare in residences and small businesses. It is considerably accelerated by external heat such as sunshine, steampipes, hot air ducts, and friction from wind or vibration. Spontaneous ignition is rather mysterious, because of many unknowns. Therefore, it is often used as a catch-all explanation.

The usual time required to produce spontaneous ignition by oxidation or fermentation runs from several hours to several days or months. This form of ignition is characterized by internal charring of a mass of combustibles, and some of the remains of this material usually are found at the point of origin (if the firefighters have been careful and especially if fog was used), because it normally takes a considerable mass—several inches of fairly dense material—to create the factors necessary for spontaneous heating. Sometimes when material of the appropriate type is suspected and found to be deeply charred all the way through, investigators must satisfy themselves that external heat was not responsible. When not heated internally, sacks of meals, flour, and the like usually survive fire with only an inch or two of charring on the exposed surface.

Dust and polishing mops have often been accused of causing spontaneous ignition and probably have in some rare cases. Most fires originating near a mop in a closet or on a back porch are caused by a child playing with matches.[8] It is debatable whether the average mop would have enough bulk to provide the necessary insulation to raise the temperature to the ignition point, although with favorable conditions—such as a large mop, saturated with fast-drying oils, pressed in a corner with other brooms, and receiving outside heat from a steampipe or the sun's rays through a window—ignition could occur. During the several hours required for the material to ignite, it gives off very acrid odors. Linseed and similar oils are especially odorous. People in the area during that time usually would be aware of these odors.

BURN INDICATORS

Burn indicators are the effects of heat or partial burning that indicate a fire's rate of development, points of origin, temperature, duration, and time of occurrence, as well as the presence of flammable liquids. Interpretation of burn indicators is a principal means for determining the causes of fires, especially arson. Some of the burn indicators used are the following.[9]

▲ **FIGURE 19-2 Alligatoring**
This is the charring and cracking that gives wood the appearance of alligator skin. (©Alexey Romanov/Getty Images RF)

ALLIGATORING

Alligatoring is the charring and cracking that gives wood the appearance of alligator skin. In the past, the appearance of charring and cracking of wood has been given meaning by the fire investigation community beyond what has been substantiated by controlled testing. Contrary to previous and erroneous assumptions, the presence of large, shiny blisters (alligator char) is not evidence that a liquid accelerant was present during the fire or that a fire spread rapidly or burned with greater intensity. These types of blisters can be found in many different types of fires[10] (Figure 19-2).

DEPTH OF CHAR

Analysis of the depth of char is most reliable for evaluating fire spread, rather than for establishing specific burn times or intensity of heat from adjacent burning materials. By measuring the relative depth and extent of charring, the investigator may be able to determine which portions of a material or construction were exposed the longest to a heat source. The relative depth of char from point to point is the key to appropriate use of **charring**—locating the places where the damage was most severe owing to exposure, ventilation, or fuel placement. The investigator may then deduce the direction of fire spread, with decreasing char depths being farther away from the heat source (Figure 19-3).

Depth of char is often used to estimate the duration of a fire. The rate of charring of wood varies widely depending on such variables as:

- rate and duration of heating;
- ventilation effects;
- surface area-to-mass ratio;
- direction, orientation, and size of wood grain;
- species of wood (pine, oak, fir, and so on);
- moisture content;
- nature of surface coating.[11]

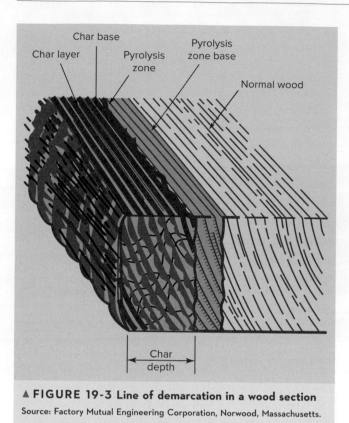

▲ FIGURE 19-3 Line of demarcation in a wood section
Source: Factory Mutual Engineering Corporation, Norwood, Massachusetts.

BREAKING OF GLASS

If a pane of glass is mounted in a frame that protects the edges of the glass from the radiated heat of a fire, a temperature difference occurs between the unprotected portion of the glass and the protected edge. Researchers estimate that a temperature difference of about 158°F (70°C) between the center of the pane of glass and the protected edge can cause cracks that start at the edge of the glass. The cracks appear as smooth, undulating lines that can spread and join together. Depending on the degree of cracking, the glass may or may not collapse from its frame. If a pane of glass has no edge protection from the radiated heat or fire, the glass breaks at a higher temperature difference. Research findings suggest that fewer cracks are formed and the pane is more likely to stay whole.

Glass that has received an impact will have a characteristic "cobweb" pattern: numerous cracks in straight lines. The glass may have been broken before, after, or during the fire.

If flame suddenly contacts one side of a glass pane while the unexposed side is relatively cool, a stress can develop between the two faces and the glass can fracture between the faces. *Crazing* is a term used in the fire investigation community to describe a complicated pattern of short cracks in glass arising from this condition. These cracks may be straight or crescent-shaped and may or may not extend through the thickness of the glass. While crazing is still a theory and has not yet been confirmed, research has established that it can be created by the rapid cooling of glass brought on by the application of water spray in a hot environment. Occasionally with small-size panes, differential expansion between the exposed and the unexposed faces may result in the pane's popping out of its frame.[12]

COLLAPSED FURNITURE SPRINGS

The collapse of furniture springs may provide the investigator with various clues concerning the direction, duration, or intensity of the fire. However, the collapse of the springs cannot be used to indicate exposure to a specific type of heat source or ignition, such as smoldering ignition or the presence of an ignitable liquid. The results of laboratory testing indicate that the annealed springs, and the associated loss of tension (tensile strength), are a function of the application of heat. The tests revealed that short-term heating at high temperatures and long-term heating at moderate temperatures over 750°F (400°C) can result in the loss of tensile strength and in the collapse of the springs. The tests also revealed that the presence of a load or weight on the springs while they are being heated increases the loss of tension.

By analyzing furniture springs, the investigator can compare the differences between the springs and other areas of the mattress, cushion, frame, and so forth. Comparative analysis of the springs can assist the investigator in developing hypotheses concerning the relative exposure of various items or areas to a particular heat source. For example, if the springs at one end of a cushion or mattress have lost their tension and those at the other end have not, then hypotheses may be developed. The hypotheses should take into consideration other circumstances, effects (such as ventilation), and evidence at the scene concerning the duration or intensity of the fire, the area of origin, direction of heat travel, and the relative proximity of the heat. Areas characterized by the loss of tensile strength may indicate greater relative exposure to heat than do areas without the loss of strength.

Other circumstances and effects to consider are the loss of mass and material; the depth of char in a wood frame; and color changes, possibly indicating intensity, in metal frames. Comparative analysis should also include consideration of the covering material of the springs. The absence of material may indicate a portion closer to the source of heat, while the presence of material may indicate an area more remote from the heat source. The investigator should also consider the condition of the springs before the fire.[13]

Spalling is the breakdown in the surface tensile strength of concrete, masonry, or brick that occurs when exposure to high temperatures and rates of heating produces mechanical forces within the material. These forces are believed to result from one or more of these factors:

- moisture present in uncured or "green" concrete;
- differential expansion between reinforcing rods or steel mesh and the surrounding concrete;
- differential expansion between the concrete mix and the aggregate (this is most common with silicon aggregates);
- differential expansion between the fine-grained surface or finished layers and the coarser-grained interior layers;
- differential expansion between the fire-exposed surface and the interior of the slab.

Spalling of concrete or masonry surfaces may be caused by heat, freezing chemicals, or abrasion. It may be induced more readily in poorly formulated or finished surfaces. Spalling is characterized by distinct lines of striation and the loss of surface material, resulting in cracking, breaking, and chipping or in the formation of craters on the surface. Spalled areas may appear lighter in color than adjacent areas. This lightening can be caused by the exposure of clean subsurface material. Also, adjacent areas may tend to be sooted.

Spalling of concrete, masonry, brick, or painted surfaces (such as plaster) has often been linked to unusually high temperatures caused by burning accelerants.

Although spalling can result from high rates of heat release or a rapid change in temperature, an accelerant need not be involved. The primary mechanism of spalling is the expansion or contraction of the surface while the rest of the mass expands or contracts at a different rate. Another factor in the spalling of concrete is the loading and stress in the material at the time of the fire. Since high-stress or high-load areas may not be related to the fire, spalling of concrete on the underside of ceilings or beams may not be directly positioned over the origin of the fire.[14]

DISTORTED LIGHT BULBS

Heat can also have an effect on the glass of a light bulb. The investigator can examine the distortion of a light bulb, for instance, to determine the direction of head impingement. Bulbs over 25 watts expand toward the heat, and bulbs that are 25 watts or less pull inward on the side of the heat; the bulbs in Figure 19-4 demonstrate this phenomenon. The bulb in the middle is greater than 25 watts, and the bulb on the right is less than 25 watts.[15]

TEMPERATURE DETERMINATION

If the investigator knows the approximate melting temperature of a material, an estimate can be made of the temperature to which the melted material was subjected. This knowledge may be of help in evaluating the intensity and duration of the heating, the extent of heat movement, or the relative rates of heat release from fuels.

When using such generic materials as glass, plastics, and white pot metals for making temperature determinations, the investigator must be aware of the wide variety of melting temperatures for these materials.

The best approach is to take a sample of the material and have its melting temperature ascertained by a competent laboratory, materials scientist, or metallurgist. Wood and gasoline burn at essentially the same flame temperature. The turbulent diffusion flame temperatures of all hydrocarbon fuels (plastics and ignitable liquids) and cellulosic fuels are approximately the same, although the fuels release heat at different rates.

The temperature achieved by an item at a given location within a structure or fire area depends on how much the item is heated. The amount of heating depends on the temperature and velocity of the airflow, the geometry and physical properties of the heated item, its proximity to the source of heat, and the amount of heat energy present. Burning metals and highly exothermic chemical reactions can produce temperatures significantly higher than those created by hydrocarbon- or cellulosic-fueled fires.

Identifiable temperatures achieved in structural fires rarely remain above 1,900°F (1,040°C) for long periods of time. These temperatures are sometimes called **effective fire temperatures,** because they reflect physical effects that can be defined by specific temperature ranges. The investigator can use the analysis

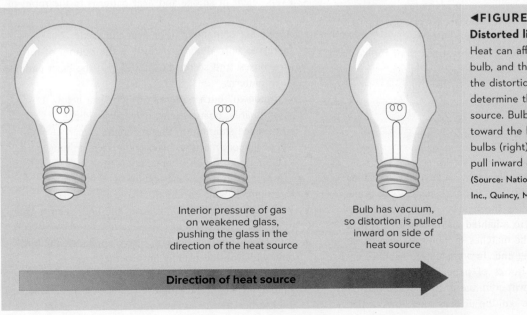

Interior pressure of gas on weakened glass, pushing the glass in the direction of the heat source

Bulb has vacuum, so distortion is pulled inward on side of heat source

Direction of heat source

◄ **FIGURE 19-4**
Distorted light bulbs
Heat can affect the glass of a light bulb, and the investigator can examine the distortion of a light bulb to determine the direction of the heat source. Bulbs over 25 watts expand toward the heat (middle bulb), and bulbs (right) that are 25 watts or less pull inward on the side of the heat. (Source: National Fire Protection Association, Inc., Quincy, MA)

of the melting and fusion of materials to assist in establishing whether higher-than-expected heat energy was present.[16]

FIRE SETTING AND RELATED MECHANISMS

It is the duty of an arson investigator to search the debris of a suspicious fire, particularly around the point of origin, to gather evidence pointing to the mechanism used by the fire setter in the arson effort.[17]

An arsonist may use the simplest of methods, a match and some paper, or elaborate mechanical or chemical methods. An **incendiary mechanism** may be mechanical or chemical, and consists of an ignition device, possibly a timing device, one or more "plants" to feed or accelerate the initial flame, and, frequently, "trailers" to spread the fire about the building or from plant to plant. Interestingly, some researchers have found differences between firesetters and non-firesetters on almost all psychological and mental health variables for both males and females.

QUICK FACTS

Gender Difference in Firesetting Patterns for Children and Adolescents

Firesetting behavior in children and adolescents is approximately two to three times more prevalent in males when compared to females.[18] Despite the research largely failing to adequately investigate characteristics of females and potential gender differences within firesetting regulations, a few studies do suggest that males and females may differ in terms of risk factors and motives.

For those children and adolescents who displayed serious antisocial behaviours, firesetting in both males and females was associated with extreme antisocial behavior. For males, drug use, suicide plans, and suicide attempts, along with a history of sexual abuse, were associated with firesetting. In females, perceived school failure and having negative expectations about their future were associated with firesetting.[19]

IGNITION DEVICES

Matches

Only juvenile arsonists and **pyromaniacs** seem to favor striking matches. Other fire setters want some delay, so they adapt the ordinary match to some timing mechanism. For example, several matches may be affixed to a lighted cigarette with a rubber band or tape, the heads of the matches set about halfway down the cigarette from its glowing end. In some cases, matches are laid alongside a cigarette. Books of paper matches are also popular. Because cigarettes will continue to burn when laid on their sides, they are effective ignition devices; the slow-burning

cigarette allows the fire setter a few minutes to get away from the scene before the fire makes any headway.

Gasoline and Other Accelerants

Gasoline and other **accelerants** ("boosters" that speed the progress of a fire) are very popular with many different types of arsonists (Figure 19-5). The investigator should remember that gasoline and many types of liquid accelerants burn at about 3,000°F as opposed to ordinary combustibles, which burn at 1,600°F. If, for example, the investigator observes a metal door melted in a pile, gasoline was probably used as an accelerant because steel generally reaches its melting point at 3,000°F.

TELLTALE SIGNS OF ACCELERANTS

- Distinct burn/damage pattern
- Witness observations (smelling gasoline, and so on)
- Explosion
- Burns to the hands, face, legs, or hair of a suspect/witness
- Unnatural fire spread (downward, very fast, and so on)
- Flames appear suddenly in an entire room followed by heavy black smoke
- Bright yellow/orange flames with black smoke
- Flames seen burning directly from the floor
- Intense localized rusting/warping (especially to the undersides and lower portions) of metal appliances and metal objects within the suspected liquid burn-pattern area
- Light, moderate, and heavy floor burn patterns in puddle or trailer shapes corresponding to the original shape of the accelerant pool on tight or non-porous floors (burn patterns vary with the type of accelerant, surface texture, and ventilation)
- Gapping of wood or vinyl floor seams within the pour burn pattern that may be caused by a liquid accelerant burning inside the seam
- Rainbow-colored sheen on the surface of suppression water over the pour area
- Even height of smoke and heat patterns in the room of origin
- Accelerant containers in or near the scene
- Increased burn damage pattern at the bottom of furniture, boxes, and so on, on the floor in the burn pattern
- Burn patterns
  - "Rundown" burn patterns on floor just below loose floorboards, board seams, or edge moldings
  - Localized staining on the underside of carpet padding
  - Pool-shaped, mottled, black-and-brown staining on a concrete floor with a tendency for the mottled portion to repel water—area may retain odor of accelerant
- Fire damage with no identifiable point of origin
- Wall burn patterns running from the floor seam upward, or appearing in corners
- Burned-out flooring beneath heavy appliances or furniture, which would usually protect the floor
- Localized "clean burn" areas on a wall, appliance, or similar vertical surfaces above the floor pattern where intense heat burned away soot deposits

▲ FIGURE 19-5 Gasoline used as an accelerant
These photographs depict in sequential order an incendiary device involving a plastic milk jug, a birthday candle, and gasoline. The cap of the milk jug was drilled to the proper size to hold the candle. As the candle burned it eventually fell into the gasoline and ignited the vapors at the level of the hole. The burning vapors then expanded which in turn intensified the fire. The delay time for the device was approximately 20 to 25 minutes. These photographs depict a test that was done before the upcoming trial of a person who allegedly used the device in the interior of a car. The results of the tests supported investigators' suspicions that the car had been intentionally burned. (Courtesy of Dave Crosbie, Burnsville, MN, Fire Department)

- Sharp line of char demarcation in a cross section of wood stud or a sharp line of calcination (color change) in plaster or drywall—indicates rapid (rather than smoldering) heat buildup
- Window glass that has melted down like "ribbon candy" and has a clean interior face (little or no soot) on the side with the accelerant

- Spring annealing in furniture/bedding—sometimes results from liquid accelerant being poured on, or adjacent to, furniture
- "Inverted cone" burn/scald patterns on vertical surfaces with the pour pattern[20]

Chemicals

Various chemical combustions have been used to set fires. Saboteurs have used such means for years. Units that provide for an acid to be released on some combination of chemicals are favorite devices, with the acid releasing itself by eating its way through the cork or even the metal of its container. The time lag from setting to ignition can be estimated with some certainty by an arsonist with a little knowledge of chemistry.

Various rubber receptacles—such as hot water bottles, ice bags, or contraceptives—have been used for a phosphorus and water ignition device. A pinhole is made in the rubber container, allowing the water to seep out. Once it drains below the level of the phosphorus, ignition takes place. As this chemical ignites upon contact with air, a time lag is secured by controlling the amount of water and the size of the hole in the container.

Even the ordinary fire setter sometimes uses a chemical that ignites on contact with water. The device can also be activated by rain. Holes in a roof or a connection to the building's gutter system have been used to trigger such devices. Another device is used to divert the sewage line in a building. It is set up at night to trigger the next morning when the toilet is flushed for the first time.

Most chemical ignition units leave some residue, have a distinctive odor, or both. Debris must be analyzed at a laboratory if it is suspected that chemicals have been used as ignition devices. Fortunately, most arsonists do not know enough to use chemical ignition or timing devices, and the machinery and tools necessary for the construction of some of these devices are not always readily available. The devices usually are fairly simple. Most complex devices, in contrast, are used only in a time of war by enemy agents.

Gas

Although not commonly encountered, the use of a combination of gas and the pilot light on the kitchen stoves of many residences is always a possibility. Illuminating gas rises to the ceiling, being lighter than air, and then slowly moves to floor level as it continues to escape. When it reaches a combustion buildup, it is close to the pilot-light level. An explosion, usually followed by fire, takes place. A candle placed in a room adjoining the kitchen has also been used as a means of ignition. Therefore, arson investigators must remember that although such explosions usually follow suicide attempts or accidents, arsonists may use an ordinary gas range as a tool.

In such cases, investigators should get help from an engineer at the local public utility. The time lag between the initial release of the gas and the explosion can be estimated from the size of the room involved, the number of openings, the type of gas, and related data. For example, a kitchen 10 by 15 feet with a ceiling 9 feet high equals a total volume of 1,350 cubic feet. When 71 cubic feet of gas are introduced into the room, the lowest limit of explosive range will have been reached. In a well-ventilated room, it is almost impossible to build up to this limit, but an arsonist can seal off the room so that the gas builds up. In a fairly well-sealed room, a single burner left open on a kitchen gas stove will deliver enough gas to explode in about 5 hours.

The oven jets will build up the same volume in 2 hours; an oven plus four burners, 30 minutes to 1 hour.

The widespread use of gas as an arson tool has been thwarted because of its smell. Neighbors usually detect the smell, call the police or the fire department, or break in themselves, and turn off the gas thereby ruining a carefully planned arson attempt.

Electrical Systems

Any wiring system, including doorbell and telephone circuits, can be used as a fire-setting tool. Ignition devices hooked to the wiring systems of buildings have been used throughout the country by arsonists. The time can be established by a study of the habits of those using the premises. Possibly a security guard switches on the light every hour while inspecting the various portions of the building, or employees turn on the lights at opening time, and so on.

Although a doorbell system can be used to trigger an ignition device, the bell may be rung by some chance visitor and the plans of the fire setter thwarted. Telephone timing devices have the same limitations. A wrong number or an unexpected call can start the fire, possibly days ahead of schedule.

Electrical appliances have also been used to set fires. An open heater is placed close to a flimsy set of curtains, and an apparently accidental fire results. An electrical circuit is deliberately overloaded with several appliances until it heats up. Sometimes an accelerant such as kerosene is dropped into a switch box. In a few cases, a length of normal wiring is removed and lighter wire substituted so that it overheats and, without blowing the fuses, serves as an ignition device.

Investigators generally discover physical traces of electrical ignition devices after a fire.

Mechanical Devices

Mechanical alarm clocks were once a favored weapon of arsonists. With a simple alarm clock, some wire, and a small battery, a fire setter was "in business." But a search of the fire debris usually sent the arsonist to prison. Some arsonists used the lead hammer in the clock to break a glass tube that fed flammable matter to a fixed flame. This action pushed one container of chemicals into another, closing an electrical circuit. Some arsonists attached matches to the hammer, where they were pressed against an abrasive surface to ignite flammable material. The clock was activated by setting the alarm for a certain time. The weights in a grandfather's clock have been used in a similar manner.

Some mechanical devices are childlike in construction while others are worthy of a master craftsperson, and others are truly fiendish. Unfortunately for many of these ingenious incendiaries, their machines do not burn and can later be used in their prosecution.

PLANTS

A **plant** is the material placed around the ignition device to feed the flame. Newspapers, wood shavings, rags, clothing, curtains, blankets, and cotton waste are some plants. Newspapers are the most frequently used; cotton waste is used extensively in factory or industrial fires.

Accelerants are also usually part of the plant. Kerosene and gasoline are favored accelerants; alcohol, lighter fluid, paint thinners, and other solvents are also popular. However, any flammable fluid or compound may be used to accelerate the blaze.

TRAILERS

Trailers are used to spread the fire. A trailer is ignited by the blaze from the plant. It carries the fire to other parts of a room or building. Usually a trailer ends in a second plant, another pile of papers, or excelsior sprinkled with gasoline, kerosene, or some other booster. From the primary plant, the fire setter may lay four trailers to four secondary plants. Four separate fires thus result from one ignition device.

Rope or toilet paper soaked in alcohol or similar fluid, motion picture film, dynamite fuses, gunpowder, and other such substances have been used as trailers. Sometimes rags or newspapers are soaked in a fire accelerant and twisted into rope. Some arsonists use a liquid fire accelerant such as kerosene as a trailer by pouring a liberal quantity on the floor in a desired path.

MISSING ITEMS

Sometimes items that are missing from the fire scene can prove valuable. For example, does it appear that many of the building's contents, especially furniture, clothing, irreplaceable family photo albums, DVDs, or valuable items, were removed before the fire? Were house pets removed? Moving a pet to a kennel or the home of friends just before a fire should raise the suspicions of the investigator.

ARSON FOR PROFIT

Understanding the motive of the arsonist is extremely important if the investigation is to be successful. There are several common motivations among arsonists for setting fires. The motive behind committing arson for profit is economic gain, whether it be the enormous gain derived from inflating insurance coverage beyond the building's value or the limited economic gain derived from cutting one's losses before oncoming financial disaster.[21]

To decide where and how to begin the investigation, the investigator needs to determine whether the arson in question was due primarily to financial stress, to a fraud scheme (without much stress), or to a combination of some stress and the profitability of fraud.

FINANCIAL STRESS AS THE PRIMARY CAUSE

The home owner or business owner who decides to arrange an arson fraud may do so out of submission to financial stress. In general, two primary factors influence the insured person's decision to commit arson fraud: (1) the desire for financial relief and (2) greed—the desire for easily obtained financial assistance. One way to conceive of an arson-fraud scheme is to view it as the result of the interplay between these two factors. Experience in cases where owners have been caught in arson-fraud schemes

indicates that the more extreme and immediately pressing the financial stress, the more desperate the insured becomes. Certainly, the number of insureds who are not persuaded to commit arson—no matter how severe their financial stress—is great, and the swelling bankruptcy court dockets reflect the prevailing honesty of most citizens. However, a rapidly developing situation of financial stress can place the insured in a position where he or she desperately examines all kinds of options both legal and illegal.

Perhaps we can understand the arson-fraud motive of a home owner who has just been fired or who faces a mortgage foreclosure (an event which has become endemic in recent years) and burns a home or business. It is important to conduct a search for evidence for those forms of stress. The investigator is likely to find a great deal about such matters in court papers associated with divorces, foreclosures, bankruptcies, and liens. Although it is not fully accepted as a rule of thumb, the more severe the financial stress of an insured, the more likely the person is to either personally set the fire or to involve a minimum number of people—usually a professional arsonist—in the crime.

Investigators often view real estate arson schemes as purely the result of the fraudulent motives of the owners. Actually, the motives for committing real estate arson split between those that are pure scams (discussed later) and those that result from the owner's or landlord's deteriorating financial position. Financial stress in the latter instance can result from any number of factors: strong net migration out of the neighborhood, a long and expensive backlog of code violation citations and fines, or a steady deterioration in the quality of the housing—sometimes by design of the landlords. Whatever the specific reasons, housing that no longer produces net income for the owner or landlord can help place the person (and perhaps the coinvestors) in a financially precarious position. The clues to determining whether the financial condition of a building or a real estate corporation would make arson-fraud attractive lie in the financial records of investment, income, and tax depreciation.

Short-Term Business Problem

The businessperson on the brink of insolvency faces financial stress that is more severe than the one who faces a short-term problem, such as a slack period in a seasonal business or an unforeseen problem of cash flow. Because of the regularity with which insurance settlements occur (when claims are not denied), the businessperson who selects arson can be fairly sure of having much of the money or all of it in hand within a short period of time. One reason to suspect that a short-term business problem, rather than a more serious one, led to the arson is the absence of creditors threatening to force the owner into bankruptcy, and thus the absence of a bankruptcy filing. An examination of the business's books enables the investigator (or accountant) to infer better whether the cash-flow problem was the likely motive for arson.

Desire to Relocate or Remodel. Arsons do occur in businesses that are subject to quickly shifting consumer tastes, and this type of arson-fraud scheme may be motivated by the desire of the owner to secure enough money to remodel or move. In this way, the insured feels able to keep up with changing tastes or to move to a more fashionable location with better market potential. Examples of businesses vulnerable to these trends are beauty salons, "theme" restaurants, and furniture stores. Frequently, such owners arrange for the arson because they realize that shifting tastes have caught them unprepared. However, an owner may also sense the onset of a new trend in its early stages and try to avoid financial distress and arrange for the arson to occur early enough to remodel or move by using the insurance proceeds. In cases in which an inventory no longer sells because of shifting tastes, a variety of internal business and supplier records can help establish whether this was the motive. In this type of arson for profit, as in many other types, the actual discomfort of financial distress may not be the motive as much as the perception that the insured will soon be in such distress—unless he/she acts immediately.

Buildup of Slow-Moving Inventory. A short-term cash-flow problem can be caused by an unusually large buildup of slow-moving inventory. Although the inventory problem may not appear to the investigator to be a logical motive for the arson, this issue may be easier to understand if the investigator becomes familiar with what are normal or abnormal levels of inventory for a particular type of business, for certain periods of the year. If an inventory problem led to the arson, it is likely the insured has filed a full and possibly even inflated claim to recoup the value of the allegedly destroyed inventory. For this reason, such documentation may point toward the motive but in itself be insufficient to establish the motive. The investigator should look also for multiple points of fire origin and the attempt to destroy all inventory.

Outmoded Technology. Several years ago, two of the largest arson-for-profit cases prosecuted in this country involved companies that failed to keep pace with the technological progress of their competitors. The arson frauds involving the Sponge Rubber Products Company and the Artistic Wire Products Company originated partly because the technologies for making the respective products had changed to more efficient, profitable forms. For whatever reasons, the owners had not kept pace. Where an industrial concern may be destroyed because of these technological problems, tell-tale signs of arson for profit are usually present. First, professional arsonists, even good ones, can rarely destroy a large industrial facility simply by burning it. Incendiary devices, sometimes involving explosives, may be required. Remnants and residues of these can often point to a "professional" arson job. Second, books and business records of the companies often reveal financial stress in ways such as corporate debt reorganizations as well as documented searches for new capital or drastic changes in marketing strategies before the arson. Third, since an owner involved in an industrial arson may claim that a labor-management grievance led to it, investigators should search for documentation on formally filed labor grievances, both with the local union and with state and federal regulatory bodies, in order to confirm or deny the validity of such a claim.

Satisfaction of a Legal or Illegal Debt

The businessperson or home owner whose property is destroyed by fire does not always broadcast clear signals of financial stress. One reason for this is that the source of the stress may not be apparent. It may not show up in the books of a business or in other indicators such as divorce or bankruptcy records. For example, if the owner incurred an illegal loan-sharking debt that the lender has called in, the tremendous pressure and threats of violence can make an incendiary fire an acceptable risk to the business owner. On many occasions, the owner either sets the fire or arranges for it to be set. In others, however, the loan shark sets it or has it set, knowing that the businessperson has fire and perhaps other (for example, business interruption) insurance in force.

Evidence of an illegal debt will be difficult to locate if the investigator follows only the "paper trail" from the insured to his or her business and personal records of transactions. If arson to satisfy an illegal debt is suspected, it is important for the investigator to seek out information on the owner's actions that led to the indebtedness—for example, a recent gambling junket, heavy betting during the sports season, or borrowing from a loan shark for a highly speculative venture that initially appeared to have enormous profit potential but later failed to meet expectations. When the trail leads to an illegal debt involving the insured but his or her denial of any involvement is convincing, the investigator should examine the possibility that the loan shark arranged the fire without the insured's knowledge or consent.

Purely Fraud Schemes as the Primary Motive

Many types of arson occur because of the actual or anticipated problem of financial stress; others result from schemes where there was not, and probably would not be, any financial problem. These types of arson-fraud schemes result from the planning and plotting of professional fraud schemers and their associates. Their objective is to defraud insurance companies, as well as banks and even creditors, of as much money as possible. Some of the common types of frauds encountered by investigators follow.

Redevelopment. In cases where a defined tract has been designated for receipt of federal redevelopment funds, owners and investors may stand to make more money if existing buildings on the tract are razed at no cost to themselves. Arson is a convenient vehicle, for although it may not destroy the building, the city or redevelopment authority will usually raze the damaged property at no cost to the owner, especially if the building is a safety hazard. Investigators who study tracts designated for redevelopment can often plot which blocks and even which buildings may burn as a result of redevelopment fraud schemes. Owners who decide to arrange this type of arson realize that if the building is only partly damaged, the adjusted insurance settlement may pay for repairs (which they do not want) but not for rebuilding. Therefore, in the interest of ensuring maximum destruction, professional arsonists are likely to be called on for their expertise.

Building Rehabilitation. To improve the condition of old or run-down dwellings, a variety of federal and state loan and loan insurance programs are available for housing rehabilitation. Certain unscrupulous owners, contractors, and others who know the "rehab" business realize that they stand to reap huge profits by obtaining funds to make repairs and then claiming that fire destroyed the rehabilitated unit. In most cases, the claimed repairs were not made, or they were only partially completed, or they were done with inferior (cheaper) materials. Therefore, in addition to reaping a profit from that portion of the loan that was not used to buy materials and pay laborers, this type of arsonist often files insurance claims for the full amount of the allegedly completed work. In addition to arson and insurance fraud, such persons commit a variety of frauds against the federal or state government that provides the rehabilitation program assistance. Financial records should indicate the cost of the work actually done.

Real Estate Schemes. In many core urban areas, the most common form of arson for profit involves the destruction of dilapidated multifamily housing. Because such housing is usually in an advanced state of disrepair, there may be little if any financial stress facing the owners. This is so because either the owner recouped the investment through depreciation of the building and through rent gouging or the owner recently purchased the building for a small fraction of the amount for which it was insured. The typical MO involves an owner purchasing the housing for a small cash down payment, often accompanied by a large, unconventional mortgage. The owner then sells the building to another speculator (usually an associate) for an inflated amount, again with little money down and a large mortgage. Often the building is insured not only for the inflated, artificial value of the second sale but for the replacement value of the building, which is even greater. Then the building burns, the policyholder is almost routinely paid, and the speculating schemers split the proceeds according to a preset formula.

To reap the maximum profit from this type of scheme, the speculators often involve one or more kinds of specialists:

- Several arsonists, so that one arsonist will not know all the plans or be easily recognized because of repeated trips to the neighborhood
- A public insurance adjuster to help inflate the claim on the building
- A realtor who scouts around for "bargain" properties to buy
- An insurance agent who may be corrupted and who is helpful in insuring buildings far beyond what normal, reasonable underwriting standards would permit

This type of real estate–arson scheme is very lucrative, and its perpetrators realize that the greater the number of buildings burned, the greater the profits. Soon, another speculator, perhaps in league with a contractor or realtor, sees how "well" the first speculator is doing, and out of greed the latter begins the same type of arson scheme, creating a chain reaction. The idea spreads to still other speculators, and shortly an entire city can find itself in the midst of a real estate arson-for-profit epidemic.

Planned Bankruptcy. Although this variation of arson for profit is not encountered often, its incidence does seem to be growing. In a typical bankruptcy fraud, the owner establishes a business and buys quantities of goods on credit. The owner pays the first few creditors quickly and in cash in order to increase the volume of merchandise he or she can then buy on credit. The inventory is then sold, often surreptitiously through another company or to a fence, and then the business declares bankruptcy. Often the creditors are left with large numbers of unpaid bills. One way to satisfy them is by paying them off with insurance proceeds obtained after a "mysterious" fire in the business. Additional money is generated from such a fraud scheme because the owner represents in the fire insurance claim that substantial amounts of inventory were destroyed, when in fact merchandise was purposely moved out before the fire. Occasionally, a cheaper grade of merchandise is substituted in its place. Because the creditors are paid, their incentive to complain or report the probable fraud is reduced. Because the destroyed records of such inventory are hard to reconstruct, it is difficult to determine exactly what was destroyed in the fire, and hence its value. Also, since bankruptcy-fraud fires always seem to destroy the office and files where the books are kept, it is difficult for the investigator to reconstruct the flow of money into and out of the business, as well as the flow of merchandise.

ARSON GENERATED BY THIRD PARTIES

This is another broad category of arson for profit, where the beneficiary of the fire is not the owner-insured but a third party who arranges for the fire out of some economic motive. Because the insured is really the major victim here, rather than the culprit, the investigator must determine whether a third-party arson for profit did occur in order to avoid targeting the wrong individual. The following are some examples of major forms of third-party arson.

Elimination of Business Competition

This type of scheme is motivated by someone who seeks to create a business monopoly or at least to maintain a competitive edge. Businesses most prone to this type of arson are those that stand to suffer from too great a concentration of similar businesses in a limited geographic area. Examples include restaurants, taverns, and sex-oriented establishments (for example, topless bars, adult bookstores, and massage parlors), which need to generate a large volume of business in order to make a profit. Increased competition can pose an economic problem to similar businesses in a limited area, which can cause some or all of them a degree of financial distress. Consequently, the financial records of a burned business may indicate the existence of financial problems that could lead the investigator to the mistaken assumption that the owner arranged the fire in order to obtain relief from that condition. Actually, in this example, a competitor is more likely to set the arson in order to improve his or her business situation.

The following case illustrates the type of arson in this category.

A brand-new nightclub had recently been opened in fairly close proximity to an older nightclub. The new nightclub was highly successful and started to draw business away from the old nightclub. Two employees of the old nightclub thought they would take matters into their own hands and "torch" the new nightclub one night after it closed, in hopes that this would help get back some of the old club's customers. Sometime during the early morning hours these two individuals broke into the new nightclub and set out eight $2\frac{1}{2}$-gallon cans of gasoline at strategic locations throughout the business. Three 12-inch pipe bombs were then inserted into three of the cans of gasoline. The fuses were lit, and the individuals quickly fled the business and drove away. Unbeknown to the would-be arsonists, the gasoline-soaked black powder could not be ignited. Thus, when the fuse finally made contact with the black powder, nothing happened. The following morning, when the business was reopened, the unexploded devices and cans of gasoline were found (Figures 19-6 and 19-7).

▲ FIGURE 19-7
Internal view of pipe bomb found at nightclub
This photograph depicts the pipe bomb that was used in conjunction with the can of gasoline in Figure 19-6. Pipe bombs have been a favorite device of arsonists for years, owing to the inexpensive costs of the materials used to construct them. International and domestic terrorists have also used pipe bombs in their efforts. (Courtesy of Michael Gonzalez)

During the initial investigation, it was suspected that at least one of the possible motives for this attempted arson was to eliminate competition with the older nightclub. Thus, the investigators focused their efforts on the owners and employees

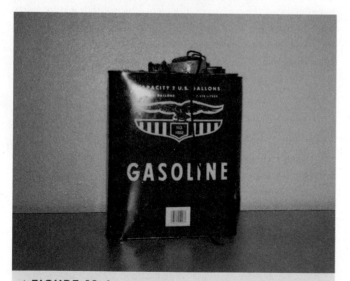

▲ FIGURE 19-6
Pipe bomb and gasoline found at nightclub
A pipe bomb intended to be used in conjunction with a can of gasoline. A hole was cut out of the top of the gasoline can between the handle and the lid to allow the bomb to be inserted into the can. The pipe bomb was immersed into the can. It was at this point that the gasoline saturated the inner workings and got the gunpowder wet, therefore making it impossible to ignite. (Courtesy of Michael Gonzalez)

associated with the older nightclub. Several days after the attempted arson, an investigative inquiry was made at the nightclub, and it was determined that two employees had recently left town and were working in a companion business of the old club 260 miles away. Not surprisingly, the sudden departure of these individuals caused them to emerge as major suspects. Their fingerprints, which were on file, were compared with fingerprints found on the gasoline cans, and a positive fingerprint identification was made of both suspects. Unfortunately, the suspects had assumed that any fingerprints they left on the cans would be destroyed once the cans were ignited, so they failed to take any precautions to ensure their fingerprints were not left on the cans. They were subsequently arrested and convicted of attempted arson. An interesting sidelight to this was the presence of a handwritten number on one of the pipes. After checking with several local hardware stores in the general area of both businesses, the investigators determined that the number was actually the price of the pipe and had been handwritten on it by one of the hardware store employees (Figure 19-8). The employee who had written the number on the pipe was not able to make an identification of the individuals who had purchased it, nor were there cameras present in the store thus eliminating the possibility of an identification.

Although this was not considered to be an organized crime–related arson attempt, the same category of arson is fairly common when an organized-crime figure maintains a financial interest in this type of business and either seeks a monopoly or

offers to hire out his or her services to create the monopoly for a client or associates in that business. In either case, it is important to involve investigators who are familiar with organized-crime intelligence gathering and investigation when elimination of business competition is suspected as a motive for arson.

Extraction of Extortion Payments

The identity of the criminal who drives out competitors by burning them out may not be known to the victim. However, offenders who demand extortion payments to let someone remain in business will necessarily identify themselves (if only through their collectors) in order to effect timely payment. In this motive pattern, the arson may be a warning signal to a businessperson to "pay up or else," or it may be a signal to similar businesstypes to either pay or wind up like the burned-out victim. This pattern is similar to that found in the elimination of business competition, in that an organized-crime figure or someone who wants to appear to victims as such a figure (for example, a juvenile gang leader) is often behind this type of scheme. Investigators who suspect this motive should examine the possibility of extortion payments being demanded of similar businesses in the locality.

Labor-Management Grievances

Arsons in business establishments may be the result of an unresolved labor-management grievance for which the perpetrator felt there was insufficient redress or resolution. Investigators should be careful to distinguish whether this type of arson is part of a more regularized pattern of violent activity in the industry or whether it could have resulted from a lone disgruntled employee. It is important to approach the possibility of this motive pattern carefully, because it can occur in an industry that is feeling the effects of an economic downturn, and thus the management logically may be reluctant to accede to labor demands because of their cost. Therefore, the financial records of the business, as well as of the entire industry, may signal financial stress. In reality, the arson may have been caused by an employee unsympathetic to that economic condition. Investigators who suspect this motive pattern should examine the history of labor-management grievances in the business by reviewing records of complaints filed with state and federal labor regulatory agencies.

OTHER MOTIVES FOR ARSON

REVENGE-MOTIVATED ARSON

Revenge-motivated fires are set in retaliation for some injustice, real or imagined, perceived by the offender. Often revenge is an element of other motives. Concept of mixed motives is discussed later in the chapter. The primary motive of revenge can be divided into four subgroups.

Personal Revenge

The subgroup with a personal revenge motive, as the name implies, uses fire to strike at an individual owing to a personal grievance. This one-on-one retaliation may be a one-time occurrence and not the product of a serial arsonist. Triggering such retaliation may be an argument, a fight, a personal affront, or any of an infinite array of events perceived by the offender to warrant retaliation. Favorite targets include the victim's vehicle, home, or property possessions.

Societal Retaliation

Perhaps the most dangerous of the revenge-motivated arsonists is the one who feels he/she has been betrayed by society in general. This type of person generally suffers from a life-long feeling of inadequacy, loneliness, persecution, and/or abuse and strikes out in revenge against a society perceived to have wronged him/her. Such a person may suffer from a congenital condition affecting appearance or health. The targets are random and fire-setting behavior often escalates. All known cases involve serial arsonists.

Institutional Retaliation

Arsonists with retaliation against institutions in mind focus on such institutions as government, education, military service(s), medical facilities, especially women's clinics that perform abortions as part of the services they provide, religion, or any other entity reflecting and representing the establishment. Often these arsonists are serial arsonists, striking repeatedly at these institution(s). The offender, in such cases, uses fire to settle grievances with the institution and to intimidate those associated with it. Buildings housing the institutions are the most frequently selected targets.

Group Retaliation

Targets for group retaliation may be religious, racial, fraternal (such as gangs or fraternal orders), or other groups. The offender tends to feel anger toward the group or members of the group collectively, rather than anger at a specific individual within the group. The target may be the group's headquarters, church, or meeting place, or symbolic targets such as emblems or logos, regardless of what they are attached to. Arsonists motivated by group retaliation sometimes become serial offenders.[22]

DETECTION AND RECOVERY OF FIRE-ACCELERANT RESIDUES

Because flammable liquids flow to the lowest level, heat travels from this level up, and the charring on the bottom of the furniture, ledges, and shelves will be as deep as, or deeper than, the charring on the top.[23]

After a fire has been extinguished, the floor should be carefully cleaned. Many signs may be found there, such as charred, inkblot-like outlines of flammable liquids. A rug that appears charred all over may, when dried out and swept with a stiff broom, show a distinct pattern of the flammable liquid. This pattern occurs because the liquid is absorbed into the nap of the rug and burns more heavily. Flammable liquid usually soaks into the joints of wooden flooring, and as a result the joints will be heavily burned.

The baseboards and sills should be checked, because flammable liquid often runs under and chars them on the bottom. Corners of the rooms should also be checked, because few floors are perfectly level, and flammable liquid often runs into and burns out the corners. In most common household fires, the corners at floor level are least damaged. The depth of charring in the floor and ceiling should be compared. If the floor is charred as much as or more than the ceiling, this indicates a flammable material directly at floor level. In the average fire, the floor temperature is only about one-third that of the ceiling.

When gasoline or similar material is suspected to have been thrown on porches or buildings without basements, especially those with single constructed flooring, the soil beneath the burned area should be checked. The investigator should dig 1 or 2 inches into the earth and smell for the odor of flammable liquids. A vapor tester is better for this purpose, because flammables such as alcohol have little or no odor in cold, wet earth.

If recovered material is suspected of containing flammable liquids, it should be sealed in an uncoated metal paint can, not in plastic bags or plastic containers. Uncoated metal paint cans can be purchased at almost any hardware store. Plastic should never be used because it gives off hydrocarbons that contaminate the material. The container should be tightly sealed to minimize evaporation or contamination. Evidence tape should be used to ensure integrity of the chain of evidence. The container may also be marked for identification purposes with permanent ink. Before they can be analyzed, accelerant residues must first be separated from the ashes, wood, carpeting, or other material in which they are found. This extraction is usually accomplished by simple, steam, or vacuum distillation. These are listed in increasing order of efficiency, particularly for petroleum products, and increasing complexity of apparatus. Steam distillation and vacuum distillation are capable of extracting 65% of any gasoline from debris; for fuel oil, the efficiencies are 30% and 90%, respectively.[24]

ALTERNATIVE FUELS IN FIRE DEBRIS ANALYSIS

Alternative fuels are becoming more prominent on the market today and soon, fire debris analysts will start seeing them in liquid samples in fire debris samples.[25] Thus, it is important for crime lab analysts to have a basic knowledge of the composition and characteristics of this fuel and the unique properties it has that are different than traditional fuels used in the commission of arsons. Biodiesel fuel is one of the most common alternative fuels and is now readily available in many parts of the United States and around the world. Biodiesel is manufactured from vegetable oils and/or animal oil/fats. When present in the fire debris, it is recommended that the samples should be analyzed by the use of the gas liquid chromatograph,[26] discussed later in this chapter.

SCIENTIFIC METHODS IN ARSON INVESTIGATION

The presence of flammable liquids may establish arson and sometimes link a suspect to the fire.[27] The objection is sometimes raised that identifiable amounts of liquid fire accelerants rarely survive a fire, and efforts to detect them would be largely wasted. But arson investigators often find accelerant residues, and accelerants can survive fires. One expert, for example, performed the following experiment: He poured 2½ gallons of kerosene over furniture and rugs in one room of a wooden building, and 1 gallon of gasoline over straw in another room, and then he left a trail of gasoline as a fuse. The building was allowed to burn freely and completely. He was able to extract identifiable amounts (more than 1 milliliter) of both kerosene and gasoline from the debris.[28]

The areas most likely to contain residues of liquid fire accelerants—floors, carpets, and soil—are likely to have the lowest temperatures during the fire and may have insufficient oxygen to support the complete combustion of the accelerant.

Porous or cracked floors may allow accelerants to seep through to underlying earth. Numerous instances have been recounted of the excellent retention properties of soil for flammable liquid.[29] Another place where accelerants may be discovered is on the clothes and shoes of a suspect.

Because each method of accelerant detection (including the human nose) has a threshold of sensitivity, another question that arises is the vapor concentration that is produced by accelerant residues. Some idea of the order of magnitude can be obtained from the experiment of two experts. They burned small (2-milliliter) samples of various accelerants for 30 seconds and then measured vapor concentrations ranging upward from 60 parts vapor per million of air—within the range of detection of currently available portable detectors and generally, but not always, well above readings produced by hydrocarbons from such things as burnt wood and burnt mattresses.[30]

Another way of looking at the potential vapor concentration is illustrated by the following hypothetical case: Suppose that a gallon of gasoline is used to accelerate a fire in a 15-by-15-by-8-feet room and that 1% (39 milliliters) survives the fire in cracks in the floor. (The residue would consist of higher boiling-point components, such as naphthalene.) The subsequent evaporation of 1 milliliter (3%) of the residue would produce an average vapor concentration of 2.7 parts per million throughout the entire room. Such a concentration can be detected with available equipment. Ventilation of the room, of course, dissipates the vapor and generally causes the vapor concentration to be highest at the points where the residues are located, a situation that can be used to advantage in locating evidence samples to be preserved for laboratory analysis.

DETECTION OF FIRE ACCELERANTS

Several types of portable equipment are available to the arson investigator for detecting residues of flammable liquids at fire scenes. Some of these use chemical color tests, catalytic combustion, flame ionization, gas liquid chromatographs, and infrared spectrophotometers and ultraviolet fluorescence. The sensitivities, limitations, advantages, and disadvantages of each of these are discussed next.

Olfactory Detection

The sensitivity of the human nose to gasoline vapor is about one part per 10 million. Gasoline is a complex mixture of chemical compounds, the proportions of which vary with the source of the crude oil and the type of process used in its manufacture. Benzene and other aromatic hydrocarbons, for example, may constitute from 0.1% to 40% of the mixture. Although no conclusive data on the sensitivity of the nose to gasoline are available, the sensitivity of the nose to benzene vapor is 0.015 parts per million. Assuming that 15% (or more) of gasoline vapor consists of aromatic hydrocarbons to which the nose is as sensitive as it is to benzene, then the sensitivity to gasoline is one part in 10 million (or greater). Thus, the nose is as sensitive as any of the currently available detecting equipment. But there are flammable liquids to which the nose is not sensitive. Another problem is the tendency of the nose to lose its sensitivity to an

odor after prolonged or intense exposure to it. Further, the odor of fire accelerants may be masked by another strong odor, such as that of burnt debris. In fact, in one case an arsonist attempted to camouflage gasoline by mixing it with vanilla.[31] Finally, it may be impractical or impossible to search with the nose for accelerant odors along floors or in recessed areas.[32]

Increasingly, agencies are using specially trained canines for the detection of accelerants. They have proved to be quite effective. On occasion such dogs are even brought to the scene of the arson while the fire is occurring in the hopes that the dogs will be able to detect accelerants on individuals who may have set the fire and are in the crowd watching it.

Chemical Color Test Detectors

Chemical color tests may be used to detect both liquid accelerant residues and their vapors. Certain dyes indicate the presence of hydrocarbons by turning red. Dyes are less sensitive and less specific to flammable liquids than other available methods. Dyes also may interfere with laboratory identification of the accelerant. Hydrocarbon vapors can be detected by pumping a suspected sample through a glass container of reagent that changes color in the presence of hydrocarbons. The reported sensitivity of this method is on the order of one part per 1,000. Again, the method is less sensitive and less specific (reacting to hydrocarbons that are not fire accelerants) than others available. Its main advantages are low cost and simplicity.[33]

Catalytic Combustion Detector

The most common flammable vapor detector operates on the catalytic combustion principle and is popularly known as a sniffer, combustible-gas indicator, explosimeter, or vapor detector. A **catalytic combustion detector** is portable, moderate in cost, and fairly simple to operate. Vapor samples are pumped over a heated, platinum-plated coil of wire that causes any combustible gas present to oxidize. The heat from the oxidation raises the electrical resistance of the coil, and this change in resistance is measured electronically. A sensitivity (to hexane vapor) on the order of a few parts per million can be achieved with this method. Because oxygen is required for the operation of the detector, its sensitivity is reduced in oxygen-deficient areas, but these are unlikely to occur in arson investigations. (An internal source of oxygen could be fitted to a detector if required.) Another problem is the gradual loss of sensitivity when this type of detector is exposed to gasoline containing lead. Lead deposits form on the platinum catalyst and interfere with its operation.[34]

Flame Ionization Detector

In the **flame ionization detector,** the sample gas is mixed with hydrogen, and the mixture is burned. Ionized molecules are produced in the flame in proportion to the amount of combustible organic gases in the sample. (Pure hydrogen, air, and water vapor produce little ionization.) The degree of ionization is then measured by electrometer. The sensitivity of this method (to methane) is on the order of one part in 10 million. It is thus more sensitive but more complex and expensive than the catalytic combustion method.

Gas Liquid Chromatograph

The portable **gas liquid chromatograph (GLC)** adapted for field use (sometimes called the *arson chromatograph*) is one of the most common detectors in arson investigations. The sample gas is first separated into components on the basis of the speed with which they travel through a tube filled with packing material. The amounts of each component are then measured by either a catalytic combustion or flame ionization detector. The sensitivity ranges from a few hundredths of a part per million to a few parts per million, depending on the type of detector used. The main advantage is specificity because of the preliminary separation process. The main disadvantages are its size, weight, and cost. Also, the time required for the analysis of each sample is about 12 hours, a disadvantage in some situations. In addition, there is a setup time of about 1 hour. The operation of the gas chromatograph requires a certain amount of technical training.

Infrared Spectrophotometer

Infrared spectrophotometers can achieve high specificity to flammable liquids and high sensitivity (on the order of hundredths of a part per million). Infrared light of varying wavelengths is directed through the sample, and the amount of light passing through is plotted on a pen recorder. The recording is compared with those of known compounds to determine the identity of the sample. Because the chemical bonds in a compound determine how it absorbs infrared radiation, these recordings (called spectrograms) are unique for different compounds. However, evidence mixed with impurities must be purified before it can be successfully identified. In particular, since water vapor absorbs infrared light, it interferes with the identification of flammable vapors. This is a disadvantage in arson investigation, where water is commonly present. A final disadvantage is the high cost of this type of detector.

Ultraviolet Fluorescence

Ultraviolet fluorescence consists of illuminating the darkened fire scene with an ultraviolet lamp. Certain substances, including constituents of gasoline and its residue, absorb the ultraviolet light and release it as visible light. They appear to glow against the darkened background. The color of the glow is affected by exposure to heat, and so the method also can be used to locate the point of origin of a fire. The only equipment required is an ultraviolet lamp and a portable power supply. The sensitivity of the method appears comparable to that of other methods of detection. The main disadvantage of the method is that it requires extensive testing, particularly to identify fire accelerants to which it does not respond.[35]

INTERVIEWS

To establish possible motives and develop suspects, the arson investigator must interview people who might know about the fire and how it started. The following kinds of people may provide information.[36]

POSSIBLE WITNESSES

Prospective witnesses include tenants, businesspeople, and customers from the burnt building or surrounding buildings, as well as passersby such as bus drivers, taxi drivers, delivery people, sanitation workers collecting garbage, police patrols, and people waiting for buses and taxis.

Questions to Ask

Did you observe the fire? At what time did you first observe the fire? In what part of the building did you observe the fire? What called your attention to the building? Did you see any people entering or leaving the building before the fire? Did you recognize them? Can you describe them? Did you observe any vehicles in the area of the fire? Can you describe them? Can you describe the smoke and the color of the flame? How quickly did the fire spread? Was the building burning in more than one place? Did you detect any unusual odors? Did you observe anything else?

FIREFIGHTERS AT THE SCENE

Firefighters can be an invaluable source of information to arson investigators because of their technical knowledge and what they observe at a fire.

Questions to Ask

What time was the alarm received? What time did you arrive at the scene of the fire? Was your route to the scene blocked? What was the extent of burning when you arrived? Were doors and windows locked? Were the entrances or passageways blocked? What kind of fire was it? What was the spread speed of the fire? In what area(s) did the fire start? How near was the fire to the roof? Was there evidence of the use of an accelerant? Was any evidence of arson recovered? Did the building have a fire alarm system? Was it operating? Was there any evidence of tampering with the alarm system? Did the building have a sprinkler system? Did it operate? Was there any evidence of tampering with the sprinkler system? Was there anyone present in the building when you arrived? Who was the person in the building? Did that person say anything to you? Were there any people present at the scene when you arrived? Who were they? Did you observe any vehicles at or leaving the scene when you arrived? Can you describe them? Were there contents in the building? Was there evidence that contents had been removed? Was the owner present? Did the owner make a statement? What did the owner say? What is the fire history of the building? What is the fire history of the area?

INSURANCE PERSONNEL

The profit in many arson-for-profit cases is an insurance payment. Three people may be interviewed to determine if the profit centers on an insurance claim: the insurance agent or broker, the insurance adjuster, and the insurance investigator.

There may be restrictions on the amount of information insurance personnel can turn over without a subpoena, but the investigator should be able to determine enough to indicate whether a subpoena or search warrant would prove fruitful.

Questions to Ask the Agent or Broker

Who is the insured? Is there more than one person insured? Is the insured the beneficiary? What type of policy was issued? What is the amount of the policy? When was it issued? When does it expire? What is the premium? Are payments up-to-date? Have there been any increases in the amount of coverage? What amount? When did the increase take effect? What was the reason for the increase? Are there any special provisions in the policy (for example, interruption of business or rental income)? What are they, and when did they take effect? Does the insured have any other policies? Were there previous losses at the location of the fire? Were there losses at other locations owned by the insured?

Questions to Ask the Insurance Claims Adjuster

Did you take a sworn statement from the insured? Did the insured submit documents regarding proof of loss, value of contents, bills of lading, value of building, and the like? Did you inspect the fire scene? Did you inspect the fire scene with a public insurance adjuster? Did you and the public adjuster agree on the cost of the loss? Have you dealt with this public adjuster before? Has he or she represented this owner before? Has the insured had any other losses with this company? (If so, get details.)

Questions to Ask the Insurance Investigator

Were you able to determine the cause of the fire? Did you collect any evidence? Who analyzed the evidence? What were the results of the analysis? Was the cause of the fire inconsistent with the state of the building as known through an underwriting examination? Have you investigated past fires at the location? Have you investigated past fires involving the insured? What were the results of the investigations? Have you had previous investigations involving the public adjuster? Have you had prior investigations involving buildings handled by the same insurance agent or broker? What were the results of these investigations? Does this fire fit into a pattern of fires of recent origin in this area? What are the similarities? What are the differences? Have you taken any statements in connection with this burning? Whose statements did you take? What do they reveal?

Property Insurance Loss Register

The insurance industry maintains a modern computerized data bank, the **Property Insurance Loss Register (PILR),** to keep track of fire, burglary, and theft claims. PILR is a listing of everyone who has an insurable interest in fire claims and a listing of *only* the insureds in burglary and theft claims. Thus, PILR is one of the most effective routes for determining a repeated pattern of claim activity on the part of individuals and organized rings. Most insurance companies are members of PILR and routinely submit data, listing insureds and claim details, to the registry after fire and burglary losses. The information is immediately entered into the PILR data bank; should the name of an insured (or of a person with an insurable interest, in the case of fire losses) have been entered before, a "hit" will be reported to the insurance company that submitted the entry. Hits can vary widely in significance, as shown by the following examples:

- *Probably insignificant:* A major landlord or mortgagee experienced a minor fire at another location 12 months before the immediate loss.
- *Inconclusive:* A home owner experienced a $4,000 burglary loss 18 months before the immediate fire loss.
- *Suspicious:* A business owner made two expensive burglary loss claims against two other insurers during the 12 months preceding the immediate, very suspicious fire loss under investigation. (Why is the owner having such bad luck, and why is he or she changing insurance companies so frequently?)
- *Highly suspicious:* A home owner or tenant experienced two expensive and suspicious fire losses at previous addresses during the 24 months before the immediate loss.
- *Probably incriminating:* An insured has made claims against two different insurers for the same immediate loss under investigation. There can be legitimate circumstances in which double claims are made; for example, the building and some of its contents may be insured by one carrier, while special inventory or equipment is insured by another.[37]

The insurance company that has made an entry is notified only when a hit occurs. Thus, the lack of a PILR response in the claim file may indicate either that there was no hit or that no entry was made. When obtaining the claim file, the investigator should ask the claims adjuster whether PILR entries were submitted and, if so, which individuals were listed on the entries. If no PILR entries were made or if the names of some of the possible suspects with an insurable interest were not included, the National Insurance Crime Bureau (NICB) can request PILR data if it is a party to the investigation.[38] If previous fire, burglary, or theft losses are reported by PILR, it then becomes possible to compare the claimed losses to see whether the same furnishings, inventory, or equipment were already reported lost, stolen, or destroyed. Likewise, PILR's records can be a means of constructing the "big picture" for an arson-for-profit conspiracy. By running the names of every possible suspect in one suspicious fire through PILR and/or the NICB's database, a dozen or more interrelated claims may be uncovered and used to develop evidence against the entire ring. In some states, model arson laws may allow the investigator to easily obtain the claim files for the previous losses from the insurance companies involved. In instances where such laws do not apply or where suspicious prior burglary claims are not covered by the laws, the NICB may be able to secure copies of the previous claims when it is a party to the investigation.[39]

OTHER WITNESSES CONCERNING FINANCES OF THE INSURED

A number of other people may have information on the finances of the owner, including business associates, creditors, and competitors. This information may indicate how the owner stood to profit from the burning.

Questions to Ask

How long have you known the owner/insured? What is the nature of your relationship with the owner/insured? Do you have any information on the financial position of the business? Is the owner/insured competitive with similar businesses? Have there been recent technological advances that would threaten the owner/insured's competitive position? Has there been a recent increase in competition that would affect the owner's/insured's position? Have changes in the economy affected the owner/insured's position? Has the owner/insured had recent difficulty in paying creditors? Has the owner/insured's amount of debt increased recently? Has the owner/insured lost key employees lately? Has the location where the owner/insured does business changed for the worse recently? Has the owner/insured increased the mortgage or taken out a second or third mortgage? Has the owner/insured had difficulty making mortgage payments? Do you have any other information about the owner's/insured's financial position?

NEWS MEDIA PERSONNEL

This category includes both the print and electronic media. Individuals affiliated with these groups may have noticed something of value to the investigator or perhaps have video footage of the fire and fire scene. For example, if the arsonist remained in the area after the fire and mingled with spectators, his or her presence may be captured on video and prove quite valuable in an investigation.

THE MEDICAL EXAMINER

The autopsy should reveal whether any victim found dead in the fire was dead or alive before the fire started and what the cause of death was. It is not uncommon for a person to be murdered and the scene made to appear as if the person had been killed by fire. (See Chapter 9, "Injury and Death Investigations," for a detailed discussion of fire deaths.)

INTERVIEWING A SUSPECT

The following questions are based on the assumption that the person to be interviewed is involved in arson for profit, that the investigator has enough evidence to make an arrest or to convince the subject that he or she is liable to arrest and that the subject is more valuable to the investigation in a cooperative role than as a defendant.

Questions to Ask the Suspect

What method was used to accomplish the arson? Specify whether what was used was an incendiary device, gasoline or another inflammable fluid, or some other means. If an incendiary device was used, be specific as to the type of device. Where did you obtain the incendiary device? If it was improvised, who made it? How much did it cost? Who paid for the incendiary device? Was it paid for by cash or check? If gasoline or another flammable fluid was used, where was it obtained? How much

was obtained and used? Were any special techniques used in setting the fire (or causing an explosion) to avoid detection?

Questions to Ask the Torch, Specifically

Are you willing to cooperate in this investigation? How many other people are involved in the arson-for-profit scheme? How are they involved? What role does each person play in the scheme? Explain (in detail) how the scheme works. How did you first become involved in the scheme? How did you meet the other participants? Where did you meet the other participants? Are you still in contact with the other participants? How often do you see them? Where do you see them? What do you talk about when you meet with them? Would you be able to record your conversations with them? Are you willing to record your conversations with them? Would you be willing to introduce an undercover investigator into the group? Could you introduce an undercover investigator into the group without the other participants' becoming suspicious? How far in advance of an arson are you told about it? What role do you play in connection with the arson (torch, driver, fence, and so forth)? Are you willing to swear to an affidavit for a search warrant? Are you willing to testify before a grand jury? Are you willing to testify at trial? Do you have information on other arson-for-profit schemes?

INTERVIEWING THE TARGET AND THE OWNER

The target of the investigation may be an owner, a landlord, a fire broker, or the like. The interview should take place after obtaining the background information on the fire and after interviewing the individuals previously listed.

Questions to Ask the Target

Tell me in your own words what you know about this fire. When did you first hear of the arson? Who told you? Where were you and what were you doing before, during, and after the arson? Who was with you? Do you know who committed the arson? Do you have any knowledge of any previous fire at the building? Do you have any knowledge of any previous incidents of any kind and at any location owned or rented by the owner/occupant of the building? Do you know of any recent changes in insurance coverage? Do you know the owner of the arson property? Describe your relationship to the owner. Do you have any financial interest in the burned property?

Questions to Ask the Owner

Tell me in your own words what you know about this fire. How long have you owned the burned property? What was the purchase price? What was the total amount of the mortgage? Who is your insurance company? Agent? Broker? Public adjuster? How much insurance do you carry? Is there more than one policy on this property? On its contents? On rental or business interruption? Have you increased your insurance coverage on the property in the past year? If so, why and at whose suggestion? Have you ever received an insurance cancellation notice on this property? Where were you at the time of the fire? When did you first hear of the arson? Who told you? When were you last in the building? Was the building secured? If so, in what manner? Who else has access to, or keys, to the building? Who was the last person to leave the building? Do you have any knowledge that the sprinkler system or burglar alarm system was on and working? Indicate the name and address of all lienholders. What is the amount of each lien? What was the value of the inventory on hand immediately before the fire? Can you provide documentation for this value? Was any inventory removed from the premises before the fire? If yes, by whom and for what purposes? Where did it go, and why was it removed? Was any inventory removed from the premises after the fire? If yes, by whom and for what purpose? List the inventory removed and its value. Did you set the fire or cause it to be set? Do you know who set it?

INTERVIEWING A POTENTIAL INFORMANT WHO IS NOT A SUSPECT

Before interviewing a potential informant who is not a suspect, investigative efforts should be made to determine if the informant has any police record and, if so, if it could have any bearing on the reliability of the information provided. For example, if a potential informant was previously convicted of arson and perjury, then the investigator should be cautious about acting on that person's information.

Questions to Ask a Potential Informant

How are you currently supporting yourself? Do you have any pending prosecutions against you? Where? What are you charged with? Do you have any information about arson for profit in this city, county, state? How did you acquire this information? Do you know anyone engaged in arson for profit? What roles does that person play in the scheme? How do you know this? What is your relationship with this person or persons—loan shark, bookmaker, fence, other? Where does this person live, frequent? Who are his/her associates? Do you know them? Are they part of the scheme? Have you been asked to involve yourself in the scheme? In what way? Have any of these people talked freely to you about their activities? Have they talked in your presence? What was said? Can you engage them in conversation about past arsons? Future arsons? Would they be suspicious of you? Could you wear a concealed recorder during conversation? Could you introduce an undercover officer into the group? Would you be willing to testify before a grand jury? Would you be willing to testify at trial? Would you be willing to swear to an affidavit for a search warrant? What do you expect in return for your help?

THE ARSON SUSPECT

In some arson investigations, a single prime suspect may emerge and investigative efforts will be focused accordingly. However, in most cases, a number of suspects emerge, and merely establishing that one or more of them had a motive to set the fire is not proof enough for an arrest and conviction. The investigator must also determine which of the suspects had the opportunity and the means to commit the crime. This determination must be related to the background, personal characteristics, past activities, and financial status of each of the suspects. For example, 10 people may have had a chance to set the fire, but only four or five may have had a motive, and of this number, perhaps only one or two would risk an arson conviction for the expected profit or satisfaction.

In probing an arson fire, seldom does direct evidence link a suspect with a fire. Because arsonists tend to take elaborate precautions not to be seen near the fire, they are seldom caught in the act. It may be best for the investigator to concentrate on gathering circumstantial evidence and some provable facts from which valid conclusions can be drawn. For example, let us assume that a warehouse fire was ignited by a timing device—a slow-burning candle attached to some flammable material triggered 2 hours before the fire actually started. The owner, who is also a prime suspect, is identified but can prove his whereabouts at the time of the fire. However, he cannot prove where he was 2 hours before the fire. In addition, the structure was locked when the fire department arrived to fight the fire, and the owner is the only one with a set of keys. The owner also took a large insurance policy out on the warehouse a short time ago.

Although far more evidence would likely be needed to arrest and convict the owner, there is sufficient justification for focusing a considerable amount of the investigation in his direction. If some other evidence is found to link him more directly to the fire (say, candles and flammable material found in the trunk of his/her car), then the circumstantial evidence becomes significant.

PHOTOGRAPHING THE ARSON SCENE

STILL PHOTOGRAPHY

Photographing a fire scene can be a challenge. Adverse conditions—poor lighting, time constraints, inconvenient angles, and so forth—necessitate the use of camera equipment that is reliable and quick. High-end digital cameras for professionals are frequently the types that are used for this. The advantages of digital cameras are that the images can be immediately viewed, printed, and if necessary quickly transmitted and disseminated.

The photo session should take at least as long as the physical examination; however, it is not necessary to photograph every step. The investigator should follow the same path in photographing the structure as is followed in the physical examination—the path of the burn trail from the least to the greatest amount of damage. The photos are as important as the written report because they show what happened rather than merely telling what happened.

Ideally, the investigator should be concerned with photographing things and areas that show, in detail, what happened. For example, if there are severely darkened ventilation patterns out of a window or a door, the investigator should photograph them. The investigator should also photograph burn patterns at lower levels and those that show distinct lines of demarcation, melted or stained glass, areas where explosions occurred, broken locks, and areas where the electric service enters the building. If the investigator does not know what happened, detailed photos will help in assessing what took place.

In some cases, it is necessary to compile a panoramic view. This can be accomplished with a composite of several photos that are taped together to create a much larger overview. The area of the fire's origin should be photographed twice, first before the rubble is disturbed and then after the debris has been removed. Severe burn patterns should be documented, especially patterns that show how the fire burned. Burn patterns at the base of doors and underneath door moldings are a strong indication that flammable liquids were used. This is because a fire spreading of its own accord burns upward, not downward.

If clocks are present, the investigator should always photograph the faces of the clocks showing the times they stopped. Fires often cause interruptions in electricity, which means electrical clocks will usually stop within 10 minutes to an hour after the time the fire started. Knowing when the fire started is crucial to the case.

VIDEO RECORDING

Another form of visual documentation is videorecording, discussed in Chapter 3, "Investigators, the Investigative Process, and the Crime Scene." Although the average fire investigation does not require videorecording, it should be done if the investigator reasonably believes that the case will involve litigation.[40]

EXPLOSIVES INVESTIGATION

Under the fire and explosion investigation definition, an **explosion** is a physical reaction characterized by the presence of four major elements: high-pressure gas; confinement or restriction of the pressure; rapid production or release of that pressure; and change or damage to the confining (restricting) structure, container, or vessel that is caused by the pressure release. Although an explosion is almost always accompanied by the production of a loud noise, the noise itself is not an essential element of an explosion.[41] The generation and violent escape of gases are the primary criteria of an explosion.

KNOW YOUR EXPLOSIVES

The earliest explosive was black powder or gunpowder, made of sulfur, charcoal, and potassium nitrate (also called saltpeter).[42]

Nitroglycerin came along a bit later. It has a greater energy density than black powder, but its sensitivity to shock makes it difficult to work with, and it is rarely used today for anything except as a vasodilator medication for individuals with heart problems who experience angina.

Alfred Nobel invented dynamite by combining nitroglycerin with sodium carbonate and diatomaceous earth. The latter ingredient is available at any garden nursery, made of ancient decomposed seashells. Dynamite was the first commercially viable explosive, and made Nobel wealthy enough to endow an annual prize for advancements in science and peacemaking.

Dynamite is usually formed into sticks and wrapped in paper. Over time, the nitroglycerine in the dynamite will "weep" or "sweat," forming unstable crystals on the wrappers. Proper storage of dynamite dictates the packages be turned periodically to prevent this.

Some people think trinitrotoluene or TNT and dynamite are the same things, but they are not. TNT starts with toluene, a common solvent used in model airplane glue, among other things. The explosive is produced by repeatedly nitrating it with nitric and sulfuric acids. TNT is more stable than dynamite, and can be poured (it melts at 176°F) into molds or combined with other explosives. It is the most common explosive used in conventional military munitions such as artillery and mortar shells.

TNT is the standard for measuring the destructive power of other compounds and weapons. The "Little Boy" atomic bomb dropped on Hiroshima in World War II was equivalent to about 15,000 tons (15 kilotons) of TNT. To provide perspective, a kiloton of solid TNT would be a cube measuring about 10 yards on each side. TNT is yellow, and skin that's in repeated contact with it turns the same color.

Terrorist bomb makers prefer plastic explosives. These are compounds containing one or more of the explosives already described, plus pentaerythritol tetranitrate (PETN) or RDX, plus wax or some other plasticizer. The resulting compound is a moldable, castable substance that can take almost any shape. PETN is a major ingredient of Semtex, while RDX is used in Torpex and C-4.

Umar Abdulmytallab (discussed in greater detail later in this chapter) stashed PETN in his underwear in December 2009 in his unsuccessful attempt to destroy Northwest Airlines Flight 253 on route from Amsterdam to Detroit. RDX was the primary explosive in the 2006 railroad bombings in Mumbai, India, and in the bombing of the Moscow Metro in March 2010.

Most, if not all, explosives developed since black powder have nitrate compounds as a base component. It is these nitrate molecules and ions that high-tech bomb "sniffers" (discussed later in this chapter) look for. Plastic explosives tend to be denser than other common materials carried by travelers, and the explosives are sometimes surrounded by wires, batteries, or electronics that complete the bomb. These are detectable with X-rays and other visual scanning methods.

When these methods fail, or when the gadget locates a suspicious lump that might be a bomb, it must be examined visually or examined by a remotely operated device.

COMPUTERIZED TOMOGRAPHY (CT)

One method used to identify explosives is a CT scan. The "CT" stands for computerized tomography, which is a method for generating a three-dimensional image from multiple 2-D X-ray images captured from multiple angles.

Modern CT scanners use multiple emitters to fire X rays through an object to a sensor on the opposite side. The sensor records the gross structures it "sees" as well as the amount of energy received, giving an indication of the density of the material it passed through. The computer combines all of these images into one virtual object that appears on a computer display. The virtual object can be rotated on any axis and zoomed in or out to inspect details of interest.

Contraband objects with telltale shapes, like guns, are fairly easy to spot. The latest equipment stores data on densities of objects, both common and deadly, and uses X-ray diffraction to identify and display those in a telltale color. An operator at an airport or other high-threat location can pay closer attention to a container colored in red and determine whether it's plastic explosive or cold cream.

There are several limitations to CT as an explosives detector. The software that flags an explosive may give a false positive alert on something innocuous, like a child's Play-Doh. CT scanners are large—typically, the size of a small truck—and expensive.

SNIFFERS

Not all explosives detectors rely on the sense of sight. Some are called "sniffers" but do not exactly rely on the sense of smell. The more formal name for sniffers is Ion Mobility Spectrometry (IMS). This might be a blasphemy to an analytical chemist to call it a sniffer but it is much easier to say.

In an IMS instrument typically used for explosives detection, a sample is heated to produce a vapor, which is then ionized (ions are atoms or molecules containing an unequal number of protons and electrons, so they have a positive or negative charge) by a radiation source, something similar to smoke detectors in a house.

The ions move through a drift chamber and an electric field that causes them to separate by size, mass, and geometry. As the ions arrive at a detector at the far end of the drift chamber, those size, mass, and shape characteristics form a signature unique to the compound from whence they came. If the signature matches what the device is programmed to detect, similar to PETN, it sounds an alarm.[43-45]

TYPES OF EXPLOSIONS

There are two major types of explosions: mechanical and chemical. These types are differentiated by the source or mechanism by which the explosive pressures are produced.

Mechanical Explosions

In **mechanical explosions,** the high-pressure gas is produced by purely physical reactions. None of the reactions involves changes in the basic chemical nature of the substances. The most commonly used example of a mechanical explosion is the bursting of a steam boiler. The source of overpressure is the steam created by heating and vaporizing water. When the pressure of the steam can no longer be confined by the boiler, the vessel fails and an explosion results.

Chemical Explosions

In **chemical explosions,** the generation of high-pressure gas is the result of reactions in which the fundamental chemical nature of the fuel is changed. The most common chemical explosions are those caused by the burning of combustible hydrocarbon fuels such as natural gas, liquified petroleum gas, gasoline, kerosene, and lubricating oils.

An example of a chemical explosion is the one that destroyed the Alfred P. Murrah Federal Building in Oklahoma City several years ago. In this case, the convicted and subsequently executed bomber, Timothy McVeigh, loaded a van with 4,000 pounds of ammonium nitrate (commonly used as a fertilizer) that had been soaked in fuel oil and detonated with high explosives. The destructive force of such a device is enormous. The explosion killed 167 people[46] (Figure 19-9).

▲ FIGURE 19-9

Damage resulting from a chemical explosion

The effects of a chemical explosion that destroyed the Alfred P. Murrah Federal Building in Oklahoma City. The destructive force of this chemical explosion killed 167 people. Timothy McVeigh was eventually convicted and executed for committing the crime. (©Ralf-Finn Hestoft/Corbis/Getty Images)

IMPROVISED EXPLOSIVE DEVICES (IEDS)

An **improvised explosive device (IED)** is a combination of items or components that are neither designed nor produced to be used in conjunction with each other but, when placed together or assembled, constitute a mechanism that has the capability of exploding and causing personal injuries and property damage.[47]

BASIC COMPONENTS OF THE IED

IEDs have two very basic components, the main charge explosive and the fuzing system. The main charge, either low or high explosive, can be combined with other materials to create a more lethal device. These materials include an incendiary to create an explosive-incendiary device or chemical, biological, or nuclear materials to fashion a weapon of mass destruction.

The fuzing system is designed to provide the required stimulus or energy to cause the main charge to function or explode. Fuzing systems do not need to be complex in order to function and most are not. Indeed, the more complex the fuzing system, the greater the chances it will not work as designed. However, of all the components used in the construction of the fuzing system, one is essential—the initiator, which is any device that may be used to start a detonation or deflagration.[48]

THE UNITED STATES AS A TARGET OF IEDS

Boston Marathon Bombers

One of the most recent cases of the use of IEDs in the United States occurred in Boston, Massachusetts on April 15, 2013. On this date at 2:50 PM two IEDs were placed in close proximity to the Boston Marathon finish line where hundreds of people were observing the race. The IEDs were two specially improvised metal pressure cookers which contained B.B.-like pellets and nails along with explosive powder and a timed ignition device. The bombs were left in two backpacks approximately 50 to 100 yards apart and were set to go off 8 to 12 seconds apart (Figure 19-10). These two explosions killed three people and injured at least 264 people.[49]

Shortly thereafter, FBI agents recovered video surveillance footage from a nearby bar and restaurant called Whiskey's Smokehouse. The surveillance video showed the crowd at the outdoor section of the business as well as people walking along and lining up at the street to watch the marathon runners go by. There was also a spectator at the scene who took a still photo that showed the finish line and Whiskey's Smokehouse along with the crowd from across the street, giving investigators another valuable perspective. The still photo also showed a black backpack on the ground in the precise place where the bomb had exploded. It had been placed next to a tree just behind an 8-year-old boy, who was killed in the blast. Standing over the backpack was a white male wearing a white baseball cap backward, minutes before the bomb went off.

Armed with this still photo and surveillance video the FBI agents were able to cross-reference the images. The surveillance video depicted 174 people walking in and out of the frame but the investigators' attention was drawn to a man wearing a white ball cap backwards standing near a backpack.

The FBI agents in the Computerized Analysis Response Team (CART) lab also played the surveillance video backward and were able to determine from which direction the man with the white ball cap had come. This portion of the surveillance video footage also led to a second suspect.[50] The FBI then posted images of the crowd on their website and asked the public to see if they recognized any individuals, and if so, to contact them (Figure 19-11). Shortly thereafter, information was provided to the FBI by individuals who recognized and personally knew the

▲ **FIGURE 19-10**

Improvised explosive device used in the boston marathon bombings

Images of a pressure cooker bomb and duffel bag found at blast site of Boston Marathon. (*Source:* Federal Bureau of Investigation)

◀FIGURE 19-11
Boston marathon bombing suspects
This photo from Whiskeys Smokehouse surveillance cameras shows Tamerlan, wearing the black ball cap and Dzhokhar wearing the white ball cap backwards. (*Source: United States Department of Justice*)

two brothers, Tamerlan Tsarnaev and Dzhokhar Tsarnaev. They would later be identified as ethnic Chechens who were adherents to the philosophy of radical Islam. Both brothers had legally emigrated to the United States in 2002 with their parents.

Later the same day as the bombing, a Massachusetts Institute of Technology campus police officer, Sean Collins, was shot and murdered by Tamerlan Tsarnaev. Soon after the shooting the two brothers carjacked a Mercedes SUV and abducted the driver. After driving around for approximately 90 minutes the two men and the abducted driver stopped at a convenience store. One of the men exited the SUV and went into the convenience store while the second one was playing around with the GPS in the car. The victim saw his opportunity to escape, jumped from the vehicle and ran to a convenience store across the street where he called the police. Shortly thereafter a police officer in a marked vehicle traveling in the opposite direction spotted the stolen car with the two brothers and turned around to follow them. Upon observing the police vehicle behind them the two brothers stopped their vehicle, exited, and started firing at the police vehicle. The officer ducked behind his dashboard and threw his cruiser into reverse to get some distance. He also advised police radio that shots had been fired. The officer eventually stopped his vehicle, got out, used his driver's door for cover and concealment, and returned fire. A second officer who also responded to the scene came under fire with a bullet crashing through his windshield. The brothers then started throwing bombs at the officers. More officers arrived at the scene and more gunfire was exchanged. During the shooting episode Tamerlan's pistol malfunctioned whereupon he threw it at one of the officers, striking him in the arm. Tamerlan then started running toward the officer he had struck with the pistol but was tackled by the officer. He resisted violently. A second officer at the scene tried to handcuff Tamerlan but by then Dzhokar had gotten back in the stolen SUV and drove it straight at the two officers, who managed to roll out of its path. However, Tamerlan

who was in the path of the SUV was struck with such force that his body was pulled into the wheel well and dragged 25 ft. In the process the SUV had also slammed into the police cruiser. Tamerlan would subsequently die as a result of his injuries. Dzhokar sped away from the scene but additional shots were fired by the officers as he fled. He did manage to escape and abandoned the vehicle a short distance away from the shooting scene. He was discovered 16 hours later hiding in a small boat on private property at a single-family residential home. The discovery was made when the homeowner went out to his boat to check it and found Dzhokhar hiding under a tarp in his boat bleeding. The police were called and Dzhokhar was arrested.[51]

The autopsy of Tamerlan revealed that he not only sustained fatal injuries from being struck by the SUV but also had bullet wounds and injuries from the bombs he and his brother had thrown at the law enforcement officers.

On January 5, 2015 the trial for Dzhokhar started and on April 11, 2015 a jury found him guilty of all thirty charges that had been placed against him. On May 15, 2015 he was sentenced to death, and on January 15, 2016 he was ordered to pay $101,000 in restitution and his request for a new trial was denied.[52]

The Times Square Bomber

A second sensational case involving attempts to use IEDs in the United States in recent years occurred in May, 2010, on Broadway in New York City. At that time, an IED was left in a Nissan Pathfinder SUV right in the heart of downtown Manhattan. The device, which was found in the back seat, consisted of two red plastic five gallon gasoline containers, three canisters of propane gas, similar to those used for barbeque grills, fire crackers described as super grade M88s, sold legally in some states, and a 55-inch-long metal gun container weighing about 75 pounds, which contained eight bags of nonexplosive grade fertilizer. With the bags the locker weighed in excess of 200 pounds. There was also a wire from the battery powered fluorescent clock that

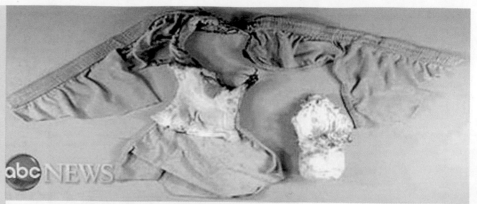

▶ **FIGURE 19-12**
Underwear bomber
The improvised explosive device concealed in the underwear of Omar Farouk Abdlumutallab involved the use of a syringe in a soft plastic container filled with pentaerythritol tetranitrate which is a highly volatile, colorless crystal which is hard to detect. The device was strapped to his legs by a substantial portion of the explosive and was more than likely in a syringe filled with nitroglycerin which was converted into an electrical detonator. The device was intended to blow a large hole in the side of the plane and cause immediate decompression thereby tearing the aircraft apart. (©ABC News/ Getty Images)

ran into the gun locker, where a metal pressure cooker pot contained many more M88s. The bomber planned to ignite the cans of gasoline which in turn would explode the propane tanks and then the fertilizer. (Apparently he was not aware the fertilizer he was using was a non-explosive grade fertilizer).

The presence of the vehicle was first noted by a vendor selling T-shirts nearby who noticed the vehicle at the curb with its engine running and its hazard lights on. The man saw smoke coming from the vehicle and immediately notified a nearby New York City mounted police officer. The bomb never did explode and upon examination was characterized by bomb experts as amateurish.

A suspect was arrested a couple of days later. His name was Faisal Shazad, he was 30 years old, had been born in Pakistan and became a naturalized American citizen in 2009. After being arrested, he confessed to having planted the bomb, and also to having received his bomb making training in Pakistan by the Taliban. In 2010, after pleading guilty to all charges against him, he was sentenced in federal district court in Manhattan to life in prison.

The Underwear Bomber

Certainly one of the more unusual improvised explosive devices used in the United States occurred in December, 2009. In this case the attempted use of an IED occurred on a Northwest Airlines flight that was approaching Detroit, Michigan. The terrorist in this case was a Nigerian national named Umar Farouk Abdlumutallab, a 22-year-old Nigerian national who had left behind a martyrdom statement in Arabic. It was believed that the attack was planned by the Yemen-based branch of Al-Qaida. This case, which was dubbed by the media as "the underwear bomber" involved the use of an improvised explosive device (Figure 19-12). The device involved the use of a syringe in a soft plastic container filled with PETN, which is a highly volatile, colorless crystal and is hard to detect if carried in the container. Part of the device was strapped to his legs but a substantial portion of the explosives

was more than likely in a syringe filled with nitroglycerin which was converted into an electrical detonator. The idea was to blow a large hole in the side of the plane and cause immediate decompression, thereby tearing the aircraft apart. For reasons which have not yet been determined, he did not attempt to ignite the device until they were approaching Detroit at a much lower altitude. Explosives experts believe there was almost certainly a failure between the primary and main charge of the IED, which meant the PETN did not fully detonate. Speculation by aviation specialists are that if the IED had gone off it would have likely not caused sufficient damage to bring the plane down and although badly damaged it would have been able to make it to the airport. The attempted use of the bomb was spotted by passengers who saw smoke emanating from the seat occupied by the terrorist, at which time he was overpowered.[53]

INVESTIGATING THE EXPLOSION SCENE

The objectives of the explosion scene investigation are no different from those for a regular fire investigation: to determine the origin, identify the fuel and ignition sources, determine the cause, and establish the responsibility for the incident. A systematic approach to the scene examination is just as important in an explosion investigation as in a fire investigation—or even more so—because explosion scenes are often larger and more disturbed than fire scenes. Without a preplanned, systematic approach, explosion investigations become more difficult or even impossible to conduct effectively.[54]

The first duty of the investigator is to secure the scene of the explosion. First responders to the explosion should establish and maintain physical control of the structure and surrounding areas. Unauthorized persons should be prevented from entering the scene or touching blast debris remote from the scene itself because the critical evidence from an explosion (whether accidental or criminal) may be very small and may be easily disturbed or moved by people passing through. Evidence is also easily picked up on shoes and tracked out. Properly securing the scene also tends to prevent additional injuries to unauthorized and/or curious persons who may attempt to enter an unsafe area. As a general rule, the outer perimeter of the incident scene should be established at one and a half times the distance of the farthest piece of debris found. Significant pieces of blast debris can be propelled great distances or into nearby buildings or vehicles, and these areas should be included in the scene perimeter. If additional pieces of debris are found, the scene perimeter should be widened.

The investigator should establish a scene pattern. Investigation team members should search the scene from the outer perimeter inward toward the area of greatest damage. The final determination of the location of the explosion's epicenter should be made only after the entire scene has been examined. The search pattern itself may be spiral, strip/line, grid, zone/quadrant, or pie/wheel. (See Chapter 3, "Investigators, the Investigative Process, and the Crime Scene," for a detailed description of these patterns.) Often the particular circumstances of the scene dictate the nature of the pattern. In any case, the assigned areas of the search pattern should overlap so that no evidence is at the edge of any search area.

It is often useful to search areas more than once. When this is done, a different searcher should be used on each search to help ensure that evidence is not overlooked. The number of actual searchers will depend on the physical size and complexity of the scene. The investigator in charge should keep in mind, however, that too many searchers can often be as counterproductive as too few. Searchers should be briefed as to the proper procedures for identifying, logging, photographing, marking, and mapping the location of evidence. The location of evidence may be marked with chalk marks, spray paint, flags, stakes, or other marking means. After being photographed, the evidence may be tagged, moved, and secured.

Structures that have suffered explosions are often more structurally damaged than those burned in a fire. The possibility that a floor, wall, ceiling, roof, or entire building will collapse is much greater and should always be considered. Explosion scenes that involve bombings or explosives have added dangers. Investigators should be on the lookout for additional devices and undetonated explosives. The modus operandi (MO) of some bomber-arsonists includes using secondary explosive devices specifically targeted for the law enforcement or fire service personnel who will be responding to the bombing incident.

LOCATING AND IDENTIFYING ARTICLES OF EVIDENCE

Investigators should locate, identify, note, log, photograph, and map any of the many and varied articles of physical evidence. Because of the propelling nature of explosions, the investigator should keep in mind that significant pieces of evidence may be found in a wide variety of locations, including outside the exploded structure, embedded in the walls or other structural members of the exploded structure, in nearby vegetation, inside adjacent structures or vehicles, or embedded in adjacent structures. In the case of bombing incidents or incidents involving the explosion of tanks, appliances, or equipment, significant pieces of evidence debris may have pierced the bodies of victims or be contained in their clothing.

The clothing of anyone injured in an explosion should be obtained for examination and possible analysis.[55] Larger, more massive missiles should be measured and weighed for comparison of the forces necessary to propel them.[56]

SUSPICIOUS PACKAGES AND LETTERS

Note that items do not have to be delivered by a carrier. Most bombers set and deliver the bombs themselves. The following are precautions that should be followed when encountering a suspicious package or letter:

- If delivered by carrier, inspect for lumps, bulges, or protrusions, without applying pressure.
- If delivered by carrier, do a balance-check to determine if package is lopsided or heavy-sided.
- If there is a handwritten address or label from a company, check to see if the company exists and if it sent the package or letter.[57]

Any of the following characteristics could denote a suspicious package or letter:

- Packages wrapped in string—modern packaging materials have eliminated the need for twine or string.
- Excess postage on small packages or letters, which indicates that the object was not weighed at a post office.
- Any foreign writing, address, or postage.
- Handwritten notes, such as "To Be Opened in the Privacy of . . . ," "Confidential," "Your Lucky Day Is Here," and "Prize Enclosed."
- Improper spelling of common names, places, or titles.
- Generic or incorrect titles.
- Leaks, stains, or protruding wires, string, tape, and so on.
- Hand delivery or a "drop-off for a friend."
- No return address or a nonsensical return address.
- Delivery before or after a phone call from an unknown person asking if the item was received[58] (Figure 19-13).

USE OF ROBOTIC DEVICES IN MOVING AND DESTROYING DANGEROUS OBJECTS

Because handling suspicious packages can be quite dangerous to law enforcement personnel, they have increasingly resorted to the use of robots to move and destroy such objects. The two photos shown depict dual-purpose robots. The first photo shows a robot designed to move potentially dangerous objects; the second depicts a robot engineered to detonate a suspicious object (Figures 19-14 and 19-15).

TERRORIST BOMB THREAT STAND-OFF

Law enforcement officers should be aware of what the bomb threat stand-off distances are in order to maximize the safety for both uninvolved citizens as well as themselves. Figure 19-16 provides a detailed description of these distances along with other relevant information.

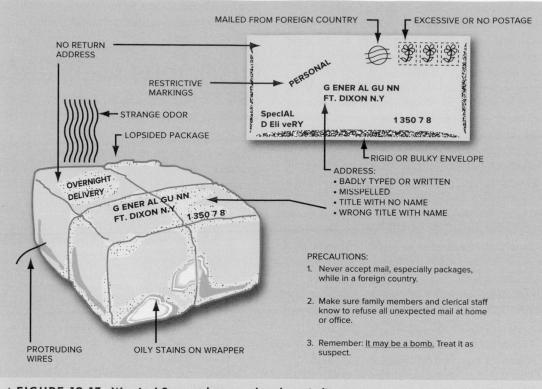

▲ FIGURE 19-13 Warning! Suspect letter and package indicators
(Source: U.S. Department of the Treasury, Bureau of Alcohol, Tobacco and Firearms)

► FIGURE 19-14
Robot for moving potentially dangerous objects
This photograph depicts a MAX A robot removing a potentially dangerous object. This model robot permits law enforcement personnel to safely remove a potentially dangerous device while minimizing danger to themselves and others who might be in the area.
(©David Duprey/AP Images)

◀FIGURE 19-15
A robot configured to destroy objects remotely.
This radio-controlled manipulator, also known as a "bomb robot," can get close to a dangerous object, inspect it, and destroy or diffuse it without a law enforcement officer having to risk his or her life. (©Morris Mac Matzen/Reuters/ Alamy)

◀FIGURE 19-16
Terrorist bomb threat stand-off
These two cards depict the terrorist bomb stand-off distances that can be used as a guide for law enforcement personnel. (Source: U.S. Government Bookstore, 2007)

Terrorist Bomb Threat Stand-Off

THREAT	THREAT DESCRIPTION	EXPLOSIVES CAPACITY[1] (TNT EQUIVALENT)	BUILDING EVACUATION DISTANCE[2]	OUTDOOR EVACUATION DISTANCE[3]
	PIPE BOMB	5 LBS/ 2.3 KG	70 FT/ 21 M	850 FT/ 259 M
	BRIEFCASE/ SUITCASE BOMB	50 LBS/ 23 KG	150 FT/ 46 M	1,850 FT/ 564 M
	COMPACT SEDAN	500 LBS/ 227 KG	320 FT/ 98 M	1,500 FT/ 457 M
	SEDAN	1,000 LBS/ 454 KG	400 FT/ 122 M	1,750 FT/ 534 M
	PASSENGER/ CARGO VAN	4,000 LBS/ 1,814 KG	640 FT/ 195 M	2,750 FT/ 838 M
	SMALL MOVING VAN/DELIVERY TRUCK	10,000 LBS/ 4,536 KG	860 FT/ 263 M	3,750 FT/ 1,143 M

This card supersedes any previous undated versions 11/99

THREAT	THREAT DESCRIPTION	EXPLOSIVES CAPACITY[1] (TNT EQUIVALENT)	BUILDING EVACUATION DISTANCE[2]	OUTDOOR EVACUATION DISTANCE[3]
	MOVING VAN/ WATER TRUCK	30,000 LBS/ 13,608 KG	1,240 FT/ 375M	6,500 FT/ 1,982 M
	SEMI-TRAILER	60,000 LBS/ 27,216 KG	1,570 FT/ 475 M	7,000 FT/ 2,134 M

All personnel must evacuate (both inside of buildings and out).

Building Evacuation Distance

Outdoor Evacuation Distance

Threat

All personnel must either seek shelter inside a building (with some risk) away from windows and exterior walls, or move beyond the Outdoor Evacuation Distance.

Preferred area (beyond this line) for evacuation of people in buildings and mandatory for people outdoors.

[1] Based on maximum volume or weight of explosive (TNT equivalent) that could reasonably fit in a suitcase or vehicle.
[2] Governed by the ability of an unstrengthened building to withstand severe damage or collapse.
[3] Governed by the greater of fragment throw distance or glass breakage/ falling glass hazard distance. Note that pipe and briefcase bombs assume cased charges which throw fragments farther than vehicle bombs.

CONNECTING THE BOMBING DOTS

The U.S. Bureau of Alcohol, Tobacco, Firearms, and Explosives (ATF) has been collecting, storing, and analyzing records on explosives and arson incidents since 1975. In 1996, the ATF Arson and Explosives National Repository Branch was established to satisfy a congressional mandate for the secretary of the treasury to establish a national repository of information on arson and explosives incidents.[59]

With the passage of the Homeland Security Act of 2002 and the movement of ATF to the Department of Justice (DOJ), U.S. attorney general John Ashcroft—in his August 2004 memorandum to the heads of the Federal Bureau of Investigation (FBI), ATF, and the Drug Enforcement Administration—delegated the collection of the information required by section 846(b) of the act to ATF. The attorney general states in his memorandum, "The Department's arson and explosives incident databases, including, but not limited to, the FBI's Automated Incident Reporting System and ATF's Bomb and Arson Tracking System, are to be combined into a single database.

The attorney general further said, "All consolidated arson and explosives incident databases shall be maintained by ATF and shall be accessible to all Department law enforcement components. No Department component may maintain any database that contains arson or explosives incident information that would otherwise be maintained in the consolidated database."[60]

Following the attorney general's direction to consolidate DOJ explosives databases, ATF changed the name of the Arson and Explosives National Repository Branch to the U.S. Bomb Data Center (USBDC). The name was chosen specifically so that any government entity–within or outside the United States–would recognize it as the one site in the United States for reporting incidents and for seeking information to prevent or investigate acts involving explosives.

The USBDC has since consolidated the information contained in the FBI's Automated Incident Reporting System into ATF's Bomb Arson Tracking System (BATS).

SHARING INTELLIGENCE GLOBALLY

Through the USBDC, ATF is a founding member of the International Bomb Data Center Working Group and serves as the group's secretary. A member of the USBDC also serves as a dedicated representative for the Americas.

The International Bomb Data Center Working Group is a collaborative body of bomb data centers and recognized government agencies focused on the efficient and effective sharing of technical intelligence on explosives as well as other information related to the lawful use of explosives. There are currently 32 member nations, with four other countries participating with observer status. According to protocols adopted by the group, the roles and functions of nations' international bomb data centers vary considerably. However, all members must be legitimate agencies responsible for the management of technical intelligence and information related to the unlawful use of explosives.

As the primary source for explosives-related intelligence and information in the United States, the USBDC will continue to work with both domestic and international law enforcement agencies to ensure the dissemination of information vital to combating violence and assisting in the fight against terrorism.[61,62]

KEY TERMS

accelerant
alligatoring
blast fragmentation
bomber's signature
burn indicators
charring
chemical explosion
effective fire temperatures
explosion

flame ionization detector
gas liquid chromatograph (GLC)
improvised explosive device
incendiary mechanism
infrared spectrophotometer
layer-checking technique
mechanical explosion
plant
Property Insurance Loss Register (PILR)

pyromaniacs
shaped charge
spalling
spontaneous heating
spontaneous ignition
trailer
ultraviolet fluorescence

REVIEW QUESTIONS

1. If arson is suspected, why should firefighters not alter the premises, such as by mopping up or overhauling the scene of the fire, especially at the point of origin?
2. What two factors are needed to cause a fire?
3. What is the layer-checking technique, and how can it assist in determining the cause and the origin of a fire?
4. What are some of the more common causes of accidental or natural fires?

5. What types of burn indications can be examined by the arson investigator to assist in determining whether a fire is accidental or incendiary in nature?

6. What are some of the most commonly used ignition and timing devices in the commission of arsons?

7. Why can items missing from the fire scene be as valuable as things remaining at the scene?

8. What are some of the most common motives for arson?

9. Why should uncoated metal paint cans (or similar containers), not plastic bags or containers, be used for the storage of material suspected of containing flammable liquids?

10. What are some of the advantages and disadvantages of olfactory detection in determining the presence of fire accelerants at the scene of a fire?

11. What types of individuals might be able to provide information relevant to the fire?

12. What is the purpose of the National Insurance Crime Bureau?

13. What are the two basic types of explosions? Briefly describe each.

14. What are the principal objectives of an explosion scene investigation?

15. What is the first duty of the investigator at the scene of an explosion?

16. What criteria should be employed in order to make a determination as to the types of containers that should be used for storage of evidence at the bomb scene?

17. What are the minimum details that should be placed on an evidence container?

18. Once the origin, or epicenter, of the explosion has been identified, the investigator should determine what type of fuel has been employed. How is this typically done?

19. What is the definition of an improvised explosive device (IED)?

20. What are the basic components of an improvised explosive device?

21. What kind of data is available within the ATF's US Bomb Data Center (USBDC)?

INTERNET ACTIVITIES

1. The Bureau of Alcohol, Tobacco and Firearms provides updates and statistics concerning arson and explosion incidents. Go to the bureau's website at *www.atf.gov*. Search the site for information on fire and explosion incidents for your state. The website also has information about arson and explosion training for police officers. What topics are covered in the training curriculum?

2. Many large police agencies and/or states have investigative units specializing in arson and bomb detection. Check several municipal and state police agencies in your region by using websites such as *www.officer.com* and *www.leolinks.com*. What are the functions and the responsibilities of these units? Under what conditions do they respond (arson investigation, bomb threats, and so on)? Are any statistics provided concerning the number of cases they have responded to and/or investigated?

► *Joaquin "El Chapo" Guzman* is one of the most notorious Mexican cartel leaders in the world today. According to some DEA reports, El Chapo (the head of the notorious Sinaloa Cartel) was responsible for the death of millions of people across the globe through drug addiction, violence, and corruption. On January 8, 2016, he was re-captured in Mexico after multiple escapes from Mexican prisons and was extradited to the United States to stand trial for organized crime and racketeering, drug trafficking, and murder.

(©Charles Reed/U.S. Immigration and Customs Enforcement/Getty Images)

20

RECOGNITION, CONTROL, AND INVESTIGATION OF DRUG ABUSE

CHAPTER OBJECTIVES

1. Identify and describe several opium-derived drugs.

2. List and describe synthetic narcotics.

3. Identify and distinguish among stimulants, depressants, and hallucinogens.

4. Outline techniques used in investigating dangerous drugs and narcotics.

5. Assess the motives, methods, and management of drug informants.

6. Describe several sources of information for undercover officers conducting drug investigations.

7. Identify and describe the four major categories of drug-buy operations.

8. Discuss the legal exceptions to a search warrant.

9. Describe the process of identifying and conducting raids on clandestine labs.

10. Discuss drug evidence handling and potential security problems.

11. Articulate the paradigm shift related to drug enforcement in the United States.

Currently, every major police department in the United States has assigned—with ample justification—a top priority to the control of drug abuse and related offenses. Most of the departments have narcotics or drug units that specialize in the identification, arrest, and prosecution of drug traffickers, ranging from low-level street dealers to leaders of organized-crime syndicates. As a result, most police agencies have allocated significant resources for narcotics officers, undercover agents, drug surveillance and recovery equipment, and agreements with drug informants. The illegal importation, manufacture, sale, and use of drugs, however, have increased more rapidly than the resources for combating them.

Explanations for the phenomenal growth of drug abuse abound in the literature on this subject. Many cite variables associated with socioeconomic and political conditions. Others suggest that the inability of some individuals to deal with personal stress and emotional problems has led to the increase in drug abuse. Regardless of the contributing factors, police must deal with the violation itself, not the motivations and human conditions that produce it.

This chapter focuses on the categories of drugs that are most commonly encountered by law enforcement officers in their enforcement activities: opium-derived drugs, synthetic narcotics, stimulants, depressants, and hallucinogens. The procedures involved in narcotics investigations are also addressed. Most of the techniques used in investigating dangerous drug and narcotics cases are the same as those used in investigating other cases. The identification of the source of the drug and the risk factors in apprehending a drug suspect, however, make investigations of these cases unique.

Another aspect of drug and narcotics cases that makes the investigation process atypical is the use of drug informants. Drug informants can provide valuable information on various types of drug activity, but compared with informants used in other investigations, they are perhaps the most difficult to manage. Drug informants have different motivations for helping the police, such as fear of punishment for criminal acts, revenge against their enemies, money, repentance, or altruism. Regardless of the motivation, informants who have entered into agreements with police agencies should initially be screened carefully and then, subsequently, be monitored. The chapter concludes with discussions on clandestine laboratories, search warrants, evidence handling, and gangs and drugs.

DRUGS AND SCHEDULING

Officers and agents charged with investigation and interdiction of illegal drug activities are responsible for a vast array of information in order to properly carry out their duties. Although many facts about drugs never change, synthetic drugs provide opportunities for new formulations, higher potency, and more difficult identification by law enforcement. Further complicating the jobs of drug investigators is the fact that the flow of illegal drugs is constantly changing and adapting in response to law enforcement practices, socioeconomic circumstances, market conditions, and availability of product. Therefore, those involved in drug interdiction must stay on top of current information regarding source countries and the types of drugs that may be encountered in the field by law enforcement officers. Frequent updates are available from federal agencies, such as the National Drug Intelligence Center, which publishes drug identification guides with updated photographs and new information.[1] Before undertaking any drug investigation, investigators should also familiarize themselves with the street slang. Commonly used terms often change over time and are different in different parts of the country. Up-to-date information about drug trafficking trends and common or emerging drugs is essential to the credibility of those working with informants or undercover. This type

of information also helps law enforcement agencies target and prioritize investigations.

Title II of the Comprehensive Drug Abuse Prevention and Control Act of 1970, also known as the Controlled Substances Act (CSA), consolidated a number of laws related to the manufacture and sale of drugs. **Narcotics,** stimulants, depressants, hallucinogens, steroids, and chemicals that could be used in the illicit production of those drugs were classified by federal law as belonging to one of five schedules (Figure 20-1).

OPIATES

Several drugs are derived from the opium poppy (*Papaver somniferum*). Known as **opiates,** they include opium, morphine, heroin, codeine, and other drugs less well known.

OPIUM

One of the first drugs of abuse was **opium.** Its pleasurable effects were known to many ancient civilizations, including the Egyptians, as early as 1500 B.C.E. During the Renaissance in Europe, opium was employed in the treatment of hysteria, making it one of the early therapeutic agents in treating mental disorders.

In the seventeenth century, opium smoking spread throughout China, and opium dependence was recognized as a problem. Opium eating was known in the United States and England during the Revolutionary War. Opium was later used by eighteenth-century doctors to treat venereal disease, cancer, gallstones, and diarrhea and to relieve pain at childbirth.

Opium comes from the poppy plant, whose pod is carefully cut to allow a milky white fluid to ooze onto the surface of the pod. Thereafter, it air-dries into tan beads. It is then carefully scraped by hand and allowed to further air-dry, after which it turns a blackish brown color. Raw opium has a pungent odor and may be smoked, making the user appear sleepy and relaxed. Prolonged use creates both physical and psychological dependence. Raw opium is the source of morphine, heroin, and codeine (Figure 20-2).

MORPHINE

Morphine is obtained from raw opium; 10 pounds of raw opium yield 1 pound of morphine. A German named Sertner first isolated the substance in 1804 and a few years later named it "morphine" after the Greek god of sleep, Morpheus. The drug was later used in medicine in 1825 as a painkiller and is still used as such today. Morphine is one of the most effective pain relievers known to man.[2]

The use of morphine increased considerably with the invention of the hypodermic syringe by an Englishman around 1843. The syringe was introduced to this country about 1853 and was used extensively for wounded Union troops during the American Civil War. Some developed physical and psychological dependence, because doctors did not clearly understand the addictive nature of opiates until around 1870.

Schedule I

a. The drug or other substance has a high potential for abuse.

b. The drug or other substance has no currently accepted medical use in treatment in the United States.

c. There is a lack of accepted safety for use of the drug or other substance under medical supervision.

Examples: Heroin, LSD, marijuana.

Schedule II

a. The drug or other substance has a high potential for abuse.

b. The drug or other substance has a currently accepted medical use in treatment in the United States or a currently accepted medical use with severe restrictions.

c. Abuse of the drug or other substances may lead to severe psychological or physical dependence.

Examples: Morphine, cocaine, methadone.

Schedule III

a. The drug or other substance has a potential for abuse less than the drugs or other substances in schedules I and II.

b. The drug or other substance has a currently accepted medical use in treatment in the United States.

c. Abuse of the drug or other substance may lead to moderate or low physical dependence or high psychological dependence.

Examples: Anabolic steroids, ketamine, OxyContin.

Schedule IV

a. The drug or other substance has a low potential for abuse relative to the drugs or other substances in schedule III.

b. The drug or other substance has a currently accepted medical use in treatment in the United States.

c. Abuse of the drug or other substance may lead to limited physical dependence or psychological dependence relative to the drugs or other substances in schedule III.

Examples: Valium, Xanax.

Schedule V

a. The drug or other substance has a low potential for abuse relative to the drugs or other substances in schedule IV.

b. The drug or other substance has a currently accepted medical use in treatment in the United States.

c. Abuse of the drug or other substance may lead to limited physical dependence or psychological dependence relative to the drugs or other substances in schedule IV.

Example: Cough medicine with codeine, such as Robitussin AC.

◀ **FIGURE 20-1**
Federal schedule of controlled substance
Source: 21 United States Code, Section 812

◀ **FIGURE 20-2 Traditional method of gathering opium**
Historically, one of the first drugs to be abused was opium. Opium comes from the poppy plant. The poppy pod is cut to allow the milky, white fluid to come to the surface of the pod. After it is dried, it is hand scraped and allowed to be further air-dried after which it turns a blackish brown color. (©Adam Butler/AP Images)

Morphine appears in tablet, capsule, and liquid forms, has no distinguishing color and provides the medical standards by which other narcotics are evaluated. It is usually administered by injection. The drug creates both physical and psychological dependence in the user, who feels euphoric and seems sleepy or relaxed. The pupils of the eyes may constrict.[3]

HEROIN (DIACETYLMORPHINE)

Heroin was developed in England in 1874, but it evoked little interest until about 1890, when it was found to be considerably stronger than morphine. Commercial production of heroin was begun in 1898 in Germany by the Bayer Company. Heroin was advertised as a cure for morphine dependence, but it was soon learned that heroin dependence was even more difficult to cure.

Heroin is an odorless, crystalline, white powder. It is usually sold in glassine paper packets, aluminum foil, or capsules. The darker the color, the more impurities it contains. Being about four to five times stronger than morphine, heroin is the principal drug of addiction among the opium derivatives. It is generally injected.

Heroin purity has evolved significantly over the past decade. At one point (in the 1960s), heroin that was 5% to 20% "pure" was common; today, much of it is around 80% pure due to increased supply and falling prices. The more pure product of heroin means increased levels of overdose.[4] Deaths from overdoses are not uncommon and ordinarily occur because a dose was more pure than that to which the addict's body was accustomed. Addicts may also have a fatal allergic reaction to the drug or some substance used to "cut," or reduce, the purity level of the drug, such as powdered milk, sugar, or quinine. Such incidents have routinely been documented at emergency rooms, since hundreds of juveniles and young adults from around the country have been admitted for heroin overdoses and allergic reactions to the "cut" placed in snorted heroin, known as **chiva**.[5] Spanish for heroin, chiva (goat) hit the streets across America in the late 1990s, originating primarily from Colombia. It has a very high concentration level made from clandestine laboratories that normally process cocaine. In addition, the powders are cut with various substances, from ground-up metal, crushed wood, sand, and cyanide to strong nasal constrictors and/or stimulants such as ephedrine and caffeine. Allergic reactions to the "cut substances" have been attributed to hundreds of deaths, as well as to the exceptionally strong concentration of heroin causing accidental overdose. The numbers continue to rise as chiva use escalates along with a spike in smoking black tar heroin (Figure 20-3) derived from chiva processing.[6] The fatal overdose is not always accidental. On occasion, addicts suspected of being police informers have been given "hot shots"—pure heroin—to eliminate them.

In addition to facing the perils of the law, withdrawal, and other aspects of addiction, the drug addict also faces the serious health problems associated with dirty needles. Many suffer STDs (sexually transmitted diseases) and hepatitis B. These are

▲ **FIGURE 20-3** **Powder and black tar heroin**
On the street, heroin is most commonly observed in the powder form, ranging in color from dark brown to white, depending on cultivation location and the level of impurities in the sample. Black tar heroin is named for its characteristic dark color and sticky touch. It is often snorted, smoked, or ingested rather than taken through intravenous injection. Smugglers often transport heroin in concentrated amounts that are "stepped-on" or diluted before individual sales.
(©ermingut/Getty Images RF)

transmitted diseases, so people sharing needles with other drug abusers run the risk of injecting themselves with traces of blood from a disease carrier and thus becoming infected. Drug users who administer their drugs through intravenous injections and share their needles with others face the additional danger of contracting the human immunodeficiency virus (HIV) and potentially developing acquired immune deficiency syndrome (AIDS).[7]

Colombia remains a major source of heroin to the United States, with much of its output supplying heroin markets in large East and Southeast Coast cities (New York City, NY; Baltimore, MD; Newark, NJ: Boston, MA; Philadelphia, PA; Washington, D.C.; Atlanta, GA; Tampa and Miami, FL; New Orleans, LA; and Houston, TX) within the U.S. Colombian heroin is usually a light brown or tan powder. The poppies are being grown in the mountains of the Cauca Province around Popayan. It is anticipated that within the next several years Colombia will become an even more important source of heroin in the United States, because existing organized crime cartels in Colombia have well-established routes developed from years of cocaine smuggling. The high-purity concentration of new heroin derivatives (chiva and black tar) from Colombia is a significant factor in recent heroin overdoses.[8] In Latin America, Mexico is also a chief exporter of heroin. Elsewhere in the world, Southeast Asia (mostly Myanmar) is a major supplier. However, Afghanistan sets the standard worldwide for heroin exportation. The country is responsible for a staggering 90% of the world's heroin production.[9]

Further, with the war in Afghanistan and its related political instability, significant exportation of heroin from the historical "Golden Crescent" area (Iran, Pakistan, and Afghanistan) is on the rise. For years under the Taliban rule in Afghanistan, opium poppy growing and production were severely limited. The offense was punishable by death, often accompanied by the confiscation of private property and land. The rule was often ruthlessly enforced by the Taliban government. Since the U.S. invasion into Afghanistan (in 2002) forcing the ouster of the Taliban government, opium poppy cultivation is again thriving.[10] Unfortunately, continued unrest and revolution are often ripe conditions for drug, gun, and human smuggling. These have been particularly interesting subjects with a strong financial nexus to terrorism. In Chapter 21 (Terrorism), we discuss the financing of terrorism from such sources.

"CHEESE" HEROIN

In the past few years the Dallas, Texas, Police Department has raised the alarm about a new and dangerous combination of drugs. Called **"cheese" heroin,** it is a combination of heroin, approximately 8% (sometimes black heroin), and a large quantity of crushed Tylenol-PM® tablets. Teens have named the drug *cheese* because of its yellowish color (it is really tannish in color). It generally comes in powder form and is administered by snorting through the nose through a tube much in the same way that cocaine is often used (discussed later in this chapter). It costs approximately $2 per dose, turning the hardest of narcotics into a "gateway drug" for teenagers. The potency of the drug makes addiction imminent for its young users, and combined with its low price, cheese has quickly become a particularly worrisome substance for authorities and parents alike. Withdrawal symptoms often begin within six hours of use, and include:

- Bloodshot eyes;
- Runny/bloody nose;
- Unexplainable cough;
- Sleeping a lot;
- Changes in behavior;
- Disorientation;
- Lethargy;
- Hunger;
- Severe headaches;
- Chills;
- Abdominal pain;
- Muscle pain and anxiety so severe the user may return to using the drug regularly within one to three days.

Furthermore, the drug contains what can be a toxic level of acetaminophen. Acetaminophen overdoses can lead to liver damage or failure. However, the relative ease of overdose due to the purity of the heroin involved is the most likely cause of death or serious injury by this drug. Nearly 40 deaths in the Dallas area alone have been attributed to the drug since 2010, and police in places like New York City are beginning to see the effects of the drug, dubbed "starter heroin."[11] Most of the victims of fatal cheese overdoses died in their sleep after a night of partying and were found by their family members.

"EL DIABLITO" HEROIN

One of the newest iterations of heroin is "el diablito," or "little devil," a heroin product that is laced with fentanyl. **Fentanyl** is a powerful synthetic opioid, 30 times more powerful than heroin itself, and 100 times more potent than morphine. The result of a heroin/fentanyl mix is a powerful high—and an increased potential for overdose. In 2015, the DEA issued an urgent alert to law enforcement as a number of deaths related to this drug cocktail began to cluster; 28 people in Philadelphia died, while there were at least 50 deaths in Pennsylvania, Maryland, and Michigan.[12] Like many other heroin mixtures, ingestion can be taken intravenously, inhaled or swallowed; the preferred method with "el diablito" is intravenously by needle. Users frequently are unaware that they are ingesting a dose of heroin with the additive, and fatal overdoses can occur with even miniscule doses, resulting in thousands of deaths per year.[13]

CODEINE

The alkaloid **codeine** is found in raw opium in concentrations from 0.7% to 2.5%. It was first isolated in 1832 as an impurity in a batch of morphine. Compared to morphine, codeine produces less analgesia, sedation, and respiratory depression. It is widely distributed in products of two general types. Codeine to relieve moderate pain may consist of tablets or be combined with other products such as aspirin; liquid codeine preparations for the relief of coughs (antitussives) include Robitussin AC, Cheracol, and terpin hydrate with codeine. Codeine is also manufactured in injectable form for pain relief.

Codeine is also a major ingredient in a popular concoction known by several different monikers, including **"drank,"** "purple drank," "Texas tea," "syrup," or "lean." Originating from the hip-hop scene in Houston, Texas, the drink is a mixture of soda such as Sprite or Big Red, pieces of Jolly Rancher candy, and prescription cough medicine containing codeine and promethazine. Promethazine is an antihistamine, which is actually added to deter abuse of the codeine element of the drug by causing extreme weakness and sleepiness in large quantities. However, in the smaller quantities used for drank, it actually enhances the opiate effect. The result is a feeling of euphoria characterized by slow movement and motor skill impairment that causes the user to lean to one side.

The drink has been celebrated in rap culture, particularly by DJ Screw of Houston who died of a codeine overdose in 2000 and by popular artists Three 6 Mafia and Lil' Wayne. Drank is a fairly expensive cocktail, costing $40 to $80 an ounce, but is relatively easy to obtain across the Southern United States, especially in Texas and Florida.[14]

BOX 20-1 | POLICE USING NALOXONE (NARCAN) TO SAVE VICTIMS OF HEROIN OVERDOSE

Though we typically think of the interaction between drug users and police as one based in enforcement, law enforcement officials are increasingly being called to intervene medically in overdose situations.

Naloxone, or Narcan, is an antidote countering the effects of opium-based narcotics, like heroin. It is used in emergency situations to revive victims of overdose. The drug blocks or reverses the effects of opioid medication, including drowsiness, depressed respiration, or loss of consciousness. Typically, paramedics or emergency room physicians administer the drug through an intramuscular injection, IV, or a nasal spray. The drug works quickly, and is highly successful at reviving patients in early stages of overdose.

Recently, there has been a push to equip law enforcement officers with the nasal spray version of the drug, in order to provide timely intervention in the case of an overdose, particularly given the national increase in heroin overdoses and the increased presence of fentanyl in heroin. Currently, there are 971 law enforcement agencies in the United States that encourage their officers to carry naloxone—and in 2014, the Office of National Drug Control Policy issued a statement encouraging police departments to participate in naloxone administration programs in order to save lives.[15]

Though this sounds like a win-win from a public health perspective, it does carry some risks. Police officers are not medical professionals, and there a number of conditions that mimic opioid overdoses. For example, paramedics and physicians will evaluate a patient for possible hypotension, hyperglycemia, and even trauma before administering the drug; police officers are not trained to do so. Further, there is little clinical evidence that police administration of the drug changes the patient outcome.

Ultimately, the program is well-intentioned and, anecdotally anyway, is credited with saving lives, particularly juvenile victims of overdose. As long as heroin continues to kill via overdose, police officers will likely aid in addressing this issue outside of traditional law enforcement parameters.

(Courtesy of The Wakefield Police Department)

OXYCONTIN

Another powerful narcotic that is presently sold legally is **OxyContin.** This drug, which is usually prescribed for cancer patients, has pushed aside marijuana, cocaine, and other narcotics as the drug of choice for addicts and teenage abusers. The active ingredient in OxyContin is a morphinelike substance called oxycodone, which is also found in the prescription drugs Percodan and Tylox. But unlike those drugs, which need to be taken in repeated dosages, OxyContin is a time-released formulation that is effective for up to 12 hours. Experts say, however, that addicts can achieve an intensely pure high by crushing the pills and snorting or injecting them. A telltale piece of paraphernalia among adolescent users is a pill crusher, sold by drugstores to help elderly people swallow their medication.[16]

With the abuse of OxyContin on the rise, police in at least three states are reporting a record number of pharmacies being broken into. The homes of people with legitimate OxyContin prescriptions are being robbed, and home invasions are targeting the pills. These patients are often tracked down by relatives who know what is inside their medicine cabinets or by neighbors who hear them talk about their prescriptions. Illegal users are even accosting drugstore customers in parking lots on the hunch that they might be carrying this sought-after drug.[17]

In an effort to deal with this growing problem, the manufacturer of OxyContin has developed a tamper-proof pill containing a newly designed polymer.[18] This polymer makes the pill extremely difficult to crush for the purposes of snorting and injecting the drug, and when pill fragments are heated, it turns into a gel-like substance. Though the FDA has stated that the benefits of this "tamper proof" pill are limited, the new pill does offer a level of difficulty to the misuse of OxyContin that the FDA calls "advantageous" (Figure 20-4).

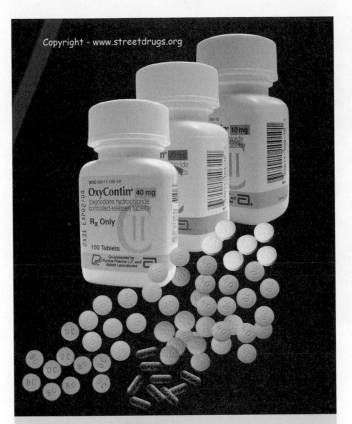

▲ FIGURE 20-4   OxyContin

OxyContin is a powerful narcotic that is sold legally. This drug is usually prescribed for cancer patients. There is some evidence that it is more popular among addicts and teenagers than is marijuana and cocaine. Addicts can achieve an intensely pure high by crushing the pills and snorting or injecting them. OxyContin is often the target sought in pharmacy burglaries.

(©streetdrugs.org)

QUICK FACTS

The Politics of Painkillers

A 2015 study found that the drug makers that produce opioid painkillers (like OxyContin, Fentanyl, and Vicodin), spent more than $880 million on campaign contributions and lobbying efforts nationally to promote the "aggressive prescription" of these drugs by doctors between 2006 and 2015. These efforts were in spite of the fact that these types of powerful painkillers claimed the lives of over 165,000 people in the United States due to abuse and overdose during the same time. To put this into perspective, the opioid lobby spent *eight times more than the gun lobby* during this timeframe, contributing to over 7,100 candidate races with an army of over 1,350 lobbyists.

Source: Feoff Mulviihill, Liz Essley Whyte and Ben Wieder, "Drug Makers Fought State Opioid Limits Amid Crisis," Associated Press and Center for Public Integrity, September 18, 2016. See: http:// bigstory.ap.org/article/4d69f4b41cbc475ca42f424524003d21 /drugmakers-fought-state-opioid-limits-amid-crisis

---

OTHER OPIUM DERIVATIVES

Other opium derivatives abused and stolen from pharmacies, hospitals, and physicians are Dilaudid, Papaverine, and Pantopon.

OPIATE OVERDOSES

The importation of heroin is of particular interest to lawmakers and law enforcement as a resurgence in heroin use among suburban teenagers has recently come about. South American drug lords strategically market the drug to a younger audience by stamping packets of the drug with recognizable and popular "brands" such as Prada and Chevrolet and have even used pop culture references to promote their product and create a foothold in the teenage marketplace. Small bags of the drug sell for as little as $5, making the drug easily accessible for high schoolers and middle schoolers. The Drug Enforcement Agency reports that overdoses, common with the potent varieties of the drug, are on the rise (Figure 20-5). Charlotte, NC, for example, has experienced a five-fold increase in deaths from heroin overdoses as part of this new wave of popularity.[19] A significant rise in opiate overdoses has also been reported in Boston, New York, Miami, San Francisco, and Los Angeles. In fact, with the exception of alcohol, heroin and other opiates account for the largest portion of drug-related hospital admissions; they average approximately 300,000 per year.[20]

Victims of opiate overdose are often young, averaging 18–22 years of age and exhibiting specific characteristics such as a "foam cone," tinged orange or red with blood, around their nostrils and mouth. Heroin and other opiates are powerful central nervous system depressants that essentially slow the body's ability to pump blood and breathe. Fluid often gathers within the lungs and the victim expels this pulmonary fluid with blood causing the "foam cone."[21] Other signs of an opiate overdose may include the common bluish tint from lack of oxygen and resulting swelling in the extremities, particularly in the lips, tongue, arms, and hands. Pupils may be constricted to a pinpoint, and many heroin users inject the substance into their veins. Look for bruising and varicose veins in the arms, the result of damaged and leaking blood vessels. Some users try to hide such use and inject in the legs, eyelids, rectal area, penis or vaginal areas, and in between their toes. Others also attempt to mask their needle marks by injecting into a tattoo. Although only medical personnel (or an autopsy in the case of death) can determine the problem, investigators can use these outward signs to initially determine an opiate overdose.[22]

SYNTHETIC NARCOTICS

Synthetic narcotics, though chemically related to the opium alkaloids, are produced entirely within the laboratory. A continuing search for a drug that kills pain but does not create tolerance and dependence has yet to yield a drug that is not susceptible to abuse.

▶ **FIGURE 20-5**
Opiate-related overdose deaths continue to climb
In 2014, the Drug Enforcement Agency (DEA) estimated that over 10,500 Americans died from heroin-related overdoses. This number represents three times the number of such deaths in 2010.
(©Reed Kaestner/Corbis/Getty Images RF)

MEPERIDINE (DEMEROL)

The commercial name for **meperidine** is Demerol, and it was the first synthetic narcotic. Next to morphine, it is probably the most widely used drug for the relief of intense pain. It is available in pure form and in combination products. The drug is administered by mouth or by injection; the latter is the more common method of abuse.[23]

METHADONE

Methadone is known by the commercial names Dolophine Hydrochloride and Methadone HCl Diskets. A heroin-dependent person can be treated with doses of methadone as a replacement for heroin. Methadone is manufactured in a solid form and administered orally. It's considered a "maintenance drug" and is used to maintain a heroin addict at a stable level of opiate use, protecting the addict from the incidental dangers of heroin use.

The beneficial properties of methadone are that it is longer acting than most opiates and addicts do not build up tolerance as fast as with heroin. Also, oral administration is less potentially hazardous than injection, since it significantly reduces the addict's risk for diseases such as hepatitis B, hepatitis C, and AIDS. On average, it takes about three weeks on methadone before a heroin addict completes the withdrawal stage and moves to the maintenance stage. However, it must be noted that the simultaneous use of methadone and heroin do not totally negate the physiological effect of the heroin on the user.

There is considerable controversy over the adoption of methadone maintenance programs. Critics argue that drug dependence is not cured. Proponents argue that it presents a cheaper way of supporting drug dependence and gets abusers out of crime and back to a conventional life. Proponents recognize that the programs need to include appropriate psychiatric help for overcoming the psychological dependence.[24]

STIMULANTS

Drugs falling into the **stimulants** group directly stimulate the central nervous system, producing excitation, alertness, wakefulness, and, in some cases, a temporary rise in blood pressure and respiration rate. The major stimulants abused are cocaine, amphetamines, phenmetrazine, and methylphenidate. The effects of an overdose are agitation, an increase in body temperature, hallucinations, convulsions, and possibly death. The withdrawal symptoms are apathy, long periods of sleep, irritability, depression, and disorientation.[25]

COCAINE

Cocaine is a naturally occurring stimulant that is extracted from the leaves of the coca plant (*Erythroxylon coca*). The leaves of this western South American shrub have been chewed by Colombian, Bolivian, and Peruvian Indians since antiquity for religious, medicinal, and other reasons. Allegedly, the chewing of coca leaves has enabled the Indians to work in high altitudes and on inadequate diets. The chewing of the coca leaf, which continues to the present day, should not be confused with the use of the extracted drug, cocaine. Coca leaves contain only about 0.5%–1% cocaine; the cocaine contained within them is released more slowly, and the route of administration (oral) is different from that in most cocaine use[26] (Figure 20-6).

Because reports of native coca use generated considerable interest in Europe, efforts were made in the nineteenth century to isolate the purified psychoactive ingredient in coca leaves. When success was achieved in the 1880s, cocaine's potential value as a tonic, its general stimulant properties, its possible value for specific ailments, and its local anesthetic properties were explored. Its use as an anesthetic was particularly important because it could be used in eye surgery, for which no

▲ FIGURE 20-6 Cocaine powder and leaves
Leaves from the coca plant grown in South America are
harvested and dried. The leaves are crumbled and mixed with
high distillant chemicals that extract the cocaine from the plant
material. The liquid chemicals are then evaporated causing
the cocaine alkaloid to form into chunks or rocks. Cocaine is
usually shipped in pressed kilo (2.2-pound) bricks of highly
concentrated material. (©streetdrugs.org)

previous drug had been suitable. Cocaine also constricted
blood vessels and limited bleeding in an anesthetized area.
This property made it valuable for surgery of the nose and
throat, areas that are richly supplied with blood. Although
many of cocaine's uses as a therapeutic drug have been abandoned, it continues to be used as a local anesthetic.[27]

Illicit cocaine is sold as a white, translucent, crystalline powder, frequently adulterated to about half its volume. The most
common adulterants are sugars (especially lactose and glucose)
and local anesthetics (Lidocaine, Procaine, and Tetracaine)
similar in appearance and taste to cocaine. Amphetamines,
other drugs with stimulant properties, are also used. Given the
high cost of cocaine, the temptation to adulterate at each level
of sale is great. The combination of high price and the exotic
properties attributed to it have contributed to cocaine's street
reputation as the status drug.

Cocaine is most commonly inhaled, or snorted, through the
nose. It is deposited on the mucous linings of the nose, from
which it is readily absorbed into the bloodstream. Repeated use
often results in irritation to the nostrils and nasal mucous
membranes. Symptoms may resemble those of a common cold—
that is, congestion or a runny nose. Users therefore often resort
to cold remedies, such as nasal sprays, to relieve their chronic
nasal congestion. They may be unable to breathe comfortably
without habitually using a spray.

A less common route of administration for cocaine is intravenous injection. The solution injected may be cocaine or a combination of heroin and cocaine. This route of administration
carries the dangers of any intravenous use. Furthermore, intravenous injection introduces unknown quantities of cocaine or
cocaine and heroin directly and suddenly into the bloodstream,
leaving body organs wholly unprotected from the toxic effects
of the drug. Cocaine deaths from intravenous injection are more
numerous than from snorting, despite the greater prevalence of
the latter method.

Freebasing

The practice of freebasing cocaine involves the dissolving of
cocaine in a base solution, usually distilled water and calcium
carbonate or lactose. The mixture is then shaken so that cocaine
is dissolved completely. Several drops of ether are then added,
and the mixture is shaken again. The cocaine is attracted to the
ether, while the other additives are attracted to the base solution.

The ether-cocaine solution separates from the base (like oil
and water), with the ether rising to the surface. An eyedropper
is commonly used to suction off the ether-cocaine solution,
which is then placed on an evaporating dish or crucible and
allowed to evaporate naturally. This process can be accelerated
by the use of a flame; however, this practice is extremely dangerous, because the ether is highly flammable.

The cocaine crystals are then scraped off the dish with a
metal spatula, placed in a glass pipe or bong (water pipe),
and smoked. The resultant high is alleged to be greater than
that from simple snorting, although users remark that injection of the drug provides a more intense high than does freebasing.

The pleasant effects of freebasing begin to decrease in duration as usage increases, and users display changes in moods and irritability if a high cannot be maintained. As freebasing usage becomes chronic, a person can experience the same symptoms as a chronic nonfreebasing abuser of cocaine.

Crack or Rock Cocaine

A relatively inexpensive form of cocaine called **crack (rock) cocaine** has grown tremendously in popularity among cocaine users (Figure 20-7). The drug is made by mixing ordinary cocaine with baking soda and water and then heating the solution in a pot. The material, which is somewhat purer and more concentrated than regular cocaine, is dried and broken into tiny chunks that dealers sell as crack rocks. These little pellets are usually smoked in glass pipes and are frequently sold in tiny plastic vials. Rock cocaine is 5–10 times more potent than powdered cocaine; the high lasts about 5 minutes and leaves the user wanting more. According to mental health specialists, crack users are more likely to show serious psychiatric consequences, including intense paranoia, extreme depression, and often suicidal and even violent behavior. Part of the attraction to the dealer is the enormous profit that can be made by the sale of crack. For example, in Los Angeles an ounce of cocaine can sell for $1,000–$1,500. Since each ounce contains 28 grams, and each gram can produce up to

▲ FIGURE 20-7 Crack or rock cocaine
Crack, the smokable form of cocaine, provides an immediate "rush." This form of cocaine is relatively inexpensive and very popular among cocaine users. The drug is made primarily by mixing ordinary cocaine with baking powder and water and then heating the solution in a pot. The resulting crack rocks are purer and more concentrated than regular cocaine.
(©streetdrugs.org)

six rocks selling for $25 each, the dealer can realize a profit of around $2,700.

AMPHETAMINES

Amphetamine, dextroamphetamine, and methamphetamine are so closely related chemically that they can be differentiated from one another only in the laboratory. These compounds resemble the natural body hormones of epinephrine and norepinephrine. As a result of this similarity, they can act directly, by mimicking the natural hormones in their effects on nerve endings, and/or indirectly, by causing increased release of the natural hormones. In either case, the **amphetamines** stimulate certain areas of the nervous system that control blood pressure, heart rate, and respiratory and metabolic rates, all of which are increased. Appetite is markedly decreased, and the senses are hyperalert. The body is in a general state of stress, as if it were extremely threatened or expecting a violent fight. This group of drugs artificially intensifies and prolongs such stimulation, keeping the body in a state of tension for prolonged periods of time.[28] Many different classes of people employ amphetamines in abusive quantities, including middle-aged businesspeople, housewives, students, athletes, and truck drivers. Government studies indicate that young people are the greatest abusers. Drivers take them to stay awake on long trips; students take them while cramming for exams; and athletes take them for extra energy and stamina.[29] When the drug is prescribed, the dose frequently ranges between 2.5 and 15 milligrams per day. Abusers have been known to inject as much as 1,000 milligrams every 2–3 hours. Medical use of amphetamines is now limited to control of narcolepsy, appetite control, and control of hyperactivity in children.

PHENMETRAZINE (PRELUDIN), METHYLPHENIDATE (RITALIN), AND PEMOLINE (CYLERT)

Phenmetrazine is related chemically to the amphetamines, and its abuse produces similar effects. Like phenmetrazine, methylphenidate (Ritalin) is related chemically to amphetamines. It is prescribed for treatment of mild depression in adults and attention deficit disorder in children. Pemoline, like amphetamines, is a stimulant. These stimulants were developed and approved for marketing as a drug to be used in the treatment of hyperactive children.

CRYSTALLIZED METHAMPHETAMINE

Crystallized methamphetamine, better known as *crystal meth* and *speed* during the 1960s and 1970s, was originally taken as pills or injected.

Currently, the drug is most typically either injected or smoked using a glass pipe similar to those employed by crack cocaine users. Crystal meth first appeared in Hawaii, possibly via Korea, but has spread throughout the United States and has become particularly problematic in rural areas of Texas, Oklahoma, Missouri, Kansas, and Arkansas owing to the ease of manufacturing and the inherent availability of anhydrous ammonia from agricultural fertilizer.[30] The other ingredients for the drug, such as lithium (found in batteries), ether (found in antifreeze), and pseudoephedrine (found in cold medicine), are relatively easy to obtain, even with federal restrictions that limit the availability of pseudoephedrine to potential cookers. The **Combat Methamphetamine Epidemic Act of 2005** took several steps toward containing the pseudoephedrine problem by requiring that:

- Medications containing pseudoephedrine must be either "behind the counter" or in lockbox displays requiring a key from store personnel at retail outlets;
- Purchasers must show valid identification to the seller;
- Sellers must maintain a log with the purchaser's signature, name, and address along with the quantity purchased;
- Purchasers are limited to 3.6 grams of pseudoephedrine per day and 9 grams within a 30-day period—of that 9-gram total, no more than 7.5 grams can be purchased via mail order.[31]

However, despite the strict federal regulations, pseudoephedrine can still be obtained in large quantity often by using a network of "smurfers," or individuals who visit a number of different pharmacies or retail stores. Furthermore, guides to the manufacture of the drug can be found on the Internet and manufacturers can set up shop in motel rooms, abandoned houses or trailers, or even cars.[32]

Crystal meth, also known as *ice* and *glass,* owes its special appeal to several factors (Figure 20-8):

▲ **FIGURE 20-8 Ice**
Made from powdered methamphetamine, "ice" is often observed as a crystalline substance. Users usually smoke ice, resulting in an intense high for as long as 12–14 hours.
(©streetdrugs.org)

- A puff of crack cocaine buoys its user for approximately 20 minutes, but the high from smoking ice endures for 12–24 hours. It does, however, share crack's addictive properties, and it produces similar bouts of severe depression and paranoia as well as convulsions.
- Ice can be manufactured in clandestine speed labs, whereas cocaine must be extracted from the leaf of the coca plant, refined, and imported by smugglers at considerable risk.
- Because it is odorless, ice can be smoked in public virtually without detection.

In its solid form, the drug resembles rock candy or a chip of ice. When lighted in a glass pipe, the crystals turn to liquid and produce a potent vapor that enters the bloodstream directly through the lungs. Ice reverts to its solid state when it cools, thus becoming reusable and highly transportable.[33] One gram of crystal meth is enough for 15–20 hits, making it extremely cost-effective to many users.

Crystal meth or "ice" production has several obvious hallmarks, owing to the fact that many of the ingredients can be found in discount stores. Large purchases of items containing ingredients required for crystal meth production, such as cough medicine and batteries, may indicate illicit activity. Furthermore, the use of anhydrous ammonia in the production of crystal meth produces a noxious odor that is noticeable by neighbors and visitors. Clandestine meth labs and special considerations for officers going into such labs are discussed later in the chapter.

Strawberry Quick Meth

Reports of candy-flavored methamphetamine are emerging around the nation, stirring concern among police and abuse prevention experts that drug dealers are marketing a new drug to younger people. According to intelligence gathered by the Drug Enforcement Administration (DEA) agents from informants, local police, and drug counselors, the flavored crystals have shown up in California, Idaho, Kansas, Minnesota, Missouri, Nevada, New Mexico, Texas, and Washington. The DEA has concluded that drug traffickers are trying to lure in new customers, no matter what their age, by making the meth seem less dangerous. Normally methamphetamine is a white or brownish, bitter-tasting crystalline powder that dissolves in water and that, as already indicated, is usually smoked or snorted. The new version looks like the "Pop Rocks" candy that sizzles in the mouth. Among the new flavors are Strawberry Quick, chocolate, cola, and other soda flavors (Figure 20-9). One DEA agent reported a red amphetamine that had been marketed as a powered form of an energy drink. **Strawberry Quick meth** is reportedly popular among new users who snort it because the flavoring can cut down on the drug taste. Teenagers who have been taught that meth is bad may see this flavored version as less harmful. Law enforcement officials have concluded that Strawberry Quick is definitely designed for the younger crowd. As methamphetamine's popularity has waned, drug dealers have found it necessary to create new ways to market it.

▲ **FIGURE 20-9**
Strawberry-Colored Crystal methamphetamine
Crystals of methamphetamine, colored with a strawberry-flavored children's drink mix, are a prime example of the new line of drugs. (Courtesy of Community Partnership)

Strawberry Quick came to prominence in January 2007 after the Nevada Department of Public Safety issued a bulletin describing the type of meth discovered in their state. It certainly has spread to other states.[34]

Ya-Ba or Nazi Speed

Ya Ba, also known as *Nazi Speed,* is a highly pure methamphetamine pill originating from Southeast Asia. The brightly colored pills are candylike and often flavored (for example, cherry-red, grape-purple, white-vanilla), apparently to make them more appealing to young people. As could be predicted, ya-ba pills are fast becoming a favorite drug at all-night rave parties, since their high is much stronger and longer lasting than that of other club drugs such as ecstacy and gamma hydroxy butrate (GHB), a drug commonly used in the crime of date rape. (See Chapter 10, "Sex-Related Offenses," for a more detailed discussion.) Users generally take a pill orally or place it in foil, heat it, and inhale the smoke. The high commonly lasts up to 10 hours.[35]

METHCATHINONE

Methcathinone, called *cat* or *goob,* is a psychomotor stimulant with a chemical structure similar to methamphetamine.[36] Originally patented in Germany in 1928 and later used in the Soviet Union in the late 1930s and 1940s for the treatment of depression, methcathinone was all but unknown in the United States until 1957, when an American pharmaceutical firm received a patent for it and began animal studies to determine its potential as an appetite suppressant.

Because initial testing revealed that methcathinone was approximately one and a half times as potent as methamphetamine, clinical trials were never initiated and testing was discontinued. The formula for methcathinone languished in the archives of the pharmaceutical firm until 1989, when it was rediscovered and "liberated" by a college intern working for the firm. He shared the formula, and in 1990 a close friend set up a clandestine laboratory on the campus of Northern Michigan University (NMU) and attempted to develop a market for cat.

Although cat use did not take hold among the students at NMU, it rapidly found acceptance among the local population of Michigan's upper peninsula. The relative ease with which cat is manufactured made it readily available, and its use and abuse rapidly spread throughout the peninsula and northern Wisconsin.

Methcathinone first came to the attention of law enforcement in the winter of 1990, when the Michigan State Police in the peninsula purchased a sample of what was purported to be a "new" drug more powerful than crack. The substance was analyzed to be methcathinone, closely related to, but more powerful than, methamphetamine. In January 1991 the Michigan State Police seized the first clandestine methcathinone lab ever discovered in the United States, in a college dormitory room in Marquette, Michigan. Six months later, the DEA raided another methcathinone lab in Ann Arbor, Michigan. However, much to the surprise of law enforcement authorities, methcathinone was not a controlled substance under either Michigan state law or federal statute.

On May 1, 1992, under the DEA's emergency scheduling authority, methcathinone was placed in Schedule 1 of the Controlled Substances Act. After a scientific and medical evaluation, this classification was made permanent on October 7, 1993.

The effects of methcathinone on the human body are very similar to those of methamphetamine. Cat is reported by users to induce feelings of omnipotence and euphoria, marked by increased energy. Other reported effects include relief from fatigue, increased self-assurance, acute alertness, hyperactivity, talkativeness, a sense of invincibility, confidence, and increased sexual stimulation.

Cat is usually a white or off-white powdered substance, very similar in appearance to methamphetamine. It is usually sold in gram quantities for $75–$100 and snorted in lines ranging from 1/10 to 1/4 of a gram. Because cat is usually sold in pure form, it reportedly can produce an immediate "rush," with a high that lasts 4–6 hours or more. There is typically a delay of 1–2 hours between dosages.

Users rapidly develop a tolerance for cat, requiring them to use larger amounts more frequently. Because cat destroys the sinus membranes, causing chronic nosebleeds and sinusitis, users may eventually resort to intravenous injection or oral ingestion.

Chronic cat use is characterized by binging. Addicts often go for days without sleep—eating very little, if at all—until they finally collapse. The onset of the "crash" occurs 4–6 hours after the last instance of use. Users often sleep for several days before beginning the cycle again.

Undesirable side effects reported by users include loss of appetite, weight loss, dehydration, stomachaches, profuse sweating, temporary blindness, deterioration of the nasal membranes, dry mouth, and an increased heart rate. Other side effects include anxiety, nervousness, depression, and hallucinations. The most

◀ **FIGURE 20-10** Khat
In the United States, khat use is most prevalent among immigrants from Somalia, Ethiopia, and Yemen. The drug is usually smuggled while wrapped in wet newspapers or banana leaves in order to keep the leaves moist, since khat's chemical composition begins to deteriorate quickly when the leaves are dried too fast. (©Simon Maina/AFP/Getty Images)

consistently reported side effect—one with a serious implication for law enforcement officers—is extreme paranoia. In one case, a cat abuser killed himself when he thought he was about to be arrested.

Symptoms of methcathinone intoxication can include profuse sweating, sweaty palms, increased heart rate, restlessness, increased body temperature, and uncontrollable shaking. Officers encountering suspected cat users should be particularly aware of withdrawal symptoms, which include irritability and argumentativeness. Other withdrawal symptoms include convulsions, hallucinations, and severe depression.

KHAT

Not to be confused with the previously described methcathinone (street name *cat*), **khat** (pronounced "cot") is a leafy import from a large flowering shrub that grows in northeast Africa and the southern Arabia peninsula. The active ingredients in khat are cathinone and cathine. Fresh khat leaves are a glossy brown color and contain an ingredient chemically similar to amphetamine. The cathinone in khat begins to degrade 48 hours after the plant has been cut. Thus, khat has to be refrigerated and kept moist or frozen to retain its potency for a longer period. Drying the leaves too fast causes the active ingredient (cathinone) to dissipate[37] (Figure 20-10).

The plant has been cultivated for centuries and is in widespread use today, primarily in Yemen, Somalia, and parts of Ethiopia and the Middle East. References to khat first appeared in the United States as American soldiers encountered rebels in Somalia, high on the drug during combat encounters. Ingestion of the drug does not impair motor skills but rather creates a mild, amphetamine-like euphoria that heightens the senses, self-esteem, and aggressiveness. The drug is also known as *Abyssinian Tea, African Tea*, and *African Salad*.

While khat is legal in countries such as the United Kingdom and Canada, it was recently classified as a Schedule I drug carrying penalties similar to heroin and cocaine in the United States. Khat is often transported into the United States from Europe, Canada, and North Africa wrapped in plastic bags or, as mentioned, in banana leaves to retain moistness. It is commonly sold by word of mouth or in ethnic specialty shops in cities such as Boston, Dallas, Houston, Los Angeles, Detroit, Buffalo, Philadelphia, Washington, D.C., and New York.[38]

DEPRESSANTS (SEDATIVES)

Depressants (sedatives) depress the central nervous system and are prescribed in small doses to reduce both restlessness and emotional tension and to induce sleep. The drugs most frequently abused are **barbiturates,** glutethimide, methaqualone, and meprobamate. Chronic use produces slurring of speech, staggering, loss of balance and falling, faulty judgment, quick temper, and quarrelsomeness. Overdoses, particularly in conjunction with alcohol, result in unconsciousness and death unless proper medical treatment is administered. Therapeutic doses cause minimal amounts of psychological dependence; chronic excessive doses result in both physical and psychological dependence. Abrupt withdrawal, particularly from barbiturates, can produce convulsions and death. Barbiturates are frequently nicknamed after the color of the capsule or tablet or the name of the manufacturer. The barbiturates most frequently abused are secobarbital and amobarbital,[39] which are among the short- and intermediate-acting barbiturates. The onset time is from 15 to 40 minutes, and the effects last for up to 6 hours.

GLUTETHIMIDE (DORIDEN)

When introduced in 1954, glutethimide was wrongly believed to be a nonaddictive barbiturate substitute. The sedative effects of glutethimide begin about 30 minutes after oral administration and last 4–8 hours. Because the effects of this drug last for a long time, it is exceptionally difficult to reverse overdoses and many result in death.

Glutethimide used with 16-milligram codeine tablets is one of the most popular pill combinations on the black market today. This combination gives a heroin-like effect and is known as *dors and 4s* or *Ds and Cs*. It is commonly taken by oral ingestion.

METHAQUALONE

Methaqualone was at one time very popular in the United States but has since been significantly reduced in the market. The drug was widely abused, because it was mistakenly thought to be safe and nonaddictive and to have aphrodisiac qualities. Methaqualone caused many cases of serious poisoning. When administered orally, large doses produce a coma that may be accompanied by thrashing or convulsions. It was marketed in the United States under various names, including Quaalude, Parest, Optimil, Somnafac, and Soper. Most methaqualones found on the street today are counterfeit and usually test as diazepam (Valium).

SPEEDBALLING

Speedballing is a slang term that refers to the simultaneous ingestion, usually through injection, of heroin (a depressant) and cocaine (a stimulant). The cocaine provides the user with a tremendous euphoric "rush," after which a drowsy or depressing sensation arises. An overdose of either drug can cause convulsions and death. Death by overdose using this type of drug mix was reportedly instrumental in the demise of several well-known rock musicians and celebrities. See Box 20.2.

HALLUCINOGENS

Hallucinogenic drugs, natural or synthetic, distort the perception of objective reality. In large doses, they cause hallucinations. Most of these drugs are processed in clandestine laboratories and have yet to be proved medically valuable. The effects experienced after taking hallucinogens are not solely related to the drug. They are modified by the mood, mental attitude, and environment of the user. The unpredictability of their effects is the greatest danger to the user. Users may develop psychological dependence but not physical dependence, so far as is known. The most commonly abused hallucinogens are PCP (phencyclidine), LSD 25 (lysergic acid diethylamide), mescaline (peyote), psilocybin, and psilocyn.

PHENCYCLIDINE (PCP)

Phencyclidine, commonly called **PCP,** in its pharmaceutically pure form is a solid white powder. Because the hydrochloride salt readily dissolves in water, and as a street drug is often adulterated or misrepresented as other drugs, its appearance is highly variable. It is sold in powder form and in tablets, both in many colors. Often it is placed on parsley or on other leaf mixtures to be smoked as cigarettes (joints).[40]

When misrepresented, PCP is commonly sold as THC (the main psychoactive ingredient in marijuana, which is rarely available on the street). But phencyclidine has also been sold as cannabinol (another marijuana constituent), mescaline, psilocybin, LSD, and even amphetamine or cocaine. Because of the variability in street names and appearance, and because PCP is sometimes found in combination with barbiturates, heroin, cocaine, amphetamine, methaqualone, LSD, and mescaline, users may be mistaken about its true identity. The mixture of marijuana and PCP has been thought to be common, but it has rarely been reported by street-drug analysis laboratories.

Significantly adding to the risk of using PCP, especially when it is taken orally, is the wide variability in purity of the street drug. Even when PCP is not misrepresented, the percentage of PCP has been found to be quite variable. Depending on how carefully PCP is synthesized, it may contain impurities, including potassium cyanide. Generally, samples represented as "crystal" or "angel dust" tend to be purer than those sold under other names or misrepresented as different drugs.

In addition to phencyclidine, over 30 chemical analogues, some of which are capable of producing similar psychic effects, can also be synthesized and may appear on the street. Thus the problems of identifying and tracking the use of PCP and related drugs is unusually difficult.

Phencyclidine is used legally in veterinary medicine to immobilize large animals. Although it was originally developed as an anesthetic for humans, it was later abandoned, because it produced psychological disturbances and agitation in some patients. PCP made its first illicit appearance in the United States in 1965 on the West Coast. At that time it rapidly developed a bad street reputation and had only limited popularity.

Because of its great variation in appearance, PCP is difficult to identify by sight. It is found in powder and tablet forms; on parsley, mint, oregano, or other leafy material; as a liquid; and in 1-gram "rock" crystals. When PCP is sold as a granular powder ("angel dust"), it may consist of 50%–100% phencyclidine. Sold under other names and in other guises, the purity varies from 10% to 30%; leafy mixtures contain still smaller amounts of the drug.

PCP is most commonly smoked or snorted. By smoking a leafy mixture on which the drug has been sprinkled, users can better regulate the dose. Because of the longer period before the drug takes effect and the greater purity, overdoses are probably worse when the drug has been taken orally.

The effects of PCP include feeling weightless, smaller, out of touch with the immediate environment, and dying or being already dead. Common signs of PCP use include flushing of the skin, profuse sweating, involuntary eye movements, muscular incoordination, double vision, dizziness, nausea, and vomiting. Another common indicator of PCP use is that the user has a desire to shed their clothes. Often times, police respond to a call similar to "a naked man running down the street," only to find that subject is high on PCP. Police officers report that individuals under the influence of PCP can be extremely violent and almost superhumanly strong.

BOX 20-2 | CELEBRITY DRUG USE AND DEATH: WHY THE HEROIN-COCAINE "SPEEDBALL" MIXTURE IS SO DANGEROUS?

Hardly a month passes without headline news reporting the death of another celebrity to a drug overdose. The endemic struggle within Hollywood is pervasive. Many of these overdoses are a result of the "speedball" combination of cocaine, and either heroin, or morphine. In some instances, this mixture is referred to as "powerballing." The list of Hollywood celebrity deaths is sadly long and includes such talented people as River Phoenix, Chris Farley, Phillip Seymour Hoffman, John Belushi, Jimi Hendrix, and Janis Joplin. Several sports figures have also succumbed to speedball overdoses including San Diego Padres pitcher Eric Show and power hitter Ken Caminiti.

So, why is the mixture so deadly? There are several factors involved in fatal speedball overdoses. First, according to users, the psychological effect ("high" or "nod") from the deadly combination is supposedly superior to any other single drug use or combination, peaking curiosity as well as return use. The combination is highly addictive, and most deaths are a result of multiple IV doses over a limited period of time, after a significant period of addiction. In other words, the body is weak and already showing significant effect of prolonged drug use to include enlarged heart, inefficient circulation, and most importantly, tolerance for both drugs is increased. The body requires increased quantities or strengths to achieve the previous effects of the drugs; larger and more potent doses are being used by long addicted addicts with weaker cardiovascular systems. Second, both drugs are expensive and unfortunately pervasive within the Hollywood culture. Third, the combination is taken intravenously, most often with cocaine and heroin in the same syringe, resulting in an immediate impact to body systems and organs. Cocaine acts on the body as a very strong stimulant and by itself is cardio-toxic; that is, it causes strong vasoconstriction of the arteries resulting in increased heart rate and blood pressure. There have been numerous cases of fatal overdose on cocaine use alone. Heroin is a strong central nervous system (CNS) depressant that slows down the heart...heart rates decrease and most importantly, breathing rates decrease...the amount of oxygen supplied to the brain and the rest of the body is severely reduced. Again, there have been numerous cases of fatal overdose on heroin use alone. Finally, the combination of cocaine and heroin places the body in a unique form of stress, often with fatal consequences. The physiologic result of the "speedball" is an extremely overworked cardiovascular system being supplied with a weak level of oxygen. Heart failure, rupture of an artery or vein (aneurysm), unconsciousness, and brain coma are all

Oscar Award Winner Philip Seymour Hoffman died of an apparent "speedball" overdose of heroin and cocaine in 2014. (©Francis Specker/Bloomberg/Getty Images)

common. The body simply shuts down and all autonomic nervous system functions that control heart rate, brain activity, and respiration cease—the immediate impact is death.

Sadly, in an industry that is replete with a history of caring and giving to various philanthropic causes, Hollywood manifests the American epidemic of drug and alcohol abuse. The list of celebrities lost to addiction of all types is staggering; with the deadly "speedball" overdose representing only one avenue of death. Arguably, many more have succumbed to alcoholism and other types of drug overdoses throughout the years, as individual "stars" have struggled to maintain normalcy within a culture that promotes fame and fortune over drug and alcohol sobriety.

METHYLENEDIOXY METHAMPHETAMINE

Methylenedioxy methamphetamine (MDMA or ecstasy) is a bitter white powder related to amphetamine and mescaline. It enjoys a high popularity among ravers and has now become a very common drug of abuse in the nightclub and party scene. The drug's popularity has grown at an alarming rate. Although it is difficult to say exactly how many people are experimenting with it, law enforcement officials consider ecstasy to be one of the most troubling illicit drugs because of its widespread use (Figure 20-11).

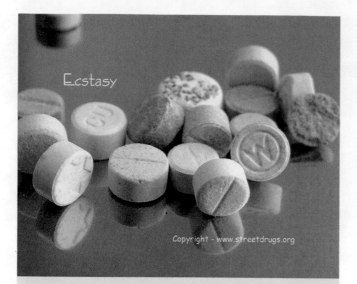

▲ **FIGURE 20-11 Ecstasy**
Ecstasy pills come in a variety of colors with unique markings, including shamrocks, stars, letters, and skull/crossbones, depending on where the drug was manufactured. The use of ecstasy is very popular in the nightclub and party scene. This drug has become increasingly popular among juveniles and is commonly used as a recreational drug at raves.
(©streetdrugs.org)

Many ecstasy users are drawn to the drug by its ability to reduce inhibitions, promote euphoria, produce light hallucinations, and suppress the need to eat or sleep. One pill's effects can last as long as 6 hours, but users build up a tolerance. An overdose can cause an accelerated heart rate, high blood pressure, aching muscle cramps, and panic attacks. According to many experts, ecstasy is psychologically addictive and can result in paranoia and psychosis.

The drug is manufactured to a large extent in laboratories in Belgium and the Netherlands. It can be created for as little as 50 cents, sold in the country of origin, and then smuggled into the United States, where it is sold for as much as $40 a pill. For the most part, Israeli organized-crime syndicates have been implicated as the main source of the drug's distribution in the United States. This so-called club drug has become increasingly popular among juveniles and is commonly used as a recreational drug at raves.[41]

LYSERGIC ACID DIETHYLAMIDE (LSD 25)

Lysergic acid diethylamide (LSD) is a semisynthetic compound produced from lysergic acid, a natural substance found in ergot fungus, a disease that affects rye and wheat. An average dose of 30–50 micrograms—about the size of a pinpoint—will take the user on a "trip" lasting 10–12 hours. Drops of the solution are taken on a lump of sugar or on blotted paper. Along with experiencing mental changes, the user may have dilated pupils, a lowered body temperature, nausea, goose bumps, profuse perspiration, increased blood sugar levels, and a rapid heart rate. Subsequent flashbacks are not uncommon.

Before 1972 there was no way to detect LSD in the body chemically. However, scientists at Collaborative Research, Inc., in Waltham, Massachusetts, developed a means for detecting it in small amounts in human blood and urine and for measuring the amount present. This discovery made it possible to study the distribution of LSD in the bodies of animals to determine the residual effect of the drug.[42] The DEA reports that LSD is making a comeback with juvenile circles and is also used frequently at raves.[43]

MESCALINE (PEYOTE)

The primary active ingredient of the peyote cactus is the hallucinogen **mescaline,** which is derived from the buttons of the plant. Mescaline has been used by the Indians of Central America and the southwestern United States for centuries in religious rites. Generally ground into a powder, it is taken orally. A dose of 350–500 milligrams of mescaline produces illusions and hallucinations for 5–12 hours. Like LSD, mescaline is not likely to produce physical dependence but may produce psychological dependence.

PSILOCYBIN AND PSILOCYN

Psilocybin and **psilocyn** are obtained from mushrooms generally grown in Mexico. Like mescaline, they have historically been used in Indian rites. They are taken orally, or placed in tea, and their effect is similar to mescaline's, except that a smaller dose—4 to 8 milligrams—produces effects for about 6 hours. Psilocybin has also become a popular drug on the party scene and at raves (Figure 20-12).

FOXY AND 5-MEO-AMT

Foxy became a controlled substance via emergency scheduling by the Drug Enforcement Agency in the spring of 2003. This Schedule I hallucinogen is a synthetic compound with chemical properties similar to those of psilocybin and psilocin. The drug is found in powder form, which is then often used to fill capsules or create tablets. The tablets may be imprinted with graphics. Most often, the drug appears at clubs and raves and is used primarily by teenagers and young adults. Effects begin to manifest in the user within about 30 minutes, and they include visual and auditory hallucinations, extreme talkativeness, and decreased inhibitions. These effects peak between 1 and 2 hours after administration and can last 3–6 hours.[44]

More commonly called *AMT, alpha,* or *alpha-O,* 5-MeO-AMT shares many similarities with Foxy. Both have similar chemical properties, induce hallucinogenic effects, and are generally used within the club or rave scenes. Additionally, the powdered AMT may be dissolved in water and distributed onto blotter paper, sugar cubes, or candy. AMT is longer-lasting than Foxy, often producing hallucinations for up to 18 hours.[45]

KETAMINE

Ketamine hydrochloride is a synthetic drug that was developed in the mid-1960s and is an anesthetic agent that has legitimate uses, mostly in veterinary medicine. Ketamine was used extensively in the Vietnam War because it is fast-acting and has a relatively short duration, making it a drug of choice for

▲ **FIGURE 20-12** **Psilocybin**

Another popular drug among adolescent youth is psilocybin. The mushrooms are eaten, causing hallucinations, disorientation, impaired coordination, and confusion on the part of the user. Mushrooms covered in chocolate, as observed in this photo set, look like candy and are often found at raves. (©streetdrugs.org)

"battlefield medicine." However, it soon became obvious that many humans who were anesthetized with ketamine often became agitated and suffered hallucinations when they awoke. It has since been replaced as an anesthetic for humans by other, more efficient agents with fewer side effects.

Ironically, the side effects that made ketamine unpopular and unsafe as a legitimate medical drug have spawned its use in the illegitimate market. On the street, ketamine is called *Vitamin K, Special K,* or *K.* It has also been closely associated with the all-night rave party phenomenon. Ketamine causes hallucinations, excitement, and delirium similar to the drugs phencyclidine (PCP) and LSD; however, the effects are not as pronounced or as long in duration. Hallucinations caused by ketamine may last only an hour or two, but the intoxication-like effects of the drug may be noticeable for several hours. Because ketamine is an anesthetic, it may temporarily mask the feeling of pain. Users of ketamine can injure themselves and not know it.

Because ketamine is so difficult to produce, it is not manufactured in clandestine laboratories. Most of the ketamine abused today comes from stolen veterinary stock and is known by brand names such as Ketalar and Ketaset. The legitimate drug is usually supplied in vials of liquid, although it can be in the form of white powder or pills.

In liquid form, ketamine may be injected into a large muscle. This route allows for a slower absorption and longer duration than the intravenous route. In powder form, ketamine is usually snorted in the same manner as cocaine. Both powder and liquid can be sprayed or sprinkled on vegetable matter and smoked or mixed with a drink. While it is not known if a person can become physically dependent on ketamine, tolerance and psychological dependence are distinct possibilities with frequent use.

The average street dose of ketamine ranges from 0.2 to 0.5 gram. The size and weight of the abuser, the desired effects, and the presence of other drugs in the abuser's system determine the ultimate effect. A vial of liquid ketamine is equivalent to approximately 1 gram of powder and sells for $100–$200. A 0.2-gram dose of powder, or a *bump,* commonly sells for $20. Ketamine may be packaged for sale in small plastic bags, aluminum foil, paper folds, or gelatin capsules.[46] Obviously, an abuser must also possess hypodermic syringes and needles to administer the drug by injection (Figure 20-13).

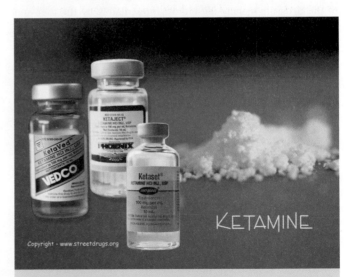

▲**FIGURE 20-13** **Ketamine**

Ketamine hydrochloride is a synthetic drug developed in the mid-1960s as an anesthetic agent. Two of the street names used for this drug are Vitamin K and Special K. Ketamine causes hallucinations, excitement, and delirium similar to LSD or PCP. Because it is an anesthetic, it may temporarily mask pain—so much so that users can even injure themselves and not be aware of it. (©streetdrugs.org)

CANNABIS

MARIJUANA

Although classified as a mild hallucinogen, the Schedule I substance **cannabis** is often considered separately owing to its wide availability and popularity. Drugs obtained from the cannabis plant include **marijuana** and hashish. Marijuana is found in the flowering tops and leaves of the cannabis-sativa (also known as *hemp*) plant. The leaves of the plant always grow in odd numbers. The plant thrives in mild climates around the world, but the principal sources of import into the United States are Colombia, Mexico, and Jamaica. Its most common nicknames are *pot, reefer, grass, weed, Maryjane,* and *a joint.* Marijuana is made by crushing or chopping the dried leaves and flowers of the plant into small pieces. The cleaned or manicured leaves are then rolled into a cigarette and smoked, smoked in some other fashion, or mixed with food and eaten. The principal psychoactive substance is thought to be delta-9-tetrahydrocannabinol (THC), a chemical found nowhere else in nature. Most marijuana is found to have less than 5% THC, but improvements in horticulture and chemistry in the cultivation process have led to much more concentrated varieties. Hybrid varieties, such as those found in the potent sinsemilla strain of the plant, and plants grown in carefully controlled indoor operations may yield up to 20% THC[47] (Figure 20-14).

Although the effects of the drug vary among users, in many cases low dosages of marijuana produce an initial restfulness and well-being, followed by a dreamy, carefree state of relaxation and food cravings. Larger dosages can result in altered perceptions, impaired memory, and rapid changes of emotion. Effects of the drug are usually felt almost immediately by the user and may last several hours.

As of this writing (2018), marijuana is actually legal for recreational use in eight U.S. states and the District of Columbia. They are Colorado, Washington, Oregon, Alaska, California, Massachusetts, Maine and Nevada. Twenty-nine other states have broadly expanded the use of marijuana for medical usage. There are also several other states with bills in process to decriminalize or legalize marijuana as well. While national sentiment reflects the sentiment that the drug is no more dangerous than alcohol, the Drug Enforcement Administration has so far refused to reclassify the drug from its Schedule 1 status. The federal government's position is very controversial and remains the same: Marijuana is a dangerous and addictive drug, has no accepted medical use in treatment as proscribed by the Food and Drug Administration, and poses a significant risk to the general public and specifically adolescent teenagers.[48] Perhaps the main reason for the unwillingness of the federal government to legalize marijuana for medicinal use is the drug's reputation as a "gateway" drug. The gateway theory states that the use of marijuana causes an eventual graduation by users to harder drugs such as cocaine and heroin. However, this idea is controversial. Several studies have recently disproved this association, but marijuana remains a Schedule I drug at this time.[49]

▲ **FIGURE 20-14   Manicured marijuana and seeds**
Manicured marijuana and buds. The manicured leaves of the marijuana plant are used to fill "joints" that are smoked similar to tobacco cigarettes. Buds of marijuana, like those in the cellophane envelope here, are placed in a pipe and smoked. The user inhales the smoke deep into the lungs and holds it for a long period of time, increasing the amount of active ingredient absorbed by the body. Low doses of the smoked drug tend to produce a sense of well-being, including an alteration of sensory perceptions and illusory expansion of time and space. Several states have recently legalized marijuana for recreational and/or medical use. Marijuana can also be manufactured into a liquid or edible form, such as in tinctures, cookies, brownies, and even gumdrops.
(©Eskymaks/Shutterstock RF)

Marijuana Grow Houses

Marijuana grow houses are normal houses in residential areas that are converted for the purposes of growing marijuana. Large houses are often used, because they provide greater capacity for growing marijuana, but such operations may be found in any home, in any neighborhood.

To make a house suitable for cultivating marijuana, significant changes are made to the home's structure. High-intensity lighting is needed to grow the plants (which is costly), so many home grow operations bypass the electricity illegally, putting the neighborhood at risk of fire and electrocution. Combined with construction to provide water and ventilation for the grow operation, the house becomes uninhabitable for future residents. Unless major repairs are made, the house is ruined, and the property value of other houses in the area is lowered.

Marijuana grow houses often have links to criminal elements and organized crime. Individuals associated with grow operations have been found to carry weapons and may be considered dangerous. Also, there is a risk of increased violence and residual crime in neighborhoods associated with illegal activity. Marijuana grow houses are not only a police concern; they are also a public safety issue.[50]

BOX 20-3 | MARIJUANA LEGALIZATION AND NEW CHALLENGES FOR LAW ENFORCEMENT

In November 2012, Colorado became the first state to overturn marijuana prohibition, with about 55% of the electorate in that state voting in favor of legalization of marijuana. The controversial vote marked a major shift in the United States; a country that has spent years waging a war on drugs and whose top drug enforcement officials still consider marijuana a dangerous substance.[51]

In theory, legalization in Colorado (and subsequently in the states of Oregon, Washington and Alaska) should free police and other law enforcement agencies to focus on more serious drugs and crimes, but the reality has been a bit more complex. There have been unanticipated consequences of legalization that required significant changes on the part of law enforcement, policy makers, and officers alike. The most obvious issue was the conflict between the state legalizing the drug and the continued federal prohibition of marijuana as a *Schedule 1 Prohibited Substance*; meaning that marijuana may be legal at the state level, however, was still illegal at the federal level. Police agencies were required to navigate complex policy issues, which necessitated that they form partnerships with agencies at the local, state, and federal level, legal groups, and police associations. Interesting conflicts erupted, like a city department not enforcing the marijuana prohibition because of new state legislation, but officers from that same department working in Drug Enforcement Administration task forces required to enforce federal marijuana laws, within law enforcement agencies. In some cases, the District or State Attorney refused to prosecute cases at the local level, while local and state law enforcement agencies still continued to arrest people for trafficking in marijuana.

Another major problem that has occurred as a result of legalization is a sharp increase in armed robberies, burglaries, and theft aimed at legitimate marijuana shops and dispensaries. Since marijuana remains a controlled substance at the federal level, legitimate companies and individuals involved in any aspect of the marijuana business (sales, manufacturing, farming, transportation, and the like) cannot use the federal banking system. Originally designed to thwart money laundering operations from large illegal drug trade, federal law prohibits the involvement of any federally-insured bank or institutions from receiving money from an enterprise that is involved in drug trade (whether legal or not at the state level). The result has been that legitimate retail establishments were relegated to a cash business. Not only was this a significant hardship on the business venture itself, the situation marks these businesses for criminals seeking to steal cash money via armed robberies, burglaries, theft, and a host of white collar crimes. Legal marijuana businesses have become veritable fortresses in an effort to prevent such crimes,

however, incidents of robbery, burglary, and theft aimed at such businesses continues to grow. Further, the legal intricacies detailing what constitutes a legal marijuana operation versus an illegal one has created significant confusion among police agencies themselves within a specific community, requiring new agencies to take on the licensing, certification, and/or inspection of these facilities at the state level. The result has been, unfortunately, a number of compromised investigations, improper investigations, and issues with determining probable cause, and mistakes related to search and seizure warrants. Other problems arising from the legalization of marijuana for police also include difficult identification and prosecution of those suspected of driving under the influence of marijuana; a lack of data on the public safety impact of legalization; increased overdoses from legally purchased marijuana products due to a lack of potency regulations; and a marked increase in marijuana use among youths and adolescents.

As more and more states move toward the legalization of marijuana, law enforcement will continue to struggle with these types of policy and operational changes. Criminal justice think tanks and police organizations recommend that law enforcement establish data collection systems and institute robust research projects in states that have already legalized marijuana, in order that other states can learn from their lessons, challenges, and successes.

The Herb Center is a legal and popular dispensary for marijuana in Bend, Oregon. Note the alarm system sign and re-enforced iron grates on the door and windows aimed at deterring robberies and burglaries of the establishment. (Courtesy of Robert W. Taylor)

What Are the Dangers?

There are many dangers associated with marijuana grow houses and problems that can result from having one in a neighborhood. These include:

- *Poisonous fumes:* Noxious fumes from the growing operation can build up inside the house or be vented outside (which affect the neighboring homes).
- *Fires:* Electricity is bypassed, by being diverted from neighboring homes. This increases the chance of fires starting owing to the amateurish rewiring jobs.
- *Electrocution:* People inexperienced with rewiring electrical systems may electrocute themselves, or people exposed to the wiring may be electrocuted.
- *Violence:* To protect distribution and production of marijuana, those involved in a growing operation may be armed, and have been known to carry out assaults or homicides.
- *Increased crime:* Marijuana from home grow operations are sold to children and other members of the community. The money raised from these sales is used to fund organized crime.
- *Booby traps:* Traps may be set by growers to protect their product from unauthorized persons entering the home or property. These traps can be life-threatening and expose emergency responders (and others entering the property) to hazardous conditions.
- *Environmental damage:* Chemicals used in the grow operation are improperly disposed of by being drained into the ground and water system.
- *Hazard to children:* Children in the neighborhood are exposed to the dangers mentioned above, and may be sold marijuana. Police have found children living in or brought by their parents to the grow houses, exposing them to these hazards.[52]

What Are the Signs of a Marijuana Home Grow Operation?

There are a number of factors that may indicate the presence of a marijuana home grow operation. These include:

- Residents rarely appear to be at home and may be in the house only for brief periods of time (such as a few hours) before leaving. Despite this, radios or televisions may be left on all night, making it sound as if someone were there.
- Visitors behave strangely or visit at odd hours.
- Entry into the home is often made through the garage or side/back entrance, to conceal activities.
- Windows are boarded or covered up, preventing light from entering the house and concealing activities inside. The glare of bright lights may be seen escaping from the windows, and the windows may have a layer of condensation on them. Even though the windows are always closed, air conditioners never run.
- Equipment used in the growing operation (such as large fans, lights, plastic plant containers, and other items) is carried into the home.
- Sounds of construction or electrical humming from equipment may be heard.
- Exterior appearance of the property is untidy. There is little outside maintenance done (unshoveled snow, uncut grass, and so on), and garbage bags containing used soil and plant material may be discarded in areas surrounding the house. Mail delivered to the house may be left unchecked, so that flyers and junk mail pile up in the mailbox.
- Warning signs are posted in windows or around the outside the house. These may warn people to "Beware of the Dog" or that "Guard Dogs" are on the property.

Cash Value

The amount of money that marijuana grow houses generate is well into the billions. For example, recently the Riverside County, California Sheriff's Department conducted raids on nine houses and found a total of 14,000 plants with an estimated value of $60–$80 million.[53] This clearly is a very lucrative criminal enterprise (Figure 20-15).

HASHISH

A drug-rich resinous secretion from the flowers of the cannabis plant, **hashish** is processed by drying to produce a drug several times as potent as marijuana. The resin from the flowers is richer in cannabinols than the leaves and tops, and THC content is 5%–12%. (The leaves range from 0.27% to 4% in THC content.) Hashish is most commonly smoked in a small "hash pipe."

HASHISH OIL

The Middle East is the main source of hashish entering the United States. Liquid hashish, or **hashish oil,** is produced by concentrating THC. The liquid hashish so far discovered has varied between 20% and 65% THC. There is reason to suspect that methods are now being employed to make an even more powerful concentrate. The purity of the final product depends on the sophistication of the apparatus used.

Like other forms of the drug, liquid hashish can be used several ways. Because of its extraordinary potency, one drop of the material can produce a high. A drop may be placed on a regular cigarette, used in cooking, added to wine, and even smeared on bread. When smoked, a small drop of hashish oil is smeared inside the glass bowl of a special pipe with a flattened side. The user exhales deeply, tilts the bowl, and holds the flame from a match under the oil. In one inhalation, the smoker draws slowly on the pipe as the oil begins to bubble, continuing as it chars and burns.

There are many ways to produce hashish oil, but most clandestine operations use a basket filled with ground or chopped marijuana suspended inside a larger container, at the bottom of which is contained a solvent, such as alcohol, hexane, chloroform, or petroleum ether. Copper tubing or similar material is arranged at the top, and cold water circulates through it. The solvent is heated, the vapors rise to the top, they condense, and then they fall into the basket of marijuana. As the solvent seeps

through the plant materials, the THC and other soluble chemicals are dissolved, and the solution drops back to the bottom of the container. Continued heating causes the process to recur. The solution becomes increasingly stronger until the plant material is exhausted of its THC.

SYNTHETIC MARIJUANA

Synthetic marijuana, otherwise known as **K2** or "spice," is actually a mixture of herbs and spices treated with a chemical additive and marketed as a type of incense. The substance contains synthetic cannabinoids, mimicking some of the effects of marijuana but also resulting in some nasty side effects. Popular among young adults as "legal marijuana," the drug contains chemicals more potent and potentially dangerous than THC. While it does result in a high for the user, it can also cause hallucinations, increased heart rate, increased blood pressure, and respiratory distress. Long-term effects can include delusional thoughts and depression. A rash of emergency room visits by K2 users experiencing these and other symptoms in 2009 and 2010 raised alarms across the country.[54]

The availability of K2 is being sharply curtailed as of this writing. Once available in head shops, tobacco shops, gas stations, and over the Internet, K2 has been the target of citywide and statewide bans across the United States. The substance is also now the target of an emergency DEA action that places the drug temporarily on the Schedule I list of controlled substances beginning in 2011, pending further research.[55] Because the popularity of K2 was driven mostly by its reputation as being a legal alternative to pot, it remains unseen whether it will continue to be sought after once it is banned.

DRUG PARAPHERNALIA

Under federal law, *drug paraphernalia* refers to "any equipment, product, or material of any kind which is primarily intended or designed for use in manufacturing, compounding, converting, concealing, producing, processing, preparing, injecting, ingesting, inhaling, or otherwise introducing into the human body a controlled substance." This equipment can include roach clips, glass and ceramic pipes, water pipes, bongs, miniature spoons, and hypodermic needles. Since 1990 it has been illegal for anyone to sell, transport, or import/export drug paraphernalia, and people violating this federal law can be sentenced to up to 3 years in prison.[56]

Drug paraphernalia are readily available in retail establishments and from Internet sites, often tailored with trendy designs or references to popular music acts that appeal directly to young consumers. In an attempt to skirt federal law, paraphernalia are usually sold with disclaimers that indicate they are to be used only with tobacco products. However, the law states that there is no requirement to prove that a merchant has to have direct knowledge that the products are being used for illegal purposes.

Recently, targeting the supply of drug paraphernalia has become an increasingly popular initiative among federal and state agencies. Taking the position that purchasers of paraphernalia are generally involved in the abuse, production, or distribution of illegal drugs, and are therefore a valuable target in drug investigations, there has been a renewed focus on paraphernalia. Recently, law enforcement agencies in 11 states seized nearly 130 metric tons of paraphernalia, shut down several websites, and arrested 55 people during the Operation Pipedreams initiative.[57] Similar initiatives are ongoing nationally to target manufacturers and distributors of paraphernalia.

INHALANTS

A common misconception about inhalant *sniffing, snorting, bagging* (fumes inhaled from a plastic bag), or *huffing* (inhalant-soaked rags placed in the mouth) is that it is a childish fad similar to youthful experiments with cigarettes. But inhalant abuse is deadly serious and one of the most dangerous of "experimental behaviors." Sniffing volatile solvents, which includes most inhalants, can cause severe damage to the brain and nervous system. By starving the body of oxygen or forcing the heart to beat more rapidly and erratically, inhalants can kill adolescent sniffers.

Inhalant abuse came to public attention in the early 1950s when the news media reported that young people who were seeking a cheap high were sniffing glue. The term *glue sniffing* is still widely used, often to include inhalation of a broad range of common products besides glue. Although different in makeup, nearly all abused inhalants produce effects similar to anesthetics, which act to slow down the body's functions. When inhaled via the nose or mouth in sufficient concentrations, inhalants can cause intoxicating effects that can last a few minutes or several hours if taken repeatedly. Similar to alcohol, users initially may feel slightly stimulated; with successive inhalations, they may feel less inhibited and less in control; in severe cases, the user loses consciousness. Sniffing highly concentrated amounts of the chemicals in solvents or aerosol sprays can directly induce heart failure and death. This is especially common from the abuse of fluorocarbon and butane-type gases. High concentrations of inhalants also cause death from suffocation by displacing oxygen in the lungs, and in the central nervous system causing breathing to cease.

MAJOR COUNTRIES OF ORIGIN AND TRAFFICKING PATTERNS

The history of drug abuse in the United States is intertwined with trends and patterns of not only use but also illicit traffic. As world affairs change, so do the patterns of drug use and trafficking. For instance, after World War II and up through the early 1960s, most heroin entering the United States originated from the Middle East; was refined in either Italy or Marseilles, France; and was imported by major American Mafia and La Cosa Nostra organizations through major east coast cities such as New York and Philadelphia (for example, *The French Connection*). However, with American involvement in Southeast Asia (Vietnam, Cambodia, and Laos) from 1965 on into the 1970s, heroin trafficking patterns significantly changed, utilizing new source countries and organizations. The 1980s witnessed an explosion of cocaine onto the American continent giving rise to the crack epidemic of the 1990s. Today heroin and cocaine trafficking patterns have again changed, with sophisticated criminal organizations and cartels working more closely together. In addition, clandestine methamphetamine labs have become a major domestic problem giving rise to new criminal elements and raising environmental safety issues for local police officers. With the war in Afghanistan, expected increases in heroin and marijuana production may once again characterize changes in trafficking patterns (Figures 20-16 and 20-17).

The following geographical areas provide a summary of today's existing trafficking patterns.

MEXICO

Mexico has the distinction of being not only a major source of heroin, methamphetamine, and cocaine but also the major pathway for drugs from South America into the United States. The country has almost 2,000 miles of border shared with the United States, most of which is unsecured, making transport of drugs from Mexico a challenge to United States law enforcement at all levels. Furthermore, United States Customs officials are able to inspect only about 2% of commercial shipments from foreign countries, including Mexico.[58]

Mexico produces the majority of the marijuana consumed in the United States. The drug is smuggled into the United States via ports of entry located along the border and is generally dispersed throughout the country in private and commercial vehicles along major interstates and highways, particularly to large markets, such as Chicago, Los Angeles, New York, Miami, and Dallas.[59]

Mexico is also the principal source of foreign-produced methamphetamine in the United States. Because the United States has enacted measures to control many of the ingredients found in methamphetamine, Mexican labs have taken advantage of the lack of regulation on such items within their own country, as well as the ease of importing chemicals such as pseudoephedrine from Canada and the Middle East.[60] As a result, methamphetamine labs in Mexico have increased their capacity to export to the Southwestern United States in the past decade. Most methamphetamine trafficked from Mexico enters the United States via pedestrian couriers and both private and commercial vehicles, particularly through points of entry in Arizona, Texas, and California.[61] However, other more sophisticated means have also been discovered. For instance, in San Diego, California, a mile-long tunnel was discovered that led from a kitchen in a home in Tijuana, Mexico, to two warehouses in San Diego's Otay Mesa industrial district[62] (Figure 20-18). The cinder-blocked tunnel travelled under the U.S.-Mexican border and dropped 80–90 feet to a wood-lined floor, equipped

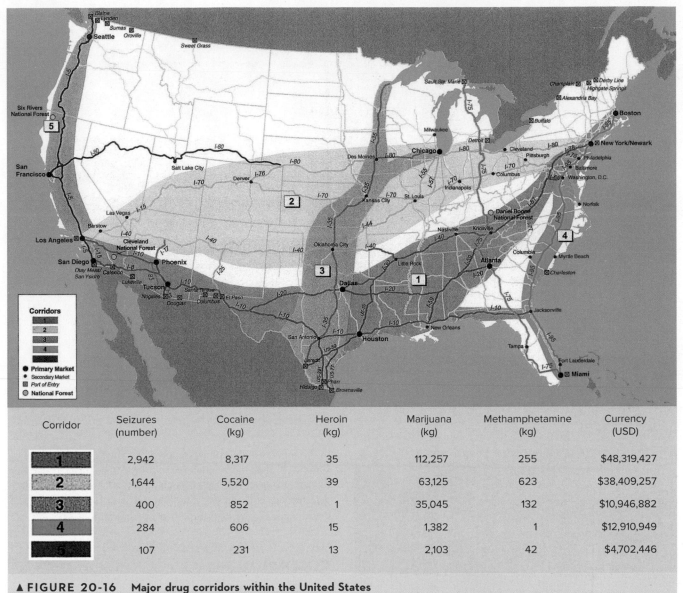

Corridor	Seizures (number)	Cocaine (kg)	Heroin (kg)	Marijuana (kg)	Methamphetamine (kg)	Currency (USD)
1	2,942	8,317	35	112,257	255	$48,319,427
2	1,644	5,520	39	63,125	623	$38,409,257
3	400	852	1	35,045	132	$10,946,882
4	284	606	15	1,382	1	$12,910,949
5	107	231	13	2,103	42	$4,702,446

▲ **FIGURE 20-16** Major drug corridors within the United States

Source: Adapted from the United States National Drug Intelligence Center.

with a rail system, ventilation and fluorescent lighting. The tunnel represented one of the most sophisticated in design and was used extensively for the transportation of heroin, cocaine, methamphetamines, and marijuana smuggling. The tunnel was also suspected to have been used to transport illegal aliens and human-trafficking victims exploited for sexual purposes inside the United States. (Refer to Chapter 12, "Human Trafficking," for more information on this subject.) As a result of this tunnel, the San Bernardino County Sheriff's Office, San Diego Police Department, Immigration and Customs Enforcement (ICE) and the Drug Enforcement Administration (DEA) have developed a new unit (The San Diego Tunnel Task Force) focused on the discovery of tunnels.

Mexico also exports nearly 7 tons of heroin a year into the United States. Black tar heroin, a powerful yet inexpensive variety of the opiate, is made exclusively in Mexico.[63] The drug is smuggled into the United States mostly via pedestrian couriers and commercial and private vehicles. The most common points of entry are in Texas, particularly at Laredo and El Paso, and California at San Ysidro.[64]

Drug Violence in Mexico

Mexico's prolific drug export business has had an increasingly violent effect on the country. Since Mexican President Felipe Calderon launched an offensive on drug cartels in 2006, more than 100,000 people have died in drug-related violence. Those killed include federal troops and police fighting an offensive against organized trafficking, politicians, cartel members who have run afoul of their own organizations, cartel members in conflict with other cartels, and scores of innocent bystanders. Calderon directly blames the United States for the turmoil and violence in his country, stating "The origin of our violence problem begins with the fact that Mexico is located next to the country that has the highest levels of drug consumption in the world."[65]

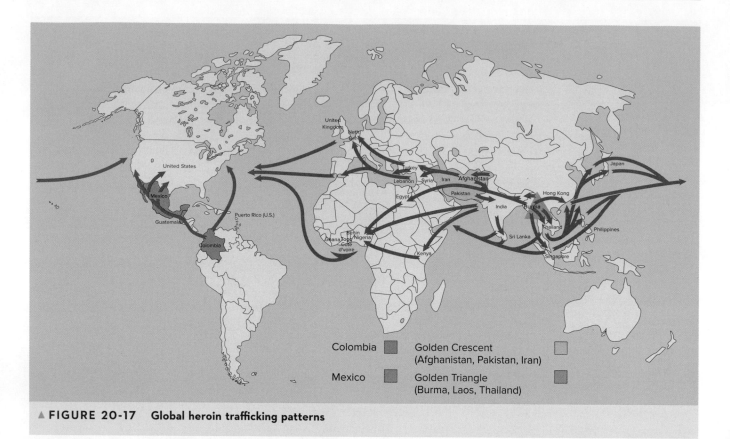

▲ FIGURE 20-17   **Global heroin trafficking patterns**

▲ **FIGURE 20-18**
Drug tunnel discovered in San Diego, California, in 2015
(©U.S. Immigration and Customs Enforcement/AP Images)

The hardest hit areas of Mexico are those in the northern border area, with Ciudad Juarez—just miles from El Paso, Texas—as one of the most notable. There are also high levels of violence in Michoacán and Guerrero states. Travel advisories to Mexico have been extended by the U.S. State Department for tourists as a result of the turmoil within the country. That turmoil has officials watching border states closely for an uptick in violence that may have spilled over the border. Authorities in Arizona and Texas have reported an increase in home invasions and abductions related to the Mexican drug trade, and bodies of cartel foes have been found over the border.[66] However, El Paso—one of the American cities closest to the chaos—was recently named the safest city in the United States.[67]

COLOMBIA

The country of Colombia, located in South America, has a political and environmental climate perfectly suited for the production and distribution of cocaine, heroin, and marijuana. Fertile valleys, which are generally removed from populated areas, are ideal for cultivation of opium poppies, marijuana plants, and coca leaves. Colombia also imports the coca plant, from Peru (the world's main source of the plant) and Bolivia for manufacture. Government corruption and political unrest in the country has created an atmosphere where clandestine cocaine production facilities can operate without fear of government intervention. These labs, in turn, are able to manufacture more cocaine than any other country in the world.[68] The drug is then generally delivered to Mexican traffickers for delivery into the United States through Texas, California, Arizona, and New Mexico. After the drug reaches the United States, it is transported to either Mexican or Colombian trafficking groups for distribution into markets such as Baltimore, Boston, Detroit, Newark, and Phoenix. Marijuana and heroin are transported similarly, often through complex maritime shipments to Mexico. Heroin may be shipped directly into the United States by couriers aboard commercial airline flights.[69]

THE GOLDEN CRESCENT

The Golden Crescent is the moniker adopted for three countries in Southwest Asia: Afghanistan, Pakistan, and Iran. Currently, these countries contribute a large percentage of the heroin imported into the United States, with Afghanistan holding a virtual monopoly on the heroin market. Afghanistan cultivates nearly 90% of the world's opium poppy supply, especially since war and political turmoil in the region makes opium one of the few viable and profitable crops.[70] Most of the crops, along with those from Pakistan and Iran, are exported into Turkey, where traffickers then use couriers to bring the drugs into the United States via commercial airlines. Most of these smuggled shipments are bound for New York and Chicago, where they are either sold locally or transported to other markets.[71] Pakistan and Afghanistan are also the largest producers of hashish.

THE GOLDEN TRIANGLE

Burma, Laos, and Thailand make up the area referred to as the Golden Triangle, known mainly for heroin and marijuana production. Thailand is also a major producer of methamphetamine. Drugs from this area are transported to the United States by Thai nationals, as well as Nigerian and Chinese traffickers. The main modes of transport include couriers on commercial flights, mail, and by concealment in cargo containers. Most of the shipments to the United States are bound for the East Coast, particularly to the Baltimore, Washington D.C., New York, and Chicago areas. Another route for drugs from the Golden Triangle into the United States is through the U.S./Canadian border, particularly at Detroit and Buffalo, New York.[72]

EUROPE

Western Europe remains the biggest producer of MDMA, or ecstasy. The DEA estimated that nearly 80% of the ecstasy coming into the United States came from Western Europe, particularly Belgium and the Netherlands.[73] This drug is often directly transported by couriers into major U.S. airports such as JFK International in New York and Los Angeles International.

DRUG INVESTIGATIONS

Narcotics investigations are particularly challenging to law enforcement because most investigations begin before a crime actually occurs. The goal of any narcotics investigation, then, is to establish that there is probable cause that an individual or group is breaking the law by using, manufacturing, or selling drugs. Once probable cause has been established by methods such as surveillance, informant use or undercover work, search warrants may be granted and arrests can be made.

GATHERING INFORMATION

Drug investigations must rely heavily on information from outside sources in order to develop a case. In fact, initiating a drug case depends on how well investigators can locate and identify leads that will strengthen their case against an identified target. Sources of information relevant to drug investigation targets can include telephone complaints, confidential informants, patrol officers, private sector sources, outside agencies, and internal police records.

Anonymous Tips

Anonymous tips can come from people with varying motives: relatives or neighbors may be concerned about a loved one's health or about their own safety if drug manufacture or other such activity is taking place near their home; the exgirlfriend or boyfriend of a drug dealer may turn them in for the sake of revenge; or a disgruntled customer may anonymously tip off police if he or she feels cheated by a dealer.

Telephone calls to law enforcement agencies are the most common form of anonymous tip. Because anonymous tipsters generally prefer to remain anonymous, great care must be taken by those who answer such phone calls to capture as much relevant information as possible. Narcotics investigators should train telephone operators to consistently ask specific information that will help to prioritize complaints. Narcotics complaints are different from others in that there is often no obvious victim or evidence that a drug crime has happened after it has been committed. It is therefore important that those taking telephone reports of a drug crime ascertain whether the information is more than hearsay.[74] When taking a telephone complaint about a drug crime, one should note whether the complainant has actually witnessed the crime that he or she is reporting. One should also note whether or not the complainant has personally been involved in a narcotics transaction with the person he or she is registering the complaint against and is willing to assist in the investigation or talk to police or prosecutors if necessary. If a complainant is merely reporting what he or she heard from a third party, the report will take a lower priority than one from a caller who reports specific, first-hand information relating to drug manufacture or sale. However, any information that might corroborate an existing investigation should be a priority.

CONFIDENTIAL INFORMANTS

Although legitimate telephone or walk-in complaints from the public are valuable to drug investigators, they are relatively rare. Narcotics investigators have to rely heavily on the use of confidential informants, who generally know dealers, manufacturers, and users personally. Confidential informants are useful because they are able to gather information not usually available to law enforcement officers through their personal knowledge and familiarity with narcotics offenders. They are often able to gain first-hand and up-to-the-minute information about drug crimes that can be the basis of warrants for searches and arrests if properly corroborated by the investigator.[75] However, the ability of informants to gather such information often means that they are criminals themselves, making their motivations suspect and the management of such informants difficult. The career of a narcotics investigator often depends on how well he or she is able to recruit, develop, and manage informants. As a result, it is crucial that investigators understand motivations and types of informants.

INFORMANTS: MOTIVATIONS AND TYPES

Like most people, informants need motivation to produce. The more motivated they are, the more likely they are to apply themselves to the task at hand and remain committed to achieving success. Therefore, by identifying an informant's true motives, an investigator greatly enhances the potential success of an investigation. Initially, informants commonly voice a specific motive for providing assistance. However, as a case proceeds and a relationship with an investigator develops, other reasons may surface. Some of the more common motivational factors encountered by drug enforcement investigators are fear, revenge, money, repentance, and altruism.[76]

The most frequently encountered motivational factor may be the confidential informant's (CI's) fear of punishment for criminal acts. Severe criminal penalties tend to increase the number of persons wanting to cooperate with drug-enforcement authorities. Informants may also fear their criminal associates. Individuals wrongly accused by drug dealers of being informants may then become informants for self-preservation, money, or both.

Informants frequently cooperate with the government to seek revenge against their enemies. Jealousy may also prompt their acts of vengeance.

Some individuals provide information or services for money. These money-motivated informants, known as *mercenaries*, are usually the most willing to follow the directions of their handlers. Mercenaries frequently possess other motives as well.

Repentance can be a motivating factor. Informants often claim they cooperate in order to repent for past crimes. However, this is seldom their only motive for cooperating.

Some individuals are motivated by a sense of altruism. People with professional obligations or feelings of responsibility frequently provide information to the police. Examples of altruistic informants include airline ticket agents and private mail-service carriers.

Problem Informants

Some informants have personalities that make them difficult, if not impossible, to manage. These individuals may also have questionable motives for offering their services to a law enforcement agency. Investigators who misjudge the true motives of informants experience tremendous control problems, which can create safety issues and place department resources and personnel in jeopardy. Therefore, investigators should avoid recruiting certain types of individuals, if possible.

Egotistical Informants

Egotistical informants, who are encountered frequently, may not have received positive reinforcement from their parents or schoolmates when growing up. Consequently, they seek positive feedback from their handlers as their primary reward. Investigators who provide this positive reinforcement motivate egotistical informants to continue supplying information. Unfortunately, these informants are often the hardest to handle, because their egos prevent them from relinquishing control of the investigation entirely to their handlers.

Informants with "James Bond Syndrome"

Some persons see their roles as informants as a way to have their lives imitate art. While working as informants, they imagine themselves in a police or spy drama. Sometimes they even attempt to orchestrate events to parallel a scene from a movie or novel. Frequently hard to handle, these informants often exaggerate their knowledge of criminal activity to enhance the likelihood of their becoming informants.

Wannabe Informants

Wannabe informants are people who, for whatever reason, failed to qualify for a law enforcement position and now seek to become involved in law enforcement as informants. Because they lack criminal associates, these individuals usually cannot provide specific information about drug dealing. Therefore, they do not make good informants.

Perversely Motivated Informants

The most dangerous and disruptive informants in drug law enforcement are perversely motivated CIs. They offer their services in order to identify undercover agents; learn the department's methods, targets, and intelligence; or eliminate their own competition in drug sales. Sometimes criminal organizations instruct these individuals to infiltrate departments and learn whatever they can to assist the traffickers. These individuals may even provide genuine information about specific events as a decoy to divert resources from more significant trafficking activity.

Therefore, investigators must question all walk-in and call-in informants (that is, individuals who volunteer their services without prompting), because they may be, or have the potential to be, perversely motivated. After completing a thorough background investigation of CIs, investigators must constantly guard against providing more information than informants furnish in return. Furthermore, investigators should not discuss specific details of methods and techniques used during drug investigations with informants.

Restricted-Use Informants

In addition to problem informants certain other informants, by virtue of their criminal background or other status, pose special management challenges to both investigators and supervisors.[77] Department managers should carefully scrutinize these individuals before using them as CIs. Examples include juveniles, individuals on probation or parole, individuals currently or formerly addicted to drugs, felons with multiple convictions, and individuals known to be unreliable.

Investigators should not use these individuals as informants until a supervisor approves them. In fact, because these informants require special scrutiny, only senior investigators should handle them. Furthermore, investigators must constantly reevaluate the motives of these individuals.

DEPARTMENT POLICY

Agencies should not leave the management of drug informants exclusively to investigators. Formulating a written policy ensures consistency in the use and management of CIs and serves as a guide for inexperienced investigators.[78]

The policy should indicate which investigators may maintain informants, as well as who will supervise these CIs. In addition, the policy should clearly establish that informants are assets of the department, not of individual investigators. In this regard, management should both authorize and encourage investigators to share informants. Also, checks and balances must be in place to ensure that the policy is followed.

Policy concerning the management of confidential informants should establish procedures in several areas. These include creating and documenting informant files, debriefing and interacting with informants, and determining methods and amounts of payments for services rendered.

The Informant File

Investigators should formally establish files for CIs who regularly furnish information, as well as for those who expect compensation for information they supply. Informant files document investigators' interactions with CIs. In fact, investigators should not use any source that cannot be documented.

Although investigators should document their contacts with CIs, not everyone in the department needs to know an informant's identity or have access to informant files. Access should be on a need-to-know basis, including only the investigators and their supervisors who deal directly with the informant.

To further protect informants' identities, investigators should use code numbers in lieu of informants' names in investigative reports. Informants should keep the same number throughout their working relationships with the department.

The informant file should include information pertaining to the CI's vital statistics, such as physical description, work and home addresses, vehicles driven, contact telephone numbers, next of kin, and so forth. National Crime Information Center searches, performed before the informant is used and then systematically thereafter, ensure that the informant has no outstanding warrants. These records should be kept in the informant's file, along with the CI's photograph, fingerprints, and FBI and state "rap" sheets.

Establishing an informant file sends a not-so-subtle message to CIs that investigators document every encounter and verify all information that CIs supply. Such documentation may also deter a perversely motivated informant. In addition, informant files enhance the credibility of the department in the eyes of the court and the public, who view CIs as inherently unreliable and who may believe that the agency fabricated information. Therefore, every time an informant provides information concerning an actual or a potential criminal matter, the agency should include a written report detailing this information in the CI's file. The original report should remain in that file, and a copy should be maintained in the case file.

The department must also document what steps it takes to corroborate information provided by a CI. This is especially important when informants act unilaterally. As a matter of policy, all CI information should be verified regardless of the CI's past reliability.

Informant Debriefings

Each time investigators initiate investigations on the basis of information received from a CI, the designated handler should interview and debrief the CI in order to ascertain the informant's motive(s) and to advise the informant of the department's rules. For example, informants should know that they carry no official status with the department, that the department will not tolerate their breaking the law or entrapping suspects, and that the department cannot guarantee that they will not be called as witnesses in court.

At the end of the interview, the investigator should put this information in writing in an "informant agreement." This agreement should be signed by the informant, witnessed by the handler, and placed in the informant's file. Investigators should debrief their informants on a regular basis—for example, every 30, 60, or 90 days—to keep them active or, if necessary, to terminate their association with the department because of lack of productivity.

Investigator-Informant Contact Procedures

The department must establish investigator-informant contact procedures and train employees in their use. For example, the handler should meet with the informant in private, if possible, but always in the presence of another investigator. In fact, the department should either strongly discourage or prohibit investigators from contacting informants alone, especially if the officer plans to pay the informant. Meeting with or paying a drug informant alone leaves the officer and the department vulnerable to allegations of wrongdoing.

Although informant handlers often develop special working relationships with their informants, department policies should preclude contact with informants outside the scope of official business. Investigators must keep their relationships with CIs strictly professional. This is particularly important when the informant and the investigator are not of the same sex. Policies should also expressly prohibit such contact as socializing with informants and/or their families, becoming romantically involved with informants, conducting nonpolice business with them, and accepting gifts or gratuities from them.[79]

To ensure adherence to department policy, supervisors should review informant files regularly. In addition, they need to attend debriefings periodically to oversee the entire informant management process.

Finally, department administrators must establish procedures for investigating alleged policy violations by investigators or informants. Thorough investigations of this type maintain the integrity of the department by dispelling any notion that the department does not enforce its own policies.

Informant Payments

Payments to CIs can be divided into two distinct categories—awards and rewards. Awards take a monetary form. They are based on a percentage of the net value of assets seized during a drug investigation as a result of information provided by a CI. Advising the informant of the exact amount of the percentage at the beginning of the case provides incentive for the CI to seek out hidden assets that might otherwise go undetected. However, because payments based on seized assets are not universally accepted in the courts, the investigator should consult the case prosecutor before promising a specific amount to the informant.

Rewards, however, do not represent a percentage of the value of the seized assets. Amounts are usually determined by the type and the quantity of drugs seized, the quality of the case produced, the number of defendants indicted, the amount of time and effort the CI exerted, and the danger faced by the CI during the course of the investigation. Unlike awards, rewards come directly from an agency's budget.

While an informant might receive money as a reward, many informants cooperate with law enforcement agencies to receive a reduced sentence for a pending criminal matter. Regardless of the form of compensation, the department's policy must address (1) the circumstances under which an informant qualifies for an award and/or reward, (2) who can authorize such payments, and (3) the conditions under which payments will be granted.

Although many informants receive substantial awards when they locate the assets of drug dealers, agency budgets may limit the dollar amount of rewards paid to informants. For this reason, investigators should exercise caution when explaining the payment policy to informants. They should avoid mentioning a specific dollar amount that the informant will receive. Otherwise, the informant may try to hold the department to that amount, regardless of future budgetary constraints.

In addition to providing awards and rewards, departments can reimburse informants for expenses incurred during an investigation. In fact, the department may want to reimburse the CI with small amounts of money beyond actual expenses as added incentives to continue working.

It is highly recommended that informants be paid only in the presence of witnesses, with the final payment being made after all court proceedings have been completed to help ensure the informant's presence at the trial. Once a payment is made, a record documenting the date, exact amount, and payer must be included in the CI file in anticipation of future court inquiries.

OTHER SOURCES FOR INFORMATION

Patrol officers are a valuable asset to narcotics investigators, and every effort should be made by investigators to foster a good relationship with them. Patrol officers have inherent advantages over investigators because they already have a routine presence in neighborhoods where drug activity takes place, allowing them to collect specific information without arousing suspicion. Furthermore, patrol officers are familiar with the layout of neighborhoods and, on occasion, specific houses or buildings, making them invaluable in planning surveillance or raids.[80] Patrol officers may also have unofficial informants who may be parlayed into formal informants for narcotics investigators. Because of the additional resources that they offer, developing relationships with patrol officers is a sound strategy in drug investigations.

Information from Private Sector Sources

The private sector can provide a wealth of information valuable to drug cases about suspects and their behavior. Drug offenders tend to come into contact with a predictable group of private sector businesses, such as travel agents, car rental employees, hotel clerks, retail clerks, and pharmacists, who may volunteer information to investigators.[81] Travel agents can show investigators patterns of travel that may outline trafficking destinations. Retail clerks may be able to tell officers about customers who repeatedly purchase large quantities of the materials found in crystal meth. Realtors are often able to obtain floor plans for homes they have sold, aiding in the planning of raids or searches.

Telephone/cellular phone providers and Internet service providers are also valuable tools to investigators. Internet service providers can pull and track e-mails that may be pertinent to investigations. This generally requires a court order. Lists of telephone calls made from a phone must also be obtained via subpoena. This information is one of the most important tools available to a narcotics investigator as it allows them to track communications between drug offenders, leading to identification of other involved parties or triangulation of hiding places, clandestine labs, and the like.[82]

Outside Agencies

Outside agencies can also offer a wealth of information about a suspect in a narcotics investigation. Outside police agencies, such as the Drug Enforcement Administration (DEA), the Federal Bureau of Investigation (FBI), the Internal Revenue Service (IRS), Immigration and Customs Enforcement (ICE), and others, may have useful information or resources to offer investigators. For example, the IRS may be investigating a suspect on money laundering charges and could provide information pertinent to that suspect's drug activities. Investigators should keep in mind, however, that not all outside law enforcement agencies are forthcoming with information that they have obtained about a suspect. Often, developing relationships with agents in organizations that an investigator has frequent contact with is a good way to obtain information that would not normally be shared with other agencies.

Many agencies use shared databases where information about ongoing cases, upcoming busts, and suspects is available at the click of a mouse. Police agencies may subscribe to such databases or may obtain access by way of task forces or other forms of interagency cooperation.

Internal Records

One of the best sources of information for investigations is the drug unit's own police department. Investigators should look for the following types of information when searching for intelligence on a suspect, criminal organization, or geographical area: police intelligence reports organized by suspect name, address, or type of criminal activity; incident reports that contain records of previous offenses; National Crime Information Center (NCIC) records, which contain in-depth information on a person's criminal history; field interview cards filled out routinely by patrol officers investigating criminal activity; traffic citations, which are helpful in obtaining physical descriptions and other identifiers; fingerprint files; arrest records; and warrant files, which include detailed information about a suspect or a physical location.[83]

SURVEILLANCE

Surveillance, defined as the "surreptitious observation of persons, places, objects, or conveyances for the purpose of determining criminal involvement,"[84] is an excellent tool used by narcotics investigators to gather information about a suspect. Surveillance is required to corroborate intelligence from informants, confirm criminal activity, obtain probable cause and to gather intelligence about a suspect's routines and behaviors that may be of use in planning apprehension.

Surveillance is an expensive and very time-consuming activity. It requires the efforts of multiple officers at a time, including a supervisor. Equipment required for surveillance, such as binoculars, cameras with telephoto lenses, communication systems, and night-vision devices is costly. Furthermore, officers may spend long periods of time trying to achieve the objectives of any surveillance operation. Anywhere from a few hours to a couple of weeks may be spent watching a subject, depending on the complexity of an investigation.

Before any type of surveillance begins, officers should have already gathered basic information about a suspect. Physical descriptions of the suspect and his or her vehicle are crucial, as well as descriptions of associates. The suspect's home and business address should be ascertained, in addition to the addresses of locations he or she frequents.

Once this basic information has been determined, investigators should scout out the locations where surveillance will take place. Investigators should map out the area, finding the best places from which to conduct surveillance. It is also a good idea to become familiar with the layout of the area, noting street names and traffic conditions to ensure maximum mobility. Officers should also determine what types of vehicles are more likely to go unnoticed in the area, and how they should dress so that they don't look suspicious or out of place while conducting surveillance.

Electronic Surveillance

Electronic surveillance is often used to supplement mobile and stationary surveillance and is also very useful as supporting evidence in court cases. However, electronic surveillance is also subject to a number of legal considerations because of its intrusive nature. Officers should familiarize themselves with case law relevant to electronic surveillance and always consult with prosecutors before utilizing these types of surveillance.

The most prominent method of electronic surveillance is wiretapping, using third-party eavesdropping devices placed on telephone lines to capture conversations. As often as wiretaps are seen as investigative tools on fictional law enforcement television shows, they are actually used as a last resort in many cases. They are very expensive and time-intensive. Furthermore, they are quite complex, legally speaking. In *Katz* v. *United States,* 389 U.S. 347 (1967), the United States Supreme Court held that wiretaps create an intrusion into a person's reasonable expectation of privacy and therefore constitute a "search and seizure" as defined by the Fourth Amendment to the Constitution of the United States. As a result, wiretaps require probable cause and a warrant to authorize the intrusion. However, they are a very useful tool in many complex investigations.

When an officer is a party to a conversation with a suspect, generally in cases in which undercover officers are being utilized, he or she can record the conversation without violating the suspect's reasonable expectation of privacy. Recording telephone conversations between an officer and a suspect is allowable then, as is use of a concealed microphone.

Pen registers are another means of telephone surveillance. These tools decode the dialed impulses on phone lines in order to record all numbers dialed from that phone. They record the date and time of all phone calls and thus are effective tools when the suspect routinely uses his/her phone to conduct drug transactions. However, the information gained is of little value unless investigators invest time into following up information obtained by the pen registers.

Video and Photo Surveillance

Known as *visual surveillance*, the use of both still and video cameras to corroborate audio surveillance and officer observation is important to drug investigations and their prosecution. When using still photography, investigators can use 35-mm or small digital cameras to document criminal activity. Although basic camera setups are sufficient, attachments such as telephoto lenses and night-vision equipment can enhance photographs. Date and time stamps on cameras may also be helpful for purposes of corroboration.

Video cameras provide a more complete document of surveillance activity than photographs do and can also be fitted with night-vision or infrared equipment for nighttime surveillance.[85]

Trash

Searching through discarded trash is another supplement to surveillance. Often suspects may discard documents or materials that are helpful to investigators trying to establish probable cause. For example, crystal meth manufacturers often discard telltale signs that they are operating a meth lab, such as large quantities of empty blister packs that contained pseudoephedrine pills or battery packages. Investigators should take care to remain surreptitious when retrieving and going through a suspect's

► FIGURE 20-19
Drug dog in action
Canines provide an invaluable service to police officers in detecting the presence of drugs in clandestine places. They are often used during search warrant executions as well as during routine checks of international flights to detect smuggled drugs and paraphernalia.
(©Daniel Munoz/Reuters/Alamy)

trash. *Trashing,* as it is sometimes called, does not require a warrant, because there is no expectation of privacy with discarded trash that is essentially in plain view for all to see.

UNDERCOVER OPERATIONS

Often portrayed by popular television and movies, undercover drug operations are actually used quite sparingly by law enforcement. These operations are very dangerous and can take a large toll on the personal lives of undercover officers. However, they are quite useful in identifying participants in drug conspiracies, whether they involve manufacturers, distributors, or users. Undercover officers can often predict which participants may be cooperative with law enforcement and are able to identify evidence for prosecution of drug crimes. They are often privy to locations of drugs or other evidence and usually know the locations of drug proceeds as well. The undercover officer is also very useful in determining the time and place appropriate for search and seizures and arrests[86] (Figure 20-19).

The officers selected for undercover work ultimately determine the success of the operation. They should be intelligent, reliable, confident, resourceful, and have good judgment and excellent communication skills. They should also have a solid knowledge base of the types(s) of drug they are investigating. Training is essential to the success of the undercover officer. Experienced undercover officers should always be the first choice for assignments, unless a less-experienced officer has a special skill required in the investigation that other officers do not (such as Spanish-language proficiency).[87]

Undercover operations may be as simple as a one-off purchase from a dealer or as in-depth as posing as someone who possesses a special skill needed by a drug trafficker, such as a truck driver or a pilot. The amount of preparation and back story needed will vary depending on the complexity of the operations. Smaller operations are the norm in drug investigations, and minimizing the contact between undercover officers and suspects is ideal, because the longer a suspect and officer have contact, the more likely it is that the officer will be discovered. Long-term undercover operations are expensive and dangerous, and generally are not used by local law enforcement entities.

Buying drugs from a suspect is the best means of gathering evidence about a drug operation. When an undercover officer develops a relationship with a suspect, he or she will generally have many opportunities to purchase drugs as evidence. Officers should have some type of monitored surveillance, such as a hidden microphone, ongoing throughout the transaction, allowing for corroboration as well as officer safety. This is a situation unique to drug investigations, because the officer is actually participating in the commission of a crime. This is lawful, provided that it can be shown that the suspect would have committed the act with or without the presence of the officer.[88] **Drug buy operations** by undercover officers generally fall under one of four categories.

Buy-Walk

These types of buys are usually made as part of an ongoing investigation whereby investigators attempt to make cases against distributors by working up the ladder to the source or merely attempting to gain the confidence of the seller. In buy-walk cases, the undercover officer purchases drugs from the suspect but does not initiate an arrest after completion of the deal. The officer often makes multiple buys from the suspect. This method fosters a business relationship with the suspect and generates a number of investigative leads. Once the suspect feels comfortable with the officer, the officer may get an opportunity to identify places of residence and observe other associates.[89] Small, multiple purchases may be chemically analyzed for purity and for signatures that can be traced back to distributors. Furthermore, with each drug purchase, larger quantities may be negotiated in order to pinpoint the source of the drugs. One successful technique is to work up to requesting a quantity that the dealer is incapable of

◀FIGURE 20-20
Undercover officer making an immediate narcotics arrest on the street
"Buy/Bust" operations are commonly used by the police to control drug traffic. Most often, they yield low amounts of drugs and cash but are designed to have an immediate impact on the visible trade in a specific area or neighborhood. (©ChameleonsEye/ Shutterstock RF)

providing without traveling to his or her supplier and then conducting vehicle surveillance to identify the supplier.[90]

Buy-Bust

In the buy-bust, the undercover officer completes a drug buy, resulting in the immediate arrest of the seller (Figure 20-20). These operations generally take place only with small amounts of drugs or cash and are considered very dangerous to the undercover officer, owing to the proximity between the officer and the suspect when the arrest commences. Undercover officers should not be physically involved with the arrest and should in fact back away from the situation as much as possible once they have completed the transaction. This method is generally used in small cases, where conspiracies are not involved.[91]

Buy(Flash)/Bust

This is the most commonly used technique in undercover drug enforcement operations. The "flash" is a large quantity of money that an undercover officer shows to a suspect without actually giving it to them. It serves as a guarantee that the undercover officer can pay for a large quantity of drugs upon delivery. This operation is very dangerous; undercover officers have been murdered for the flash money, which can range from $5,000 to $100,000. Following is a list of considerations essential to ensuring safe management of the buy(flash)/bust:[92]

1. Whenever possible, isolate the suspects and get them on neutral ground to do the transaction.
2. Do not allow the suspects to isolate the undercover officer. The best way to avoid this is by staying on neutral ground. The undercover officer should dictate the time and the place to the suspects.
3. Flash the money in an open location, isolating suspects from one another if possible. Do not flash the money twice in the same location.

4. Minimize the vulnerability of the undercover officer during the bust.
5. The undercover officer should always be armed.

Flash busts are very effective but must be carefully managed to ensure the safety and the integrity of the investigation. Informants should never be allowed to handle flash rolls, and if possible, two undercover officers should be used in these types of transactions. If one officer handles the money, he/she can leave as soon as the flash is completed, increasing the safety of both officers.[93] Flash busts require extensive training and a consistent policy on the part of police departments, and should only be attempted by experienced undercover officers.

Reverse Operations

The final type of undercover operation is the reverse operation. Reverse undercover operations are those in which the officer acts as the seller of the drug, in an effort to obtain probable cause against drug buyers. This type of operation is more controversial than the buy/busts previously discussed, because of the element of entrapment bound to be brought up in defense claims. Investigators must take care to show other evidence that the buyer was predetermined to commit the crime, with or without the presence of the officer.[94]

Undercover operations are far more complex than a few pages in a textbook can convey. Entire books have been written about the factors involved in such operations, and undercover officers receive careful and in-depth training to help them prepare for all levels of undercover work. Undercover work in narcotics investigation is a valuable tool but requires immense operational planning to be successful and safe.

Informant Purchases

A tool similar to undercover purchases of drugs involves confidential informants obtaining drugs via a controlled purchase. This usually occurs when use of an undercover officer would be impractical. If a peddler will sell only to an informant and not to an undercover officer, the informant must be searched before the sale to make sure that he/she has no narcotics already on his/her person. Officers should ensure that the informant has no money on him, except official funds with recorded serial numbers for the purchase. The informant should be wired with a hidden microphone in order to corroborate the transactions. Surveillance teams should monitor the informant constantly throughout the transaction, and the informant should go to a designated location immediately after the transaction in order to be searched. At that time, evidence should be recovered from the informant, and he or she should be thoroughly debriefed. Evidence obtained through "informant buys" is admissible in court, but the testimony of the informant may be required.

Drug Canines

Drug dogs are extremely useful to narcotics investigations; a positive alert by a canine can provide probable cause to further search a suspect. Dogs have a keen sense of odor, with nearly 30 times more olfactory cells than humans. When properly trained, canines can be used in a variety of settings to detect the presence of drugs. Drug dogs are usually used to provide passive alerts that drugs are present. This means that the dog either sits or uses some other signal (such as a bark) when the odor of drugs is detected. Canines can be used in vehicle examinations, freight examinations, consensual encounters between suspects and officers in homes, airports, businesses, bus stations, and storage facilities. Canines may also be used in limited person examinations.[95]

The Supreme Court ruled in *U.S.* v. *Place*, 462 US 696 (1983) that use of a drug canine to sniff property is not considered a search. However, use of a drug dog to sniff a person is less clear legally. Many courts have ruled that using canines to sniff a person for presence of drug odors requires reasonable suspicion and that random and suspicionless dog sniffs are not reasonable.[96]

Drug dogs differ from track-and-bite canines, which are taught to be aggressive upon apprehension of a subject. Drug dogs must never use aggression toward a suspect. Canines are a very expensive undertaking for a police department. They must be carefully trained, and a handler must be selected and trained. The training of a drug dog is ongoing and is critical to the admissibility to the any evidence obtained through its use.

Field Testing

A variety of field testing kits are available to law enforcement to give valuable clues about the identity of substances. Field tests can test for the presence of specific substances, including marijuana, cocaine, amphetamine, and heroin. Investigator kits usually include vials of chemicals in small pouches. When small samples of a substance are put into the pouch and then the chemicals in the vials are released, the mixture will produce certain colors. Those colors indicate the presence of controlled substances.[97]

Field tests are easy to perform. They are, however, only presumptive because they may produce false positives. Any drug that will be used as evidence must be positively identified by a qualified chemist. Additionally, a negative test does not preclude the possibility that another similar drug may be present.[98]

HIGH-INTENSITY DRUG TRAFFICKING AREA (HIDTA) PROGRAMS

HIDTA programs are an invaluable resource to narcotics investigations. HIDTA programs were created by the Anti-Drug Abuse Act of 1988 and provide federal assistance to better coordinate and enhance counterdrug law enforcement efforts of local, state, and federal agencies in areas where major drug activity occurs. Currently, there are 31 HIDTAs in the nation, including Puerto Rico and the U.S. Virgin Islands (Figure 20-21). HIDTAs are joint efforts of regional, local, and federal agencies, whose leaders work

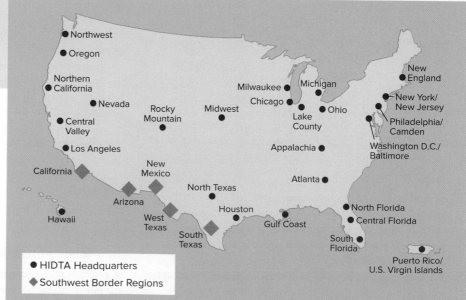

▶ **FIGURE 20-21**
High-intensity drug trafficking area—HIDTA task force locations
(Office of National Drug Control Policy; see www.whitehousedrugpolicy.gov/hidta/)

together to assess regional drug threats, to design strategies to combat those threats, and to develop initiatives to implement the strategies. Regional strategies include building multiagency task forces. HIDTA legislation also provides for investigative support centers in designated areas that create a communications infrastructure that can facilitate information-sharing between agencies.[99] For example, the Washington/Baltimore area HIDTA offers software for participating agencies that provides case management functions and also notifies agencies if another agency is collecting information on the same suspect. They also grant access to a number of databases that allow investigators to access law enforcement records and financial information.[100] The North Texas HIDTA analyzes information from participating departments, and identifies major drug trafficking organizations, including patterns and trends of these organizations. The North Texas HIDTA's Investigative Support Center prepared 644 intelligence profiles and conducted over 10,000 database searches in 2012. That same year, the North Texas HIDTA seized 23 pounds of methamphetamine in the course of one investigation in the Dallas area, and indicted 24 participants in a crack-cocaine distribution ring in Denton, TX.[101]

HIDTAs are just one example of a task force in action. Each jurisdiction may have its own drug task forces, involving a variety of law enforcement or outside agencies, which are valuable to narcotics investigations. Investigators should take full advantage of these resources, when available.

SEARCHES, SEIZURES, AND WARRANTS

Drug investigations are useless without evidence. Therefore, it is vitally important that an investigator be knowledgeable of the latest legal guidelines that govern the search for, and seizure of, evidence. Case law in the United States provides literally thousands of decisions that affect how officers may handle searches and seizures. There are some major principles, however, that every narcotics investigator should be familiar with in order to present a legally sound case against drug criminals. Things that are commonly searched for and seized in drug crimes include the drugs themselves or other contraband; instrumentalities of a crime, meaning those items that are not necessarily illegal on their own but that are used to carry out a crime; fruits of a crime, such as things bought with drug proceeds; and mere evidence of a crime.

PROBABLE CAUSE

The general requirements for searches and seizures of evidence or persons are a search warrant or recognized exception to the warrant requirement (to be discussed later) and probable cause. Probable cause to search and seize exists when "facts and circumstances in a given situation are sufficient to warrant a person of reasonable caution to believe that seize-able objects are located at the place to be searched."[102] Generally, a single fact cannot establish probable cause; it is usually several facts and

circumstances taken together that do. Probable cause may also be established by hearsay, which is typically the case with informants. This information may be used as long it can be shown that the totality of the circumstances surrounding the information suggests that it is reliable. Information should be verifiable, and corroborating information is helpful in establishing probable cause.[103]

SEARCH WARRANTS

The search warrant is one of the most valuable tools available to a narcotics investigator. The warrant authorizes searches of homes, businesses, and automobiles of subjects and generally results in the arrest of multiple suspects, expediting the investigation and its closure.[104]

Searches require search warrants, or a recognized exception to a warrant in order to be legal. There are four requirements for the valid issuance of a search warrant. The first is that a neutral and impartial magistrate authorizes the warrant. The second requirement is that probable cause exists to search the place described in the warrant. Third, the warrant must be precise in describing both the places and persons to be searched and the items to be seized. Fourth, the warrant requires a supporting oath or affirmation by the requesting officer. Narcotics officers requesting a warrant should follow additional guidelines when requesting warrants, since so much of the information provided to law enforcement officers comes from confidential informants.

PAST RELIABILITY OF THE CONFIDENTIAL INFORMANT

The past reliability of the confidential informant is of considerable importance, especially when the effort to determine probable cause to obtain a search warrant is based exclusively on such information. One should consider the length of time the applicant has known the informant and the number of occasions on which reliable information was supplied. For example, how many times before did the confidential informant's information result in the seizure of contraband or paraphernalia on persons, on premises, or in vehicles, and how many of these offenses resulted in a conviction? To confirm that the confidential informant has been reliable, the officer should be prepared to cite specific instances of reliable information. Other considerations are the informant's familiarity with the type of offense involved in the affidavit and familiarity with paraphernalia used in connection with the offense.

INFORMATION SUPPLIED BY THE INFORMANT

Information to be considered in this area includes the date, time, and place of the meeting between police and the informant; the substance and content of the information; and the date, time, and place that the information was obtained.

The law enforcement officer should try to elicit from the informant as many facts as possible that can be corroborated— for example, the telephone number and address of the suspect's residence, a physical description of the suspect, the occupation of the suspect, vehicles owned or operated by the suspect, a description of the vehicle and the tag number, and the time at which the suspect may be observed at the premises or within the described vehicle.

CORROBORATION OF THE INFORMATION SUPPLIED

All efforts should be made to corroborate information supplied by a confidential informant. In some instances, corroboration is a simple check of the accuracy of portions of the information, such as the suspect's address, associates, vehicle, hangouts, patterns of behavior, and criminal record. When information is corroborated, careful records should be kept, including the date, time, and method of corroboration. Some jurisdictions have found it useful to attach a mug shot of the suspect along with a photograph, diagram, or sketch of the property, vehicle, store, or other place to be searched.

There are also requirements for the valid execution of a search warrant. The first is that time limits set out in the warrant or by statute are observed. This requirement ensures that probable cause remains until the warrant is executed. Next, time-of-day limits should be observed. This means that officers should serve warrants at a reasonable hour, mostly because of safety and privacy concerns. Officers must knock and announce their presence before gaining entry to a home or business, unless an exigency exists. Another requirement states that police can not go beyond the terms spelled out in the search warrant. Finally, officers must leave an inventory of items seized with both the suspect and the judge who issued the search warrant.

THE EXCLUSIONARY RULE

This rule states that courts will exclude any evidence that is obtained in violation of the Fourth Amendment's provisions against unreasonable searches and seizures, no matter how pertinent it is to the case at hand. This includes *Fruit of the Poisoned Tree* items. This means that evidence recovered from constitutionally sound methods may be excluded if the initial action was proven to be illegal. For example, an officer may legally search a person incident to their arrest. However, if that initial arrest is later determined to be illegal, the items recovered during the postarrest search may be thrown out.[105] There are exceptions to the exclusionary rule, however. The first is the *Good Faith Exception.* This states that if officers act in reasonable reliance on a search warrant that is issued by a neutral magistrate but is ultimately found to be invalid, the evidence may still be used.[106] The second is the *doctrine of inevitable discovery.* This doctrine holds that evidence that would have been discovered with or without the illegal search or seizure is allowed into court.[107] The computer errors exception allows evidence to be admitted even though the search or seizure was based on an erroneous piece of information.[108]

WARRANTLESS SEARCHES

There are cases where warrants are not necessary, although these are each fairly narrowly defined by the courts. The first is the consent search. These types of searches are permissible without a warrant and without probable cause as long as consent has been voluntarily given by a person who has authority to give consent and that the scope of the search doesn't exceed the consent given. Narcotics officers should keep in mind that the scope of a consent search must be consistent with the nature of the consent given and that the consenter can place limitations on the search.

Vehicle searches are also exempt from the warrant requirement. This is a boon to narcotics officers, because many drug traffickers conceal drugs within their vehicles. The logic behind allowing warrantless searches of vehicles is that there is a reduced expectation of privacy in vehicles because they are mobile and used in public areas, their interiors are visible to the outside, and because vehicles are highly regulated by the government.

Vehicles also create an exigency in that they are inherently moveable. In other words, by the time a narcotics officer is able to write an affidavit and obtain a warrant, the vehicle may be gone. As a result, a narcotics officer may stop a car based on reasonable suspicion and then search that vehicle, including all passenger areas, containers, and the trunk when they have probable cause to believe evidence or contraband is contained.[109]

Vehicles that have been lawfully impounded may also be searched without a warrant, but the search may not be a pretense for further investigation. Searches of impounded vehicles are allowed for the safety of officers and the impounding agency, and as a result must take place within agency guidelines and procedures.

Open-field searches are another type of search that can take place without a warrant. The Supreme Court has held that open fields outside the curtilage surrounding buildings or homes are not constitutionally protected and are therefore allowable without a search warrant. There is no reasonable expectation of privacy in an open field.[110] This particular exception is useful to narcotics officers who might encounter marijuana fields in their investigations.

Another situation in which a search warrant is not required is an exigent situation known as the evanescent evidence exception. In this case, evidence is likely to disappear in the time it would take to get a warrant. In drug cases, this could involve drugs that may be flushed down the toilet in the time needed to secure a warrant. The evanescent evidence exception requires a rough approximation of probable cause and the evidence must be seized in a reasonable manner. Officers may also search without a warrant if there is a threat of a subject escaping in the time it would take to get a warrant, or if there is danger to a person's life.[111]

Plain-view searches may also be conducted without a warrant. Officers may confiscate evidence that they find in plain sight, which is a useful tool to narcotics officers. Often, drug paraphernalia that may be useful evidence are left in plain view. The Supreme Court has ruled that "objects falling in the plain view of an officer who has a right to be in the position to have that view are subject to seizure and may be used as evidence."[112] However, officers may not move other objects to gain a better view of evidence otherwise hidden from view, and the objects

◄ FIGURE 20-22
Officer searching a "crack house." Once an arrest is made, additional drugs may be seized if found in plain sight. Here, officers enter a known drug house through an open door looking for drugs and drug paraphernalia.
(©Michael Matthews - Police Images/Alamy)

cannot be in a position where officers would have to dislodge or move it to examine it closely.

Stop-and-frisk searches are another example of the warrantless search. These are conducted in the interest of officer safety and/ or crime prevention. To stop a suspect, the officer must have articulable facts and reasonable suspicion that criminal activity is afoot. For further procession to a frisk, which is essentially a pat-down of a suspect's outer clothing, there must be reasonable facts to suggest that the individual is presently armed and dangerous.[113] If the officer happens to come across drug paraphernalia during the frisk, that evidence would be admissible in court.

Finally, searches incident to arrest are allowable without a search warrant. In these cases, officers are allowed to search the area under the immediate control of the suspect, which is essentially their armspan.[114] In an automobile, this includes the entire passenger compartment of the vehicle, including the glove box if it is unlocked.[115] If the arrest occurs in the suspect's home, then the officers are allowed to make a protective search of the home to look for additional suspects. (See Figure 20-22). Plain view doctrine would apply in such a case.[116]

SEARCH PROCEDURES

Once a search begins, narcotics officers should survey the entire site and make a determination as to the best way to conduct the search, keeping the legal aspects of searches in mind. The leader of the search should establish a work station where paperwork can be filled out and evidence collected.

Searches should be careful, thorough, systematic, and within the limitations of the search warrant. Most drug searches permit the opening of packages, checking the insides of light fixtures, and looking in ceiling panels and other potential hiding places. Other places that should be checked are attics and crawl spaces; furnace ducts; plumbing access panels; furniture (including mat-

tresses and boxsprings); dresser drawers; kitchen appliances; food containers; children's furniture and toys; and personal property such as cameras, storage sheds, garages, and other outbuildings. Each room should be subject to two separate searches by different individuals to ensure that all areas are covered. Drug criminals are extremely good at hiding money and drugs, making searching for drugs a skill that requires quite a bit of patience and experience.[117]

The following items are generally related to drug crimes and should be listed in the warrant and included in the search:[118]

1. Drugs, in any quantity;
2. Cash, which should be checked against money lists for buy money from undercover and controlled buys;
3. Drug packaging and processing materials, such as plastic baggies, balloons, and so on;
4. Drug paraphernalia;
5. Weapons;
6. Paperwork, which can include address books with drug contacts, personal correspondence, notes, telephone bills, and other records of possible drug transactions;
7. Financial records;
8. Computers;
9. Keys (a key to a target location may prove a suspect's direct connection to it);
10. Surveillance equipment;
11. Other items specifically relevant to the investigation at hand.

Searches should be well documented, with photographs taken of evidence in its original place and with narratives detailing where evidence was found and who found it. The suspect and the warrant judge, as noted earlier, should receive a detailed inventory of anything removed from the location as evidence.

▶ **FIGURE 20-23   Drug seizures**
Large seizures of drugs pose special problems and considerations for testing the concentration and holding of evidence for trial. In most cases, samples of the large seizure are tested, and only a small portion of the drugs are actually kept as evidence. Most courts allow a sample of the drugs to be admitted as evidence along with officer/agent testimony linking the sample with the confiscated seizure. The remaining drugs are then destroyed after testing. (©Davide Karp/AP Images)

EVIDENCE HANDLING

Aside from the burglaries, larcenies, and other crimes committed because of narcotics, additional related problems sprout from the drug-culture vine. Some of these growths entwine the individual police officer and the overall police function. One offshoot, the handling and securing of narcotics and dangerous drugs after they are collected and seized, has emerged as an area of growing concern to police administrators for a number of reasons (Figure 20-23).

Once seized by the police, narcotic and dangerous-drug evidence requires protection so that it may be preserved in its original state until it is brought before a court or destroyed through a legal process. It is during this period that the greatest demands are placed on personnel of the law enforcement agency

concerned. Narcotic and dangerous-drug evidence must be protected not only against loss and outside threats of incursion but, unfortunately, sometimes from internal theft as well.

Although relatively uncommon, there have been occasions when narcotic and dangerous-drug evidence, as well as large caches of money, has disappeared from a "secure" area under the control and within the confines of a police agency (Figure 20-24). The following methods for handling drug evidence will go far in addressing this concern and minimizing its occurrence.[119]

There are two recognized methods for introducing narcotic and dangerous-drug evidence into the processing sequence immediately after it is seized and marked. Neither method omits any of the processing steps; the difference is found in the manner in which the sequential steps are arranged.

▶ **FIGURE 20-24
Money and Drugs**
During sophisticated investigations involving large-scale operations, it is not uncommon to seize huge caches of cash. Literally, millions of dollars are bartered each year in the drug trade, making for high-stake risks and potentially dangerous situations.
(©Nam Y. Huh/AP Images)

The first method (the laboratory-first method) requires that all seized evidence (after it is field tested, marked, photographed, weighed, and initially inventoried) be transported immediately to the laboratory for analysis. Drop boxes are provided in the laboratory for the deposit of evidence during periods when the facility is not operational. All seized narcotic and dangerous-drug evidence is taken directly to a room in the vicinity of the laboratory. This room, known as an inventory room or a display room, is specially equipped for inventorying narcotic and dangerous-drug evidence and is not used for any other purpose. Weighing scales, cameras, film holders, lighting equipment, evidence seals, evidence containers, appropriate forms, desks, typewriters, tables or counters, and necessary administrative supplies are maintained in the room. When not in use, the room is locked, and the keys (two) are retained in a secure location (normally, one key is kept in the laboratory and the other is controlled by the watch supervisor or desk officer). To achieve even greater control over inventory rooms, departments that have a high volume of narcotic evidence are employing more sophisticated entry-control systems, including "entry" or "swipe" cards on a system that records the cardholder's identity and time of entry and departure. Video cameras may also be used to record all behavior in the inventory room.

After seizure of the evidence and while en route to police headquarters, the seizing officer requests a witnessing officer of supervisory grade (at least one grade above that held by the seizing officer) and a member of the laboratory staff (technician on duty) or a technician from the mobile laboratory unit, if available, to meet with him or her at the narcotic and dangerous-drug inventory room. When the supervisory official arrives at the inventory room, the seizing officer displays the material seized (the witnessing officer does not handle any of the evidence). After the evidence package has been marked and displayed in the manner best suited for a photographic inventory, the laboratory technician photographs the evidence (the photographer does not handle any of the evidence). When photographs of the evidence have been taken, the evidence is weighed and inventoried under the direct supervision of the supervisory officer. Appropriate forms are then completed and witnessed, and the evidence is sealed in containers or envelopes provided for that purpose.

After these steps have been accomplished, in company with the witnessing officer and the laboratory technician, the seizing officer carries the evidence to the laboratory drop box and deposits it therein. If the drop box cannot accommodate the evidence package, the laboratory evidence-room custodian or an alternate is requested to come to the laboratory, assume custody of the evidence, and store it in the laboratory evidence room. If the evidence is taken to the laboratory during normal operational hours, the drop box is not used; the evidence is turned over directly to the laboratory evidence custodian or alternate.

On completion of the analytical process by the laboratory, the evidence is delivered to the narcotic and dangerous-drug evidence room in the property room. Here, the evidence custodian assumes control of the evidence and provides for its preservation and subsequent processing as required.

In the second method (the evidence-room-first method), seized narcotic and dangerous-drug evidence, after being field tested, marked, photographed, weighed, and inventoried, is sealed in an appropriate container and deposited in a drop box or delivered directly to the evidence room in the property room. There are variations to the procedure; in some cases, certain intermediate steps (photographing the evidence, for example) are omitted or the initial processing (weighing, photographing, and inventorying) may be accomplished in the property room or evidence room. The single difference between the two methods is that in one the evidence is analyzed before it is stored, whereas in the other the evidence is taken directly to the narcotic and dangerous-drug evidence room (or to an adjunct depository), receipted, and then removed to the laboratory for analysis.

Of the two methods used for introducing narcotic and dangerous-drug evidence into the processing sequence, the laboratory-first procedure is preferred and should be followed whenever possible. The main advantage of this method is that it reduces actual handling of the evidence and decreases the number of custody transfer points. By first delivering the evidence to the laboratory, the evidence must undergo only one journey to the narcotic and dangerous-drug evidence room—that is, after analysis, rather than before and after. Consequently, the exposure of the evidence to various loss hazards is reduced and its security is enhanced.

It must be recognized, however, that establishment of the laboratory-first method depends on the existence of certain features that are not available to many law enforcement agencies. The laboratory-first method requires that a mobile laboratory unit or laboratory technician be on call for around-the-clock operation. Also, this method requires an easily accessible laboratory—preferably located in the same building housing the headquarters of the police agency itself.

PHARMACEUTICAL DIVERSIONS

The diversion of pharmaceutical drugs is considered an increasing problem within the drug enforcement community, especially with the popularity of narcotic drugs such as Oxy-Contin. Health care professionals are sometimes involved with the distribution of controlled substances from hospitals, clinics, pharmacies, and doctor's offices. In fact, the DEA has estimated that around 13,000 practicing physicians or pharmacists may be involved in the illegal diversion of drugs.[120] Investigation of these types of activities are difficult because doctors and other health professionals are usually seen as highly educated, productive members of society. Diversions are also easy to cover up. Careful records regarding controlled substances are required to be kept by doctors and pharmacists, but suspicious fires, break-ins, and robberies may act as covers for drug shortages or the destruction of records. Furthermore, many investigators are unfamiliar with the problem of diversion and how to deal with it.

Doctors and Diversion

There are generally four types of doctors who divert drugs. The first is the dishonest physician, who profits from the illegal sale of controlled substances. The second is the impaired doctor, who diverts drugs for his or her own use and addiction. The third type is the dated doctor. The dated doctor has been in practice for a number of years and may be willing to hand out drugs to anyone who appears to have a legitimate reason. These doctors are generally unwilling to conform to new rules and regulations about prescription drugs. Finally, there's the gullible physician who falls victim to scams by patients regarding prescription drugs. Gullible physicians are not considered criminals.[121]

Among the most common indications that a physician may be unlawfully diverting drugs are these:

- A physician places excessively frequent orders for narcotics.
- A physician picks up and pays for filled narcotics prescriptions from a pharmacy.
- A physician places an emergency call for a narcotic medication to a pharmacy and requests delivery. The deliverer is met by the physician and given a prescription for the drugs. In some instances, no patient exists, or if one does exist, the narcotics are retained by the physician, and other medication is substituted.
- A narcotics prescription is issued to a patient by a physician with instructions to have it filled and to return with the drug for administration. Substitute medication is then given to the patient.
- In narcotics records, a physician uses fictitious or deceased people's names and addresses.
- The physician frequently requests that a prescription for an alleged patient be taken to the pharmacy by a nurse, a receptionist, or a member of the family and be returned to the doctor personally.
- While other physicians are in the operating room or making hospital rounds, the addict-physician searches their vehicles or medical bags for narcotics.
- A physician obtains a key to the narcotics locker in a hospital and has a duplicate made.
- A physician may place an order for a patient in a hospital; when the drug is prepared by a nurse, the doctor takes it over and either uses a substitute syringe containing a placebo or administers only a small portion of the drug.

Nurses and Diversion

Nurses tend to be more likely to divert drugs for their personal use than to divert drugs for resale. Investigators may choose to deal with personal diversions far differently than they would diversions that are destined for resale.

CLANDESTINE DRUG LABORATORIES

Clandestine drug laboratories throughout the United States produce a variety of illegal drugs for sale and distribution. The processes used in production of these drugs range in their degree of sophistication from primitive to advanced. By the same token, those who operate such laboratories may range in expertise from the novice experimenter to the professional

chemist. These factors alone can have a serious impact on the safety of the general public and on police and fire department personnel who may deal with these laboratories in enforcement and emergency situations.[122]

Raids conducted on clandestine drug laboratories are inherently dangerous, irrespective of the dangers associated with taking suspects into custody. The degree of danger is based largely on the types of chemicals that are typically used and the chemical processes employed. These dangers may be heightened by the operator's lack of expertise and experience and by the physical limitations and restrictions of the facility being used, as well as by weather conditions and other factors. Such dangers cannot be overemphasized. Major accidents resulting in loss of life have occurred during raids conducted on such facilities by those who are untrained, inexperienced, or careless in the dismantling, handling, transportation, storage, or disposal of the involved chemicals.

Normally, direct physical involvement with drug laboratories takes place during the execution of a search warrant on a suspect property. Under these circumstances, there is generally enough information to forewarn police officers about the nature of the operations and the types of chemicals that are most likely involved. Adequate safety precautions can thus be developed and employed. However, police officers may inadvertently encounter a laboratory operation while conducting other enforcement or investigatory operations. In such instances, unless there is imminent danger of loss of life, police officers and civilians alike should be restricted from entering laboratory premises. Clandestine laboratories typically employ processes using chemicals that are toxic, corrosive, caustic, and flammable. The laboratory environment may pose explosive toxic or carcinogenic risks that should be dealt with only by specially trained and equipped personnel.

IDENTIFYING LABORATORY OPERATIONS

Clandestine laboratory operations are typically identified in one of four ways. In some instances, fire departments responding to the scene of a fire or explosion find evidence of laboratory operations. Positive determinations, however, depend on the ability of emergency service personnel to recognize the type of substances and equipment typically used in such operations. Therefore, these personnel must be trained in identification of clandestine lab operations. Since fire departments should be close at hand during police raids of drug laboratories, responsible personnel from both agencies should develop a working relationship in dealing with problems that arise from these types of operations.

Evidence of drug laboratory operations may also be generated through informants. Laboratory operators who are attempting to establish operations in a new community often need to determine sources for the purchase of specific chemicals. Plans for development of a lab and related involvement of suppliers or distributors frequently are revealed by confidential informants and intelligence gathered from arrestees.

The community at large may also provide valuable tips on laboratory operations on the basis of observations of unusual activities or circumstances. Many drug labs operate in urban or suburban residential communities where citizens who are alerted to the common signs of laboratory operations can provide valuable information to the police. These indicators include:

- A residence where one or more individuals visit but where no one lives. Laboratory operators are generally cautious about the risks of fire, explosion, or contamination and attempt to limit their exposure and risk.
- Residences or other buildings that have sealed doors and windows, although they are not abandoned facilities.
- The presence of ventilating fans that operate irrespective of weather conditions.
- A strong ammonia or related odor.
- An unfurnished "residence."
- A "resident" who frequently goes outside for a cigarette or to get some air.

Although these circumstances do not prove the existence of an illegal drug manufacturing operation, several of these factors together may be suggestive enough to warrant establishment of low-profile police surveillance.

METH LABS

Meth labs have been around since the 1960s, when they were organized and operated by outlaw motorcycle gangs. To stop the spread of "clan labs," chemicals such as ether and ephedrine were restricted by the Chemical Diversion and Trafficking Act of 1988. Rogue chemical companies that sold to clan-lab precursors were prosecuted and put out of business by the DEA and other local, state, and federal law enforcement agencies.[123]

In the late 1980s and early 1990s, the biker manufacturers began to be edged out of the market by new and very violent methamphetamine manufacturers—the Mexican national methamphetamine organizations. Today, they dominate the meth manufacturing market. Their industrial-size labs are producing methamphetamine in mass quantities for distribution across the United States. This is evidenced by recent DEA operations that resulted in methamphetamine arrests in California, Texas, and North Carolina.

With the restriction of methamphetamine manufacturing chemicals, lab seizures started to decline in the late 1980s. Since then, however, the trend has been reversed with a vengeance, and lab seizures have started to skyrocket. One of the reasons for this increase is the Internet. Now all a methamphetamine manufacturer has to do is turn on his or her computer, point and click to find a recipe, and point and click again to find the chemicals. If the "meth cook" has any questions during the manufacturing process, he/she can simply visit one of the methamphetamine-manufacturing chat pages. These small "tweeker"-type labs are capable of making anywhere from ounce to pound quantities of methamphetamine. Size does not matter when it comes to clan labs; these small labs are just as dangerous for law enforcement officers as are the biker and Mexican national labs.

Meth labs can be broken down into six different styles:

- Biker or traditional;
- Mexican national;
- Cold-cook;
- Pressure cooker;
- Hydrogenation;
- Tweeker.

Chemicals used to manufacture methamphetamine are easily obtainable, even with chemical restrictions. Laboratory equipment used to manufacture methamphetamine runs the full spectrum from the scientific to the yard-sale purchase. Heating mantles, condensers, vacuum pumps, buchner funnels, and 22-liter reaction vessels are regularly seized at clandestine labs. Not wanting to attract attention of law enforcement, clandestine laboratory equipment manufacturers are turning to other types of clan-lab equipment. They now use pressure cookers, hot plates, mason jars, sun tea dispensers, nalgene containers, homemade compressed-gas cylinders, Pyrex bowls, sports bottles, microwave ovens, and other such material.[124]

A new method for producing meth without the elaborate laboratories traditionally associated with the drug has many law enforcement agencies concerned. Rather than complex systems of tubing, glassware, and burners, the new method requires only a 2-liter soda bottle, cold pills, and noxious chemicals. Manufacturers shake the bottle and the volatile reaction produces methamphetamines. Known as **shake and bake,** this new approach requires a much smaller amount of pseudoephedrine, allowing the manufacturer to slip under the radar and avoid the repercussions of the Combat Meth Act. Unlike the laboratory method, no flame is required to produce the drug and it can be made in a home, car, or even a space as small as lavatory stall.[125] This is particularly worrisome, because it allows meth addicts to make their own supply at home, instead of buying mass produced quantities from a dealer. As a result of this popular new method, meth arrests that had been declining ever since the Combat Meth Act was implemented are on the rise again.

Shake and bake scenarios are not only quick and easy for meth addicts to use, they are exceedingly dangerous. While there is no open flame, the chemical reaction taking place inside the 2-liter bottle is extremely violent and volatile. Opening the cap too soon, for example, can result in a huge flash fire causing extreme burns on unlucky addicts.

CATCHING COOKS: METH MONITORS

After the Combat Methamphetamine Epidemic Act of 2005 was enacted, the availability of ingredients used in the manufacture of methamphetamines became much more difficult to assemble. The legislation required pharmacies and retailers to limit access to, and record sales of, over-the-counter products containing pseudoephedrine, ephedrine, and phenylpropanolamine. However, the large paper log books used by many retailers initially were a cumbersome means of tracking manufacturers. Often—and particularly during cold and flu season where sales of those ingredients for legitimate purposes are highest—there were thousands of records to maintain, and the books presented a threat for identity theft for those who had to sign it. Furthermore, there was no way that pharmacies, retailers, or law enforcement could see whether or not those purchasing the medications were "smurfing"—that is, visiting a number of retail establishments in the area in order to obtain the quantity needed.

However, several companies have introduced database systems that allow retailers to enter information and identifiers for those purchasing pseudoephedrine medications. A pharmacy can enter in an individual's information into the database and determine immediately if he or she has already reached the limits proscribed in the Combat Meth Act at other locations. This also allows law enforcement to track suspects, recognize patterns, and develop leads to identify meth laboratories in real time. *Leadsonlabs.com* is one such database, and users of the software report that the ability to network and receive information in real time has helped to stem the tide of meth in their areas. After widespread implementation in the state of Arkansas, law enforcement officials there credit the database with helping narcotics officers track meth labs, as well as help deny high volume manufacturers the quantities they need to make this dangerous drug.

LAB SEIZURE AND FORFEITURE

Laboratory operators may be arrested under a wide variety of circumstances, only the most typical of which are discussed here. Most laboratory operations are closed as the result of police raids following intensive investigative work.

On occasion, police officers will inadvertently discover a clandestine lab operation while responding to other public safety situations. It is essential that officers take only those steps necessary to protect their lives and the lives of bystanders and that they make arrests only if entry into the laboratory is not required. Normally, if the officer's presence has not been detected, this involves relaying information to supervisory personnel and/or other appropriate personnel in the department who have received specialized training in handling clandestine laboratories.

Once the scene is secure, it may be possible to interview neighbors in order to determine information on occupancy. Officers should make note of all vehicles parked in the immediate area of the laboratory.

Another means of interdiction involves the civil forfeiture of illicit chemicals and drug-manufacturing paraphernalia. This procedure, which pertains to individual laboratory operators as well as chemical suppliers, allows federal agents to seize anything used or intended to be used to illegally manufacture, deliver, or import drugs. Most states have similar prohibitions, and officers should be familiar with the provisions and limitations of these laws. Use of the forfeiture statutes may be a reasonable alternative to attempts to establish a criminal case, particularly where staffing constraints limit surveillance and other operations, when suspects' discovery of surveillance may necessitate terminating the investigation, or when it is feared that the laboratory operation is preparing to relocate quickly. Often the circumstances that justify a civil seizure will lead thereafter to successful prosecution under criminal statutes relating to conspiracy or the attempt to manufacture controlled substances.

When making a decision concerning civil seizure of illegal drugs and manufacturing materials, officers should contact their local prosecuting attorney for advice. Evidence not sufficient to support criminal prosecution may be adequate for a civil seizure. Normally, successful seizure requires that officers demonstrate the suspect's probable intent to manufacture a controlled substance. This can be accomplished by reference to the type and combination of chemicals and paraphernalia on hand, furtive activity, use of subterfuge, or other questionable practices.

Those who supply materials to clandestine laboratories with knowledge of their use are also subject to civil and criminal penalties under various federal and state laws. Chemical companies or supply houses may knowingly sell chemicals to laboratory operators without reporting the sales to the police, disguise sales records, assist buyers in using the chemicals, or otherwise assist in the preparation or merchandising process. It is normally possible to apply seizure and forfeiture actions to such merchants if investigation can establish any factor that shows the suppliers' "guilty knowledge" of the illegal uses of their merchandise.

An undercover purchase of chemicals from suspected suppliers is the most typical means of developing criminal cases against them. In addition, chemicals seized at drug laboratories may display manufacturers' labels, including lot numbers, and equipment may have manufacturers' plates and serial numbers that can be used to trace their sales or transfers.

Under proper circumstances, therefore, civil seizure may be an acceptable, if not preferred, approach to termination of illegal drug-manufacturing operations. Additionally, once such actions are taken, perpetrators will often cooperate with the police and provide intelligence that assists in additional enforcement operations.

CONDUCTING A LABORATORY RAID

Conducting a raid on an occupied laboratory requires careful planning. Normally, a planning meeting involves the police tactical unit, bomb squad, hazardous-material or chemical-waste disposal personnel, a chemist, and fire department representatives—all of whom are specially trained. The nature of the operation from initial entry to dismantling should be reviewed with particular attention to the types of chemicals most likely being used, the nature of the suspects involved, and contingency plans for emergency services should a fire, explosion, or toxic reaction take place.

The initial entry team should be outfitted with Nomex clothing, body armor, and goggles. Nomex provides short-term protection from fire, and goggles protect one's eyes from airborne fumes and thrown chemicals. The tactical unit is responsible only for securing the suspects and exiting the laboratory as quickly as possible and with the minimum amount of force.

To avoid unduly restricted movements, the tactical team should wear the minimum amount of protective clothing necessary; therefore, the team's exposure to the laboratory environment must be extremely limited. The team should make a mental note of the laboratory environment and report its findings to the assessment team members who follow. Laboratory operators, in anticipation of possible raids, sometimes booby-trap the facility in order to destroy evidence. The ability

Meth-lab raids and assessment
The methamphetamine cooking process is extremely dangerous owing to fumes and the volatility of ingredients. After the site is secured, an assessment team enters the lab, segregates the various compounds used to make "meth" and secures them as evidence. Team members should wear Nomex disposable suits, as well as chemical resistant gloves and boots. Each team member should be equipped with a self-contained breathing apparatus with an air-monitoring device as well.
(©Mark Allen Johnson/ZumaPress/Newscom)

to recognize traps and other potential hazards depends on the training and experience of team members, a factor that underscores the importance of special training for such operations. After leaving the facility, the tactical team should undergo decontamination.

After the site is secured, the assessment team is free to enter. Team members should wear Nomex clothing covered with disposable protective suits, as well as chemical-resistant gloves and boots covered with disposable gloves and boots. All seams of the suits should be taped with nonporous adhesive tape, and each team member should be equipped with a self-contained breathing apparatus. The team should also be outfitted with two air-monitoring devices—a combustible-gas indicator and indicator tubes.

The combustible-gas indicator is an essential air-monitoring device that tests for oxygen levels, airborne gas particle levels, and the combustibility of the environment. The indicator tubes test for the presence and quantity of specific types of chemical vapors. A pump is used to force air through the individual tubes.

Assessment team members test the lab environment at several locations and make notes of instrument readings. They should also make a diagram of the interior, noting any dangers or problems that may be encountered. When their work is completed, the assessment team should leave the facility, decontaminate, and give their report to the dismantling team.

The dismantling team should wear the same type of protective clothing as the assessment team (Figure 20-25.) Even though dangerous substances may not have been found, there is always the possibility of spills and damage during dismantling, which could create a hazardous situation. A chemist trained in laboratory dismantling should be on hand to take samples of chemicals and of products being manufactured so that informed judgments can be made on safety in packaging, transportation, storage, disposal, and handling of evidence samples.

Crime scene personnel, under the close supervision of the dismantling team supervisor, should conduct standard crime scene processing procedures, including taking photographs and searching for latent fingerprints. Videotaping of laboratory operations is also helpful for evidentiary purposes and for court presentation.

The chemist can direct the proper packaging of chemical substances. Care must always be taken that only compatible chemicals are packaged together. Typically, chemicals are placed in drums filled with vermiculite or a similar absorbent, nonflammable substance. A waste disposal company approved by the Environmental Protection Agency (EPA) can be of great value in the packaging process.

Chemicals that are not being used in court because of potential hazards, together with contaminated clothing and equipment, must be packaged, transported, and stored or disposed of according to EPA guidelines.

CONSPIRACY INVESTIGATIONS

A **conspiracy** is defined as two or more people entering into an agreement to violate the law with a commission of one or more overt acts in furtherance of the agreement. Drug investigators undertake conspiracy cases when they desire to get the leaders of a drug organization who may not handle drug transactions and would otherwise be too insulated from the day-to-day operations by associates operating further down the chain of command. The law of conspiracy makes it possible for each conspirator to be held accountable for the actions of anyone else involved.[126]

There are three main types of conspiracies. The first is the *chain conspiracy*. In a chain conspiracy, the investigator must show that a group of conspirators are all working toward a common goal, depending on one another to further the success of the scheme. Each participant must be aware that their success depends on each member of the conspiracy.

In the more complex *wheel conspiracy,* there is a central or primary conspirator called the *hub.* The hub makes an agreement with other conspirators, referred to as *spokes.* Each spoke is aware of everyone else's role in the scheme. All are bound together by the *rim,* which is a common agreement, tying each person to the conspiracy.

Finally, the *enterprise conspiracy* is defined by federal statutes. In this type of conspiracy, the enterprise may have a number of different criminal activities going on. These activities are called *racketeering* and include such things as drug violations, loan-sharking, mail fraud, bribery, counterfeiting, and obstruction of justice. The members of an enterprise do not have to be aware of one another's roles, and investigators have to show only that members have agreed to participate in the enterprise. Enterprise conspiracies in narcotics investigations must obviously include drug violations, as well as one other activity defined under racketeering.[127]

GANGS AND DRUGS

Street gangs, outlaw motorcycle gangs, and prison gangs are the main distributors of drugs in the United States. Currently, there are about 31,000 gangs and 850,000 active gang members in the country.[128] Gangs present numerous problems for narcotics investigators, because they are difficult to infiltrate. Their use of violence makes confidential informants scarce, and undercover operations are exceptionally risky to the officer.

Street gangs arc located throughout the country in cities of various sizes and characteristics. Large, well-organized gangs are the most likely to be involved with drug trafficking, because their networks allow for the manufacture, sale, transportation, and distribution of drugs throughout the nation. These gangs are mostly involved with drugs such as cocaine, heroin, and marijuana. Violence is employed regularly within these gangs in an effort to control and expand distribution activities.

Outlaw motorcycle gangs are smaller than street gangs but are highly organized. The three main outlaw motorcycle gangs are the Hell's Angels Motorcycle Club, the Banditos, and the Outlaws Motorcycle Club. The primary drugs associated with outlaw motorcycle gangs are methamphetamine, marijuana, and cocaine. Like street gangs, outlaw motorcycle gangs have been known to use violence to further distribution activities.

Prison gangs are much smaller than street or outlaw motorcycle gangs and are aligned along racial or ethnic lines. The most prominent prison gangs include the Aryan Nation, Mexican Mafia, and Nuestra Familia. These gangs consist of a select group of inmates who are organized into a hierarchy and operate within prisons and on the streets to distribute cocaine, marijuana, methamphetamine, and heroin. These gangs are notoriously difficult to infiltrate and are considered extremely violent and dangerous.[129]

PARADIGM SHIFT

For decades, police have fought a "war against drugs," the efforts of which you have read about throughout this chapter. However, at this point in U.S. history, a paradigm shift in drug interdiction may be on the horizon. The Obama administration has begun to consider drug use in this country as a public health issue rather than as a strictly criminal one. The Office of National Drug Control Policy has recently acknowledged that prevention and treatment (not interdiction and arrest) may be the only ways to effectively curb the problem of drug abuse and addiction. Thus federal funds are being earmarked for programs that fit under the prevention and treatment umbrellas versus police interdiction and arrest strategies.[130] These types of programs include training primary-care physicians to help them to identify patients with drug problems, funding for advanced-treatment facilities, and mentoring/prevention programs for children. These programs have little to do with the law enforcement strategies addressed in this chapter, but they do herald changes that may affect the funding and implementation of such strategies.

In the last edition of this book, we wrote that "it remains doubtful that legalization or decriminalization of any drug will occur in the United States anytime soon." Since that time, eight states plus the District of Columbia have legalized marijuana and many more have relaxed regulations for the medical use of marijuana. The federal government remains firm that they are not ready or willing to do so. Though public attitudes toward marijuana have softened significantly, it remains clear that drugs are still largely seen as a dangerous and destructive force in American society.

| KEY TERMS

amphetamines	Combat Methamphetamine Epidemic	fentanyl
barbiturates	Act of 2005	hallucinogenic drugs
cannabis	conspiracy	hashish
cheese heroin	crack (rock) cocaine	hashish oil
chiva	crystallized methamphetamine	heroin (diacetylmorphine)
clandestine drug laboratories	depressants (sedatives)	HIDTA
cocaine	drank	K2
codeine	drug buy operations	ketamine

khat
lysergic acid diethylamide (LSD)
marijuana
marijuana grow houses
meperidine (Demerol)
mescaline
meth labs
methadone
methaqualone

methcathinone
methylenedioxy methamphetamine
   (MDMA) (ecstasy)
morphine
narcotics
opiates
opium
OxyContin
phencyclidine (PCP)

psilocybin and psilocin
shake and bake
speedballing
stimulants
Strawberry Quick meth
surveillance
synthetic narcotics

REVIEW QUESTIONS

1. What major drugs of abuse are derived from opium?
2. What role does the drug methadone play in treating heroin addicts?
3. What are the acute and chronic effects of cocaine use?
4. What is freebasing?
5. According to the Drug Enforcement Administration, what are drug traffickers attempting to accomplish by introducing Strawberry Quick meth to the market?
6. What is methcathinone?
7. Why is the drug OxyContin so attractive to drug addicts?
8. What is speedballing?
9. What are some of the known side effects of PCP?
10. What are the signs of a Marijuana Grow House Operation?
11. What are the major exceptions to searching without a search warrant?
12. How are clandestine drug laboratory operations typically identified?
13. Which major factors should be considered when attempting to secure a search warrant solely on the basis of information supplied by a confidential informant?
14. What is a HIDTA?
15. Define a conspiracy, and give examples of conspiracy cases.
16. What are the two recognized methods for introducing narcotics and dangerous drugs into the processing sequence immediately after they are seized and marked?

INTERNET ACTIVITIES

1. The U.S. Drug Enforcement Agency website, *https://www .dea.gov/index.shtml,* provides a variety of statistics and information on drug trafficking and use in various countries around the world. For the most recent drug-trafficking intelligence, log on to the website and click "Programs," then "Southwest Border Initiative." Find the most recent reports about Mexico. See how enforcement efforts have recently affected the drug cartels operating on the U.S.-Mexico border.

2. Find out about the changes in abused drugs commonly found on the party scene or at all-night raves. Visit the National Institute of Drug Abuse website at *https:// www.drugabuse.gov/drugs-abuse/club-drugs,* and browse the site for information pertaining to "club drugs" and teenagers. What new drugs are becoming popular among America's youth? How pervasive is inhalant abuse? What are the so-called club drugs?

► Officers look over the evidence of the San Bernardino terrorist attack on December 2, 2015. Fourteen people were killed and twenty-two were wounded. FBI Director James B. Comey described the terrorists Syed Rizwan Farook and Tashfeen Malik as "homegrown violent extremists" inspired by ISIS (Islamic State in Iraq and Syria).

(©Mario Anzuoni/Reuters/Alamy)

21

TERRORISM

CHAPTER OBJECTIVES

1. Identify the three radical movements within Islam.

2. Provide a brief history of Osama bin Laden and the evolution of the al-Qaeda terrorist organization.

3. Discuss the recent development of the Islamic State and the role of Abu Musab al-Zarqawi in it's inception.

4. Be familiar with different terrorist groups that threaten the United States and its allies; describe the term *homegrown terrorism*.

5. Distinguish between right-wing and left-wing domestic terrorists.

6. Describe the prominent national structures involved in terrorist intelligence, and outline their responsibilities.

7. List and explain several ways terrorist organizations finance themselves.

8. List and describe some of the steps every police agency and/or officer can take to prevent terrorism in the United States.

9. Describe some of the suspicious factors to consider that may indicate a possible terrorist threat.

10. Describe the type of attacks conducted by homegrown, lone wolf terrorists that may describe the future.

The events of September 11, 2001, were clearly the most horrendous and devastating terrorist acts ever to occur on U.S. soil. Few people would take issue with the proposition that 9/11 forever changed the lives of all Americans. The events of that day evoked a sense of national outrage, caused profound losses, and created a sense of vulnerability.

This chapter discusses various aspects of terrorism and their relation to the work of a criminal investigator. It opens with an overview of international terrorism and the international groups that have committed terrorist acts against the United States and its allies. There is specific focus on Middle Eastern groups, since they pose perhaps the greatest threat against America. Increasingly, Middle Eastern groups are recruiting terrorists from American soil, and these "home-grown" terrorists represent an emerging threat to national security. The chapter then turns to an examination of domestic terrorism and its perpetrators, including right-wing and left-wing domestic groups. Right-wing terror groups, along with extremist groups, are responsible for high-profile incidents in the past, such as the Oklahoma City bombing in 1995 and the Charleston, S.C. church shooting in 2015. Current political and economic climates have many experts worried that terror acts from such groups may see a resurgence. The next section addresses the financing of terrorism, with a focus on drug, arms, and human smuggling, credit card and charities fraud, and theft. This is followed by a discussion of several U.S. national agencies charged with the task of gathering information on terrorism, terrorism prevention and investigation, and counterterrorism.

Although federal agencies are clearly important in assessing the threat of future terrorist acts, the role of criminal investigators at both the state and the local law enforcement levels should not be underestimated. The remainder of the chapter outlines the ways that criminal investigators can assist in the fight against terrorism. Confronting terrorism is not an occasional or a seasonal venture; it is an ongoing responsibility. Now, more than ever, criminal investigators must be prepared to encounter and handle terrorist-incident crime scenes.

The world and the United States are not strangers to terrorism. The first U.S. plane hijacking occurred in 1961, when Puerto Rican Antuilo Ortiz, armed with a gun, diverted a National Airlines flight to Cuba, where he was given asylum.[1] A rebel faction in Guatemala assassinated U.S. Ambassador John Mein in 1968 after forcing his car from the road. Black September terrorists struck in Munich at the Olympics in 1972 and the following year killed U.S. Ambassador Cleo Noel in the Sudan. The Baader-Meinhof group and the Popular Front for the Liberation of Palestine (PFLP) seized a French airliner in 1976 and flew the 258 passengers to Uganda, precipitating the Entebbe hostage crisis. In 1979 the Italian Prime Minister was kidnapped and killed by Red Brigade members; the U.S. Embassy in Tehran was seized by Iranian radicals; and Mecca's Grand Mosque was taken over by 200 Islamic terrorists who took hundreds of pilgrims hostage, an incident that left 250 people dead and 600 wounded. By the turn of the century, we witnessed almost daily occurrences of suicide bombings in Israel, new plots of violence against airliners in London, the horrible destruction of 9/11, and the gruesome beheadings of innocent civilians by the Shiite al-Mahdi Army in Iraq. Today, the violence continues, with apparently random shootings and bombings aimed at mass carnage and destruction of people worldwide. For example, the National Counterterrorism Center indicates that over 11,700 terrorist attacks occurred throughout the world in 2015. Although the number of attacks decreased from 2014, the acts resulted in a substantial number of deaths and injuries. Over 28,300 people, including suicide attackers were killed worldwide.[2] A majority of these victims were Muslim and living in Afghanistan, Iraq, Pakistan, and Syria.[3]

Nevertheless, across the United States, people continue to wonder if terrorism is still the province of the future or simply anomalies observed in the unrest of foreign countries. They are not anomalies: the United States is opposed by international and domestic terrorist groups, and the likelihood of additional incidents is quite real. Together, globally and locally, police have to be smarter and work harder using better tools to eliminate, disrupt, minimize, and investigate terrorist attacks.

INTERNATIONAL TERRORISM

"**International terrorism** involves violent acts or acts dangerous to human life that are the violation of the criminal laws of the United States or any state, or that would be a criminal act if committed within the jurisdiction of the United States or any state. Acts of international terrorism are intended to intimidate a civilian population, influence the policy of a government, or affect the conduct of a government. These acts transcend national boundaries in terms of the means by which they are accomplished, the persons they intend to intimidate, or the locale in which perpetrators operate."[4] The FBI further defines terrorism as the unlawful use of force or violence against persons or property to intimidate or coerce a government, the civilian population, or any segment thereof, in furtherance of political or social objectives. It is impossible to discuss all of the groups around the world now labeled "terrorist"; however, it is important to give a brief description of those groups that pose the most significant threat to the United States. Many originate from the Middle East, where anti-American tensions have recently escalated, primarily because of the wars in Syria, Afghanistan, and Iraq. For that reason, this discussion focuses on groups stemming from that area.

RADICAL ISLAM

Radical Islam has long been a component of terrorist activity throughout the world (Figure 21-1). Groups with ties to radical Islamic beliefs have been at the forefront of the news since

▲ **FIGURE 21-1**

Revolutionary Shiite leader, Grand Ayatollah Ruhollah Khomeini represented one of the most influential radical Islamic thinkers in the world. After masterminding the overthrow of the Pahlavi monarchy in Iran, he supported the Iran hostage crisis in 1979. (©Sayaad/AP Images)

BOX 21-1 | THE ISLAMIC STATE: VIOLENCE AND CARNAGE THAT CHARACTERIZES AN ELUSIVE NAME

To most of the American public, the Islamic State seemingly came out of nowhere in 2014. The radical Islamic terrorist group became an international threat previously known as the **Islamic State in Iraq and Syria—ISIS** and the **Islamic State in Iraq and the Levant—ISIL** (the Levant is a geographical area in the Middle East composed of modern-day Syria, Lebanon, Jordan, and Israel). Today, the group is referred to simply as the Islamic State—IS.

The Islamic State is so violent that it is "disowned" by al-Qaeda. The grisly tactics that included mass executions of captured soldiers and beheading of Western captives, including aid workers and journalists, marked an era of violence previously unseen in the modern world. The Islamic State justifies the extensive use of violence, savagery, and rage through misinterpretation of Islamic scripture and prophesies. Hence, beheadings, assassinations, stoning, public executions, and rape (e.g., the 2014–16 mass kidnapping and rape of captured Yasidi women in Iraq and Syria) are justified by selected passages taken out of context. Make no doubt about it . . . the Islamic State is fighting a Medieval war in modern times.

(Photo credits: (left photo) ©Universal History Archive/UIG/Getty Images; (right photo) ©AY-Collection/SIPA/Newscom)

Source: Robert W. Taylor and Charles R. Swanson, *Terrorism, Intelligence and Homeland Security* (Columbus, OH: Pearson, 2016) Graeme Wood, "What ISIS Really Wants," *The Atlantic* (March 2015).

the late 1970s, when the Islamic revolution in Iran reached its peak and led to the capture of the U.S. embassy in Tehran. Terrorist organizations that lay claim to radical Islamic beliefs, whether from the Sunni tradition (making up over 92% of the Islamic world) or the Shi'ite tradition (centered primarily in Iran, Lebanon, and Iraq), have garnered widespread press attention over the past 30 years, particularly since al-Qaeda claimed responsibility for the September 11, 2001 attacks and more recent attacks in Europe by the Islamic State (ISIS).

Radical Islamic groups are generally characterized by a belief that is not shared by mainstream Muslims: violence is a means to an end. See Box 21-1. These radical groups believe that Western culture poses an imminent threat to the sanctity of the Muslim religion, corrupting morals and threatening to overtake the Muslim way of life. In the past, western interventions in Israeli/Palestinian affairs and in Iraq have served as prime examples of Western "colonialization" in the minds of Muslim terrorist groups, further fueling their resolve to take action against the United States and its allies.[5] More recently, several attempted and completed terrorist acts perpetrated by radical Islamists have occurred on U.S. soil. Most notably, the country was stunned when Army Major Nidal Hasan shot and killed 13 people at a U.S military base in Fort Hood, Texas, in November 2009. Colleagues of Nidal reported that he appeared to be fixated on the notion that the military equated with a war on Islam. Thirty-two additional individuals were also injured in that incident.[6] In 2010, federal authorities arrested Faisal Shahzad for attempting to detonate an explosives-filled SUV in New York City's Time

Square. Shahzad later admitted that he received explosives training in Pakistan and would have attempted to set off another bomb in New York City had he not been arrested.[7] The information about the Orlando massacre being the worst shooting will now have to be updated because of Las Vegas. And in 2015 and 2016, two ISIS-inspired attacks in the U.S. again shook the American public. Following a series of attacks in Europe (Paris and Brussels), Syed Rizwan Farook and Tashfee Malik (a married couple of Pakistani descent) killed 14 people and wounded another 20 when they opened fire at a holiday party on December 2, 2015 at the Inland Regional Center in San Bernardino, California. Just six months later in the early morning hours of June 12, 2016, a lone gunman, Omar Mateen, entered the crowded Pulse nightclub in Orlando, Florida with an assault rifle and several pistols. He opened fire, killing 49 people and wounding another 50. The incident represents the deadliest mass shooting massacre on U.S. soil.[8]

Some factions that help compose three major radical and fundamentalist movements within Islam pose a direct threat to the interests of the West, and specifically to the United States. They are discussed next.

The Wahhabi Movement

An Islamic orientation owing much of its basic ideology to the writings of Abd al-Wahhab (1703–1792),[9] who espoused a very conservative form of Sunni Islam. His teachings are commonly referred to as *salafi*, which fundamentally means adhering to the ways of the earliest Islamic generations. The basic concept of the **Wahhabi movement** is that the teachings of Islam were corrupted after the time of the Prophet Muhammad. Much like the early Christian Inquisition during the twelfth and thirteenth centuries, the Wahhabis dealt harshly with those nonobservant of their Muslim traditions. Thus the early Wahhabi focus was internal, on other nominally devout Muslims. The Wahhabi tradition today is centered in Saudi Arabia, with followers primarily on the Arabian Peninsula, including Qatar and Yemen. It is a conservative, closed-society tradition that is intolerant of nonbelievers. Some believe this stance encourages violence against the West.

Many practitioners of Wahhabism prefer to be called *muwahhidun* (unifiers of Islamic practice) or *salafists*. There is no single approach to salafism, which in part accounts for the variety of orientations associated with it, such as: (1) the *shumuliyas*, who believe that religion, politics, and government are inseparable; (2) the *wasatiyyans*, who are reformers/moderates but not necessarily anti-Western and entertain ideas about how to simultaneously accommodate some Western values with those of Islam; and (3) the Islamic revivalists/fundamentalists, which includes the Muslim Brotherhood and radical Jihadist Salafism.

The Muslim Brotherhood

The **Muslim Brotherhood** movement was formed in 1928 as an Egyptian youth organization and grew into a political party by 1939, influenced by the writings of Hasan al-Banna (1906–1949) and Sayyid Qutb (1906–1966) in Egypt.[10] Building on the tenets of Wahhabism, al-Banna believed that the Islamic faith is not just a religion, but an all-encompassing way of living and governing. As such, its focus included not only a rejection of the secularization of Islam but a renunciation of Western colonialization and the modern views and values that often accompanied it throughout the Middle East. The Muslim Brotherhood supports the use of violence to return the entire Middle East to its original and purest form of Islam under the rule of the Shari'a, the first books of the Holy Koran. The term **jihad** is interpreted as an obligation for all Muslims to engage in a "holy war" against the West.

The Muslim Brotherhood has a past history of attempted and successful assassinations of Arabic leaders, including Egyptian President Anwar-al-Sadat (1918–1981), who was seen as too moderate following his 1979 signing of peace accords with Israel. Some of its members helped found al-Qaeda, have been elected to parliamentary seats throughout the Middle East, and have established banks, including one in the Bahamas and several in the Middle East that helped finance terror activities worldwide. Brotherhood members have fought with al-Qaeda in Afghanistan against the Russians and in support of radical Muslims in Kashmir, Chechnya, and Iraq. Today, much of the Muslim Brotherhood leadership supports the activities of the Islamic State, and is active in Syria and Iraq.

QUICK FACTS

Sunni Versus Shi'a or Shiite Traditions

There are two primary traditions in Islam:

Sunni: The "True Path of Allah" and the larger of the two groups, making up approximately 90% of the entire Muslim population and rapidly growing throughout the Middle East, Africa, and Southeast Asia.

Shi'a or Shiite: Followers of the Shi'a tradition, often called the "Shi'at Ali" or Party of Ali, believe that Ali (the son-in-law of the Prophet Muhammad) was given a divine right of successorship to lead the Muslim community after the 7th century. Shi'a population is primarily concentrated in Iran, Iraq, Lebanon, and Yemen.

Jihadist Salafism

This is the radical branch of **Salafism,** whose ideology rocketed during the 1980s and 1990s as a direct result of the Soviet-Afghan War (1980–1989). It embraces a strict, literal interpretation of Islam combined with an emphasis on jihad as a holy war against all Western influences in the Middle East (Figure 21-2). This was the ideology of the al-Qaeda and Jemaah Islamiah terrorist groups.

◄ FIGURE 21-2   Jihad
For nearly 1.3 billion people, Islam is a religion of discipline and peace. However, radical elements within Wahhabism and Jihadist Salafism promote violence and jihad against the United States, modernization, and the West in general. (©Ali Fraidoon/AP Images)

RADICAL ISLAMIC GROUPS

Radical Islamic groups and their history, goals, leaders, tactics, and operational methods were for the most part unknown to state and local investigators before 9/11. However, the new imperative is to master such knowledge. Sun Tzu, who lived around 400 B.C.E., observed that "if you are to win a war, you must know your enemy."[11] Of necessity then, the first part of this chapter deals with who terrorist enemies are, their history, what they want, what they've done, and why they are a threat to us. With this overview, the subsequent portions of the chapter dealing with responses to terrorism and its investigation assume greater meaning. Although there are several Islamic terrorist organizations that are active, the following groups pose the most significant, dangerous, and continued threat to U.S. interests.

The Islamic State (ISIS)

Although most people associate the birth of the **Islamic State** or the **Islamic State in Iraq and Syria (ISIS)** with the renewed war in Northern Iraq in 2014, the actual beginnings of the organization come at least a decade earlier in Middle East history. **Abu Musab al-Zarqawi** was a militant Islamist from Jordan who operated a large training camp for al-Qaeda in Afghanistan during the last 1990s. He was a loyal and successful follower of Osama bin Laden and met with him as well as other leadership of al-Qaeda often. When the United States went to war with Iraq in 2003, al-Zarqawi abandoned his camp in Afghanistan and proceeded to Iraq. He formed the *al-Tawhid wal-Jihad* group and took responsibility for several high-profile bombings and executions.

Although he was openly opposed to Western influence in the Middle East, the American invasion of Iraq and the existence of Israel as a recognized state, al-Zarqawi's main focus of enmity was the Shi'a population in Iraq. In September 2005, he declared war on the United States and the new government of Iraq (then highly organized around the majority Shi'a population) and began a vicious series of attacks on the Shi'a militias and politicians that had developed in an effort to gain control of the country. By end of that year, al-Zarqawi was the most wanted man in the world, having conducted numerous raids and murders on Shi'a civilians and leaders in Iraq, and having a reward of $25 million (offered by the United States) on his head for capture . . . the same amount offered for the capture of bin Laden just one year earlier. Al-Zarqawi had taken the opportunity to turn the U.S. war in Iraq into the genocide of the Shi'a population in that country . . . an extension of a war between Iraq and Iran that had lasted over ten years during the 1970s when Saddam Hussein was supported by the United States in an effort to curb the outgrowth of radical Shi'a Islam from Iran. On June 7, 2006, al-Zarqawi was killed during a U.S. bombing run on a safe house in Hibhib, Iraq.

Although his tenure was short as a leader of Sunni radicals in Iraq, al-Zarqawi's impact was huge. Many of the radical Sunni fighters loyal to al-Qaeda (like al-Zarqawi) had suffered dramatic losses to U.S. forces during the Iraq War. Coupled with the loss of political power (through the death of Saddam Hussein and his Sunni-influenced Ba'athist Party) and, most importantly, the establishment of a majority Shiite-led and U.S.-supported government in Iraq, many fighters fled to neighboring countries, and in particular Syria, where violent revolution already in progress was pitting Sunnis against a Shiite-backed al-Assad government. The early name of this new group, composed primarily of remnant fighters loyal to al-Zarqawi, became widely known as **ISIS** (or the Islamic State in Iraq and Syria). Syrian rebel groups quickly welcomed these hardened fighters; however, they soon realized that the Iraqi group had a much larger goal than toppling the al-Assad regime—their goal was to establish a new "Islamic State."

ISIS succeeded in carving out a portion of land in the heart of the Middle East (from Syria across Iraq to Iran) in which to build a new country and recruit other like-minded Sunnis worldwide. The rise of the ISIS was quick and historical, occurring along the banks of the Tigris and Euphrates Rivers, a region commonly known as the cradle of civilization.

In July 2014, the leader of ISIS, Abu Bakr al-Baghdadi, declared himself "caliph" over the area he controlled and announced the establishment of the new "**caliphate.**" He then changed the name of the group to the **Islamic State**, and within a month (August 2014), he led attacks on Kurdish territories in northern Iraq, prompting an immediate response by the United States—retaliatory air strikes and bombing of IS-held areas. He called upon all Muslims around the world to pledge support and allegiance to him and his country. These were powerful words in the Muslim world, and ones that positioned al-Baghdadi and the Islamic State as a unique challenge to Western nations and a direct threat to the stability of the entire Middle East. This became particularly true as other radical Islamic groups aligned with the Islamic State. Boko Harem (Nigeria), Abu Sayyaf (The Philippines), Ansar al-Tawhid (Pakistan/Afghanistan), al-Qaeda on the Arabian Peninsula—AQAP (Yemen), Answar al-Sharia (Libya), and others recognized and became affiliates to al-Baghdadi's proclamation.

The Islamic State is not just another radical Islamic group; rather it is a significant movement across the world (some scholars estimate the movement includes over 8 million people) that sees itself as the provocateurs of the coming apocalypse, paving the way for the final Islamic rule in the Middle East and the rest of the world.[12] The Islamic State rules by fear and demands obedience to conservative Islamic law by citizens within its control. The group quickly became so powerful and so violent in its application of the law that many individuals formally associated with the leadership of al-Qaeda, such as Ayman al-Zawahiri, have disavowed any associations with ISIS.[13]

Although this wholesale violence has driven small wedges in the proliferation of the overall Islamic State, it continues to flourish as a movement. American soldiers are the continual targets of ISIS, as well as government buildings, security positions, and non-Islamic schools throughout the Middle East. ISIS bombers and soldiers continue to strike at locations both in the Middle East (Saudi Arabia, Yemen, Tunisia, and Turkey) as well as in Europe (Madrid, London, Brussels and Paris) and the United States. From website announcements and flyers to the recruitment of new fighters in the Middle East, the Islamic State continues to grow in sustained acts of violence against Western interests. Most alarming are the numbers of attacks being planned or those implemented over the past two years from U.S.-born, radical Islamic terrorists loyal to the Islamic State cause. Certainly, the attacks in San Bernardino, California (2015) and Orlando, Florida (2016) reveal that the threat of radical Islamic terrorism is no longer a phenomenon that impacts only large cities, but now threatens all communities across America. See Box 21-2.

QUICK FACTS

Islamic State Loses Territory in Syria and Iraq, Poses Threat to the West

In 2016, a renewed military push by U.S.-led allies including Great Britain, France, Germany, Jordan, and Turkey caused a significant loss of territory for the Islamic State caliphate. While the coalition actions were lauded as severely limiting the military actions of the Islamic State in Syria and Iraq, the actions may pose a serious future threat. As the Islamic State loses ground in Syria and Iraq, an estimated 30,000 hardened fighters return to their home countries. Former FBI Director James Comey has argued that these individuals will continue the fight through the development of individual cells carrying out terrorist strikes in their home countries. Such strikes could destabilize some Middle East countries like Turkey and Jordan, as well as cause significant loss of life, carnage, and property damage in countries like Great Britain, France, and Belgium. Indeed, some sources indicate that the Islamic State actually anticipated the loss of territory in Syria and Iraq, fighting a ground war against superior air and land forces led by the United States. Accordingly, the Islamic State suggested early in 2015 that new fighters stay in their native countries to continue strikes and suicide bombings in these countries rather than travel to Syria and Iraq. Further, the Islamic State indicated in 2016 that it would return to its primary operations of guerrilla warfare and terrorist strikes as its territory continues to shrink under military attack in Syria and Iraq, posing significant threat to Western nations worldwide.

Source: Eric Schmitt, "With Caliphate in Peril, Threat Abroad May Rise," *New York Times* (September 18, 2016)

Al-Qaeda

Al-Qaeda ("the base") has its basis in the mujahedin, or "holy warriors," who fought against the Russians when they invaded Afghanistan in 1979. During the 1970s Afghanistan's leaders were dependent on the Soviet Union for economic and political support. As a result, Islamic movements in Afghanistan were suppressed in favor of Soviet Marxism. When the pro-communist government faltered in the late 1970s, Russia invaded in a doomed attempt to prop it up.[14] The invasion caused Afghanistan's tribal and religious leaders to abandon their infighting and band together to resist the Russians. The U.S. government, eager to undermine the Soviet Union's power, offered assistance in the form of funding and personnel. The result was a jihad against the Soviet Union, fought by a coalition consisting of Afghans, Central Intelligence Agency operatives, and scores of young Arab men, drawn from places such as Saudi Arabia, who were eager to fight for Islam.[15]

BOX 21-2 | ATTACKS IN CHARLESTON AND ORLANDO: ACTS OF HATE OR ACTS OF TERRORISM

Hate crimes are harms inflicted on a victim by an offender whose motivation derives primarily from hatred directed at a perceived characteristic of the victim (e.g., the person's race, religion, ethnicity, gender, and/or sexual orientation). These crimes are particularly heinous because of their unique impact on victims as well as on the community. Victims often suffer physical injury caused by assault or property damage associated with vandalism. But they are also victimized by the thought that such acts were *not* random, that at least some people in our society detest them because of who they are—African American, Jewish, Islamic, Catholic, Irish, gay-lesbian-transgender, and so on.

Around 8:00 pm on Wednesday, June 17, 2015 a young white man, Dylann Storm Roof, entered the Emanuel A.M.E. Church in Charleston, South Carolina and began shooting African-Americans in a Bible study group, resulting in nine deaths.[16] Roof initially fled the scene, but was quickly arrested and subsequently confessed to the grotesque massacre of the church members. Roof's motive was to start a race war and in that context he saw himself as a heroic figure, doing what others did not dare to do. His website was filled with comments about Nazis and rants about African Americans, Jews, Hispanics, and Asians. A survey taken 10 days after the massacre revealed that 87% of Americans saw the murders as a hate-based crime.[17]

In the early morning hours of June 12, 2016 Omar Seddique Mateen, an American-born man of Pakistani descent, entered a crowded, gay nightclub called "Pulse" in Orlando, Florida. He was armed with an assault rifle and a pistol and began firing indiscriminately into the groups of openly homosexual men embracing each other on the crowded dance floor of the club. The resulting gunfire left 49 people killed and over 50 wounded, marking it one of the deadliest attacks in U.S. history since 9/11.[18] Mateen was ultimately killed by police responding to the scene in a protracted shootout at the club.

Both Roof's and Mateen's actions were characteristic of lone wolf attacks, commonly associated with acts of terrorism. These acts of random violence seemingly come out of nowhere, with no warning and result in mass carnage, death, and destruction. Both of the suspects had voiced earlier allegiance to specific known terrorist groups operating in the United States. Roof's website was littered with pictures of him wearing emblems associated with the white supremacy movement, including him adorned in a jacket sporting two flags, one from apartheid-era South Africa and the other from white-ruled Rhodesia. He was, according to friends, enamored with the white supremacist movement as expressed by groups such as the Ku Klux Klan and the neo-Nazi party and openly bragged about these associations in his manifesto. In Orlando, Mateen had made a telephone call to the police just minutes before the attack, pledging

(©Carlo Alegri/Reuters/Alamy)

his allegiance to ISIS, and previously had glorified the 2013 Boston Marathon bombers. While neither a specific white supremacist group nor ISIS claimed direct responsibility for the attacks, they did praise the attacks on various media and Internet forums. Both attacks were aimed at individuals based on hate directed at a perceived characteristic of the victims; in Charleston the victims were chosen based on race—they were all black—and in Orlando the victims were chosen based on sexual orientation—they were all gay. However, in both cases, the perpetrators acted in an effort to stoke fear, anger, and social strife in service of their extremist ideologies.[19] Both of these heinous acts could be technically classified as a hate crime, however, they also met the definition of a terrorist attack. President Obama called the Orlando shooting "an act of terror and an act of hate" and charged the FBI with investigating the incident as an act of terrorism.[20]

Does it make a difference how the incident is classified? It is an important question and issue and impacts the potential investigation, how offenders are charged, and the severity of their sentences. More importantly, these labels are highly symbolic acknowledgments by the government of the harms inflicted on individuals by terrorists, and on specific social groups by hate crimes. Essentially, these labels shape the public agenda and response surrounding extremist crimes.[21]

Legal definitions of hate crimes vary. The federal definition addresses civil rights violations under 18 U.S.C. Section 245. A hate crime is a criminal offense committed against persons, property, or society that is motivated, in whole or in part, by an offender's bias against an individual's or a group's perceived race, religion, ethnic/national origin, gender, age, disability, or sexual orientation.[22] Most states have a hate crime statute that provides enhanced penalties for crimes in which victims are selected because of the perpetrator's bias against the victims' perceived race, religion, or ethnicity; some states include the victim's sexual orientation, gender, and disability in this list. However, in the Charleston case, South Carolina does *not* have such a statute; passage of a hate crime statute in some states has been controversial as politicians have debated the constitutionality of enhanced penalties based on a suspect's association with an extremist group or the inclusion of homosexuality as a protected class.

The tragic incidents in Charleston and Orlando raise a number of important questions and issues: Are terrorists who commit acts of hate radicalized the same way? Do they have the same motivations? Are perpetrators of hate crimes motivated by far-right extremist views in the same manner that others are motivated by radical Islamic extremism? What factors push perpetrators to act out with such indiscriminate violence and carnage? And most importantly, what can be done by law enforcement to identify, investigate, prosecute, and ideally thwart those who would wantonly conduct such incidents of hate and terror on innocent civilians?[23] Indeed, some incidents do fit the definitions of both hate crime and terrorism. These should be classified as both, in order for us to remember that such crimes and acts of terror are the province not only of those espousing radical and foreign religious beliefs, but also of those that were born American and bred in the United States but adhere to wildly different visions of our culture.

One such Saudi citizen was Osama bin Laden, who came from a wealthy family and who had studied civil engineering before arriving in Afghanistan. He set up the organization known as "the base," or *al-Qaeda*, in order to track the movements of fighters and money coming into the Afghan resistance. The United States and Saudi Arabia both applauded the efforts of bin Laden, whose efficiency and strategic knowledge led Afghan fighters toward victory. Soviet troops withdrew from Afghanistan in 1989, and bin Laden returned, victorious and a hero, to Saudi Arabia, where he rejoined his family.[24] Bin Laden quickly came into disfavor with the Saudi Arabian government as a result of his vocal opposition to the Saudi alliance with the United States during the first Gulf War. He fled Saudi Arabia and returned briefly to Afghanistan in 1991, finally settling in Sudan in 1992, a country that welcomed his arrival.[25] It was there that bin Laden stepped up his sponsorship of training camps for fundamental Islamic young men, particularly those who subscribed to Jihadist Salafism.[26] Because of these and other activities, the Saudis revoked his citizenship in 1994, and his family, at least publicly, disowned him.

Following the 1993 World Trade Center bombings, American interest in bin Laden escalated, although he denied involvement in the attack. The United States was also interested in his training camps in Sudan, believing that graduates from bin Laden's schools were responsible for attacks on U.S. forces in Somalia and Riyadh. Sudan, acting under pressure from the United States and Egypt, finally expelled him in 1996.[27]

Bin Laden again returned to Afghanistan, where the Taliban, a strict Muslim faction, had united Afghanistan under their harsh rule. The Taliban offered sanctuary to bin Laden and benefited greatly from his wealth. In return, bin Laden and his al-Qaeda organization were protected and allowed to recruit hundreds of followers in his pursuit of jihad against the United States.

The goals of the jihad were to drive U.S. forces out of the Arab peninsula, overthrow the pro-Western Saudi government, thereby liberating the holy sites Mecca and Medina, and support radical Islamic groups throughout the world. By the late 1990s al-Qaeda's training camps were turning out hundreds of "graduates" annually.[28]

In 1998 al-Qaeda made its first strike against the United States. A suicide bomber drove a truck into the U.S. embassy compound in Nairobi, Kenya, killing 216 people and injuring over 4,500. Eight minutes later, another truck bomb detonated in Dar-es-Salaam, Tanzania, killing 11 and injuring over 100. The United States reacted by launching cruise missiles on the training sites in Afghanistan, attempting to kill bin Laden. As a result of the embassy bombings, bin Laden made his way onto the list of America's most wanted men.[29] He was also indicted for the attacks, along with 17 other al-Qaeda members.

The October 12, 2000, bombing of the *U.S.S. Cole* has also been attributed to al-Qaeda. Although bin Laden never formally took responsibility for the suicide attack, which killed 17 U.S. Navy personnel, the key suspect in the case told Yemini authorities that he and the suicide bombers were acting under the directions of Osama bin Laden.[30]

On September 11, 2001, planes hijacked by al-Qaeda cells crashed into the Twin Towers in New York City and the Pentagon. Aboard another hijacked flight, passengers unsuccessfully fought to retake the plane to prevent its use in another attack, resulting in its crash in rural Pennsylvania and the loss of everyone aboard. The United States promptly declared war against the terrorist groups responsible and went after bin Laden and his supporters in Afghanistan.

The subsequent wars in Afghanistan and Iraq have resulted in the killing or capture of hundreds of al-Qaeda fighters and operatives. Hundreds of documents linking al-Qaeda to the September 11 attacks have been found, and other documents suggest future plans to attack U.S. interests. By December of 2001 the Taliban rule in Afghanistan had been toppled. However, bin Laden and many of his closest cohorts within al-Qaeda were still at large.

USAMA BIN LADEN

▲ **FIGURE 21-3   Osama bin Laden**

Osama bin Laden was one of the most wanted persons in the world with a $50 million reward for his capture. However, in June 2011, bin Laden was finally located living inside a walled compound in Abbottabad, Pakistan. Elite members of the U.S. Joint Special Operations Command (Navy SEAL Team Six) attempted to secure bin Laden; a brief firefight ensued and bin Laden was killed. (*http:// www.fbi.gov/wanted/topten/usama-bin-laden*) (*Left:* ©Mark Wilson/Getty Images; *Right:* ©Getty Images)

Nearly a decade after the September 11 attacks, Osama bin Laden was finally located in a small town in Pakistan by ongoing intelligence operations. A small team of U.S. Navy commandos (Navy SEAL Team 6) approached the compound in an attempt to apprehend bin Laden, however a firefight broke out and bid Laden was killed. The body was taken into custody and subsequent DNA tests confirmed the identity of the body as that of Osama bin Laden (Figure 21-3). The core leadership of al-Qaeda had been destroyed in previous U.S. military actions in Afghanistan and Iraq, and the death of bin Laden only further depreciated the potential of one of the world's most notorious terrorist groups. The leadership of al-Qaeda has now fallen to bin Laden's top lieutenant and personal cleric, Dr. Ayman al-Zawarahi.[31] America has become familiar with this new leader, and the many video tapes that deride the American "invasion" into Iraq and Afghanistan that he has presented to the public.

Al-Qaeda's activities in Somalia and Yemen have become a great concern to the United States in the past few years. On Christmas Day 2009 a 23-year-old Nigerian man named Umar Farouk Abdulmutallab was discovered with a bomb on a Northwest Airlines flight to Detroit. Abdulmutallab was unsuccessful in his attempt, but as details emerged about his motivations, homeland security officials became increasingly alarmed about what they had previously thought was just a regional outpost of al-Qaeda in Yemen. Abdulmutallab trained in Yemen, and a martyrdom statement by him was released by al-Qaeda's Yemeni operation. It is becoming clear that the Yemeni network has an international reach. The group has taken advantage of a weakened central government in Yemen, mobilizing an impoverished and angry population and establishing training camps in remote areas. U.S. intelligence officials have warned that a number of Americans have travelled to Yemen and disappeared, possibly to train in these camps.

Al-Qaeda is also expanding its presence in war-torn Somalia. The open borders, lack of central government, and emergence of Al-Shabab, a militant Islamic group, have all contributed to a hospitable environment for al-Qaeda operatives. Al-Qaeda fighters have moved to the southern region of Somalia to train Al-Shabab fighters in al-Qaeda techniques.[32] These camps have become a magnet for foreign fighters coming from all over the Middle East and potentially even the United States. In 2010, 14 people (mostly located in Minnesota, home of the largest Somali population in the U.S.), were charged with providing financial support or recruits to Al-Shabab.[33] Their close ties to al-Qaeda continue to worry U.S. intelligence and law enforcement, afraid that Al-Shabab operations are merely another pipeline to terror against the United States.

Several cases have raised concerns about the extent to which al-Qaeda has new operatives functioning within the United States. In the last few years alone, investigators have uncovered a number of plots perpetrated by al-Qaeda affiliates living in the country. For instance, Oussama Abdullah Kassir was sentenced to life in prison in 2009 for operating a training camp in Bly, Oregon that was designed to provide Muslims with military-like jihad training. In addition, officials revealed that Kassir was also operating several terrorist websites.[34] The presence of al-Qaeda operatives in the U.S. was further substantiated when officials recently indicated that members of the group considered poisoning the U.S. food supply by putting ricin and cyanide in the food at restaurant and hotel buffets.[35]

Al-Qaeda has also been linked to numerous other terrorist organizations throughout the Middle East and Asia, such as Hizbollah, Al-Jihad, Harakat al-Mujahedeen, the Islamic Movement of Uzbekistan, HAMAS, the Chechens, and Jemaah Islamiayah; it is due partly to its wide reach that al-Qaeda remains powerful. Despite the fact that its power center has been disrupted in the past and hidden, al-Qaeda communicates regularly with the Arab world through the media. Al-Queda continues to condemn U.S. involvement in Muslim affairs and urges jihad and violent terrorist attacks against the United States and its allies. The basis of their threat to the United States is in their ideology, past actions, continuing intent, and capability, and their financial resources help to make such plans a reality. In 2009 al-Qaeda leaders in Yemen boasted of their ability to defeat U.S. intelligence and airport security in an attempted bombing involving an American passenger jet.[36]

Although most of the news attention today has focused on the rapid expansion and extreme acts of violence associated with the Islamic State, it is important to understand that al-Qaeda remains a dangerous group in the world. While much smaller in years past, the group still has hardcore loyalists and remains uniquely separate from the Islamic State; their primary goal being the expulsion of Western powers from the Islamic world. In January 2016, al-Qaeda's Saharan Chapter, known as al-Qaeda in the Islamic Maghreb (AQIM), attacked the Splendid Hotel in the West African country of Burkina Faso, killing over 30 people and wounding another 50.[37] The hotel was the meeting site of many foreign visitors and business leaders to the capital city of Ouagadougou in the former French colony of Burkina Faso. Other such activities in western Africa by AQIM included a similar attack on a Radisson Blu hotel in Bamako, Mali in 2015 killing 22 people, and the overt backing of Boko Haram in Nigeria that has waged a war in that country claiming more than 27,000 people dead and the destabilization of the government. While al-Qaeda supported and help develop Boko Haram for many years, the group became a self-declared province of the Islamic State in 2015.[38]

Jemaah Islamiyah

Jemaah Islamiyah (JI) began when two radical Indonesian clerics named Abdullah Sungkar and Abu Bakar Ba'asyir established a pirate (unauthorized) radio station in 1960, which advocated Shari'a, strict Muslim law. Subsequently, they opened an Islamic school, which taught a hard-line version of Salafi Wahhabism. Increasingly in conflict with their government, both men were arrested in 1978 and sentenced to four years imprisonment. The two men eventually fled to Malaysia, where they developed a large following of other refugee Indonesians. Two prominent radical Islamics, Riduan Isamuddin (a.k.a., Hambali) and Abu Jibril, became part of JI's leadership.[39] Together, the core group of four men preached jihad and the establishment of an Islamic republic across Malaysia, Indonesia, southern Thailand, and the southern Philippines[40] and were able to develop cells in these target countries.[41]

In 2000 JI carried out a series of bombings in Indonesia and Manila, resulting in the deaths of 27 people.[42] There were also plans for large-scale attacks against the United States in Singapore and the Philippines, but these plans were foiled by the arrests of several key JI members. Angered by these circumstances, Hambali began to focus JI's efforts on smaller strikes against places frequented by Western tourists. This planning culminated in the 2002 bombing of a Bali nightclub. Two hundred and two people died in the attacks.[43] Although key leaders were subsequently arrested, JI's operations continued, thereby resulting in another fatal bombing in 2003. The networks established by JI throughout Southeast Asia have resulted in a seemingly strong backbone of Islamic terrorists who are willing to carry on JI's flight, with or without its original leaders. JI's dangerousness to the United States and its allies is due to its al-Qaeda-trained operatives, its strong network, good resources, and its ability to strike at "soft" targets.

Through 2016, most of the members of Jemaah Islamiyah remain separate from the Islamic State has developed a strong transnational organization throughout Southeast Asia, in the countries of Thailand, Singapore, Malaysia and the Philippines. Their single point of division with ISIS being the development of a regional Islamic caliphate in Southeast Asia and not the Middle East.[44]

Hizbollah

Hizbollah, also transliterated Hezbollah, or "the Party of God," was founded in 1982 in reaction to the Israeli invasion of Lebanon. This invasion was generally precipitated by continuing Palestinian military action from Lebanon in Northern Israel and more particularly by the unsuccessful assassination attempt on the life of Israel's Ambassador to the United Kingdom by the Abu Nidal organization. During the invasion, Israel battled Palestinian Liberation Organization (PLO), Syrian, and Muslim Lebanese forces, driving halfway across Lebanon to Beirut.

The roots of Hizbollah go back to the late 1970s, when hundreds of Shi'ite clerics and students were forced to leave Iraq and settle in Lebanon. These exiles recruited young militants and formed the Committee Supportive of the Islamic Revolution, which identified closely with the Shi'ite Muslim government in Iran. The group was also loosely associated with a Lebanese Shi'ite militia, known as Amal,[45] led by Nabih Berri.

The 1982 invasion of Lebanon by Israel damaged or destroyed more than 80% of the villages in southern Lebanon with 19,000 Lebanese killed and another 32,000 injured. The invasion caused a mass exodus from the southern areas of Lebanon, owing mostly to the total destruction of Lebanese agriculture by the Israelis. The exiles flooded into northern Lebanon, settling into refugee camps that were also occupied by displaced Palestinians. These refugee camps quickly became a hotbed of discontent against Israel and Western Zionist sympathizers, such as the United States. Militant groups such as Amal organized a Lebanese resistance front to fight the Israelis, but it wasn't until Iran sent 1,500 troops to the aid of the Lebanese fighters that the development of Hizbollah truly began. The Iranian fighters further fostered the desire among the Lebanese Shi'ites to model their government after Iran's, where Muslim clerics and disciples of the Ayatollah Khomeni ruled. The Shi'ites wanted the same for Lebanon.[46]

The final stage of Hizbollah's development occurred when a schism arose within Amal. Nabih Berrie (the leader of Amal) had begun to participate in a committee whose head was pro-Israeli. Others within Amal felt this was a manipulation conceived of by Americans who wished to water down Lebanese militancy. They also considered it a betrayal of Islam. As a result, the more radical Islam faction of Amal broke free and joined the smaller radical groups and the Iranian forces to establish the *Committee of Nine,* Hizbollah's first decision-making council. Hizbollah eventually absorbed all the smaller Shi'ite resistance groups, becoming a powerful force against the Israeli occupation.[47] Guerrilla attacks were conducted against the Israelis, which included the use of car bombs, sniper attacks, and suicide bombers.

Hizbollah's terrorist activity began to escalate. On April 18, 1983, a suicide bomber drove into the U.S. embassy in Beirut, Lebanon, killing 63 people, including the top-level American intelligence officials in Lebanon at the time.[48] On October 23, 1983, another suicide bomber drove at least 6 tons of dynamite into a U.S. Marine command center located at Beirut's International Airport, killing 241 Marine and Navy personnel (Figure 21-4). Twenty seconds later, another blast erupted at the barracks of a French military contingent. Fifty-eight French soldiers died in the attack. Hizbollah claimed responsibility for both attacks, claiming them to be retaliation for French and U.S. support of Christian governmental factions in the Lebanese civil war.[49]

U.S. troops were ordered out of Lebanon in early 1984 by President Ronald Reagan, a move that did not lead to a drop in the violence. Malcolm Kerr, President of the American University of Beirut (AUB), was assassinated on January 18, 1984; another American embassy bombing occurred on September 20, 1984, which killed 14 people; and kidnappings of Westerners by Hizbollah escalated. The rising toll of the dead and missing led the United States to stage a complete withdrawal from Lebanon, leaving only six diplomats in the country by November of 1984.[50]

Again, retreat by the United States did not mean an end to terrorist attacks against U.S. and Western interests. In 1985 TWA flight 847 was hijacked by Hizbollah affiliates, resulting in the death of one American on board. Hizbollah also claimed responsibility for the kidnappings of 18 American and British journalists and church officials, three of whom were killed, including Beirut Central Intelligence Agency (CIA) Station Chief William Buckley, who was held 19 days and then executed. In 1992 the Israeli embassy in Buenos Aires, Argentina, was bombed, killing 29 people. Although Hizbollah never directly claimed responsibility, they did release a surveillance tape of the embassy that overtly implied their responsibility. In 1994 a Jewish community center in Buenos Aires was bombed, killing 95 people. Hizbollah was also responsible for this act.[51]

In 2000 faced with mounting casualties, Israel ordered a complete retreat from Lebanon after nearly 18 years of occupation. This act served to legitimize Hizbollah not only in the Shi'ite community but also the Arab world at large. No other Arab group had been able to successfully drive Israel from occupied lands. Palestinians waging the current Intifada (or uprising) cite Hizbollah as a major inspiration in their battles. Furthermore, Hizbollah holds 12 seats in the Lebanese parliament and has built an extensive educational and social aid network within the Lebanese Shi'ite community.[52]

Although the 1994 Jewish community center attack in Buenos Aires is the last terrorist act directly linked to Hizbollah, the organization remains a risk to the United States and Israeli interests. Attacks against Israeli troops have continued in the Sheeba area, which Israel claims is a part of Syria and therefore not subject to withdrawal. Hizbollah forces claim that Sheeba is part of Lebanon and has continued to launch missile attacks against Israeli forces.[53]

Although initially dismissed because of the religious differences between the groups, evidence has been found linking Hizbollah to al-Qaeda. Leaders of both groups apparently met several times in the 1990s, and there is some evidence that the groups have been coordinating logistics and training for specific operations.[54] Investigators of a 2002 bombing of an Israeli-owned hotel in Mombasa that killed 16 people have found clues that point to such a collaboration. Materials and techniques used in the attack, formally blamed on al-Qaeda, are the same as those used by the Hizbollah suicide bombers in the attacks on the U.S. Marine barracks and embassy in the 1980s. Furthermore, the only claim of responsibility for the attack was made on Hizbollah radio. Also, missiles found after an attempt to shoot down an Israeli charter jet by al-Qaeda were identified as SAM-7s, used almost exclusively by Hizbollah fighters against Israeli targets.[55]

More recent intelligence also indicates that Hizbollah provided aid to al-Qaeda operatives fleeing Afghanistan at the end of 2001. Between 80 and 100 al-Qaeda fighters were given fake passports by Hizbollah, allowing their safe passage into Saudi Arabia and Yemen. Some 10 to 20 senior al-Qaeda commanders are believed to have settled within Lebanon since 2001, as well.[56] As a result, Hizbollah remains a designated foreign terror

▲ **FIGURE 21-4   Sayyad Hassan Nasrallah**
The head of Hizbollah in Lebanon; aside from involvement in the 1983 suicide bomber attack on the Marine barracks in Beirut which killed 241 Marines, Hizbollah is very active in the financing of various terrorist operations through trafficking of drugs, arms, and human beings. (©Patrick Baz/AFP/Getty Images)

organization, classified as having a high activity level by the U.S. State Department. During his 2002 State of the Union address, President George W. Bush singled the organization out as a target of the U.S. War on Terror.[57]

In 2004 Hizbollah won nearly a quarter of the parliamentary seats in the Lebanese government and was largely responsible for starting the Second Lebanon War in July 2006 by firing rockets into northern border towns of Israel and capturing several IDF soldiers. The incident became an international topic of debate as over a thousand civilians were killed in the ensuing bombing and ground invasion by Israel. The war ended after a short but deadly 34 days, rendering Lebanon's infrastructure in chaos and parts of southern Lebanon uninhabitable because of unexploded cluster bombs. Hizbollah and Nasrallah emerged as "victors" against the Israeli forces and boasted that their armed forces were now much stronger than before, and much better armed with missiles supplied by Iran. Over a million people attended Nasrallah's speech in Beirut in late August 2006 declaring "victory" over the Zionist state. The war was something of a public relations disaster for Hizbollah, causing it to lose favor among many pro-Western Lebanese. However, it retains several seats in Lebanon's parliament and has ministers in the national unity government formed in 2009. Though the Bush administration classified Hizbollah as a primary target in the War on Terror, the Obama administration has recognized that it has evolved somewhat from a "purely a terrorist organization" to a more legitimate political operation, and has expressed hopes that it can tap into the more moderate elements of the organization.[58] However, many believe that Hizbollah remains one of the most dangerous terrorist organizations in the world, by virtue of their size, training, discipline, financing, and their arms cache. In March of 2009 retired chief of operations for the DEA Michael Braun stated that Hizbollah had become involved in the operation of Mexico's drug cartels.

Hizbollah's involvement in Mexico raises two separate issues: the first is that the organization is connected to drugs and arms trafficking, as well as money laundering in an effort to fund their objectives in Lebanon. In August of 2010 a major Hizbollah-connected drug trafficking organization in South America was targeted by a DEA operation, and officials say that currently Hizbollah is aligning itself with powerful Mexican syndicates who are responsible for nearly 90% of cocaine trafficking into the US.[59] The implications of a 2009 indictment in a New York federal court against alleged Hizbollah member Jamal Yousef are quite telling: Yousef had a cache of weapons, including military rifles, rocket-propelled grenades, C-4 plastic explosives and surface to air missiles. He offered to sell those weapons to a narco-terror organization, the Revolutionary Armed Forces of Colombia (FARC), which we discuss later in this chapter. This case underscores the fact that Hezbollah maintains operations in Mexico and is a participant in arms and drug trafficking; Hezbollah is willing to join forces with narco-terrorist organizations that seek to destabilize American interests; and these weapons could have just as easily been smuggled into the United States for use in a terrorist plot.[60]

The second issue is that of immigration. Hizbollah relies on the same document traffickers and transportation experts that the Mexican drug cartels do to smuggle humans into the United States. In 2008 Salim Boughader Mucharrafille, a Mexican of Lebanese descent, was sentenced to 60 years in prison by Mexican authorities for smuggling 200 people, including Hizbollah supporters, into the United States. Others, including Mahmoud Yossef Kourani, have used the Mexican border to cross into the United States in order to generate support and resources for Hizbollah. Kourani was caught in Dearborn, Michigan, and pled guilty in 2006 to supporting the organization.

Currently, Hizbollah's presence in the United States is primarily limited to fundraising, technology purchases, recruiting, and arms smuggling. We will discuss the Holy Land Foundation and other fund-raising schemes later in the chapter, but it is worth noting that Hizbollah has a long history of fundraising in the United States. For example, the Hammoud brothers in North Carolina were purchasing large quantities of cigarettes in their state, which were cheaper than other states owing to lower taxes, and shipping them into states where taxes were much higher. By selling the cigarettes on the black market, the Hammouds were able to funnel millions back to Lebanon.

It should be noted that Hizbollah's presence in the United States is also one of intelligence-gathering and reconnaissance. Former CIA head James Woolsey told a Senate committee in February of 2009 that Hizbollah has identified 29 key targets in the United States and other parts of the "Western World" whose destruction would cripple Western civilization. Because their intelligence-gathering force is supplemented and trained by Iran's Ministry of Intelligence Service (MOIS), this is particularly worrisome.

Hizbollah maintains sleeper cells throughout the United States and Canada to carry out fundraising and reconnaissance activities, but do they pose a direct threat of a terrorist attack on American soil? The answer is quite possibly. The most likely trigger of a Hizbollah attack on America by sleeper cells is an American attack on Iran, Syria, or Lebanon. Continued tensions with Iran, an influential ally of Hizbollah, are in fact the greatest risk for such an attack.[61] Likely targets would include synagogues or other Jewish centers; civilian targets like malls or hotels; economic infrastructure such as banks or financial institutions; symbolic American landmarks; or other infrastructure like power or water supply. As such, continued monitoring of Hizbollah by United States intelligence and law enforcement organizations is essential to homeland security.

Palestinian Terrorist Groups

The current conflict between the Israelis and the Palestinians is a decades-old dispute regarding land rights that grows increasingly complex by the day. The issues arose with the creation of Israel in 1948, which eventually resulted in the loss of the Palestinian state and the displacement of the Palestinian people. This conflict is worsened owing to the two fundamentally different ideologies of both sides and a general unwillingness of both to compromise. The most dangerous manifestation of this conflict comes in the form of terrorist groups that are often willing to go to any length to draw attention to their cause. Palestinian terrorist groups, whether secular or grounded in Islamic fundamentalism, are known throughout the world for their extreme tactics (including suicide bombing) used against the

Israelis and their supporters. These organizations focus their attacks on civilian and political targets within Israel, often in reaction to Israeli aggression upon Palestinians.

The Popular Front for the Liberation of Palestine (PFLP).

The PFLP is a Christian-led Marxist-Leninist group founded in 1967 by George Habash as a direct response to the Six-Day War of 1967. George Habash, code-named "al-Hakim," or "the doctor," is a Christian-Marxist Palestinian. Under his leadership, the PFLP essentially established the concept of skyjacking an airplane, back in the late 1960s. Their motivation was relatively benign: to make the world aware of the plight of the Palestinian people. Killing passengers and using skyjacked planes as weapons (for example, the attacks on September 11, 2001) were *not* PFLP tactics. However, PFLP did conduct other violent attacks aimed directly at Israel. For instance, in 1972, working in conjunction with the PFLP, Japanese Red Army terrorists killed 25 people at Lod (now Ben Gurion International Airport) in Haifa; and in 1976, during their last skyjacking attempt, PFLP terrorists died at the hands of Israeli Special Forces at the now famous Entebbe raid in Uganda. In recent years, and particularly after the retirement of George Habash in 2000 as leader of the PFLP, the group has been relatively quiet, responsible only for a few suicide bombings in the West Bank. And, after more than 50 years of involvement in various Palestinian terrorist groups, George Habash died of a heart attack in a hospital in Amman, Jordan on January 26, 2008. Habash was 81 years old at time of his death.

The Abu-Nidal Organization (ANO).

This organization was formed by Sabri al-Banna, code-named Abu Nidal (meaning "father of the Holy Struggle"). The group formed after it split from the Palestinian Liberation Organization as a result of perceived moderation on the part of Yassir Arafat in 1972. Al-Banna was strictly antimoderation and adhered strongly to the doctrine that Israel must be destroyed at any cost, branding Arafat, the PLO, and the rest of the al-Fatah as traitors. Al-Banna continued to launch international terrorist operations against Israeli interests and even struck at pro-Arafat groups and moderate Arab countries in his list of targets. The Abu Nidal organization has been financially backed by Syria, Libya, Iraq, and Iran.[62]

The Abu Nidal Organization has attacked more foreign and Arab interests than any other Palestinian terrorist organization to date, and at one point was considered the most dangerous group in the world, having been accused of killing or wounding nearly 1,000 people in 20 different countries. Over the past 30 years ANO attempted or carried out assassinations of Arab government officials and high-ranking PLO officers. This is one of the few Palestinian groups to have actually claimed an attack within the United States, having conducted a robbery in St. Louis, Missouri, in the mid-1980s. In August 2002 Sabri al-Banna's body was found in an Iraqi apartment with multiple gunshot wounds. Reports state that he committed suicide, but intelligence sources believe he was killed by Iraqis so Saddam Hussein could have access to the Abu Nidal Organizational network, which is still active, yet diminished, throughout the world.

The Palestinian Islamic Resistance Movement (HAMAS).

HAMAS, a radical fundamentalist organization, came to prominence as the foremost opponent of the Oslo peace accords following the first major Palestinian Intifada in the 1990s (Figure 21-5). The primary modus operandi of HAMAS is **suicide bombings** against civilian targets. HAMAS has been directly responsible for over 90% of the suicide bombings against Israel. The bombings have been notoriously ruthless, often aimed at inflicting the most civilian damage possible. For example, on March 27, 2002, in the Israeli resort of Netanya, a bomber blew himself up at a hotel, killing 28 Israelis who were

◄ **FIGURE 21-5   HAMAS**
This group is responsible for over 90% of the suicide bombings in Israel, with most bombs being relatively crude homemade devices aimed at killing a relatively small number of people.
(©Enric Marti/AP Images)

celebrating Passover. This attack remains one of the most deadly HAMAS actions to date.[63]

Deconstructing the Suicide Bomber. For most Americans, trying to understand the motivation behind suicide bombing is very difficult. In our culture, such actions are often labeled unpredictable, irrational, and fanatical. However, a careful analysis of the phenomenon shows that suicide bombings are not spontaneous outbursts of emotion but rather calculated, strategic moves by a specific group for a specific purpose. Indeed, suicide bombers are actually trained in the actions. They undergo a relatively long period of indoctrination filled with group pressure, pep talks, organizational support, and personal commitment. Quite interestingly, suicide is strictly forbidden in the Holy Quran; however, when deemed by a religious edict to protect the Kingdom of Islam, suicide bombing serves as a means to an end. Some argue that the huge difference in might between Israel and the Palestinian people militarily gives legitimacy to the act, while others suggest that people who have little political power in the present or no hope for the future engage in the ultimate desperate measure.[64]

Under the religious and ideological leadership of radical Islamic cleric, Sheikh Ahmed Yassin, people who engage in suicide bombing became a *shahid*, or martyr fulfilling a religious command. Most suicide bombers in Israel fit a specific profile: young men between 18 and 24 years old, born in relative poverty with little or no education and with no real understanding of the outside world or of the geopolitical issues surrounding the Middle East. For the most part, the shahid is a victim of some personal tragedy or event from the Israeli occupation in the West Bank or Gaza. This person seeks honor, praise, and financial reward for his family after the action has been completed, as well as the personal religious rewards of seeing the face of Allah and the temporal love and servitude of 72 virgins in heaven. Most suicide bombers in Israel kill themselves and two other individuals. They often walk less than two miles from their home before engaging in their deadly action. For the most part, their "weapon" is crude: TNT or dynamite wrapped with iron nuts and bolts, or metal ball bearings worn in a vest or around their waist (Figure 21-6). In a crowded café or on a bus, or in a shopping center, suicide bombers wreak havoc on their unsuspecting victims. However, on March 22, 2004, Yassin was killed by the Israeli Moussad returning from prayer services at a West Bank mosque. The radical leader was gone, and the number of suicide bombings in Israel dramatically decreased.

U.S. intelligence officials have consistently warned that HAMAS may strike U.S. interests or American gathering places in Israel and throughout the Middle East. The report does not rule out attacks on American soil. The FBI has long suspected there are HAMAS sympathizers among Islamic extremists in the United States. Federal and local law enforcement officers are closely tracking thefts of explosives (like those used in HAMAS backpack bombs) and unusual sales of fertilizer, chemicals, and fuel that could be used to make a truck bomb.[65]

HAMAS' activities within the United States, much like Hizbollah, focus on recruiting and fundraising. American freedoms

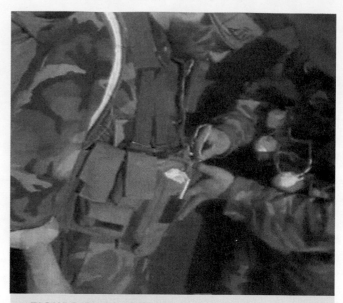

▲ **FIGURE 21-6** **Shahid**
Suicide bomber wearing a satchel-style bomb of TNT wrapped with metal ball bearings and ignited by a simple finger push device. The bomber wears a jacket or coat over the deadly cargo upon entering a crowded café or night spot. (©APTV/AP Images)

have allowed HAMAS to mobilize intellectual support for their cause in universities and via the Internet. This, in turn, allows for an increased flow of funds to HAMAS. As such, it is not in the best interest of HAMAS to "cause troubles in the American theater."[66] However, HAMAS leadership has sometimes countered that assertion with anti-American rhetoric. And like Hizbollah, American tensions with Iran are a major trigger for potential sleeper cell activation on American soil. Because Iran indirectly funds HAMAS, any attack or hostilities visited on that country by the United States could stimulate a HAMAS response. Furthermore, HAMAS has a history of independent cells that do not always fall in line with the parent organization. For example, a rogue cell broke an Israeli-HAMAS ceasefire in 2003. Such a cell could certainly instigate a terror operation within the United States based on a different set of motivations than HAMAS' "legitimate" organization.

HAMAS is clearly one of the most interesting groups in the Middle East. Although it has been responsible for the vast majority of suicide bombings and radical violence in Israel (particularly under the leadership of Yassin), it enjoys a favorable opinion among the Palestinian people. HAMAS has consistently tried to focus on helping the people within the occupied territories of the West Bank and Gaza, collecting millions of dollars in aid and rebuilding schools, mosques, and hospitals. In fact, in 2006 it was elected the governing body for the Palestinian territories of the West Bank and Gaza in Israel.

Today, however, after a violent conflict in 2006-09, HAMAS shares administrative governmental control over the Palestinian territory with the largest Palestinian political group, al-Fatah, now headed by Chairman Mahmoud Abbas. The unity government of the Palestinian Authority was negotiated by Egypt in June 2014 with al-Fatah maintaining control over the West Bank and HAMAS effectively governing the Gaza Strip within the country of Israel.[67]

HOMEGROWN TERRORISM

For many years the United States government and its intelligence and law enforcement arms have focused on terror threats from outside the United States. The men who hijacked the planes on 9/11 were all exports from other nations, sent here to perpetrate attacks. But it is becoming obvious that al-Qaeda has shifted its tactics to recruit terror operatives from right here in the United States. The organization, fractured by the ongoing U.S. war in Afghanistan and military presence in Iraq, may be less able to pull together a "spectacular" attack on the scale of 9/11. That attack required years of organization and planning from al-Qaeda, something they are less likely to be able to do with the constant relocation and turmoil they are currently faced with. Many experts feel that this means al-Qaeda may have begun a sea-change in their tactics, focusing on the recruit, indoctrination and support of "homegrown terrorists." Homegrown terrorists include those who plot to carry out attacks at home in the United States and those who provide material support to foreign terrorist organizations via financial, intellectual, or other means. Between September 11 and the end of 2009, a total of 46 cases of domestic recruitment and radicalization to jihadist terrorist groups were reported.[68] By the end of 2010 there had been several more high-profile terrorist stings involving domestic terrorists. Clearly, this is a disturbing trend that has commanded the attention of law enforcement, homeland security forces, and the general public.

WHO IS THE "HOMEGROWN TERRORIST"?

The majority of homegrown terrorists are American citizens, although others may be immigrants to this country. American citizens are particularly attractive recruits for a couple of reasons. First, they are able to travel quite extensively largely without questioning or investigation. This allows recruited jihadists the ability to fly overseas, travel to a terrorist training camp, and return without raising any eyebrows, particularly if they take less direct routes. Second, they are also ideal candidates for jihadist organizations because of their innate knowledge of the English language, and of American cultural norms. This allows these individuals to blend into crowds, as well as to identify potential targets and weaknesses for terrorist organizations. Finally, open access to the Internet is another advantage to terrorist organizations who recruit Americans. This medium allows for easy radicalization via Internet propaganda; a sense of community or solidarity with people halfway around the world; and a means to communicate plot details. One of the more active and vocal examples of the Internet recruiter is Anwar al-Awlaki, an extremist English-speaking Muslim cleric based out of Yemen, who has been linked to many Muslim extremists including the Christmas Day bomber, Umar Farouk Abdulmutallab, and Major Nidal Hassan of the Ft. Hood shootings.

Immigrants to the United States who feel disenfranchised or disenchanted with their new homeland are also a target for jihadist recruiters. Several recent plots have involved immigrants or recent American citizens.

Prisoner radicalization is also a concern for United States law enforcement. The insides of prisons have long been a place where inmates converted to Islam, but increasingly, those inmates are identifying with jihadist beliefs. Violent inmate culture, a feeling of institutional and governmental oppression, and limited education combined with religious fervor makes prisoners easy targets for extremist recruiters. "Jailhouse Islam" has been cited as a factor in the radicalization of several homegrown terrorists, and officials have warned that the world's largest prison system could be a potential breeding ground for homegrown terrorists.[69]

ATTACKS FROM INSIDE THE UNITED STATES

Unfortunately, there have been a number of homegrown terrorists identified in the past few years. But fortunately, they have all been caught either before their plots were carried to fruition or because their plots failed. While this speaks to the tenacity of law enforcement and intelligence operations, it also points to the fact that the homegrown phenomenon is now a crucial concern in the war against terrorism. What follows are examples of some of these homegrown terrorists, their motivations, and their modus operandi in assisting jihadist organizations.

- Colleen LaRose, more commonly known as "Jihad Jane," is a U.S. citizen apprehended for conspiracy to provide material support to terrorists, conspiracy to kill in a foreign country, attempted identity theft and making false statements to a government official. LaRose had been exchanging emails for years attempting to recruit fighters for "violent jihad" in South Asia and Europe. Her U.S. citizenship and Caucasian appearance made her appealing to the Islamic extremists she had been in contact with. She had also made posts on various online message boards expressing sympathy with terrorists and expressing a desire to help in any way possible to help ease the suffering of the Muslim people in their "holy war." She planned to use her European looks to blend into the Swedish population, and to carry out the killing of a Swedish artist who depicted the face of Mohammed on a dog.[70]
- In November 2009 five young men from Virginia were arrested in Pakistan for attempting to join Jihadist terrorist groups, specifically al-Qaeda. They had been reported missing by their parents in Virginia on the advice of the local Muslim community after the men had traveled to the Middle East without informing their parents. The "Virginia 5" was reported to have been arrested in a safe

▲ **FIGURE 21-7** **Jihadist**

Abu Mansoor Al-Amriki, a jihadist born and raised in Daphe, Alabama. Al-Amriki trained with Somali terrorist organization Al-Shabab, which is linked to al-Qaeda. (©Newscom)

house of an anti-India terrorist group in possession of Jihadist literature who were building schematics and maps of local areas. Officials believe they may have been in the planning stages of an attack.[71]

- Abu Mansoor Al-Amriki, or "The American," was born Omar Hammami in the small town of Daphne, Alabama, to his Syrian-born father and Caucasian Southern-Baptist mother (Figure 21-7). Al-Amriki has become the celebrity of the Al-Shabab group in Somalia, promoting Jihad and his group to youth through the Internet, video and hip-hop lyrics. He alone has greatly advanced the image of the violent Islamist insurgency group. Al-Amriki left the country several years ago for Somalia and has quickly moved through the ranks of Al-Shabab, now directing forces in the field, organizing attacks and developing strategy with other top al Quaeda officials. His role as a high profile recruitment tool is what makes him such a concern for U.S. law enforcement officials. He is able to connect to a younger generation through effective and attractive means like hip-hop lyrics, demonstrating Al-Shabab's attempt to recruit not only young foreign nationals but specifically English-speaking Americans and westerners.[72] Al-Amriki's influence is particularly worrisome, given that in June 2010 two Americans were stopped by FBI officials from boarding separate flights to Egypt to join Al-Amriki in Somalia.

- A North Carolina man, Daniel Boyd, along with six other individuals, was arrested in the summer of 2009 for operating a terrorism training camp in North Carolina. Daniel Boyd, a U.S. citizen, his two sons and four others had allegedly been training in their rural lakeside home for "violent jihad." Mr. Boyd had traveled to Afghanistan nearly 20 years earlier to train at terrorist camps in Pakistan and Afghanistan, and he fought the Soviets for three years before returning to the United States. It was reported that members of the group

traveled to Israel in 2007 with the intent of joining the jihad movement but returned with no success. The seven men were charged with providing material support to terrorism.[73]

- In 2009 Major Nidal Malik Hasan, a psychiatrist for the United States army, killed 13 people and wounded 30 at Fort Hood, Texas, in a processing center for soldiers about to be deployed. Hasan was reportedly unhappy about the continuing wars in Iraq and Afghanistan and was afraid of being deployed to Afghanistan. Hasan showed many signs throughout his career in the Army of resistance to the war efforts in the Middle East, and he disagreed with American foreign policies related to Israel and the Middle East. He had been in contact with Anwar al-Awlaki, as well.[74] Unfortunately, Hasan's behavior went largely unnoticed by the U.S. Army, who failed to connect the dots and predict potential terrorist activity before it was too late.

- The Times Square bomber, Faisal Shahzad, is another example of a U.S. resident who was radicalized, exposed to training overseas, and then used that training to plot an attack on U.S. soil. On May 1, 2010, Shahzad left a vehicle parked in Times Square that contained a large quantity of explosives. Fortunately, the devices inside the vehicle did not detonate, but smoke coming from the vehicle led to a quick response by authorities and an evacuation of a large swath of the tourist attraction. Shahzad had been living in the United States for 11 years and had even become a naturalized U.S. citizen in 2009. Shahzad was married with two children and by all accounts lived a normal life as a financial analyst with an MBA, living in a Connecticut suburb. In 2009 Shahzad lost his job and had become very committed to his religion. Shahzad had reportedly spent nearly five months in Pakistan where, according to him, he had been getting training from the Pakistan Taliban. The Pakistan Taliban claimed responsibility for the botched attack in Times Square.[75] Shahzad's terrorist activity seems to have been triggered, by many reports, after he lost his job, had his house foreclosed on, and was reportedly being sued by an energy company. After that he and his family made trips to Pakistan where his wife eventually stayed. Shahzad returned to the United States and rented a small apartment in a Connecticut suburb where he planned his attack. Shahzad was able to travel with ease for extended periods of time in foreign countries without raising suspicion. After the attempted Times Square attack, he was even able to purchase a single one-way ticket to Saudi Arabia in cash with no luggage checked. This is a prime example of how terrorist organizations can use U.S. citizens and residents to carry out their goals.

- In late 2010 a few plots involving homegrown terrorist raised the alarms even higher. On November 28 Mohamed Osman Mohamud, a 19-year-old naturalized U.S. citizen from Somalia, planned to detonate explosives during a Christmas tree lighting ceremony in downtown Portland, Oregon. Mohamud was working with two people he thought were al-Qaeda agents, but he was in fact dealing with undercover FBI operatives. Mohamud submitted articles to extremist magazines and online publications, and confided to the undercover operatives that he wanted to wage war on America, and that the 9/11 attacks were "awesome."[76] A little over a week later, on December 9, another plot involving a U.S. citizen in Baltimore was foiled after he praised violent jihad on Facebook. Antonio Martinez, a 21-year-old construction worker, tried to blow up a U.S. military recruitment center. He, too, was working with undercover FBI operatives.[77] Much discussion from these two FBI-involved stings, as well as a similar plot in Dallas to blow up a skyscraper also involving the FBI, has revolved around the concept of entrapment. Some believe that without collaboration and active participation from undercover FBI agents, these attacks would have never come to fruition. However, the willingness of the participants to go so far as to push the trigger in these plots speaks to the fact that they felt strongly enough in their jihadist beliefs to kill hundreds, possibly thousands of American citizens on their own soil.

- The Boston Marathon bombing on April 15, 2013 marked the first time that radical Islamic terrorists struck at an American sports event or venue. This type of attack was specifically outlined in the al-Qaeda training manual and has been a major concern for security officials since 9/11.[78] At Boston, Chechen-born brothers Tamerlan and Dzhokhar Tsarnaev used two homemade pressure cooker bombs to kill 4 people and wound another 170 on the crowded street side near the finish line of the race. While Tamerlin was killed during a shootout with police, Dzhokhar was subsequently arrested having been discovered hiding in a boat in the Boston suburb of Watertown just hours after the bombing. Dzhokhar Tsarnaev was found guilty and sentenced to death by a federal jury on May 15, 2015. He is currently awaiting execution at the ADX Federal Supermax prison in Florence, Colorado.
- In Chattanooga, Tennessee on July 16, 2015, Mohammad Youssuf Abdulazeez shot five people at two different military facilities in Chattanooga, Tennessee. Abdulazeez was killed in the attack. He had been influenced by writings and speeches made by Anwar al-Awlaki, and material relating to the cleric were found on Abdulazeez's computer.[79] See Box 21-3.
- On December 2015 28 year old U.S. citizen, Syed Rizwan Farook and his wife, Tashfeen Malik (age 29), a legal immigrant to the United States, walked into a morning holiday party for disabled persons at the Inland Regional Center in San Bernardino, California and opened fire with semi-automatic weapons and pistols. The attack left 14 individuals dead and another 17 wounded. Farook and Malik were later killed in a shoot-out with police later that evening. Interestingly, Farook was recently married, a graduate student at California State University-Fullerton, and worked for

the county as an environmental health specialist. Neighbors and friends refereed to Farook as a "normal guy;" however, both Farook and Malik had expressed allegiance to ISIS leader Abu Bakir Bashir in recent Facebook posts.[80]

- One of the most deadly attacks on U.S. soil since 9/11 occurred on June 12, 2016 in Orlando, Florida when Omar Mateen, a 29-year-old American born citizen of Pakistani descent entered the crowded and popular Pulse nightclub in Orlando, Florida. Armed with an assault rifle and a pistol, Mateen indiscrimently opened fire on gay patrons of the nightclub, killing 49 people and wounding another 53. Mateen was killed in a shootout with police earlier that morning. He had made a telephone call to 9-11 just before the shooting in Orlando and claimed allegiance to ISIS.

THE THREAT

With the uptick in homegrown terrorist incidents, it is obvious that this is the next phase of terrorism in the United States. Recent reports by the former heads of the September 11 Commission indicate that the government and law enforcement were slow to take this threat seriously and have failed to put strategies into place to deal with the issue.[81] Currently there is no federal agency specifically charged with identifying and preventing radicalization and related attacks. There are also no set legal or legislative procedures specific to the phenomenon, leading to problems like the accusations of entrapment leveled at FBI agents in the Portland, Dallas, and Baltimore cases discussed previously. The FBI has reached out to Muslim populations, in an effort to identify potential extremists, and relies heavily on tips from vigilant citizens. However, experts warn that the rapid increase in Syrian refugees, as well as the radicalization of disenfranchised Muslim youth pledging allegiance to the Islamic State, are likely the biggest threats to homeland security in the coming years, and advises interagency cooperation and community outreach to stem the growth of the homegrown terrorist threat.[82]

DOMESTIC TERRORISM

As defined by the FBI, **domestic terrorism** is the unlawful use, or threatened use, of violence by a group or an individual based and operating entirely within the United States or its territories, without foreign direction, committed against persons or property to intimidate or coerce a government, the civilian population, or any segment thereof, in furtherance of political or social objectives.[83] Its perpetrators can be divided into two groups: right-wing terrorists and left-wing terrorists.

RIGHT-WING TERRORISTS

Domestic **right-wing terrorist** groups often adhere to the principles of racial supremacy and embrace antigovernment, anti-regulatory beliefs.[84] They may also cling to anti-abortion and

BOX 21-3 | SHEIKH ANWAR AL-AWLAKI: THE INSPIRATIONAL VOICE OF RADICAL ISLAM

(©Dennis Brack/Newscom)

Born in Las Cruces, New Mexico in 1971, Anwar al-Awlaki was one of the world's leading radical Islamic ideologues. He was a U.S. citizen and attended high school and college in Colorado and California. He lived much of his adult life in the Washington, D.C. area of Virginia and the Middle East country of Yemen. He was married and had at least one son, Abdulrahman al-Awlaki. He was the first Muslim cleric to ever address the Congressional Muslim Staffer Association at the U.S. Capitol by invitation in 2002.[85] He was very charismatic, had excellent English-speaking skills, and used the Internet to attract disenfranchised Muslim youth living in the West. He encouraged them to use "violent jihad" to accomplish their goals. Al-Awlaki, more commonly known as "Sheikh Anwar," represented the inspirational voice of Islamic radicalization in the United States.

Al-Awlaki met with Umar Fouk Abdulmutallab (the Christmas Day bomber), who in late 2009 attempted to blow up a Northwest Airlines planes with a bomb concealed in his underwear. He also exchanged at least 18 emails with Major Nidal Malik Hassan, who killed 13 people at Fort Hood, Texas in 2009. Faisal Shahzad, who tried in 2010 to set off a car bomb in New York City's Times Square, also called Sheikh Anwar for "inspiration."

Because al-Awlaki was linked to at least 19 terrorist operations inside the United States, the federal government took the unprecedented action of placing him on a 2010 "capture or kill list" approved by President Barack Obama.[86] After several attempts to capture him failed, al-Awlaki was killed in Yemen (September 30, 2011) by a Hellfire missile fired from a remotely flown drone.[87] Al-Awlaki's death caused significant controversy. The "targeted killing" of an American citizen was unprecedented in the Unites States. He was never charged nor convicted of a crime yet was killed by a CIA-led drone attack. The same attack killed three other individuals linked to al-Qaeda, and al-Awlaki's son, Abdulrahman was killed in a similar attack just two weeks after the killing of his father, again in Yemen. The U.S. response to critics was swift and certain as President Obama announced:

> "The death of al-Awlaki is a major blow to al-Qaeda's most active operational affiliate. He took the lead in planning and directing efforts to murder innocent Americans and he repeatedly called on individuals in the United States and around the globe to kill innocent men, women, and children to advance a murderous agenda. [The strike] is further proof that al-Qaeda and its affiliates will find no safe haven anywhere in the world.[88]

Today, the digital legacy of Sheikh Anwar continues to influence thousands of young, radical Islamists worldwide, but particularly inside the United States. Type his name into YouTube's search bar and you get 40,000 hits. His lectures and sermons are powerful and speak directly to those seeking a means to violent jihad. His "martyrdom" is openly expressed in Islamic websites and continues to be the inspirational voice that calls homegrown terrorists to action.[89] Mohammad Youssuf Abdulazeez, the shooter in two incidents in Chattanooga, Tennessee, vigilantly watched CDs of al-Awlaki weeks before the shootings. The brothers Tsarnaev owed part of their pressure cooker, bomb-making skills and ideological training in preparation for the 2013 Boston Marathon bombing to online instruction given by al-Awlaki. And several of the terrorists involved in the attack on newpaper headquarters Charlie Hebdo in Paris in 2015 were devoted followers of Sheikh Anwar on the Internet. The list of plots, attacks, and successful operations influence by al-Awlaki, sadly goes on and on.[90] Over six years after his death, al-Awlaki continues to inspire radical Islamic activities.

survivalist views and the need for paramilitary training in "militias." In general, right-wing militias believe that inevitably there will be a "showdown" with the federal government, so they stockpile weapons and food. In contrast, patriot groups tend to be more focused on the overthrow and destruction of the federal government. There has been some movement toward "leaderless resistance," which is enacted by small groups autonomously. The Montana Freemen illustrate the antiregulatory attitude of some right-wing groups. They refused to register their cars or pay income taxes, filed liens on government property, established their own court system, announced rewards for the arrest of government officials, and forged financial documents such as money orders. A 960-acre farm was declared sovereign territory and named "Justus Township." The 21 armed freemen surrendered after being under siege from authorities for roughly 90 days in 1996.[91]

Similarly in early 2016, several people seized and held the Malheur National Wildlife Refuge in central Oregon for 41 days. The leader, Ammon Bundy, had participated in early stand-offs with authorities in 2014 at his father's ranch in Nevada. The occupational leaders were careful not to hurt anyone and were originally protesting the imprisonment of two Oregon ranchers convicted of setting fires on public land. However, the convicted ranchers distanced themselves from the occupiers and the cause soon broadened. Ammon Bundy (See Figure 21-8) and others contended that the U.S. Constitution limited the federal government's power to acquire and manage property within a state's border, revealing the much larger dispute between ranchers and the federal government, over the federal government's ownership and control of vast expanses of land, which had been freely used by ranchers for decades, and now newly controlled with grazing fees and penalties. The militants were heavily armed and attempted to use the media to garner wider support for their cause. However, on January 26, 2016 as the main leaders of the group were driving from the refuge for supplies, they were intercepted in a roadblock by members of the FBI Hostage-Rescue Team and the Oregon State Police (OSP). The driver of one of the pick-up trucks, Robert "LaVoy" Finicum, was subsequently shot by OSP officers at the roadblock as he reached for a concealed weapon. Soon thereafter, the remaining militants surrendered their occupation of the wildlife refuge. Investigation of the refuge by the FBI later revealed significant damage and vandalism to the refuge as well as the willful destruction of Native American artifacts held within the refuge buildings.

▲ FIGURE 21-8 AMMON BUNDY
Meets with law enforcement officials during the occupation of the Malheur National Wildlife Refuge in Oregon in 2016. (©Beth Nakamura/The Oregonian/AP Images)

More traditional right-wing groups have included the Ku Klux Klan and the Neo-Nazi Party. Although these anti-Semitic and hate-oriented groups have continued to plague American society, they have been relatively quiet over the last five years, primarily owing to the success of civil litigation against specific groups brought about by the Southern Poverty Law Center, the focused attention given by law enforcement to such groups, and the natural death of several leaders within the movement.[92]

Domestic right-wing groups have been around for years, and have always thrived on insecurities about the economy and politics. The second wave of the Ku Klux Klan was born in the early 1900s out of fears that waves of immigrants and Southern migrants were taking industrial jobs from white Americans. We can see parallels to that in the modern economy, where tight jobs markets have ratcheted up tensions toward immigrant groups that are perceived as pushing Americans out of jobs. The multiracial makeup of the newest White House administration has further increased fears among white supremacist groups that white Americans will be marginalized.

A paradigm change in American politics has also increased anxiety toward the government. Health care reform has many Americans afraid of increased government intervention in their everyday lives, and rumors of planned gun control legislation have increased concerns among some parts of the population that Americans will be unable to defend themselves against an out-of-control government. Some legitimate political and economic concerns are feeding the rhetoric that is espoused by extremist groups, and as a result, both racist groups and anti-government groups are experiencing a surge in interest among Americans feeling disenfranchised or fearful of what the future holds.

Fueling that interest is the availability of information about extremist groups on the Internet. Many of the groups have a web presence, either formally or informally, that allows people with similar views to feel connected to a legitimate cause. Stormfront is a white supremacist-themed site with message boards, news stories, content aimed at children, fundraising mechanisms, and even merchandise. Those who post on Stormfront can interact and connect with up to 100,000 other users per day and are treated to a host of links to other extremist groups on the World Wide Web. Furthermore, the advent of social networking sites such as Facebook and Twitter have enabled extremist groups to reach out to people who identify with their cause. These sites allow almost instantaneous communication between members, allowing conspiracy theories, rhetoric, and calls to action to reach an unprecedented audience in a matter of moments at any given time.

The Southern Poverty Law Center, which researches extremist and hate groups in America extensively, reports that there are currently over 900 extremist groups operating in the United States. This number has nearly doubled in the past decade, a result of the "perfect storm" phenomenon.

It would be difficult to stay up to speed on all 900-plus groups, each of which can splinter and implode on a regular basis. White supremacists groups such as the National Socialist Movement, which is America's largest neo-Nazi organization, and Volksfront, which attracts a large following of young men, are among the most active and consistent extremist groups in the country. The most popular antigovernment militia groups, such as the Kentucky State Militia and the Michigan Militia, are also a regular presence among right-wing extremist organizations.[93] One of the most potentially violent of these is the Hutaree or Christian Warrior militia, based in eastern Michigan. Established in 2008, the group is heavily inclined to the paramilitary, training extensively for an "end times battle." Nine members of this group were indicted by a grand jury in Detroit for conspiring to murder police officers and civilians using explosives and firearms in a plot to replace all factions of the government.[94]

QUICK FACTS

The Southern Poverty Law Center-SPLC

The Southern Poverty Law Center located in Birmingham, Alabama was founded in 1971. The center is dedicated to fighting hate and bigotry in America and seeks justice for those harmed by individuals espousing such doctrines. The SPLC monitors hate groups and other extremists throughout the United States, providing continuous publications aimed at informing citizens of such threats. The SPLC maintains and publishes several online resources: *Hatewatch* (monitors and exposes the activities of the far right), *Intelligence Report* (a monthly periodical monitoring the radial right in the U.S.), *Extremist Files* (dossiers on individual extremists in the U.S), *Case Docket* (summaries on current and historical civil rights cases), *Hate Map* (on ongoing depiction of current hate groups and/or extremists operating in the United States), and a variety of educational and law enforcement resources aimed at teaching tolerance and keeping citizens actively involved in the fight against hate.

Visit the Southern Poverty Law Center website at: https://www.splcenter.org/.

Extremist groups are not known for subtlety, which can be a boon to law enforcement officials assessing everyday situations for potential extremist ties. Most white supremacists want to be identified as such, and thus have adopted a certain style and symbology that makes their beliefs clear to anyone who sees them. White supremacists and other racist extremists often tattoo these symbols prominently on their arms, neck, chest, back, and legs. As a result, men are often seen without shirts in order to give others the best view of their ideology. Hallmarks of racist extremism include the rune, which looks a lot like an upside-down peace sign; SS Bolts, which signify neo-Nazi beliefs and resemble two side-by-side lightning bolts; swastikas; the Iron Cross, which can identify National Socialist Movement sympathizers; and spider webs, which can identify racist convicts and are becoming tattooed more and more on people unaware of their meaning. The number 14 is a neo-Nazi favorite, as is 88,

which is shorthand for "Heil Hitler." The acronyms "ZOG" (Zionist Occupied Government), "ROA" (Race Over All), and "ORION" (Our Race Is Our Nation) are also white supremacist identifiers.

Names of white supremacist bands may also be featured as tattoos, bumper stickers, and T-shirts that identifies a person's extremist ideology. Many extremist groups have used music as a way to reach out to disaffected youth and as a highly effective recruiting tool. Some of the most popular extremist bands include Skrewdriver, Blue Eyed Devils, Bound for Glory, Rahowa, Extreme Hatred, Angry Aryans, Aggravated Assault, Nordic Thunder, Blood and Honour, Brutal Attack, Berserkr and Max Resist.

These symbols, numbers, band names, song lyrics, and acronyms can also crop up in graffiti found at the scene of a crime, sometimes tying what may seem like a simple incident of vandalism to a hate crime or terrorist threat.[95] Police officers should be aware of the most common signs and symbols of extremism as a matter of routine.

This became particularly clear in a 2010 incident where two officers in West Memphis, Arkansas, were killed by extremists and "sovereign citizens" Jerry Kane and his 16-year-old son Joe. Officers Brandon Paudert and Bill Evans noticed a white minivan with unusual license plates, and pulled it over. Jerry Kane argued with the officers before his son got out of the car and shot them with an AK-47. **"Sovereign citizens"** are right-wing extremists who believe that they get to choose which laws to obey and are independent of the rule of courts, law enforcement, the IRS, juries, and elected officials[96] (Figure 21-9).

Although we traditionally think of terrorists as those who perpetrate large-scale attacks on populations, extremists are considered terrorist threats as well. Right-wing and racist groups and individuals are using violence to further their ideologies and political agendas, and they are increasing in frequency. In 2009 the mother of 23-year-old Richard Poplawski called police complaining that she wanted her son out of the house after an

▲ **FIGURE 21-9** **Death on the interstate**
A traffic stop turns deadly. Jerry and Joe Kane, who identified themselves as sovereign citizens, killed two Arkansas policemen.
(©West Memphis Police Dept/AP Images)

argument. She told dispatchers that Poplawski did have several weapons, but that information was never passed down to the first responders.

Officer Paul Sciullo III, Officer Stephen Mayhle and Officer Eric Kelly were gunned down by the young man, who had a history of violent behavior. Most unnerving was the revelation that he had been active on the Stormfront website in the months before his attack. Under his Internet monikers "Rich P" and "Braced for Fate," Poplawski had been posting about his fears that the economic crisis heralded a "Zionist occupation"; that the Obama administration was going to strip citizens of their right to bear arms; and that police would round up political dissenters and bus them to camps. His Stormfront and MySpace accounts also contained derogatory references to African-Americans, Hispanics, Asians, and Jews, as well as photographs of his tattoos, which have symbolic roots in white supremacy movements.[97]

Nativist movements are also on the rise. **Nativists** are extremist immigration opponents who go beyond advocating immigration policy and actually harass or confront immigrants. The Southern Policy Law Center estimates an 80% increase in these groups, which include various factions of the Minuteman Project and Federal Immigration Reform and Enforcement (FIRE) Coalition.[98] In 2009 Minuteman American Defense members in Arizona were accused of shooting and killing a Latino man and his 9-year-old daughter. These groups are also known for staging protests, propagating conspiracy theories (such as the Obama citizenship theory) and acting as vigilantes in immigration issues.

LEFT-WING TERRORISTS

Left-wing terrorists generally profess a revolutionary socialist doctrine and view themselves as protectors of the people against the "dehumanizing effects" of capitalism and imperialism.[99] They advocate revolution as the means of transforming society; from the 1960s to the 1980s, leftists were the most serious domestic terrorist threat.[100] Their demise as a threat was brought about by law enforcement efforts and the fall of communism in Eastern Europe, which deprived them of ideological support.[101]

The traditional left-wing extremist was replaced in the 1990s by a right-wing opposite as the most dangerous domestic terrorist, but subgroups of the left have developed that are potentially just as dangerous as the right and arguably more economically destructive.[102] A resurgence of anarchist groups, including those associated with Anarchist International, have dramatically increased since September 11, 2001. Most of these groups are relatively small and confine their activities to "rallies" against what they see as incursions of the government into the individual rights of people. Several "Black Bloc" (Figure 21-10) rallies in protest of the USA PATRIOT Act and the increased security associated with terrorism prevention have been held. However, unlike the anarchist groups of the 1960s (for example, the Weather Underground and the Symbionese Liberation Army), there have been few violent acts attributed to these newly formed groups.

Today's extreme-left movements are best represented by modern ecoterrorists.[103] The FBI defines **ecoterrorism** as the use, or threatened use, of violence of a criminal nature against innocent victims or property by an environmentally oriented, national group for environmental-political reasons, or aimed at an audience beyond the target, which is often chosen for its symbolic nature.[104]

Although these groups are considered left-wing extremists, they are most often referred to as "special interest or single-issue extremists."[105] Special-interest extremists are seen as different from traditional right- and left-wing, because they are not trying to effect a more widespread political change but instead seek to resolve specific issues. These issues include animal rights and environmentalism on the left, and prolife, antigay, and antigenetic on the right.[106] In attempting to understand these groups,

▲ **FIGURE 21-10** **Left-wing extremists**
Black Bloc groups often demonstrate while prepared for encounters with the police by wearing gas masks and latex protective suits. The Anarchist A is a common symbol associated with left-wing groups. (*Left:* ©Tim Uhlman/Newsmakers/Getty Images; *right:* ©Charles Dharapak/AP Images)

one's judgment should not be clouded by the political rhetoric of the left or the right, since these groups typically step outside discourse and attempt to change one aspect of the social or political arena through terrorism.[107]

Many special-interest groups try to claim that they are not terrorist groups, because they do not harm any animal, human or nonhuman by their actions. Because of this, they often enjoy a sympathetic welcome from many liberal affluent Americans unaware of the true actions of these groups. Although in the United States to date, no murders have been directly attributed to environmental activists, they have used intimidation tactics on those they see as enemies and have caused millions of dollars in damage. The FBI estimates that the Animal Liberation Front (ALF) and the Earth Liberation Front (ELF) have committed more than 600 criminal acts in the United States since 1996, resulting in damages that exceed $43 million.[108] Left-wing groups have stayed fairly low-profile in the past decade, choosing to stage most of their attacks digitally via cyberattacks. The most common left-wing attacks included deletion of user accounts, flooding servers with e-mails, and other types of e-mail assaults designed to overload system capacities and exhaust company resources.[109] These cyberattacks also affect secondary businesses; for example, in an attack on Huntingdon Life Sciences by animal rights extremists, Wachovia Bank, which was a shareholder in Huntingdon, and Staples Office Supply, who provided their office supplies, were also targeted.[110] Experts predict that cyberattacks will be one of the primary modus operandi for left-wing groups in the next decade.

Contrary to the claims of their partisans that ecogroups of this sort are not terrorists because they have not killed or injured any living being, thus making their acts mere vandalism and not terrorism, their use of arson and pipe bombs challenges such claims. A great part of the intent of these groups, too, is to influence policy by intimidation and coercion.[111]

Special-Interest Groups: ELF and ALF

The Animal Liberation Front (ALF), established in Great Britain in the mid-1970s, is a loosely organized movement committed to ending the "abuse and exploitation of animals." The American branch of ALF began its operations in the late 1970s. Similar to the right-wing's leaderless resistance orientation, individuals become members of ALF by simply engaging in direct action against those who utilize animals for research or economic gain. *Direct action* is generally defined by the group as criminal activity, which is aimed at causing economic loss or destroying company operations. ALF activists have engaged in a steadily growing campaign of illegal activity against fur companies, mink farms, restaurants, and animal research centers.[112]

In 1980 Tucson resident Dave Foreman created Earth First! and began a campaign of civil disobedience and monkey-wrenching (vandalism) at construction sites and logging locations. One tactic involved driving nails into trees, which broke chain saws and foiled logging operations but that also injured innocent workers.[113] In 1992, when some members wanted to mainstream Earth First! and back away from violence, others broke away to continue their illegal tactics; these splinter groups eventually founded the Earth Liberation Front (ELF). ELF has since been responsible for numerous ecoterrorism attacks in this country. One of the more infamous examples of these was the $12 million in damages that occurred when they set fire to a Vail, Colorado, ski lodge in 1998[114] (Figure 21-11).

(©Peter Fredin/AP Images)

▶ **FIGURE 21-11**
Picture of Vail fire and map of arson incidents

Since 1987 over $70 million in damage has been attributed to special-interest terrorists ALF and ELF owing to arson, primarily in the western states, including the 2000 arson of the Vail Ski Resort shown here.

In 2004 several cases highlighted the continuing ecoterrorism of ELF and ALF. In Utah, a man sprayed "ELF" at a lumber yard where he set a fire that resulted in some $1.5 million in damages. Seven people associated with ALF were arrested for allegedly setting fire to the cars of Huntington Sciences Lab employees, vandalizing shareholders' homes, and threatening families.[115] The company was targeted because they used animals for product testing.

In January 2006, after nine years of investigation, the FBI indicted 11 people in connection with a five-year wave of arson and sabotage claimed by the ELF and ALF groups. The indictment named 17 separate attacks conducted by the ecoterrorists, which occurred from 1996 to 2001, resulting in no deaths but an estimated $23 million in damage, including the Vail, Colorado, ski resort arson.[116] Clearly, members within each group collaborated on specific actions and crimes. The arrests and ensuing conspiracy cases have made a dramatic dent in the leadership and activity of both organizations. Arson and vandalism cases attributed to both groups have dramatically declined, and although their websites and blogs continue to expound on the righteousness of their actions, most certainly, from an operational standpoint, both ELF and ALF have been dealt a significant setback.

FINANCING TERRORIST ORGANIZATIONS

After 9/11, U.S. agencies shifted gears, from identifying and thwarting individual terrorists/cells to adopting a broader strategy that includes targeting the financial operations and networks supporting terrorism.

In response to this new focus, steps were taken to strengthen America's ability to combat the flow of funds into terrorist organizations. In late 2001 President Bush issued Executive Order 13224 on Terrorist Financing.[117] It authorized the seizure of assets that belong to terrorist or terrorist supporters and dovetailed with the Anti-Terrorism and Effective Death Penalty Act of 1996, which established penalties for people who finance terrorism.[118] Later in 2001 the USA PATRIOT Act was enacted, which strengthened U.S. measures to prevent, detect, and prosecute terrorist financing and money laundering.

NEW LAWS AND LEGAL TOOLS

In the United States, a number of initiatives were created to help combat the financing of terrorism. These include the Foreign Terrorist Asset Tracking Center (FTAT), which brings together members of the Treasury Department, FBI, and CIA to identify terrorist financial infrastructures and focus on eliminating the ability of terrorists to obtain funds through the international financial system. Operation Green Quest is an initiative out of the Treasury Department aimed at denying terrorist groups access to the international financial system and is the investigative arm of FTAT and FinCen. The Financial Review Group (FRG) was originally formed to analyze the terrorist financing as it related

to the 9/11 attacks. It now works to investigate all financial and fundraising activities related to terrorism.[119]

On the international front, the United Nations passed UN Resolution 1373, which imposed binding measures on all member states to help prevent terrorism worldwide including the suppression of the financing of terrorism. The United Nations also created the Counter-Terrorism Committee (CTC) to monitor, assist, and promote the implementation of this resolution.[120] In 2001 the task of creating standards in the fight against terrorism was added to the mission of the FTAT.[121]

DRUG SMUGGLING

Although the illegal drug trade has been around for centuries, recently much attention has been given to the link between the illegal drug trade and terrorism. The term **narco-terrorism** has been used to define this linkage. Some estimates are that terrorist organizations in as many as 30 different countries finance a significant portion of their operations through the use of profits obtained trading in the drug market. Many of the increases came about at the end of the Cold War, which was accompanied by a decline in state-sponsored terrorism. New countries, many of which belonged to the former Soviet Union, were grappling with conflicts both from inside and outside influences. This provided the opportunity for many criminal organizations, particularly those from Central Asia to take advantage of these unstable conditions and become more active in illegal activities such as drug trafficking.[122] Terrorist groups known to be involved with drug trafficking include al-Qaeda, Hizbollah, HAMAS, Sendero Luminoso, the PPK, and the Basque group, ETA.[123]

In Colombia, the current government finds itself in a long-standing struggle with the procommunist group the Revolutionary Armed Forces of Colombia (Fuerzas Armadas Revolucionarias de Colombia, or FARC). This terrorist organization seeks to replace the current government with a leftist, anti-American regime. It is one of the largest and best-equipped insurgent organizations in the world, controlling large portions of Colombia and producing much of the cocaine that is distributed around the world. These drugs allow the FARC to generate large sums of money so they can purchase arms and other commodities to support their cause. It is estimated that as much as $400–$600 million a year is generated through drug trafficking.[124] In 2002 the United States indicted several members of FARC, which marked the first time that members of a terrorist organization had been charged with engaging in illegal drug trafficking.[125]

Al-Qaeda obtained much of its initial financial support through the illegal opium trade in Taliban-controlled Afghanistan. This was an example of a state-sponsored narcotic operation openly supporting a known terrorist organization. The U.S.-led invasion of Afghanistan and the subsequent dismantling of the Taliban as the ruling party forced groups such as al-Qaeda to seek other funding sources. Often the groups simply changed tactics from an open environment to a more clandestine operation similar to those in Colombia. Lately, however, because of the international focus on Iraq, reports have surfaced that the opium trade is returning to higher levels across

Afghanistan. A recently released UN report stated that over one-half million people were involved in the illegal trafficking of drugs in Afghanistan, generating more than $25 billion annually.[126] In 2006, the government offered Afghan farmers $500 per acre to destroy their fields, but drug processors and traffickers are believed to have given farmers $6,400 per acre in profits for growing poppies. More than 225,000 acres are believed to have been cultivated in 2006. In addition, U.N. figures in September 2007 reveal that Afghanistan's poppy production has risen 15% since 2006. The higher yields brought world production to a record high of 7,286 tons (in 2006), 43% more than in 2005.[127] This emphasizes the difficulty in eradicating something that, to a particular region, is its primary cash crop. In addition, the desire to obtain profits from such crops usually invigorates terrorist organizations to try and gain a foothold in the country.

According to the Drug Enforcement Administration (DEA), there are three critical elements to attacking narco-terrorism: law enforcement efforts, intelligence gathering, and international cooperation.[128] Rarely do terrorist organizations operate within one specific country. Instead, they tend to be more global in their boundaries, particularly when it comes to fundraising. Attacking the problem of terrorist use of the drug market to fund their operations requires international cooperation. Law enforcement across the globe must work together to eliminate the petty territorial wars of the past. Even within the United States there is an attempt to dismantle many of the obstacles that had plagued previous efforts at cooperation. The most notable is the creation of the Department of Homeland Security (DHS), which was the biggest governmental reorganization since the creation of the Department of Defense.

In April of 2004 the Congressional Research Services (CRS) office issued a report to the U.S. Congress outlining the links between illicit drugs and the terrorist threat. The findings indicated that the international drug market contributes to terrorist risk through at least five mechanisms:

- supplying cash for terrorist operations;
- creating chaos in countries where drugs are produced and through which they pass, or in which they are sold at retail and consumed—chaos sometimes deliberately cultivated by drug traffickers—which may provide an environment conducive to terrorist activity;
- generating corruption in law enforcement, military, and other governmental and civil-society institutions in ways that either build public support for terrorist-linked groups or weakens the capacity of the society to combat terrorist organizations and actions;
- providing services also useful for terrorist actions and movements of terrorist personnel and material, and supporting a common infrastructure, such as smuggling capabilities, illicit arms acquisition, money laundering, and the production of false identification or other documents, capable of servicing both drug-trafficking and terrorist purposes;
- competing for law enforcement and intelligence attention.[129]

There are several cases within the United States that highlight drug smuggling as a major method of operation for Middle Eastern terrorist groups operating within the United States. For instance, Operation Mountain Express (Figure 21-12) culminated in 2002 with the arrest of over 136 persons and the seizure of 36 tons of pseudoephedrine, 179 pounds of methamphetamine, $4.5 million in cash, 8 real-estate properties, and 160 vehicles. The operation was conducted over a year and

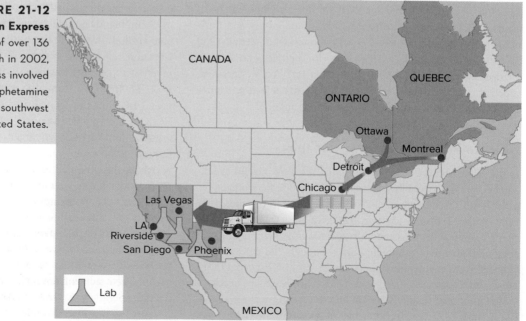

▶ **FIGURE 21-12**
Operation Mountain Express
Culminating in the arrest of over 136 people linked to Hizbollah in 2002, Operation Mountain Express involved the smuggling of methamphetamine from Canada to cities in the southwest United States.

focused on two very large Middle Eastern drug trafficking groups: the Jaffar organizations out of Detroit, Michigan, and the Yassoui organization in Chicago, Illinois. This sophisticated, multinational trafficking operation was primarily involved in the smuggling of pseudoephedrine (the precursor to methamphetamine) from Canada through Michigan to several West Coast labs operated by Mexican cartels. Much of the organization, resources, and profits from this operation were directly linked to various Middle Eastern terrorist groups, primarily Hizbollah.

In 2002 and 2003 several Middle Eastern subjects were arrested for attempting to sell 600 kilos of heroin and 5 tons of hashish to fund the purchase of four Stinger antiaircraft missiles for al-Qaeda. The negotiations with undercover officers for this deal transpired in San Diego, Hong Kong, and other cities in Southeast Asia. And finally, Operation White Terror culminated in 2004–2005 with the arrest of four people (two in Houston, Texas, and two in San Jose, Costa Rica) associated with FARC in Colombia. The individuals attempted to trade $19 million (nearly 17 tons) in cocaine and cash for five containers of "Warsaw Pact" weapons stored in Cuba. The arms cache consisted of 9,000 AK-47 assault rifles, over 1,000 grenade launchers and over 300,000 grenades, hundreds of shoulder-fired SAM-7 missiles, and over 50 million rounds of ammunition.

With an estimated annual yield of over 500 metric tons of opium, Afghanistan alone provides over $60 billion in revenue mainly directed to the financing of the Islamic State in Iraq and Syria, and the remnants of al-Qaeda working throughout the Middle East.[130] All too often this opium is illegally smuggled into the United States for heroin production. In 2015 and 2016, several cases revealed Islamic extremists embedded in the United States, posing as Hispanic nationals and partnering with violent Mexican drug gangs to finance terrorist networks. Several of these cases centered around Laredo, Texas on the border with Mexico. According to the DEA and the U.S. Department of State, Middle Eastern terrorists have crossed the border and adopted Hispanic surnames.[131] And as discussed earlier, Mexican and other Latin American cartels are collaborating with Hezbollah terrorists out of Lebanon to finance terrorism. In February 2016, DEA arrested several members of Hezbollah on suspicion of using millions of dollars from cocaine sales in the U.S. and Europe to buy weapons in Syria.[132] While Hezbollah supports the incumbent al-Assad regime in Syria, the arrests clearly reveal that both sides of the Syrian and Iraqi conflicts use illicit drug trafficking and sales to finance their terrorist operations worldwide.

ARMS SMUGGLING

One of the main goals of a terrorist organization is to inflict would-be victims with paralyzing fear. Often this can be done with only the implied threat of the use of force. However, to maintain a level of fear and to demonstrate their capabilities, inevitably violence is used as an object lesson. This can be done by kidnappings, bombings, and the torture and/or execution of prisoners, hostages, and anyone who is, or may be, a threat. To do these things, terrorists must buy, capture, or trade for weapons. Thus,

there is a lively illicit international market for conventional weapons as well as a desire for sophisticated arms, such as stinger missiles. In addition to being buyers of weapons on the international market, terrorist groups may use their knowledge of drug or other types of smuggling routes to sell arms to anyone with the requisite cash. Trades of weapons for commodities, such as drugs that can profitably be sold, are also part of the arms smuggling landscape. The collapse of the Soviet Union late in the twentieth century created an influx of weapons into the market.[133] The former Soviet republics are in need of funds, and the terrorist organizations desire weapons. The result is that terrorist groups across the globe are increasingly better equipped with more dangerous weapon systems, often purchased with drug trafficking profits.

In 2000 FARC (Revolutionary Armed Forces of Colombia) bought some 10,000 rifles using a timber export business as a cover. Most of the weapons were Russian-made Kalashnikov (AK-47) and AKM rifles and were flown to Central America by a Russian transport plane. Once on site, the weapons were dropped by parachute into the dense jungle that serves as the operating area for FARC. The operation was foiled by the Peruvian government. Later, it was determined that the weapons were purchased with profits obtained from FARC's extensive drug-dealing network.[134] In yet another case in 2004, agents of the Immigration and Customs Enforcement (ICE) agency arrested a Colombian for attempting to purchase over $4 million worth of weapons for FARC. A portion of the payment was to be paid with 15,000 kilos of cocaine, again solidifying the connection between terrorist organizations and the drug trade.[135]

The arms smuggling network is not limited to Latin America. In 2004 the U.S. government was able to stop a plot to purchase high-tech weapons, including 200 Stinger missiles for private buyers in Pakistan. The suspects, residents of New Jersey, met with undercover agents and expressed an interest in buying 200 missiles at a cost of several millions of dollars. A third U.S. citizen was arrested in connection with the case and charged with money laundering. The suspect intended to launder the profits from the weapons sale through his job as a Wall Street trader.[136] According to court documents, a portion of the purchase was to be made with the use of heroin.[137] And in 2016, a reported $1.2 billion dollars worth of weapons were discreetly sold and traded in the Middle East from East European countries like Bulgaria, the Czech Republic, and Romania, and the Balkan countries of Bosnia, Croatia, Montenegro, Slovakia and Serbia. Most of these weapons were trafficked illegally by rogue criminal groups through Saudi Arabia, Jordon, and Turkey with delivery to a wide variety of terrorist groups working in Syria, Iraq and Yemen.[138]

As governments around the world began to give more scrutiny to financial institutions, groups such as ISIS and al-Qaeda have to look for alternate ways to move financial resources. Al-Qaeda purchased diamonds with cash from both Liberia and Sierra Leone, creating easily moved, convertible, and untraceable assets. The two countries used the cash to purchase weapons and to support its security forces. Estimates of the value of diamonds purchased are generally $19 million. These transactions occurred in 2000, and the 9/11 attacks happened the following year. In a similar manner, ISIS now uses the vast oil reserves captured in northern Iraq and Syria to finance much of their operations. An estimated $3 million per day is derived from the sale of illegally seized oil.[139] This money is used to fund the "black flag" of the Islamic State worldwide.

CREDIT CARD FRAUD AND THEFT

The problems of identity theft and follow-on crimes such as credit, credit card, and ATM frauds were covered in Chapter 15, "White-Collar Crime and Larceny."

In 2004 the French government announced that it had detected ten suspected Islamic militants who were stealing more than $100,000 a month from ATM-accessed accounts in several European countries. Shoulder surfing and other techniques (Chapter 15) were being used to acquire the information needed to execute these crimes. Although no exact figure is available on the amount of money terrorists acquire each year through such frauds, law enforcement has found significant direct links between terrorist missions and credit fraud.

When the 9/11 hijackers entered America, many did so with false identification or engaged in credit card fraud. In the failed plot to blow up Los Angeles International Airport, two of the three Algerian terrorists admitted they engaged in credit card fraud and used those proceeds to finance their operation. A fourth accomplice was caught in London in possession of a credit card duplicating machine, laminating equipment, and several cards from a local department store. A few weeks after 9/11, authorities in Spain arrested several individuals who were members of a suspected Algerian Islamic terrorist group. They explained that they used credit fraud to support their mission, which involved shipping computers to Algeria and propaganda equipment to others in Chechnya.[140]

In Chicago, a joint terrorism task force secured indictments against two businesses that allegedly used credit fraud to defraud about $1.7 million from banks and credit card companies. These individuals were suspected of having ties to Hizbollah, the Iranian-backed Lebanese terror group.[141] Also, during testimony to a Senate subcommittee on technology, terrorism and government information, a former Secret Service agent gave testimony concerning two Middle Eastern groups who had known affiliations to Islamic terrorist organizations (Hizbollah and al-Qaeda). These two groups had allegedly bilked financial institutions out of $21 million.[142]

Another major funding source for many terrorist organizations has been the illicit sale of cigarettes and other commodities. Traffickers can make as much as $60 per carton sold illegally. Although not yet reaching the scope of the drug trade, the risks and penalties are far lighter. This is making the illicit cigarette trade a new method of choice for financing terrorist operations. Federal investigators have uncovered traffickers who are providing material support to Hizbollah, as well as having ties to al-Qaeda, HAMAS, and the Islamic State, among others. Many terrorist organizations are working in concert with traditional organized crime groups to establish supply routes and business contacts. Many states are reporting losses in their state taxes from cigarettes in excess of $1.4 million, demonstrating the significant amount of proceeds that can be generated from the illegal sale of cigarettes.[143]

Refugees Arrested in Connection with Terrorism Plots in the United States

Between 2014 and 2016, well over 100 Middle Eastern refugees have been arrested by police (Joint Terrorism Task Forces) on terrorism-related charges. The following are some of those documented cases:

- June 2016: An unidentified Middle Eastern woman described as an "Islamic refugee" by the Luna County Sheriff's Office was arrested on terrorism-related charges. At the time of her arrest, she was in possession of the region's gas pipeline plans.
- January 2016: Omar Faraj Saeed al-Hardan, a 24 year old Palestinian-Iraqi refugee living in Houston (TX), was arrested and charged with attempting to provide material support to the Islamic State (ISIS).
- January 2016: Aws Mohammed Younis al-Jayab, a 23 year old Syrian refugee living in Sacramento (CA), was arrested and charged with making a false statement involving international terrorism.
- June 15, 2016: In Luna County, New Mexico near the Mexican border, a Middle Eastern woman (refugee) was arrested during a routine traffic stop. In her possession, were plans and maps of gas pipelines and pump stations in the nearby area.
- April 2015: Somalia refugees Zacharia Abdurahman, Hamza Ahmed, Hanad Musse, and eight others loyal to al Shababb from Minneapolis (MN) pled guilty to providing material support to a foreign terrorist group (ISIS), and aspiring to travel to Syria to join ISIS.
- February 2015: Bosnian refugee Ramiz Zijad Hodzic and his wife Sedina were arrested in St. Louis (MO) and charged with gathering money to buy military equipment for ISIS fighters. He was charged with attempting to finance a terrorist organization. Five others were eventually charged from the investigation: two more from Missouri, two from Illinois, and one from New York were arrested and charged with sending money and military equipment to ISIS in Syria and to the al-Qaeda affiliate, al-Nusra Front.
- May 2014: Yemini-born Mufid Elfgeeh was arrested in Rochester (NY) for plotting to send men and materials in support of ISIS in Syria. At the time of his arrest, the heavily armed Elfgeeh was recruiting others to join ISIS in an attempt to kill U.S. soldiers.

Source: Anti-Defamation League, "2015 Sees Dramatic Spik in Ilamic Extemism Arrests," April 27, 2015. See: http://www.adl.org/combating-hate/domestic-extremism-terrorism/c/2015-terror-arrests-30-april.html?referrer=https://www.google.com/#.V9Cqs5grKVM

Catherine E. Shoichet, "Feds Arrest 2 Middle East Refugees on Terror-Related Charges." *CNN News* (January 8, 2016).

Ben Ashford, "America's Enemies Within," *The Daily Mail,* November 18, 2015

CHARITIES FRAUD AND LINKAGES

During the past 20 years alone, several groups (including HAMAS, Hizbollah, the Palestinian Islamic Jihad, al-Qaeda and ISIS) have used a variety of charities, educational think tanks and religious studies programs to raise tens of millions of dollars. In a 1996 report the CIA claimed that there were more than 50 Islamic nongovernmental organizations operating within the United States, and of these "approximately one third support terrorist groups or employ individuals suspected of terrorist connections."[144] Some of those identified since 9/11 as having connections to terrorist organizations include the Benevolence International Foundation (BIF), the Muslim World League, the Qatar Charitable Society, the Holy Land Foundation (HLF), and the International Islamic Organization. These groups have used some funds for charitable purposes but have also diverted millions of dollars to terrorist activities.

BIF and its companion, Illinois-based charity, the Global Relief Foundation (GRF), have been publicly accused of providing financial support to al-Qaeda and other international terrorist organizations. The BIF had offices in ten countries and raised millions of dollars in the United States for humanitarian aid but funneled a portion of other proceeds directly to terrorist groups. The GRF operated in 25 countries and also raised millions of dollars, sending a large percentage of it to Islamic extremists with significant links to terrorist groups. The FBI was conducting an investigation into both groups before 9/11 but was stymied by a lack of coordination and an unwillingness to assign the necessary resources. However, after the 2001 attacks, the government aggressively moved to seize the assets of both groups on terrorism-related charges, effectively shutting them down.[145]

The Al Haramin Islamic Foundation (HIF) was widely known as the "United Way" of Saudi Arabia. It was established in the early 1990s and exists to promote Wahhabi Islam by funding the construction of mosques, religious education, and humanitarian projects. Although considered to be a private organization, it has been supported by the government of Saudi Arabia both publicly and privately since its inception. Since 1996 the U.S. government has been gathering information on HIF leading to the belief that certain parts of the group were funneling funds to terrorist organizations. The U.S. requested assistance from the Saudi government but failed to receive any meaningful cooperation. Following 9/11 there were increased efforts to obtain information about those connected with HIF. Several well-publicized meetings took place ending in a commitment from the Saudi government to cooperate in the investigation. However, real help failed to occur until a bombing in Riyadh, Saudi Arabia, killed many westerners and Saudi Arabians. Since then, the Saudi government has taken significant steps to curtail the flow of funds to terrorists. It remains to be seen if the Saudi government is willing to make the difficult political and religious decisions necessary to significantly affect the flow of funds to terrorists from their kingdom.[146]

The Holy Land Foundation (HLF) was originally founded to assist Palestinians affected by the intifada, the Palestinian uprising against the Israeli occupation of Gaza and the West Bank. Headquartered in Texas, HLF had been under investigation for several years. However, as with the HIF, only limited measures were taken against the group until 9/11. Using new legislation, law enforcement developed a case against HLF and accused them of sending approximately $12.4 million dollars to HAMAS.[147] HLF has since had its assets seized and its leaders indicted on charges of providing assistance to a known terrorist organization. In addition, the head of the HLF was linked to the INFOCOM Corporation, which was subsequently charged with supplying computers and computer parts to Libya and Syria, both of which are designated state sponsors of terrorism.[148]

Another front has recently opened up against these "charities" in the form of civil judgments. A federal appeals court ruled in 2002 that the U.S. antiterrorism law permitted suits to be brought against the organizations that have been identified as supplying funds to terrorist organizations. In 2004 the first major case was won against the HLF, granting the family of a terrorist victim $156,000,000 in damages. According to the ruling, not only the organization but also contributors can now be held liable. This was a major part of the 2007 case in Dallas, Texas, against the HLF, proving that donors as well as the suspect knew that donations would be used to fund terrorist activities. The defendants were subsequently convicted in November 2008 of all 108 counts. The complexity of such a case often lies in providing financial records that prove knowledge and association with a terrorist group (Figure 21-13) as well as understanding charitable giving in Islamic cultures.

One of the five pillars of Islamic faith is known as *zakat,* or charitable giving. It is much broader in its reach into Islamic society than giving is in Western cultures. It can also function as a form of income tax, educational assistance, foreign aid, and political influence. The Western idea of the separation of civic duty and religious duty does not exist in many Islamic cultures. Thus, charitable organizations take advantage of the Islamic sense of religious duty to raise significant amounts of money.[149] Another unique aspect of the Islamic faith that played a role in the difficulty of tracking expenses was the use of the system known as **hawala.** This system is based on individual trust, family relationships, and regional affiliation. It is an integral part of the economies of many countries in the Middle East and Southeast Asia. It is a method that has been used for centuries to transfer funds from one person or place to another without the issue of federal banking or monetary reporting systems.[150] Since hawala is based largely on trust, there is an absence of the traditional paper trail used in most forensic financial investigations (Figure 21-14). The difficulty for law enforcement is to promote regulation of the hawalas in order to prevent their abuse by terrorist organizations without harming the financial centers of the populations they serve. One approach being tried in the UAE is to require that hawalas be licensed and regulated.[151] It is not known how many hawalas operate within the United States, but many believe that they have existed in America since the 1980s. Based on a 1994 law, hawalas were supposed to register with the government, but no enforcement activity was ever created. Following 9/11, Congress quickly

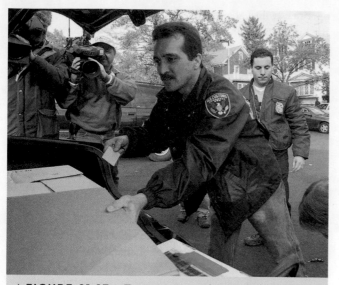

▲ FIGURE 21-13   **Terrorists records**

Information about al-Qaeda and its allies being unloaded by FBI personnel. The boxes contain videotapes, maps, notebooks, and other documentary sources seized by military, intelligence, and law enforcement personnel in Afghanistan and brought to the United States for closer investigation. The proof for investigators in linking specific terrorist organizations to charities, foundations, and state sponsorship are often found in financial records, an often time-consuming and tedious investigative process that may yield an important conviction.

(©C.J. Gunther/AFP/Getty Images)

NATIONAL COUNTERTERRORISM INTELLIGENCE STRUCTURES

The National Infrastructures Protection Center (NIPC) is responsible for protecting and investigating unlawful acts against U.S. computer and information technologies and unlawful acts, both physical and electronic, that threaten or target critical U.S. infrastructures.[154] NIPC manages computer intrusion technologies, coordinates specialized training related to its spheres of interest, and supports national security authorities when unlawful attacks go beyond crimes and become foreign-sponsored events. Founded in 1998, NIPC is housed by the FBI. In addition to protecting national security information, NIPC is engaged in preventing and investigating **cyberterrorism,** the use of electronic tools to disrupt or shut down critical components of our infrastructure, including energy, transportation, and government operations. For example, massive thefts of credit card numbers and other such acts could do serious harm to the public's confidence in using e-commerce transactions.[155]

The U.S. PATRIOT Act of 2001 provides law enforcement with new, broadened electronic surveillance authority; using DCS 1000, an Internet surveillance program formerly designated as "Carnivore," the FBI can intercept e-mail messages. Other methods of communication that the PATRIOT Act allows surveillance of include digital pagers, wireless telephones, fax machines, and videoconferencing. Terrorists, child molesters, pornographers, drug traffickers, spies, money launderers, hostile governments, hackers, and nations waging information warfare against the United States all use these means of comunication.[156]

The Departments of Justice, Defense, Energy, and Health and Human Services, the Environmental Protection Agency, and the Federal Emergency Management Agency form the National Domestic Preparedness Office (NDPO). Established in 1998, it is responsible for assisting state and local authorities with the planning, equipment, and training (including health and medical support), needed to respond to weapons of mass destruction attacks.

passed the USA PATRIOT Act, part of which requires that hawalas operating within the U.S. register with the Treasury department and report any suspicious activities.[152] Failure to comply with this law gives law enforcement a justification for investigation. This is similar to the tactic that resulted in the 1930 indictment and conviction of Chicago gangster Al Capone for tax evasion.[153]

▶ FIGURE 21-14

Checklist of items common in an illegal hawala operation

- Spiral notebooks, scraps of paper, or diaries listing information for numerous financial transactions, which generally include the date, payer name, amount received, exchange rate, and payment method or remittance code
- An unusually high number of phone lines at a residence or business; short incoming calls and lengthy overseas calls
- Fax transmittal logs/receipts, which may contain name of sender, beneficiary, or a code
- Wire transfer receipts/documents
- Phone records/documents; multiple calling cards
- Multiple financial ledgers (one for legitimate transfers, one for criminal activity, and one possibly for settling accounts)
- Bank account information, particularly multiple accounts, under same name
- Multiple forms of identification (false ID for the subject and for several other individuals)
- Third-party checks
- Evidence of other fraud activity

(Adapted from Dean T. Olson, "Financing Terror," *FBI Bulletin*, Volume 76, Number 2, February 2007)

The FBI Counterterrorism Center has steadily expanded since its creation in 1996. It operates on three fronts: international terrorism operations both within the United States and abroad, domestic terrorism operations, and counterterrorism measures at home and abroad.[157] The center is staffed by 18 participating agencies, including the Department of State, the Central Intelligence Agency, and the Secret Service.

OTHER CRIMINAL ACTIVITIES LINKED TO TERRORIST GROUPS

In addition to the major types of terrorist financing already mentioned, there are many smaller operations that raise funds. Some of these include selling baby formula on the black market for a significant markup, coupon scamming involving hundreds of stores,[158] and counterfeit goods including cheap copycat designer clothes, purses, and CDs.[159] Interpol has issued a report indicating strong links between terrorist organizations and intellectual property crime.[160] Even the music industry has its own dark side with the racist genre of "hatecore" music that is producing millions of dollars in profits, most of which goes to the neo-Nazi movement in Germany.[161] Each of these actions may not garner the attention that more high-profile actions like drug or weapons smuggling do, but each represents a part of the financial portfolio of many terrorist organizations.

The creation of the Department of Homeland Security represents one of the largest federal reorganizations since the modern Defense Department was developed in 1947. The 170,000-employee department absorbed the U.S. Coast Guard; the Immigration and Naturalization Service; the Customs Department; the Secret Service; much of the Bureau of Alcohol, Tobacco, and Firearms; the Federal Emergency Management Agency; the Border Patrol; and a host of other enforcement agencies.

Created in 2001 as an immediate response to the 9/11 attacks, the Department of Homeland Security (DHS) was established by President Bush to develop and coordinate the implementation of a comprehensive national strategy within the federal executive branch needed to prevent, respond to, and recover from terrorist acts within the United States (Figure 21-15). The DHS thus absorbed the U.S. Coast Guard; the Immigration and Naturalization Service; the Customs Department; the Secret Service; much of the Bureau of Alcohol, Tobacco, and Firearms; the Federal Emergency Management Agency; the Border Patrol; and a host of other enforcement agencies.

Among its responsibilities are facilitating the exchange of information across agencies, reviewing and assessing the adequacy

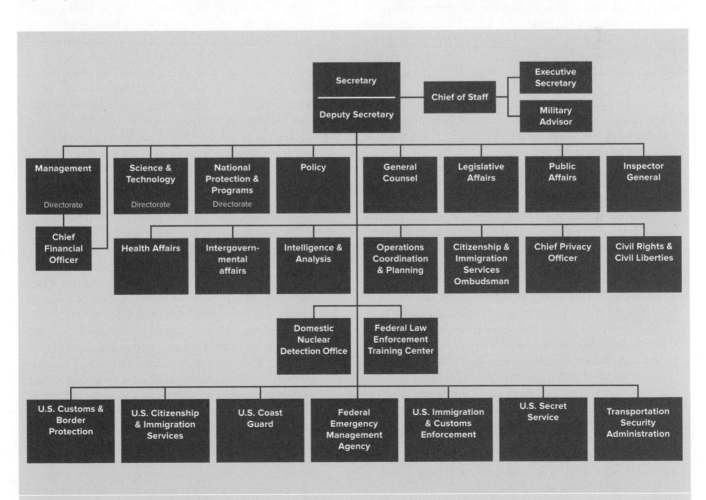

▲ **FIGURE 21-15   Organizational chart—Department of Homeland Security, 2017**

(*Source:* https://www.dhs.gov/sites/default/files/publications/Department%20Org%20Chart.pdf)

of federal plans relating to terrorism, and increasing, as necessary, vaccine and other pharmaceutical stockpiles. The Department of Homeland Security also plays a significant role in intelligence gathering and analysis. The development of Homeland Security Operation Centers across the United States places significant emphasis on information and intelligence analysis.

INVESTIGATION OF TERRORIST ACTIVITIES

The role for local and state officers in combating terrorism has greatly expanded since 9/11. Terrorists may be operating alone, or in concert with sophisticated narcotics cartels, insurgent organizations in foreign countries, or state sponsors. In any event, they are often involved in criminal activity directly affecting state and local officers. Analysis of terrorist operations has revealed a pattern of activity—actions that typically precede major incidents. These *pre-incident indicators* have become a primary subject of training for law enforcement officers. Coupled with knowledge of group ideology and stated goals, pre-incident indicators provide insight concerning group behavior and plans. They provide a framework to monitor and analyze group activities and to assess potential threats against the United States. The Institute for Intergovernmental Research (IIR), sponsored by the Bureau of Justice Assistance, has been actively training law enforcement officers in this area for the past ten years. The SLATT (State and Local Anti-Terrorism Training) Program provides free terrorist investigation and intelligence-related training for street officers as well as officers assigned to narcotics, organized crime, and terrorism task forces.

While the role of state and local agencies in combating domestic and international terrorism is rapidly evolving, there are several steps that police agencies and their officers can take immediately to thwart attacks:

- *Participate in joint terrorism task forces.* Joint terrorism task forces (JTTFs) are responsible for gathering and acting on intelligence related to international and domestic terrorism, conducting investigations related to planned terrorist acts, preventing such acts, and investigating terrorist acts in their geographic areas of responsibility. Consisting of representatives of federal agencies and state and local enforcement officers, JTTFs are directly supervised by the FBI. JTTFs represent a collage of highly trained federal, state, and local law enforcement officers and agents committed to gathering intelligence, investigating specific activities, making arrests, and responding to threats at a moment's notice. The task forces are based in 104 cities nationwide, including one in each of the 56 FBI field offices. As of 2016, a total of 71 of these JTTFs have been created since 9/11, composed of more than 4,200 members from over 600 state and local agencies and 50 federal agencies (e.g., U.S. Marshals Service, Secret Service, Immigration and Customs Enforcement, Drug Enforcement Administration, Transportation Security Administration, and U.S. Military).[162]
- *Be aware of suspicious activity and keep a log.* Some terrorist events have been prevented by individual, astute officers recognizing that "something was wrong," as in

the case with Ahmed Ressam (See Box 21-4). It is easy to forget details, especially if they seem only a little suspicious and probably inconsequential. To combat this possibility, keep a separate log of suspicious activities.[163] Using the disparate entries, it may be possible for you or others to "connect the dots" and foil an attack or some criminal activity. Do not just make records of events; apply critical thinking to them.

- *Use critical thinking.* Critical thinking involves rigorously challenging your own views and those of others. "Challenging" does not mean being verbally confrontational at every encounter; rather, it means reasonably assessing the basis of assumptions and beliefs. There are two generally recognized components of critical thinking: (1) possessing the knowledge and skills to be able to look at data and see it in a new light and (2) having the personal and mental discipline to use the "new light" as a guide. Things are not always what they seem at first glance. For instance, the person running out of a bank where a robbery is in progress may be the robber, or she may not be. Occasionally, police officers have shot innocent civilians fleeing from the crime.
- *Be alert for reconnaissance operations.* The execution of an attack is predated by reconnaissance, often involving multiple efforts, although not necessarily by the same person. While some of these efforts are carried out in stealth at night, many occur during normal business hours. Operatives may rent rooms that give them a view of the target and recruit insiders to provide them with drawings or copies of plans. They may also take legitimate jobs that allow them to have access to the sites (for example, driving a delivery truck).
- An analysis of past terrorist attacks (both domestically and internationally) reveals significant planning by the terrorist group. Indeed, members of the group often visit the scene ("case") on multiple occasions and even rehearse the event before it actually occurs. It is at this point that terrorists are most vulnerable! For instance, counterintelligence information and analysis reveal that organized groups and terrorists plan their attacks very well. This includes multiple visits to the scene (up to 20 time involving 3-person teams) before the incident. During these visits to the scene, the terrorists make notes on the behaviors of law enforcement officers and private security guards, photograph the location of surveillance cameras, sketch the presence of targets (such as fuel depots at airports), assess maximum casualty and damage potentials (such as the times of services at local synagogues), and map escape routes. It is important that street officers and investigators be aware of pre-attack behaviors and surveillance activities by terrorist in an effort to prevent the attack. Following a specific and thorough guideline is imperative. The FBI has developed a Terrorism Quick Reference Card for first responders as have many individual police agencies. For instance, the New York State Intelligence Center has provided all sworn officers in their state a Terrorism Indicator Reference Card designed to provide officers and investigators with a list of factors that

BOX 21-4 | PROFILE OF A TERRORIST: THE JOURNEY OF AHMED RESSAM

(©Montreal Police/Zuma Press/Newscom)

Born May 19, 1967, in Algeria, Ahmed Ressam grew up as an ordinary young man, attending school and helping his father in the family business. He fished in the Mediterranean Sea, frequented local discotheques, and wanted to attend college. By all appearances, he was a typical young man.

In 1998, Ressam attended a basic training camp in Afghanistan sponsored by al-Qaeda. It consisted of four months of intensive training, concentrating on the use of firearms; physical exercise; basic concepts in intelligence gathering and warfare; targeting; and surveillance, as well as bomb-making, a subject to which Ressam was particularly drawn. The true identities of his classmates were hidden by code names and false identities, although they were from all parts of Asia, Europe, and the Middle East.

After graduating from the camp, Ressam went to a "Kurdish camp" in northern Iraq, where he sharpened his terrorist skills and was formally indoctrinated into radical Islam. His final training came several months later at a camp known as Durenta, located in Afghanistan. Ressam was further schooled on various bomb compounds, bomb mechanisms, target selection, and placement of explosives for maximum damage.

Upon graduation, Ressam was given $12,000, a large sum by Middle Eastern standards, and sent to Montreal to develop a plan for a specific target within the United States. He lived a modest life in Montreal, remaining in constant contact with a known Arab cell operating there.

From Montreal, he flew to Vancouver, British Columbia, and rented a small, one-bedroom apartment. Authorities believe Ahmed made relatively large quantities of nitroglycerin in his apartment. This conclusion is based on a large chemical burn on his leg noted at the time of his arrest, which was similar to burns found on his apartment furniture.

Ressam's plan targeted Los Angeles International Airport (LAX) on the eve of the millennium (January 1, 2000). He would explode a large suitcase bomb in one of the terminals. Fortunately, on December 12, 1999, an observant and cautious U.S. Customs Inspector in Port Angeles, Washington, noticed something odd about the slightly built, dark-complected, profusely sweating Middle Eastern businessman attempting to cross into the United States from Canada. Further investigation revealed contraband material and explosives, which led to Ressam's arrest. On March 13, 2001, Ahmed Ressam was convicted of nine counts of conspiracy to commit international terrorism and sentenced to 130 years in a federal penitentiary.

(For additional information regarding Ahmed Ressam, view the 2001 Frontline video, *Trail of a Terrorist* and visit www.pbs.org/wgbh/pages/frontline/shows/trail on the web.)

---

may be indicative of a possible terrorist threat. Further, they have provided a reference card to interpret responses from a check through the NCIC Violent Gang Terrorist Organization File (VGTOF).

- *Coordinate and disseminate intelligence information through the use of advanced technology.* In Chapter 7 we discussed fusion centers, intelligence units, and analytical technologies as part of the investigative process. These technologies are also critical in efforts designed to *prevent* terrorism and criminal activity. The detection of trends and patterns that are real-time coupled with an immediate police response may well prevent a horrible event from ever occurring. However, to maximize their

effectiveness, intelligence and analytic operations must be fully supported by line and investigative officers. A routine traffic stop, a random individual encounter, or even a mundane investigative tip may be the final part of a much larger puzzle that will indicate a possible terrorist strike! Officers and investigators need to be aware that intelligence information can no longer be held in the minds of a single detective or jotted down in a small books held in the breast pocket of a senior beat officer. Intelligence information must be disseminated to other individuals and entities so that it may be analyzed in light of thousands of other "tips" and "pieces" of information.

- The use of advanced technology also provides community support for a new Department of Homeland Security program entitled Suspicious Activity Reporting—SAR. Modeled after a long and successful program with the IRS (also called SAR) aimed at thwarting money laundering and terrorist funding that requires banks and lending companies to report suspicious activity by clients, the new DHS SAR program is aimed at providing a mechanism of "force multiplier"; that is, the program provides a mechanism for community members at large to report suspicious activity to the police, particularly activity that may be associated with terrorism. SAR is a program designed specifically for officers on the street that allows a uniform methodology for reporting tips and suspicious activity within a specific region or state. In some cases, the SAR program is quite advanced, as in New York and Texas, where agencies provide easy ways to report activity directly to area fusion centers. For instance, in Dallas, Texas, community members are asked to use their smart phones to capture video and still pictures of individuals that pose suspicious activity related to terrorism or crime in general; that information is then reviewed by fusion center members for immediate follow-up or forwarded for future intelligence (Figure 21-16).

- *Apply and update your knowledge base.* Just as terrorist groups study our precautions and design countermeasures to defeat them, investigators must continually update their knowledge and skills. The "shelf life" of knowledge is growing increasingly shorter as the pace of change quickens. Thus, to stay on top of things, it requires continual training, ongoing learning from other investigators, a program of personal development through professional reading, and memberships in specialized investigative associations. Additionally, absolute mastery of your agency's critical incident policies and procedures is required, and is the final word on how to conduct yourself.

▶ **FIGURE 21-16**
I Watch Dallas. Do You?
The Dallas Police Department has created an innovative program asking all members of the community to be vigilant against terrorism and crime. Individuals can use their smart cell phones to not only report suspicious circumstances directly to the police, but also photograph and video such activity. (The iWatch Application and the iWatch Logo were created by and are property of iThinQware, Inc., *http://www.ithinqware.net*) (Courtesy of The Dallas Police Department)

TERRORIST CRIME SCENES

It is beyond the scope of this section to cover crime scene safety issues for every type of terrorist attack, particularly those that might include WMDs (weapons of mass destruction). Therefore, the section focuses on two areas of major concern: limited biological attacks and chemical attacks that produce mass casualties. Nuclear and radiological weapons are not discussed in depth, because the use of these types of weapons would have a catastrophic national impact and fall squarely within the realm of national security and defense, not the police.[164]

In early 2011 the Washington, D.C., and Baltimore, Maryland, area was hit by a number of package bombs that resulted in the disruption of mail service, traffic jams, and some social chaos and disorder, but relatively minor physical damage and no serious injuries or deaths. However, the pattern of incidents reminded officials of past letters and packages that contained lethal biological agents[165] (Figure 21-17). Fire departments have extensive training, appropriate equipment, and experience in handling hazardous-material (HAZMAT) situations. Because of this, they, along with public health officials and other specialists, play major roles in processing biological and chemical threats and attack sites. In addition, the FBI has developed a number of Hazardous Materials Response Teams (HMRTs), which are situated in sensitive locations around the country. HMRTs are composed of special agents uniquely trained and equipped to collect evidence in hazardous environments. They are a crucially important part of the FBI's responsibility to investigate acts of terrorism involving weapons of mass destruction.[166]

LIMITED BIOLOGICAL ATTACKS: ANTHRAX

Biological agents include both living microorganisms and the toxins produced by organisms. Their effect on humans ranges from various degrees of illness to death. Compared with chemical agents, biological agents are generally slower-acting. Among the biological agents that could be used in a terrorist attack are smallpox, anthrax, plague, botulism, tularemia, hemorrhagic fevers, and Q fever.

Anthrax (Figure 21-18) is an acute infectious disease caused by a bacterium;[167] it has a one- to six-day incubation period, although in some unusual cases incubation may take as long as eight weeks. In nonwarfare situations, it most commonly occurs in hoofed animals, but it can also infect humans. There are three types of anthrax, each with its own means of transmission.

In *cutaneous anthrax*, a cut or abrasion in the skin allows the anthrax bacterium to enter the body. This type of anthrax develops fairly rapidly: the incubation period can be one to seven days but is usually two to five days. There is no latent period for its development. Starting as a raised itchy patch resembling the site of an insect bit, it progresses into a red-brown bump that becomes filled with fluid and may be accompanied by local swelling. This ruptures the skin, creating a painless ulcer 1–3 centimeters wide. At the center, a black area emerges, caused by dying flesh. The affliction may be accompanied by fever and

Some characteristics of suspicious packages and envelopes include the following:

◄ FIGURE 21-17
Identifying suspicious packages and envelopes

- **Inappropriate or unusual labeling**
  - Excessive postage
  - Handwritten or poorly typed addresses
  - Misspellings of common words
  - Strange return address or no return address
  - Incorrect titles or title without a name
  - Not addressed to a specific person
  - Marked with restrictions, such as "Personal," "Confidential," or "Do not X Ray"
  - Marked with any threatening language
  - Postmarked from a city or state that does not match the return address

- **Appearance**
  - Powdery substance felt through or appearing on the package or envelope
  - Oily stains, discolorations, or odor
  - Lopsided or uneven envelope
  - Excessive packaging material such as masking tape, string, and so on

- **Other suspicious signs**
  - Excessive weight
  - Ticking sound
  - Protruding wires or aluminum foil

If a package or envelope appears suspicious, DO NOT OPEN IT.

Source: Centers for Disease Control and Prevention: Emergency Preparedness and Response.

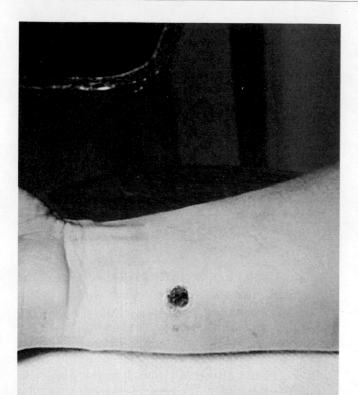

▲ FIGURE 21-18   Cutaneous anthrax on victim's arm
Note the darker spot, which is an area of dying flesh.
Anthrax is an acute infectious disease caused by a
bacterium. It is one of the biological agents that terrorists
could use in an attack against the United States. In
cutaneous anthrax, a cut or abrasion in the skin allows the
anthrax bacterium to enter the body. Death is rare with
appropriate antibiotic treatment. (©CDC/Arthur E. Kaye/Smith
Collection/Gado/Getty Images)

sweating. The affected skin dries and falls off in one to two
weeks, often leaving no scar.[168] Cutaneous anthrax can spread
via the substantially clear fluid that oozes from the rupture site.
Death is rare with appropriate antibiotic treatment, and even
without it there is an 80%–95% recovery rate.[169]

Intestinal anthrax is contracted by eating anthrax-contaminated
meat that has been insufficiently cooked; it produces an acute
inflammation of the intestines. Initial symptoms are nausea, vomiting (including vomiting of blood), fever, abdominal pain, and
severe, bloody diarrhea. The incubation period is one to seven
days.[170] The mortality rate is estimated to be 25%–75%;[171] the
latter figure may indicate a lack of timely diagnosis and treatment.

Inhalation anthrax enters the body through the respiratory
system; its usual incubation period is one to six days, but there
have been a few latent cases that did not reveal themselves until
six weeks after exposure. During the first one to three days after
exposure, the physical symptoms are similar to those of a cold
or flu; thus they are not very specific. They may include a sore
throat, fever, fatigue, muscle aches, mild chest discomfort, and
a dry, hacking cough. A period of brief improvement may follow,

lasting from several hours to days. Then the symptoms return
and quickly advance to severe respiratory distress, shock, and,
typically, death. Death usually results within 24 to 36 hours after
the onset of respiratory distress. Therefore, it is important to
begin antibiotic treatment early. The effectiveness of treatment
started after the onset of significant symptoms is limited,[172] and
mortality rates at this stage are estimated to be 90%–100%.

Inhalation anthrax is extremely unlikely to occur through per-
son-to-person contact, so communicability is not a concern. The
disease is spread by a deliberate act. Large amounts of high-quality, weapon-grade inhalation anthrax delivered in an aerosol form
could produce horrific mass casualties. The Centers for Disease
Control (CDC) recommends getting annual flu shots to facilitate
early differential diagnosis because flu presents many of the same
symptoms as does inhalation anthrax. There is a vaccination for
the anthrax virus, but it is not yet available to the general public.

Biological Scene with No Overt Dissemination: Unopened Suspicious Letters and Packages

In the past, workers have died from handling unopened mail containing inhalation anthrax, so new precautions have been implemented to reduce the potential for receiving anthrax-tainted mail
through the U.S. Post Office and other major carriers. For instance,
guidelines have been issued to help spot suspicious mail, postal
workers are being trained to identify such mail (Figure 21-19), and
many post offices are using electronic beams to kill biological bacteria such as anthrax. However, even at a **biological scene with no
overt dissemination**—such as one in which suspicious mail is
unopened, the situation is well controlled, and there is no known
dissemination of a biological agent—precautions are warranted:

1. If individuals at the scene are not symptomatic—which is
   the most likely scenario—extensive PPE (personal protection equipment) (Figure 21-20) and respiratory protection
   may not be needed.[173] The Centers for Disease Control
   recommends that the minimum level of respiratory protection for first responders at a biological-hazard site is the
   use of a half-mask or full-face-piece air-purifying respirator
   with particulate filters from N95 to P100.[174] Disposable
   hooded coveralls, shoe covers, and gloves are also warranted.[175] Currently, this equipment is not routinely carried
   in police cars. Therefore, wait for support specialists, such
   as a HAZMAT or public health team, if they are needed.
2. Control the scene and assess the threat (for example, is it
   credible?). If the threat is credible, let other responding
   officers know what the situation is; the 911 dispatch center will notify the appropriate federal, state, and local
   agencies, which, in turn, will determine whether they
   accept the threat as credible. Direct people to leave the
   room, and close windows and doors. Have all people
   from the room in which the suspicious mail was discovered stay together in a room some distance away or,
   preferably, outside the building.
3. Allow only qualified emergency personnel to enter the scene.
4. You and other responders should not smell, shake, or handle
   the mail (except as necessary when seizing it as evidence).

5. The person handling the evidence should triple-bag the suspicious mail in heavy plastic evidence pouches; limit handling of it to an absolute minimum, and do not drop the mail. When sealing the pouches, avoid creating a puff of air that could spread pathogens. This is most likely to happen if the pouches are sealed too vigorously or if they are noticeably larger than the size actually needed.[176]

6. Mark "Biohazard" on each evidence pouch. Place the evidence in a rigid, leak-proof container, seal the container, and mark it "Biohazard." Repeat this process two more times. The evidence should then be taken by police courier to the appropriate public health laboratory.

7. Get the names of and locator information for everyone who was in the room, anyone who came into the room, and the primary handler of the mail. Determine how the mail traveled through the organization before it reached the point at which it was discovered. Consider the possibility of additional contaminated mail.

8. Do not conduct your preliminary investigation in or near the room where the suspicious mail was found.

9. Have the organization's health and safety officer advise persons who have been exposed to the biological threat about the precautions they should take and any follow-up health measures they should pursue.

10. Do not allow site decontamination to take place until the crime scene is released.

11. Inspect the ventilation system to see if it was tampered with, since other attack modes and agents could also be in operation.

12. Follow standard procedures for discarding disposable PPE items and for decontamination.

▶ FIGURE 21-20   PPE
Officers use personal protection equipment with special sensing devices to make sure the air is free from potentially harmful chemical or biological agents before entering a building. (©Mike Stone/Getty Images)

Biological Scene with Limited Dissemination: Opened and Easily Bagged Letters and Packages

A somewhat higher level of personal protection equipment (PPE) is required at a **biological scene with limited dissemination**—such as one in which dissemination occurs only through an opened letter or package—even if the situation is still fairly contained:

1. A full-face-piece respirator, giving facial coverage roughly from the hairline to the chin, with a P100 filter or air-purifying respirator (PAPR) with a high-efficiency particulate air (HEPA) filter and appropriate PPE are needed for safety.[177] Disposable hooded coveralls, shoe covers, and gloves are sufficient for this situation.[178]
2. Control the scene and assess the threat; communicate the facts to other responders. If the threat is credible, close windows and doors; direct people to leave the room immediately without taking anything with them or touching anything.
3. Ask the organization's health and safety officer to attend to the people who have been exposed and to consider turning off the ventilation system.
4. Proceed with your investigation along the lines outlined in the previous list.

QUICK FACTS

What Is the Possibility of the Islamic State (or other terrorist group) Using a Biological Attack Against the United States?

It is commonly known within intelligence circles that al-Qaeda experimented with sending squads of "bio-martyrs" infected with human transmittable strains of bird flu to the United States. Further, there are reports that the group tried to weaponize a number of highly virulent pathogens, again to use against the United States. However, the prob-ability of successfully carrying out such a biological attack is relatively low for several reasons: (1) Acquisition of deadly pathogens is very difficult; (2) The scientific skill to weapon-ize a biological agent is either non-existent or very rudi-mentary within most terrorist groups, including al-Qaeda and ISIS; and (3) The large-scale dissemination of such weapons (via some sort of aerosol mechanism or even by personal infection) is also very difficult.

A recent statement found on a laptop recovered at an ISIS hideout in Syria has once again raised the specter of such an attack. The message stated, "The advantage of bio-logical weapons is that they do not cost a lot of money, while the human casualties can be huge." Even though the Islamic State is better resourced, more brutal, and more organized than any terrorist movement or group to date, their ability to successfully carry out a biological attack against the United States is still relatively low. Authorities classify such an attack as a low probability, high impact event and as such, continue in the development of preven-tative strategies and biological safeguards aimed at severely limiting the possibility of such an attack in the United States.

Source: Amanda Vicinanzo, "Biological Terrorist Attack on US an 'Urgent and Serious Threat'," *Homeland Security Today* (April 23, 2015). See: http://www.hstoday.us/briefings/daily-news-analysis/sin-gle-article/biological-terrorist-attack-on-us-an-urgent-and-serious-threat/0ce6ebf3524d83c537b1f4f0cc578547.html

CHEMICAL ATTACKS: MASS CASUALTIES

Chemical attacks may be accomplished with V agents, mustard gas, sarin, soman, and tabun. With some **chemical agents,** inca-pacitation of victims occurs in only 1 to 10 minutes. We have no experience dealing with mass casualties from a chemical-agent attack. Depending on the size of the jurisdiction, the nature of the chemical agent, the method of dispersal, the time-liness of any warning that might be given, weather conditions, and other factors, casualties could number in the hundreds of thousands or even higher. Atropine autoinjectors are available to the military, emergency first responders, and civilians for use as an antidote for most nerve gases. They should not be used on children, who require a pediatric dose. Within the context of what we presently understand, the actions discussed next are appropriate if a chemical attack occurs and produces mass casualties.

Initial Response to the Scenes

There may or may not be a warning before the attack; you must be on the alert for signs of danger when you patrol or are assigned to the scene of a possible chemical threat or to a **chemical attack scene.** If assigned to such a site, always approach with the wind at your back and from the high ground.[179] To achieve these favorable conditions, you may find it necessary to drive across open areas; remember, you are not restricted to driving on roads. Watch for the following signs of chemical attacks:

1. Lack of insects.
2. Birds falling from the sky, dying animals acting in an unusual manner, and dead animals.
3. Discoloration and withering of some types of grass, plants, shrubs, and trees. (These signs may become evident a few minutes to several days after the attack. The discoloration may be light or dark.)
4. Unexplained casualties, multiple victims, or victims with confused behavior, nausea, headaches, severe twitching, burning, or runny eyes, nose, or mouth, extremely small pupils, labored breathing, reddened or blistered skin, loss of bladder or bowel control, convulsions, or cardiac arrest.
5. Unusual liquid droplets with an oily film. (Liquids may be any of several colors—for example, clear, amber, or dark.)
6. Unexplained odors such as the smell from bitter almonds, freshly mown grass or hay, onions, sulfur, geraniums, garlic, mothballs, fruit, or fish. (Nerve gas has no odor.)
7. Vapor, mist, thin fog, or low clouds unrelated to the weather.
8. Unusual metal debris or unusual equipment such as abandoned sprayers and unexplained munitions.[180]

Protection Measures

1. The most important thing you can do is resist the urge to rush in and help. First protect yourself; put on the highest level-PPE you have, including respiratory protection, immediately. Control the scene and assess the threat. The greatest contribution you can make is keeping others advised of conditions. You must be prepared to operate in somewhat of a standoff mode. Use binoculars, if you have them, to assess the scene.
2. In the absence of appropriate PPE, turn off your car's air conditioner and ventilation system, make sure windows are completely shut, and work from inside the car. It is crucial that you protect your respiratory system. Even

placing a cloth or your sleeve over your mouth is beneficial.
3. Inform other responders about the dangerous conditions, as well as the direction in which suspicious plumes and clouds are moving, the color and odor of such plumes and clouds, the scene condition, and the numbers, symptoms, and conditions of casualties.[181] Identifying the chemical agent or giving others sufficient information to do so is a high priority.
4. You will not be alone long; an integrated team will soon be there to help. Standing plans will immediately go into effect, and key federal agencies such as the Environmental Protection Agency (EPA), the Department of Defense (DoD), the Federal Emergency Management Agency (FEMA), and the Centers for Disease Control (CDC) will handle tasks appropriate to their responsibilities regarding terrorist attacks. The FBI is designated as the lead federal agency for such incidents. At the same time, state and local terrorist plans, which are coordinated with the federal efforts, will go into effect. Fairly quickly, additional officers, public health officials, the fire department, and rescue and medical personnel will be arriving to help control the scene and to consider decontamination, triage, treatment, and transportation of living casualties.
5. Deny entry to the area to all but emergency responders.
6. Identify a staging area for responders.
7. Direct survivors to a single area; assure them that help is on its way.
8. Be alert to the possibility of secondary devices being present—for example, command-detonated car bombs to kill rescuers. Watch for suspicious people.

After emergency responders arrive at the chemical attack scene, these better-equipped and trained specialists will enter and work the "hot zone." Your responsibilities then will be to help maintain the scene perimeter and to write the incident/offense report. When you are relieved from duty at the scene, follow your agency's post-incident decontamination procedures.

Ideally, contingency planning, disaster preparedness drills, and the rapid arrival of an incident commander will relieve officers from the responsibility of making some of the decisions discussed earlier. If traffic or other conditions delay or prevent their arrival, officers must make the best decisions they can based on their training and experience, the available resources, and the situation.

TERRORISM AND THE FUTURE

In addition to the dangers already discussed, other types of terrorist acts are possible, including agroterrorism, threats to water supplies, and the use of high-energy radio frequency (HERF) and electromagnetic pulse (EMP) weapons. **Agroterrorism** is the deliberate and malicious use of biological agents as weapons against the agricultural and food supply industries.[182] HERF weapons direct a high-energy radio signal at particular targets, such as computers and networks. They are essentially Denial-of-Service weapons (Chapter 17). EMP bombs can destroy electromagnetic systems over a wide area when detonated.[183] Then, too, there is the possibility of a nuclear device or a much less sophisticated **dirty bomb** that renders an isolated area inhabitable for a period of time. Such dirty bombs involve combining nuclear waste from medical X rays or commercial, low-level nuclear material with high explosives, sending the radioactive material into the nearby environment.

Confronting terrorism is not an occasional or seasonal venture; it is an ongoing responsibility. With the help of allies, the United States has the capacity to significantly disrupt terrorist groups and their finances and operations. Information systems must be improved and the products shared; genuine teamwork across numerous agencies will ensure such progress. The United States must have the political will to be decisively and continuously engaged, and the public must help sustain the effort and provide information. The greatest untapped resource in the fight against terrorism is local public safety officers: they are an army of eyes and ears on the nation's streets, and the first line in preventing the next terrorist attack.

In assessing future terrorist threats, we must look at thing that we didn't consider post 9/11. At that time, reeling from shock, homeland security consisted of looking for and identifying major plots against American interests. In the years following, many of those types of intricate plots have been foiled, but by and large, we may not have been seeing the forest for the trees. Homegrown terrorists acting as lone wolves have become a huge threat to American interests. For the most part, the attacks of the past five years have been composed of one or two individuals (or in some instances groups of individuals, as in the 2016 attacks in Paris and Brussels) that have used crude devices and non-sophisticated weapons. The bombs used in the Boston Marathon attacks in 2013 by the Tsarnaev brothers were essentially made from two pressure cookers. And the attacks on the Inland Regional Center in San Bernardino, California (2015) and on the gay Pulse nightclub in Orlando, Florida (2016) were conducted by individuals using semi-automatic pistols and assault rifles. Most experts expect these types of attacks to dominate the future because they can be accomplished with very little planning, and virtually no training, yet sadly result in massive numbers of deaths and casualties.[184] Further, the sporadic nature of such attacks heightens fear and distrust among the greater public as common and popular entertainment and gathering places like sports events, theatres, restaurants, and night clubs become favorite targets.

Most certainly, al-Qaeda was devastated and splintered by the wars in Iraq and Afghanistan. However, new factions of al-Qaeda and now the Islamic State reach out to disenfranchised and sympathetic, young, often first-generation Americans from Middle Eastern counties. While U.S. and allied forces continue to used direct efforts against the Islamic State in Syria, their influence and call to Muslims worldwide as a global caliphate continues. Despite significant losses in fighters and territory in Iraq and Syria in 2016 and 2017, the Islamic State continues to be a dangerous threat to Western nations.

Finally, domestic right-wing groups inside the United States appear to be escalating in terms of rhetoric and numbers, reacting to a paradigm shift in American politics and economics. Indeed, these challenges facing American law enforcement at all levels are, quite frankly, unprecedented in our nation's history.

| KEY TERMS

Abu Musab al-Zarqawi

agroterrorism

al-Qaeda

anthrax

Anwar al-Awlaki

biological agents

biological scene with limited dissemination

biological scene with no overt
  dissemination

caliphate

chemical agents

chemical attack scene

cyberterrorism

dirty bomb

domestic terrorism

ecoterrorism

HAMAS

hate crime

hawala

Hizbollah (Hezbollah)

international terrorism

Islamic State (IS) or Islamic State in Iraq
  and Syria (ISIS)

Jemaah Islamiyah (JI)

jihad

left-wing terrorists

Muslim Brotherhood

narco-terrorism

nativist

right-wing terrorists

Salafism

Shi'a or Shiite

sovereign citizens

suicide bombings

Sunni

Wahhabi movement

REVIEW QUESTIONS

1. How does the FBI define *terrorism*?
2. What are the three major radical or fundamental movements within Islam?
3. How did the Islamic State become the predominant movement in the Middle East? Why is it so violent?
4. How did Osama bin Laden vault to power in Afghanistan? Name some of the important terrorist incidents that al-Qaeda has conducted in the last decade.
5. What does *Hizbollah* mean?
6. What types of events are associated with the Palestinian group known as HAMAS?
7. Explain how the current political and economic climate has affected the resurgence of right-wing organizations.
8. What is ecoterrorism? Name two important special-interest groups associated with ecoterrorism that are active in the United States.
9. Discuss how the violence in Mexico relates to terrorism.
10. Assess the threats from domestic and foreign terrorists.
11. Discuss how terrorist organizations are financed. Give examples.
12. List several steps that every police agency and/or officer can do to help prevent terrorism.
13. What is anthrax, and how does it relate to terrorism?
14. List some of the signs that a chemical attack may have taken place. How can officers protect themselves from such attacks?

INTERNET ACTIVITIES

1. Since September 11, 2001, several police departments and law enforcement institutes throughout the country have begun to offer training for police personnel on preparing for, investigating, and responding to terrorist crime incidents. Search the web for information on this training. What types of training are available? What topic areas do they cover? Do you think the training would be helpful to a criminal investigator? Why or why not? Is there any specific type of training that you think should be provided but is not available?

2. Visit the home page for the Department of Homeland Security at *www.dhs.gov/index.shtm* and determine what the National Threat Level is. Click on "Countering Violent Extremism" and read about the various resources as well as examples of effective tools and programs to build strong and safe communities. Also, click on "Get a Homeland Security Job" on the sidebar and learn about the myriad job opportunities existing with the Department of Homeland Security.

Design Element: (crime scene tape): ©UpperCut Images/Getty Images RF

► British Prime Minister William Gladstone (1809–1898) famously declared, "Justice delayed is Justice denied." There may be some truth to it. One in 20 cold case investigations results in an arrest and only one in 100 cold case trials concludes with a conviction. In a case that defied the odds, Ira Einhorn, shown here, went on the run for 23 years after killing his girlfriend. He was arrested at the Philadelphia Airport and subsequently convicted of murder.

(©Roger Bacon/Reuters/Alamy)

22

THE TRIAL PROCESS AND THE INVESTIGATOR AS A WITNESS

CHAPTER OBJECTIVES

1. Briefly outline the steps in a trial process.
2. Assess the importance of a criminal investigator's knowing the rules of evidence.
3. Describe the hearsay rule and the philosophy under which the exceptions to this rule have evolved.
4. Explain the impact of *Crawford v. Washington* on the rules of evidence.
5. Explain the reason for the existence of evidentiary privileges.
6. Discuss the role of an investigator as a witness in a criminal trial.
7. Explain the purpose of cross-examination.

At some point during the investigation of a crime, the investigator will decide to invoke the processes of the judicial system. If preparing for and taking a case to court were not the goal or, at least, one of the goals of a criminal investigation, there would be little point to investigating. That goal, however, may not always mesh with reality. Sometimes, despite the high level of investigative work done by the law enforcement agency, cases may not be prosecutable. First, even if a case is investigated as thoroughly as possible, many investigators at some time throughout their careers will be faced with the fact that the suspect simply cannot be identified. Second, if there is a suspect, investigators may not have enough evidence to arrest and later to convict him/her. Third, there may be situations in which legal requirements, such as probable cause, *Miranda* rights, and evidence-collection rules, are violated. Finally, because of certain rules of evidence or evidentiary privileges, some information garnered in an investigation may not be admissible. In short, investigators should always be aware of potential factors that may prevent or impede the prosecution of a criminal case.

The time at which the judicial system becomes involved during the course of an investigation is not uniform. The decision to begin involving the judicial system may come at the conclusion of the investigation, or it may occur at some earlier point. That decision will be based on a variety of factors, including identification of a suspect, collection of essential evidence and information for the case, and cooperation of witnesses and victims. Regardless of when the decision is made, the first step is bringing the accused before the court. How, when, where, and why this is done is called *evaluating the case*. This chapter discusses the trial process, including the order in which a trial is conducted and the elements of a criminal trial. This is followed by the rules of evidence, evidentiary privileges, and the investigator as a witness.

EVALUATING A CASE

THE INVESTIGATOR

The decisions investigators must make involve a great deal of discretion. Investigators must consider what may be termed risk factors. As suggested by Figure 22-1, the fact that probable cause exists does not require that the arrest be made at the moment, nor does it mean that the investigation is complete. Certain disadvantages may result from a premature arrest, even one that is valid. In Figure 22-1, B1 through B7 represent the alternative times when arrest may take place between the establishment of **probable cause** and the existence of certainty requiring

CHAPTER OUTLINE

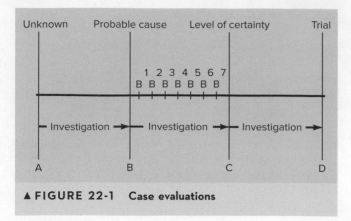

▲ FIGURE 22-1   Case evaluations

arrest as a prerequisite to prosecution. (The spacing and numbering are arbitrary and are intended for graphic purposes only.)

One prime consideration is whether the suspect is likely to flee if allowed to remain free. If there is a high risk of this, the investigator should make an arrest as soon as probable cause can be established and complete the investigation while the suspect is in custody. In evaluating the likelihood of flight, the investigator will consider such factors as the nature and seriousness of the offense, whether the suspect is a transient or an established member of the community, the suspect's occupation and income, and whether the suspect has a family to support.

Another risk that must be considered by the investigator deals with the potential danger posed to others if the suspect is allowed to remain free. Again, the nature of the offense along with any past criminal record or history of the suspect must be carefully evaluated. If the case under investigation involves a violent crime or one that tends to reveal violent propensities on the part of the suspect, early arrest is most probably the wisest course of action.

The investigator should also consider the hardships imposed on the suspect by early incarceration. Is the suspect gainfully employed? Is the suspect supporting a family or dependent children as a single parent? Does the suspect suffer from a serious illness or unique malady that will cause serious medical or psychological concerns for the jail staff and other inmates, thus making early arrest a less desirable choice? Although this is often overlooked, it is one additional portion of the investigator's responsibility in evaluating the case.

THE PROSECUTOR

While the investigator is investigating and deciding to make an arrest, the prosecutor is also evaluating the case to determine whether the investigator has provided enough information, verbally and in written case (incident) reports to enable the prosecutor to believe he/she can prove a case. This is the standard the prosecutor is held to in deciding whether there is a sufficient basis on which to file formal criminal charges.

If the prosecutor files formal charges, the next step in the evaluation process is to determine whether the investigation has produced enough needed evidence to prove the case before a jury. Investigators need to know what is required for this proof

so that investigative time can be spent wisely gathering needed evidence, rather than gathering "nice to have" evidence but disregarding something essential to the case.

Prosecutors rely heavily on police incident reports and follow-up investigation reports. Reports must be accurate, complete and thorough. This applies to the fill-in-the- blanks part of the report and the narrative (Chapter 6, "Field Notes and Reporting").

The prosecutor will review officer/investigator conduct to determine whether arrests have been lawful, searches and seizures were reasonable (Chapter 2), and if *Miranda* requirements were satisfied in case there is a confession or other statement involved (Chapter 5).

Three other legal issues will be evaluated by the prosecutor: discovery, jurisdiction, and venue. The case of *Brady* v. *Maryland*[1] requires the prosecution in state courts to disclose the names of all its witnesses and list all its evidence to the defense in ample time before trial to allow the defense to examine evidence and depose witnesses. This enables the defense to prepare. Conversely, the defense must advise the prosecution of any alibi it intends to raise, any witnesses it intends to call and any evidence it intends to introduce. This is called *reciprocal discovery*.

Jurisdiction is composed of three parts but is generally not a problem in a criminal prosecution. First, territorial jurisdiction would generally be the state in which the charged crime was committed. Jurisdiction over the person is satisfied if the accused is in court and courts don't care how the defendant got to the court even if the defendant was kidnapped from another state. If such a case happened, there may be criminal and civil liability for the kidnappers, but the court can proceed with the defendant present. The third aspect is subject matter jurisdiction. The court must have the authority to dispose of the case in front of it. Again, this generally presents no problem, but, for example, the state's highest court does not have jurisdiction to hold the initial trial of a person charged with burglary since the state's highest court is empowered only to hear cases on appeal.

QUICK FACTS

149 Wrongfully Convicted People were Exonerated in 2015

Even though police processes, criminal investigative procedures, and prosecutorial standards have dramatically improved over the years, there is still a large number of individuals who have been wrongly convicted of crimes they simply did not commit. According to the University of Michigan Law School's National Registry of Exonerations, there were 149 people who were either declared innocent or cleared of the consequences of their convictions or guilty pleas in 2015. Sadly, their study shows that police and prosecutorial misconduct (official misconduct) was the leading cause of the wrongful convictions.

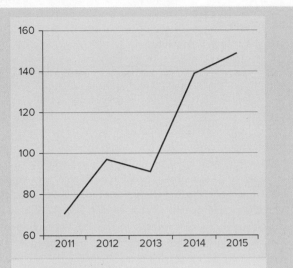

▲ FIGURE 22-2

Number of Exonerations per Year

Sources: Stephanie Mencimer, "A Record Number of Wrongfully Convicted People were Exonerated in 2015" *Mother Jones* (February 3, 2016). See: http://www.motherjones.com/politics/2016/02/record-number-exonerations-2015

The National Registry of Exonerations, "Exoneration in 2015" (Ann Arbor, MI: University of Michigan Law School, February 3, 2016). See: http://www.law.umich.edu/special/exoneration/Documents/Exonerations_in_2015.pdf

THE TRIAL PROCESS

Some law enforcement officers and criminal investigators are not fully aware of the order in which a trial is conducted, because time often prohibits them from attending a complete trial from beginning to end. Also, witnesses are often sequestered from the courtroom before and after giving testimony and are instructed not to discuss the case with anyone other than the attorneys representing the prosecution or defense. This very common practice is used to minimize the possibility that a witness's testimony might be affected by other witnesses' testimony.

JURY SELECTION

The courtroom process begins with the selection and swearing in of a jury. Jury selection is more of an art than a science, although there may be jury selection "experts" who would disagree. Jury selection can last a few hours or a few weeks, depending on the selection process and the nature of the case. The more serious the case, the longer the selection process normally lasts, as can be seen in some of the more notorious and publicized cases, such as the O. J. Simpson trial and the Scott Peterson trial. No matter how much time and effort are expended on jury selection, one still can't predict how a jury will decide a case. The jury panel from whom the jurors in the trial are eventually picked is called a **venire.** Some general questions are asked of each prospective juror concerning whether he/she knows anyone involved in the trial, including the attorneys; any witnesses to be called; any of the court personnel, including the judge; any relationships to a law enforcement officer; prosecutor or defense attorney; what is his/her occupation; spouse's occupation; information about any children; hobbies; any potential conflicts with the date(s) of the trial; physical infirmities that might interfere with the prospective juror's ability to see, hear, sit, or understand what will happen during the trial; and inquiry as to whether any prospective juror has been convicted of a crime and whether each person can follow the law as the judge will give it to them (Figure 22-3).

Following the general questions, the prosecutor and the defense attorney get to ask questions to determine attitudes of

◀ FIGURE 22-3

A defense attorney (L) consults with his intently listening client (R) during jury selection. The woman was charged with the first degree murder of her 2-year-old daughter. The disappearance of the daughter was reported to authorities by grandparents who said they had not seen her in 31 days and the mother's car smelled like a dead body. The defendant was found not guilty of all felony charges, but was convicted of several misdemeanor charges, such as lying to investigators. There was widespread outrage at the verdict in a trial that was widely followed nationally.

(©Gary W. Green/Orlando Sentinel/MCT/Newscom)

prospective jurors on any number of topics. What they cannot do, however, is to talk about the facts of the case to be tried. They may say that the defendant is charged with murder and, if the jurisdiction has the death penalty, ask if any of the prospective jurors would be unable to vote for the death penalty should that decision be presented to them. Although both the prosecutor and the defense attorney say they are trying to pick a fair and impartial jury, each side, of course is trying to pick jurors they believe will support their side of the case.

Once the questioning is done, the judge meets with the attorneys to pick the trial jury. Each side may challenge for cause any prospective juror it believes has demonstrated an obvious bias for or against one side of the case, an obvious lack of understanding or indifference to what the jury selection process is about, or what the trial process will involve. A language barrier may also occasionally be a basis for a **challenge for cause.** There is no limit on the number of challenges for cause but the judge is the ultimate source for deciding whether to excuse a prospective juror for cause. Each side then has a specific number of **peremptory challenges.** These are challenges that may be used for any reason as long as the reason is race and gender neutral and is not a pretext for racial or gender motivation. Again, the judge has the final authority whether to allow the challenge.

Once the final jury is selected, which frequently includes one or more alternates in case something happens to one of the jurors during the trial, the jury is sworn to try the case fairly, listen to all the testimony and consider all evidence, along with the instructions on the law to be given by the judge, before making a decision. The swearing of the jury is an important point in the process because, in many jurisdictions, this is the point when jeopardy attaches. This means that, if the prosecution decides it cannot proceed for some reason, such as a defect in the formal charging document that needs to be corrected, the defense can claim that any such change creates double jeopardy for the defendant and, if the prosecution is unable to proceed, the defendant is freed and cannot be retried for the same offense.

QUICK FACTS

Scientific Jury Selection

Prosecutors and defense attorneys often employ scientific jury selection (SJS) on high profile cases. The process almost always involves an expert in the social sciences who advises the attorney regarding their use of peremptory challenges (the right to reject a potential juror from the jury panel without stating a reason). The challenges are based on community surveys conducted by the SJS expert relating to race, ethnicity, gender, marital status, age, income, and employment that tests the beliefs and attitudes likely associated with a favorable or unfavorable verdict. The success of SJS is highly controversial without the support of any rigorous methodological study, still, criticisms have been leveled against the practice as being racially and ethnically biased, very expensive, and thus benefiting only those that have the money to pay for such expensive consulting.

Sources: Matthew Hutson, "Unnatural Selection" *Psychology Today* (March/April 2007)
See "Jury Zoom: Intelligence Solutions by Litigation Success. Visit their site at: http://www.juryzoom.com/ (Retrieved December 12, 2016).
See also, the seminal case forbidding the use of peremptory challenge based solely on race or gender: *Batson v. Kentucky*, 476 U.S. 79 (1986).

THE TRIAL

The trial starts with opening statements by the prosecutor and the defense attorney (Figure 22-4). These statements acquaint the jury with the allegations in the case. The prosecutor tells the jury how he/she will attempt to prove that a crime was committed and that it was committed by the defendant. The defense tells how it will attempt to convince the jury that either no crime was committed or the crime was not committed by this defendant.

▶ **FIGURE 22-4**
Attorney giving an opening statement before a jury
A prosecutor attempts to tell the jury what he intends to present to convince the jury that a crime was committed and that the defendant committed the offense. However, in an opening statement by a defense attorney, the emphasis is usually that no crime was committed or that the defendant did not commit the offense.
(©John Neubauer/PhotoEdit)

Then the prosecution presents its case in chief, calling witnesses and introducing evidence to establish that a crime was committed and that it was committed by the defendant. While the prosecution is presenting its case, the questioning of witnesses it calls to testify on behalf of the prosecution is called **direct examination.** When the same witness is questioned by the defense attorney, the process is called **cross-examination.** In most jurisdictions, the scope of cross-examination is limited to matters brought up during direct examination. If on cross-examination the defense attorney manages to confuse a point raised on direct examination, the prosecutor has the opportunity to conduct a **redirect examination** after the defense attorney has completed cross-examination, and likewise the defense later has an opportunity to conduct a **re-cross-examination** of each witness.

When the prosecution finishes introducing all its evidence and presenting all its witnesses, the defense attorney usually moves to dismiss the charge on the grounds that the state failed to prove that a crime was committed or that the defendant committed it. This is a normal procedural response to the state's case by the defense attorney. If, in fact, the judge is convinced that the prosecution did substantially fail to establish that a crime was committed or that the defendant is guilty, charges are dismissed and the trial ends. But if the judge feels that the jury could reasonably decide that the defendant is guilty after hearing the defense case, the motion is denied, and the defense attorney is permitted to present the case for the defendant.

The presentation of the defense case in chief follows the same pattern as that for the state. Evidence is introduced at the appropriate time, and witnesses are called. Witnesses called by the defense are directly examined by the defense attorney and cross-examined by the prosecutor. The procedures for redirect and re-cross-examination are applicable. Note that a defendant is not required to testify, and this failure may not be mentioned or commented on by the prosecutor. The burden to prove the defendant's guilt beyond a reasonable doubt is on the prosecution. The defendant is never required to prove his or her innocence.

After the defense rests its case, the prosecution has an opportunity for **rebuttal.** New evidence may be presented, or witnesses may be reexamined to clarify earlier testimony. If the prosecutor uses the opportunity to present rebuttal evidence, then the defense is given equal opportunity to rebut this, through the process called **surrebuttal.**

After the introduction of all evidence by both sides, both attorneys may make a closing argument. They summarize for the jury the evidence they have presented. The prosecutor attempts to show the jury that sufficient evidence has been presented to indicate that the defendant is guilty of the particular crime charged, and that it should find guilt. The defense attorney attempts to persuade the jury that the prosecution has failed to prove its case against the defendant beyond and to the exclusion of a reasonable doubt and the jury should acquit.

Once closing statements are completed, the judge has the responsibility of instructing the jury on the law applicable to the case and of advising the jury of its responsibilities: to weigh the testimony of witnesses and the evidence presented (Figure 22-5). The judge also tells the jury the various decisions it may reach in terms of guilt or innocence and the elements of the crimes—including lesser offenses—of which they may find the

defendant guilty. The judge advises the jurors of the degree to which they must be convinced of guilt or acquit the defendant.

THE RULES OF EVIDENCE

Every law enforcement officer must have a working knowledge of the rules of evidence. This requirement is particularly true for the criminal investigator, on whose shoulders falls the responsibility of collecting and preserving evidence that will be useful to presenting the prosecution's case in court. Therefore, the investigator must be able to distinguish between factual material that is admissible in court and that which is worthless as evidence. The rules govern what evidence the jury will be allowed to hear or see and what evidence must be excluded from a jury's consideration.

The language and terminology used in the field of law are quite different from those that most of us are accustomed to using. In the rules of evidence, many terms have specific meanings that investigators must know and understand. Many of these are set forth in this chapter.

EVIDENCE DEFINED

Evidence can be defined as anything that tends logically to prove or disprove a fact at issue in a judicial case or controversy. Simply put, anything that might have the slightest bearing on the outcome of a case can be broadly classified as evidence, provided it has a logical tendency to relate to the outcome of the case. In a criminal case, if the matter has a bearing on the guilt or innocence of the defendant, it is evidence. The word "anything" should be emphasized because, in its broadest sense, anything can be evidence.

THE FIRST RULE OF EVIDENCE

The rules of evidence are designed primarily to keep a jury from hearing or seeing improper evidence, and the first rule of evidence is designed to set parameters on the preceding definition of evidence. Because evidence can be anything that has a bearing on the outcome of the case, the first rule of evidence provides that anything is admissible as evidence unless there is some rule that prohibits its admissibility. Thus, this first rule provides that all the other rules of evidence may limit the things that a jury is entitled to hear, see, and decide on. From this, it can be surmised that most of the rules are stated in negative form.

PROOF

Many people confuse proof with evidence. They are separate but related elements of the judicial process. As noted, evidence consists of individual facts submitted to the jury for its consideration. **Proof** may be defined as the combination of all those facts—of all the evidence—in determining the guilt or innocence of a person accused of a crime. Thus, in referring to Figure 22-6 one can see that the entire pie might constitute proof of guilt, while slices of the pie are matters of evidence.

TESTIMONY

Although testimony and evidence often are considered to be interchangeable, they are distinct. **Testimony** is simply evidence

► **FIGURE 22-5**
A judge instructs a jury
The jury is considered the finder of fact in a trial. The jury is not expected to know the law. After closing arguments by both the prosecution and defense, the judge is responsible for instructing the jury on the procedures it must follow and the applicable law in the case. When the jury retires to deliberate, it will have the applicable law, procedures, and facts as heard and seen from the evidence and testimony to decide the case. (©Fuse/Corbis/Getty Images RF)

given in oral form. It consists of spoken facts of which witnesses have knowledge. Even though the gun found at the scene, fingerprints, and tire treads are evidence, they require testimony to explain their significance to the case. In Figure 22-6, it is apparent that all six segments of the pie constitute evidence. But only segments 2, 3, and 5 are testimonial evidence.

Admissibility

Admissibility is the essence of the rules of evidence. The rules of admissibility protect the trier of fact, generally a jury, from hearing improper evidence that may be unreliable or untrustworthy and that may prejudice the case unjustifiably against the defendant. The majority of the rules of evidence deal with what is admissible. Questions of admissibility are decided by the judge, and these decisions are made outside of the hearing of the jury.

RELEVANCE

One of the rules governing the admissibility of evidence requires that the evidence be relevant. The evidence must have a bearing on the issues in the case being tried. The relevance of a particular piece of evidence can easily be determined by the answer to this question: "Does this piece of evidence have probative value?" Alternatively stated, "Will it aid in proving or disproving a particular point that the jury should consider in determining the guilt or innocence of the defendant?" If it cannot throw some light on the case, it is irrelevant.

▲ **FIGURE 22-6**   **The relation of evidence and proof**

Materiality

Admissibility is also governed by the test of materiality. Even assuming that a particular piece of evidence is relevant, if it is such an insignificant and unimportant point that its admissibility will not affect the outcome of the case, it may be inadmissible. Thus, materiality deals with the importance of the item of evidence in question.

Competence of Evidence

The test of competence of evidence relates to evidence's legal significance to the case. Because of certain statutory requirements or other rules of evidence, a particular item of evidence may not be admissible. For example, there is a rule of evidence to the effect that the defendant's character cannot be attacked by the prosecution unless and until the defendant tries to show that he/she is of good character. Hence, unless the defendant did proceed in this direction, any attempt by the prosecution to introduce evidence of the defendant's character would be inadmissible on the grounds of incompetence.

The competence of physical evidence must also be established as a condition of admissibility. This is done through a process known as laying a foundation. For instance, the admissibility of an electronically recorded conversation would have to be prefaced by testimony about the date, time, place, and circumstances under which the recording was made; the satisfaction of legal requirements in the making of the recording; proper identification of the voices on the tape; assertions about the functioning of the recorder and tape at the time of the recording; and assurances about the absence of editing or modification of the tape.

Competence of Witnesses

Regardless of their knowledge of the facts of a case, certain individuals are not permitted by law to testify for or against a defendant in a criminal case. For example, the rules of evidence generally prohibit people who have been declared legally insane from testifying in a criminal case. A child "of tender years" may or may not be declared a competent witness. A person intoxicated by alcohol or drugs at the time of testifying will not be permitted to relate his/her knowledge in court. In some circumstances, a witness may be competent to testify regarding particular aspects but be held incompetent to testify regarding other matters. One spouse may be competent to testify for or against the other spouse on certain matters but not others. This aspect of the competence of a witness is discussed in greater detail later in the chapter.

WEIGHT OF EVIDENCE

Once evidence has been admitted into the trial, it must be weighed by the jury. The object of the attorney for either side in a case is to persuade the jury to believe his or her side's view of the facts at issue and the responsibility of the defendant. The jury must then weigh all the evidence and determine which is the more believable. Guilt or innocence is then determined. **Weight** then deals with the elements of persuasion and believability. Within certain guidelines, discussed next, the jury is free to give whatever weight it desires to the evidence presented to it. In essence, the entire judicial system in the United States is directed toward persuading the jury to weigh one side more favorably than the other.

PRESUMPTIONS

Among the guidelines that the jury is required to follow in weighing and applying evidence are those regarding presumptions. There are two types of presumptions: conclusive and rebuttable. A conclusive presumption is one that the jury must follow without alternatives. For example, when the prosecution creates a reasonable belief in guilt, and the defense does not contradict any of the prosecution's case, the jury must follow a conclusive presumption that guilt has been established and must find the defendant guilty. A rebuttable presumption requires that a specific conclusion be drawn unless that conclusion has been dispelled or rebutted by evidence presented to the jury for its consideration. The presumption that one is innocent until proven guilty is an example of a rebuttable presumption. Another presumption of this type is that all persons are presumed sane at the time they commit criminal acts. This presumption can be rebutted by the introduction of evidence to the contrary indicating insanity.

INFERENCES

An inference is similar to a presumption but differs in that the jury has more latitude in accepting or rejecting an inference. Thus an inference is a permissible deduction that the jury may make. An inference is a natural conclusion arrived at by deduction, in logical sequence, from given facts. For example, if fact A—the gun found at the scene of the crime belongs to the defendant—and fact B—testimony by a witness placing the defendant near the scene just before the shots were fired—are both known facts, this is not conclusive proof that the defendant committed the crime. However, on the basis of these known facts, the jury may logically infer that the defendant did in fact commit the crime. But it is equally free to reject that inference if it feels that the evidence is not sufficient for that conclusion.

BURDEN OF PROOF

In each criminal case, the prosecution has the responsibility of affirmatively proving the allegations on which it has based its accusation. This is known as the **burden of proof.** The burden of proof rest on the prosecution and never shifts to the defense. The defendant is never required to prove innocence. Innocence is presumed. The state must prove guilt. Assuming that both the prosecution and the defense present evidence in the trial in support of their theories of the case, the prosecution must establish proof beyond, and to the exclusion of, every reasonable doubt. The jurors must be convinced that the prosecution has proved the defendant guilty beyond any doubt to which they can attach a reason. Often only the defendant knows positively whether he/she is guilty or innocent. Because juries are composed of human beings, they are subject to some doubt in every case and must rely on testimony and physical evidence in reaching their decision. However, if the prosecution so thoroughly convinces the jurors of the defendant's guilt that they cannot give a reasonable explanation of why they doubt that guilt, then the burden of proof has been satisfied beyond, and to the exclusion of, every reasonable doubt. The word "reasonable" is included to separate human fallibility from the alleged infallibility of machines.

There is one exception to the requirement that the state prove its case beyond reasonable doubt. When the prosecution

▶ **FIGURE 22-7**
Relations among burden of proof, burden of going forward, and preponderance of evidence

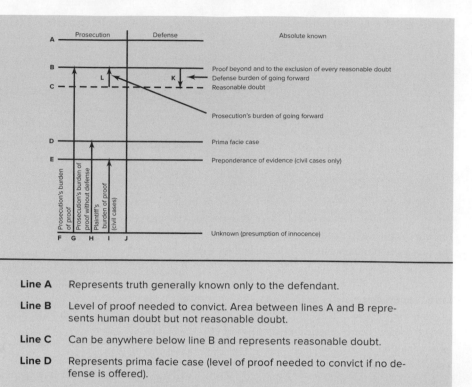

Line A	Represents truth generally known only to the defendant.
Line B	Level of proof needed to convict. Area between lines A and B represents human doubt but not reasonable doubt.
Line C	Can be anywhere below line B and represents reasonable doubt.
Line D	Represents prima facie case (level of proof needed to convict if no defense is offered).
Line E	Level of proof needed for decision in civil case.
Line F	Starting point—presumption of innocence.
Arrow G	Represents prosecution's burden of proof.
Arrow H	Represents prosecution's burden of proof necessary to convict if no defense is offered.
Arrow I	Plaintiff's burden of proof in civil cases.
Line J	Represents the continuum between unknown and absolute known.
Arrow K	Defense burden of going forward with evidence to create a reasonable doubt (line C).
Arrow L	Prosecution's burden of going forward with evidence to overcome reasonable doubt created by defense, thereby elevating level of proof (pushing line C up to overlie line B).

QUICK FACTS

Prima Facia Cases and Evidence

The term **prima facia** is often used to describe the apparent nature of something upon initial observation. In legal parlance, the term generally describes one of two things: First, the presentation of sufficient evidence to support the indictment or charge, (or claim in a civil case). It is important to understand that the concept of prima facia need not be conclusive or irrefutable, simply that the case has enough merit to take the issue to a full trial. Second, a specific piece of evidence that directly supports a particular proposition or fact, such as probable cause to make an arrest, or a witness that places a suspect at the scene of the crime, is often referred to as prima facia evidence because it supports the original legal proposition or claim.

Source: Farlex, *The Free Dictionary (Legal Dictionary)*. See: http://legal-dictionary.thefreedictionary.com/prima+facie

shows sufficient facts to indicate that the defendant more likely did commit the crime than did not, it has a prima facie case. The prosecution has satisfied its burden of proof if it presents a prima facie case, provided that there is no contradiction by the defense. Figure 22-7 illustrates these relationships.

BURDEN OF GOING FORWARD

The requirements concerning burden of proof do not mean that a defendant has no responsibility for convincing the jury of his or her innocence. The defense carries a **burden of going forward** with evidence. That responsibility is a great deal less than the burden of proof carried by the prosecution. The burden of going forward with evidence is placed on the defense so that it will present evidence that creates a reasonable doubt of guilt. In other words, the defense need present only enough evidence to overcome the prosecution's contentions and create a reasonable doubt of guilt in the minds of the jurors.

When a unanimous decision by the jury is necessary to find the defendant guilty, the burden is even lighter, for the defense need create that reasonable doubt in the mind of only one juror to avoid a verdict of guilty.

This explanation sounds as though every benefit is being given to the defendant, and it is. The very essence of our entire criminal justice system is to place the heaviest responsibility on the accuser—the prosecution.

The prosecution also has the burden of going forward with evidence. If the prosecution presents a prima facie case that is contradicted by evidence presented on behalf of the defendant, the state must then erase the reasonable doubt by presenting evidence that contradicts that offered by the defense.

PREPONDERANCE OF EVIDENCE

In a civil case, the party allegedly wronged is called the **plaintiff.** The plaintiff may be an individual, a group, a business, or a representative of some other private concern. The plaintiff in a civil action is not required to prove allegations beyond and to the exclusion of every reasonable doubt. All that is required is a **preponderance of evidence**—that is, that the evidence the plaintiff presents be considered weightier by the jury than the contrary evidence presented by the defendant. Thus, if the civil jury believes that the plaintiff's story offers a higher probability of being true than does the defendant's contention, the plaintiff will win the case. But the defendant wins if the jury gives greater credibility to the defense. In nonlegal terms, if evidence had to be weighed on a 100-point scale of probability, 50% plus a feather believability would win.

ORDER OF PROOF

Court procedures generally require that the prosecuting attorney prove the existence of the corpus delicti at trial before attempting to show the guilt of the defendant. The **corpus delicti** is the combination of all the elements of the crime. It is, of course, only logical that the prosecution be required to show that a crime has been committed before it can begin proving the defendant's guilt. Trial judges rarely exercise their discretionary power to allow evidence to be submitted to prove a point out of order. The judge has the prerogative of allowing the introduction of evidence to establish the guilt of the defendant prior to the prosecution's showing the existence of all the elements of the crime. However, this is done only on rare occasions, when to maintain the order of proof might be a major inconvenience to a particular witness. Permission is given only on the condition that the prosecution guarantees it will later establish the corpus delicti. If the guarantee is made and the prosecution later cannot show the corpus delicti, grounds exist for a mistrial or a directed verdict of acquittal.

JUDICIAL NOTICE

The doctrine of judicial notice is an evidentiary shortcut. Judicial notice is designed to speed up the trial and eliminate the necessity of formally proving the truth of a particular matter when that truth is not in dispute. **Judicial notice,** then, is proof without evidence and may be taken in three situations:

1. Judicial notice may be taken of matters of common knowledge that are uniformly settled and about which there is no dispute. If the fact is known to most reasonably informed people in the community where the trial is being held, judicial notice may be taken of that fact. For example, the fact that a particular intersection, located in a city where an accident occurred, is a business district might well be a matter of common knowledge of which judicial notice could be taken if the trial is held in that city. Since most reasonably informed people in a community would know that a particular intersection was a business area, the court would accept that as a given fact without requiring formal proof.

2. Judicial notice may be taken of laws. A state court, for example, is required to take judicial notice of the state statutes of the jurisdiction in which the court operates; a municipal court takes judicial notice of municipal ordinances.

3. Judicial notice may be taken of matters that may be ascertained as true by referring to common authoritative sources such as books or official agencies. Included in this category are scientific facts, medical facts, historical facts, and meanings of words, phrases, and abbreviations. Examples would include the official time of sunset on a particular date by reference to a weather bureau; the fact that the abbreviation "M.D." following a name stands for "medical doctor"; the fact that the hair and blood types of human beings differ from those of animals; and the fact that no two individuals have identical fingerprints or DNA.

Judicial notice must be distinguished from judicial knowledge. The latter refers to knowledge possessed by a judge. The fact that the judge may know a fact is not material in applying the doctrine of judicial notice. Personal knowledge may not be substituted for common knowledge in the community or for facts capable of being ascertained.

Judicial notice may be taken only on a collateral or minor point of fact in a case. Judicial notice may never be used to prove a fact that the jury is required to decide in determining the proper charge and verdict. For example, in the case of a defendant on trial for stealing a car, the court may not take judicial notice of the value of the car if that value will determine the seriousness of the charge against the defendant. Even if it is a matter of common knowledge that a brand new Cadillac El Dorado is worth more than $100, judicial notice may not be taken, because the value is an important element that the prosecution must prove to ensure the propriety of the charge placed against the defendant.

TYPES OF EVIDENCE

There are many ways of classifying evidence. Not all authorities agree on the classifications, but the differences are immaterial as long as the principles are understood. Five types of evidence are defined next.

▲ FIGURE 22-8   Witness examining a gun during trial
This weapon is a piece of real evidence or physical evidence
involved in the offense being tried. Here, an investigator
examines the weapon closely to be able to positively state that it
was the weapon found at the scene. (©Bill Greene/Reuters/Alamy)

Direct Evidence

Direct evidence usually is the testimony of witnesses that ties the
defendant directly to the commission of the crime, such as the
testimony of an eyewitness who can positively state that the
defendant committed the crime. It is based on the firsthand
knowledge of the witness regarding the guilt of the defendant.

Real Evidence

Sometimes referred to as *physical evidence*, *real evidence* is connected with the commission of the crime and can be produced
in court. Items of physical evidence found at a crime scene, such

as a weapon used to commit a homicide (Figure 22-8), a crow-
bar used to pry open a window, and fingerprints, all constitute
real evidence that can be observed by the jury.

Demonstrative Evidence

Demonstrative, or *illustrative*, *evidence* is not identical to real evidence even though the items introduced are tangible (Figure
22-9). It consists of maps, diagrams, sketches, photographs, tape
recordings, videotapes, X rays, and visual tests and demonstrations produced to assist witnesses in explaining their testimony.
When testimony alone would be inadequate to describe a victim
or crime scene, photographs taken by police officers are used
to help the jury understand the conditions that existed.

The use of demonstrative evidence is governed by complex
and highly restrictive rules to ensure that the jury is not prejudiced against the defendant.

Circumstantial Evidence

It is a myth that one cannot be convicted of a crime based solely
on circumstantial evidence. The broad definition of circumstantial evidence encompasses all evidence other than direct evidence, provided that it logically connects the defendant to the
crime. Circumstantial evidence is sometimes referred to as *indirect evidence* for this reason. Circumstantial evidence is used in
a criminal case by inferring from a series of known facts the
existence of an unknown fact. In other words, by the process of
deductive reasoning, inferences are logically drawn from a series
of known facts, and a conclusion is reached. For example, the
fact that the defendant's fingerprints are detected on a weapon
found at the scene of a homicide does not necessarily mean that
the defendant committed the crime. The fingerprints tie the
defendant to the gun, and finding the gun at the scene of the
crime may be a circumstance relating the gun to the commission
of the crime. Likewise, testimony that the defendant was seen

► FIGURE 22-9
Introduction of demonstrative
evidence at trial
Demonstrative evidence is sometimes
referred to as *illustrative evidence*.
Demonstrative evidence consists of
visual tests and demonstrations such as
pictures produced to assist the witness
with the testimony. (©Joe Burbank-Pool/
Getty Images)

near the scene of the crime shortly after its commission does not necessarily constitute guilt; but again, it may lead the jury to infer guilt.

It is possible that an accumulation of circumstantial evidence may be nothing more than a series of unfortunate coincidences for which the defendant may have a logical and truthful explanation. How much circumstantial evidence is required for a jury to convict someone of a crime varies from case to case and depends largely on the composition of the jury.

Circumstantial evidence can be considered analogous to links in a chain. Each link might be an unfortunate coincidence, but the greater the number of links, the more a jury is likely to infer guilt by joining the links into a chain of overwhelming circumstantial evidence.

Opinion Evidence

Witnesses ordinarily are not permitted to give their opinions or draw conclusions on matters about which they are testifying. Their function is to present the facts about which they have firsthand knowledge. It is within the province of the jury to determine the truthfulness of those facts and to draw whatever conclusions it believes are necessary. However, there are a few exceptions to that general rule. Everything a human being perceives through the senses is generally expressed in the form of a conclusion. It is difficult, if not impossible, to describe something perceived as an absolute fact without expressing it in the form of a conclusion. The only things on which a nonexpert may give opinion evidence are matters of description in which fact and opinion are so interwoven that they cannot be separated without losing most of their probative value. Matters of description in which a nonexpert may give an opinion include color, size, shape, speed, mental condition, identity, race, and language.

An expert is someone with special skills or knowledge not ordinarily possessed by others. The skills or knowledge may be acquired through experience, study, observation, or education. To be an **expert witness,** one need not necessarily have a formal education. The expert witness is permitted to interpret facts and give opinions about their significance; the lay witness may present only facts that are a matter of firsthand knowledge. The expert witness is called on to assist the jurors in understanding facts that they are ordinarily not sufficiently trained to understand, such as the results of medical examinations, chemical analyses, ballistics reports, and findings from questioned documents. Results of DNA analysis, for example, would certainly require the supporting testimony of an expert witness.

THE HEARSAY RULE

Most people have heard a story from several different sources and recognized how different the versions sound. Whether these alterations are caused by poor memory or deliberate attempts to spice up the truth is immaterial in a legal context. The fact that stories tend to be changed when they are repeated makes their reliability and truthfulness questionable. For this reason, the hearsay rule was created. **Hearsay** is

derived from "heard say." Testimony in court that repeats what others were heard to say means testifying to a second version of what actually happened. The witness has no personal knowledge of the facts in question. Thus, the truth of the testimony depends on the truthfulness and the competence of the person from whom the information was heard rather than of the person testifying. For these reasons, the hearsay rule is perhaps one of the most important yet most confusing rules of evidence.

Inaccuracy, unreliability, and untrustworthiness are only some of the reasons why hearsay evidence is excluded. The inability of the judge and jury to observe the demeanor or conduct of the person who actually has firsthand knowledge of the information is another.

Other reasons for generally excluding hearsay rely on protections guaranteed in the Constitution. The Sixth Amendment guarantees a defendant the right to be confronted by the witnesses against him or her and the right to cross-examine those witnesses. Because the person with firsthand knowledge is not present in court, that person cannot be confronted or cross-examined by the defendant.

Hearsay is a version of the truth repeated in court by one who does not know whether the assertion is true. People may assert things lightly and casually out of court without being overly concerned about the truth; but they would likely be more careful about speaking truthfully in court, when an individual's life or liberty may be at stake and when they are testifying under oath.

The hearsay rule also excludes written statements by people not in the courtroom to testify. Because the writer's personal knowledge is in his or her head, writing that knowledge makes it secondhand information.

If the out-of-court assertion is being offered as evidence not to prove the truth of a matter but only to show that it was said, it is not hearsay and thus may be admissible. This is one of the rare occasions in which the hearsay rule would not be applicable. For example, a homicide victim may have made threats against the defendant. These threats can be repeated in court to show the defendant's state of mind when he/she killed the victim and to support a claim of self-defense. The truth or falsity of the threats is not the issue.

A second exception deals with reputation. The reputation of a defendant or a witness in a trial may be questionable. A third party may testify about what he/she has heard concerning another's reputation. Because an individual's reputation is representative not of actual character but, rather, of what other people think of that person, the truth of the reputation is immaterial. But the fact that such a reputation exists is admissible. For example, if the defendant presents evidence in a trial for assault that he/she is a calm individual, a witness may testify to having heard that the defendant is extremely short-tempered.

In these situations, evidence is offered to show only that the statements were made, not that they are true. Because the witness has personal knowledge, it is not hearsay, and because the statements are not offered for the truth of their contents, they are admissible.

BOX 22-1 | EXPERT OPINON AND THE *DAUBERT STANDARD*

In Chapter 8, The Crime Laboratory, we discuss the admissibility of expert testimony as part of the rules of evidence in a trial that helps the judge or jury understand the scientific and technical evidence in a case, or determine a fact in issue. The acceptance of an expert witness as well as the acceptance of expert opinion rests squarely on the shoulders of the trial judge. In essence, trial judges act as the gatekeepers of admissibility of expert opinion.

In a series of three cases,[2] the Supreme Court has developed a basic guideline known as the "Daubert Standard" in deciding if specific scientific, technical, or other specialized knowledge presented by an expert should be permitted to be given in testimony to a jury. The Daubert Standard includes a number of factors that may be considered in determining admissibility:

- What is the basic theory to be presented and has it been, or can it be tested?
- Are the standards controlling the technique or theory based on the scientific method? In other words, is the testimony relevant to the task at hand and rests on a reliable foundation?
- Has the theory or technique been subjected to peer review and publication?
- What is the known or potential error rate?
- Is there general acceptance within the relevant scientific community of the theory or issue?
- Has the research been conducted independently and neutral to the litigation or case in question?
- Has the expert adequately accounted for alternative explanations?
- Has the expert unjustifiably extrapolated from an accepted premise to an unfounded conclusion?
- Is the witness indeed an "expert" based on knowledge, skill, experience, training, education, publication, and/or other evidence that distinguishes him or her as an expert?

▲ FIGURE 22-10
Expert witnesses are often used to assist the court and jury in understanding complex issues or techniques often observed in the admissibility of forensic evidence such as questioned documents, fingerprint analysis, DNA analysis, ballistics, and the like.
(©ssuaphotos/Shutterstock RF)

The *Daubert Standard* is used in all federal courts and in many state courts. A Daubert hearing or motion is often used to examine the above questions before the trial judge. In such hearings, the qualifications of the expert as well as the expert's opinion and testimony can be rigorously cross-examined. Further, contrary experts and opinions can be proffered by opposing counsel.

The hearsay rule is based on the recognition that human beings have weaknesses and that the testimony of human witnesses provides the majority of evidence presented to juries in modern trials. Because we will continue to rely on the testimony of human beings as the principal source of information for trying cases, the law must continue to impose standards to ensure the most accurate and reliable testimony possible. Unequivocal application of the hearsay rule to all situations does, however, present certain injustices in our modern judicial system. For this reason, a number of specific exceptions to the hearsay rule have developed.

EXCEPTIONS TO THE HEARSAY RULE

The sheer number of exceptions often creates doubt about whether the hearsay rule has any merit. Among the many reasons for the existence of the hearsay rule, two stand out as the most critical: the unreliability and the untrustworthiness of declarations repeated under oath in court. Until March 8, 2004, the exceptions to the rule could be justified only if these two major drawbacks could be overcome. If the circumstances surrounding the hearsay evidence could ensure a high degree of trustworthiness and reliability, that evidence was admissible as an exception to the rule in order to minimize any injustice. Each exception had to meet many tests to satisfy the criteria of reliability and trustworthiness before it was admissible. Supreme Court decisions eliminated concern over the constitutional issues by holding that the exceptions did not violate the Sixth Amendment guarantees of confrontation and cross-examination,[3] and did not violate the due process guarantees of the Fourteenth Amendment.

In the 2004 case of *Crawford* v. *Washington*,[4] the U.S. Supreme Court decided that some hearsay evidence, that which contains "testimonial" statements, is inadmissible in a criminal prosecution if the original declarant who made the out-of-court statement is unavailable to testify unless the defendant had the opportunity to confront and cross-examine the witness in an earlier proceeding. Thus, with one decision, the Court unraveled many years of judicial precedents that justified many of the exceptions on the basis of trustworthiness and reliability. The Court, in overturning its previous decisions that found the exceptions did not violate those constitutional principles, is now saying that the Constitution does require confrontation and the opportunity for cross-examination if the hearsay evidence is a testimonial statement.

The question of what qualifies as a testimonial statement, was not answered by the Court when it said

> We leave for another day any effort to spell out a comprehensive definition of "testimonial." Whatever else the term covers, it applies at a minimum to prior testimony at a preliminary hearing, before a grand jury, or at a former trial; and to police interrogations. These are the modern practices with closest kinship to the abuses at which the Confrontation Clause was directed.[5]

Although it appears that the general consensus is that if it is conceivable an out-of-court statement might later be used in court against the defendant, it is testimonial and the *Crawford* decision does apply, but, since the *Crawford* decision, many thousands of federal and state cases have been decided interpreting the application of the decision to differing factual scenarios and many of the decisions conflict with one another. As is typical for U.S. Supreme Court decisions, time and many court decisions, including more from the high court, will result in a clearer picture of the requirements for adhering to this change of philosophy.

Some hearsay exceptions apply in both civil and criminal cases; others apply only to civil or criminal cases. The following paragraphs discuss several exceptions applicable in criminal cases. In each case, note is made of whether the *Crawford* decision is potentially involved. It should be noted that examples of applications of *Crawford* to specific fact situations will serve no purpose at this point because of many different interpretations of *Crawford*'s applicability in the thousands of cases in state and federal courts.

Confessions

A **confession** is an acknowledgment by a person accused of a crime that he/she is guilty of that crime. To constitute a confession, the admission of guilt must incorporate all the elements of the crime and exclude any reasonable doubt about the possibility of innocence. Confessions are generally of two types. A judicial confession is an in-court confession made before a judge. A judicial confession can also take the form of a guilty plea. Judicial confessions do not fall within the hearsay rule, because they are in-court assertions of the truth of the matter asserted by the person directly involved.

Confessions made out of court fall within the hearsay rule. For such confessions to be admissible, they must meet the tests of admissibility and overcome the assumptions of unreliability and untrustworthiness.

The admissibility of a confession usually raises questions about constitutionality. First, it must be shown that the confession satisfies constitutional requirements of voluntariness. A confession that is obtained involuntarily certainly would not be admissible under modern law. Second, courts admit confessions as an exception to the hearsay rule on the theory that it is highly unlikely that a person will say something against his or her own interest unless it is true. Therefore, a confession tends to establish the reliability and trustworthiness of the truth of the matter asserted. People do not often deliberately make statements that jeopardize their own life or liberty unless those statements are true. Based on this assumption, the major objections to admitting confessions, as hearsay, are overcome. (See the discussion in Chapter 5, "Documenting the Interview and Interrogation.")

Since a confession is made by the defendant, confrontation and cross-examination are not an issue, and the *Crawford* decision is not applicable.

Admissions

One who makes an **admission** does not acknowledge all the facts surrounding the crime necessary to constitute guilt but does admit to certain facts or circumstances from which guilt may be inferred by the jury. For example, without confessing to the crime, an accused may admit having been at or near the scene of the crime at the time it occurred, having a motive to commit the crime against the victim, possessing the gun used in the crime, having foot impressions that match those found outside the window of the victim's house, and leaving town the day after the crime was committed. These admissions may be introduced in the trial by a witness who overheard the accused make these statements or in the form of a written document or electronic recording repeating these statements. They may be introduced for basically the same reasons as confessions are admissible. The contents of the admissions are certainly against the interest and welfare of the defendant and, like confessions, must have been made voluntarily to be admissible. If these factors exist, it is unlikely that a defendant would make such admissions unless they were true. Therefore, the courts allow the admissions on the basis that the principal objections to the hearsay rule—unreliability and untrustworthiness—have been overcome. Here again, the *Crawford* decision is not applicable for the same reasons that it does not apply to confessions.

Spontaneous and Excited Utterances

Human nature is such that speaking the truth is an instinctive reaction. Therefore, if one makes a spontaneous or excited utterance after something startling or unusual has happened, the utterance may be admissible as an exception to the hearsay rule when testified to by one who heard it made. It may be offered to prove the truth of the matter asserted. The spontaneity of the utterance and its declaration under startling and unusual circumstances lend credence to its reliability and trustworthiness. To illustrate, a 5-year-old girl, observing a playmate struck at a railroad crossing, was heard by a passerby to scream, "The engine runned over Billy!" The passerby was permitted to testify in court about what he had heard the girl say. If the little girl is available and qualified, she can be cross-examined as to what she said. Since a third person is testifying to what the girl said, it is most likely that the girl is unavailable for an acceptable reason. This is one of those instances when the applicability of *Crawford* has resulted in conflicting decisions.

It is under this exception that electronic recordings of 911 emergency calls are sought to be introduced. The impact of *Crawford* on the admissibility of 911 recordings have been extremely varied, even within a single jurisdiction and are evaluated on such things as the length of time after the occurrence before the 911 call was made. Was it the first call made? Where was the call made from? Was there a questionable underlying purpose of the call? In other words, courts look to all the circumstances to determine if they think the caller had prosecution in mind when the call was made. If so, it could be considered "testimonial" and be excluded under *Crawford*.

Dying Declarations

A declaration concerning the facts and circumstances of the fatal injury made by the victim of a homicide who is about to die, expects to die, and does not hope to recover is admissible as an exception to the hearsay rule. The theory is that a person about to die has no reason to lie. Statements admissible under this exception must concern the injury inflicted to the declarant and are admissible only in the trial of the person charged with the declarant's death.

Former Testimony

Written or oral testimony in a hearing or trial falls within the hearsay rule if that testimony is sought to be introduced in a later judicial proceeding. For example, if a witness testifies against the defendant in a preliminary hearing to determine probable cause to hold the defendant for trial, the court record is not admissible in the later trial unless it meets the tests of the former-testimony exception to the hearsay rule. Because the testimony was given in a court under oath, it is presumed reliable and trustworthy and is admissible provided the two judicial proceedings involve the same defendant, who is charged with committing the same act, under the same circumstances. In addition, the witness who originally testified at the former hearing must be unavailable for testimony before the transcript of the hearing is admissible, and, to show that constitutional requirements have been satisfied, it must be proved that the defendant had the right to cross-examine the witness in the former hearing or trial. As the Supreme Court pointed out, this is one of the specific instances when the *Crawford* decision is applicable. The requirement that the defendant must have had the opportunity to cross-examine the declarant has been a long-standing test to satisfy the reliability element of this exception to the hearsay rule.

EVIDENTIARY PRIVILEGES

Defendants and other witnesses have a right to have certain matters of communication barred from disclosure in court—for example, confidential communications between husband and wife, confidential communications between attorney and client, and grand jury proceedings that are confidential requirements of law are barred.

The **evidentiary privileges** may vary from state to state. Some are universally recognized as necessary and have existed since the early days of common law. Others exist only if the state legislature has created the privilege by statute. Some of the more common evidentiary privileges fall into four basic categories. The first might be called professional privileges and includes those that exist between attorney and client, physician and patient, priest and penitent, and journalist and informant. Government communications and information, state secrets, and matters of diplomacy are classified as political privileges. The third category is social privileges and includes confidential communications between husband and wife or between a guidance counselor and a child. Finally, judicial privileges include grand jury proceedings, communications among jurors deliberating a verdict, and the privilege against self-incrimination guaranteed by the Fifth Amendment.

All these privileges can be waived by the person against whom the evidence is to be used or who would suffer from its disclosure. Thus, an attorney cannot disclose evidence of a confidential communication between attorney and client unless so directed by the client. Likewise, a spouse cannot testify against a mate without the latter's express permission, unless the spouse is the victim of the mate's crime.

Although only confidential communications are excluded by the privilege, it is the relationship, not the communications, that is privileged. The theory underlying evidentiary privileges creates a balance between the disclosure of truth and the welfare of society. The assumption is that the public benefits more by protecting these relationships than it does by requiring disclosure of the truth to seek to convict one defendant.

WITNESSES

Until a few hundred years ago, witnesses appeared at a trial voluntarily. There were no legal means to compel attendance. With the advent of the rules of evidence, procedures had to be established for requiring the presence of people who possessed knowledge of the facts of the case. The **subpoena** is used for this purpose. It is a written order commanding the person named to appear in court at a specified date and time to testify, under oath, before a judicial tribunal, to facts within the witness's personal knowledge that are pertinent to the case. A *subpoena duces tecum* commands the individual to bring certain records or documents in his or her possession. Refusal to obey subjects the individual to punishment for contempt. Likewise, refusal to testify or answer specific questions may be grounds for contempt unless valid grounds exist, such as the self-incrimination protections guaranteed in the Constitution.

People who possess firsthand knowledge have a duty, not a right, to appear in court.

In early common law, defendants had no right to call witnesses on their behalf. Therefore, the prosecution was required to call all witnesses having knowledge of facts, regardless of which side those facts favored. Today, the defense has an equal right to compel the attendance of witnesses. Hence, the state may use only those witnesses it chooses. Witnesses may also be called by the judge, but this power is rarely exercised.

Once in court, the witness's competence to testify must be ascertained. Competence of witnesses was discussed earlier in this chapter. If the witness is not insane, intoxicated, or excluded for other reasons, and if the testimony will not fall within any of the evidentiary privileges, he/she will be presumed competent to testify, though this must first be asserted by taking an oath or affirmation.

In common law, taking an **oath** was a process by which individuals swore to tell the truth on the basis of their sacred belief in a supreme being. Today, of course, the oath is still a recognized means of establishing a witness's competence, but it is no longer the only method. The affirmation is also used for people who refuse, for personal reasons, to take the oath. Because they are otherwise competent to testify, some guarantee that they will tell the truth is necessary. A witness may be declared competent if he/she understands and undertakes the obligation of an oath. This obligation is to tell the truth with a realization of the penalties for perjury. As long as the witness understands and undertakes the obligation, even without swearing to a supreme being, the witness is considered competent to testify. This process is called **affirmation.**

A declaration of a witness's competence in no way guarantees the credibility of the testimony. Credibility deals with believability, which, like the weight of any other evidence, is determined by the jury. Attitude, personality, appearance, hygiene, and general demeanor all affect a witness's credibility, along with the substance of the testimony.

THE INVESTIGATOR AS A WITNESS

The success or failure of a criminal investigation is often ultimately measured in terms of the quality and effectiveness of an officer's presentation of evidence to a court and jury. Because one aim of the entire process of criminal investigation is to bring about the apprehension and prosecution of violators of the criminal laws, the presentation of the case in court must be of paramount concern to the investigator from the moment of arrival at the crime scene. Inability to understand and appreciate this crucial role in the judicial process not only adversely affects the investigator's performance as a witness but also reflects on the investigator's overall professional effectiveness.

Every law enforcement witness, whether a uniformed officer or criminal investigator, must become skilled at testifying on the witness stand. Preparation should include knowledge of the rules of evidence so that the officer not only can perform in the field more effectively but also can have a better understanding of courtroom procedures and the functions of the prosecution and the defense. To prepare a case adequately, the investigator must understand the rules of admissibility and the relevance of evidence collected. The best witnesses are those who have an understanding and appreciation of their role in the courtroom and their relationship to other participants in the judicial process.

The Role of the Law Enforcement Witness

The function of any witness in the courtroom, including the investigator, is to present firsthand knowledge of facts to the jury for its consideration. The investigator must inform the jury of the matters investigated in the case and present this information so that the jury understands the sequence of events and their significance. But the investigator may not offer personal conclusions.

To understand his/her role in the courtroom completely, the witness must also understand the functions of the other participants in the criminal process. Specifically, the witness must understand the functions of the judge and the jury in relation to the role of a witness.

As mentioned earlier, the function of any witness is to present facts from firsthand knowledge. The jury's function is to weigh the facts presented by witnesses from both prosecution and defense and to interpret these facts, giving appropriate weight and credibility to the evidence and to the witnesses for the purpose of reaching a decision regarding the guilt or innocence of the defendant. The responsibility of the judge is twofold. The judge functions as a referee to ensure compliance with the rules of evidence and interprets the law as applicable to the facts of a case.

Credibility

A law enforcement officer is not entitled to any more credibility in the courtroom than is any other witness. The officer has an equal responsibility, through presentation, appearance, demeanor, and the substance of testimony, to persuade the jury to believe the facts being related.

The issue of credibility is of special concern to the law enforcement witness. Few people from the general population ever view a criminal offense or act as witnesses in court. It is likely that the trauma of such an event would be so vivid for them that remembering it would not be difficult. However, police officers regularly deal with criminal cases and investigate some with striking similarities. Thus, for officers, the frequency and similarities of, and the time lag between, investigations and court appearances may create difficulties in the presentation of testimony.

A related area that may affect the credibility of the law enforcement witness stems from public expectations and perceptions of the law enforcement role. Many citizens expect nothing less than perfection from law enforcement officers in both the performance of their duties and their presentation of testimony in court. They often lose sight of the fact that law enforcement officers are subject to human frailties. An officer's credibility may suffer if his/her recall is less than perfect.

Another issue in the investigator's credibility relates to the perceptions of the jurors. Some individuals regard as suspect any statements made by police officers. The predisposition of jurors with this attitude may be reinforced by defense attorneys

BOX 22-2 | LYING AND OFFICER CREDIBILITY AS A WITNESS

In Chapter 2, we discussed the impact of the 1963 landmark case, *Brady v. Maryland*.[6] Based on the due process clause of the U.S. Constitution, the Supreme Court held that the prosecution, including the police, cannot suppress or withhold any evidence that may be favorable to the accused. Such evidence is often called, "exculpatory evidence" and includes any information concerning the credibility of the individual police officer. *Brady* has had a dramatic impact on the credibility of police officers as witnesses. Because the prosecution must reveal any possible impeachment evidence regarding its own witness, an officer's internal affairs records and any documented report where the officer lied or was untruthful must be presented to

the defense. Such officers simply cannot testify in court without being impeached; hence, their ability to work as a police officer is seriously compromised. For this reason, most departments have policies that terminate an employee (officer) for lying.[7] In those cases, when such officers are retained by the agency even after a major violation is discovered and corrected, the officers cannot testify in court and are relegated to non-sworn duties in communications, call-taking, records, and the like. These officers are often called, "*Brady* officers" and are essentially barred from patrol and investigative functions where there is a strong possibility that the officers could make an arrest and be required to act as a witness.

who, on cross-examination, seek to discredit the testimony of the officer on the basis of his or her occupation.

The law enforcement witness can overcome all these barriers by preparing meticulously for testimony and by giving straightforward, unemotional responses (Figure 22-11).

Characteristics of a Good Witness: Preparation, Preparation, and Preparation

The successful testimony of the investigator is based on adequate preparation of the case, familiarity with the rules of evidence and with how juries think and react, knowledge of trial processes, and maintenance of proper appearance and conduct at all times.

Preparation for testimony, as has already been indicated, is of extreme importance and cannot be overemphasized. For the law enforcement witness, the first step in preparation is to ensure that a complete investigation was conducted, that all leads were followed and all avenues explored. It must be remembered that the prime responsibility of the investigator is not to convict but to ascertain the facts objectively. The investigator must also prepare complete and accurate notes on information obtained and evidence gathered. Before appearing in court, the investigator must review all notes, reports, electronic recordings, and physical evidence; on the stand, he/she must recall events in as much detail as possible with minimal referral to notes. In addition to reviewing notes, investigators must thoroughly review all

▶ FIGURE 22-11
Officer on the witness stand
In the American criminal justice system, cases that ultimately result in trials are relatively few. However, for those that do go to trial, the courtroom testimony by investigators can be very important. The success or failure of a criminal investigation may ultimately be measured in terms of the quality and the effectiveness of an officer's presentation of evidence to the court and jury. Every police witness, whether a uniformed officer or criminal investigator, must become skilled at testifying on the stand.
(©Spencer Grant/PhotoEdit)

written reports, all evidence, and any deposition that may have been given before trial to ensure that his/her memory is complete and accurate.

Many prosecution offices have sworn law enforcement investigators. How these investigators function in criminal investigation cases depends on their authority, the role of the prosecutor during the investigation and the working relationships with the officers and investigators from the initiating agency. In some jurisdictions, once the case is referred for prosecution, the prosecutor's investigators take over and assist in getting the case ready for trial. In other jurisdictions, the prosecutor's investigators are there to assist the local agency investigators or assist in doing some follow-up investigation asked for by the prosecuting attorney as he/she prepares for trial. The working relationship between the investigators from the local agency and the prosecutor's office may take a completely different form from those described, and some communities may not have investigators employed full time but rather have an investigator hired for a specific case.

The investigator should review the case with prosecuting officials so that they will know the testimony the investigator can offer and the evidence available. This review also gives the investigator a chance to learn the nature of the questions that might be asked on direct examination. Admittedly investigators rarely can spend much time with the prosecutor before a trial. The demands on prosecutors' time and the caseloads that most prosecutors carry make in-depth preparation with each witness a virtual impossibility. This is also true because of the caseloads and time demands on the investigator. But even a short time spent in preparation is valuable. It is true that the more serious the case, the more time investigators and uniformed officers will spend with the prosecutor. It is not uncommon for investigators to spend less than an hour with the prosecutor before trial in many less serious cases, but a lot can be accomplished during that time.

Understanding the Jury

The jury's task is unique. In theory, it is constrained in what it may consider by rules of evidence and other procedural requirements. In practice, juries are composed of human beings who are subject to influences other than those that might appear in written rules and regulations. The study of jury psychology is fascinating, because it points out the flexibility and the fallibility of the human mind and, in turn, the absurdity of some of the procedural requirements imposed on the jury. The good law enforcement witness, at the very least, understands and appreciates the fact that juries do not make their determination of guilt or innocence solely on the substance of testimony and evidence offered. The appearance and demeanor of the defendant, attorneys, and witnesses; the manner in which witnesses make their presentations and answer questions; the professionalism displayed by law enforcement officers while in the courtroom; and the way in which witnesses respond to cross-examination all bear on the reactions of individual jurors. A good witness is conscious of these factors at all times.

Appearance and Demeanor

Law enforcement authorities disagree as to whether officers should wear uniforms or civilian clothes to court. Some believe that a law enforcement officer should always wear a uniform when testifying in court for immediate identification by the jurors. Others contend that civilian clothing is proper dress, because the uniform presents an authoritarian appearance that may be offensive to the jury. A third group takes the view that the officer should wear the type of dress—that is, uniform or civilian clothes—worn at the time of the arrest. Often this decision is largely a matter of departmental policy.

In any event, dress should be clean and neat. If civilian clothes are worn, a degree of formality is appropriate. Conservative clothes are less likely to offend members of the jury than are wild, flashy outfits, even though neat. Identifying items such as jewelry representing a specific occupation or association membership should be avoided. Lapel pins from specific civic clubs or tie tacks with emblems of handcuffs or service revolvers should not be worn. Although these are extremely small points, one can never predict who might be offended. Additionally, all the fundamentals pertaining to personal hygiene should be scrupulously observed.

Law enforcement witnesses should be conscious of their demeanor from the time they arrive at the courthouse. Before trial or during recesses, jurors may be standing around the courthouse. If an officer makes a bad impression through his or her appearance or actions, this may be remembered by a juror when the officer takes the stand and may adversely affect the credibility of the officer in that juror's mind. Consequently, any actions that could be offensive to jurors are to be avoided. The law enforcement officer should avoid talking to the prosecutor, court clerks, or judges and should refrain from acting overly friendly to anyone involved in the trial. Although there is nothing inherently wrong with idle talk or friendliness, jurors may perceive it as collusion.

Taking the Witness Stand

From the moment the law enforcement witness enters the courtroom, people are forming opinions. The officer should walk naturally when approaching the witness stand, not look at or speak to the prosecutor, and not frown at the defendant. If the jury sees these expressions, it interprets them as signs of partiality. The law enforcement witness should stand erect while being sworn in and, when permitted to be seated, should sit erect, facing the jury. The investigator should not continually cross his/her legs or fidget uncomfortably. Hands should be kept comfortably in the lap or on the arms of the chair.

Nervousness is natural for anyone who appears as a witness. Usually it disappears with experience. However, if the law enforcement witness is properly prepared and answers all questions accurately and truthfully to the best of his/her knowledge, nervousness is minimized.

Eye contact and speaking voice are extremely important. Many authorities contend that the witness should maintain eye contact with the jury while answering questions rather than watching the prosecutor or defense attorney. But this skill must be developed. It is difficult for most people to look at the jury when responding to a question from an attorney who may be standing on the opposite side of the courtroom. If the jury cannot hear or understand what the witness is saying, the testimony is worthless. Witnesses should speak loudly enough for people in the back of the courtroom to hear clearly and understand what they are saying. Then they can be sure that the jury, the attorneys, and the judge also can hear them.

Answering Questions

The ability to answer questions under direct and cross-examination is usually developed through experience. The law enforcement witness must answer without emotion or partiality. Sarcasm, witty remarks, or an attitude of "I'm out to get the defendant" must be avoided at all times. The good law enforcement witness must be positive and firm in answering all questions and should readily admit not knowing an answer if this is the case. The witness who constructs an answer to avoid embarrassment jeopardizes the case for the prosecution. Even the slightest fabrication of testimony is perjury and is likely to be discovered on cross-examination. It should be remembered that to err is human. It is not impossible for law enforcement witnesses to make mistakes in their testimony. Although it is slightly embarrassing, the witness should not hesitate to admit having made a mistake. This acknowledgment should be accompanied by an explanation. Even if the mistake is not discovered until after testimony is complete, the witness should immediately advise the prosecutor of the mistake so that the prosecutor will have the opportunity to correct it before the conclusion of the trial.

The requirement of being positive and firm in responding to questions also means that the witness must avoid the use of such expressions as "I think," "I believe," or "as I recall." It is difficult to avoid using expressions such as these, because they are part of everyday usage of the English language, but in court they can raise questions as to the definitiveness of the officer's testimony and can be a factor in the degree of credibility given to the testimony by the jury.

There are two basic methods by which witnesses are examined. The narrative technique allows the witness to tell the facts in his/her own words as they are known to be, in response to a question such as "Now tell us what you found at 1234 Elm Street." This technique is used if the examiner knows the witness well and has confidence that the witness will relate only relevant, unobjectionable matters. The advantage of the narrative technique is that it permits the witness to relate details chronologically and make them clearer to the jury. The obvious disadvantage is that an inexperienced witness may ramble, give objectionable or irrelevant testimony, or expose the jury to tainted evidence, potentially causing a mistrial. Hence, prosecutors use this technique sparingly.

Usually attorneys use the question-and-answer technique for examining witnesses. They ask a single, pointed question and receive an answer to it. When the question-and-answer technique is used, the law enforcement witness should hesitate momentarily before answering. This allows time for the opposing attorney to raise any objections. It also gives the witness an opportunity to digest the question to make sure it has been clearly understood. If not, the witness should ask that the question be repeated as many times as necessary. If the question does not make any sense after several repetitions, the witness

may ask that the question be phrased in different terms. The witness should not volunteer information.

Courtesy and respect are important qualities of an effective witness. The judge should always be addressed as "Your Honor." The witness's language should be intelligible and understandable to the jury. Police witnesses should deliberately avoid the use of slang and words unique to the police service, for these may not be understood by the jury. Profanity should not be used in the courtroom unless the witness is repeating a direct quote. If such is the case, the officer should not hesitate in repeating the exact words used during the investigation.

Occasionally a yes or no answer may be demanded of a witness, particularly on cross-examination. Sometimes such an answer is not an appropriate response to the question. If this occasion arises, the witness should not be pressured into an inaccurate response for the sake of brevity. The witness is always permitted to qualify answers and should persist in this right, if necessary asking the judge for permission to qualify the answer. But if the question can be accurately answered with a simple yes or no, the witness should respond accordingly.

Cross-Examination

The purpose of cross-examination is to ensure that testimony given under direct examination has been accurate and truthful. Through cross-examination the attorney attempts to impeach witnesses called by the opposing side. **Impeachment** is the process of discrediting or contradicting the testimony of the witness to show that the witness is unworthy of belief. It is designed to weaken or destroy the effect of the testimony presented under direct examination and thus to destroy the credibility of the witness in the eyes of the jury. Cross-examination tests the reliability of the witness by attempting to detect whether testimony was intentionally slanted or whether an error or misstatement was made.

The five basic methods for attacking the credibility of a witness are these:

1. Showing that the witness's previous statements, personal conduct, or conduct of the investigation is inconsistent with the witness's testimony in court;

2. Showing that the witness is biased or prejudiced for or against the state or the defendant because of a close relationship, personal interest in the outcome of the case, hostility toward the opposing party, or similar biases;

3. Attacking the character of the witness—revealing previous criminal convictions or other irrefutable characteristics that would render testimony unworthy of belief, such as documented evidence that the officer has lied in previous reports or testimony (refer to Box 22-2 on "Brady Officers");

4. Showing the witness's incapacity to observe, recollect, or recount owing to mental weakness, a physical defect, influence of drugs or alcohol, or the like;

5. Showing that the witness is in error, that the facts are otherwise than as testified.

Cross-examination tactics used by attorneys vary widely, but they fall into two basic categories. Browbeating or belligerent cross-examination is designed to put the witness under pressure to provoke an unprofessional reaction. The attorney may ask a series of questions rapidly in an attempt to confuse the witness and force inconsistent responses. The attorney may try to reverse the witness's words or may continually repeat the same questions in an attempt to elicit inconsistent or conflicting answers.

The cross-examiner who assumes a friendly, condescending role attempts to lull the witness into a false sense of security to bring about less caution in listening to and answering questions. Once the witness's guard is down, the cross-examiner often resorts to leading questions. Leading questions suggest the answer desired. Although leading questions are not permitted in direct examination, they are permitted in cross-examination.

Another danger that should be avoided in cross-examination involves questions regarding whether the officer has talked with anyone about the case. Law enforcement witnesses often have the impression that this kind of question is designed to attack their integrity by attempting to show that they discussed the details of the case with the press or others in an attempt to create prejudice toward the defendant. In fact, discussing the case with the prosecutor before the trial is perfectly permissible. If the officer answers no to the question and this later turns out to be false, his/her credibility suffers. Likewise, if the witness responds no to the question, "Did the prosecutor tell you how to testify?" the answer is only partly complete. Obviously, the prosecutor generally has instructed the witness to testify to firsthand knowledge of facts and to tell the truth. But the question is designed in such a manner as to imply that an affirmative response means the prosecutor told the witness exactly how to answer each question. The best way of handling this type of situation is to respond, "Yes, I talked with the prosecutor about the case. The prosecutor advised me to relate the facts about which I had first-hand knowledge."

Use of Notes and Reports on the Stand

It is permissible for witnesses to use notes and reports to help refresh their memory while testifying; the human mind can retain only so much information. The witness is not and cannot be expected to remember minute details such as dates and numbers that are of lesser importance than the major facts of the case. However, the witness should constantly be aware of the proper use of notes and reports and the ramifications of their use.

There are two reasons why a witness may refer to notes and reports. The first is a need to remember a particular fact in question. In this case, the officer does remember the case and is permitted to use the notes and reports to help recall minor details. This use of notes and reports is perfectly permissible.

However, if the officer's references to the notes and reports are necessitated by an inability to remember anything about the events preceding the trial, the consequences of referring to notes and reports are entirely different.

In the rules of evidence, using notes and reports simply to refresh the memory is referred to as *past recollection refreshed*. As indicated, this is permissible but should be used with restraint, because it may indicate a lack of pretrial preparation. When notes or reports are used by a law enforcement officer in direct examination, the defense attorney has an absolute right to examine those notes and reports and test the witness's memory before allowing the witness to continue testifying under direct examination. This is done to ensure that the witness is, in fact, testifying from memory.

In the event that the witness cannot remember the facts of the case but uses the notes or reports as the sole basis of testimony without any independent recall, the term applied is *past recollection recorded*. In this instance the oral testimony of the law enforcement officer becomes worthless, as the knowledge is entirely based on the notes or reports. Should this occur, the prosecutor most likely will, at the insistence of the defense attorney, dismiss the officer as a witness and introduce the notes or reports as evidence in the trial. If the notes are meaningless to everybody but the law enforcement officer who took them and the report contains inaccuracies, the entire substance of the knowledge will be excluded from evidence.

For the various reasons just described, it is highly recommended that officers use loose-leaf notebooks during their investigations. In this way, materials not relevant to the particular case at hand can be removed before the trial and only the notes that are pertinent will be brought into the courtroom. If this is not done, the defense attorney may question the officer on any irrelevant part of the contents of the notebook and perhaps, by embarrassment, decrease the officer's credibility with the jury.

Leaving the Witness Stand

How witnesses leave the witness stand is just as important as how they enter, because the eyes of the jury follow them. It is improper for the witness to rise and leave the witness stand on completion of cross-examination. The prosecutor may conduct a redirect examination, or the defense attorney may think of a last-minute question. During this time, the witness should be careful not to be caught off guard. A common tactic in cross-examination is to ask a last-minute question while the witness is preparing to leave the stand, in hopes of catching the witness in an error after the pressure of testifying seems over. The witness should wait to be excused by the judge and should leave the courtroom without smiling, speaking, or glaring at anyone.

| KEY TERMS

admissibility	burden of proof	direct examination
admission	challenge for cause	evidence
affirmation	confession	evidentiary privileges
Brady officers	corpus delicti	expert witness
burden of going forward	cross-examination	hearsay

impeachment	prima facia	subpoena
judicial notice	probable cause	surrebuttal
oath	proof	testimony
peremptory challenge	rebuttal	venire
plaintiff	re-cross-examination	weight (of evidence)
preponderance of evidence	redirect examination	

REVIEW QUESTIONS

1. During an ongoing criminal investigation, what factors must the criminal investigator consider in deciding whether to make an arrest and when to make it?

2. Why must a criminal investigator know the rules of evidence?

3. Define the following concepts:
   (a) evidence
   (b) proof
   (c) testimony
   (d) admissibility
   (e) relevancy
   (f) materiality
   (g) competency of evidence
   (h) competency of witnesses
   (i) weight

4. Distinguish between *burden of proof* and *burden of going forward with evidence.*

5. What is the purpose of judicial notice?

6. Describe the manner in which circumstantial evidence is used in a criminal prosecution.

7. Why does the opinion rule of evidence exist?

8. What is the hearsay rule, and why does it exist?

9. What is the philosophy under which exceptions to the hearsay rule have evolved?

10. For what proposition does the U.S. Supreme Court case of *Crawford* v. *Washington* stand?

11. Describe the philosophy underlying the existence of evidentiary privileges.

12. What is the role of the investigator as a witness?

13. What factors affect the credibility of the investigator as a witness?

14. What are the characteristics of a good witness?

15. How important are a witness's appearance and demeanor to credibility?

16. What is the function of cross-examination?

17. When and how may a witness use notes and reports on the witness stand?

INTERNET ACTIVITIES

1. Explore the crime scene investigator network at: http://www.crime-scene-investigator.net/index.html. Search for the article by Doris Wells on "Testifying in Court as a Forensic Expert." What tips does the author provide for testifying in court? How do these tips compare with the standards relating to other witnesses in court?

2. Visit the Innocence Project's Website at: http://www.innocenceproject.org. Select ONE case/person/profile of interest to you listed under "The Cases" tab. Feel free to do additional research on this case via the Internet (for example, read newspaper articles about the case, search out other articles that may be presented on the case). What were the contributing causes to the person being falsely convicted? In your opinion, what should be done for both the exonerated person and the original victim in the case? What role did "official misconduct" on either the part of the prosecutor or the police have in this case?

3. Search your state statutes for information on privileged communications. Legal research websites such as *www.megalaw.com* and *www.Findlaw.com* are good places to start. What types of communication are privileged in your state?

Design Element: (crime scene tape): ©UpperCut Images/Getty Images RF

A

A Child Is Missing (ACIM) This program, started in 1997, was created to assist law enforcement officers in locating missing children, as well as disabled and mentally challenged individuals, and elderly persons, such as those suffering from Alzheimers.

AAMVANET Maintained by the American Association of Motor Vehicle Administrators, this computerized network allows U.S. and Canadian agencies to share information about driver's licenses and motor vehicle matters.

accelerant In fire starting, any flammable fluid or compound that speeds the progress of a fire. Also called a *booster*.

account takeover A follow-on crime to identity theft. In this scenario, the possessor of your identity changes where your bill is being mailed to and quickly runs up charges before you are aware of the problem.

Accurint for Law Enforcement (ALE) A provider of information and information services that go beyond credit reports. Approximately 3,000 government entities use Accurint, which has access to 12 billion public records. It can quickly retrieve information about businesses and individuals, including current and former addresses, and links, such as to family members, neighbors, and associates. Among its capabilities is Person Alerts (PA); each time an individual who is a person of interest or fugitive appears in the database, the investigator is automatically notified.

action stereotyping Occurs when an officer expects an event to unfold in a particular way; it can result in the officer's failure to see the event the way it actually occurred.

active system A type of vehicle antitheft device which requires that the driver do something to activate and deactivate the system every time the vehicle is parked or driven.

administrative log A written record of the actions taken by the crime scene coordinator, including assignments and release of the scene.

admissibility A legal criterion used to determine whether an item of evidence can be presented in court; requires that the evidence have relevance, materiality, and competence.

admissions A person's acknowledgment of certain facts or circumstances that tend to incriminate him or her with respect to a crime but are not complete enough to constitute a confession.

advance-fee scheme These are operated in a bewildering variety of ways; goods, services, or a portion of a fortune are promised contingent upon the person being contacted paying an advanced or "up-front" fee. The essence of these is always (1) you pay before receiving anything, and (2) you never receive anything, unless it is a smaller amount designed to "hook" you into coming up with a really large advanced fee.

affidavit A sworn, written statement of the information known to an officer that serves as the basis for the issuance of an arrest warrant or a search warrant.

affinity fraud These include many different types of frauds perpetrated upon groups such as church members who know and trust each other, and have an affinity for one another. Often, a person of high status in the group, such as its pastor, president, or a member of the governing board will be recruited and will unknowingly help further the scheme by endorsing it.

affirmation The process in which a witness acknowledges that he or she understands and undertakes the obligation of an oath (i.e., to tell the truth with a realization of the penalties for perjury); a means of establishing a witness's competence.

agrichemicals Any of various chemical products used on farms; includes pesticides, fertilizers, and herbicides.

agroterroism The use of biological agents as weapons against the agricultural and food supply industries.

al-Awlaki, Anwar An extremist English-speaking Muslim cleric based out of Yemen, who had been linked to many Muslim extremists including Umar Farouk Abdulmutallab, and Major Nidal Hassan. Al-Awlaki was the first American citizen killed by U.S. military forces as an *enemy combatant* in the Iraqi War.

algor mortis The decrease in body temperature that occurs after death.

alligatoring The checking of charred wood, which gives it the appearance of alligator skin.

alternative light sources (ALSs) Separates out a specific wave length of light to examine a crime scene. When shined on a surface, the surface can absorb, reflect, or transmit light. In some situations, a surface that absorbs light may re-emit a different wave length, meaning it fluoresces. Also called a forensic light.

al-Zarqawi, Abu Musab A militant Islamist from Jordan who operated a large training camp for al-Qaeda in Afghanistan during the late 1990s. He was a loyal follower of Usama bin Laden, and after his death, al-Zarqawi formed the al-Tawhid wal-Jihad group and conducted several high-profile bombings and executions.

amateur burglar Burglars who operate on the basis of impulse or opportunity, with no planning. Often use sheer force to enter, ransacking the premises for anything of value. May become violent if detected and commit secondary crimes (e.g., murder, rape).

Amber Plan A voluntary partnership between law enforcement agencies and broadcasters to activate an urgent news bulletin in the most serious child abduction cases.

ambush A robbery that involves virtually no planning and depends almost entirely on the element of surprise.

American Society of Crime Laboratory Directors (ASCLD) An international society devoted to maintaining the highest standards of practice at crime laboratories; conducts an accreditation program for laboratories and education programs for lab personnel.

Americans with Disabilities Act (ADA) A federal law which establishes the workplace rights of those with perceived or actual disabilities.

amido black A dye that is sensitive to blood and thus is used in developing fingerprints contaminated with blood.

amphetamines Stimulants that increase blood pressure as well as heart, respiratory, and metabolic rates; produces decreased appetite, hyperalert senses, and a general state of stress that lasts a prolonged period.

anger-excitation rape-murder This crime is designed to inflict pain and terror on the victim for the gratification of the perpetrator. The prolonged torture of the victim energizes the killer's fantasies and temporarily satisfies a lust for domination and control.

anger-retaliatory rape-murder This type of planned murder involves overkill. It is an anger-venting act that expresses symbolic revenge on a female victim.

anthrax An acute infectious disease with three forms (cutaneous, intestinal, and inhalation), which differ in the means of their transmission, symptoms, and lethality; also, a biological agent.

anthropometry Developed by Alphonse Bertillon in the late 19th century, the study and comparison of body measurements as a means of criminal identification.

archaeological looting The illegal, unscientific removal of archaeological resources from public, tribal, or private land.

arrest The process of taking a person into legal custody to answer a criminal charge.

arrest warrant A judicial order commanding that a particular person be arrested and brought before a court to answer a criminal charge.

assignment sheets Written reports completed by persons assigned tasks at a crime scene that document what they have done and found.

associative evidence Bidirectional evidence that connects the perpetrator to the scene or victim, or connects the scene or victim to the perpetrator.

ATM attacks The seizure and removal of ATMs from their rightful location to another place where they can be broken into, or the attempted or successful act of breaking into them where they are located. Applicable state statutes vary, so such attacks may be charged as a larceny or a burglary depending on the location of the crime.

attack code A malicious software program intended to impair or destroy the functioning of a computer or a network resource.

auction fraud Involves the misrepresentation of a product advertised for sale through an Internet auction site or the non-delivery of products purchased through an Internet auction site.

autoerotic death Death from accidental asphyxiation as a result of masochistic activities of the deceased. Also called *sexual asphyxia*.

Automated Fingerprint Identification System (AFIS) A computerized system, maintained by the FBI, that stores and compares millions of fingerprints and is used to find matches for identification purposes.

autopsy The medical examination of a body to determine the time, and cause, of death; required in all cases of violent or suspicious death.

avionics The electronic equipment (e.g., radio, navigation) on an aircraft.

B

B3Ms *see smash and grab*

bait money Cash with sequential serial numbers that are recorded by a bank and inserted with the cash that is stolen by the bank robber.

bandit barrier This is the bullet-resistant glass often used by banks to separate the tellers from the customers. These devices are fairly common in conveniences stores, especially those that operate 24-hours a day and are in high-crime areas.

bank examiner con A tried-and-true trick to separate unwary people from their money. The scam usually unfolds this way: A con identifying themselves as a bank examiner or police officer approaches a person with a tale about how someone is embezzling money at the bank and help is needed to identify that person. The victim is asked to withdraw money from their account and then meet the bank examiner who gives them a "cashier's check" for the money withdrawn. The victim is told not to deposit the check for a week in order that the investigation not be compromised. This action is repeated with other victims during the week and then the cons disappear along with the money they collected, leaving the victims holding worthless "cashier" checks.

barbiturates Short-, intermediate-, and long-lasting depressants (e.g., secobarbital, amobarbital) that when stopped abruptly can cause convulsions and death; nicknamed after the capsule or pill color, or the manufacturer's name.

basic yellow 40 Used after superglue fuming, a dye that causes latent prints to fluoresce under alternative lighting.

battered-child syndrome The clinical term for the mental difficulties sustained by a physically abused child.

behavioral evidence analysis (BEA) A deductive and evidence-based method of criminal profiling.

be-on-the-lookout (BOLO) Part of the preliminary investigation, a notification broadcast to officers that contains detailed information on suspects and their vehicles.

Bertillon, Alphonse Recognized worldwide as the father of personal identification; he developed anthropometry.

Biggers-Brathwaite Factors Test A test that balances the reliability of eyewitness identification (as determined by five factors specified by the Supreme Court) with the corrupting effect of any suggestive procedures; enables a highly reliable identification to be used in court even if something jeopardized the fairness of the identification procedure.

biological agents Certain microorganisms and toxins produced by organisms (e.g., smallpox, anthrax, plague, botulism) that cause human illness or death and could be used as terrorist weapons; typically slower acting than chemical agents.

black market peso exchange (BMPE) A sophisticated method of money laundering which is typically operated to convert drug or other illicitly gained money into funds which appear to be from legitimate sources.

blast fragmentation Devices may be constructed with high or low explosives. They use a hard case container such as a metal pipe or other suitable enclosure or have fragmentation shrapnel added to or around the main charge explosive. These types of IEDs use the explosive to propel casualty-producing fragmentation and shrapnel throughout the scene.

bobbies A colloquial term used in reference to British police constables; derived by the public from the first name of Sir Robert Peel, whose efforts led to the creation of the first metropolitan police force in London.

body language Gestures, demeanor, facial expressions, and other nonverbal signals that convey, usually involuntarily, a person's attitudes, impressions, truthfulness, and so on.

bomber's signature This refers to an identifiable pattern or characteristic of using essentially the same or similar bomb construction components and construction fabrication and design techniques for multiple bombs.

bone rustlers Unauthorized fossil hunters, who loot public and private lands.

bore The diameter of a gun barrel's interior between its opposing high sides (the lands).

Bow Street Runners Established by Henry Fielding in 1748, a group of volunteer, nonuniformed home owners who helped catch thieves in London by rushing to crime scenes and beginning investigations, thus acting as the first modern detective force. By 1785, some were paid government detectives.

Brady officers Comes from *Brady v. Maryland*, 373 U.S. (1963), in which the Supreme Court held that the prosecution, including the police, cannot suppress or withhold any evidence that may be favorable to the accused. Such evidence is often called "exculpatory evidence" and includes any information concerning the credibility of the individual police officer. *Brady* has had a dramatic impact on the credibility of police officers as witnesses because the prosecution must reveal any possible impeachment evidence regarding its own witness, including an officer's internal affairs records. In addition, any documented report where the officer lied or was untruthful <u>must</u> be presented to the defense. Such officers simply cannot testify in court without being impeached; hence, their ability to work as a police officer is seriously compromised. These officers are often called "*Brady* officers" and are essentially barred from patrol and investigative functions where there is a strong possibility that the officers could make an arrest and be required to act as a witness.

Brady Violation *see Brady Officers*

brands On livestock, registered combinations of numbers, letters, marks, and shapes that establish unique identifications.

brothel A house or other structure which is used primarily for the business of prostitution.

Brown v. Mississippi The first notable case in which the U.S. Supreme Court intervened in the interrogation practices of local law enforcement officers. In 1936 the U.S. Supreme Court held that under no circumstances could a confession be considered freely and voluntarily given when it was obtained as a result of physical brutality and violence inflicted by a law enforcement officer.

buccal swab Sterile cotton swabs used to obtain saliva from the mouth of a suspect for DNA analysis.

bumping—key bumped or a bump key gun Lock picking techniques adopted by a growing number of burglars. Both methods require lower skill levels and can be effective against pin tumbler locks, which are commonly installed in many homes and businesses. Key bumping is a manual approach and the bump key gun is battery automated. Also see snap gun.

burden of going forward In a criminal trial, the responsibility of the defense to present enough evidence to create a reasonable doubt of guilt in the jurors' minds; an optional burden, as the defense is not required to present any evidence.

burden of proof In a criminal trial, the requirement that the prosecution establish the defendant's guilt beyond, and to the exclusion of, every reasonable doubt.

burglary The crime of breaking and entering a house or other building belonging to another with the intent to commit a crime therein.

burglary checklist A police-generated written list of investigative steps which begin with the arrival of the first officer at the scene through prosecution.

burglary tools Tools used in the commission of a burglary; often are ordinary household tools, but may be modified for increased effectiveness in breaking and entering.

burn indicators Any effects of heat or partial burning that indicate a fire's rate of development, points of origin, temperature, duration, and time of occurrence and the presence of flammable liquids.

C

cadaveric spasm The instantaneous tightening of an extremity or other part of the body at the time of death. Also called *death grip*.

caliber The diameter of a bullet; somewhat larger than the bore of the weapon from which the bullet is fired.

caliphate A geographic area controlled by a "caliph" or Muslin leader; a social and governmental form based on Muslim beliefs.

car, recreational vehicle, and trailer burglaries The act of breaking and entering such places to commit an unlawful act therein. These acts may, depending on the state and fact situation, be chargeable as a burglary or as a larceny. Their inclusion in the burglary chapter is predicated by the fact that regardless of what charge is actually made, the techniques used to gain entry and the investigation of these acts is kindred to burglaries generally.

cargo theft The theft of items from or in commercial motor vehicles.

carjacking The crime of taking a motor vehicle from the motorist or passenger, or from his or her immediate presence, by use of force, fear, or threat of force, with the intent to temporarily or permanently deprive the owner of its use.

catalytic combustion detector A portable device that oxidizes any combustible gases in a sample; used to detect residues of flammable-liquid accelerants at fire scenes. Also called *sniffer, combustible-gas indicator, explosimeter,* and *vapor detector.*

chain of custody The witnessed, unbroken, written chronological record of everyone who had an item of evidence, and when each person had it; also accounts for any changes in the evidence.

charging The act of formally asserting that a particular person is to be prosecuted for a crime.

charring The scorching of materials by fire; used to deduce the direction of fire spread by comparing relative depths of char throughout the scene.

check kiters People who open accounts at several banks and then knowingly write a bad check on their account at bank 1 and then cover it with a bad check written on their account at bank 2 and so on. Eventually the scheme falls apart because the sums keep getting larger and larger and cannot be maintained indefinitely.

chemical agents Rapidly acting substances (e.g., mustard gas, sarin, V agents) that produce a variety of incapacitating symptoms or death; as weapons, can cause mass casualties and devastation.

chemical explosions Explosions in which a high-pressure gas is produced by reactions that involve changes in the basic chemical nature of the fuel; commonly caused by the burning of hydrocarbon fuels (e.g., natural gas, gasoline, lubricating oils)

child pornography The sexually explicit visual depiction of a minor (as defined by statute); includes photographs, negatives, slides, magazines, movies, videotapes, and computerized images.

chop shop An illegal operation at which stolen cars are disassembled and their traceable parts altered or disposed of so that untraceable parts can be sold to repair shops, salvage yards, and indiscriminate buyers.

Christian Identity theology A right-wing philosophy expressing the superiority of the white Aryan race over the forces of Satan (people of color and Jews). Central to the CI belief is a distortion of the Bible supporting the creation of "pre-Adamites," or people of color, the sexual union of Eve and Satan in the Garden of Eden giving rise to the Jewish race, and the future physical battle of Armageddon between Aryan people and the forces of Satan (Jews and non-whites).

clandestine drug laboratories Illicit operations that produce a variety of illegal drugs for sale and distribution; due to the chemicals, processes used, and workers' inexperience, police and firefighters, as well as the public, can face severe danger on location.

class characteristics Characteristics of physical evidence that are common to a group of objects or persons.

cleared by arrest The classification assigned to an offense when the suspect has been arrested and there is sufficient evidence to file a formal charge.

cloning (1) The creation of a second legitimate vehicle by counterfeiting or duplicating identification numbers and ownership documents.

cloning (2) The illegal programming of cellular phones by overwriting their access codes with the codes of legitimate cellular customers; done through a personal computer or cloning "black box."

cocaine A natural stimulant extracted from the leaves of the coca plant; illegally sold as a white, translucent, crystalline powder, which is often adulterated.

codeine An opiate in tablet, liquid, and injectable forms that produces less analgesia, sedation, and respiratory depression than morphine.

CODIS *See* **Combined DNA Index System.**

coerced-compliant false confession This includes individuals who are induced to confess through the process of police interrogation as a result of certain specific concrete initiatives on the part of the police. This includes not being allowed to sleep, eat, make a phone call, go home, or in the case of drug addicts, feed a drug habit.

cognitive interview technique An interviewing approach in which a witness is asked to recall events and details in different ways as a means of fostering the witness's recollections.

cold case Assigning detectives to examine cases that went unsolved, which includes using new advanced technology that was unavailable before to analyze old evidence, and re-interviewing witnesses who were previously hostile. In some cases, the original detectives assigned the case were simply overworked and could not allocate enough time to properly work it.

Combined DNA Index System (CODIS) Developed by the FBI, a database of convicted-offender and known- and unknown-subject DNA profiles that is used to find matches and to link unsolved crimes in multiple jurisdictions.

commercial-vehicle theft The theft of vehicle tractor units and trailers.

competency (of a witness) A witness's qualification for testifying in court, which depends on circumstances that affect the person's legal ability to function as a sworn witness (e.g., age, mental state).

component swapping A fraudulent practice in which manufacturers (e.g., of computers) use parts from the lowest-cost supplier but do not inform consumers that the parts are nonstandard.

computer abuse Any intentional act involving knowledge of computer use or technology in which the perpetrator could have made a gain and the victim could have experienced a loss; includes acts that may not be covered by criminal laws.

computer crime Any illegal act in which knowledge of computer technology is used to commit the offense.

computer manipulation crime Any act that involves changing data or creating records in an electronic system for the purpose of facilitating another crime, typically fraud or embezzlement.

computer vandalism The unauthorized removal of valuable information from a computer system, thereby preventing the legitimate user or owner from having access to that information.

Computer Voice Stress Analyzer (CVSA) A method of lie detection originally developed in 1988 by the National Institute for Truth Verification (NITV). By 2004, some 1,400 agencies were using it instead of the polygraph. The CVSA notes microvariations in the audible and non-audible portions of speech to identify deception. The CVSA is presently the first significant challenge to the dominance of the polygraph in 85 years.

concentric fracture Multiple radial fractures in glass, shooting away from the point of impact, which occur when glass is penetrated by a violent force. Concentric fracture lines roughly circle the point of impact; each arc of the concentric circle is broken at right angles to two opposing radial fractures.

confabulation In hypnosis, the subject's fabrication of recollections to fill in gaps in his or her actual memory.

confession The acknowledgment by a person accused of a crime that he or she is guilty of that crime and committed every element of the offense; must exclude any reasonable doubt about the possibility of innocence.

confidential VIN A duplicate vehicle identification number stamped into a vehicle's frame or body in a place known only to the manufacturer and law enforcement specialists in vehicle identification and auto theft investigation.

consensual contact Mutually voluntary contacts that can be made by police at any time from wherever they can legally be made. There is no need for an articulable police purpose in a consensual contact. As an example, an officer approaches someone getting out of a just-parked car and says, "Hi, I'm Officer Gonzales. As you pulled to the curb I noticed your left rear tire is nearly flat. It still looks new. However, it may be ruined by further driving. So, you may want to get it fixed." In this consensual contact, the driver is free to depart without explanation at any time of his/her own choosing.

contact bullet wound This involves the weapon being placed right up against the skin. The entrance wound is often star-shaped with flaps directed outward.

contact burns Burns on the skin caused by contact with flames or hot solid objects (e.g., irons, cigarettes).

contaminated/visible prints Prints created when fingers contaminated with blood, face powder, or a similar material touch a clean surface.

corpus delicti evidence Evidence that substantiates elements whose commission or omission must be demonstrated to have occurred in order to prove a case.

crack or rock cocaine *See* rock cocaine.

cramming The intentional process of placing unauthorized, misleading, inaccurate or deceptive charges on the victims' telephone bills. While telephone companies may legally place such charges on your bill on behalf of other companies, it is also a method by which scams can also be run by those other companies.

credibility (of a witness) That quality of a witness that renders his or her testimony worthy of belief; established in terms of presence, consciousness, and attentiveness during interviews.

credit repair scam A type of advanced fee scam in which people with bad or poor credit are promised their records can be cleansed of negative entries. New credit cards may also be promised as part of the scam.

crime The commission of any act that is prohibited, or the omission of any act that is required by the penal code of an organized political state.

crime analysis The use of systematic analytical methods to acquire timely and pertinent information on crime patterns and trend correlations; subdivided into administrative, strategic, and tactical analysis.

crime laboratory A scientific organization that analyzes material collected from crime scenes and suspects to help determine whether a crime was committed and, if so, how, when, and by whom it was committed.

crime scene The location at which a crime was committed.

crime scene control The procedure of limiting and documenting access to the crime scene to ensure that physical evidence is not accidentally or deliberate altered or removed. The procedure begins with the arrival of the first officer at the scene and continues until the scene is released from police control.

crime scene entry log sheet A written chronological record of all persons who enter and leave the crime scene and the times they do so, along with their reason for entering.

crime scene reconstruction Involves analysis of complex crime scenes, integrates data from various sources, and uses a rigorous methodology to reach conclusions. The scientific method is at the heart of CSR.

crime scene release The end of crime scene processing and the return of the premises or area to the owner or another responsible person; determined by the scene coordinator.

crime scene search patterns Used to locate physical evidence at a crime scene; there are five patterns: spiral, strip/line, grid, zone/quadrant, and pie/wheel.

criminal enterprise homicide A murder committed for material gain.

criminalistics The application of scientific disciplines, such as geology, physics, chemistry, biology, and mathematics, to criminal investigation and the study of physical evidence.

crimogen (1) An individually known offender who is responsible for a large number of crimes; (2) one victim who reports a large number of crimes.

cross-contamination In a trial, the questioning of a witness who was initially called by the opposing party.

cross-examination In a trial, the questioning of a witness who was initially called by the opposing party.

cryptanalysis software Software used to intrusively access secured information by breaking down encryption.

crystal violet A dye used to develop latent prints on the adhesive side of almost any kind of tape.

crystallized methamphetamine A long-acting stimulant originally in pill or injectable form (*crystal meth, speed*) but now in a smokable, odorless version (*ice*); in solid form, resembles an ice chip but liquifies when lighted.

cyberstalking The crime of harassing or threatening victims by means of electronic technologies (e.g., through e-mail and Internet chat rooms or news groups).

cyberterrorism A premeditated, politically or ideologically motivated attack against information systems, networks, programs, and/or data; often includes the use of electronic tools to disrupt or shut down critical infrastructure components, such as energy, transportation, or other government operations.

D

dactylography The study and comparison of fingerprints as a means of criminal identification; first used systematically for that purpose in England in 1900, but a means of identification since the first century.

dark or deep web A vast uncharted part of the world wide web, not accessible through regular Internet browsing or search engines. Most of the information in the deep web is hidden and encrypted with a unique software application called *Tor*.

date-rape drugs Drugs that render a victim unconscious for the purpose of sexual abuse or rape by an offender; Rohypnol, GHB (gamma hydroxybutyrate) and MDMA-ecstasy (methlenedioxy-methamphetamine) are common date-rape drugs.

Daubert v. Merrell Dow Pharmaceuticals, Inc. A 1993 case in which the Supreme Court held that the admissibility of an expert's testimony or a scientific technique's results depends on a preliminary assessment, made by the trial judge, of the principles and methodology involved.

debt bondage Type of debt that occurs when a person provides a loan to another and then uses the person's labor or services to repay the debt.

decoys A police officer who is disguised to resemble the type of victims who are being targeted for robbery. This is especially true for street robberies.

deductive reasoning The thought process that moves from general premises to specific details—for example, a hypothesis about the crime is developed and then tested against the factual situation to arrive at a conclusion.

defense wounds Wounds suffered by victims while attempting to protect themselves from an assault; often inflicted by a knife or club.

delay-in-arraignment rule Based on a 1943 Supreme Court decision, the principle that the failure to take a prisoner before a committing magistrate without unnecessary delay will render his or her confession inadmissible even if it was freely obtained.

dental identification The identification of an individual on the basis of dental records (or, sometimes, "smiling" photographs); performed by a forensic dentist, who compares before-death records with after-death findings to see if there is a match.

dental stone The preferred material for casting tire, footwear, and foot impressions; stronger and faster setting than plaster of paris and provides more detailed impressions.

deoxyribonucleic acid (DNA) A nucleic acid consisting of the molecules that carry the body's genetic material and establish each person as separate and distinct.

depressants or sedatives Drugs that depress the central nervous system, reducing tension and inducing sleep; can cause, in chronic use, loss of balance, faulty judgment, quick temper, and in overdose, unconsciousness and death.

detection of deception The ability to read non-verbal behaviors with clarity and reliability in order to assess truthfulness or deception during the interviewing or interrogation process.

detention A temporary and limited interference with a person's freedom for investigative purposes. Also called *investigative detention, street stop,* and *field interrogation.*

DFO (diazafluren-9-one) A very effective chemical for developing latent prints on paper; produces red prints that may be visible to the naked eye and that fluoresce under most laser and alternative lighting.

digital forensic analysis The process of acquiring, preserving, analyzing, and presenting evidentiary electronic data relevant to an investigation or prosecution.

digital videography Digital video cameras used to document crime scenes. They are relatively inexpensive, they incorporate audio, their use can be quickly learned, the motion holds the attention of viewers, and they give prosecutors a much better sense of the scene than just still photographs can.

direct examination In a trial, the questioning of a witness by the party that calls the witness to testify.

disorganized burglaries Burglaries which often result in a crime scene that is left in a state of disarray. These offenders may smash windows to force entry into a premises, and ransack it while searching for goods, drugs, or cash. The disorganized burglar may dump out a jewelry box, often taking its entire contents. However, in many disorganized burglaries no items are stolen, suggesting the offender did not find an item of interest, had no way to sell large desirable items they found and left them behind, the motivation for the crime was not property based, they panicked, or their crime was interrupted and they fled.

disposition of incident reports The supervisory review of subordinates' incident reports to ensure they meet police department quality control standards.

document Anything on which a mark is made for the purpose of transmitting a message.

documented vessel A boat that is registered by the U.S. Coast Guard.

domestic terrorism The use or threatened use of violence against persons or property by a group (or an individual) whose operations are entirely within the victims' nation, without foreign direction, and are done to further political or social objectives.

double swab A method which is used before any attempts are made in the development of identifiable latent fingerprints (LFP). It maximizes the possibility of recovering useful biological evidence at a crime scene, such as DNA.

drones Have been used to plan burglaries. For example, drones can be used to take photographs of alarm systems, and other security measures, identify potential escape routes, and surveille the police while the burglaries are in progress or the perpetrators are fleeing the scene.

Drug Enforcement Administration (DEA) Created in 1973, this federal agency is responsible for enforcing laws on illicit drugs and fighting international drug traffic; also trains state and local police in investigative work regarding illegal drugs, surveillance, and use of informants.

dual safes Consist of two major protection categories, fire and burglary protection. Dual safes provide both fire and burglary protection at different levels of performance. Fire safes are used in some homes and many businesses. Homeowners buy them to protect birth certificates, marriage licenses, cash, titles to vehicles, insurance policies, investment reports, tax returns, and similarly important documents. A number of "safes" do provide 30 minutes or more of fire protection from specified temperatures. However, their burglary protection needs to be examined closely because it may be limited to resisting an attack by common hand tools for five minutes. Also see **Residential Security Container**.

due process Fairness.

due process clause The title of clauses appearing in both the Fifth and Fourteenth amendments to the Constitution of the United States.

dumpster diving Going through people's trash for the purpose of finding sufficient sensitive information to commit identity theft.

dye packs Widely used by banks to prevent stolen money from being used. Dye packs explode thereby staining both the robber and the cash, preventing the use of the money and aiding in the detection of the robber.

E

EDTA A preservative used to prevent coagulation.

effective fire temperatures In structural fires, identifiable temperatures which reflect physical effects that can be defined by specific temperature ranges.

El Paso Intelligence Center - EPIC A regional intelligence center which collects and disseminates information about aliens, drugs, weapons smuggling, and other activities committed by criminal suspects.

embezzlement The misappropriation or misapplication of money or property entrusted to one's care, custody, or control.

emotional approach An interrogation technique in which the interrogator appeals to the suspect's sense of honor, morals, family pride, religion, and so on; works better with women and first-time offenders.

encryption A means of data security in which the data are scrambled into nonsense for storage or transmission and then unscrambled, as needed, by legitimate users.

Enderby cases Two rape-murder cases in England that involved the first use of DNA typing, in 1987, in a criminal case. DNA samples recovered from both victims led to the release of an innocent man and the subsequent arrest and conviction of the killer.

environmental crime Encompasses roughly 18 major federal environmental laws that form the basis for four Environmental Protection Agency (EPA) programs. This includes chemical safety and site security, clean air and water or pollution, toxic substance control, emergency planning, and environmental cleanup.

e-selling The selling of stolen goods by burglars through private websites such as Craigslist or through online sites such as eBay. This gives thieves access to buyers they would not otherwise reach. Alternatively, some fences will buy stolen goods from offenders and dispose of at least some of them by e-selling.

estate locators and research specialists These cons approach people by mail, purporting to be looking for heirs to a substantial fortune. In order to determine their eligibility, victims are asked to pay an "estate assessment fee" up-front, another variation on an advanced-fee scheme. This scam may also be operated as part of an identity theft operation.

evidence Anything that tends logically to prove or disprove a fact at issue in a judicial case or controversy.

evidence recovery log A chronological record of each item of evidence, listing who collected it, where and when it was collected, who witnessed the collection, and whether it was documented by photos or diagrams.

evidential intelligence Factual, precise information that can be presented in court.

evidentiary privileges Certain matters of communication that defendants and other witnesses can rightfully have barred from disclosure in court; classified as professional, political, social, and judicial.

exceptionally cleared The classification assigned to an offense when a factor external to the investigation results in no charge being filed against a known suspect (e.g., the death of the suspect).

exchangeable traces Particulates, lubricants, and spermicide added to condoms by manufacturers; can help identify particular brands and indicate condom use.

excusable homicide Someone who, to some degree, is at fault but the degree of fault is not enough to constitute a criminal homicide.

exigent circumstances An exception to the requirement that law enforcement officers have a search warrant; occurs when there is a compelling need for official action and there is no time to get a warrant.

expert witness A person who is called to testify in court because of his or her special skills or knowledge; permitted to interpret facts and give opinions about their significance to facilitate jurors' understanding of complex or technical matters.

exploits Software programs written to take advantage of security holes or "back doors" and thereby provide the user with illegal access to computer files.

explosion A physical reaction characterized by the presence of high-pressure gas, confinement of the pressure, rapid release of the pressure, and change or damage to the confining structure, container, or vessel as a result of the pressure release.

eyewitness identification The identification of someone or something involved in a crime by a witness who perceives the person or thing through one or more senses.

F

facial identification systems Manual kits or computer programs for preparing a likeness of a suspect; creates a composite from individual facial features.

facial recognition software Any of various computer programs that compare video images of persons' faces (taken by cameras at arenas, airports, hotels, and so on) with mug shots of known offenders for the purpose of identifying and apprehending wanted persons.

false-theft scheme An insurance fraud in which the owner of a vehicle reports it stolen but has actually hidden or disposed of it.

false-vehicle scheme An insurance fraud in which a person insures a vehicle that: does not exist; has already been salvaged; or belongs to someone else and later reports the vehicle stolen.

farm equipment Motorized equipment used on farms and on lawns; usually does not require a title or registration. Also called *off-road equipment*.

FBI Child Abduction and Serial Murder Investigative Center (CAS-MIRC) Provides investigative support through coordination and providing federal resources, training and application of multidisciplinary expertise, and to assist federal, state, and local authorities in matters involving child abductions, mysterious disappearances of children, child homicide, and serial murders across the country.

FBI Crime Laboratory A comprehensive forensic laboratory that conducts a broad range of scientific analyses of evidence and provides experts to testify in relation to analysis results; offers its services without charge to state and local law enforcement agencies.

federal safety standards certification sticker The sticker certifying a vehicle's safety, including its VIN; usually located on the driver's door or doorpost.

felonious assaults An assault committed for the purpose of inflicting severe bodily harm or death; usually involves use of a deadly weapon.

felonious homicides Killings that are treated and punished as crimes; includes murder and manslaughter.

felony A serious violation of the criminal code; punishable by imprisonment for one or more years or by death.

fences/receivers Individuals & businesses which knowingly buy, sell, or dispose of stolen merchandise, vehicles, financial instruments, and other things of value.

fentanyl A powerful synthetic opioid, 30 times more powerful than heroin, and 100 times more potent than morphine; when mixed with heroin, the drug combination becomes a highly potent and lethal injection attributing to numerous overdoses throughout the U.S.

field interview/information report A form on which a patrolling officer notes details about a person or vehicle that seems suspicious but is not connected with any particular offense.

field notes The shorthand written record made by a police officer from the time he or she arrives at a crime scene until the assignment is completed.

Fielding, Henry Chief Magistrate of Bow Street in London beginning in 1748. In 1750, he formed a group of volunteer, non-uniformed homeowners, who hurried to the scene of crimes to investigate them. These "Bow Street Runners" were the first modern detective unit. In 1752, he created *The Covent Garden Journal,* which circulated the descriptions of wanted persons.

Fielding, John The brother of Henry Fielding. Following Henry's death in 1754, John carried on his work for 25 years, making Bow Street a clearing house for crime information.

Financial Crimes Enforcement Network (FinCen) Part of the Department of the Treasury, an agency responsible for investigating major financial crimes (e.g., money laundering); provides assistance to law enforcement agencies.

fingerprint classification A system used to categorize fingerprints on the basis of their ridge characteristics.

fingerprint patterns Patterns formed by the ridge detail of fingerprints; primarily loops, whorls, and arches.

fingerprints Replicas of the friction ridges (on palms, fingers, toes, and soles of the feet) that touched the surfaces on which the prints are found.

flame ionization detector A device that produces ionized molecules in proportion to the amount of combustible organic gases in a sample; used to detect residues of accelerants at fire scenes.

fluorescent powders Powders, dusted on areas being examined, that chemically enhance latent prints viewed under UV, laser, or alternative light illumination.

follow-up investigation The process of gathering information after the generation of the incident report and until the case is ready for prosecution; undertaken for cases receiving a supervisory disposition for further investigation.

foot and mouth disease A disease which causes painful blisters on the tongues, hooves, and teats of cloven-hoofed animals, rendering them unable to walk, give milk, eat or drink.

footwear impressions Impressions that result when footwear, feet, or tires tread on a moldable surface such as earth, clay, or snow.

footwear prints Prints that result when footwear, feet, or tires contaminated with foreign matter such as mud, grease, or blood are placed on a smooth, firm surface (e.g., a floor, a chair, paper). Also called *residue prints.*

forensic entomology The study of insects associated with a dead body in order to determine the elapsed time since death.

forensic odontology A specialty that relates dental evidence to investigation.

forensic palynology The study of pollen and spores. It is not often used because it is labor intensive and requires considerable expertise and experience.

forensic pathology The study, by physicians, of how and why people die; can also include examination of the living to determine physical or sexual abuse.

forensic photograph analysis The comparison of photos from a security surveillance camera with file pictures of suspects to identify a perpetrator or acquire information about him or her.

forensic science The examination, evaluation, and explanation of physical evidence in terms of law.

fracture match The alignment of the edges of two items of evidence, thereby showing that both items were previously joined together.

franchise fraud Scam in which people are conned into believing they are purchasing a legitimate franchise, such as a copy shop, convenience store, fast food restaurant, or other business.

free inspection fraud Most often, this type of fraud is associated with home repair or improvement scams, although it is also operated using automobiles. A person appears at your home promising a free inspection of your heating and cooling system, gutters, chimney, roof shingles, or your entire home. Serious defects are found and scare tactics are used to maneuver victims into correcting the situation "right away." Any actual damage is caused by the inspector, who may ask for an advance fee to buy materials or who offers a great deal because they have "just finished a job nearby and have some materials left over." Any work actually done is shoddy, uses inferior materials, and does not meet local building codes.

free-and-voluntary rule Based on a number of Supreme Court decisions since 1936, the principle that the exertion of any kind of coercion, physical or psychological, on a suspect to obtain a confession will render the confession inadmissible.

freehand forgery Written in the forger's normal handwriting, with no attempt to mimic the style of the genuine signature.

freezer crimes Thefts of livestock (usually only one or a few animals) in which the motivation is food rather than profit.

Frye v. United States A 1923 federal case which established that the results of a scientific technique would be admissible only if the technique had gained general acceptance in its field. (Per *Daubert,* this was superceded by the federal rules of evidence.)

furrows The low areas between ridges in fingerprints. They are a sort of miniature valley.

fusion centers Formed after 9/11 to pool resources and information from various governing agencies. FCs are staffed by multiple federal, state, tribal, and local agencies and private-sector entities. In 2015, 78 FCs were operational. Fusion is defined as turning information and intelligence into actionable knowledge. It is the fundamental process by which homeland security and crime-related information and intelligence are shared.

G

Galton, Francis Galton published, in 1892, the first definitive book on dactylography, *Finger Prints,* which presented statistical proof of their uniqueness and many principles of identification by fingerprints. Charles Darwin's cousin.

gamma hydroxybutyrate (GHB) A central nervous system depressant used to perpetrate sexual attacks; mixed into a victim's food or drink, can induce relaxation or unconsciousness, leaving the victim unaware of the attack; can also cause seizures or death.

gas liquid chromatograph (GLC) A portable device that separates a sample gas into measurable components; used to detect residues of accelerants at fire scenes.

geographic profiling An investigative strategy in which the locations of a series of crimes (or, sometimes, the scenes of a single crime) are used to determine the most probable area of the offender's residence.

Girard, Stephen Bequeathed $33,190 to Philadelphia to develop a competent police force. In 1833, the city passed an ordinance creating America's first paid daytime police department.

glanders A disease caused by bacteria which primarily affects dogs, mules, and monkeys but is also seen in animals like goats, and cats.

Goddard, Calvin A U.S. World War I veteran and physician, he is widely considered to be most responsible for raising firearms identification to a science and for perfecting the bullet-comparison microscope.

Goddard, Henry One of the last Bow Street Runners, who in 1835 made the first successful identification of a murderer by studying a bullet recovered from a murder victim. In the case, a bullet mold with a noticeable defect was found at the suspect's home; this defect corresponded to a defect found on the recovered bullet.

grand larceny A felonious theft that is generally classified based upon the dollar value of a specific item. The dollar amount necessary to constitute a grand larceny varies from state to state.

gray hatters Computer hackers with exceptional skills, who when they find vulnerability in a system, rather than exploit it or sell it to others for financial gain, attempt to fix it for a fee.

gray-market vehicles Vehicles purchased abroad and shipped to the United States; may require modifications to meet U.S. emission control and safety standards.

grooves In a firearm's rifled bore, the low cuts that separate the higher lands.

Gross, Hans Austrian prosecutor who wrote the first major book on the application of science to investigation in 1893.

group cause homicide Involves two or more people with a common ideology, who sanction an act committed by one or more of the group's members that results in another person's death.

guides Residents who are familiar with a poaching area and will provide their services to non-residents in exchange for money.

H

hacker's dictionary A software program that provides unauthorized access to computer systems by generating millions of alphanumeric combinations until it finds one that matches a password.

hacking or cracking The process of gaining unauthorized entry into a computer system.

hallucinogenic drugs Natural or synthetic drugs that distort perception of objective reality and, in large doses, cause hallucinations; can lead to unpredictable effects based on user and environment.

hard and soft frauds Hard fraud is when a person fakes an injury, loss, accident, theft, arson, or other loss to illegally collect from an insurance company. Soft frauds are when people tell "little white lies" to increase the amount of an actual loss for which they will be compensated by their insurer.

hash values Are forensic evidence which acts as the electronic fingerprints of the hard drive used during analysis (also called the bench drive). A hash value is a numeric value that ensures data integrity by use of a fixed length that uniquely identifies data on a specific drive.

hashish A natural hallucinogen, derived from resinous secretions of the cannabis plant, that is more potent than marijuana; sold in soft lumps and usually smoked in a small hash pipe.

hashish oil An extremely potent hallucinogen, derived by distilling THC from marijuana, that produces a high from a single drop; smoked in a cigarette or glass-bowled pipe, or ingested in food or wine.

hate crime Are harms inflicted on a victim by an offender whose motivation derives primarily from hatred directed at a perceived characteristic of the victim (e.g., the person's race, religion, ethnicity, gender, and/or sexual orientation).

hawking A strategy by which offenders sell stolen items directly to "consumers," sometimes to people they have just met in a bar or other setting. The advantage to the burglar is they cut out the fence and therefore make a larger profit.

hazardous wastes May be solids, liquids, sludges, or by-products of manufacturing process. They may also be commercial products such as battery acid and household cleaning supplies.

hearsay Testimony by a witness that repeats something which he or she heard someone say out of court and which the witness has no personal factual knowledge of; inadmissible in court.

heavy equipment Heavy construction equipment; usually does not require a title or registration. Also called *off-road equipment*.

Hemident A reagent used in preliminary or presumptive field tests to check for the presence of blood.

Henry system Devised by Edward Henry, the fingerprint classification system that facilitated the use of fingerprints in criminal identification; adopted in England in 1900 and today used in almost every country.

hepatitis B (HBV) and hepatitis C (HCV) Viruses present in blood (and, for HBV, other bodily fluids) that attack the liver and can lead to death; a health hazard at scenes where bodily fluids are exposed.

heroin (diacetylmorphine) An opiate that is much stronger than morphine and often causes death due to its purity or diluents; an odorless, crystalline white powder, which is usually sold diluted and is injected.

Hizbollah (Hezbollah) "The Party of God (Allah)"; the largest Shi'a terrorist group in the world, led by Hassan Nasrallah and headquartered in Lebanon.

home-invasion robbery (HIR) A crime in which one or more offenders deliberately enter a home to commit robbery; characterized by gangs who target individuals rather than residences and use violence to terrify and control their victims.

homicide The killing of a human being by another human being; can be felonious or nonfelonious.

hot prowl A burglary taking place with people on the premises. They can be intended by the burglar or unintended. One example of unintended is when, unknown to the burglar, a child may be sick and staying at home instead of going to school. In other burglaries, the breaking and entering may only be a prelude to the primary crime they came to commit: e.g., sexual assault or murder of a competitor or a witness.

hot spot A location where various crimes are committed on a regular basis, usually by different offenders. Also called a *hot dot*.

hull identification number (HIN) Identification number assigned to boats.

human immunodeficiency virus (HIV) The blood-borne pathogen, also present in other bodily fluids, that can progress into AIDS, which reduces the body's defenses against diseases and leaves victims vulnerable to infections from which they die; a health hazard at scenes where bodily fluids are exposed.

hypercompliance In hypnosis, the situation in which the desire to please the hypnotist or others leads the subject to provide information that does not reflect his or her actual memories.

hypersuggestibility In hypnosis, the subject's heightened degree of suggestibility, which creates the possibility of the hypnotist's influencing the subject, intentionally or inadvertently, to give false information.

hypnosis A state of heightened awareness in which subconscious memories may surface that can be of help to an investigation.

I

identity theft The assumption of another person's identity for use in fraudulent transactions that result in a loss to the victim; accomplished by acquiring personal information about the victim (e.g., date of birth, address, credit card numbers).

illegal dumping The unauthorized disposal of hazardous waste material that can generally do considerable damage to the environment.

immersion burns Burns on the skin that occur when part or all of the body falls into, or is placed into, a tub or other container of hot liquid.

improvised explosive device This is a combination of items or components that are neither designed nor produced to be used in conjunction with each other, but when placed together or assembled, constitute a mechanism that has the capability of exploding and causing personal injuries and property damage.

impeachment In a trial, the process of discrediting or contradicting the testimony of a witness to show that he or she is unworthy of belief.

incendiary mechanism A fire-starting mechanism that consists of an ignition device, possibly a timing device, one or more plants to accelerate the flame, and, often, trailers to spread the fire; can be mechanical or chemical.

incest Broadly, any sexual abuse of a minor by an adult who is perceived by the minor to be a family member; also, under some statutes, sexual activity between closely related adults.

incident/Offense reports The first written investigative record of a crime. The uniformed officer assigned to the call conducts a preliminary investigation, which is the basis for preparing the incident/offense report. It is written in such a manner that someone reading that report can understand what happened.

incised and stab wounds Wounds inflicted with a sharpedged instrument such as a knife or razor; typically narrow at the ends and gaping at the center, with considerable bleeding. Also called *cutting wounds.*

in-custody interrogation The legal condition under which the *Miranda* warnings are required, although case decisions vary on the definitions of "custody" and "interrogation."

indicative intelligence Information pertaining to emerging and new criminal developments; may include fragmentary or unsubstantiated information, as well as hard facts.

individual characteristics Characteristics of physical evidence that can be identified as coming from a particular person or source.

inductive reasoning The thought process that moves from specific details to a general view; e.g., the facts of a case are used to arrive at a logical explanation of the crime.

infant abduction The taking of a child less than one year of age by a nonfamily member; classified by the FBI as kidnapping, although the motive is usually to possess the child rather than to use the child as a means for something else (e.g., money, sex, revenge).

inflated-theft-loss scheme An insurance fraud in which the owner of a stolen vehicle reports a greater financial loss—based on alleged current value, damage, or stolen parts—than is the case.

infrared spectrophotometer A device that identifies samples by recording the amount of infrared light that passes through them; used to detect residues of flammable-liquid accelerants at fire scenes.

The Innocence Lost Initiative A collaboration of federal, state, and local law enforcement authorities as well as victim assistance providers that focus on combating the prostitution of children.

Instant Street View Google's Instant Street View is used for surveillance by a burglar to identify a potential target, such as a home. When a target is picked out, surveillance can be used to identify the potential victim's living patterns and other information, such as the presence of alarms.

intangible property Items with value such as stocks, bonds, checking and savings accounts and other types of financial instruments as well as patent and copyrights.

Integrated Automated Fingerprint Identification System (IAFIS) Maintained by the FBI, a national online fingerprint and criminal-history database with identification and response capabilities; may be accessed by local law enforcement agencies.

intelligence/analytical cycle A five-part process designed to produce usable information for the client.

international terrorism The use or threatened use of violence against persons or property by a group (or an individual) whose operations transcend national boundaries and are done to further political or social objectives.

interpersonal burglaries Burglaries which are deliberately committed when some particular person is present. The target of the crime is not property, but the victim. This act implies that the actual purpose of the burglary is to instill fear in the victim and to display the offender's power over them.

interrogation A conversation between an investigator and a suspect that is designed to match acquired information to the suspect and secure a confession.

interrogatory questions Who? What? Where? When? How? And Why?

interviewing The process of obtaining information from people who have knowledge that might be helpful in a criminal investigation.

investigative plan Method that shows which lines of inquiry will be pursued and any special resources which will be needed—for instance, the assistance of a surveillance unit. As the investigation progresses, many factors may cause IPs to be revised, such as a newly identified witness who names a suspect or can describe where unrecovered physical evidence—for example, a handgun—is located.

investigative psychology A criminal-profiling approach based on interpersonal coherence, significance of time and place, criminal characteristics, and the offender's criminal career and forensic awareness.

investigator An official who gathers, documents, and evaluates evidence and information in the investigation of a crime.

iodine A dye used in developing latent prints on porous (particularly paper) and nonporous surfaces; one of the oldest and most proven means of locating prints.

Islamic State (IS) or Islamic State in Iraq and Syria (ISIS) A radical Islamic terrorist group which has become an international threat, justifying its existence, extensive use of violence, savagery, and rage through misinterpretation of Islamic scripture and prophesies.

J

jacklighting A technique used by law enforcement officers that involves nighttime aircraft patrols to pinpoint places where it appears artificial light is being used by poachers to take game.

Jacob Wetterling Crimes against Children and Sexually Violent Offender Registration Act A 1994 federal act requiring that states create and maintain registries of sex offenders. See also **Megan's law.**

jail booking report A document containing complete personal information about a suspect, including a photograph, fingerprints, and a list of the suspect's personal property at the time of booking.

Johns The male customers who pay for the services of a prostitute.

joyriding The theft and use of a motor vehicle solely to drive it, after which it is abandoned; usually committed by teenagers.

judicial notice An evidentiary shortcut whereby the necessity of formally proving the truth of a particular matter is eliminated when that truth is not in dispute.

justifiable homicide The necessary killing of a person in the performance of a legal duty or the exercise of a legal right when the slayer is not at fault.

K

ketamine A synthetic hallucinogen that produces hallucinations, excitement, and delirium of less intensity and shorter duration than the effects of PCP and LSD; sold as liquids, tablets, or white powder, and injected, smoked, or ingested in a drink.

key bumping *see bumping*

kinesics The relationship between body language (limb movements, facial expressions, and so on) and the communication of feelings and attitudes.

Kirk, Paul A biochemist, educator, and criminalist; wrote *Criminal Investigation* in 1953; helped to develop the careers of many criminalists.

known samples (1) Standard or reference samples from known or verifiable sources; (2) control or blank samples from known sources believed to be uncontaminated by the crime; (3) elimination samples from sources who had lawful access to the crime scene.

L

lacerations Wounds inflicted by blunt objects such as clubs, pipes, and pistols; typically open and irregularly shaped, bruised around the edges, and bleeding freely.

lands The high sides in a firearm's rifled bore.

laser illumination A method of developing latent prints in which lasers are used to illuminate a crime scene, causing otherwise-undetectable fingerprints to fluoresce when viewed through a special lens.

latent/invisible prints Fingerprints created when friction ridges deposit body perspiration and oil on surfaces they touch; typically invisible to the naked eye.

Lattes, Leone Made a key discovery in forensic serology in 1915, which permits blood typing from a dried blood stain.

Law Enforcement Intelligence Unit (LEIU) Formed in 1956 by 29 local and state law enforcement agencies to exchange information about organized crime which was not available through normal police channels.

Law Enforcement Online (LEO) Maintained by the FBI, an intranet system through which enforcement officers can communicate, obtain critical information, and participate in educational programs and focused dialogs.

layer-checking technique In arson investigation, the process of examining the strata of debris, working through to the floor; may indicate the sequence of burning.

left-wing terrorists Terrorists who usually profess a revolutionary socialist doctrine and view themselves as protecting the people against capitalism and imperialism.

LEO *See* **Law Enforcement Online.**

letter of transmittal In the context of criminal investigation, it is the letter which accompanies physical evidence to the crime laboratory; its elements include the identity and locator information of the submitting individual, the case facts, examinations requested, and other related information.

lifted-prints log A written record of lifted-prints evidence that contains the same type of information as that listed in the evidence recovery log.

lifters Various materials and devices used to "lift" evidence, especially fingerprints and footwear prints, from a surface and preserve it; include flap, electrostatic, rubber-gelatin, and clear-tape lifters.

ligature strangulation Pressure on the neck applied by a constricting band that is tightened by a force other than body weight; causes death by occluding the blood vessels that supply oxygen to the brain.

lineup A procedure in which a number of similar-looking persons, including the suspect, are shown simultaneously or sequentially to a witness who may be able to identify one of them as the perpetrator; can also be conducted with photos.

link analysis The process of charting or depicting temporal and other data gathered during a criminal investigation to uncover and help interpret relationships and patterns in the data.

link/association diagram A drawing, which represents the relationships between individuals involved in illegal activity.

live lineup A process in which a series of "real people" are shown to an eyewitness to establish whether they can pick out the suspect.

livestock Farm and ranch animals raised for profit.

livestock identification The establishment of a particular animal as the property of a specific owner.

livor mortis Soon after death, a purplish color that appears under the skin on the portions of the body that are closest to the ground; caused by settling of the blood.

Locard, Edmond Researcher interested in microscopic evidence; all crime sense today comes under the presumption of Locard's Principle—that there is something to be found.

Locard's exchange principle The fundamental assumption on which crime scene searches are conducted, which can be simplified to: There is something to be found.

logic bomb A computer program that uses illegitimate instructions or misuses legitimate instructions to damage data structures; operates at a specific time, periodically, or according to other instructions.

loiding The act of using a credit card or a similar plastic item to slip open or shim a spring-bolt lock that does not have an anti-shim device.

lookout Accomplices of a robber who watch for police and may provide armed backup for the offender.

lysergic acid diethylamide (LSD) A semisynthetic hallucinogen that produces mental changes lasting up to 12 hours; taken as drops on a sugar lump or blotted paper, was popular in the 1960s and is now making a comeback among juveniles.

M

macroscopic scene The "large view" of a crime scene, including things such as locations, the victim's body, cars, and buildings.

Mandatory Restitution Act Provides for the monetary re-payment of victims by the defendant in an amount commensurate with the servitude into which they were forced.

The Mann Act Also known as the White Slave Traffic Act, prohibits the transportation of individuals across state lines for purposes of engaging in prostitution or other criminal sexual activity.

manslaughter A criminal homicide that is committed under circumstances not severe enough to constitute murder but that cannot be classified as justifiable or excusable.

marijuana A natural hallucinogen, derived from certain hemp plants, that produces a dreamy, carefree state and an alteration of sensory perceptions; in the form of crushed dried leaves and flowers, it is smoked or eaten in food.

marine theft The theft of boats, boat trailers, outboard motors, jet skis, and all equipment associated with boating or water activities.

mass murder Consists of intentionally killing a group of people at one time (four or more), frequently in a public place.

McNabb v. United States 1943 U.S. Supreme Court case that held that a failure to comply with procedural requirements regarding the unnecessary delay in taking someone before a magistrate would render a confession inadmissible, regardless of whether or not it was obtained freely or voluntarily.

mechanical explosions Explosions in which a high-pressure gas is produced by purely physical reactions; commonly caused by steam (e.g., the bursting of a steam boiler).

medico-legal examination Brings medical skill to bear on injury and death investigations.

Megan's law An amendment to the Jacob Wetterling act, legislation requiring that states disclose information about registered sex offenders to the public.

meperidine (Demerol) A synthetic narcotic that in illicit use is usually injected but can be taken orally; the first synthetic opiate.

mescaline A natural hallucinogen, derived from the peyote cactus, that produces hallucinations for up to 12 hours; ground into a powder and taken orally.

meth labs Illegal laboratories that manufacture methamphetamine; range from industrial-size organizations to oneperson tweeker labs, with prevalence skyrocketing due to the availability of "recipes" and chemicals via the Internet.

methadone A synthetic narcotic used to maintain a heroin addict at a stable level of opiate use during and after withdrawal from heroin; administered orally, thus reducing dangers from injection.

methaqualone A strong depressant that can cause poisoning and convulsive comas; removed from the legal U.S. market; street versions are usually counterfeit.

methcathinone A psychomotor stimulant chemically similar to methamphetamine but more potent, often producing extreme paranoia; usually a white or off-white powder that is sold pure and snorted. Also called *cat* and *goob*.

methylenedioxy methamphetamine (MDMA) or ecstasy A hallucinogen that produces reduced inhibitions, euphoria, light hallucinations and can result in paranoia and psychosis; sold as a white powder, with usage increasing alarmingly.

Metropolitan Police Act (1829) An act of Parliament that created the London Metropolitan Police, the first centralized, professional police force in Britain, which soon became the international model of professional policing.

microscopic scene A crime scene viewed in terms of specific objects and pieces of evidence associated with the crime, such as knives, guns, hairs, fibers, and biological fluids.

minimal fact interview A preliminary or first interview with the victim of sexual assault, which is intended to be brief and non-intrusive, establishing basic facts of the assault and general elements of the crime.

Minnick v. Mississippi 1990 U.S. Supreme Court case that held that once counsel has been requested interrogation must cease; officials may not re-initiate interrogation without counsel being present, whether or not the accused has consulted with his or her attorney.

minutiae The characteristics of friction ridges on palms, fingers, toes, and soles of the feet.

Miranda v. Arizona The 1966 case in which the Supreme Court established that law enforcement officers must advise a person of his or her constitutional rights before beginning an in-custody interrogation.

mirror To match a person's words, actions, and mannerisms in order to eliminate communication barriers, foster trust, and create the flow of desired information.

misdemeanor A violation of the criminal code that is less serious than a felony; often punishable by imprisonment for no more than one year and/or a fine of no more than $500.

missing person frauds A particularly cruel type of advancedfee scam. Cons gather information on missing persons and then contact relatives explaining how they might be able to find the person for an up-front fee.

mitochondrial DNA (mtDNA) DNA found in the mitochondria of a cell; inherited only from the mother, it thus serves as an identity marker for maternal relatives.

mobile data terminal (MDT) An electronic system in a police car that provides features such as secure communication with 911, and among police units, direct access to national and local databases, and computer functions (e.g., e-mail, Internet access, computing, word processing).

mobile device Any small, computer device, typically small enough to be held in the hand such as media players, notebook computers, computer tablets, and "smartphones"—cell phones.

money laundering The process of making illegally obtained money seem legitimate by filtering it through a business and falsifying the business's accounts and invoices.

morgue A crime lab that determines cause of death; when the cause is questionable or is other than a known disease, conducts analyses that produce investigative information.

morphine An opiate in tablet, capsule, and liquid form (but usually injected) that produces euphoria, drowsiness, and relaxation; provides the medical standards by which other narcotics are evaluated.

Motor Vehicle Theft Law Enforcement Act (1984) Federal legislation requiring that manufacturers place permanent identification numbers on major parts of certain car lines.

mugging *See* **strong-armed robbery.**

Mulberry Street Morning Parade Instituted by Chief Detective Thomas Byrnes in New York City in the late 1800s, an innovative approach to criminal identification in which all new arrestees were marched each morning before detectives so that the detectives could make notes and later recognize the criminals.

multi-agency task forces The combined efforts of local, state, and federal law enforcement agencies to deal with a specific problem.

Munchausen syndrome by proxy (MSBP) A psychological disorder in which a parent or caretaker attempts to elicit medical attention for himself or herself by injuring or inducing illness in a child.

murder Defined in law as killing of any human being by another with malice of forethought.

N

narrative style In incident reports, the officer's written chronological account of events at the crime scene from the time he or she arrived until the assignment was completed.

NAIS see *U.S. Department of Agriculture's National Animal Identification System (NAIS)*

National Center for the Analysis of Violent Crime (NCAVC) Operated by the FBI, an organization that provides investigative and operational assistance to agencies dealing with violent crimes; consists of the BEA, CASMIRC, and VICAP.

National Counter-Improvised Explosives Device Capabilities Analysis Database – NCCAD Seeks ways in which to improve the capabilities, training, and equipment of those responsible for responding to IED threats. These improvements are aimed at: (1) the IED responders at the unit, local, state, regional, and national levels and (2) informing decision-makers on policy decisions, resource allocation, and crisis management.

National Drug Pointer Index Begun in 1997, promotes agent safety and prevents duplication of effort. Permitted system users can ensure that different agencies are not running investigations on the same subjects and operations.

National Incident-Based Reporting System (NIBRS) An FBI program for crime reporting that features a detailed report format documenting far more data than does a basic incident report; involves voluntary participation, but made mandatory by some states.

National Institute-Based Reporting System The FBI's *Uniform Crime Reporting System (UCR)* began in 1929 and its focus is on reporting the types and numbers of crimes.

National Integrated Ballistic Information Network Program (NIBIN) A joint program of the ATF and the FBI, a computerized database of crime gun information that stores images of ballistic evidence (projectiles and casings), against which new images are compared for identification.

National Law Enforcement Telecommunication System – NLETS Handles some 1.5 billion transactions daily for law enforcement and other criminal-justice agencies. In addition to providing secure channels for members' communication, NLETS also is a conduit for information and alerts flowing from the U.S. Department of Homeland Security (DHS).

National Motor Vehicle Title Information System (NMVTIS) Under development; a computerized database that will include complete histories of vehicles in all states and will prevent title laundering between states.

NCAVC *See* **National Center for the Analysis of Violent Crime.**

NCIC *See* **National Crime Information Center.**

neighborhood canvas A systematic approach to interviewing residents, merchants, and others who were in the immediate vicinity of a crime and may have useful information.

neuro-linguistic programming (NLP) An approach used in interviewing and interrogating that emphasizes establishing rapport, through mirroring, as a means of improving communication and thus obtaining useful information.

Next Generation Identification Program (NGI) Program started in 1999 by the FBI that produces the world's largest set of biometric data to supplement its fingerprint records. "Biometric" simply means measuring living things, in this case people. NGI released its first enhancement, Advanced Fingerprint Identification Technology (AFIT), in 2011, which provided faster, more accurate fingerprint handling than its aging predecessor AFIS.

NIBRS *See* **National Institute-Based Reporting System.**

night pickers Criminals who attack orchards and groves after dark, sometimes picking entire stocks of fruit and then selling them to local farmers markets.

ninhydrin A chemical used in developing latent prints on paper and cardboard; produces purplish prints, making it unsuitable for use with money.

NMVTIS *See* **National Motor Vehicle Title Information System.**

non-felonious homicides May be justifiable or excusable. Justifiable homicide is the necessary killing of another person in the performance of a legal duty or the exercise of a legal right when the slayer was not at fault.

nuclear DNA DNA found in the nucleus of a cell; inherited from both the mother and the father.

O

oath A formal attestation in which a witness swears to tell the truth on the basis of his or her belief in a supreme being and acknowledges a realization of the penalties for perjury; a means of establishing a witness's competence.

ocular changes Changes that occur in the eyes after death and can be valuable in determining the time of death.

odometer fraud The crime of rolling back a vehicle's odometer so that it shows a lower mileage than is the case, and obtaining or altering paperwork to support the fraud. Also called *odometer tampering, rollback,* and *clocking.*

off-road equipment Heavy construction equipment and farm equipment.

off-shore accounts Accounts in so-called safe-haven foreign banks, often operated by small island-nations which promise untraceable financial services.

one-year callable certificates of deposit Unscrupulous sellers tout these certificates of deposit (CDs) (which trumpet high rates of interest), but mislead or do not explain to investors about the actual terms of the investment.

opiates Drugs derived from the opium poppy (e.g., opium, morphine, heroin, codeine).

open source intelligence - OSINT Sources of information that are available to everyone. It is publicly available information that anyone can lawfully order, observe, or purchase.

opium An opiate in the form of blackish-brown, pungentsmelling beads of dried fluid, which are smoked; produces drowsiness and relaxation and is the source of morphine, heroin, and codeine.

opportunistic burglaries A burglary which occurs when offenders select a target and quickly strike because they perceived that some type of immediate opportunity exists. In almost all opportunistic burglaries the amount of force used to gain entry is not great. The offender "takes the easy path" and enters through a window or door which is unlocked or easily defeated. Often, the premises are an unoccupied residence.

organized burglaries Are burglaries characterized by being very professionally executed. They also show signs of premeditation to reduce the burglar's risks and increase his/her gains.

organized/disorganized offender patterns A criminalprofiling approach in which offenders are categorized as organized or disorganized on the basis of personal and crime scene characteristics. Mixed organized-disorganized crimes reflect aspects of both patterns.

organized retail theft Refers to the problem of significant losses to retailers caused by crews or rings of often mobile professional shoplifters.

Osborn, Albert In 1910, wrote *Questioned Documents,* still considered one of the definitive works on document examinations.

outfitters *See guides.*

overpayment fraud In this type of crime a seller advertises a high-value item such as a car or computer on the Internet. A scammer contacts the seller to purchase the item then sends the seller a counterfeit check or money order for an amount greater than the price of the item. The purchaser asks the seller to deposit the payment, deduct the actual sale price and then return the difference to the purchaser.

OxyContin A powerful narcotic consisting of oxycodone, a morphine-like drug, in a time-release formulation that, when crushed and snorted or injected, produces an intense heroinlike high; the latest drug of choice among addicts and teenage abusers.

P

packet sniffers Computer programs designed to monitor network communications and selectively record sensitive information (e.g., passwords, credit card numbers); used by hackers and, with a court order, by the FBI.

palo verde seedpod case A 1992 murder case in Phoenix, Arizona in which DNA analysis of plant evidence was used for the first time in criminal proceedings to help secure a conviction.

paper accident An automotive incident in which no actual auto accident has taken place. Collusion is required by a body shop owner who may even provide a wrecked car for the adjuster to inspect. By only filing the cost of repairs, which are not done, the amount paid by the insurance is not out of line and therefore not scrutinized closely.

"paper vehicle" A vehicle that does not exist but is insured on the basis of a counterfeit title or manufacturer's certificate of origin so that it can later be reported stolen.

paralanguage Characteristics of speech—such as volume, pitch, tone, and tempo—that communicate, often unconsciously, meanings and attitudes of the speaker that may not be evident in the words themselves.

parts marking The process, mandated by law, of attaching VIN labels to the major parts of vehicles in high-theft lines.

passive system (theft deterrent) A type of vehicle antitheft device which activates automatically but may require that the driver do something to deactivate the system.

patent prints Fingerprints which may immediately be wholly visible, or may be latent. Visible/residue patent prints form when blood, dirt, ink, paint, etc., is transferred from the surface of a finger or thumb to another surface. Patent prints can be left on many surfaces, including smooth or rough and porous (such as paper, cloth, or wood) or nonporous (such as metal, glass, or plastic). Patent prints become latent prints when the fingerprint is not formed by residue, but by the body's natural oils and sweat on the skin that are deposited onto another surface.

PDQ Paint Data Query A global automotive paint database, based on original manufacturer finishes. PDQ is used by 102 labs in 24 countries.

Peel, Robert *See* **bobbies.**

peremptory challenge The limited number of race and gender-neutral challenges each side has in a criminal case to excuse a juror for any other reason.

personal cause homicide Homicide motivated by a personal cause, which ensues from interpersonal aggression. The slayer and the victim(s) may not be known to each other.

personal protection equipment (PPE) Equipment and clothing designed to protect individuals at high-risk crime scenes from injury and infection.

perspective one of the 4 types of sketching and mapping which requires drawing the object of interest in three dimensions.

petit or petty larceny A misdemeanor theft in which cash or the dollar value of an item stolen falls below the specific amount necessary to constitute a felony. The dollar value is designated by state statute.

phencyclidine (PCP) A hallucinogen in powder (angel dust), tablet, liquid, leafy mixture, and rock-crystal forms that produces unpleasant effects and can cause extreme violence and strength; as a street drug, often adulterated and misrepresented, yet usage is increasing notably.

phenotyping provides a genomic-based, probabilistic estimation of the image of a person of interest.

phishing E-mails or letters soliciting personal and account information with which the collector can commit identity fraud or sell the information to someone who will commit that crime.

photo array lineup A procedure in which a series of usually six photographs, each in a separate folder, are shown sequentially to a witness to determine if he/she can identify the perpetrator of a crime.

photographic log A written record listing the photographs taken at a crime scene and detailing who took them, where and when they were taken, and under what conditions.

photographing The primary means of documenting a crime scene.

phreakers People who misuse telephone systems through a variety of fraudulent methods that make it seem as if long-distance service and airtime are being legitimately purchased.

physical stereotyping Occurs when an officer expects that the robber will fit a preconceived description; can result in the escape of a suspect or harm to the officer.

pigeon drop con Another old, but effective scam in which one con strikes up a conversation with someone on the street. Another con approaches them with a bag of money, which is from some illicit source, which he/she just found. After talking about what they could do with the money, one of the cons calls his/her boss, an "attorney" who meets them. The attorney says they will be able to keep the money after they do a reasonable search for the owner, but that "good faith money" must be put up. After the mark puts up his/her money, the cons disappear with it.

pimps Individuals who control, exploit, and benefit from the money earned by prostitutes who specifically work for them.

PIN *See* **product information number.**

Pinkerton, Allan Formed the Pinkertons in 1850 along with Edward Rucker; the only consistently competent detectives in the United States for over 50 years.

placement, layering, and integration The three main phases of laundering money from illicit sources so it can take on the appearance of legitimate income.

plaintiff In a civil case, the party that was allegedly wronged and that files the lawsuit.

planned operation A robbery that involves careful planning and no planned use of force; has less likelihood of apprehension and generates a large score.

plant In arson, the material placed around the ignition device to feed the flame.

plastic prints Finger impressions left in pliable, soft surfaces, such as wax, soap, wet paint, or fresh caulk, putty, and explosives. Those surfaces give the print the quality of being three dimensional.

poaching The illegal taking or possessing of game, fish, and other wildlife.

police sexual violence (PSV) An egregious form of sexual misconduct that involves sexual aggressiveness and violence, including rape and other sexual assault perpetrated by police officers.

"police spies" In early nineteenth-century England, a derogatory term used in reference to plainclothes detectives; coined by persons who feared that the use of such officers would reduce civil liberties.

polygraph A mechanical device that records physiological changes that occur in a person while he or she is being questioned, with deviations from normal readings indicating deception; can be used only with subject's voluntary consent. Also called a lie detector.

Ponzi/pyramid fraud Basically this involves recruiting people who are promised great returns on their money. The early investors are paid with the money from later investors. The scheme always collapses because the recruitment of investors cannot be sustained and the cons will ultimately steal the funds for their personal use.

Popay, Sergeant Dismissed from London's Metropolitan Police in 1833 for infiltrating a radical group and advocating the use of violence after he acquired a leadership position. Today, we would call Popay's call for violence entrapment.

positive match In DNA analysis, an identical match of a suspect's DNA with that found on evidence at the crime scene.

post-traumatic stress disorder (PTSD) A term that describes a mental health disorder caused, in part, by exposure to one or more traumatic events.

power-assertive rape-murder A series of acts in which the rape is planned but the murder is an unplanned response of increasing aggression to ensure control of the victim. The acts within the rape assault are characterized by forceful aggression and intimidation.

power-reassurance rape A planned single rape attack followed by an unplanned overkill of the victim. Motivated by an idealized seduction and consequent fantasy, the killer focuses on acting out a fantasy and seeks verbal reassurance of his sexual adequacy.

preferential child molester A person who molests children because he or she has a definite sexual preference for children.

preliminary investigation The process undertaken by the first officer (usually a patrol officer) to arrive at the scene of a crime; includes assessment, emergency care, scene control, a BOLO, scene determination, incident report, and, sometimes, evidence procedures.

preponderance of evidence The burden of proof in civil cases; requires only that the evidence presented by one side be seen by the jury as more believable than the evidence presented by the opposing side.

prima facia A term used to describe the apparent nature of something upon initial observation. In legal parlance, the term generally describes one of two things: First, the presentation of sufficient evidence to support the indictment or charge, (or claim in a civil case); simply that the case has enough merit to take the issue to a full trial. Second, a specific piece of evidence that directly supports a particular proposition or fact, such as probable cause to make an arrest, or a witness that places a suspect at the scene of the crime, is often referred to as prima facia evidence because it supports the original legal proposition or claim.

primary fusion center Typically provides information sharing and analysis for an entire state. These centers are the highest priority for the allocation of available federal resources, including the deployment of personnel and connectivity with federal data systems.

primary scene The location at which the initial offense was committed.

probable cause A condition in which an officer has suspicion about an individual and knowledge of facts and circumstances that would lead a reasonable person to believe that a crime has been, is being, or is about to be, committed.

procedural criminal law That branch of criminal law that defines what can and cannot be done with, or to, people.

product identification number (PIN) PIN stands for product identification number.

professional poachers Individuals who poach exclusively for profit.

professional theft (of vehicle) The theft of a vehicle to fill a specific order or to resell the parts.

promissory notes Essentially short term I.O.U.s which promise to pay its holder, the investor, the fixed amount invested, plus a fixed interest at some future specified date. While these may be operated legally, many such investments are simply frauds and the money disappears.

proof The combination of all the evidence in determining the guilt or innocence of a person accused of a crime.

Property Insurance Loss Register (PILR) An insurance industry database that lists the insureds in burglary and theft claims and everyone with an insurable interest in fire claims; detects repeated patterns of claim activity.

proximity The amount of space between the participants in a conversation—neither too close, which causes discomfort, nor too far apart, which causes a loss of connectivity.

psilocybin and psilocin Natural hallucinogens, derived from certain mushrooms, that produce hallucinations for about 6 hours; taken orally.

psychological autopsy An analysis of a decedent's thoughts, feelings, and behavior, conducted through interviews with persons who knew him or her, to determine whether a death was an accident or suicide.

pump and dump A scheme where glowing, but false, information about a stock is widely distributed, often through the Internet, and the rapid buying of it "pumps" the price of the stock up. Once pumped, the fraudsters "dump" the stock for a quick profit.

puncture wounds Wounds inflicted with piercing instruments such as leather punches, screwdrivers, and ice picks; typically small, with little or no bleeding.

pyromaniacs Arsonists who lack conscious motivation for their fire setting.

Q

quick strip (of vehicle) The process of removing from a stolen vehicle valuable parts (e.g., seats, stereos, tires) that have no identifying numbers and thus can be easily sold.

R

radial fracture lines Lines that move away from the point of impact in a glass window.

Racketeer Influenced and Corrupt Organizations Act (RICO) Passed in 1970 by Congress to "seek the eradication of organized crime."

rape or sexual battery The crime of having sexual relations with a person against her or his will; with a person who is unconscious or under the influence of alcohol; or with someone who is insane, feeble-minded, or under the age of consent.

rape-murder Murder that results from or is an integral part of the rape of the victim; either an unplanned response (of increasing aggression or panic over sense of failure) or a planned act (of revenge or sadism).

rapid response deployment or quick action deployment (QUAD) An intervention approach in which patrol officers are trained in the principles and tactics of rapid deployment for critical incidents so that responding officers can take action immediately rather than wait for a SWAT team.

rapport In interviews and interrogations, the harmonious relationship with the witness or suspect that must be established by the investigator to foster trust and meaningful communication.

rebuttal In a trial, the optional process in which the prosecution, after the defense has closed its case, presents new evidence or calls or recalls a witness; it occurs at the discretion of the prosecution.

recognized fusion center Typically provides information sharing and analysis for a major urban area. As the federal government respects the authority of state governments to designate fusion centers, any fusion center not designated as a primary fusion center is referred to as a recognized fusion center.

re-cross-examination In a trial, the requestioning of a witness initially called by the opposing party.

redirect examination In a trial, the requestioning of a witness by the party that called the witness.

reflected ultraviolet imaging system (RUVIS) Lighting and imaging system in which ultraviolet light applied to undetected fingerprints is "bounced" back, highly intensifying the prints.

refurbishment fraud A practice in which working components from damaged or returned items (e.g., a computer) are used in the construction of new items or are resold as new items.

repeat victimization Homes or businesses attacked multiple times, usually within 30 days. The likelihood is estimated at 17%, although for houses some estimates reach as high as 40%.

Residential Security Container (RSC) Low-cost home dual purpose safes will often have a reasonable degree of fire protection, but the burglary protection may be the Residential Security Container (RSC) rating. The RSC rating offers burglary protection analogous to a TL-5 rating. The RSC designation gives protection from an attack by one person using common hand-held tools, no powered tools, no hammer with a head weight more than three pounds, or tool longer than 18".

revenge-motivated arson Fires set in retaliation for some injustice, real or imagined, that is perceived by the offender.

reverse sting A special police operation using one or more female officers serving as decoys who pose as prostitutes and wait for men to approach them for the purpose of purchasing sex.

rhodamine 6G An excellent fluorescing chemical for enhancing developed latent prints and revealing others; used on metal, glass, plastic, wood, and other nonabsorbent surfaces.

ridges The raised portions of the finger skin, atop which are miniscule sweat pores.

rifling The lands and grooves in the rifled bore of a firearm.

rigor mortis The stiffening of the muscles after death. It can be useful in determining the approximate time of death.

right-wing terrorists Terrorists who usually espouse racial supremacy and antigovernment or antiregulatory beliefs; they often hold antiabortion and survivalist views and call for paramilitary training in "militias."

robbery The crime of taking and carrying away the personal property of another by means of force, fear, or threat of force, with the intent to permanently deprive the owner of its use.

rogues' gallery Instituted by the New York City Police Department in 1857, a display in which photographs of known offenders were arranged by criminal specialty and height for detectives to study so that they might recognize criminals on the street.

Rohypnol A benzodiazapine used to perpetrate sexual attacks; mixed into a victim's food or drink, can induce sedation, memory impairment, or unconsciousness, leaving the victim unaware of the attack. Also called *flunitrazepam*.

root kits Exploit packages that enable computer-system intruders to maintain the highest level of access by installing back doors and secret accounts and altering logs and basic system services.

rough sketch A drawing made at the crime scene; not drawn to scale, but indicates accurate dimensions and distances.

rules of evidence Federal evidentiary rules which state that scientific, technical, or other specialized knowledge is admissible if it will help the trier of fact understand the evidence or determine a fact at issue.

S

safes Locked receptacles for protecting valuables; classified as fire-resistant safes (offering protection from fire but minimum security) or money chests (providing security and reasonably good protection from fire).

salami slice A computerized-theft technique in which dollar amounts are automatically rounded down and the difference is diverted to the perpetrator's special account.

salvage switch A method of disguising a stolen vehicle whereby the title and VIN plate of a salvage vehicle are transferred to an identical stolen vehicle, which can then be sold in the legitimate market.

salvage title The title issued to an insurance company after it has paid a total-loss claim; remains with the vehicle until it is destroyed.

salvage vehicle A vehicle that has been damaged to such an extent that the cost of repairing it is more than its fair market value.

scald burns Burns on the skin caused by contact with hot liquids, either through spills/splashes or immersion; most common type of burn injury to children.

scientific method The blending of empirical knowledge, gained from observation and deduction, and rationalism, inductive thought and reasoning, particularly critical thinking.

Scotland Yard The original headquarters of the London Metropolitan Police, so-called because the building formerly housed Scottish royalty. Since 1890, the headquarters have been located elsewhere, but have been still known as New Scotland Yard.

script kiddies Computer jargon for individuals that used existing computer codes, tools, and/or scripts rather than write their own to exploit vulnerabilities during the early developmental years of computers, bulletin board systems and the Internet, and then boasted openly about their "computer attacks."

search The process of looking for evidence of a crime.

search and seizure The process of looking for evidence of a crime and taking that evidence into the custody of a law enforcement agency.

search warrant Written authorization by a judge allowing law enforcement officers to look for specified items of evidence of a crime in a specified place.

seasoning A technique employed to break a victim's will and separate her from her previous life so she does not know where to turn for help.

secondary scenes The locations of all events subsequent to, and connected with, the event at the primary scene.

selective raid A robbery that involves a minimal amount of casual planning and may be repeated several times in rapid succession.

semen A grayish-white fluid produced in the male reproductive organs and ejaculated during orgasm; has a chlorinelike odor and dries to a starchlike consistency.

serial burglar Burglaries which are episodic victimization of the same premises or a series of burglaries committed at various locations by the same offender, small group, or large burglary crew.

series A crime characteristic in which crimes of the same type are committed over a short period of time, usually by the same offender.

sex offenses Crimes related to sexual activity; classified as serious (e.g., rape), nuisance (e.g., voyeurism, exhibitionism), and mutual consent (e.g., adultery, prostitution).

Sexting Sending by cell phone or posting sexually explicit photos, images, or videos.

Sextortion Threats of exposing a sexual image in order to make a person do something (most often pay money as a bribe) or for other reasons, such as revenge, embarrassment, or humiliation.

sexual homicide In sexual homicide, a sexual element (activity) is the basis, or the sequence of, acts leading to the death.

shaken-baby syndrome (SBS) Severe intracranial trauma caused by the deliberate application of violent force (shaking) to a child.

shaped charge Explosives specifically designed and constructed to achieve a very specific result, namely the blasting of a hole through metal and other types of hardened material.

Shi'a or Shiite Followers of the Shi'a tradition, often called the "Shi'at Ali" or Party of Ali, who believe that Ali (the son-in-law of the Prophet Muhammad) was given a divine right of successorship to lead the Muslim community after the 7th century. The Shi'a population is primarily concentrated in Iran, Iraq, Lebanon, and Yemen.

Shoeprint Image Capture and Retrieval System (SICAR) Computer software that classifies, archives, and identifies shoeprints.

shopping cart fraud A computer crime in which the offender selects purchases at an online store, saves a copy of the purchase page and lowers the prices, and then submits the altered page and continues the checkout process.

shoulder surfing When identity thieves stay close enough to people using their credit cards, pins, telephone calling cards, and writing checks that they can gather sensitive identity information.

show-up A process by which the police conduct an immediate eyewitness identification of someone they have temporarily detained. The practice permits the immediate clearing of a wrongfully suspected person, and detention is kept to a minimum. One witness at a time is brought to view the person temporarily detained.

Silk Road An underground website that traded in goods and services. Most everything traded on the sprawling network was illegal, for example: the sale of drugs, weapons, forged documents, exploit kits in which to attack computer networks, and even body parts, to the services of prostitutes, computer hackers, money launderers, and hit men. While the site has been "closed" by recent FBI sting operations, the site still remains on the dark web.

situational child molester A person who molests children because the opportunity exists to do so or because of his or her inadequacy, regressed personality, or desire for experimentation; does not have a sexual preference for children.

situational poachers Individuals who may not be going out specifically to poach but have the opportunity to do so and take advantage of that opportunity. Some may also poach to feed their families because of economic hardship.

situational stereotyping Occurs when an officer's knowledge and experience with a location creates the expectation that the present situation will be the same as past situations; increases the officer's vulnerability.

sketching The process of drawing a crime scene using rudimentary methods; sketches made can be "rough" or "smooth."

skimmers Data collection devices through which credit cards are passed. When used illegally, they are employed to obtain the credit card numbers used by customers so credit card and/or identity theft can be committed.

small-particle reagent (SPR) A chemical used in developing latent prints on objects that have been immersed in water, dew- or rain-soaked cars, surfaces covered with a residue such as ocean salt, waxed materials, plastics, tile, and glass.

smash and grab B3Ms "Smash and grab" burglaries sometimes called B3M (3 minute burglaries). That is the approximate time it takes for offenders to break a glass door or window of a jewelry or other retail store, grab whatever is available, and flee.

smiling photographs Forensic dentists may be able to establish individual identity by comparing the teeth displayed in a smiling photograph of an otherwise unidentifiable person with dental records.

smooth bore A bore without rifling; characteristic of most shotguns.

smooth sketch A finished sketch of the crime scene, often drawn to scale using information contained in the rough sketch.

smuggling Occurs when someone is paid to assist another in the illegal crossing of borders.

smurfing A method associated with money laundering. Multiple deposits of cash are made at different accounts in different banks or bank drafts are bought; the transactions are kept under $10,000 to avoid the bank rendering a required report of the transaction to federal authorities.

snap gun Are electric lock picks. A snap gun operates by inserting what is called a "needle" into the lock.

snow print wax An aerosol wax sprayed on footwear impressions in snow to tint the highlights so that the impressions can be photographed before being cast.

social network sites A category of websites that contain personal profiles and that may offer dating or other such services—one example of such a site is FaceBook.

soft targets Lightly protected sites targeted by burglars, such as many homes.

solvability factors Used to screen and evaluate the information in an offense/incident report to determine if there is sufficient information to warrant a follow-up investigation. Such factors include whether suspects are named, the existence of significant physical evidence, the use or display of deadly weapons, and similarities to recently reported crimes.

spalling The breakdown in the surface tensile strength of concrete, masonry, or brick that occurs when exposure to high temperatures and rates of heating produces mechanical forces within the material.

speedballing The simultaneous ingestion of heroin (a depressant) and cocaine (a stimulant); produces a euphoric rush followed by a drowsy or depressing effect. Can cause convulsions and death.

sperm Tadpolelike organisms that are contained in, and travel through, semen to fertilize the female egg.

spill/splash injuries Burns on the skin that occur when a hot liquid falls from a height and splashes onto the body.

spontaneous heating An increase in temperature that results from a natural process; caused by chemical action, fermentation, or oxidation.

spontaneous ignition The catching afire of materials subjected to spontaneous heating; usually requires several hours to several months of oxidation or fermentation.

sprees A crime characteristic in which crimes of the same type are committed at almost the same time by the same offender.

spree killer An individual who embarks on a murderous rampage. The killings take place within a given period of time, generally, hours or days without an interval.

staged crime scene Used to misdirect investigators, usually away from the actual perpetrator of a crime. It may also be done for other reasons, such as protecting a family from embarrassment or financial hardship—for example, trying to make a suicide appear as an accident or a murder.

STAR *See* **Stolen Auto Recovery System.**

stimulants Drugs that directly stimulate the central nervous system, producing excitation, alertness, wakefulness, and, sometimes, a temporary increase in blood pressure and respiration rate; in overdose, can cause hallucinations, convulsions, and death.

sting operations In combating fences, this is a tactic in which undercover officers pose as fences in a "front" business to gain information. Such operations have proven to be an effective means of identifying criminals, penetrating criminal organizations, and recovering property.

Stockholm Syndrome A group of psychological symptoms that occur in some persons in a captive or hostage situation.

Stolen Auto Recovery System (STAR) A method of examining and photographing the contents of shipping containers, by means of gamma rays, while they are entering a port or being loaded onto a vessel; used to identify stolen vehicles being shipped abroad.

stop The use of police authority to limit a person's liberty of movement, communicated in a manner that a reasonable person understands he/she is not free to go until the officer's business is completed. Examples include: "Please turn your ignition off" and "Please show me your driver's license".

stop and frisk A limited pat down of the outer clothing of a person encountered by a law enforcement officer when the person is acting suspiciously, and the officer, concerned about safety, seeks to determine if the person has a weapon.

storage forensics Data and information retrieved from physical media connected to a computer.

strategic intelligence Information gathered and analyzed over time that usually confirms new or recently discovered patterns of criminal activity.

striae Tiny furrows made by the action of a tool on an object's surface (e.g., marks left on a door's hinge from an attempt to force the door open with a pry bar).

strong-armed robbery A robbery in which the perpetrator attacks and beats the victim but no weapons are involved.

subpoena A written order commanding a particular person to appear in court at a specified date and time to testify as a witness.

substantive criminal law That branch of criminal law dealing with the elements that describe and define a crime.

sudden infant death syndrome (SIDS) The sudden and unexpected death of an apparently healthy infant, usually during sleep, the cause of which has yet to be determined.

Sunni Followers of the Prophet Muhammad, the "True Path of Allah," focused in Saudi Arabia. Approximately 90% of the Muslim population is Sunni, and it is rapidly growing throughout the Middle East, Africa, and Southeast Asia.

superglue fuming The process of heating cyanoacrylate in a high-humidity chamber so that the condensing of the resultant fumes develops any latent prints.

supplemental reports Provide additional information relevant to the crime reported in the initial incident/offense report. They may be prepared by other officers who responded to the call in support of the officer assigned to it and have collected important information, such as interviews from some witnesses. The investigator(s) assigned to follow-up the case will ordinarily file one or more additional supplemental reports.

surface impression Two-dimensional impressions, having a length and width and lacking any appreciable height. They are often called "prints" or "residual prints." They are formed when the soles of the feet, footwear, or tires are contaminated with foreign matter such as blood, oil, or dust and leave a print on a firm base, such as a linoleum floor, a piece of paper, or cloth. They may also be found on doors that have been kicked in during burglaries and home invasion robberies.

surrebuttal In a trial, the process in which the defense, after a rebuttal by the prosecution, presents new evidence or calls or recalls a witness; permitted only if the prosecution conducts a rebuttal.

surreptitious entries Burglaries in which no apparent force is used and thus a point of entry or exit cannot be established; may indicate loiding, picking, an unlocked door, a perpetrator with authorized access, or an occupant-staged crime.

surveillance The secretive and continuous observation of persons, places, and things to obtain information concerning the activities and identity of individuals.

Survival Identification Syndrome An alternate name used for Stockholm Syndrome.

survival sex Individuals who engage in prostitution in order to obtain the basic necessities of life such as food, shelter, or money.

swoop and squat One of several varieties of auto fraud. In this version, a person suddenly swoops in front of the car you are driving and hits his/her breaks, causing you to rear-end them. The person then claims medical injuries were caused by you and your insurer usually pays the "victim."

synthetic narcotics Narcotics that are chemically related to opiates but that are produced entirely within laboratories; primarily used as painkillers.

T

tack The equipment used with horses (e.g., saddles, bridles, horse blankets).

tactical intelligence Information that implies immediate action and can lead to arrests or the collection of additional information; may be derived from surveillance, informants, and intelligence analysis.

tangible personal property Means things that have a physical existence such as jewelry, lawnmowers, cameras, laptops, computers, televisions, furniture, clothing, and collectibles such as old rare coins.

taxidermists Individuals who mount the heads and antlers of game animals for hunters.

taxonomy A classification system. Its categories are formed by empirically studying observable and measurable characteristics.

telephone record analysis time-event charting An intelligence technique in which telephone records are compiled and analyzed to obtain information on the relationships between the subscriber and the numbers called.

testimony A witness's oral presentation of facts about which he or she has knowledge.

theft by conversion Involves the elements of embezzlements and are the same as the traditional larceny charge with the addition that a person who has been entrusted with something valuable converts it to their own purpose or use in contravention of his/her legal obligation.

theft by deception Such as removing a price sticker from one item for sale and replacing it with a less expensive price sticker.

theft by fraud Such as the unauthorized use of another's credit card, using someone else's medical insurance card or social security number to get benefits, and "pump and dump" stock schemes, whereby a stock is heavily promoted then after the stock runs up in price, its promoters dump it.

theft of services Covers such things as "skipping out" on hotel, restaurant, and bar bills or illegally connecting or reconnecting an electrical meter.

theft by trick Involve such things as con games and swindles.

threat assessment The process of determining the risk level posed by a threat and whether law enforcement should be called in and a criminal prosecution pursued; includes evaluation of the threatener.

three-dimensional impression (3DI) Impressions that have a significant depth, in addition to having a length and width. 3DI may be found impressed into soil, sand, snow, or other materials. The level of detail is affected by the material in which the impression is made, as well as its degrading due to weather, contamination, or other conditions.

timber theft Can result from the cutting down of trees which are rare and have unique value for making furniture, even guitars and musical instruments. Some urban areas, particularly along parkways and expressways in the month leading up to the Christmas holiday, have Christmas-type trees disappear as motorists cut them down and cart the trees home to decorate.

time event charting An investigative tool which depicts the major events involving an offender. Time is shown as intervals between major events.

title fraud For motor vehicles, any act that involves altering, laundering, or counterfeiting a title or title reassignment form; often engaged in to support and cover up odometer rollbacks.

T-men Agents of the Bureau of Internal Revenue (which enforced Prohibition), so-called because the bureau was part of the Department of the Treasury.

tool mark Any impression, cut, gouge, or abrasion made when a tool comes into contact with another object.

Tor Network A synonym for the dark or deep web, a secretive online world which remains mostly untraceable and difficult to access for regular Internet users and even traditional law enforcement, which unfortunately permits a large criminal domain to exist and thrive today. This underground world is the Internet's secret black market where criminals, rogue agents, and even terrorists can conduct criminal and illegal activities.

totality of the circumstances In determining the applicability of the *Miranda* warnings, an approach that takes all the circumstances into consideration, rather than imposing a strict interpretation based on formal procedures.

touch DNA A person's skin sheds some 400,000 dead cells daily, although there may be only a few that are suitable for DNA analysis. People may also transfer DNA bearing material to their hands from picking their nose or other activities. As someone handles an object, such as a baseball bat, the mere touching of it may transfer material viable for DNA analysis. The more a person handles an object, the greater the potential for touch DNA to be present. Secondary transfers may occur when someone deposits both their DNA and yours on a object, potentially implicating you in a crime.

toxicologist The scientist who specializes in the identification and recognition of poisons, their physiological effects on humans and animals, as well as their antidotes.

trace evidence Evidence that is extremely small or microscopic in size or is present only in limited amounts.

trace evidence vacuum A vacuum which gathers small (even microscopic) evidence at the crime scene. Examples of evidence gathered by it include hairs and fibers.

traced forgery Created by tracing over a genuine signature, commonly found on fraudulent (questioned) documents such as contracts, checks, and monetary instruments.

tracing evidence Evidence that helps identify and locate the suspect.

traditional amateur burglar Type of burglar who tends to work in a small area. Sometimes they borrow the family car or one from a friend. About 21% of apprehended burglars are under 18 years of age. Some of these don't yet have a driver's license because they aren't old enough, others can't afford a car and insurance so they don't drive, and members of a third group have had their licenses suspended. Others know their local "territory" much better and feel more comfortable in it as compared to offending at locations that are greater distances away in unfamiliar surroundings.

traditional powders The basic powders, available in a number of colors, that have been used for decades for developing latent fingerprints.

traditional professional burglar Burglars who may operate alone or with others in "crews." They often work in multiple cities and the connection of their crimes may not be made for longer periods of time. They may commit fewer burglaries annually than amateurs due to their larger "scores," but that is not iron clad and perhaps only true for the highest echelon of professionals.

trafficking Occurs when a person is forced into a situation of exploitation whereby their freedom is taken away.

Trafficking Victims Protection Act 2000 The law that makes trafficking a federal crime, establishes resources to combat human trafficking and issues measures for the protection of victims, thereby squarely targeting human trafficking for federal prosecution.

Trafficking Victims Protection Reauthorization Act 2003 Passed by Congress in order to meet the increasing challenges posed by deficiencies of TVPA 2000 and includes new legal resources against trafficking such as allowing victims to bring civil lawsuits against traffickers.

Trafficking Victims Protection Reauthorization Act 2005 Law that gives jurisdiction to U.S. courts over government employees who become involved in human trafficking abroad.

trailer In arson, any substance used to spread the fire from the plant to other parts of a room or building.

transgender A person who experiences incongruence between the sex that they were assigned at birth and their internal gender identity, or who experiences binary gender as restrictive or inaccurate.

trauma bonding See *Stockholm Syndrome*.

trauma-informed response The practice of responding to a victim of sexual violence in a compassionate, sensitive, and non-judgmental manner in order to reduce the physical and psychological trauma the victim as already suffered.

The Travel Act Federalizes the crime of operating a prostitution business.

trophy poaching Hunting those animals which are particularly prized for display in homes and typically dens in homes.

trends A general tendency in the occurrence of crime across a large geographic area over an extended period of time.

Trojan horse Any computer program that is altered or designed to perform an unwanted or malicious function while appearing to perform a routine or benign function.

Truth in Mileage Act (1986) Federal legislation that requires more tightly controlled documentation and recording of odometer readings each time ownership of a vehicle changes.

T/S/D crimes Any illegal acts involving the treatment, storage, and disposal of hazardous wastes.

T-visa Available for trafficking victims who self-petition to stay in the U.S. for up to 4 years, after meeting certain conditions.

tuberculosis A chronic bacterial infection, spread by air, that usually infects the lungs and can lead to death if untreated; a health hazard for anyone in contact with high-risk individuals such as drug addicts and homeless persons.

tumbling The illegal altering of a cellular phone's microchip so that its access codes change after each call, making it difficult to trace the fraudulent user; done through a personal computer.

turned out Term used to describe the time at which the victim is allowed to begin the prostitution process. This is generally preceded by physical and verbal abuse.

typology A classification system that rationally creates categories into which similar things are respectively placed.

U

ultraviolet fluorescence A technique in which a darkened fire scene is illuminated with an ultraviolet lamp so that certain substances glow; used to detect residues of accelerants and to locate the point of a fire's origin.

unbundling A medical fraud technique in which each component of service is separated and billed separately, creating a higher charge than if properly billed as a single category of service.

Uniform Crime Report (UCR) An annual FBI publication containing crime data for the United States. It is released each fall and covers the 12 months of the preceding year.

unknown or questioned samples (1) Recovered crime scene samples whose sources are in question; (2) questioned evidence that may have been transferred to an offender during the commission of a crime and may have been taken away by him or her; (3) questioned evidence recovered at multiple crime scenes that associates a particular tool, weapon, or person with each scene.

upcoding A type of medical fraud in which patients and insurers are billed for longer office visits than occurred, or are billed for more expensive tests which were never done.

U.S. Department of Agriculture's National Animal Identification System (NAIS) Provides all agricultural animals with a 15-digit Animal Identification Number (AIN) which ultimately could track them from birth to death.

U-visa Available to immigrants who have been the victim of a wide range of serious crimes and provides victims with a means to stabilize their legal status.

V

vehicle canvass A systematic approach to documenting every vehicle in the immediate vicinity of a crime as a means of locating the suspect's vehicle.

vehicle fraud Any fraudulent activity involving motor vehicles; includes theft of vehicles, fraud perpetrated on purchasers of vehicles, and fraud committed by owners (or persons acting on their behalf) against insurance companies.

vehicle identification number (VIN) The 17-character identification number assigned to every car manufactured or sold in the United States.

venire The large panel of potential jurors from which a trial jury will be picked.

viatical settlements Though some viatical settlements are operated legally, many are scams. An example of a viatical settlement is when people's life insurance policies are bought for less than face value. The seller thus has access to cash and the buyer makes a profit on the difference between the face value of the policy and the amount paid to the insured.

victim-centered response A law enforcement investigation technique that focuses on the actions and choices of the offender—not the actions or inactions of the victim.

VIN *See* **vehicle identification number.**

violation In some states, this is a minor transgression of the law, often punishable by a fine of no more than $250 (e.g., littering).

Violent Criminal Apprehension Program (VICAP) FBI unit whose mission is to facilitate cooperation, communication, and coordination between law enforcement agencies and to provide support in their efforts to investigate, identify, track, apprehend, and prosecute violent serial offenders.

virus A malicious program that is secretly inserted into normal software or a computer's active memory and runs when the host runs; causes effects ranging from annoying messages and deletion of data to interference with the computer's operation.

Vollmer, August Often thought of as an administrator, Vollmer's other contributions are towering: he helped John Larson develop the first workable polygraph in 1921 and established in Los Angeles in 1923 America's first full forensic laboratory.

Vucetich, Juan Worked on the use of fingerprints in Argentina. In 1894, he published his own book on the subject, *Dactiloscopia Comparada.*

W

washing (of title) The process of fabricating a vehicle's sale to a purchaser in a jurisdiction that does not issue salvage titles or carry title brands forward, thereby obtaining a clean title on the vehicle.

weight (of evidence) The amount of believability a jury gives to the testimony of a witness or the presentation of an item of evidence.

West case A 1903 incident in which two criminals with the same name, identical appearances, and nearly identical measurements were distinguished only by fingerprints, thus significantly advancing the use of fingerprints for identification in the United States.

white-collar crime Any illegal act committed by concealment or guile, rather than physical means, to obtain money or property, avoid payment or loss of money or property, or obtain business or personal advantage. While these may be operated legally, many such investments are simply frauds and the money disappears.

WiFi A wireless local area network in a specific location which allows multiple access to the Internet; based on IEEE 802.11 standards and technology.

wildlife crimes Generally involves the illegal hunting of wildlife which are prized for their food value or trophy value.

William Wilberforce Trafficking Victims Protection Reauthorization Act 2008 Law authorizing the appropriations for 2008–2011 for the TVPA and establishing a system to monitor and evaluate all assistance under the act.

wire transfer schemes Type of crime that starts with fraudulent and misleading ads for the sale of high-value items. When buyers take the bait they are directed to wire money to crooks using a money transfer company. Once the money changes hands the buyer never hears from them again.

witness A person who has firsthand knowledge regarding a crime or who has expert information regarding some aspect of the crime.

worm A malicious program that attacks a computer system directly, rather than infecting a host program; spreads rapidly through the Internet or e-mail.

Chapter 1

1. Material on the evolution of criminal investigation is drawn, in part, from Thomas R. Phelps, Charles R. Swanson, Jr., and Kenneth Evans, *Introduction to Criminal Justice* (New York: Random House, 1979), pp. 42–55.

2. T. A. Critchley, *A History of Police in England and Wales,* 2nd ed. (Montclair, NJ: Patterson Smith, 1972), p. 34.

3. Loc. cit.

4. A. C. Germann, Frank D. Day, and Robert J. Gallati, *Introduction to Law Enforcement and Criminal Justice* (Springfield, IL: Charles C. Thomas, 1970), pp. 54–55.

5. Melville Lee, *A History of Police in England* (Montclair, NJ: Patterson Smith reprint, 1971), p. 240.

6. Thomas A. Reppetto, *The Blue Parade* (New York: Free Press, 1978), p. 26.

7. Ibid., pp. 26–28.

8. Ibid., p. 29.

9. James F. Richardson, *The New York Police* (New York: Oxford, 1970), p. 37.

10. James D. Horan, *The Pinkertons* (New York: Bonanza Books, 1967), p. 25.

11. Ibid., p. 23.

12. Ibid., p. 25.

13. Jurgen Thorwald, *The Marks of Cain* (London: Thames and Hudson, 1965), p. 129.

14. Reppetto, *The Blue Parade,* p. 257. There are disputes whether a real threat existed or if Pinkerton or the New York City Police discovered it.

15. Ibid., pp. 257–258.

16. Ibid., p. 258. It is argued Pinkerton was a failure as a military analyst. His overestimates of enemy strength may have made General McClellan too cautious, for which President Lincoln dismissed him.

17. No author, "Pinkerton National Detective Agency-For 150 Years," Legends of America, September 2017, p. 1, www.legendsofamerica.com/pinkertons, accessed December 4, 2017.

18. Loc. cit.

19. The Blue Parade, pp. 257-258.

20. William J. Bopp and Donald Shultz, *Principles of American Law Enforcement and Criminal Justice* (Springfield, IL: Charles C. Thomas, 1972), pp. 70–71.

21. Thorwald, *The Marks of Cain,* p. 131.

22. Reppetto, *The Blue Parade,* p. 259, notes that in two separate instances a total of eight Reno gang members arrested by the Pinkertons were subsequently lynched. In the first instance, three gang members reportedly were taken from Pinkerton custody.

23. Thorwald, *The Marks of Cain,* p. 131.

24. Ibid., p. 263.

25. Clive Emsley, *Policing and Its Context 1750-1870* (New York: Schocken Books, 1983), p. 106.

26. Augustine E. Costello, *Our Police Protectors* (Montclair, NJ: Patterson Smith, 1972 reprint of an 1885 edition), p. 402.

27. Richardson, *The New York Police,* p. 122.

28. Bopp and Shultz, *Principles of American Law Enforcement and Criminal Justice,* p. 66.

29. William J. Mathias and Stuart Anderson, *Horse to Helicopter* (Atlanta: Community Life Publications, Georgia State University, 1973), p. 22.

30. Thorwald, *The Marks of Cain,* p. 136.

31. Ibid.

32. Reppetto, *The Blue Parade,* p. 263.

33. Ibid., p. 267.

34. Ibid., p. 278.

35. Ibid., p. 282.

36. Ibid., p. 283.

37. Richard Saferstein, *Criminalistics* (Englewood Cliffs, NJ: Prentice Hall, 1977), p. 5.

38. Jurgen Thorwald, *Crime and Science* (New York: Harcourt, Brace & World, 1967), p. 4.

39. Thorwald, *The Century of the Detective,* p. 6.

40. Ibid.

41. Ibid., p. 7.

42. Ibid., p. 9.

43. Ibid.

44. Ibid., p. 10.

45. Ibid., p. 12.

46. Ibid., pp. 83–84.

47. Anthony L. Califana and Jerome S. Levkov, *Criminalistics for the Law Enforcement Officer* (New York: McGraw-Hill, 1978), p. 20; also see Frederick R. Cherrill, *The Finger Print System at Scotland Yard* (London: Her Majesty's Stationery Office, 1954), p. 3.

48. Ibid.

49. Cherrill, *The Finger Print System at Scotland Yard,* p. 2.

50. Califana and Levkov, *Criminalistics for the Law Enforcement Officer,* p. 20.

51. Cherrill, *The Finger Print System at Scotland Yard,* p. 4.

52. Thorwald, *The Century of the Detective,* pp. 14–16.

53. Ibid., p. 18.

54. Ibid.

55. Ibid., p. 32.

56. Ibid., p. 33.

57. Saferstein, *Criminalistics,* p. 4.

58. Thorwald, *The Marks of Cain,* p. 81.

59. Thorwald, *The Century of the Detective,* p. 58.

60. Ibid.

61. Ibid., p. 60.

62. Ibid., p. 62.

63. Thorwald, *The Marks of Cain,* p. 138.

64. Ibid.

65. Ibid.

66. Ibid., p. 139.

67. Ibid.

68. Saferstein, *Criminalistics,* p. 281.

69. Thorwald, *The Century of the Detective,* p. 88.

70. Ibid.

71. Ibid., p. 87.

72. Ibid., p. 88.

73. Richard Saferstein, *Criminalistics: An Introduction to Forensic Science,* 5th ed. (Englewood Cliffs, NJ: Prentice Hall, 1995), p. 384.

74. Tod W. Burke and Walter F. Row, "DNA Analysis: The Challenge for Police," *The Police Chief,* Oct. 1989, p. 92.

75. Saferstein, *Criminalistics,* 5th ed., p. 383.

76. "British Police Use Genetic Technique in Murder Arrest," *The Atlanta Constitution,* Sept. 22, 1987, p. A3.

77. David Bigbee et al., "Implementation of DNA Analysis in American Crime Laboratories," *The Police Chief,* Oct. 1989, p. 86.

78. Saferstein, *Criminalistics,* 5th ed., p. 384.

79. Bigbee et al., "Implementation of DNA Analysis," p. 86.

80. The account of the role of DNA in solving the Mann-Ashworth murders is drawn, in part, from Clare M. Tande, "DNA Typing: A New Investigatory Tool," *Duke Law Journal,* April 1989, p. 474.

81. This information is from Ricki Lewis, "DNA Fingerprints: Witness for the Prosecution," *Discover,* June 1988, pp. 44, 46.

82. Bigbee et al., "Implementation of DNA Analysis," p. 88.

83. This account is drawn from several sources: Jim Erickson, "Tree Genes: UA Professor's DNA Work Helps Convict Killer," *The Arizona Daily Star,* May 28, 1993, Metro/Region Section, p. 1; and Tim Henderson, "Report on Analysis of Palo Verde Samples," University of Arizona, April 14, 1993.

84. Saferstein, *Criminalistics,* 5th ed., p. 438.

85. Ibid., p. 30.

86. Thorwald, *The Marks of Cain,* p. 161.

87. Ibid.

88. Thorwald, *The Century of the Detective,* pp. 418–419.

89. Ibid., p. 419.

90. Thorwald, *The Marks of Cain,* p. 164.

91. Ibid.

92. Thorwald, *The Century of the Detective*, p. 434.

93. These points are drawn with restatement from Joe Minor, "Touch DNA: From the Crime Scene to the Crime Laboratory," *Forensic Magazine*, April 12, 2013, www.forensicmag.com/article/2013/04/touch-dna-crime-scene-crime-laboratory, accessed July 5. 2016; David Spraggs, "Just a Touch: Using Touch DNA Evidence," *Police Magazine*, December 2008, http://www.policemag.com/channel/technology/articles/2008/12/just-a-touch.aspx, accessed July 3, 2016; Suzanna Ryan, "Trace DNA: If Your DNA Is on Evidence, Did You Really Touch It?" Ryan Forensic, http://ryanforensicdna.com/trace-dna-analysis, accessed July 3, 2016; and Matthew Phillips and Susan Petricevic, "The Tendency of Individuals to Transfer DNA to Handled Items," *Forensic Science International*, Vol. 169, Issue 2/3, May 2007, pp. 162–168.

94. For example, see Cynthia M. Cale, "Forensic DNA Is Not Infallible," *Nature*, October 29, 2015, Vol. 526, Issue 775, p. 61.

95. Matthew Shaer, "The False Promise of DNA Testing," *The Atlantic*, June 2016, www.theatlantic.com/magazine/archive/2016/06/a-reasonable-doubt/480747, accessed July 1, 2016.

96. "Forensic DNA Is Not Infallible," p. 61.

97. Panayiotis Manoli and Antonis Antoniou, "Sex-Specific Age Association with Primary DNA Transfer," *International Journal of Legal Medicine*, Vol. 130, Issue I, January 2016, p. 103.

98. No Author, "Welcome to the Biometric Center for Excellence," Federal Bureau of Investigation, undated, https://www.fbi.gov/about-us/cjis/fingerprints_biometrics/biometric-center-of-excellence, accessed July 2, 2016.

99. No author, "The World Identifies with Us," CrossMatch, p. 1, 2016, http://www.crossmatch.com, accessed July 2, 2016.

100. See Robert C. Davis, et. al., "Working Smarter on Cold Cases: Identifying Factors Associated with Successful Cold Case Investigations," Journal of Forensic Sciences, Vol. 59, Issue 2, March 2014, pp. 375–382.

101. Loc. Cit.

102. Loc. Cit.

103. C. E. MacLean and A. Lamparello, "Forensic DNA Phenotyping in Criminal Investigations and Criminal Courts: Assessing and Mitigating the Dilemmas Inherent in the Science," *Recent Advances in DNA and Gene Sequencing*, Vol. 8, No. 2, 2014, p. 104. This journal was listed in 2015 as being discontinued.

104. The material from this paragraph is drawn from Jack A. Gilbert and Josh D. Neufeld, "Life in World without Microbes," *PLOS Biology*, Vol. 12, No. 12, December 16, 2014, and National Institutes of Allergy and Infectious Diseases, "Microbes," July 9, 2015. *PLOS Biology* is an on-line, peer-reviewed journal.

105. Drawn from National Institute of Allergy and Infectious Diseases, "Diseases and Infections Caused by Microbes," November 2, 2010, p. 1, www.niaid.nih.gov/topics/microbes/pages/diseases.aspx, accessed July 5, 2016; and Smruti Ranjan Singh, Krishnamurthy N. B., and Blessy Baby Mathew, "A Review of Recent Diseases Caused by Microbes," *Journal of Applied & Environmental Microbiology*, Vol. 2, No. 4, 2014, pp. 106–115, pubs.sciepub.com/jaem/2/4/4/, accessed July 5, 2016.

106. Tia Ghose, "At 3.5 Billion Years Old, They're Among the Oldest Life Forms Ever," NBC news, November 13, 2013, www.nbcnews.com/science/science-news/3-5-billion-years-old-theyre-among-oldest-life-forms-f2D11591109, accessed January 11, 2018.

107. The sentences pertaining to life without microbes is taken with reorganization and restatement from "Life in World without Microbes," PDF document, no page numbers.

108. Loc. Cit.

109. Life in World without Microbes.

110. Jessica Metcalf, "Microbial Communities Could Be a New Tool for Forensic Science," *University of Colorado News*, Boulder, December 10, 2015, p. 1.

111. David O. Carter, et al., "Seasonal Variations of Postmortem Microbial Communities," *Forensic Science, Medicine, and Pathology*, Vol. 11, Issue 2, June 2015, p. 202.

Chapter 2

1. Neil C. Chamelin, Vernon B. Fox, and Paul M. Whisenand, *Introduction to Criminal Justice*, 2nd edition, (Upper Saddle River, NJ: Prentice Hall, 1979), p. 236.

2. Ibid.

3. See *Brady v. Maryland*, 373 U.S. 83 (1963).

4. See *Giglio v. United States*, 405 U.S. 150 (1972) and expansion of the *Brady duty* in *United States* v. *Agurs*, 427 U.S. 97 (1976); *United States* v. *Bagley*, 473 U.S. 667 (1985); *Kyles* v. *Whitley*, 514 U.S. 419 (1995); and *Youngblood* v. *West Virginia*, 547 U.S. (2006), *Connick v. Thompson* (2011).

5. Pam McDonald and Randy Means, "Brady/Giglio Disclosure Requirements," *Law and Order*, March 2016.

6. *Brady* v. *Maryland*, 373 U.S. 83 (1963).

7. Ibid., pp. 236–237.

8. 110 U.S. 516 (1884).

9. Ibid., pp. 237–238.

10. Ibid., p. 242.

11. Wayne LaFave, *Arrest: The Decision to Take a Suspect into Custody* (Boston: Little, Brown, 1965), pp. 3–4.

12. *Terry* v. *Ohio*, 392 U.S. 1 (1968).

13. See Ryan Devereaux, "Scrutiny Mounts as NYPD "Stop and Frisk" Searches Hit Record High," *The Guardian*, February 14, 2012, and New York Civil Liberties Union, "Stop-and-Frisk Data" at www.nyclu.org/content/stop-and-frisk-data.

14. Jim Dwyer, "What Donald Trump Got Wrong on Stop-and-Frisk," *The New York Times*, September 27, 2016.

15. 129 S.Ct. 695; 172 L.Ed.2d 496 (2009).

16. See, for example, Section 901.15, Florida statutes, for these and other circumstances when arrest by an officer without a warrant is lawful.

17. The majority of this section is taken verbatim from Neil C. Chamelin, Vernon B. Fox, and Paul M. Whisenand, *Introduction to Criminal Justice*, 2nd edition. (Upper Saddle River, NJ: Prentice Hall, 1979), pp. 244–246.

18. 232 U.S. 383 (1914).

19. *Elkins* v. *United States*, 364 U.S. 206 (1960).

20. 338 U.S. 25 (1949).

21. 367 U.S. 643 (1961).

22. 374 U.S. 10 (1963).

23. *Jones* v. *State*, 895 So,2d 1246

24. *Hudson* v. *Michigan*, 126 S.Ct. 2159 (2006).

25. *Muehler* v. *Mena*, 544 U.S. 93, 125 S.Ct. 1465 (2005).

26. *United States* v. *Robinson*, 414 U.S. 218 (1973).

27. 395 U.S. 752 (1969).

28. 494 U.S. 325 (1990).

29. *Maryland* v. *Buie*, 108 L.Ed.2d 276 (1990).

30. Ibid., p. 277.

31. Ibid., p. 283.

32. 267 U.S. 132 (1925).

33. *Chambers* v. *Maroney*, 399 U.S. 42 (1970).

34. 527 U.S. 465 (1999).

35. *Husty* v. *United States*, 282 U.S. 694 (1931).

36. 453 U.S. 454 (1981).

37. 75CrL 177 (U.S. 2004).

38. 129 S.Ct. 1210; 173 L.Ed.2d 485 (2009).

39. 553 U.S. 164; 128 S.Ct. 1598; 170 L.Ed.2d 559 (2008).

40. *United States* v. *Halloway*, 290 F.3d 1331 (C.A. 11) (Ala.) (2002). See also *Johnson* v. *United States*, 333 U.S. 10, 14–15 (1948), listing situations falling within exigent circumstances exception.

41. 387 U.S. 294 (1967).

42. *United States* v. *Holloway*, 290 F.3d 1331 (C.A. 11) (Ala.) (2002).

43. *Brigham City* v. *Stuart*, 126 S.Ct. 1943 (2006).

44. 130 S.Ct. 546; 175 L.Ed.2d 410 (2009).

45. 392 U.S. 1 (1968).

46. 508 U.S. 366 (1993).

47. *Hiibel* v. *Sixth Judicial Circuit Court of Nevada*, 124 S.Ct. 2451 (2004).

48. Ibid., pp. 2457–2458.

49. *Wong Sun* v. *United States*, 371 U.S. 471 (1963).

Chapter 3

1. Justin Zaremba, "Lab Tech Allegedly Faked Result in Drug Case; 7,827 Cases in Question, NJ.com, March 2, 2016, http://www.nj.com/passaic-county/index.ssf/2016/03/state_police_lab_tech_allegedly_faked_results_in_p.html, accessed December 23, 2016.

2. Portions of the information on the preliminary investigation are drawn, with considerable additions by the authors, from the Technical Working Group on Crime Scene Investigation, Crime Scene Investigation: A Guide for Law Enforcement (Washington, D.C.: U.S. Department of Justice, 2013), pp. 1–9.

3. Fox Butterworth, "A Boston Tragedy: The Stuart Case," The New York Times, January 15, 1990, http://www.nytimes.com/1990/01/15/us/boston-tragedy-stuart-casespecial-case-motive-remains-mystery-deaths-that-haunt.html? pagewanted=all, accessed December 18, 2016.

4. Tyler Vazquez, "Alligator Kills Florida Burglary Suspect Hiding from Cops, USAToday, December 8, 2015, http://www.usatoday.com/story/news/nationnow/2015/12/08/alligator-kills-florida-burglary-suspect-hiding-cops/76966512, accessed January 12, 2016.

5. Henry C. Lee, Timothy Palbach, and Marilyn T. Miller, Crime Scene Handbook (San Diego,)CA: Academic Press, 2001), pp. 2–3.

6. No author, "Lori Hacking's Remains Found in Utah Landfill," Fox News, October 1, 2004, http://www.foxnews.com/story/2004/10/01/lori-hacking-remains-found-in-utah-landfill.html, accessed December 19, 2016.

7. Crime Scene Handbook, p. 4.

8. Loc. cit.

9. Ibid., pp. 4-5 from which some points have been taken.

10. Barry A. J. Fisher, Techniques of Crime Scene Investigation, 6th ed. (Boca Raton, FL: CRC Press, 2000), p. 46, with some restatement.

11. Ibid., p. 32.

12. Some of the points in this paragraph are restatements from Crime Scene Investigation, pp. 19–23.

13. Jeffrey Dailey and Lou Martin, "Smart Briefs: Digital Evidence," National Institute of Justice, July 2005, p. 1, https:// www.justnet.org/pdf/SMART_Brief_1.pdf, accessed January 2, 2016.

14. Technical Working Group on Crime Scene Investigation, Crime Scene Investigation, pp. 11-12, with additions by the coauthors.

15. Information on media relations was drawn from various law enforcement policies, including Baltimore (Maryland) Police Department, Policy 601, "Member Confidentiality and Media Releases,| August 9,2016, , accessed January 1, 2017, Seattle (Washington) Police Department, Police Manual, Policy 1.110, Media Relations, March 21, 2012, http://www.seattle.gov/police-manual/general-policy-information/preface, accessed January 2, 2017, Urbana (Illinois) Police Department, Policy Manual, Policy 326, December 3-, 2016, http://www.urbanaillinois.us/sites/default/files/attachments/326-media-relations.pdf, accessed January 3, 2017, and Town of Shalimar (Florida) Police Department Policy Manual, Policy 15.01, December 13, 2016, https://townofshalimar-public.sharepoint.com/Pages/Meetings/2016/20161213%20Meeting/15.01%20SPD%20Media%20Relations%20(20161206).pdf, December 13, 2016, accessed January 3, 2016.

16. Bill Berkeley, "Wrong Assumptions Ruined Probe, "Atlanta Journal and Constitution, Feb. 17, 1982, pp. A1, A13.

17. "But Some Have Ins and Outs," St. Petersburg (Florida) Times, Feb. 24, 1979, p. A1.

18. "Man Accused of Shipping Self to Bank," Atlanta Journal and Constitution, May 10, 1979, p. A18.

19. John Lester, "Forensic Expert Uses Tiny Clues to Solve Crimes," Tampa Tribune, Sept. 9, 1992, pp. 1–2.

20. "Real Estate Agent Pleads Guilty to 5 'Lock Box' Thefts," Washington Post, Sept. 12, 1978, p. B5.

21. Centers for Disease Control and Prevention (CDC), HIV/AIDS, HIV Transmission, June 16, 2017, p. 1, www.cdc.gov/hiv/basics/transmission.html, accessed December 23, 2017.

22. Loc. cit. and HIV/AIDS, HIV Risk Behaviors, December 4, 2015, calculated from p. 1 data, www.cdc.gov/hiv/risk/estimates/riskbehaviors.html, accessed December 23, 2017.

23. Centers for Disease Control and Prevention, HIV Risk Reduction Tool (Beta Version), undated, https://wwwn.cdc.gov/hivrisk/transmit/needles/getting_hiv_needle.html, accessed December 23, 2017.

24. HIV/AIDS, HIV Transmission, p. 1.

25. CDC, HIV/Aids, Opportunistic Infections, May 30, 2017, https://www.cdc.gov/hiv/basics/livingwithhiv/opportunisticinfections.htm, accessed December 23, 2017.

26. NAM AIDsMap, "Survival Outside the Body, 2017, https://www.aidsmap.com/Survival-outside-the-body/page/1321278, accessed December 23, 2017 and AIDs/HIV.

27. American Cancer Society, Kaposi's Sarcoma, Causes, Risk Factors, and Prevention, February 9, 2016, https://www.cancer.org/content/dam/CRC/PDF/Public/8655.00.pdf, accessed December 23, 2017.

28. CDC, HIV/AIDS, HIV in the United States, at a Glance, November 29, 2017, https://www.cdc.gov/hiv/statistics/overview/ataglance.html, accessed December 23, 2017.

29. John Marzulli, "Four Cops on Job: Ruling," (NY) Daily News, October 2, 2008, http://www.nydailynews.com/news/cops-hiv-job-ruling-article-1.300312, accessed December 23, 2017.

30. Centers for Disease Control and Prevention, "HIV/AIDS, PEP," July 12, 2016, https://www.cdc.gov/hiv/basics/pep.html, accessed January 1, 2017.

31. These points are drawn from a variety of sources, which often had repetitive content, For example, See Boston Police Department, Policy 810, Bloodborne Pathogens and Human Bites, July 1, 2016, http://www.baltimore-police.org/sites/default/files/policies-and-procedures/810_Bloodborne_Pathogens_And_Human_Bites.pdf, accessed January 3, 2017, No author, Guidelines for Standard Precautions and Pathogen Occupational Exposure Control (Atlanta: Georgia Department of Public Health), February, 2015, p. 4, and Fort Lauderdale Police http://www.flpd.org/home/showdocument?id=4116 Department, Policy 403.1, Infectious/Communicable Disease Control Plan, February 2016, accessed January 2, 2017, Woodbury County (IOWA) Sheriff's Office, Policy 5, Bloodborne Pathogen and other Infectious Diseases, July 15, 2015, http://www.woodburycountyiowa.gov/attachments/article/2831/WCSO%20Directive%20Manual%207-14%20Sheriff%20Drew.pdf , accessed January 1, 2017, and No author, Facts on Aids: A Law Enforcement Guide, Minnesota Department of Health, undated, http://www.health.state.mn.us/divs/idepc/diseases/hiv/factsonaids.html, accessed January 2, 2017.

32. Centers for Disease Control and Prevention, "Viral Hepatitis," May 26, 2016, p. 1 and supporting pages, www.cdc.gov/hepatitis/abc/index.htm, accessed December 31, 2016.

33. loc. cit.

34. San Francisco Department of Public Health, "Hepatitis A," 2018, p. 1, www.sfcdcp.org/infectious-diseases-a-to-z/d-to-k/hepatitis-a, accessed January 11, May 26, 2016, p. 1.

35. No author, "Police: Woman Spit Hepatitis A-Infected Blood on Officers Face," CBS 46.com, https://www.google.com/webhp?sourceid=chrome-instant&ion=1&espv=2&ie=UTF-8#q=Police%3A+Woman+Spit+Hepatitis+A-Infected+Blood+on+Officers+Face%2C%E2%80%9D, accessed January 1, 2017.

36. Centers for Disease Control and Prevention, "Hepatitis A Questions and Answers for the Public," November 27, 2017, www.cdc.gov/hepatitis/hav/afaq.htm#transmission, accessed January 11, 2018.

37. "Viral Hepatitis," p. 1 and supporting pages.

38. Hepatitis B Foundation, "Hepatitis B Basics," 2010, hepb.org.

39. Aimee Green, "18-year-old Who Acquires A Hepatitis C from his mom—acop—Gets $89k from City," The Oregonisn/Oregon Live, September 30, 2016. http://www.oregonlive.com/portland/index.ssf/2016/09/18-year-old_son_of_portland_co.html, accessed January 1, 2017.

40. Centers for Disease Control, "Hepatitis C," www.cdc.gov/hepatittis/hcv, June 2010, no page number.

41. Centers for Disease Control and Prevention, "Viral Hepatitis."

42. Centers for Disease Control and Prevention, "Questions and Answers: 2014 Ebola Outbreak," February 18, 2016, https://www.cdc.gov/vhf/ebola/outbreaks/2014-west-africa/qa.html, accessed January 5, 2017.

43. Centers for Disease Control and Prevention, "Ebola (Ebola Virus Disease)," February 18, 2016, pp. 1–2, https://www.cdc.gov/vhf/ebola/outbreaks/2014-west-africa/qa.html, accessed January 12, 2017.

44. Centers for Disease Control and Prevention, "Questions and Answers: 2014 Ebola Outbreak,"

45. Centers for Disease Control and Prevention, "Zika Virus: Case Counts in the United States," January 19, 2017, https://www.cdc.gov/zika/geo/united-states.html, accessed January 21, 2017.

46. Centers for Disease Control and Prevention, "Zika Virus: Transmission and Risks," January 20 2017, https://www.cdc.gov/zika/transmission, accessed January 22, 2017.

47. Centers for Disease Control and Prevention, "Zika Virus: Zika and Sexual Transmission," December 1, 2016. https://www.cdc.gov/zika/transmission/sexual-transmission.html, accessed December 23, 2017.

48. Loc. cit.

49. Centers for Disease Control and Prevention, "Zika Virus: Preventing Mosquito Bites," January 17, 2017, https://www.cdc.gov/zika/prevention/prevent-mosquito-bites.html, accessed January 20, 2017.

50. Centers for Disease Control and Prevention, "Tuberculosis: Data and Statistics," December 9, 2016, https://www.cdc.gov/tb/statistics, accessed January 1, 2017.

51. Centers for Disease Control and Prevention, "Tuberculosis: How TB Spreads," March 11, 2016, https://www.cdc.gov/tb/topic/basics/howtbspreads.htm, accessed November 2, 2016.

52. Loc. cit.

53. Centers for Disease Control and Prevention, "TB in Special Populations," April 16, 2013, https://www.cdc.gov/tb/topic/populations/default.htmApril Accessed December 25, 2016.

54. Centers for Disease Control and Prevention, "Tuberculosis: Data and Statistics."

55. Centers for Disease Control and Prevention, "Tuberculosis: Signs and Symptoms," January 7, 2015, https://www.cdc.gov/features/tbsymptoms, accessed July 11, 2016.

56. Associated Press, "Police File Casualty Reports Contact with Man with TB, The Denver Post, November 25, 2007, p. 1, http://www.denverpost.com/2007/11/25/police-file-casualty-reports-contact-with-man-with-tb, accessed December 10, 2016.

57. These points are drawn, often with restatement, from No author, "Physical Evidence Handbook,"PEH-02-01, p. 1, August 16, 2016. (Austin: Texas Department of Public Safety" and Physical No author Crime Scene Investigation: "A Guide for Law Enforcement, Crime Scene Procedures III," (Largo, FL: National Forensic Science Technology Center, 2013), pp. 2–6 and 27–38.

58. Austin (Texas) Police Department "Crime Scene Technical Manual," Photography, October 1, 2014, pp. 7–8.

59. Steve Staggs, "Crime Scene and Evidence Photography-Camera and Lighting, Crime Scene Investigator Network, undated, p. 2, http://www.crime-scene-investigator.net/csp-cameraandlighting.html, accessed January 23, 2017. This article is based on Steve Staggs 4+ star book, Crime Scene and Evidence Photography, 2nd edition 2014). Visit http://www.staggspublishing.com for more details about it.

60. Oregon State Police, Physical Evidence Manual, General Evidence Handling, June 3, 2014 and Austin (Texas) Police Department "Crime Scene Technical Manual," August 16, 2016. p. 7

61. No author Crime Scene Investigation: "A Guide for Law Enforcement, pp. 27–34.

62. Scientific Working Group on Digital Evidence (SWGDE), "Crime Scene/Critical Incident Videography Recommendations and Guidelines," October 8, 2016, p. 4.

63. Crime Scene Investigation: "A Guide for Law Enforcement, pp. 35–38.

64. No author, Physical Evidence Handbook, 8th edition, 2009, p. 45 (WILNET) Wisconsin Law Enforcement Network, Wisconsin Attorney General.

65. Ross Gardner generously reviewed the section on major mapping methods and made several suggestions. He is the lead coauthor of Practical Crime Scene Processing, 2nd Edition, 2013, CRC Press, Boca Raton, Florida.

66. Ross Gardner, Practical Crime Scene Processing (Boca Raton, FL, CRC Press), 2005. Pp. 173–174.

67. Ibid., pp. 174–175.

68. Ibid., p. 178.

69. Forensic Services Policy and Procedures Manual, p. 4.

70. Gardner, Practical Crime Scene Processing, p. 178.

71. Mike Byrd, "Unearthing New Technology in Crime Scene Responses with Forensic Mapping," (www.Crime-Scene-Investigation.net//Forensic Mapping.HTML), undated, p. 4.

72. Gardner, Practical Crime Scene Processing, pp. 181–183.

73. Ibid., p. 188.

74. Kent J. Buehler, "The Role of Archaeological Techniques in Forensic Settings" (Norman: University of Oklahoma, College of Arts and Sciences, Oklahoma Archaeological Survey Newsletter), Vol. 23, No. 1, July 2003, p. 1.

75. Gardner, Practical Crime Scene Processing, p. 188.

76. Ibid., p. 190.

76. Jennifer Coleman, editor, Handbook of Forensic Science (Quantico, VA: Federal Bureau of Investigation, 2013), pp. 1–2.

77. Ibid., p. 3

Chapter 4

1. Kevin Lothridge, Crime Scene Investigation: A Guide for Law Enforcement (Largo, FL: National Forensic Science Technology Center, 2013), Appendices, p. iii.

2. Texas Department of Public Safety, Physical Evidence Handbook, PEH-02-09, Version 5, August 16, 2016, https://www.dps .texas.gov/CrimeLaboratory/documents/PEHmanual.pdf, accessed February 17, 2017.

3. Loc. cit.

4. Federal Bureau of Investigation, Handbook of Forensic Science (Washington, D.C.: Government Printing Office, 1978), p. 2.

5. Crime Scene Investigation: A Guide for Law Enforcement, Appendices, p. iii.

6. Raymond Murray and John Tedrow, Forensic Geology (New Brunswick, NJ: Rutgers University Press, 1975), pp. 17–19.

7. Crime Scene Investigation: A Guide for Law Enforcement, pp. iii–iv.

8. Washington State Patrol, Forensic Service Bureau, Forensic Services Guide, September 2015, pp. 51.

9. Loc. cit.

10. See Chelsea Wald, "Forensic Science: The Soil Sleuth," Nature. com, April 21, 2015, no page numbers, http://www.nature .com/news/forensic-science-the-soil-sleuth-1.17373, accessed February 17, 2017; and Sandrine Demaneche et al., "Microbial Soil Community Analysis for Forensic Science: Application to a Blind Test," Forensic Science International, January 2017, Vol. 270, pp. 153–158.

11. Patricia E. J. Wiltshire, "Protocols for Forensic Palynology," Palynology, March 2016, Vol. 40, Issue 1, pp. 4–24.

12. Kevan A. J. Walsh and Mark Horrocks, "Palynology: Its Position in the Field of Forensic Science," Journal of Forensic Science, September 2008, Vol. 53, Issue 5, pp. 1053–1060.

13. Vaughn M. Bryant and Gretchen D. Jones, "Forensic Palynology: Current Status of a Rarely Used Technique in the United States," Forensic Science International, November 2006, Vol. 163, Issue 3, pp. 183–197. The value of pollen may increase with the development of a semi-automated method of classifying it. See Kimberly C. Riley et. al, "Progress Towards Establishing Collection Standards for Semi-Automated Pollen Classification in Forensic Geo-Historical Location Applications," Review of Palaeobotany and Palynology, October 2015, Vol. 221, pp. 117–127

14. Missouri State Highway Patrol, Forensic Service Handbook (MSHP: Jefferson City, MO, 2012) p. 31.

15. No author, "Pollen Provides Crucial Clue in 1976 Cold Case Murder, CBS News, March 28, 2016, www.cbsnews.com/news/pollen-provides-crucial-new-clue-in-1976-cold-case-murder-of-woodlawn-jane-doe, accessed February 17, 2017.

16. Federal Bureau of Investigation, Handbook of Crime Scene Forensics (New York City: Skyhorse Publishing, 2015), "Soil Samples," Kindle version, no page number.

17. Handbook of Forensic Sciences, p. 133.

18. Oregon State Police, Forensic Services Division, Physical Evidence Manual, September 10, 2015, Impression Evidence, p. 82, http://www.oregon.gov/osp/FORENSICS/docs/Physical %20Evidence%20Manual%20(3940_2).pdf, accessed February 17, 2017.

19. Barry A. J. Fisher, Techniques of Crime Scene Investigation, 8th ed. (Boca Raton, FL: CRC Press, June 15, 2015).

20. Oregon State Police, Forensic Services Division, Physical Evidence Manual, p. 82.

21. National Forensic Science Technology Center, A Simplified Guide to Footwear and Tire Track Examination (Largo, FL: National Forensic Science Technology Center), p. 4, www.forensicsciencesimplified.org/fwtt/FootwearTireTracks .pdf, accessed February 17, 2017. This is source is undated but is supported by a 2009 grant. The material from this source was restated.

22. Florida Department of Law Enforcement, Crime Laboratory Evidence Submission Manual, 2013, p. 50, www.flaccreditation.org/docs/resources/2013ev idencesubmissionm anuel.pdf, accessed February 17, 2017.

23. These guidelines are mentioned consistently in crime laboratory manuals. Some of them are from Ibid., p. 50, and Oregon State Police, Forensic Services Division, Physical Evidence Manual, pp. 82–83.

24. Some of the thoughts in this paragraph are from Oregon State Police, Forensic Services Division, Physical Evidence Manual, p. 84.

25. These guidelines are commonly found in physical evidence or crime scene handbooks prepared by state crime laboratories, for example, Texas Department of Public Safety, Physical Evidence Handbook, PEH-02-05, pp. 8–9 and Oklahoma State Bureau of Investigation, Evidence Collection Manual, 2011, p. 73, https://www.ok.gov/osbi/documents/Crime%20Scene%20Manual.pdf, accessed February 19, 2017. Also see Dick Warrington, "Casting: Beyond the Basics," Forensic Magazine, May 6, 2015, https://www.forensic-mag.com/article/2015/05/casting -beyond-basics, accessed February 17, 2017. For the most part these guidelines have been restated.

26. Handbook of Crime Scene Forensics (2015), no page number, and "Casting: Beyond the Basics," p. 3, with restatement.

27. Oklahoma State Bureau of Investigation, Evidence Collection Manual (2011), p. 74 and "Casting: Beyond the Basics," p. 3, with restatement.

28. This content is drawn from materials that appear on portions of the pages cited: Wisconsin State Crime Laboratories, Physical Evidence Handbook (Madison, WI; 8th edition, 2013), pp. 93–98.

29. Brenda B. Christy, "The Use of the PDQ (Paint Data Query) Database Along with Other Resources to Provide Vehicle Information for Hit and Run Vehicles within Virginia," undated, http://projects.nfstc.org/trace/docs/Trace%

20Presentations%20CD-2/christy.pdf, accessed December 26, 217. The author is a Forensic Scientists Senior, in the Trace Evidence Section, Eastern Laboratory, Virginia Department of Forensic Science, Norfolk.

30. Kim Waggoner, *Handbook of Forensic Science* (Washington, D.C.: Government Printing Office, 1977), p. 101.

31. Texas Department of Public Safety, *Physical Evidence Handbook*, PEH-02-05, p. 5.

32. Oregon State Police, *Physical Evidence Manual*, p. 69.

33. Texas Department of Public Safety, *Physical Evidence Handbook*, PEH-02-05, p. 5.

34. Oregon State Police, *Physical Evidence Manual*, p. 68.

35. Ibid., p. 69.

36. Ibid., p. 68.

37. Loc. cit.

38. Maureen C. Bottrell, "Forensic Glass Comparison: Background Information Used in Data Interpretation, *FBI Forensic Science Communications,* April 2009, Vol. 11, No. 2, p. 3. https://archives.fbi.gov/archives/about-us/lab/forensic-science-communications/fsc/april2009/review/2009_04_review01.htm, accessed December 28, 2017.

39. Loc. cit.

40. Ibid., 2

41. *Handbook of Forensic Science,* (2015) pp. 69–71.

42. Ibid., p. 71

43. Mignon Dunbar and Terence M. Murphy, "DNA Analysis of Natural Fiber Rope," *Journal of Forensic Sciences,* January 2009, Vol. 54, Issue 1, pp. 108–113.

44. Robert C. Chisnall, "Knot Tying Habits, Tier Handedness, and Experience," *Journal of Forensic Sciences,* September 2010, Vol. 55, No. 5, pp. 1232–1244.

45. Although the fingerprints of twins may have a high degree of similarity, variations still occur that make identification possible. C. H. Chin et al., "Fingerprint Comparison I: Similarity of Fingerprints," *Journal of Forensic Sciences,* 1982, Vol. 27, No. 2, pp. 290–304.

46. Phillip Jones, "Friction Ridges Make a Lasting Impression," *Forensic Magazine,* October 1, 2006, p. 5, www.forensicmag.com/article/2006/10/friction-ridges-make-lasting-impression, accessed February 21, 2017. National Forensic Sciences Technology Center, "A Simplified Guide to Fingerprint Analysis" (NFSTC: Largo, FL, 2011), p. 2.

47. Nitin Kaushal and Purnima Kaushal, "Human Identification and Fingerprints: A Review," Journal of Biometrics and Biostatistics, November 15, 2011, www.omicsonline.org/human-identification-and-fingerprints-a-review-2155-6180.1000123.php?aid=2581, accessed December 27, 2017.

48. National Institute of Science and Technology, U.S. Department of Commerce, "Who, What, and When: Determining the Age of Fingerprints," August 15, 2015, https://www.nist.gov/news-events/news/2015/08/who-what-when-determining-age -fingerprints, accessed February 21, 2017.

49. "A Simplified Guide to Fingerprint Analysis," p. 5. Similar content is found elsewhere, including *The Sourcebook for Fingerprints* (2012). The information was drawn with restatement, added examples, and reorganization.

50. Karley Hujet and Diana Tabor, "Chicken or the Egg: Process for Latent Prints or DNA First, Wisconsin State Crime Laboratory-Madison, http://docplayer.net/20662014-Chicken-or-the-egg-process-for-latent-prints-or-dna-first-karley-hujet-diana -tabor.html, accessed February 22, 2017.

51. Information in this paragraph was influenced or drawn with restatement from the Georgia Bureau of Investigation's "Latent Prints Overview" (Georgia Bureau of Investigation: Atlanta, GA), 2011, 10 pp; Alan McRoberts, ed., *The Source Book of Finger Prints* (Washington, D.C.: National Institute of Justice, U.S. Department of Justice, 2011); Brian Yamashita et al., Chapter 7, "Latent Print Development," Laura Hutchins with Robert E. May, Chapter 8, "The Preservation of Friction Ridges," and John R. Vanderkolk, Chapter 9, "The Examination Process," and the Federal Bureau of Investigation, and The West Virginia State Police, *Forensic Laboratory Field Manual* (West Virginia State Police; Charleston, WV, October 8, 2010), pp. 112–130.

52. A. J. Brooks, "The Search for Latent Prints When an Offender Wears Gloves," Fingerprint and Identification Magazine, Vol. 53, No. 12, 1972, pp. 3–7 and 15–16.

53. Sara Fieldhouse, Eliska Oravcova, and Laura Walton-Williams, "The Effect of DNA Recovery on the Subsequent Quality of Latent Fingerprints," *Forensic Science International,* October 2016, Vol. 267, pp. 78–88.

54. James Osterburg and Richard H. Ward, *Criminal Investigation* (Cincinnati: Anderson Publishing, 1992), p. 109. For general information on the subject, see S. Clark, "Chemical Detection of Latent Fingerprints," *Journal of Chemical Education,* July 1993, Vol. 70, No. 7, pp. 593–595.

55. K. B. Rozman, M. Trapecar, and B. Dobovsek, "Fingerprint Recovery from Human Skin by Finger Powder," *Journal of Forensic Science and Criminology,* 2014, Vol. 2, Issue 3, p. 1.

56. Matej Trapecar and Jose Balazic, "Fingerprint Recovery from Human Skin Surface," *Science and Justice,* 2007, Vol. 46, pp. 136–140.

57. Final Report ISEC Project, "Optimisation of Recovery of Fingerprints and DNA on Human Skin," German Federal Police, 2nd edition, May 21, 2014, pp. 4–8, http://www.csofs.org/write/MediaUploads/News/Optimisation _of_recovery_of_Latent_Fingerprints_and_DNA_on_Human_Skin_EU _ISEC_project.pdf, accessed February 22, 2017.

58. C. Michael Bowers, "Who is a Qualified Forensic Dentist?" in C. Michael Bowers, editor, Forensic Dental Evidence (Boston: Elsevier, 2011), p. 30.

59. See Adriana Balan et al., "Orofacial Trauma Patterns in Child Victims of Violence and Abuse," *Romanian Society of Legal Medicine,* 2014, Vol. 22, pp. 187–192 and Arturo Garrocho-Rangel, et. al., "Dentist Attitudes and Responsibilities Concerning Child Sexual Abuse. A Review and Case Report," Journal of Clinical and Experimental Dentistry," Vol. 7, No. 3, July 2015.

60. Panarat Thepgumpanat, "Thai Tsunami Forensic Centre Produces First IDs," Reuters, January 18, 2005 , www.alertnet.org

61. C. Stavrianos et al., "Applications of Forensic Dentistry: Part I," *Research Journal of Medical Sciences,* 2010, Vol. 4, Issue 3, p. 179.

62. G. Sung et. al, "Smile Photographs as a Tool for Forensic Identification," *Journal of Dental Specialties,* September 2014, Vol. 2, Issue 2, pp. 11–17.

63. I. A. Pretty and D. Sweet, "A Look at Forensic Dentistry—Part 1: The Role of Teeth in the Determination of Human Identity," *British Dental Journal,* April 14, 2001, Vol. 190, No. 7, p. 362.

64. C. Michael Bowers, "Recognition, Documentation, Evidence Collections, and Interpretation of Bite Marks," in C. Michael Bowers, ed., *Forensic Dentistry: A Field Investigator's Handbook* (Academic Press: Burlington, MA, 2004), p. 106.

65. Roger W. Byard et al., "Locard's Principle of Exchange, Dental Examination and Fragments of Skin," *Journal of Forensic Sciences,* March 2016, Vol. 66, Issue 2, pp. 545–547.

66. American Board of Forensic Odontology, "Bite Mark Methodology, Standards, and Guidelines," March 16, 2016, 10 pp., http://abfo.org/wp-content /uploads/2016/03/ABFO-Bitemark -Standards-03162016.pdf, accessed February 23, 2016. Qw3z.6. Also see S. A. Blackwell et al., "Three-Dimensional Comparative Analysis of Bitemarks," *Journal of Forensic Sciences* May 2009, Vol. 54, Issue 3, pp. 658–661.

67. Rachana V. Prabhu et al., "Cheiloscopy: Revisited," *Journal of Forensic Dental Science,* 2012, Vol. 4, No. 1, pp. 47–52.

68. Janardhanam Dineshshankar et al., "Lip Prints: Role in Forensic Odontology," *Journal of Pharmacy and Bioallied Sciences,* June 2013, Vol. 5, Issue 5 (Supplement), pp. 95–97.

69. "Cheiloscopy: Revisited," pp. 47–52.

70. Marin Vodanovic and Hrvoje Brkic, "Dental Profiling in Forensic Science," *Medicinske Znanost,* 2012, Vol. 522. Issue 38, p. 153.

71. Karen A. Lanning et al., "Scientific Working Group on Materials Analysis Position Paper on Hair," *Journal of Forensic Sciences,* September 2009, Vol. 54, Issue 5, p. 1198.

72. Many of the points in this list are drawn, with restatement and the addition of examples, from Scientific Working Group on Materials Analysis (SWG-MAT), "Forensic Human Hair Examination Guidelines," April 2005, PDF document, no page numbers, https://www.nist.gov/sites/default/files/documents /2016/09/22/forensic_human_hair_examination_guidelines.pdf, accessed December 30, 2017.

73. On dyed hair, see Julie A. Barrett, Jay Siegel, and John V. Goodpaster, "Forensic Discrimination of Dyed Hair Color," *Journal of Forensic Sciences,* March 2010, Vol. 55, Issue 2, pp. 323–333.

74. Karen A. Lanning et al., "Scientific Working Group on Materials Analysis Position Paper on Hair," *Journal of Forensic Sciences,* September 2009, Vol. 54, Issue 5, p. 1198. Also see Terry Melton, "Mitochondrial DNA Examination of Cold Case Crime Scene Hairs," Forensic Journal, April 1, 2009, pp.1–3.

75. Oregon State Police, Forensic Services Division, *Physical Evidence Manual,* p. 80.

76. Loc. cit.

77. Annapolis (Maryland) Police Department, "Collection of Trace Evidence and DNA Evidence," General Order K.7, April 2007, pp. 3–4,www.annapolis.gov/DocumentCenter/Home/View/4873, accessed December 30, 2017.

78. Lily Huang and Diane Beauchemin, "Ethnic Background and Gender Identification Using Electrothermal Vaporization Coupled to Iinductively Coupled

Plasma Optical Emission Spectrometry for Forensic Analysis of Hair," Journal of Analytical Atomic Spectrometry, Also see Ewelina Mistek et al., "Race Differentiation by Raman Spectroscopy of a Blood Stain for Forensic Purposes,"," *Analytical Chemistry,* Vol. 88, Issue 2016, 15, pp. 7453–7456.

79. Donald J. Johnson et al., "A Molecular Method to Correlate Bloodstains with Wound Site at Crime Scene Reconstruction," *Journal of Forensic Sciences,* 2014, Vol. 59, Issue 3, pp. 735–742.

80. J. Chang and S. Michielsen, "Effect of Fabric Mounting Method and Backing Material on Bloodstain Patterns of Drip Stains on Textiles,*" International Journal of Legal Medicine,* 2016, Vol. 130, Issue 3, pp. 649–659.

81. N. Kabaliuk et al., "Experimental Validation of Numerical Model for Predicting the Trajectory of Blood Drops in Typical Crime Scene Conditions, Including Droplet Deformation and Breakup, with Study of the Effect of Indoor Wind Currents and Wind on Typical Blood Splatter Drop Trajectories," *Forensic Science International,* 2014, Vol. 245, pp. 107–120.

82. For example, see Hancheng Lin, et. al., Scientific Reports, "Estimation of the Age of Human Bloodstains Under the simulated Indoor and Outdoor Crime Scene Conditions by ATR-FTIR Spectroscopy," October 16, 2017, https://www. nature.com/articles/s41598-017-13725-1, accessed December 3, 2017.

83. Edward Hueske, *Practical Analysis & Reconstruction of Shooting Incidents* (Boca Raton, FL: CRC Press, 2006), p. 226.

84. Henry C. Lee, Timothy Palmbach, and Marilyn T. Miller, *Crime Scene Handbook* (San Diego: Academic Press, 2001), p. 282.

85. S. Shanan et al., "Evaluation of Six Presumptive Tests for Blood: Their Specificity, Sensitivity, and Effect on High-Molecule-Weight DNA," *Journal of Forensic Sciences,* January 2007, Vol. 52, Issue 1, pp. 102–109.

86. Waggoner, Handbook of Forensic Services, pp. 45–46.

87. Muchael S. Adamowicz, "The Potential of Cosmetic Applicators as a Source of DNA for Forensic Analysis," *Journal of Forensic Sciences,* July 2015, Vol. 60, Issue 4, pp. 1001–1011.

88. O. C. Smith, L. Jantz, H. E. Berryman, and S. A. Symes, "Effects of Human Decomposition on Striations," *Journal of Forensic Sciences,* 1993, Vol. 38, No. 3, pp. 593–598.

89. See R. Thomas, "Contribution to the Identification of Smooth Bore Firearms," *International Criminal Police Review,* 1974, Vol. 28, No. 280, pp. 190–193.

90. Aylin Saribey, Abigail Hannam, and Celik Tarimci, "An Investigation into Whether or Not Class and Individual Characteristics of Five Turkish Manufactured Pistols Change During Extensive Firing," *Journal of Forensic Sciences,* September 2009, Vol. 54, Issue 5, pp. 1068–1072.

91. John W. Bond and Chuck Heidel, "Visualization of Latent Fingerprint Corrosion on a Discharged Brass Shell Casing," *Journal of Forensic Sciences,* July 2009, Vol. 54, Issue 4, pp. 892–894.

92. Michael D. Clark, "Tool Identification from a Clod of Soil from a Grave," *Journal of Forensic Sciences,* January 2011, Vol. 56, Issue 1, pp. 241–243.

93. Nebraska State Patrol, Crime Laboratory, Crime Laboratory Manual, Toolmarks, January 5, 2015, p. 1, www.statepatrol.nebraska.gov/vimages/shared/ vnews/stories/56a799f237860/toolmarks.pdf, accessed December 31, 2017.

94. Ibid., pp. 1–4.

95. Benjamin Bachrach et al., "Statistical Evidence of the Individuality and Repeatability of Striated Tool Marks: Screwdrivers and Tongue and Groove Pliers," *Journal of Forensic Sciences,* March 2010, Vol. 55, Issue 2, pp. 348–357.

96. Georgia Bureau of Investigation's "Tool Mark Examination" (Georgia Bureau of Investigation: Atlanta, GA), 2011, p. 1, \, accessed February 16, 2017.

97. E'lyn Bryan, "Questioned Document Examination," *Evidence Technology Magazine,* May/June 2010, Vol. 8, No. 3. Accessed January 10, 2011, p. 1, with additions.

98. Carolyne Bird, Bryan Found, and Doug Rogers, "Forensic Document Examiners' Skill in Distinguishing between Natural and Disguised Handwriting Behaviors," *Journal of Forensic Sciences,* September 2010, Vol. 55, Issue 5, pp. 1291–1295.

99. No author, "Tool for Document Examination," *Tech Beat,* Spring 2010, National Law Enforcement and Corrections Center, Spring 2010, 2 pp., http://www.cedar.buffalo.edu/pub_docs/article134_full.pdf, accessed February 17, 2017.

100. Loc. cit.

Chapter 5

1. Marshall Houts, *From Evidence to Proof* (Springfield, IL: Charles C. Thomas, 1956), pp. 10–11.

2. John E. Hess, *Interviewing and Interrogation for Law Enforcement* (Cincinnati: Anderson, 1997), p. 33.

3. Ibid., pp. 81–84; Charles L. Yeshke, *The Art of Investigative Interviewing* (Boston: Butter-worth-Heinemann, 1997), pp. 56–68.

4. Paul B. Weston and Kenneth M. Wells, *Criminal Investigation: Basic Perspectives* (Englewood Cliffs, NJ: Prentice Hall, 1970), p. 151.

5. *First Response to Victims of Crime,* U.S. Department of Justice, Office of Justice Programs; www.ojp.usdoj.gov.

6. Hess, *Interviewing and Interrogation for Law Enforcement,* p. 84.

7. William Hart, "The Subtle Art of Persuasion," *Police Magazine,* January 1981, p. 10.

8. Stan B. Walters, *Principles of Kinesic Interview and Interrogation,* 2nd edition (New York: CRC Press, 2003), p. 2.

9. Yeschke, *The Art of Investigative Interviewing,* pp. 25–40, 113–134.

10. *First Response to Victims of Crime,* U.S. Department of Justice, p. 17.

11. U.S. Department of Labor, Office of Disability Employment Policy; the Medial Project, Research and Training Center on Independent Living, University of Kansas, Lawrence, KS; and the National Center for Access Unlimited, Chicago, IL. About 9% of the American population is either deaf or hard of hearing. And as baby boomers reach their senior years, the percentage is going to increase. So the chance of an officer dealing with a deaf person or someone who is hard of hearing is a distinct possibility, which the officer should be prepared to deal with. Retrieved from *http:// www.dol.gov/odep/pubs/fact/comucate.htm,* accessed February 17, 2014.

12. Amaury Muragado, "Dealing with the Deaf," *Police Beat,* September 20, 2013; http://www.policemag.com/channel/careers-training/articles/2013/09/dealing-with-the-deaf.aspx, accessed February 17, 2014.

13. U.S. Department of Labor, Office of Disability Employment Policy.

14. "Police Officer's Guide for Working with People with Developmental Disabilities and Achieving Positive Come, Community Mental Health for Central Michigan; http://www.thearcofmidland.org/wordpress/wp-content/ uploads/2013/11/A-Police-Officers-Guide-for-Working-with-People-with-Developmental-Disabilities-and-Achieving-Positive-Outcome.pdf, accessed February 17, 2014.

15. U.S. Department of Labor, Office of Disability Employment Policy.

16. Brian L. Cutler and Steven D. Penrod, *Mistaken Identification: The Eyewitness, Psychology, and the Law* (New York: Cambridge University Press, 1995), p. 6.

17. Ibid., p. 7.

18. Robert L. Donigan, Edward C. Fisher, et al., *The Evidence Handbook,* 4th edition (Evanston, IL: Traffic Institute, Northwestern University, 1980), p. 205.

19. Robert Buckhout, "Eyewitness Testimony," *Scientific American,* December 1974, Vol. 231, No. 6, p. 23. Also see Elizabeth F. Loftus, Edith L. Greene, and James M. Doyle, "The Psychology of Eyewitness Testimony," in *Psychological Methods in Criminal Investigation and Evidence,* David C. Raskin, ed. (New York: Springer, 1989), pp. 3–45; Hunter A. McAllister, Robert H. I. Dale, and Cynthia E. Hunt, "Effects of Lineup Modality on Witness Credibility," *Journal of Social Psychology,* June 1993, Vol. 133, No. 3, p. 365.

20. Cutler and Penrod, *Mistaken Identification,* p. 112.

21. Janet Reno, "Message from the Attorney General," *Introduction at the National Institute of Justice, Office of Justice Programs, Eyewitness Evidence: A Guide for Law Enforcement* (Washington, D.C.: U.S. Department of Justice, Oct. 1999), p. iii.

22. Siegfried Ludwig Sporer, Roy S. Malpass, and Guenter Koehnken, *Psychological Issues in Eyewitness Identification* (Mahwah, NJ: Lawrence Erlbaum, 1996), p. 23.

23. Cutler and Penrod, *Mistaken Identification,* p. 113.

24. Buckhout, "Eyewitness Testimony," p. 24. See also, Steven Wallace, "The Puzzle of Memory: Reflections on the Divergence of Truth and Accuracy," *The Florida Bar Journal,* October 2005, pp. 24–28.

25. Elizabeth Loftus, "Incredible Eyewitness," *Psychology Today,* December 1974, Vol. 8, No. 7, p. 118.

26. Sporer, Malpass, and Koehnken, *Psychological Issues,* pp. 26–29.

27. Ibid., pp. 34–35.

28. Ibid., pp. 36–39.

29. Buckhout, "Eyewitness Testimony," pp. 24–26.

30. Kelly Dedel, "Witness Intimidation," *Problem-Oriented Guides for Police Problem-Specific Guides Series No. 42* (Washington, D.C.: U.S. Department of Justice, Office of Community Oriented Policing Services, 2006), pp. 2–30. (This discussion was adapted from this source.)

31. In this chapter, the term "witness" is used to refer both to victims and to bystanders who could provide information to police. The term "victim" is used to denote the victim of the initial crime.

32. C. Johnson, B. Webster, and E. Connors, *Prosecuting Gangs: A National Assessment,* NIJ Research in Brief Series (Washington, D.C.: U.S. National Institute of Justice, 1995).

33. P. Finn and K. Healey, *Preventing Gang and Drug-Related Witness Intimidation*, NIJ Issues and Practices Series (Washington, D.C.: U.S. National Institute of Justice, 1996); R. Elliott, "Vulnerable and Intimidated Witnesses: A Review of the Literature," in *Speaking Up for Justice* (London: Home Office, 1998).

34. N. Fyfe and H. McKay. "Police Protection of Intimidated Witnesses: A Study of the Strathclyde Police Witness Protection Programme," *Policing and Society*, 2000a, Vol. 10, No. 3 pp. 277-299.

35. J. Tomz and D. McGillis, *Serving Crime Victims and Witnesses*, 2d edition (Washington, D.C.: U.S. Department of Justice, National Institute of Justice, 1997).

36. Elliott, "Vulnerable and Intimidated Witnesses"; Finn and Healey, *Preventing Gang and Drug-Related Witness Intimidation*.

37. C. Gaines, "Witness Intimidation," *United States Attorneys' Bulletin*, 2003, Vol. 51, No. 1, pp. 5-10.

38. K. Healey, *Victim and Witness Intimidation: New Developments and Emerging Responses*, Research in Action Series (Washington, D.C.: U.S. National Institute of Justice, 1995).

39. Thomas P. Sullivan, "Police Experiences with Recording Custodial Interrogations," *North-western University School of Law* Summer 2004, Vol. 1, p. 4.

40. See the discussion of camera angles in G. Daniel Lassiter et al., "Criminal Confessions on Videotape: Does Camera Perspective Bias Their Perceived Veracity?" *Current Research in Social Psychology*, 2001, Vol. 7, No. 1, *at* www.uiowa.edu/~grpproc/crisp/crisp.7.1.htm.

41. Sullivan, "Police Experiences with Recording Custodial Interrogations," pp. 5-10.

42. See Timothy T. Burke, "Documenting and Reporting a Confession: A Guide for Law Enforcement," *FBI Law Enforcement Bulletin*, Feb. 2001, Vol. 70, No. 2, pp. 17-21.

43. Fred E. Inbau and John E. Reid, *Criminal Interrogation and Confessions* (Baltimore: Williams & Wilkins, 1962), p. 1.

44. Saul M. Kassin, "The Psychology of Confessions," *Annual Review of Law in Social Science*, 2008, Vol. 4, pp. 194-196.

45. The Innocence Project is a national litigation and public policy organization dedicated to exonerating wrongfully convicted people through DNA testing and reforming the criminal justice system to prevent future injustice; available from http://www.innocenceproject.org/; Internet.

46. Kassin, "The Psychology of Confessions."

47. S. M. Kassin et al., "Police Interviewing and Interrogation: A Self-Reporting Survey of Police Practices and Beliefs," *Law and Human Behavior* 2007, Vol. 31, pp. 381-400.

48. S. M. Kassin and L. S. Wrightsman, "Confession Evidence," in *The Psychology of Evidence and Trial Procedure*, S. M. Kassin and L. A. Wrightsman, eds. (Beverly Hills, CA: Sage, 1985), pp. 67-94.

49. G. H. Gudjonsson, *The Psychology of Interrogations and Confessions: A Handbook* (Chichester, UK: Wiley, 2003).

50. C. F. Karlsen, *The Devil in the Shape of a Woman: Witchcraft in Colonial New England* (New York: Vintage, 1989).

51. S. M. Kassin, "Internalized False Confessions," in *Handbook of Eyewitness Psychology: Vol. 1: Memory for Events*, M. Toglia, J. Read, D. Ross, and R. Lindsay, eds (Mahwah, NJ: Erlbaum, 2007).

52. S. A. Drizin and B. Colgan, "Tales from the Juvenile Confession Front: A Guide to How Standard Police Interrogation Tactics Can Produce Coerced and False Confessions from Juvenile Suspects," in *Interrogations, Confessions and Entrapment*, G. D. Lassiter, ed. (New York: Kluwer Acad., 2004), pp. 127-162.

53. Thomas P. O'Connor, *False Confessions*, at the 115th IACP Conference held in 2008 in San Diego; the Police Investigative Operations Committee, the Police Image and Ethics and the Forensics Committee adopted a resolution supporting research of wrongful convictions and recommended that Congress support and fund efforts to review and develop recommendations to reduce and eventually eliminate wrongful convictions. (This discussion is based upon these recommendations.)

54. 297 U.S. 278 (1936).

55. *Payne* v. *Arkansas*, 356 U.S. 560 (1958).

56. *Miranda* v. *Arizona*, 384 U.S. 436 (1966).

57. Ibid.

58. Donigan et al., *The Evidence Handbook*, pp. 47-48. See also *Frazier* v. *Cupp*, 394 U.S. 731 (1969); *Oregon* v. *Mathiason*, 429 U.S. 492 (1977).

59. 318 U.S. 332 (1943).

60. 354 U.S. 449 (1957).

61. *Miranda* v. *Arizona*, 384 U.S. 436 (1966).

62. *Escobedo* v. *Illinois*, 378 U.S. 478 (1964).

63. 384 U.S. 436 (1966).

64. 451 U.S. 477, 101 S.Ct. 1880 (1981).

65. 498 U.S. 146 (1990).

66. 559 U.S. ____. 1305 S. Ct. 1213(2010).

67. 423 U.S. 96, 96 S.Ct. 321 (1975).

68. 492 U.S. 195, 109 S.Ct. 2875 (1989).

69. 130 S.Ct. 1195, 175 L.Ed.2d 1009 (2010).

70. 82 L. Ed. 317 (1984).

71. 430 U.S. 387 (1977).

72. 446 U.S. 291, 100 S.Ct. 1682 (1980).

73. *United States* v. *Clark*, 982 F.2d 965, at 968 (6th Cir. 1993).

74. Jonathan L. Rudd, "You Have to Speak Up to Remain Silent: The Supreme Court Revisits the *Miranda* Right to Silence," *FBI Law Enforcement Bulletin*, September 2010, pp. 25-31.

75. *Berghuis* v. *Thompkins*, 560 U.S.____(2010).

76. *Id.* "Notification of Constitutional Rights and Statement: (1) You have the right to remain silent. (2) Anything you say can and will be used against you in a court of law. (3) You have the right to talk to a lawyer before answering any questions and you have the right to have a lawyer present with you while you are answering questions. (4) If you cannot afford to hire a lawyer, one will be appointed to represent you before any questioning, if you wish one. (5) You have the right to decide at any time before or during questioning to use your right to remain silent and your right to talk with a lawyer while you are being questioned."

77. Ibid.

78. Ibid.

79. Thompkins also filed a motion for a new trial claiming ineffective assistance of counsel. This motion was likewise denied and followed the appeal regarding alleged *Miranda* violations to the Supreme Court.

80. The Sixth Circuit Court also ruled in favor of Thompkins on the ineffective-assistance-of-counsel claims.

81. *Miranda* at 446. In *Michigan* v. *Mosley*, 423 U.S. 96 (1995), the Court explained that when a subject invokes his right to silence, all questioning must cease. However, the Court further held that the invocation of the right to remain silent does not mean that police never may resume questioning. Indeed, in *Mosley*, the Court held that the police had scrupulously honored the suspect's Fifth Amendment rights when a different officer questioned the subject in a different location about a different crime after 2 hours had elapsed since the subject invoked his right to remain silent. (Note, this differs from an invocation of the right to counsel, wherein officers would not be allowed to reinitiate contact after merely the passage of time. See *Edwards* v. *Arizona*, 451 U.S. 477 (1981) and *Maryland* v. *Shatzer*, 559 U.S. __(2010).

82. Justice Kennedy delivered the 5-4 opinion of the Court, in which Chief Justice Roberts and Justices Scalia, Thomas, and Alito joined. Justice Sotomayor filed a dissenting opinion, in which Justices Stevens, Ginsberg, and Breyer joined.

83. *Davis* v. *United States*, 512 U.S. 452 (1994).

84. *Berghius*.

85. *Miranda*, at 475

86. Ibid.

87. *Davis*, at 460; *Moran* v. *Burbine, 475 U.S.* 412, at 427 (1986).

88. *Dickerson*, at 443-444.

89. Joe Navarro, with Marin Karlins, *What Every BODY Is Saying* (New York, NY: HarperCollins, 2008), pp. 207-229.

90. C. V. Ford, *Lies!, Lies!!, Lies!!! The Psychology of Deceit* (Washington, DC: American Psychiatric Press, Inc., 1996), p. 217. P. Ekman, *Telling Lies: Clues to Deceit in the Marketplace, Politics, and Marriage* (New York: W.W. Norton & Co., 1991), p. 162.

91. P. Ekman and M. O'Sullivan, "Who Can Catch a Liar?" *American Psychologist*, 1991, Vol. 46, pp. 913-920.

92. Ekman, *Telling Lies*, pp. 187-188.

93. Ibid., pp. 162-189.

94. Ekman, *Telling Lies*, pp. 170-173.

95. R. B. Cialdini, *Influence: The Psychology of Persuasion* (New York: William Morrow and Company, Inc., 1993), pp. 167-207.

96. Ekman, *Telling Lies*, p. 185.

97. In the study of nonverbal communications, the limbic brain is where the action is ___ because it is the part of the brain that reacts to the world around us reflexively and instantaneously, in real time, and without thought. For that reason, it gives off a *true* response to information coming in from the environment [D. G. Myers, *Exploring Psychology*, 2nd edition (New York: Worth Publishers, 1993), pp. 35-39]. Because it is uniquely responsible for our survival, the limbic brain does not take breaks. It is always "on." The limbic brain is also our emotional center. It is from there that signals go out to various other parts of the brain, which in turn orchestrate our behaviors as they relate

to emotions or our survival [J. LeDoux, *The Emotional Brain: The Mysterious Underpinnings of Emotional Life* (New York: Touchstone, 1996), pp. 104–137]. These behaviors can be observed and decoded as they manifest physically in our feet torso, arms, hands, and faces. Since these reactions occur without thought, unlike words, they are genuine. Thus, the limbic brain is considered the "honest brain" when we think of nonverbal [D. Goleman, *Emotional Intelligence* (New York: Bantam Books, 1995), pp. 13–29].

98. G. de Becker, *The Gift of Fear* (New York: Dell Publishing, 1997), p. 133.
99. Ekman, *Telling Lies*, pp. 101–133.
100. D. J. Lieberman, *Never Be Lied to Again* (New York: St. Martin's Press, 1998), p. 24.
101. Ekman, *Telling Lies*, pp. 158–169.
102. J. Navarro and J. R. Schafer, "Detecting Deception," *FBI Law Enforcement Bulletin,* July 2001, pp. 9–13.
103. A. Virj, *Detecting Lies and Deceit* (Chichester, UK: John Wiley & Sons, Ltd., 2003), pp. 38–39.
104. R. R. Johnston, "Race and Police Reliance on Suspicious Non-Verbal Cues," *Policing: An International Journal of Police Strategies & Management,* 2007, Vol. 20, No. 2, pp. 280–281.
105. Saul M. Kasin and Gisli H. Gudjonsson, "True Crimes, False Confessions," *Scientific American Mind,* June 2005, Vol. 16, pp. 24–31.
106. S. M. Kassin, "A Critical Appraisal of Modern Police Interrogations," in *Investigative Interviewing: Rights, Research, Regulation*, Tom Williamson, ed. (Devon, UK: Willian Publishing, 2006), pp. 207–228.
107. Virj, *Detecting Lies and Deceit*, pp. 25–27.
108. These points are found on the Internet site for the American Association of Police Polygraphists, p. 2, January 21, 2005; see www.policepolygraph.org/standards.htm.
109. Based on information supplied by Captain John P. Slater (Ret.), Law Enforcement Training Coordinator, National Institute for Truth Verification, 2007.

Chapter 6

1. Michael Biggs, *Just the Facts: Investigative Report Writing* (Upper Saddle River, NJ: Prentice Hall, 2001), p. 16.
2. Amy Hyman Gregory et. al., "A Comparison of U.S. Police Interviewers' Notes and Their Subsequent Reports," *Journal of Investigative Psychology & Offender Profiling,* June 2011, Vol. 8, Issue 2, p. 203.
3. Gary Cordner, "The Problem with People with Mental Illness," Center for Problem-Oriented Policing, 2016 POP Conference, Tempe, AZ, October 22–24, 2016, p. 1.
4. Loc. cit.
5. Ibid., p. 22.
6. Brian A. Reaves, Local Police Departments, 2015: Equipment and Technology (Washington, D.C.: Bureau of Justice Statistics, July 2015), p. 1.
7. Major Cities Chiefs and Major County Sheriffs, Technology Needs-Body Worn Cameras (Vienna, Virginia: Lafayette Group, December 2015), p. 1.
8. Loc. cit.
9. No author, "State Body-Worn Camera Laws," National Conference of State Legislatures, June 11, 2016, p. 1, http://www.ncsl.org/meetings-training.aspx, accessed July 9, 2016.
10. Roseanna Sommers, "Will Putting Cameras on Police Reduce Polarization" Yale Law Journal, Vol. 125, Issue 5, March 2016, pp. 1304–1362.
11. San Diego (California) Police Department Procedure 1.49 Administration, Subject: Axon Body Cameras, July 8, 2015, pp. 11–12.
12. David K. Bakardjiev, "Officer Body-Worn Cameras-Capturing Objective Evidence with Quality Technology and Focused Policies," Jurimetrics, The Journal of Law, Science, and Technology, Vol. 56, Issue 1, Fall 2015, pp. 79–112.
13. Federal Bureau of Investigation, "About the Uniform Crime Report (UCR) Program," 2016, p.5, https://ucr.fbi.gov/nibrs/2016/resource-pages/aboutucrmain_nibrs-2016_final.pdf, accessed November 11, 2017.
14. Loc. cit.
15. Ibid., p. 5.
16. Ibid., p. 6.
17. Federal Bureau of Investigation, 2016 National Incident Based Reporting System (NIBRS), p. 1., https://ucr.fbi.gov/nibrs/2016, accessed December 11, 2017.
18. No author, Incident-Based Reporting Resource Center, 2016, p.1, http://www.jrsa.org/ibrrc/background-status/nibrs-states.html, accessed December 11, 2017.
19. 2016 National Incident Based Reporting System (NIBRS), p. 1.
20. Brian A. Reaves, "Local Police Departments, 2013: Equipment and Technology" (Washington, D.C.: Bureau of Justice Statistics, July 2015), p. 5.

21. These points were drawn from Christy Mallory, Amira Hasenbush, and Brad Sears, "Discrimination and Harassment by Law Enforcement Officers on the LGBT Community," The Williams Institute, School of Law, University of California, Los Angeles, March 2015, p. 1; https://williamsinstitute.law.ucla.edu/wp-content/uploads/LGBT-Discrimination-and-Harassment-in-Law-Enforcement-March-2015.pdf, accessed December 12, 2017 and Emily Swanson, et. al., "Law Enforcement and Violence: The Divide Between Black and White Americans," The University of Chicago, The Associated Press-NORC Center for Public Affairs Research, July 2015, accessed December 12, 2017.
22. "Discrimination and Harassment by Law Enforcement Officers on the LGBT Community," p. 1.
23. "Discrimination and Harassment by Law Enforcement Officers on the LGBT Community," p. 2.
24. Federal Bureau of Investigation, 2016 National Incident-Based Report, Hate Crimes, Table 2, https://ucr.fbi.gov/hate-crime/2016/tables/table-1, accessed December 12, 2017.
25. These qualities of reports are found in many documents, including police academy handouts. However, the original source appears to be Allen Z. Gammage, Basic Report Writing (Springfield, Illinois: Charles C. Thomas Publisher, 1966), pp. 13–14.
26. No author, "Overview of the Discipline Process," Minneapolis Police Department, Minneapolis, MN, January 14, 2014, pp. 4–5., http://www.ci.minneapolis.mn.us/www/groups/public/@civilrights/documents/, accessed December 7, 2017.accewebcontent/wcms1p-119255.pdf, accessed August 15, 2017.

Chapter 7

1. When solvability factors first emerged, there was little variation between departments in what factors were on their lists. While there is still some commonality, many departments have developed their own factors based on their own experiences and research. This list of factors was developed from a sample of the policies of 16 different departments from various geographic regions and sizes. For example, see University of Wisconsin-Madison Police Department, Policy 42.1, "Investigations-Administrative," May 15, 2015, p. 2 and Greenville, North Carolina Police Department, "Criminal Investigations," Chapter 42, March 12, 2015. p. 10.
2. Security Info Watch, Report: Installed Base of Security Cameras to Reach 62 Million in 2016, www.securityinfowatch.com/news/12251875/report-installed-base-0f-security-cameras-in-north-america-expected-to-reach-62m-in-2016, accessed December 18 2017.
3. An experienced officer could produce a list like this. Law enforcement agencies normally have a shorter list of the responsibilities for officers conducting follow-up list, perhaps because, they use broader language. Among the most comprehensive set of tasks for a follow-up investigation is found in endnote 1 above.
4. See Robert G. Lowery, Jr and Robert Hoever, "Long-Term Missing Child Guide for Law Enforcement, National Center for Missing and Exploited Children, 2016, www.missingkids.com/ourwork/publications/missing/long-termmissingguide, accessed December 18, 2017.
5. Department of Homeland Security, National Counter-Improvised Device Capabilities Analysis Database, January 12, 2017, www.dhs.gov/nccad, accessed February 7, 2017.
6. Department of Homeland Security, Immigration and Customs Enforcement Pattern Analysis and Information Collection System (ICEPIC), January 1, 2008, www.ice.gov/factsheets/icepic, accessed February 6, 2017.
7. Stephanie L. Britt, "NCIC 2000," FBI Law Enforcement Bulletin, July 2000, Vol. 69, No. 7, p. 14.
8. Ibid., p. 13.
9. Federal Bureau of Investigation, Next Generation Identification (NGI), www.fbi.gov/services/cjis/fingerprints-and-other-biometrics/ngi, undated, accessed December 18, 2017.
10. Federal Bureau of Investigation, National Crime Information Center (NCIC), undated, www.fbi.gov/services/cjis/ncic, accessed February 6, 2017.
11. The information on WIN is drawn from Chelsea S. Keefer, "The Western Identification Network: A Multi-State AFIS," The Police Chief, Vol. 77, No. 5, May 2010, www.PoliceChiefMagazine.org , and No author, Western Identification Network Service Strategy, January 2008, www.WINID.org, accessed May 23, 2016.
12. Law Enforcement Teletype System, "Our Mission," www.nlets.org/about/who-we-are, 2017, accessed February 1, 2017.
13. LeadsOnLine," Success Stories," undated, www.LeadsOnLine.com/main/default.aspx, accessed November 28, 2010.
14. See the U.S. Supreme Court's 1986 decision in California v. Ciraolo, 476 U.S. 207.

15. There is no shortage of ways to categorize surveillance, including, fixed versus mobile and covert versus overt, and physical versus technical. The authors have elected to use three types of physical surveillance (casual, formal, and long-term) that combine the elements of time and intensity. About a dozen police and procedure manuals were consulted prior to the preparation of the surveillance section.

16. American Civil Liberties Union, "Stingray Tracking Devices: Who's Got Them" 2017, p. 1, https://www.aclu.org/map/stingray-tracking-devices-whos-got-them, accessed February 10, 2017.

17. Jonah Engel Bromwich, Daniel Victor, and Mike Isac, "Police Use Surveillance Tool to Scan Social Media, A.C.L.U. Says," The New York Times, October 11, 2016, www.nytimes.com/2016/10/12/technology/aclu-facebook-twitter-instagram-geofeedia.html, accessed December 18, 2017.

18. Loc. cit.

19. Elizabeth Dwoskin, "Facebook Says Police Can't Use Its Data for 'Surveillance,' March 13, 2017, www.google.com/search?q=elizabeth+Dwoakin%2C+facebook+says+can%27t+use&oq=elizabeth+Dwoakin%2C+facebook+says+can%27t+use+&aqs=chrome..69i57.23997j0j4&sourceid=chrome&ie=UTF-8, accessed December 19, 2017.

20. See, for example, Palm Beach Gardens (Florida) Police Department, Policy 3.2.10, "Surveillance Operations," July 30, 2015, https://egov.pbgfl.com/cp/data/pdpolicies/3.2.10%20surveillance%2007302015.pdf, accessed December 20, 2017.

21. These points are taken with restatement from No author, Law Enforcement and Eyewitness Identifications: A Policy Writing Guide, State Bar of Michigan, December 22, 2015, p. 9, www.michigan.gov/documents/mcoles/State_Bar_Eyewitness_Law_Enforcement_Policy_Writing_Guide_410867_7.pdf, accessed February 10, 2017.

22. See Virginia General Assembly House Bill Number 207, introduced January 13, 2010. This bill was an attempt to implement the recommendations of the Innocence Project. Instead a bill was passed requiring law enforcement agencies to have written policies on witnesses.

23. No author, Reevaluating Lineups: Why Witnesses Make Mistake s (New York: Cardozo School of Law, Yeshiva University, 2009), Appendix, p. 4.

24. Best Practices Committee, Lineup Guidelines (New York State District Attorneys Association, May 17, 2010), p. 2.

25. Ibid., p. 3

26. See Virginia General Assembly House Bill Number 207, introduced January 13, 2010., p. 19

27. Virginia State Crime Commission, "Law Enforcement Lineups," 2014, p. 2., http://vscc.virginia.gov/Lineups.pdf, accessed February 10, 2017.

28. Kevin Johnson, "Eyewitness Rules Ignored, Wrongful Convictions Result," USAToday, June 11, 2013, https://www.usatoday.com/story/news/nation/2013/06/11/eyewitness-wrongful-convictions-exonerate-dna/2411717/, accessed December 20, 2017.

29. Robert R. Hazelwood and Michael R. Napier, International Journal of Offender Therapy and Comparative Criminology, 2004, 48: p. 744. On this topic also see Brent E. Turvey, "Staged Crime Scenes: A Preliminary Study of 25 Cases," Journal of Behavioral Profiling , December 2000,Vol. 1, No. 3, pp. 1–9 and W. Jerry Chisum and Brent E. Turvey, Crime Reconstruction (New York: Applied Press, 2007), pp. 441–480. More recently see Seth Augenstein, "Staged Crime Scenes: Suicide, Murder, or Disappearance?" Forensic Magazine, December 8, 2016.

30. Hazelwood and Napier, p. 746.

31. Ibid., p. 755.

32. Edgar Sentell, "Suicide and the Life Insurance Death Claim," FDCC Quarterly, Spring 2008, p. 364. Also see Ibid., pp. 754–755.

33. Claire Ferguson, The Defects of the Situation: Typology of Staged Crime Scenes, Dissertation, Bond University, Australia, 2010, p. 3 and Hazelwood and Napier, pp. 746–747.

34. The Defects of the Situation, pp. 62-63 and Hazelwood and Napier, pp. 747–751.

35. Hazelwood and Napier., p. 756.

36. Ibid., p. 756, from which several of these points are taken with change and additional comment.

37. Harper J. Jackson, and C. Munn, "The Detection of Staging and Personation at the Crime Scene," in A. Burgess, J. Douglas, and R. Ressler, editors, Crime Classification Manual (New York: Lexington Books, 1992), with restatement from p. 253.

38. Federal Bureau of Investigation, Crime in the United States (2014, 2015, 2016), murder and non-negligent homicide cases and clearances (Known offenses and exceptionally cleared), accessed December 20, 2017.

39. Tsiaperas and Julie Fancher, "Unsolved," The Dallas Morning News, 2015, no day or month indicated, http://interactives.dallasnews.com/2015/cold-cases/Tasha, accessed February 11, 2017.

40. James Cronin, et. al., Promoting Effective Homicide Investigations, Office of Community Policing and Police Executive Research Forum, August 2007, p. 103.

41. Tracy Bloom and Steve Kuzj, "Photos Released in Effort to ID Victims in 1980 Cold Case (Warning: Graphic Images," September 30, 2015, Television Station KTLA, Los Angeles, California, http://ktla.com/2015/09/30/photos-released-in-effort-to-id-victims-in-1980-cold-case-warning-graphic-images, accessed February 9, 2017.

42. Promoting Effective Homicide Investigations, p. 105.

43. 2015 National Network of Fusion Centers Final Report, p.i, https://www.dhs.gov/sites/default/files/publications/2015%20Final %20Report%20Section%20508%20Compliant.pdf, accessed February 9 2017.

44. Department of Homeland Security, Fusion Center Locations and Contact Information, January 12, 2017, p. 1, accessed February 11, 2017.

45. David L. Carter, Law Enforcement Intelligence: A Guide for State, Local, and Tribal Law Enforcement Agencies 2nd Edition, (Washington, D. C.: Office of Community Oriented Policing Services, January 13, 2017, p. 12.

46. Chandler (Arizona) Police Department, General Order D-14, Criminal Intelligence Unit, April 15, 2009, 6 pp, www.chandlerpd.com/about/general-orders/d-14-100-intelorg, accessed December 21, 2017.

47. A Guide for State, Local, and Tribal Law Enforcement Agencies 2nd Edition, p. 10.

48. Ibid., pp. 283–284.

49. Chris Pallaris, "Open Source Intelligence: A Strategic Enabler of National Security," Center for Security Studies, Vol. 3, Np. 32, April 2008, p. 1.

50. Ibid., p. 2.

51. Iowa Department of Public Safety, Division of Intelligence, "The Intelligence Production Cycle," 2017, p. 3, http://www.dps.state.ia.us/intell/intellcycle.shtml, accessed February 15, 2017.

52. Ibid., pp. 3–4.

53. Ibid., p. 4.

54. Jessica B. LeBlanc, Definition and Types of Crime Analysis, International Association of Crime Analysts, 2014, pp. 4–5 with restatement. http://www.iaca.net/Publications/Whitepapers/iacawp_2014_02_definition_types_crime_analysis.pdf, accessed February 13, 2017.

55. Ibid., p. 2.

56. See Massachusetts Association of Crime Analysts, "Crime Analysis," October 18, 2001, www.macrimeanalysts.com/aboutca.html, accessed December 16, 2017.

57. Ross M. Gardner and T. Bevel, "Theoretical and Practical Considerations in Crime Scene Reconstruction," Journal of Forensic Identification , Vol. 57, No. 6, p. 894 and Michael A. Knox, "A Philosophy of Crime Scene Reconstruction," Crime Scene Journal, February 15, 2017, p. 1, http://www.crimescenejournal.com/content.php?id=0007, accessed February 15, 2017.

58. "Theoretical and Practical Considerations in Crime Scene Reconstruction," p. 899.

59. Ross M. Gardner and Tom Bevel, Practical Crime Scene Analysis and Reconstruction (Boca Raton, Florida: CRC Press, 2009), p. 18.

60. Loc. Cit.

61. W. Jerry Chisum and Brent E. Turvey, Crime Reconstruction (Academic Press: Burlington, MA, 2007), p. 107.

62. Practical Crime Scene Analysis and Reconstruction, p. 37.

63. Ibid., pp. 37–38.

64. Ibid., p. 38.

65. "New York's Mad Bomber," njnj.essortment.com/madbomber_rwid.htm, December 3, 2001, pp. 1–2.

66. Christopher Devery, "Criminal Profiling and Criminal Investigation," Journal of Contemporary Criminal Justice, Vol. 26, Issue 4, November 2010, pp. 393–409.

67. Louis B. Schlesinger, "Psychological Profiling: Investigative Implications from Crime Scene Analysis," Journal of Psychiatry and Law, Spring 2009, Vol. 37, Issue 1, pp. 73–84.

68. J. Amber Scherer and John P. Jarvis, "Criminal Investigative Analysis: Practitioner Perspectives (Part One of Four)," FBI Law Enforcement Bulletin, June 10, 2014, p. 2, https://leb.fbi.gov/articles/featured-articles/criminal-investigative-analysis-practitioner-perspectives-part-one-of-four, accessed December 21, 2017.

69. David Canter, "Prioritizing Burglars: Comparing the Effectiveness of Geographical Profiling Methods," Police Practices and Research, Vol.8, Issue 4, September 2007, p. 371.

70. Shengyi, Li, et al., "Geographic Profiling Methods: Improvement and Combination," *Applied Mechanics and Material*, Vol. 34–35, October 2010. Pp. 157–1511.

71. Robert Sanderson, *Introduction to Remote Sensing*, New Mexico Space Grant Consortium, New Mexico State University, undated.

72. The first balloonist photograph is credited to a Frenchman in 1858, Felix Tournachon; the oldest surviving photograph from a balloon was by James Wallace Black, who took an aerial shot of Boston in 1860.

Chapter 8

1. Florida Bureau of Law Enforcement, "Crime Laboratory," unpublished document, 2007, p. 2.

2. Paul L. Kirk, "The Ontogeny of Criminalistics," *Journal of Criminology and Police Science*, Vol. 54, 1963, p. 238.

3. Richard Fox and Carl L. Cunningham, *Crime Scene Search and Physical Evidence Handbook* (Washington, DC: U.S. Department of Justice, 1985), p. 1.

4. Statement of Kevin L. Lothridge, President, American Society of Crime Laboratory Directors, National Forensic Science Technology Center, before the House Judiciary Committee, Subcommittee on Crime, May 13, 1997.

5. Ibid.

6. www.nfstc.org/aboutus.htm (graciously supplied by NFSTC)

7. Kevin Rayburn, "U of L Teams with FBI, Other Agencies to Stop Digital Crime," *University of Louisville News*, KY, November 3, 2006, http://php.louisville.edu/ news/news.php?news+727, accessed September 1, 2007.

8. James W. Osterburg, *The Crime Laboratory* (Bloomington: Indiana University Press, 1968), p. 3.

9. Marc H. Caplan and Joe Holt Anderson, *Forensics: When Science Bears Witness*, National Institute of Justice (Washington, DC: Government Printing Office, October 1984), p. 2.

10. For a discussion of working relationships between police investigators and crime laboratory personnel, see Joseph L. Peterson, *The Utilization of Criminalistics Services by the Police: An Analysis of the Physical Evidence Recovery Process*, Law Enforcement Assistance Administration, National Institute of Law Enforcement and Criminal Justice (Washington, DC: Government Printing Office, March 1974).

11. National Research Council of the National Academies of Science, *Strengthening Forensic Science in the United States: A Path Forward* (Washington, DC: The National Academies Press, February 2009).

12. Sara Frueh, "Badly Fragmented Forensic Science System Needs Overhaul; Evidence to Support Reliability of Many Techniques is Lacking," *News from the National Academies*, February 18, 2009.

13. National Advisory Commission on Criminal Justice Standards and Goals, *Police* (Washington, DC: Government Printing Office, 1973), p. 303.

14. See Kenneth S. Field, Oliver Schroeder, Jr., Ina J. Curtis, Ellen L. Fabricant, and Beth Ann Lipskin, *Assessment of the Forensic Sciences Profession: Assessment of the Personnel of the Forensic Sciences Profession*, Vol. II, National Institute of Law Enforcement and Criminal Justice, Law Enforcement Assistance Administration, U.S. Department of Justice (Washington, DC: Government Printing Office, March 1977), pp. I-4–I-9.

15. National Advisory Commission, *Police*, p. 302.

16. Ibid.

17. Peterson, *Utilization of Criminalistics Services*, p. 6.

18. American Society of Crime Laboratory Directors, *180-Day Study: Status and Needs of United States Crime Laboratories*, May 28, 2004, p. iii.

19. Candace Rondeaux and Ernesto Londoño, "As Requests for DNA Tests Soar, So Do Lab Backlogs," *Washington Post*, July 15, 2007.

20. 293 Fed. 1013 (D.C. Cir. 1923).

21. 507 U.S. 904 (1993).

22. *United States v. Mitchell*, 365 F. 3d 215 (3rd Circ. 2004).

23. Matthew Durose, "Census of Publicly Funded Forensic Crime Laboratories, 2005," *Bureau of Justice Statistics Bulletin*, July 2008.

24. Jeffrey M. Prottas and Alice A. Noble, "Use of Forensic DNA Evidence in Prosecutor's Offices," *Journal of Law, Medicine and Ethics*, Summer 2007, pp. 310–315.

25. www.fbi.gov/kids/dna/dna.htm, July 17, 1998.

26. National Commission on the Future of DNA Evidence, National Institute of Justice, "What Every Law Enforcement Officer Should Know about DNA Evidence," pamphlet (Washington, DC: U.S. Department of Justice, no publication date).

27. Theresa F. Spear, "Sample Handling Considerations for Biological Evidence and DNA Extracts," California Department of Justice, California Criminalistics Institute.

28. Ibid.

29. T. Spear, "Sample Handling Considerations for Biological Evidence and DNA Extracts," and T. Spear and N. Khoshkebarr, "Analysis of Old Biological Samples: A Study on the Feasibility of Obtaining Body Fluid Identification and DNA Typing Results," California Department of Justice, California Criminalistics Institute.

30. Notes from the seminar "Supporting Your Case Using DNA Evidence," Altamonte Springs, Florida, August 23–24, 2001.

31. Ronald Bailey, "Criminal Kinship: Slouching Toward a DNA Database Nation," *Reason Magazine*, May 19, 2006. www.reason.com/news/show/116487.html.

32. Shaila K. Dewan, "New York Works on a Better DNA Trap to Catch Burglars," *The New York Times*, May 26, 2004, p. 1 and p. 23.

33. Frederick R. Bieber, Charles H. Brenner, and David Lazer, "Human Genetics: Finding Criminals through DNA of Their Relatives," *Science*, Vol. 312, Issue 5778 June 2, 2006, pp. 1315–1316.

34. Ibid.

35. Ibid.

36. Ronald Bailey, "Criminal Kinship."

37. Ibid.

38. Ker Than, "Family DNA Helps Cops Catch Criminals," *Live Science*, May 11, 2006, and William J. Cromie, "Catching Criminals through Their Relatives' DNA; Finding Genetic Needles in Database Haystacks," *Harvard University Gazette*. May 11, 2006, www.news.harvard.edu/gazette/daily/2006/05/11-dna.html.

39. www.fbi.gov/hq/org/dnau/htm

40. Ibid.

41. Office of Justice Programs, *National Institute of Justice Journal* (Washington, DC: U.S. Department of Justice, Dec. 1997), pp. 17–19.

42. Cromie, "Catching Criminals."

43. The Innocence Project, http://innocenceproject.org/, accessed November 15, 2010.

44. Ibid.

45. Ibid.

46. Ibid.

47. Scott Cooper, "Judge Releases McCarty; Rips Former Chemist," *OKC News*, May 11, 2007.

48. Ibid.

49. Ibid.

50. www.atf.treas.gov/labs

51. www.atf.treas.gov/explarson

52. www.fbi.gov/labs

53. Spencer Hsu (April 18, 2015). "FBI Admits Flaws in Hair Analysis over Decades." *The Washington Post*. Retrieved from https://www.washingtonpost.com/local/crime/fbi-overstated-forensic-hair-matches-in-nearly-all-criminal-trials-for-decades/2015/04/18/39c8d8c6-e515-11e4-b510-962fcfabc310_story.html

54. Roma Khanna and Steve McVicker, "'Troubling' Cases Surface in Report on HPD Crime Lab," *Houston Chronicle*, July 17, 2007, and Mike Glenn, "Police DNA Lab under the Microscope," *Houston Chronicle*, July 11, 2006.

55. *Education and Training in Forensic Science: A Guide for Forensic Science Laboratories, Educational Institutions, and Students*, National Institute of Justice, June 2004, p. 25.

56. Richard Saferstein, *Criminalistics: An Introduction to Forensic Science*, 6th ed. (Upper Saddle River, NJ: Prentice Hall, 1998), p. 17.

57. Randolf Jonakait, "Forensic Science: The Need for Regulation," *Harvard Journal of Law and Technology*, Spring 1999, p. 6.

58. Saferstein, *Criminalistics*, p. 243.

59. Paul Gianelli, "Crime Labs Need Improvement," *Issues in Science and Technology*, 2003, p. 2.

60. Ibid., p. 3.

61. Robert Tanner, "Crime Labs Under a Microscope: Miscues Lead to Calls for Changes in Forensic Labs," *Washington Post*, July 27, 2003, p. 2.

62. John F. Kelly and Phillip K. Wearne, *Tainting Evidence: Inside the Scandals of the FBI Crime Lab* (Denver: Free Press, 2003), www.bioforensics.com/conference/Examiner%20Bias/Tainting%20Evidence.pdf, accessed March 15, 2011.

63. "Document Says Police Chemist Falsified Evidence," *Dallas Morning News*, April 21, 2004, p. 2A.

64. Barry Fisher, *Techniques of Crime Scene Investigation*, 6th ed. (Boca Raton, FL: CRC Press, 2000), p. 15.

65. Ruth Teichroeb, "Rare Look Inside State Crime Labs Reveals Recurring DNA Test Problems," *Seattle Post Intelligencer*, July 22, 2004, p. 2.

66. "Chief Hopes Computers Restore Faith in Crime Lab," *Dallas Morning News*, p. 4A.

67. Jack King, "DOJ Aware of Problems in FBI's DNA Lab," *NADCL News Release*, p. 1-2.

68. Matthew Durose, "Census of Publicly Funded Forensic Crime Laboratories, 2005," *Bureau of Justice Statistics Bulletin*, July 2008.

69. Mark Nelson, "Making Sense of DNA Backlogs—Myth vs. Reality," *National Institute of Justice Special Report*, June 2010.

70. Nicholas P. Lovrich, Travis Pratt, Michael Gaffney, Charles Johnson, Christopher Asplen, Lisa Hurst, and Timothy Schellberg, "National Forensic DNA Study Report," February 2004, p. 3. See www.ojp.usdoj.gov/nij/pdf/dna _studyreport_final.pdf.

71. Ibid., p. 63.

72. Ibid., p. 4.

73. Ibid., p. 17.

74. United States Department of Justice, "Background to the OIG Investigation," *FBI Labs Report*, March 1997, p. 1.

75. Ibid., p. 4.

76. Excerpted from an affidavit led by FBI Special Agent Richard K. Werder in support of an arrest warrant for Brandon Mayfield. The warrant was signed by U.S. District Judge Robert Jones on May 6, 2004.

77. The AFIS system analyzed the print against a widely accepted 45-million fingerprint database yielding 20 possible matches.

78. Excerpted from testimony of Mr. Ken Moses, FBI Forensic Identification Services, May 19, 2004 (*U.S.* v. *Brandon Mayfield*).

79. Steven T. Wax and Christopher J. Schatz, "A Multitude of Errors: The Brandon Mayfield Case," *The Champion*, September/October 2004, National Association of Criminal Defense Lawyers, www.nacdl.org.

80. Ibid.

81. Associated Press, "FBI Apologizes to Lawyer Held in Madrid Bombings," *MSNBC.com*, May 25, 2004.

82. Excerpted from the motion to dismiss material witness led in U.S. District Court, Oregon on May 4, 2004.

83. Alan John Bayle, as quoted in Wax and Schatz, "A Multitude of Errors: The Brandon Mayfield Case." Note that Bayle's finding of fundamental error by the FBI analysts was consistent with the view held by the Spanish police authorities regarding the print.

84. *United States* v. *Mitchell*, 365 F.3d 215, 244-47 (3rd Circuit, 2004).

85. Excerpted from Wax and Schatz, p. 8. See also *Kumho Tire Co., Ltd.* v. *Carmichael*, 526 U.S. 137 (1999), criticizing purported expert's application of his methodology.

86. Peter Barnett, *Ethics In Forensic Science: Professional Standards for the Practice of Criminalistics* (Boca Raton, FL: CRC Press, 2001), p. 163.

87. H. Dale Nute, "An Ethical Code for Forensic Science," www.southernforensic.org/ethics%20code.htm, accessed August 10, 2010, pp. 2-3.

88. Teichroeb, "Oversight for Crime Lab Staff," p. 2.

89. Excerpted from testimony of Mr. Ken Moses, FBI Forensic Identification Services, May 19, 2004 (*U.S.* v. *Brandon Mayfield*).

90. Steven T. Wax and Christopher J. Schatz, "A Multitude of Errors: The Brandon Mayfield Case," *The Champion*, Sept./Oct. 2004, National Association of Criminal Defense Lawyers, *www.nacdl.org*.

91. Ibid.

92. Associated Press, "FBI Apologizes to Lawyer Held in Madrid Bombings," *MSNBC.com*, May 25, 2004.

93. Excerpted from the motion to dismiss material witness filed in U.S. District Court, Oregon on May 4, 2004. Alan John Bayle, as quoted in Wax and Schatz, "A Multitude of Errors: The Brandon Mayfield Case." Note that Bayle's finding of fundamental error by the FBI analysts was consistent with the view held by the Spanish police authorities regarding the print.

94. See Radley Balko and Roger Koppl, "C.S.Oy: Forensic Science is Badly in Need of Reform." *The Slate* (August 12, 2008). See www.slate.com/articles/news_and_ politics/jurisprudence/2008/08/csoy.singlse.html; and Conor Friedersdorf, "CSI is a Lie," *The Atlantic* (April 20, 2015). See: www.theatlantic.com/politics /archive/2015/csi-is-a-lie/390897/.

95. *United States* v. *Mitchell*, 365 F.3d 215, 244-47 (3 rd Circuit, 2004).

96. Alan John Bayle, as quoted in Wax and Schatz, "A Multitude of Errors: The Brandon Mayfield Case." Note that Bayle's finding of fundamental error by the FBI analysts was consistent with the view held by the Spanish police authorities regarding the print.

97. Excerpted from Wax and Schatz, p. 8. See also *Kumho Tire Co., Ltd.* v. *Carmichael*, 526 U.S. 137 (1999), criticizing purported expert's application of his methodology.

98. Peter Barnett, *Ethics in Forensic Science: Professional Standards for the Practice of Criminalistics* (Boca Raton, FL: CRC Press, 2001), p. 163.

99. H. Dale Nute, "An Ethical Code for Forensic Science," *www.southernforensic. org/ethics%20code.htm* (accessed August 10, 2010), pp. 2-3.

100. Ruth Teichroeb, "Oversight for Crime Lab Staff has Often been Lax" *Seattle Post Intelligencer* (July 22, 2004) p. 2.

Chapter 9

1. Bureau of Justice Assistance, U.S. Department of Justice, *10 Things Law Enforcement Executives Can Do to Positively Impact Homicide*, 2009, pp. 2-17.

2. Neil C. Chamelin and Andrew Thomas, *Essentials of Criminal Law* (Englewood Cliffs, NJ: Pearson/Prentice Hall, 2009), pp. 116-130.

3. Ibid.

4. Jay Dix and Robert Calaluce, *Guide to Forensic Pathology* (Columbia: University of Missouri, 1998), p. 3.

5. Wisconsin Crime Laboratory, *Criminal Investigation and Physical Evidence Handbook* (Madison: Department of Justice, State of Wisconsin, 1968), p. 10.

6. John J. Horgan, *Criminal Investigation* (New York: McGraw-Hill, 1974), p. 292.

7. This information was obtained at *www.crime-scene-investigator.net/dead bodyevidence.html.*

8. James L. Luke, "The Estimation of Time of Death in the Early Postmortem Period," *The American Journal of Forensic Medicine and Pathology* 17, no. 3 (September 1996): 270.

9. Ibid.

10. Dix and Calaluce, *Guide to Forensic Pathology*, pp. 35-36.

11. Cyril J. Polson, David J. Gee, and Bernard Knight, *The Essentials of Forensic Medicine*, 4th ed. (Oxford: Pergamon Press, 1985), p. 11.

12. Keith Simpson and Bernard Knight, *Forensic Medicine*, 9th ed. (London: Butler & Tanner Ltd., 1988), p. 9.

13. I. Gordon, H. A. Shapiro, and S. D. Berson, *Forensic Medicine: A Guide to Principles*, 3rd ed. (Edinburgh: Churchill Livingstone, 1988), p. 18.

14. Johnnie Bennett, *Introduction to Forensic Science*; available at *http:// bennettkids.homestead.com/autopsies.html.*

15. Ibid.

16. Dix and Calaluce, *Guide to Forensic Pathology*, pp. 33-34.

17. Francis E. Camps, ed., *Gradwohl's Legal Medicine*, 3rd ed. (Bristol: Wright and Sons, 1976), p. 83.

18. For a more detailed discussion, see Ask Dr. Baden at *www.hbo.com /autopsy/baden.*

19. Dix and Calaluce, *Guide to Forensic Pathology*, pp. 38-40.

20. Gail S. Anderson, Forensic Entomology, British Columbia, Canada, Simon Fraser University, School of Criminology, 2005. (This discussion was specifically developed by Dr. Anderson for this chapter. She is also a court-qualified expert and may be contacted at ganderso@sfu.ca.)

21. "Insect Evidence," *Catching Killers*, season 1, episode 3, Smithsonian Channel, originally aired: Jul 8, 2012. The summary of this case was adapted from this TV program.

22. Vernon J. Geberth, *Practical Homicide Investigation* (Boca Raton, FL: CRC, 2006), pp. 325, 327.

23. Barry A. J. Fisher, *Techniques of Crime Scene Investigation* (New York: Elsevier, 1992), pp. 452-458.

24. The information on shotgun wounds was obtained from material developed by Vincent J. M. DiMaio, M.D., Medical Examiner, Dallas County, Texas.

25. The information on firearm residue included in this chapter was developed by the Southwestern Institute of Forensic Sciences at Dallas, Texas.

26. R. C. Harrison and R. Gilroy, "Firearms Discharge Residues," *Journal of Forensic Sciences*, 1959, No. 4, pp. 184-199.

27. Dominic J. DiMaio and Vincent J. M. DiMaio, *Forensic Pathology* (New York: Elsevier, 1989), p. 87.

28. Ibid.

29. Ibid., pp. 231-243.

30. Jacques Charon, *Suicide* (New York: Scribner's, 1972), p. 56.

31. Centers for Disease Control and Prevention (CDC). Web-based Injury Statistics Query and Reporting System (WISQARS) [Online]. (2013, 2011) National Center for Injury Prevention and Control. CDC (producer). Available from http://www.cdc.gov/injury/wisquars/index.html.

32. Ibid.

33. S. E. Parks, L. L. Johnson, D. D. McDaniel and M. Gladden, *Surveillance for Violent Deaths - National Violent Deaths Reporting System, 16 states, 2010*. MMWR 2014: 63(ss01): 1-33; http://www.cdc.gov/mmwr/preview /mmwrhtml/ss6301a1.htm.

34. Centers for Disease Control and Prevention (CDC), Web-based Injury Statistics Query and Reporting System, p. 2.

35. Charon, *Suicide*, p. 39.

36. Lemoyne Snyder, *Homicide Investigation* (Springfield, IL: Charles C. Thomas, 1973), p. 228.

37. Donna Newson, "Doctors Perform Rare Surgery," *Tampa Tribune,* July 25, 1980, pp. A1, A10.

38. Richard H. Fox and Carl L. Cunningham, *Crime Scene Search and Physical Evidence Handbook* (Washington, D.C.: Government Printing Office, 1973), pp. 124, 126. This discussion of poisons was taken from this source.

39. John Harris Trestrail, III, *Criminal Poisoning* (Totowa, NJ: Humana Press Inc., 2000-2001), p. 29.

40. Todd F. Prough, "Investigating Opiate-Overdose Deaths," *FBI Law Enforcement Bulletin,* April 2009; available from *www.thefreelibrary.com/Investigating+opiate-overdose+deaths-a0197673510.*

41. U.S. Department of Health and Human Services, Substance Abuse and Mental Health Services, *www.dasis.samhsa.gov/webt/information.htm.*

42. Werner U. Spitz, ed., *Spitz and Fisher's Medicolegal Investigation of Death* (Springfield, MA: Charles C. Thomas, 1993).

43. J. Tuckman et al., "Credibility of Suicide Notes," *American Journal of Psychiatry,* June 1960, No. 65, pp. 1104–1106.

44. David Lester, *Why People Kill Themselves* (Springfield, IL: Charles C. Thomas, 1972), p. 36.

45. Z. G. Standing Bear, *The Investigation of Questioned Deaths and Injuries—Conference Notes and Outline* (Valdosta, GA: Valdosta State College Press, 1988), pp. 78–82.

46. John J. O'Conner, *Practical Fire and Arson Investigation* (Boca Raton, FL: CRC Press, 1993), pp. 160–161.

47. Ibid.

48. Camps, *Gradwohl's Legal Medicine,* p. 358; Lester Adelson, *The Pathology of Homicide* (Springfield, IL: Charles C. Thomas, 1974), p. 610; Richard Lindenberg, "Mechanical Injuries of the Brain and Meninges," in Spitz, *Spitz and Fisher's Medicolegal Investigation of Death,* pp. 447–456.

49. George B. Palermo, "Homicidal Syndromes: A Clinical Psychiatric Perspective," in *Criminal Profiling: International Theory, Research, and Practice,* ed. R. N. Kocsis (Totowa, NJ: Humana Press Inc., 2007), 14–15.

50. Ibid., pp. 16–18.

51. *Serial Murder: Multi-Disciplinary Perspectives for Investigators* (Washington, D.C.: U.S. Department of Justice, Federal Bureau of Investigation, 2005), pp. 8–9. (This discussion was adapted from this source.)

52. Ibid., pp. 11–12.

53. National Center for the Analysis of Violent Crime, Behavioral Science Unit, FBI Academy (Quantico, VA: 1985), p. 5.

54. ViCAP Crime Analysis Report Form used by the FBI for profiling, 1999.

55. Eric W. Witzig, "The New ViCAP," *FBI Law Enforcement Bulletin,* January 16, 2003.

56. David McLemore, "Aliases, Trainhopping Obscure Suspect's Trail," *Dallas Morning News,* June 17, 1999, sec. A1, p. 16.

57. Pauline Arrillaga, "Town Copes after Slayings by Suspected Rail Rider," *Dallas Morning News,* June 11, 1999, sec. A., p. 29.

58. *Supra* note 12, sec. A., p. 17.

59. Michael Pearson, "Railroad Killer," *Associated Press,* June 22, 1999.

60. Mark Babineck, "Railroad Killer," *Associated Press,* July 2000.

61. "Railroad Killer," *Associated Press,* July 2000.

62. Ibid.

63. Scott Glover, "FBI Database Links Long-Haul Truckers, Serial Killings," *PoliceOne.com News,* April 6, 2009, p. 2.

Chapter 10

1. Black, M.C, Basile, K.C, Breiding, M.J., et al. (2011) *The National Intimate Partner and Sexual Violence Survey: 2010 Summary Report.* Retrieved from: Centers for Disease Control and Prevention, National Center for Injury and Violence Prevention: https://www.cdc.gov/violenceprevention/pdf/nisvs_report2010-a.pdf

2. See Rennison, CA (2002). Rape and Sexual Assault: Reporting to the Police and Medical Attention. 1992-2000. Retrieved from http://www.bjs.gov/content/pub/pdf/rcp00.pdf, and Kilpatrick, Dean G., Ph.D., Heidi S. Resnick, Ph.D., Kenneth J. Ruggiero, Ph.D., Lauren M. Conoscenti, M.A., and Jenna McCauley, M.S., "Drug-Facilitated, Incapacitated, and Forcible Rape: A National Study," July 2007. (https://www.ncjrs.gov/pdffiles1/nij/grants/219181.pdf).

3. Human Rights Watch. "Improving Police Response to Sexual Assault." (2013) Retrieved from: https://www.hrw.org/sites/default/files/reports/improvingSAInvest_0.pdf

4. Ibid.

5. Michigan Domestic and Sexual Violence Prevention and Treatment Board. (2015) "Michigan Model Policy: The Law Enforcement Response to Sexual Assault." Retrieved from: http://www.bwjp.org/assets/documents/pdfs/2015-michigan-model-policy-the-law-enforcement-respo.pdf

6. Hollandsworth, Skip. "If the Serial Killer Gets Us, He Gets Us". (December 2011) Texas Monthly. Retrieved from: http://www.texasmonthly.com/articles/if-the-serial-killer-gets-us-he-gets-us/

7. Michigan Domestic and Sexual Violence Prevention and Treatment Board. (2015) "Michigan Model Policy: The Law Enforcement Response to Sexual Assault." Retrieved from: http://www.bwjp.org/assets/documents/pdfs/2015-michigan-model-policy-the-law-enforcement-respo.pdf

8. ibid

9. Morton Bard and Katherine Ellison, "Crisis Intervention and Investigation of Forcible Rape," *Police Chief,* May 1974, Vol. 41, No. 5, pp. 68–74.

10. This discussion and accompanying references came from R. R. Hazelwood, "The Behavior-Oriented Interview of Rape Victims: The Key to Profiling," *FBI Law Enforcement Bulletin,* Sept. 1983, pp. 13–15.

11. L. L. Holmstrom and A. W. Burgess, "Sexual Behavior of Assailants during Rape," *Archives of Sexual Behavior,* 1980, Vol. 9, No. 5, p. 437.

12. Ibid., p. 427.

13. L. L. Holmstrom and A. W. Burgess, "Rapist's Talk: Linguistic Strategies to Control the Victim," *Deviant Behavior,* 1979, Vol. 1, p. 101.

14. C. LeGrande, "Rape and Rape Laws: Sexism in Society and Law," *California Law Review,* 1973, p. 929.

15. Office for Victims of Crime. "Responding to Transgender Victims of Sexual Assault." (June 2014). Office of Justice Programs. Retrieved from: http://www.ovc.gov/pubs/forge/transgender.html

16. ibid

17. ibid

18. Lauren R. Taylor and Nicole Gasken-Laniyan, Study Reveals Unique Issues Faced by Deaf Victims of Sexual Assault, 2007, U.S. Department of Justice: Office of Justice Programs, National Institute of Justice, pp. 24–26.

19. J. Obinna, S. Krueger, C. Osterbaan, J. M. Sandusky, and W. DeVore, *Understanding the Needs of the Victims of Sexual Assault in the Deaf Community,* final report submitted to the National Institute of Justice, Washington, D.C.: February 2006 (NCJ 212867), *www.ncjrs.gov/pdffiles1/nij/grants/212867.pdf.*

20. Ann Wolbert Burgess, Robert A. Prentky and Elizabeth B. Dowdell, "Sexual Predators in Nursing Homes," in *Practical Aspects of Rape Investigation,* 4th ed., Robert R. Hazelwood and Ann Wolbert Burgess, eds. (Boca Raton, FL: CRC Press, Taylor & Francis Group, 2009), pp. 484–499.

21. U.S. General Accounting Office, *Nursing Homes: Complaint Investigation Processes Often Inadequate to Protect Residents* (No. 6AO/HEHS-99-80) (Washington, D.C.: Health Education and Human Services, 2002).

22. A. W. Burgess, E. B. Dowdell and R. A. Prentky, "Sexual Abuse of Nursing Home Residents," *Journal of Psychosocial Nursing* 38, No. 6 (June) 2000: 10–18.

23. Queens Bench Foundation, *Rape Victimization Study* (San Francisco, 1975), pp. 81–87; E. L. Willoughby and James A. Inciardi, "Estimating the Incidence of Crime," *Police Chief,* 1975, Vol. 42, No. 8, pp. 69–70; President's Commission on Law Enforcement and the Administration of Justice, *Task Force Report: Crime and Its Impact* (Washington, D.C.: Government Printing Office, 1967), p. 80; Eugene J. Kanin, "False Rape Allegations," *Archives of Sexual Behavior,* 1994, Vol. 23, No. 1, pp. 81–90.

24. The state of Florida repealed its previous statute, Forcible Rape and Carnal Knowledge 794, replacing it with a new statute, titled Sexual Battery 794. The new law provides for various penalties for sexual battery depending on the amount of force used and the injuries sustained by the victim. In addition, the statute provides that specific instances of previous sexual activity between the victim and any person other than the defendant cannot be admitted into evidence.

25. Queens Bench Foundation, *Rape Victimization Study,* p. 86.

26. Levin, Sam. "Ex-Stanford swimmer gets jail and probation for sexual assault." (June 2, 2016) The Guardian. Retrieved from: https://www.theguardian.com/us-news/2016/jun/02/stanford-swimmer-sexual-assault-brock-allen-turner-palo-alto

27. Kadvany, Elena. "Stanford sex-assault victim: 'You took away my worth." (June 3, 2016). Palo Alto Online. Retrieved from: http://www.paloaltoonline.com/news/2016/06/03/stanford-sex-assault-victim-you-took-away-my-worth.

28. Lavigne, Paula. "Baylor faces allegations of ignoring sex assault victims." (February 2, 2016). *ESPN.* Retrieved from: http://espn.go.com/espn/otl/story/_/id/14675790/baylor-officials-accused-failing-investigate-sexual-assaults-fully-adequately-providing-support-alleged-victims.

29. U.S. Department of Justice, Civil Rights Division, *Investigation of the Baltimore City Police Department* (Washington, D.C.: USGPO) August 10, 2016.

30. See Sheryl Gay Stolberg and Jess Bidgood, "Another Side of Policing Bias: Gender." (August 11, 2016). *New York Times*

31. Ibid.

32. National Sexual Violence Report Center. "Statistics About Sexual Violence." (2015) Retrieved from: http://www.nsvrc.org/sites/default/files/publications_nsvrc_factsheet_media-packet_statistics-about-sexual-violence_0.pdf.

33. "Crime in the United States: 2000 Uniform Crime Reports," *www.fbi.gov/ucr/cius_00/00 crime3.pdf.*

34. Sofi Sinozich and Lynn Langton, *Rape and Sexual Assault Victimization Among College-Age Females, 1995-2013* (Washington, D.C.: USDOJ, December 2014).

35. Ibid., p. 2

36. C. P. Krebs, C.H. Lindquist, T.D. Warner, B.S. Fisher, and S. L. Martin, *The Campus Sexual Assault (CSA) Study (*Washington, D.C.: National Institute of Justice, 2007)

37. See: Centers for Disease Control and Preventions, *Prevention and Characteristics of Sexual Violence, Stalking an Intimate Partner Violence Victimization - The National Intimate Partner and Sexual Violence Survey, United States, 2011* (Atlanta, GA: CDC, 2011), and White House Task Force to Protect Students from Sexual Assault, *Not Alone* (Washington, D.C.: The White House, April 2014). See: https://www.notalone.gov/assets/report.pdf.

38. See "The Realities of Sexual Assault on Campus" at http://www.bestcolleges.com/resources/preventing-sexual-assault/

39. Spaulding and Bigbee, "Physical Evidence in Sexual Assault Investigations."

40. Ibid.

41. A. N. Groth and A. W. Burgess, *Rape, a Sexual Deviation,* paper presented to the American Psychological Association Meeting, Washington, D.C., Sept. 5, 1976, p. 4.

42. J. H. Davis, "Examination of Victims of Sexual Assault and Murder," material developed for a homicide seminar offered by the Florida Institute for Law Enforcement, St. Petersburg, Florida, 1965.

43. Ibid.

44. Arne Svensson and Otto Wendel, *Techniques of Crime Scene Investigation* (New York: American Elsevier, 1973).

45. William Watson, "Forensic Serology and DNA Analysis," lecture given at the University of North Texas, 2001.

46. Joe Nickell and John Fischer, *Crime Science: Methods of Forensic Detection* (Lexington: University Press of Kentucky, 1999).

47. Watson, "Forensic Serology and DNA Analysis."

48. Spaulding and Bigbee, "Physical Evidence in Sexual Assault Investigations."

49. Thomas B. Carney, *Practical Investigation of Sex Crimes* (Boca Raton, FL: CRC Press, 2004) p. 55.

50. Ibid., p. 55.

51. Ibid., p. 57.

52. Ibid., pp. 57-58.

53. Ibid., p. 58.

54. Robert D. Blackledge, "Condom Trace Evidence: A New Factor in Sexual Assault Investigations," *FBI Bulletin,* May 1996, pp. 12-16. This discussion was adapted from this article.

55. R. D. Blackledge and L. R. Cabiness, "Examination for Petroleum-Based Lubricants in Evidence from Rapes and Sodomies," *Journal of Forensic Sciences,* 1983, Vol. 28, pp. 451-462.

56. R. D. Blackledge, "Collection and Identification Guidelines for Traces from Latex Condoms in Sexual Assault Cases," *Crime Laboratory Digest,* 1994, Vol. 21, pp. 57-61.

57. Michigan Domestic and Sexual Violence Prevention and Treatment Board. (2015) "Michigan Model Policy: The Law Enforcement Response to Sexual Assault." Retrieved from: http://www.bwjp.org/assets/documents/pdfs/2015-michigan-model-policy-the-law-enforcement-respo.pdf

58. Michigan Domestic and Sexual Violence Prevention and Treatment Board. (2015) "Michigan Model Policy: The Law Enforcement Response to Sexual Assault." Retrieved from: http://www.bwjp.org/assets/documents/pdfs/2015-michigan-model-policy-the-law-enforcement-respo.pdf

59. Tamantha Chapman, "Drug-Facilitated Sexual Assault," *Police Chief,* June 2000, pp. 38-39.

60. Bureau of Justice Statistics, *Violence against Women: Estimates from the Designed Survey* (Washington, D.C.: U.S. Department of Justice, Aug. 1995).

61. Hoffman-LaRoche, Inc., "Rohypnol Fact Sheet"; Drug Enforcement Administration, "Intelligence Report (Rohypnol)," July 1995.

62. A. G. Gardiner, Jr., "Rohypnol: The New Stealth Weapon," *Police Chief,* April 1998, p. 37.

63. Drug Enforcement Administration, "Fact Sheet (GHB)," Aug. 1998; Food and Drug Administration, "Training Bulletin," Office of Criminal Investigations, San Diego, CA.

64. Executive Office of the President's Office of National Drug Control Policy, "Gamma Hydroxybutyrate (GHB) Fact Sheet," Oct. 1998.

65. Chapman, "Drug-Facilitated Sexual Assault," p. 41.

66. Nora Fitzgerald and K. Jack Reilly. *Assessing Drug Facilitated Rape.* The U.S. Department of Justice, Office of Justice Programs, National Institute of Justice. April 2000, p. 14.

67. American Prosecutors Research Institute, *The Prosecution of Rohypnol- and GHB-Related Sexual Assaults* (Alexandria, VA: April 1999).

68. R. Crooks and K. Baur, *Our Sexuality,* 4th ed. (Redwood City, CA: Benjamin/Cummings, 1990), pp. 317, 324, 332-333, 340.

69. R. R. Hazelwood, *Autoerotic Deaths* (Quantico, VA: Behavioral Science Unit, FBI Academy, 1984).

70. J. Rupp, "The Love Bug," *Journal of Forensic Science,* 1973, pp. 259-262.

71. H. L. P. Resnick, "Eroticized Repetitive Hangings: A Form of Self-Destructive Behavior," *American Journal of Psychotherapy,* January 1972, p. 10.

72. R. Litman and C. Swearingen, "Bondage and Suicide," *Archives of General Psychiatry,* July 1972, Vol. 27, p. 82.

73. Vernon J. Geberth, *Practical Homicide Investigation,* 4th ed. (Boca Raton, FL: CRC Press, 2006), pp. 375-377.

74. N. Hibbler, "The Psychological Autopsy," *Forensic Science Digest,* Sept. 1978, Vol. 5, pp. 42-44.

Chapter 11

1. C. J. Flammang, *The Police and the Unprotected Child* (Springfield, IL: Charles C. Thomas, 1970), p. 90; Harold E. Simmons, *Protective Services for Children* (Sacramento, CA: General Welfare Publications, 1968), p. 45.

2. S. Maguire, M. K. Mann, J. Sibert, and A. Kemp, "Are There Patterns of Bruising in Childhood Which Are Diagnostic or Suggestive of Abuse? A Systematic Review," *Archives of Disease in Childhood,* 2005, Vol. 90, pp. 182-186.

3. H. Dubowitz and S. Bennett, "Physical Abuse and Neglect of Children," *Lancet,* 2007, Vol. 369, pp. 1891-1899.

4. Phylip J. Peltier, Gary Purdue, and Jack R. Shepherd, *Burn Injuries in Child Abuse* (Washington, D.C.: U.S. Department of Justice, 1997), pp. 1-9.

5. D. Finkelhor and R. Ormrod. "Homicides of Children and Youth," *Juvenile Justice Bulletin.* Office of Justice Programs, Office of Juvenile Justice and Delinquency Prevention, October 2001, *www.ncjrs.gov/pdffiles1/ojjdp/187239.pdf.*

6. *A Resource Handbook: Sudden Infant Death Syndrome* (Tallahassee, FL: Department of Health and Rehabilitative Services, 1978), pp. 1-2. Much of the information dealing with SIDS was taken from this source.

7. Ann L. Ponsonby, Terrence Dwyer, Laura E. Gibbons, Jennifer A Cochrane, and You-gan Wang, "Factors Potentiating the Risk of Sudden Infant Death Syndrome Associated with Prone Position," *New England Journal of Medicine,* Aug. 1993, Vol. 329, No. 6, p. 373. The scientists conducted the study (58 infants with SIDS and 120 control infants) and perspective cohort study (22 infants with SIDS and 233 control infants) in Tasmania. Interactions were examined and math analyses done with a multiplicative model interaction.

8. J. L. Emery and J. A. Thornton, "Effects of Obstruction to Respiration in Infants with Particular Reference to Mattresses, Pillows, and Their Coverings," *BMJ,* 1968, Vol. 3, pp. 309-313.

9. David S. Paterson et. al., "Multiple Serotonergic Brainstem Abnormalities in Sudden Infant Death Syndrome," *Journal of American Medical Association,* Nov. 1, 2006, Vol. 296; pp. 2124-2132.

10. Vincent J. DiMaio and Dominick DiMaio, *Forensic Pathology* (Boca Raton, FL: CRC Press, 2001), pp. 330-331. The following are online resources for providing additional information on SIDS: First Candle, *www.firstcandle.org*; Interagency Panel on Sudden Infant Death Syndrome, "Guidelines for Death Scene Investigation of Sudden, Unexplained Infant Deaths," *www.cdc.gov/mmwr/preview/mmwrhtml/00042657.htm*; Office of Juvenile Justice and Delinquency Prevention "Recognizing When a Child's Injury or Illness is Caused by Abuse," *www.ncjrs.gov/pdffiles1/ojjdp/160938.pdf*; Canadian Association of Chiefs of Police "Code of Police Practice: A Guide for First-Line Officers," *www.rcmplearning.org/copp/encopp/d_infant.htm.*

11. Vincent J. DiMaio and Dominick DiMaio, *Forensic Pathology* (Boca Raton, FL: CRC Press, 2001), pp. 349-350.

12. David P. Southall, "Covert Video Recording of Life-Threatening Child Abuse: Lessons for Child Protection," *Pediatrics*, Nov. 1997, Vol. 100, No. 5, pp. 735–760; Sharon Begley, "The Nursery's Littlest Victim," *Newsweek*, September 22, 1997, p. 72.

13. Begley, "The Nursery's Littlest Victim," p. 67.

14. Randell Alexander and K. Kleinmann, *Diagnostic Imaging of Child Abuse* (Washington, D.C.: U.S. Department of Justice, 1996), pp. 6–9.

15. Bill Walsh. "Investigating Child Fatalities," Office of Justice Programs, Office of Juvenile Justice and Delinquency Prevention. August 2005, *www.ncjrs.gov/pdffiles1/ojjdp/209764.pdf*.

16. Rob Parrish, *Battered Child Syndrome: Investigating Physical Abuse* (Washington, D.C.: U.S. Department of Justice, 1996), pp. 9–10.

17. Stephen J. Boros and Larry C. Brubaker, "Munchausen Syndrome by Proxy: Case Accounts," *FBI Law Enforcement Bulletin*, 1992, Vol. 61, No. 6, pp. 16–20. These case reports were taken from this article.

18. James D. Regis, "The Battered Child," *Police Work*, April 1980, pp. 41–42.

19. Nicholas Kristof, "Seduction, Slavery and Sex," *The New York Times*, July 16, 2010.

20. Kenneth V. Lanning, *Child Molesters: A Behavioral Analysis for Law Enforcement Officers Investigating Cases of Child Sexual Exploitation*, 3rd ed. (Arlington, VA: National Center for Missing and Exploited Children, 1992), pp. 6–10. This entire discussion of child molesters has been reproduced (with minor changes) with permission. No part of this may be reproduced without the express written permission of the National Center for Missing and Exploited Children, 1-800-843-5678.

21. Ibid.

22. Debra Whitcomb, *When the Victim Is a Child* (Washington, D.C.: National Institute of Justice, 1992), pp. 15–20.

23. D. Floyd, testimony before President's Task Force on Victims of Crime, Final Report, December 1982, p. 51.

24. J. Waterman, "Development Considerations," in K. MacFarlane and J. Waterman, eds., *Sexual Abuse of Young Children* (New York: Guilford Press, 1986), pp. 15–29.

25. W. M. Friedrich, J. Fischer, D. Broughton, D. Houston, and C. R. Shafran, "Normative Sexual Behavior in Children: A Contemporary Sample," *Pediatrics*, Vol. 101, No. 4, April, p. 9.

26. A. Warren-Leubecker et al., "What Do Children Know about the Legal System and When Do They Know It? First Steps Down a Less-Traveled Path in Child Witness Research," S. J. Ceci, D. F. Ross, and M. P. Toglia, eds., *Perspectives on Children's Testimony* (New York: Springer Verlag, 1989), pp. 158–183.

27. M. A. Young, "Working with Victims Who Are Children or Adolescents: Using the Lessons of Child Development with Young Trauma Victims," *NOVA Newsletter*, 1989, Vol. 13.

28. Warren-Leubecker et al., "What Do Children Know about the Legal System"; K. J. Saywitz, "Children's Conceptions of the Legal System: 'Court Is a Place to Play Basketball,'" in Ceci et al., *Perspectives on Children's Testimony*, pp. 131–157. Also see S. P. Limber, G. B. Melton, and S. J. Rahe, "Legal Knowledge, Attitudes, and Reasoning Abilities of Witnesses," paper presented at AP-LS Division 41 Biennial Convention, Williamsburg, Virginia, March 1990.

29. R. Pynoos and S. Eth, "The Child Witness to Homicide," *Journal of Social Issues*, 1984, Vol. 40, p. 98.

30. K. J. Saywitz and C. Jaenicke, "Children's Understanding of Legal Terms: A Preliminary Report of Grade-Related Trends," paper presented at the Society for Research on Child Development Biennial Meeting, Baltimore, Maryland, April 1987.

31. Warren-Leubecker et al., "What Do Children Know about the Legal System?"

32. Whitcomb, *When the Victim Is a Child*, pp. 33–38. This discussion was adapted from this source.

33. Alabama, Connecticut, Michigan, New Jersey, New York, Pennsylvania, West Virginia, and Wyoming.

34. See, for example, *Cleveland v. State*, 490 N.R. 2nd 1140 (Ind. App. 1986); *People v. Garvie*, 148 Mich. App. 444, 384 N.W. 2d 796 (1986); *State v. Jenkins*, 326 N.W. 2d 67 (N.D. 1982).

35. E. Gray, "Children as Witnesses in Child Sexual Abuse Cases Study," Final Report submitted to the National Center on Child Abuse and Neglect under Grant No. 90-CA-1273, by the National Council of Jewish Women, New York, New York, 1990, p. 51. (Henceforth referred to as NCJW Study.)

36. K. R. Freemand and T. Estrada-Mullany, "Using Dolls to Interview Child Victims: Legal Concerns and Interview Procedures," *Research in Action*, National Institute of Justice, January/February 1988, p. 2.

37. White, pp. 472–473.

38. S. White and G. Santilli, "A Review of Clinical Practices and Research Data on Anatomical Dolls," *Journal of Interpersonal Violence*, Dec. 1988, Vol. 3, pp. 437–439.

39. L. Berliner, "Anatomical Dolls," *Journal of Interpersonal Violence*, Dec. 1988, Vol. 3, pp. 468–470; also see B. W. Boat and M. D. Everson, "Normative Data: How Non-Referred Young Children Interact with Anatomical Dolls," paper presented at the Symposium of Interviewing Children, cited in Berliner, "Anatomical Dolls," p. 469.

40. White and Santilli, "A Review of Clinical Practices," p. 431.

41. B. Boat and M. Everson, "Use of Anatomical Dolls among Professionals in Sexual Abuse Evaluations," *Child Abuse and Neglect*, 1988, Vol. 12, pp. 171–179.

42. K. MacFarlane and S. Krebs, "Techniques for Interviewing and Evidence Gathering," in MacFarlane and Waterman, *Sexual Abuse of Young Children*, pp. 74–75.

43. Ibid.

44. White and Santilli, "A Review of Clinical Practices," pp. 439–440.

45. MacFarlane and Krebs, "Techniques for Interviewing and Evidence Gathering," p. 87.

46. NCJW Study, pp. 439–440.

47. S. J. Ceci, D. Ross, and M. Toglia, "Age Differences in Suggestibility: Narrowing the Uncertainties," in S. J. Ceci, M. P. Toglia, and D. F. Ross, eds., *Children's Eyewitness Memory* (New York: Springer-Verlag, 1987), pp. 79–91.

48. H. Wakefield and R. Underwager, "Techniques for Interviewing Children in Sexual Abuse Cases," *VOCAL Perspective*, Summer 1989, pp. 7–15.

49. K. Saywitz et al., "Children's Memories of Genital Examinations: Implications for Cases of Child Sexual Assault," paper presented at the Society for Research in Child Development Meetings, Kansas City, Missouri, 1989.

50. J. R. Conte and J. R. Schuerman, "The Effects of Sexual Abuse on Children: A Multidimensional View," *Journal of Interpersonal Violence*, December 1987, Vol. 2, pp. 380–390.

51. W. N. Friedrich, R. L. Beilke, and A. J. Urquiza, "Children from Sexually Abusive Families: A Behavioral Comparison," *Journal of Interpersonal Violence*, Dec. 1987, Vol. 2, pp. 391–402.

52. J. Conte et al., "Evaluating Children's Report of Sexual Abuse: Results from a Survey of Professionals," unpublished manuscript, University of Chicago, undated, cited in J. E. B. Myers et al., "Expert Testimony in Child Sexual Abuse Litigation," *Nebraska Law Review*, 1989, Vol. 68, p. 75.

53. Whitcomb, *When the Victim Is a Child*, pp. 6–11.

54. D. Jones and J. McGraw, "Reliable and Fictitious Accounts of Sexual Abuse to Children," *Journal of Interpersonal Violence*, March 1987, Vol. 2, pp. 27–45.

55. Ibid.

56. J. Paradise, A. Rostain, and M. Nathanson, "Substantiation of Sexual Abuse Charges When Parents Dispute Custody or Visitation," *Pediatrics*, June 1988, Vol. 81, pp. 835–839.

57. See, for example, E. P. Benedek and D. H. Schetky, "Allegations of Sexual Abuse in Child Custody and Visitation Disputes," in D. H. Schetky and E. P. Benedek, eds., *Emerging Issues in Child Psychiatry and the Law* (New York: Brunner/Mazel, 1985), pp. 145–158; A. H. Green, "True and False Allegations of Sexual Abuse in Child Custody Disputes," *Journal of the American Academy of Child Psychiatry*, 1986, Vol. 25, pp. 449–456.

58. For an excellent summary of the drawbacks of such studies, see D. Corwin et al., "Child Sexual Abuse and Custody Disputes: No Easy Answers," *Journal of Interpersonal Violence*, March 1987, Vol. 2, pp. 91–105; also see L. Berliner, "Deciding Whether a Child Has Been Sexually Abused," in E. B. Nicholson, ed., *Sexual Abuse Allegations in Custody and Visitation Cases* (Washington, D.C.: American Bar Association, 1988), pp. 48–69.

59. N. Thoennes and J. Pearson, "Summary of Findings from the Sexual Abuse Allegations Project," in Nicholson, *Sexual Abuse Allegations*, pp. 1–21.

60. D. Finkelhor, L. M. Williams, and N. Burns, *Nursery Crimes: Sexual Abuse in Day Care* (Newbury Park, CA: Sage, 1988).

61. Kenneth V. Lanning, *Child Molesters: A Behavioral Analysis for Law Enforcement Officers Investigating Cases of Child Sexual Exploitation*, 3rd ed. (Arlington, VA: National Center for Missing and Exploited Children, 1992), pp. 24–31. This entire discussion of child pornography has been reproduced (with minor changes) with permission. No part of this may be reproduced without the express written permission of the National Center for Missing and Exploited Children, 1-800-843-5678.

62. R. W. Taylor, E. J. Fritsch, J. Liederbach, and T. J. Holt, *Digital Crime and Digital Terrorism*, Chapter 7: Sex Crimes, Victimization and Obscenity on the World Wide Web, 2nd ed. (Upper Saddle River, NJ: Prentice Hall, 2011), pp. 143, 183.

63. Defined as part of the United Nations General Assembly on the Promotion and Protection of the Rights of Children, September 20, 1995. Document

available at *www.unhchr.ch/Huridocda/Huridoca.nsf/0/97dd6479be18883f80 256719005e5661?Opendocument.*

64. "Review of the US Department of State Office to Monitor and Combat Trafficking in Persons TIP Report 2007." *The Protection Project* (Washington, D.C.: Johns Hopkins University, June 2007), p. 28, *www.theprotectionproject.org.*

65. E. Klain, "Prostitution of Children and Child-Sex Tourism: An Analysis of Domestic and International Responses" (Washington, D.C.: Office of Juvenile Justice and Delinquency Programs and National Center for Missing and Exploited Children, 1999) p. 37.

66. "State Seeks to Close Dutchess and Queens Based Travel Agency." Press release from the New York State Attorney General, August 20, 2003, *www .oag.state.ny.us/press/2003/aug/aug20a_03.html.*

67. "Child Sex Tourism," *Child Exploitation and Obscenity of the U.S. Department of Justice, www.justice.gov/criminal/ceos/sextour.html,* November 10, 2010.

68. E. Klain, "Prostitution of Children and Child-Sex Tourism: An Analysis of Domestic and International Responses" (Washington, D.C.: Office of Juvenile Justice and Delinquency Programs and National Center for Missing and Exploited Children, 1999) pp. 33–35.

69. F. Miko, "Trafficking in Persons: The U.S. and International Response," Congressional Research Service, Library of Congress (Washington D.C.: July 7, 2006).

70. E. Klain, "Prostitution of Children and Child-Sex Tourism: An Analysis of Domestic and International Responses" (Washington, D.C.: Office of Juvenile Justice and Delinquency Programs and National Center for Missing and Exploited Children, 1999) p. 33.

71. *The Paedo File,* End Child Prostitution, Child Pornography and Trafficking of Children for Sexual Purposes (EPCAT) Newsletter (EPCAT International: Bangkok, Thailand, April 1996), pp. 4–5.

72. E. Klain, "Prostitution of Children and Child-Sex Tourism: An Analysis of Domestic and International Responses" (Washington, D.C.: Office of Juvenile Justice and Delinquency Programs and National Center for Missing and Exploited Children, 1999) p. 37.

73. V. Silverman, "US Law Enforcement Targets Child Sex Tourism" (Washington D.C.: U.S. Department of State, December 17, 2003*). http://usinfo .state.gov/gi/Archive/2003/Dec/17-227348.html.*

74. "The Facts about Child Sex Tourism," Fact sheet from the U.S. Department of State Office to Monitor and Combat Trafficking in Persons, August 19, 2005, *www.state.gov/g/tip/rls/fs/2005/51351.htm.*

75. "Child Sex Tourism," Child Exploitation and Obscenity of the U.S. Department of Justice, *www.justice.gov/criminal/ceos/sextour.html.*

76. S. K. Andrews, U.S. Domestic Prosecution of the American International Sex Tourist: Efforts to Protect Children from Sexual Exploitation," *The Journal of Criminal Law and Criminology,* 2004, Vol. 94, 415–454.

77. The Child Pornography Prevention Act, U.S. Code Title 18, Section 2252: Certain Activities Relating to Material Involving the Sexual Exploitation of Minors.

78. U.S. Code, Title 18, Section 2251: Sexual Exploitation of Children.

79. In the Supreme Court of the United States, *John D. Ashcroft, Attorney General of the United States et al., Petitioners,* v. *The Free Speech Coalition et al., www.usdoj.gov/osg/briefs/2000/3mer/2mer/2000-0795.mer.aa.html.*

80. Supreme Court of the United States, *www.supremecourtus .gov/index.html.*

81. Donald M. Kerr, "Internet and Data Interception Capabilities Developed by the FBI," Statement for the Record, U.S. House of Representatives, Committee on the Judiciary, Subcommittee on the Constitution, *www.cdt.org/ security/carnivor/000724fbi.shtml,* July 24, 2000.

82. Kind Holger, "Combating Child Pornography on the Internet by the German Federal Criminal Police Office (BKA)."

83. "14 Nations Join to Bust Huge Internet Child Porn Ring," *www.cnn.com/ WORLD/europe/9809/02/internet.porn.02/.*

84. National Sex Offender Public Website. "Raising Awareness About Sexual Abuse: Facts and Statistics." Retrieved from: https://www.nsopw.gov/en-us/ Education/FactsStatistics?AspxAutoDetectCookieSupport=1

85. J. Wolak et al., "Online Victimization of Youth: 5 Years Later" (Washington, D.C.: Office of Juvenile Justice and Delinquency Programs, Crimes Against Children Research Center, and National Center for Missing and Exploited Children, 2006) p. 17.

86. Ibid., p. 18.

87. San Diego County District Attorney. "Protecting Children Online." Retrieved from: http://www.sdcda.org/preventing/protecting-children-online/facts-for-parents.html.

88. Information taken from Internet Crimes Against Children Task Force website, *www.icactraining.org/,* September 10, 2007.

89. J. Wolak, D. Finkelhor, and K. Mitchell, "Trends in Arrests of 'Online Predators,'" Crimes Against Children Research Center, 2009.

90. M. Huffman, "MySpace Deletes More Sex Offenders." ConsumerAffairs. com, July 25, 2007, *www.consumeraffairs.com/news04/2007/07/myspace _more.html.*

90. Vaas, Lisa. (July 16, 2012) "How Facebook catches would-be child molesters by analyzing relationships and chat content." Sophos.com. Retrieved from https://nakedsecurity.sophos.com/2012/07/16/facebook-child-molester/.

91. Facebook. "Information for Law Enforcement Authorities." Retrieved from https://www.facebook.com/safety/groups/law/guidelines

92. V. Coleman-Wright, "For Detective, Kids' Safety Is First and Foremost."

93. National Conference of State Legislatures. School Bullying: Overview, *www. ncsl.org/Default.aspx?Tabld=12952.*

94. U.S. Department of Education, *Exploring the Nature and Prevention of Bullying, www2.ed.gov/admins/lead/safety/training/bullying/bullying_pg11.html.*

95. Hinduja, S. and Patchin, J. (January 2016) "State Cyberbullying Laws: A Brief Review of State Cyberbullying Laws and Policies". Cyberbullying Research Center. Retrieved from: http://cyberbullying.org/Bullying-and-Cyberbullying-Laws.pdf

96. Hinduja, S. and Patchin, J. (January 2016) "State Cyberbullying Laws: A Brief Review of State Cyberbullying Laws and Policies". Cyberbullying Research Center. Retrieved from: http://cyberbullying.org/Bullying-and-Cyberbullying-Laws.pdf

97. J. O. Beasley, A. S. Hayne, K. Beyer, G. L. Cramer, S. B. Berson, Y. Muirhead, and J. I. Warren, "Patterns of Prior Offending by Child Abductors: A Comparison of Fatal and Non-Fatal Outcomes," *International Journal of Law and Psychiatry,* 2009, Vol. 32, pp. 273–280.

98. Amanda Lenhart, "Pew Internet and American Life Project." <u>Data Memo</u> (June 27, 2007) Pew Research Center. See: http://www.pewinternet.org

99. See http://www.cyberbulling.org

100. National Crime Prevention Council at: http://www.ncpc.org/newsroom/current-campaigns/cyberbullling

101. Janis Wolak and David Finkelhor, <u>Sextortion: Findings from an Online Survey about Threats to Expose Sexual Images</u> (University of New Hampshire: Crimes Against Children Research Center, June 2016). See: https:// www.wearethorn.org/sextortion/1880/

102. Sameer Hinduja and Justin W. Patchin, <u>Sexting: Advise for Teens.</u> Cyberbullying Research Center (May 2016). See: http://cyberbullying.org/sexting-advice-teens

103. K. Hanfland, R. Keppel, and J. Weis, "Case Management for Missing Children: Homicide Investigation," Washington State Attorney General's Office, 1997.

104. Adapted from the FBI's *Child Abduction Response Plan,* Critical Incident Response Group, National Center for the Analysis of Violent Crime (Quantico, VA), pp. 15–16.

105. For more information, agencies can contact the NCAVC coordinator at their local FBI field office.

106. Interview with Supervisory Special Agent Mark Hilts, Federal Bureau of Investigation, NCAVC, Mar. 2, 1999.

107. W. D. Lord, M. C. Boudreaux, and K. V. Lanning, "Investigating Potential Child Abduction Cases: A Developmental Perspective," FBI Law Enforcement Bulleting, April 2001, Vol. 70, pp. 1–10.

108. W. D. Lord, M. C. Boudreaux, and K. V. Lanning, "Investigating Potential Child Abduction Cases: A Developmental Perspective," *FBI Law Enforcement Bulletin,* April 2001, Vol. 70, pp. 1–10.

109. L. G. Androm and C. J. Lent, "Cradle Robbers: A Study of the Infant Abductor," FBI Law Enforcement Bulletin, Sept. 1995, pp. 12–17.

110. W. D. Lord, M. C. Boudreaux, and K. V. Lanning, "Investigating Potential Child Abduction Cases: A Developmental Perspective," *FBI Law Enforcement Bulletin,* April 2001, Vol. 70, pp. 1–10.

111. Ibid.

112. Ibid.

113. Ibid.

114. Ibid.

115. J. Robert Flores, *When Your Child Is Missing: A Family Guide to Survival,* Department of Justice, 2002, pp. 21–22.

116. For more information about the AMBER alert, visit *www.amberalert.gov.*

117. Federal Bureau of Investigation, *Child Abduction Response Plan,* p. 17.

118. 42 U.S.C. 14071; National Criminal Justice Association, *Sex Offender Community Notification Policy Report* (Washington, D.C.: Oct. 1997), p. 5.

119. The Edward Byrne Memorial State and Local Law Enforcement Assistance Program provides grants to states to "improve the functioning of the criminal justice system, with emphasis on violent crimes and serious offenders," *www.ojp.usdoj.gov/BJA/html/byrnef.htm,* accessed Feb. 22, 2000.

120. Scott Matson and Roxanne Lieb, *Sex Offender Registration: A Review of State Laws* (Olympia: Washington State Institute for Public Policy, July 1996), p. 5.

121. Edward Byrne Memorial, p. 1.

122. Ibid.

123. 104. P.L. 145, 100 Stat. 1345; Wetterling, "The Jacob Wetterling Story," p. 8.

124. C. L. Scott and J. B. Gerbasi, "Sex Offender Registration and Community Notification Challenges: The Supreme Court Continues," *The Journal of the American Academy of Psychiatry and the Law,* 2003, Vol. 31, 494–501.

125. 42 U.S.C 14072; Wetterling, ibid., pp. 8–9. Congress named the act after Lychner when she and her two daughters died in the TWA Flight 800 explosion off the coast of Long Island in July 1996.

126. The National Sex Offender Registry (NSOR), which became operational in 1997, initially served as a pointer system for a convicted sex offender's record in the Interstate Identification Index. The permanent registry–part of NCIC (National Crime Information Center) 2000–went online in 1999, replacing the earlier version. The NSOR flags sex offenders when agencies request authorized, fingerprint-based, criminal-history checks. Information provided by the Crimes against Children Unit, Criminal Investigative Division, FBI Headquarters, Washington, D.C., Feb. 24, 2000.

127. The U.S. attorney general set October 2001 as the date by which all states should comply with DOJ standards relating to the Jacob Wetterling Act. To date, all states have developed sex offender registries.

128. National Institute of Education, *Violent Schools–Safe Schools: The Safe School Study Report to the Congress,* Washington, D.C.: U.S. Department of Education, 1978.

129. National School Safety Center, "School Crime: Annual Statistical Snapshot," *School Safety* (Winter 1989).

130. J. Hall, "The Knife in the Book Bag," *Time* (May 22, 1993); T. Toch, T. Guest, and M. Guttman, "Violence in Schools: When Killers Come Home." *U.S. News and World Report* (Nov. 8, 1993).

131. "The School Shooter: A Threat Assessment Perspective." National Center for the Analysis of Violent Crime, FBI National Academy, Quantico, VA, 2000, pp. 2–9. (Much of this discussion on crime in school was adapted from this source.)

132. C. Malmquist, Homicidal Violence, malq001@atlas.socsci.umn.edu.

133. "The School Shooter: A Threat Assessment Perspective," pp. 16–21.

134. Glenn Stutzky, "How to Battle the School Bully," an interview with *ABC News, www.abcnews.go.com/sections/community/DailyNews/chat_bullying11298.html,* Nov. 29, 2001.

135. James Blair, "The Ethics of Using Juvenile Informants: Murder in California Prompts New Bill, Raises Questions about Whether Minors Should Be Operatives," *Christian Science Monitor, www.csmonitor.com/durable/1998/04/14/p3s1.htm,* Apr. 14, 1998.

136. Michael Dorn, Senior Public Safety and Emergency Analyst–Janes Consultancy, "Home Searches: A Valuable Tool." *Campus Safety Journal,* Training Bulletins–Training Bulletin #8, 2003.

Chapter 12

1. In May 2014, The International Labour Organization released a groundbreaking report estimating that victims of this crime generate a staggering $150 billion in profits per year for the private global economy: $99 billion in the sex industry and $51 billion in other sectors. See U.S. Department of State, *Trafficking in Persons Report,* June 2014, Closing Note, p. 432; http://www.state.gov /j/tip/rls/tiprpt/2014/index.htm.

2. Trafficking victims can be either foreign nationals or natives. Under U.S. law, persons are placed in conditions of **forced labor** if they are forced to work against their will through actual or implied threats of serious harm, physical restraint, or abuse of the law. If they are forced to work through physical force or threats of physical force, they are victims of *involuntary servitude*. A person is subjected to **peonage** if that person is compelled by force, threat of force, or abuse of the law to work against his/her will in order to pay off a debt. If the value of a person's work is never reasonably applied toward payment of the debt, the person has been subjected to *debt bondage*. The term "forced labor" is also often used to describe all of these forms of modern slavery.

3. For a more detailed discussion on this topic see Leonard Territo and Rande Matteson, eds., *The International Trafficking of Human Organs: A Multi-Disciplinary Perspective* (Boca Raton, FL: CRC Press, 2012).

4. Pamela Chen and Monica Ryan, "Federal Prosecution of Human Traffickers," in Jill Laurie Goodman and Dorchen A. Leidholdt, eds., *Lawyer's Manual on Human Trafficking: Pursuing Justice for Victims* (Supreme Court of the State of New York, Appellate Division, First Department, New York State Judicial Committee on Women in the Courts, 2011), pp. 275–277.

5. See 18 U.S.C. §§ 2421 and 2423.

6. *18 U.S.C. § 2421.*

7. *18 U.S.C. § 2423.*

8. The Travel Act criminalizes travel for the purpose of engaging in other criminal activity such as acts of violence, gambling, and extortion. *See* 18 U.S.C. § 1952. In addition, as later discussed, the Travel Act also criminalizes the use of certain interstate facilities to commit crimes.

9. 18 U.S.C. § 1952(a)(3) and (b).

10. United States v. Mukovsky, 863 F.2d 1319, 1327 (7th Cir. 1988); see United States v. Bates, 840 F.2d 858, 863 (11th Cir. 1988) (same); United States v. Davis, 666 F.2d 195, 202 n. 10 (5th Cir. Unit B 1982) (same); *United States v. Corbin,* 662 F.2d 1066, 1073 (4th Cir. 1981) (same); United States v. Cozzetti, 441 F.2d 344, 348 (9th Cir. 1971) (same). However, the "business enterprise" need not be sophisticated nor prolific. See, e.g., Cozzetti, 441 F.2d at 347–48.

11. For a more detailed discussion of the Trafficking Victim Protection Act, 2000 and the Reauthorization Acts of 2003, 2005, and 2008 see Leonard Territo and Nataliya Glover, *Criminal Investigation of Sex Trafficking in America* (Boca Raton, FL: CRC Press, Taylor & Francis Group, 2014), pp. 34–52.

12. Stacey Ivie and Natalie Nanasi, "The U Visa: An Effective Resource for Law Enforcement, *FBI Law Enforcement Bulletin,* October 2009, http://www.fbi.gov/publications/leb/2009/october2009/visa_feature.htm; Internet.

13. http://www.uscis.gov/files/pressrelease/U-visa_05Sept07.pdf

14. The U visa is available to individuals with temporary immigration status (e.g., student, employment-based, and tourist visas or Temporary Protected Status), as well as undocumented persons with no legal status.

15. Organized Crime Control Act of 1970, Pub. L. No. 91-452, 84 Stat. 922, 923.

16. Kendal Nichole Smith, "Human Trafficking and RICO: A New Prosecuting Hammer in the War on Modern Day Slavery," *George Mason Law Review,* Vol. 18, Issue 3, 2011, pp. 776–777.

17. G. Robert Blakey & Brian Gettings, "Racketeer Influenced and Corrupt Organizations (RICO): Basic Concepts–Criminal and Civil Remedies," *Temple Law Quarterly,* Vol. 53, 1980, pp., 1009, 1014.

18. Ibid., p. 1013.

19. Smith, "Human Trafficking and RICO," pp. 785–786.

20. See 18 U.S.C. § 1963(a) (2006). The Organized Crime and Racketeering Section will approve a RICO count seeking a sentence beyond 20 years if: (1) the count charges against the defendant a racketeering act for which the penalty includes life imprisonment; (2) the racketeering act charges the necessary facts to trigger the life imprisonment penalty, tracking that portion of the statute that sets forth the factors supporting a penalty of life imprisonment; and (3) the racketeering act cites the appropriate statute or statutes the racketeering act violates. Organized crime and Racketeering Section, U.S. Dept. of Justice, Criminal RICO: 18 U.S.C. §§ 1961-1968, A Manual for Federal Prosecutors 159 (ed. Frank J. Marine, 5th rev. ed., 2009) [hereinafter *RICO Prosecutor's Manual*]. Online at: http://www.justice.gov/usao/eousa/foia_reading_room/usam/title9/rico.pdf.

21. Ibid. at 177; *see infra* Part V.B.

22. 18 U.S.C. § 1963(a); *see* Gerard E. Lynch, "RICO" The Crime of Being a Criminal, Parts III & IV, 87," *Columbia Law Review,* 1987, pp. 920, 924. ("In some cases, the impetus for the use of RICO in criminal enterprise cases appears to be, as in the white collar and labor cases, its extreme, mandatory and procedurally simple financial penalties.")

23. Blake and Gettings, "Racketeer Influenced and Corrupt Organizations (RICO)," p. 1036.

24. *See, e.g., United States v. Segal,* 495 F.3d 826, 838 (7th Cir. 2007) (finding that a defendant who owned the entire enterprise was properly required to forfeit the full enterprise, despite the jury's finding that only 60% of his interests were "tainted" by racketeering activity); *United States v.*

Busher, 817 F.2d 1409, 1413 (9th Cir. 1987) ("[F]forfeiture is not limited to those assets of a RICO enterprise that are tainted by use in connection with the racketeering activity, but rather extends to the convicted person's entire interest in the enterprise."); *see also RICO Prosecutor's Manual,* pp 189-192.

25 18 U.S.C. § 1963(a)(2)(D).

26 Leonard Territo and Nataliya Glover, *Criminal Investigation of Sex Trafficking in America* (Boca Raton, FL: CRC Press, 2014), pp. 30-31.

27 Natalie M. McClain and Stacy E. Garrity, "Sex Trafficking and the Exploitation of Adolescent," *Journal of Obstetrics, Gynecology and Neonatal Nursing,* Vol. 40, Issue 2 March-April 2011, pp. 243-52.

28 Beth E. Molnar et al., "Suicidal Behavior and Sexual/Physical Abuse Among Street Youth," *Child Abuse Neglect,* Vol. 22, Issue 3, 1998, pp. 213-214; Maggie O'Neill, "Prostitute Women Now," in Graham Scambler and Annette Scambler, eds., *Rethinking Prostitution: Purchasing Sex in the 1990s* (London: Routledge, 1997), p. 19; Debra Whitcomb and Julie Eastin, *Joining Forces Against Child Sexual Exploitation: Models for a Multijurisdictional Team Approach* (United States: Office of Juvenile Justice and Delinquency Prevention, 1998).

29 *See* Debra Whitcomb, Edward De Vos, and Barbara E. Smith, *Program to Increase Understanding of Child Sexual Exploitation, Final Report* at 3 (Washington, DC: Education Development Center, Inc., and ABA Center on Children and the Law, 1998) (since much of the literature is "based on the same (or related) research efforts by the same (or collaborating) authors, the actual research base is even smaller. Many of these studies lack scientific rigor and are based on extremely small sample sizes.").

30 Ibid.

31 *Report of the Special Rapporteur on the Sale of Children, Child Prostitution and Child Pornography,* United Nations Economic and Social Council, Commission on Human Rights, 52d Sess., Agenda Item 20, ¶ 35, U.N. Doc. E/CN.4/1996/100 (1996) [hereinafter *Report of the Special Rapporteur*].

32 In one study of 200 prostitutes in San Francisco, about 60% were 16 and younger, many were 10, 11, and 12 years old. Mimi H. Silbert and Ayala M. Pines, "Entrance into Prostitution," *Youth Society,* Vol. 13, Issue 4, 1982, pp. 471, 473. A more recent sample of 83 sexually- exploited youth interviewed in shelters in Dallas, Pittsburgh, and San Diego showed a majority (62%) between the ages of 14 and 17, and 12% between 10 and 13. Twenty-six percent were older than 18. Whitcomb et al., *Program to Increase Understanding of Child Sexual Exploitation,* p. 66.

33 Whitcomb and Eastin, *Joining Forces Against Child Sexual Exploitation,* 36 (citing *Community Consultation on Prostitution in British Columbia, Overview of Results* (March 1996)); Mimi H. Silbert and Ayala M. Pines, "Occupational Hazards of Street Prostitutes," *Criminal Justice and Behavior,* Vol. 8, 1981, p. 397.

34 *Program to Increase Understanding of Child Sexual Exploitation, Assessment Report, Volume II* (Education Development Center, Inc., and ABA Center on Children and the Law 1994) [hereinafter *Assessment Report*].

35 Byron Fassett and Bill Walsh, "Juvenile Prostitution: An Overlooked Form of Child Sexual Abuse," *The APSAC Advisor,* Vol. 7, Issue 1, 1994, pp. 9-10 (American Professional Society on the Abuse of Children 1994).

36 Whitcomb and Eastin, *Joining Forces Against Child Sexual Exploitation,* 36 (citing *Community Consultation on Prostitution in British Columbia, Overview of Results* (March 1996)).

37 Whitcomb et al., *Program to Increase Understanding of Child Sexual Exploitation,* 65 (76% of exploited youth interviewed in shelters were girls).

38 *Assessment Report.* Some service providers also mentioned an increase in the number of homeless boys, which they sometimes linked to cutbacks in other community services.

39 *Assessment Report.*

40 David Barrett and Wilma Beckett, "Child Prostitution: Reaching out to Children Who Sell Sex to Survive," *British Journal of Nursing,* Vol. 5, Issue 18, October 12, 1996, pp. 1120-1125, note 18.

41 Silbert and Pines, "Occupational Hazards of Street Prostitutes," p. 485.

42 Alex H. Kral et al., "Prevalence of Sexual Risk Behavior and Substance Use Among Runaway and Homeless Adolescents in San Francisco, Denver and New York City," *International Journal of STD and AIDS,* 1997, p. 109.

43 Kathryn V. Wurzbacher et al., "Effects of Alternative Street School on Youth Involved in Prostitution," *Journal of Adolescent Health,* Vol. 12, 1991, pp. 549-554.

44 Silbert and Pines, "Occupational Hazards of Street Prostitutes," p. 490.

45 Linda A. Smith, Samantha Healy Vardaman and Melissa A. Snow, *The National Report on Domestic Minor Sex Trafficking: America's Prostituted Children,* Shared Hope International, May 2009. Accessed July 9, 2012, http://www.sharedhope.org/Resources/TheNationalReport.

46 Kacie L. Macdonald, "Human Trafficking: A Service Provider's Guide to Recognizing and Assisting Victims of Modern Day Slavery (paper presented at North American Association of Christians in Social Work (NACSW), Indianapolis, IN, October 2009). Accessed January 17, 2013, http://www.nacsw.org.

47 Magnus J. Seng, "Child Sexual Abuse and Adolescent Prostitution: A Comparative Analysis," *Adolescence,* Vol. 24, 1989, pp. 665, 671.

48 Wurzbacher et al., "Effects of Alternative Street School on Youth Involved in Prostitution," 549. *See also* Whitcomb et al., *Program to Increase Understanding of Child Sexual Exploitation,* 21 (of sexually-exploited youth interviewed in a Dallas shelter, 81% had been truants, 34% had been suspended or expelled, and 12% were drop-outs).

49 Augustine Brannigan and Erin Gibbs Van Brunschot, "Youth Prostitution and Child Sexual Trauma," *International Journal of Law and Psychiatry,* Vol. 20, Issue 3, 1997, pp. 337-354.

50 Silbert and Pines, "Occupational Hazards of Street Prostitutes," p. 490.

51 Brannigan and Gibbs van Brunschott, "Youth Prostitution and Child Sexual Trauma," p. 350.

52 Wurzbacher et al., "Effects of Alternative Street School on Youth Involved in Prostitution," p. 549.

53 Among girls, 14% reported exchanging sex for money; 11% for drugs or alcohol; and 10% for food, shelter, or clothing. Among boys, 23% reported exchanging sex for money; 7% for drugs or alcohol; and 10% for food, shelter, or clothing. Kral et al., "Prevalence of Sexual Risk Behavior and Substance Use Among Runaway and Homeless Adolescents in San Francisco, Denver and New York City," 113. Various studies have found that 22% of boys and 7% of girls on New York City streets had engaged in prostitution at some time, while 26 to 28% of boys and 26 to 31% of girls in Los Angeles did so. Mary Jane Rotheram-Borus et al., "Sexual Abuse History and Associated Multiple Risk Behavior in Adolescent Runaways," *American Journal of Orthopsych,* Vol. 66, 1996, pp. 390-391. Although less than 1% of minority nonhomeless youth at a medical clinic in a New York City public high school reported using sex to obtain money or drugs, 13% of homeless youth in Chicago had recently engaged in prostitution. Prostitution was also reported by 54% of street youth in Toronto, 26.4% of a sample of runaways in Los Angeles, and 19% of runaway and homeless youth in Houston. T. P. Johnson et al., "Self-Reported Risk Factors for AIDS Among Homeless Youth," *AIDS Education and Prevention* 8, no. 4 (August 1996): 308, 318 (citing numerous studies). See also Gary L. Yates et al., "A Risk Profile Comparison of Runaway and Non-Runaway Youth," *American Journal of Public Health* 78 (1988): 820-821.

54 Seng, "Child Sexual Abuse and Adolescent Prostitution," p. 671.

55 Whitcomb et al., *Program to Increase Understanding of Child Sexual Exploitation,* p. 74.

56 Gary L. Yates et al., "A Risk Profile Comparison of Homeless Youth Involved in Prostitution and Homeless Youth Not Involved," *Journal of Adolescent Health,* Vol. 12, 1991, pp. 545, 547.

57 Seng, "Child Sexual Abuse and Adolescent Prostitution," p. 673.

58 M. Alexis Kennedy and Nicole Joey Pucci, *Domestic Minor Sex Trafficking Assessment Report—Las Vegas, Nevada* (Springfield, VA: Shared Hope International, August 2007), p. 106.

59 Ibid.

60 Kelli Stevens et al., *Domestic Minor Sex Trafficking Assessment Report—Fort Worth, Texas* (Springfield, VA: Shared Hope International, July 2008, p. 35.

61 Jennifer Bayhi-Gennaro, *Domestic Minor Sex Trafficking Assessment Report—Baton Rouge/New Orleans, Area Assessment* (Springfield, VA: Shared Hope International, April 2008), p. 13, citing E. Fitch, "Grand Jury Indicts Murder Suspect." *The News-Star,* June 14, 2006.

62 Silbert and Pines, *Occupational Hazards of Street Prostitutes, Criminal Justice and Behavior,* p. 481. After leaving school and before getting into prostitution, the vast majority of young women in the study reported being either isolated, with no friends (40%), or deeply involved with friends exhibiting deviant behavior (80%).

63 M.A. Morey and L.S. Friedman, "Health Care Needs of Homeless Adolescents," *Current Opinion in Pediatrics,* Vol. 5, Issue 4, 1993, pp. 395-399.

Self-identified homosexual or bisexual homeless teenagers are five times more likely to engage in survival sex than heterosexual homeless youth.

64 Silbert and Pines, "Occupational Hazards of Street Prostitutes," p. 485.

65 Linda A. Smith, Samantha Healy Vardaman, and Melissa A. Snow, *The National Report on Domestic Minor Sex Trafficking* (Springfield, VA: Shared Hope International, 2009).

66 Ibid.

67 Ibid.

68 Definition of Stockholm syndrome. Accessed June 7, 2012, http://medical-dictionary.thefreedictionary.com.

69 Remarks by K. Childs. Shared Hope International National Training Conference on the Sex Trafficking of America's Youth. Transcript on file with authors.

70 Evelina Giobbe, "Juvenile Prostitution: Profile of Recruitment," in Ann Wolbert Burgess, ed., *Chile Trauma I: Issues and Research* (New York: Garland Publishing, Inc. 1992), p. 118.

71 O'Neill, "Prostitute Women Now," p. 14.

72 Children of the Night, *Training Manual,* Vol. 11, February 1993.

73 Fassett and Walsh, "Juvenile Prostitution: An Overlooked Form of Child Sexual Abuse," p. 30.

74 *Assessment Report*, p. 162; Kathleen Barry, *The Prostitution of Sexuality* (New York: New York University Press 1995), p. 208.

75 Barry, "Juvenile Prostitution: An Overlooked Form of Child Sexual Abuse," p. 106.

76 Jean Faugier and Mary Sargeant, "Boyfriends, 'Pimps' and Clients," in Graham Scambler and Annette Scambler, eds., *Rethinkinng Prostitution: Purchasing Sex in the 1990s* (London: Routledge 1997), p. 123.

77 Neal K. Katyal, "Men Who Own Women: A Thirteenth Amendment Critique of Forced Prostitution," p. 103 *Yale Law Journal,* Vol. 103, 1993, pp. 791, 793.

78 Barry, "Juvenile Prostitution: An Overlooked Form of Child Sexual Abuse," p. 208.

79 Annette U. Rickel and Marie C. Hendren, "Aberrant Sexual Experiences," in Gullotta, Adams and Montemayor, eds., *Adolescent Sexuality* (Newbury Park, CA: Sage Publications 1993).

80 Ibid., p. 153.

81 Fassett and Walsh, "Juvenile Prostitution: An Overlooked Form of Child Sexual Abuse," p. 30.

82 Barry, "Juvenile Prostitution: An Overlooked Form of Child Sexual Abuse," p. 200.

83 Evelina Giobbe, "An Analysis of Individual, Institutional and Cultural Pimping," *Michigan Journal of Gender and Law,* Vol. 1, Issue 1, 1993, pp. 33, 46. Others have also come to this conclusion: "By listening to survivors describe the tactics of control that kept them trapped in the sex industry and comparing this to our knowledge about battering, we've come to recognize that prostitution is violence against women." Holly B. Fechner, "Three Stories of Prostitution in the West: Prostitutes' Groups, Law and Feminist 'Truth'," *Columbia Journal of Gender and Law, Vol.* 4, 1994, pp. 26, 36–37 (citing WHISPER Progress Report 1985–1989 at 1 (WHISPER, Minneapolis, MN)). WHISPER endorses abolition of all laws that penalize women and children in prostitution and seeks enhanced penalties for pimps and customers as well as increased enforcement of existing laws. Ibid.

84 Giobbe, "An Analysis of Individual, Institutional and Cultural Pimping," p. 47.

85 Ibid., p. 48.

86 Ibid., p. 50.

87 Minouche Kandel, "Whores in Court: Judicial Processing of Prostitutes in the Boston Municipal Court in 1990," *Yale Journal of Law and Feminism,* Vol. 4, 1992, p. 329. The Council for Prostitution Alternatives found that 53% of prostitutes they interviewed were "horribly" beaten by pimps an average of 58 times per year. Barry, "Juvenile Prostitution: An Overlooked Form of Child Sexual Abuse," p. 202.

88 Fassett and Walsh, "Juvenile Prostitution: An Overlooked Form of Child Sexual Abuse," p. 30; Giobbe, "An Analysis of Individual, Institutional and Cultural Pimping," p. 48.

89 *See* expert testimony presented in State v. Simon, 831 P.2d 139 (Wash. 1992).

90 Ibid.

91 Pierce v. United States, 146 F.2d 84 (5th Cir. 1944); People v. Kent, 96 Cal. App. 3d 130 (1979) (prostitute beaten for not bringing in enough money).

92 Ibid. *See also* Giobbe, "An Analysis of Individual, Institutional and Cultural Pimping," p. 124.

93 Margaret A. Baldwin, "Pornography and the Traffic in Women: Brief on Behalf of Trudee Able-Peterson, et al. Amici Curiae in Support of Defendant and Intervenor-Defendants, Village Books v. City of Bellingham," *Yale Journal of Law and Feminism,* Vol. 1, 1989, pp. 111, 130.

94 Ibid., p. 128. *See also* Rickel and Hendren, "Aberrant Sexual Experiences," p. 151.

95 Baldwin, "Pornography and the Traffic in Women," p. 140.

96 Ibid., p. 132. Runaways who "come under the control of pornographers and pimps become susceptible to subsequent physical and sexual victimization by pimps and customers." Widom, Cathy S. Widom and Joseph B. Kuhns, "Childhood Victimization and Subsequent Risk for Promiscuity, Prostitution and Teenage Pregnancy: A Prospective Study, American Journal of Public Health, Vol. 86, Issue 11, 1996, pp. 1607–1612

97 Giobbe, "An Analysis of Individual, Institutional and Cultural Pimping," p. 43. Another commentator analyzes forced prostitution as slavery under the 13th Amendment's prohibition against slavery and involuntary servitude, advocating that government officials act unconstitutionally under the 13th Amendment if they fail to enforce laws against pimps. Katyal, "Men Who Own Women."

98 Richard J. Estes and Neil Alan Weiner, *Commercial Sexual Exploitation of Children in the U.S., Canada, and Mexico* (Philadelphia: University of Pennsylvania, Executive Summary, 2001).

99 Graeme R. Newman, *The Exploitation of Trafficked Women* (Washington, DC: U.S. Department of Justice, Office of Community Oriented Policing Services, February 2006), pp. 10–51. Much of this discussion was adapted with minor modifications from this source.

100 MiraMed Institute, "Who is Trafficking CIS Women?" *Preliminary Survey Report on Sexual Trafficking in the CIS* (Moscow: MiraMed Institute, June 1999).

101 International Organization for Migration, *Information Campaign Against Trafficking in Women from Ukraine-Research Report* (Geneva, Switzerland: International Organization for Migration, July 1998).

102 Donna M. Hughes, "Sex Tours via the Internet." *Agenda: A Journal about Women and Gender,* Vol. 28, 1996, pp. 71–76.

103 J. Raymond and D. Hughes, *Sex Trafficking of Women in the United States: International and Domestic Trends* (North Amherst, MA: Coalition Against Trafficking in Women, 2001), http://action.web.ca/home/catw/attach/sex_traff_us.pdf.

104 One study found that over 50% of trafficked women entered the Unites States with tourist visas and overstayed their visas. Raymond and Hughes, *Sex Trafficking of Women in the United States.*

105 Jim Walters and Patricia H. Davis, "Human Trafficking, Sex Tourism, and Child Exploitation on the Southern Border," *Journal of Applied Research on Children: Informing Policy for Children at Risk,* Vol. 2, Issue 1 (Article 6), 2011, pp. 3–8.

106 "Rise in the Numbers of Border-Crossers Dying Along the U.S.-Mexico Border," *Homeland Security News Wire,* March 20, 2013, http://www.homelandsecuritynewswire.com/dr20130320-rise-in-the-number-of-border-crossers-dying-along-the-u-s-mexico-border.

107 M. Jiminez, "Humanitarian Crisis: Migrant Deaths at the U.S.–Mexico Border," ACLU of San Diego & Imperial Counties/ Comisión Nacional de los Derechos Humanos, October 2009. Accessed January 15, 2009, http://www.aclu.org/immigrants-rights/humanitarian-crisis- migrant-deaths-us-mexico-border.

108 D. Hughes, *The Impact of the Use of New Communications and Information Technologies on Trafficking in Human Beings for Sexual Exploitation: A Study of the Users* (Strasbourg: Council of Europe, Committee for Equality between Women and Men, 2001).

109 When a person provides a loan to another who uses his or her labor or services to repay the debt; when the value of the work, as reasonably assessed, is not applied towards the liquidation of the debt.

110 In the pre-Civil War South, replacing a slave cost the modern equivalent of $40,000. Slaves in the twenty-first century can be purchased for as little as $90. For example, a family in Thailand was reported to have sold a daughter into the sex trade in order to buy a television set (Florida State University, Center for the Advancement of Human Rights, 2003), p. 14.

111 United Nations Economic and Social Commission for Asia and the Pacific (UNESCAP) (2003). *Combating Human Trafficking in Asia: A*

Resource Guide to International and Regional Legal Instruments, Political Commitments and Recommended Practices. Bangkok, Thailand: UNESCAP. www.unescap.org/publications/detail.asp?id=841.

112   Donna Hughes, "The 'Natasha' Trade: Transnational Sex Trafficking," *National Institute of Justice Journal*, no. 246, January 2001.

113   Todd S. Fogelsong and Peter H. Solomon, *Crime, Criminal Justice and Criminology in Post-Soviet Ukraine*—A Report (Washington, DC: National Institute of Justice, August 30, 1999).

114   PERESTROIKA—From modest beginnings at the Twenty-Seventh Party Congress in 1986, perestroika, Mikhail Gorbachev's program of economic, political, and social restructuring, became the unintended catalyst for dismantling what had taken nearly three-quarters of a century to erect: the Marxist-Leninist-Stalinist totalitarian state.

115   Chris Bird, "100,000 Ukrainians Slaves of West's Sex Industry," *Reuters*, July 6, 1998.

116   *Post Guidelines on Law Enforcement Response to Human Trafficking 2014*, Sacramento, California. Online at. Accessed October 6, 2015, http://lib.post.ca.gov/Publications/human_trafficking.pdf.

117   Advanced Investigative Techniques of Human Trafficking Offenses, May 10, 2007, Instructor Guide, Florida Criminal Justice Advanced Course 1166, Criminal Justice Standards and Training Commission Florida Department of Law Enforcement, Unit 2, Lesson 1, pp. 10–15.

118   *Post Guidelines on Law Enforcement Response to Human Trafficking 2014*, p. 12.

119   International Association of Chiefs of Police, *The Crime of Human Trafficking: A Law Enforcement Guide to Identification*, p. 11, http://www.vaw.umn.edu/documents/completehtguide/completehtguide.pdf.

120   *Anti-Human Trafficking Task Force Strategy and Operations e-Guide*, p. 68, http://www.ovcttac.gov/TaskForceGuide.

121   For more information about demand reduction programs review Leonard Territo and Nataliya Glover, "The John Factor," in Chapter 5, *Criminal Investigation of Sex Trafficking in America* (Boca Raton, FL: CRC Press, 2014), p. 187.

122   Michael Shively, Kristina Kliorys, Kristin Wheeler, and Dana Hunt, *A National Overview of Prostitution and Sex Trafficking Demand Reduction Efforts*, Final Report, April 30, 2012 prepared for the National Institute of Justice by Abt Associates Inc., Document number 238796 (Cambridge, MA: Abt Associates Inc.)

123   Ibid., p. 79.

124   M. Dodge, D. Starr-Gimeno and T. Williams, "Puttin' on the Sting: Women Police Officers' Perspectives on Reverse Prostitution Assignments," *International Journal of Police Science and Management*, Vol. 7, Issue 2, 2005, pp. 71–85; L. Jetmore, "The Oldest Profession: Investigating Street-level Prostitution," *Law Officer Magazine*, Vol. 4, Issue 10, 2008.

125   Other parts of the demand reduction effort include forfeiture programs, driver's license suspension, shaming, "Dear John" letters and "John" Schools. For a more detailed discussion of each of these subjects see Leonard Territo and Nataliya Glover, *Criminal Investigation of Sex Trafficking in America* (Boca Raton, FL: CRC Press, 2014), pp. 179–220.

126   Anti-Human Trafficking Task Force Strategy and Operations e-Guide, Bureau of Justice Assistance (U.S. Department of Justice, 2011), p. 27.

127   Ibid.

128   Ibid., p. 29.

Chapter 13

1.   Federal Bureau of Investigation, *Crime in the United States—1999* (Washington, D.C.: Government Printing Office, 2000), p. 28.

2.   Ibid.

3.   Ibid., p. 29.

4.   Bureau of Justice Statistics, *Criminal Victimization in the United States—1999* (Washington, D.C.: Bureau of Justice Statistics, 2000), p. 79, table 75.

5.   Ibid., p. 80.

6.   Ibid., p. 27, table 27.

7.   Ibid., p. 39, table 37.

8.   Bureau of Justice Statistics, *Criminal Victimization in the United States*, p. 32, table 32.

9.   Bureau of Justice Statistics, *Criminal Victimization in the United States*, p. 41, table 43.

10.   FBI, *Crime in the United States*, p. 29.

11.   Matt Nelson, "Note, Tipster Help in Search for Bank Robber," *Duluth News-Tribune* (Minnesota), March 1, 2000.

12.   "Two Plead Guilty in Robbery Try," *Las Vegas Review-Journal*, May 25, 2001.

13.   "Deer River," *Duluth News-Tribune* (Minnesota), February 21, 2001.

14.   See Werner J. Einstadter, "The Social Organization of Armed Robbery," *Social Problems*, 1969, Vol. 17, No. 1, p. 76. The broad categories are those identified by Einstadter; some of the content has been extended by the authors.

15.   FBI, *Crime in the United States*, p. 28.

16.   Bureau of Justice Statistics, *Criminal Victimization in the United States*, p. 38, table 36.

17.   Ibid., p. 68, table 64.

18.   Ibid., p. 69, table 65.

19.   Ira Sommers and Deborah R. Baskin, "The Violent Context of Violent Female Offending," *Journal of Research in Crime and Delinquency*, May 1993, Vol. 30, No. 2, p. 147.

20.   Bureau of Justice Statistics, *Criminal Victimization in the United States*, p. 39, table 37.

21.   Michael J. Feeny, "Cameras Monitor Streets for Paterson Police," *Herald News* (Passaic, County, NJ, 31307), p. B-03.

22.   Tod W. Burke and Charles O'Rear, "Armed Carjacking: A Violent Problem in Need of a Solution," *Police Chief*, January 1993, Vol. 60, No. 1, p. 18.

23.   FBI, *An Analysis of Carjackings*, p. 3.

24.   James T. Hurley, "Violent Crime Hits Home," *FBI Law Enforcement Bulletin*, June 1995, p. 10.

25.   Howie Padilla, "Two Men Beat Up Couple in Their Home," *Star Tribune* (Minneapolis, MN), September 6, 2001.

26.   Bureau of Justice Administration, U.S. Department of Justice, "Smartphone Thefts and Robberies Growing Trends and Promising Practices," 2015, (accessed November 23, 2015).

27.   Aaron Smith, "Smartphone Ownership 2013," *Pew Internet* (June 5, 2013) Web, September 5, 2013. Online at; http://pewinternet.org/Reports/2013/Smartphone-Ownership-2013.aspx (accessed October 4, 2015).

28.   Smith, "Smartphone Ownership 2013," p. 3

29.   James Brehm, "Apple Picking . . . and the Epidemic of Smartphone Theft," Web log post, The Pulse of the Market, Compass Intelligence, Strategy Acceleration Experts, May 25, 2012, Web, March 18, 2013. Online at; http://blog.compassintelligence.com/post/2012/05/25/Apple-Pickingand-the-Epidemic-of-Smartphone-Theft.aspx (accessed October 4, 2015).

30.   Nicole Goodkind, "The Top 10 Cities for Smartphone Theft and Loss," *CNBC*, Yahoo Finance, November 8, 2012, Web, March 18, 2013. Online at; http://www.cnbc.com/id /49751093/The_Top_10_Cities_for_Smartphone_Theft_and_Loss (accessed October 4, 2015).

31.   Yarti, "141 Arrested by NYPD in Stolen iPhone, iPad Sting Operation," *iPhone Hacks* (December 20, 2011), Web, April 12, 2013. Online at; http://www.iphonehacks.com/2011/ 12/141-arrested-by-nypd-in-stolen-iphone-ipad-sting-operation.html (accessed October 4, 2015).

32.   "U.S. Couple Made $4 Million From Stolen Smartphone," India TV, Associated Press, March 13, 2013, Web 18, 2013. Online at; http://www.indiatvnews.com/crime/news/us-couple-made-million-from-stolen-smartphones-2877.html (accessed October 4, 2015).

33.   Office of Public Affairs, U.S. Department of Justice, "Arrests Made in Case Involving Conspiracy to Procure Weapons, Including Anti-Aircraft Missiles," U.S. Department of Justice, November 23, 2009. Online at; http://www.justice.gov/opa/pr/2009/November/09/-nsd-1270.html (accessed October 5, 2015). (This discussion was adapted from this source.)

34.   Prince George's County Code Section 5-234, Secondhand Dealer and Pawn Dealer's and Employee Licenses, September 5, 2013. Online at; http://www.princegeorgescountymd.gov/sites/ DPIE/Permits/Licenses/LicensingCenter/Pages/default.aspx (accessed October 5, 2015).

35.   Daniel J. Mahoney, "Smartphone Device Crime Response," Message to Hilary Rios, March 17, 2013, E-mail.

36.   Jordan Usdan and Kevin Almasy, "FCC and Public-Private Partners Launch Smartphone *Security* Checker to Help Consumers Protect Mobile Devices This Holiday Season," Web log post, *Official FCC Blog*, Federal Communications Commission, December 17, 2012. Online at: http://www.fcc.gov/blog/fcc-and-public-private-partners-launch-smartphone-security-checker-help-consumers-protect-mobil (accessed October 5, 2015).

37.   "Stolen Smart Phone? Brick It!" Metropolitan Police Department, District of Columbia, n.d. Online at; http://mpdc.dc.gov/page/stolen-smart-phone-brick-it (accessed October 5, 2015).

38.   Christina Farr, "My Stolen iPhone Could End Up in Your Stocking This Christmas," Security, VentureBeat. Online at: http://venturebeat.com/2012/12/10/smartphone-theft/ (accessed October 5, 2015).

39. Josh Saul, "NYPD's iTheft Buster," *New York Post*, February 13, 2012. Online at; http://nypost.com/2012/02/13/nypds-ithief-buster/ (accessed October 5, 2015).

40. CTIA-The Wireless Association7 "Before It's Gone: Steps to Deter Smartphone Thefts & Protect Personal Info," n.d. Online at; http://www.ctia.org/consumer_info/safety/index.cfm/ AID/12084 (accessed October 5, 2015).

41. Michael Medaris, "Baltimore Cell Phone Unit Material," Message to Doug Bordero, April 4, 2013, E-mail.

42. Raymond V. Clark, "Hot Products: Understanding, Anticipating and Reducing Demand for Stolen Goods Policies," United Kingdom, Home Office, Policing and Reducing Crime Unit, *Police Research Series*, Paper 112 (1999).

43. "Top 5 Ways to Protect Your Smartphone Data in Case of Loss or Theft," Web log post, *Helpful How-To's*, Support.com June 7, 2011. Online at; http://www.stage.support.com/blog/post/top-5-ways-protect-your-smartphone-data-case-loss-or-theft (accessed October 5, 2015).

44. Farr, "My Stolen iPhone Could End Up in Your Stocking This Christmas."

45. David Morrison, "3 Million ATMs Worldwide by 2015: ATM Association," *Credit Union Times* (July 28, 2014); available from: http://www.cutimes.com/2014/07/28/3-million-atms-worldwide-by-2015-atm-association (accessed December 8, 2015).

46. Michael S. Scott. *Robbery at Automated Teller Machines* (U.S. Department of Justice, Office of Community-Oriented Policing Services, September 2001), pp. 3-24. (Much of this discussion was adapted from this source.)

47. W. Boyle, *ATM Security* (Rolling Meadows, IL: Bank Administration Institute, 1983).

48. Anne Arundel County (Maryland) installed ATMs in all its police stations in response to a rash of ATM robberies. K. Morgan "Banking Under the Watchful Eye of the Law," *American City and County* 112 (1997): 16.

49. R. Hudak, "How Safe Is Your ATM (Automated Teller Machine)?" *Security Management* 32, no. 6 (1998): 34, 37.

50. W. Wipprecht, "Strike Back at ATM Crime," *Journal of California Law Enforcement* 25, no. 3 (1991): 53-58; Hudak, "How Safe Is Your ATM?"; F. Schreiber, *ATM Security in the 1990s: The Final Report of the Electronic Funds Transfer Association's ATM Security Task Force* (Alexandria, VA: Electronic Funds Transfer Association, 1990).

51. Office of Banks and Real Estate, State of Illinois, "ATM Report," wwwobre.state.il.usa/agency/atmrpt.htm, 1999, p. 4.

52. Ibid.

53. *ATM Security in the 1990s: The Final Report of the Electronic Funds Transfer Association's ATM Security Task Force* (Alexandria, VA: Electronic Funds Transfer Association, 1990).

54. S. Morrison and I. O'Donnell, "An Analysis of the Decision-Making Practices of Armed Robbers," in *The Politics and Practice of Situational Crime Prevention*, Crime Prevention Studies Series, Vol. 5 (Monsey, New York: Criminal Justice Press, 1996).

55. For a thorough discussion of the principles of repeat offender programs and descriptions of model programs, see W. Spelman, *Repeat Offender Programs for Law Enforcement* (Washington, DC: Police Executive Research Forum, 1990).

56. J. Eck, *Solving Crimes: The Investigation of Burglary and Robbery* (Washington, DC: Police Executive Research Forum, 1983).

57. J. Stockdale and P. Gresham, *Tackling Street Robbery: A Comparative Evaluation of Operation Eagle Eye*, Crime Detection and Prevention Series, (London: Home Office, 1998).

58. F. Schreiber, "The Future of ATM Security," *Security Management* 38, no. 3 (1994): 18A-20A.

59. Jayme Fraser, "Fulshear Offers Safe Place to Meet Craigslist Buyers After Killings Nationwide," *Houston Chronicle*, February 20, 2015; http://www.chron.com/neighborhood /katy/news/article/Fulshear-offers-safe-place-to-meet-Craigslist-6090093.php.

60. Martha J. Smith, "Robbery of Taxi Drivers," U.S. Department of Justice, Office of Community Oriented Policing, 2005, pp 2, 5-36. (This discussion was adapted from this source.)

61. B. Schaller, "Causes and Solutions to Service Refusals," *GothamGazette.com* December 1999, www.schallerconsultant .com/taxi/refusal.htm.

62. Alicia Altizio and Diana York, "Robbery of Convenience Stores," *Problem-Oriented Guides for Police Problem-Specific Guides Series No. 49*, (Washington, D.C.: U.S. Department of Justice, Office of Community Oriented Policing Services, April 2007), pp. 6-32. (This discussion was adapted from this source.)

63. R. Hunter, "Convenience Store Robbery Revisited: A Review of Prevention Results," *Journal of Security Administration* 22, Nos. 1 & 2 (1999), pp. 1-13.

64. S. Lins and R. Erickson, "Stores Learn to Inconvenience Robbers," *Security Management* 42, No. 11 (1998): 49-53.

65. U.S. Department of Labor, OSHA, *Recommendations on Workplace Violence Prevention Programs in Late-Night Retail Establishments* OSHA 3153 (Washington, D.C.: Justice Research and Statistics Association, 1998).

66. F. Schreiber, "The Future of ATM Security," *Security Management* 38 (March Suppl., 1994): 18A-20A.

67. "Pharmacy Robberies: What do Do," United States Drug Enforcement Administration, Press Release, February 15, 2012; www.dea.gov/pubs/pressrel/pr021512.html; accessed August 21, 2015.

68. "Fighting Cargo Theft," *Transportation Topics, Trucking's Electronic Newsletter*, September 8, 1999: 4.

69. Ibid.

70. Deborah Lamm Weisel, U.S. Department of Justice, Office of Community Oriented Policing Services, March 2007, pp. 13-49. (This discussion of bank robbery was adapted from this source.)

71. M. Gill and R. Matthews. "Robbers on Robbery: Offenders Perspectives," in *Crime and Work: Studies in Security and Crime Prevention*, Vol. 1, M. Gill, ed. (Leicester: Perpetuity Press, 1994).

72. M. Gill and K. Pease, "Repeat Robbers: How are They Different?" in *Crime and Work: Increasing the Risk for Offenders*, Vol. II, M. Gill, ed. (Leicester: Perpetuity Press, 1998).

73. T. Gabor and A. Normandeau, "Preventing Armed Robbery through Opportunity Reduction: A Critical Analysis," *Journal of Security Administration* 12(1) (1989): 3-18.

74. H. Leineweber and H. Buchler. "Preventing Bank Robbery: The Offense from the Robber's Perspective," *Police Research in the Federal Republic of Germany*, E. Kube and H. Storzer, eds. (Berlin: Springer-Verlag, 1991).

75. J. Haran, "The Losers Game: A Sociological Profile of 500 Armed Robbers" (Ph.D. diss., Fordham University, 1982), University Microfilms.

76. T. Gabor and A. Normandeau, "Preventing Armed Robbery through Opportunity Reduction: A Critical Analysis," *Journal of Security Administration* 12(1) (1989): 3-18.

77. G. Camp, "Nothing to Lose: A Study of Bank Robbery in America" (Ph.D. diss., Yale University, 1968), Ann Arbor: Michigan University Microfilms.

78. D. Johnston, "Psychological Observations of Bank Robbery," *American Journal of Psychiatry* 135:11 (1978): 1377-1379.

79. M. Borzychki, "Bank Robbery in Australia," *Trends and Issues in Crime and Criminal Justice*, No. 253 (Canberra: Australian Institute of Criminology, 2003).

80. R. Matthews, *Armed Robbery: Police Responses*. Crime Detection and Prevention Series, Paper 78 (London: Home Office, Police Research Group, 1996).

81. J. Vardalis and T. Cox, "A Descriptive Analysis of Bank Robberies in Dade County, Florida, During 1994," *Journal of Security Administration* 21(2) (1998): 1-18.

82. Leineweber and Buchler, "Preventing Bank Robbery."

83. P. Van Koppen and R. Jansen, "The Time to Rob: Variations in Time and Number of Commercial Robberies," *Journal of Research in Crime and Delinquency* 36(1) (1999): 7-29.

84. P. Van Koppen and R. Jansen, "The Road to Robbery: Travel Patterns in Commercial Robberies," *British Journal of Criminology* 38(2) (1998): 230-247.

85. R. Erickson, *Armed Robbers and Their Crimes* (Seattle, WA: Athena Research Corporation, 1996).

86. F. Desroches, *Force and Fear: Robbery in Canada* (Toronto: Nelson Canada, 1995).

87. Johnston, "Psychological Observations of Bank Robbery."

88. Gabor et al., "Armed Robbery."

89. R. Erickson and A. Stenseth "Crimes of Convenience." *Security Management* 40(10) (1996).

90. Leineweber and Buchler, "Preventing Bank Robbery."

91. E. Kube, "Preventing Bank Robbery: Lessons from Interviewing Robbers," *Journal of Security Administration* 11(2) (1988): 78-83.

92. W. D. Nugent, P. Burns, and D. Cappell, *Risks and Rewards in Robbery Prevention and the Offender's Perspective* (Sydney, Australia: Australian Bankers Association, 1989).

93. W. Tiffany and J. Ketchel, "Psychological Deterrence in Robberies of Banks and Its Application to Other Institutions," *The Role of Behavioral Science in Physical Security*, NBS Special Publication 480-38 (Washington, D.C.: U.S. National Bureau of Standards, 1978).

94. Ibid.

95. S. Morrison and I. O'Donnell, *Armed Robbery: A Study in London* (Oxford, United Kingdom: Centre for Criminological Research, 1994).

96. S. Barancik, "FBI Data on Bank Robbery Contradict Movie Myths," *American Banker* 163(232) (1998): 2.

97. Tiffany and Ketchel, "Psychological Deterrence."

98. T. Hannan, "Bank Robberies and Bank Security Precautions," *Journal of Legal Studies* 11(1) (1982): 83–92.

99. Nugent et al., *Risks and Rewards in Robbery Prevention and the Offender's Perspective.*

100. Hannan, "Bank Robberies and Bank Security Precautions."

101. W. Saylor and M. Janus, *Bank Robberies: A Study of Bank Characteristics and Probabilities of Robbery.* Unpublished study, (Washington, D.C.: Office of Research, Federal Bureau of Prisons, 1981).

102. T. Baumer and M. Carrington, *The Robbery of Financial Institutions: Executive Summary* (Washington, D.C.: U.S. Department of Justice, National Institute of Justice, 1986).

103. Hannan, "Bank Robberies and Bank Security Precautions."

104. Nugent et al., *Risks and Rewards in Robbery Prevention and the Offender's Perspective.*

105. Kube, "Preventing Bank Robbery."

106. Gill and Pease, "Repeat Robbers: How are They Different?"

107. Vardalis and Cox, "A Descriptive Analysis."

108. J. Wise and B. Wise, *Bank Interiors and Bank Robberies: A Design Approach to Environment Security* (Rolling Meadows, IL: Bank Administration Institute, 1985).

109. Barancik, "FBI Data on Bank Robbery."

110. Ibid.

111. Gill and Matthews, "Robbers on Robbery."

112. J. Archea, "The Use of Architectural Props in the Conduct of Criminal Acts," *Journal of Architectural and Planning Research* 2(4) (1985): 245–259.

113. Charles Remsberg, *The Tactical Edge: Surviving High Patrol* (Northbrook, IL: Calibre Press, 1986), p. 251.

114. Ibid.

115. Ibid., p. 248.

116. Ibid., p. 253.

117. Ibid., p. 252.

118. Ibid.

119. The distinction between these types of stereotyping is taken from Jerry W. Baker and Carl P. Florez, "Robbery Response," *Police Chief,* October 1980, Vol. 47, No. 10, pp. 46–47.

120. Ibid., p. 47.

121. Ibid.

122. Kevin B. O'Leary, "Robbery 'Hoax': Shootings Real," *Boston Globe,* November 19, 1993, p. 1.

123. Richard Perez-Pena, "Teller Machine Robbery Was a Hoax, Police Say," *The New York Times,* February 19, 1994, p. A25.

124. For more information, see the website for Sirchie's ComphotoFitPlus Color, *http://sirchie.com/detail.asp?product_ID=CCID200.*

Chapter 14

1. Federal Bureau of Investigation (FBI), 2014 Crime in the United States, Burglary, p. 1, https://ucr.fbi.gov/crime-in-the-u.s/2014/crime-in-the-u.s.-2014/offenses-known-to-law-enforcement/browse-by/national-data,accessed August 26, 2015.

2. Loc. cit.

3. Loc. cit.

4. FBI, 2014 Crime in the United States, Persons Arrested, Table 41, p. 1, https://ucr.fbi.gov/crime-in-the-u.s/2014/crime-in-the-u.s.-2014/tables/table-41, released 2015, accessed August 26, 2016.

5. Shannan Catalano, "Victimization During Household Burglary," (Washington, D.C.: Bureau of Justice Statistics, September 2010), pp. 1 and 9.

6. Rana Sampson, *False Burglar Alarms,* 2nd Edition (Washington, D.C.: Office of Community Oriented Policing Services, August 2011), pp. 11–13.

7. Examples of this include state statutes in Texas, Florida, and North Carolina. States may charge a misdemeanor for a first offense of this type, but upon any subsequent offense violating the same statute it advances to a felony charge.

8. C. Bennell and N. J. Jones, "Between a ROC and a Hard Place: A Method for Linking Serial Burglaries by Modus Operandi," Journal of Investigative Psychology and Offender Profiling, Vol. 2, No. 1, pp. 23–41, 2005.

9. See Ronald V. Clarke, Elizabeth Perkins, and Donald J. Smith, Jr., "Explaining Repeat Residential Burglaries: An Analysis of Property Sto-

len," in Graham Farrell and Ken Pease, Editors *Repeat Victimization,* Vol. 12 (Monsey, NY: Criminal Justice Press, 2001) pp. 119–132.

10. Mike Springer, "Police Arrest Accused Serial Burglar," Albuquerque Television Station KOAT, March 21, 2016, p. 1, http://www.koat.com/news/apd-arrest-alleged-serial-burglar/38608186, accessed August 29, 2016.26.

11. No author, *Historical Census of Housing, House Heating Fuel,* U.S. Census Bureau, October 31, 2011, p. 1, https://www.census.gov/hhes/www/housing/census/historic/fuels.html, accessed October 1. 2016.

12. For more information see the Longhorn Lockpicking Club, http://www.longhornlockpicking.com, accessed December 11, 2017.

13. Richard Wright and Scott H. Decker, Burglars on the Job: Streetlife and Break-ins (Boston: Northeastern University Press,1994), p. 37.

14. Ibid., p. 36.

15. Ibid., p. 58.

16. Ibid., p. 37.

17. The information in this paragraph is drawn with restatement from Kristie R. Blevins, Joseph B. Kuhns, and Seungmug "Zech" Lee, "Understanding Decisions to Burglarize from the Offender's Perspective," University of North Carolina at Charlotte, Department of Criminal Justice and Criminology, December 2012, p. 2.

18. Ibid., p. 26

19. Loc. cit.

20. Ibid., p. 24.

21. Ibid., p. 32.

22. Ibid., pp. 28–29.

23. Mark Duell, "Burglars are Buying Drones to Identify Targets: Police Fear Gadgets Are Being Used to Take Undetected Surveillance Photos of Alarm Systems and Getaway Routes," The Daily Mail (London, England), May 19, 2015, http://www.dailymail.co.uk/news/article-3087264/Burglars-buying-drones-identify-targets-Police-fear-gadgets-used-undetected-surveillance-photos-alarm-systems.html and Pierluigi Paganani, "Law Enforcement Warns Thieves Are Use Mini-Helicopters and Commercial Drones to Carry Out Reconnaissance on Homes to Burgle," Security Affairs, May 22, 2015, http://securityaffairs.co/wordpress/37050/cyber-crime/thieves-using-commercial-drones.html, accessed September 13, 2016

24. No author, "NJ Burglars Caught in PA Are Suspected of Using Drone to Take Crime to New Heights," September 30, 2014, http://newjersey.news12.com/news/nj-burglars-caught-in-pa-are-suspectcd-of-using-drone-to-take-crime-to-new-heights-1.9450872, accessed Oct 12, 2016.

25. "Understanding Decisions to Burglarize from the Offender's Perspective," p.5.

26. Ibid., p. 38.

27. No author, "How Burglars Use Social Media," http://www .pwcgov.org/government/dept/police/pages/how-burglars-use-social-media.aspx, Prince William County (VA) Police Depart-ment site, accessed October 13, 2016.

28. Kiristy Smorol, "Deputies Say Suspects Used Craiglist to Find Burglary Targets," CNYCentral.com, October 12, 2012, http://cnycentral.com/news/local/deputies-say-suspects-usedcraigslist-to-find-burglary-targets, accessed Oct 22, 2016.

29. "Understanding Decisions to Burglarize from the Offender's Perspective," p. 41.

30. Ibid., p. 5.

31. Ibid., p. 38.

32. Ibid., pp.8–9.

33. Ibid., p. 5.

34. Ibid., p. 37.

35. Ibid. p. 40

36. Loc. cit.

37. Loc. cit.

38. Loc. cit.

39. Ibid., p. 2

40. Loc. cit.

41. Loc. cit.

42. Ibid., p. 24.

43. Ibid., p. 3.

44. Dr. Fox provided the authors with the manuscript submitted for publication in the FBI Law Enforcement Bulletin (See Bryanna Fox, David P. Farrington, Michael Chitwood, and Edith James, "Developing a Profile for Burglary," FBI Law Enforcement Bulletin, February 2013). Citations of the Fox Study are drawn from the manuscript copy

45. David Robson, "The Strange Expertise of Burglars," *BBC,* J June June 18, 2015, p. 3, accessed October 1, 2016.

46. David O'Reilly and Julie Shaw, "40-Year Old Theft Vexes FBI: $1M Rockwell Gone from Cherry Hill," *Philly.com* (Philadelphia Media Network, PBC), July 2, 2016, http://articles.philly.com/2016-07-02/news/74153692_1_art-theft-robert-grant-painting, accessed July 31, 2016.

47. Frank Main and Annie Sweeney "Burglary Ring's Formula Worked for Decades," Chicago Sun-Times, January 2, 2005.

48. Jessica Rice, "Gang Members Arrested in Connection with 5,000 Home Burglaries," NBC Los Angeles, August 26, 2016, http://www.nbclosangeles.com/news/local/More-Than-Dozen-Gang-Members-Arrested-in-Connection-With-5000-home-Burglaries-391427671.html, accessed October 2, 2016.

49. No author, "Loot Jams Home of Alleged Super Thief," Atlanta Constitution, December 16, 1980.

50. See Table 14-1 in this manuscript.

51. The content in this section is drawn with some restatement from "Developing a Profile for Burglary," pp. 3-6.

52. "Developing a Profile for Burglary," p. 8.

53. Loc. cit.

54. D.L. Weisel, "Burglary of Single-Family Houses," Center for Problem-Oriented Policing, State University of New York, Albany, 2002, p. 1.

55. David DeMille, "Will Your House Be Broken into This Year?" Home Security, October 2, 2016, p. 7, http://www.asecurelife.com/burglary-statistics, accessed October 24, 2016.

56. Ronald V. Clarke, "What Does Research Tell Us About Burglary?" Center for Problem-Oriented Policing, State University of New York, Albany, 2002, p. 1

57. William D. Moreto, "Risk Factors of Urban Residential Burglary," Center for Public Policy, Rutgers University, New Brunswick, New Jersey, Issue 4, October 2010, p. 2.

58. Shannan Catalano, "Victimization During Household Burglary," (Washington, D.C.: Bureau of Justice Statistics, September 2010), pp. 1.

59. Ibid., p. 7 and from data in Table 11.

60. David DeMille, "Will Your House Be Broken into This Year?" Home Security, October 2, 2016, p. 4, http://www.asecurelife.com/burglary-statistics, accessed October 24, 2016.

61. Foti Kallergis, "Largest Closet in America Burglarized in Woodlands," ABC13, Houston (Texas), August 2, 2014, http://abc13.com/fashion/largest-closet-in-america-burglarized-in-woodlands/235548, accessed November 22, 2016.

62. No author, Crisp Report: Preventing Burglary in Commercial and Institutional Settings (Alexandria, Virginia: ASIS Research Foundation, 2015), p. 6.

63. Crime in the United States-2015, Washington, D.C.: Federal Bureau of Investigation: September 26, 2016, Table 23, https://ucr.fbi.gov/crime-in-the-u.s/2015/crime-in-the-u.s./tables/table23/, accessed November 1, 2016.

64. "Understanding Decisions to Burglarize from the Offender's Perspective," p. 1.

65. Ronald V. Clarke, "Burglary of Retail Establishment," Washington, D.C.: Office of Community Oriented Policing Services, No. 15, March 13, 2002, p. 4

66. Loc. cit.

67. Deborah Lamm Weisel, *Analyzing Repeat Victimization* (Center for Problem-Oriented Policing, Tool Guide 4, 2005), p. 3.

68. Burglary of Retail Establishments," p. 3.

69. No author, *Crisp Report: Preventing Burglary in Commercial and Institutional Settings*, (Alexandria, Virginia: ASIS Research Foundation, 2015), p. 6.

70. Loc. cit.

71. Loc. cit.

72. Loc. cit.

73. Scott F. Guginsky, et. al., *Jewelers' Security Alliance 2015 Annual Crime Report* (New York, NY: Jewelers' Security Alliance, March 2, 2015), p. 4.

74. Ibid., p. 8.

75. Loc. cit.

76. Loc. cit.

77. Ibid., p. 9.

78. Loc. cit.

79. Benjamin Weiser, "3-Are Charged in Hollywood-Style Bank Burglaries in New York," The New York Times, July 26, 2016, http://www.nytimes.com/2016/07/27/nyregion/3-charged-in-brooklyn-bank-burglaries.html, accessed October 11, 2016.

80. Benjamin Weiser, "3-Are Charged in Hollywood-Style Bank Burglaries in New York," The New York Times, July 26, 2016, www.nytimes.com/2016/07/27/nyregion/3-charged-in-brooklyn-bank-burglaries.html, accessed January 12, 2016.

81. Federal Bureau of Investigation, Bank Crime Statistics January 1, 2015-December 31, 2015, file:///Users/charles1155/Downloads/BCS-ANNUAL-2015%20(2).pdf, accessed November 11, 2016. Jewelers' Security Alliance 2014 Annual Crime Report, p. 7.

82. Laura Carroll, "Burglaries Not Uncommon at Las Vegas Hotels," Las Vegas Review Journal, May 29, 2013, http://www.reviewjournal.com/business/tourism/burglaries-not-uncommon-las-vegas-hotels, accessed November 22, 2016.

83. Calculated on the basis of 17 burglaries weekly and the Las Vegas Convention and Visitors Authority estimate of 42,312,216 visitors in 2015.

84. No author, *Crisp Report: Preventing Burglary in Commercial and Institutional Settings* (Alexandria, Virginia: ASIS Research Foundation, 2015), p. 6 and FBI, Uniform Crime Reports-2015, https://ucr.fbi.gov/crime-in-the-u.s/2015/crime-in-the-u.s.-2015/offenses-known-to-law-enforcement/burglar, accessed November 3, 2016. With respect to burglary statistics, the UCR defines the term "unlawful entry" as entry made without force by someone lacking authorization to on the premises.

85. "Understanding Decisions to Burglarize from the Offender's Perspective," p.35

86. Sam Webb, "The Secret Language of Crime: Police Revel Symbols Used by Burglars to Help Fellow Criminals Target Rich and Vulnerable," Daily Mail, January 9, 2013, http://www.dailymail.co.uk/news/article-2259445/Police-reveal-symbols-used-burglars-help-fellow-criminals-target-rich-vulnerable-homes.html, accessed October 31, 2016.

87. No author, "Safecracking Returns to Texas; Dallas Reports 165 Safe Burglars This Year," The Crime Report, John Jay College, Center on Media Crime and Justice, July 9, 2013, http://thecrimereport.org/our-mission, accessed November 10, 2016.

88. Jodi Weinberger, "Gresham RV Dealer Hit with 20 Burglaries This Week," The Portland (Oregon) Tribune, November 6, 2015, http://portlandtribune.com/pt/9-news/280379-156644-gresham-rv-dealer-hit-with-more-than-20-burglaries-this-week, accessed November 14, 2016.

89. Mike Sutton, "How Prolific Thieves Sell Stolen Goods," Internet Journal of Criminology, 2008, p. 5, http://www.internetjournalofcriminology.com/Sutton%20-%20How%20Prolific%20Thieves%20Sell%20Stolen%20Goods.pdf, accessed October 22, 2016.

90. Ibid., p. 1

91. Ibid., p. 4

92. Ibid., p. 4 with restatement.

93. National Retail Federation, *Organized Retail Crime Survey*, October 2016, p. 4.

94. Kimberly Alt, "Security Infographic: A Burglar's Quest" A Secure Life, August 10, 2016, p.1, http://www.asecurelife.com/security-infographic, accessed November 27, 2016.

95. No author, "Top 10 Reasons to Get A Security System," *Simpson Security Systems, Inc.,* undated, http://simpsonsecurity.com/Blog/top-10-reasons-get-security-system, accessed November 17, 2016. This figure is often quoted by security companies.

96. Some of these ideas were drawn with restatement from sources consulted. Those sources were: Glendale (Wisconsin) Police Department, "Home Security Handbook," which has a very good checklist; San Jose (California) Police Department, "Crime Preventions Tips"; Pennsylvania State Police, "Home Burglary Prevention Guide," Sacramento (California) Police Department; District of Columbia Metropolitan Police Department, "Burglary Prevention"; Albuquerque (New Mexico) Police Department, "Home Burglary"; City of Coventry (Connecticut), "Home Burglaries"; and City of Yonkers (New York), "Home Burglary Protection Tips."

97. Ideas were taken from multiple excellent sources and restated and/or added to develop this list of precautions. Sources consulted are: Montgomery County (Maryland) Police Department, "Commercial Burglary Prevention," which is in the form of a substantial slide presentation; San Diego (California) Police Department, "Business Robbery and Burglary Prevention," which provides detailed information about various aspects of security, such as deterring crime, preventing unauthorized entry, protecting assets, and recovering stolen property; and one-page "Commercial Burglary Prevention" from the Lake Stevens (Washington) Police Department, which despite its brevity had some strong points.

Chapter 15

1. This paragraph is restated with additions from John S. Baker, *The Sociological Origins of White Collar Crime* (Washington, D.C.: The Heritage Foundation, October 4, 2004), pp. 1-2.

2. To learn more about theft by deception, see such sources as the New Jersey Statutes Annotated (N.J.S.A.) 2C:20-4.

3. Ronald V. Clarke and Gohar Petrossian, "Shoplifting, 2nd Edition," *Problem-Specific Guides Series, Problem-Oriented Guides for Police No. 11*, (Washington,

D.C.: U.S. Department of Justice, Community Oriented Policing Services, April 2013), pp. 33–35.

4. Kristin M. Finklea, *Organized Retail Crime*, CRS Report to Congress, (Washington, D.C.: Congressional Research Service, 2012).

5. Charles Miller, *Organized Retail Theft: Raising Awareness, Offering Solutions* (Washington, D.C.: National Retail Foundation, 2005).

6. Charlotte-Mecklenburg Police Department, "The Home Depot Project," Submission for the Herman Goldstein Award for Excellence in Problem-Oriented Policing, 2003.

7. Colorado Springs Police Department, "Pikes Peak Retail Security Association: Decreasing the Level of Shoplifting Citywide." Submission for the Herman Goldstein Award for Excellence in Problem-Oriented Policing, 2009.

8. Hampshire Constabulary (U.K.), "Operation Kensington: Bringing the Business Community and the Police Together." Submission for the Herman Goldstein Award for Excellence in Problem-Oriented Policing, 2007.

9. Boise Police Department, "Organized Retail Crime Interdiction: A Partnership that Works." Submission for the Herman Goldstein Award for Excellence in Problem-Oriented Policing, 2012.

10. Walter E. Palmer and Chris Richardson, *Organized Retail Crime: Assessing the Risk and Developing Effective Strategies. An ASIS Foundation Research Council CRISP Report* (Alexandria, VA: American Society for Industrial Security Foundation, Inc., 2009).

11. U.S. Government Accountability Office, "Organized Retail Crime: Private Sector and Law Enforcement Collaborate to deter and Investigate Theft." GAO-11-685. Report to the Ranking Member, Subcommittee on Crime, Terrorism, and Homeland Security, Committee on the Judiciary, House of Representatives (Washington, D.C.: General Accountability Office, 2011).

12. Amber Virgillo, "Are Retailers to Blame?" *LP Magazine* (July–August, 2012).

13. Retail Industry Leaders Association, Crime Trends and Leading Practices Survey, October 2011.

14. Ronald V. Clarke and Gohar Petrossian, "Shoplifting, 2nd Edition," Problem-Specific Guides Series, Problem-Oriented Guides for Police No. 11, (Washington, D.C.: U.S. Department of Justice, Community Oriented Policing Services, April 2013), pp. 11–15.

15. Ronald V. Clarke, *Hot Products: Understanding, Anticipating and Reducing the Demand for Stolen Goods. Police Research Series,* Paper 112 (London: Home Office, 1999). Clarke notes that certain analgesics contain ingredients that can be used in making other drugs, and that decongestants help to produce a high when taken together with some illegal drugs. See Problem- Specific Guide No. 16, *Clandestine Methamphetamine Labs,* 2nd edition, for further information. He also notes that some frequently stolen products, such as hemorrhoid remedies and condoms, can be embarrassing to buy. Self-checkout systems that allow customers to scan and bag their own goods might provide a solution.

16. Read Hayes, *Organized Retail Crime: Describing a Major Problem* (Tallahassee, FL: Loss Prevention Research Council, University of Florida, 2005).

17. Clarke, *Hot Products.*

18. See the forthcoming Problem-Solving Tool Guide, *Understanding Theft of 'Hot Products,'* for further information.

19. Paul Ekblom, *The Prevention of Shop Theft: An Approach Through Crime Analysis. Crime Prevention Unit,* Paper 5 (London: Home Office Crime Prevention Unit, 1986).

20. Michigan Retailers Association, "How Do I Spot Shoplifters?" February 16, 2005, p. 1 *www.retailers.com/eduandevents/ask/askshoplifters.html.*

21. Ibid.

22. John W. Kolberg, "Shoplifting Prevention," *www.safetycops.com/shoplifting. htm* (accessed March 1, 2016).

23. Even so, retailers might be advised to take account of the finding that shoplifters do not think that "young, skater type teen" store associates are effective place managers because they "are kind of lax...and they really don't care," from Caroline A. Cardone, "Opportunity Makes the Thief: Analysis of the Physical Cues that Influence Shoplifter Perceptions of the Retail Interior and the Decision to Steal," (master's thesis, University of Florida, 2006).

24. Adrian Beck, "Self-Scan Checkouts and Retail Loss: Understanding the Risk and Minimizing the Threat," *Security Journal* 24, no. 3 (2011): 199–215.

25. Ekblom, The Prevention of Shop Theft.

26. Candy Carmel-Gilfilen, "Advancing Retail Security Design: Uncovering Shoplifter Perceptions of the Physical Environment," *Journal of Interior Design* 36, no. 2 (2011): 21–38.

27. Michael Sutton, "Stolen Goods Markets," Community Oriented Policing Services Problem- Specific Guide No. 57 (Washington, D.C.: U.S. Department of Justice, 2010).

28. Liz Parks, "Uniting Against ORC: LP Execs Work with Each Other: Law Enforcement and Legislatures to Battle Crime," *Stores Magazine* (May 2008): 12.

29. Hayes, *Organized Retail Crime.*

30. David P. Farrington, "Measuring, Explaining and Preventing Shoplifting: A Review of British Research," *Security Journal* 12, no. 1 (1999): 9–27.

31. Shane D. Johnson, Aiden Sidebottom, and Adam Thorpe, "Bicycle Theft," *Problem-Oriented Guides for Police Problem-Specific Guides Series,* No. 52, U.S. Department of Justice, Office of Community Oriented Policing Services, June 2008, pp. 4–6. (This discussion of bicycle theft was adapted from this source.)

32. K. Bryan-Brown and T. Saville, "Cycle Theft in Britain," *TRL Report 284* (Crowethorne, England: Transport Research Laboratory, 1997).

33. Federal Bureau of Investigation, *Crime in the United States 2014.*

34. R. Svensson, "Bicycle Theft," *Crime Trends in Sweden 1998–2000* (Stockholm, Sweden: BRA (Swedish National Council for Crime Prevention, 2002).

35. For evidence of this view the films Bike Thief, by Casey Neistat. Available at https://www.youtube.com/watch?v=UGttmR2DTY8 (accessed December 17, 2015), and Stop Nicking My Bike, by Dominic Waugh. Available at http://www.channel4.com/culture/microsites/0-9/3MWbicycle/dom _waugh.html (accessed December 17, 2015).

36. Michael S. Scott, *Clandestine Drug Labs,* 2002. ISBN: 1-932582-15-0.

37. Rana Sampson, *Acquaintance Rape of College Students,* 2002. ISBN: 1-932582-16-9.

38. Expanded typology of bicycles can be found at: www.bikeoff.org (accessed December 17, 2015).

39. Sean B. Hoar, "Identity Theft: The Crime of the New Millennium," *United States Attorneys' USA Bulletin,* Vol. 49, No. 2, March 2001, p. 1.

40. Ibid., p. 1.

41. Erika Harrell, "Victims of Identity Theft, 2014," Bureau of Justice Statistics, U.S. Department of Justice, NCJ 248991, September 2015, p. 1; http://www.bjs.gov/content/pub/pdf/vit14.pdf (accessed March 21, 2016).

42. United States General Accounting Office, *Identity Theft: Prevalence and Cost Appear to Be Growing* (Washington, D.C.: March 2002), p. 8.

43. Bill Husted, "Database Raid Fallout Escalates" *The Atlanta-Journal Constitution,* February 17, 2005.

44. Federal Trade Commission, *Identity Crime: When Bad Things Happen to Your Good Name* (Washington, D.C.: September 2002), p. 3, with some restatement and additions.

45. See (no author) "Protect Your Identity," *PC World,* Vol. 22, No. 12, Dec. 2004, pp. 107–112.

46. Federal Trade Commission, *Identity Crime: When Bad Things Happen to Your Good Name,* pp. 2 and 9.

47. Richard Hamilton, *The Police Notebook* (Norman, OK: University of Oklahoma), January 7, 2005, pp. 14–17.

48. Cindy Maggiulli, "Identity Theft Is a Risk on Campus," *The Ranger* (Amarillo College Newspaper), September 20, 2007.

49. Federal Trade Commission, *Identity Crime: When Bad Things Happen to Your Good Name,* p. 4.

50. Linda and Jay Foley, Executive Directors, Identity Theft Resource Center, "Identity Theft: The Aftermath 2003," Summer 2003, p. 5.

51. National Conference of State Legislatures, Identity Theft, 2007, *www.ncsl. org/programs/lis/privacy/idt-statures.htm.*

52. Linda and Jay Foley, "Identity Theft: The Aftermath 2003," p. 4.

53. Ibid., p. 8.

54. No author, "Credit Card Fraud" (Fairmont, WV: National White Collar Crime Center), Jan. 2003, p. 2.

55. Ibid., p. 1.

56. Ibid., pp. 1–2.

57. Laura Czekaj, "Card Scam Bust," *The Ottawa Sun,* July 23, 2004, p. 1.

58. No author, "Check Fraud" (Fairmont, WV: National White Collar Crime Center), September 2002, p. 1.

59. Barbara Hurst, Financial Institution Fraud Statistics," BankersOnLine.com, February 5, 2005, *http://BankersOnLine.com/security/gurus_sec090202c. html.*

60. Ian Dempsky, "Theft Operation 'Staggering,' SayPolice," Tennessean.com, December 30, 2004, *www.Tennnessean.com/local/archives/04/12/63484418.shtml.*

61. Kara Platoni, "Trailers Are for Travelers," *East Bay Express* (Weekly Newspaper, Emeryville, CA), September 10, 2003, p. 2.

62. Ibid.

63. For information relating to the increase in fraud and con activity over the past three to five years, see the FBI website focused on fraud, *www.fbi.gov/scams-safety/fraud.*

64. No author, "Insurance Fraud," (Fairmont, WV: National White Collar Crime Center), September 2002, p. 1.

65. No author, "San Jose Father, Son Arrested on Auto Fraud Charges," *Insurance Journal*, Feb. 7, 2005, *www.insurancejournal.com/news/west/2005/02/07/50896.htm.*

66. No author, "Insurance Fraud: The Crime You Pay For," Coalition Against Insurance Fraud, February 9, 2005, p. 3.

67. No author, "Health Care Fraud" (Fairmont, WV: National White Collar Crime Center), September 2002, p. 2. For an overview of this subject, see Malcolm K. Sparrow, "Fraud Control in the Health Care Industry," (Washington, D.C.: National Institute of Justice), December 1998.

68. Ibid., p. 3.

69. Ibid., p. 1

70. Ibid.

71. Ibid., pp. 1–2, and Oxford Health Plan, "Healthcare Fraud," 2005, p. 1, *www.oxhp.com/main/fraud/fraud.html.*

72. No author, "Insurance Fraud," (Fairmont, WV: National White Collar Crime Center), p. 3.

73. Ibid., p. 1.

74. Federal Bureau of Investigation, *2009 Financial Crimes Report, www.fbi.gov/stats-services/publications/financial-crimes-report-2009.*

75. No author, "Fraud and Organized Crime Intersect: Eurasian Enterprise Targeted" (Washington, D.C.: FBI), October 13, 2010, *www.fbi.gov/news/stories/2010/October/medicare-fraud-organized-crime-bust/medicare-fraud-organized-crime-bust.*

76. Statement of John M. Taylor, Food and Drug Administration (no title), United States Senate's Special Committee on Aging, John B. Breaux, Chair, September 10, 2001, p. 1.

77. No author, "Big Apple Selects 10 'Rotten Apples'," *Insurance Journal*, April 5, 2004, p. 1, *http://insuranceJournal.com/magazines/east/2004/04/05/fraud.*

78. Federal Bureau of Investigation, *2009 Financial Crimes Report, www.fbi.gov/stats-services/publications/financial-crimes-report-2009.*

79. Ibid.

80. Ibid.

81. Ibid.

82. Jillian Deam, "Police Say Thieves are Posing as Pest Control Workers, Planning to Rob Homes," Fox 59, June 3, 2015; available at: http://fox59.com/2015/06/03/police-say-thieves-are-posing-as-pest-control-workers-planning-to-rob-homes/(accessed December 14, 2015).

83. See Internet Crime Complaint Center, *www.ic3.gov/default.aspx.*

84. Ibid.

85. Ibid.

86. Several Internet companies, such as eBay and PayPal, have extensive fraud alert and prevention programs aimed at educating would-be victims. For example, eBay has taken a proactive approach by sending their own email to customers, *http://reviews.ebay.com/NEWEST-eBay-SCAM-ALERT-via-Email-see-detailed-pics-W0QQugidZ10000000003241637, accessed* December 18, 2010.

87. Modified from an actual report; however, the names and locations have been changed to protect the victim.

88. This information was provided by Bill Flowers, United States Secret Service, via e-mail on December 20, 2010. Agent Flowers correctly points out that most Nigerians are hard-working and honest and that these scams do not represent them as a whole.

89. There are a number of websites that discuss the bank examiner and pigeon drop schemes. For example, see this website, sponsored by the State of Missouri Attorney General's Office: *http://ago.mo.gov/publications/bankexamine.htm, accessed* December 25, 2010.

90. There are a number of social science surveys that reflect conservative and patriotic values of senior citizens. See The Senior Citizen League for such surveys at *www.seniorleague.org.*

91. Federal Bureau of Investigation, Fraud Target: Senior Citizens, *www.fbi.gov/scams-safety/fraud/seniors.*

92. No author, "Money Laundering," (Montreal, Canada: Royal Canadian Mounted Police), January 26, 2005, p. 2.

93. Mark Motivans, Money Laundering Offenders, 1994–2001 (Washington, D.C.: Bureau of Justice Statistics), July 2003, p. 1.

94. No author, "Money Laundering," (Fairmont, WV: National White Collar Crime Center), August 2003, p. 1.

95. No author, "Economic Perspectives: The Fight against Money Laundering" (Washington, D.C.: U.S. Department of State), Vol. 6, No. 2, May 2001.

96. Ibid., p. 1.

97. No author, "Money Laundering," Aug. 2003, p. 1. Use only short cite

98. Ibid., p. 2.

99. Bonni Tischler, Assistant Commissioner U.S. Customs Service, "The Columbian Black Market Peso Exchange," Statement before the Senate Caucus on International Drug Control, June 21, 1999, and no author, "Black Market Peso Exchange," *Dictionary of Financial Scam Terms,* January 26, 2005, p. 1.

100. Ibid., p. 1.

101. Ibid.

102. No author, "Money Laundering: Extent of Money Laundering through Credit Cards Is Unknown," Report to the Chairman, Permanent Subcommittee on Governmental Affairs, U.S. Senate (Washington, D.C.: United States General Accounting Office), July 2002, p. 3.

103. No author, "Securities/Investment Fraud" (Fairmont, WV: National White Collar Crime Center), June 2003, p. 1.

104. Ibid.

105. Ibid.

106. Federal Bureau of Investigation, *2009 Financial Crimes Report, www.fbi.gov/stats-services/publications/financial-crimes-report-2009;* Stephen Gandel, "Wall Street's Latest Downfall: Madoff Charged with Fraud," *Time Magazine,* December 12, 2008.

107. Scott Burns, "Madoff's Case Topples Measures," *Dallas Morning News,* December 28, 2008, p. D-1.

108. Federal Bureau of Investigation, *2009 Financial Crimes Report, www.fbi.gov/stats-services/publications/financial-crimes-report-2009;* see also "Madoff Victims Win Biggest Settlement So Far," *Wall Street Journal,* December 17, 2010, p.1.

109. No author, "Pump and Dump Schemes," U.S. Securities and Exchange Commission, March 12, 2001, p. 1, *www.sec.gov/answers/pumpdump.htm.*

110. Ibid.

111. No author, "Microcap Stock: A Guide for Investors," U.S. Securities and Exchange Commission, Aug. 2004, pp. 1–2 is the source of information in this paragraph.

112. No author, "Securities/Investment Fraud" (Fairmont, WV: National White Collar Crime Center), June 2003, pp. 2–3.

113. No author, "Affinity Fraud: How to Avoid Scams that Target Groups," U.S. Securities and Exchange Commission, p. 2, *www.sec.gov/investor/pubs/affinity.htm;* also see *SEC v. A.B. Financing and Investments, Inc.,* and Anthony Blissett, Case No. 02-23487-CIV-Ungaro-Benages (South District, Florida, Dec. 6, 2002).

114. No author, "Certificates of Deposit: Tips for Savers," Federal Deposit Insurance Corporation, February 12, 2005, p. 1.

115. Ibid.

116. No author, "Broken Promises: Promissory Note Fraud," U.S. Securities and Exchange Commission, January 11, 2005, p. 1.

117. Ibid.

118. Ibid.

119. Ibid.

120. Ibid.

121. No author, "Common Fraud Schemes," Federal Bureau of Investigation, February 12, 2005, p. 7, http://FBI.gov/majcases/fraud/fraudschemes.htm.

122. No author, "Prime Investment Schemes," (Montreal, Canada: Royal Canadian Mounted Police), October 16, 2003, p. 1.

123. No author, "Insurance-Agent Scams," Consumer Reports, August 2004, p. 4.

124. Ibid.

125. Ibid.

126. No author, "FCC Consumer Advisory: 809 Phone Scam-Beware," (Washington, D.C.: Federal Trade Commission), Oct. 6, 2003, p. 1.

127. Family Safe Media, "Pornography Statistics 2008," *www.familysafemedia.com/pornography_statistics.html, accessed* December 22, 2010.

128. United States Postal Service, "Get Rich Quick? Don't Count on It!" Press Release, February 2, 2004, p. 1.

129. Ibid., p. 20

130. Ibid., p. 22.

131. Ibid., p. 16.

132. Ibid., p. 13.

Chapter 16

1. Federal Bureau of Investigation, "Crime in the United States 2014", September 2016, https://ucr.fbi.gov/crime-in-the-u.s/2014/crime-in-the-u.s.-2014/figs/crime-clock.jpg.

2. National Insurance Crime Bureau, "Historical Look at Vehicle Theft in the US," December 2015, https://www.nicb.org/newsroom/news-releases/historical-look-at-vehicle-theft-in-the-u-s-.

3. Federal Bureau of Investigation, "Crime in the United States 2014," September 2016, https://ucr.fbi.gov/crime-in-the-u.s/2014/offenses-known-to-law-enforcement/motor-vehicle-theft.

4. Progressive Insurance, "Press Release: Car Theft Stats, Tips for Keeping Cars Safe," August 2013, http://www.autoblog.com/2013/08/16/best-worst-states-for-vehicle-theft-recovery/.

5. Federal Bureau of Investigation, "Crime in the United States 2014," September 2016, https://ucr.fbi.gov/crime-in-the-u.s/2014/crime-in-the-u.s.-2014/offenses-known-to-law-enforcement/clearances/main.

6. Insurance Information Institute, "Auto Theft." July 2016, http://www.iii.org/issue-update/auto-theft.

7. National Insurance Crime Bureau, "Motorcycles Offer a Tempting Target for Criminals," https://www.nicb.org/theft_and_fraud_awareness/fact_sheets.

8. National Insurance Crime Bureau, "2014 Heavy Equipment Theft Report," October 2015, https://www.nicb.org/newsroom/news-releases/2014-heavy-equipment-theft-report.

9. Matt Cole, *Cargo Theft Numbers Down in 2015,* FreightWatch Reports." February 17, 2016, http://www.overdriveonline.com/cargo-theft-numbers-down-in-2015-freightwatch-reports/.

10. National Insurance Crime Bureau, "NICB's Hot Wheels: America's Most Stolen Vehicles," August 1, 2016, https://www.nicb.org/newsroom/nicb_campaigns/hot%E2%80%93wheels.

11. Insurance Information Institute, "Auto Theft," July 2016, http://www.iii.org/issue-update/auto-theft.

12. Gohar Petrossian and Ronald Clarke, "The Problem of Export of Stolen Vehicles Across Land Borders," 2012. Center for Problem-Oriented Policing, http://www.popcenter.org/problems/export_stolen_vehicles/.

13. Ibid.

14. National Insurance Crime Bureau, "Hot Spots 2015," June 2016, https://www.nicb.org/newsroom/nicb_campaigns/hot_spots.

15. Gohar Petrossian and Ronald Clarke, "The Problem of Export of Stolen Vehicles Across Land Borders," 2012. Center for Problem-Oriented Policing, http://www.popcenter.org/problems/export_stolen_vehicles/.

16. Speech by Lt. Greg Terp, Commander, Miami-Dade Police Department Auto Theft Task Force, Summit on Auto Theft in Florida 2002, Tampa, Florida, September 16, 2002.

17. NICB, "Doing a Double Take: Vehicle Clones Are a Street-Level Problem for Insurers," *Strategic Analysis Report,* Vol. 1, October 10, 2004.

18. Ibid.

19. Ibid.

20. National Auto Theft Bureau, 1990 Annual Report, p. 15.

21. National Equipment Register and National Insurance Crime Bureau, "2014 Theft Report," 2014, https://www.nicb.org/File%20Library/Public%20Affairs/NICB-NER2014-HE_FINAL.pdf.

22. Comments by David Shillingford, President, National Equipment Register, Summit on Auto Theft in Florida 2002, Tampa, Florida, September 16, 2002.

23. Gene Rutledge, "7 Character PIN for Off-Road Equipment Is Here," *APB,* July 1999, pp. 17–19.

24. "There's More than One Way to Stop a Thief," *APB,* March 2001, pp. 52, 58–59.

25. FIA International Research, "Contraband, Organized Crime, and the Threat to the Transportation and Supply Chain Function." Study conducted on behalf of the National Cargo Security Council, a coalition of public and private transportation organizations, September 2001, Executive Summary, p. 1.

26. Joseph Weherle, CEO, NICB, opening remarks, 58th Annual Conference, International Association of Auto Theft Investigators, Orlando, Florida. Mr. Wherele stated that there is no good data available on cargo theft losses and estimates range from $10 billion–$60 billion.

27. Remarks of Joseph Weherle, CEO, NICB.

28. Brian Shockley, "Automated License Plate Recognition," *APB,* the official publication of the International Association of Auto Theft Investigators, November 2008, p. 47. See also "Automated License Scan: The Ultimate 'Multi-Task' Tool for Patrol," *The Sheriff's Star,* official publication of the Florida Sheriff's Association, May/June 2009, p. 3, and Norman Gaumont,

"The Role of Automatic License Plate Recognition Technology in Policing: Results from the Lower Mainland of British Columbia," *The Police Chief,* IACP, November 2008, pp. 50–59.

29. National Insurance Crime Bureau, *2010 Passenger Vehicle Identification Manual, 81st Edition* (Palos Hills, IL: NICB, 2010).

30. Ibid.

31. National Insurance Crime Bureau, *2010 Commercial Vehicle Identification Manual* (Palos Hills, IL: NICB, 2004).

32. National Insurance Crime Bureau, *2010 Passenger Vehicle Identification Manual, 81st Edition,* front matter (Palos Hills, IL: NICB, 2010).

33. Federal Bureau of Investigation, "The New Generation of NCIC," *CJIS: A Newsletter For the Criminal Justice Community,* Vol. 3, Issue 2, 1999, pp. 5–6.

34. Ibid.

35. Ibid.

36. Information provided in a conversation with Sgt. Chris Bimonte, Miami-Dade Police Department, who represents the department on the North America Export Committee.

37. Comments by Senator Bill Nelson, Florida, Summit on Auto Theft in Florida 2002, Tampa, Florida, September 15, 2002.

38. Information provided by Sgt. Chris Bimonte.

39. Information provided by Sgt. Chris Bimonte.

40. Glenn Wheeler, "North American Export Committee Update," *APB,* March 2001, p. 11.

41. "NICB, ISO, and NER Form Industry Alliance to Combat Equipment Theft," Industry News Section, *APB,* International Association of Auto Theft Investigators, July 2008, p. 13.

42. Ibid.

43. "Attorney General Issues Report on Component Part Markings," IAATI Legal News Column, *APB,* November 2000, pp. 59, 61.

44. Ibid.

45. Ibid.

46. Ibid.

47. "Restoration of Altered or Obliterated Numbers," training bulletin, Alabama Department of Public Safety.

48. Jeff Bennett, "Thieves Go High-tech to Steal Cars." *Wall Street Journal,* July 5, 2016, http://www.wsj.com/articles/thieves-go-high-tech-to-steal-cars-1467744606.

49. National Insurance Crime Bureau, *Fire Investigation Handbook* (Palos Hills, IL: NICB, 1995), pp. 31–67; National Fire Protection Association International, *NFPA 921 Guide for Fire and Explosion Investigations,* 2001 Edition (Quincy, MA: NFPA International, 2001), pp. 921–171 to 921–182.

50. Hiawatha Bray, "Technology Making Car Theft Obsolete." *Boston Globe,* September 8, 2014, https://www.bostonglobe.com/business/2014/09/07/how-tech-making-car-theft-obsolete/4qzCXHQHiQPvcjqewQWIZJ/story.html.

51. "OnStar by GM," Industry News Section, *APB,* International Association of Auto Theft Investigators, November 2008, p. 67.

52. Federal Bureau of Investigation, "FBI 100: First Strike Global Terror in America," https://archives.fbi.gov/archives/news/stories/2008/february/tradebom_022608.

53. Jerry Capeci and Tom Robbins, "How Agents Caught the First Suspect in the First World Trade Center Bombing in 1993," *New York Daily News,* March 3, 2015, http://www.nydailynews.com/new-york/agents-caught-wtc-bomber-1993-article-1.2130082.

54. Much of the material on this topic is drawn from Phillip J. Crapeau, "Photo Inspection Helps Deter Auto Theft," *National Underwriter,* September 18, 1990.

55. Ibid.

Chapter 17

1. Larry Ponemon, *2015 Cost of Data Breach Study: Global Analysis* (New York: Ponemon Institute and IBM, 2015), https://securityintelligence.com/media/2015-ponemon-cost-of-a-data-breach-study/

2. Limor Kessem, "Carbanak: How Would You Have Stopped a $1 Billion APT Attack?" *Security Intelligence Bulletin by IBM,* February 23, 2105, https://securityintelligence.com/carbanak-how-would-you-have-stopped-a-1-billion-apt-attack/

3. Federal Bureau of Investigation (FBI), Internet Crime Complaint Center, *2015 Internet Crime Report,* https://pdf.ic3.gov/2015_IC3Report.pdf

4. James Moar, *The Future of Cybercrime and Society: Financial and Corporate Threats and Mitigation 2015–2020* (London: Juniper Networks, 2015).

5. FBI, op. cit., p. 5.

6. U.S. Attorney's Office, Western District of Washington, "Financial Fraud Crime Victims," 2016, https://www.justice.gov/usao-wdwa/victim-witness/victim-info/financial-fraud

7. Internet Live Stats. See: http://www.internetlivestats.com/one-second/

8. Points 2, 5, and 8 are drawn from Olasanmi Omoneye Olufunke, "Computer Crimes and Counter Measures in the Nigerian Banking Sector," *Journal of Internet Banking and Commerce,* Vol. 15, Issue 1 April 2010, p. 5.

9. Much of this section on organized crime and the Silk Road is adapted from Robert W. Taylor, Eric J. Fritsch and John Liederbach, *Digital Crime and Digital Terrorism,* 3rd edition (New York: Pearson, 2015), Chapter 5.

10. The boon of hacking came after the 1983 film, War Games; and one of the first major arrests for hacking was on the 414 Gang (from Milwaukee-area code 414), a group of teenagers that penetrated and vandalized the secure military data systems at Los Alamos in that same year.

11. These cases are well documented in the popular media as well as in Michael Newton, *The Encyclopedia of High-Tech Crime and Crime-Fighting* (New York: Checkmark Books, 2004).

12. Mad Macz, *Internet Underground: the Way of the Hacker* (PageFee Publishing Inc., 2002)

13. See Robert W. Taylor, Eric J. Fritsch, and John Liederbach, *Digital Crime and Digital Terrorism,* 3rd edition (New York: Pearson, 2015), Chapter 5

14. George Silowash, Dawn Cerappelli, Andrew Moore, Randall Trzeciak, Timothy Shimeall, and Lori Flyn, *Common Sense Guide to Mitigating Insider Threats,* 4th edition. (Pittsburgh, PA: Software Engineering Institute—Carnegie Mellon University, CERT Program, December 2012).

15. Ibid.

16. Chris Hadnagy, Social Engineering Defined. Social-Engineer.org. September 2009, http://www.social-engineer.org/framework/Social_Engineering_Defined.

17. Federal Bureau of Investigation, *Organized Crime Overview* (Washington, DC: FBI, 2012, http://www.fbi.gov/about-us/investigate/organized crime/overview.

18. Jerome Bjelopera, *Organized Crime: An Evolving Challenge for US Law Enforcement* (Washington, DC: Congressional Research Service, 2012).

19. See Benjamin Weiser, "Online Drug Bazaar's Founder Gets Life in Prison," *New York Times,* May 30, 2015; Andy Greenberg, "An Interview with a Digital Drug Lord: The Silk Road's Dread Pirate Roberts (Q&A)," *Forbes,* August 14, 2013, and Andy Greenberg, "End of the Silk Road: FBI Says It's Busted the Web's Biggest Anonymous Drug Black Market," *Forbes,* October 2, 2013.

20. See Mark Pollit, "Cyberterrorism—Fact or Fancy?" Proceedings of the 20th National Information Systems Security Conference," October 25, 1999, pp . 285–289; and Dorthy E. Dennin, "Cyberterrorism," www.cs.georgetown.edu/~denning/infosec/cyberterror-DG.doc.

21. United Nations Office on Drugs and Crime, The Use of the Internet for Terrorist Purposes, 2012, http://www.unodc.org/documents/frontpage /Use_of_Internet_for_Terrorist_Purposes.pdf

22. See Robert W. Taylor and Charles R. Swanson, *Terrorism, Intelligence and Homeland Security* (New York: Pearson Publishing, 2016), p. 141.

23. Liam Tung, 2012. Judgment of 4 May 2012 of the Tribunal de Grande Instance de Paris. Jihadists get world-class encryption kit (29 January 2008). See: www.zdnet.com.au/jihadists-get-world-class-encryption-kit-339285480.htm

24. United Nations Office on Drugs and Crime, "The Use of the Internet for Terrorist Purposes," 2012, http://www.unodc.org/documents/frontpage /Use_of_Internet_for_Terrorist_Purposes.pdf

25. Stefano Mele, "Cyberwarfare and its Damaging Effects on Citizens," CSIG-Foggia Center for the Study of the Legal Aspects of Computing, 2010

26. Michael Sheets, "The Rise of Tech-Savvy Global Terrorism Networks," *CNBC Explains,* December 2016, http://www.cnbc.com/2015/12/04/the -everyday-technology-helping-terrorists-plot-evil.html

27. Bill Chu, Thomas J. Holt, and Gail Joon Ahn, *Examining the Creation, Distribution, and Function of Malware Online,* (Washington, DC: U.S. Department of Justice, March 2010), p. 5.

28. Ibid., pp., 41, 23.

29. Ibid., p. 42.

30. See Daniel Regalado, Shon Harris, Allen Harper, Chris Eagle, Jonathon Ness, Branko Spasejevic, Ryan Linn, and Stephen Sims, *Gray Hat Hacking: The Ethical Hacker's Handbook,* 4th edition (New York: McGraw-Hill, 2015)

31. Mustaque Ahamad et al., "Emerging Cyber Threats for 2009," Georgia Institute of Technology, p. 2. Also see Reid Goldsborough, "Computer Zombies an Increasing Concern," *Tech Directions,* Vol. 69, Issue 8, March 2010, p. 15.

32. Rafael Etges and Emma Sutcliffe, "An Overview of Transnational Organized Cyber Crime," p. 92.

33. EMSISoft Blog, Slade, "How to Stay Safe on Facebook and Avoid the Top 5 Scams," April 16, 2015, http://blog.emsisoft.com/2015/04/16/how-to-stay-safe-on-facebook-and-avoid-the-top-5-scams/

34. Hassan Wahshat, Yasir Khalil, and Takialdin, "Computer Virus, Survey Study," *International Journal of Computer Science and Network Security,* Vol. 7, Issue 4, April 2007, p. 308.

35. No author, "The 12 Costliest Computer Viruses Ever," Insure.com, August 3, 2010, http://insure.com/2010/08/03/The-12-Costliest-Computer-Viruses-Ever/.

36. Tom Zeller, Jr., "Protecting Yourself from Keylogging Thieves," *The New York Times,* February 27, 2006, p. 16.

37. Jean Thilmany, "Stealth Worms," *Mechanical Engineering,* Vol. 132, Issue 5, May 2010, p. 15 and Mark Bowden, "The Enemy Within," *Atlantic Monthly,* Vol. 305, Issue 5, June 2010, and Robert McMillan, "After One Year, 7 Million Conficker Infections," *AllThingsDigital, Network-World.com,* October 30, 2009, p. 1.

38. No author, "Defense Security Report , VeriSign, Distributed Denial of Service Attacks," July 11, 2008, p. 12.

39. Xin Luo and Qinyu Liao, "Awareness Education as the Key to Ransomware Prevention," *Information Security Systems,* Vol. 16, 2007, p. 195.

40. Ibid., p. 197.

41. No author, "A Cyber Crime Report," p. 6.

42. Jim Wingate, The Perfect Dead Drop, White Paper, Back-Bone Security, 2004.

43. Symantec, Trojan Horse, April 20, 2010, pp. 1–2, www.Symantec.com /security-response/writeup.jsp?docid=2004-021914-2822-99, August 16, 2010.

44. Ibid.

45. Arik Hesseldahl, "Spyware's Growing Arsenal," *Business Week,* online edition, August 16, 2006, p. 6.

46. Thorsten Holtz, Markus Engelberth, and Felix Freiling, "Learning More about the Underground Economy: A Case Study of Keyloggers and Drop-zones," Laboratory for Dependable System, University of Mannheim, Germany, December 18, 2008, pp. 7–8.

47. Aaron Emigh, "The Crimeware Landscape: Malware, Phishing, Identity Theft, and Beyond," IronKey, Los Altos, California, September 19, 2006, p. 5.

48. David E. Sanger, "Obama Order Sped Up Wave of Cyberattacks Against Iran," *New York Times,* June 1, 2012, p. 1.

49. Michael Kelley, "The Stuxnet Attack on Iran's Nuclear Plant was Far More Dangerous than Previously Thought," *Business Insider,* November 2013, http://www.businessinsider.com/stuxnet-was-far-more-dangerous-than-previous-thought-2013-11

50. Danielle Veluz, "Stuxnet Malware Targets SCADA Systems," *Trend Micro,* October 1, 2012, http://www.trendmicro.com/vinfo/us/threat-encyclopedia /web-attack/54/stuxnet-malware-targets-scada-systems

51. Ellen Nakashima, "U.S., Israel developed Flame Computer Virus to Slow Iranian Nuclear Efforts," *Washington Post,* June 19, 2012.

52. Joel Hruska, "Windows PCs Vulnerable to Stuxnet Attack—Five Years after Patch," *ExtremeTech,* March 11, 2015, http://www.extremetech.com/ computing/200898-windows-pcs-vulnerable-to-stuxnet-attack-five-years -after-patches

53. See Michael Landi, "The Methods of Windows Rootkits," *Journal of Applied Security Research,* Vol. 4, Issue 2, 2009, pp. 389–426.

54. University of Pennsylvania, Wharton School of Business, "Mobile Devices and Cybercrime: Is Your Phone the Weakest Link?" *Knowledge Technology,* June 5, 2013, http://knowledge.wharton.upenn.edu/article/mobile-devices -and-cybercrime-is-your-phone-the-weakest-link/

55. Chris Mitchell, "The Cyber Crime Threat on Mobile Devices," http://www .chrismitchell.net/Papers/tcctom.pdf

56. Statista, http://www.statista.com/statistics/330695/number-of-smartphone -users-worldwide/

57. University of Pennsylvania, op. cit., p. 1.

58. Ellen Nakashima, "The FBI's Most Powerful, and Controversial, High Tech Tools," *Washington Post,* December 10, 2015.

59. With restatement and additions, these points are drawn from Hollis Stambaugh et al., *Electronic Crime Needs Assessment for State and Local Law Enforcement* (Washington, DC: National Institute of Justice, 2001).

60. For a more extended view of this subject see Nathan Judish et al. (Washington, DC: U.S. Department of Justice, Computer Crime and Intellectual Property Section, 2009).

61. People v. Ledesma, 39 Cal 4th, 657, 703–704, 2006.

62. United States v. Bolin, 514 F.2d 554, 560–561, 1975, United States v. Ivy, 165 F.3rd, 397, 403, 1998 and United States v. Tibbs, 49 F.Supp.2d 47, 48–49, 53.

63. United States v. Sanchez, 32 F.3d 1330, 1994.

64. Jones v. State, 648 So.2d 669 (FL, 1994).

65. The impact of Georgia v. Randolph is discussed in greater detail in Renee E. Williams, "Third Party Consent Searches after Randolph: Dueling Approaches to Dueling Roommates," *Boston Law Review,* Vol. 87, Issue 4, October 2007, pp. 937–968.

66. Georgia v. Randolph, 547 U.S. 103, 2006.

67. For a fuller treatment of this subject see Yule Kim, *Protecting the U.S. Perimeter: Border Searches under the Fourth Amendment* (Washington, DC: Congressional Research Service, June 29, 2009).

68. With changes and consolidation of points, the content in this and the remaining sections of this chapter are drawn from various portions of Katrina Rose, *Electronic Crime Scene Investigation: An On-the-Scene Reference for First Responders* (Washington, DC: National Institute of Justice, November 2009), most of it from pp. 6–22.

69. Much of this section is adapted from Robert W. Taylor, Eric J. Fritsch, and John Liederback, *Digital Crime and Digital Terrorism*, 3rd edition (New York: Pearson Publishing, 2015); Chapter 13: Digital Forensics.

70. Microsoft Developer Network, "Ensuring Data Integrity with Hash Codes," https://msdn.microsoft.com/en-us/library/f9ax34y5(v=vs.110).aspx

71. Pavitra Shankdhar, "22 Popular Computer Forensics Tools," *InfoSec Institute Forensics,* August 26, 2014, http://resources.infosecinstitute.com/computer-forensics-tools/

Chapter 18

1. Patricia Leigh Brown, "Someone Is Stealing Avocados," The New York Times, Jan. 26, 2004.

2. E-mail, Laurie Hill to Charles Swanson, California Avocado Commission, October 2, 2007.

3. "Lake Wales Man Charged with Stealing Tangerines," The Ledger November 7, 2014.

4. Christine Souza, "Vineyard Thieves Target Grapes, Harvest Supplies," California Farm Bureau Federation, September 19, 2007, p. 2.

5. Jesse McKinley, "Authorities Work to Crack Nut Crime Ring," The New York Times, October 2006.

6. Catherine E. Shoicet, "Thieves Strip Park's Palms," St. Petersburg Times, September 21, 2007.

7. Ibid.

8. FBI, Crime in the United States, 2010 (Washington, D.C.: FBI, 2010), Table 24. No page number in the Internet version of this document, available at, https://www.fbi.gov/about- us/cjis/ucr/crime-in-the-u.s/2010/crime-in-the-u.s.-2010/tables/10tbl24.xls.

9. U.S. Department of Agriculture, Economic Research Service, U.S, Beef and Cattle Industry 2002-2005: Background Statistics and Information, p. 1. www.ers.usda.gov/news/BSECoverage.htm. For 2005, the National Agricultural Statistics Service (NASS) reported 190,000 cattle and calves lost to predation: 9.4% were attacks by mountain lions or bobcats, 12.9% involved dogs, 32.4% were killed by coyotes, and 45.3% "other or unknown predators." In contrast, that same year NASS accounted for only 21,000 head lost due to thefts, which seems very low; that same year Wyoming authorities reported 3,700 heads of cattle lost due to theft for just that state. That would mean Wyoming, one of the smaller cattle-producing states, had 17.6% of all cattle stolen, or nearly one in five.

10. Nelson Hernandez, "$75,000 in Bull Semen Stolen from Frederick Farm," The Washington Post, November 3, 2005.

11. Garance Burke and Olivia Munoz, "Hormone Theft Worries Rural Police, Redding (California) Record, February 23, 2007.

12. Mike Toner, "Brazen Fossil Hunters Are Cleaning Out U.S. Dinosaur Heritage," Atlanta Journal Constitution, Aug. 23, 2001.

13. William L. Hamilton, "Jurassic Bark," The New York Times, December 1, 2005, and No author, "Petrified Wood Stolen on Federal Land," The Associated Press State and Local Wire, January 29, 2007.

14. Joe Corcoran, "High-Tech Measures Thwart Ginseng Poachers," Voice of America News, April 12, 2006, p. 1.

15. Ibid., p. 2 with additions.

16. Janet Heimlich, "Thorny Problem," Texas Parks and Wildlife Magazine, June 2003, p. 1.

17. No author, "Thieves Steal Hundreds of Millions of Dollars Worth of Trees," USA Today, May 18, 2003.

18. Chuck Hayes, "Pennsylvania: Stop Theft! Timber Theft Growing Concern in Allegheny National Forest," Times Observer (Warren, Pennsylvania), July 14, 2006.

19. Warren Cornwall, "Maples Falling Victim to Backwoods Thieves," The Seattle Times, May 17, 2007.

20. No author, "Two Charged with Timber Theft from Medicine Bow National Forest," Associated Press, February 12, 2004.

21. David Windsor, "Timber Theft: A Solvable Crime," Indiana Woodland Steward, Spring 2001, vol. 10, no. 1, pp. 1–3; retrieved from www.fnr.purdue.edu/inwood/past%20issues/timberth.htm.

22. For a more detailed discussion on wildfire investigations see National Wildlife Coordinating Group Fire Investigation Working Team, *Wildfire Origin & Cause Determination Handbook,* (National Wildlife Coordinating Group Fire Investigation Working Team, May 2005). This publication is available at www.nwcg.gov. Copies may be ordered from the Great Basin Cashe Supply Office, 3833 S. Development Ave., Boise, ID 83705. Order NFES 1874.)

23. Ibid., pp. 65–91.

24. These points are drawn from Sgt. William Bacon, *Livestock Theft Investigation,* Los Angeles County Sheriff's Department, undated, p. 2, with modifications made by the authors.

25. Ibid., which is the source for the information in this paragraph.

26. Ibid.

27. Some of the information in this paragraph is drawn from ibid., pp. 5–6.

28. For further discussion on this subject see Fred Grimm, "Stolen and Butchered Horses Not So Shocking in South Florida," Miami Herald, October 28, 2015, retrieved from: www.miamiherald.com/news/local/news-columns-blogs/fred-grimm/article41719107.html (accessed March 6, 2016).

29. Bacon, *Livestock Theft Investigation*, p. 5.

30. Ibid.

31. E.N. Smith, "Modern Rustlers Steal Livestock via the Highway," Seattle Times Com, June 7, 1998, p. 1.

32. Ibid., p. 1.

33. Ibid., p. 12.

34. Ibid.

35. Bacon, *Livestock Theft Investigation*, p. 16, from which this paragraph was obtained with restatement.

36. Ibid., 24.

37. See *Utah Livestock Brand Book*, Utah Department of Agriculture, 2006.

38. These methods are identified in virtually all discussions of this topic. In preparing this edition we reviewed and drew a limited amount of restated content from Michael Neary, *Methods of Livestock Identification,* Purdue University Cooperative Extension, December 2002.

39. On this subject see No author, *A Sampling of Thoughts and Opinions on Electronic Identification.* The University of Tennessee, Center for Profitable Agriculture, 2004. In a small survey of farmers and ranchers it was found that among those who used a method of identification, 14.2% employed tattoos, 4.5% used brands, 77.4% used plastic ear tags, 1.8% relied on RFID devices, and 1.2% used other methods.

40. Several of these points were taken from Bacon, *Livestock Theft Investigation*, p. 17.

41. Daniel P. Mears, Michelle L. Scott, Avinash S. Bhati, John Roman, Aaron Chalfin and Jessie Jannetta, *Policy, Theory, and Research Lessons from and Evaluation of an Agricultural Crime Prevention Program*, Urban Institute, Justice Policy Center, Florida State University College of Criminology and Criminal Justice (Washington, DC: U.S. Department of Justice, 2007), pp. 27–28.

42. Dean Olson, "Agroterrorism: Threats to America's Economy and Food Supply," *FBI Law Enforcement Bulletin,* February 2012, pp. 1–8. (This discussion was adapted from this source.)

43. U.S. Census Bureau, *Statistical Abstract of the United States: 2004–2005* (Washington, DC: 2004), 234.

44. Office of the United States Trade Representative, Fact Sheet: Expanding Food and Agricultural Exports: Successes in Reducing Sanitary and Phytosanitary Barriers, 04/01/2013; retrieved from http://www.ustr.gov/about-us/press-office/fact-sheets/2013/april/expanding-food-agricultural-exports (accessed March 12, 2014).

45. Jim Monke, Congressional Research Service Report for Congress, *Agroterrorism: Threat and Preparedness*; retrieved from http://www.fas.org.sgp/crs/terror/RL32521.pdf (accessed May 25, 2011).

46. Terry Knowles,, James Lane, Gary Bayens, Nevil Speer, Jerry Jaax, David Carter, and Andra Bannister, *Defining Law Enforcement's Role in Protecting American Agriculture from Agroterrorism;* retrieved from http://www.ncjrs.gov/pdffiles1/nij/grants/212280.pdf (accessed May 25, 2011, p. 22).

47. Bruce Hoffman, "Al Qaeda Has a New Strategy. Obama Needs One, Too"; retrieved from http://www.washingtonpost.com/wp- dny/content/article/2010/01/08/AR201010803555.html?sid=ST2010031703003 (accessed on May 25, 2011).

48. Peter Chalk, "Hitting America's Soft Underbelly: The Potential Threat of Deliberate Biological Attacks Against the U.S. Agricultural and Food Industry"; retrieved from http://www.rand.org/pubs/monographs/2004/RAND_MG135135.pdf (accessed on May 25, 2011).

49. Peter Chalk, "The U.S. Agricultural System: A Target for al Qaeda?" *Terrorism Monitor* 3, no. 5 (2005).

50. Chalk, "The U.S. Agricultural System: A Target for al Qaeda?"

51. Knowles et al., *Defining Law Enforcement's Role in Protecting American Agriculture from Agroterrorism,* 3.

52. U.S. Department of Agriculture, Animal and Health Inspection Service, *APHIS Factsheet: Foot-and-Mouth Disease;* retrieved from http://www.aphis.usda.gov/publications/animal_health/ content/printable_versions/fs_foot_mouth_disease07.pdf (accessed on May 25, 2011).

53. Glenn R. Schmitt, "Agroterrorism—Why We're Not Ready: A Look at the Role of Law Enforcement"; retrieved from http://www.nim.gov/journals/257/agroterrorism.html (accessed on May 25, 2011).

54. Anthrax is a serious infectious disease caused by gram-positive, rod-shaped bacteria known as *Bacillus anthracis.* Anthrax can be found naturally in soil and commonly affects domestic and wild animals around the world. Although it is rare, people can get sick with anthrax if they come into contact with infected animals or contaminated animal products. Available at: http://www.cdc.gov/anthrax/basics/.

55. Glanders is a disease caused by bacteria which primarily affects horses, mules and donkeys, but is also seen in animals like goats, dogs and cats. Glanders is rare in humans - no human cases have been reported in the U.S. since 1945. However, people can become infected through direct contact with infected animals. Minnesota Department of Health, Bioterrorism Factsheet, 9/11/2006; available at: http://www.health.state.mn.us/divs/idepc/diseases/glanders/glanders. html#def.

56. For a more detailed discussion of the efforts by the German saboteurs in World War I to introduce both anthrax and glanders into American horses and mules being shipped to Europe see Howard Blum, *Dark Invasion: 1915-Germany's Secret War and the Hunt for the First Terrorist Cell in America* (New York, NY: Harper Collins Publishers, 2014).

57. Janice P. Morgan, "Overview of a Foreign Animal Disease Response"; retrieved from http://www.agr.state.ne.us/division/bai/overview_foreign_animal_disease_response_ .pdf (accessed on May 25, 2011).

58. Knowles et al., *Defining Law Enforcement's Role in Protecting American Agriculture from Agroterrorism,* 4.

59. Ibid., p. 92.

60. U.S. Department of Agriculture, *Economic Impact of a Foreign Animal Disease (FAD) Outbreak Across the United States.*

61. Knowles et al., *Defining Law Enforcement's Role in Protecting American Agriculture from Agroterrorism,* 92.

62. Randal C. Archibold, "Poachers in West Hunt Big Antlers to Feed Big Egos," The New York Times, December 9, 2006.

63. For example, see No author, "Thrill Killings Adding to Boost in Poaching of Nevada's Big Game," The Associated Press State and Local Wire, November 29, 2006.

64. Archibold, "Poachers in West Hunt Big Antlers to Feed Big Egos,"

65. Ingrid Peritz, "Rich Hunters Used Copter to Stalk Terrified Moose," The Globe and Mail, Canada, December 7, 2006.

66. "Poachers Enlisted to Save Big Game," The New York Times, Dec. 26, 1990, p. A28.

67. Press release, New Mexico Department of Game and Fish, March 16, 2005.

68. Wency Leung, "Asia's Bile Trade Takes Its Toll of Canadian Bears," South China Morning Post, August 26, 2007.

69. Ibid.

70. Press release, The Humane Society of the United States, "Congress Aims to End the Black Market Trade in Bear Parts," July 18, 2007; see www.hsus.org/press_and_publications/press_releases.

71. Stephen L. Eliason, "Trophy Poaching: A Routine Activities Perspective," Deviant Behavior 33 (2012), p. 1.

72. Ibid., p. 76.

73. Ibid., 77.

74. Ibid., 78.

75. Ibid., pp. 78-79.

76. U.S. Fish & Wildlife Service Forensics Laboratory, available at: http://www.fws.gov/lab/about.php.

77. There are a number of articles on the use of DNA in wildlife investigations; as an illustration, see "Wildlife Officers Use of DNA Evidence to Solve Cold Case," US States News, August 21, 2006, no author.

Chapter 19

1. K. D. Moll, *Arson, Vandalism, and Violence: Law Enforcement Problems Affecting Fire De-partments* (Washington, D.C.: Government Printing Office, 1977), pp. 20-21.

2. "Arson," Insurance Information Institute, n.d., retrieved from; http://www.iii.org/fact-statistic/arson (accessed April 30, 2016).

3. This information was obtained from "Stop Arson Now," a brochure published by the Florida Advisory Committee on Arson Prevention.

4. C. W. Stickney, "Recognizing Where Arson Exists," *Fireman Magazine,* September-December 1960, p. 3.

5. *Touched Off by Human Hands,* 1979. This booklet was originally published by the Illinois Ad-visory Committee on Arson Prevention in cooperation with the Illinois Chapter of the Interna-tional Association of Arson Investigation and was reprinted for distribution by the State Farm Fire and Casualty Company, Bloomington, Illinois. Much of the information in this section was taken from this source, pp. 7-11.

6. Stickney, "Recognizing Where Arson Exists," 1960, p. 4.

7. Ibid., p. 8.

8. Ibid.

9. C. W. Stickney, "Recognizing Where Arson Exists," *Fire and Arson Investigator,* October-December 1970; W. A. Derr, "Wildland Fire Investigation: Information from Objects," paper presented at the 18th Annual Fire and Arson Investigators Seminar, Palm Springs, California, June 14-18, 1971.

10. National Fire Protection Association, *921 Guide for Fire and Explosives Investigation,* (Quincy, MA: NFPA, 2008, pp. 921-40.

11. National Fire Protection Association, *921 Guide for Fire and Explosion Investigations* (Quincy, MA: NFPA, 2001), pp. 921-27, 921-28.

12. Ibid., p. 921-33.

13. Ibid., p. 921-33.

14. Ibid., p. 921-29.

15. *User's Manual for NFPA 921—Guide for Fire and Explosion Investigation* 2nd edition, (Quincy, MA) National Fire Protection Association, Inc. 2005, p. 46.

16. Ibid., pp. 921-30.

17. B. P. Battle and P. B. Weston, *Arson: A Handbook of Detection and Investigation* (New York: Arco, 1972), pp. 19-28.

18. Ian Lambie,, Julia Ioane, and Isabel Randell, "Understanding Child and Adolescent Fireset-ting," in *The Psychology of Arson: A Practical Guide to Understanding and Managing Deliber-ate Firesetting,* eds. Rebekah M. Doley, Geoffrey L. Dickens and Theresa A. Gannon (Routledge, Taylor & Francis: London and New York), 32-33.

19. G. Martin, H. Bergen, A.S. Richardson, L. Roegar, and S. Allison, "Correlates of firesetting in a community sample of young adolescents," *Australian and New Zealand Journal of Psychiatry* 38, 2004, pp. 32-33.

20. Joseph Toscano. *"Motive, Means & Opportunity: A Guide to Fire Investigation,"* American Re-Insurance Company, Princeton, N.J., 1996, pp. 87-88.

21. C. L. Karchmer, M. E. Walsh, and J. Greenfield, *Enforcement Manual: Approaches for Com-bating Arson for Profit Schemes* (Washington, D.C.: U.S. Department of Justice, 1981), pp. 15-31. This discussion was adapted from this source.

22. Joseph Toscano. *"Motive, Means & Opportunity: A Guide to Arson Investigation,"* American Re-Insurance Company, 1996, Princeton, N.J., pp. 10-23.

23. Stickney, "Recognizing Where Arson Exists," 1960, pp. 11-12.

24. B. B. Caldwell, "The Examination of Exhibits in Suspected Arson Cases," *Royal Canadian Mounted Police Quarterly,* 1957, Vol. 22, pp. 103-108.

25. Stauffer, Eric and Doug Byron, "Alternative Fuels in Fire Debris Analysis: Biodiesel Basics," *Journal of Forensic Science* 52, no. 2 (March 2007): 371-379.

26. Ibid.

27. J. F. Bordeau, Q. Y. Kwan, W. E. Faragker, and G. C. Senault, *Arson and Arson Investigation* (Washington, D.C.: Government Printing Office, 1974), pp. 77-83. Much of the information in this section was taken from this source.

28. J. D. Nicol, "Recovery of Flammable Liquids from a Burned Structure," *Fire Engineering,* 1961, Vol. 114, p. 550.

29. D. Q. Burd, "Detection of Traces of Combustible Fluids in Arson Cases," *Journal of Criminal Law, Criminology, and Police Science,* 1960, Vol. 51, pp. 263-264; P. Rajeswaran and P. L. Kirk, "Identification of Gasoline, Waves, Greases, and Asphalts by Evaporation Chromatog-raphy," *Microchemical Journal,* 1962, Vol. 6, pp. 21-29.

30. R. Milliard and C. Thomas, "The Combustible Gas Detector (Souffer), an Evaluation," *Fire and Arson Investigator,* January-March 1976, pp. 48-50.

31. D. M. Lucas, "The Identification of Petroleum Products in Forensic Science by Gas Chroma-tography," *Journal of Forensic Sciences,* 1960, Vol. 5, No. 2, pp. 236-243.

32. P. L. Kirk, *Fire Investigation* (New York: Wiley, 1969), pp. 43-44; E. C. Crocker and L. B. Sjostrom, "Odor Detection and Thresholds," *Chemical Engineering News,* 1949, Vol. 27, pp. 1922-1931; and H. Zwaardemaber, "Camera Inoorata," *Perfumery and Essential Oil Record,* 1921, Vol. 12, pp. 243-244.

33. P. L. Kirk, *Crime Investigation, Physical Evidence, and the Police Laboratory* (New York: Interscience, 1966), p. 717; H. P. Wonderling, "Arsonists—Their Methods and the Evidence," *International Association of Arson Investigators Newsletter,* October–December 1953, reprinted in *Selected Articles for Fire and Arson Investigators,* International Association of Arson Investigators, 1975; K. Ol'Khosvsbaya, "Colormetric Determination of Hydrocarbons, Gasoline, Kero-sene and White Spent in the Air of Industrial Installations," *Gigiena Truda i Professional'nye Zabolevaniza,* 1971, Vol. 15, No. 11, pp. 57–58.

34. J. W. Girth, A. Jones, and T. A. Jones, "The Principle of Detection of Flammable Atmos-pheres by Catalytic Devices," *Combustion and Flame,* 1973, Vol. 21, pp. 303–312.

35. C. M. Lane, "Ultra-Violet Light . . . Gem or Junk," *Fire and Arson Investigator,* Dec. 1975, Vol. 26, No. 2, pp. 40–42.

36. C. L. Karchmer, M. E. Walsh, and J. Greenfield, *Enforcement Manual: Approaches for Com-bating Arson for Profit Schemes* (Washington, D.C.: U.S. Department of Justice, 1981), pp. 249–252.

37. National Insurance Crime Bureau, *Fire Investigation Handbook* (Palos Hills, IL: NICB, 1995), pp. 24, 25.

38. The purpose of the National Insurance Crime Bureau is to investigate questionable insurance claims and cooperate with public law enforcement agencies in securing the prosecution of insurance criminals.

39. National Insurance Crime Bureau, *Fire Investigation Handbook,* p. 26.

40. John Barracato, *Burning: A Guide to Fire Investigation* (Stamford, CT: Aetna Casualty and Surety, 1986), pp. 14–16.

41. National Fire Protection Association, *Guide for Fire and Explosion Investigations,* pp. 921-94–921-100.

42. Tim Dees, "Things That Go Boom in the Night," *Police* 34, no. 6 (2010): pp. 44, 46–47. (This discussion was adapted from this source.)

43. Smiths Detection is one of the largest manufacturers of IMS instruments for explosives detec-tions, are typically found at airport security checkpoints. In most cases an operator uses a glori-fied coffee filter to swab luggage or some other suspicious item and places it in a recess for analysis. More often than not a green light comes on and the traveler is free to go.

44. Spectrafluidics has developed a new detection technology that is a combination of Free Sur-face Microfluidics (FSF) and Surface Enhanced Raman Spectroscopy (SERS).

45. A Raman Laser, which works by measuring activity on the surface exposed or excited by the laser, produces a profile that is compared to that of the target substance. The effect is a detector that can be either fixed or handheld and costs a fraction of the IMS instrument. The microfluidic chips are consumed in the analysis process. The company plans to ship its first operational units this year.

46. George Buck, *Preparing for Terrorism* (Albany, NY: Delmar, 1998), pp. xi–xii.

47. James T. Thurman, *Practical Bomb Scene Investigation* (Boca Raton, FL: CRC Press, 2006): p. 123.

48. Ibid., p. 125.

49. "Boston Marathon Terror Attack Fast Facts," March 29, 2017, CNN Library, pp. 1–4; http://www.cnn.com/2013/06/03/us/boston-marathon -terror-attack-fast-facts/.

50. Brian Ross, "Boston Bombing Day 2: The Improbable Story of How Authorities Found the Bombers in the Crowd," ABC News; retrieved from http://www.abcnews.go.com/US/boston-bombing-day-improbable-story -authorities-found-bombers/story?

51. Tom Winter, Andy Thibault, and Joh Schuppe, "Cops Recall Deadly Shoot-out with Boston Bombing Suspects," March 16, 2015, NBC News; http://www.nbcnews.com/storyline/boston-bombing-trial/boston-bombing-trial-jury-inspects-boat-where-dzhokhar-tsarnaev-hid-n324231.

52. "Boston Marathon Terror Attack Fast Facts," CNN Library.

53. Ian Sample, *The Guardian,* Co, UK, 27 December 2009; retrieved from http://www.guardian.co.uk/world/2009/dec/27/petn-pentaerythritol-trinitrate -explosive.

54. National Fire Protection Association, *Guide for Fire and Explosion Investigations,* 1992, (Quincy, MA: NFPA) pp. 921-103–921-107.

55. James T. Thurman, *Practical Bomb Scene Investigation* (Boca Raton, FL: CRC Press, 2006); (For a more detailed discussion of locating, identifying, and collecting items of evidence from bomb scenes see pages 137–159).

56. Detail packaging instructions for different types of evidence can be found in the FBI Labora-tory Division Publication, *Handbook for Forensic Services,* as revised in 2003.

57. This checklist was provided by the U.S. Department of the Treasury, Bureau of Alcohol, To-bacco, and Firearms, 1999.

58. Ibid.

59. Donald G. Robinson, "U.S. Bomb Data Center: A Central Source for Explosives Incident In-formation," *The Police Chief LXXVI,* no. 2 (February 2009), p. 26.

60. "The Attorney General's August 11, 2004, Memorandum Regarding the Coordination of Ex-plosives Investigations and Related Matters," cited in Office of the Inspector General, "Bureau of Alcohol, Tobacco, Firearms and Explosives' and Federal Bureau of Investigation's Arson and Explosives Intelligence Databases," Audit Report 05-01, October 2004, retrieved from; http://www.usdoj.gov/oig/reports/ATF/a0501/app6.htm (accessed December 29, 2008).

61. Robinson, "U.S. Bomb Data Center," p. 27.

62. Process of requesting BATS access may be initiated by e-mailing the USBDC at USBDC@atf.gov or by calling 800-461-8841.

Chapter 20

1. The National Drug Intelligence Center (NDIC), established in 1993, is a component of the U.S. Department of Justice. The General Counterdrug Intelligence Plan, implemented in February 2000, designated NDIC as the nation's principal center for strategic domestic counterdrug intelligence. The NDIC produces national, regional, and state drug threat assessments, various drug information bulletins, and a series of pamphlets providing detailed information on specific drugs. The NDIC is a very valuable resource for local and state police officers engaged in drug enforcement in this country, and much of the description, usage, and abuse of drugs in this chapter is supported and grounded within the NDIC publications. See www.usdoj.gov/ndic.

2. Gregory Lee, *Global Drug Enforcement: Practical Investigative Techniques* (Boca Raton, FL: CRC Press, 2004), p. 19.

3. Several references and books have been developed to categorize individual drugs of abuse and articulate their specific effects on the physical body over the last 50 years. One of the first of these references was the landmark text by Samuel F. Levine, *Narcotics and Drug Abuse* (Cincinnati, OH: The W. H. Anderson Company, 1973). For additional references, see Erich Goode, *Drugs in American Society,* 5th ed. (New York: McGraw-Hill, 2000); James Inciardi and Karen McElrath's, *The American Drug Scene,* 4th ed. (Los Angeles, CA: Roxbury Press, 2004); and Carl Hart, Charles Ksir, and Oakley Ray, *Drugs, Society and Human Behavior,* 12th ed. (New York: McGraw-Hill, 2010).

4. Mark Potter. "Ground Zero: Tracking Heroin From Colombia to America's Streets." (November 23, 2014). NBC News. See: http://www.nbcnews.com/news/world/ground-zero-tracking-heroin-colombia-americas-streets-n250791.

5. David Holthouse, *The Chiva Game* (Denver, CO: Westworld, October 7, 2004).

6. Jane C. Maxwell, *Drug Abuse Trends* (Austin, TX: Texas Commission on Drug and Alcohol Abuse, June 1998).

7. Clyde B. McCoy and James A. Inciardi, *Sex, Drugs and the Continuing Spread of AIDS* (Los Angeles, CA: Roxbury Press, 1995).

8. David Holthouse, "The Chiva Game."

9. United Nations Office on Drugs and Crime, "The Global Heroin Market," *World Drug Report 2010,* www.unodc.org/documents/wdr/WDR_2010/1.2 _The_global_heroin_market.pdf.

10. David Holthouse, *The Chiva Game.*

11. Daniel Bates. "Police Warning over 'Cheese': Lethal Combination of Heroin and Cold Medicine behind 20 Deaths," *Daily Mail,* October 12, 2010, www.dailymail.co.uk/news/article-1319865/Cheese-Heroin-cold-medicine -drug-20-school-childrens-deaths-NY.html.

12. Partnership for Drug-Free Kids. "DEA Issues Alert on Fentanyl-Laced Heroin as Overdose Deaths Surge Nationwide," March 19, 2015, http://www.drugfree.org/news-service/dea-issues-alert-fentanyl-laced-heroin-over-dose-deaths-surge-nationwide/.

13. Christina Costanini, Daren Foster and Marian Van Zeller, The Naked Truth, "Death by Fentanyl, http://interactive.fusion.net/death-by-fentanyl /intro.html.

14. Donna Leinwand. "DEA Warns of Soft Drink-Cough Syrup Mix," *USA Today,* October 19, 2006, www.usatoday.com/news/nation/2006-10-18 -lean_x.htm?csp=34.

15. North Carolina Harm Reduction Coalition. "US Law Enforcement Who Carry Naloxone," http://www.nchrc.org/law-enforcement/us-law-enforcement -who-carry-naloxone/.

16. "Prescription Cancer Drug Is a Narcotic of Choice," *Law Enforcement News,* February 14, 2001, p. 5.

17. Timothy Roche, "Potent Perils of a Miracle Drug," *Time,* January 8, 2001.

18. Matthew Perrone, "FDA: Limited Benefit with Tamper-Proof OxyContin," *Associated Press,* September 22, 2009, www.physorg.com/news172847086.html.

19. "Heroin Use in Suburbs on the Rise," *ABCnews.com*, March 29, 2010, http://abcnews.go.com/WN/heroin-suburbs- rise/story?id=10230269&page=1.

20. U.S. Department of Health and Human Services, Substance Abuse and Mental Health Services Administration, www.dasis.samhsa.gov/webtv/information.htm, accessed December 16, 2010.

21. Todd F. Prough, "Investigating Opiate-Overdose Deaths," *FBI Law Enforcement Bulletin*, April 2009, pp. 27–31.

22. Ibid.

23. Carl Hart, Charles Ksir, and Oakley Ray, *Drugs, Society and Human Behavior*.

24. The controversy surrounding methadone treatment continues to be a hot topic in the drug research literature. See Charles E. Faupel, *Shooting Dope: Career Patterns in Hard-Core Heroin Users* (Gainesville, FL: University of Florida Press, 1991); James A. Inciardi, Frank M. Tims, and Bennet W. Fletcher, *Innovative Approaches in the Treatment of Drug Abuse: Program Models and Strategies* (Westport, CT: Greenwood Press, 1993); and *About Methadone*, 2nd ed. (Washington, DC: Drug Policy Alliance, 2004).

25. Hart et al., *Drugs, Society and Human Behavior*.

26. Robert C. Petersen and Richard C. Stillman (eds.), *Cocaine-1977*, NIDA Research Monograph #13. (Washington, DC: Department of Health, Education and Welfare, May 1977). See: https://archives.drugabuse.gov/sites/default/files/monograph13.pdf

27. Hart et al., *Drugs, Society and Human Behavior*.

28. Ibid.

29. National Drug Intelligence Center, *Amphetamines—Fast Facts* (Washington, DC: U.S. Department of Justice, 2010), www.usdoj.gov/ndic.

30. "Hawaii's Problems with 'Ice,'" *Police*, October 1989, p. 14.

31. See Combat Methamphetamine Epidemic Act 2005, Title VII of Public Law 109–177, May 2006, www.deadiversion.usdoj.gov/meth/cma2005_general_info.pdf, accessed December 18, 2010.

32. Patrik Jonsson, "Appalachia's New Cottage Industry: Meth," *Christian Science Monitor*, March 21, 2003.

33. Adapted and excerpted from "The Menace of Ice," *Time*, September 18, 1989, p. 28.

34. For a more detailed discussion of Strawberry Quick meth, see Donna Leiwand, "DEA: Flavored Meth Use on the Rise," *USA Today*, accessed http://usatoday.printthis.clickability.com/pt/cpt?action=cpt&title-DEQ%3A+Flavored+meth; "Strawberry Meth: Email Fliers Warn of a New, Candy-Flavored Form of Methamphetamine Targeted at Young People Called Strawberry Meth or Strawberry Quick Meth," http://urbanlegends.about.com/library/bl_strawberry_meth.htm; "Candy-Flavored Meth Targets New Users," *MY 2*, 2007, http://cbsnews.com/stories/2007/05/02/health/printable2752266.shtml.

35. Donna Leinwand, "10 Held in Smuggling of 'Nazi Speed,'" *USA Today*, August 21, 2002, p. 1-A.

36. James McGiveny, "'Made in America': The New and Potent Methcathinone," *Police Chief*, April 1994, pp. 20–21 Methcathinone is also known as 2-methylamino-1-phenylpropan-1-one, n-methcathinone, monomethylproprion, and ephedrone; street names include *go, goob, sniff, crank, star, wonder star, bathtub speed, gaggers, wildcat,* and *cat.*

37. Todd Bensman, "Ancient Use, New Import," *Dallas Morning News*, June 27, 2002, p. A-21 and A-28. Also, see National Drug Intelligence Center, *Khat—Fast Facts* (Washington, DC: U.S. Department of Justice, 2004), www.usdoj.gov/ndic.

38. Ibid.

39. National Drug Intelligence Center, *Barbiturates—Fast Facts* (Washington, DC: U.S. Department of Justice, 2010), www.usdoj.gov/ndic.

40. Robert C. Petersen and Richard C. Stillman, "Phencyclidine Abuse," in *Drug Enforcement* (Washington, DC: Government Printing Office, 1978), pp. 19-20. See National Drug Intelligence Center, *PCP—Fast Facts* (Washington, DC: U.S. Department of Justice, 2010), www.usdoj.gov/ndic.

41. Raymond Hernandez, in "New Drug Battles, Use of Ecstasy among Young Soars," *The New York Times* on the Web, August 2, 2000.

42. "Way Found to Detect LSD in Humans," *Tampa Tribune*, September 8, 1972.

43. National Drug Intelligence Center, *LSD—Fast Facts* (Washington, DC: U.S. Department of Justice, 2010), www.usdoj.gov/ndic.

44. National Drug Intelligence Center, *Foxy—Fast Facts* (Washington, DC: U.S. Department of Justice, 2010), www.usdoj.gov/ndic.

45. National Drug Intelligence Center, *5-MeO-AMT—Fast Facts* (Washington, DC: U.S. Department of Justice, 2010), www.usdoj.gov/ndic.

46. National Drug Intelligence Center, *Ketamine—Fast Facts* (Washington, DC: U.S. Department of Justice, 2010), www.usdoj.gov/ndic.

47. Lee, *Global Drug Enforcement: Practical Investigative Techniques*, p. 43.

48. Carrie Johnson. "DEA Rejects Attempt To Loosen Federal Restrictions on Marijuana," August 10, 2016. National Public Radio, www.npr.org/2016/08/10/489509471/dea-rejects-attempt-to-loosen-federal-restrictions-on-marijuana.

49. Drug Policy Research Center, *Research Brief: Using Marijuana May Not Raise the Risk of Doing Harder Drugs* (Santa Monica, CA: RAND Corporation, 2002), www.rand.org/publications/RB/RB6010/.

50. "Marijuana Home Grow Operation," *Crime Prevention and Information, Niagara Regional Police Service*, http://nrps.com/community/marijuana.asp.

51. Mora Fiedler, Jim Specht, Mary DeStefano, and Mary Sigler, "Colorado's Legalization of Marijuana and the Impact on Public Policy: A Practical Guide for Law Enforcement," The Police Foundation, 2015, www.policefoundation.org/projects/colorados-legalization-of-marijuana-and-the-impact-on-public-policy-a-practical-guide-for-law-enforcement/.

52. Ibid., pp. 2–3.

53. Wes Woods II, "Authorities Seize 14,000 Plants Worth $60 Million to $80 million," *Inland Valley Daily Bulletin*, California, 2007.

54. Pierre Thomas and Lisa Jones, "Synthetic Marijuana: 'Legal' High a Dangerous Thrill for Young Americans," *ABC News*, November 22, 2010, http://abcnews.go.com/US/synthetic-marijuana-legal-drug-scary-consequences/story?id=12211253&page=1.

55. Ryan Grim, "K2 Crackdown: DEA Using Emergency Powers to Ban Fake Pot," *The Huffington Post*, November 24, 2010, www.huffingtonpost.com/2010/11/24/dea-using-emergency-power_n_788149.html.

56. See U.S. Code Title 21, Section 863.

57. National Drug Intelligence Center, "Drug Paraphernalia Prosecution: Stopping Criminal Facilitators of Drug Use," Information Brief (Washington, DC: U.S. Department of Justice, July 2003).

58. Lee, *Global Drug Enforcement: Practical Investigative Techniques*, p. 11.

59. National Drug Intelligence Center, National Drug Threat Assessment 2010: Domestic Drug Flows (Washington, DC: U.S. Department of Justice, May 2010).

60. Lee, *Global Drug Enforcement: Practical Investigative Techniques*, p. 12.

61. National Drug Intelligence Center, *National Drug Threat Assessment 2010: Domestic Drug Flows*.

62. See Washington Post Online, www.washingtonpost.com/wp-dyn/content/video/2010/11/05/VI201010110501962.html, accessed December 18, 2010.

63. National Narcotics Intelligence Consumers Committee, *The NNICC Report 1995: The Supply of Illicit Drugs to the United States* (Washington, DC: U.S. Government Printing Office, 1996).

64. National Drug Intelligence Center, *National Drug Threat Assessment 2010: Domestic Drug Flows*.

65. William Booth, "Mexico's Deadly Drug Violence Claims Hundreds of Lives in Past 5 Days," *Washington Post*, June 16, 2010, www.washingtonpost.com/wp-dyn/content/article/2010/06/15/AR2010061503174.html.

66. Randal C. Archibold, "Mexican Drug Cartel Spills Over, Alarming U.S." *The New York Times*, March 22, 2009, www.nytimes.com/2009/03/23/us/23border.html.

67. See Morgan Quitno, *America's Safest (and Most Dangerous) Cities* (Washington, DC: CQ Press, 2010); also, interview with Chief Gregory Allen by Dr. Robert W. Taylor on December 14, 2010. Dr. Taylor has been a consultant to the City of El Paso, Texas for the past 15 years.

68. Lee, *Global Drug Enforcement: Practical Investigative Techniques*, p. 7.

69. National Drug Intelligence Center, *National Drug Threat Assessment 2010: Domestic Drug Flows*.

70. United Nations Office on Drugs and Crime, "The Global Heroin Market," *World Drug Report 2010*, www.unodc.org/documents/wdr/WDR_2010/1.2_The_global_heroin_market.pdf.

71. National Drug Intelligence Center, *National Drug Threat Assessment 2010: Domestic Drug Flows*.

72. Ibid.

73. Jason Burke, "Europe Supplies World's Ecstasy," *The Observer*, September 1, 2002, www.guardian.co.uk/drugs/Story/0%2C2763%2C784304%2C00.html.

74. Paul Mahoney, *Narcotics Investigative Techniques* (Springfield, IL: Thomas Books, 1992), p. 5.

75. *New York v. Belton*, 452 US 454 (1981).

76. Gregory D. Lee, "Drug Informants, Motives, and Management," *FBI Law Enforcement Bulletin*, September 1993, pp. 10–15. This information was obtained with some modifications from this article.

77. Drug Enforcement Administration, *Agent's Manual*, Appendix B: "Domestic Operations Guideline, 2004."

78. Several police agencies have general orders, special guidelines, and/or policies relating to investigator-informant relationships. Such guidelines include specific direction on confidential informant management and control. Topics

that should be addressed in these types of policies include (1) procedures to establish a person as a CI; (2) documenting contacts with the CI; (3) debriefing the CI; (4) restricting the use of the CI and protecting the identity of the CI; (5) designation of an informant control officer or supervisor; (6) documentation and registration of the CI; (7) documentation of payment to the CI and receipts; (8) developing control unit records on the CI; (9) using the CI in controlled purchases; and (10) using the CI in a search warrant affidavit. In addition, many departments require officers to attend special training on the management and control of confidential informants previous to their assignment in a narcotics or drug unit.

79. *DEA Integrity Assurance Notes*, 2004.
80. Mahoney, *Narcotics Investigative Techniques*, p. 17.
81. Lyman, *Practical Drug Enforcement*, pp. 10–13.
82. Lee, *Global Drug Enforcement: Practical Investigative Techniques*, pp. 92–93. Mahoney, *Narcotics Investigative Techniques*, pp. 92–93.
83. Lyman, *Practical Drug Enforcement*, pp. 6–7.
84. Ibid., p. 113.
85. Ibid., p. 127.
86. Lee, *Global Drug Enforcement: Practical Investigative Techniques*, p. 116.
87. Ibid., p. 123.
88. Lyman, *Practical Drug Enforcement*, p. 31.
89. Ibid., p. 34.
90. Lee, *Global Drug Enforcement: Practical Investigative Techniques*, p. 147.
91. Mahoney, *Narcotics Investigative Techniques*, pp. 309–310.
92. Ibid., p. 311.
93. Lyman, *Practical Drug Enforcement*, pp. 156–159.
94. Mahoney, *Narcotics Investigative Techniques*, pp. 312–314.
95. George Steffen and Samuel Candelaria, *Drug Interdiction: Partnerships, Legal Principles, and Investigative Methods for Law Enforcement* (Boca Raton, FL: CRC Press, 2003), pp. 73–84.
96. *B. C. v. Plumas Unified School District*, 192 F.3d 1260 (1999).
97. Lee, *Global Drug Enforcement: Practical Investigative Techniques*, pp. 164–165.
98. Drug Enforcement Administration, *Field Testing for Controlled Substances* (Washington, DC: National Training Institute, U.S. Department of Justice, 2000), pp. 1–6.
99. Office of National Drug Control Policy, "The High In-tensity Drug Trafficking Area Program: An Overview," www.whitehousedrugpolicy.gov/hidta/frames_overview.html.
100. Washington/Baltimore HIDTA, www.hidta.org.
101. Office of National Drug Control Policy, "North Texas HIDTA," www.whitehousedrugpolicy.gov/hidta/frames_ntex.html.
102. Charles Whitebread and Christopher Slobogin, *Criminal Procedure: An Analysis of Cases and Concepts* (New York: Foundation Press, 2000), p. 150.
103. *Illinois* v. *Gates*, 462 US 213 (1983).
104. Lyman, *Practical Drug Enforcement*, p. 138.
105. Whitebread and Slobogin, *Criminal Procedure: An Analysis of Cases and Concepts*, p. 37.
106. *U.S.* v. *Leon*, 468 US 897 (1984).
107. Nix v. *Williams*, 467 US 431 (1984).
108. *Arizona* v. *Evans*, 514 US 1 (1995).
109. *California* v. *Acevado*, 500 US 565 (1991).
110. *Oliver* v. *U.S.*, 466 US 170 (1984).
111. Lee, *Global Drug Enforcement: Practical Investigative Techniques*, p. 148.
112. *Harris* v. *United States*, 390 US 234 (1968).
113. Terry v. *Ohio*, 392 US 1 (1968).
114. *Chimel* v. *California*, 395 US 752 (1969).
115. *New York* v. *Belton*, 452 US 454 (1981).
116. *Maryland* v. *Buie*, 494 US 395 (1990).
117. Mahoney, *Narcotics Investigative Techniques*, p. 206.
118. Ibid., pp. 206–209.
119. There are a number of different techniques and methods for securing drug evidence. These two methods have been adapted from Lee, *Global Drug Enforcement: Practical Investigative Techniques*, p. 12.
120. Lyman, *Practical Drug Enforcement*, p. 227.
121. Ibid.
122. Training Key 388, *Clandestine Laboratories* by L. Ray Brett. International Association of Chiefs of Police, Inc.
123. Michael Cashman, "Meth Labs: Toxic Timebombs," *Police Chief*, February 1998, p. 44.
124. Ibid., pp. 44–45.
125. "New Meth Formula Avoids Anti-Drug Laws," *Associated Press*, August 24, 2009, www.msnbc.msn.com/id/32542373/ns/us_news-crime_and_courts/.
126. Lyman, *Practical Drug Enforcement*, p. 45.
127. Ibid., pp. 45–46.
128. National Drug Intelligence Center, "Gangs and Drugs in the United States," *Drugs and Crime* (Washington, DC: U.S. Department of Justice, July 2003).
129. Ibid.
130. Presentation by Director R. Gil Kerlikowske at the Caruth Police Institute, Dallas Police Department, Lieutenant's Series II Final Training Session in Dallas, Texas on December 14, 2010.

Chapter 21

1. Office of the Historian, *Significant Terrorist Incidents, 1961–2001* (Washington, DC: U.S. Department of State, 2002), 10 pp. The information in this paragraph was extracted, with restatement, from this source.
2. U.S. Department of State, "Statistical Information on Terrorism in 2015," http://www.state.gov/j/ct/rls/crt/2015/257526.htm.
3. Ibid.
4. Phillip W. Thomas (Special Agent in Charge, Memphis Division, Federal Bureau of Investigation), "Statement for the Record before the House Committee on Government Reform, Subcommittee on Government Efficiency, Financial Management, and Intergovernmental Relations," March 1, 2002, p. 1.
5. The role of religion as a motivator or causation of terrorism has been argued by several scholars, with a recent focus on radical Islam and terrorism. See David C. Rapport, "Fear and Trembling: Terrorism in Three Religious Traditions," *American Political Science Review*, Vol. 78, Issue 3, September 1984; Walter Laqueur, *The Age of Terrorism* (Boston: Little, Brown, Inc., 1987); Mark Juergensmeyer, "Terror Mandated by God," *Terrorism and Political Violence*, Vol. 9, Issue 2, Summer 1997; Mark Juergensmeyer, *Terror in the Mind of God: The Global Rise of Religious Terrorism* (Berkeley and Los Angeles: University of California Press, 2000); Bruce Weitzman, *Religious Radicalism in the Greater Middle East. Volume 4* (New York: Frank Cass Publications, 1997), p. 10; Jonathon R. White, "Political Eschatology: A Theology of Antigovernment Extremism," *American Behavioral Scientist*, Vol. 44, pp. 937–956 and *Terrorism: An Introduction*, 3rd ed. (Belmont, CA: Wadsworth Thomson Learning, 2003), pp. 46–61; Bruce Hoffman, "Holy Terror: The Implications of Terrorism Motivated by a Religious Imperative," *Studies in Conflict and Terrorism*, Vol. 18, 2008, pp. 271–284; John Murphy, *The Sword of Islam* (Amherst, MA: Prometheus Books, 2002); Lawrence Davidson, *Islamic Fundamentalism* (Westport, CT: Greenwood Press, 1998); and John Esposito, *Islam and the Straight Path* (New York: Oxford University Press, 1991); Bernard Lewis, *The Crisis of Islam: Holy War and Unholy Terrorism* (New York: Random House, 2004); Mark A. Gabriel, *Islam and Terror* (Lake Mary, FL: Frontline Books, 2002); Neil J. Kressel, *Bad Faith: The Days of Religious Extremism* (Amherst, NY: Prometheus Books, 2009); Eli Berman, *Radical, Religious and Violent: The New Economics of Terrorism* (Boston, MA: MIT Press, 2009); Moorthy S. Muthuswamy, *Defeating Political Islam: The New Cold War* (Amherst, NY: Prometheus Books, 2009); R. Joseph Hoffman (ed.), *The Just War and Jihad: Violence in Judaism, Christianity, and Islam* (Amherst, NY: Prometheus Books, 2010).
6. Lee Hancock, "Hasan's Hearing Resumes Monday as Focus Shifts to His Defense Team," *The Dallas Morning News*, November 14, 2010.
7. No author, *The Times Square Case* (Washington, DC: FBI), May 4, 2010, www.fbi.gov/news/stories/2010/may/timessquare_050410/times-square-case; No author, *Faisal Shahzad Sentenced in Manhattan Federal Court to Life in Prison for Attempted Car Bombing in Times Square* (Washington, DC: FBI, October 5, 2010), http://newyork.fbi.gov/dojpressurel/pressrel10/nyfo100510.htm.
8. Dan Berry. "Orlando Shooting: Realizing It's a Small, Terrifying World After All," *New York Times*, June 20, 2016.
9. Lansine Kaba, *The Wahhabiyya* (Evanston, IL: Northwestern University Press, 1974) and Lawrence Davidson, *Islamic Fundamentalism* (Westport, CT: Greenwood Press, 1998).
10. Henry Munson, *Islam and Revolution in the Middle East* (New Haven, CT: Yale University Press, 1989) and Ziyad Abu Amr, *Islamic Fundamentalism in the West Bank and Gaza* (Indianapolis, IN: Indiana University Press, 1994). In addition, Sayyid Qutb wrote over a hundred books mainly focusing on social justice and Islam. One of his central themes is the Islamic concept of tawhid (the singularity of God and, therefore, of the universe). See Sayyid Qutb, *Milestones* (Beirut, Lebanon: The Holy Quoran Publishing House, 1980).

11. Sun Tsu, *The Art of War*, translated by Lionel Gates (London: British Museum, 1910).

12. Graeme Wood, "What ISIS Really Wants," *The Atlantic*, March 2015, https://www.theatlantic.com/features/archive/2015/02/what-isis-really-wants/384980/?fb_ref=Default.

13. Some of this section has been adapted from Taylor and Swanson, *Terrorism, Intelligence and Homeland Security.*

14. Malis Ruthven, *A Fury for God* (London: Hanover Books, 2002), pp. 170–171.

15. John Esposito, *Unholy War: Terror in the Name of Islam* (New York: Oxford University Press, 2002), pp. 9–11.

16. Federal Bureau of Investigation, "Seeking Suspect in Church Shootings in Charleston, South Carolina," June 18, 2015, p. 1, https://www.fbi.gov/news/news_blog/seeking-suspect-in-church-shootings-in-charleston-south-carolina.

17. Janell Ross, "Why Blacks See Dylann Roof as a Terrorist and Whites Don't," *The Washington Post*, July 3, 2015, p. 1, https://www.washingtonpost.com/news/the-fix/wp/2015/07/03/why-blacks-see-dylann-roof-as-a-terrorist-and-whites-don't.

18. Ralph Ellis, Ashley Fantz, Faith Karimi, and Eliott C. McLaughlin, "Orlando Shooting: 49 Killed, Shooter Pledged ISIS Allegiance," *CNN*, June 13, 2016, http://www.cnn.com/2016/06/12/us/orlando-nightclub-shooting/.

19. Connor Friedersdorf, "Why IT Mattes That the Charleston Attack was Terrorism," *The Atlantic*, June 22, 2015, http://www.theatlantic.com/politics/archive/2015/06/was-the-charleston-attack-terrorism/396329/.

20. President Barack Obama, "Address on Mass Shooting in U.S. History," June 13, 2016, http://www.cnn.com/2016/06/12/us/orlando-nightclub-shooting/.

21. Joshua D. Freilich, Jeff Gruenewald, Steven Chermak, and William Parkin, "Was the Orlando Shooting a Hate Crime or Terrorist Act? The Answer Matters." *The New Republic*, June 15, 2016, https://newrepublic.com/article/134319/orlando-shooting-hate-crime-terrorist-act-answer-matters.

22. Responding to Hate Crimes: A Police Officer's Guide to Investigation and Prevention (Washington, DC: U.S. Department of Justice and International Association of Chiefs of Police, 1999).

23. Freilich et al. "Was the Orlando Shooting a Hate Crime..."

24. Ibid.

25. Congressional Research Service, *Terrorism: Near Eastern Groups and State Sponsors, 2002* (Washington, DC: Library of Congress, 2002), p. 16.

26. Esposito, pp. 13–14.

27. Ibid., pp. 18–21.

28. Dilip Hiro, *War Without End* (London: Routledge, 2002), pp. 267–274.

29. ABC News report, January 8, 2001, "Orders from Osama," http://abcnews.go.com/sections/world/DailyNews/yemen010108.html.

30. Zachary Abuza, *Militant Islam in Southeast Asia: A Crucible of Terror* (London: Rienner Publishers, 2003), pp. 127–128.

31. Tom Lasseter and Jonathan S. Landay, "Conditions Ripe for bin-Laden's Survival." *Dallas Morning News*, September 9, 2007.

32. "Al Qaeda in Yemen and Somalia: A Ticking Time Bomb," *United States Senate: Report to the Committee on Foreign Relations* (Washington, DC: U.S. Government Printing Office, January 21, 2010).

33. Greg Miller, "US Charges 14 with Giving Support to Somali Insurgent Groups," *Washington Post*, August 6, 2010, www.washingtonpost.com/wp-dyn/content/article/2010/08/05/AR2010080503683.html?sid=ST2010080504294.

34. "Al Qaeda Supporter and Organizer of Jihad Training Camp in Oregon Sentenced in Manhattan Federal Court to Life in Prison" (Washington, DC: FBI), September 15, 2009, http://newyork.fbi.gov/dojpressrel/pressrel09/nyfo091509.htm.

35. Mike M. Ahlers and Brian Todd, "Al Qaeda Group Contemplated Poisoning Food in U.S., Officials Say," *CNN*, December 21, 2010, http://edition.cnn.com/2010/US/12/21/al.qaeda.poison.plot/?htp=T2.

36. Richard Esposito and Brian Ross, "Exclusive: Photos of the Northwest Airlines Flight 253 Bomb," *ABC News*, December 28, 2009, http://abcnews.go.com/Blotter/northwestairlines-flight-253-bomb-photos-exclusive/story?id=9436297.

37. See Drew Hinshaw and Zoumana Wonogo, "Al-Qaeda Attacks in Burkina Faso Kill at Least 30," *The Wall Street Journal*, January 17, 2016, http://www.wsj.com/articles/operation-ends-at-burkina-faso-hotel-seized-by-al-qaeda-1452936866.

38. Ibid.

39. Craig Whitlock, "Al-Qaeda Is Rebuilt, Restored and Renewed," *Washington Post*, September 10, 2007.

40. Ibid., pp. 128–132.

41. Ibid., pp. 133–136.

42. Ibid., pp. 153–166.

43. BBC News report, October, 9, 2003. "Timeline: Bali Bomb Trials," http://news.bbc.co.uk/2/hi/asia-pacific/3126241.stm.

44. Uppsala Conflict Data Program (UCDP) Encyclopedia, http://ucdp.uu.se/#country/850.

45. Ibid., pp. 12–14.

46. Ibid., pp. 15.

47. Robin Wright, *Sacred Rage: The Wrath of Militant Islam* (New York: Simon and Schuster, 2001), p. 16.

48. Ibid., pp. 73–76.

49. Ibid., pp. 102–106.

50. Congressional Research Service, 2002, p. 6.

51. Council on Foreign Relations, "Terrorism Q and A: Hezbollah," www.terrorismanswers.com/groups/hezbollah_print.html.

52. BBC News report, February 16, 2001, "Israeli Killed in Hizbollah Attack," http://news.bbc.co.uk/1/hi/world/middle_east/1173682.stm.

53. Congressional Research Service, 2002, p. 7.

54. Associated Press report, December 8, 2002, "Mombasa Bombing Reveals Possible al-Qaeda-Hizbollah Link," www.lebanonwire.com/0212/02120805TGR.asp.

55. Ibid.

56. Council on Foreign Relations, "Terrorism Q and A: Hezbollah."

57. International Policy Institute for Counter-Terrorism, "Terrorist Organizations: The Abu Nidal Organization," www.ict.org.il/.

58. BBC News, "Who Are Hezbollah?" July 4, 2010, http://news.bbc.co.uk/2/hi/middle_east/4314423.stm.

59. Reuters, "US Wants to Build Up Hezbollah Moderates: Advisor," May 18, 2010, www.reuters.com/article/idUSTRE64I0UM20100519.

60. Ben Conery, "Hezbollah Uses Mexican Drug Routes into U.S.," *The Washington Post*, March 27, 2009, www.washingtontimes.com/news/2009/mar/27/hezbollah-uses-mexican-drug-routes-into-us/?page=1.

61. Joan Neuhaus Schaan, "Case Outlines Potential Terror Threat to U.S.," *Houston Chronicle*, September 19, 2009, www.chron.com/disp/story.mpl/editorial/outlook/6627377.html and John C. Thompson, "The New World Expansion of Hezbollah," The *Mackenzie Institute*, August 2010, http://mackenzieinstitute.com/2010/hezbollah081810.htm.

62. BBC Online, "Israel's History of Bomb Blasts."

63. United Press International, "Report: HAMAS Attacks Possible in the U.S.," March 16, 2003.

64. See Bruce Hoffman, "The Logic of Suicide Terrorism," *Atlantic Monthly*, June 2003, and The Palestinian Report, "An Interview with Eyad Sarraj," *Media Monitors Network*, 2001.

65. Dennis M. Lormel (Chief, Financial Crimes Investigations, FBI), "Statement for the Record before the House Committee on Financial Services, Subcommittee on Oversight and Investigations," February 12, 2002, p. 9.

66. Justin Walker and Leila Golestrani, "Threat Analysis: Hamas and Hezbollah Sleeper Cells in the United States," *Urban Warfare Analysis Center*, March 18, 2009, www.uwac-ok.com/research.html.

67. Daniel L. Byman, "HAMAS or the Palestinian Authority: Who Will Fail First?" Brookings Institute, September 21, 2015, https://www.brookings.edu/blog/markaz/2015/09/21/hamas-or-the-palestinian-authority-who-will-fail-first/.

68. Brian Michael Jenkins, *Would-Be Warriors: Incidents of Jihadist Terrorist Radicalization in the United States Since September 11, 2001* (Arlington, VA: RAND Corporation 2010).

69. The George Washington University Homeland Security Policy Institute, "Out of the Shadows: Getting Ahead of Prisoner Radicalization," September 2006, www.gwumc.edu/hspi/policy/PrisonerRadicalization.pdf.

70. U.S. Department of Justice, "Pennsylvania Woman Indicted in Plot to Recruit Violent Jihadist Fighters and to Commit Murder Overseas" (Philadelphia Office Press Release: Federal Bureau of Investigation, March 9, 2010), http://philadelphia.fbi.gov/dojpressrel/pressrel10/ph030910a.htm.

71. S. Ackerman, "Pakistani Court Indicts 'Virginia Five,'" *The Washington Independent*, March 17, 2010, http://washingtonindependent.com/79446/pakistani-court-indicts-virginia-five.

72. Andrea Elliot, "The Jihadist Next Door," *The New York Times*, January 27, 2010, www.nytimes.com/2010/01/31/magazine/31Jihadist-t.html?hp=&pagewanted=all.

73. M. J. Stephey, "Daniel Boyd: A Homegrown Terrorist?" *Time Online*, July 30, 2009, www.time.com/time/nationa/article/0,8599,1913602,00.html.

74. Rick "Ozzie" Nelson and Ben Bodurian, "A Growing Terrorist Threat? Assessing 'Homegrown Extremism' in the United States," *Center for International and Strategic Studies*, March 8, 2010, www.csis.org/files/publication/100304_Nelson_GrowingTerroristThreat_Web.pdf.

75. Associated Press, "Faisal Shahzad Kept Low Profile in U.S.," *CBS News*, May 4, 2010, www.cbsnews.com/stories/2010/05/04/national/main6459360.shtml.

76. Bob Drogin and April Choi, "Teen Held in Alleged Portland Bomb Plot," *Los Angeles Times*, November 28, 2010, http://articles.latimes.com/2010/nov/28/nation/la-na-portland-bomb-plot-20101128.

77. Bob Drogin and Richard Serrano, "Baltimore Man Arrested in Foiled Terrorism Plot," *Los Angeles Times*, December 9, 2010, http://articles.latimes.com/2010/dec/09/nation/la-na-bomb-plot-arrest-20101209.

78. *The Al-Qaeda Training Manual*, originally found as a computer file by the Manchester (England) Metropolitan Police in 2000, https://www.justice.gov/sites/default/files/ag/legacy/2002/10/08/manualpart1_1.pdf.

79. See International Security Data website: http://securitydata.newamerica.net/extremists/terror-plot.html?id=1675298532.

80. Saeed Ahmed, "Who Were Syed Rizwan Farook and Tashfeen Malik?" *CNN Reports*, December 4, 2015, http://www.cnn.com/2015/12/03/us/syed-farook-tashfeen-malik-mass-shooting-profile/.

81. Lolita C. Baldor, "Home-Grown Terror Threat Not Taken Seriously, Report Says," *The Washington Times*, September 15, 2010, www.washingtontimes.com/news/2010/sep/15/homegrownterror-threat-not-taken-seriously/.

82. See Chapter 15: The Future in Robert W. Taylor and Charles R. Swanson, *Terrorism, Intelligence and Homeland Security*, pp. 361–375.

83. Under current United States law, set forth in the USA PATRIOT ACT of 2005, acts of domestic terrorism are those which: "(A) involve acts dangerous to human life that are a violation of the criminal laws of the United States or of any State; (B) appear to be intended—(1) to intimidate or coerce a civilian population; (2) to influence the policy of a government by intimidation or coercion; or (3) to affect the conduct of a government by mass destruction, assassination, or kidnapping; and (C) occur primarily within the territorial jurisdiction of the United States." See also the FBI Terrorism Research and Analysis Center Memo, *Domestic Terrorism*, 1994.

84. Federal Bureau of Investigation, *Terrorism in the United States* (Washington, DC: FBI, 1996), p. 7.

85. Jana Winter, "Some Muslims Attending Capitol Hill Prayer Group Have Terror Ties, Probe Reveals," *Fox News*, April 7, 2010.

86. Brian Ross, "How Anwar-al-Awlaki Inspired Terror From Across the Globe," September 30, 2011, www.ABCNews.go.com/Blotter/Anwar-al-Awlaki-Inspired-Terrorism/Story?Id=14643383#UDA1KLGNFI.

87. No author, "Anwar al-Awlaki," *New York Times*, July 18, 2012, www.NYTimes.com/Topics/Reference/Timetopics/people/A/Anwar_al_Awlaki/Index.html.

88. Jennifer Griffin, "Two U.S.-Born Terrorists Killed in CIA-led Drone Strike," *Fox News*, April 7, 2010 and Kimberly Dozier, "Drones: Obama Administration's Weapon of Choice in the War on al-Qaeda," *The Washington Post*, October 30, 2011.

89. Scott Shane, "The Lessons of Anwar al-Awlaki," *The New York Times*, August 30, 2015, http://www.nytimes.com/2015/08/30/magazine/the-lessons-of-anwar-al-awlaki.html?_r=0.

90. Ibid.

91. Several important and relatively recent developments have helped to reduce the impact of right-wing, Christian Identity theology in the United States. First, the natural deaths of prominent leaders in the movement, including William Pierce, author of the Turner Diaries and a leader in the National Alliance and American Nazi Party, and the Reverend Richard Butler, pastor of the Church of Christ's Christians of Hayden Lake, Idaho, who died on September 8, 2004. In addition, several civil suits have been successfully litigated by Mr. Morris Dees and the Southern Poverty Law Center against the Christian Identity movement and the Ku Klux Klan.

92. Michael Barkum, *Religion and the Racist Right: The Origins of the Christian Identity Movement* (Chapel Hill, NC: The University of North Carolina Press, 1997).

93. Much of this discussion is informed by Anti-Defamation League, "Extremism in America," www.adl.org/learn/ext_us/default.asp?LEARN_Cat=Extremism&LEARN_SubCat=Extremism_in_America&xpicked=1&item=0.

94. See *United States v. Hutaree Members*, copy of federal indictment, http://commons.wikimedia.org/wiki/File:Federal-hutaree-indictment-mar-2010.pdf.

95. Much of this discussion is informed by the Southern Poverty Law Center, "Intelligence Project: Monitoring Hate and Extremist Activities," www.splcenter.org/what-we-do/hate-and-extremism.

96. J. J. McNabb, "Sovereign Citizen Kane," *Intelligence Report* (Birmingham, AL: Southern Poverty Law Center, Fall 2010), pp. 13–19.

97. Jerome Sherman, "Poplawski Called Unremorseful, *Pittsburgh Post Gazette*, April 8, 2009, www.post-gazette.com/pg/09098/961304-53.stm.

98. Heidi Beirich, "The Year in Nativism," *Intelligence Report* (Birmingham, AL: Southern Poverty Law Center, Spring 2010), www.splcenter.org/get-informed/intelligence-report/browse-all-issues/2010/spring/the-year-in-nativism.

99. See Federal Bureau of Investigation, *Terrorism in the United States*, 1994.

100. Ibid.

101. James F. Jarboe (Domestic Terrorism Section Chief, Federal Bureau of Investigation), "The Threat of Ecoterrorism," speech before the House of Resources Committee, Subcommittee on Forests and Forest Health, February 12, 2002.

102. Ibid.

103. Louis J. Freeh (Director, FBI), "Threat of Terrorism to the United States," speech before the U.S. Senate, Committees on Appropriations, Armed Services, and Select Committee on Intelligence, May 10, 2001.

104. Brent L. Smith, *Terrorism in America: Pipe Bombs and Pipe Dreams* (Albany, New York: State University of New York Press, 1994), p. 125.

105. Freeh, *Threat of Terrorism to the United States*.

106. Smith, *Terrorism in America: Pipe Bombs and Pipe Dreams*.

107. Jarboe, "The Threat of Ecoterrorism."

108. Center for the Defense of Free Enterprise (CDFE), "Ecoterrorism," www.cdfe.org/ecoterror.hml.

109. See U.S. Department of Homeland Security, "Leftwing Extremists Likely to Increase Use of Cyber Attacks over the Coming Decade," www.fas.org/irp/eprint/leftwing.pdf.

110. Ibid.

111. Jarboe, "The Threat of Ecoterrorism."

112. Off-Road.com, "A Short History of Ecoterrorism," www.off-road.com/land/ecoterrorism_history.html, viewed July 2003.

113. Jarboe, "The Threat of Ecoterrorism."

114. Off-Road.com, "A Short History of Ecoterrorism."

115. Larry Copeland, "Domestic Terrorism: New Trouble at Home," p. 3.

116. See Blaine Harden, "11 Indicted in Eco-Terrorism Case," *Washington Post*, January 13, 2006; and U.S. Department of Homeland Security, Office of Intelligence and Analysis, *Domestic Extremism Digest*, March 2006.

117. Center for Arms Control and Non-Proliferation, "Financial Actions Against Terrorists," www.armscontrolcenter.org/terrorism/issues/Financing.html.

118. United States Mission to the United Nations, statement by James Shinn, Special Adviser to the U.S. Mission to the United States, on Agenda Item 160, Measures to Eliminate International Terrorism, in the Sixth Committee of the Fifty-Seventh Session of the United Nations General Assembly, October 2, 2002. USUN Press release #142-2 (02) October 3, 2002, www.un.int/usa/02_142-2.htm.

119. Financial Action Task Force on Money Laundering, "FATF Cracks Down on Terrorist Financing," October 31, 2001, www1.oecd.org/fatf/pdf/PR-20011031_en.pdf.

120. Canadian Foundation for Drug Policy, "The Scope of the Problem: The Value of Illegal Drugs for Terrorist and Criminal Organizations, 2001," www.cfdp.ca/eoterror.htm.

121. U.S. Drug Enforcement Administration, Drug Intelligence Brief, "Drugs and Terrorism; A New Perspective," p. 4.

122. Canadian Foundation for Drug Policy, "The Scope of the Problem: The Value of Illegal Drugs for Terrorist and Criminal Organizations."

123. U.S. Drug Enforcement Administration, Drug Intelligence Brief, "Drugs and Terrorism; A New Perspective," p. 5.

124. Ibid.

125. Ibid.

126. United Nations Office of Drugs and Crime, *The 2007 World Drug Report* (New York: UN Publications, 2007).

127. Jerry Seper, "Afghanistan Leads Again in Heroin Production," *The Washington Times*, August 12, 2003, www.washingtontimes.com/functions/print.php?StoryID=20030811-100220-8928r.

128. U.S. Drug Enforcement Administration, Drug Intelligence Brief, "Drugs and Terrorism; A New Perspective," p. 5.

129. Mark A. R. Kleiman, "Illicit Drugs and the Terrorist Threat: Causal Links and Implication for Domestic Drug Control Policy," *Congressional Research Service*, April 2004, pp. 1–2.

130. Pamela Falk, "U.N.: Afghan's $61B Drug Trade Funding Terrorism" *CBS News*, June 23, 2011.

131. See "Thugs, Drugs and Coyotes on the U.S.-Mexican Border" (Austin, TX: Stratford Reports, March 14, 2010), and U.S. Department of State, *2016 International Narcotics Control Strategy Report – INCSR* (Washington, DC: USGPO, 2016).

132. Guy Taylor, "Hezbollah Moving Tons of Cocaine in Latin America, US, and Europe to Finance Terror Operations," *Washington Times*, June 8, 2016, http://www.washingtontimes.com/news/2016/jun/8/hezbollah-moving-tons-of-cocaine-in-latin-america-/.

133. International Policy Institute for Counter-Terrorism, "Peru Breaks Up FARC Arms Smuggling Ring," Press release, August 2000, www.ict.org.il/spotlight/det.cfm?id=474.

134. Eric Green, "U.S. Arrests Colombian for Trying to Buy Arms from Terrorist Groups," Embassy of the United States to Japan, http://japan.usembassy.gov/e/p/tp-20040406-10.html.

135. Terry Frieden, "Federal Agents Charge Four with Arms Smuggling," *CNN.com*, June 15, 2001, http://archives.cnn.com/2001/LAW/06/15/arms.smuggling/.

136. Jon Burstein, "Former Boca Jewelers Might Be Crucial to Arms Smuggling Case," *The South Florida Sun-Sentinel*, August 7, 2001, http://billstclair.com/911timeline/2002/sunsentine1080701.html.

137. Ibid.

138. Ivan Angelovski, Miranda Patrucic, and Lawrence Marzouk, "Revealed: The $1B of Weapons Flowing from Europe to Middle East," *The Guardian*, London, July 27, 2016, https://www.theguardian.com/world/2016/jul/27/weapons-flowing-eastern-europe-middle-east-revealed-arms-trade-syria.

139. Karen Leigh "ISIS Makes Up to $3 million per Day Selling Oil, Say Analysts," *ABC News*, August 2, 2015.

140. From Internet discussion forum: Discussion42, "Terrorist Using ATMs and Fake Credit Cards for Financing," December 11, 2004, www.secularislam.org/discussion42/_disc42/000001fd.htm.

141. "Fraud, ID Theft Finance Terror," *Chicago Tribune*, November 4, 2001, www.chicagotribune.com/news/specials/chi-011104identity,0,5867496,print.story?.

142. FBI Terror Task Force Probed Credit Card Fraud Case, *The Detroit News*, May 27, 2004, www.detnews.com/2004/metro/0405/27/metro-165657.htm.

143. William Billingslea, "Illicit Cigarette Trafficking and the Funding of Terrorism," *The Police Chief*, February 2004.

144. United States Action, remarks by President Bush in his announcements on the financial aspect of terrorism.

145. National Commission on Terrorist Attacks upon the United States, "Monograph on Terrorist Financing," pp. 87–113.

146. Ibid., pp. 114–130.

147. U.S. Immigration and Customs Enforcement—news release, "Holy Land Foundation, Leaders Accused of Providing Material Support to HAMAS Terrorist Organization," July 27, 2004, www.ice.gov/graphics/news/newsreleases/articles/072704hamas.htm.

148. U.S. Department of State, Office of International Information Programs, "U.S. Government Indicts 7 for Helping Finance Terrorist," December 19, 2002, http://usinfo.org/wf-archive/2002/021219/epf405.htm.

149. *The 9/11 Commission Report: Final Report of the National Commission on Terrorist Attacks Upon the United States* (New York: W.W. Norton & Company, 2004), p. 372.

150. Ibid., p. 172.

151. U.S. Department of State, Office of International Information Programs, Embassy of the United States of America, Jakarta, Indonesia. "Tracking Informal Terrorist Financing Next Task of U.S.-Led Coalition," speech by Kenneth W. Dam Deputy Secretary of the Treasury delivered to the Council on Foreign Relations New York, New York on June 8, 2002, June 11, 2002, p. 4, www.usembassyjakarta.org/terrorism/coalition2.html.

152. Kathleen Day, "Hawalah Cash Outlets Investigated as Source for Terror Funds," *Washington Post*, November 7, 2001. Obtained through the Internet site for United States action, January 12, 2005, www.unitedstatesaction.com/islam-money-changing.htm.

153. Sina Lehmkuhler, "Countering Terrorist Financing: We Need a Long-Term Prioritizing Strategy," April 2003, p. 8, www.homelandsecurity.org/journal/articles/Lehmkuhler.html.

154. National Infrastructure Protection Center, www.nipc.gov, March 12, 2001, p. 1.

155. Watson, "Statement for the Record," pp. 7–8.

156. Donald M. Kerr (Assistant Director, Laboratory Division, Federal Bureau of Investigation), "Statement for the Record on Carnivore Diagnostic Tool" before the Senate Committee on the Judiciary, pp. 1–12, September 6, 2000.

157. Ibid., p. 8.

158. United States Action, remarks by President Bush in his announcement on the financial aspect of terrorism.

159. Kathleen Millar, "Financing Terror: Profits from Counterfeit Goods Pay for Attacks," U.S. Customs Today, November 2002, www.customs.ustreas.gov/xp/CustomsToday/2002/November/interpol.xml.

160. Text of public testimony by Ronald K. Noble, Secretary General of Interpol on the links between intellectual property crime and terrorist financing, July 16, 2003, www.interpol.com/Public/ICPO/speeches/SG20030716.asp?HM=1.

161. United States Action, U.S. NEO-Nazi Group: National Alliance, January 12, 2005, p. 1, www.unitedstatesaction.com/national-alliance-nazi.htm.

162. See FBI website: https://www.fbi.gov/investigate/terrorism/joint-terrorism-task-forces.

163. International Association of Chiefs of Police, *Leading from the Front: Law Enforcement's Role in Combating Terrorism* (Alexandria, VA: IACP, 2001), p. 7.

164. For an important discussion of WMDs regarding the police, refer to Daniel R. Symonds, "A Guide to Selected Weapons of Mass Destruction," *Police Chief*, March 2003, pp. 19–29.

165. In January 2011, a series of incendiary letters were sent to government buildings in Washington, D.C., and Baltimore, Maryland. The letters were often addressed to high-level government officials, such as Janet Napolitano (Secretary of the Department of Homeland Security), but none of the packages exploded; rather they sparked and ignited causing significant disruption of services and chaos. Some postal workers reported minor burns to their fingers and hands, but no serious injuries resulted from these incidents, unlike the attacks sent to celebrities (e.g. Tom Brokaw) after 9/11 in 2001, which resulted in several postal workers dying from handling letters filled with inhalation anthrax.

166. Christopher Rigopoulos, "The FBI Philadelphia Division's Hazardous Materials Response Team," *Police Chief*, March 2003, p. 20.

167. The singular of "bacteria."

168. Thomas v. Inglesby et al., "Anthrax as a Biological Weapon," *Journal of the American Medical Association*, Vol. 281, 1999, p. 7.

169. U.S. Department of Defense, "Information Paper: Anthrax as a Biological Warfare Agent," June 1998, p. 2, www.defenselink.mil/other_info/agent.html.

170. Centers for Disease Control, "Use of Anthrax Vaccine in the United States," *Morbidity and Mortality Report*, Vol. 49, Issue. RR-15, December 15, 2000, p. 3.

171. Centers for Disease Control, "Anthrax," www.cdc.gov/ncidod/dbmd/diseaseinfo/anthrax_t.htm, accessed January 10, 2011, p. 1.

172. Ibid.

173. National Domestic Preparedness Office, "On-Scene Commanders Guide for Responding to Biological and Chemical Threats" (Washington, DC: November 1, 1999), p. 19.

174. Centers for Disease Control, "Interim Guidelines for Firefighters and Other First Responders for the Selection and Use of Protective Clothing and Respirators," www.bt.cdc.gov/docuementsapp/anthrax/protective/10242001.asp, January 10, 2011, p. 2.

175. Ibid.

176. Ibid., p. 3.

177. Ibid.

178. Ibid., p. 4.

179. National Domestic Preparedness Office, "On-Scene Commanders," p. 4, with minor additions by the authors.

180. Ibid., pp. 9–10.

181. Ibid., p. 10.

182. Steve Cain, *Agroterrorism: A Purdue Extension Backgrounder* (West Lafayette, IN: Purdue University 2001), p. 1.

183. Federal Bureau of Investigation, Terrorism in the United States, 1999, p. 240.

184. See Robert W. Taylor and Charles R. Swanson, *Terrorism, Intelligence, and Homeland Security*, Chapter 15.

Chapter 22

1. 373 U.S. 83 (1963).

2. The "Daubert Trilogy" Cases Are: *Daubert* v. *Merrell Dow Pharmaceuticals, Inc.* 509 U.S. 579 (1993); *General Electric Company* v. *Joiner*, 522 U.S. 1356 (1997); and *Kumho Tire Company* v. *Carmichael*, 526 U.S. 137 (1999).

3. *Ohio v. Roberts*, 488 U.S. 56 (1982).

4. 124 S.Ct. 1354 (2004).

5. Crawford, 124 S.Ct. 1354, at 1374.

6. See *Brady v. Maryland*, 373 U.S. 83 (1963)

7. Charles R. Swanson, Leonard Territo, and Robert W. Taylor, *Police Administration: Structures, Processes and Behaviors*, 9th ed. (Upper Saddle River, NJ: Pearson Publishing, 2017)